LABOR LAW:
A PROBLEM BASED
APPROACH

LABOR LAW: A PROBLEM BASED APPROACH

Paul M. Secunda
Associate Professor of Law
Marquette University Law School

Jeffrey M. Hirsch
Associate Professor of Law
University of North Carolina School of Law

ISBN: 978-1-4224-8530-9 (casebook)
ISBN: 978-0-7698-5868-5 (looseleaf)

Library of Congress Cataloging-in-Publication Data
Secunda, Paul M.
Labor law : a problem based approach / Paul M. Secunda, Associate Professor of Law, Marquette University Law School, Jeffrey M. Hirsch, Associate Professor of Law, University of North Carolina School of Law.
p. cm.
Includes index.
ISBN 978-1-4224-8530-9
1. Labor laws and legislation—United States. I. Hirsch, Jeffrey M. II. Title.
KF3319.S43 2012
344.7301—dc23
2012034603

NOTE TO USERS
To ensure that you are using the latest materials available in this area, please be sure to periodically check the LexisNexis Law School web site for downloadable updates and supplements at www.lexisnexis.com/lawschool.

Editorial Offices
121 Chanlon Rd., New Providence, NJ 07974 (908) 464-6800
201 Mission St., San Francisco, CA 94105-1831 (415) 908-3200
www.lexisnexis.com

MATTHEW◆BENDER

DEDICATION

PMS: To my grandfather, Joseph B. Godick, for instilling in me a life-long desire to fight the good fight for workers' rights, and with love to Mindy, Jake, and Izzy

JMH: With love to Lynn, Noah, and Naomi

PREFACE

Labor law is facing challenging times in the first part of the 21st Century. This is especially true in the American private sector, which largely comes under the federal, Wagner-model based, National Labor Relations Act (NLRA). Just over 75 years after its enactment, both employers and unions are seriously questioning the continuing viability of the Wagner model.

Regardless of which side they take in labor law debates, it is important for students to have a model of learning that mirrors the type of problems that newly-minted labor attorneys will face in practice. The problem-based approach we take in this book derives from prescient statements made by Professor Pavel Wonsowicz of the UCLA Law School. In discussing why moving beyond lectures and the Socratic method would be a pedagogical improvement over the way law students have traditionally been taught, Professor Wonsowicz commented: "I tell my students at the outset of a course that there's an unfairness going on in the way classes have been traditionally handled. It's this: We teach you on the case method and test on the problem method." We also believe strongly that the problem-based pedagogical method will directly help students in their eventual practice of labor law by synchronizing the way labor law is taught with the way it is tested in the law school environment.

A typical chapter in this book commences with a clear synopsis of the materials to be covered in the chapter. Second, introductory materials relate the basic thrust of the materials about to be covered. Third, in most sections, a problem is presented based on scholarly articles in the area, recent case law, and current events. Fourth, students are given problem materials to work through to solve the hypothetical presented; these materials include case excerpts, public documents, and law review articles and other secondary materials. Fifth, and finally, the students are presented with a section entitled, "Post Problem Discussion." Similar in structure to the Notes section of more traditional casebooks, this section seeks to highlight important areas in the primary and secondary materials, while providing additional materials for consideration of the problem. We hope that professors will engage in classroom teaching based on the problem(s) assigned for class. Indeed, this material lends itself well to classroom role-playing exercises and other experiential learning techniques.

To be clear, *Labor Law: A Problem Based Approach*, still features the most important cases, documents, and articles for students to study in order to become proficient in the practice of American private-sector labor law. But rather than attempting to have students glean the important facets of the law solely through the traditional case method, this book's problem-based approach requires students to act like attorneys. In short, this book provides a pedagogical alternative that we believe many professors and students will embrace as more compatible with the challenges that labor law practitioners will face in the coming decades. In our view, engagement with both the theoretical foundations and practical implications of labor law is essential for any labor law student who wishes to think critically about these issues and become a more effective advocate for their clients.

Throughout this book, we also hope to bring to bear our familiarity with the Internet, blogs, and social media to make our book one of the most interactive for students yet. In this vein, students will find relevant links to government websites, links to the Workplace

PREFACE

Prof Blog (which we co-edit along with three other law professors), and links to other relevant information on the web.

We offer thanks to all who helped us with this project, especially to the law professors who gave us permission to reproduce their works and to our families for putting up with our long hours in bringing this book to publication. A special thanks goes to Alana Leffler, Marquette University Law School Class of 2013, and Casey Turner, University of North Carolina School of Law Class of 2013, for their exceptional and tireless editorial assistance on this Casebook. It would not have been possible to complete this book without them. Also, thanks to Leslie Levin who was our initial contact with the publisher and to Pali Parekh who was our principal editor for this edition.

Paul M. Secunda
Milwaukee, Wisconsin

Jeffrey M. Hirsch
Chapel Hill, North Carolina

May 2012

TABLE OF CONTENTS

TABLE OF CONTENTS

TABLE OF CONTENTS

TABLE OF CONTENTS

TABLE OF CONTENTS

TABLE OF CONTENTS

TABLE OF CONTENTS

TABLE OF CONTENTS

TABLE OF CONTENTS

TABLE OF CONTENTS

Chapter 1

THE STRUGGLE FOR CONTROL OVER THE EMPLOYMENT RELATIONSHIP

Synopsis

SECTION 1   WHAT IS LABOR LAW AND IS IT STILL RELEVANT?

In starting a discussion about labor law in the United States, it is necessary to first ask the most basic of questions: What is labor law? One way to answer this question is by pointing out that labor law focuses on employees acting collectively to gain economic advantages for the group as a whole. More specifically, labor law focuses on the organization of unions, collective bargaining between management and unions over terms and conditions of employment, and other protected activities that parties undertake (including strikes, lockouts, pickets, and boycotts). Labor law is not limited to unions, however, as it also protects nonunion employees who attempt to act together to improve their work conditions.

This book is for general use in an introductory course in labor law and, for the most part, limits its focus to private-sector labor law. But your law school may offer other labor law courses that include topics such as public-sector labor law, labor arbitration, internal union governance, and multiemployer benefit plans.

So what is labor law not? There are many other labor and employment law courses that are offered at your law school that do not involve the regulation of collective activity. For example, one can study Employment Law (employment at-will doctrine, employee handbooks, common law tort actions, whistleblower actions, Fair Labor Standards Act (FLSA) claims, Family and Medical Leave Act (FMLA) claims, unemployment compensation schemes, and Occupational Safety and Health Act (OSHA) enforcement); Employment Discrimination Law (Equal Employment Opportunity Commission (EEOC), Title VII of the Civil Rights Act of 1964 and other civil rights and anti-discrimination laws); Employee Benefits Law (Employee Retirement Income Security Act (ERISA) claims involving pension and welfare benefit plans); or Workers' Compensation Law (involving injuries in the workplace).

A third question might be: What about labor law is different from the legal principles learned in other classes? Most of the other classes in law school focus on the American notion of individual rights. Labor law, on the other hand, is group-oriented and asks that individuals allow group concerns to trump their own. Indeed, labor law looks with suspicion on individual advantage. At the same time, American labor law is not a type of political communism or socialism, but rather a bread-and-butter unionism which seeks to give employees a larger share of the profits produced by corporations.

A final introductory question: What are unions and what are some examples of unions with which you may have already become familiar? Unions are labor organizations which assist workers in organizing, collective bargaining, and engaging in concerted activities. Unions bring to bear the collective voice of their employee members in negotiating with their employers.

Union adherents believe unions are necessary to balance the unequal bargaining power between individual employees and their employers, to prevent industrial strife, and to place "economic warfare" between the union and management within a well-defined procedural mechanism to control the economic strife that would otherwise result. The existence of a union in a workplace may also lead to improved working conditions, better pay, and worker participation in workplace decisions ("industrial democracy").

Examples of unions include the United Steelworkers, United Autoworkers, Service Employees International Union, the American Federation of Teachers, and Teamsters. In this book, we focus primarily on private-sector unions, which fall under the major legislation in this course, the National Labor Relations Act (NLRA).

PROBLEM #1: IS LABOR LAW STILL RELEVANT?

Prior to diving into a brief history of labor law relations in this country, we should pause to discuss the presence and relevance of labor law in modern American society. A couple of noteworthy issues that have danced across the pages of major newspapers and websites in this country include: the UAW's decision to take over its employees' retiree health coverage using a voluntary employee benefits association (VEBA); the ongoing labor disputes within professional sports unions (especially lockouts in the professional football and basketball leagues); the attack against public sector unions in Wisconsin and other states; the case brought against Boeing; and the battles over enacting the Employee Free Choice Act, which among other things, would have instituted card-check recognition for unions. Card-check recognition permits a union to be formally recognized based on signed employee authorization cards, rather than based on a secret ballot election (much more on this topic later). Some of the current challenges facing the federal agency that administers the NLRA, the National Labor Relations Board (NLRB or Board), are highlighted in the following excerpts from a law review essay by former Board Chairman Wilma Liebman:

> Labor law policy has been marginalized for too long, and public dialogue on these issues has too long been absent. Public consideration of labor policy, in which the Board plays a positive role, is sorely needed if we are to protect

the rights of workers to organize and bargain collectively in a competitive global economy. How do we achieve a proper balance between market freedom and democratic values? How do we preserve a middle-class society? Today, the story of faded trust in American labor law lies in the gap between early hopes and later results. Like dinosaur DNA, however, the promise of the Act is worth preserving. The stakes are too high to do otherwise.

If you were the general counsel for a non-profit group interested in general labor law reform, what strategy would you pursue today? Does the Liebman excerpt influence your thinking? What is the proper role of the NLRB?

PROBLEM MATERIALS

Wilma B. Liebman, *Decline and Disenchantment: Reflections on the Aging of the Aging of the National Labor Relations Board*, 28 BERKELEY J. EMP. & LAB. L. 569 (2007)

The Dunlop Commission on the Future of Worker-Management Relations — Final Report (1995)

Wilma Liebman, *Decline and Disenchantment: Reflections on the Aging of the National Labor Relations Board*
28 BERKELEY J. EMP. & LAB. L. 569 (2007)[1]

I. Introduction

Today, more than seventy years after passage of a law intended to encourage collective bargaining and equalize bargaining power between labor and capital, there is rapidly rising income inequality, and organized labor, as a percentage of the private sector workforce, is at a historic low point.

Various commentators describe the National Labor Relations Act, enacted in 1935 (the Wagner Act), and "essentially unchanged since 1947" (the Taft-Hartley Act amendments), as dead, dying, or at least "largely irrelevant to the contemporary workplace" — a doomed legal dinosaur. In their view, the Act has failed to protect workers' rights to organize and to promote the institution of collective bargaining. Scholars contend that labor law suffers from "ossification." Some even say that it is "contributing to the demise of the very rights it was enacted to protect." Collective action seems "moribund." Supporters of the Act are "in despair." The National Labor Relations Board, charged with administering the Act, is "isolated and politicized." "What went wrong?" and "Can we fix it?" are the questions of the day.

Meanwhile, the Board's case intake has plummeted. Increasingly disillusioned with the law's ability to protect worker rights, labor unions have turned away from the Board, and especially from its representation procedures. This disenchantment has intensified in recent years as the Board, in case after case, has narrowed the

---

statute's coverage, cut back on its protections, and adopted an increasingly formalistic approach to interpreting the law. More and more, unions are seeking to negotiate recognition in the workplace rather than use the Board's election machinery. And, in a historical twist, organized labor has turned increasingly to state and local governments for help in protecting workers, with diminished hope that the federal government can be a guarantor of important rights. Whether labor is right or wrong about the Board makes little difference. In this case, the perception of the law's failure is what matters.

Something has indeed gone wrong. Somewhere along the way, New Deal optimism has yielded to raw deal cynicism about the law's ability to deliver on its promise. The National Labor Relations Act, by virtually all measures, is in decline if not dead. Nor, at least until recently, has there been any real prospect for labor law reform.

In this context, what remains of the Act's original promise to achieve "economic advance and common justice"? Is the NLRB destined to operate on the legal margins of a failed statute? Certainly, the Board operates under significant constraints: a judicial, political, and economic climate indifferent or even hostile to collective bargaining; an arguably antique statute; and a lack of administrative will. Yet I would suggest that the Board, even under the current statutory scheme, can play a modest but meaningful role in preserving the values of this Act and in furthering its aims. Its failure to do even that is an unfortunate lost opportunity.

II.

. . . The story of faded trust in the law unfolded gradually. By 1983, Harvard Law School Professor Paul Weiler lamented that "[c]ontemporary American labor law more and more resembles an elegant tombstone for a dying institution." By then, organized labor was in steady decline. In 1981, President Reagan fired striking air-traffic controllers, a watershed event. The economy was changing dramatically. Foreign trade had begun to surge; technology was beginning to transform ways of communicating and doing business; oil prices were climbing; a major recession had hit the nation; and real wages were stagnating. In collective bargaining, concessions were frequently sought and two-tier wage structures became common.

What followed over the next two decades is familiar. The Cold War ended; technological innovation accelerated; relentless competition, both domestic and global, grabbed the economy; major industries were deregulated; manufacturing declined and the service sector exploded; shifting demographics changed the composition of the workforce; and a fourth wave of immigrants crossed our borders. All of this flux has put severe strains on the collective-bargaining system created by the Act, and on labor and business, both struggling to adapt to and survive in a changing economy.

Through the late 1970s, management's priority in employment practice was to build a stable, loyal workforce. The existing system of labor law was designed with a particular workplace model in mind. This workplace was characterized by a stable contract of hire between a single employer and employees engaged in work of a continuing nature at a fixed location, with hierarchical organization of work and promotion ladders. This model — exemplified by the manufacturing plants of the 1930s and 1940s — is increasingly anachronistic in a post-industrial and fiercely competitive global economy that has led firms to place a premium on flexibility instead of stability in employment patterns. The social contract that governed employment for decades has been broken . . . .

III.

. . . B. How the Board Has Lost Its Way and Its Will

Constrained or not, as an administrative agency responsible for enforcing Congressional policy, the Board does have discretion — indeed, it has a fundamental duty — to "adapt [its] rules and practices to the Nation's needs in a volatile, changing economy." Surely, "the primary function and responsibility of the Board . . . is that of applying the general provisions of the Act to the complexities of industrial life." But today, the perceived obsolescence of the Board is linked in substantial part to its seeming lack of administrative will.

The Board is not only failing to maximize its available discretion, but its recent decisions are marginalizing statutory rights. While any one decision standing alone may not be cataclysmic in impact, viewed together, they represent a pattern of weakening the protections of the Act. Where decisional choices are available to the Board, the choice too often selected narrows statutory coverage or protection. Fewer workers have been afforded fewer rights; employee rights are subordinated to countervailing business interests; meaningful remedies are denied; and recent decisions that tried to update the law have been overruled. Increasingly, the Board has adopted a formalistic approach to interpreting the law, turning away from the real world and the challenges it poses for labor policy. This approach threatens to result in a loss of confidence in the Board's decisionmaking, not simply in terms of the results reached, but also in the way those results are reached . . . .

IV. What Comes Now?

. . . The good news from the past year is that labor law issues have once again entered the public domain. In the summer of 2006, extensive news coverage surrounded the then-expected issuance of the *Oakwood* decision on supervisory status, especially as applied to nurses. Indeed, on July 18, 2006, the Comedy Central cable television network program Colbert Report even included a segment on the issue. And there has been wide coverage of the Employee Free Choice Act, approved by the House of Representatives on March 1, 2007, but filibustered in the Senate. With this publicity, Americans are being educated about the erosion of the right to organize and the danger posed to our society as a consequence, especially in the context of growing income inequality.

The Dunlop Commission on the Future of Worker-Management Relations — Final Report
(1995)

The Role of Unions in Society

The preamble to the National Labor Relations Act declares it to be the policy of the United States to 'encourage the practices and procedure of collective bargaining and [to] protect . . . the exercise by workers of full freedom of association, self-organization and designation of representatives of their own choosing, for the purpose of negotiating the terms and condition of their employment or other mutual aid or protection.'

The Collective Bargaining Forum, a group of leading corporate chief executives and national labor leaders, reflecting on this policy, has stated:

> "The institution of collective bargaining is an integral part of American economic life and has proved capable of helping our society and adjust through periods of prosperity and recession. A democratic society must provide workers with effective rights to join and be represented by unions of their own choosing." New Directions for Labor and Management, The Collective Bargaining Forum, Washington, D.C.: U.S. Department of Labor, 1988.

Unions contribute to the economic health of the nation by 'leveling the field between labor and management,' as Senator Orrin Hatch has stated. 'If you didn't have unions,' Senator Hatch continued, 'it would be very difficult for even enlightened employers to not take advantage of workers on wages and working conditions because of rivals.'. . . . Indeed, as we noted in the Fact Finding Report, and as the President's Council of Economic Advisors also has concluded, the recent decline in the proportion of workers represented by unions has 'contributed to the rise in inequality' in the United States.

Unions likewise contribute to the political health of the nation by providing a legitimate and consistent voice to working people in the broader society. As former Secretary of State George P. Shultz has stated, 'free societies and free trade unions go together.' Societies that lack a vibrant labor movement which will 'really get up on its hind legs and fight about freedom' are sorely wanting.

The import of the worst features of political campaigns into the workplaces by managers and unions creates confrontation and is not conducive to achieving the goals outlined in Section I. The Commission remains persuaded that, as we said in our Fact Finding Report, 'All participants — employees, management, and unions — would benefit from reduction in illegal activity and de-escalation of a conflictual process that seems out of place with the demands of many modern workplaces and the need of workers, their unions, and their employers.'

The Commission cannot hope to do more than propose first steps on the necessary road to achieving a new direction and approach to labor-management relations. The process of change will require a long, sustained effort. But we believe that American society — management, labor, and the general public — does support the principle that workers have the right to make a free, uncoerced and informed choice as to whether to join a union and to engage in collective bargaining. Our recommendations seek to, as we said at the outset, 'turn down the decibel count' and to effectuate this fundamental principle of our democracy . . . .

Established Collective Bargaining Relationships

Not all aspects of collective bargaining are in need of repair. The Fact Finding Report concluded that 'In most workplaces with collective bargaining, the system of labor-management negotiations works well.' Mr. Howard Knicely, speaking for the Labor Policy Association, would elevate this observation to a principal finding: 'collective bargaining where it exists, is working very well.'

The majority of managers and workers with experience under collective bargaining agree with this assessment. Both the Worker Representation and Participation Survey and others before it report that about 90 percent of union members would vote to retain their membership if asked.

Approximately 70 percent rate their experience with their union as good or very good. Sixty-four percent of the managers surveyed agreed that the union in their companies makes the work lives of its members better. When asked how the union relationship affects their companies, managers' views vary considerably. Twenty-seven percent believe the union helps their company's performance; 38 percent believe it hurts performance, and 29 percent believe the union neither helps nor hurts organizational performance. By a two to one margin (32 to 16 percent) managers report that in recent years their relations with unions have become more cooperative rather than confrontational.

In general, though there are notable exceptions, collective bargaining appears to be adapting to its changing economic and social setting. Work stoppages have declined significantly, many grievance procedures are experiencing more settlements through informal discussions or mediation without resort to arbitration. The AFL-CIO's February 1994 report, The New American Workplace: A Labor Perspective . . . is a significant statement endorsing workplace cooperation and labor-management partnerships.

A number of collective bargaining agreements in 1994 extend the frontiers of labor-management partnerships to new issues, new levels of decision-making, and new workers. Among the more notable recent examples are the Levi-Strauss and Amalgamated Clothing and Textile Worker agreement governing manufacturing innovations in union and non-union Facilities and the Bath Iron Works and International Association of Machinists agreement providing for significant restructuring of jobs, training, and pay systems among multiple trades, and the NYNEX and Communications Workers of America agreement that provides for voluntary procedures governing the organizing of new work units and the negotiation and arbitration of initial contracts.

Innovations such as these need to be encouraged and extended to more bargaining relationships. But additional changes will be needed in the attitudes and policies of many labor organizations and managers if the goals of the workplace of the future outlined in Section I are to be achieved. One area in need of greater focus is the responsiveness of workplace practices to the needs of working women. A large scale survey of working women published by the Women's Bureau of the Department of Labor in October 1994 reported that, while most women are breadwinners and many are the sole support of their households, 'they are not getting the pay and benefits commensurate with the work they do, the level of responsibility they hold, or the societal contribution they make.'

. . . Collective bargaining will need to continue to evolve and adapt in the future as the diversity of the workforce increases in terms of gender, race, ethnic background, education, and location of work. The Women's Bureau Survey, the Worker Representation and Participation Survey, and many others document the desire of workers for more say over a wide range of workplace issues as well as a desire for cooperative rather than conflictual processes for addressing their concerns. It is in the national interest to encourage continued growth in the range of issues and workplaces governed by cooperative labor-management partnerships. The Commission believes that existing collective bargaining relationships are progressing in this direction, and considers it important that new bargaining relationships achieve this same level of cooperation and effectiveness as soon as possible.

POST PROBLEM DISCUSSION

1.   Former Chairman Liebman mentions that some commentators believe that the NLRB is hopelessly "isolated and politicized." For more information on how the Board enforces the NLRA and how political affiliation is important to Board Member nominations, see Chapter 2 on the Organization, Procedures, and Jurisdiction of the NLRB. Although Board Members from both political parties appear to be in general agreement on most well-settled Board doctrines there does seem to be politics at play in decisions involving some of the more controversial labor issues. *See* Ronald Turner, *Ideological Voting on the National Labor Relations Board*, 8 U. Pa. J. Lab. & Emp. L. 707, 711 (2006) ("The only claim made in this Article is that ideology has been a persistent and, in many instances, a vote-predictive factor when the Board decides certain legal issues."); Paul M. Secunda, *Politics Not as Usual: Inherently Destructive Conduct, Institutional Collegiality, and the National Labor Relations Board*, 32 Fla. St. U. L. Rev. 51, 53-54 (2004) (arguing that in straightforward cases, the concept of institutional collegiality explains the unusual amount of decisional consistency in Board cases involving the amorphous "inherently destructive" legal standard) (discussed in Chapter 9). To what extent does the at-least-sometimes political nature of the Board make labor law reform less possible? Should Board Members be appointed without regard to their political party affiliation?

2.   Chairman Liebman also points out that unions and their allies are increasingly turning to state government for meaningful workplace remedies in the labor context. Is this a good or bad development? Does your view depend on your historical understanding on what role states and their courts played in the past?

This argument over whether to permit states a greater role in regulating labor law is discussed further in Jeffrey M. Hirsch, *Taking States out of the Workplace*, 117 Yale L.J. Pocket Part 225, 225 (2008), http://yalelawjournal.org/content/view/

659/14/; and Paul M. Secunda & Jeffrey M. Hirsch, *Workplace Federalism*, 157 U. PA. L. REV. PENNumbra 26 (2008), http://www.pennumbra.com/debates/pdfs/WorkplaceFederalism.pdf (debate between Secunda and Hirsch regarding whether the federal government or the states can best protect worker rights). *See also* Paul M. Secunda, *Toward the Viability of State-Based Legislation to Address Workplace Captive Audience Meetings in the United States*, 29 COMP. LAB. L. & POL'Y J. 209, 214 (2008) (arguing for more state authority to prohibit workplace captive audience meetings). One example of a state trying to expand its role in labor law is Oregon's enactment of legislation seeking to keep employers from requiring employees to attend mandatory meetings about their employer's views of unions during a union organizing campaign. In 2010, the Chamber of Commerce sought to invalidate the law on both labor preemption and First Amendment free speech grounds, but a federal district court ruled that the lawsuit was premature because Oregon had not sought to enforce the law at that point. *See Associated Oregon Industries v. Avakian*, No. CV 09-1494-MO (D. Or. May 6, 2010).

For discussion on the limits of state labor law regulation, see Chapter 11, Labor Law Preemption Doctrines.

3.   As of the writing of this casebook, the United States is still dealing with the aftermath of the Great Recession. Does it necessarily follow that bad economic times are bad for unions? Consider this study reported by Nate Silver at the website, http://www.fivethirtyeight.com/2009/09/as-unemployment-rises-support-for.html (Sept. 7, 2009):

> Gallup recently found sympathy toward labor unions is at an all-time low, at 48 percent, but then again, unemployment is close to its post-WWII highs. Gallup did not happen to ask this question in late 1982 or early 1983, when unemployment exceeded 10 percent. They did ask in August 1981, when unemployment was up to 7.4 percent and rising rapidly, and at that point support for labor was at 55 percent, which was the lowest figure it had achieved before this year's survey.

> The regression line finds that, for every point's worth of increase in the unemployment rate, approval of labor unions goes down by 2.6 points. Alternatively, we can add a time trend to the regression model, to account for the fact that participation in labor unions has been declining over time. This softens the relationship slightly, but still implies a decrease in approval of 2.1 points for unions for every point increase in unemployment. Both relationships are highly statistically significant.

So why does support for labor unions go down when the unemployment rate rises? Here are some possibilities:

a.   Fear of Losing Job: "I will lose my job and not be able to find another one, especially in these difficult economic times."

b.   The Blame Game: "It is because of unions and their unreasonable demands for higher wages and benefits that American companies are losing jobs to global competition."

c. We Need More Unions: "The decrease is union support has actually caused higher unemployment rates, not vice versa. If there was more support for unions, we would have a large middle class, greater consumer spending, and more jobs for everyone."

d. We Need More Safety Nets: "Unions have shot themselves in the foot. Rather than working for safety net legislation like their European peers, American unions get blamed by the unemployed for not providing enough help to negotiate this difficult economic climate."

e. Resentment of Unions: "When unemployment is high, the non-unionized working class resent unions for giving their members greater job security while they're left out in the cold."

As you consider the current plight of unions throughout your study of labor law, consider which of these theories (or possibly others) represent the most plausible explanation for unions' continued struggle in America's private sector.

4. If the President were to appoint a new "Dunlop Commission" to recommend labor law reforms, what issues do you think the new commission would have to consider? Are the issues the same as they were almost two decades ago?

5. On the issue of unionization's effect on wage inequality, economists Richard B. Freeman & James L. Medoff observed:

> [U]nion wage policies appear to contribute to the equalization of wages by decreasing the differential between covered blue-collar workers and non-covered white-collar workers. If we add the apparent decrease in inequality due to wage standardization and the apparent decrease due to reduction in the white-collar/blue-collar differential to the apparent increase due to the greater wages of blue-collar union workers, we find that the apparent net effect of unionism is to reduce total wage inequality.

FREEMAN & MEDOFF, WHAT DO UNIONS DO? 55 (1984). How does that argument resonate in today's economic environment?

6. What role does the NLRB have in assuring the continuing relevancy of its own historical mission? Do present trends suggest that the NLRB is playing less of a role with unions and collective bargaining in the United States? Consider the problems outlined by former Chairman Liebman and her outlook for the NLRB's future. Is there a need for a more aggressive NLRB, and if so, what issues should it tackle first? Again, consider these issues as you examine the various aspects of labor law throughout this book.

SECTION 2   A BRIEF OVERVIEW OF THE AMERICAN LABOR MOVEMENT

To help the student fully appreciate American labor law today, it is necessary to consider where labor relations stood in the United States before the modern system. To be clear, this is an area rich in material and could easily be part of a 14-week labor history course. Here, we attempt to cover merely the important points in labor history in summary fashion.

This book will occasionally include film recommendations that provide a different, and possibly more entertaining, way to understand certain material. In that light, a good movie that illustrates the historical context of labor law regulation is *Germinal* (1993), a French film based on a novel by Émile Zola and starring Gérard Depardieu. The film describes the severe conditions in a mid-19th Century coal mining town and the labor uprising that eventually occurs. Although it's a novel and not directly related to American labor law, Zola based the story on his research into coal mining towns and his depiction of the miners' work conditions would sound familiar to American miners of the same period.

A.   The Roots of American Labor Law

Labor law can be conceived of as the struggle among three parties (employees/unions, employers, and the government) vying to control the contours of the employment relationship. Throughout American history, this struggle has often been expressed as a violent confrontation among the parties.

For much of this country's history, what little law of "labor relations" that existed was almost entirely judge-made, largely borrowed from the English common law. As the 19th Century approached, the fighting issue was whether England's common law had extended the doctrine of criminal conspiracy to combinations of workers, and, if so, whether that doctrine should be transported into American law. In the earliest American labor cases, various forms of collective action by workers, such as strikes, were subjected to the doctrine of criminal conspiracy. One question under this doctrine was whether all activities of groups of workers were to be condemned as criminal, regardless of the group's purposes. For instance, employees may have sought only to bargain collectively for themselves or sought workplace solidarity by insisting that employers hire only their members at wages set by the group.

Although many courts of this time utilized the law of criminal conspiracy to deal with "unsavory assemblages" of workers attempting to make their workplaces more bearable, it was no match for the Industrial Revolution in the mid- and late-18th Century, which saw the American economy transform from its reliance, in part, on native-born, highly-skilled craftsman to immigrant, highly compartmentalized, semi-skilled factory workers. Due to the harsh conditions that resulted from the Industrial Revolution — including miniscule wages and abhorrent hours and work conditions — workers sought to gain security through protective workplace legislation, such as new federal maximum hour and minimum wage laws.

In response to these workers demands, a conservative Supreme Court in the early 1900s elevated "freedom of contract" to a constitutional right in *Lochner v. New York*, 198 U.S. 45 (1905) (striking down N.Y. maximum hour law for bakers), and *Adair v. United States*, 208 U.S. 161 (1908) (striking down federal law prohibiting "yellow-dog" contracts).[2] It was not until the 1930s that the Court

---

[2] A "yellow-dog" contract is an employment agreement that prohibits an employee from joining a union. Employers used these contracts to sue unions who tried to organize their workers by claiming that the unions were intentionally interfering with contractual relations.

began to consistently uphold legislation regulating the workplace. *See West Coast Hotel v. Parrish*, 300 U.S. 379 (1937) (upholding Washington minimum wage law for women under the rationale that a state's interest in redressing inferior bargaining power of women outweighed "freedom of contract" — some commentators refer to this case as the "switch in time that saved nine" after Justice Owen Roberts changed sides in this debate); *see also U.S. v. Carolene Products Co.*, 304 U.S. 144, 152 (1938) (making clear a presumption of constitutionality would apply in all economic substantive due process challenges; this case contains the famous footnote 4 and its discussion of heightened review for discrete and insular minorities).

B.   Events Leading up to the Enactment of Modern Labor Laws

Unable to ease the harsh realities of the late 19th Century and early 20th Century workplace through protective legislation, organized labor groups started to engage in economic warfare against the powerful corporations through strikes and other concerted activities. Initially, the Knights of Labor were formed in 1869 as a secret artisan society centered on changing conditions through political activity; however, these skilled workers later formed the American Federation of Labor (AFL) in 1886. Led by Samuel Gompers until his death in 1924, the AFL was one of the first significant labor unions in the American workplace. The AFL focused on economic power, as opposed to political activity, to enlarge the bargaining power of workers against employers in order to ease the burden of industrial employment. This type of unionism was referred to as Bread & Butter unionism, as opposed to the labor movements of Europe which were more socialistic in orientation. By 1914, the AFL had over 2 million members. While the AFL mobilized skilled workers, other groups formed to address the needs of unskilled workers. These groups tended to be more ideologically motivated by communist and socialistic ideologies. Chief among them was the International Workers of the World (IWW), also known as the Wobblies, formed in 1905. With the rise of the labor movement came strikes and labor violence often resulting in employers calling for military help. This social unrest brought to the forefront of debate what has become known as "The Labor Question."

Because of the lack of protective workplace legislation in the early parts of the 20th Century, workers continued to form unions to advance their mutual aim of achieving better working conditions. Yet, employers and their allies on state courts had come to rely on the law of civil conspiracy to undermine the union's collective actions. Employers sought judicial intervention first from state courts and then from federal courts exercising either diversity jurisdiction — developing a body of labor-related federal common law — or subject-matter jurisdiction under the Sherman Antitrust Act.

For instance, in the well-known case of *Vegelahn v. Guntner*, 167 Mass. 92 (1896), a company sought to enjoin union members picketing in front of the company store by arguing the labor combinations were pursuing "unlawful objectives" by "unlawful means," i.e., they were trying to gain equal bargaining strength by threatening to engage in strikes and other collective actions against intransient employers. Although the majority in *Vegelahn* granted the full injunction, Oliver Wendell Holmes, in a famous dissent, presciently recognized that there was an economic war between management and workers, and in order for industrial peace to be assured, workers needed equal bargaining power.

Employers preferred injunctions like those used in *Vegelahn* because they could usually obtain broad orders quickly, often through *ex parte* motions, and without having to take the case before a jury which may be sympathetic to the workers. Other forms of relief included criminal charges and civil liability.

Another weapon used by employers against unions during this time period was the antitrust laws. Initially passed to combat illegal monopolies and trusts, the Sherman Antitrust Act of 1890 was employed by a conservative Supreme Court to enjoin the formation of labor organizations. A famous example of this type of case is *Loewe v. Lawlor*, 208 U.S. 274 (1908). Also known as the *Danbury Hatters* case, it provides a classic example of how the Court sought to hold down worker mobilization. In *Loewe*, the Court found a union's threat not to do business with a non-union hat maker to be a "combination in restraint of trade" in violation of the Sherman Act. Even more significant, the Sherman Act and its treble damages provision allowed companies to take huge judgments against labor organizers, which left them bankrupt and homeless (though their union allies helped raise money for them to pay off the debt). Needless to say, union organizing was discouraged by this aggressive application of antitrust laws.

Not only were there increasing use of civil conspiracy and antitrust laws against union efforts during this time period, but organizing efforts were also marked by widespread turbulence and violence. In one display of the government's use of violence to control labor relations, the Colorado National Guard was called upon to end a coal miners strike in Ludlow, Colorado. On April 20, 1914, Guardsmen set up a machine-gun on a ridge overlooking the strikers' tent encampment. Strikers had been evicted from company housing and had built a tent city to house themselves and their families. A firefight broke out between Guardsmen and miners, and the miners attempted to flank the gun's position. While the battle continued, the Guardsmen burned the tent encampment as they searched for miners. Eleven children and four women hiding in a pit were killed when the tent above them was set on fire. Several miners were found shot to death in the camp. Three agents from the private Baldwin-Felts detective agency,[3] which was hired by the mine owner, were also killed in what came to be known as the Ludlow Massacre. Eventually President Wilson sent in federal troops to disarm both sides and stop the bloodshed.

Action favorable to the interests of workers and organized labor, however, did occur during the period leading up to World War I, at both federal and state levels. For example, in 1914, Congress enacted the landmark Clayton Antitrust Act, which sought to revise hostile judge-made law by declaring generally that unions were not to be regarded as illegal combinations in restraint of trade, and by imposing

---

[3] At this time, employers frequently hired private detective agencies to act as "union busters." The most well know of these was the Pinkerton National Detective Agency (which is still in operation as Pinkerton Government Services, Inc.). "Pinkertons" frequently infiltrated unions and were involved in many of the most infamous and violent labor battles in the early 20th Century.

what appeared to be substantial restrictions on the issuance of labor injunctions. Nevertheless, restrictive interpretation of this legislation by the Supreme Court disappointed labor unions, which had expected more freedom from court injunctions and relief from antitrust suits.

For instance, in *Duplex Printing Press Co. v. Deering*, 254 U.S. 443 (1921), the Supreme Court greatly undermined unions' ability to organize and exert pressure on employers by limiting the terms of the Clayton Act to union actions that were "proximately and substantially" concerned with a party to the labor dispute. Thus, under *Duplex Printing*, workers at another facility or another employer could not support another union's strike, making it more difficult for the striking union to have the desired economic effect on the employer. In dissent, Justice Brandeis famously stated that the purpose of the Clayton Act was to equalize before the law the position of workingmen and employer as "industrial combatants."

Comparable state protective enactments proved more lasting, including legislation dealing with child labor, women's hours, workers' compensation systems, and minimum wage obligations. And another clear benefit realized by the labor movement in this World War I period was the National War Labor Board's legitimization of unionization by recognizing "the rights of workers to organize in trade unions and to bargain collectively through chosen representatives." Even though this affirmation of organizational and collective-bargaining rights was not formally carried forward after the Great War, it survived in the railroad industry, and the idea shaped the national labor policy legislated a decade later during the Great Depression.

In the wartime years, union membership growth remained concentrated in the skilled or craft trades; large numbers of unskilled workers were yet to be organized, especially in such heavy industries as steel. There were several factors involved with the dearth of unskilled organizing, including the usual forms of employer resistance. In addition, the overall prosperity in the 1920s generated by increased productivity made possible a general lift in wages and a reduction in the standard workweek, which for many employees lessened the need for unions. Also, employers' greater attention to such workplace benefits as insurance and profit sharing plans, and to programs for involving workers in decisions about conditions in the workplace ("employee councils" or "committees"), encouraged unorganized workers to shun organization. Finally, at least some of the explanation for labor's setbacks during this period can be attributed to the unions themselves, such as the graft and corruption that tainted some unions. This was part of a broader problem that arose as unions moved away from a volunteer-based model to one that gave more centralized power to full-time union officials, who did not always use their power to promote working class interests or solidarity.

C. The First Attempts at Federal Labor Legislation

Despite these setbacks, the 1920s and 1930s marked the pinnacle of federal legislative success for unions in the United States.

The Railway Labor Act of 1926, 45 U.S.C. §§ 151-188 (RLA) was agreed upon in advance by railroads and unions, with Congress making only minor changes (today the RLA also applies to airlines). The emphasis of the RLA was the peaceful settlement of labor disputes because of the strategic importance of the transportation industry. In order to achieve peaceful settlements, the RLA set-up adjustment boards, grievance procedures, and mediation procedures. We will note throughout this book the many similarities, and important differences, between interpretations of the RLA and the NLRA.

As a result of *Duplex Printing*, by the 1920s labor unions were being besieged by injunctions brought under civil conspiracy and antitrust laws. But by the 1930s, there was a growing opposition in Congress to the intervention of the federal courts into labor disputes.

Congress's response was the Norris-LaGuardia Act of 1932, 29 U.S.C. §§ 101-115, which generally prevented federal courts from enjoining nonviolent union activity and from enforcing yellow-dog contracts. Norris-LaGuardia later served as the model for a number of state anti-injunction acts, so-called baby Norris-LaGuardia acts, which have exceptions for state injunctions including the seizure of property (also called mass picketing). Those in support of eliminating federal court intervention in labor disputes made the following points:

> *Substantive Considerations* — the granting or denial of an injunction bore no relation to the merits of the underlying labor dispute.

> *Procedural Objections* — *ex parte* restraining orders, based only on the employer's side of the case, at least temporarily broke strikes and halted unions' ability to exert economic pressure.

> *Considerations of Judicial Administration* — because labor disputes turned on questions of social and economic policy, these disputes were more suitable for legislative rather than judicial determination.

A key provision of the Norris-LaGuardia Act was Section 2, which provides a broad declaration of the need to protect workers' ability to join unions, pursue collective bargaining, and resort to concerted activities. Section 2 was an important precursor to Section 7 of the NLRA.

In *United States v. Hutcheson*, 312 U.S. 219 (1941), the U.S. Supreme Court narrowed the application of the Sherman Act even further through an expanded interpretation of the Norris-LaGuardia Act. The machinist union in *Hutcheson* went on strike and boycotted Anheuser-Bush's products after the company hired members of the carpenters union. The Court found the union activity was protected under the Norris-LaGuardia Act because that Act removed federal courts' power to enjoin several types of union activity that are related to "labor dispute[s]," including strikes. The Court also made clear that judicial intervention was not needed when unions act in their self-interest and do not combine with other unions. Much later, in *Jacksonville Bulk Terminals, Inc. v. International Longshoremen's Association*, 457 U.S. 702 (1982), the Court held that the definition of "labor dispute" should be interpreted broadly to apply to politically motivated work stoppages.

D. Modern Day Labor Legislation

The National Labor Relations Act or Wagner Act of 1935 (NLRA), 29 U.S.C. §§ 151-169, had a tremendous impact on unionism thanks in large part to its active encouragement of unionization and collective bargaining. For example, in 1933, there were 3 million unionized workers, but by 1942, a mere nine years later, there were over 12 million.

Section 1[4] of the NLRA builds on the theme established in the Norris-LaGuardia Act that the legislature is in a better position to reduce industrial strife than the judiciary. As a result, Section 1 provides that the NLRA's aim is to reduce industrial strife and promote the flow of commerce by creating a structure that provides for the "friendly adjustment of industrial disputes." By encouraging collective bargaining and unionization, the Act looks to "restor[e] equality of bargaining power between employers and employees." The full Section 1 is well worth a read, as its explicit and strong promotion of collective representation and labor rights may come as a surprise to you.

The heart of the Wagner Act is Section 7, which provides employees with three distinct statutory rights: 1) to organize; 2) to bargain collectively through a representative of their own choosing; and 3) to engage in concerted activities for mutual aid and protection (e.g., pickets, boycotts, and strikes, which are also protected by Section 13). Section 8 was the NLRA's enforcement section and it prohibited certain unfair labor practices (ULPs) by employers, which violated employees' Section 7 rights. For instance, Section 8(1) outlawed employer coercion of employees who exercised their Section 7 rights or employer interference with the exercise of those rights; Section 8(2) outlawed company unions (i.e., unions dominated or assisted by employers); Section 8(3) forbade discrimination against an employee with the intent to encourage or discourage union membership; and Section 8(5) required employers to bargain in good faith with representatives of their employees' choosing.[5] Any violation of these provisions constitutes a ULP, which were ruled on by the NLRB and enforced through the federal appellate courts. The Board, in turn, was created under Sections 3 & 4 of the Act. The procedures the Board must follow are set forth in Section 10, whereby the Board acted as both the prosecutor and the judge. Under Section 9, Congress set forth the basic provisions for selecting and designating an employee representative by a union, including the process of the Board-run election. See Chapter 2 for more discussion of the NLRB's operations.

The Wagner Act was a conscious, carefully thought out program for minimizing labor disputes without undue sacrifice of personal and economic freedom. Characteristics of the Wagner Act include: 1) concern primarily with organizational phase of labor relations, not the post-organizational phase; 2) concern exclusively with employer wrongdoing, not union wrongdoing — which were addressed in the Taft-Hartley Amendments of 1947; and 3) leaving substantive provisions of

---

[4] As is the practice in labor law, this book will refer to the NLRA's sections rather than the formal U.S. Code citations. To obtain those citations, just remember that Section 1 of the NLRA is found at 29 U.S.C. § 151, Section 7 is at 29 U.S.C. § 157, Section 8 is at 29 U.S.C. § 158, and so on.

[5] As noted below, these provisions are now Sections 8(a)(1), 8(a)(2), 8(a)(3), and 8(a)(5) of the NLRA.

collective contracts to private negotiation between the parties.

In *NLRB v. Jones & Laughlin Steel Corp.*, 301 U.S. 1 (1937), the Court upheld the constitutionality of the NLRA based on an expansive view of Congress's power under the federal Constitution's Commerce Clause to regulate the manufacturing sector of the economy.

Along with the enactment of the Wagner Act, the 1930s' second major labor development, a breakthrough from within the union movement, was the formation of the Congress of Industrial Organizations (CIO) and the emergence of the large industrial union. The American Federation of Labor (AFL), primarily made up of skilled craftsmen unions, had earlier formed, and chartered, local industrial unions in some industries (e.g., automobiles and rubber), affiliating them with the AFL rather than existing national unions. Because these AFL locals aimed to achieve "wall to wall" bargaining rights for all workers in the plants involved, there was conflict with the organizing claims of both the established craft unions and the established industrial unions, such as the United Mine Workers (UMW) headed by John L. Lewis. When the AFL, in convention in 1935, took the side of the craft unions, Lewis led the industrial unionists into the formation of the Committee for Industrial Organization (later changed to the Congress of Industrial Organizations), which, in competition with the AFL, operated as a rival federation until the AFL-CIO merger in 1955.

The conclusion of World War II was followed by a wave of strikes affecting many of the nation's important industries. In 1946, the federal government took dramatic action to end the damaging strikes in coal and railroads, including seizure of mines and the imposition of fines on John L. Lewis and the UMW for violating a court injunction. (The story is told in *United States v. United Mine Workers of America*, 330 U.S. 258 (1947).) These widespread strikes during the postwar reconversion period contributed to the growing belief that there was need to curb the power of organized labor. Congress acted to do just that in the Taft-Hartley Act of 1947, over the veto of President Truman. Taft-Hartley, formally entitled the Labor Management Relations Act (LMRA), 29 U.S.C. §§ 141–187, made major additions to the original Wagner Act, a number of which sought to restrict certain union economic weapons.

The Taft-Hartley Act started from the premise that the Wagner Act was too union-friendly, finding many union abuses had occurred since the passage of the Wagner Act. These alleged abuses included: 1) strikes that threatened public health and safety, such as in coal mines and public utility industries; 2) unions being used as vehicles for racketeering; 3) violence involved with strikes and picketing; 4) high union membership fees; 5) increased jurisdictional disputes among unions; 6) increased use of the secondary boycott by unions to ensnare neutral employers in labor disputes; and 7) increased abuse of closed and union shops contracts that required workers immediately (closed shop), or soon thereafter (union shop), to become member of the union if they wanted to work for employers with these types of union security arrangements.

In addition to these abuses, Congress appeared to fear powerful labor bosses such as John L. Lewis of the United Mine Workers, who seemed to have the ability and the will to throw the country's economy into chaos every time they called a strike. As a result, the Taft-Hartley Act instituted changes that made federal labor law less encouraging to unionism and the government more neutral. "Employee free choice" became the buzz words. Nevertheless, union numbers continued to increase for a significant period of time after Taft-Hartley.

So what were the major features of this legislation?:

1. Taft-Hartley abandoned the notion that courts had no role to play in deciding labor disputes; as a result, the Act revived the labor injunction in a modified and restricted form under Sections 10(j) and 10(l) of the Act — basically to allow for preliminary court enforcement of an NLRB order.

2. Section 8(b) outlawed union abuses including violence and intimidation; secondary boycotts; strikes to compel an employer to commit an unfair labor practice, such as discharging an employee for not belonging to a union; and jurisdictional strikes over work assignments. Employer ULPs were re-labeled under Section 8(a).

3. Marked a period of significant change in the government's attitude toward unions, which no longer encouraged unionization, instead allowing the government to stand in the center of a labor dispute. Section 7 was also modified to give employees the right to refrain from organizing, collective bargaining, and engaging in concerted activities for mutual aid and protection.

4. Taft-Hartley ratified the NLRB's regulation of collective bargaining, extended government regulation of collective bargaining, and imposed a new duty to bargain in good faith on unions. Section 8(d) regulated the renewal or reopening of collective bargaining agreements; Section 8(a)(3) outlawed the closed shop and permited only limited forms of the union shop; and Section 14(b) afforded individual states the right to outlaw any union security agreement, such as agency-shop provisions. Currently, there are twenty-four so called "right-to-work" states.

5. Taft-Hartley added new sections completely separate from the existing Wagner Act, including provisions allowing parties to sue over collective-bargaining agreements in federal court (Section 301), providing regulations for union trust funds (Section 302), and providing for damages in federal court for unlawful secondary boycotts by unions (Section 303).

In addition to the passage of Taft-Hartley in 1947, congressional investigations ("the McClennan Committee") of corruption and other misconduct in some unions were undertaken soon after the AFL-CIO merger. The disclosures that resulted were a major news item in the 1950s. The AFL-CIO took immediate steps toward self-regulation, including the adoption of codes on conflicts of interest and various forms of misconduct. Acting pursuant to this authority, it expelled three unions in 1957, including its largest affiliate, the Teamsters. The move against the Teamsters stemmed from that union's refusal to oust its president, James Hoffa, who had become a controversial figure. These actions cost the AFL-CIO a million and a half members and untold annual revenues. The growth of the Teamsters, with Hoffa remaining in power, continued at a rate faster than that of the AFL-CIO.

The principal consequence of the congressional investigations in the 1950s was the enactment, in 1959, of the Landrum-Griffin Act (also called Labor Management Reporting and Disclosure Act (LMRDA) 29 U.S.C. §§ 401-531, a first-time entry by the federal government into comprehensive regulation of internal union affairs.

Because the Landrum-Griffin Act deals generally with internal union affairs, it is not a major subject of this introductory course. Nevertheless, the student should know that the LMRDA requires union elections to be held periodically for local and national unions' officers. It also assures union members the right to vote, to run for union office, to comment upon and nominate candidates, to attend membership meetings, and to participate and vote at such meetings. Unions must also file extensive information with the Department of Labor on the financial affairs of the union and its officers. Further, it prohibits both the embezzlement of union funds and the making of loans of certain amounts by a union to its officials.

More relevant to this course, the Landrum-Griffin Act placed substantial limitations on the ability of union to picket for the purposes of organizing workers or obtaining recognition from the employer under Section 8(b)(7) of the NLRA. It also allows workers replaced in the course of an economic strike to vote in union elections.

E.   The Global Workplace, Intra-Union Disputes, and Present Day Attacks of Unions

From the 1960s forward to the present, unions' influence and power has been waning. The union density rate (i.e., the percentage of workers who are members of unions) which had at one time been between 31 to 35 percent dropped to 24 percent by 1979. It has decreased continuously since that period and, by 2011, stood at just under 12 percent of the nonagricultural workforce (some 17 million workers were union members, and perhaps an additional two million wage and salary workers were represented by unions). The union membership rate for private-sector industry workers in 2011 was 6.9 percent, while public-sector workers (who are not covered by the NLRA) weighed in at a substantially higher 37 percent rate. *See* Barry T. Hirsch & David A. Macpherson, *Union Membership and Coverage Database* (2011), www.unionstats.com. Indeed, in the last couple of decades, unions have achieved their principal organizing successes in the governmental sector (federal, state, and local).

Numerous reasons have been offered to explain the fall in union membership. Consider this passage from Chairman Leibman's article excerpted above:

> Various commentators describe the National Labor Relations Act . . . as dead, dying, or at least "largely irrelevant to the contemporary workplace" — a doomed legal dinosaur. In their view, the Act has failed to protect workers' rights to organize and to promote the institution of collective bargaining. Scholars contend that labor law suffers from "ossification." Some even say that it is "contributing to the demise of the very rights it was enacted to protect." Collective action seems "moribund." Supporters of the Act are "in despair." The National Labor Relations Board, charged with administering the Act, is "isolated and politicized." "What went wrong?"

and "Can we fix it?" are the questions of the day.

Meanwhile, the Board's case intake has plummeted. Increasingly disillusioned with the law's ability to protect worker rights, labor unions have turned away from the Board, and especially from its representation procedures. This disenchantment has intensified in recent years as the Board, in case after case, has narrowed the statute's coverage, cut back on its protections, and adopted an increasingly formalistic approach to interpreting the law. More and more, unions are seeking to negotiate recognition in the workplace rather than use the Board's election machinery. And, in a historical twist, organized labor has turned increasingly to state and local governments for help in protecting workers, with diminished hope that the federal government can be a guarantor of important rights. Whether labor is right or wrong about the Board makes little difference. In this case, the perception of the law's failure is what matters.

Of course, many domestic jobs in the auto industry, steel industry, and countless other industries, have simply vanished because of global competition and the relocation of this work to the "Global South," i.e., unorganized parts of this country and other countries. The ascendant numbers of undocumented workers in this country, as well as the ever-expanding contingent workforce of part-time and leased workers, have also not helped matters for unions.

There has also been a transformation of the American economy more generally in the new millennium. The blue-collar, manufacturing jobs that used to dominate the national economy given way to white-collar, service industries. Moreover, as this book is being published, the country is just beginning to come out of the Great Recession where millions of jobs have been lost and the unemployment rate hovers near 8%. Rather than worry about good, unionized jobs, workers are worried about having jobs, period.

One of the ironic consequences of these new economic realities is that many unionized newspaper workers have lost their jobs as their companies have lost revenue in the Age of the Internet. As a result, the media coverage of labor disputes and labor issues generally has been forced to the back pages or into smaller print on news websites, if it exists at all. It is important to note that while union density has declined and the media coverage of labor disputes has also waned (with many major newspaper no longer having a designated labor reporter), significant labor disputes continue to this day. Major strikes in the last two decades have dramatically impacted employment relationships in certain industries and at times have changed the very industry itself. *See, e.g.*, the Justice for Janitors social movement which started in 1985; the Detroit News strike (lasted 583 days from 1995 to 1997 with union losing its battle and only 200 out of 2500 strikers being recalled to work and 1400 strikers permanently replaced); and the 2002 West Coast Port Strike (federal judge ordered an injunction under the emergency powers of the Taft-Hartley Act to end lockout of about 10,500 union workers at U.S. West Coast ports).

Because labor unrest is often described in terms of the different adversarial parties, it is easy to conceive of employers, government, and unions each being as monolithic or unified in their ideology. However, this is not the case. An example of intra-party dispute occurred in 2005 when four unions split from the AFL–CIO to form their own labor federation, Change to Win. The Change to Win/AFL-CIO split was motivated by very different interpretations of why organized labor was losing member density and what to do about it. AFL-CIO unions largely saw the failure of union organizing campaigns as the result of a changed legal landscape that made organizing success less likely. This prompted the AFL-CIO to favor expenditures on lobbying over organizing. Change to Win unions, while acknowledging legal impediments to widespread organizing success, felt that the legal framework would best be overcome, if not changed, by large-scale unionization.

These differences also prompted divergent representation strategies by the two groups. Change to Win unions not surprisingly advocated very aggressive organizing models which in practice favored new unit formation to enhance union density over servicing of the union contract. AFL-CIO unions, while supportive of new organizing initiatives, wanted to spend a greater proportion of union time and money on servicing existing contracts to prevent loss of existent member density. As of the writing of this book, it still remains to be seen whether the conflicted organizations can mend their differences.

In the meantime, new attacks again the labor movement have been mounted by corporate and conservative forces in the United States. In 2011, Wisconsin's Act 10 stripped most public-sector unions in that state of their collective-bargaining rights. But not before over 100,000 thousand Wisconsinites took to the streets in front of the Capitol in Madison protesting the bill. Similar anti-public union legislative efforts were undertaken in Ohio, Michigan, Indiana, and New Jersey.

On the private-sector side, 2011 marked a bitter battle between the NLRB and Republicans in Congress over the NLRB General Counsel's decision to pursue a case against Boeing Corp. for moving work from Washington State to South Carolina. The General Counsel alleged that the work was moved from the union facility in Washington to a non-union shop in South Carolina in retaliation for previous strikes by the Machinist Union. Before the dispute was finally settled by the parties, Republicans in Congress attempted to interfere with the ongoing investigation through document requests, threats to hold the General Counsel in contempt when he did not comply, and introduction of a number of pieces of legislation that would have either defunded the NLRB or would have completely eliminated it.

To say that labor law in the United States has reached a defining moment in 2012 is not in any way an overstatement.

SECTION 3 UNIONIZATION AND COLLECTIVE BARGAINING: JUSTIFICATION AND CRITIQUE

In this American age of individual rights and social entitlement programs, it may be hard to recall what brought about the ideas that led to the enactment of the Wagner Act some seventy-five years ago. As you review some of the writings below, consider whether these same issues still remain today and whether labor law needs to be merely reformed to meet some of these new challenges or whether a more radical transformation of American labor relations law is required.

PROBLEM #2: SHOULD I SEEK UNIONIZATION?

Blake Carney lives in a rural area of North Carolina and works in a large textile mill, S.J. Cotton, that her family had worked at for as long as she could remember. The working conditions are awful. There is cotton dust in the air, the machines are so loud that they can cause hearing loss, and employees are not even able to get to the bathroom during their shifts. On a more personal level, Blake's mother works in the same textile plant and appears to have suffered substantial hearing loss and his father, also a plant worker, has been suffering from severe chest pains.

Alan Carr is an organizer for the Textile Workers Union of America and would like nothing better than to organize the S.J. Cotton textile workers in this part of North Carolina. The company has faced numerous union organizational campaigns over the years, and through both fair and foul methods, it has been able to keep the union out of its facility. Alan is hoping to find conscientious textile workers who will help him to organize this S.J. Cotton facility from the inside out.

1. What are the advantages for Blake if he decides to work with Alan to bring the Union into the textile mill?

2. What are the disadvantages?

3. Will Blake be able to argue that the union could provide benefits to both the company and the workers?

PROBLEM MATERIALS

Movie, *Norma Rae* (1979) (story involving the struggle to unionize a textile mill in North Carolina)

POST PROBLEM DISCUSSION

1. While some economists claim that unions are a net positive, and add to social welfare, others reach the conclusion that unions act as "monopolists" of labor, and are inefficient. In a well-known book, two economists, Professors Freeman and Medoff, have maintained that unions improve society. *See* RICHARD B. FREEMAN & JAMES L. MEDOFF, WHAT DO UNIONS DO? (1984); *see also* Richard B. Freeman & James L. Medoff, *The Two Faces of Unionism?*, 57 THE PUBLIC INTEREST 69 (1979). Rather than view unions as organizations whose primary concern is to exert monopolistic power to increase wages, Freeman and Medoff argue that unions provide a broader basket of service to its members that creates value for both workers and society at large. For example, not only do unions secure fair wage rates, but they can also provide job security, due process via a grievance and arbitration system, a means for employees to provide input at work, and political participation outside the workplace. Taking all of these services into consideration, Freeman and Medoff conclude that unions offer benefits that are socially desirable. Moreover, they also claim that under ideal circumstances "unionism can be a significant plus that improves managerial efficiency" of the company.

2. Other economists and jurists, however, have questioned the conclusions reached by Freeman and Medoff. For instance, Judge Richard Posner, has written:

It is inconsistent with the fundamental assumption of economics: that people, in this case employers, are rational profit or utility maximizers. . . . If granting his employees tenure will increase their productivity, the rational employer will do so, for this will reduce his costs of production. Even if the whole productivity gain is paid to the employee in the form of a higher wage, the employer will be better off. He will have lower total costs than his competitors and will therefore be able to expand his output relative to theirs and increase his profits. . . . [Also,] for every older worker whom job security encourages to share his knowhow, casual observation suggests that there is at least one other older worker, and probably several, whom job security protects at the expense of a more efficient younger worker. Most important of all, for many generations now employers have expended substantial resources to prevent unionization of their plants expenditures that would be irrational if it were true that unions enhanced labor productivity. Such *persistent* irrationality by American businessmen is very hard to credit, but it is a proposition entailed by the productivity enhancement theory of unionization.

See Richard Posner, *Some Economics of Labor Law*, 51 U. Chi. L. Rev. 988, 1000-1002 (1984).

3.   Taking a different tact, Professor Cynthia Estlund observes:

As long as it remains feasible for a firm to remain nonunion, to de-unionize, or to relegate unions to a shrinking base of operations within the firm, managers have little motivation to make the great leap from the familiar ground of managerial prerogatives and mistrust toward unions to the unfamiliar ground of joint decision-making and mutual trust. And as long as few managers have made that leap, it is hard for unions to demonstrate their ability and willingness to serve as productive partners.

Cynthia Estlund, *The Ossification of American Labor Law*, 102 Colum. L. Rev. 1527, 1596 n. 296 (2002).

4.   What are the best arguments that Posner makes about why unions do not make employers better off? What would be a possible response to his argument? Similarly, what is the best argument Freedman & Medoff make about why unions are a productivity-enhancing feature of the workplace? How does Posner seek to undermine their premises?

What responses are there to the problems Estlund outlines? What types of law or regulations could be passed to make it harder for firms to remain non-union or de-unionize? How do we give managers the incentive to take the risk of sharing decision-making responsibilities with a union? Keep considering all of these questions as you study the materials in the rest of this book.

Chapter 2

THE ORGANIZATION, PROCEDURES, AND JURISDICTION OF THE NLRB

Before examining the substance of NLRA law, it is important to consider how the statute is enforced. That inquiry focuses on the agency with primary responsibility for interpreting and enforcing the NLRA: the National Labor Relations Board (NLRB or Board). The NLRB is an independent agency that operates in an unusual fashion. As discussed below, most of the NLRB's policymaking occurs through adjudication — an approach that helps explain much of the Board's organization and operations.

SECTION 1   THE NLRB'S ORGANIZATIONAL STRUCTURE

The NLRB is a relatively old agency, having started in 1935 at the height of the New Deal. This fact, in combination with the lack of substantive updates to the NLRA in over 50 years, makes the NLRB look unusual compared to most other independent agencies. In particular, the NLRB's method of enforcing the statute under its purview is much different than most agencies'. What you might be used to seeing from agencies like the Environmental Protection Agency or the Department of Labor are the promulgation of regulations that flesh out various aspects of the statutes the agencies are entrusted by Congress to enforce. These agencies may also engage in adjudication to enforce those rules, but most policy decisions come from published regulations. In contrast, the NLRB largely takes the opposite approach; although it issues regulations on occasion, most of its work is done through adjudication. *See NLRB v. Bell Aerospace Co.*, 416 U.S. 267, 294 (1974) (approving the NLRB's use of adjudicatory policymaking); Samuel Estreicher, *Policy Oscillation at the Labor Board: A Plea for Rulemaking*, 37 Admin. L. Rev. 163 (1985). The structure and operations of the NLRB reflects this reliance on adjudicatory policymaking.

The NLRB is divided into three basic parts: the NLRB members and their staffs, the Office of General Counsel, and the Division of Judges. These parts can be categorized as an investigatory and prosecutorial section (the Office of General Counsel) and two levels of adjudication (the NLRB members and the Division of Judges). In particular, the General Counsel investigates and prosecutes cases that are decided first by an administrative law judge ("ALJ") from the Division of Judges and then by the NLRB members. The final two levels of review are the federal appellate courts and the Supreme Court.

You might be curious how a single agency can act as both the prosecutor and judge in cases brought under the NLRA. One analogy, albeit an imperfect one, is a criminal prosecution in which the police and prosecutors who investigate and bring cases, and the judges who oversee or decide the cases, are all officials in the same government. Like these players in a criminal matter, the three parts of the NLRB are all independent of each other.

A.   Office of General Counsel

The Office of General Counsel is headed by a single General Counsel who, since 1947, is appointed by the President and needs Senate confirmation to serve a full four-year term. When, as has frequently been the case in recent years, an appointee is unable to obtain Senate confirmation, the President can either make a recess appointment or designate an individual under the Federal Vacancies Act as the "Acting General Counsel."[1] In both of these cases, the General Counsel will be able to serve only until the end of the current congressional session. Although there is only a single General Counsel, the employees under him or her make up the bulk of the agency's workforce. This is primarily because of the number of employees who work in various offices throughout the country. These 32 "regional offices," along with a handful of smaller "resident offices" that operate under the supervision of a regional office, do most of the Office of General Counsel's work.[2]

The work of the regional offices reflects the two primary types of matters that the NLRB handles: representational issues and unfair labor practice cases. For the most part, "representational issues" refers to running elections. As described in more detail in Section 2.02(A), when a union files a valid petition for an election, the regional office is the entity that receives the petition and holds the election. Among the tasks associated with running an election are: resolving any pre-and post-election disputes; determining the location and time of the election; ensuring that informational notices are posted; and overseeing the actual voting and counting of ballots. A similar process exists when there is a "decertification" election — that is, an election to determine whether an incumbent union will remain as the collective-bargaining representative. After the regional office has finished running the election and issued findings regarding any disputes, appeals of those decisions go to the NLRB members.

As described below, parties also file unfair labor practice charges with the relevant regional office. Employees at the regional office then investigate a charge and, if it is found to be meritorious, the region issues an unfair labor practice complaint. Regional attorneys then act as the prosecutor for the case as it is litigated before an ALJ and the NLRB. Attorneys in a different office, the

---

[1] Since 1971, there have been 19 separate General Counsel terms (a few of which were held by the same individual at different times). Of those terms, 15 were recess or acting appointments, and 8 of those terms lasted for approximately 6 months or less. *See* National Labor Relations Board, *General Counsels Since 1935*, https://www.nlrb.gov/who-we-are/general-counsel/general-counsels-1935.

[2] For a list of all Regional and Resident Offices, see https://www.nlrb.gov/who-we-are/regional-offices.

Appellate and Supreme Court Litigation Branch, which is located at NLRB headquarters in Washington, D.C., handle the case if it goes to a federal circuit court or is the subject of a certiorari petition at the Supreme Court. If the Supreme Court hears an NLRB case, the Solicitor General's Office generally handles the litigation, albeit with input from NLRB attorneys.[3]

B. Division of Judges

The Division of Judges is made up of 40 ALJs (previously called "Trial Examiners") who conduct unfair labor practice proceedings in various places across the county. These hearings are very similar to trials, with the General Counsel's attorney, the alleged unfair labor practice perpetrator, and often a representative of the alleged victims (for instance, a union attorney) litigating the case. Like a trial, there are witnesses and evidence, which the ALJ uses to issue a recommended decision and order. These decisions state an ALJ's belief about what happened; whether unfair labor practices occurred; and what the remedies, if any, should be. The NLRB members often adopt ALJs' recommended decisions, especially their factual determinations, but the NLRB does not have to give any deference to ALJs' conclusions.

ALJs act independently of each other, and of the NLRB members and General Counsel. *See* 5 U.S.C. § 554(d) (Administrative Procedure Act). Indeed, ALJs are hired outside of the NLRB; they are hired through another agency, the Office of Personnel Management, and assigned to the NLRB. Moreover, the NLRB cannot assign cases to particular ALJs. *See generally NLRB v. Permanent Label Corp.*, 657 F.2d 512, 527-28 (3d Cir. 1981) (discussing independence of NLRB ALJs).

C. NLRB Members

The NLRB (or "Board-side" as it is often referred to within the agency) consists of the NLRB members and their staffs. When at full strength, the NLRB has five members. By tradition, three members are designated as appointees of the party that controls the White House, and the other two members come from the other party. As you will see throughout the semester, one of the ramifications of this system is that the NLRB often flip-flops back and forth on contentious issues as control of the White House changes.

Both the NLRB and appellate courts hear most cases in three-person panels but, similar to most courts' en banc process, all of the NLRB members will decide especially important cases. Like judges, NLRB members are presidential appointees. However, unlike Article III judges' lifetime appointments, NLRB members are supposed to serve five-year terms. NLRB members can have longer tenures if they are appointed to additional terms. Each NLRB member is

---

[3] Several decades ago, before the Supreme Court substantially reduced the number of cases it hears, thereby prompting the Solicitor General's Office to argue more agency cases, the NLRB litigated its own Supreme Court cases. Indeed, the NLRB's long-time Supreme Court litigator, Norton Come, argued the second-most cases before the Court (56) of any government attorney — a particularly impressive feat for an attorney who did not work in the Solicitor General's office. *See Longtime NLRB Official Dies*, DAILY LAB. REP. (BNA) No. 53, at A-9 (Mar. 19, 2002).

appointed to a specific seat which has its own term; the terms are staggered so that, if everything works as it was intended, only one seat would change each year.

Recently, the reality of NLRB appointments have not been close to this intent. The main problem has been an increased politicization of NLRB nominations over the last few decades. Often acrimonious political maneuvering has resulted in many nominations being delayed or abandoned. Even when the Senate does confirm a nominee, it often occurs only as part of package with other NLRB nominees. The frequent result is that multiple NLRB members start at the same time, although each will have terms that expire on different dates. *See* NLRB, Members of the NLRB Since 1935 (showing each identified seat and every past and current Member), *available at* https://www.nlrb.gov/members-nlrb-1935.

This system has been problematic for the NLRB's operation. It is now typical to have an NLRB with fewer than five members. *See id.* The lack of all five members not only deprives the NLRB of its intended level of experience and policymaking deliberations, it also increases delay as the Board has fewer members to do the same amount of work. This problem becomes critical when the NLRB falls to fewer than three members. Under a 2010 Supreme Court decision, the NLRB is unable to issue decisions if it lacks its quorum of at least three members. *See New Process Steel, LP v. NLRB*, 130 S. Ct. 2635 (2010) (not addressing special circumstances such as one NLRB member dying after deliberations on a case have begun). The *New Process* case arose when the NLRB, on the eve of several members' terms expiring, delegated authority to the two remaining members. Those remaining members issued almost 600 decisions during the 27 months before new members were appointed. Following a circuit split on the issue, the Supreme Court ultimately decided that the NLRB's power to delegate decision-making authority to panels of fewer than five members did not permit indefinite delegation to a panel that lacked three members. This means that the political inability to confirm members can prevent the NLRB from issuing decisions, and possibly a few other agency functions.

On January 3, 2012, the NLRB again fell to only two members. This time, however, the lack of quorum did not last long because the next day President Obama made three recess appointments; the NLRB officially returned to full strength several days later when the new members were sworn into office. Recess appointments occur when the Senate is in recess and require no Senate confirmation. However, recess appointees can serve only until the end of the current legislative year. These appointments have become increasingly common, but the January 2012 appointments were especially contentious because of the surrounding circumstances. The year and a half prior to the recess appointments was a tumultuous one for the NLRB, as it was a frequent target of Republicans politicians, particularly after the General Counsel issued an unfair labor practice complaint against Boeing (see Problem #2 in Chapter 3). This was part of a trend in which various labor issues had become highly politicized. Particularly noteworthy examples were new restrictions against public-sector bargaining in Wisconsin and other states, and the Employee Free Choice Act which, as discussed below, would have made it easier for employees to unionize. In other words, Obama had about the same chance of getting his NLRB nominees confirmed by a Senate in which Republicans were capable of filibustering any nominee as he did of winning the

Republican presidential primaries that year. Rather than allow the NLRB to fall to only two members, Obama appointed two Democrats and one Republican to the NLRB (the Republican, Terrence Flynn, has since resigned following an NLRB Inspector General report finding that he had improperly released confidential information to private parties). There was a great deal of controversy regarding the legality of these recess appointees because the Senate had been engaging in "pro forma" sessions during Congress's winter break in order to prevent recess appointments. This issue is beyond the scope of this book, but should a court address it, there could be significant ramifications for the NLRB if this situation happens again.

Even when the NLRB has at least three members, the uncertainty that now surrounds the nomination and confirmation process can hinder the agency's ability to plan for the future. The politicization itself also creates issues, because the agency's budget is regularly threatened by certain blocks in Congress. *See, e.g.*, Jeffrey M. Hirsch, *Attack on the NLRB*, Workplace Prof Blog (Feb. 16, 2011) (describing Amendment 578 to Full-Year Continuing Appropriations Act, 2011, H.R. 1, 112th Cong. (2011), which would have completely defunded the NLRB if it had not failed by a vote of 260-176), http://lawprofessors.typepad.com/laborprof_blog/2011/02/attack-on-the-nlrb.html. All of this means that this is a very interesting time to be studying labor law!

SECTION 2   NLRB PROCEDURES

A.   Representation Questions

One of the most important duties of the NLRB is to hold elections. Election issues can arise when there is a "question concerning representation." In other words, there is a question about whether employees want a collective-bargaining representative and, if so, who that representative should be. This question can arise when employees express interest in unionizing for the first time, or when unionized employees express interest in representation by a different union or no longer having any union representation.

You will learn more about this process in Chapter 6, which discussed the issue of selecting a bargaining representative, but the main threshold for the NLRB is whether at least 30% of a group or "unit" of employees express interest in holding an election. Once that level is met, a petition for an election can be filed with the relevant regional office; these petitions can seek an election for a new union ("certification election") or seek to remove an incumbent union ("decertification election"). The regional office investigates the petition and determines whether the accompanying expression of employee interest is valid. This expression of interest usually comes in the form of a petition or cards signed by employees. If valid, the regional office will direct that an election be held, and then it contacts the union and employer to set up the details of the election. Most of the time the parties reach a stipulated agreement on the details, but there are frequently disputes about the appropriate scope of the unit of employees, whether workers alleged to be part of the unit are eligible to vote, and other legal issues. The regional office hears these arguments and makes the initial decision. The Board can review some of these decisions, but its method for doing so is the subject of a recent, controversial change.

As noted earlier, the NLRB rarely issues regulations. However, the NLRB made a recent exception with a new regulation that addressed election dispute procedures. A frequent complaint about the NLRB's election processes is that parties have too many opportunities both to delay the holding of an election and delay the NLRB's "certification" of the results of a completed election. The regulation attempted to mitigate this problem by reducing parties' ability to file challenges to the regional office's election-related determinations and create delay before the election. This delay can be significant, especially for a union that is struggling to maintain support from employees, a topic we will look at in Chapter 6. One significant example of this delay was a mandatory 25-day waiting period for the NLRB to engage in a pre-election review of the regional office's decision — something the NLRB almost never did. Thus, in 2011, the NLRB issued a new election rule that, among other things, eliminated this waiting period and required parties to raise most issues in a post-election challenge. The NLRB's theory was that many of these disputes will become moot if the party raising them "won" the election. The new election rule also allowed the regional office to limit issues discussed in a pre-election hearing to those that are directly related to whether an election should be held. *See* Representation-Case Procedures, 76 Fed. Reg. 80,138 (Dec. 22, 2011) (to be codified at 29 C.F.R. §§ 101-02).

The controversy over these changes was the result of several factors. One was the context in which the regulation was promulgated. Early after President Obama's inauguration in 2009, unions and their Democratic supporters pushed the Employee Free Choice Act ("EFCA") bill. EFCA would have allowed unions to become representatives based solely on a majority showing of support from employees as shown by authorization cards — even without an election. The reason for this push was unions' belief that the current NLRB election process allowed too much employer interference. Opponents countered that EFCA's "card check" requirement was just an attempt by unions to bolster their membership and that it sacrificed the sanctity of the secret-ballot election. Although EFCA passed the House by a 241-185 vote, it died in the Senate. As you read the material in Chapters 5 and 6, ask yourself who has the better argument on this issue.

The arguments over EFCA may be considered the beginning of the tumultuous period referred to earlier. A further aspect of the political disputes swirling around the NLRB at this time was strong opposition to one of the Democratic NLRB nominees, the former union attorney (and law professor) Craig Becker. Eventually, Becker received a recess appointment, but that appointment was due to expire as the NLRB was contemplating the new election regulation. Initially, the NLRB published a larger set of proposed changes, but once it became clear that no one was likely to replace Becker soon, the NLRB pursued a smaller set of reforms in the hope that it could be finalized before Becker's term expired. Further controversy ensued as many opponents of the changes urged the only Republican on the NLRB at that time, Brian Hayes, to resign and deprive the NLRB of the three-member quorum that was arguably necessary to implement the proposed regulation. However, Hayes did not resign; instead, he expressed his opposition and refused to sign on to the final approval of the regulation. Opponents quickly challenged this new regulation in court and, at the time of publication of this book, one district court has held that Hayes' refusal to sign made the rule's promulgation improper. The NLRB is appealing, but the issues may be moot. The current NLRB has expressed an interest in implementing a more robust set of election rules now that it has four members, so there may be an entirely new regulation in force.

One challenge procedure that the new regulation does not address is the litigation that follows an NLRB decision on a representation matter. After the NLRB issues such a decision, or refuses to review a region's determination, the employer must take an odd procedural route to maintain the challenge. Essentially, in order to take advantage of the judicial review process that applies only to the NLRB's unfair labor practice decisions, which is discussed below, an employer must convert a representational issue into an unfair labor practice one. This is because appellate courts have jurisdiction only over unfair labor practice cases. The means to make this conversion is called a "technical 8(a)(5)." As you will learn later, Section 8(a)(5) of the NLRA establishes employers' duty to bargain with a union that represents the employer's employees. Thus, when an employer believes that the regional office improperly decided that a majority of employees wanted the union to represent them, the employer simply refuses to recognize the union as its employees' representative and refuses to bargain with the union. By openly refusing to bargain, the case turns into a possible violation of Section 8(a)(5), which courts have the authority to review under Section 9(d) of the NLRA. *See* Boire v. Greyhound Corp., 376 U.S. 473, 477-79 (1964). The court's determination whether the employer violated Section 8(a)(5) will be based on its evaluation of the employer's objections to the regional office's or NLRB's representation decision.

When courts review the NLRB's representational decisions, the agency is entitled to even more deference then normal (see below for a discussion "normal" NLRB deference). Because one of the NLRB's primary tasks is to establish the "safeguards necessary to insure the fair and free choice of bargaining representatives by employees," and this task is not one particularly well-suited for courts, the NLRB is entitled to a "wide degree of discretion" in representational cases. *NLRB v. A.J. Tower Co.*, 329 U.S. 324, 330 (1946); *see also Family Serv. Agency San Francisco v. NLRB*, 163 F.3d 1369, 1377 (D.C. Cir. 1999). Moreover, by overturning a union's victory and ordering a new election, a court may enable the employer to use the delay to frustrate employees' right to organize. *Amalgamated Clothing & Textile Workers Union v. NLRB*, 736 F.2d 1559, 1562-64 (D.C. Cir. 1984). As a result of this risk and the NLRB's expertise, court review of representational decisions is "extremely limited," and a court should not reverse the NLRB unless the agency abused its discretion or acted irrationally. *Id.* at 1562; *Sitka Sound Seafoods, Inc. v. NLRB*, 206 F.3d 1175, 1178 (D.C. Cir. 2000); *Colquest Energy, Inc. v. NLRB*, 965 F.2d 116, 119 (6th Cir. 1992).

Unlike employers, unions have almost no options to challenge the NLRB's representational decisions. At most, they can argue that the NLRB's determination was "contrary to a specific provision" of the NLRA and exceeded the agency's statutory authority. *See Leedom v. Kyne*, 358 U.S. 184 (1958). But this option is very limited and, in practice, means that unions rarely have recourse if the NLRB rejects their arguments in representational matters.

B.   Unfair Labor Practices

The start of an unfair labor practice proceeding occurs with the filing of a charge with the relevant regional office. Under Section 10(b) of the NLRA, there is a six-month statute of limitations for unfair labor practice charges. After notifying the employer or union that it is the subject of a charge, the region investigates the allegations, often interviewing participants and reviewing documents. If the region finds enough evidence to find that the charge has merit, it issues an unfair labor practice complaint. If the region finds that such evidence is lacking, it will dismiss a complaint — an outcome that occurs approximately 30% of the time. *See* NLRB, *Analysis of Methods of Disposition of Unfair Labor Practice Cases Closed, Fiscal Year 2010*, Table 7, https://www.nlrb.gov/sites/default/files/documents/3580/table_7.pdf. A similar proportion of charges are withdrawn (about 35%) or settled (about 34%) without the region filing a complaint. *Id.* The complaining party may challenge the region's refusal to issue a complaint before the NLRB's Office of Appeals; the challenge basically acts as a request for the Office of General Counsel to reconsider the region's decision. This reconsideration is final, and no further challenges are available.

If a charge is not dismissed, withdrawn, or settled, it is assigned to an ALJ who schedules a hearing. ALJ hearings are similar to trials, albeit less formal, and include discovery and witness testimony. *See NLRB v. Augusta Bakery Co.*, 957 F.2d 1467, 1479 (7th Cir. 1992) (noting that although administrative adjudications are not bound by the Federal Rules of Evidence, agencies must strive to follow the federal rules as much as practicable). Reaching this stage is rare, as only approximately 2% of charges ever develop far enough to have a hearing or a decision by an ALJ. *See* NLRB, *Disposition by Stage of Unfair Labor Practice Cases Closed, Fiscal Year 2010*, Table 8, https://www.nlrb.gov/sites/default/files/documents/3580/table_8.pdf. After the ALJ issues a recommended decision and order, parties may challenge that decision to the NLRB by filing "exceptions" to certain findings or recommendations. This is merely an appeal by another name. A bit fewer than 2% of unfair labor practice charges ever lead to a NLRB decision. *Id.*

Although the NLRB can hold oral arguments prior to issuing a decision, it very rarely does so and only in extremely high-profile cases. In the vast majority of cases, the NLRB reviews exceptions based solely on the record developed in the ALJ hearing and the parties' briefs. Because the NLRB is the entity with authority to enforce the NLRA, it is the official decisionmaker. This means that, although the NLRB members and staffs were not present at the hearing, it owes no deference to the ALJ. *See Local 702, IBEW v. NLRB*, 215 F.3d 11, 15 (D.C. Cir. 2000). This is true for both factual and legal issues, although the NLRB must explain its differences with the ALJ and will generally defer to credibility determinations because the ALJ was able to view witnesses' demeanor. *See id.; Paragon Paint Corp.*, 317 N.L.R.B. 747, 747 (1995).

This structure, as well as the NLRB's often-antiquated decision format, can make many NLRB decisions difficult to read. When researching NLRB cases, be mindful that the NLRB has several options for how it treats an ALJ decision, and it will often elect more than one option in the same case. For instance, the NLRB can simply adopt the ALJ's recommended findings and order. It can also adopt the

ALJ's decision, but provide additional language. When adding its own language, the NLRB may simply be providing further reasoning to support the ALJ's decision, or it might be modifying or rejecting part of the ALJ's reasoning. This makes citation to NLRB cases difficult, because it can take a lot of effort to determine what parts of an ALJ decision the NLRB adopted and are therefore citable.

One important feature of NLRB orders is that they are not self-enforcing. What that means is that if the NLRB finds that an employer or union committed an unfair labor practice and issues an order to remedy that violation, the NLRB has no power to make the employer or union comply with that order. This fact explains one of the two ways in which an NLRB decision comes to a federal court of appeals. The losing party can always seek an appeal by filing a "petition for review" of the NLRB decision. Appeals can be filed in either the D.C. Circuit, which has jurisdiction over all NLRB cases, or any circuit that covers the activity at issue in the case or an area in which the union or company has offices. However, if the losing party does not file a petition for review and does not comply with the NLRB's order, the Appellate Litigation and Supreme Court Branch, which is part of the Office of General Counsel, will file an "application for enforcement" with an appropriate appellate court. By practice, the NLRB, unlike many parties, will not forum-shop; it will instead file with the court that covers the area where most of the relevant activity occurred. *See* Jeffrey M. Hirsch, *Defending the NLRB: Improving the Agency's Success in the Federal Courts of Appeals*, 5 F.I.U. L. REV. 437, 454 (2010). Finally, a party will frequently file cross-petitions for either review or enforcement if the other filed first. If the appellate court agrees with the NLRB and enforces its order, then the losing party's failure to comply constitutes a failure to comply with a court order. For that reason, the NLRB has a Contempt Branch that seeks contempt of court orders against recalcitrant parties, and on some occasions, parties have faced imprisonment for more brazen refusals to comply.

The final step for review of an NLRB case is the Supreme Court. Although the Supreme Court used to hear many NLRB cases in the 1940s-1970s, the number of cases has declined since then. Indeed, the last decade or so has seen very few cases. Part of this decline may be related to the Court's overall reduction in the number of petitions for certiorari that it grants. But the NLRB also seems less interested in having cases heard by a conservative Court that many view as hostile to the agency's positions.

Although the courts of appeals have the duty to review the NLRB's decisions, the Board has the primary responsibility to resolve issues under the NLRA. Thus, like court review of other agencies, the NLRB's decisions are entitled to deference. Under Section 10(e) of the NLRA, courts must defer to the NLRB's factual findings as long as they are "supported by substantial evidence on the record considered as a whole." Deference only extends so far, however. Under the substantial evidence test, courts must still "take into account whatever in the record fairly detracts from [the finding's] weight." *Universal Camera Corp. v. NLRB*, 340 U.S. 474, 488 (1951). That said, substantial evidence review still places significant weight on the NLRB's findings. Courts do not ask whether the NLRB's factual findings are correct; rather, they look to whether evidence exists that could reasonably support the agency's findings. *See Allentown Mack Sales & Service, Inc. v. NLRB*, 522 U.S. 359, 370 (1998); *Consolidated Edison Co. v. NLRB*, 305 U.S. 197, 229 (1938). Moreover, substantial evidence review is not limited to pure factual findings. Instead, the Supreme Court has applied the test to instances where the NLRB decides how to apply the law to a given set of facts, which is a crucial element of most NLRB cases. *See Fall River Dyeing & Finishing Corp. v. NLRB*, 482 U.S. 27, 42 (1987). In addition, when the NLRB's factual findings differ from the ALJ's, many circuits will give the evidence more careful review. *See, e.g., Joy Silk Mills, Inc. v. NLRB*, 185 F.2d 732, 742 (D.C. Cir. 1950). However, the Sixth Circuit recently stated that this enhanced review was a "misleading" and "meaningless standard" that should be put "out to pasture." *NLRB v. Galicks, Inc.*, 671 F.3d 602 (6th Cir. 2012).

One subset of factual findings — credibility determinations — are given especially heightened deference. Appellate courts extend a particularly high degree of deference to credibility determinations and will typically reverse them only in "extraordinary circumstances." *See J.C. Penney Co. v. NLRB*, 123 F.3d 988, 995 (7th Cir. 1997). Yet, where the NLRB has reversed an ALJ's credibility determination, the appellate court will take into account that the agency did not observe the relevant witnesses and give a less deferential review. *See Ewing v. NLRB*, 732 F.2d 1117, 1120-21 (2d Cir. 1984).

When the NLRB is deciding a purely legal issue, a different standard applies. Under the Supreme Court's "*Chevron* doctrine," an agency's interpretation of the statute it has authority to enforce is "given controlling weight unless [it is] arbitrary, capricious, or manifestly contrary to the statute." *Chevron U.S.A., Inc. v. Natural Resources Defense Council, Inc.*, 467 U.S. 837, 843-44 (1984). Thus, when the NLRB is interpreting the NLRA, and only the NLRA, *Chevron's* two-step analysis applies. Under the first step, a court examines whether the NLRA directly answers the question at issue. *Id.* at 842. If it does, Congress's clear intent ends the inquiry, and both the agency and court are bound to the express statutory command. However, if the NLRA does not directly address the precise question at issue, the NLRB's interpretation takes center stage. The appellate court must defer to that interpretation as long as it is merely "a permissible construction of the statute." *Id.* In other words, if the NLRB's "choice represents a reasonable accommodation of conflicting policies that were committed to the agency's care by the statute, we should not disturb it unless it appears from the statute or its legislative history that the accommodation is not one that Congress would have sanctioned." *Id.* at 845. As you read the cases in this book, especially ones that were decided after *Chevron*, ask yourself whether courts are actually giving the NLRB the level of deference that it is owed.

SECTION 3   JURISDICTIONAL LIMITS OF THE NLRB

An important feature of all labor and employment statutes are their coverage. If the statute doesn't apply to a certain worker, firm, or situation, then there is no case to be had. This means that if the NLRB lacks jurisdiction in a given situation, the workers involved have no NLRA right to unionize and no protection against termination or other forms of retaliation made because of the workers' collective activity. However, it is possible that the workers might be covered by other labor statutes, such as the Railway Labor Act (applies to railroad and airline employees), the Federal Labor Relations Act (FLRA) (applies to federal employees), and state equivalents to the FLRA.

The NLRA gives the NLRB broad authority to regulate labor activity over most of the U.S.' private workforces. However, there are several important limitations to this jurisdiction. The following material will explore some of the more litigated issues, many of which are related to the fact that the NLRA gives rights only to "employees" who are not considered supervisors or managers. In addition, the NLRA excludes several different categories of employers, some of which are covered by other labor laws and others that lack any labor protections.

A.   Who is an "Employer" Under the NLRA?

The NLRA's definition of employer is relatively broad: under Section 2(2), "employer" is defined as including "any person acting as an agent of an employer, directly or indirectly, but shall not include the United States or any wholly owned Government corporation, or any Federal Reserve Bank, or any State or political subdivision thereof, or any person subject to the Railway Labor Act . . . or anyone acting in the capacity of officer or agent of such labor organization." In addition to the explicit exclusions under Section 2(2), such as public employers and employers covered by the RLA, there have been other implicit exclusions added. Most notable are NLRB-created exclusions for certain small employers and constitutional-based exclusions for certain religious employers.

1.   Private-Sector Employers

One of the more significant limitations to the NLRA's jurisdiction is that it applies only to the private sector. *See* Section 2(2) of the NLRA (stating that "employer" shall not include federal, state, or local governments). Federal employers are covered by the Federal Labor Relations Act, which is similar to the NLRA. Coverage for state and local employers varies widely. Some states, like New York, have a robust public labor relations law. Other states have no labor relations law and leave protection for state employees' labor activity and collective bargaining up to public employers' whim. Two states — North Carolina and Virginia — actually ban public-sector collective bargaining; public employers in these states cannot bargain with unions even if they wanted to. *See* MARTIN H. MALIN, JOSEPH SLATER & ANN C. HODGES, PUBLIC SECTOR EMPLOYMENT 284-85 (2d ed. 2011). As noted above, state labor law has been a hot political topic recently as several Republican governors and legislatures, most notably in Wisconsin, have made heavily publicized attempts to restrict public-sector unionism. Those attempts have been largely successful, but whether the trend continues in a more restrictive direction remains to be seen.

2.   Railway and Airline Exclusion

Another limitation under Section 2(2) is the exclusion of any employer regulated by the Railway Labor Act ("RLA"). As discussed in Chapter 1, the RLA was enacted in 1926, although its predecessor statutes reach as far back as the late 1800s. Because of the importance of railroads to the nation's commerce, Congress enacted a series of laws to regulate labor activity as a means to reduce the threat of costly strikes and other labor unrest. In 1936, airlines were added to the RLA's jurisdiction. As a result, labor matters that arise in either the railway or airline industries are governed by the RLA rather than the NLRA. *See* 45 U.S.C. § 151.

3.   Monetary Threshold

Although the NLRA does not establish a minimum threshold for the size of covered employers, the NLRB has been mindful of the fact that the statute was enacted pursuant to the Constitution's Interstate Commerce Clause. *See* Sections 9(c) & 10(a) of the NLRA; *NLRB v. Jones & Laughlin Steel Corp.*, 301 U.S. 1, 31 (1937). As a result, the NLRB has created a policy that looks to an employer's finances to ensure that truly small employers who might engage in only intrastate commerce are not covered.

Under the NLRB's rules, the agency will extend its jurisdiction to employers who engage in retail business if their annual gross receipts are $500,000 or more. The NLRB considers apartments and condominiums, cemeteries, casinos, home building, hotels, restaurants, taxi, and amusement to be retail businesses. Shopping centers and office buildings are also classified as retail, but they must only have annual gross receipts of $100,000.

An employer engaged in non-retail business is measured by the sales outside of the employer's state or the employer's purchases from a different state. If annual sales or purchases, including those through a third party, exceed $50,000 the NLRB will assert jurisdiction over the employer. There are numerous special thresholds that apply to various industries including essential links of transportation, such as trucking and private buses ($50,000); health care and child care ($250,000); nursing homes ($100,000); legal services ($250,000); and cultural and educational institutions ($1,000,000). The NLRB has described these and other jurisdictional rules in Chapter 1 of its *An Outline of Law and Procedure in Representation Cases*, which is available at https://www.nlrb.gov/sites/default/files/documents/44/rc_outline_ 2008_full.pdf.

4.   Religion Exception

The NLRA says nothing about religious employers. Yet, as has been the case in other areas of labor and employment law, First Amendment concerns have allowed certain religious employers to avoid coverage under the NLRA. *Cf. Hosanna-Tabor Evangelical Lutheran Church and School v. EEOC*, 132 S. Ct. 694 (2012) (holding that the First Amendment requires an exception for ministerial employees in employment discrimination cases). The main case under the NLRA is *NLRB v. Catholic Bishop of Chicago*, 440 U.S. 490, 499 (1979). In *Catholic Bishop*, the Supreme Court rejected the NLRB's rule that it would exclude teachers in religious schools only when the schools were "completely religious," because the rule created too much risk of violating the First Amendment. In order to avoid this constitutional problem, the Court interpreted the NLRA as lacking the intent to extend jurisdiction to teachers of religious schools.

The Court declined to establish a test for avoiding the problems with the First Amendment that existed under the NLRB's approach. Instead, the Court inter- preted the NLRA as not applying to church-operated schools like the one in

Catholic Bishop. Appellate courts have attempted to fill this analytical gap. One frequently cited case is *University of Great Falls v. NLRB*, 278 F.3d 1335, 1347 (D.C. Cir. 2002), in which the D.C. Circuit held that a school will be exempt from the NLRB's jurisdiction if it "(a) holds itself out to the public as a religious institution; (b) is non-profit; and (c) is religiously affiliated." The NLRB has not expressly followed or rejected *University of Great Falls*, but has applied the test "assuming [that it] governs the Board's assertion of jurisdiction over religious, educational institutions." *Catholic Social Services*, 355 N.L.R.B. No. 167, at *1 (2010).

Typically, the NLRB limits the religious exception to educational institutions and pure religious organizations, as it has found that other employers with religious affiliation do not present the same threat to the First Amendment. *See id.* (finding that child care services were secular); *The Salvation Army*, 345 N.L.R.B. 550 (2005) (finding that ex-convict rehabilitative services were secular). When the NLRB finds the employer to be purely religious in nature, it will deny jurisdiction over all employees, whether or not they perform religious duties. *See St. Edmonds Roman Catholic Church, Brooklyn*, 337 N.L.R.B. 1260, 1260 (2002) (noting refusal to assert jurisdiction over "religious institutions which operate in a conventional sense using conventional means" and "over secular employees of religious institutions, without whom the employers could not accomplish their religious missions").

B. Who is an "Employee" Under the NLRA?

If you've taken other employment-related courses, you've no doubt discovered one of the bizarre facets of labor and employment law: the definition of "employee." Many of these statutes' definitions of employee are based on the NLRA, although given the NLRA's basic definition, you'd be forgiven for wondering why. This is because Section 2(3) defines employee in the most circular terms possible: "The term 'employee' shall include any employee." As you will see in the following material, the NLRB and courts have developed a multi-factored approach for dealing with this unhelpful definition, but that approach is often criticized for its own lack of predictability.

In addition to the basic definition of employee, Section 2(3) adds more gloss to the term:

> The term "employee" shall include any employee, and shall not be limited to the employees of a particular employer, unless the Act explicitly states otherwise, and shall include any individual whose work has ceased as a consequence of, or in connection with, any current labor dispute or because of any unfair labor practice, and who has not obtained any other regular and substantially equivalent employment, but shall not include any individual employed as an agricultural laborer, or in the domestic service of any family or person at his home, or any individual employed by his parent or spouse, or any individual having the status of an independent contractor, or any individual employed as a supervisor, or any individual employed by an employer subject to the Railway Labor Act . . . or by any other person who is not an employer as herein defined.

This additional language does several things. First, it makes clear that job applicants and terminated workers are still considered employees under the NLRA. Second, it creates several explicit exclusions of certain categories of workers. We will discuss several of the most relevant issues surrounding these exclusions below. *See generally* Anne Marie Lofaso, *The Vanishing Employee: Putting the Autonomous Dignified Union Worker Back to Work*, 5 F.I.U. L. REV. 495, 524-25 (2010) (providing history and development of NLRA's definition of "employee").

1.   Employee or Independent Contractor?

PROBLEM #1: "FREELANCE" SOFTWARE ENGINEERS

CompuWare is a major computer software company. In addition to its thousands of regular employees, CompuWare hired hundreds of software designers that the company classified as "freelancers." These freelancers were initially hired to work on specific projects, but most ended up working on several new projects and stayed at CompuWare for a year or more. The freelancers worked alongside regular employees, had the same supervisors, did the same type of work in the same places, and worked the same hours. However, freelancers had badges of a different color than regular employees, were given different e-mail addresses, and had less training and orientation. Unlike regular software designers, the freelancers were not able to assign work to other workers or attend official company functions. CompuWare treated the freelancers as independent contractors for tax purposes, did not pay them overtime or provide them with benefits, and paid them through submitted invoices rather than the payroll department. At the time freelancers began their work, CompuWare made these differences clear to them and had them sign statements stating that "as an Independent Contractor to CompuWare, you are self-employed and you alone are responsible for paying your taxes, insurance, and benefits."

The freelancers have become upset with CompuWare's treatment of them and, after initial discussion with a union, have filed a petition to have an election on whether to unionize. CompuWare has responded by firing several of the more pro-union freelancers; the company argues that the firings are legal, and that the freelancers cannot seek an election, because the workers are not "employees" under the NLRA.

Ask yourself whether that argument has merit as you read the next case. As you consider both sides of this question, make sure to think about which factors seem the most relevant to you.

PROBLEM MATERIAL

Roadway Package System, Inc., 326 N.L.R.B. 842 (1998)

ROADWAY PACKAGE SYSTEM, INC.
326 N.L.R.B. 842 (1998)

. . . Roadway, a Delaware corporation, operates a nationwide pickup and delivery system for small packages throughout the United States. This system currently is comprised of approximately 317 terminals and hub facilities. The sole issue to be decided here is whether the drivers at Roadway's Ontario and Pomona terminals are employees under Section 2(3) of the Act or independent contractors not subject to the Board's jurisdiction.

Almost a decade ago, the Board addressed a similar issue for the pickup and delivery drivers at Roadway's terminals located at Louisville, Kentucky, and Redford, Michigan. The Board found employee status for the drivers in those cases. Specifically, in [*Roadway Package System (Roadway I)*, 288 N.L.R.B. 196 (1988)], the Board stated that the drivers "bear few of the risks and enjoy little of the opportunities for gain associated with an entrepreneurial enterprise" and Roadway had "substantial control over the manner and means" of performance by their drivers.

In *Roadway I*, Roadway controlled, inter alia, the customer service areas and the number of packages and stops that were assigned to the Louisville drivers. The drivers had no proprietary interest in their customer service areas, and their compensation was controlled by Roadway. Roadway also maintained a "core zone supplement rate" to balance the Louisville drivers' income across various zones and thus minimize their risk and opportunity for gain. In addition, Roadway had a "flex" program to allow for the temporary transfer of packages or areas among the Louisville drivers to equalize their workload. The drivers received no commission for any customer sales leads, but they were eligible for a startup loan of $650 in gross income per week for the first 13 weeks of delivery for Roadway. Most of the Louisville drivers purchased or leased their vehicles from a source sponsored by Roadway. On the termination of their service to Roadway, the drivers were simultaneously released from their financial obligations to that source. Finally, Roadway had significant control over the daily work schedule of the Louisville drivers, and it required that drivers wear a uniform and use the Roadway color and logo on their vehicles.

At oral argument in the instant cases, counsel for Roadway argued that, commencing in 1994, Roadway made nationwide changes in its driver operations. He argued that those particular changes support a finding of independent contractor status for the Ontario and Pomona drivers. In this connection, counsel emphasized, inter alia, that Roadway no longer: (1) requires a uniform starting time; (2) maintains a fleet of vehicles for its drivers' use; (3) maintains forms for the drivers to lease or purchase vehicles; (4) releases terminated drivers from their financial obligations; (5) terminates drivers' agreements at will and without cause; and (6) assigns customer service areas without giving the drivers a proprietary interest in these areas.

As fully described below, we find that these 1994 changes do not require a different result from *Roadway I*. Applying the common-law agency test as interpreted by the Supreme Court in *NLRB v. United Insurance Co. of America*, 390 U.S. 254 (1968), we have considered all the incidents of Roadway's relationship with its Ontario and Pomona drivers, including the 1994 changes cited by Roadway, and we find that the factors, as a whole, weigh in favor of finding employee status for these drivers. . . .

Section 2(3) of the Act, as amended by the 1947 Labor Management Relations Act (the Taft-Hartley Act), provides that the term "employee" shall not include "any individual having the status of independent contractor." The meaning and ramifications of this 1947 amendment were first considered by the Supreme Court in *NLRB v. United Insurance Co. of America*, 390 U.S. 254 (1968).[4] In that case, the Court declared that

> [t]he obvious purpose of this amendment was to have the Board and the courts apply general agency principles in distinguishing between employees and independent contractors under the Act. [Footnote omitted.] And both petitioners and respondents agree that the proper standard here is the law of agency. Thus there is no doubt that we should apply the common-law agency test here in distinguishing an employee from an independent contractor. [390 U.S. at 256.]

The Court, however, recognized that the application of the common-law agency test may be challenging at times because "[t]here are innumerable situations which arise in the common law where it is difficult to say whether a particular individual is an employee or an independent contractor." The Court further stated that there is no "shorthand formula" or "magic phrase" associated with the common-law test. Instead, the Court specifically instructed that under the common-law agency test "all the incidents of the relationship must be assessed and weighed with no one factor being decisive. What is important is that the total factual context is assessed in light of the pertinent common-law principles." 390 U.S. at 258.

In *United Insurance*, the Court upheld the Board's determination of employee status for the debit agents of the respondent insurance company. In doing so, the Court emphasized the following "decisive factors" present in that case:

> [T]he agents do not operate their own independent businesses, but perform functions that are an essential part of the company's normal operations; they need not have any prior training or experience, but are trained by company supervisory personnel; they do business in the company's name with considerable assistance and guidance from the company and its managerial personnel and ordinarily sell only the company's policies; the "Agent's Commission plan" that contains the terms and conditions under which they operate is promulgated and changed unilaterally by the company; the agents account to the company for the funds they collect under an elaborate and regular reporting procedure; the agents receive the benefits of the company's vacation plan and group insurance and pension fund; and the agents have a permanent working arrangement with the company under which they may continue as long as their performance is satisfactory. [390 U.S. at 259-260.]

---

[4] [n.30] This amendment was added in response to Congressional disagreement with the standard applied by the Board to determine employee status in *NLRB v. Hearst Publications, Inc.*, 322 U.S. 111 (1944).

For a long time, *United Insurance* has been the preeminent guidance to the lower courts and the Board on what standard should be applied in differentiating employee status from independent contractor status in the NLRA context. Recent Supreme Court precedent reinforces *United Insurance*'s observations about the appropriateness of using the common law of agency as the test for determining employee status. See *NLRB v. Town & Country Electric*, 516 U.S. 85 (1995); *Nationwide Mutual Insurance Co. v. Darden*, 503 U.S. 318 (1992); and *Community for Creative Non-Violence v. Reid*, 490 U.S. 730 (1989). Furthermore, these cases teach us not only that the common law of agency is the standard to measure employee status but also that we have no authority to change it. . . .

In each situation, the Court turned, as it had previously done in *United Insurance*, to traditional common-law agency criteria to identify whether an employer-employee relationship existed. In this connection, the Court in *Reid*, supra at 752 fn. 31, further high-lighted the importance of the multifactor analysis of the Restatement (Second) of Agency, Section 220 (dealing with the definition of a servant).[5] . . .

The Supreme Court has clearly stated that "all of the incidents of the relationship must be assessed and weighed with no one factor being decisive." See *United Insurance*, 390 U.S. at 258; *Reid*, 490 U.S. at 752; and *Darden*, 503 U.S. at 324. While we recognize that the common-law agency test described by the Restatement ultimately assesses the amount or degree of control exercised by an employing entity over an individual, we find insufficient basis for the proposition that those factors which do not include the concept of "control" are insignificant when compared to those that do. Section 220(2) of the Restatement refers to 10 pertinent factors as "among others," thereby specifically permitting the consideration of other relevant factors as well, depending on the factual circumstances presented. In addition, Comment c to Section 220(1) of the Restatement states that "[t]he factors in Subsection (2) are *all* considered in determining the question [of

---

[5] [n.32] This section provides, in pertinent part:

(1) A servant is a person employed to perform services in the affairs of another and who with respect to the physical conduct in the performance of the services is subject to the other's control or right of control.

(2) In determining whether one acting for another is a servant or an independent contractor, the following matters of fact, among others, are considered:

(a) The extent of control which, by the agreement, the master may exercise over the details of the work.

(b) Whether or not the one employed is engaged in a distinct occupation or business.

(c) The kind of occupation, with reference to whether, in the locality, the work is usually done under the direction of the employer or by a specialist without supervision.

(d) The skill required in the particular occupation.

(e) Whether the employer or the workman supplies the instrumentalities, tools, and the place of work for the person doing the work.

(f) The length of time for which the person is employed.

(g) The method of payment, whether by the time or by the job.

(h) Whether or not the work is part of the regular business of the employer.

(i) Whether or not the parties believe they are creating the relation of master and servant.

(j) Whether the principal is or is not in the business.

employee status], and it is for the triers of fact to determine whether or not there is *a sufficient group of favorable factors* to establish the employee relationship." (Emphasis added.) Thus, the common-law agency test encompasses a careful examination of all factors and not just those that involve a right of control. As the Board stated in *Austin Tupler Trucking*, 261 NLRB 183, 184 (1982): "Not only is no one factor decisive, but the same set of factors that was decisive in one case may be unpersuasive when balanced against a different set of opposing factors. And though the same factor may be present in different cases, it may be entitled to unequal weight in each because the factual background leads to an analysis that makes that factor more meaningful in one case than in the other." . . .

To summarize, in determining the distinction between an employee and an independent contractor under Section 2(3) of the Act, we shall apply the common-law agency test and consider all the incidents of the individual's relationship to the employing entity.

Guided by [these] legal principles . . . we now apply the common-law agency test to the present situation involving the Ontario and Pomona drivers. We find that the dealings and arrangements between these drivers and Roadway, including those reflective of the changes made by the 1994 Agreement, have many of the same characteristics of the employee-employer relationship presented in *United Insurance*. Reviewing the factors relied on by the Board in *Roadway I*, we see insignificant change pointing to independent contractor status.

As in *United Insurance*, the drivers here do not operate independent businesses, but perform functions that are an essential part of one company's normal operations; they need not have any prior training or experience, but receive training from the company; they do business in the company's name with assistance and guidance from it; they do not ordinarily engage in outside business; they constitute an integral part of the company's business under its substantial control; they have no substantial proprietary interest beyond their investment in their trucks; and they have no significant entrepreneurial opportunity for gain or loss. All these factors weigh heavily in favor of employee status . . . .

The Ontario and Pomona drivers devote a substantial amount of their time, labor, and equipment to performing essential functions that allow Roadway to compete in the small package delivery market. . . . None of the drivers are required to have prior delivery training or experience. Those unfamiliar with Roadway's system can gain assistance and guidance from the new driver orientation meetings that are conducted by Roadway's personnel. While a few operate as incorporated businesses, all the Ontario and Pomona drivers do business in the name of Roadway. Wearing an "RPS-approved uniform," the drivers operate uniformly marked vehicles. In fact, the vehicles are custom designed by Roadway and produced to its specifications by Navistar. The vehicles are identical as to make, model, internal shelving, and rear door, differing only as to chassis and payload (three choices depending on the size of the driver's primary service area). All the vehicles clearly display Roadway's name, logo, and colors. . . .

The drivers have a contractual right to use this customized truck in business activity outside their relationship with Roadway, though none of the Ontario and Pomona drivers (and only 3 out of Roadway's 5000 drivers nationwide) have used their vehicles for other commercial purposes. This lack of pursuit of outside business activity appears to be less a reflection of entrepreneurial choice by the Ontario and Pomona drivers and more a matter of the obstacles created by their relationship with Roadway.

Roadway's drivers are prohibited under the 1994 Agreement from conducting outside business for other companies throughout the day. The drivers' commitment to Roadway continues through the evening hours when they must return their vehicles to the terminal to interface with Roadway's evening line-haul operations. Typically, most drivers then take their vehicles out of circulation. They leave their vehicles overnight at the terminal to take advantage of loading of the next day's assignments by Roadway's package handlers. As a consequence, their vehicles remain out of service during these off-work hours. Even if the drivers want to use their vehicles for other purposes during their off-work hours, there are several obvious built-in hindrances. First, the vehicles are not readily available. Second, before the driver can use his vehicle for other purposes, he must mask any marking reflecting Roadway's name or business. Every vehicle utilized by the driver has been dictated in detail-color, size, internal configuration including the internal shelving and door-by Roadway's operations. The vehicles are also not easily flexible or susceptible to modifications or adaptations to other types of use. Thus, these constraints on the drivers' use of their vehicles during their off-work hours "provide minimal play for entrepreneurial initiative and minimize the extent to which ownership of a truck gives its driver entrepreneurial independence." [*NLRB v Amber Delivery Service*, 651 F.2d 57, 63 (1st Cir. 1981).] Roadway has simply shifted certain capital costs to the drivers without providing them with the independence to engage in entrepreneurial opportunities.

Truck ownership can suggest independent contractor status where, for example, an entrepreneur with a truck puts it to use in serving his or another business' customers. But, the form of truck ownership, here, does not eliminate the Ontario and Pomona drivers' dependence on Roadway in acquiring their vehicles. Roadway's indirect control is further seen in that it requires the drivers to acquire and maintain their own specialty vans, and Roadway eases the drivers' burden through its arrangement and promotion of Navistar vans sold or leased through Bush Leasing. Although it does not directly participate in these van transfers, Roadway's involvement in these deals undoubtedly facilitates and ensures that a fleet of vehicles, built and maintained according to its specifications, is always readily available and recyclable among the drivers.

Roadway also encourages the sale of used vehicles from former to new drivers. In this way, Roadway eases the new driver's responsibility for obtaining a qualified vehicle. It further decreases the former driver's risk of repossession by Bush Leasing and increases the likelihood that there will be a qualified buyer for a costly specialty van no longer needed by the former driver. There is simply no ready market for these vehicles. Every feature, detail, and internal configuration has been dictated by Roadway's specifications. In short, Roadway has created a system which makes the necessary, custom vehicles readily available to prospective drivers, and enables drivers who want to end their relationship with it to easily transfer their vehicles to incoming drivers. By the same token, the specialized vehicles required by Roadway are of no further use to former drivers who naturally sell the vehicles to incoming Roadway drivers when their relationship with Roadway is over.

Roadway is also a ready source for replacement vans when the drivers' vehicles are unavailable because of needed maintenance or repair. Roadway arranges for the rental of vehicles from national rental companies and negotiates rental prices favorable to its drivers. At most terminals, Roadway also maintains spare vehicles purchased from former drivers that can be used by current drivers on a short-term basis when their vehicles break down. In addition to this vehicle assistance, the "business support package" helps ensure that the drivers' vehicles are properly maintained and covered by specific warranties. Roadway reminds the drivers that certain essential maintenance is needed by placing charts on the windows of the drivers' vehicles. The brochure to prospective drivers also advertises Roadway's maintenance "assistance" and further notes that "RPS provides warranty recovery assistance" to its drivers. The "business support package" also gives the drivers easy access to clean work uniforms. This assistance by Roadway points in the direction of finding employee status for the Ontario and Pomona drivers.

Other support for employee status can be found in Roadway's compensation package for the drivers. Here, Roadway establishes, regulates, and controls the rate of compensation and financial assistance to the drivers as well as the rates charged to customers. Generally speaking, there is little room for the drivers to influence their income through their own efforts or ingenuity. Whatever potential for entrepreneurial profit does exist, Roadway suppresses through a system of minimum and maximum number of packages and customer stops assigned to the drivers. For example, when a driver becomes busier and the number of packages or customer stops grows, his territory may be unilaterally reconfigured, and the extra packages or stops are reassigned if the driver has already attained the maximum level for his primary service area that has been already determined by Roadway.
. . .

[A] temporary core zone settlement subsidizes the driver's income. With the 1994 Agreement, the driver receives this supplement until he reaches the "normal" range of pickups and deliveries for his service area. In this way, the temporary core zone settlement serves as an important safety net for the fledging driver to shield him from loss, and it guarantees an income level predetermined by Roadway, irrespective of the driver's personal initiative and effort in his service area.

Income from each delivery and pickup, the last major compensation component, may vary among the drivers. This variance stems not from the drivers' entrepreneurial efforts but from the differences in customer bases that were assigned to the drivers. . . . Although Roadway states that drivers can, and have, secured new customers, there is no evidence that such additional customers have significantly affected the earnings of any driver.

Roadway stresses that two items in the 1994 Agreement — the driver's proprietary interest in his service area and his right to sell all or part of his area to the "highest bidder" — allow the drivers to influence their profits like entrepreneurs. We disagree because Roadway has imposed substantial limitations and conditions on both new features of the driver's relationship such that neither one retains any significant entrepreneurial characteristics.

Under the terms of the Agreement, Roadway has considerable control over whether the driver may sell at all, to whom, and under what circumstances. Roadway can and has influenced, if not forced, complete or partial sales of service areas. Regarding the few sales to which participants testified, it appears that the drivers had little choice, entrepreneurial or otherwise, but to sell. The evidence establishes that these drivers were pressured to sell by Roadway's warning or threat that their service areas would be reconfigured and customer accounts reassigned, or worse, that their entire relationship with Roadway would be terminated. . . .

POST PROBLEM DISCUSSION

1. After reading *Roadway*, what do you think about the freelancers in our problem — should they be classified as employees who can unionize under the NLRA or excluded independent contractors? How important are the agreements that the freelancers signed stating that they acknowledged that they were independent contractors? *See Vizcaino v. Microsoft*, 120 F.3d 1006, 1010 (9th Cir. 1997) (en banc) (holding, in the case upon which our problem is based, that the court must make its own interpretation of the employment relationship, including agreements between the parties). Also consider *Roadway's* companion case, *Dial-A-Mattress Operating Corp.*, 326 N.L.R.B. 884 (1998) (concluding that owner-drivers were independent contractors).

2. The employee/independent contractor question is a significant one in all areas of labor and employment law. *See* U.S. Gov't Acc. Office, *Employee Misclassification: Improved Outreach Could Help Ensure Proper Worker Classification* (2007), http://www.gao.gov/new.items/d07859t.pdf. Employers have become aggressive about trying to classify workers as independent contractors because of the consequences. As we've already seen, one consequence is that labor and employment laws do not apply to independent contractors. For our purposes, this means that workers classified as independent contractors have no right to unionize and no legal protection for their labor-related activity. But perhaps an even greater reason is that employers do not have to make payroll tax contributions for independent contractors. The push to treat workers as independent contractors has spurred several legislative efforts to reform this problem across many different areas of law, but none of these proposals have been enacted. *See, e.g.*, Employee Misclassification Act, S. 3254, 111th Cong. (2010) (attempting to amend the Fair Labor Standards Act).

3. As footnote 30 in *Roadway* mentions, Section 2(3)'s exclusion of independent contractors was a reaction to an earlier case in which the Supreme Court affirmed the NLRB's inclusion of such workers under the NLRA. *NLRB v. Hearst Publications, Inc.*, 322 U.S. 111 (1944). *Hearst* involved workers whose job it was to sell papers on street corners (referred to as "newsboys," although they were typically adults). The NLRB concluded that the newsboys should be considered employees even though the newspaper publisher lacked the amount of control that is typically needed under the common-law test. In the Taft-Hartley Amendments, Congress rejected that ruling and expressly excluded independent contractors in Section 2(3). Do you agree with that change, or do you think that the NLRA should protect more workers than would be considered employees under the common-law

test? Does it affect your opinion once you realize that this common-law test was originally developed to determine when a principal would be responsible for the misconduct of its agent ("vicarious liability")?

4.   One aspect of the common-law test that has become a key issue in some NLRA cases is the workers' opportunity to act as entrepreneurs. It is but one of many factors in the NLRB's test. *See Dial-A-Mattress Operating Corp.*, 326 N.L.R.B. 884, 891 (1998). However, the D.C. Circuit has recently held that the entrepreneurial factor should be the central focus of independent contractor inquiries. *See FedEx Home Delivery, Inc. v. NLRB*, 563 F.3d 492, 497 (D.C. Cir. 2009) (holding that the emphasis of the common law test has shifted to the "animating principle" of "whether the 'putative independent contractors have significant entrepreneurial opportunity for gain or loss.'") (quoting *Corporate Express Delivery System v. NLRB*, 292 F.3d 777, 780 (D.C. Cir. 2002)). Moreover, the court determined that only a few instances of workers taking advantage of entrepreneurial opportunities, despite restrictions by the company that made most workers unable to actually take advantage of those opportunities, was enough to establish independent contractor status. *See id.* at 502-503; *see generally* Micah Prieb Stoltzfus Jost, Note, *Independent Contractors, Employees, and Entrepreneurialism Under the National Labor Relations Act: A Worker-by-Worker Approach*, 68 WASH. & LEE L. REV. 311 (2011). The new Restatement of Employment Law stresses the importance of entrepreneurial opportunity, but appears to view actual entrepreneurialism as the key factor, rather than mere theoretical opportunity. *See* RESTATEMENT (THIRD) OF EMPLOYMENT LAW § 1.01 (2009) (defining "employee" as a worker who does not render services as an "independent business").

5.   The distinction between employee and independent contractor is one that touches on many different laws that affect the workplace. Although most of those areas follow a rule similar to the common law, others do not. Most notable of those exceptions are the Fair Labor Standards Act and Family and Medical Leave Act which have a more expansive definition of "employee." *See Secretary of Labor v. Lauritzen*, 835 F.2d 1529 (7th Cir. 1987) (noting use of "economic realities" test that looks to a worker's economic dependence on the employer); Commission on the Future of Worker-Management Relations (commonly known as the "Dunlop Commission"), Report and Recommendations Executive Summary 36 (1994) (arguing for extension of economic realities test to the NLRA). Similarly, other countries take different approaches, including a classification of "dependent contractors" who are not formally considered employees, but are given similar coverage because of their economic dependence. *See St. Joseph News-Press and Teamsters Union Local 460*, 345 N.L.R.B. 474, 486 (2005) (Member Liebman, dissenting) (noting use of this classification by Canada, Germany, and Sweden); Katherine V.W. Stone, *Legal Protections for Atypical Employees: Employment Law for Workers Without Workplaces and Employees Without Employers*, 27 BERKELEY J. EMP. & LAB. L. 251, 284 (2006) (proposing dependent contractor classification for NLRA). Many commentators have provided other options:

- Define employment relationships as covering a service provider and recipient. *See* Marc Linder, *Dependent and Independent Contractors in Recent U.S. Labor Law: An Ambiguous Dichotomy Rooted in Simulated Statutory Purposelessness*, 21 COMP. LAB. L. POL'Y J. 187, 223 (1999);

- Cover workers who sell labor to a firm that uses the labor in combination with capital investment — in contrast to individuals who sell a product or service that consists of their labor and their own capital. *See* Michael C. Harper, *Defining the Economic Relationship Appropriate for Collective Bargaining*, 39 B.C. L. REV. 329, 341 (1998);

- Use the current common-law test to further emphasize entrepreneurial independence and dependence on the firm. *See* Ruth Burdick, *Principles of Agency Permit the NLRB to Consider Additional Factors of Entrepreneurial Independence and the Relative Dependence of Employees when Determining Independent Contractor Status under Section 2(3)*, 15 HOFSTRA LAB. & EMP. L.J. 75 (1997); and

- Base liability on a firm's duty to ensure compliance throughout its supply chain, rather than on an individual worker's status. *See* Timothy P. Glynn, *Taking the Employer Out of Employment Law? Accountability for Wage and Hour Violations in an Age of Enterprise Disaggregation*, 15 EMPLOYEE RTS. & EMP. POL'Y J. 201, 235 (2011); Brishen Rogers, *Toward Third-Party Liability for Wage Theft*, 31 BERKELEY J. EMP. & LAB. L. 1 (2010).

Which alternative do you think best fit the purpose of the NLRA, or do you think the current common-law test is best? Do you have a proposal of your own?

6.   Note that Section 2(3) also specifically excludes individuals who work as agricultural laborers, as domestic helpers in a home, or for a parent or spouse. The agricultural exclusion, which exists in other workplace statutes such as Title VII of the Civil Rights Act, has been controversial, particularly because those workers often face poor working conditions that unions can attempt to rectify. *See* Michael H. LeRoy & Wallace Hendricks, *Should "Agricultural Laborers" Continue to be Excluded from the National Labor Relations Act*, 48 EMORY L.J. 489 (1999); *see also* Peggie R. Smith, *Organizing the Unorganizable: Private Paid Household Workers and Approaches to Employee Representation*, 79 N.C. L. REV. 45 (2000).

2.   Employee or Student?

Although independent contractors are the largest class of non-employee workers, there are others. One of the more contentious groups under the NLRA has been various graduate-level students who also do work for their universities. These students are essentially hybrids; they act as both students and workers. The question boils down to which role predominates. Thus, are medical residents who are required to work at a hospital to become doctors more like employees covered by the NLRB or more like unprotected students? Similarly, are graduate students who both take classes and work as research or teaching assistants the type of workers that the NLRA should cover, or are they more like students who do not enjoy protection under the NLRA? For the NLRB's most recent take on these questions, read on. Although, as you will see, the following cases are unlikely to be the NLRB's final word on these issues.

PROBLEM #2: LAW STUDENTS UNITE!

You are one of a group of 75 "Wagner Scholars" at your private law school. The law school designates 25 entering students out of a class of approximately 200 students to be Wagner Scholars for their full three years at law school. Wagner Scholars are selected based on several varying characteristics, including financial need, academic success, and diversity considerations. Participation in the Wagner Scholars program is optional for all selected students and, in most years, a few students decline to participate and simply matriculate as regular law students. A key benefit of the Wagner Scholars program is a $2,400 tuition stipend for each academic year. In order to keep that stipend, Wagner Scholars must maintain a 3.0 grade point average and work for 10 hours a week during the 30-week academic year. Most Wagner Scholars meet this work requirement by serving as research assistants to members of the law school faculty, although some do other work such as providing assistance in the law library or serving as teaching assistants for large classes. Failure to work the necessary hours can result in removal from the Wagner Scholars program and the need to pay back the entire stipend for the deficient academic year.

Although there is a certain amount of prestige associated with the Wagner Scholars program, participants have begun to question the fairness of the work requirement. In particular, you and other Wagner Scholars have been complaining about receiving only $8 an hour for having to work with obnoxious faculty members. After hearing your complaint, the law school dean refused to increase the stipend, saying "you don't have to take the money if you don't want it." You decided to talk about this issue with your labor law professor, who is slightly less obnoxious than most of her colleagues, and she suggested that the Wagner Scholars consider talking to a union. You follow her advice and get a union to agree to represent you and the rest of the Wagner Scholars. After getting support from the majority of the Wagner Scholars, the union filed a petition with the NLRB for an election. However, the dean argued to the NLRB that the Wagner Scholars are students and, therefore, have no right under the NLRA to unionize. The dean also threatens you with expulsion if you don't stop agitating for a union.

Read the next two cases to see if you need to start looking at transfer applications to other law schools. After reaching your conclusion, ask yourself whether it fits with your understanding of the NLRA and its intended scope.

PROBLEM MATERIALS

Boston Medical Center Corp., 330 N.L.R.B. 152 (1999)

Brown University, 342 N.L.R.B. 483 (2004)

BOSTON MEDICAL CENTER CORP.
330 N.L.R.B. 152 (1999)

. . . [Boston Medical Center ("BMC")] operates a 432-bed, nonprofit, acute-care teaching hospital in Boston, Massachusetts. It provides both inpatient and outpatient services, maintains a 24-hour emergency care facility, and serves as the primary teaching facility for the Boston University School of Medicine. As such,

BMC sponsors some 37 different residency programs varying in length from 3 to 5 years, with some lasting longer. Fellowships last from 1 to 4 additional years. There are about 430 house officers in the unit sought by the Petitioner [union]. . . .

BMC, like all institutions sponsoring medical residency programs, begins its academic year on July 1 of each year. Students halfway through their fourth year of medical school decide what area of medicine they would like to pursue and apply to appropriate medical programs. Out of hundreds or thousands of applications received, a small percentage of applicants are picked to interview for particular residency programs at BMC. Thereafter, BMC, like other teaching hospitals, ranks the individual applicants and submits its top candidates to a national matching program. At about the same time, applicants submit a list of residency programs that they would like to attend. In March, the national matching program generates a "match" list that sets forth which applicants will attend which residency programs. There is no matching process for fellowships. Applicants for fellowships are hired directly by the teaching hospitals.

House officers enter a residency or fellowship program in order to become certified specialists in their chosen medical specialty. [Residents and interns (who are residents in their first year) have obtained their medical decrees. After completion of the first year of their residency and passage of a required exam, they can practice as fully licensed physicians. Some residents moon-light at other institutions to make extra money after their first year. After completion of their full residency program, residents are eligible to take an exam to become certified in a given specialty.] . . .

House officers work notoriously long hours, which vary depending on the specialty and the rotation. They are trained by and work under the medical direction of attending physicians who are referred to as "attendings" or faculty. . . . Attendings are physicians on the staff of BMC, 99 percent of whom are also faculty members of the Boston University School of Medicine. . . .

Residency programs have essentially two elements: didactic lectures and clinical training. Medical residents attend didactic lectures on a variety of topics relevant to their particular residency program. In addition, residents gain experience in performing direct patient care by working in teams that include third- and fourth-year medical students, interns, junior and senior residents, and attending physicians. Each intern on an inpatient ward is generally assigned 12 to 15 patients. A more senior resident is responsible for overseeing the work of the interns, and the interns oversee the medical students. An attending physician must be the physician of record for every patient. . . .

As residents progress through the program, they are given increased responsibility commensurate with their level of experience. For example, internal medicine interns see patients 80 to 90 percent of the time outside the presence of an attending physician. Interns do, however, discuss all patients with attending physicians, who are primarily responsible for their patients' care plans and who see their patients daily. . . .

In addition to their time spent in direct patient care, house staff also attend so-called "didactic" conferences. In some residencies, such conferences take place at noon and cover various topics. Residents spend varying amounts of time in conferences, ranging in some estimates from 5 to 8 hours per week. House staff also engage in rounds, a 1-hour "morning report" conference (6 days a week), clinic talks, and the like.

Residents in each program are required to take an annual "in-training" exam offered by their specialty board, which is used to make comparisons with other programs throughout the country, to identify the residents' academic strengths and weaknesses, and to indicate the likelihood that they will pass the Boards. . . . In addition to the in-training exam, residents in the surgery residency program take weekly or biweekly exams and are constantly quizzed by attendings using the Socratic method. . . .

Unlike other BMC employees, house officers are not recruited, interviewed, or hired by BMC's human resources department. They receive, however, annual compensation ranging from about $34,000 to over $44,000, depending on the number of years in the residency program. They also receive paid vacation and sick, parental, and bereavement leave. Like other BMC employees, house officers are entitled to health, dental, and life insurance, and they may use the employee health service. BMC also provides malpractice insurance at its expense for its house staff.

BMC deducts Federal and state taxes from house officers' pay. House staff receive W-2 forms for income tax purposes. BMC also maintains a workers compensation policy that applies to all employees, including house staff, and treats house staff as covered by the various state and Federal laws that regulate employment, such as the Family and Medical Leave Act, the Americans with Disabilities Act, and other state and Federal laws that prohibit various forms of discrimination in employment.

There are, however, some differences in the treatment of house officers as compared to other BMC physicians and/or employees in general. House officers are much lower paid than attending physicians, and their compensation is generally unrelated to the number of hours they work. House officers cannot participate in the retirement program, which is made available to other employees, although about 24 of them participate in a tax-sheltered annuity. The group malpractice insurance policy maintained by BMC for its house staff is separate from the individual policies provided for the faculty and paid for by their department practice plans. Other benefits available to other BMC employees but not to house officers include vision care, disability insurance, health care and dependent care reimbursement accounts, extended sick leave, and earned time. Unlike other BMC employees, residents are allowed to defer payments of some of their Federal and bank loans for medical school during a portion of their residency because they are still considered to be training for a job. . . .

Over 20 years ago, this Agency — despite the dissent of one member — concluded that hospital house staff were "primarily" students, and thus were not employees within the meaning of Section 2(3) of the Act. *Cedars-Sinai*, 223 NLRB at 253. The Board "clarified" its position shortly thereafter to explain that it did not mean to find that private sector house staff were not covered by the statute, but that as a particular type of student they were not entitled to collective-bargaining rights. *St. Clare's Hospital*, 229 NLRB at 1003.

We are convinced by normal statutory and legal analysis, including resort to legislative history, experience, and the overwhelming weight of judicial and scholarly opinion, that the Board reached an erroneous result in *Cedars-Sinai.* Accordingly, we overrule that decision and its offspring, conclude that house staff are employees as defined by the Act, and find that such individuals are therefore entitled to all the statutory rights and obligations that flow from our conclusion. . . .

We begin our analysis with reference to Section 2(3) of the Act. That key statutory language is as follows:

> The term "employee" shall include any employee . . . unless the Act [this subchapter] explicitly states otherwise . . . but shall not include any individual employed as an agricultural laborer, or in the domestic service of any family or person at his home, or any individual employed by his parent or spouse, or any individual employed as an independent contractor . . . .

The "breadth of § 2(3)'s definition is striking. The Act specifically applies to 'any employee.' " *Sure-Tan, Inc. v. NLRB,* 467 U.S. 883, 891-892 (1984) (undocumented aliens "plainly come within the broad statutory definition of 'employee' "). The exclusions listed in the statute are limited and narrow, and do not, on their face, encompass the category "students." Thus, unless there are other statutory or policy reasons for excluding house staff, they literally and plainly come within the meaning of "employee" as defined in the Act. We find no such reasons. . . .

At common law, a servant was one who performed services for another and was subject to the other's control or right of control. Consideration, i.e., payment, is strongly indicative of employee status. . . .

The Supreme Court in *Town & Country*[, 516 U.S. 85 (1995),] echoed the same logic in its analysis of Section 2(3). Specifically, the Court noted that the Board's definition of the term "employee" as used in the Act reflected the common law agency doctrine of the conventional master-servant relationship. In this recent case, the Court reiterated that the language of this section of the statute is "broad":

> The ordinary dictionary definition of "employee" includes any "person who works for another in return for financial or other compensation." American Heritage Dictionary 604 (3d ed. 1992). See also Black's Law Dictionary 525 (6th ed. 1990) (an employee is a "person in the service of another under any contract of hire, express or implied, oral or written, where the employer has the power or right to control and direct the employees in the material details of how the work is to be performed"). The phrasing of the Act seems to reiterate the breadth of the ordinary dictionary definition, for it says "[t]he term 'employee' shall include *any* employee." 29 U.S.C. § 152(3) (1988 ed.) [Emphasis added.]

> [T]he Board's broad, literal interpretation of the word "employee" is consistent with several of the Act's purposes, such as protecting "the right of employees to organize for mutual aid without employer interference" . . . and "encouraging and protecting the collective-bargaining process." . . .

[*Town & Country Electric,* 516 U.S. at 90-91 (some citations omitted).]

Ample evidence exists here to support our finding that interns, residents and fellows fall within the broad definition of "employee" under Section 2(3), notwithstanding that a purpose of their being at a hospital may also be, in part, educational. That house staff may also be students does not thereby change the evidence of their "employee" status. As stressed above, nothing in the statute suggests that persons who are students but also employees should be exempted from the coverage and protection of the Act. The essential elements of the house staff's relationship with the Hospital obviously define an employer-employee relationship.

First, house staff work for an employer within the meaning of the Act. Second, house staff are compensated for their services. The house staff, as noted, receive compensation in the form of a stipend. . . . Further, the interns, residents, and fellows receive fringe benefits and other emoluments reflective of employee status. . . . Third, house staff provide patient care for the Hospital. Most noteworthy is the undisputed fact that house staff spend up to 80 percent of their time at the Hospital engaged in direct patient care. . . .

Additionally, while house staff possess certain attributes of student status, they are unlike many others in the traditional academic setting. Interns, residents, and fellows do not pay tuition or student fees. They do not take typical examinations in a classroom setting, nor do they receive grades as such. They do not register in a traditional fashion. Their education and student status is geared to gaining sufficient experience and knowledge to become Board-certified in a specialty. . . .

We cannot subscribe to dissenting Member Brame's forecast of doom to medical education as a consequence of our decision today. We simply cannot say, either as a matter of law or as a matter of policy, that permitting medical interns, residents and fellows to be considered as employees entitled to the benefits of the Act would make them any less loyal to their employer or to their patients. Nor can we assume that the unions that represent them will make demands upon them or extract concessions form their employers that will interfere with the educational mission of the institutions they serve, or prevent them from obtaining the education necessary to complete their professional training. If there is anything we have learned in the long history of this Act, it is that unionism and collective bargaining are dynamic institutions capable of adjusting to new and changing work contexts and demands in every sector of our evolving economy. We have no doubt that they can also adjust to accommodate the special functions of medical house staff. To assume otherwise is not only needlessly pessimistic, but gives little credit to the intelligence and ingenuity of the parties. . . .

MEMBER HURTGEN, dissenting.

. . . The majority goes to some length to establish that house staff fall within the statutory definition of employee. They thereby miss my essential point. I am *not* necessarily suggesting that house staff cannot fall within the statutory definition. Rather, I conclude that, as a policy matter, the Board should continue to exercise its discretion to exclude them for purposes of collective bargaining.

No case has held that the Act *compels* a conclusion that house staff are employees for purposes of collective bargaining. Nor does the language of Section

2(3) compel that result. That section provides that "the term 'employee' shall include any employee." Thus, the Act defines the word "employee" by reference to the word itself. This is hardly a statutory command that house staff must be regarded as employees for bargaining purposes.[6]

Second, I note that all courts considering the matter have upheld the Board's discretion to exclude house staff from the status of employees who are entitled to the collective-bargaining provisions of the Act.

Further, I note that, in 1979, Congress was presented with a bill that would have specifically overruled *Cedars-Sinai/St. Clare's*, and would have *required* the Board to treat house staff as unit employees. The proposed legislation was rejected. . . .

The majority observes that no problems have developed in the public sector where house staff are involved in collective bargaining. I would remind them that these governmental employees do not have the right to strike. The majority would now thrust house staff into the NLRA sector where there is a right to strike. In these circumstances, it surely does not follow that the absence of strikes in the public sector will translate to an absence of strikes under the NLRA. . . .

Although the Board has the power to change longstanding precedent, that change should be grounded in experience. An agency can change its rules and policies if there are "change[d] circumstances."[7] But, there is no record evidence herein of "change[d] circumstances." More particularly, there is no record evidence that the essentially educational nature of the house staff experience has changed to any appreciable degree in the past 20 years. Indeed, the Regional Director found, in the instant case, that the graduate medical programs of Respondent are substantially the same as those in *Cedars-Sinai and St. Clare's*.

In essence, there is no change in circumstances, but only a change in Board member composition. I would not alter longstanding and workable precedent simply because of a change in Board membership. In my view, the interests of stability and predictability in the law require that established precedent be reversed only upon a showing of manifest need. There is no such showing here. . . .

[Dissent by MEMBER BRAME omitted.]

BROWN UNIVERSITY
342 N.L.R.B. 483 (2004)

. . . The case presents the issue of whether graduate student assistants who are admitted into, not hired by, a university, and for whom supervised teaching or research is an integral component of their academic development, must be treated as employees for purposes of collective bargaining under Section 2(3) of the Act. The Board in *NYU* [*New York University*, 332 N.L.R.B. 1205 (2000),] concluded that graduate student assistants are employees under Section 2(3) of the Act and

---

[6] [n.4] The section contains explicit exceptions (e.g., agricultural laborers). These persons *must* be excluded. As explained above, others *may* be excluded. . . .

[7] [n.7] See *Permian Basin Area Rate Cases*, 390 U.S. 747, 784 (1968).

therefore are to be extended the right to engage in collective bargaining. That decision reversed more than 25 years of Board precedent. That precedent was never successfully challenged in court or in Congress. In our decision today, we return to the Board's pre-*NYU* precedent that graduate student assistants are not statutory employees.

Until *NYU*, the Board's principle was that graduate student assistants are primarily students and not statutory employees. See [*Leland Stanford Junior University*, 214 N.L.R.B. 621 (1974)]. The Board concluded that graduate student assistants, who perform services at a university in connection with their studies, have a predominately academic, rather than economic, relationship with their school. Accordingly, the Board held that they were not employees within the intendment of the Act.

This longstanding approach towards graduate student assistants changed abruptly with *NYU*. The Board decided that graduate student assistants meet the test establishing a conventional master-servant relationship with a university, and that they are statutory employees who necessarily have "statutory rights to organize and bargain with their employer." 332 N.L.R.B. at 1209. . . .

The Petitioner [union] sought to represent a unit of approximately 450 graduate students employed as teaching assistants (TAs), research assistants (RAs) in certain social sciences and humanities departments, and proctors. The Petitioner, relying on *NYU* . . . contended to the Regional Director that the petitioned-for TAs, RAs, and proctors are employees within the meaning of Section 2(3) and that they constitute an appropriate unit for collective bargaining.

Brown contended to the Regional Director that the petitioned-for individuals are not statutory employees because this case is factually distinguishable from *NYU*. Brown asserted that, unlike *NYU*, where only a few departments required students to serve as a TA or RA to receive a degree, most university departments at Brown require a student to serve as a TA or RA to obtain a degree. Brown contended that these degree requirements demonstrate that the petitioned-for students have only an educational relationship and not an employment relationship with Brown. Brown also argued that the TA, RA, and proctor awards constitute financial aid to students, emphasizing that students receive the same stipend, regardless of whether they "work" for those funds as a TA, RA, or proctor, or whether they receive funding for a fellowship, which does not require any work. . . .

The Regional Director, applying *NYU*, rejected Brown's arguments. She also concluded that the petitioned-for unit was appropriate, and she directed an election. The election was conducted on December 6, 2001, and the ballots were impounded pending the disposition of this request for review. . . .

Although varying somewhat among the departments, a teaching assistant generally is assigned to lead a small section of a large lecture course taught by a professor. Although functions of research assistants vary within departments, these graduate students, as the title implies, generally conduct research under a research grant received by a faculty member. Proctors perform a variety of duties for university departments or administrative offices. Their duties depend on the individual needs of the particular department or the university administrative office in which they work and, thus, include a wide variety of tasks. Unlike TAs and RAs, proctors generally do not perform teaching or research functions. Fellowships do not require any classroom or departmental assignments; those who receive dissertation fellowships are required to be working on their dissertation. . . .

In their pursuit of a Ph.D. degree, graduate students must complete coursework, be admitted to degree candidacy (usually following a qualifying examination), and complete a dissertation, all of which are subject to the oversight of faculty and the degree requirements of the department involved. In addition, most Ph.D. candidates must teach in order to obtain their degree. Although these TAs (as well as RAs and proctors) receive money from the Employer, that is also true of fellows who do not perform any services. Thus, the services are not related to the money received.

The faculty of each department is responsible for awarding TAs, RAs, or proctorships to its students. To receive an award, the individual usually must be enrolled as a student in that department. . . .

The amount of funding for a fellowship, TA, RA, and proctorship generally is the same. The basic stipend for a fellowship, TA, RA, or proctorship is $12,800, although some fellowships, RAs, and TAs are slightly more. Tuition remission and health fee payments generally are the same for TAs, RAs, proctors, and fellows, although the amount of tuition remission depends on the number of courses taken by a student.

Brown treats funds for TA, RAs, proctors, and fellowships as financial aid and represents them as such in universitywide or departmental brochures. Graduate student assistants receive a portion of their stipend award twice a month, and the amount of stipend received is the same regardless of the number of hours spent performing services. The awards do not include any benefits, such as vacation and sick leave, retirement, or health insurance. . . .

The Supreme Court has recognized that principles developed for use in the industrial setting cannot be "imposed blindly on the academic world." *NLRB v. Yeshiva University*, 444 U.S. 672, 680-681 (1980), citing *Syracuse University*, 204 N.L.R.B. 641, 643 (1973). While graduate programs may differ somewhat in their details, the concerns raised in *NYU*, supra, and here forcefully illustrate the problem of attempting to force the student-university relationship into the traditional employer-employee framework. After carefully analyzing these issues, we have come to the conclusion that the Board's 25-year pre-*NYU* principle of regarding graduate students as nonemployees was sound and well reasoned. It is clear to us that graduate student assistants, including those at Brown, are primarily students and have a primarily educational, not economic, relationship with their university. Accordingly, we overrule *NYU* and return to the pre-*NYU* Board precedent. . . .

In Section 1 of the Act, Congress found that the strikes, industrial strife and unrest that preceded the Act were caused by the "inequality of bargaining power between employees who do not possess full freedom of association or actual liberty of contract, and employers who are organized in the corporate or other forms of ownership . . . ."[8] To remove the burden on interstate commerce caused by this industrial unrest, Congress extended to and protected the right of employees, if they so choose, to organize and bargain collectively with their employer, encouraging the "friendly adjustment of industrial disputes arising out of differences as to wages, hours or other conditions . . . ." *Id.* The Act was premised on the view that there is a fundamental conflict between the interests of the employers and employees engaged in collective-bargaining under its auspices and that " '[t]he parties . . . proceed from contrary and to an extent antagonistic viewpoints and concepts of self-interest' ":[9]

> [T]he damage caused to the nation's commerce by the inequality of bargaining power between employees and employers was one of the central problems addressed by the Act. A central policy of the Act is that the protection of the right of employees to organize and bargain collectively restores equality of bargaining power between employers and employees and safeguards commerce from the harm caused by labor disputes. *The vision of a fundamentally economic relationship between employers and employees is inescapable.*[10] . . .

We emphasize the simple, undisputed fact that all the petitioned-for individuals are students and must first be enrolled at Brown to be awarded a TA, RA, or proctorship. Even students who have finished their coursework and are writing their dissertation must be enrolled to receive these awards. Further, students serving as graduate student assistants spend only a limited number of hours performing their duties, and it is beyond dispute that their principal time commitment at Brown is focused on obtaining a degree and, thus, being a student. Also, as shown below, their service as a graduate student assistant is part and parcel of the core elements of the Ph.D. degree. Because they are first and foremost students, and their status as a graduate student assistant is contingent on their continued enrollment as students, we find that that they are primarily students.

We also emphasize that the money received by the TAs, RAs, and proctors is the same as that received by fellows. Thus, the money is not "consideration for work." It is financial aid to a student. The evidence demonstrates that the relationship between Brown's graduate student assistants and Brown is primarily educational. . . .

[I]n light of the status of graduate student assistants as students, the role of graduate student assistantships in graduate education, the graduate student assistants' relationship with the faculty, and the financial support they receive to attend Brown, we conclude that the overall relationship between the graduate student assistants and Brown is primarily an educational one, rather than an economic one. . . .

Imposing collective bargaining would have a deleterious impact on overall educational decisions by the Brown faculty and administration. These decisions

---

[8] [n.17] Sec. 1, 29 U.S.C. § 151.

[9] [n.19] *NLRB v. Insurance Agents*, 361 U.S. 477, 488 (1960).

[10] [n.20] *WBAI Pacifica Foundation*, 328 N.L.R.B. 1273, 1275 (1999) (emphasis added).

would include broad academic issues involving class size, time, length, and location, as well as issues over graduate assistants' duties, hours, and stipends. In addition, collective bargaining would intrude upon decisions over who, what, and where to teach or research — the principal prerogatives of an educational institution like Brown. Although these issues give the appearance of being terms and conditions of employment, all involve educational concerns and decisions, which are based on different, and often individualized considerations.

Based on all of the above-statutory and policy considerations, we concluded that the graduate student assistants are not employees within the meaning of Section 2(3) of the Act. Accordingly, we decline to extend collective bargaining rights to them, and we dismiss the petition. . . .

Our [dissenting] colleagues argue that graduate student assistants are employees at common law. Even assuming arguendo that this is so, it does not follow that they are employees within the meaning of the Act. The issue of employee status under the Act turns on whether Congress intended to cover the individual in question. The issue is not to be decided purely on the basis of older common-law concepts. For example, a managerial employee may perform services for, and be under the control of, an employer. Indeed, the Supreme Court used the term "managerial *employee*" in *Bell Aerospace Co.*, 416 U.S. 267 (1974). And yet, the Court held that these persons were not statutory employees. . . .

MEMBERS LIEBMAN and WALSH, dissenting.

Collective bargaining by graduate student employees is increasingly a fact of American university life. Graduate student unions have been recognized at campuses from coast to coast, from the State University of New York to the University of California. Overruling a recent, unanimous precedent, the majority now declares that graduate student employees at private universities are not employees protected by the National Labor Relations Act and have no right to form unions. The majority's reasons, at bottom, amount to the claim that graduate-student collective bargaining is simply incompatible with the nature and mission of the university. This revelation will surely come as a surprise on many campuses — not least at New York University, a first-rate institution where graduate students now work under a collective-bargaining agreement reached in the wake of the decision that is overruled here.

Today's decision is woefully out of touch with contemporary academic reality. Based on an image of the university that was already outdated when the decisions the majority looks back to . . . were issued in the 1970's, it shows a troubling lack of interest in empirical evidence. Even worse, perhaps, is the majority's approach to applying the Act. It disregards the plain language of the statute — which defines "employees" so broadly that graduate students who perform services for, and under the control of, their universities are easily covered — to make a policy decision that rightly belongs to Congress. The reasons offered by the majority for its decision do not stand up to scrutiny. But even if they did, it would not be for the Board to act upon them. The result of the Board's ruling is harsh. Not only can universities avoid dealing with graduate student unions, they are also free to retaliate against graduate students who act together to address their working conditions. . . .

We would adhere to the Board's decision in *NYU* and thus affirm the Regional Director's decision in this case.

In *NYU*, applying principles that had recently been articulated in *Boston Medical Center*, the Board held that the graduate assistants involved there were employees within the meaning of Section 2(3) of the Act, because they performed services under the control and direction of the university, for which they were compensated by the university. The Board found "no basis to deny collective-bargaining rights to statutory employees merely because they are employed by an educational institution in which they are enrolled as students." 332 N.L.R.B. at 1205. It was undisputed, the Board observed, that "graduate assistants are not within any category of workers that is excluded from the definition of 'employee' in Section 2(3)." Id. at 1206.

In turn, the Board rejected policy grounds as a basis for effectively creating a new exclusion. Rejecting claims that graduate assistants lacked a traditional economic relationship with the university, the Board pointed out that the relationship in fact paralleled that between faculty and university, which was amenable to collective bargaining. The university's assertion that extending collective-bargaining rights to graduate students would infringe on academic freedom was also rejected. Such concerns, the Board explained, were speculative. Citing 30 years of experience with bargaining units of faculty members, and the flexibility of collective bargaining as an institution, the Board concluded that the "parties can 'confront any issues of academic freedom as they would any other issue in collective bargaining.'" Id., quoting *Boston Medical Center*, 330 N.L.R.B. at 164. . . .

Here, the Regional Director correctly applied the Board's decision in *NYU*. She concluded that the teaching assistants (TAs), research assistants (RAs), and proctors were statutory employees, because they performed services under the direction and control of Brown, and were compensated for those services by the university. With respect to the TAs, the Regional Director rejected, on both factual and legal grounds, Brown's attempt to distinguish *NYU* on the basis that teaching was a degree requirement at Brown. Finally, she found that the TAs, RAs, and proctors were not, as Brown contended, merely temporary employees who could not be included in a bargaining unit. Accordingly, she directed a representation election, so that Brown's graduate students could choose for themselves whether or not to be represented by a union. . . .

"[W]e declare the federal law to be that graduate student assistants are not employees within the meaning of Section 2(3) of the Act," says the majority. But the majority has overstepped its authority, overlooked the economic realities of the academic world, and overruled *NYU* without ever coming to terms with the rationale for that decision. The result leaves graduate students outside the Act's protection and without recourse to its mechanisms for resolving labor disputes. The developments that brought graduate students to the Board will not go away, but they will have to be addressed elsewhere, if the majority's decision stands. That result does American universities no favors. We dissent.

POST PROBLEM DISCUSSION

1.   How do you think you and the other Wagner Scholars in our problem will be classified? How does your answer to that question affect the dean's threat to expel you? (Hint: when considering this question, note that the NLRA prohibits retaliation against an employee's pro-union activity — you'll read more about this prohibition in Chapter 3's discussion of Section 8(a)(3) of the NLRA).

2.   Are *Boston Medical* and *Brown University* consistent or do they merely represent two different political lineups on the NLRB? At the time of this book's publication, graduate students at various universities are already pursuing cases that seek to reverse *Brown University*. Moreover, the NLRB recently invited briefs on whether to overrule *Brown University. See NYU* (2-RC-23481), and *Polytechnic Institute of New York University* (29-RC-12054), Notice and Invitation to File Briefs (June 22, 2012). It's possible that by the time you read this, those arguments may have already been successful.

3.   In his *Boston Medical* dissent, Member Hurtgen laments the NLRB's reversal of precedent without an obvious change in circumstances. Think about that argument as you read various flip-flops in NLRB case law throughout the semester. Is the NLRB limiting its policy changes to situations where circumstances appear to be different? Should it?

4.   Do you agree with the general conclusions in these cases: that medical residents are more like employees than students and that graduate assistants are more like students than employees? Is your answer "it depends"? Do *Boston Medical* and *Brown University* allow for different results given a different set of facts, or are the decisions setting forth firm rules about medical residents and graduate students?

5.   What do you think of Member Hurtgen's argument in his dissent in *Boston Medical* that the NLRB has the ability to exclude workers who meet the definition of "employee" under Section 2(3) of the NLRA? Do you think that Congress intended to give the NLRB that level of discretion? If so, do you think the exercise of that discretion warranted in *Boston Medical*?

6.   What do you make of the NLRB's statement in *Brown University* that graduate students' classification as under the common law test doesn't necessarily apply to the NLRA? Is this consistent with *Roadway* and its reliance on the Supreme Court's *United Insurance* decision?

7.   The dissent in *Brown University* argues, in a portion of the decision not included here, that graduate students in most modern universities have a far more substantial role in teaching than they used to. Based on your experiences as an undergrad, how do you view the role of graduate students, especially TAs? Did you view them more as teachers, along the lines of your professors and other full-time instructors? Or did they seem more like other students?

8.   The NLRB's approach in both *Boston Medical* and *Brown University* provides a binary choice: the workers are either employees or students under the NLRA, but not both. Does this make sense? Is there a better approach? *See* Anne Marie Lofaso, *The Vanishing Employee: Putting the Autonomous Dignified Union*

Worker Back to Work, 5 F.I.U. L. REV. 495, 524-25 (2010) (criticizing NLRB's categorical approach in *Brown University*); Ellen Dannin, *Understanding How Employees' Rights To Organize Under the National Labor Relations Act Have Been Limited: The Case of Brown University*, AM. CONST. SOC'Y FOR L. & POL. (2008) (same). For instance, as some states and countries do, why not explicitly allow unionization and some limited form of bargaining for students, no matter their classification under the common-law test? *See* Coalition of Graduate Employee Unions, *Frequently Asked Questions: Union Rights of Graduate Students by State* (listing 14 states that expressly permit graduate students at public universities to unionize), http://cgeu.org/faq.php#12.

9.   Imagine a situation in which a company participates in a program that provides various training, educational, and rehabilitative services to mentally and physically disabled adults. As part of that program, the company had ten disabled individuals work as janitors along with five non-disabled janitors. All of these janitors were supervised by two non-disabled "leadpersons." The disabled and non-disabled janitors performed the same duties, were expected to meet the same quality standards, worked the same hours, and received the same wages and benefits. Disabled workers, however, were permitted to work at their own pace. A trainer came once a week to train new disabled janitors and to retrain those whose performance had slipped. A mental health counselor was also available to provide counseling as needed. Although non-disabled workers were subject to a progressive discipline policy, the disabled workers were not disciplined for any conduct related to their disabilities. Rather, the trainer worked with them to correct the problems or they were assigned to a different team. Are the disabled janitors employees under the NLRA? *See Brevard Achievement Center, Inc.*, 342 N.L.R.B. 982 (2004) (finding, under similar facts, that janitors were not employees because their relationship with the company was primarily rehabilitative, not economic).

What if the workers were part of a "workfare" program in which they were required to work to receive welfare benefits? *See* David L. Gregory, *Br(e)aking the Exploitation of Labor?: Tensions Regarding the Welfare Workforce*, 25 FORDHAM URB. L.J. 1, 22-25 (1997) (describing approaches under non-NLRA employment statutes); Craig L. Briskin & Kimberly A. Thomas, Note, *The Waging of Welfare: All Work and No Pay?*, 33 HARV. C.R.-C.L. L. REV. 559, 570-72 (1998) (describing uncertainty regarding how NLRB will classify workfare participants). What if the workers were volunteers? *See* Mitchell H. Rubinstein, *Our Nation's Forgotten Workers: The Unprotected Volunteers*, 9 U. PA. J. LAB. & EMP. L. 147 (2006) (describing varied approaches to addressing volunteers' classification).

3.   Unions Salts

In Chapter 5, you will read about the employers' ability to exclude union organizers from worksites. A simple preview of that issue is that an employer has extraordinary freedom to bar from its property any union organizers who are not employees. The Supreme Court solidified this result in its 1992 *Lechmere* decision. *See Lechmere, Inc. v. NLRB*, 502 U.S. 527 (1992). This is a significant problem for unions, as getting initial face-to-face discussions with employees is often a key factor in gaining support. However, note the condition placed on that rule: an employer's ability to bar organizers from its property hinges on the organizers *not being employees.* As you might imagine, unions have increasingly taken advantage of that condition by getting its organizers to apply for jobs at companies they were trying to organize. This strategy is called "salting."

For our purposes in this chapter, the central question is whether union salts are employees. Employers argued that they were not, because the salts' primary employment was with the union rather than with the targeted employer. Unions countered that the salts were merely trying to moonlight, which doesn't typically eliminate an individual's employee status at either of her employers. The NLRB concluded that salts were employees; as the excerpt describes below, the Supreme Court ultimately agreed. Later, in Chapter 4, we will consider how to analyze cases alleging that an employer unlawfully refused to hire salts. Therefore, as you read the Court's holding in *Town & Country* ask yourself whether, even if you agree with the Court's holding, there are any differences between salts and other applicants that might warrant distinct treatment in other contexts.

NLRB v. TOWN & COUNTRY ELECTRIC, INC.
516 U.S. 85 (1995)

JUSTICE BREYER delivered the opinion of the Court.

Can a worker be a company's "employee," within the terms of the National Labor Relations Act, if, at the same time, a union pays that worker to help the union organize the company? We agree with the National Labor Relations Board that the answer is "yes."

The relevant background is the following: Town & Country Electric, Inc., a nonunion electrical contractor, wanted to hire several licensed Minnesota electricians for construction work in Minnesota. Town & Country (through an employment agency) advertised for job applicants, but it refused to interview 10 of 11 union applicants (including two professional union staff) who responded to the advertisement. Its employment agency hired the one union applicant whom Town & Country interviewed, but he was dismissed after only a few days on the job.

The members of the International Brotherhood of Electrical Workers, Locals 292 and 343) (Union), filed a complaint with the National Labor Relations Board claiming that Town & Country and the employment agency had refused to interview (or retain) them because of their union membership. An Administrative Law Judge ruled in favor of the Union members, and the Board affirmed that ruling.

In the course of its decision, the Board determined that all 11 job applicants (including the two Union officials and the one member briefly hired) were "employees" as the Act defines that word. The Board recognized that under well-established law, it made no difference that the 10 members who were simply applicants were never hired. See *Phelps Dodge Corp. v. NLRB*, 313 U.S. 177, 185-186 (1941) (statutory word "employee" includes job applicants, for otherwise the Act's prohibition of "'discrimination in regard to hire'" would "serve no function"). Neither, in the Board's view, did it matter (with respect to the meaning of the word "employee") that the Union members intended to try to organize the company if they secured the advertised jobs, nor that the Union would pay them while they set about their organizing. The Board then rejected the company's fact-based explanations for its refusals to interview or to retain these 11 "employees" and held that the company had committed "unfair labor practices" by discriminating on the basis of union membership.

The United States Court of Appeals for the Eighth Circuit reversed the Board. It held that the Board had incorrectly interpreted the statutory word "employee." In the court's view, that key word does not cover (and therefore the Act does not protect from antiunion discrimination) those who work for a company while a union simultaneously pays them to organize that company. . . .

The relevant statutory language is the following:

> *"The term 'employee' shall include any employee, and shall not be limited to the employees of a particular employer, unless this subchapter explicitly states otherwise*, and shall include any individual whose work has ceased as a consequence of, or in connection with, any current labor dispute or because of any unfair labor practice, and who has not obtained any other regular and substantially equivalent employment, but shall not include any individual employed as an agricultural laborer, or in the domestic service of any family or person at his home, or any individual employed by his parent or spouse, or any individual having the status of an independent contractor, or any individual employed as a supervisor, or any individual employed by an employer subject to the Railway Labor Act, as amended from time to time, or by any other person who is not an employer as herein defined."
> § 152(3) (emphasis added).

We must specifically decide whether the Board may lawfully interpret this language to include company workers who are also paid union organizers. . . .

Several strong general arguments favor the Board's position. For one thing, the Board's decision is consistent with the broad language of the Act itself — language that is broad enough to include those company workers whom a union also pays for organizing. The ordinary dictionary definition of "employee" includes any "person who works for another in return for financial or other compensation." American Heritage Dictionary 604 (3d ed.1992). See also Black's Law Dictionary 525 (6th ed.1990) (an employee is a "person in the service of another under any contract of hire, express or implied, oral or written, where the employer has the power or right to control and direct the employee in the material details of how the work is to be performed"). The phrasing of the Act seems to reiterate the breadth of the ordinary dictionary definition, for it says "[t]he term 'employee' shall include *any* employee." 29 U.S.C. § 152(3) (1988 ed.) (emphasis added). Of course, the Act's definition also contains a list of exceptions, for example, for independent contractors, agricultural laborers, domestic workers, and employees subject to the Railway Labor Act; but no exception applies here.

For another thing, the Board's broad, literal interpretation of the word "employee" is consistent with several of the Act's purposes, such as protecting "the right of employees to organize for mutual aid without employer interference," *Republic Aviation Corp. v. NLRB*, 324 U.S. 793, 798, (1945); see also 29 U.S.C. § 157 (1988 ed.); and "encouraging and protecting the collective-bargaining process." *Sure-Tan,*

Inc. v. NLRB[, 467 U.S. 883, 892]. And, insofar as one can infer purpose from congressional reports and floor statements, those sources too are consistent with the Board's broad interpretation of the word. It is fairly easy to find statements to the effect that an "employee" simply "means someone who works for another for hire," and includes "every man on a payroll." At the same time, contrary statements, suggesting a narrow or qualified view of the word, are scarce, or nonexistent — except, of course, those made in respect to the specific (here inapplicable) exclusions written into the statute.

Further, a broad, literal reading of the statute is consistent with cases in this Court such as, say, *Sure-Tan, Inc. v. NLRB, supra* (the Act covers undocumented aliens), where the Court wrote that the "breadth of § 2(3)'s definition is striking: the Act squarely applies to 'any employee.'" 467 U.S., at 891. See *NLRB v. Hendricks County Rural Elec. Membership Corp.*, 454 U.S. 170, 189-190 (1981) (certain "confidential employees" fall within the definition of "employees"); *Phelps Dodge Corp. v. NLRB*, 313 U.S., at 185-186 (job applicants are "employees"). Cf. *Chemical Workers v. Pittsburgh Plate Glass Co.*, 404 U.S. 157, 166 (1971) (retired persons are not "employees" because they do not "work for another for hire"). . . .

Finally, at least one other provision of the 1947 Labor Management Relations Act seems specifically to contemplate the possibility that a company's employee might also work for a union. This provision forbids an employer (say, the company) to make payments to a person employed by a union, but simultaneously exempts from that ban wages paid by the company to "any . . . employee of a labor organization, who is *also* an employee" of the company. 29 U.S.C. § 186(c)(1) (emphasis added). If Town & Country is right, there would not seem to be many (or any) human beings to which this last phrase could apply.

Town & Country believes that it can overcome these general considerations, favoring a broad, literal interpretation of the Act, through an argument that rests primarily upon the common law of agency. It first argues that our prior decisions resort to common-law principles in defining the term "employee." And it also points out that the Board itself, in its decision, found "no bar to applying common law agency principles to the determination whether a paid union organizer is an 'employee.'"

Town & Country goes on to argue that application of common-law agency principles *requires* an interpretation of "employee" that excludes paid union organizers. It points to a section of the Restatement (Second) of Agency (dealing with *respondeat superior* liability for torts), which says:

> "Since . . . the relation of master and servant is dependent upon the right of the master to control the conduct of the servant in the performance of the service, giving service to two masters at the same time normally involves a breach of duty by the servant to one or both of them. . . . [A person] cannot be a servant of two masters in doing an act as to which an intent to serve one necessarily excludes an intent to serve the other." Restatement (Second) of Agency § 226, Comment *a*, p. 499 (1957).

It argues that, when the paid union organizer serves the union — at least at certain times in certain ways-the organizer is acting adversely to the company.

Indeed, it says, the organizer may stand ready to desert the company upon request by the union, in which case, the union, not the company, would have "the right . . . to control the conduct of the servant." *Ibid.* Thus, it concludes, the worker must be the servant (*i.e.*, the "employee") of the union alone.

As Town & Country correctly notes, in the context of reviewing lower courts' interpretations of statutory terms, we have said on several occasions that when Congress uses the term "employee" in a statute that does not define the term, courts interpreting the statute " 'must infer, unless the statute otherwise dictates, that Congress means to incorporate the established meaning of th[at] ter[m]. . . . In some cases, there may be a question about whether the Board's departure from the common law of agency with respect to particular questions and in a particular statutory context, renders its interpretation unreasonable. See *NLRB v. United Ins. Co., supra,* at 256, ("independent contractor" exclusion). But no such question is presented here since the Board's interpretation of the term "employee" is consistent with the common law.

Town & Country's common-law argument fails, quite simply, because, in our view, the Board correctly found that it lacks sufficient support in common law. The Restatement's hornbook rule (to which the quoted commentary is appended) says that a

> "person *may* be the servant of two masters . . . *at one time as to one act,* if the service to one does not involve *abandonment* of the service to the other." Restatement (Second) of Agency § 226, at 498 (emphasis added).

The Board, in quoting this rule, concluded that service to the union for pay does not "involve abandonment of . . . service" to the company.

And, that conclusion seems correct. Common sense suggests that as a worker goes about his or her *ordinary* tasks during a working day, say, wiring sockets or laying cable, he or she *is* subject to the control of the company employer, whether or not the union also pays the worker. The company, the worker, the union, all would expect that to be so. And, that being so, that union and company interests or control might *sometimes* differ should make no difference. . . . Moreover, union organizers may limit their organizing to nonwork hours. If so, union organizing, when done for pay but during *nonwork* hours, would seem equivalent to simple moonlighting, a practice wholly consistent with a company's control over its workers as to their assigned duties.

Town & Country's "abandonment" argument is yet weaker insofar as the activity that constitutes an "abandonment," *i.e.*, ordinary union organizing activity, is itself specifically protected by the Act. This is true even if a company perceives those protected activities as disloyal. After all, the employer has no legal right to require that, as part of his or her service to the company, a worker refrain from engaging in protected activity.

Neither are we convinced by the practical considerations that Town & Country adds to its agency law argument. The company refers to a Union resolution permitting members to work for nonunion firms, which, the company says, reflects a union effort to "salt" nonunion companies with union members seeking to organize them. Supported by *amici curiae*, it argues that "salts" might try to harm the company, perhaps quitting when the company needs them, perhaps disparaging the company to others, perhaps even sabotaging the firm or its products. Therefore, the company concludes, Congress could not have meant paid union organizers to have been included as "employees" under the Act.

This practical argument suffers from several serious problems. For one thing, nothing in this record suggests that such acts of disloyalty were present, in kind or degree, to the point where the company might lose control over the worker's normal workplace tasks. Certainly the Union's resolution contains nothing that suggests, requires, encourages, or condones impermissible or unlawful activity. For another thing, the argument proves too much. If a paid union organizer might quit, leaving a company employer in the lurch, so too might an unpaid organizer, or a worker who has found a better job, or one whose family wants to move elsewhere. And if an overly zealous union organizer might hurt the company through unlawful acts, so might another unpaid zealot (who may know less about the law), or a dissatisfied worker (who may lack an outlet for his or her grievances). This does not mean they are not "employees."

Further, the law offers alternative remedies for Town & Country's concerns, short of excluding paid or unpaid union organizers from all protection under the Act. For example, a company disturbed by legal but undesirable activity, such as quitting without notice, can offer its employees fixed-term contracts, rather than hiring them "at will" as in the case before us; or it can negotiate with its workers for a notice period. A company faced with unlawful (or possibly unlawful) activity can discipline or dismiss the worker, file a complaint with the Board, or notify law enforcement authorities. . . .

For these reasons the judgment of the Court of Appeals is vacated, and the case is remanded for further proceedings consistent with this opinion.

POST PROBLEM DISCUSSION

1.   Who do you think has the better argument, the Court or the employer? In particular, what about the employer's concern about the disloyalty issue? Once salts are classified as employees, employers must treat them in most respects the same as any other employee or job applicant (we'll see some exceptions in Chapter 3). Is this fair? In other words, should an employer be required to hire or keep someone who is actively working against the employer's interests by trying to unionize the workforce? Do the NLRA's policies help answer this question?

2.   One less obvious benefit of salts is that, in addition to their value as organizers, they can help ensure that employers are not discriminating against job applicants with union ties. For more on this "tester" role, see Michael C. Duff, *Union Salts as Administrative Private Attorneys General*, 32 BERKELEY J. EMP. & LAB. L. 1 (2011).

C. Excluded Employees

1. Managers

PROBLEM #3: COMPUWARE'S PURCHASING CONTROLLER

Consider again CompuWare, the software company in Problem #1. Following the unionization attempt by CompuWare's freelancers, the union involved began seeking other groups of CompuWare workers to organize. One group consisted of employees who worked in CompuWare's new tablet manufacturing facility. This facility is where CompuWare manufactured its new competitor to the iPad: the MicroTab. The union sought to organize all hourly workers at the facility and managed to get enough support to seek an election. However, the election looked like it was going to be close, and the union was worried in particular about an openly anti-union employee, Bill, who was the facility's "purchasing controller." Bill's primary responsibility was to purchase supplies needed by the facility to make and ship the MicroTab — a task that involved approximately $5 million in expenditures the previous year.

Like other employees, Bill is paid by the hour, although he earns slightly more than virtually all of the other hourly employees. Bill's direct supervisor is the facility's general manager, in contrast to other employees, who have intermediate-level supervisors. Bill also works mostly separate from other employees, except to communicate regarding needed supplies. Most of Bill's purchases are for regularly needed supplies that he obtains from an established set of suppliers. However, Bill is permitted to change suppliers if he believes the change would improve the cost, quality, or timeliness of the supply orders. Before making such a change, Bill will consult other employees who have any relevant technical expertise. Any change from the normal suppliers and their established prices must be approved by the general manager. But the general manager almost never overrules Bill's decisions; in fact, Bill is so trusted that the general manager usually doesn't even look at his change requests unless the amount of money involved is substantial.

The union is now arguing that Bill should not be allowed to vote in the upcoming election because he is a "manager" under the NLRA. After reading the following, do you agree? What, in particular, influenced your decision?

PROBLEM MATERIALS

NLRB v. Yeshiva University, 444 U.S. 672 (1980)

NLRB v. YESHIVA UNIVERSITY
444 U.S. 672 (1980)

Mr. Justice Powell delivered the opinion of the Court.

Supervisors and managerial employees are excluded from the categories of employees entitled to the benefits of collective bargaining under the National Labor Relations Act. The question presented is whether the full-time faculty of Yeshiva

University fall within those exclusions. Yeshiva is a private university which conducts a broad range of arts and sciences programs at its five undergraduate and eight graduate schools in New York City. On October 30, 1974, the Yeshiva University Faculty Association (Union) filed a representation petition with the National Labor Relations Board (Board). The Union sought certification as bargaining agent for the full-time faculty members at 10 of the 13 schools. The University opposed the petition on the ground that all of its faculty members are managerial or supervisory personnel and hence not employees within the meaning of the National Labor Relations Act (Act). A Board-appointed hearing officer held hearings over a period of five months, generating a voluminous record.

The evidence at the hearings showed that a central administrative hierarchy serves all of the University's schools. Ultimate authority is vested in a Board of Trustees, whose members (other than the President) hold no administrative positions at the University. The President sits on the Board of Trustees and serves as chief executive officer, assisted by four Vice Presidents who oversee, respectively, medical affairs and science, student affairs, business affairs, and academic affairs. An Executive Council of Deans and administrators makes recommendations to the President on a wide variety of matters.

University-wide policies are formulated by the central administration with the approval of the Board of Trustees, and include general guidelines dealing with teaching loads, salary scales, tenure, sabbaticals, retirement, and fringe benefits. The budget for each school is drafted by its Dean or Director, subject to approval by the President after consultation with a committee of administrators. The faculty participate in University-wide governance through their representatives on an elected student-faculty advisory council. The only University-wide faculty body is the Faculty Review Committee, composed of elected representatives who adjust grievances by informal negotiation and also may make formal recommendations to the Dean of the affected school or to the President. Such recommendations are purely advisory.

The individual schools within the University are substantially autonomous. Each is headed by a Dean or Director, and faculty members at each school meet formally and informally to discuss and decide matters of institutional and professional concern. At four schools, formal meetings are convened regularly pursuant to written bylaws. The remaining faculties meet when convened by the Dean or Director. Most of the schools also have faculty committees concerned with special areas of educational policy. Faculty welfare committees negotiate with administrators concerning salary and conditions of employment. Through these meetings and committees, the faculty at each school effectively determine its curriculum, grading system, admission and matriculation standards, academic calendars, and course schedules.

Faculty power at Yeshiva's schools extends beyond strictly academic concerns. The faculty at each school make recommendations to the Dean or Director in every case of faculty hiring, tenure, sabbaticals, termination and promotion. Although the final decision is reached by the central administration on the advice of the Dean or Director, the overwhelming majority of faculty recommendations are implemented. Even when financial problems in the early 1970's restricted Yeshiva's budget, faculty recommendations still largely controlled personnel decisions made within the constraints imposed by the administration. Indeed, the faculty of one school recently drew up new and binding policies expanding their own role in these matters. In addition, some faculties make final decisions regarding the admission, expulsion, and graduation of individual students. Others have decided questions involving teaching loads, student absence policies, tuition and enrollment levels, and in one case the location of a school.

A three-member panel of the Board granted the Union's petition in December 1975, and directed an election in a bargaining unit consisting of all full-time faculty members at the affected schools. The unit included Assistant Deans, senior professors, and department chairmen, as well as associate professors, assistant professors, and instructors. Deans and Directors were excluded. The Board summarily rejected the University's contention that its entire faculty are managerial, viewing the claim as a request for reconsideration of previous Board decisions on the issue. Instead of making findings of fact as to Yeshiva, the Board referred generally to the record and found no "significan[t]" difference between this faculty and others it had considered. The Board concluded that the faculty are professional employees entitled to the protection of the Act because "faculty participation in collegial decision making is on a collective rather than individual basis, it is exercised in the faculty's own interest rather than 'in the interest of the employer,' and final authority rests with the board of trustees."

The Union won the election and was certified by the Board. The University refused to bargain, reasserting its view that the faculty are managerial. In the subsequent unfair labor practice proceeding, the Board refused to reconsider its holding in the representation proceeding and ordered the University to bargain with the Union. When the University still refused to sit down at the negotiating table, the Board sought enforcement in the Court of Appeals for the Second Circuit, which denied the petition. . . . We granted certiorari, and now affirm.

There is no evidence that Congress has considered whether a university faculty may organize for collective bargaining under the Act. Indeed, when the Wagner and Taft-Hartley Acts were approved, it was thought that congressional power did not extend to university faculties because they were employed by nonprofit institutions which did not "affect commerce." Moreover, the authority structure of a university does not fit neatly within the statutory scheme we are asked to interpret. The Board itself has noted that the concept of collegiality "does not square with the traditional authority structures with which th[e] Act was designed to cope in the typical organizations of the commercial world." *Adelphi University*, 195 N.L.R.B. 639, 648 (1972). . . .

The absence of explicit congressional direction, of course, does not preclude the Board from reaching any particular type of employment. Acting under its responsibility for adapting the broad provisions of the Act to differing workplaces, the Board asserted jurisdiction over a university for the first time in 1970. Within a year it had approved the formation of bargaining units composed of faculty members. The Board reasoned that faculty members are "professional employees" within the meaning of § 2(12) of the Act and therefore are entitled to the benefits of collective bargaining.

Yeshiva does not contend that its faculty are not professionals under the statute. But professionals, like other employees, may be exempted from coverage under the Act's exclusion for "supervisors" who use independent judgment in overseeing other employees in the interest of the employer, or under the judicially implied exclusion for "managerial employees" who are involved in developing and enforcing employer policy. Both exemptions grow out of the same concern: That an employer is entitled to the undivided loyalty of its representatives. Because the Court of Appeals found the faculty to be managerial employees, it did not decide the question of their supervisory status. In view of our agreement with that court's application of the managerial exclusion, we also need not resolve that issue of statutory interpretation.

Managerial employees are defined as those who " 'formulate and effectuate management policies by expressing and making operative the decisions of their employer.' " [*NLRB v. Bell Aerospace Co.*, 416 U.S. 267, 288 (1974)] (quoting *Palace Laundry Dry Cleaning Corp.*, 75 N.L.R.B. 320, 323, n. 4 (1947)). These employees are "much higher in the managerial structure" than those explicitly mentioned by Congress, which "regarded [them] as so clearly outside the Act that no specific exclusionary provision was thought necessary." 416 U.S., at 283. Managerial employees must exercise discretion within, or even independently of, established employer policy and must be aligned with management. Although the Board has established no firm criteria for determining when an employee is so aligned, normally an employee may be excluded as managerial only if he represents management interests by taking or recommending discretionary actions that effectively control or implement employer policy.

The Board does not contend that the Yeshiva faculty's decisionmaking is too insignificant to be deemed managerial.[11] Nor does it suggest that the role of the faculty is merely advisory and thus not managerial. Instead, it contends that the managerial exclusion cannot be applied in a straightforward fashion to professional employees because those employees often appear to be exercising managerial authority when they are merely performing routine job duties. The status of such employees, in the Board's view, must be determined by reference to the "alignment with management" criterion. The Board argues that the Yeshiva faculty are not aligned with management because they are expected to exercise "independent professional judgment" while participating in academic governance, and because they are neither "expected to conform to management policies [nor] judged according to their effectiveness in carrying out those policies." Because of this independence, the Board contends there is no danger of divided loyalty and no need for the managerial exclusion. In its view, union pressure cannot divert the faculty from adhering to the interests of the university, because the university itself expects its faculty to pursue professional values rather than institutional interests. The

---

[11] [n.16] The Board has found decisions of far less significance to the employer to be managerial when the affected employees were aligned with management. *Swift & Co.*, 115 N.L.R.B. 752, 753 (1956) (procurement drivers who made purchases for employers); *Firestone Tire & Rubber Co.*, 112 N.L.R.B. 571, 573 (1955) (production schedulers); *Peter Kiewit Sons' Co.*, 106 N.L.R.B. 194, 196 (1953) (lecturers who indoctrinated new employees); *Western Electric Co.*, 100 N.L.R.B. 420, 423 (1952) (personnel investigators who made hiring recommendations); *American Locomotive Co.*, 92 N.L.R.B. 115, 116–117 (1950) (buyers who made substantial purchases on employer's behalf).

Board concludes that application of the managerial exclusion to such employees would frustrate the national labor policy in favor of collective bargaining. . . .

The controlling consideration in this case is that the faculty of Yeshiva University exercise authority which in any other context unquestionably would be managerial. Their authority in academic matters is absolute. They decide what courses will be offered, when they will be scheduled, and to whom they will be taught. They debate and determine teaching methods, grading policies, and matriculation standards. They effectively decide which students will be admitted, retained, and graduated. On occasion their views have determined the size of the student body, the tuition to be charged, and the location of a school. When one considers the function of a university, it is difficult to imagine decisions more managerial than these. To the extent the industrial analogy applies, the faculty determines within each school the product to be produced, the terms upon which it will be offered, and the customers who will be served.

The Board nevertheless insists that these decisions are not managerial because they require the exercise of independent professional judgment. We are not persuaded by this argument. There may be some tension between the Act's exclusion of managerial employees and its inclusion of professionals, since most professionals in managerial positions continue to draw on their special skills and training. But we have been directed to no authority suggesting that that tension can be resolved by reference to the "independent professional judgment" criterion proposed in this case. Outside the university context, the Board routinely has applied the managerial and supervisory exclusions to professionals in executive positions without inquiring whether their decisions were based on management policy rather than professional expertise. Indeed, the Board has twice implicitly rejected the contention that decisions based on professional judgment cannot be managerial.[12] Since the Board does not suggest that the "independent professional judgment" test is to be limited to university faculty, its new approach would overrule *sub silentio* this body of Board precedent and could result in the indiscriminate recharacterization as covered employees of professionals working in supervisory and managerial capacities.

Moreover, the Board's approach would undermine the goal it purports to serve: To ensure that employees who exercise discretionary authority on behalf of the employer will not divide their loyalty between employer and union. In arguing that a faculty member exercising independent judgment acts primarily in his own interest and therefore does not represent the interest of his employer, the Board assumes that the professional interests of the faculty and the interests of the institution are distinct, separable entities with which a faculty member could not simultaneously be aligned. The Court of Appeals found no justification for this distinction, and we perceive none. In fact, the faculty's professional interests — as applied to governance at a university like Yeshiva — cannot be separated from those

---

[12] [n.26] *University of Chicago Library*, 205 N.L.R.B. 220, 221–222, 229 (1973), enf'd, 506 F.2d 1402 (CA7 1974) (reversing an Administrative Law Judge's decision which had been premised on the "professional judgment" rationale); *Sutter Community Hospitals of Sacramento*, [227 N.L.R.B. 181, 193 (1976)] (excluding as managerial a clinical specialist who used interdisciplinary professional skills to run a hospital department).

of the institution. . . . Faculty members enhance their own standing and fulfill their professional mission by ensuring that the university's objectives are met. But there can be no doubt that the quest for academic excellence and institutional distinction is a "policy" to which the administration expects the faculty to adhere, whether it be defined as a professional or an institutional goal. It is fruitless to ask whether an employee is "expected to conform" to one goal or another when the two are essentially the same.

The problem of divided loyalty is particularly acute for a university like Yeshiva, which depends on the professional judgment of its faculty to formulate and apply crucial policies constrained only by necessarily general institutional goals. . . . The large measure of independence enjoyed by faculty members can only increase the danger that divided loyalty will lead to those harms that the Board traditionally has sought to prevent.

We certainly are not suggesting an application of the managerial exclusion that would sweep all professionals outside the Act in derogation of Congress' expressed intent to protect them. The Board has recognized that employees whose decision-making is limited to the routine discharge of professional duties in projects to which they have been assigned cannot be excluded from coverage even if union member-ship arguably may involve some divided loyalty.[13] Only if an employee's activities fall outside the scope of the duties routinely performed by similarly situated profes-sionals will he be found aligned with management. We think these decisions accurately capture the intent of Congress, and that they provide an appropriate starting point for analysis in cases involving professionals alleged to be manage-rial.[14]

Affirmed.

MR. JUSTICE BRENNAN, with whom MR. JUSTICE WHITE MR. JUSTICE MARSHALL, and MR. JUSTICE BLACKMUN join, dissenting.

. . . Unlike the purely hierarchical decisionmaking structure that prevails in the typical industrial organization, the bureaucratic foundation of most "mature" universities is characterized by dual authority systems. The primary decisional

---

[13] [n.30] For this reason, architects and engineers functioning as project captains for work performed by teams of professionals are deemed employees despite substantial planning responsibility and authority to direct and evaluate team members. See *General Dynamics Corp.*, 213 N.L.R.B., at 857–858; *Wurster, Bernardi & Emmons, Inc.*, 192 N.L.R.B. 1049, 1051 (1971); *Skidmore, Owings & Merrill*, 192 N.L.R.B. 920, 921 (1971). See also *Doctors' Hospital of Modesto, Inc.*, 183 N.L.R.B. 950, 951–952 (1970), enf'd, 489 F.2d 772 (CA9 1973) (nurses); *National Broadcasting Co.*, 160 N.L.R.B. 1440, 1441 (1966) (broadcast newswriters). . . .

[14] [n.31] We recognize that this is a starting point only, and that other factors not present here may enter into the analysis in other contexts. It is plain, for example, that professors may not be excluded merely because they determine the content of their own courses, evaluate their own students, and supervise their own research. There thus may be institutions of higher learning unlike Yeshiva where the faculty are entirely or predominantly nonmanagerial. There also may be faculty members at Yeshiva and like universities who properly could be included in a bargaining unit. It may be that a rational line could be drawn between tenured and untenured faculty members, depending upon how a faculty is structured and operates. But we express no opinion on these questions, for it is clear that the unit approved by the Board was far too broad.

network is hierarchical in nature: Authority is lodged in the administration, and a formal chain of command runs from a lay governing board down through university officers to individual faculty members and students. At the same time, there exists a parallel professional network, in which formal mechanisms have been created to bring the expertise of the faculty into the decisionmaking process.

What the Board realized — and what the Court fails to apprehend — is that whatever influence the faculty wields in university decisionmaking is attributable solely to its collective expertise as professional educators, and not to any managerial or supervisory prerogatives. Although the administration may look to the faculty for advice on matters of professional and academic concern, the faculty offers its recommendations in order to serve its own independent interest in creating the most effective environment for learning, teaching, and scholarship. And while the administration may attempt to defer to the faculty's competence whenever possible, it must and does apply its own distinct perspective to those recommendations, a perspective that is based on fiscal and other managerial policies which the faculty has no part in developing. The University always retains the ultimate decisionmaking authority and the administration gives what weight and import to the faculty's collective judgment as it chooses and deems consistent with its own perception of the institution's needs and objectives.

Moreover, insofar as faculty members are given some say in more traditional managerial decisions such as the hiring and promotion of other personnel, such discretion does not constitute an adequate basis for the conferral of managerial or supervisory status. Indeed, in the typical industrial context, it is not uncommon for the employees' union to be given the *exclusive* right to recommend personnel to the employer, and these hiring-hall agreements have been upheld even where the union requires a worker to pass a union-administered skills test as a condition of referral.

The premise of a finding of managerial status is a determination that the excluded employee is acting on behalf of management and is answerable to a higher authority in the exercise of his responsibilities. The Board has consistently implemented this requirement — both for professional and non-professional employees — by conferring managerial status only upon those employees "whose interests are closely aligned with management *as true representatives of management.*" (Emphasis added.) *E.g., Sutter Community Hospitals of Sacramento,* 227 N.L.R.B. 181, 193 (1976); *Bell Aerospace,* 219 N.L.R.B. 384, 385 (1975); *General Dynamics Corp.,* 213 N.L.R.B. 851, 857 (1974). Only if the employee is expected to conform to management policies and is judged by his effectiveness in executing those policies does the danger of divided loyalties exist.

Yeshiva's faculty, however, is not accountable to the administration in its governance function, nor is any individual faculty member subject to personal sanction or control based on the administration's assessment of the worth of his recommendations. When the faculty, through the schools' advisory committees, participates in university decisionmaking on subjects of academic policy, it does not serve as the "representative of management." Unlike industrial supervisors and managers, university professors are not hired to "make operative" the policies and decisions of their employer. Nor are they retained on the condition that their interests will correspond to those of the university administration. Indeed, the notion that a faculty member's professional competence could depend on his undivided loyalty to management is antithetical to the whole concept of academic freedom. Faculty members are judged by their employer on the quality of their teaching and scholarship, not on the compatibility of their advice with administration policy. . . .

It is no answer to say, as does the Court, that Yeshiva's faculty and administration are one and the same because their interests tend to coincide. . . . Ultimately, the performance of an employee's duties will always further the interests of the employer, for in no institution do the interests of labor and management totally diverge. Both desire to maintain stable and profitable operations, and both are committed to creating the best possible product within existing financial constraints. Differences of opinion and emphasis may develop, however, on exactly how to devote the institution's resources to achieve those goals. When these disagreements surface, the national labor laws contemplate their resolution through the peaceful process of collective bargaining. And in this regard, Yeshiva University stands on the same footing as any other employer. . . .

POST PROBLEM DISCUSSION

1. As noted in *Yeshiva*, the Supreme Court's recognition of the managerial exception first occurred in NLRB v. Bell Aerospace Co., 416 U.S. 267 (1974). Although the Court in *Bell Aerospace* agreed with the NLRB's long-standing rule that managers should not be covered by the NLRA, the Court rejected the NLRB's "labor nexus" requirement, which only excluded managerial workers who were involved with the formulation and implementation of the employer's labor policies. *Id.* at 272, 289 (remanding case to NLRB). Following the Court's rejection of its labor-nexus requirement, the NLRB reconsidered its conclusion in *Bell Aerospace* and again found that the employees in question were not managers because their discretion was significantly limited by their employer's manuals and instructions. *Bell Aerospace Corp.*, 219 N.L.R.B. 384, 386 (1975). In that decision the NLRB also restated its analysis of managerial cases:

> The Board long has defined managerial employees as those who formulate and effectuate management policies by expressing and making operative the decisions of their employer, and those who have discretion in the performance of their jobs independent of their employer's established policy . . . . [M]anagerial status is not conferred upon rank-and-file workers, or upon those who perform routinely, but rather it is reserved for those in executive-type positions, those who are closely aligned with management as true representatives of management.

Id. at 385 (internal quotations omitted).

2. Given the NLRB's definition of managers, as well as the Supreme Court's holding in *Yeshiva*, do you think the union will be successful in arguing that Bill is a manager? *See NLRB v. Bell Aerospace Co.*, 416 U.S. 267 (1974); *Concepts & Designs, Inc.*, 318 N.L.R.B. 948, 956-57 (1995) (concluding that employee in charge of purchasing, with unreviewed discretion involving substantial amounts of credit, was a manager).

3.   As you see from the views of the majority and dissent in *Yeshiva*, the extent to which faculty or other workers can control managerial decisions is often in the eye of the beholder. For faculty, this issue is frequently difficult because of the contrast between the administration's formal authority to make most managerial decisions and the reality that, most of the time, the administration follows the collective opinion of the faculty. Which do you think is more important for deciding whether workers are covered employees or excluded managers: the formal hierarchy of the workplace or workers' actual influence in most instances? *See Bosart Co.*, 314 N.L.R.B. 245, 247 (1994) (concluding that power to effectively recommend hiring of unionized employees is a factor in favor of managerial status). The NLRB may shed more light on this issue, as it invited briefing on which factors should be most relevant in determining whether faculty should be considered managers. *See Point Park University* (6-RC-12276), Notice and Invitation to File Briefs (May 22, 2012).

4.   How important is the fact that faculty are professionals? As you will see in the next section on supervisors, there has been concern that an expansive interpretation of the managerial and supervisory exceptions will effectively eliminate professionals' ability to organize, although the NLRA clearly contemplates that some professionals will be covered employees. *See* Section 2(12) of the NLRA; *see generally* Marion Crain, *The Transformation of the Professional Workforce*, 79 CHI.-KENT L. REV. 543 (2004) (discussing collective action by professionals).

2. Supervisors

As you will see in the following readings, Congress added Section 2(11) in the Taft Hartley amendments to exclude supervisors from the NLRA's coverage. One of the difficulties in applying that exclusion is that many workplaces have changed dramatically in the ensuing decades. Section 2(11) was enacted in a time where employees and their bosses were relatively easy to distinguish. But that distinction is now frequently blurred. For instance, nurses have become a focal point in the debate regarding Section 2(11)'s scope, in large part because more experienced nurses often give some direction and oversight to less experienced nurses and lower-trained nursing assistants. As you read the following material, think about the impact of the Section 2(11) tests and whether the outcomes under those tests make sense given the policy aims of the NLRA.

PROBLEM #4: RESTAURANT CAPTAINS

One evening you are approached by a worker while eating at your favorite restaurant, Royal East. Evelyn told you that she had heard of your extensive labor law knowledge and wanted to ask you whether she should be worried for her job. Apparently, Evelyn has been instrumental in attracting a union to start an organizing drive at the restaurant, and the owner of the restaurant is furious with her.

Royal East serves food from certain regions in China and is well known for its ability to host large banquets. The restaurant employs 30 dining room workers, including wait staff; busers; and two "captains," including Evelyn. The captains were originally wait staff, and still spend approximately a third of each shift performing waiting and busing duties. However, the captains also unlock the restaurant before other workers arrive and, when the restaurant's managers or owners are not present, the captains are the highest ranking worker. The captains' other duties include assigning wait staff and busers to sections of the restaurant; the assignments are based on a pre-determined schedule that rotates each day. Once a shift's work begins to decrease and the captains believe that less staff is needed, the captains can send workers home — again, based on a rotating schedule. The captains assist in training new dining room workers, although the majority of training is done by senior wait staff or busers. Moreover, during a shift, captains can tell wait staff or busers to address a problem that has arisen, but the captains are supposed to inform managers of anything that is out of the ordinary. If dining room staff call in sick, the captains seek a replacement by making calls to workers from a directory designed for that purpose that lists staff in order of seniority. The captains cannot hire, fire, or discipline workers, although they can and do notify a manager if they believe there is a problem. After listening to the captain's recommendation, the manager will look into the matter and make a decision about possible corrections, discipline, or termination.

Given that the owner of Royal East is angry about the union campaign, how worried should Evelyn be? Read the following material to determine whether the NLRA will provide her protection. Make sure to keep track of the areas in which the Supreme Court has given the NLRB room to interpret the meaning of Section 2(11) and the areas in which it has not. Where the NLRB is exercising discretion, ask yourself whether you agree with its conclusions.

PROBLEM MATERIALS

Section 2(11) of the NLRA

Brief of the NLRB General Counsel, in *Oakwood Healthcare, Inc.*, NLRB Case #7-RC-22141

Oakwood Health Care, Inc., 348 N.L.R.B. 686 (2006)

SECTION 2(11) OF THE NLRA

The term "supervisor" means any individual having authority, in the interest of the employer, to:

- hire,
- transfer,
- suspend,
- lay off,
- recall,
- promote,
- discharge,
- assign,

- reward, or

- discipline other employees, or

- responsibly to direct them, or

- to adjust their grievances, or

- effectively to recommend such action,

if in connection with the foregoing the exercise of such authority is not of a merely routine or clerical nature, but requires the use of independent judgment.

BRIEF OF THE NLRB GENERAL COUNSEL, IN OAKWOOD HEALTHCARE, INC.
NLRB Case #7-RC-22141

. . . Although not formally a party, the General Counsel has a substantial interest in these proceedings in view of his role in administrating the National Labor Relations Act (Act). Since the Board has posed questions aimed at determining the scope of supervisory status in light of the Supreme Court's decision in [*NLRB v. Kentucky River Community Care*, 532 U.S. 706 (2001)], the General Counsel is vitally concerned that his views be considered. . . .

The recurring and important question of who is a supervisor within the meaning of Section 2(11) of the Act has long been a source of disagreement among Board members and between the Board and the reviewing courts. The disagreement has largely centered on the relationship of the terms "responsibly to direct" and "assign" with the term "independent judgment."

The conflict with the courts has always been pronounced in the power industry, where the Board has resisted finding dispatchers and similar controllers to be supervisors. See, e.g., *Ohio Power*, 80 N.L.R.B. 1334 (1948), *enforcement denied*, 176 F.2d 385, 387 (6th Cir.) (rejecting Board finding that control operators were not 2(11) supervisors where they were responsible in emergencies); *Maine Yankee Atomic Power Co.*, 239 N.L.R.B. 1216 (1979), *enforcement denied*, 624 F.2d 347, 366 (1st Cir. 1980) (same).

Since the enactment of the Health Care Amendments in 1974, the disagreement between the Board and the courts has become particularly important in the health care industry. In the 1970s, the Board adopted the "patient care analysis," which examined "whether the alleged supervisory conduct of the charge nurses is the exercise of professional judgment incidental to patient care or the exercise of supervisory authority in the interest of the employer." *Eventide S., a Div. of Geriatrics, Inc.*, 239 N.L.R.B. 287, 289 (1978) . . . . After many years of conflict within the Board and circuit courts, the Supreme Court rejected the "patient care analysis" in *NLRB v. Health Care & Ret. Corp. of Am.*, 511 U.S. 571, 579 (1994).

After *Health Care & Retirement*, the Board focused on refining its definition of "independent judgment" in nursing and other contexts, reasoning that the exercise of professional or technical judgment or expertise by professional and technical workers was routine and not the exercise of "independent judgment." See, e.g., *Providence Hosp.*, 320 N.L.R.B. 717, 729 (1996), *enforced* 121 F.3d 548 (9th Cir.

1997). After another lengthy conflict in the circuit courts, the Supreme Court in *Kentucky River* rejected the Board's position that independent judgment does not include the exercise of professional or technical judgment in directing less skilled employees. Although the Court agreed with the Board's allocation of the burden of proof in supervisory cases and held that the Board had authority to decide whether the degree of delegated discretion sufficed to constitute "independent judgment," the Court found that the Board's "categorical exclusion" of a particular kind of judgment, namely, professional or technical judgment, inserted a "startling categorical exclusion into statutory text that does not suggest its existence." *Id.* at 713-714. While recognizing the Board's asserted tension between Section 2(12)'s definition of professional employees as those who use discretion and judgment and Section 2(11)'s definition of supervisors, the Court found the Board's solution could not "be given effect through [the] statutory text." *Id.* at 720. The Court did, however, suggest that the Board could "offer a limiting interpretation of the supervisory function of responsible direction by distinguishing employees who direct the manner of others' performance of discrete *tasks* from employees who direct other *employees*," citing *Providence. Ibid.* (emphasis in original). The Court, however, declined to consider the distinction because interpretation of "responsibly to direct" was not at issue. *Id.* at 720-721.

It is in light of the Supreme Court's *Kentucky River* decision that the Board now revisits the problem of devising a construction of "assign," "responsibly to direct," and "independent judgment." . . .

OAKWOOD HEALTH CARE, INC.
348 N.L.R.B. 686 (2006)

. . . On July 25, 2003, the Board issued a notice and invitation to the Employer, the Petitioner, and interested amici curiae to file briefs addressing the supervisory issue in this case in light of the Supreme Court's decision in *NLRB v. Kentucky River Community Care*, 532 U.S. 706 (2001). The Board sought, inter alia, comments relating to (1) the meaning of "assign," "responsibly to direct," and "independent judgment," as those terms are used in Section 2(11) of the Act; and (2) an appropriate test for determining the unit placement of employees who take turns or "rotate" as supervisors. . . .

Having considered the record and briefs of the parties and amici, and the Supreme Court's decision in *Kentucky River*, we refine the analysis to be applied in assessing supervisory status. That refined analysis honors our responsibility to protect the rights of those covered by the Act; hews to the language of Section 2(11) and judicial interpretation thereof, most particularly the guidance provided by the Supreme Court in *Kentucky River* and other decisions; and endeavors to provide clear and broadly applicable guidance for the Board's regulated community. Applying that analysis in the instant case we reverse the decision of the Acting Regional Director and find that certain charge nurses should be excluded from the unit as statutory supervisors.

I. Facts

The Employer has approximately 181 staff RNs who provide direct care to patients in 10 patient care units at Oakwood Heritage Hospital, an acute care hospital with 257 licensed beds. The patient care units are behavioral health, emergency room, intensive care, intermediate care, medical/surgical east, medical/surgical west, operating room, pain clinic, post-anesthesia care/recovery and rehabilitation. The RNs report to the on-site nursing manager, clinical managers, clinical supervisors, and assistant clinical managers-all stipulated supervisors. In providing patient care, RNs follow the doctors' orders and perform tasks such as administering medications, running blood tests, taking vital signs, observing patients and processing admissions and discharges. RNs may direct less-skilled employees to perform tasks such as feeding, bathing, and walking patients. RNs may also direct employees to perform tests that are ordered by doctors for their patients.

Many RNs at the hospital serve as charge nurses. Charge nurses are responsible for overseeing their patient care units, and they assign other RNs, licensed practical nurses (LPNs), nursing assistants, technicians, and paramedics to patients on their shifts. Charge nurses also monitor the patients in the unit, meet with doctors and the patients' family members, and follow up on unusual incidents. Charge nurses may also take on their own patient load, but those who do assume patient loads will sometimes, but not always, take less than a full complement of patients. When serving as charge nurses, RNs receive an additional $1.50 per hour.

Twelve RNs at the hospital serve permanently as charge nurses on every shift they work, while other RNs take turns rotating into the charge nurse position. In the patient care units of the hospital employing permanent charge nurses, other RNs may serve as charge nurses on the permanent charge nurses' days off or during their vacations. Depending on the patient care unit and the work shift, the rotation of the charge nurse position may be worked out by the RNs among themselves, or it may be set by higher-level managers. The frequency and regularity with which a particular RN will serve as a "rotating" charge nurse depends on several factors (i.e., the size of the patient care unit in which the RN works, the number of other RNs who serve as rotating charge nurses in that unit, and whether the unit has any permanent charge nurses). However, some RNs do not serve as either rotating or permanent charge nurses at the hospital. Most individuals who fit in this category are either new employees at the hospital or those who work in the operating room or pain clinic units. There are also a handful of RNs at the hospital who choose not to serve as charge nurses.

. . . The Employer, joined by other amici, seeks to exclude the permanent and the rotating charge nurses from the unit on the basis that they are supervisors within the meaning of Section 2(11) because they use independent judgment in assigning and responsibly directing employees. The Acting Regional Director found that none of the charge nurses are 2(11) supervisors and directed an election in the RN unit including them.

II. Legal Principles

In 1947, the Supreme Court held in *Packard Motor Car Co. v. NLRB*, 330 U.S. 485, that supervisors were included in the definition of "employee" as used in Section 2(3) of the Act. In response, Congress amended the National Labor Relations Act that same year, adding Section 2(11) to specifically exclude supervisors from the Act's definition of "employee."

Section 2(11) defines "supervisor" as

> any individual having the authority, in the interest of the employer, to hire, transfer, suspend, lay off, recall, promote, discharge, assign, reward, or discipline other employees, or responsibly to direct them, or to adjust their grievances, or effectively to recommend such action, if in connection with the foregoing the exercise of such authority is not of a merely routine or clerical nature, but requires the use of independent judgment.

Pursuant to this definition, individuals are statutory supervisors if (1) they hold the authority to engage in any 1 of the 12 supervisory functions (e.g., "assign" and "responsibly to direct") listed in Section 2(11); (2) their "exercise of such authority is not of a merely routine or clerical nature, but requires the use of independent judgment;" and (3) their authority is held "in the interest of the employer." Supervisory status may be shown if the putative supervisor has the authority either to perform a supervisory function or to effectively recommend the same. The burden to prove supervisory authority is on the party asserting it.

Both the drafters of the original amendment and Senator Ralph E. Flanders, who proposed adding the term "responsibly to direct" to the definition of supervisor, agreed that the definition sought to distinguish two classes of workers: true supervisors vested with "genuine management prerogatives," and employees such as "straw bosses, lead men, and set-up men" who are protected by the Act even though they perform "minor supervisory duties." *NLRB v. Bell Aerospace Co.*, 416 U.S. 267, 280-281 (1974) (quoting S. Rep. No. 105, 80th Cong., 1st Sess., 4 (1947)). Thus, the dividing line between these two classes of workers, for purposes of Section 2(11), is whether the putative supervisor exercises "genuine management prerogatives." Those prerogatives are specifically identified as the 12 supervisory functions listed in Section 2(11) of the Act. If the individual has authority to exercise (or effectively recommend the exercise of) at least one of those functions, 2(11) supervisory status exists, provided that the authority is held in the interest of the employer and is exercised neither routinely nor in a clerical fashion but with independent judgment.

Whether an individual possesses a 2(11) supervisory function has not always been readily discernible by either the Board or reviewing courts. Indeed, in applying Section 2(11), the Supreme Court has recognized that "[p]hrases [used by Congress] such as 'independent judgment' and 'responsibly to direct' are ambiguous."[15]

As a general principle, the Board has exercised caution "not to construe

---

[15] [n.17] *See NLRB v. Healthcare & Retirement Corp. of America*, 511 U.S. 571, 579 (1994).

supervisory status too broadly because the employee who is deemed a supervisor is denied rights which the Act is intended to protect." *Chevron Shipping Co.*, 317 NLRB 379, 381 (1995) (internal quotations omitted). However, in applying that principle, the Board has occasionally reached too far. Indeed, on two occasions involving the healthcare industry, the industry at issue in this case, the Supreme Court rejected the Board's overly narrow construction of Section 2(11) as "inconsistent with the Act."[16] Accordingly, although we seek to ensure that the protections of the Act are not unduly circumscribed, we also must be mindful of the legislative and judicial constraints that guide our application and interpretation of the statute. Thus, exercising our discretion to interpret ambiguous language in the Act and consistent with the Supreme Court's instructions in *Kentucky River*, we herein adopt definitions for the terms "assign," "responsibly to direct," and "independent judgment" as those terms are used in Section 2(11) of the Act. . . .

B. Assign and Responsibly to Direct

1. Assign

The ordinary meaning of the term "assign" is "to appoint to a post or duty." *Webster's Third New International Dictionary* 132 (1981). Because this function shares with other 2(11) functions — i.e., hire, transfer, suspension, layoff, recall, promotion, discharge, reward, or discipline — the common trait of affecting a term or condition of employment, we construe the term "assign" to refer to the act of designating an employee to a place (such as a location, department, or wing), appointing an employee to a time (such as a shift or overtime period), or giving significant overall duties, i.e., tasks, to an employee. That is, the place, time, and work of an employee are part of his/her terms and conditions of employment. In the health care setting, the term "assign" encompasses the charge nurses' responsibility to assign nurses and aides to particular patients. It follows that the decision or effective recommendation to affect one of these — place, time, or overall tasks — can be a supervisory function.

The assignment of an employee to a certain department (e.g., housewares) or to a certain shift (e.g., night) or to certain significant overall tasks (e.g., restocking shelves) would generally qualify as "assign" within our construction. However, choosing the order in which the employee will perform discrete tasks within those assignments (e.g., restocking toasters before coffeemakers) would not be indicative of exercising the authority to "assign." To illustrate our point in the health care setting, if a charge nurse designates an LPN to be the person who will regularly administer medications to a patient or a group of patients, the giving of that overall duty to the LPN is an assignment. On the other hand, the charge nurse's ordering an LPN to immediately give a sedative to a particular patient does not constitute an assignment. In sum, to "assign" for purposes of Section 2(11) refers to the charge

---

16 [n.18] *Kentucky River*, supra at 721-722 (holding that the Board erred in finding no "independent judgment" where nurses use ordinary professional or technical judgment in directing less-skilled employees); *Healthcare & Retirement Corp.*, 511 U.S. at 576, 584 (holding that the Board erred in finding a nurse's supervisory activity that was incidental to patient care was not exercised "in the interest of the employer").

nurse's designation of significant overall duties to an employee, not to the charge nurse's ad hoc instruction that the employee perform a discrete task. . . .

The dissent says that our interpretation of "assign" to include the assignment of employees to significant over-all tasks violates the canon against redundancy by failing to draw a line between assigning and directing. That is not so. As discussed below, direction may encompass ad hoc instructions to perform discrete tasks; assignment does not. . . .

2. Responsibly to Direct

We now address the term "responsibly to direct." The phrase "responsibly to direct" was added to Section 2(11) after the other supervisory functions of Section 2(11) already had been enumerated in the proposed legislation. Senator Flanders, who made the proposal to add "responsibly to direct" to Section 2(11), explained that the phrase was not meant to include minor supervisory functions performed by lead employees, straw bosses, and setup men. Rather, the addition was designed to ensure that the statutory exemption of Section 2(11) encompassed those individuals who exercise basic supervision but lack the authority or opportunity to carry out any of the other statutory supervisory functions (e.g., where promotional, disciplinary and similar functions are handled by a centralized human resources department). Senator Flanders was concerned that the person on the shop floor would not be considered a supervisor even if that person directly oversaw the work being done and would be held responsible if the work were done badly or not at all.[17] Consequently, the authority "responsibly to direct" is not limited to department heads as the dissent suggests. The "department head" may be a person between the personnel manager and the rank and file employee, but he or she is not necessarily the only person between the manager and the employee. If a person on the shop

---

[17] [n.27] In proposing his amendment adding the phrase "responsibly to direct," Senator Flanders commented:

> The definition of "supervisor" in this act seems to cover adequately everything except the basic act of supervising. Many of the activities described in [Section 2(11)] are transferred in modem practice to a personnel manager or department. The supervisor may recommend more or less effectively, but the personnel department may, and often does, transfer a worker to another department or other work instead of discharging, disciplining or otherwise following the recommended action.

> In fact, under some modern management methods, the supervisor might be deprived of authority for most of the functions enumerated and still have a personal judgment based on personal experience, training, and ability. He is charged with the responsible direction of his department and the men under him. He determines under general orders what job shall be undertaken next and who shall do it. He gives instructions for its proper performance. If needed, he gives training in the performance of unfamiliar tasks to the worker to whom they are assigned.

> Such men are above the grade of "straw bosses, lead men, set-up men, and other minor supervisory employees" as enumerated in the report. Their essential managerial duties are best defined by the words "direct responsibly", which I am suggesting.

> In a large measure, the success or failure of a manufacturing business depends on the judgment and initiative of these men. The top management may properly be judged by its success or failure in picking them out and in backing them up when they have been properly selected. See NLRB, Legislative History of the Labor Management Relations Act of 1947, 1303. Nothing in the text of the amendment passed by Congress is at variance with Senator Flanders' remarks.

floor has "men under him," and if that person decides "what job shall be undertaken next or who shall do it," that person is a supervisor, provided that the direction is both "responsible" (as explained below) and carried out with independent judgment. In addition, as the statute provides and Senator Flanders himself recognized, the person who effectively recommends action is also a supervisor.

Since the enactment of Senator Flanders' amendment, the Board rarely has sought to define the parameters of the term "responsibly to direct." In *Providence Hospital*,[18] the Board majority summarized past efforts on the part of several courts of appeals . . . to ascertain the limits of this term. The Board majority in *Providence Hospital* concluded that these courts endorsed, for the most part, an accountability definition for the word "responsibly" that was consistent with the ordinary meaning of the word. The majority cited to the Fifth Circuit's interpretation, which is set forth in *NLRB v. KDFW-TV, Inc.*, [790 F.2d 1273, 1278 (5th Cir. 1986)], as follows:

> "To be responsible is to be answerable for the discharge of a duty or obligation." . . . In determining whether "direction" in any particular case is responsible, the focus is on whether the alleged supervisor is "held fully accountable and responsible for the performance and work product of the employees" he directs. . . . Thus, in *NLRB v. Adam [&] Eve Cosmetics, Inc.*, 567 F.2d 723, 727 (7th Cir. 1977), for example, the court reversed a Board finding that an employee lacked supervisory status after finding that the employee had been reprimanded for the performance of others in his Department.

The majority in *Providence Hospital*, however, found it unnecessary to pass on the courts' accountability definition. We have decided to adopt that definition.

We agree with the circuit courts that have considered the issue and find that for direction to be "responsible," the person directing and performing the oversight of the employee must be accountable for the performance of the task by the other, such that some adverse consequence may befall the one providing the oversight if the tasks performed by the employee are not performed properly. This interpretation of "responsibly to direct" is consistent with *post-Kentucky River* Board decisions that considered an accountability element for "responsibly to direct."

Thus, to establish accountability for purposes of responsible direction, it must be shown that the employer delegated to the putative supervisor the authority to direct the work and the authority to take corrective action, if necessary. It also must be shown that there is a prospect of adverse consequences for the putative supervisor if he/she does not take these steps.

Our dissenting colleagues express the concern that our definition of "responsibly to direct" will result in supervisory authority being extended to "every 'person on the shop floor.' " In our view, however, the emphasis on accountability contained in the definition will prevent such an occurrence.

Significantly, the concept of accountability creates a clear distinction between those employees whose interests, in directing other employees' tasks, align with

---

[18] [n.29] 320 N.L.R.B. 717 (1996) . . . .

management from those whose interests, in directing other employees, is simply the completion of a certain task. In the case of the former, the dynamics of hierarchical authority will arise, under which the directing employee will have, if and to the extent necessary, an adversarial relationship with those he is directing. The directing employee will rightly understand that his interests, in seeing that a task is properly performed, are to some extent distinct from the interests of those under his direction. That is, in directing others, he will be carrying out the interests of management disregarding, if necessary, employees' contrary interests. Excluding from coverage of the Act such individuals whose fundamental alignment is with management is at the heart of Section 2(11).

C. Independent Judgment

In *Kentucky River*, . . . the Supreme Court took issue with the Board's interpretation of "independent judgment" to exclude the exercise of "ordinary professional or technical judgment in directing less skilled employees to deliver services." That is, in the Board's then extant view, even if the Section 2(11) function is exercised with a substantial degree of discretion, there was no independent judgment if the judgment was of a particular kind, namely, "ordinary professional or technical judgment in directing less-skilled employees to deliver services." While recognizing that the Board has the discretion to resolve ambiguities in the Act, the Supreme Court found that the Board had improperly inserted "a startling categorical exclusion into statutory text that does not suggest its existence." The Court said that the Board had gone "beyond the limits of what is ambiguous and contradicted what in our view is quite clear." *Id.* at 714. The Court held that it is the *degree* of discretion involved in making the decision, not the *kind* of discretion exercised — whether professional, technical, or otherwise — that determines the existence of "independent judgment" under Section 2(11). Id. We are guided by these admonitions.

Consistent with the Court's *Kentucky River* decision, we adopt an interpretation of the term "independent judgment" that applies irrespective of the Section 2(11) supervisory function implicated, and without regard to whether the judgment is exercised using professional or technical expertise. In short, professional or technical judgments involving the use of independent judgment are supervisory if they involve one of the 12 supervisory functions of Section 2(11). Thus, for example, a registered nurse who makes the "professional judgment" that a catheter needs to be changed may be performing a supervisory function when he/she responsibly directs a nursing assistant in the performance of that work. Whether the registered nurse is a 2(11) supervisor will depend on whether his or her responsible direction is performed with the degree of discretion required to reflect independent judgment. . . .

[A]s a starting point, to exercise "independent judgment" an individual must at minimum act, or effectively recommend action, free of the control of others and form an opinion or evaluation by discerning and comparing data. As more fully explained below, however, these requisites are necessary, but not in all instances sufficient, to constitute "independent judgment" within the meaning of the Act. As we said above, although we start with the "ordinary meaning of the words used,"

INS v. Phinpathya, supra, 464 U.S. at 189, we also consider the Act as a whole, its legislative history, policy considerations, and judicial precedent. Here, we must interpret 'independent judgment" in light of the contrasting statutory language, "not of a merely routine or clerical nature." It may happen that an individual's assignment or responsible direction of another will be based on independent judgment within the dictionary definitions of those terms, but still not rise above the merely routine or clerical. . . .

In our view, and that of the Supreme Court, actions form a spectrum between the extremes of completely free actions and completely controlled ones, and the degree of independence necessary to constitute a judgment as "independent" under the Act lies somewhere in between these extremes. As the Court indicated in *Kentucky River*, supra at 713-714, there are, at one end of the spectrum, situations where there are detailed instructions for the actor to follow. At the other end, there are other situations where the actor is wholly free from constraints. In determining the meaning of the term "independent judgment" under Section 2(11), the Board must assess the *degree* of discretion exercised by the putative supervisor.

Consistent with the Court's view, we find that a judgment is not independent if it is dictated or controlled by detailed instructions, whether set forth in company policies or rules, the verbal instructions of a higher authority, or in the provisions of a collective bargaining agreement. Thus, for example, a decision to staff a shift with a certain number of nurses would not involve independent judgment if it is determined by a fixed nurse-to-patient ratio. Similarly, if a collective-bargaining agreement required that only seniority be followed in making an assignment, that act of assignment would not be supervisory.

On the other hand, the mere existence of company policies does not eliminate independent judgment from decision-making if the policies allow for discretionary choices. Thus a registered nurse, when exercising his/her authority to recommend a person for hire, may be called upon to assess the applicants' experience, ability, attitude, and character references, among other factors. If so, the nurse's hiring recommendations likely involve the exercise of independent judgment. Similarly, if the registered nurse weighs the individualized condition and needs of a patient against the skills or special training of available nursing personnel, the nurse's assignment involves the exercise of independent judgment. As Senator Flanders remarked, the supervisor determines "who shall do [the job]" and in making that determination the supervisor makes "[a] personal judgment based on personal experience, training, and ability."

As stated above, Section 2(11) contrasts "independent judgment" with actions that are "of a merely routine or clerical nature." Thus, the statute itself provides a baseline for the degree of discretion required to render the exercise of any of the enumerated functions of 2(11) supervisory. The authority to effect an assignment, for example, must be independent, it must involve a judgment, and the judgment must involve a degree of discretion that rises above the "routine or clerical." See, e.g., *J.C. Brock Corp.*, 314 NLRB 157, 158 (1994) (quoting *Bowne of Houston*, 280 NLRB 1222, 1223 (1986)) ("[T]he exercise of some supervisory authority in a merely routine, clerical, perfunctory, or sporadic manner does not confer supervisory status."). If there is only one obvious and self-evident choice (for example, assigning the one available nurse fluent in American Sign Language (ASL) to a patient dependent upon ASL for communicating), or if the assignment is made solely on the basis of equalizing workloads, then the assignment is routine or clerical in nature and does not implicate independent judgment, even if it is made free of the control of others and involves forming an opinion or evaluation by discerning and comparing data. By contrast, if the hospital has a policy that details how a charge nurse should respond in an emergency, but the charge nurse has the discretion to determine when an emergency exists or the authority to deviate from that policy based on the charge nurse's assessment of the particular circumstances, those deviations, if material, would involve the exercise of independent judgment. . . .

D. Persons Who Are Supervisors Part of the Time

Where an individual is engaged a part of the time as a supervisor and the rest of the time as a unit employee, the legal standard for a supervisory determination is whether the individual spends a regular and substantial portion of his/her work time performing supervisory functions. Under the Board's standard, "regular" means according to a pattern or schedule, as opposed to sporadic substitution. The Board has not adopted a strict numerical definition of substantiality and has found supervisory status where the individuals have served in a supervisory role for at least 10-15 percent of their total work time. We find no reason to depart from this established precedent.

[In applying its new tests, the NLRB concluded that permanent charges nurses were supervisors because they assigned other nurses with independent judgment under 2(11); however, the NLRB found that the charge nurses did not responsibly direct. The NLRB did not find the rotating charge nurses to be supervisors because the employer could not show that those nurses exercised supervisory authority for a substantial portion of their work time.]

MEMBERS LIEBMAN and WALSH, dissenting in part and concurring in part in the result.

Today's decision threatens to create a new class of workers under Federal labor law: workers who have neither the genuine prerogatives of management, nor the statutory rights of ordinary employees. Into that category may fall most professionals (among many other workers), who by 2012 could number almost 34 million, accounting for 23.3 percent of the work force. "[M]ost professionals have some supervisory responsibilities in the sense of directing another's work — the lawyer his secretary, the teacher his teacher's aide, the doctor his nurses, the registered nurse her nurse's aide, and so on."[19] . . .

In this case, a narrow focus on dictionary definitions of individual words in isolation leads the majority astray. If we read the whole statutory text, consider the context and purpose of the National Labor Relations Act, and consult authoritative legislative history, then the majority's statutory interpretation is revealed as untenable. Despite its claim to the contrary, the majority proceeds as if the

---

[19] [n.2] *NLRB v. Res-Care, Inc.*, 705 F.2d 1461, 1465 (7th Cir. 1983) (opinion by Circuit Judge Posner).

"ordinary meaning of the words used" in Section 2(11) can dictate a choice among potential alternative interpretations. But where the words of a statute are ambiguous, the text alone cannot tell us which interpretation is best and why. The majority never offers a clear and carefully reasoned explanation of its choices. . . .

As we will explain, our disagreement with the majority on the interpretation of "assign" focuses on the treatment of task assignments made to employees, which we view as a quintessential function of the minor supervisors whom Congress clearly did *not* intend to cover in Section 2(11). As to responsible direction, we differ principally concerning the scope and scale of the authority required to satisfy the statutory test. In our view, the phrase "responsibly to direct" was intended to reach persons who were effectively in charge of a department-level *work unit*, even if they did not engage in the other supervisory functions identified in Section 2(11). Our differences with the majority might seem arcane and insignificant. But the real-world consequences of the competing interpretations, in terms of who is (and is not) a statutory supervisor, could prove dramatic. . . .

Using the dictionary definition of "assign" adopted by the majority ("to appoint to a post or duty"), the more natural reading would limit the phrase "assign employees" to a significant employment decision on the order of determining (1) an employee's position with the employer (in most settings, identified by job classification); (2) designated work site (i.e., facility or departmental unit), or (3) work hours (i.e., shift). This limited reading better fits the idea of appointing an employee to a post or duty. . . .

Reading the phrase "assign . . . other employees" in its statutory context confirms that it contemplates something beyond mere task assignment. The majority recognizes the need for such a contextual interpretation, but its actual reading misses the mark. The majority asserts that each of the supervisory functions listed in Section 2(11) — "hire, transfer, suspend, lay off, recall, promote, discharge, *assign*, reward, or discipline" — "affect[s] a term or condition of employment." In fact, the listed functions do more. The terms in this series speak either to altering employment tenure itself ("hire," "suspend," "lay off," "recall," "discharge") or to actions that affect an employee's overall status or situation ("promote," "reward," "discipline," "transfer").

Viewed as a member of this series, "assign" must denote authority to determine the *basic* terms and conditions of an employee's job, i.e., position, work site, or work hours. Indeed, no other Section 2(11) duty in the series addresses this elementary supervisory function. "Assign" is the corollary to the authority to "transfer" employees (i.e., to *reassign* them to a different classification, location, or shift). By contrast, the act of assigning tasks — whether on a daily basis or task-by-task — from among those already included within an employee's overall job responsibilities effects no real change in basic terms and conditions of employment. That employees may perceive certain tasks to be more onerous or more desirable is a fact that appropriately is considered in relation to the Section 2(11) authority to "discipline" or "reward." . . .

[T]he phrase "responsibly to direct" refers to the general supervisory authority delegated to foremen overseeing an operational department and the accountability that goes with it, in contrast to the kind of one-on-one task direction (mistakenly covered by the majority's interpretation of "assign") that would be given by minor supervisory employees (persons who themselves answered to the foreman) to other employees. What is missing from the majority's interpretation, then, is the recognition of the scope and scale of the supervisory function that "responsibly to direct" was intended to capture. More than simply the responsible oversight of another worker's performance of a task is involved.

Rather, the test proposed by the General Counsel in this case accurately captures the intent of Congress in articulating the analytical factors for determining the existence of "responsibly to direct" authority:

> An individual responsibly directs with independent judgment within the meaning of Section 2(11) when it is established that the individual:
>
> a. has been delegated substantial authority to ensure that a work unit achieves management's objectives and is thus "in charge";
>
> b. is held accountable for the work of others; and
>
> c. exercises significant discretion and judgment in directing his or her work unit.

This test differs crucially from the majority's construction in requiring oversight with respect to a work unit . . . .

POST PROBLEM DISCUSSION

1. Which Section 2(11) categories do you think Evelyn's employer will most likely argue she falls under? Do you think the restaurant will succeed in making any of those arguments?

2. What are the differences between the tests for the majority and dissent in *Oakwood*? The dissent believes that these differences will have a substantial impact in many cases; do you agree? Which test do you think better reflects the language of Section 2(11)? No matter what you think about the best interpretation of Section 2(11), what do you think the proper scope of the supervisory exclusion *should* be?

3. One difference between the majority and dissent in *Oakwood* is their approach to statutory construction. The majority, as it did in *Brown University*, seemed to take a more textual view of "employee." In contrast, the dissent criticized the majority's overreliance on the dictionary, arguing that the NLRA's statutory aims should have played a more important role. What's your take on these two approaches? *See* Michael C. Harper, *Judicial Control of the National Labor Relations Board's Lawmaking in the Age of* Chevron *and* Brand X, 89 B.U. L. REV. 189, 241-48 (2009) (criticizing NLRB for failing to consider impact of *Oakwood's* interpretation on supervisors); Daniel P. O'Gorman, *Construing the National Labor Relations Act: The NLRB and Methods of Statutory Construction*, 81 TEMP. L. REV. 177 (2008) (analyzing Board's statutory construction in *Brown University* and *Oakwood*, and arguing for a more policymaking approach).

4. Although *Oakwood* is considered a more pro-employer decision, the fact that not all of the employees involved in the case were classified as supervisors is a reminder that even *Oakwood's* broad interpretation of Section 2(11) will always be

case-specific. Indeed, in *Oakwood's* two companion cases, the NLRB concluded that all of the challenged workers were employees rather than supervisors. *See Croft Metals, Inc.*, 348 N.L.R.B. 717 (2006) (concluding that manufacturing plant lead persons lacked authority to assign and their authority to responsibly direct was too routine to be considered supervisory); Golden Crest Healthcare Center, 348 N.L.R.B. 727 (2006) (concluding that charge nurses lacked the authority to assign and their authority to responsibly direct nurse assistants lacked the accountability needed for supervisor status).

5.   Imagine that you are a worker in a similar work situation as the charge nurses in *Oakwood*. Would you rather be considered a supervisor who is not covered by the NLRA, or would you rather trade supervisory status for NLRA protection? Should it matter what you, or other workers, want? For a humorous take on this question — and to hear Stephen Colbert state that he is a "labor law fanatic" who "can't get enough of [] National Labor Relations Board decisions" — see The Colbert Report, *The Word: Solidarity* (July 18, 2006), http://www.colbertnation.com/the-colbert-report-videos/71890/july-18-2006/the-word---solidarity.

6.   As you saw in *Yeshiva*, the *Oakwood* decision exhibits a tension between excluding workers with managerial or supervisory power and the NLRA's express inclusion of professional employees. In a portion of *Oakwood* not excerpted here, the dissent worried that a substantial portion of the professional workforce will be excluded from NLRA by what it views as an overly expansive interpretation of Section 2(11). *See* 348 N.L.R.B. at 700; *see also* Anne Marie Lofaso, *The Vanishing Employee: Putting the Autonomous Dignified Union Worker Back to Work*, 5 F.I.U. L. Rev. 495, 541 (2010). The majority responded by stressing that not all professionals will exercise one of the twelve Section 2(11) duties with independent judgment. *Id.* at 693. Think about professionals whom you know (or the attorney you imagine becoming). Do you believe that they would meet the definition of supervisor? Should they?

3.   Confidential Employees

Much like managerial workers, the NLRB has created some type of exclusion for confidential employees, which are not mentioned in the NLRA. Under the NLRB's policy, confidential employees are not permitted to be members of the same bargaining unit as other employees. You can best understand why by considering how confidential employees are defined.

In contrast to managerial workers, the Supreme Court has approved of the NLRB's labor nexus requirement for confidential employees. *See NLRB v. Hendricks County Rural Electric Membership Corp.*, 454 U.S. 170, 190 (1981). Therefore, excluded confidential employees must have access to confidential information that is related to the employer's labor relations. Take, for example, an administrative assistant to Coca-Cola's CEO. If the assistant had access to the secret formula for Coke, that employee would not be considered confidential under the NLRA, despite the obvious value and importance of the secret formula. If instead, the assistant had access to Coke's bargaining strategy in negotiations with a union, then the confidential employee exception would apply. The reason is that the assistant's access to information about the employer's labor relations would create a conflict of interest if the assistant was in the same unit with other employees. *See Hendricks County*, 454 U.S. at 179 (noting concern that "management should not be forced to negotiate with a union that includes employees "who in the normal performance of their duties may obtain advance information of the [c]ompany's position with regard to contract negotiations, the disposition of grievances, and other labor relations matters"). This concern is similar to the one that is embodied in the NLRA rule that keeps guards in a separate unit. *See* Section 9(b) (stating that the NLRB shall not "decide that any unit is appropriate . . . if it includes, together with other employees, any individual employed as a guard to enforce against employees and other persons rules to protect property of the employer or to protect the safety of persons on the employer's premises" and "no labor organization shall be certified as the representative of employees in a bargaining unit of guards if such organization admits to membership, or is affiliated directly or indirectly with an organization which admits to membership, employees other than guards").

Although it is clear that confidential employees cannot be in a unit with other employees, what is less clear is whether confidential employees are protected at all by the NLRA. The Supreme Court expressly refused to answer that question in *Hendricks County. See* 454 U.S. at 186-87 n.19. However, the NLRB has concluded that confidential employees' concerted activity should be protected, but not all appellate courts have agreed. *Compare Grove Valve & Regulator Co.*, 262 N.L.R.B. 285, 304 (1982) (citing Ford Motor Co., 66 N.L.R.B. 1317 (1946)), *with Peerless of America v. NLRB*, 484 F.2d 1108, 1112 (7th Cir. 1973); *Wheeling Electric Co.*, 444 F.2d 783 (4th Cir. 1971). Because so few employees at a given workplace are classified as confidential, this question doesn't get raised very often.

4.   Foreign Jurisdictions and Extraterritoriality

PROBLEM #5: A BAD BUSINESS TRIP

Mike is an accountant at a major U.S. accounting firm, Anderson Arthurs. Last year, he created a website called "Greedy Accountants," which collected salary information from accountants across the country. This information helped junior accountants negotiate for better salaries, as the accounting firms started raising their wage structures in an attempt to attract the best accountants. However, the firms were not pleased with this development and the additional costs it imposed. Realizing that antitrust laws prevented them from agreeing to cap salaries, the firms put pressure on Anderson Arthurs to keep its employee in check. Anderson Arthurs' General Counsel cautioned against going after Mike, as his operation of Greedy Accountants could be viewed as concerted activity that is protected by the NLRA (you will see why that might be so in Chapter 4). Later, as Anderson Arthurs began considering which accountants it would send to an international accounting conference in London, the General Counsel thought of a way to get rid of Mike. Pursuant to the General Counsel's plan, Mike's manager flew on the same plane with Mike to London. As soon as they arrived at their hotel, the manager turned to Mike and said, "I've got good news for you. You'll have a lot of extra time to visit London's museums." After Mike asked why, the manager responded, "Because you're fired and no longer need to go to the conference."

If you assume that Mike was fired for NLRA-protected work on Greedy Associates, why did the General Counsel come up with this plan, and do you think it will work for Anderson Arthurs? As you're reading the case that follows, ask yourself whether the court accurately interpreted the NLRA and, if so, whether you think this aspect of the statute should be changed.

PROBLEM MATERIAL

Asplundh Tree Expert Co. v. NLRB, 365 F.3d 168 (3d Cir. 2004)

ASPLUNDH TREE EXPERT CO. v. NLRB
365 F.3d 168 (3d Cir. 2004)

McKee, Circuit Judge.

Asplundh Tree Expert Company petitions for review of a decision of the National Labor Relations Board ("NLRB" or "Board") wherein the NLRB ruled that Asplundh committed unfair labor practices by threatening to lay off Dennis Brinson and by discharging Brinson and Eric Crabtree in response to their concerted complaint about working conditions while on temporary work assignment in Ottawa, Canada. Those employees also briefly withheld their services in support of their job related complaints. . . . However, we hold that since the National Labor Relations Act ("NLRA") does not apply outside the territorial jurisdiction of the United States, the Board did not have jurisdiction over the unfair labor practices charge. . . .

Asplundh provides tree trimming services throughout the eastern United States and maintains its principal place of business in Willow Grove, Pennsylvania. Much of Asplundh's work is performed for utility companies that need to keep their power lines cleared of tree limbs. One of Asplundh's operations is based in Cincinnati, Ohio, where it primarily performs line clearance work for the Cincinnati Gas & Electric Company. Asplundh's employees are represented by Local 171 of the International Brotherhood of Electrical Workers ("IBEW"). A collective bargaining agreement between Asplundh and IBEW covers Asplundh's workers when they are engaged in line clearance work on the property of Cincinnati Gas & Electric Company or its subsidiaries.

Asplundh also offers its services to utilities and other entities in other states. In that capacity, it assigns its employees to perform work related to storms, natural disasters and natural emergencies. Several provincial governments in Canada retained Asplundh to assist in clearing electrical lines, trimming tree limbs and cleaning streets after a major ice storm struck eastern Canada in January 1998. Ottawa, Ontario was among the entities that contracted for Asplundh's services following that storm, and on January 12, Asplundh's Cincinnati operation prepared to send 10 crews of 2 employees each to that Canadian city.

Asplundh does not require its employees to travel outside of their locality for emergency storm cleanup work like the Ottawa assignment. Instead, employees volunteer for such work, and are compensated in part by a per diem covering their food and lodging while working away from home.

On January 13, a group of 20 employees met in a parking lot before leaving for Ottawa. At the meeting, Supervisor Darrell Lewis told the employees that they would receive per diem payments in the amount of $25 for food and that Asplundh would pay up to $75 per day for hotel rooms.

The group left for Ottawa later that day in a caravan of Aslpundh trucks. Lewis did not travel to Ottawa, and Foreman Ronald Lacey was therefore left in charge of the assignment. On the 31 hour trip to Ottawa, the employees did not take any breaks lasting longer than 3 hours. They also experienced a number of problems including malfunctioning heaters and taillights. Several crews became lost when they were unable to keep pace with Lacey, who was leading the caravan. Some employees received no per diem or food money for the uninterrupted travel time. By the time the employees arrived in Ottawa on the evening of January 14, many of them were hungry, fatigued and disgruntled.

Once in Ottawa, Lacey reserved hotel rooms for all of the employees which he paid for at a negotiated price of $61 per room per night. That rate was obviously less than the $75 per night Lewis had told the employees was available for their lodging. Concomitantly, some of the employees began to feel that the $25 per diem for food was insufficient to cover the high cost of food in Ottawa.

At least four employees — Brinson, Crabtree, Shane Duff and Ron Noble — met on the first night in Ottawa and discussed their dissatisfaction with the problems they had encountered en route as well as the amount of their per diem. They discussed augmenting the per diem with the $14 remaining from the difference between the $75 that Asplundh was willing to spend per hotel room and the $61 that Lacey was actually paying. They agreed that they should discuss the matter with Lacey and decided that Brinson would be the spokesperson. [Duff also learned that Asplundh employees in Quebec received more paid expenses than the Ottowa employees, as well as an occasional free steak dinner.] . . .

On the morning of January 17, Brinson phoned Lacey and told him that the employees wanted a $14 increase in their per diem payments — the difference between the $75 authorized for hotel rooms and the actual $61 room cost. Brinson also indicated that the employees might not work if their per diem payments were not increased. Lacey then called Cincinnati and spoke with Lewis, the supervisor. Lacey told Lewis of the employees' request and of the possibility that they might not work if their concerns were not addressed. Lewis instructed Lacey not to raise the per diem payments and told Lacey that "if they're not going to take the trucks out, that means they quit."

Lacey went to the hotel lobby to meet with the employees, placed another call to Lewis, then handed Brinson the phone. Lewis told Brinson that the employees were "whiny cry babies" and were "making the Company look bad." Lewis then told Brinson that a number of crews would be laid off when they returned to Cincinnati and that the Ottawa employees were making it easier for Lewis to decide whom to lay off.

Brinson relayed his conversation with Lewis to a group of crew members, told them it was time to decide what they wanted to do, and then left to let them make a decision. A short time later, Brinson realized that most of the crew members had left to go to their work assignment.

Lacey then approached Brinson, who was standing with Crabtree, Duff and Noble, and asked them what they were going to do. Brinson replied that they still wanted to discuss their situation before going to work. Lacey responded by demanding Brinson's truck keys. After Brinson handed over his keys, Lacey asked Crabtree what he wanted to do. Crabtree replied: "I'm with Dennis [Brinson]. I still think we need to have something done about this." Lacey then asked Crabtree for his keys, and after Crabtree gave them to Lacey, Lacey said "this means you quit." Lacey also admonished Brinson and Crabtree for sticking up for their fellow employees and then told them to "get home the best way you f . . . g can." Duff and Noble briefly considered joining Brinson and Crabtree in their refusal to work, but Brinson, concerned about Duff's and Noble's job security, convinced them that they ought to go to work.

Soon thereafter, Brinson and Crabtree returned to Cincinnati by bus. Once back in Cincinnati, Brinson repeatedly offered to return to work, but neither he nor Crabtree were ever allowed to return to their jobs with Asplundh.[20] . . .

Asplundh argues that the Board's finding of violations of § 8(a)(1) of the NLRA was not supported by substantial evidence. However, we must first resolve Asplundh's challenge to the Board's exercise of jurisdiction over an unfair labor practices charge arising from "offending" conduct that occurred in Canada.[21]

Although Congress undoubtedly has the authority "to enforce its laws beyond the territorial boundaries of the United States[,] . . . [w]hether Congress has in fact exercised that authority . . . is a matter of statutory construction." *EEOC v. Arabian American Oil Co.,* ("*ARAMCO*"), 499 U.S. 244, 248 (1991) (citations omitted).[22] Moreover, "[i]t is a longstanding principle of American law 'that legislation of Congress, unless a contrary intent appears, is meant to apply only within the territorial jurisdiction of the United States.' " *Id.* (quoting *Foley Bros., Inc. v. Filardo,* 336 U.S. 281 (1949)).

This canon of construction is a valid approach whereby unexpressed congressional intent may be ascertained. It serves to protect against unintended clashes

---

[20] [n.2] The Board and Asplundh agree that because the collective bargaining agreement between IBEW Local 171 and Asplundh was limited to work on the property of Cincinnati Gas & Electric Company and its subsidiaries, Local 171 was not the employees' exclusive representative for the purposes of employment in Ottawa.

[21] [n.4] Asplundh argued before the ALJ and the Board, that because the conduct giving rise to the unfair labor practices charge occurred outside the United States, the Board did not have jurisdiction. Both the ALJ and the Board rejected Asplundh's argument. However, we owe no deference to the NLRB's view because the extraterritorial application of a statute is purely a matter of statutory construction not involving agency expertise. *Cleary v. United States Lines, Inc.*, 728 F.2d 607, 610 n. 6 (3d Cir.1984).

[22] [n.5] In *ARAMCO*, the Supreme Court held that protections against employment discrimination of Title VII of the Civil Rights Act of 1964 did not extend extraterritorially to protect United States citizens employed abroad by United States employers. 499 U.S. at 248–59. However, in the wake of ARAMCO, Congress amended Title VII to protect United States citizens employed abroad by United States employers. *Spector v. Norwegian Cruise Line Ltd.*, 356 F.3d 641, 646 n. 4 (5th Cir.2004) (citing 42 U.S.C. § 2000e(f) (2000)).

between our laws and those of other nations which could result in international discord.

> In applying this rule of construction, we look to see whether language in the relevant Act gives any indication of a congressional purpose to extend its coverage beyond places over which the United States has sovereignty or has some measure of legislative control. We assume that Congress legislates against the backdrop of the presumption against extraterritoriality. Therefore, unless there is the affirmative intention of the Congress clearly expressed, we must presume it is primarily concerned with domestic conditions.

ARAMCO, 499 U.S. at 248. . . .

[T]he Board now contends that the assumption of jurisdiction over the unfair labor practices charge at issue here is "entirely compatible" with the presumption against extraterritoriality. In the Board's view, it is appropriate for it to assume jurisdiction when a United States citizen is working on a short-time, temporary assignment outside the United States, with the clear expectation of returning to the United States upon completion of the assignment. This argument is not without some force and certainly appears consistent with the labor policy endemic in the NLRA. However, as noted above, our task is one of statutory interpretation. Accordingly, sound policy positions advocated by either side neither constrain nor influence our inquiry. *See ARAMCO*, 499 U.S. at 248.

As *ARAMCO* teaches, we begin our analysis with the language of the NLRA. Section 10 of that Act provides that "[t]he Board is empowered, as hereinafter provided, to prevent any person from engaging in any unfair labor practice (listed in section 158) affecting commerce." 29 U.S.C. § 160(a). Admittedly, the NLRA defines the jurisdictional terms "affecting commerce" and "commerce" very broadly. " '[A]ffecting commerce' means in commerce, or burdening or obstructing commerce or the free flow of commerce, or having led or tending to lead to a labor dispute burdening or obstructing commerce or the free flow of commerce." 29 U.S.C. § 152(7). Similarly, the NLRA broadly defines "commerce" as:

> trade, traffic, commerce, transportation, or communication among the several States, or between the District of Columbia or any Territory of the United States and any State or other Territory, or *between any foreign country* and any State, Territory, or the District of Columbia, or within the District of Columbia or any Territory, or between points in the same State but through any other State or any Territory or the District of Columbia or any foreign country.

29 U.S.C. § 152(6) (1988) (emphasis added).

Thus, a literal reading of the jurisdictional and definitional provisions of the NLRA seems to not only favor the NLRB's extraterritorial exercise of jurisdiction, it seems to dictate that result and end our jurisdictional inquiry. However, in interpreting this seemingly broad language, we are not free to ignore the Supreme Court's interpretation of the similarly broad jurisdictional reach of Title VII in *ARAMCO*. Title VII then stated that "[a]n employer is subject to Title VII if it has employed 15 or more employees . . . and is engaged in an industry affecting commerce." *ARAMCO*, 499 U.S. at 249. . . . "Commerce," in turn, was defined as "trade, traffic, commerce, transportation, transmission, or communication among the several States; or *between a State and any place outside thereof*, or within the District of Columbia, or a possession of the United States; or between points in the same State but through a point outside thereof." *Id.*

The petitioners in *ARAMCO* argued that the broad definition of "employer" and "commerce" in Title VII reflected Congress' intent to give the EEOC extraterritorial jurisdiction. The Court rejected that argument reasoning that such broad jurisdictional terms were nothing more than "boilerplate language" that Congress had used in numerous other enactments. The Court held that such "boilerplate" was simply not enough to defeat the presumption against the extraterritorial application of Title VII. *Id.* (cited statutes omitted). In doing so, the Court reiterated, "we have repeatedly held that even statutes that contain broad language in their definitions of 'commerce' that expressly refer to '*foreign* commerce' do not apply abroad." *Id.*, at 251. (emphasis in original).

The Court held that the wording of Title VII was not sufficient to rebut the presumption against extraterritoriality and support a conclusion that Congress intended to empower the Equal Employment Opportunity Commission to exercise jurisdiction beyond the United States, despite the broad definitions suggesting the contrary. The Court buttressed reliance on presumption against extraterritorial jurisdiction by noting that Congress had not included any mechanism for the extraterritorial enforcement of the Act's protections. . . . Similarly, in enacting the NLRA, Congress included no mechanism for extraterritorial enforcement, and did not provide a method for resolving any conflicts with labor laws of other nations. Given the obvious potential for conflict where United States companies employ workers oversees, this omission strikes us as more than a mere oversight. It is consistent with the Supreme Court's conclusion that broad definitional language is little more than "boilerplate" in the absence of an express manifestation of extraterritorial intent.

Therefore, absent more, we can not interpret the "boilerplate language" before us in the NLRA in a manner that would inject the expression of congressional intent required to stretch it to cover the employees Asplundh temporarily detailed to Canada. Moreover, the Board is not able to point to any language in the NLRA that would support its position given the rationale of *ARAMCO*. In fact, the Board seems to completely ignore the fact that we are confronted with an issue of statutory construction rather than policy. Instead, the Board advances a number of reasons why the NLRA *should* apply to United States citizens working temporarily abroad. Although we are sympathetic to the argument that the NLRA *should* apply abroad under the circumstances here, we must determine if the NLRA *does* apply abroad. As noted above, that is an inquiry governed by statutory construction as guided by Supreme Court precedent; it is not an inquiry governed by the kind of policy considerations the NLRB urges upon us.

The NLRB contends that its assertion of jurisdiction was appropriate for three reasons. First, the unfair labor practices charge "involves an employment relationship that has been shown to be primarily within the territorial boundaries of the United States." Second, its "remedial order has no extraterritorial reach, as it will only require a U.S. employer to take action — namely, reinstatement, backpay and a notice posting — in the United States." Third, "failure to assert jurisdiction would not only deny Brinson and Crabtree relief to which they would otherwise unquestionably be entitled;" it would also frustrate the remedial and deterrent purposes of the NLRA. Accordingly, the Board argues that it was reasonable for it to assume jurisdiction over the unfair labor practices charge because the "fact that Brinson and Crabtree were briefly in Canada . . . when they staged their short-lived protest was little more than a fortuity for U.S. workers employed by a U.S. enterprise."

We do not disagree that the Board's exercise of jurisdiction can be seen as "reasonable," however, that is not tantamount to determining if it was authorized. As noted above, given the Court's holding in *ARAMCO*, the language of the NLRA simply can not be read as an expression of the congressional intent required to empower the Board to exercise jurisdiction over Asplundh's conduct here.

Moreover, although the Board's argument to the contrary has significant appeal at first blush, we believe the Board's "policy" argument is nothing more than a "balancing of contacts" test that the Supreme Court has already rejected in a case it decided before *ARAMCO* [(citing *McCulloch v. Sociedad Nacional de Marineros de Honduras*, 372 U.S. 10 (1963).] . . .

Simply put, under that balancing test, if the Board found that the American contacts in the dispute were substantial, it asserted jurisdiction under the NLRA; however, if it found that the foreign contacts outweighed the American contacts, the Board concluded the NLRA did not apply and would not assert jurisdiction. . . . [T]he Supreme Court rejected the Board's "balancing of contacts" test and concluded that the question before it was "more basic; namely, whether the Act *as written* was intended to have any application to foreign registered vessels employing alien seamen." *Id.* at 19. (emphasis added). In other words, the inquiry turned on statutory construction rather than an analysis of the comparative impact the Board's exercise of jurisdiction would have on the jurisdictions potentially affected by the underlying dispute or the Board's action. . . .

Thus, after *McCulloch*, the Board's "balancing of contacts" cannot be used to manufacture jurisdiction in the absence of clearly expressed congressional intent to extend the NLRA to United States citizens temporarily working abroad for a United States employer. Perhaps realizing this, the Board attempts to craft a new jurisdictional test to justify its assertion of jurisdiction here. It argues that the employee's "work station" determines whether the NLRA applies. According to the Board, Brinson's and Crabtree's "work station" was the United States. . . .

The Board claims that the major advantage of its new "work station" theory is that the assertion of jurisdiction under the test has no extraterritorial effect because the permanent "work station" remained the United States. However, the Board's "work station" rule also spawns a policy driven analysis at the expense of one driven by statutory interpretation. Adopting the Board's "work station" inquiry also requires an examination of the specific impact of the extraterritorial application to the acts in question. Nothing in *McCulloch* suggests that such a case by case inquiry can overcome the presumption against extraterritoriality in the absence of express jurisdictional language. . . . Moreover, the Board has cited no authority to support its claim that a "work station" rule even exists under the NLRA. . . .

Finally, we are mindful of the fact that Congress knows how to provide for extraterritorial application of its enactments when it intends them to operate outside of the United States. For example in 1984, after a number of courts of appeals held that the ADEA did not operate extraterritorially, Congress expressly amended the ADEA to provide for limited extraterritorial application. In 1991, following the Supreme Court's decision in *ARAMCO*, Congress amended both Title VII and the Americans with Disabilities Act to similarly provide for limited extraterritorial application. However, Congress has never amended the NLRA to provide for extraterritorial application under any circumstances despite the Court's decision in *McCulloch* over 40 years ago expressly limiting the territorial reach of the NLRA. . . .

Despite the broad "boilerplate" definitions in the NLRA, we can discover no clearly expressed congressional intention that that Act was intended to apply to employees working temporarily outside of the United States for United States employers. Therefore, we hold the Board did not have jurisdiction over the unfair labor practices charge here. Accordingly, we will vacate the Board's decision and dismiss the petition for review and cross-application for enforcement.[23]

POST PROBLEM DISCUSSION

1.   How bad is *Asplundh* for Mike's situation in our problem? Does the case give an absolute rule against any enforcement of the NLRA for facts that happen outside of the U.S.? If so, does Mike have any other options to challenge his termination under the NLRA? (A related question/hint: would it have mattered in *Asplundh* if the court had interpreted Supervisor Lewis' statement that "if they're not going to take the trucks out, that means they quit" as part of the allegedly unlawful termination?).

2.   See footnote 4 of *Asplundh*. Is the court's description of the deference it owes to the NLRB consistent with what you learned in Section 2(B) of this chapter?

3.   Should it have mattered in *Asplundh* whether Canadian labor laws applied to the employees? It apparently didn't to the court, because the Canadian laws don't apply to foreign employees like those in *Asplundh*. Therefore, the fired employees were in a labor law no-man's land. Given this, should the requirement of an express

---

[23] [n.16] As we have noted throughout our discussion, the Board's position that the employees here should be afforded the protection of the NLRA given the temporary and limited nature of their assignment is not without force. Extraterritorial application of the NLRA here certainly does not appear to create the potential for international discord that was so evident from the circumstances in *McCulloch*. . . .

The presumption against extraterritorial application of congressional enactments is, in large measure, based upon the notion that legislation is nearly always enacted in response to domestic concerns. The difficulties we have already discussed with an *ad hoc* approach to these difficult issues certainly mitigates against creating exceptions to the extraterritorial reach of the NLRA to accommodate the kind of dispute before us here. However, given the seemingly incongruous result we believe the text of the NLRA and prior decisions require, Congress can amend the NLRA to extend its protections to these kinds of work assignments if that is what it intended. However, given the current wording of the NLRA, "the [NLRB's] arguments should be directed to Congress rather than to us." *McCulloch*, 372 U.S. at 22.

statement of congressional intent be loosened somewhat?

4. Note that the NLRB has expressly refused to follow the court's rejection of its approach in *Asplundh. See California Gas Transport Co.*, 347 N.L.R.B. 1314, 1316 n.11 (2006) ("We respectfully disagree with the Third Circuit's analysis. The Third Circuit's opinion failed to address the Supreme Court's post-*Aramco* weakening of the strict presumption against extraterritoriality . . . . Further, the Third Circuit did not address the Eleventh Circuit's conflicting decision in *Dowd v. Longshoremen ILA*, 975 F.2d 779 (11th Cir. 1992)). Although the NLRB usually follows court rejections of its rules, it will occasionally refuse to do so under its "non-acquiescence" policy. Under this policy, which usually arises when there is a circuit-split, the NLRB will assert its responsibility as the primary interpreter of the NLRA to pursue its own view of an issue despite its disagreement with a court. *See generally* Samuel Estreicher & Richard L. Revesz, *Nonacquiesence by Federal Administrative Agencies*, 98 YALE L.J. 679 (1989). A recent example of the NLRB's use of the non-acquiescence policy occurred with regard to the two-member Board issue discussed earlier. Although most courts held that the two-member NLRB had authority to issue decisions, the D.C. Circuit disagreed. *See New Process Steel, LP v. NLRB*, 130 S. Ct. 2635 (2010) (describing split). The NLRB invoked its non-acquiescence policy to continue issuing decisions until the Supreme Court agreed with the D.C. Circuit in *New Process.*

Under this non-acquiescence policy, "the Board, in selected cases, has chosen to adhere to its view of the law, where it respectfully disagrees with an appellate court's adverse decision. This step enables the Board's position to be presented to other Circuits and, where appropriate, to the Supreme Court." *See* Statement of Chairman Wilma B. Liebman and Member Peter C. Schaumber Concerning the District of Columbia Circuit's *Laurel Baye Healthcare* Decision, May 18, 2009, http://mynlrb.nlrb.gov/link/document.aspx/09031d45801e3933. What practical effect, if any, does this have if the NLRB needs the courts to enforce its orders?

5. For a general discussion of extraterritorial issues in labor law by a former Chairman of the NLRB, see William B. Gould IV, *Labor Law Beyond U.S. Borders: Does What Happens Outside of America Stay Outside of America?*, 21 STAN. L. & POL'Y REV. 401 (2010). For a discussion of related issues of extraterritoriality in the employee benefits law context, see Paul M. Secunda, *"The Longest Journey, With a First Step": Bringing Coherence to Sovereignty and Jurisdictional Issues in Global Employee Benefits Law*, 19 DUKE J. COMP. & INT'L L. 107 (2008).

Chapter 3

DOMINATION AND DISCRIMINATION

Synopsis

Section 1 Employer Domination of a Labor Organization

Section 2 Anti-Union Discrimination

As you will see in later chapters, much of the NLRA is concerned with the process of selecting a union and establishing a duty on both employers and unions to bargain in good faith. However, the NLRA also reflects the fact that employees' right to choose collective representation means little if employers are able to influence that choice through inappropriate means. The NLRA establishes what it considers to be inappropriate in Section 8's list of unfair labor practices (see Chapter 1 for more detail).

In this chapter, we will focus on two unfair labor practices. The first is Section 8(a)(2)'s prohibition against an employer's domination of, or assistance to, a labor organization. This is usually described as a ban on "company unions" that give employees a false sense of independent representation.

The second unfair labor practice is Section 8(a)(3) (and its twin, Section 8(b)(2) for unions). Section 8(a)(3) may be the most familiar unfair labor practice because it mirrors other types of anti-discrimination workplace laws, many of which were modeled after the NLRA. Section 8(a)(3)'s prohibition against discrimination based on union conduct or sympathies is an obvious necessity for a statute that seeks to promote unionization and to give employees the freedom to choose whether collective representation is right for them.

SECTION 1   EMPLOYER DOMINATION OF A LABOR ORGANIZATION

Early in the history of the American labor movement, and well before the NLRA's enactment, employers created "company unions." Employers used these sham unions to make employees think they were getting meaningful representation as a way to ward off organizing drives from truly independent unions. One of the key features of the NLRA was to prohibit this practice.

Section 8(a)(2) of the NLRA makes it an unfair labor practice for an employer to "dominate or interfere with the formation or administration of any labor organization or contribute financial or other support to it." This prohibition has been effective at eliminating many of the most egregious company unions. Perhaps too effective. As you will see in the following case, the NLRB has broadly interpreted both Section 8(a)(2) and Section 2(5)'s definition of "labor organization." The result has been to prohibit many workplace organizations that fall well short of the sham unions of old. Many commentators and legislators have attempted to relax this interpretation to give employers more options to discuss various issues with non-unionized employees. However, many others have resisted this change because of a fear that it will deprive many employees of the opportunity to obtain truly independent representation.

PROBLEM #1: THERE'S NO SUCH THING AS A FREE LUNCH

Partridge Mountain Resort caters to skiers and other vacationers that visit nearby Partridge Mountain in the Colorado Rockies. The resort contains a hotel, restaurant, and bar. Recently, a local chapter of the United Food and Commercial Workers union began a campaign to organize employees at the resort. One thing that piqued the interest of the union organizers was something called the Quality Committee. The resort created the Quality Committee over ten years ago, soon after the resort opened. After a couple of years, it had stopped meeting because of a lack of interest from employees; however, four years ago, some employees asked to have it restarted, which the resort did. The Quality Committee is part of an overall program by the resort to hear from its employees. The two major pieces of the program are a suggestion box for employee comments and the Quality Committee meetings that all employees may, and are encouraged to, attend.

One of the resort's managers, Noah, ran the Quality Committee meetings, which occurred once a month. Generally, between five to twenty of the resort's one-hundred employees attended each meeting, and the resort paid attendees if they were on shift at the time. Noah opened every meeting, introduced discussion topics, prepared minutes, and posted those minutes throughout the resort. Noah also provided copies of the minutes to the resort's owner. During the meetings, Noah would initially raise issues, including those that the resort's owners wanted further input on, and he would sometimes participate in discussions. Those discussions involved employee ideas and suggestions on issues that included the dates of new paid holidays, daycare for employees' children, employee meals, employee parking, and smoking in the employee cafeteria. Supervisors and managers occasionally attended meetings and voiced their opinion.

The resort's owner would either accept or reject employees suggestions from the Quality Committee meetings, or request further input from the committee. For example, after employees complained about the lack of hot entrée options during the free lunch provided to employees every day at the resort, the owner asked the Quality Committee to report back on meal options that employees would like. Ultimately, the owner provided several of those options at the free lunch.

After reading the following material, can you answer why the union organizers were so interested in the Quality Committee? Make sure to carefully consider all of the steps involved with answering this question, and think about which ones are at issue here.

PROBLEM MATERIALS

Electromation, Inc., 309 N.L.R.B. 990 (1992)

Michael H. LeRoy, *Employee Participation in the New Millennium: Redefining a Labor Organization Under Section 8(a)(2) of the NLRA*, 72 S. CAL. L. REV. 1651 (1999)

ELECTROMATION, INC.
309 N.L.R.B. 990 (1992)

. . . This case presents the issue of whether "Action Committees" composed, in part, of the Respondent's employees constitute a labor organization within the meaning of Section 2(5) of the Act and whether the Respondent's conduct vis á vis the "Action Committees" violated Section 8(a)(2) and (1) of the Act. In the notice of hearing . . . the Board framed the pertinent issues as follows:

(1)   At what point does an employee committee lose its protection as a communication device and become a labor organization?

(2)   What conduct of an employer constitutes domination or interference with the employee committee?

For the reasons below, we find that the Action Committees were not simply "communication devices" but instead constituted a labor organization within the meaning of Section 2(5) of the Act and that the Respondent's conduct towards the Action Committees constituted domination and interference in violation of Section 8(a)(2) and (1). These findings rest on the totality of the record evidence, and they are not intended to suggest that employee committees formed under other circumstances for other purposes would necessarily be deemed "labor organizations" or that employer actions like some of those at issue here would necessarily be found, in isolation or in other contexts, to constitute unlawful support, interference, or domination.

The Respondent is engaged in the manufacture of electrical components and related products. It employs approximately 200 employees. These employees were not represented by any labor organization at the time of the events described herein.

In late 1988 the Respondent concluded that it was experiencing unacceptable financial losses. It decided to cut expenses by altering the existing employee attendance bonus policy and, in lieu of a wage increase for 1989, distributed year-end lump-sum payments based on length of service. Shortly after these changes were announced, the Respondent became aware that employees were displeased with the reduction in benefits. In early January 1989, the Respondent received a petition signed by 68 employees expressing displeasure with the new attendance policy. Upon receipt of this petition, the Respondent's president, John Howard, met with the Respondent's supervisors to discuss the petition and the employees' complaints. At this meeting, the Respondent decided to meet directly with employees to discuss their problems. Thereafter, on January 11, the Respondent met with a selected group of eight employees and discussed with them a number of issues, including wages, bonuses, incentive pay, attendance programs, and leave policy.

After the January 11 meeting, President Howard again met with his supervisors and concluded that the Respondent had serious problems with its employees. Howard testified that it was decided at that time that "it was very unlikely that further unilateral management action to resolve these problems was going to come anywhere near making everybody happy . . . and we thought that the best course of action would be to involve the employees in coming up with solutions to these issues." Howard testified further that management came up with the idea of "action committees" as a method to involve employees.

The Respondent next met with the same group of eight employees on January 18. Howard explained to the assembled group that management "had distilled the employees' complaints into five categories. Howard testified that he proposed the creation of Action Committees that "would meet and try to come up with ways to resolve these problems; and that if they came up with solutions that . . . we believed were within budget concerns and they generally felt would be acceptable to the employees, that we would implement these suggestions or proposals." Howard testified further that the reaction of the assembled employees to the concept of action committees was "not positive." Howard explained to the employees that because "the business was in trouble financially . . . we couldn't just put things back the way they were . . . we don't have better ideas at this point other than to sit down and work with you on them." According to Howard, as the meeting went on, the employees "began to understand that that was far better than leaving things as they were, and that we weren't going to just unilaterally make changes. And so they accepted it." Howard agreed that employees would not be selected at random for the committees based on seniority and that, instead, sign-up sheets would be posted.

On January 19, the Respondent posted a memorandum directed to all employees announcing the formation of five Action Committees and posted sign-up sheets for each Action Committee. The memorandum explained that each Action Committee would consist of six employees and one or two members of management, as well as the Respondent's Employees Benefits Manager, Loretta Dickey, who would coordinate all the Action Committees. The sign-up sheets explained the responsibilities and goals of each Committee. No employees were involved in the drafting of the policy goals expressed in the sign-up sheets. The Respondent determined the number of employees permitted to sign-up for the Action Committees. The Respondent informed two employees who had signed up for more than one committee that each would be limited to participation on one committee. After the Action Committees were organized, the Respondent posted a notice to all employees announcing the members of each Committee and the dates of the initial Committee meetings. The Action Committees were designated as (1) Absenteeism/Infractions, (2) No Smoking Policy, (3) Communication Network, (4) Pay Progression for Premium Positions, and (5) Attendance Bonus Program.

The Action Committees began meeting in late January and early February. The Respondent's coordinator of the Action Committees, Dickey, testified that management expected that employee members on the Committees would "kind of talk back and forth" with the other employees in the plant, get their ideas, and that, indeed, the purpose of the Respondent's postings was to ensure that "anyone [who] wanted to know what was going on, they could go to these people" on the Action Committees. Other management representatives, as well as Dickey, participated in the Action Committees' meetings, which were scheduled to meet on a weekly basis in a conference room on the Respondent's premises. The Respondent paid employees for their time spent participating and supplied necessary materials. Dickey's role in the meetings was to facilitate the discussions.

On February 13, the Union made a demand to the Respondent for recognition. There is no evidence that the Respondent was aware of organizing efforts by the Union until this time. On about February 21, Howard informed Dickey of the recognition demand and, at the next scheduled meeting of each Action Committee, Dickey informed the members that the Respondent could no longer participate but that the employees could continue to meet if they so desired. The Absenteeism/Infraction and the Communication Network Committees each decided to continue their meetings on company premises; the Pay Progression Committee disbanded; and the Attendance Bonus Committee decided to write up a proposal they had discussed previously and not to meet again. The Attendance Bonus Committee's proposal was one of two proposals that the employees had developed concerning attendance bonuses. The first one, developed at the committee's second or third meeting, was pronounced unacceptable by the Respondent's controller, a member of that committee, because it was too costly. Thereafter the employees devised a second proposal, which the controller deemed fiscally sound. The proposal was not presented to President Howard because the Union's campaign to secure recognition had intervened.

On March 15, Howard informed employees that "due to the Union's campaign, the Company would be unable to participate in the committee meetings and could not continue to work with the committees until after the election," which was to be held on March 31. . . .

Section 2(5) of the Act defines a "labor organization" as follows:

> The term "labor organization" means any organization of any kind, or any agency or employee representation committee or plan, in which employees participate and which exists for the purpose, in whole or in part, of dealing with employers concerning grievances, labor disputes, wages, rates of pay, hours of employment, or conditions of work.

Section 8(a)(2) provides that it shall be an unfair labor practice for an employer:

> to dominate or interfere with the formation or administration of any labor organization or contribute financial or other support to it: *Provided*, That subject to rules and regulations made and published by the Board pursuant to section 6, an employer shall not be prohibited from permitting employees to confer with him during working hours without loss of time or pay.

Whenever we are attempting to determine the application of the statute to particular facts, we must first determine whether the statutory language standing alone answers the question. Here, we cannot properly limit our analysis to the statutory language because the terms are not all self-defining. For example,

although the "Action Committees" are committees in which "employees participate," the parties have raised questions about the meaning of "representation" in
the phrase "employee representation committee." We therefore seek guidance from
the legislative history to discern what kind of activity Congress intended to prohibit
when it made it an unfair labor practice for an employer to "dominate or interfere
with the formation or administration of any labor organization" or to contribute
support to it.

The legislative history reveals that the provisions outlawing company dominated
labor organizations were a critical part of the Wagner Act's purpose of eliminating
industrial strife through the encouragement of collective bargaining. . . . Because
of the Wagner Act's purpose to eliminate employer dominated unions, the term
"labor organization" was defined broadly. Indeed, even though the original Senate
Bill (S. 2976) broadly defined "labor organization" as "*any organization, labor
union, association, corporation, or society of any kind in which employees
participate to any degree whatsoever* and which exists for the purpose . . . of
dealing with employers concerning grievances, labor disputes, wages, rates of pay,
or hours of employment, or conditions of work" [emphasis added], the Wagner Act,
as finally enacted, expanded the initial part of the definition in order to encompass
common forms of company dominated unions that had arisen following passage of
the National Industrial Recovery Act. . . .

With respect to employer conduct that was to come within the ambit of Section
8(a)(2) itself, it is noteworthy that the original Senate bill (S. 2926) made it an unfair
labor practice for an employer to "initiate, participate in, supervise, or influence the
formation, rules, and other policies of a labor organization." After considering
testimony that certain unaffiliated employee organizations confined to representing
employees on a single employer basis often operated in an amicable and cooperative
atmosphere, the Senate sponsors modified Section 8(a)(2) specifically to permit
employees to confer with their employer during working hours without loss of time
or pay. In this regard it is also noteworthy that the modified version contained in S.
1958 substituted the term "to dominate or interfere with the formation or
administration" for the terms "initiate, participate in, supervise, or influence." . . .

Thus, Congress concluded that ridding collective bargaining of employer-
dominated organizations, the formation and administration of which had been
fatally tainted by employer "domination" or "interference," would advance the
Wagner Act's goal of eliminating industrial strife. That conclusion was based on the
nation's experience under the NIRA, recounted by witnesses at the Senate
hearings, that employer interference in setting up or running employee "representation" groups actually robbed employees of the freedom to choose their own
representatives. . . . In sum, Congress brought within its definition of "labor
organization" a broad range of employee groups, and it sought to ensure that such
groups were free to act independently of employers in representing employee
interests.

Before a finding of unlawful domination can be made under Section 8(a)(2) a
finding of "labor organization" status under Section 2(5) is required. Under the
statutory definition set forth in Section 2(5), the organization at issue is a labor
organization if (1) employees participate, (2) the organization exists, at least in part,

for the purpose of "dealing with" employers, and (3) these dealings concern "conditions of work" or concern other statutory subjects, such as grievances, labor disputes, wages, rates of pay, or hours of employment. Further, if the organization has as a purpose the representation of employees, it meets the statutory definition of "employee representation committee or plan" under Section 2(5) and will constitute a labor organization if it also meets the criteria of employee participation and dealing with conditions of work or other statutory subjects. Any group, including an employee representation committee, may meet the statutory definition of "labor organization" even if it lacks a formal structure, has no elected officers, constitution or bylaws, does not meet regularly, and does not require the payment of initiation fees or dues. Thus, a group may be an "employee representation committee" within the meaning of Section 2(5) even if there is no formal framework for conducting meetings among the represented employees (i.e. those employees whose conditions of employment are the subject of committee dealings) or for otherwise eliciting the employees' views.

As noted in our discussion of the Wagner Act's legislative history, Congress viewed the abolition of employer-dominated organizations as essential to the Act's purpose. After Congress passed the Act in 1935, a first order of business for the Board, backed by the Supreme Court, was to weed out employer-dominated organizations. Indeed, the very first unfair labor practice case decided by the Board raised the issues of whether an organization was a labor organization under Section 2(5) and whether the employer had dominated that organization in violation of Section 8(a)(2) and (1). . . .

In considering the interplay between Section 2(5) and Section 8(a)(2), we are guided by the Supreme Court's opinion in *NLRB v. Cabot Carbon Co.*, 360 U.S. 203 (1959). In *Cabot Carbon* the Court held that the term "dealing with" in Section 2(5) is broader than the term "collective bargaining" and applies to situations that do not contemplate the negotiation of a collective-bargaining agreement. The Court also found that the 1947 amendment of Section 9(a),[1] and the defeat of a proposed amendment to the 1947 Taft-Hartley Act that would have permitted an employer to form or maintain a committee of employees to discuss with it conditions of employment in the absence of an established bargaining representative, demonstrated that there was nothing in the 1947 amendments indicating that Congress intended to eliminate dominated employee representation committees from the term "labor organization" as defined in Section 2(5) and as used in Section 8(a)(2). . . .

Notwithstanding that "dealing with" is broadly defined under *Cabot Carbon*, it is

---

[1] [Section 9(a) currently states that:

Representatives designated or selected for the purposes of collective bargaining by the majority of the employees in a unit appropriate for such purposes, shall be the exclusive representatives of all the employees in such unit for the purposes of collective bargaining in respect to rates of pay, wages, hours of employment, or other conditions of employment: Provided, That any individual employee or a group of employees shall have the right at any time to present grievances to their employer and to have such grievances adjusted, without the intervention of the bargaining representative, as long as the adjustment is not inconsistent with the terms of a collective-bargaining contract or agreement then in effect: Provided further, That the bargaining representative has been given opportunity to be present at such adjustment.]

also true that an organization whose purpose is limited to performing essentially a managerial or adjudicative function is not a labor organization under Section 2(5). In those circumstances, it is irrelevant if the impetus behind the organization's creation emanates from the employer. See *General Foods Corp.*, 231 N.L.R.B. 1232 (1977) (employer created job enrichment program composed of work crews of entire employee complement); *Mercy-Memorial Hospital*, 231 N.L.R.B. 1108 (1977) (committee decided validity of employees' complaints and did not discuss or deal with employer concerning the complaints); *John Ascuaga's Nugget*, 230 N.L.R.B. 275, 276 (1977) (employees' organization resolved employees' grievances and did not interact with management).

Although Section 8(a)(2) does not define the specific acts that may constitute domination, a labor organization that is the creation of management, whose structure and function are essentially determined by management, . . . and whose continued existence depends on the fiat of management, is one whose formation or administration has been dominated under Section 8(a)(2). In such an instance, *actual* domination has been established by virtue of the employer's specific acts of creating the organization itself and determining its structure and function. However, when the formulation and structure of the organization is determined by employees, domination is not established, even if the employer has the potential ability to influence the structure or effectiveness of the organization. Thus, the Board's cases following *Cabot Carbon* reflect the view that when the impetus behind the formation of an organization of employees emanates from an employer and the organization has no effective existence independent of the employer's active involvement, a finding of domination is appropriate if the purpose of the organization is to deal with the employer concerning conditions of employment. . . .

As noted previously (fn. 24), Board precedent and decisions of the Supreme Court indicate that the presence of antiunion motive is not critical to finding an 8(a)(2) violation. Instead, our inquiry is two-fold. First, we inquire whether the entity that is the object of the employer's allegedly unlawful conduct satisfies the definitional elements of Section 2(5) as to (1) employee participation, (2) a purpose to deal with employers, (3) concerning itself with conditions of employment or other statutory subjects, and (4) if an "employee representation committee or plan" is involved, evidence that the committee is in some way representing the employees. Second, if the organization satisfies those criteria, we consider whether the employer has engaged in any of the three forms of conduct proscribed by Section 8(a)(2).

Of course, Section 2(5) literally requires us to inquire into the "purpose" of the employee entity at issue because we must determine whether it exists "for the purpose of dealing" with conditions of employment. But "purpose" is different from motive; and the "purpose" to which the statute directs inquiry does not necessarily entail subjective hostility towards unions. Purpose is a matter of what the organization is set up to do, and that may be shown by what the organization actually does. If a purpose is to deal with an employer concerning conditions of employment, the Section 2(5) definition has been met regardless of whether the employer has created it, or fostered its creation, in order to avoid unionization or whether employees view that organization as equivalent to a union.

Applying these principles to the facts of this case, we find, in agreement with the judge, that the Action Committees constitute a labor organization within the meaning of Section 2(5) of the Act; and that the Respondent dominated it, and assisted it, i.e., contributed support, within the meaning of Section 8(a)(2).

First, there is no dispute that employees participated in the Action Committees. Second, we find that the activities of the committees constituted dealing with an employer. Third, we find that the subject matter of that dealing — which included the treatment of employee absenteeism and employee remuneration in the form of bonuses and other monetary incentives — concerned conditions of employment. Fourth, we find that the employees acted in a representational capacity within the meaning of Section 2(5). Taken as a whole, the evidence underlying these findings shows that the Action Committees were created for, and actually served, the purpose of dealing with the Respondent about conditions of employment.

[T]he Action Committees were created in direct response to the employees' disaffection concerning changes in conditions of employment that the Respondent unilaterally implemented in late 1988. These changes resulted in a petition that employees presented to the Respondent. President Howard testified that after a January 11 meeting with a group of employees selected by management, he realized that the Respondent had serious problems with the employees and that "it was very unlikely that further *unilateral* management action to resolve these problems" would succeed. (Emphasis supplied.) Accordingly, the Action Committees were created in order to achieve a *bilateral* solution to these problems. Employees on the Action Committees, according to Howard, were to meet with their management counterparts and, "try to come up with ways to resolve these problems." Howard also explained what would happen to any solutions that came out of the Action Committees. Howard testified that if the Committee's solutions satisfied the Respondent's budgetary concerns, "we would implement those suggestions or proposals." . . .

The evidence thus overwhelmingly demonstrates that a purpose of the Action Committees, indeed their *only* purpose, was to address employees' disaffection concerning conditions of employment through the creation of a bilateral process involving employees and management in order to reach bilateral solutions on the basis of employee-initiated proposals. This is the essence of "dealing with" within the meaning of Section 2(5) . . . .

It is also clear that the Respondent contemplated that employee-members of the Action Committees would act on behalf of other employees. Thus, after talking "back and forth" with their fellow employees, members were to get ideas from other employees regarding the subjects of their committees for the purpose of reaching solutions that would satisfy the employees as a whole. This could occur only if the proposals presented by the employee-members were in line with the desires of other employees. In these circumstances, we find that employee-members of the Action Committees acted in a representational capacity and that the Action Committees were an "employee representation committee or plan" as set forth in Section 2(5).

There can also be no doubt that the Respondent's conduct vis a vis the Action Committees constituted "domination" in their formation and administration. It was the Respondent's idea to create the Action Committees. When it presented the idea to employees on January 18, the reaction, as the Respondent's President Howard admitted, was "not positive." Howard then informed employees that management would not "just unilaterally make changes" to satisfy employees' complaints. As a result, employees essentially were presented with the Hobson's choice of accepting the status quo, which they disliked, or undertaking a bilateral "exchange of ideas" within the framework of the Action Committees, as presented by the Respondent. The Respondent drafted the written purposes and goals of the Action Committees which defined and limited the subject matter to be covered by each Committee, determined how many members would compose a committee and that an employee could serve on only one committee, and appointed management representatives to the Committees to facilitate discussions. Finally, much of the evidence supporting the domination finding also supports a finding of unlawful contribution of support. In particular, the Respondent permitted the employees to carry out the committee activities on paid time within a structure that the Respondent itself created.

On these facts, we find that the Action Committees were the creation of the Respondent and that the impetus for their continued existence rested with the Respondent and not with the employees. Accordingly, the Respondent dominated the Action Committees in their formation and administration and unlawfully supported them. . . .

In sum, this case presents a situation in which an employer alters conditions of employment and, as a result, is confronted with a work force that is discontented with its new employment environment. The employer responds to that discontent by devising and imposing on the employees an organized Committee mechanism composed of managers and employees instructed to "represent" fellow employees. The purpose of the Action Committees was, as the record demonstrates, not to enable management and employees to cooperate to improve "quality" or "efficiency," but to create in employees the impression that their disagreements with management had been resolved *bilaterally*. By creating the Action Committees the Respondent imposed on employees its own *unilateral* form of bargaining or dealing and thereby violated Section 8(a)(2) and (1) as alleged.

MEMBER DEVANEY, concurring [opinion omitted].

MEMBER OVIATT, concurring.

American companies, their employees, and labor unions representing those employees are at present confronted with diverse competitive forces requiring an array of different responses if those companies are to remain competitive in the world economy. To the extent present laws are interpreted to apply restrictions and roadblocks to companies' ability to perform more efficiently and to respond promptly to competitive conditions, the more difficult will be the common task of achieving or retaining equality. This is a time of testing for the American and world economies and we must proceed with caution when we address the legality of innovative employee involvement programs directed to improving efficiency and productivity. I view the violations found here as clear cut, however. Accordingly, I join in the majority opinion, but I do so as much for what the opinion does *not* condemn as an unfair labor practice as for what it *does* find to be a violation of Section 8(a)(2) and (1). Thus, I write separately to stress the wide range of lawful activities which I view as untouched by this decision.

In my view, the critical question in most cases of alleged violations of Section 8(a)(2) through domination or support of an entity that includes employees among its membership is whether the entity is created with any purpose to deal with "grievances, labor disputes, wages, rates of pay, hours of employment, or conditions of work" as set forth in the Section 2(5) definition of "labor organization." In this case, I have no doubt that the subject matter of the Action Committees falls comfortably within the definition. The Committee's purpose was to address and find solutions for issues related to absenteeism, pay progression, attendance bonuses, and no-smoking policies. These are plainly among the subject matters about which labor organizations traditionally bargain since they involve "wages" or "conditions of work."

There is, however, an important area of industrial relations where committees and groups of employees and managerial personnel act together with the purpose of communicating, addressing and solving problems in the workplace that do not implicate the matters identified in Section 2(5). Among the employee-participation groups that may be established by management are so-called "quality circles" whose purpose is to use employee expertise by having the group examine certain operational problems such as labor efficiency and material waste. Other such committees have been dubbed "quality-of work-life programs." These involve management's attempt to draw on the creativity of its employees by including them in decisions that affect their work lives. These decisions may go beyond improvements in productivity and efficiency to include issues involving worker self-fulfillment and self-enhancement. Others of these programs stress joint problem-solving structures that engage management and employees in finding ways of improving operating functions. And then there are employee-management committees that are established by a company with the purpose of creating better communications between employer and employee by exploring employee attitudes, communicating certain information to employees, and making management more aware of employee problems. . . .

Certainly, I find nothing in today's decision that should be read as a condemnation of cooperative programs and committees of the type I have outlined above. The statute does not forbid direct communication between the employer and its employees to address and solve significant productivity and efficiency problems in the workplace. In my view, committees and groups dealing with these subjects alone plainly fall outside the Section 2(5) definition of "labor organization" since they are not concerned with grievances, labor disputes, wages, rates of pay, hours of employment or conditions of work. Indeed, in this age of increased global competition I consider it of critical importance that management and employees be able, indeed, are encouraged, to engage in cooperative endeavors to improve production methods and product quality. . . .

MEMBER RAUDABAUGH, concurring.

My colleagues find a violation of Section 8(a)(2) in this case. I concur. However, because I believe that this case genuinely raises the broader issue of whether Section 8(a)(2) should be reinterpreted and because of the significance of this issue as applied to employee participation programs, I write this separate concurrence. . . .

The question before me is how to interpret the[] words ["dominate, interfere with, or support"] in a way that will accommodate labor-management cooperation and the Section 7 rights of employees. In my view, the answer to the question turns on the following factors: (1) the extent of the employer's involvement in the structure and operation of the committees; (2) whether the employees, from an objective standpoint, reasonably perceive the EPP ["employee participation programs"] as a substitute for full collective bargaining through a traditional union; (3) whether employees have been assured of their Section 7 right to choose to be represented by a traditional union under a system of full collective bargaining, and (4) the employer's motives in establishing the EPP. I would consider all four factors in any given case. No single factor would necessarily be dispositive.

With respect to the first factor, the fact that an employer initiates the idea of an EPP is not sufficient to condemn it. Under Section 8(c) of the Act, an employer is free to voice an opinion on labor-management matters. Thus, for example, an employer can tell its employees that it favors or disfavors traditional union representation. By the same token, an employer should be able to tell its employees that it favors an EPP. I also note that the original version of the Wagner Act made it unlawful for an employer to "initiate" or "influence the function of" a labor organization. The provision was rejected. Thus, even under the Wagner Act, it would appear that such conduct was lawful.

However, the employer cannot coerce an employee into becoming part of an EPP. Consistent with Taft-Hartley, the choice must be that of the employee. Similarly, if the employees on a committee are to be the representatives of other employees, they must be selected by the employees, not by the employer.

In addition, although the employer can set forth the broad purpose of the committee, the committee must be free to consider any and all matters that are germane to that purpose. Thus, for example, the employer may say that the purpose of the committee is to enhance product quality or improve production efficiency. However, the committee must be free to consider any and all matters which are germane to those broad goals.

Further, managers and supervisors can be on the committee. In this regard, I note that the original version of the Wagner Act made it unlawful for the employer to "participate in" the labor organization. The provision was rejected. Thus, even under the Wagner Act, such conduct was lawful. However, managers and supervisors cannot be given a dominant role.

In addition, the employer can give support to the committee by providing it with meeting rooms, writing materials, secretarial assistance, etc., and it would be permissible to allow the committee to meet on company time.

Finally, the mere fact that the employer may suggest the rules and policies of the labor organization is not sufficient to condemn the EPP. In this regard, I note that the original version of the Wagner Act made it unlawful for an employer to "influence . . . the rules and other policies of a labor organization." The provision was rejected.

The second factor seeks to accommodate the Section 7 right of employees to choose traditional unions to represent them in resolving their disputes with their employer. If the committee is set up in response to employee grievances and complaints, and if it functions as a vehicle for presenting those matters to the employer, it can reasonably be viewed as a substitute for traditional union representation. However, if the committee is set up by the employer to accomplish *its own entrepreneurial interests*, e.g., enhanced product quality and improved production efficiency, it can reasonably be viewed as a vehicle for addressing *employer interests*, rather than as a substitute for traditional union representation. Similarly, to the extent that employees reasonably perceive the committee as their representative concerning employment related matters, the committee may be viewed as a substitute for collective bargaining. Conversely, to the extent that the employees do not view the committee in this way, the committee would not be viewed as a substitute for collective bargaining.

The third factor also seeks to accommodate Section 7 rights. I would consider it significant that the employer expressly assures its employees that, notwithstanding the EPP, they are free to select traditional union representation and full collective bargaining.

As to the fourth factor, if the employer establishes the EPP for a purpose of stifling an ongoing union campaign, the impact on Section 7 rights is obvious. Conversely, if the employer's motive in establishing the committee is solely to enhance lawful entrepreneurial goals, there would be no impact, under this factor, on Section 7 rights.

I believe that these four factors properly balance interests in labor-management cooperation and employee Section 7 rights. In addition, they reflect the Taft-Hartley goals of (1) insuring employee free choice and (2) promoting harmony and cooperation in the sphere of labor-management relations. Finally, they reflect the national interest in taking steps to insure that American firms successfully compete in a global economy. . . .

Michael H. LeRoy, *Employee Participation in the New Millennium: Redefining a Labor Organization Under Section 8(a)(2) of the NLRA*
72 S. Cal. L. Rev. 1651 (1999)[2]

. . . Employee participation programs are often misunderstood to be a recent innovation inspired by Japanese work practices. In fact, they have existed in the American workplace for more than a century. Some early programs were remarkably progressive. However, recent studies show that there was a tension early on

---

[2] Copyright © 1999 by Michael H. LeRoy. All rights reserved. Reprinted by permission.

between nonunion participation programs and the labor movement's efforts to represent workers covered by these plans. In the 1930s, this conflict intensified. The focus of employee participation shifted from creating positive social and psychological conditions for workers to forming sham unions. Employers widely adopted employee participation programs in anticipation of Congress enacting a law favoring collective bargaining. Employers hoped that by already having a "union" and "labor agreement" in place, real labor unions would be barred from organizing and otherwise representing employees.

Congress prohibited employers from installing sham unions by a two-step process. Section 8(a)(2) prohibits employer domination of or interference with a labor organization. To make this effective in the nonunion setting, Congress defined labor organization very broadly, so that it covers any employee group that "deals with" employers concerning one or more aspects of the employment relationship.

Controversies surrounding Section 8(a)(2) continued into the 1950s. In 1947, when the Taft-Hartley Act substantially amended many parts of the NLRA, Congress considered a proposal to limit the definition of a labor organization to unionized workplaces. This proposal was rejected, and, in a key Supreme Court decision, employer efforts to achieve this limitation failed again.[3] For the next twenty-five years, Section 8(a)(2) disappeared as a major policy concern, but recently returned to the fore as more employers began to experiment with participatory work organizations.

Renewed "ferment in theoretical approaches to labor law" was prompted in the 1980s and 1990s by "[e]xperiments in 'cooperative' workplace arrangements [that] began . . . with relatively superficial innovations such as quality circles and joint labor-management committees, and deepened . . . with the spread of full-blown cooperationist models of labor-management relations."[4]

Where are these participatory models headed? Recent history suggests that many of these efforts still have a narrow and instrumental focus, which is related to improving organizational performance. These programs reduce turnover, and improve profitability, productivity, and product quality. Related efforts focus on employee compensation. These include gainsharing plans, profit sharing plans, and Employee Stock Ownership Plans ("ESOP").

These participation systems continue to evolve and appear even more removed from company unions of the 1930s. The use of information technology ("IT"), an unimagined workplace asset in the 1930s, illustrates this point. Work teams are increasingly integrated with emerging IT systems. Xerox Corporation, for example, is developing an Internet-based system to enable front-line employees around the world to answer their own human resources ("HR") questions.

This cross-fertilization of technology, organizational systems, and human resource practices is aimed at improving the firm's performance. Hewlett Packard uses employee empowerment to limit conflict. Hewlett Packard democratized the

---

[3] [n. 42] *See NLRB v. Cabot Carbon*, 360 U.S. 203 (1958).

[4] [n. 43] *See* Mark Barenberg, *The Political Economy of the Wagner Act: Power, Symbol, and Workplace Cooperation*, 106 Harv. L. Rev. 1381, 1384 (1993).

workspace for all employees by requiring all employees, including the CEO, to work in standard cubicles. As an integrated element of this flattened corporate hierarchy, employees are given authority to make on-the-job decisions.

Another distinction between today's employers and those of the 1930s is the current fierce competition for quality employees. Company unions arose in the midst of this nation's worst depression, when people were desperate for any work. Today, unemployment is extremely low and employers are competing for talent by trying to win model employer awards.

This has two implications for the Section 8(a)(2) policy debate. First, any employer who institutes a coercive work group may risk losing quality employees to competitors. Second, employers increasingly believe that they must offer employees a genuine degree of involvement in managing their work. This notion extends to other organizational goals, such as improving career advancement for women by increasing leadership opportunities in participation groups.

Of course, these new versions of employee groups are certainly not a panacea. Abusive forms still exist, and a few even become ensnared by Section 8(a)(2). Even groups designed for legitimate purposes may fail in their mission and alienate employees. This particularly occurs when firms layoff workers. Other groups are embroidered with buzz words but lack substance. Additionally, breakdown of internal controls, and even business failures, can confront some groups.

In sum, participation programs are distinctly different from the company unions of the 1930s. Information technology alone differentiates past and present participation groups because of its democratizing influence. In addition, current workplaces integrate people with diverse characteristics and backgrounds in a way that was almost unimaginable in 1935. This has important implications for encouraging employers to empower work teams as well. Therefore, these cultural changes require reconsideration of the fact premises that justified Section 8(a)(2).

The Section 8(a)(2) policy debate is strangely parochial, focusing primarily on contemporary American experience. Proponents for maintaining Section 8(a)(2) believe that this public policy is a vital element in maintaining employee freedom to choose union representation. Professor Michael Harper's 1998 article in the Michigan Law Review offers a typical statement of this view:

> In sum, the critics of section 8(a)(2) are wrong to claim that modern employee-involvement programs pose no threat to American workers comparable to the pre-Wagner Act company union movement. Modern programs, like their pre-Wagner Act antecedents, are often designed and used to secure greater managerial control of the work force, perhaps through the avoidance of an independent union movement or other forms of collective employee resistance to managerial control, perhaps through the neutralization of an incumbent independent union.[5]

Lawmakers, union officers, labor lawyers, and other scholars agree with this view.

---

[5] [n.64] Michael C. Harper, *The Continuing Relevance of Section 8(a)(2) to the Contemporary Workplace*, 96 Mich. L. Rev. 2322, 2375–76 (1998).

However, these views are strongly challenged. America's foremost industrial relations scholar, Professor Thomas Kochan, believes that "the National Labor Relations Act no longer serves the purposes for which it was originally enacted."[6] He proposes a two-track system that allows "progressive" employers to set up employee governance systems outside the bounds of traditional collective bargaining.

Many eminent labor law professors agree. Professor Charles Craver advocates mandatory employee representation in nonunion settings — precisely the concept that Section 8(a)(2) was intended to outlaw.[7] Professor Samuel Estreicher bluntly condemns the NLRA, stating that it "confine[s] workers to the choice of independent representation or no representation at all."[8] Professor Paul Weiler, who served as general counsel to President Clinton's Commission on The Future of Worker Management Relations (commonly called the Dunlop Commission), was notably outspoken in his condemnation of the Commission's failure to advocate a more thorough overhaul of Section 8(a)(2).[9]

The remarkable aspect of this policy debate is that it overlooks the Canadian experience, where collective bargaining laws are mostly similar to American laws. Notably, however, Canada lacks the equivalent of a statutory prohibition against company unions. . . .

[Professor LeRoy then examined a Canadian company union, the "Norman Wells JIC," which he argues would have violated Section 8(a)(2) of the NLRA. He then states that:]

Assuming that many Canadian company unions are structured like the Norman Wells JIC, these organizations are a paradox by American standards. They are aimed at providing a substitute for a traditional union, but they are implemented in the absence of a union organizing campaign. In contrast, the participation groups that violated Section 8(a)(2) in the cases following *Electromation* were belated and manipulative employer efforts to create superficial or sham forms of employee participation.

Adding to this incongruity, the Norman Wells JIC actually stimulated effective

---

[6] [n.69] Thomas A. Kochan, *Labor Policy for the Twenty-First Century*, 1 U. Pa. J. Lab. & Emp. L. 117 (1998).

[7] [n.71] See Charles B. Craver, *Mandatory Worker Participation Is Required in a Declining Union Environment to Provide Employees with Meaningful Industrial Democracy*, 66 Geo. Wash. L. Rev. 135 (1997). Recognizing that his proposal would essentially erode Section 8(a)(2), Craver notes: "Many labor leaders undoubtedly would oppose mandatory worker participation legislation out of concern that such employee involvement arrangements would become a substitute for traditional union representation." Id. at 158.

[8] [n.72] Samuel Estreicher, *The Dunlop Report and the Future of Labor Law Reform*, 12 Lab. Law. 117, 132 (1996). He adds: "A substantial repeal of § 8(a)(2) would create opportunities for alternative forms of workplace representation." *Id.*

[9] [n.73] *See Labor Law Reform: Dunlop Panel Did Not Go Far Enough in 8(a)(2) Proposal, Weiler Says*, Daily Lab. Rep. (BNA) No. 11, at D-13 (Jan. 18, 1995). In its final report, the Commission urged Congress to "clarify" Section 8(a)(2) so as to give nonunion employee participation programs more freedom without breaking the law. Weiler said this was a move "in the right direction," but he favored a "total repeal" of Section 8(a)(2). *Id.*

union organizing. This is directly contrary to the public policy presumptions for maintaining the Section 8(a)(2) status quo. Taras and Copping assessed the transformation of the Norman Wells JIC from a company to an independent union and suggest that Canadian-style company unions benefit employees in three vital respects. [Daphne Gottlieb Taras & Jason Copping, *The Transition from Formal Nonunion Representation to Unionization: A Contemporary Case*, 52 Indus. & Lab. Rel. Rev. 22 (1998).].

First, in contrast to their American counterparts at companies such as Aero Detroit or Ryder, they genuinely allow employees to share power with management. In addition, employees are able to leverage this internal democracy with a credible threat to unionize. While this occurs to a degree in the U.S., Section 8(a)(2) prohibits the kind of participation organization that the Norman Wells workers had in their pre-union experience. By permitting such an agreement, Canadian law puts unions and company unions on a much more competitive footing. For the Norman Wells workers, the issue was not whether they would have a collective agreement, but what would the bargaining structure be to arrive at a contract. Finally, Canadian policy allowed the Norman Wells workers to develop a collective identity and voice that was essential to self-organization. . . .

The American policy debate over nonunion forms of employee participation must consider this question: How can Sections 2(5) and 8(a)(2) be modeled after the Canadian experience with company unions so as to promote more than one form of industrial democracy? . . .

This Article proposes a new structure for nonunion employee participation groups . . . . The following would be inserted immediately after the existing language in Section 8(a)(2):

> Notwithstanding any other provision of this Section, it shall not constitute or be evidence of an unfair labor practice for an employer to form or maintain a committee in which employees participate to at least the same extent practicable as representatives of management participate to discuss with it matters of mutual interest, including grievances, wages, hours of employment and other working conditions, and which does not have, claim, or seek authority to be the exclusive bargaining representative of the employees or to enter into collective bargaining agreements between the employer and any labor organization, except that in a case in which a labor organization is the representative of such employees as provided in section 9(a), this proviso shall not apply. . . .

This article's proposal for broadening lawful employee participation draws from [] historical and transnational precedents. It also offers these advantages:

(1)   Current enforcement of Section 8(a)(2) is woeful. Countless American employers use participation groups that go beyond *Electromation*, but only an infinitesimal fraction are held accountable for breaking this law. This raises the question: Why use such a law when such underwhelming enforcement trivializes its legitimacy? This Article's proposal would more closely align the NLRA with current employer practices.

(2) The amendment proposed in this Article would satisfy a large majority of working Americans who prefer some form of employee participation.

(3) The amendment would permit employees to discuss and even decide on a broad range of work-related issues, but it would prohibit formal bargaining. Moreover, it would remove the ambiguity in the current law surrounding the "dealing with" provisions of a Section 2(5) labor organization. The treatment of this critical aspect of employee participation in the *du Pont* decision was conceived before e-mail and on-line systems came into vogue. The bilateral interaction doctrine and the endorsement of employee suggestion boxes are untested in this new age of information technology. The proposed amendment recognizes that the "dealing with" concept is intractably vague and creates a more distinct line between lawful and unlawful participation. . . .

POST PROBLEM DISCUSSION

1. Consider the Quality Committee in our problem — is there a Section 8(a)(2) violation? In *Electromation*, the NLRB provides a roadmap for analyzing this issue: first, you must determine if the committee is a labor organization; and, second, if it is a labor organization, you must address whether the resort dominated it or gave it unlawful assistance.

a. The first issue, whether the committee is a labor organization, looks to Section 2(5). As noted in *Electromation*, that definition has several elements:

  i. Did employees participate? This one is easy given the facts of our problem.

  ii. Was a purpose of the committee to deal with the employer? Think about how the NLRB in *Electromation* defined "dealing with" and how the Quality Committee fares under that definition. Is it more like a suggestion box, or does it involve the bilateral exchanges that are the hallmark of "dealing with"? *See Grouse Mountain Associates II*, 333 N.L.R.B. 1322, 1336 (2001), *enforced*, 56 Fed. Appx. 811 (9th Cir. 2003) (concluding, in similar case to problem, that the committee dealt with the employer); *Polaroid Corp.*, 329 N.L.R.B. 424, 425 (1999) (stating that "dealing with" does not include unilateral suggestion box-like communications); *E. I. du Pont de Nemours & Co.*, 311 NLRB 893, 894 (1993) (concluding that " 'dealing with'. . . ordinarily entails a practice in which a group of employees, over time, makes proposals to management, management responds to these proposals by acceptance and rejection by word or deed, and compromise is not required. If the evidence establishes such a pattern or practice . . . the element of dealing is present."). Note, as did the NLRB in *Electromation*, that the Supreme Court has held that "dealing with" does not require actual collective bargaining or an attempt to reach a collective-bargaining agreement. *See NLRB v. Cabot Carbon Co.*, 360 U.S. 203, 210-14 (1959).

iii. Did the committee concern itself with conditions of employment? Discussions about paid holidays are clearly within Section 2(5)'s list of subjects: "grievances, labor disputes, wages, rates of pay, hours of employment, or conditions of work." But what about daycare for employees' children and the type of food provided in a complementary lunch?

iv. If the committee is considered an "employee representation committee or plan," is there evidence that it represented employees? Should we care? Based on the facts of the problem, there's a good case to be made that the committee acted on behalf of other employees' interests, especially if there was evidence that participants at the meetings represented the views of employees who did not attend.

A broader question is whether it matters. Section 2(5) doesn't appear to require representation, although it mentions an employee representation committee as a possible labor organization. The NLRB thus far has refused to provide an answer to this question *See Polaroid*, 329 N.L.R.B. at 424 (citing *Electromation*, 309 N.L.R.B. at 994 n.20; *Webcor Packaging*, 319 N.L.R.B. 1203, 1204 n.6 (1995), *enforced*, 118 F.3d 1115 (6th Cir. 1997)).

b. If the committee is classified as a labor organization under Section 2(5), did the employer dominate, assist, or support it in a manner that violated Section 8(a)(2)? (The NLRB typically describes Section 8(a)(2)'s prohibition against "interfer[ing]" with a labor organization in terms of unlawful "assistance" or "support.") What factors would you consider in determining this question? *See, e.g., NLRB v. Pa. Greyhound Lines, Inc.*, 303 U.S. 261, 268-69 (1938) (finding unlawful interference, domination, and support because, in part, employer presided over meetings, and initiated and actively promoted employee representation plan); *NLRB v. Ampex Corp.*, 442 F.2d 82, 84–85 (7th Cir. 1971) (finding unlawful interference, support, and domination where "nothing . . . suggest[s] that the [committee] would continue if left up to the employees;" employer decided when meetings would be held, presided at meetings, and took minutes; and committee had no function other than meetings).

What's the difference in domination versus support or interference, and does it matter? There is no firm test for differentiating the different types of unlawful Section 8(a)(2) conduct. Largely, it boils down to a matter of degree, with "domination" existing where the level of support and interference is substantial. *Compare Webcor Packaging, Inc.*, 118 F.3d at 1124 (finding domination where labor organization "was created by management and could have been disbanded by management," and "lacked independent means of support, met on company property during work hours, [and] never met independent of management"), *with Grouse Mountain*, 333 N.L.R.B. at 1337 (finding unlawful assistance and support, but not domination, because the employer did not "devise[] the structure of or prepare[] formative documents for the conduct of the" committee or exert "any control over which employees attend meetings or over the subjects raised and discussed").

Where the difference really matters is the remedy. If an employer has merely given unlawful assistance or support, the NLRB will order it to cease and desist from continuing to do so in the future. In contrast, a finding of unlawful domination requires the labor organization at issue to be disbanded, as the level of interference is so high that the organization is too tainted to continue. *See NLRB v. Newport News Shipbuilding Co.*, 308 U.S. 241, 250 (1939).

2.   There are some additional issues that you might consider with regard to the Quality Committee in our problem. For instance, Section 2(5) covers "organization[s] of any kind," agencies, or employee representation committees or plans. Does the fact that the Quality Committee lacked a set membership, bylaws and other governing rules, or any real structure, mean that it cannot qualify as a labor organization? *See Sahara Datsun, Inc. v. NLRB*, 811 F.2d 1317, 1320 (9th Cir. 1987) (holding that "organizations without written constitutions, by-laws, dues or initiation fees" may be labor organizations if they are organized in part to deal over work conditions).

3.   What about the fact in *Electromation* that the employer wasn't aware of the union campaign when it set up the committees? Does Section 8(a)(2) require a bad motivation by the employer? *See International Ladies' Garment Workers v. NLRB* (Bernhard-Altmann), 366 U.S. 731, 739 (1961) (stating that "[w]e find nothing in the statutory language prescribing scienter as an element [of Section 8(a)(2) and] . . . [i]t follows that prohibited conduct cannot be excused by a showing of good faith").

4.   What if employees like the committee at issue? In our problem, isn't it likely that the employees appreciated having a voice in the workplace? *See* RICHARD B. FREEMAN & JOEL ROGERS, WHAT WORKERS WANT 32-33, 81-84 (1999) (finding strong support among American workers for increased voice in the workplace). Given that a major policy goal of Section 8(a)(2) is to prevent employees from being fooled into thinking that they have an independent representative, should employer support of a committee be unlawful if the employees like the committee and are aware that it does not serve a true representative role? *See Electromation, Inc. v. NLRB*, 35 F.3d 1148, 1166 (7th Cir. 1994) (examining circuit split and affirming NLRB's rule that the Section 8(a)(2) analysis can consider employees' subjective beliefs, but does not require dissatisfaction) (citing, among other cases, *Newport News Shipbuilding*, 308 U.S. at 249). How would Member Raudabaugh, in his *Electromation* concurrence, approach this question?

5.   Consider a workplace in which the employer has set up teams of workers that address issues of production quality, training, safety, and discipline. These teams are given authority to make some decisions on their own, such as halting production because of a safety concern. In *Crown Cork & Seal Co.*, 334 N.L.R.B. 699 (2001), the NLRB concluded that such teams may not be considered labor organizations when they exercise authority that is equivalent to a front-line supervisor. When such authority exists, the teams are considered managerial organizations, not labor ones. *Id.* at 701 ("[T]he seven committees in issue do not "deal with" management within the meaning of Section 2(5). Rather, the evidence

shows that, within their delegated spheres of authority, the seven committees *are* management.")

6.   Section 8(a)(2) may also be implicated in circumstances not involving the typical company union context. For instance, an employer will also violate Section 8(a)(2) if it recognizes a union as employees' collective-bargaining representative when the union lacks support from a majority of employees. *See Bernhard-Altmann*, 366 U.S. at 737-38; *Dairyland USA Corp.*, 347 NLRB 310, 311 (2006) (noting that unlawful assistance to union in getting cards can lead to Section 8(a)(2) violation).

7.   There has been much criticism of the broad interpretation of "labor organization" and its application in Section 8(a)(2) cases. In particular, some have argued that the prohibition extends further than necessary to prevent sham unions and results in limiting employees' opportunity to provide input, and employers' ability to benefit from employee input, in nonunion workplaces. Congress made an attempt to address this issue in a bill called The Teamwork for Employees and Managers Act of 1995, H.R. 743, 104th Cong. (1996) (TEAM Act), which would have made it lawful for:

> an employer to establish, assist, maintain, or participate in any organization or entity of any kind, in which employees who participate to at least the same extent practicable as representatives of management participate, to address matters of mutual interest, including, but not limited to, issues of quality, productivity, efficiency, and safety and health, and which does not have, claim, or seek authority to be the exclusive bargaining representatives of the employees or to negotiate or enter into collective bargaining agreements with the employer or to amend existing collective bargaining agreements between the employer and any labor organization, except . . . a case in which a labor organization is the representative of such employees as provided in section 9(a).

Id. The House and Senate passed the TEAM Act, which President Clinton vetoed. *See* 142 Cong. Rec. H8816 (1996).

How do the concurrences in *Electromation* compare to the TEAM Act? What about Professor LeRoy's proposal? And how do these alternative approaches differ from current law? Which approach do you find more convincing, or do you have your own take?

For a sample of the many writings on this issue, including historical accounts of company unions and the pros and cons of Section 8(a)(2) and its alternatives, see: NONUNION EMPLOYEE REPRESENTATION: HISTORY, CONTEMPORARY PRACTICE, AND POLICY (Bruce E. Kaufman & Daphne Gottlieb Taras eds., 2000); Jeffrey M. Hirsch & Barry T. Hirsch, *The Rise and Fall of Private Sector Unionism: What Next for the NLRA?*, 34 FLA. ST. L. REV. 1133 (2007); Charles B. Craver, *Mandatory Worker Participation is Required in a Declining Union Environment To Provide Employees with Meaningful Industrial Democracy*, 66 GEO. WASH. L. REV. 135 (1997); Rafael Gely, *Where Are We Now? Like After* Electromation, 15 HOFSTRA LAB. & EMP. L.J. 45 (1997); Samuel Estreicher, *Employee Involvement and the "Company Union" Prohibition: The Case for Partial Repeal of Section 8(a)(2) of the NLRA,*

69 N.Y.U. L. REV. 125, 135-39 (1994); Clyde W. Summers, *Employee Voice and Employer Choice: A Structured Exception to Section 8(a)(2)*, 69 CHI.-KENT L. REV. 129, 133-35 (1993).

SECTION 2 ANTI-UNION DISCRIMINATION

One of the central unfair labor practices under the NLRA is Section 8(a)(3) and its prohibition against union-based discrimination. Section 8(a)(3) will appear familiar to anyone with exposure to other anti-discrimination laws, such as Title VII of the Civil Rights Act which prohibits workplace discrimination based on race, sex, color, national origin, and religion. Indeed, Section 8(a)(3) is the predecessor to Title VII; although the two provisions now have many differences, their basic structures are still quite similar.

Section 8(a)(3) states that an employer commits an unfair labor practice "by discrimination in regard to hire or tenure of employment or any term or condition of employment to encourage or discourage membership in any labor organization." A significant number of Section 8(a)(3) cases arise when employers fire or otherwise punish employees because of their union activity. This type of situation was an obvious concern to Congress as it enacted the Wagner Act because employees must be given protection against employer retaliation if they are to have a genuine opportunity to seek unionization. However, as we shall see, Section 8(a)(3) encompasses other scenarios. But before we get to the specifics of the Section 8(a)(3) analysis, it is worth taking a brief detour to make clear what Section 8(a)(3) does not involve.

A. What Section 8(a)(3) is Not: A Very Brief Introduction to Section 8(a)(1)'s Prohibition Against Interference with Employees' Labor Rights

It probably seems odd to begin a discussion of one unfair labor practice by addressing an entirely different provision. Yet, one way to explain what Section 8(a)(3) does is to examine what it does not do. In particular, Section 8(a)(3)'s focus on whether an employer acted with an unlawful intent stands in sharp contrast to Section 8(a)(1) — an unfair labor practice that is often confused with Section 8(a)(3).

Section 8(a)(1) acts as the enforcer for Section 7 of the NLRA. Under Section 7, employees are given the right to "self-organization, to form, join, or assist labor organizations, to bargain collectively through representatives of their own choosing, and to engage in other concerted activities for the purpose of collective bargaining or other mutual aid or protection . . . ." Section 8(a)(1) gives those rights teeth by providing that "[i]t shall be an unfair labor practice for an employer to interfere with, restrain, or coerce employees in the exercise" of their Section 7 rights. In Chapter 4 we will discuss the Section 8(a)(1) analysis in more detail, but for our purposes now, we need only to focus on the basic Section 8(a)(1) test, which asks whether an employer's actions would tend to make a reasonable employee believe that her Section 7 rights are being interfered with, restrained, or coerced (there's also a balancing of employer and employee interests that comes into play).

Unlike cases brought under Section 8(a)(3), the General Counsel does not have to provide evidence of anti- or pro-union intent to establish a violation of Section 8(a)(1).

Given the difference between the two sections, it may come as a surprise to learn that the two analyses are often mixed up, particularly by courts that do not see a lot of NLRB cases. One reason for the confusion may be that the facts underlying a Section 8(a)(1) or 8(a)(3) violation will often look similar; indeed, at times an identical set of facts may lead to violations of both sections (we will explain what we mean by that in a moment). For instance, a typical case under both Section 8(a)(1) and 8(a)(3) involves an employer firing an employee who engaged in some sort of NLRA-related conduct. Which unfair labor practice is most appropriate turns on whether the employer acted with an intent to discourage union activity.

Another basis for confusion is that evidence of an employer's improper motivation is often presented in Section 8(a)(1) cases. This is not inconsistent with Section 8(a)(1)'s analysis because an employer's bad faith could affect whether a reasonable employee would tend to think that her Section 7 rights are being chilled. Take, for example, a pro-union employee whose hours are cut during bad economic times. Based solely on that fact, the employees might not think that the change in hours had anything to do with their Section 7 rights. However, if the change occurred around the same time as other unfair labor practices by the employer, such as terminations of particularly vocal union supporters, the change may no longer seem as innocuous. The trouble occurs when courts occasionally use the fact that an employer's intent is *relevant* in a Section 8(a)(1) case to mistakenly believe that such intent is *necessary*. We'll see this concept in action soon in the *Darlington* case, but for now remember that although motivation can play a role in a Section 8(a)(1) case, it is not necessary to find a violation of that section.

Finally, one other possible source of confusion is that the NLRB has two different types of Section 8(a)(1) unfair labor practices: independent and derivative. Almost all of the Section 8(a)(1) cases you'll see in this book, primarily in Chapters 4 and 5, are "independent 8(a)(1)s." These are violations of 8(a)(1) that stand on their own, such as the hypothetical hour reduction discussed above. In contrast, a "derivative 8(a)(1)" piggybacks off of another unfair labor practice, such as Section 8(a)(3). Consider the hour reduction again. Instead of a situation where there is no proof that the employer intended to punish the employee for her union activity by cutting her hours, imagine that another employee overheard a supervisor saying that they were cutting the hours or terminating all pro-union employees so "we can get rid of all the union troublemakers." That's a pretty clear violation of Section 8(a)(3). Notice, however, that Section 8(a)(1) is implicated as well. If we were willing to find that reasonable employees would believe that their Section 7 rights are chilled after a pro-union employees' hours were cut while other unfair labor practices were occurring, wouldn't we reach the same finding if we had proof that the employer acted to retaliate against the employees' support for the union? A derivative 8(a)(1) reflects the reality that all unfair labor practices also have the tendency to chill employees' Section 7 rights. Therefore, the NLRB has a practice of adding a derivative Section 8(a)(1) violation to all other unfair labor practices found in a case. It is possible that some courts see Section 8(a)(1) listed in connection with a finding of improper motive and conflate the two. If your professor is anything like this book's authors, that is a mistake that you do not want to make.

In sum, the most basic difference to keep in mind is that Section 8(a)(3) is intent-based and Section 8(a)(1) is not. Accordingly, the purpose of the Section 8(a)(3) analysis is to determine whether the employer acted with an improper motivation. As you will see, this is often a difficult task.

B. What Section 8(a)(3) Is: Prohibition Against Union-Based Discrimination

Think again about the language of Section 8(a)(3), which makes it an unfair labor practice for an employer "by discrimination in regard to hire or tenure of employment or any term or condition of employment to encourage or discourage membership in any labor organization." There are two central components to this violation. First, there must be some type of adverse employment action. In other words, the employer must have done something with "regard to hire or tenure of employment or any term or condition of employment." Termination is a typical adverse employment action, but there are no shortage of others.

The second major part of Section 8(a)(3) is that the adverse employment action must have been motivated by "discrimination" that is intended "to encourage or discourage membership in any labor organization." The NLRB and courts have broadly interpreted this phrase to cover an intent to affect employees' willingness to engage in a wide range of union-related activity, such as expressing support for a union or assisting a union campaign. In addition, the original version of Section 8(a)(3) under the Wagner Act only addressed discouraging union activity. But since being amended by the Taft-Hartley Act, Section 8(a)(3) also prohibits an employer's attempt to *encourage* union activity. In cases involving encouragement, you will typically see a union being charged under the equivalent to Section 8(a)(3), which is Section 8(b)(2). (There is a Section 8(a)(1) for unions too, which is Section 8(b)(1).) Although this may seem straightforward at first blush, things can get complicated easily. Therefore, we must consider the basic analysis for determining whether a Section 8(a)(3) violation exists — an analysis that the NLRB refers to as its *Wright Line* test.

1. The *Wright Line* Test

PROBLEM #2: BOING TRAMPOLINES AND POGO STICKS

Boing, Inc. in an international corporation that manufactures trampolines and pogo sticks. Its headquarters are in Wisconsin, where the company also maintains a large production facility. For decades, Boing's Wisconsin employees have been represented by the International Association of Bouncy Toy Workers (IABTW). Boing and IABT have entered into numerous collective-bargaining agreements, including one that is still in effect. However, these agreements were not always easy to come by, as the parties' long bargaining history was often contentious and involved numerous strikes, including during negotiations over the current agreement. During the most recent strike, one Boing official told a newspaper that the labor unrest could affect where the company would build its products in the future.

About six months after the end of the most recent strike, Boing began corporate deliberations about its need to expand production capabilities to handle a large number of orders for its newest pogo stick model, the 999 Dreammaker. Boing had the capabilities to fulfill these orders by adding another production line at its Wisconsin facility and asked the union for a twenty-year no-strike agreement. Although the union responded that twenty years was too long, it said that it would be willing to extend the current four-year agreement. But the parties could not reach an agreement. Ultimately, the company decided instead to open a new plant in North Carolina. Boing officials told the media that the reason for the decision was to obtain an additional set of suppliers that were not involved with the Wisconsin plant and because "we've had strikes happening every three to four years in Wisconsin and we've got to get to a position where we can ensure our customers that they're not going to have a protracted shutdown every three years." One of Boing's executive vice presidents also told a reporter that "[t]he overriding factor was not the business climate. And it was not the wages we're paying today. It was that we cannot afford to have a work stoppage, you know, every three years. We cannot afford to continue the rate of escalation of wages."

Following a charge filed by the IABTW, the NLRB's General Counsel issued a complaint alleging that Boing violated Section 8(a)(3). Because of the political climate at the time, the complaint became a rallying cry for both business and labor interests in Wisconsin and North Carolina, with Boing supporters arguing that the General Counsel had no reason to file the complaint.

Read the following material and see whether you think that criticism is appropriate. One important thing to focus on is how the General Counsel will try to prove a violation of Section 8(a)(3). In other words, what will the central inquiry and facts be in this case?

PROBLEM MATERIALS

NLRB v. Transportation Management Corp., 462 U.S. 393 (1983)

Textile Workers Union of America v. Darlington Manufacturing Co., 380 U.S. 263 (1965)

NLRB v. TRANSPORTATION MANAGEMENT CORP.
462 U.S. 393 (1983)

Mr. Justice White delivered the opinion of the Court.

The National Labor Relations Act (NLRA or Act), makes unlawful the discharge of a worker because of union activity, [Section 8(a)(3) and (a)(1)] but employers retain the right to discharge workers for any number of other reasons unrelated to the employee's union activities. When the General Counsel of the National Labor Relations Board (Board) files a complaint alleging that an employee was discharged because of his union activities, the employer may assert legitimate motives for his decision. In *Wright Line*, 251 N.L.R.B. 1083 (1980), *enforced*, 662 F.2d 899 ([1st Cir.] 1981), the National Labor Relations Board reformulated the allocation of the burden of proof in such cases. It determined that the General Counsel carried the burden of persuading the Board that an anti-union animus contributed to the employer's decision to discharge an employee, a burden that does not shift, but that the employer, even if it failed to meet or neutralize the General Counsel's showing, could avoid the finding that it violated the statute by demonstrating by a preponderance of the evidence that the worker would have been fired even if he had not been involved with the Union. The question presented in this case is whether the burden placed on the employer in *Wright Line* is consistent with §§ 8(a)(1) and 8(a)(3), as well as with § 10(c) of the NLRA, which provides that the Board must prove an unlawful labor practice by a "preponderance of the evidence."[10]

Prior to his discharge, Sam Santillo was a bus driver for respondent Transportation Management Corp. On March 19, 1979, Santillo talked to officials of the Teamster's Union about organizing the drivers who worked with him. Over the next four days Santillo discussed with his fellow drivers the possibility of joining the Teamsters and distributed authorization cards. On the night of March 23, George Patterson, who supervised Santillo and the other drivers, told one of the drivers that he had heard of Santillo's activities. Patterson referred to Santillo as two-faced, and promised to get even with him.

Later that evening Patterson talked to Ed West, who was also a bus driver for respondent. Patterson asked, "What's with Sam and the Union?" Patterson said that he took Santillo's actions personally, recounted several favors he had done for Santillo, and added that he would remember Santillo's activities when Santillo again asked for a favor. On Monday, March 26, Santillo was discharged. Patterson told Santillo that he was being fired for leaving his keys in the bus and taking unauthorized breaks.

Santillo filed a complaint with the Board alleging that he had been discharged because of his union activities, contrary to §§ 8(a)(1) and 8(a)(3) of the NLRA. The General Counsel issued a complaint. The administrative law judge (ALJ) determined by a preponderance of the evidence that Patterson clearly had an anti-union animus and that Santillo's discharge was motivated by a desire to discourage union activities. The ALJ also found that the asserted reasons for the discharge could not withstand scrutiny. Patterson's disapproval of Santillo's practice of leaving his keys in the bus was clearly a pretext, for Patterson had not known about Santillo's practice until after he had decided to discharge Santillo; moreover, the practice of leaving keys in buses was commonplace among respondent's employees. Respondent identified two types of unauthorized breaks, coffee breaks and stops at home. With respect to both coffee breaks and stopping at home, the ALJ found that Santillo was never cautioned or admonished about such behavior, and that the employer had not followed its customary practice of issuing three written warnings before discharging a driver. The ALJ also found that the taking of coffee breaks during working hours was normal practice, and that respondent tolerated the

[10] [n.2] Section 10(c) provides, in relevant part: ". . . No order of the Board shall require the reinstatement of any individual as an employee who has been suspended or discharged, or the payment to him of any back pay, if such individual was suspended or discharged for cause."

practice unless the breaks interfered with the driver's performance of his duties. In any event, said the ALJ, respondent had never taken any adverse personnel action against an employee because of such behavior. While acknowledging that Santillo had engaged in some unsatisfactory conduct, the ALJ was not persuaded that Santillo would have been fired had it not been for his union activities.

The Board affirmed, adopting with some clarification the ALJ's findings and conclusions and expressly applying its *Wright Line* decision. It stated that respondent had failed to carry its burden of persuading the Board that the discharge would have taken place had Santillo not engaged in activity protected by the Act. The First Circuit Court of Appeals, relying on its previous decision rejecting the Board's *Wright Line* test, *NLRB v. Wright Line*, 662 F.2d 899 (CA1 1981), refused to enforce the Board's order and remanded for consideration of whether the General Counsel had proved by a preponderance of the evidence that Santillo would not have been fired had it not been for his union activities.

Under [Section 8(a)(1) and (a)(3),] it is undisputed that if the employer fires an employee for having engaged in union activities and has no other basis for the discharge, or if the reasons that he proffers are pretextual, the employer commits an unfair labor practice. He does not violate the NLRA, however, if any anti-union animus that he might have entertained did not contribute at all to an otherwise lawful discharge for good cause. Soon after the passage of the Act, the Board held that it was an unfair labor practice for an employer to discharge a worker where anti-union animus actually contributed to the discharge decision. This construction of the Act — that to establish an unfair labor practice the General Counsel need show by a preponderance of the evidence only that a discharge is in any way motivated by a desire to frustrate union activity — was plainly rational and acceptable. The Board has adhered to that construction of the Act since that time.

At the same time, there were [NLRB] decisions indicating that the presence of an anti-union motivation in a discharge case was not the end of the matter. An employer could escape the consequences of a violation by proving that without regard to the impermissible motivation, the employer would have taken the same action for wholly permissible reasons.

The Courts of Appeals were not entirely satisfied with the Board's approach to dual-motive cases. The Board's *Wright Line* decision in 1980 was an attempt to restate its analysis in a way more acceptable to the Courts of Appeals. The Board held that the General Counsel of course had the burden of proving that the employee's conduct protected by § 7 was a substantial or a motivating factor in the discharge. Even if this was the case, and the employer failed to rebut it, the employer could avoid being held in violation of §§ 8(a)(1) and 8(a)(3) by proving by a preponderance of the evidence that the discharge rested on the employee's unprotected conduct as well and that the employee would have lost his job in any event. It thus became clear, if it was not clear before, that proof that the discharge would have occurred in any event and for valid reasons amounted to an affirmative defense on which the employer carried the burden of proof by a preponderance of the evidence. "The shifting burden merely requires the employer to make out what is actually an affirmative defense. . . ." *Wright Line, supra*, at 1088, n. 11; see also *id.*, at 1084, n. 5.

The Court of Appeals for the First Circuit refused enforcement of the *Wright Line* decision because in its view it was error to place the burden on the employer to prove that the discharge would have occurred had the forbidden motive not been present. The General Counsel, the Court of Appeals held, had the burden of showing not only that a forbidden motivation contributed to the discharge but also that the discharge would not have taken place independently of the protected conduct of the employee. The Court of Appeals was quite correct, and the Board does not disagree, that throughout the proceedings, the General Counsel carries the burden of proving the elements of an unfair labor practice. Section 10(c) of the Act expressly directs that violations may be adjudicated only "upon the preponderance of the testimony" taken by the Board. The Board's rules also state "the Board's attorney has the burden of pro[ving] violations of Section 8." 29 CFR § 101.10(b). We are quite sure, however, that the Court of Appeals erred in holding that § 10(c) forbids placing the burden on the employer to prove that absent the improper motivation he would have acted in the same manner for wholly legitimate reasons.

As we understand the Board's decisions, they have consistently held that the unfair labor practice consists of a discharge or other adverse action that is based in whole or in part on anti-union animus — or as the Board now puts it, that the employee's protected conduct was a substantial or motivating factor in the adverse action. The General Counsel has the burden of proving these elements under § 10(c). But the Board's construction of the statute permits an employer to avoid being adjudicated a violator by showing what his actions would have been regardless of his forbidden motivation. It extends to the employer what the Board considers to be an affirmative defense but does not change or add to the elements of the unfair labor practice that the General Counsel has the burden of proving under § 10(c).[11] We assume that the Board could reasonably have construed the Act in the manner insisted on by the Court of Appeals. We also assume that the Board might have considered a showing by the employer that the adverse action would have occurred in any event as not obviating a violation adjudication but as going only to the permissible remedy, in which event the burden of proof could surely have been put on the employer. The Board has instead chosen to recognize, as it insists

---

[11] [n.6] The language of the National Labor Relations Act requiring that the Board act on a preponderance of the testimony taken was added by the Labor Management Relations Act. A closely related provision directed that no order of the Board reinstate or compensate any employee who was fired for cause. Section 10(c) places the burden on the General Counsel only to prove the unfair labor practice, not to disprove an affirmative defense. Furthermore, it is clear from the legislative history of the Labor Management Relations Act that the drafters of § 10(c) were not thinking of the mixed motive case. Their discussions reflected the assumption that discharges were either "for cause" or punishment for protected activity. Read fairly, the legislative history does not indicate whether, in mixed motive cases, the employer or the General Counsel has the burden of proof on the issue of what would have happened if the employer had not been influenced by his unlawful motives; on that point the legislative history is silent. The "for cause" proviso was not meant to apply to cases in which both legitimate and illegitimate causes contributed to the discharge. The amendment was sparked by a concern over the Board's perceived practice of inferring from the fact that someone was active in a union that he was fired because of anti-union animus even though the worker had been guilty of gross misconduct.

The proviso was thus a reaction to the Board's readiness to infer anti-union animus from the fact that the discharged person was active in the union, and thus has little to do with the situation in which the Board has soundly concluded that the employer had an anti-union animus and that such feelings played a role in a worker's discharge.

it has done for many years, what it designates as an affirmative defense that the employer has the burden of sustaining. We are unprepared to hold that this is an impermissible construction of the Act.

The Board's allocation of the burden of proof is clearly reasonable in this context . . . . The employer is a wrongdoer; he has acted out of a motive that is declared illegitimate by the statute. It is fair that he bear the risk that the influence of legal and illegal motives cannot be separated, because he knowingly created the risk and because the risk was created not by innocent activity but by his own wrongdoing.

In *Mount Healthy City Board of Education v. Doyle*, 429 U.S. 274 (1977), we found it prudent, albeit in a case implicating the Constitution, to set up an allocation of the burden of proof which the Board heavily relied on and borrowed from in its *Wright Line* decision. There, we held that the plaintiff had to show that the employer's disapproval of his First Amendment protected expression played a role in the employer's decision to discharge him. If that burden of persuasion were carried, the burden would be on the defendant to show by a preponderance of the evidence that he would have reached the same decision even if, hypothetically, he had not been motivated by a desire to punish plaintiff for exercising his First Amendment rights. The analogy to *Mount Healthy* drawn by the Board was a fair one. . . .

The Board was justified in this case in concluding that Santillo would not have been discharged had the employer not considered his efforts to establish a union. At least two of the transgressions that purportedly would have in any event prompted Santillo's discharge were commonplace, and yet no transgressor had ever before received any kind of discipline. Moreover, the employer departed from its usual practice in dealing with rules infractions; indeed, not only did the employer not warn Santillo that his actions would result in being subjected to discipline, it never even expressed its disapproval of his conduct. In addition, Patterson, the person who made the initial decision to discharge Santillo, was obviously upset with Santillo for engaging in such protected activity. It is thus clear that the Board's finding that Santillo would not have been fired even if the employer had not had an anti-union animus was "supported by substantial evidence on the record considered as a whole." [Section 10(f).]

TEXTILE WORKERS UNION OF AMERICA v. DARLINGTON MANUFACTURING CO.
380 U.S. 263 (1965)

MR. JUSTICE HARLAN delivered the opinion of the Court.

. . . Darlington Manufacturing Company was a South Carolina corporation operating one textile mill. A majority of Darlington's stock was held by Deering Milliken, a New York 'selling house' marketing textiles produced by others. Deering Milliken in turn was controlled by Roger Milliken, president of Darlington, and by other members of the Milliken family. The National Labor Relations Board found that the Milliken family, through Deering Milliken, operated 17 textile manufacturers, including Darlington, whose products manufactured in 27 different mills, were marketed through Deering Milliken.

In March 1956 petitioner Textile Workers Union initiated an organizational campaign at Darlington which the company resisted vigorously in various ways, including threats to close the mill if the union won a representation election.[12] On September 6, 1956, the union won an election by a narrow margin. When Roger Milliken was advised of the union victory, he decided to call a meeting of the Darlington board of directors to consider closing the mill. Mr. Milliken testified before the Labor Board:

> I felt that as a result of the campaign that had been conducted and the promises and statements made in these letters that had been distributed (favoring unionization), that if before we had had some hope, possible hope of achieving competitive (costs) . . . by taking advantage of new machinery that was being put in, that this hope had diminished as a result of the election because a majority of the employees had voted in favor of the union
> . . . .

The board of directors met on September 12 and voted to liquidate the corporation, action which was approved by the stockholders on October 17. The plant ceased operations entirely in November, and all plant machinery and equipment were sold piecemeal at auction in December. . . .

The Board, by a divided vote, found that Darlington had been closed because of the antiunion animus of Roger Milliken, and held that to be a violation of [Section] 8(a)(3). . . . Respondent Deering Milliken was ordered to bargain with the union in regard to details of compliance with the Board order. . . .

We hold that so far as the Labor Relations Act is concerned, an employer has the absolute right to terminate his entire business for any reason he pleases, but disagree with the Court of Appeals that such right includes the ability to close part of a business no matter what the reason. We conclude that the cause must be remanded to the Board for further proceedings.

Preliminarily is should be observed that both petitioners argue that the Darlington closing violated [Section] 8(a)(1) as well as [Section] 8(a)(3) of the Act. We think, however, that the Board was correct in treating the closing only under [Section] 8(a)(3). Section 8(a)(1) provides that it is an unfair labor practice for an employer 'to interfere with, restrain, or coerce employees in the exercise of' [Section] 7 rights. Naturally, certain business decisions will, to some degree, interfere with concerted activities by employees. But it is only when the interference with [Section] 7 rights outweighs the business justification for the employer's action that [Section] 8(a)(1) is violated. A violation of [Section] 8(a)(1) alone therefore presupposes an act which is unlawful even absent a discriminatory motive. Whatever may be the limits of [Section] 8(a)(1), some employer decisions are so peculiarly matters of management prerogative that they would never constitute

---

[12] [n.3] The Board found that Darlington had interrogated employees and threatened to close the mill if the union won the election. After the decision to liquidate was made . . . Darlington employees were told that the decision to close was caused by the election, and they were encouraged to sign a petition disavowing the union. These practices were held to violate [Section] 8(a) (1) of the National Labor Relations Act . . . and that part of the Board decision is not challenged here.

violations of [Section] 8(a)(1), whether or not they involved sound business judgment, unless they also violated [Section] 8(a)(3). Thus it is not questioned in this case that an employer has the right to terminate his business, whatever the impact of such action on concerted activities, if the decision to close is motivated by other than discriminatory reasons.[13] But such action, if discriminatorily motivated, is encompassed within the literal language of [Section] 8(a)(3). We therefore deal with the Darlington closing under that section.

We consider first the argument, advanced by the petitioner union but not by the Board, and rejected by the Court of Appeals, that an employer may not go completely out of business without running afoul of the Labor Relations Act if such action is prompted by a desire to avoid unionization. Given the Board's findings on the issue of motive, acceptance of this contention would carry the day for the Board's conclusion that the closing of this plant was an unfair labor practice, even on the assumption that Darlington is to be regarded as an independent unrelated employer. A proposition that a single businessman cannot choose to go out of business if he wants to would represent such a startling innovation that it should not be entertained without the clearest manifestation of legislative intent or unequivocal judicial precedent so construing the Labor Relations Act. We find neither.

So far as legislative manifestation is concerned, it is sufficient to say that there is not the slightest indication in the history of the Wagner Act or of the Taft-Hartley Act that Congress envisaged any such result under either statute.

As for judicial precedent, the Board recognized that "(t)here is no decided case directly dispositive of Darlington's claim that it had an absolute right to close its mill, irrespective of motive." [139 N.L.R.B. 241, 250 (1962).] . . . The courts of appeals have generally assumed that a complete cessation of business will remove an employer from future coverage by the Act. Thus the Court of Appeals said in these cases: The Act "does not compel a person to become or remain an employee. It does not compel one to become or remain an employer. Either may withdraw from that status with immunity, so long as the obligations of any employment contract have been met." [325 F.2d 682, 685 (4th Cir. 1963).] . . .

The AFL-CIO suggests in its amicus brief that Darlington's action was similar to a discriminatory lockout, which is prohibited "because designed to frustrate organizational efforts, to destroy or undermine bargaining representation, or to evade the duty to bargain." One of the purposes of the Labor Relations Act is to prohibit the discriminatory use of economic weapons in an effort to obtain future benefits. The discriminatory lockout designed to destroy a union, like a "runaway shop," is a lever which has been used to discourage collective employee activities in the future. But a complete liquidation of a business yields no such future benefit for

---

[13] [n.10] It is also clear that the ambiguous act of closing a plant following the election of a union is not, absent an inquiry into the employer's motive, inherently discriminatory. We are thus not confronted with a situation where the employer "must be held to intend the very consequences which foreseeably and inescapably flow from his actions . . . ." (*National Labor Relations Board v. Erie Resistor Corp.*, 373 U.S. 221, 228 [(1963)]), in which the Board could find a violation of [Section] 8(a)(3) without an examination into motive. See *Radio Officers v. National Labor Relations Board*, 347 U.S. 17, 42–43 [(1954)]; *Local 357 International Brotherhood of Teamsters, etc. v. National Labor Relations Board*, 365 U.S. 667, 674–676 [(1961)].

the employer, if the termination is bona fide.[14] It may be motivated more by spite against the union than by business reasons, but it is not the type of discrimination which is prohibited by the Act. The personal satisfaction that such an employer may derive from standing on his beliefs and the mere possibility that other employers will follow his example are surely too remote to be considered dangers at which the labor statutes were aimed. Although employees may be prohibited from engaging in a strike under certain conditions, no one would consider it a violation of the Act for the same employees to quit their employment en masse, even if motivated by a desire to ruin the employer. The very permanence of such action would negate any future economic benefit to the employees. The employer's right to go out of business is no different.

Relevant to problem ⌐→

We are not presented here with the case of a "runaway shop," whereby Darlington would transfer its work to another plant or open a new plant in another locality to replace its closed plant. Nor are we concerned with a shutdown where the employees, by renouncing the union, could cause the plant to reopen. Such cases would involve discriminatory employer action for the purpose of obtaining some benefit in the future from the employees in the future. We hold here only that when an employer closes his entire business, even if the liquidation is motivated by vindictiveness toward the union, such action is not an unfair labor practice.[15]

While we thus agree with the Court of Appeals that viewing Darlington as an independent employer the liquidation of its business was not an unfair labor practice, we cannot accept the lower court's view that the same conclusion necessarily follows if Darlington is regarded as an integral part of the Deering Milliken enterprise.

The closing of an entire business, even though discriminatory, ends the employer-employee relationship; the force of such a closing is entirely spent as to that business when termination of the enterprise takes place. On the other hand, a discriminatory partial closing may have repercussions on what remains of the business, affording employer leverage for discouraging the free exercise of [Section] 7 rights among remaining employees of much the same kind as that found to exist

---

[14] [n.14] The Darlington property and equipment could not be sold as a unit, and were eventually auctioned off piecemeal. We therefore are not confronted with a sale of a going concern, which might present different considerations . . . . [Eds: see Chapter 13 for more discussion of the successorship doctrine referred to in this footnote.]

[15] [n.20] Nothing we have said in this opinion would justify an employer's interfering with employee organizational activities by threatening to close his plant, as distinguished from announcing a decision to close already reached by the board of directors or other management authority empowered to make such a decision. We recognize that this safeguard does not wholly remove the possibility that our holding may result in some deterrent effect on organizational activities independent of that arising from the closing itself. An employer may be encouraged to make a definitive decision to close on the theory that its mere announcement before a representation election will discourage the employees from voting for the union, and thus his decision may not have to be implemented. Such a possibility is not likely to occur, however, except in a marginal business; a solidly successful employer is not apt to hazard the possibility that the employees will call his bluff by voting to organize. We see no practical way of eliminating this possible consequence of our holding short of allowing the Board to order an employer who chooses so to gamble with his employees not to carry out his announced intention to close. We do not consider the matter of sufficient significance in the overall labor-management relations picture to require or justify a decision different from the one we have made.

in the 'runaway shop' and 'temporary closing' cases. Moreover, a possible remedy open to the Board in such a case, like the remedies available in the 'runaway shop' and 'temporary closing' cases, is to order reinstatement of the discharged employees in the other parts of the business. No such remedy is available when an entire business has been terminated. By analogy to those cases involving a continuing enterprise we are constrained to hold, in disagreement with the Court of Appeals, that a partial closing is an unfair labor practice under [Section] 8(a)(3) if motivated by a purpose to chill unionism in any of the remaining plants of the single employer and if the employer may reasonably have foreseen that such closing would likely have that effect.

While we have spoken in terms of a 'partial closing' in the context of the Board's finding that Darlington was part of a larger single enterprise controlled by the Milliken family, we do not mean to suggest that an organizational integration of plants or corporations is a necessary prerequisite to the establishment of such a violation of [Section] 8(a)(3). If the persons exercising control over a plant that is being closed for antiunion reasons (1) have an interest in another business, whether or not affiliated with or engaged in the same line of commercial activity as the closed plant, of sufficient substantiality to give promise of their reaping a benefit from the discouragement of unionization in that business; (2) act to close their plant with the purpose of producing such a result; and (3) occupy a relationship to the other business which makes it realistically foreseeable that its employees will fear that such business will also be closed down if they persist in organizational activities, we think that an unfair labor practice has been made out.

Although the Board's single employer finding necessarily embraced findings as to Roger Milliken and the Milliken family which, if sustained by the Court of Appeals, would satisfy the elements of 'interest' and 'relationship' with respect to other parts of the Deering Milliken enterprise, that and the other Board findings fall short of establishing the factors of 'purpose' and 'effect' which are vital requisites of the general principles that govern a case of this kind.

Thus, the Board's findings as to the purpose and foreseeable effect of the Darlington closing pertained only to its impact on the Darlington employees. No findings were made as to the purpose and effect of the closing with respect to the employees in the other plants comprising the Deering Milliken group. It does not suffice to establish the unfair labor practice charged here to argue that the Darlington closing necessarily had an adverse impact upon unionization in such other plants. . . . In an area which trenches so closely upon otherwise legitimate employer prerogatives, we consider the absence of Board findings on this score a fatal defect in its decision. . . .

Accordingly, without intimating any view as to how any of these matters should eventuate, we vacate the judgments of the Court of Appeals and remand the cases to that court with instructions to remand them to the Board for further proceedings consistent with this opinion. It is so ordered.

[Eds.: on remand, the NLRB found that the Supreme Court's test for a violation of Section 8(a)(3) was met. *See* Darlington Manufacturing Co., 165 N.L.R.B. 1074 (1967).]

POST PROBLEM DISCUSSION

1. The *Wright Line* analysis creates a two-step process for Section 8(a)(3) "mixed-motive" cases, which are cases that involve at least one lawful and one unlawful reason for the firing or other adverse employment action at issue. (In practice, the NLRB uses *Wright Line* for the vast majority of Section 8(a)(3) cases, as the employer almost always alleges a lawful reason for an adverse action). The General Counsel has the burden of persuasion under the first step to prove discrimination. The NLRB and courts typically break this step, often referred to as the General Counsel's "prima facie" case, into three parts: proof "(1) that the employee was engaged in protected activity, (2) that the employer was aware of the activity, and (3) that the protected activity was a substantial or motivating factor for the employer's action." *RGC (USA) Mineral Sands, Inc. v. NLRB*, 281 F.3d 442, 448 (4th Cir. 2002).

If the General Counsel fails to meet its burden, the case is over. If the General Counsel does meet that burden, then the employer has the burden of persuasion under the second step to show that the adverse action occurred in part because of "the employee's unprotected conduct . . . and that the employee would have lost his job in any event." *Transportation Management*, 462 U.S. at 400. Put another way, the second step is an affirmative defense under which an employer must show that even if it had not discriminated, it would have implemented the same adverse action. A typical argument for employers at this stage is to argue that the employee's work performance warranted termination (see Note 3 below for more on this). This is a true affirmative defense; that is, if the employer is successful, it will have no liability under Section 8(a)(3). It also means, along with the first step's requirement that the discrimination be a "substantial or motivating factor," that if an employer's discrimination plays only a minor or trivial role in an adverse action, there will not be a Section 8(a)(3) violation.

One exception to this test is the so-called "inherently destructive" case, in which the NLRB presumes that certain adverse actions were caused by discriminatory intent. The Supreme Court refers to this doctrine in footnote 10 of *Darlington* and we discuss it in more detail in Chapter 9.

2. A good test of whether you understand what Section 8(a)(3) covers and why it exists is the classic case of *Edward G. Budd Manufacturing Co. v. NLRB*, 138 F.2d 86 (3d Cir. 1943). *Budd* involved a traditional sham company union. Walter Weigand was one of the union shop stewards (an employee who acts as a low-level union representative) and, by the court's account, the position suited him:

> The case of Walter Weigand is extraordinary. If ever a workman deserved summary discharge it was he. He was under the influence of liquor while on duty. He came to work when he chose and he left the plant and his shift as he pleased. In fact, a foreman on one occasion was agreeably surprised to find Weigand at work and commented upon it. Weigand amiably stated that he was enjoying it. He brought a woman (apparently generally known as the 'Duchess') to the rear of the plant yard and introduced some of the employees to her. He took another employee to visit her and when this man got too drunk to be able to go home, punched his time-card for him and put him on the table in the representatives'

meeting room in the plant in order to sleep off his intoxication. Weigand's immediate superiors demanded again and again that he be discharged, but each time higher officials intervened on Weigand's behalf because as was naively stated he was 'a representative.' In return for not working at the job for which he was hired, the petitioner gave him full pay and on five separate occasions raised his wages. One of these raises was general; that is to say, Weigand profited by a general wage increase throughout the plant, but the other four raises were given Weigand at times when other employees in the plant did not receive wage increases.

Id. at 90. Ultimately, Weigand was fired. As should come as no surprise, the employer claimed that it fired him because of his work performance, or lack thereof. However, Weigand argued that the cause of his firing was that the employer recently discovered his membership and advocacy for an independent union. The Supreme Court held that an:

> employer may discharge an employee for a good reason, a poor reason or no reason at all so long as the provisions of the National Labor Relations Act are not violated. It is, of course, a violation to discharge an employee because he has engaged in activities on behalf of a union. Conversely an employer may retain an employee for a good reason, a bad reason or no reason at all and the reason is not a concern of the Board. But it is certainly too great a strain on our credibility to assert, as does the petitioner, that Weigand was discharged for an accumulation of offenses. We think that he was discharged because his work on behalf of the CIO [union] had become known to the plant manager. That ended his sinecure at the Budd plant. The Board found that he was discharged because of his activities on behalf of the union. The record shows that the Board's finding was based on sufficient evidence.

Notice that despite the long list of things that should have justified Weigand's termination, the employer lost because Weigand's misconduct was not its genuine motivation for firing him. Instead, the NLRB found that employer's true motivation was the desire to discourage the independent union from gaining support. Although *Wright Line* was decided much later, this result shows how the General Counsel's prima facie case turns on evidence regarding the employer's motivation. But what if *Wright Line* had applied at the time? Could the employer have successfully argued that it would have fired Weigand even if it had not wanted to punish his activity on behalf of the independent union? Finally, after Weigand returns to work following his win, is his job now protected indefinitely or is there a way for the employer to terminate him?

3. One more issue related to the *Budd* case. The employer in that case (and many other Section 8(a)(3) cases) argued that the NLRA should not prevent it from firing a bad employee. Since 1947, the NLRA explicitly gives employers the authority to terminate employees where appropriate. As noted in *Transportation Management*, Section 10(c) states that "[n]o order of the Board shall require the reinstatement of any individual as an employee who has been suspended or discharged, or the payment to him of any back pay, if such individual was suspended or discharged for cause." So why didn't Section 10(c) help the employer in

Transportation Management or, if it existed at the time, in *Budd*?

4. As you can see from the *Wright Line* analysis, the main focus of most Section 8(a)(3) cases is the employer's motivation. But if the employer never expressly states its motivation, that can be a difficult issue to determine. Among the major factors that can play into this determination are: the employer's knowledge of and hostility to its employees' union activity, the presence of other unfair labor practices, the timing of the adverse action compared to the protected activity, the implausibility of the employer's nondiscriminatory explanation, disparate treatment of alleged victims compared to others or the employer's past practices, proportionality of the adverse action to the employer's explanation, and the failure to investigate alleged misconduct by the alleged victim. *See Tellepsen Pipeline Services Co. v. NLRB*, 320 F.3d 554, 565 (5th Cir. 2003); *Grand Canyon Mining Co.*, 116 F.3d 1039, 1048 (4th Cir. 1997).

5. As you no doubt picked up on, Problem #2 is based on the General Counsel's 2011 complaint against Boeing Co. The political uproar was immense and involved, among other things, congressional hearings, Freedom of Information Act (FOIA) requests, and a subpoena issued against the General Counsel. For a running commentary on the case as it developed and ultimately settled, you can search the Workplace Prof Blog; starting with this post and following its links is a good place to begin: http://lawprofessors.typepad. com/laborprof_blog/2011/05/the-nlrbs-boeing-complaint-gops-1-issue-to-resolve-.ht ml.

But what about this facts of our problem, which are obviously a much-simplified and somewhat-altered version of the Boeing case? Assume that choosing not to give a unit of employees work in retaliation for their union activity can be an unlawful adverse action. *See Cold Heading Co.*, 332 N.L.R.B. 956, 956 n.5, 975-76 (2000) (finding Section 8(a)(3) violation when employer rerouted equipment from union facility to new nonunion facility); *see also Pittsburg & Midway Coal Mining Co.*, 355 N.L.R.B. No. 197 (2010) (finding Section 8(a)(3) violation for announced reduction in bonuses that never materialized). What facts would support the General Counsel's belief that Boing violated Section 8(a)(3)? Are they enough to meet the General Counsel's burden under *Wright Line*? If so, do you think that Boing can prove its affirmative defense? For more details on the legal arguments in the Boeing case, take a look at the NLRB's webpage dedicated to the matter: http://nlrb.gov/node/516. The Advice Memo has the most extensive analysis of the law involved.

6. Note that *Wright Line* and its genuine affirmative defense is not the only mixed-motive analysis available in labor and employment law. There are many possible variations, but the most well-known alternative is Title VII's quasi-affirmative defense test. Title VII has a similar prima facie case as *Wright Line*, which places the burden of persuasion on the employee-plaintiff to show, in a mixed motive case, that discrimination was a "motivating factor" in the challenged adverse action. It the employee meets that burden, the employee-defendant has the burden of persuasion to show that it would have made the same decision absent the discrimination. Sounds familiar so far. But the result of the employer meeting its burden is not the avoidance of all liability. Instead, the employer is considered to have violated the statute but is not liable for any monetary damages; rather, the

employer may be subject only to certain types of injunctions, attorney's fees, and litigation costs. *See* Title VII, Sections 703(m), 706(g)(2)(B) (42 U.S.C. §§ 2000e-2(m), 2000e-5(g)(2)(B)).

7.   Although in the following chapters we'll discuss in detail independent Section 8(a)(1) unfair labor practices, consider a few aspects of *Darlington* related to that violation. Why did the Supreme Court reject the NLRB's finding of a Section 8(a)(1) violation? Did the Supreme Court hold that shutting down a plant, even to retaliate against employees' vote for a union, can never violate Section 8(a)(1) or just not in cases like that one? Note that Section 8(a)(1) allegations generally require a balancing of interests — what interests were in play in *Darlington* and do you agree with the Court's decision?

8.   Do you agree with the Court that there should never be a violation of Section 8(a)(3) absent the employer having another business whose employees would feel threatened by the plant closing? Think about the reasons given for the Court's holding and whether they should absolve an employer of liability despite its discriminatory intent.

9.   What if, in our problem, Boing simply shut down its Wisconsin facility and no longer performed that work anywhere else? Would there be a Section 8(a)(3) violation under *Darlington*? Are there more facts that you would want to know about to better answer that question? If you think there was a violation, what should the remedy be?

C. Refusal-to-Hire Cases

Many Section 8(a)(3) cases involve adverse actions that occur to current employees, such as termination. But Section 8(a)(3) applies to job applicants as well. However, hiring cases pose special problems. For instance, a job applicant cannot rely on her past performance and history with an employer in an attempt to show discrimination. Additionally, there may be remedial issues related to the existence of more discriminatees than open positions. Finally, unions' use of "salts" has led to some recent controversy within the NLRB. A salt is typically a union-employer organizer who applies for a position with an employer for possibly two different purposes: 1) To get the job and organize the employer from within. This tactic is especially important given the limits that non-employees face in accessing an employer's workplace, as discussed in Chapter 5; or 2) To test the employer's willingness to hire union-affiliated applicants and/or set up the employer for a Section 8(a)(3) charge. The former tactic has been approved by the Supreme Court in its *Town & Country* decision; the latter tactic was the subject of a recent NLRB decision, *Toering*, that disapproved of the practice. Both cases will be discussed in the excerpt below.

PROBLEM #2: THE ELECTRIC COMPANY

Electro is an electrical contracting company that performs industrial and commercial work. The company does not have a bargaining relationship or agreement with the local chapter of the International Brotherhood of Electrical Workers. Indeed, the NLRB had recently found that Electro had unlawfully tried to exclude union organizers from public property near its office. The union had a well-known policy of disallowing its members to work for a non-union contractor, unless they agreed to engage in organizing activity.

Electro currently was working on a large project at a local hospital. Two of its electricians had just quit and the project manager was planning on advertising for a new electrician, but had not done so yet. One day, six members of the union submitted applications to Electro's office; the electricians' applications all listed their union membership and prior work with unionized electrical contractors. The receptionist accepted the applications and, after being asked when Electro was hiring, said that she thought it would be soon. A few days later, one of the electricians called to update his application, but no one at Electro called him back. Around the same time, an Electro electrician heard a foreman state that "I hope we don't hire anyone union."

A week and a half after the electricians submitted their applications, the hospital project manager hired an electrician, Peter Parker. Electro's president, Max Dillon, met Parker at church and recommended him to the project manager. Parker's application noted that he was a union member. A few days later, the project manager hired a second electrician who did not have any union affiliation.

The union has filed a charge with the NLRB, arguing that by not hiring any of the six union members, Electro violated Section 8(a)(3). As you read the following material, consider whether the union has a good case. Also consider how the NLRB handles the special issues that arise in a failure-to-hire case like this one.

PROBLEM MATERIALS

NLRB, Office of the General Counsel, *Guideline Memorandum Concerning Toering Electric Company*, Memorandum GC 08-04 (Revised), February 15, 2008

Michael C. Duff, *Union Salts as Administrative Private Attorneys General*, 32 BERKELEY J. EMP. & LAB. L. 1 (2011)

NLRB, OFFICE OF THE GENERAL COUNSEL GUIDELINE MEMORANDUM CONCERNING TOERING ELECTRIC COMPANY
Memorandum GC 08-04 (Revised), February 15, 2008

In *Toering Electric Company*, [351 NLRB No. 18 (September 2007),] the Board changed the burden of proof required for establishing that an individual is a Section 2(3) "job applicant" entitled to statutory protection against hiring discrimination. The purpose of this memorandum is to provide guidance for analyzing, investigating, and pleading Section 8(a)(3) refusal to hire cases under *Toering*.

I. Introduction

. . . Prior to *Toering*, the Board presumed that an individual who submitted an application for employment was a Section 2(3) employee and thus entitled to protection against discriminatory employer practices. In *Toering*, the Board "abandon[ed] its previous implicit presumption that anyone who applies for a job is protected as a Section 2(3) employee." The Board stated:

> We hold that an applicant for employment entitled to protection as a Section 2(3) employee is someone genuinely interested in seeking to establish an employment relationship with the employer . . . . We further hold that the General Counsel bears the ultimate burden of proving an individual's genuine interest in seeking to establish an employment relationship with the employer.

Although the holding in *Toering* is broadly worded, suggesting that an applicant's genuine interest in employment is an issue in all discriminatory refusal to consider and refusal to hire allegations, the Board's treatment of other refusal to hire or recall situations indicates that *Toering* is intended to apply only in the salting context.

II. Burden of Proof under *Toering*

In *FES* [*(A Division of Thermo Power)*, 331 NLRB 9, 12-13 (2000), enfd. 301 F.3d 83 (3d Cir. 2002),] the Board held that to prove that an employer engaged in Section 8(a)(3) hiring discrimination, the General Counsel has to demonstrate a prima facie case that (1) the respondent was hiring; (2) the applicant had experience or training relevant to the announced or generally known requirements; and (3) anti-union animus contributed to the decision not to hire the applicant. In *Toering*, the Board explained that although the *FES* burdenshifting framework still applies in refusal to hire and consider cases, proof of an applicant's genuine job interest is now also an element of the General Counsel's prima facie case. Specifically, under *Toering's* modified *FES* framework, the General Counsel has the burden of proving that an applicant is genuinely interested in seeking to establish an employment relationship with an employer, rather than the employer having the burden of proving the applicant had no such interest. As discussed below, this requirement embraces two components: (1) there was a bona fide application for employment; and (2) the applicant had a genuine interest in becoming employed by the employer.

(A) Application for employment

As to the first component, the General Counsel must introduce evidence either that the individual actually applied for employment or that the individual authorized someone to do so on his or her behalf. If the latter, then agency must also be shown.

With respect to agency, the Board reaffirmed that the fact that applications are submitted in batches does not itself preclude bonafide applicant status, so long as the submitter of the batched applications had the requisite authorization from the individual applicants. Thus, in cases involving batched applications, the Regions [regional offices] should investigate to determine whether the applicants had in fact authorized the submitter(s) to submit applications on their behalf. Evidence that the union regularly confirmed applicants' continuing interest in employment (such as by routinely updating applicant lists or by contacting individuals prior to submitting their applications) would support a finding of agency.

(B) Applicant had "genuine interest" in becoming employed

Once the General Counsel has demonstrated that there was an application for employment, his burden is met unless the employer raises "a reasonable question as to the applicant's actual interest in going to work for the employer." An employer may raise such a question by introducing evidence that an applicant recently refused similar employment with the employer; made belligerent or offensive comments on his or her application; engaged in disruptive, insulting, or antagonistic behavior during the application process; or engaged in other conduct inconsistent with a genuine desire to establish an employment relationship with the employer. Similarly, an application that is "stale" or incomplete may, depending on the circumstances, indicate that the applicant did not genuinely seek to establish an employment relationship with the employer.[16]

Once the employer has placed at issue the genuineness of the applicant's interest in employment, the General Counsel then bears the burden of proving by a preponderance of the evidence that the applicant in question was genuinely interested in seeking to establish an employment relationship; that is, "the ultimate burden of proof" rests with the General Counsel. Thus, an employer's motivation for making an alleged discriminatory hiring decision does not become relevant until the General Counsel satisfies his burden of proof as to the applicant's statutory employee status.

The Region may be able to prove that applicants had a genuine interest in employment through their credible, direct testimony that they would have accepted a position with the Respondent if one had been offered. In addition, the Region may rely on the following kinds of evidence:

> that an alleged discriminatee submitted an application in accordance with the employer's procedures, arrived on time to interviews, made follow-up inquiries regarding the application, had relevant work experience with other employers, and/or was also seeking similar employment with other employers. In *Cossentino Contracting Co.*, for example, the Board held that individuals were genuine applicants for employment because, although they arrived "en masse" at the request of the union, their behavior was orderly, they attempted to submit applications in a manner consistent with the respondent's established procedures, they had relevant work experience, and there was no evidence suggesting that they were there for any reason other than to apply for work.

Applicants may also present testimony refuting specific evidence proffered by the employer. For example, evidence that the applicant engaged in conduct inconsistent with a desire for an employment relationship may be refuted by demonstrating that the applicant engaged in no such conduct, or that if he did, that the conduct was in response to inappropriate actions or comments by management interviewers. Similarly, an employer's claim that an applicant would not have been able to perform his job duties because he also worked for the union may be refuted

---

[16] [n.13] . . . An application would likely be considered "stale" if a significant amount of time has elapsed since the individual authorized filing an application, or if it has been on file for a long period without being submitted to an employer for consideration.

by evidence demonstrating why his union responsibilities would not have interfered with his obligations to the employer.

III. Investigating and Pleading a Section 8(a)(3) refusal to hire allegation

In its pre-complaint investigation, the Region should question each alleged discriminatee as to whether he made or authorized an application and as to his intentions regarding employment with the employer. Further, if the employer disputes the discriminatee's genuine interest in employment during the initial investigation, or if evidence is uncovered during the investigation that would indicate that the applicant does not have a genuine interest in employment, the Region should conduct a full investigation to determine whether complaint is warranted.

If the Region concludes that a discriminatee was a genuine applicant, and decides to issue a complaint alleging a Section 8(a)(3) refusal to hire or consider, it should specifically allege in the complaint that "[name of employee] applied for [type of job] at [respondent employer] and therefore is an employee within the meaning of Section 2(3) of the Act." The Employer's admission to that assertion in its Answer will preclude litigation of the issue at trial. . . .

Michael C. Duff, *Union Salts as Administrative Private Attorneys General*
32 Berkeley J. Emp. & Lab. L. 1 (2011)[17]

. . . Salting activities may be either "overt" — the salt reveals his or her union affiliation at the time of job application, or at some point in time during the ensuing employment, or "covert" — union affiliation is never disclosed but is ultimately discovered by the employer. In either instance, the disclosed or discovered union affiliation is eventually alleged as the motive for an adverse employment action — a discharge or a refusal to hire — subsequently taken against the salt, who is either a job applicant or a hired employee, depending on the circumstances.

Salting fact scenarios are usually fairly simple. For example, an individual applies for a job by filling out a standard form in the lobby of a small business. If the individual is an overt salt, he or she may wear union insignia, or communicate in some other manner a union affiliation, placing the employer on immediate notice of some union objective. The employer thereafter refuses employment, sometimes in a strikingly obvious fashion. In some instances, overt applicants and non-union affiliated applicants with similar skill sets apply for the same job opening. The basis for arguing that the law has been violated is established when only the non-affiliated applicant is contacted for an interview.[18] In other cases, an employer with substantial hiring needs fails to contact openly union-affiliated applicants whose applications have been tendered en masse by their union. In these circumstances, the NLRB has found violations of law even though the involved applicants never

---

[18] [n.20] *FES*, 331 N.L.R.B. 9, 33 (2000).

personally appeared at the employer's facility. Sometimes an employer refuses to accept an application because of alleged "disrespectful" behavior by salt-applicants. Finally, in some scenarios salts obtain employment but are subsequently discharged — often abruptly — when their union affiliation becomes known to the employer.

As a general proposition, the union activities of salts are protected under the NLRA. That is, if salts are discriminated against with regard to hire or tenure of employment, for the purpose of discouraging membership in a labor organization, nothing with respect to applicants' or employees' status as salts should impact the finding of a violation of law.[19] Union salts who are motivated — in part or in whole — by a desire to inflict "injury" on the employer are controversial within the community of labor law scholars and practitioners, as they have objectives beyond obtaining employment with a targeted employer for the purpose of persuading employees to join a union. For example, some courts have concluded that salting "may be found to be unprotected if the purported organizational activity is a subterfuge used to further purposes unrelated to organizing, undertaken in bad faith, designed to result in sabotage, or designed to drive the employer out of the area or out of business." Nevertheless, most courts appear resigned to the now established rule that "[a]n employee does not lose his protected status merely because he is a salt."[20] . . .

Over the last decade, however, probably in response to political pressure, the NLRB has required preliminarily proof of the bona fides of a job applicant in order to establish a refusal to hire violation. This backwards analysis circumvents the Supreme Court's *Town & Country* opinion. The question of whether a salt is a "genuine" applicant is a circumlocution of the question of whether a salt is "really" a statutory employee, a question that the Court has already answered in the affirmative. No preliminary, elevated proof of employee status should be required to make out a prima facie case.[21] The NLRB's self-inflicted maneuvering revealed an alignment of the George W. Bush Labor Board with hostile circuit courts. These circuit courts equate labor tactics found repugnant on moral grounds with conduct that is unprotected for articulable statutory reasons. . . .

In *Toering Electric Company*, [51 N.L.R.B. 225 (2007)] the NLRB took up its most substantial revisiting of the salting issue since its *FES* decision in 2000, a case refining the NLRB's allocation of proof in salting cases. Perhaps the outcome of

---

[19] [n.25] *NLRB v. Town & Country Elec., Inc.*, 516 U.S. 85, 90–98 (1995) (upholding NLRB's determination that salts fall within statutory definition of employee).

[20] [n.28] *Contractors' Labor Pool, Inc., v. NLRB*, 323 F.3d 1051, 1061 (D.C. Cir. 2003).

[21] [n.46] For a useful analysis of this development, see Member Fox's partial dissent in *FES*:

> [W]hat is at stake in the allocation of burdens under [the NLRB's traditional burden shifting mechanism] is which side bears the risk that the influence of legal and illegal motives cannot be separated. Under *Wright Line* [the NLRB's seminal case on burden allocation], that risk is properly placed on the employer, because he has been shown to have acted with an unlawful motive. If he is unable to come forward with evidence sufficient to persuade the factfinder that he would have taken the same action for lawful reasons, he cannot escape liability. Under the majority's formulation for refusal-to-hire cases, at least part of the risk of nonpersuasion is on the General Counsel rather than the employer. I see no reason for such a departure from the basic principles of *Wright Line* in refusal-to-hire cases.

FES[, 331 N.L.R.B. at 31 (internal citations and quotations omitted).]

Toering was never in doubt; it was one of sixty-one decisions handed down in a single month that were adverse to the interests of organized labor. Simply put, the case severely limited the ability of the NLRB's General Counsel to prevail in salting cases. In the course of dealing that blow to salting campaigns, however, the NLRB's politically divided factions explicitly took on the issue explored here: whether salts serve a private attorney general role in a manner that is permissible under the NLRA. . . .

The central issue in *Toering* amounted to an only slightly modified rehashing of the statutory employee question considered in the Supreme Court's 1995 *Town and Country* opinion. In *Town and Country*, the most important salting case to date, the Court held that a salt could be both an employer's employee and a professional union organizer seeking to organize that employer's employees. In *Toering*, the NLRB held that its General Counsel had the burden of proving that a job applicant was "genuinely interested" in an "employment relationship" with an employer to establish entitlement to statutory protection against hiring discrimination. A corollary of the holding is that an applicant seeking employment merely for the purpose of exposing an employer's unlawful hiring practices or obtaining a backpay award is entitled to statutory protection only under unusual circumstances.

To consider the difficulty with the rule one need only think of a discharge case. Imagine an employee who has been hired but who has no genuine interest in remaining with an employer for more than a day (for whatever reason). Imagine further that the employee is discovered by the employer discussing unionization with fellow employees and that the subject employee is promptly discharged for that reason. There is no rule that would require the NLRB to prove that the employee was genuinely interested in continuing employment at the time of the discharge to make out a violation. Stated somewhat differently, I am unaware of a rule that would deny the employee the protection of the NLRA if the NLRB could not prove such genuine interest.[22]

Leaving substance aside momentarily, the parrying in *Toering* may have left casual observers of the NLRB wondering why salting has continued to provoke litigation. Two reasons predominate. First, prior to the NLRB's recent decision in *Oil Capitol Sheet Metal, Inc.,* [349 N.L.R.B. 1348 (2007),] the prospect of comparatively large back pay awards prompted litigation of many salting cases that had become relatively expensive to settle.[23] Second, and probably more importantly,

---

[22] [n.59] The NLRB has, however, placed the burden on the General Counsel to prove, after a successful adjudication, that salts unlawfully discharged from employment have continuing entitlement to backpay. See *Oil Capitol Sheet Metal, Inc.,* 349 N.L.R.B. 1348 (2007) (reversing the previous longstanding rule); *Tualatin Elec., Inc. v. NLRB,* 253 F.3d 714, 718 (D.C. Cir. 2001) ("The principle that the party who has acted unlawfully should bear the burden of producing evidence for the purpose of limiting its damages has as much force in a case involving salts as in any other.").

[23] [n.61] Under the then existing "moonlighting doctrine," wages paid to a salt by his union were earnings from secondary employment which, consistent with the NLRB's general moonlighting rule, were not offset against the salt's gross backpay. *Ferguson Elec. Co.,* 330 N.L.R.B. 514, 517 (2000). A union salt discriminatorily not hired, or discharged after hire, could limit a post-discrimination work search (necessary to establish continued eligibility for gross backpay) to non-union employers. These employers would often refuse to hire the now loudly overt union salt, creating the possibility of additional unfair labor practice charge filings, and the opportunity for multiple, often concurrent, backpay awards. In

salting provides a fertile battleground in which aggressive union agents come directly into contact with equally resistant employers. The visceral encounters between these front line emissaries is symbolic and serves as a showcase for the public of the untidy reality that labor-management conflict is alive and well, and that unions remain willing to combat anti-union employers aggressively.

Well before the recent salting controversies, the Supreme Court acknowledged that employers' refusals to hire job applicants because of union affiliation were a major impediment to union organizing and a threat to industrial peace.[24] However, *Toering* and the NLRB's "impact analysis" categorizations,[25] which provide explicit directions to NLRB investigators about which cases are deemed most important at each investigative stage, reveal the NLRB's predilection to view salting as a vaguely illegitimate union exercise in inflicting economic injury on non-union employers. The ameliorative aspects of salting campaigns which courts have recognized are, however, much more subtle.

Salting campaigns are in important respects an unintended consequence of courts' dramatic abrogation of prior labor policy by denying unions' access to employees' workplaces. The Supreme Court's 1992 opinion in *Lechmere v. NLRB*[, 502 U.S. 527 (1992),] eliminated access by non-employee union organizers to employers' property except in the very rare cases where no reasonable alternatives exist. Most commentators agree that as a practical matter the opinion banished unions from most workplaces. If experienced, professional union organizers have no access to employers' property during traditional organizing campaigns, the opportunities for unions to organize are almost by definition severely circumscribed. And the denial of access has gone even further. One court (as of this writing) has concluded that unions are forbidden from attempting to identify unorganized employees by viewing their license plates as they enter their employers' facilities, further diminishing unions' opportunities to gain access to and communicate with employees. . . .

A different and in some respects even more interesting question than the protection of union salting activity during traditional organizing campaigns is whether salting activity with no organizational objective in the traditional sense is unprotected by the NLRA. The premise underlying such a case is that a union undertakes salting activity solely because of suspicions that an employer will commit unfair labor practices, and thus filing an unfair labor practices charge will lead to backpay liability and payment of attorneys' fees. Assuming the premise to be correct, holding an employer accountable for unlawful discrimination has a fundamental organizational objective because an unfair labor practices charge could

---

some NLRB regions this practice was honed to a fine art. This writer[, who used to work as an NLRB regional attorney,] has spent many an afternoon dutifully attempting to calculate backpay awards in such tangled circumstances.

[24] [n.63] *Phelps Dodge Corp. v. NLRB*, 313 U.S. 177, 185 (1941).

[25] [n.64] Nat'l Labor Relations Bd., Office of the Gen. Counsel, Memorandum 02-02, Impact Analysis Program Modifications (Dec. 6, 2001) (concluding that allegations of unlawful refusals to hire should be given lower investigative priority than charges alleging unlawful discharges because the necessary evidence in refusal to hire cases "is generally peculiarly within the knowledge or possession of the employer, and thus not readily available. Therefore, investigations of such issues necessarily are often more time consuming and difficult than most discharge cases.").

remove an illegitimate obstacle to union organization in unorganized workplaces. Removal of such obstacles facilitates any union's ultimate organizational objective of organizing all unorganized employers in a given industry.

Even in the narrowest sense of "organizational objective," however — an organizational objective most commonly reflected in the "hot shop" workplace-by-workplace model now so widely disfavored by contemporary unions — *Toering* in effect holds that because the filing of unfair labor practice charges may be motivated by "non-organizational" objectives in some salting cases, the General Counsel carries the prima facie burden of proving the bona fides of all salts in all salting cases. This rule is in severe tension with *Town & Country*. In that case the Court never doubted that an employee's organizational objectives might come into conflict with employment duties. But, "[a] company faced with unlawful (or possibly unlawful) [worker] activity can discipline or dismiss the worker." [516 U.S. at 97.] The critical point of *Town & Country* is that employees are presumed to be employees until they have done something to remove themselves from the protection of the NLRA. "After all, the employer has no legal right to require that, as part of his or her service to the company, a worker refrain from engaging in protected activity." [*Id.* at 96.] But *Toering* insists tenaciously on a presumption that a paid union organizer applicant — an acknowledged statutory employee — is "non-genuine," and requires the General Counsel to prove otherwise as part of her case-in-chief. . . .

POST PROBLEM DISCUSSION

1.   The General Counsel's memorandum and Professor Duff's article reference the NLRB's decision in *FES (A Division of Thermo Power)*, 331 N.L.R.B. 9 (2000), *enforced*, 301 F.3d 83 (3d Cir. 2002), which is an important refusal-to-hire case. In *FES*, the NLRB concluded that:

> To establish a discriminatory refusal to hire, the General Counsel must, under the allocation of burdens set forth in [*Wright Line*], first show the following at the hearing on the merits: (1) that the respondent was hiring, or had concrete plans to hire, at the time of the alleged unlawful conduct; (2) that the applicants had experience or training relevant to the announced or generally known requirements of the positions for hire, or in the alternative, that the employer has not adhered uniformly to such requirements, or that the requirements were themselves pretextual or were applied as a pretext for discrimination; and (3) that antiunion animus contributed to the decision not to hire the applicants. Once this is established, the burden will shift to the respondent to show that it would not have hired the applicants even in the absence of their union activity or affiliation. . . .
>
> To establish a discriminatory refusal to consider . . . the General Counsel bears the burden of showing the following at the hearing on the merits: (1) that the respondent excluded applicants from a hiring process; and (2) that antiunion animus contributed to the decision not to consider the applicants for employment. Once this is established, the burden will shift to the respondent to show that it would not have considered the applicants

even in the absence of their union activity or affiliation.

Id. at 12, 15. *FES* was notable because it also concluded that an employer could violate Section 8(a)(3) even if the employer did not ultimately hire any workers. Rejecting the Sixth Circuit's contrary position, the NLRB reiterated its previous rule that such a violation was appropriate because its excludes union applicants from future openings and because it would deter other employees' willingness to engage in union activity. *Id.* at 15-15. *But see NLRB v. Fluor Daniel, Inc.*, 161 F.3d 953 (6th Cir. 1998).

How does *Toering* affect the *FES* analysis? Is it, as Professor Duff and the dissenters in *Toering* argue, a significant new burden for the General Counsel that runs counter to previous NLRA precedents and policies? Or is the *Toering* rule a reasonable reaction to unions testing employers and potentially setting them up for Section 8(a)(3) charges? Do you think the NLRB should revisit *Toering*? *See* Anne Marie Lofaso, *The Persistence of Union Repression in an Era of Recognition*, 62 ME. L. REV. 199, 206-09 (2010) (criticizing *Toering*).

2.   Consider our problem. Do you think there is a viable Section 8(a)(3) claim under *FES*? What about with the new *Toering* burden? Are there other facts that you would like to know?

D.   Remedies for Section 8(a)(3) Violations (and Section 8(a)(1) Too)

Section 10(c) states that upon finding that an employer or union committed an unfair labor practice, the Board "shall issue and cause to be served on such person an order requiring such person to cease and desist from such unfair labor practice, and to take such affirmative action including reinstatement of employees with or without back pay, as will effectuate the policies of this subchapter." The section does not permit the NLRB to levy fines or to issue awards for pain or suffering, punitive damages, or attorney's fees. *See Republic Steel Corp. v. NLRB*, 311 U.S. 7, 10 (1940). Instead, the NLRB's remedial options are limited to "make-whole relief," which can consist of a cease and desist order, and appropriate injunctive relief such as reinstatement, and backpay. *See Phelps Dodge Corp. v. NLRB*, 313 U.S. 177, 194 (1941). Typically, the regional office will hold a subsequent "compliance hearing" to determine remedial issues after the unfair labor practice proceeding has been decided by the NLRB.

1.   Cease and Desist Order/Notice Posting. Look at Section 10(c) and note that it says that the NLRB "shall" issue a cease and desist order. As a result, in every case in which the NLRB finds an unfair labor practice, there is a cease and desist order. This order is basically an injunction stating that the employer or union must stop doing whatever the NLRB found to be unlawful. This order serves multiple purposes. First, if an appellate court enforces the NLRB's order, then the cease and desist order becomes the equivalent of a judicial injunction. Failure to comply with that injunction could lead to contempt of court charges. The NLRB has a separate department called the Contempt Branch and its duty is to seek compliance with these orders — which at times has involved officials of recalcitrant

parties being sent to jail.

Second, the cease and desist order dovetails with another consistent practice of an NLRB order: the notice posting. After an unfair labor practice finding, the NLRB will order the employer or union to post a notice stating its unlawful actions and its duty to comply with the detailed cease and desist order. This ensures that all employees are aware of the NLRB's finding and the employer's or union's duty to comply in the future. As an aside, the cease and desist order is a useful shortcut when researching NLRB cases. If you want to see a quick summary of which unfair labor practices the NLRB found in a case, just look at the cease and desist order.

2. Affirmative Action. No, not *that* affirmative action (although the current meaning of that term came out of a provision in Title VII that is similar to Section 10(c)'s use of that term). Affirmative action really refers to any affirmative, make-whole injunction. Reinstatement is a common type of affirmative action that occurs in termination cases, but there are many others. We've already seen two variations in this chapter: disbanding a dominated union under Section 8(a)(2) and an "instatement" order in refusal-to-hire and refusal-to-consider cases. Similarly, violations that involve non-termination adverse actions could result in different types of affirmative orders. Examples include orders to promote, provide a raise, transfer, and numerous other actions that seek to put the victim in the position they would have been absent the unlawful act. In addition, as will be more obvious in Chapter 4, this type of relief can also apply to Section 8(a)(1) cases, such as firing non-union employees who criticize the company while on Facebook. *See* Office of the General Counsel, Division of Operations-Management, Memorandum OM 11-74 (Aug. 18, 2011) (summarizing types of social media cases considered by the General Counsel's office), http://mynlrb.nlrb.gov/link/document.aspx/ 09031d458056e743. Finally, Section 8(a)(4), which we will not address in detail, essentially mirrors Section 8(a)(3) with regard to remedies. That is because Section 8(a)(4) is also a motivation-based unfair labor practice, which makes it unlawful for an employer "to discharge or otherwise discriminate against an employee because he has filed charges or given testimony under this Act."

3. Backpay. Notice anything missing in the previous two types of relief? That's right, money. Given the lack of fines, compensatory or punitive damages, or attorney's fees, backpay orders are the only way for an employee to receive a monetary award. Very simply, backpay represents the compensation that the employee would have earned had the unlawful adverse action not occurred. In termination and refusal-to-hire cases, this involves the salary of whatever position the employee was or should have been in. But it could also involve other things, such as a loss of salary caused by an unlawful demotion, reduction of hours, or failure to promote. The backpay award is based on the time period starting from the unlawful action and ending when the employer offers a relevant remedy, such as reinstatement in termination

cases.

Backpay awards get more complicated, however. That is largely because of an important doctrine that exists for most labor and employment statutes: mitigation. This term usually refers to two issues. First, a victim who is out of work must look for a new job; this requirement is similar to individuals receiving unemployment benefits. The victim does not have to take any job, but must look for one that is "substantially equivalent." Failure to look for work, or to accept a comparable position, will make the victim ineligible for backpay during a given period of time. The second mitigation issue is one of subtraction. If the victim obtains work, then the compensation she earns is subtracted from the backpay award. *See Phelps Dodge*, 313 U.S. at 198. There is no cap to this type of mitigation and a victim could lose all backpay if she earns more in her new job. The calculations for mitigation can be much more complex than they appear from this brief summary, and regional attorneys often rely on detailed NLRB manuals to calculate awards. (See the previous section and Professor Duff's comments in footnotes 59 and 61 for another reference to backpay calculations.) For instance, the NLRB recently invited briefs on whether it should require a losing party to compensate an employee for additional taxes owed on lump-sum backpay awards. *See Latino Express, Inc.*, 358 N.L.R.B. No. 94 (July 31, 2012).

Finally, the NLRB will occasionally award "frontpay," which sounds like backpay but is really a substitute for reinstatement. For instance, if the unlawfully terminated employee's former department no longer exists and there is no job to reinstate her to, then the NLRB may award frontpay for a reasonable period of time to offset the lack of reinstatement.

PROBLEM #3: CAREER OPPORTUNITIES

Julius School of Music is a private school specializing in musical instruction. Recently, Julius has been dealing with disgruntled teaching staff, who believe that their pay is too low for what they are asked to do. These teachers all worked under annual contracts that were typically renewed every July. The teachers, who lack the faculty governance authority that exists at most universities, have been talking to unions about possibly seeking representation. The administration at Julius caught wind of these discussions and, as shown in an e-mail sent by the school president, decided not to renew the contracts of the four teachers who were leading the union drive. That decision was made in March, but the school did not inform the teachers of the decision until early July, when the school did not send the four teachers a new contract. It was only after the teachers asked about their status later in July that the school confirmed that their contracts were not renewed.

One of the affected teachers was Joe Strummer, a British citizen who was working at Julius under a valid work visa issued by the U.S. government. After learning that his contract would not be renewed, Strummer contacted three other music schools around the country, but was told by all three that no positions were available. This came as no surprise to Strummer given that the traditional hiring season for music schools was in March. Thus, Strummer decided to wait until the following March to look for a new job and vowed to start work on the symphony he had been planning on writing. However, in October, his work visa expired. Strummer had believed that he would be able to receive an extension, but because he no longer had a job, his request for a new visa was denied. According to a State Department official, if Strummer subsequently found work in the U.S., he could reapply for a work visa and would likely receive one.

Assume that Julius' refusal to renew Strummer's contract violated Section 8(a)(3). What, if any, remedy should the NLRB order? If you were counseling Strummer as soon as his contract was not renewed, what would you have told him to do differently?

PROBLEM MATERIALS

Movie, *Morristown: In the Air and Sun* (2007) (a documentary on immigrant labor in the U.S.)

Jeffrey M. Hirsch, *NLRB Reverses Backpay Burden*, Workplace Prof Blog, http://lawprofessors.typepad.com/laborprof_blog/2007/10/nlrb-reverses-b. html

Hoffman Plastic Compounds, Inc. v. NLRB, 535 U.S. 137 (2002)

Jeffrey M. Hirsch, *NLRB Reverses Backpay Burden*
Workplace Prof Blog
http://lawprofessors.typepad.com/laborprof_blog/2007/10/nlrb-reverses-b. html[26]

The NLRB, in a 3-2 decision, has reversed decades of precedent by shifting the burden in certain instances during backpay hearings. The case is *St. George's Warehouse*, 351 N.L.R.B. [961] (Sept. 29, 2007), in which the employer had been found to have violated the NLRA by firing two employees due to their union activity. In the compliance hearing, the employer challenged the Board's backpay specifications, arguing that evidence of job openings in the area showed that the employees did not properly mitigate. For the 45-plus years, the employer would have the burden of showing that the employees did not make reasonable attempts to find new work, but no longer. According to the Board:

> The contention that a discriminate has failed to make a reasonable search for work generally has two elements: (1) there were substantially equivalent jobs within the relevant geographic area, and (2) the discriminate unreasonably failed to apply for these jobs. Current Board law places on the respondent-employer the burden of production or going forward with evidence as to both elements of the defense. As to the first element, we reaffirm that the respondent-employer has the burden of going forward with the evidence. However, as to the second element, the burden of going forward with the evidence is properly on the discriminatee and the General Counsel who advocates on his behalf to show that the discriminate took reasonable steps to seek those jobs. They are in the best position to know

---

of the discriminatee's search or his reasons for not searching. Thus, following the principle that the burden of going forward should be placed on the party who is the more likely repository of the evidence, we place this burden on the discriminatee and the General Counsel. . . . [T]his burden allocation relieves a respondent of the impractical burden of proving a negative fact. Further, this burden-shifting framework is also consistent with the obligations already imposed on the General Counsel by the NLRB's Casehandling Manual [requiring the General Counsel to investigate the discriminatee's job-search efforts]. . . .

Today, we modify the principles governing the issue of willful loss of earnings in one respect only. When a respondent raises a job search defense to its backpay liability and produces evidence that there were substantially equivalent jobs in the relevant geographic area available for the discriminate during the backpay period, we will place on the General Counsel the burden of producing evidence concerning the discriminatee's job search.

[351 N.L.R.B. 961, 964, 965.] Not surprisingly, the dissent has a different view:

Departing from more than 45 years of established precedent, the majority relieves wrongdoers of their burden to produce all of the facts to substantiate the affirmative defense that a discriminate unreasonably failed to mitigate damages and, instead, requires the General Counsel to produce facts to negate it. The result is to place a stumbling block before discriminatees and, ultimately, to frustrate enforcement of the National Labor Relations Act. Unfortunately, this is just the latest in a series of cases in which the majority has sought to reduce the effectiveness of the Board's backpay and reinstatement remedies. The result, of course, is to make it less costly for an employer to violate the Act. . . .

[T]he Board's [previous] requirement that a respondent come forward with facts to substantiate affirmative defenses to backpay, including an alleged failure to mitigate, is consistent with the general rule that a party asserting an affirmative defense has the burden of producing evidence to support it. . . . The Board's approach is also consistent with the Supreme Court's oft-quoted observation that the "most elementary conceptions of justice and public policy require that the wrongdoer shall bear the risk of the uncertainty which his own wrong has created." *Bigelow v. RKO Radio Pictures*[, 327 U.S. 251, 265 (1946).] . . .

There are good reasons to question the presumption that the General Counsel will be fully informed of a discriminatee's mitigation efforts and location. As explained above, the General Counsel is not the discriminatee's lawyer, and the Board's regional offices necessarily depend on the discriminatee's cooperation in reporting efforts to find interim employment. Moreover, although discriminatees are requested to periodically complete forms regarding their mitigation efforts, those forms rarely offer complete information. . . . In any event, the majority's presumption utterly ignores the fact that a respondent is often just as likely, if not more likely, to have access to a discriminatee.

[351 N.L.R.B. 967, 969–70.] It will come as no[] surprise (especially given that I worked briefly on getting the ULP in this case enforced in the Third Circuit), that I think the dissent has the better argument. The remedies under the NLRA are weak even at their strongest. It is telling that the majority is willing to impose further remedial hurdles for workers already identified as victims of unlawful discrimination. . . .

HOFFMAN PLASTIC COMPOUNDS, INC. v. NLRB
535 U.S. 137 (2002)

CHIEF JUSTICE REHNQUIST delivered the opinion of the Court.

The National Labor Relations Board (Board) awarded backpay to an undocumented alien who has never been legally authorized to work in the United States. We hold that such relief is foreclosed by federal immigration policy, as expressed by Congress in the Immigration Reform and Control Act of 1986 (IRCA).

Petitioner Hoffman Plastic Compounds, Inc. (petitioner or Hoffman), custom-formulates chemical compounds for businesses that manufacture pharmaceutical, construction, and household products. In May 1988, petitioner hired Jose Castro to operate various blending machines that "mix and cook" the particular formulas per customer order. Before being hired for this position, Castro presented documents that appeared to verify his authorization to work in the United States. In December 1988, the United Rubber, Cork, Linoleum, and Plastic Workers of America, AFL-CIO, began a union-organizing campaign at petitioner's production plant. Castro and several other employees supported the organizing campaign and distributed authorization cards to co-workers. In January 1989, Hoffman laid off Castro and other employees engaged in these organizing activities.

Three years later, in January 1992, respondent Board found that Hoffman unlawfully selected four employees, including Castro, for layoff "in order to rid itself of known union supporters" in violation of § 8(a)(3) of the National Labor Relations Act (NLRA). To remedy this violation, the Board ordered that Hoffman (1) cease and desist from further violations of the NLRA, (2) post a detailed notice to its employees regarding the remedial order, and (3) offer reinstatement and backpay to the four affected employees. Hoffman entered into a stipulation with the Board's General Counsel and agreed to abide by the Board's order.

In June 1993, the parties proceeded to a compliance hearing before an Administrative Law Judge (ALJ) to determine the amount of backpay owed to each discriminatee. On the final day of the hearing, Castro testified that he was born in Mexico and that he had never been legally admitted to, or authorized to work in, the United States. He admitted gaining employment with Hoffman only after tendering a birth certificate belonging to a friend who was born in Texas. He also admitted that he used this birth certificate to fraudulently obtain a California driver's license and a Social Security card, and to fraudulently obtain employment following his layoff by Hoffman. Neither Castro nor the Board's General Counsel offered any evidence that Castro had applied or intended to apply for legal authorization to work in the United States. Based on this testimony, the ALJ found the Board precluded from awarding Castro backpay or reinstatement as such relief would be contrary to *Sure-Tan, Inc. v. NLRB*, 467 U.S. 883 (1984), and in conflict with IRCA, which makes it unlawful for employers knowingly to hire undocumented workers or for employees to use fraudulent documents to establish employment eligibility.

In September 1998, four years after the ALJ's decision, and nine years after Castro was fired, the Board reversed with respect to backpay. Citing its earlier decision in *A.P.R.A. Fuel Oil Buyers Group, Inc.*, 320 N.L.R.B. 408 (1995), the Board determined that "the most effective way to accommodate and further the immigration policies embodied in [IRCA] is to provide the protections and remedies of the [NLRA] to undocumented workers in the same manner as to other employees." . . . It calculated this backpay award from the date of Castro's termination to the date Hoffman first learned of Castro's undocumented status, a period of 4 1/2 years. . . .

Hoffman filed a petition for review of the Board's order in the Court of Appeals. A panel of the Court of Appeals denied the petition for review. After rehearing the case en banc, the court again denied the petition for review and enforced the Board's order. We granted certiorari, and now reverse.

This case exemplifies the principle that the Board's discretion to select and fashion remedies for violations of the NLRA, though generally broad, is not unlimited. Since the Board's inception, we have consistently set aside awards of reinstatement or backpay to employees found guilty of serious illegal conduct in connection with their employment. In *Fansteel*, the Board awarded reinstatement with backpay to employees who engaged in a "sit down strike" that led to confrontation with local law enforcement officials. We set aside the award, saying:

> "We are unable to conclude that Congress intended to compel employers to retain persons in their employ regardless of their unlawful conduct, — to invest those who go on strike with an immunity from discharge for acts of trespass or violence against the employer's property, which they would not have enjoyed had they remained at work." *NLRB v. Fansteel Metallurgical Corp.*, 306 U.S. 240, 255 (1939). . . .

Our decision in *Sure-Tan* . . . set aside an award closely analogous to the award challenged here. There we confronted for the first time a potential conflict between the NLRA and federal immigration policy, as then expressed in the Immigration and Nationality Act (INA). Two companies had unlawfully reported alien-employees to the Immigration and Naturalization Service (INS) in retaliation for union activity. Rather than face INS sanction, the employees voluntarily departed to Mexico. The Board investigated and found the companies acted in violation of §§ 8(a)(1) and (3) of the NLRA. The Board's ensuing order directed the companies to reinstate the affected workers and pay them six months' backpay.

We affirmed the Board's determination that the NLRA applied to undocumented workers, reasoning that the immigration laws "as presently written" expressed only a " 'peripheral concern' " with the employment of illegal aliens. 467 U.S., at 892, (quoting *De Canas v. Bica*, 424 U.S. 351 (1976)). "For whatever reason," Congress had not "made it a separate criminal offense" for employers to hire an illegal alien, or for an illegal alien "to accept employment after entering this country illegally."

Sure-Tan, 467 U.S., at 892–893. Therefore, we found "no reason to conclude that application of the NLRA to employment practices affecting such aliens would necessarily conflict with the terms of the INA." *Id.*, at 893.

With respect to the Board's selection of remedies, however, we found its authority limited by federal immigration policy. For example, the Board was prohibited from effectively rewarding a violation of the immigration laws by reinstating workers not authorized to reenter the United States. Thus, to avoid "a potential conflict with the INA," the Board's reinstatement order had to be conditioned upon proof of "the employees' legal reentry." *Sure-Tan*, 467 U.S., at 903. "Similarly," with respect to backpay, we stated: "[T]he employees must be deemed 'unavailable' for work (and the accrual of backpay therefore tolled) during any period when they were not lawfully entitled to be present and employed in the United States." *Ibid.* "[I]n light of the practical workings of the immigration laws," such remedial limitations were appropriate even if they led to "[t]he probable unavailability of the [NLRA's] more effective remedies." *Id.*, at 904. . . .

In 1986, two years after *Sure-Tan*, Congress enacted IRCA, a comprehensive scheme prohibiting the employment of illegal aliens in the United States. As we have previously noted, IRCA "forcefully" made combating the employment of illegal aliens central to "[t]he policy of immigration law." *INS v. National Center for Immigrants' Rights, Inc.*, 502 U.S. 183, 194, and n. 8 (1991). It did so by establishing an extensive "employment verification system," designed to deny employment to aliens who (a) are not lawfully present in the United States, or (b) are not lawfully authorized to work in the United States This verification system is critical to the IRCA regime. To enforce it, IRCA mandates that employers verify the identity and eligibility of all new hires by examining specified documents before they begin work. If an alien applicant is unable to present the required documentation, the unauthorized alien cannot be hired.

Similarly, if an employer unknowingly hires an unauthorized alien, or if the alien becomes unauthorized while employed, the employer is compelled to discharge the worker upon discovery of the worker's undocumented status. Employers who violate IRCA are punished by civil fines, and may be subject to criminal prosecution. IRCA also makes it a crime for an unauthorized alien to subvert the employer verification system by tendering fraudulent documents. It thus prohibits aliens from using or attempting to use "any forged, counterfeit, altered, or falsely made document" or "any document lawfully issued to or with respect to a person other than the possessor" for purposes of obtaining employment in the United States. 18 U.S.C. §§ 1324c(a)(1)-(3). Aliens who use or attempt to use such documents are subject to fines and criminal prosecution. There is no dispute that Castro's use of false documents to obtain employment with Hoffman violated these provisions.

Under the IRCA regime, it is impossible for an undocumented alien to obtain employment in the United States without some party directly contravening explicit congressional policies. Either the undocumented alien tenders fraudulent identification, which subverts the cornerstone of IRCA's enforcement mechanism, or the employer knowingly hires the undocumented alien in direct contradiction of its IRCA obligations. The Board asks that we overlook this fact and allow it to award backpay to an illegal alien for years of work not performed, for wages that could not lawfully have been earned, and for a job obtained in the first instance by a criminal fraud. We find, however, that awarding backpay to illegal aliens runs counter to policies underlying IRCA, policies the Board has no authority to enforce or administer. Therefore, as we have consistently held in like circumstances, the award lies beyond the bounds of the Board's remedial discretion.

The Board contends that awarding limited backpay to Castro "reasonably accommodates" IRCA, because, in the Board's view, such an award is not "inconsistent" with IRCA. The Board argues that because the backpay period was closed as of the date Hoffman learned of Castro's illegal status, Hoffman could have employed Castro during the backpay period without violating IRCA. The Board further argues that while IRCA criminalized the misuse of documents, "it did not make violators ineligible for back pay awards or other compensation flowing from employment secured by the misuse of such documents." . . . What matters here, and what sinks both of the Board's claims, is that Congress has expressly made it criminally punishable for an alien to obtain employment with false documents. There is no reason to think that Congress nonetheless intended to permit backpay where but for an employer's unfair labor practices, an alien-employee would have remained in the United States illegally, and continued to work illegally, all the while successfully evading apprehension by immigration authorities. Far from "accommodating" IRCA, the Board's position, recognizing employer misconduct but discounting the misconduct of illegal alien employees, subverts it.

Indeed, awarding backpay in a case like this not only trivializes the immigration laws, it also condones and encourages future violations. The Board admits that had the INS detained Castro, or had Castro obeyed the law and departed to Mexico, Castro would have lost his right to backpay. Castro thus qualifies for the Board's award only by remaining inside the United States illegally. Similarly, Castro cannot mitigate damages, a duty our cases require, without triggering new IRCA violations, either by tendering false documents to employers or by finding employers willing to ignore IRCA and hire illegal workers. The Board here has failed to even consider this tension.

We therefore conclude that allowing the Board to award backpay to illegal aliens would unduly trench upon explicit statutory prohibitions critical to federal immigration policy, as expressed in IRCA. It would encourage the successful evasion of apprehension by immigration authorities, condone prior violations of the immigration laws, and encourage future violations. However broad the Board's discretion to fashion remedies when dealing only with the NLRA, it is not so unbounded as to authorize this sort of an award.

Lack of authority to award backpay does not mean that the employer gets off scot-free. The Board here has already imposed other significant sanctions against Hoffman — sanctions Hoffman does not challenge. These include orders that Hoffman cease and desist its violations of the NLRA, and that it conspicuously post a notice to employees setting forth their rights under the NLRA and detailing its prior unfair practices. Hoffman will be subject to contempt proceedings should it fail to comply with these orders. We have deemed such "traditional remedies" sufficient to effectuate national labor policy regardless of whether the "spur and catalyst" of backpay accompanies them. *Sure-Tan*, 467 U.S., at 904. See also *id.*, at

904, n. 13 ("This threat of contempt sanctions . . . provides a significant deterrent against future violations of the [NLRA]"). As we concluded in *Sure-Tan*, "in light of the practical workings of the immigration laws," any "perceived deficienc[y] in the NLRA's existing remedial arsenal" must be "addressed by congressional action," not the courts. *Id.*, at 904. In light of IRCA, this statement is even truer today.

JUSTICE BREYER, with whom JUSTICE STEVENS, JUSTICE SOUTER, and JUSTICE GINS-BURG join, dissenting.

I cannot agree that the backpay award before us "runs counter to," or "trenches upon," national immigration policy. (citing the Immigration Reform and Control Act of 1986 (IRCA)). As *all* the relevant agencies (including the Department of Justice) have told us, the National Labor Relations Board's limited backpay order will *not* interfere with the implementation of immigration policy. Rather, it reasonably helps to deter unlawful activity that *both* labor laws *and* immigration laws seek to prevent. Consequently, the order is lawful.

The Court does not deny that the employer in this case dismissed an employee for trying to organize a union — a crude and obvious violation of the labor laws. And it cannot deny that the Board has especially broad discretion in choosing an appropriate remedy for addressing such violations. Nor can it deny that in such circumstances backpay awards serve critically important remedial purposes. Those purposes involve more than victim compensation; they also include deterrence, *i.e.*, discouraging employers from violating the Nation's labor laws.

Without the possibility of the deterrence that backpay provides, the Board can impose only future-oriented obligations upon law-violating employers — for it has no other weapons in its remedial arsenal. And in the absence of the backpay weapon, employers could conclude that they can violate the labor laws at least once with impunity. Hence the backpay remedy is necessary; it helps make labor law enforcement credible; it makes clear that violating the labor laws will not pay.

Where in the immigration laws can the Court find a "policy" that might warrant taking from the Board this critically important remedial power? Certainly not in any statutory language. The immigration statutes say that an employer may not knowingly employ an illegal alien, that an alien may not submit false documents, and that the employer must verify documentation. They provide specific penalties, including criminal penalties, for violations. But the statutes' language itself does not explicitly state how a violation is to effect the enforcement of other laws, such as the labor laws. What is to happen, for example, when an employer hires, or an alien works, in violation of these provisions? Must the alien forfeit all pay earned? May the employer ignore the labor laws? More to the point, may the employer violate those laws with impunity, at least once — secure in the knowledge that the Board cannot assess a monetary penalty? The immigration statutes' language simply does not say.

Nor can the Court comfortably rest its conclusion upon the immigration laws' purposes. For one thing, the general purpose of the immigration statute's employment prohibition is to diminish the attractive force of employment, which like a "magnet" pulls illegal immigrants toward the United States. To permit the Board to award backpay could not significantly increase the strength of this magnetic force, for so speculative a future possibility could not realistically influence an individual's decision to migrate illegally.

To *deny* the Board the power to award backpay, however, might very well increase the strength of this magnetic force. That denial lowers the cost to the employer of an initial labor law violation (provided, of course, that the only victims are illegal aliens). It thereby increases the employer's incentive to find and to hire illegal-alien employees. Were the Board forbidden to assess backpay against a *knowing* employer — a circumstance not before us today — this perverse economic incentive, which runs directly contrary to the immigration statute's basic objective, would be obvious and serious. But even if limited to cases where the employer did not know of the employee's status, the incentive may prove significant — for, as the Board has told us, the Court's rule offers employers immunity in borderline cases, thereby encouraging them to take risks, *i.e.*, to hire with a wink and a nod those potentially unlawful aliens whose unlawful employment (given the Court's views) ultimately will lower the costs of labor law violations. The Court has recognized these considerations in stating that the labor laws must apply to illegal aliens in order to ensure that "there will be no advantage under the NLRA in preferring illegal aliens" and therefore there will be "fewer incentives for aliens themselves to enter." *Sure-Tan, supra*, at 893–894. The Court today accomplishes the precise opposite.

The immigration law's specific labor-law-related purposes also favor preservation, not elimination, of the Board's backpay powers. See [*A.P.R.A. Fuel Oil Buyers Group, Inc.*, 320 N.L.R.B. 408, 414 (1995)] (immigration law seeks to combat the problem of aliens' willingness to "work in substandard conditions and for starvation wages"); cf. also *Sure-Tan*, 467 U.S., at 893 ("[E]nforcement of the NLRA . . . is compatible with the policies" of the Immigration and Nationality Act). As I just mentioned and as this Court has held, the immigration law foresees application of the Nation's labor laws to protect "workers who are illegal immigrants." *Id.*, at 891–893. And a policy of *applying* the labor laws must encompass a policy of *enforcing* the labor laws effectively. Otherwise, as Justice KENNEDY once put the matter, "we would leave helpless the very persons who most need protection from exploitative employer practices." *NLRB v. Apollo Tire Co.*, 604 F.2d 1180, 1184 (C.A.9 1979) (concurring opinion). That presumably is why those in Congress who wrote the immigration statute stated explicitly and unequivocally that the immigration statute does *not* take from the Board *any* of its remedial authority. H.R. Rep. No. 99–682, at 58, U.S. Code Cong. & Admin. News 1986, pp. 5649, 5662 (IRCA does not "undermine or diminish in any way labor protections in existing law, or . . . limit the powers of federal or state labor relations boards . . . to remedy unfair practices committed against undocumented employees"). . . .

The Court also refers to the statement in *Sure-Tan, Inc. v. NLRB*, 467 U.S., at 903, that "employees must be deemed 'unavailable' for work (and the accrual of backpay therefore tolled) during any period when they were not lawfully entitled to be present and employed in the United States." The Court, however, does not rely upon this statement as determining its conclusion. See And it is right not to do so. *Sure-Tan* involved an order reinstating (with backpay) illegal aliens who had left the country and returned to Mexico. In order to collect the backpay to which the order entitled them, the aliens would have had to reenter the country illegally. Consequently, the order itself could not have been enforced without leading to a violation of criminal law. Nothing in the Court's opinion suggests that the Court intended its statement to reach to circumstances different from and not at issue in *Sure-Tan*, where an order, such as the order before us, does not require the alien to engage in further illegal behavior.

Finally, the Court cannot reasonably rely upon the award's negative features taken together. The Court summarizes those negative features when it says that the Board "asks that we . . . award backpay to an illegal alien [1] for years of work not performed, [2] for wages that could not lawfully have been earned, and [3] for a job obtained in the first instance by a criminal fraud." The first of these features has little persuasive force, given the facts that (1) backpay ordinarily and necessarily is awarded to a discharged employee who may not find other work, and (2) the Board is able to tailor an alien's backpay award to avoid rewarding that alien for his legal inability to mitigate damages by obtaining lawful employment elsewhere.

Neither can the remaining two features — unlawfully earned wages and criminal fraud — prove determinative, for they tell us only a small portion of the relevant story. After all, the same backpay award that compensates an employee in the circumstances the Court describes *also* requires an employer who has violated the labor laws to make a meaningful monetary payment. Considered from this equally important perspective, the award simply requires that employer to pay an employee whom the employer believed could lawfully have worked in the United States, (1) for years of work that he would have performed, (2) for a portion of the wages that he would have earned, and (3) for a job that the employee would have held — had that employer not unlawfully dismissed the employee for union organizing. In ignoring these latter features of the award, the Court undermines the public policies that underlie the Nation's labor laws. . . .

POST PROBLEM DISCUSSION

1. Be aware that *St. George's Warehouse* may not be long for this world; indeed, it might already be overturned by the time you're reading this. That is because, in 2011, the General Counsel indicated that he would ask the NLRB to reverse *St. George's. See* NLRB, Office of the General Counsel, *Guideline Memorandum Regarding Backpay Mitigation*, Memorandum GC 11-07 (Mar. 11, 2011) (also indicating intent to ask NLRB to reverse another case decided about the same time, *Grosvenor Resort*, 350 N.L.R.B. 1197 (2007), in which the NLRB created a new rule requiring fired employees to begin their job searches within two weeks of their termination, even if they are on strike).

2. Consider our problem. Is Strummer entitled to backpay? If so, for what periods of time? Focus in particular on whether you think Strummer satisfied the requirement to mitigate. Do you think the mitigation requirement is appropriate or should employers be responsible for more robust damages? *See* James J. Brudney, *Private Injuries, Public Policies: Adjusting the NLRB's Approach to Backpay Remedies*, 5 FIU L. REV. 645 (2010) (criticizing limits on current backpay awards and proposing mandatory minimum awards). Also, what effect should his visa expiration have on a potential backpay award?

3.   Refusal-to-hire and -consider cases pose special remedial issues because of the number of affected individuals that can be involved. In *FES*, the NLRB addressed one problem in particular: what happens when the number of rejected applicants is more than the number of positions being filled? The NLRB stated that a single discriminatory rejection of applicant in this situation warrants a cease and desist order. *FES*, 331 N.L.R.B. at 14. However, if the General Counsel seeks backpay or instatement orders, it must show that there were openings for those applicants. In other words, the employer will not have to provide backpay or instatement for more positions than it had open.

4.   In another decision decided at approximately the same time as *Toering*, the NLRB altered its presumption that the backpay period continues indefinitely until the employer gives the discriminatee an offer of employment. *See Oil Capitol Sheet Metal, Inc.*, 349 N.L.R.B. 1348 (2007), *petition for review dismissed as unripe*, 561 F.3d 497 (D.C. Cir. 2009). This presumption still exists for other relevant Section 8(a)(1) and (a)(3) violations, but not for those involving salts. In salting cases under *Oil Capitol*, backpay damages will be awarded for only the period of time that the General Counsel can prove that the salt would have remained on the job.

The NLRB reasoned that most salts stay on the job only until their organizing efforts at that particular employer end. Thus, damages will be awarded only for periods of time that the General Counsel could show that the salt would have remained. The dissenters would have applied the traditional rule that it is up to the employer to show that a discriminatee would have left because unresolved factual uncertainties should go against the wrongdoer.

Now reconsider Problem #2. Remember that six union members applied for, but did not receive, jobs with Electro. Remember as well that at the time, Electro was looking for only two electricians. What, if any, remedies are appropriate if Electro refused to hire or consider the applicants because of their union membership?

5.   Following the Supreme Court's decision in *Hoffman*, some employers tried to argue that undocumented workers should not be considered employees under the NLRA. However, those attempts have failed. *See Agri Processor Co. v. NLRB*, 514 F.3d 1, 3–7 (D.C. Cir. 2008) (holding that IRCA did not change *Sure-Tan's* holding on this issue). Ask yourself what advantages an opposite holding would have given employers beyond what *Hoffman* already provides.

6.   Do you agree with the Court in *Hoffman* that the notice and cease and desist remedies are sufficient to deter future unfair labor practices by the employer in question or other employers? *See* Robert M. Worster, III, *If It's Hardly Worth Doing Right: How the NLRA's Goals Are Defeated Through Inadequate Remedies*, 38 U. RICH. L. REV. 1073, 1077–80 (2004). There has been much criticism of the NLRB's general remedies, much less the limited set of remedies available to undocumented employees after *Hoffman*. *Id. see also* Wilma B. Liebman, *Decline and Disenchantment: Reflections on the Aging of the National Labor Relations Board*, 28 BERKELEY J. EMP. & LAB. L. 569, 584–86 (2007) (former NLRB Chair); Paul C. Weiler, *Promises To Keep: Securing Workers' Rights To Self-Organization Under the NLRA*, 96 HARV. L. REV. 1769, 1777–95 (1983) (noting, in part, that the mitigation doctrine inhibits the possible deterrent effect of backpay orders).

7. Do you agree with the Court that not allowing backpay aids IRCA's policies? Or are you more persuaded by the dissent's view that the opposite is true?

8. For more background on the *Hoffman* case, see Catherine L. Fisk & Michael J. Wishnie, *The Story of* Hoffman Plastics Compounds, Inc. v. NLRB: *Labor Rights Without Remedies for Undocumented Aliens, in* LABOR LAW STORIES (Laura J. Cooper & Catherine L. Fisk, eds., 2005).

Chapter 4

PROTECTED CONCERTED ACTIVITIES UNDER SECTION 7

Synopsis

As has been discussed in previous chapters, the NLRA seeks to balance employer and employee interests in a labor-management dispute. Section 7 of the Act generally describes the legality of employee concerted activities this way: "Employees shall have the right . . . to engage in . . . concerted activities for the purpose of collective bargaining or other mutual aid or protection." This statutory provision can be seen as dividing what counts as protected conduct under Section 7 into three prongs: (1) concertedness; (2) legitimate purpose; and (3) legitimate means.

As an initial point, it is important to understand that a concerted activity need not be union-sponsored. *See NLRB v. Washington Aluminum Co.*, 370 U.S. 9 (1962). There, the United States Supreme Court held that employees who had taken part in a walkout because they claimed the plant was too cold had engaged in protected activity, even though they were not in a union or organizing to be in a union. Section 7 applies to all employees, regardless of whether they have unionized or made a demand of recognition to their employer. However, as you will see below, such activity must be deemed "concerted" and undertaken for employees' "mutual aid or protection."

The next group of cases considers these elements of protected activity under Section 7.

SECTION 1 CONCERTEDNESS OF THE EMPLOYEE CONDUCT

There is no dispute that concertedness is met when two or more employees act together to achieve a common employment-related goal. It is also true that most courts recognize that an individual employee acts in a concerted manner when he or she speaks as a spokesperson for a group of employees or is trying to persuade other employees to take group action. But what if the individual is merely referencing rights bargained for under a collective-bargaining agreement? Or, as the next problem discusses, what if an individual wants another employee to join him in a disciplinary meeting with the boss?

PROBLEM #1: FACING THE MUSIC, WITH A BUDDY

Ralph Roxy had been a decent, but not great, sales employee at Wonderful Widgets, Inc. Math is not Ralph's strong suit, and he has historically struggled with filling out and submitting expense reimbursement sheets on a timely basis as required by the company. Ralph has been warned before about turning in expense reimbursement sheets, but he continues to hand them in late. The last time, his boss, Wanda Wang, told him that there would be severe consequences the next time he was late with his expense reimbursements.

Inevitably, Ralph was late again, and he received an e-mail that Wanda wanted to see him in her office. After telling his co-worker and friend, Barry Barr, about the trouble he was in, Barry suggested that it might be helpful if he joined Ralph during his meeting with Wanda. Although Ralph eagerly agreed, Wanda told Barry that he could not stay.

Wonderful Widgets is a non-union facility, and there is no organizing drive currently taking place. Can Ralph argue that he and Barry are engaging in concerted activity protected by Section 7 and that Wanda's refusal to allow Barry into the meeting is an unfair labor practice?

PROBLEM MATERIALS

NLRB v. City Disposal Systems, Inc., 465 U.S. 822 (1984)

NLRB v. J. Weingarten, Inc., 420 U.S. 251 (1975)

IBM Corp., 341 N.L.R.B. No. 148 (2004)

NLRB v. CITY DISPOSAL SYSTEMS, INC.
465 U.S. 822 (1984)

JUSTICE BRENNAN delivered the opinion of the Court.

James Brown, a truck driver employed by respondent, was discharged when he refused to drive a truck that he honestly and reasonably believed to be unsafe because of faulty brakes. Article XXI of the collective-bargaining agreement between respondent and Local 247 of the International Brotherhood of Teamsters, Chauffeurs, Warehousemen and Helpers of America, which covered Brown, provides: "[t]he Employer shall not require employees to take out on the streets or highways any vehicle that is not in safe operating condition or equipped with safety appliances prescribed by law. It shall not be a violation of the Agreement where employees refuse to operate such equipment unless such refusal is unjustified."

"Unjustified"

The question to be decided is whether Brown's honest and reasonable assertion of his right to be free of the obligation to drive unsafe trucks constituted "concerted activit[y]" within the meaning of § 7 of the National Labor Relations Act (NLRA or Act). The National Labor Relations Board (NLRB or Board) held that Brown's refusal was concerted activity within § 7, and that his discharge was, therefore, an unfair labor practice under § 8(a)(1) of the Act. The Court of Appeals disagreed and declined enforcement. At least three other Courts of Appeals, however, have accepted the Board's interpretation of "concerted activities" as including the assertion by an individual employee of a right grounded in a collective-bargaining agreement. We granted certiorari to resolve the conflict, and now reverse.

I

The facts are not in dispute in the current posture of this case. Respondent, City Disposal System, Inc. (City Disposal), hauls garbage for the City of Detroit. Under the collective-bargaining agreement with Local Union No. 247, respondent's truck drivers haul garbage from Detroit to a land fill about 37 miles away. Each driver is assigned to operate a particular truck, which he or she operates each day of work, unless that truck is in disrepair.

James Brown was assigned to truck No. 245. On Saturday, May 12, 1979, Brown observed that a fellow driver had difficulty with the brakes of another truck, truck No. 244. As a result of the brake problem, truck No. 244 nearly collided with Brown's truck. After unloading their garbage at the land fill, Brown and the driver of truck No. 244 brought No. 244 to respondent's truck-repair facility, where they were told that the brakes would be repaired either over the weekend or in the morning of Monday, May 14.

Early in the morning of Monday, May 14, while transporting a load of garbage to the land fill, Brown experienced difficulty with one of the wheels of his own truck — No. 245 — and brought that truck in for repair. At the repair facility, Brown was told that, because of a backlog at the facility, No. 245 could not be repaired that day. Brown reported the situation to his supervisor, Otto Jasmund, who ordered Brown to punch out and go home. Before Brown could leave, however, Jasmund changed his mind and asked Brown to drive truck No. 244 instead. Brown refused, explaining that "there's something wrong with that truck. . . . [S]omething was wrong with the brakes . . . there was a grease seal or something leaking causing it to be affecting the brakes." Brown did not, however, explicitly refer to Article XXI of the collective-bargaining agreement or to the agreement in general. In response to Brown's refusal to drive truck No. 244, Jasmund angrily told Brown to go home. At that point, an argument ensued and Robert Madary, another supervisor, intervened, repeating Jasmund's request that Brown drive truck No. 244. Again, Brown refused, explaining that No. 244 "has got problems and I don't want to drive it." Madary replied that half the trucks had problems and that if respondent tried to fix all of them it would be unable to do business. He went on to tell Brown that "[w]e've got all this garbage out here to haul and you tell me about you don't want to drive." Brown responded, "Bob, what you going to do, put the garbage ahead of the safety of the men?" Finally, Madary went to his office and Brown went home. Later that day, Brown received word that he had been discharged. He immediately returned to work in an attempt to gain reinstatement but was unsuccessful.

On May 15, the day after the discharge, Brown filed a written grievance, pursuant to the collective-bargaining agreement, asserting that truck No. 244 was defective, that it had been improper for him to have been ordered to drive the truck, and that his discharge was therefore also improper. The union, however, found no objective merit in the grievance and declined to process it . . . .

II

Section 7 of the NLRA provides that "[e]mployees shall have the right to . . . join or assist labor organizations, to bargain collectively through representatives of their own choosing, and to engage in other concerted activities for the purpose of collective bargaining or other mutual aid or protection." The NLRB's decision in this case applied the Board's longstanding "*Interboro* doctrine," under which an individual's assertion of a right grounded in a collective-bargaining agreement is recognized as "concerted activit[y]" and therefore accorded the protection of § 7. See Interboro Contractors, Inc., 157 N.L.R.B. 1295, 1298 (1966), enforced, 388 F.2d 495 (2d Cir. 1967); Bunney Bros. Construction Co., 139 N.L.R.B. 1516, 1519 (1962). The Board has relied on two justifications for the doctrine: First, the assertion of a right contained in a collective-bargaining agreement is an extension of the concerted action that produced the agreement, *Bunney Bros. Construction, supra*, at 1519; and second, the assertion of such a right affects the rights of all employees covered by the collective-bargaining agreement. *Interboro Contractors, supra*, at 1298.

We have often reaffirmed that the task of defining the scope of § 7 "is for the Board to perform in the first instance as it considers the wide variety of cases that come before it," Eastex, Inc. v. NLRB, 437 U.S. 556, 568 (1978), and, on an issue that implicates its expertise in labor relations, a reasonable construction by the Board is entitled to considerable deference. The question for decision today is thus narrowed to whether the Board's application of § 7 to Brown's refusal to drive truck No. 244 is reasonable. Several reasons persuade us that it is.

A

Neither the Court of Appeals nor respondent appears to question that an employee's invocation of a right derived from a collective-bargaining agreement meets § 7's requirement that an employee's action be taken "for purposes of collective bargaining or other mutual aid or protection." As the Board first explained in the *Interboro* case, a single employee's invocation of such rights affects all the employees that are covered by the collective-bargaining agreement. This type of generalized effect, as our cases have demonstrated, is sufficient to bring the actions of an individual employee within the "mutual aid or protection" standard, regardless of whether the employee has his own interests most immediately in mind.

The term "concerted activit[y]" is not defined in the Act but it clearly enough embraces the activities of employees who have joined together in order to achieve common goals. What is not self-evident from the language of the Act, however, and what we must elucidate, is the precise manner in which particular actions of an individual employee must be linked to the actions of fellow employees in order to permit it to be said that the individual is engaged in concerted activity. We now turn to consider the Board's analysis of that question as expressed in the *Interboro* doctrine.

Although one could interpret the phrase, "to engage in concerted activities," to refer to a situation in which two or more employees are working together at the same time and the same place toward a common goal, the language of § 7 does not confine itself to such a narrow meaning. In fact, § 7 itself defines both joining and assisting labor organizations — activities in which a single employee can engage — as concerted activities. Indeed, even the courts that have rejected the *Interboro* doctrine recognize the possibility that an individual employee may be engaged in concerted activity when he acts alone. They have limited their recognition of this type of concerted activity, however, to two situations: (1) that in which the lone employee intends to induce group activity, and (2) that in which the employee acts as a representative of at least one other employee. The disagreement over the *Interboro* doctrine, therefore, merely reflects differing views regarding the nature of the relationship that must exist between the action of the individual employee and the actions of the group in order for § 7 to apply. We cannot say that the Board's view of that relationship, as applied in the *Interboro* doctrine, is unreasonable.

The invocation of a right rooted in a collective-bargaining agreement is unquestionably an integral part of the process that gave rise to the agreement. That process — beginning with the organization of a union, continuing into the negotiation of a collective-bargaining agreement, and extending through the enforcement of the agreement — is a single, collective activity. Obviously, an employee could not invoke a right grounded in a collective-bargaining agreement were it not for the prior negotiating activities of his fellow employees. Nor would it make sense for a union to negotiate a collective-bargaining agreement if individual employees could not invoke the rights thereby created against their employer. Moreover, when an employee invokes a right grounded in the collective-bargaining agreement, he does not stand alone. Instead, he brings to bear on his employer the power and resolve of all his fellow employees. When, for instance, James Brown refused to drive a truck he believed to be unsafe, he was in effect reminding his employer that he and his fellow employees, at the time their collective-bargaining agreement was signed, had extracted a promise from City Disposal that they would not be asked to drive unsafe trucks. He was also reminding his employer that if it persisted in ordering him to drive an unsafe truck, he could reharness the power of that group to ensure the enforcement of that promise. It was just as though James Brown was reassembling his fellow union members to reenact their decision not to drive unsafe trucks. A lone employee's invocation of a right grounded in his collective-bargaining agreement is, therefore, a concerted activity in a very real sense.

Furthermore, the acts of joining and assisting a labor organization, which § 7 explicitly recognizes as concerted, are related to collective action in essentially the same way that the invocation of a collectively bargained right is related to collective action. When an employee joins or assists a labor organization, his actions may be divorced in time, and in location as well, from the actions of fellow employees. Because of the integral relationship among the employees' actions, however, Congress viewed each employee as engaged in concerted activity. The lone employee could not join or assist a labor organization were it not for the related organizing activities of his fellow employees. Conversely, there would be limited utility in forming a labor organization if other employees could not join or assist the organization once it is formed. Thus, the formation of a labor organization is integrally related to the activity of joining or assisting such an organization in the same sense that the negotiation of a collective-bargaining agreement is integrally related to the invocation of a right provided for in the agreement. In each case, neither the individual activity nor the group activity would be complete without the other.

The *Interboro* doctrine is also entirely consistent with the purposes of the Act, which explicitly include the encouragement of collective bargaining and other "practices fundamental to the friendly adjustment of industrial disputes arising out of differences as to wages, hours, or other working conditions." Although, as we have said, there is nothing in the legislative history of § 7 that specifically expresses the understanding of Congress in enacting the "concerted activities" language, the general history of § 7 reveals no inconsistency between the *Interboro* doctrine and congressional intent. That history begins in the early days of the labor movement, when employers invoked the common law doctrines of criminal conspiracy and restraint of trade to thwart workers' attempts to unionize . . . .

Against this background, it is evident that, in enacting § 7 of the NLRA, Congress sought generally to equalize the bargaining power of the employee with that of his employer by allowing employees to band together in confronting an employer regarding the terms and conditions of their employment. There is no indication that Congress intended to limit this protection to situations in which an employee's activity and that of his fellow employees combine with one another in any particular way. Nor, more specifically, does it appear that Congress intended to have this general protection withdrawn in situations in which a single employee, acting alone, participates in an integral aspect of a collective process. Instead, what emerges from the general background of § 7 — and what is consistent with the Act's statement of purpose — is a congressional intent to create an equality in bargaining power between the employee and the employer throughout the entire process of labor organizing, collective bargaining, and enforcement of collective-bargaining agreements.

The Board's *Interboro* doctrine, based on a recognition that the potential inequality in the relationship between the employee and the employer continues beyond the point at which a collective-bargaining agreement is signed, mitigates that inequality throughout the duration of the employment relationship, and is, therefore, fully consistent with congressional intent. Moreover, by applying § 7 to the actions of individual employees invoking their rights under a collective-bargaining agreement, the *Interboro* doctrine preserves the integrity of the entire collective-bargaining process; for by invoking a right grounded in a collective-bargaining agreement, the employee makes that right a reality, and breathes life, not only into the promises contained in the collective-bargaining agreement, but also into the entire process envisioned by Congress as the means by which to achieve industrial peace . . . .

In practice, however, there is unlikely to be a bright-line distinction between an incipient grievance, a complaint to an employer, and perhaps even an employee's initial refusal to perform a certain job that he believes he has no duty to perform. It is reasonable to expect that an employee's first response to a situation that he believes violates his collective-bargaining agreement will be a protest to his employer. Whether he files a grievance will depend in part on his employer's reaction and in part upon the nature of the right at issue. In addition, certain rights might not be susceptible of enforcement by the filing of a grievance. In such a case, the collective-bargaining agreement might provide for an alternative method of enforcement, as did the agreement involved in this case, or the agreement might be silent on the matter. Thus, for a variety of reasons, an employee's initial statement to an employer to the effect that he believes a collectively bargained right is being violated, or the employee's initial refusal to do that which he believes he is not obligated to do, might serve as both a natural prelude to, and an efficient substitute for, the filing of a formal grievance. As long as the employee's statement or action is based on a reasonable and honest belief that he is being, or has been, asked to perform a task that he is not required to perform under his collective-bargaining agreement, and the statement or action is reasonably directed toward the enforcement of a collectively bargained right, there is no justification for overturning the Board's judgment that the employee is engaged in concerted activity, just as he would have been had he filed a formal grievance.

The fact that an activity is concerted, however, does not necessarily mean that an employee can engage in the activity with impunity. An employee may engage in concerted activity in such an abusive manner that he loses the protection of § 7. Furthermore, if an employer does not wish to tolerate certain methods by which employees invoke their collectively bargained rights, he is free to negotiate a provision in his collective-bargaining agreement that limits the availability of such methods. No-strike provisions, for instance, are a common mechanism by which employers and employees agree that the latter will not invoke their rights by refusing to work. In general, if an employee violates such a provision, his activity is unprotected even though it may be concerted. Whether Brown's action in this case was unprotected, however, is not before us . . . .

III

In this case, the Board found that James Brown's refusal to drive truck No. 244 was based on an honest and reasonable belief that the brakes on the truck were faulty. Brown explained to each of his supervisors his reason for refusing to drive the truck. Although he did not refer to his collective-bargaining agreement in either of these confrontations, the agreement provided not only that "[t]he Employer shall not require employees to take out on the streets or highways any vehicle that is not in safe operating condition," but also that "[i]t shall not be a violation of the Agreement where employees refuse to operate such equipment, unless such refusal is unjustified." There is no doubt, therefore, nor could there have been any doubt during Brown's confrontations with his supervisors, that by refusing to drive truck No. 244, Brown was invoking the right granted him in his collective-bargaining agreement to be free of the obligation to drive unsafe trucks. Moreover, there can be no question but that Brown's refusal to drive the truck was reasonably well directed toward the enforcement of that right. Indeed, it would appear that there were no other means available by which Brown could have enforced the right. If he had gone ahead and driven truck No. 244, the issue may have been moot.

Respondent argues that Brown's action was not concerted because he did not explicitly refer to the collective-bargaining agreement as a basis for his refusal to drive the truck. The Board, however, has never held that an employee must make such an explicit reference for his actions to be covered by the *Interboro* doctrine, and we find that position reasonable . . . . As long as the nature of the employee's complaint is reasonably clear to the person to whom it is communicated, and the complaint does, in fact, refer to a reasonably perceived violation of the collective-bargaining agreement, the complaining employee is engaged in the process of enforcing that agreement. In the context of a workplace dispute, where the participants are likely to be unsophisticated in collective-bargaining matters, a requirement that the employee explicitly refer to the collective-bargaining agreement is likely to serve as nothing more than a trap for the unwary . . . .

In this case, because Brown reasonably and honestly invoked his right to avoid driving unsafe trucks, his action was concerted. It may be that the collective-bargaining agreement prohibits an employee from refusing to drive a truck that he reasonably believes to be unsafe, but that is, in fact, perfectly safe. If so, Brown's action was concerted but unprotected. As stated above, however, the only issue before this Court and the only issue passed upon by the Board or the Court of Appeals is whether Brown's action was concerted, not whether it was protected . . . .

JUSTICE O'CONNOR, dissenting [opinion omitted].

NLRB v. J. WEINGARTEN, INC.
420 U.S. 251 (1975)

JUSTICE BRENNAN delivered the opinion of the Court.

The National Labor Relations Board held in this case that respondent employer's denial of an employee's request that her union representative be present at an investigatory interview which the employee reasonably believed might result in disciplinary action constituted an unfair labor practice in violation of § 8(a)(1) of the National Labor Relations Act, because it interfered with, restrained, and coerced the individual right of the employee, protected by § 7 of the Act, 'to engage in . . . concerted activities for . . . mutual aid or protection . . . .' The Court of Appeals for the Fifth Circuit held that this was an impermissible construction of § 7 and refused to enforce the Board's order that directed respondent to cease and desist from requiring any employee to take part in an investigatory interview without union representation if the employee requests representation and reasonably fears disciplinary action . . . . We reverse.

I

Respondent operates a chain of some 100 retail stores with lunch counters at some, and so-called lobby food operations at others, dispensing food to take out or eat on the premises. Respondent's sales personnel are represented for collective-bargaining purposes by Retail Clerks Union, Local 455. Leura Collins, one of the sales personnel, worked at the lunch counter at Store No. 2 from 1961 to 1970 when she was transferred to the lobby operation at Store No. 98. Respondent maintains a companywide security department staffed by "Loss Prevention Specialists" who work undercover in all stores to guard against loss from shoplifting and employee dishonesty. In June 1972, "Specialist" Hardy, without the knowledge of the store manager, spent two days observing the lobby operation at Store No. 98 investigating a report that Collins was taking money from a cash register. When Hardy's surveillance of Collins at work turned up no evidence to support the report, Hardy disclosed his presence to the store manager and reported that he could find nothing wrong. The store manager then told him that a fellow lobby employee of Collins had just reported that Collins had purchased a box of chicken that sold for $2.98, but had placed only $1 in the cash register. Collins was summoned to an interview with Specialist Hardy and the store manager, and Hardy questioned her. The Board found that several times during the questioning she asked the store manager to call the union shop steward or some other union representative to the interview, and that her requests were denied. Collins admitted that she had purchased some chicken, a loaf of bread, and some cake which she said she paid for and donated to her church for a church dinner. She explained that she purchased four pieces of chicken for which the price was $1, but that because the lobby department was out of the small-size boxes in which such purchases were usually packaged she put the chicken into the larger box normally used for packaging larger quantities. Specialist Hardy left the interview to check Collins' explanation with the fellow employee who had reported Collins. This employee confirmed that the lobby department had run out of small boxes and also said that she did not know how many pieces of chicken Collins had put in the larger box. Specialist Hardy returned to the interview, told Collins that her explanation had checked out, that he was sorry if he had inconvenienced her, and that the matter was closed.

Collins thereupon burst into tears and blurted out that the only thing she had ever gotten from the store without paying for it was her free lunch. This revelation surprised the store manager and Hardy because, although free lunches had been provided at Store No. 2 when Collins worked at the lunch counter there, company policy was not to provide free lunches at stores operating lobby departments. In consequence, the store manager and Specialist Hardy closely interrogated Collins about violations of the policy in the lobby department at Store No. 98. Collins again asked that a shop steward be called to the interview, but the store manager denied her request. Based on her answers to his questions, Specialist Hardy prepared a written statement which included a computation that Collins owed the store approximately $160 for lunches. Collins refused to sign the statement. The Board found that Collins, as well as most, if not all, employees in the lobby department of Store No. 98, including the manager of that department, took lunch from the lobby without paying for it, apparently because no contrary policy was ever made known to them. Indeed, when company headquarters advised Specialist Hardy by telephone during the interview that headquarters itself was uncertain whether the policy against providing free lunches at lobby departments was in effect at Store No. 98, he terminated his interrogation of Collins. The store manager asked Collins not to discuss the matter with anyone because he considered it a private matter between her and the company, of no concern to others. Collins, however, reported the details of the interview fully to her shop steward and other union representatives, and this unfair labor practice proceeding resulted.

II

The Board's construction that § 7 creates a statutory right in an employee to refuse to submit without union representation to an interview which he reasonably fears may result in his discipline was announced in its decision and order of January 28, 1972, in Quality Mfg. Co., 195 N.L.R.B. 197 . . . .

First, the right inheres in § 7's guarantee of the right of employees to act in concert for mutual aid and protection. In Mobil Oil, the Board stated:

> An employee's right to union representation upon request is based on Section 7 of the Act which guarantees the right of employees to act in concert for "mutual aid and protection." The denial of this right has a reasonable tendency to interfere with, restrain, and coerce employees in violation of Section 8(a)(1) of the Act. Thus, it is a serious violation of the employee's individual right to engage in concerted activity by seeking the assistance of his statutory representative if the employer denies the employee's request and compels the employee to appear unassisted at an interview which may put his job security in jeopardy. Such a dilution of the employee's right to act collectively to protect his job interests is, in our view, unwarranted interference with his right to insist on concerted protection, rather than individual self-protection, against possible adverse employer action.

Second, the right arises only in situations where the employee requests representation. In other words, the employee may forgo his guaranteed right and, if he prefers, participate in an interview unaccompanied by his union representative.

Third, the employee's right to request representation as a condition of participation in an interview is limited to situations where the employee reasonably believes the investigation will result in disciplinary action. Thus the Board stated in Quality:

> We would not apply the rule to such run-of-the-mill shop-floor conversation as, for example, the giving of instructions or training or needed corrections of work techniques. In such cases there cannot normally be any reasonable basis for an employee to fear that any adverse impact may result from the interview, and thus we would then see no reasonable basis for him to seek the assistance of his representative.

Fourth, exercise of the right may not interfere with legitimate employer prerogatives. The employer has no obligation to justify his refusal to allow union representation, and despite refusal, the employer is free to carry on his inquiry without interviewing the employee, and thus leave to the employee the choice between having an interview unaccompanied by his representative, or having no interview and forgoing any benefits that might be derived from one. As stated in Mobil Oil:

> "The employer may, if it wishes, advise the employee that it will not proceed with the interview unless the employee is willing to enter the interview unaccompanied by his representative. The employee may then refrain from participating in the interview, thereby protecting his right to

representation, but at the same time relinquishing any benefit which might be derived from the interview. The employer would then be free to act on the basis of information obtained from other sources." 196 N.L.R.B., at 1052.

The Board explained in Quality:

> This seems to us to be the only course consistent with all of the provisions of our Act. It permits the employer to reject a collective course in situations such as investigative interviews where a collective course is not required but protects the employee's right to protection by his chosen agents. Participation in the interview is then voluntary, and, if the employee has reasonable ground to fear that the interview will adversely affect his continued employment, or even his working conditions, he may choose to forego it unless he is afforded the safeguard of his representative's presence. He would then also forego whatever benefit might come from the interview. And, in that event, the employer would, of course, be free to act on the basis of whatever information he had and without such additional facts as might have been gleaned through the interview.

Fifth, the employer has no duty to bargain with any union representative who may be permitted to attend the investigatory interview. The Board said in Mobil, "we are not giving the Union any particular rights with respect to predisciplinary discussions which it otherwise was not able to secure during collective-bargaining negotiations." The Board thus adhered to its decisions distinguishing between disciplinary and investigatory interviews, imposing a mandatory affirmative obligation to meet with the union representative only in the case of the disciplinary interview. The employer has no duty to bargain with the union representative at an investigatory interview. "The representative is present to assist the employee, and may attempt to clarify the facts or suggest other employees who may have knowledge of them. The employer, however, is free to insist that he is only interested, at that time, in hearing the employee's own account of the matter under investigation." Brief for Petitioner, at 22.

III

The Board's holding is a permissible construction of "concerted activities for . . . mutual aid or protection" by the agency charged by Congress with enforcement of the Act, and should have been sustained.

The action of an employee in seeking to have the assistance of his union representative at a confrontation with his employer clearly falls within the literal wording of § 7 that "(e)mployees shall have the right . . . to engage in . . . concerted activities for the purpose of . . . mutual aid or protection." This is true even though the employee alone may have an immediate stake in the outcome; he seeks "aid or protection" against a perceived threat to his employment security. The union representative whose participation he seeks is, however, safeguarding not only the particular employee's interest, but also the interests of the entire bargaining unit by exercising vigilance to make certain that the employer does not initiate or continue a practice of imposing punishment unjustly. The representative's presence is an assurance to other employees in the bargaining unit that they, too, can obtain his aid and protection if called upon to attend a like interview. Concerted activity for mutual aid or protection is therefore as present here as it was held to be in NLRB v. Peter Cailler Kohler Swiss Chocolates Co., 130 F.2d 503, 505-506 (2d Cir. 1942), cited with approval by this Court in Houston Contractors Assn. v. NLRB, 386 U.S. 664, 668–669 (1967):

> "When all the other workmen in a shop make common cause with a fellow workman over his separate grievance, and go out on strike in his support, they engage in a 'concerted activity' for 'mutual aid or protection,' although the aggrieved workman is the only one of them who has any immediate stake in the outcome. The rest know that by their action each of them assures himself, in case his turn ever comes, of the support of the one whom they are all then helping; and the solidarity so established is 'mutual aid' in the most literal sense, as nobody doubts."

The Board's construction plainly effectuates the most fundamental purposes of the Act. In § 1, the Act declares that it is a goal of national labor policy to protect "the exercise by workers of full freedom of association, self-organization, and designation of representatives of their own choosing, for the purpose of . . . mutual aid or protection." To that end the Act is designed to eliminate the "inequality of bargaining power between employees . . . and employers." Requiring a lone employee to attend an investigatory interview which he reasonably believes may result in the imposition of discipline perpetuates the inequality the Act was designed to eliminate, and bars recourse to the safeguards the Act provided "to redress the perceived imbalance of economic power between labor and management." American Ship Building Co. v. NLRB, 380 U.S. 300, 316 (1965). Viewed in this light, the Board's recognition that § 7 guarantees an employee's right to the presence of a union representative at an investigatory interview in which the risk of discipline reasonably inheres is within the protective ambit of the section "read in the light of the mischief to be corrected and the end to be attained." NLRB v. Hearst Publications, Inc., 322 U.S. 111, 124 (1944).

The Board's construction also gives recognition to the right when it is most useful to both employee and employer. A single employee confronted by an employer investigating whether certain conduct deserves discipline may be too fearful or inarticulate to relate accurately the incident being investigated, or too ignorant to raise extenuating factors. A knowledgeable union representative could assist the employer by eliciting favorable facts, and save the employer production time by getting to the bottom of the incident occasioning the interview. Certainly his presence need not transform the interview into an adversary contest. Respondent suggests nonetheless that union representation at this stage is unnecessary because a decision as to employee culpability or disciplinary action can be corrected after the decision to impose discipline has become final. In other words, respondent would defer representation until the filing of a formal grievance challenging the employer's determination of guilt after the employee has been discharged or otherwise disciplined. At that point, however, it becomes increasingly difficult for the employee to vindicate himself, and the value of representation is correspondingly diminished. The employer may then be more concerned with justifying his actions than re-examining them.

IV

. . . The statutory right confirmed today is in full harmony with actual industrial practice. Many important collective-bargaining agreements have provisions that accord employees rights of union representation at investigatory interviews. Even where such a right is not explicitly provided in the agreement a "well-established current of arbitral authority" sustains the right of union representation at investigatory interviews which the employee reasonably believes may result in disciplinary action against him.

The judgment is reversed and the case is remanded with direction to enter a judgment enforcing the Board's order.

JUSTICE POWELL, dissenting [opinion omitted].

IBM Corp.
341 N.L.R.B. No. 148 (2004)

By CHAIRMAN BATTISTA and MEMBERS LIEBMAN, SCHAUMBER, WALSH, and MEISBURG

The sole issue in this case is whether the Respondent, whose employees are not represented by a union, violated Section 8(a)(1) of the Act by denying the Charging Parties' requests to have a coworker present during investigatory interviews. The judge, applying the Board's decision in *Epilepsy Foundation of Northeast Ohio*, 331 NLRB 676 (2000), found that the Respondent violated the Act by denying the Charging Parties' requests for the presence of a coworker.

The Respondent urges the Board to overrule *Epilepsy Foundation* and return to the principles of *E. I. du Pont & Co.*, 289 NLRB 627 (1988). In that case, the Board refused to apply the principles of *NLRB v. J. Weingarten*, 420 U.S. 251 (1975), in a nonunionized setting to permit an employee to have a coworker present at an investigatory interview that the employee reasonably believed might result in discipline . . . .

Having carefully considered the entire record in this proceeding, including the briefs of the Respondent and the various amici curiae, we have decided, for the reasons set forth below, to overrule *Epilepsy Foundation* and to return to earlier Board precedent holding that the *Weingarten* right does not extend to a workplace where, as here, the employees are not represented by a union . . . .

Facts

On October 15, 2001, the Respondent, prompted by allegations of harassment contained in a letter it received from a former employee, interviewed each of the Charging Parties. None of them requested the presence of a witness during the October 15 interviews. On October 22, the Respondent's manager, Nels Maine, denied Charging Party Bannon's request to have a coworker or an attorney present at an interview scheduled for the next day. On October 23, Maine interviewed each of the Charging Parties individually after denying each employee's request to have a coworker present during the interview. All three employees were discharged approximately a month after the interviews . . . .

Analysis and Conclusions

After careful reexamination of the rationale of *Epilepsy Foundation*, we find that national labor relations policy will be best served by overruling existing precedent and returning to the earlier precedent of *du Pont*, which holds that *Weingarten* rights do not apply in a nonunion setting.

A. The Issue of Whether to hold that Weingarten Rights Apply or do not Apply in a Nonunionized Workplace Requires the Board to Choose Between two Permissible Interpretations of the Act

We agree with the Board's conclusion in *du Pont* . . . that a holding that *Weingarten* rights do not apply in a nonunionized workplace involves a permissible construction of the Act, and that a holding that they do apply is also a permissible construction . . . .

We agree with the Board's position on remand in *du Pont*, and find that the Board's decision in that case is a permissible interpretation of the Act. By the same token, we acknowledge that the Board's decision in *Epilepsy Foundation* extending the *Weingarten* right to the nonunionized workplace is also a permissible interpretation of the Act. Because there is Board precedent in this area presenting two permissible interpretations of the statute, the decision as to which approach to follow is a matter of policy for the Board to decide in its discretion. "It is the Board's duty to choose amongst permissible interpretations of the Act to best effectuate its overarching goals."

B. The Reexamination of Epilepsy Foundation is a Proper Exercise of the Board's Adjudicative Authority

In choosing today to return to the permissible interpretation set out in *du Pont*, we engage in a process both anticipated and approved by the Supreme Court in *Weingarten*. There, the Court noted that the Board had overruled its earlier precedent by recognizing the right of an employee to refuse to submit, without union representation, to an investigatory interview that the employee reasonably believes may result in disciplinary action. The Court approved the Board's action, finding that the Board was free to reexamine past constructions of the Act. Indeed, the Court observed that it was in the nature of administrative decisionmaking to do so. Thus the Court stated:

> "Cumulative experience" begets understanding and insight by which judgments . . . are validated or qualified or invalidated. The constant process of trial and error, on a wider and fuller scale than a single adversary litigation permits, differentiates perhaps more than anything else the administrative from the judicial process."

Our reexamination of *Epilepsy Foundation* leads us to conclude that the policy considerations supporting that decision do not warrant, particularly at this time, adherence to the holding in *Epilepsy Foundation.* In recent years, there have been many changes in the workplace environment, including ever-increasing requirements to conduct workplace investigations, as well as new security concerns raised by incidents of national and workplace violence.

Our consideration of these features of the contemporary workplace leads us to conclude that an employer must be allowed to conduct its required investigations in a thorough, sensitive, and confidential manner. This can best be accomplished by permitting an employer in a nonunion setting to investigate an employee without the presence of a coworker.

C. Policy Considerations Underlying Board Precedent Concerning Application of the Weingarten Right

The history of an employee's right to have a representative present during an investigatory interview begins with the Supreme Court's decision in *Weingarten.* The Supreme Court there held that an employer violates Section 8(a)(1) of the Act by denying an employee's request to have a union representative present at an investigatory interview which the employee reasonably believes might result in disciplinary action. The Court explained that the right to the presence of a representative is derived from Section 7 of the Act giving employees the right to engage in concerted activities for mutual aid or protection. The Court stated that the union representative whom an employee seeks to include in an interview "safeguard[s] not only the particular employee's interest, but also the interests of the entire bargaining unit . . . ." The Court also recognized that the Act was designed to eliminate a perceived imbalance of power between labor and management and that "[r]equiring a lone employee to attend an investigatory interview . . . perpetuates the inequality the Act was designed to eliminate, and bars recourse to the safeguards the Act provided . . . ." Additionally, the Court observed that because an employee attending an interview by himself may not have the wherewithal to protect or defend himself, a "knowledgeable union representative could assist the employer by eliciting favorable facts, and save the employer production time by getting to the bottom of the incident occasioning the interview." The Court concluded that the right to the presence of a union representative comported with actual industrial practice, noting that collective-bargaining contracts often contained provisions affording the right of union representation at interviews.

Weingarten did not address the situation in which an employee of a nonunionized employer asks for a coworker to be present as his representative at an investigatory interview . . . .

DuPont remained the law for 12 years until it was overruled in *Epilepsy Foundation.* The Board in *Epilepsy Foundation* emphasized that the right to representation is grounded in Section 7 of the Act which protects the right of employees to engage in concerted activities for mutual aid or protection, and that "Section 7 rights are enjoyed by all employees and are in no wise dependent on union representation for their implementation." The Board also rejected, as "wholly speculative," the claims, stated in *du Pont*, that coworker representatives do not represent the interests of the whole work force, or that they lack the ability to provide effective representation, or that an employee whose employer decides to forego an interview is left without a chance to tell his story.

D. Policy Considerations Support the Denial of the Weingarten Right in the Nonunionized Workplace

In reviewing the policy considerations underlying the application of the *Weingarten* right, we follow the teaching of the *Weingarten* Court that the Board has a duty "to adapt the Act to changing patterns of industrial life . . . . [T]he Board has the 'special function of applying the general provisions of the Act to the complexities of industrial life." The years after the issuance of *Weingarten* have seen a rise in the need for investigatory interviews, both in response to new statutes governing the workplace and as a response to new security concerns raised by terrorist attacks on our country. Employers face ever-increasing requirements to conduct workplace investigations pursuant to federal, state, and local laws, particularly laws addressing workplace discrimination and sexual harassment. We are especially cognizant of the rise in the number of instances of workplace violence, as well as the increase in the number of incidents of corporate abuse and fiduciary lapses. Further, because of the events of September 11, 2001, and their aftermath, we must now take into account the presence of both real and threatened terrorist attacks. Because of these events, the policy considerations expressed in *du Pont* have taken on a new vitality. Thus, for the reasons set forth below, we reaffirm, and find even more forceful, the result and the rationale of *DuPont*. We hold that the *Weingarten* right does not extend to the nonunion workplace.

1. Coworkers do not represent the interests of the entire work force. In *Weingarten*, the Supreme Court emphasized that a union representative accompanying a unit employee to an investigatory interview represents and "safeguards" the interests of the entire bargaining unit. This is so because the unit employees have selected a union as their bargaining representative and the union has delegated to its officials the authority to act on its behalf for the entire unit. The union's officials are bound by the duty of fair representation to represent the entire unit. Whatever the union representative accomplishes inures to the benefit of the entire unit, not just to the individual employee.

A coworker in a nonunion setting, on the other hand, has no such obligation to represent the entire work force. There is no legally defined collective interest to represent, because there is no defined group, i.e., a bargaining unit, with common interests defined by a collective-bargaining contract. Additionally, because there is no group to represent, there is typically no designated representative. Rather, the choice of a representative is done on an ad hoc basis and the identity of the representative may change from one employee interview to the next. Moreover, a coworker does not have the same incentive to serve the interests of the group as does a union representative. The coworker is present to act as a witness for and to lend support to the employee being interviewed. It is speculative to find that a coworker would think beyond the immediate situation in which he has been asked to participate and look to set precedent. A coworker has neither the legal duty nor the personal incentive to act in the same manner as a union representative.

2. Coworkers cannot redress the imbalance of power between employers and

employees. In *Weingarten*, the Supreme Court recognized that one of the purposes of the Act is to protect workers in the exercise of concerted activities for their mutual aid or protection. The presence of a union representative at a meeting with an employer puts both parties on a level playing field inasmuch as the union representative has the full collective force of the bargaining unit behind him.

Additionally, a union representative has a different status in his relationship with an employer than does a coworker. The union representative typically is accustomed to dealing with the employer on a regular basis concerning matters other than those prompting the interview. Their ongoing relationship has the benefit of aiding in the development of a body of consistent practices concerning workplace issues and contributes to a speedier and more efficient resolution of the problem requiring the investigation.

This is not true in a nonunion setting. Unlike a union representative, a coworker chosen on an ad hoc basis does not have the force of the bargaining unit behind him. A coworker does not usually have a union representative's knowledge of the workplace and its politics. Because the coworker typically is chosen on an ad hoc basis, he has no "official status" that he can bring to the interview. In other words, a coworker is far less able to "level the playing field," for there is no contract from which he derives his authority and he typically has no other matters to discuss with an employer.

3. Coworkers do not have the same skills as a union representative. The Supreme Court in *Weingarten* recognized the unique skills that a union representative brings to an investigatory interview: a "knowledgeable" union representative can facilitate the interview by "eliciting favorable facts," clarifying issues, and eliminating extraneous material, all of which save the employer valuable production time. A union representative is accustomed to administering collective-bargaining agreements and is familiar with the "law of the shop," both of which provide the framework for any disciplinary action an employer might take against a unit member. A union representative's experience allows him to propose solutions to workplace issues and thus try to avoid the filing of a grievance by an aggrieved employee.

A coworker is unlikely to bring such skills to an interview primarily because he has no experience as the statutory representative of a group of employees. It is likely that a coworker is chosen out of some personal connection with the employee undergoing the interview and while that coworker may provide moral and emotional support, it should not be expected that he could skillfully assist in facilitating the interview or resolving the issues. Moreover, it is possible that a coworker, with enthusiasm but with no training or experience in labor relations matters, could actually frustrate or impede the employer's investigation because of his personal or emotional connection to the employee being interviewed.

Finally, an employee being interviewed may request as his representative a coworker who may, in fact, be a participant in the incident requiring the investigation, as a "coconspirator." It can hardly be gainsaid that it is more difficult to arrive at the truth when employees involved in the same incident represent each other. By contrast, the union representative in a unionized setting can offer more objective assistance. The *Epilepsy* result does not take into account the significant policy considerations relevant to a nonunion work force. The critical difference between a unionized work force and a nonunion work force is that the employer in the latter situation can deal with employees on an individual basis. The Board's decision in *Epilepsy* does not take cognizance of that distinction. It forbids the employer from dealing with the employee on an individual basis. Thus, for this reason as well, grounded in national labor policy, we choose not to follow *Epilepsy.* Further in this regard, our colleagues suggest that the term "dealing" is confined to the Section 2(5) definition of "labor organization." That is not true. The Board uses the phrase "dealing" to condemn direct contacts between a unionized employer and employees. Our point is that, prior to *Epilepsy*, a nonunion employer could have such contacts with individual employees. Today we return to that doctrine.

4. The presence of a coworker may compromise the confidentiality of information. Employers have the legal obligation, pursuant to a variety of Federal, State, and local laws, administrative requirements, and court decisions, to provide their workers with safe and secure workplace environments. A relatively new fact of industrial life is the need for employers to conduct all kinds of investigations of matters occurring in the workplace to ensure compliance with these legal require- ments. An employer must take steps to prevent sexual and racial harassment, to avoid the use of toxic chemicals, to provide a drug-free and violence-free workplace, to resolve issues involving employee health matters, and the like. Employers may have to investigate employees because of substance abuse allegations, improper computer and internet usage, and allegations of theft, violence, sabotage, and embezzlement.

Employer investigations into these matters require discretion and confidential- ity. The guarantee of confidentiality helps an employer resolve challenging issues of credibility involving these sensitive, often personal, subjects. The effectiveness of a fact-finding interview in sensitive situations often depends on whether an employee is alone. If information obtained during an interview is later divulged, even inadvertently, the employee involved could suffer serious embarrassment and damage to his reputation and/or personal relationships and the employer's investi- gation could be compromised by inability to get the truth about workplace incidents.

Union representatives, by virtue of their legal duty of fair representation, may not, in bad faith, reveal or misuse the information obtained in an employee interview. A union representative's fiduciary duty to all unit employees helps to assure confidentiality for the employer.

A coworker, however, is under no similar legal constraint. A coworker represen- tative has no fiduciary duty to the employee being questioned or to the workplace as a whole. Further, it is more likely that a coworker representative in casual conversation among other coworkers and friends in the workplace, could inadver- tently "let slip" confidential, sensitive, or embarrassing information. Not only is this upsetting to the employee directly affected, it also interferes with an employer's ability to conduct an effective internal investigation. The possibility that information will not be kept confidential greatly reduces the chance that the employer will get the whole truth about a workplace event. It also increases the likelihood that employees with information about sensitive subjects will not come forward.

To be sure, under *Weingarten* and *Epilepsy*, the employer can conduct the investigation without the presence of the employee. However, in many situations, the employer will want to hear the story "from the horse's mouth", i.e., directly from the employee. *Weingarten* and *Epilepsy* foreclose that approach unless the employee is granted the presence of another employee.

The presence of the other employee causes its own problems. As discussed above, the presence of the other employee may well inhibit the targeted employee from candidly answering the questions posed by the employer. And, if he does candidly respond, there is a concern that the assisting employee will reveal to others what was said. Finally, the employer may have an interest in keeping quiet the fact of the inquiry and the substance of the questions asked. There is a danger that an assisting employee will spread the word about the inquiry and reveal the questions, thereby undermining that employer interest.

We recognize that many of these same concerns exist in a unionized setting as well. However, the dangers are far less when the assisting person is an experienced union representative with fiduciary obligations and a continuing interest in having an amicable relationship with the employer . . . .

E. On Balance, Policy Considerations Favor Overruling Epilepsy Foundation

. . . Our examination and analysis of all these factors lead us to conclude that, on balance, the right of an employee to a coworker's presence in the absence of a union is outweighed by an employer's right to conduct prompt, efficient, thorough, and confidential workplace investigations. It is our opinion that limiting this right to employees in unionized workplaces strikes the proper balance between the competing interests of the employer and employees.

We recognize, as did the *du Pont* Board, that the parties to a workplace investigation have the option to forego an interview, which allows the employer to reach a conclusion and impose discipline based on its independent findings. We further recognize, however, that this approach is not optimal for either side and forces what could be an unsatisfactory conclusion based on something less than the whole truth. Further, under today's statutory schemes, foregoing the employee interview leaves an employer open to charges that it did not conduct a fair and thorough investigation, which in turn exposes the employer to possible legal liability based on a claim that unfair discipline was imposed based on incomplete information. As for the employee involved, if the interview is not held, he loses the chance to tell his version of the incident under investigation because there typically is no grievance procedure in a nonunion setting to provide an alternative forum. This, in essence, forces the employer to act on what may possibly be, at best, incomplete information and, at worst, erroneous information.

As we stated in *du Pont*, we do not deny that "an employee in a workplace without union representation might welcome the support of a fellow employee . . . [and] that, in some circumstances, the presence of such a person might aid the employee or both the employee and the employer." Our decision today, however, does not leave employees without recourse to other procedures which provide a measure of due process in the nonunionized workplace. For example, there are a variety of alternative dispute resolution processes available, such as peer mediation.

Employees also may seek the presence of an ombudsman in their workplace to investigate complaints and help achieve an equitable solution. Finally, there are "whistleblower" statutes, which protect employees from employer retribution.

. . . Applying the law we fashion today to the facts of the present case, we find that the Charging Parties were not entitled to the presence of a coworker during the interviews the Respondent conducted on October 23. Accordingly, we dismiss the complaint.

MEMBER SCHAUMBER, concurring [opinion omitted].

MEMBERS LIEBMAN and WALSH, dissenting.

Today, American workers without unions, the overwhelming majority of employees, are stripped of a right integral to workplace democracy. Abruptly overruling *Epilepsy Foundation of Northeast Ohio*, a recent decision upheld on appeal as "both clear and reasonable," the majority holds that nonunion employees are not entitled to have a coworker present when their employer conducts an investigatory interview that could lead to discipline.

Under Section 7 of the National Labor Relations Act, all workers, union represented or not, have the "right to . . . engage in . . . concerted activities for the purpose of . . . mutual aid or protection." It is hard to imagine an act more basic to "mutual aid or protection" than turning to a coworker for help when faced with an interview that might end with the employee fired. In its *Weingarten* decision, the Supreme Court recognized that union-represented workers have a right to representation. But the majority rejects the same right for workers without a union — second-class citizens of the workplace, it seems. According to the majority, nonunion workers are not capable of representing each other effectively and therefore have no right to representation. With little interest in empirical evidence, the majority confidently says that recognizing such a right would make it impossible for nonunion employers to conduct effective workplace investigations and so would endanger the workplace.

Due process in the nonunion workplace should not be sacrificed on such dubious grounds. Workers without unions can and do successfully stand up for each other on the job — and they have the legal right to try, whether or not they succeed. The majority's predictions of harm, in turn, are baseless. There is no evidence before the Board that coworker representatives have interfered with a single employer investigation since *Epilepsy Foundation* issued in 2000. We are told instead that everything has changed in "today's troubled world," following "terrorist attacks on our country," the rise of workplace violence, and an increase in "corporate abuse and fiduciary lapses." But allowing workers to represent each other has no conceivable connection with workplace violence and precious little with corporate wrongdoing, which in any case seems concentrated in the executive suite, not the employee cubicle or the factory floor. Finally, we would hope that the American workplace has not yet become a new front in the war on terrorism and that the Board would not be leading the charge, unbidden by other authorities.

As we will explain, the right to coworker representation, in nonunion workplaces as well as in unionized ones, has a strong foundation in the Act. Two of our colleagues, at least, recognize that *Epilepsy Foundation* is "a permissible interpretation of the Act," but they invoke "policy considerations" (which a third colleague joins) for refusing to adhere to it. To the extent that the majority raises any legitimate concerns, they easily can be accommodated without abandoning that right, which — as applied in unionized workplaces and as it presumably would apply in nonunion workplaces — is quite limited. Under the Board's application of *Weingarten*: the employer has the option to forego an interview; the union representative may not obstruct an investigation; the right to have a witness present does not apply to every conversation or workplace matter; and the employer has no duty to "bargain with" the representative.

I.

The right to representation in nonunion workplaces has had a surprisingly fitful history. Our colleagues now aim to bury the right forever. "[T]he matter can now be set to rest," they say. We beg to differ.

. . . What is at stake is the Act's guarantees for workers who are not represented by a union, today the great majority of American workers. The Act applies to these workers, whether they know it or not, and whether or not the Board is prepared to give full recognition to that fact. As one commentator has observed, before *Epilepsy Foundation*, the "scope of coverage of section 7 and its application to nonunion employees may have been one of the best-kept secrets of labor law." However obscure that coverage is, it is well established, if now endangered . . . .

In contrast, we adhere to the view of the *Epilepsy Foundation* Board and the *Materials Research* Board before it. We believe, in other words, that the Supreme Court's decision in *Weingarten* supports the right to representation, even in nonunion settings, because that right is grounded in Section 7 and because the "right to have a coworker present at an investigatory interview . . . greatly enhances the employees' opportunities to act in concert to address their concern 'that the employer does not initiate or continue a practice of imposing punishment unjustly.' " . . .

The majority now eliminates the *Weingarten* right for nonunion workers, leaving intact only the protection against discharge or discipline based on the mere request for a coworker representative . . . .

III.

Chairman Battista and Member Meisburg acknowledge that the Board's decision in *Epilepsy Foundation* is "a permissible interpretation of the Act," but invoke "policy considerations" for refusing to adhere to it, and Member Schaumber endorses those considerations. The decision to overrule a recent precedent, carefully reasoned and upheld in the courts, should be based on far more compelling reasons than our colleagues have articulated. Before examining the reasons actually offered, it is worth emphasizing what (besides justifying a departure from the doctrine of stare decisis) those reasons must accomplish. They must explain either why there is no Section 7 right implicated here or why, on balance, that right is outweighed — in every case, regardless of the circumstances — by other considerations that the Board legitimately can give weight. The majority appears to make arguments of both kinds, none of them persuasive.

A.

Our colleagues argue that differences in the union and nonunion settings justify denying nonunion workers the right recognized in *Weingarten*. The real question, however, is whether these differences mean that the right to representation can be grounded in Section 7 only where a union represents workers. Clearly, they do not, for reasons convincingly explained in *Epilepsy Foundation*.

From the perspective of Section 7, at least, it makes no difference whether, like union representatives, coworker representatives (1) represent the interests of the entire workforce, (2) can redress the imbalance of power between employers and employees, or (3) have the skills needed to be effective. The majority makes a powerful case for unionization, but a weak one for refusing to recognize the rights of nonunion workers. As the *Epilepsy Foundation* Board correctly observed, "Section 7 rights do not turn on either the skills or the motives of the employee's representative." The majority here simply confuses the efficacy of a right with its existence.

According to the majority, there is a "critical difference between a unionized work force and a nonunion work force" that is relevant here: "the employer in the latter situation can deal with employees on an individual basis." . . .

B.

Aside from its attempt to distinguish union and nonunion workplaces, the majority claims that employers have an overriding need to prevent interference with workplace investigations mandated by law. But there is no basis to conclude that coworker representation has had, or likely will have, any of the harmful consequences that the majority conjures up. The solution here is to strike a balance, not to pretend that nonunion employees have no Section 7 interest that must be respected.

Although the majority does not bother to detail the sources of employers' legal obligations to conduct effective workplace investigations, we will assume that employers do have such a legal obligation, in some circumstances. Further, we will assume that nonunion employees' right to representation makes it harder, in some measure, for employers to discharge that obligation — just as observing other legal requirements or moral norms does (Star Chamber proceedings, in contrast, were wonderfully efficient). Even making these assumptions, however, it is impossible fairly to reach the majority's conclusion: that nonunion workers are *never* entitled to a coworker representative in investigatory interviews.

First, to the extent that employees' rights under the Act may be in tension with legitimate employer interests or the goals of other federal statutes, the majority never explains why it is that Section 7 must give way, always and completely. Surely the process is one of balancing and accommodation, conducted case-by-case, as federal labor law has long recognized in other contexts. If, as we believe, the right to representation is guaranteed by Section 7, then any infringement of that right is presumptively a violation of Section 8(a)(1), but the presumption may be overcome, in appropriate circumstances (a point we will address).

Second, the majority has simply failed to make the case that a nonunion employer cannot conduct an effective investigation if employees are entitled to coworker representation during interviews that reasonably may lead to discipline. Here, too, the majority contrasts union representatives and coworker representatives, arguing that union representatives may actually facilitate an effective investigation and that in any case, their special legal status makes them less likely to violate confidentiality.

The majority's arguments against extending the *Weingarten* right to nonunion employees prove too much. If employers' obligation to conduct effective investigations is an overriding concern, then even the right to a union representative should be foreclosed (a radical step we hope the majority forswears). Nothing in a union's statutory duty of fair representation, which runs to *employees*, requires the union to serve the *employer's* interests, whether in imposing discipline or preserving confidentiality. Indeed, given the skill of union representatives and the power of union solidarity (factors noted by the majority), permitting union representation is, if anything, *more* likely to complicate an employer's investigation than permitting coworker representation in nonunion workplaces.

In any case, there is no evidence before the Board either that unions have interfered with employers' investigatory obligations since 1975, when *Weingarten* was decided, or that coworker representatives have caused harm since *Epilepsy Foundation* issued in 2000. Nothing in the record shows that investigations have come to a halt because of the presence of a coworker at an investigatory interview, or that information obtained during such an interview has been compromised. Rotely repeating the unsupported assertions of employer advocates in their briefs to the Board, the majority shows a startling lack of interest in what is actually happening in American workplaces.

If and when the right to representation raises legitimate concerns, they can and should be addressed by refining the right, case-by-case. For example, our colleagues have suggested that an investigation could be impeded if the employer were compelled to permit representation by a coworker involved in the same incident being investigated (a so-called "coconspirator"). That concern could be addressed specifically, by permitting an employer to deny an employee's request for representation by a possible coconspirator, under appropriate circumstances. But instead of permitting the Board's law to evolve in response to actual situations confronting employers and employees, the majority proceeds by fiat.

IV.

No one suggests that the National Labor Relations Act gives employees the same protections that are available to criminal suspects under the Constitution. The *Weingarten* right is not the equivalent of a right to counsel, and employees have no privilege against self-incrimination. Yet modest as the *Weingarten* right is, it brings a measure of due process to workplace discipline, particularly in nonunion workplaces, where employees and their representatives typically are at-will employees, who may be discharged or disciplined for any reason not specifically prohibited by law. "[T]he presence of a coworker gives an employee a potential witness, advisor, and advocate in an adversarial situation, and, ideally, militates against the imposition of unjust discipline by the employer." Needless to say, unjust discipline can provoke labor disputes. Because a purpose of the Act is to provide a vehicle for employee voice and a system for resolving workplace disputes, this due process requirement furthers the goals of the Act.

Far from being an anachronism, then, *Epilepsy Foundation* is in perfect step with the times. In nonunion workplaces, employer-imposed alternative dispute resolution (ADR) mechanisms, from grievance procedures to compulsory arbitration, are becoming increasingly common. These mechanisms, when adopted in good faith, reflect an evolving norm of fairness and due process in the workplace — a norm that should not be entirely dependent on winning union representation. The arbitrary exercise of power by employers, over their employees, no longer strikes us as either natural or desirable. Grounded in the Act's notion of "mutual aid or protection," the right to coworker representation for nonunion workers also contributes to a workplace in which employers respect something like the rule of law.

On this view, it is our colleagues who are taking a step backwards. They have neither demonstrated that *Epilepsy Foundation* is contrary to the Act, nor offered compelling policy reasons for failing to follow precedent. They have overruled a sound decision not because they must, and not because they should, but because they can. As a result, today's decision itself is unlikely to have an enduring place in American labor law. We dissent.

POST PROBLEM DISCUSSION

1. Now that you've read the problem materials, can Ralph argue that he deserves to have a friend with him during the disciplinary meeting with his employer? Why not? Whose arguments do you find more persuasive in the *IBM* case, the majority or the dissent?

2. As far as the *City Disposal* case, what sort of connection with one or more employees must an employee's activity have in order to be deemed "concerted activity" protected by the Act? Justice Brennan in *City Disposal* held that an employee's honest and reasonable assertion of his right under a collective-bargaining agreement to refuse to drive a truck he believed to be unsafe constituted "concerted activity" under the Act. Justice O'Connor dissented on the basis that even if the right the employee asserts can be grounded in the collective-bargaining agreement, it is not enough to make the individual's self-interested action concerted. In her dissent, she points out that labor laws were designed to encourage employees to act together. While it is possible for one employee to act on behalf of other employees, and his activity thus be concerted under the *Interboro* doctrine, O'Connor did not feel these particular facts suggest that the truck driver was acting for anything other than personal benefit. Who has the better argument in your opinion?

3.   Outside of the traditional labor law context, there are possible non-NLRA protections for union and non-union employees claiming rights under various federal employment statutes. For instance, there are non-retaliation provisions in the Occupational Safety and Health Act (OSHA), Title VII of the Civil Rights Act of 1964, and the Fair Labor Standards Act. Additionally, federal and state whistle-blower statues may also protect an employee reporting safety or health violations. Finally, there are state common law protections against discharges and disciplines that are contrary to public policy. *See* Chapter 4 of the Restatement (Third) of Employment Law (discussing the tort of wrongful discipline in violation of public policy).

4.   Employers defend pay secrecy rules, where employee are not permitted to discuss their salaries with another worker, on the basis that these rules lessen internal strife among employees. Discussing wages, according to employers, leads to discord among employees because a disparity in pay leads to resentment, while at the same time leaving employees without all the information they need to understand the disparity. *See* Rafael Gely & Leonard Bierman, *Pay Secrecy/ Confidentiality Rules and the National Labor Relations Act*, 6 U. PA. J. LAB. & EMP. L. 121 (2003) (arguing that business justifications do exist sometimes for promulgating pay secrecy rules, but corporate counsels historically have been too timid in expressing their justifications). Yet, such restrictions on employees discussing their salary are generally found to be unlawful. *See, e.g., Fredericksburg Glass and Mirror, Inc.*, 323 N.L.R.B. 165, 165 (1997) (holding a "no-discussion rule" formalized by the employer was a violation of the NLRA).

5.   It does appear that in particular divisive areas of labor law, such as the Weingarten context, political affiliation of Board Members still plays a predictive role in how the Board decides cases. *See* Ronald Turner, *Ideological Voting on the National Labor Relations Board*, 8 U. PA. J. LAB. & EMP. L. 707, 711 (2006) ("The only claim made in this Article is that ideology has been a persistent and, in many instances, a vote-predictive factor when the Board decides certain legal issues. The NLRB has never embraced the concept of *stare decisis*."). Does the flip-flopping of the Board in decisions like *IBM* suggest the Board should place more emphasis on precedent? What are some reasons that administrative agencies might want to be bound less by prior decisions?

6.   Is there an inconsistency with the position that allowing an employee to have a co-worker accompany them to a disciplinary investigatory interview cannot be viewed as concerted activity for mutual aid and protection under Section 7? Should it matter whether the co-employee is an effective aid and protection? Shouldn't employees be able to decide what is a legitimate purpose for acting in a concerted manner?

7.   Even if a union employee would be normally entitled to *Weingarten* rights, such rights are not available if the purpose of the meeting is not to elicit facts from the employee that would assist the employer in deciding whether to issue discipline. This scenario might arise where the employer has already made the decision to terminate the employee. *See NLRB v. Certified Grocers of California, Ltd.*, 587 F.2d 449 (9th Cir. 1978).

8.   In *Parexel International*, 356 N.L.R.B. No. 82 (2011), the employer fired a worker who had in fact not engaged in any concerted activity, but whom the employer suspected might engage in such activity in the future. Although the ALJ rejected the General Counsel's "nip in the bud" theory of NLRA violation, the Obama Board reversed the ALJ and found a violation. This holding seems in line with *Mushroom Transportation Co. v. NLRB*, 330 F.2d 683, 685 (3d Cir. 1964), where the court held that conduct is protected "if it was engaged in with the object of initiating or inducing or preparing for group action or that it had some relation to group action in the interest of the employees." For an interesting take on the *Parexel* decision, see generally Michael C. Duff, *New Nip in the Bud: Does the Obama Board's Preemptive Strike Doctrine Enhance Tactical Employment Law Strategies?* 16 EMPLOYEE RTS. & EMP. POL'Y J. (forthcoming 2012) (reassessing the *Parexel* decision based on an expanded notion of Section 7's definition of concerted activity).

SECTION 2   LEGITIMATE PURPOSE FOR CONCERTED ACTIVTY

In addition to the threshold requirement of concertedness, activity qualifying for Section 7 protection must be directed toward a legitimate purpose and carried out through legitimate means. As to purpose, Section 7 says the activity must be directed toward "mutual aid or protection."

What if the purpose for the concerted activity is not directly related to an employee's own workplace? Is that activity for a legitimate purpose?

PROBLEM #2: POLITICS AS USUAL?[1]

A union wishes to distribute on an employer's property, during nonworking hours and nonworking time, the following newsletter:

WE NEED YOU

As a member, we need you to help build the Union through your support and understanding. Too often, members become disinterested and look upon their Union as being something separate from themselves. Nothing could be further from the truth.

This Union or any Union will only be as good as the members make it. The policies and practices of this Union are made by the membership — *the active membership*. If this Union has ever missed its target it may be because not enough members made their views known where the final decisions are made — The Union Meeting.

It would be impossible to satisfy everyone with the decisions that are made but the active member has the opportunity to bring the majority around to his way of thinking. This is how a democratic organization works and it's the best system around.

---

[1] Taken and revised from the actual newsletter in *Eastex, Inc. v. NLRB*, 437 U.S. 556 (1978).

Through participation, you can make your voice felt not only in this Local but throughout the International Union.

A PHONY LABEL — *"Right to Work"*

Wages are determined at the bargaining table, and the stronger the Union, the better the opportunity for improvements. The "right to work" law is simply an attempt to weaken the strength of Unions. The misleading title of "right to work" cannot guarantee anyone a job. It simply weakens the negotiating power of Unions by outlawing provisions in contracts for Union shops, agency shops, and modified Union shops. These laws do not improve wages or working conditions but just protect free riders. Free riders are people who take all the benefits of Unions without paying dues. They ride on the dues that members pay to build an organization to protect their rights and improve their way of life. At this time there is a very well-organized and financed attempt to place the "right to work" law in our new state constitution. This drive is supported and financed by big business, namely, the National Right-To-Work Committee and the National Chamber of Commerce. If their attempt is successful, it will more than pay for itself by weakening Unions and improving the edge business has at the bargaining table. States that have no "right-to-work" law consistently have higher wages and better working conditions. Texas is well known for its weak laws concerning the working class, and the "right-to-work" law would only add insult to injury. If you fail to take action against the "right-to-work" law, it may well show up in wages negotiated in the future. I urge every member to write their state congressman and senator in protest of the "right-to-work" law being incorporated into the state constitution. Write your state representative and state senator and let the delegate know how you feel.

POLITICS AND PAID FAMILY LEAVE

A state family paid medical leave law was recently vetoed by our Governor. The Governor termed the bill as a "job killer."

It seems almost unbelievable that the Governor could say that while at the same providing corporate tax cuts to businesses in this state.

The state legislature is now proceeding with a second state family and medical leave bill that hopefully the Governor will sign into law.

As working men and women we must defeat our enemies and elect our friends. If you haven't registered to vote, please do so today.

FOOD FOR THOUGHT

In Union there is strength, justice, and moderation;
In disunion, nothing but an alternating humility and insolence.
COMING TOGETHER WAS A BEGINNING
STAYING TOGETHER IS PROGRESS
WORKING TOGETHER MEANS SUCCESS
THE PERSON WHO STANDS NEUTRAL, STANDS FOR NOTHING!

*   *   *

The union has asked you, as their counsel, whether such a distribution would be deemed "mutual aid and protection" under Section 7 of the NLRA.

PROBLEM MATERIALS

Eastex, Inc. v. NLRB, 437 U.S. 556 (1978)

EASTEX, INC. v. NLRB
437 U.S. 556 (1978)

JUSTICE POWELL delivered the opinion of the Court.

Employees of petitioner sought to distribute a union newsletter in nonworking areas of petitioner's property during nonworking time urging employees to support the union and discussing a proposal to incorporate the state "right-to-work" statute into the state constitution and a Presidential veto of an increase in the federal minimum wage. The newsletter also called on employees to take action to protect their interests as employees with respect to these two issues. The question presented is whether petitioner's refusal to allow the distribution violated § 8(a)(1) of the National Labor Relations Act by interfering with, restraining, or coercing employees' exercise of their right under § 7 of the Act, to engage in "concerted activities for the purpose of . . . mutual aid or protection."

I

Petitioner is a company that manufactures paper products in Silsbee, Tex. Since 1954, petitioner's production employees have been represented by Local 801 of the United Paperworkers International Union. It appears that many, although not all, of petitioner's approximately 800 production employees are members of Local 801. Since Texas is a "right-to-work" State by statute, Local 801 is barred from obtaining an agreement with petitioner requiring all production employees to become union members.

In March 1974, officers of Local 801, seeking to strengthen employee support for the union and perhaps recruit new members in anticipation of upcoming contract negotiations with petitioner, decided to distribute a union newsletter to petitioner's production employees. The newsletter was divided into four sections. The first and fourth sections urged employees to support and participate in the union and, more generally, extolled the benefits of union solidarity. The second section encouraged employees to write their legislators to oppose incorporation of the state "right-to-work" statute into a revised state constitution then under consideration, warning that incorporation would "weake[n] Unions and improv[e] the edge business has at the bargaining table." The third section noted that the President recently had vetoed a bill to increase the federal minimum wage from $1.60 to $2.00 per hour, compared this action to the increase of prices and profits in the oil industry under administration policies, and admonished: "As working men and women we must defeat our enemies and elect our friends. If you haven't registered to vote, please do so today." . . .

II

Two distinct questions are presented. The first is whether, apart from the location of the activity, distribution of the newsletter is the kind of concerted activity that is protected from employer interference by §§ 7 and 8(a)(1) of the National Labor Relations Act. If it is, then the second question is whether the fact that the activity takes place on petitioner's property gives rise to a countervailing interest that outweighs the exercise of § 7 rights in that location . . . .

A

Section 7 provides that "[e]mployees shall have the right . . . to engage in . . . concerted activities for the purpose of collective bargaining or other mutual aid or protection . . . ." Petitioner contends that the activity here is not within the "mutual aid or protection" language because it does not relate to a "specific dispute" between employees and their own employer "over an issue which the employer has the right or power to affect." In support of its position, petitioner asserts that the term "employees" in § 7 refers only to employees of a particular employer, so that only activity by employees on behalf of themselves or other employees of the same employer is protected. Petitioner also argues that the term "collective bargaining" in § 7 "indicates a direct bargaining relationship whereas 'other mutual aid or protection' must refer to activities of a similar nature . . . ." Thus, in petitioner's view, under § 7 "the employee is only protected for activity within the scope of the employment relationship." Petitioner rejects the idea that § 7 might protect any activity that could be characterized as "political," and suggests that the discharge of an employee who engages in any such activity would not violate the Act. We believe that petitioner misconceives the reach of the "mutual aid or protection" clause. The "employees" who may engage in concerted activities for "mutual aid or protection" are defined by § 2(3) of the Act to "include any employee, and shall not be limited to the employees of a particular employer, unless this subchapter explicitly states otherwise . . . ." This definition was intended to protect employees when they engage in otherwise proper concerted activities in support of employees of employers other than their own. In recognition of this intent, the Board and the courts long have held that the "mutual aid or protection" clause encompasses such activity. Petitioner's argument on this point ignores the language of the Act and its settled construction.

We also find no warrant for petitioner's view that employees lose their protection under the "mutual aid or protection" clause when they seek to improve terms and conditions of employment or otherwise improve their lot as employees through channels outside the immediate employee-employer relationship. The 74th Congress knew well enough that labor's cause often is advanced on fronts other than collective bargaining and grievance settlement within the immediate employment context. It recognized this fact by choosing, as the language of § 7 makes clear, to protect concerted activities for the somewhat broader purpose of "mutual aid or protection" as well as for the narrower purposes of "self-organization" and "collective bargaining." Thus, it has been held that the "mutual aid or protection" clause protects employees from retaliation by their employers when they seek to improve working conditions through resort to administrative and judicial forums, and that employees' appeals to legislators to protect their interests as employees are within the scope of this clause. To hold that activity of this nature is entirely unprotected-irrespective of location or the means employed-would leave employees open to retaliation for much legitimate activity that could improve their lot as employees.

It is true, of course, that some concerted activity bears a less immediate relationship to employees' interests as employees than other such activity. We may assume that at some point the relationship becomes so attenuated that an activity cannot fairly be deemed to come within the "mutual aid or protection" clause. It is neither necessary nor appropriate, however, for us to attempt to delineate precisely the boundaries of the "mutual aid or protection" clause. That task is for the Board to perform in the first instance as it considers the wide variety of cases that come before it. To decide this case, it is enough to determine whether the Board erred in holding that distribution of the second and third sections of the newsletter is for the purpose of "mutual aid or protection."

The Board determined that distribution of the second section, urging employees to write their legislators to oppose incorporation of the state "right-to-work" statute into a revised state constitution, was protected because union security is "central to the union concept of strength through solidarity" and "a mandatory subject of bargaining in other than right-to-work states." The newsletter warned that incorporation could affect employees adversely "by weakening Unions and improving the edge business has at the bargaining table." The fact that Texas already has a "right-to-work" statute does not render employees' interest in this matter any less strong, for, as the Court of Appeals noted, it is "one thing to face a statutory scheme which is open to legislative modification or repeal" and "quite another thing to face the prospect that such a scheme will be frozen in a concrete constitutional mandate." We cannot say that the Board erred in holding that this section of the newsletter bears such a relation to employees' interests as to come within the guarantee of the "mutual aid or protection" clause.

The Board held that distribution of the third section, criticizing a Presidential veto of an increase in the federal minimum wage and urging employees to register to vote to "defeat our enemies and elect our friends," was protected despite the fact that petitioner's employees were paid more than the vetoed minimum wage. It reasoned that the "minimum wage inevitably influences wage levels derived from collective bargaining, even those far above the minimum," and that "concern by [petitioner's] employees for the plight of other employees might gain support for them at some future time when they might have a dispute with their employer." We think that the Board acted within the range of its discretion in so holding. Few topics are of such immediate concern to employees as the level of their wages. The Board was entitled to note the widely recognized impact that a rise in the minimum wage may have on the level of negotiated wages generally, a phenomenon that would not have been lost on petitioner's employees. The union's call, in the circumstances of this case, for these employees to back persons who support an increase in the minimum wage, and to oppose those who oppose it, fairly is characterized as concerted activity for the "mutual aid or protection" of petitioner's employees and of employees generally.

In sum, we hold that distribution of both the second and the third sections of the newsletter is protected under the "mutual aid or protection" clause of § 7.

JUSTICE WHITE, concurring [opinion omitted].

JUSTICE REHNQUIST, with whom THE CHIEF JUSTICE joins, dissenting [opinion omitted].

POST PROBLEM DISCUSSION

1.   The term "mutual aid and protection" applies only to employees acting as employees, not employees seeking to be owners. The Board held in *Harrah's Lake Tahoe Resort Casino*, 307 N.L.R.B. 182 (1992), that although the employee distributing the literature was engaging in concerted activity, the thrust of the proposal contained in the literature was to fundamentally change how and by whom the casino was run. Therefore, the relationship between the literature distributed and the employees' interests was so attenuated that it would be unfair to protect the activity as being for the mutual aid and protection of the group. *See* Jeffrey M. Hirsch, *Labor Law Obstacles to the Collective Negotiation and Implementation of Employee Stock Ownership Plans: A Response to Henry Hansmann and Other "Survivalists,"* 67 FORDHAM L. REV. 957, 984-92 (1998) (criticizing *Harrah's* and arguing for coverage the "mutual aid and protection" prong for certain attempts by employees to gain an ownership stake in their employer).

2.   Should political advocacy by unions be protected and permitted on employer property? Should the Supreme Court and Board place more emphasis on the property rights of employers in these types of cases?

> In the wake of *Eastex*, the Board has issued several decisions addressing the intersection of political activity and section 7 protection . . . . [T]he present standards for defining the scope of section 7 coverage call for a determination on a case by case basis. The current decisions seem to suggest that if placed on a continuum, those activities that would be deemed not within the scope of section 7 would be those that merely tout a political candidate or party in an election. At the other end of the spectrum activity that would seem to almost always garner section 7 coverage are direct appeals by unions and employees to legislators over issues of general workplace concern.

Paul E. Bateman, *Concerted Activity-the Intersection Between Political Activity and Section 7 Rights*, 23 LAB. LAW. 41 (2007). Can you think of activities that would fall in the middle of the continuum? Should those activities be protected?

3.   In *Eastex*, the Board and the Court agreed "that 'concern by [petitioner's] employees for the plight of other employees might gain support for them at some future time when they might have a dispute with their employer.'" Do you think it's true that the employees' actions were self-serving? Should it matter whether

employees are acting in their own interest when determining whether concerted activity was for mutual aid or protection? *See also* NLRA Section 2(3) ("The term 'employee' shall include any employee, and shall not be limited to the employees of a particular employer . . . .").

SECTION 3   LEGITIMATE MEANS FOR CONCERTED ACTIVITY

The purpose of this section is to emphasize that an employee may be engaged in "concerted" activity for "mutual aid or protection," but nevertheless the activity is unprotected because it otherwise falls outside of the NLRA. This situation arises when employees have engaged in illegitimate means for accomplishing their purpose or objective. For example, employee actions that contribute to a union's refusal to bargain in good faith, illegal protests like secondary boycotts, and other employee actions contrary to the spirit of the Act, are all unprotected activities regardless of whether they are concerted and for mutual aid and protection.

Clearly, committing a crime or intentional tort is beyond the protection of the Act. Although a group of employees who blow up a plant or beat up a strike-breaker with the intent of increasing the bargaining power of the union may be acting in "concert" and for "mutual aid and protection," it doesn't mean that their actions will be protected. But where should the Supreme Court draw the line between legitimate and illegitimate means in closer cases?

PROBLEM #3: THE SIX-FOOT INFLATABLE RAT

Pogo-Sticks-R-Us is in a dispute with their certified incumbent union, Local 11 of the Pogo-Stick Makers Union. The feud is over a new collective-bargaining contract, and more specifically, about the company wanting wage concessions and additional health insurance contributions.

Although Local 11 has not called a boycott or strike, workers are manning a picket line on the sidewalk outside of the company facility. In addition to signs saying that the company is treating them unfairly with regard to wages and benefits, the workers have set up a giant six-foot inflatable rat outside the company.

The company learns that Arnie Arkel is responsible for the rat and believes that Arnie is disparaging their products by suggesting that only a rat would bother to buy such pogo sticks. Consequently, they immediately terminate Arnie's employment for disloyalty and product disparagement.

Can Arnie bring a Section 8(a)(3) claim for discrimination based on the company's activities?

PROBLEM MATERIALS

NLRB v. Local 1229, IBEW (Jefferson Standard Broadcasting Co.), 346 U.S. 464 (U.S. 1953)

Matthew W. Finkin, *Disloyalty! Does* Jefferson Standard *Stalk Still?*, 28 Berkeley J. Emp. & Lab. L. 568 (2007)

NLRB v. LOCAL 1229, IBEW (JEFFERSON STANDARD BROADCASTING CO.)
346 U.S. 464 (U.S. 1953)

JUSTICE BURTON delivered the opinion of the Court.

The issue before us is whether the discharge of certain employees by their employer constituted an unfair labor practice, within the meaning of §§ 8(a)(1) and 7 of the Taft-Hartley Act, justifying their reinstatement by the National Labor Relations Board. For the reason that their discharge was "for cause" within the meaning of § 10(c) of that Act, we sustain the Board in not requiring their reinstatement.

In 1949, the Jefferson Standard Broadcasting Company was a North Carolina corporation engaged in interstate commerce. Under a license from the Federal Communications Commission, it operated, at Charlotte, North Carolina, a 50,000-watt radio station, with call letters WBT. It broadcast 10 to 12 hours daily by radio and television. The television service, which it started July 14, 1949, representing an investment of about $500,000, was the only such service in the area. Less than 50% of the station's programs originated in Charlotte. The others were piped in over leased wires, generally from New York, California or Illinois from several different networks. Its annual gross revenue from broadcasting operations exceeded $100,000 but its television enterprise caused it a monthly loss of about $10,000 during the first four months of that operation, including the period here involved. Its rates for television advertising were geared to the number of receiving sets in the area. Local dealers had large inventories of such sets ready to meet anticipated demands.

The company employed 22 technicians. In December 1948, negotiations to settle the terms of their employment after January 31, 1949, were begun between representatives of the company and of the respondent Local Union No. 1229, International Brotherhood of Electrical Workers, American Federation of Labor. The negotiations reached an impasse in January 1949, and the existing contract of employment expired January 31. The technicians, nevertheless, continued to work for the company and their collective-bargaining negotiations were resumed in July, only to break down again July 8. The main point of disagreement arose from the union's demand for the renewal of a provision that all discharges from employment be subject to arbitration and the company's counter-proposal that such arbitration be limited to the facts material to each discharge, leaving it to the company to determine whether those facts gave adequate cause for discharge.

July 9, 1949, the union began daily peaceful picketing of the company's station. Placards and handbills on the picket line charged the company with unfairness to its technicians and emphasized the company's refusal to renew the provision for arbitration of discharges. The placards and handbills named the union as the representative of the WBT technicians. The employees did not strike. They confined their respective tours of picketing to their off-duty hours and continued to draw full pay. There was no violence or threat of violence and no one has taken exception to any of the above conduct.

But on August 24, 1949, a new procedure made its appearance. Without warning, several of its technicians launched a vitriolic attack on the quality of the company's television broadcasts. Five thousand handbills were printed over the designation "WBT Technicians." These were distributed on the picket line, on the public square two or three blocks from the company's premises, in barber shops, restaurants and busses. Some were mailed to local businessmen. The handbills made no reference to the union, to a labor controversy or to collective bargaining. They read:

Is Charlotte A Second-Class City?

You might think so from the kind of Television programs being presented by the Jefferson Standard Broadcasting Co. over WBTV. Have you seen one of their television programs lately? Did you know that all the programs presented over WBTV are on film and may be from one day to five years old. There are no local programs presented by WBTV. You cannot receive the local baseball games, football games or other local events because WBTV does not have the proper equipment to make these pickups. Cities like New York, Boston, Philadelphia, Washington receive such programs nightly. Why doesn't the Jefferson Standard Broadcasting Company purchase the needed equipment to bring you the same type of programs enjoyed by other leading American cities? Could it be that they consider Charlotte a second-class community and only entitled to the pictures now being presented to them?

WBT Technicians

This attack continued until September 3, 1949, when the company discharged ten of its technicians, whom it charged with sponsoring or distributing these handbills. The company's letter discharging them tells its side of the story . . . .

In its essence, the issue is simple. It is whether these employees, whose contracts of employment had expired, were discharged "for cause." They were discharged solely because, at a critical time in the initiation of the company's television service, they sponsored or distributed 5,000 handbills making a sharp, public, disparaging attack upon the quality of the company's product and its business policies, in a manner reasonably calculated to harm the company's reputation and reduce its income. The attack was made by them expressly as "WBT Technicians." It continued ten days without indication of abatement. The Board found that —

It (the handbill) occasioned widespread comment in the community, and caused Respondent to apprehend a loss of advertising revenue due to dissatisfaction with its television broadcasting service.

In short, the employees in this case deliberately undertook to alienate their employer's customers by impugning the technical quality of his product. As the Trial Examiner found, they did not misrepresent, at least wilfully, the facts they cited to support their disparaging report. And their ultimate purpose-to extract a concession from the employer with respect to the terms of their employment-was lawful. That purpose, however, was undisclosed; the employees purported to speak as experts, in the interest of consumers and the public at large. They did not indicate that they sought to secure any benefit for themselves, as employees, by casting discredit upon their employer.

The company's letter shows that it interpreted the handbill as a demonstration of such detrimental disloyalty as to provide "cause" for its refusal to continue in its employ the perpetrators of the attack. We agree.

Section 10(c) of the Taft-Hartley Act expressly provides that "No order of the Board shall require the reinstatement of any individual as an employee who has been suspended or discharged, or the payment to him of any back pay, if such individual was suspended or discharged for cause." There is no more elemental cause for discharge of an employee than disloyalty to his employer. It is equally elemental that the Taft-Hartley Act seeks to strengthen, rather than to weaken, that cooperation, continuity of service and cordial contractual relation between employer and employee that is born of loyalty to their common enterprise.

Congress, while safeguarding, in § 7, the right of employees to engage in "concerted activities for the purpose of collective bargaining or other mutual aid or protection," did not weaken the underlying contractual bonds and loyalties of employer and employee.

The conference report that led to the enactment of the law said:

> (T)he courts have firmly established the rule that under the existing provisions of section 7 of the National Labor Relations Act, employees are not given any right to engage in unlawful or other improper conduct. . . . Furthermore, in section 10(c) of the amended act, as proposed in the conference agreement, it is specifically provided that no order of the Board shall require the reinstatement of any individual or the payment to him of any back pay if such individual was suspended or discharged for cause, and this, of course, applies with equal force whether or not the acts constituting the cause for discharge were committed in connection with a concerted activity. H.R.Rep.No. 510, 80th Cong., 1st Sess. 38-39.

This has been clear since the early days of the Wagner Act. In 1937, Chief Justice Hughes, writing for the Court, said:

> The act does not interfere with the normal exercise of the right of the employer to select its employees or to discharge them. The employer may not, under cover of that right, intimidate or coerce its employees with respect to their self-organization and representation, and, on the other hand, the Board is not entitled to make its authority a pretext for interference with the right of discharge when that right is exercised for other reasons than such intimidation and coercion.

Many cases reaching their final disposition in the Courts of Appeals furnish examples emphasizing the importance of enforcing industrial plant discipline and of maintaining loyalty as well as the rights of concerted activities. The courts have refused to reinstate employees discharged for "cause" consisting of insubordination, disobedience or disloyalty. In such cases, it often has been necessary to identify individual employees, somewhat comparable to the nine discharged in this case, and to recognize that their discharges were for causes which were separable from the concerted activities of others whose acts might come within the protection of § 7. It has been equally important to identify employees, comparable to the tenth man in the instant case, who participated in simultaneous concerted activities for the purpose of collective bargaining or other mutual aid or protection but who refrained from joining the others in separable acts of insubordination, disobedience or disloyalty. In the latter instances, this sometimes led to a further inquiry to determine whether their concerted activities were carried on in such a manner as to come within the protection of § 7.

The above cases illustrate the responsibility that falls upon the Board to find the facts material to such decisions. The legal principle that insubordination, disobedience or disloyalty is adequate cause for discharge is plain enough. The difficulty arises in determining whether, in fact, the discharges are made because of such a separable cause or because of some other concerted activities engaged in for the purpose of collective bargaining or other mutual aid or protection which may not be adequate cause for discharge.

In the instant case the Board found that the company's discharge of the nine offenders resulted from their sponsoring and distributing the "Second-Class City" handbills of August 24-September 3, issued in their name as the "WBT Technicians." Assuming that there had been no pending labor controversy, the conduct of the "WBT Technicians" from August 24 through September 3 unquestionably would have provided adequate cause for their disciplinary discharge within the meaning of § 10(c). Their attack related itself to no labor practice of the company. It made no reference to wages, hours or working conditions. The policies attacked were those of finance and public relations for which management, not technicians, must be responsible. The attack asked for no public sympathy or support. It was a continuing attack, initiated while off duty, upon the very interests which the attackers were being paid to conserve and develop. Nothing could be further from the purpose of the Act than to require an employer to finance such activities. Nothing would contribute less to the Act's declared purpose of promoting industrial peace and stability.

The fortuity of the coexistence of a labor dispute affords these technicians no substantial defense. While they were also union men and leaders in the labor controversy, they took pains to separate those categories. In contrast to their claims on the picket line as to the labor controversy, their handbill of August 24 omitted all reference to it. The handbill diverted attention from the labor controversy. It attacked public policies of the company which had no discernible relation to that controversy. The only connection between the handbill and the labor controversy was an ultimate and undisclosed purpose or motive on the part of some of the sponsors that, by the hoped-for financial pressure, the attack might extract from the company some future concession. A disclosure of that motive might have lost more public support for the employees than it would have gained, for it would have given the handbill more the character of coercion than of collective bargaining . . . .

We find no occasion to remand this cause to the Board for further specificity of findings. Even if the attack were to be treated, as the Board has not treated it, as a concerted activity wholly or partly within the scope of those mentioned in § 7, the means used by the technicians in conducting the attack have deprived the attackers of the protection of that section, when read in the light and context of the purpose of the Act.

Accordingly, the order of the Court of Appeals remanding the cause to the

National Labor Relations Board is set aside, and the cause is remanded to the Court of Appeals with instructions to dismiss respondent's petition to modify the order of the Board. It is so ordered.

JUSTICE FRANKFURTER, whom JUSTICE BLACK and JUSTICE DOUGLAS join, dissenting.

. . . On th[e] central issue-whether the Court of Appeals rightly or wrongly found that the Board applied an improper criterion-this Court is silent. It does not support the Board in using "indefensible" as the legal litmus nor does it reject the Court of Appeals' rejection of that test. This Court presumably does not disagree with the assumption of the Court of Appeals that conduct may be "indefensible" in the colloquial meaning of that loose adjective, and yet be within the protection of § 7.

Instead, the Court, relying on § 10(c) which permits discharges "for cause," points to the "disloyalty" of the employees and finds sufficient 'cause' regardless of whether the handbill was a "concerted activity" within § 7. Section 10(c) does not speak of discharge "for disloyalty." If Congress had so written that section, it would have overturned much of the law that had been developed by the Board and the courts in the twelve years preceding the Taft-Hartley Act. The legislative history makes clear that Congress had no such purpose but was rather expressing approval of the construction of "concerted activities" adopted by the Board and the courts. Many of the legally recognized tactics and weapons of labor would readily be condemned for "disloyalty" were they employed between man and man in friendly personal relations. In this connection it is significant that the ground now taken by the Court, insofar as it is derived from the provision of § 10(c) relating to discharge "for cause," was not invoked by the Board in justification of its order.

To suggest that all actions which in the absence of a labor controversy might be "cause" — or, to use the words commonly found in labor agreements, "just cause" — for discharge should be unprotected, even when such actions were undertaken as "concerted activities for the purpose of collective bargaining", is to misconstrue legislation designed to put labor on a fair footing with management. Furthermore, it would disregard the rough and tumble of strikes, in the course of which loose and even reckless language is properly discounted.

"Concerted activities" by employees and dismissal "for cause" by employers are not dissociated legal criteria under the Act. They are like the two halves of a pair of shears. Of course, as the Conference Report on the Taft-Hartley Act said, men on strike may be guilty of conduct "in connection with a concerted activity" which properly constitutes "cause" for dismissal and bars reinstatement. But § 10(c) does not obviate the necessity for a determination whether the distribution of the handbill here was a legitimate tool in a labor dispute or was so "improper," as the Conference Report put it, as to be denied the protection of § 7 and to constitute a discharge "for cause." It is for the Board, in the first instance, to make these evaluations, and a court of appeals does not travel beyond its proper bounds in asking the Board for greater explicitness in light of the correct legal standards for judgment.

The Board and the courts of appeals will hardly find guidance for future cases from this Court's reversal of the Court of Appeals, beyond that which the specific facts of this case may afford. More than that, to float such imprecise notions as "discipline" and "loyalty" in the context of labor controversies, as the basis of the right to discharge, is to open the door wide to individual judgment by Board members and judges. One may anticipate that the Court's opinion will needlessly stimulate litigation.

Section 7 of course only protects "concerted activities" in the course of promoting legitimate interests of labor. But to treat the offensive handbills here as though they were circulated by the technicians as interloping outsiders to the sustained dispute between them and their employer is a very unreal way of looking at the circumstances of a labor controversy. Certainly there is nothing in the language of the Act or in the legislative history to indicate that only conventional placards and handbills, headed by a trite phrase such as "Unfair To Labor," are protected. In any event, on a remand the Board could properly be asked to leave no doubt whether the technicians, in distributing the handbills, were, so far as the public could tell, on a frolic of their own or whether this tactic, however unorthodox, was no more unlawful than other union behavior previously found to be entitled to protection.

Matthew W. Finkin, *Disloyalty! Does* Jefferson Standard *Stalk Still?*
28 BERKELEY J. EMP. & LAB. L. 541 (2007)[2]

. . . III. Disloyalty

A. Provenance

"Disloyalty" is a shorthand expression, a catchphrase, and as such incapable of supplying a clear guide to decision, that, at least, being the near universal judgment of contemporaneous and later students of Jefferson Standard. Loyalty can mean personal fealty, the subordination of one's ends and will to the command of another, sometimes near total as in its military usage; and personal fealty to management has sometimes been an element of corporate policy. But that feudal notion is not quite what Justice Burton seems to have had in mind. Rather, the Court's treatment of disloyalty harkens back to the common law, as it was still in the 1950s, of Master and Servant.

The law of master and servant implied on the servant's part a basic obligation of faithfulness to the master's interests. As Lord Kenyon put in 1799, "A servant while engaged in the service of his master, has no right to do any act which may injure his trade, or undermine his business . . . ." This is the obligation captured by the catchphrase "disloyalty." As the law of master and servant came to be applied in the employment setting well after the Industrial Revolution — that is to workers to whom the ascription of household service is discordant, to say the least — the obligation took firm root in legal treatises though, oddly, the actual catchphrase seems rarely to have been used. Fraser's 1882 treatise on the law of master and servant simply states as a broad principle that, "The Servant must do nothing to

---

injure his Master's Business," citing, among other decisions, Lacy v. Osbaldson, of which more will be said momentarily. Horace Wood's 1886 treatise captures the same principle and by extensive reference to authority including that decision. So, too, does Charles Manly Smith's treatise of 1906, citing the same case. And C.B. Labatt's eight volume treatise in 1913 supplies even greater detail, with even more extensive reference to authority, to illustrate the general principle that a servant's conduct that is likely to produce detriment to the master breaches the employment contract and gives cause to dismiss. Breach had been found where the servant's conduct had been calculated to offend, annoy, or alarm persons having business dealings with his master; where he had made a wilful and deliberate attempt to injure his master's business; where his acts or words had been such as to injure the master's standing as a business man; where he had acquired an interest in a business which competed with that of his master; where he had taken part in a strike affecting the employer's interests; where his behavior was calculated to excite discontent among his subordinates. The last referencing Lacy v. Osbaldson. The case is instructive.

Lacy had been hired as acting manager of Covent Garden for the theatrical season 1835-36, had been dismissed, and sued for sums due. The employer defended on several grounds one being that Lacy had excited discontent in the workplace by saying to a performer, Miss Romer, singing in the opera Zampa, "I wonder how you can perform in such rubbish." That was enough to present a question for the jury, of whether he'd conducted himself in a fashion so injurious to the employer's interests as to warrant discharge. For our purposes it is irrelevant that Lacy was a manager; an employee, Miss Romer, for example, who excited discontent among her coworkers by uttering such remarks would have been equally disloyal.

As Justice Frankfurter noted in Jefferson Standard, much that the Labor Act protects would be considered in breach of the implied obligation that a servant do nothing likely to produce detriment to the master's business. As Labatt's treatise pointed out, taking part in a strike would be just such an act and he cited authority to just that effect; but, as Frankfurter noted, an economic strike is quintessentially protected labor activity. Offending one's employer's customers breaches the duty of loyalty, but the statute allows employees to appeal to customers regarding the evils of their employer's policies; and if inciting discontent among coworkers were cause to dismiss today few unions would be able to engage in organizational activity. What needs explanation is why White's speech should fail of protection apart from the fact that economic harm might result, for economic harm might well result from any of these other disloyal but statutorily protected acts. What the Board's decision elicited instead of an explanation was the recitation of a catchphrase.

It is not surprising that the [court in] Endicott Interconnect [Technologies, Inc. v. NLRB, 453 F.3d 532 (D.C. Cir. 2006)], declined to supply a rationale for it was the want of a rationale that triggered the dissent in Jefferson Standard: the District of Columbia Circuit saw no need to be any more forthcoming on that account than the superior tribunal had been a half century before. But if one reads the opinion through the lens of Jefferson Standard, it becomes clearer that the decision tacitly rests on two grounds. The first is a conjunction of legal assumptions. The second draws from an ideology of industrial relations. Let us take each up in turn.

The legal conjunction is this: (1) that the obligation of non-disparagement of an employer's product or of its management is an immutable obligation inherent in the very nature of the employment relationship; and, (2) that Jefferson Standard permits no reading of the Labor Act that could extend statutory protection in derogation of it. Note that the strength of the conclusion rests upon the strength of the conjunction: if the meaning of "disloyalty" is mutable — if the law of employment in the United States in the first decade of the 21st century is not governed by the law of Master and Servant at the time when Dickens was young — it would be difficult to maintain that the Supreme Court's decision of a half century ago nonetheless makes it so. Accordingly, what the legal and industrial relations landscape is today must first be surveyed and how the jurisprudential foundation of Jefferson Standard relates to it needs next to be explored. Once the legal assumptions have been treated the ideological assumption will be taken up. Only after that is done can Endicott Interconnect be comprehended.

B. The Legal Landscape a Half Century On

Are employees today obligated as they were in 1953 never ever to disparage their employers or their products to third parties? Two legal developments in the public and private sectors respectively speak to the question.

1. Public Policy in Public Employment

Recall that in 1953 the law of master and servant applied to public and private employment equally; as the Tennessee Supreme Court captured it, in relation to its "servants" the public master is no more hampered by the Constitution than a private master is. The principle expounded by Fraser, Wood, Smith, and Labatt applied in both settings.

On September 24, 1964, Marvin Pickering, a teacher in Township High School District 205, in Will County, Illinois, published a letter to the editor in the local press. In it he accused the Board of Education of financial mismanagement in connection with a bond issue: "No doors on many of the classrooms, a plant room without any sunlight, no water in a first aid treatment room, are just a few of many things. Taxpayers were really taken to the cleaners." He was dismissed. Before the United States Supreme Court the school board argued to the common law duty of loyalty that Pickering owed to it. The Court rejected the claim. Howsoever time-honored, by 1964 the duty of loyalty to the employer abutted freedom of speech. Public employees were thus emancipated publicly to criticize those of their employer's actions that were of social, economic, or other concern to the community. The Court agreed that speech directed toward a person with whom the speaker would be in a close personal working relationship or that threatened the maintenance of discipline would inject a countervailing consideration. But neither of these factors was present. The questions Marvin Pickering addressed were of "legitimate public concern" and Pickering was free publicly to address them even if, in the process, he disparaged the quality of his employer's management or the educational product, which he did.

The warp and weft of public employee free speech, first framed in 1968, has become a rich tapestry of decisional law. For the purposes of this discussion it is important only to note a reversal of values: no longer do we see an employee's public utterance critical of the quality of her employer's management or service as an egregious breach of the duty of loyalty, we see it today as an act of responsible citizenship that contributes to a constitutionally valued robust debate on matters of legitimate public concern whatever the potential impact on the employer's "bottom line."

It would cabin the mind by a naked legalism to see this reversal of values as having no broader social emanation. Nor will it due to advert the public's monopoly of the service provided to distinguish it from private enterprise for public services have come to compete ever more frequently with private sector counterparts — in schooling, health care, security service, and a good deal more — or even to be privatized. The potential impact of employee speech on the employer's reputational or managerial interest cannot invariably be distinguished by the legal setting of the employment; the employer's concern for the "bottom line" may be no less today in the public than in the private sector . . . .

2. Public Policy in Private Employment

In 1971, a generation after Jefferson Standard, the chairman of the board of the General Motors Corporation lamented that,

". . . [T]he enemies of business now encourage an employee to be disloyal to the enterprise. They want to create suspicion and disharmony, and pry into the proprietary interests of the business. However this is labelled [sic] — industrial espionage, whistle blowing, or professional responsibility — it is another tactic for spreading disunity and creating conflict."

Public concern about corporate misconduct and encouragement of employee speech to disclose it grew apace nevertheless. Today, private employment is hedged 'round with whistleblower laws and common law tort doctrine protecting employees from discharge for speaking out and so encouraging them to do so, i.e., to breach their duty of loyalty. These vary enormously from state to state in coverage and technical detail, but that an employee in the private sector publicly criticizes her company's product or management can no longer be said to be such an act of disloyalty as to warrant discharge per se.

3. The Meaning of "Cause"

As it is no longer true that any public criticism of the product or of management is fatally disloyal, the question is whether Jefferson Standard must be read as stating a per se rule to the contrary — one the Labor Board is not free to modify, one only Congress can correct. The Supreme Court can give the statute a definitive if arguably erroneous reading having just that preclusive effect. It did in the Lechmere case concerning the access of union organizers to solicit employees for union support on company property. The Court, glossing its 1956 decision in Babcock & Wilcox, held that the previous decision had drawn a categorical statutory distinction between the expressive rights of employees, those in an employment relationship with the subject employer, and non-employees, those who are strangers to the enterprise for the want of that proximate relationship. The Court did so without reference in either decision to the statutory definition of an employee, which would seem to reject that distinction, or to its legislative history. This definitive reading is nevertheless binding upon the Labor Board and the lower courts; only Congress can correct it. The question is whether Jefferson Standard did the same.

The statutory basis for Jefferson Standard is § 10(c) of the Act, disallowing the Labor Board the power to afford a remedy for an employee who'd been dismissed for cause. But "cause" is not defined in the Act. As the dissent in Jefferson Standard pointed out, cause, or "just cause," is a concept borrowed from the world of industrial relations. The statutory term accordingly draws its sustenance from the common law of the workplace. If, today, speech to a third party critical of an employer or its product would not be cause to dismiss an employee under a collective bargaining agreement per se — if, that is, whether cause is presented is content and context specific — then it follows that it is well within the Labor Board's discretion to decide that the content and context is such as statutorily to privilege the speech when made in the context of labor organizing or of a labor dispute.

The common law of the workplace does recognize an implied "duty of loyalty," i.e., to "refrain from deliberately interfering with the employer's business interests." The question rhetorically put in cases of employee disparagement is whether the employee, like a dog, can "bite the hand that feeds . . . [him]." Not surprisingly, the answer often given is no. Often, but not inexorably, for cause is a fact-specific and context-driven question even when disparagement is the basis for industrial discipline. Let us turn then to the common law of industrial justice, of cause to dismiss.

Malicious or groundless disparagement of an employer's product is cause to discharge: where an employee published an article in a union newsletter accusing the employer, a defense contractor, of making "bad parts," of ordering inspectors to let them pass, and so of threatening the lives of servicemen, none of which was true, the arbitrator found just cause to discharge. And where an employee, whilst making a delivery, told the customer that his employer " 'always screws all their customers — they sell nothing but junk'," apparently out of personal hostility to the company president, the arbitrator said that such would be cause to dismiss. "[R]ights as a citizen," wrote one arbitrator, "must be balanced against his [the employee's] obligations to his employer" — necessarily to acknowledge that there could be circumstances where the balance weighs in favor of the employee. The factors to be weighed in the balance were catalogued by another arbitrator, among them consideration of: the audience to whom the employee's remarks are directed; whether the statements were "known to be or reasonably held" by the employee to be true or false; whether the " 'tone' " or actual language was malicious or inflammatory; and, whether " 'substantial personal rights of expression and citizenship' " were involved — which the arbitrator characterized as "a forceful mitigating consideration."

Consequently, a prominent arbitrator refused to sustain the discharge of an employee who'd written a letter of vitriolic criticism to the company's Operations Superintendent, copying it to his Congressman as well as several company officials.

The award relied extensively on the body of first amendment law governing labor speech in defamation cases. The arbitrator reasoned that speech insulated from reprisal by a suit for defamation as a matter of national labor policy, grounded in the nation's commitment to "'robust' debate in labor disputes," must be equally insulated from employer reprisal, by discharge, if that commitment is to have purchase in the workplace. And in a recent case reminiscent of Lacy v. Osbaldson, a Pepsi-Cola employee, identified as R., making a delivery at a Wal-Mart, encountered a Wal-Mart employee, Bev, and a Wal-Mart manager, Kevin. Bev told R that she didn't buy from the "pop machines" as they were too expensive. That prompted a colloquy in which Pepsi's employee disparaged Wal-Mart, his employer's customer. So seriously did Wal-Mart take the criticism that it notified Pepsi that it would not allow R. access to its premises. Pepsi issued R. a "Last Chance Agreement," a form of discipline that, in lieu of discharge, renders any future misconduct subject to summary termination; the union took the issuance of the latter to arbitration.

The Company argued that R. had breached the duty of loyalty he owed to Pepsi by offending Pepsi's customer; in fact, it claimed he'd "destroyed the relationship" between his employer and its customer. The arbitrator was not persuaded: "This was merely a free expression of ideas," he reasoned, the employee expressed his "political thinking." There was, he concluded, "no connection" between the content of the employee's speech and "'proper [just] cause' for termination."

By the standards laid down by Frasier (1882), Wood (1886), Smith (1906), and Labatt (1913), R's remarks were certainly contrary to his employer's business interest — in the latter's terms, it certainly "offend[ed] persons having business dealings with his master." By nineteenth century standards R's remarks were cause to dismiss and would be so today unless our appreciation of the value of free speech has changed.

From even so cursory a review it is apparent that the contemporary industrial understanding of "just cause" vis-à-vis the duty of loyalty differs meaningfully from the assumption of the Jefferson Standard Court a half century ago. The common law of the workplace recognizes an implied obligation to refrain from the deliberate infliction of economic or reputational harm — to speak maliciously, falsely, even accurately but gratuitously; but, it also recognizes that a human being does not give up all right to speak to an employer's policies or qualities upon entering upon another's employ. It recognizes that, in appropriate circumstances, a balance needs be struck the very statement of which necessarily implies that, depending upon the circumstances, the balance is not inexorably speech-suppressive . . . .

POST PROBLEM DISCUSSION

1.   Do you agree with the majority in *Jefferson Standard* that the technicians' activity itself (or the means by which they sought to achieve their purpose of winning the labor dispute) did not clearly relate to an employment practice of the employer, or otherwise address wages, hours, or working conditions? Is the situation similar or different to the use of the inflatable rat in Problem 3? Weren't the purpose of both activities, in part, to do harm to the employer's business?

2. Does the conduct in Problem 3 seem much like the disloyalty and product disparagement that took place in *Jefferson Standard*? *See Patterson-Sargent*, 115 N.L.R.B. 1627 (1956) ("We believe that the handbill was intended to, and did, publicly impugn the quality and usability of the Respondent's product. In this respect we view the conduct as quite distinguishable from the boycott of an employer's business and product which inheres in the usual strike situation."). Could it not be argued that a sophisticated observer would recognize the disparagement for what it is, i.e., just an extension of the ongoing labor dispute? *See Sierra Publishing Co.*, 889 F.2d 210 (9th Cir. 1989) (holding that letter, which was directly and overtly related to labor dispute, which did not disparage employer's product, and which disclosed no significant confidences, was not so unreasonable as to lose protection for concerted activity under the Act on grounds of disloyalty). As for the second part of this question, the Eighth Circuit held in *St. Luke's Episcopal-Presbyterian Hospital*, 268 F.3d 575 (8th Cir. 2001), that even speech that is not malicious but is false loses protection of the Act because the disparagement was guaranteed to adversely affect the hospital's business.

3. The Ninth Circuit held in *Atlantic-Pacific Construction Co. v. NLRB*, 52 F.3d 260 (9th Cir. 1995) that an employee's protest (on behalf of the group) of an especially disliked employee's promotion to a managerial position was protected activity because it was directly related to working conditions. The court therefore held that the employer violated the Act by terminating the protesting employee.

4. In *Trompler, Inc. v. NLRB*, 338 F.3d 747 (7th Cir. 2003), Judge Posner held for the Seventh Circuit that an employee walkout in protest of a supervisor's action was protected. Arguing for a broader standard in such circumstances, Judge Easterbrook wrote in concurrence that reasonableness should not apply in determining whether an employee has engaged in protected concerted activity using lawful means:

> The Board's conclusion that strikes and other walkouts are protected as concerted activity whether or not they are "reasonable" does not contradict any statute, and it is compatible with the premise that wages and working conditions grow out of a test of economic strength. Labor may resort to strikes and work-to-rule campaigns; workers may quit individually or en masse. Employers may use lockouts and permanent replacements and, after bargaining to impasse, may implement terms that workers abhor. Neither labor nor management must show that any of these steps is "reasonable."

But see Smithfield Packing Co. v. NLRB, 510 F.3d 507 (4th Cir. 2007) (holding that without reasonableness as a factor, employees could take over core managerial functions like hiring and firing managers by walking out over every change in management). But shouldn't employers and employees who engage in economic warfare be expected to suffer the consequences of their actions?

5. In *Elk Lumber Co.*, 91 N.L.R.B. 333 (1950), the Board held that employee work slowdowns, where employees purposefully slow down their work in order to place economic pressure on their employer, are unprotected concerted activities. This does not mean that slowdowns are unlawful under the Act, but that employees who engage in them can be disciplined without their employers' facing ULP

charges. The rationale is that although employees are free to go on strike or quit work, they are not protected from employer discipline when they continue to go to work, receive wages, and select in what manner they want to work. The Board reasoned that to allow otherwise would be equivalent to allowing employees to prescribe all the terms and conditions of their own employment. Do you agree with this reasoning? Isn't a slowdown just another display of economic strength which employers can respond to with their own economic weapons (e.g., with a lockout)?

6.   Is using an inflatable rat as in the Problem similar to writing a sarcastic letter critical of an employer's gift of ice cream? *See New River Industries, Inc. v. NLRB*, 945 F.2d 1290 (4th Cir. 1991) (finding employees' writing was not protected activity). Is the use of the rat, like the sarcastic letter, merely to mock the employer, not to solicit the help of other employees or improve working conditions? *But see Reef Industries, Inc. v. NLRB*, 952 F.2d 830 (5th Cir. 1991) (holding that an employee's activities in designing a cartoon for a T-shirt that suggested someone of low intelligence and sending the T-shirt with a letter to a personnel manager was a protected activity and part of an ongoing labor dispute).

7.   What is the connection between whistleblower statutes and disloyal conduct? Both the Court in *Jefferson Standard* and Professor Finkin discuss the possible connections. *See also Jolliff v. NLRB*, 513 F.3d 600 (6th Cir. 2008) (concluding that although employee's statement that local management had asked truck drivers to fix logbooks was capable of carrying defamatory meaning, NLRB's determination that employees acted with actual malice was not supported by substantial evidence); *International Union, UAW v. NLRB*, 514 F.3d 574 (6th Cir. 2008) (coming to opposite conclusion where employee sent package of complaint letters with forged name to employer).

8.   In *Five Star Transportation*, 349 N.L.R.B. 42 (2007), school bus drivers tried to convince a school board not to hire a non-union competitor for a contract because that company had hired a sex offender in previous years. When the non-union company won the contract, that same company refused to hire those union employees who had signed the letter to the school board. The employees in question were found to have failed the disparagement test of *Jefferson Standard* because they had called the non-union bus company "sub-standard" and "reckless," among other things. Should such disparaging letters, related to a labor dispute, come under *Jefferson Standard*? Member Liebman wrote in dissent in *Five Star Transportation* that an employee has no duty of loyalty to an employer for whom they currently do not work. Do you agree? Should employees in this situation be permitted to fight on behalf of their own company as part of a labor dispute?

9.   *Endicott Interconnect Technologies v. NLRB*, 453 F.3d 532 (D.C. Cir. 2006) is discussed prominently in Professor Finkin's article. Finkin argues that the opinion seems to revive the *Jefferson Standard* rule. Do you agree with Finkin that "the legal and ideological underpinnings of *Jefferson Standard* have become thoroughly eroded over the ensuing half century; that, at best, 'disloyalty' is worthless as a guide to decision, at worst, it chills speech of social value, and ought that it be abandoned?"

Chapter 5

ORGANIZING A UNION

This chapter is something of a hybrid. In one sense, it can be viewed as a continuation of the material that you've already read on various types of unfair labor practices. Every case in this chapter either was, or could have been, litigated solely as an unfair labor practice proceeding under Sections 8(a)(1) and 8(a)(3). The reason that these cases are in a separate chapter is that they are all related to a certain period of time: the period when a union is attempting to organize a group of employees. In Chapter 6, we'll discuss more of the mechanics involved with selecting a union, such as how the NLRB runs elections, how a proper group (or "bargaining unit") of employees is established, and other matters. The focus of this chapter is the conduct of both employers and unions in the lead-up to the election.

The connection to elections leads to the other part of this chapter's hybrid nature. When alleged misconduct occurs in the "critical period" before an election — the period of time that starts when a union files with the NLRB a valid petition for an election and continues until the election is held — a party can challenge the election results and ask the NLRB to re-run the election. This means that a union, where an employer engages in misconduct, or an employer where a union engages in misconduct, has two options. One option is to file an unfair labor practice charge. The second option, if the other party wins[1] the election, is to file election objections with the NLRB seeking to overturn the results of the election. Either option, or both options, are available to the "losing" party. Later, in Chapter 6, we'll discuss why a party might choose not to pursue both (spoiler alert: delay and something called the "blocking charge policy" are particularly relevant).

When a party files election objections, the NLRB must decide whether the misconduct is significant enough to warrant throwing out a completed election and taking the time to run a new election. In practice, the decision usually turns on

---

[1] Note that "winning" an election is something of a misnomer when the union fails to get a majority of votes because it's not necessarily true that the employer should be considered the "winner."

whether the "winning" party committed an unfair labor practice during the critical period because if it did, the NLRB will typically re-run the election. But that's not always the case.

The NLRB's standard for determining whether misconduct warrants overturning an election is whether the party who filed the objections can show that the misconduct has "a reasonable tendency to interfere with employee free choice." *See Randell Warehouse of Arizona, Inc.*, 347 N.L.R.B. 591, 597 (2006). *See also Westwood Horizons Hotel*, 270 N.L.R.B. 802, 803 (1984) (concluding that misconduct by a nonparty, such as an employee that is not an agent of the union, will warrant a new election only if that "misconduct was so aggravated as to create a general atmosphere of fear and reprisal rendering a free election impossible"). This inquiry can also be described as asking whether the employees were able to freely and fairly exercise their right to choose a collective-bargaining representative or to choose not to have a representative. The NLRB evaluates this question by looking at several factors, such as:

(1) the number of the incidents of misconduct;

(2) the severity of the incidents and whether they were likely to cause fear among the employees in the bargaining unit;

(3) the number of employees in the bargaining unit subjected to the misconduct;

(4) the proximity of the misconduct to the election date;

(5) the degree of persistence of the misconduct in the minds of the bargaining unit employees;

(6) the extent of dissemination of the misconduct among the bargaining unit employees;

(7) the effect, if any, of misconduct by the opposing party in canceling out the effect of the original misconduct;

(8) the closeness of the final vote; and

(9) the degree to which the misconduct can be attributed to the union [or employer].

Avis Rent-A-Car System, Inc., 280 N.L.R.B. 580, 581 (1986), *enforced sub nom. I.T.O. Corp. of Baltimore v. NLRB*, 818 F.2d 1108 (4th Cir. 1987).

As is the case for most factor tests, there is a great deal of wiggle room in determining whether a party's misconduct, given all the relevant circumstances, has gone too far.

The NLRB's original approach to that inquiry was embodied in the case, *General Shoe Corp.*, 77 N.L.R.B. 124 (1948). In *General Shoe*, the union alleged that the employer's aggressive anti-union campaign involved the commission of several unfair labor practices the day before the election — including a captive-audience meeting, which you'll learn about later in this chapter. In its decision, the NLRB primarily focused on whether the employer's actions warranted a new election, rather than analyzing whether the employer's actions actually violated the NLRA.

The NLRB stressed that "[c]onduct that creates an atmosphere which renders improbable a free choice will sometimes warrant invalidating an election, even though that conduct may not constitute an unfair labor practice. An election can serve its true purpose only if the surrounding conditions enable employees to register a free and untrammeled choice for or against a bargaining representative." *Id.* at 126. Continuing, the NLRB analogized its function in these cases as "provid[ing] a laboratory in which an experiment may be conducted, under conditions as nearly ideal as possible, to determine the uninhibited desires of the employees . . . . When, in the rare extreme case, the standard drops too low, because of our fault or that of others, the requisite laboratory conditions are not present and the experiment must be conducted over again." *Id.* at 127. Thus, even though the NLRB failed to find unfair labor practices, the employer's conduct "created an atmosphere calculated to prevent a free and untrammeled choice by the employees." *Id.* at 127.

If you ever practice or research in the area of labor law, you will frequently read about *General Shoe's* "laboratory conditions." *General Shoe* has never been overruled, and it remains true that the decision to overturn an election does not necessarily depend on the existence of an unfair labor practice. *See Contech Division, SPX Corp. v. NLRB*, 164 F.3d 297, 305 (6th Cir. 1998). However, as you read the cases in this chapter, think about the extent to which the NLRB and courts are actually following the laboratory conditions approach. Not to ruin the surprise, but if the NLRB's current election objection analysis is a laboratory, it's a messy one.

SECTION 1   THE RIGHT TO COMMUNICATE v. EMPLOYERS' PROPERTY RIGHTS

PROBLEM #1: FOOD COURT MEETING

The Northside Mall is a large, suburban shopping mall. It employs 25 janitors who clean the mall in different shifts. The janitors have increasingly been upset about their working conditions, particularly what they view as bad pay, lack of benefits, and abusive supervisors. During one of the janitors' informal discussions about their options to address these problems, one janitor suggested contacting a union. Many other janitors agreed and they ultimately contacted the local office of the Service Employees International Union (SEIU).

An SEIU organizer asked the janitors to arrange a meeting where she could talk to them about their problems at work and discuss the possibility of starting a campaign to select the SEIU as their collective-bargaining representative. The meeting took place on a slow shopping day around lunch time in the mall's food court. Attending the meeting was the organizer; janitors who were working that day, but on their lunch break; and janitors who were not working that day. The janitors and the SEIU organizer were easily able to find several tables to accommodate the group, as the food court was only about half full. During the meeting, the janitors told the organizer about their complaints. The organizer informed the janitors about how an organizational campaign might work and how the union could help them; she also gave the janitors fliers informing them about the union and their rights under the NLRA, as well as union buttons and hats.

Sarah, one of the mall's managers, noticed that the meeting was occurring. Once Sarah realized that the janitors were talking with a union, she immediately tried to break it up. Sarah told the SEIU organizer and the off-duty janitors that they needed to leave the mall; she then told the janitors working that day that if they wanted to talk about unions or any other type of solicitations, they needed to do so away from the mall.

As you read the material below, think about the various orders that Sarah made and whether any of them could lead to an unfair labor practice finding. Pay particular attention to how the legal analysis changes depending on the types of employees or situations involved.

PROBLEM MATERIALS

Movie, *Matewan* (1987) (film based on true events that illustrates the levels of violence and other extreme hostility that existed in some pre-NLRA union campaigns)

Republic Aviation Corp. v. NLRB, 324 U.S. 793 (1945)

Lechmere, Inc. v. NLRB, 502 U.S. 527 (1992)

A. Employee Communications at the Workplace

REPUBLIC AVIATION CORP. v. NLRB
324 U.S. 793 (1945)

JUSTICE REED delivered the opinion of the Court.

In the *Republic Aviation Corporation* case, the employer, a large and rapidly growing military aircraft manufacturer, adopted, well before any union activity at the plant, a general rule against soliciting which read as follows:

"Soliciting of any type cannot be permitted in the factory or offices."

The Republic plant was located in a built-up section of Suffolk County, New York. An employee persisted after being warned of the rule in soliciting union membership in the plant by passing out application cards to employees on his own time during lunch periods. The employee was discharged for infraction of the rule and, as the National Labor Relations Board found, without discrimination on the part of the employer toward union activity.

Three other employees were discharged for wearing UAW-CIO union steward buttons in the plant after being requested to remove the insignia. The union was at that time active in seeking to organize the plant. The reason which the employer gave for the request was that, as the union was not then the duly designated representative of the employees, the wearing of the steward buttons in the plant indicated an acknowledgment by the management of the authority of the stewards to represent the employees in dealing with the management and might impinge upon the employer's policy of strict neutrality in union matters and might interfere with the existing grievance system of the corporation.

The Board was of the view that wearing union steward buttons by employees did not carry any implication of recognition of that union by the employer where, as here, there was no competing labor organization in the plant. The discharges of the stewards, however, were found not to be motivated by opposition to the particular union or, we deduce, to unionism.

The Board determined that the promulgation and enforcement of the "no solicitation" rule violated § 8(1) [currently § 8(a)(1)] of the National Labor Relations Act as it interfered with, restrained and coerced employees in their rights under § 7 and discriminated against the discharged employee under § 8(3) [currently § 8(a)(3)]. It determined also that the discharge of the stewards violated § 8(1) and 8(3). As a consequence of its conclusions as to the solicitation and the wearing of the insignia, the Board entered the usual cease and desist order and directed the reinstatement of the discharged employees with back pay and also the rescission of "the rule against solicitation in so far as it prohibits union activity and solicitation on company property during the employees' own time." The Circuit Court of Appeals for the Second Circuit affirmed and we granted certiorari . . . .

In the case of *Le Tourneau Company of Georgia*, two employees were suspended two days each for distributing union literature or circulars on the employees' own time on company owned and policed parking lots, adjacent to the company's fenced-in plant, in violation of a long standing and strictly enforced rule, adopted prior to union organization activity about the premises, which read as follows:

> In the future no Merchants, Concern, Company, or Individual or Individuals will be permitted to distribute, post, or otherwise circulate handbills or posters, or any literature of any description, on Company property without first securing permission from the Personnel Department.

The rule was adopted to control littering and petty pilfering from parked autos by distributors. The Board determined that there was no union bias or discrimination by the company in enforcing the rule . . . .

The Board found that the application of the rule to the distribution of union literature by the employees on company property which resulted in the lay-offs was an unfair labor practice under § 8(1) and 8(3). Cease and desist, and rule rescission orders, with directions to pay the employees for their lost time, followed. The Circuit Court of Appeals for the Fifth Circuit reversed the Board, and we granted certiorari . . . .

These cases bring here for review the action of the National Labor Relations Board in working out an adjustment between the undisputed right of self-organization assured to employees under the Wagner Act and the equally undisputed right of employers to maintain discipline in their establishments. Like so many others, these rights are not unlimited in the sense that they can be exercised without regard to any duty which the existence of rights in others may place upon employer or employee. Opportunity to organize and proper discipline are both essential elements in a balanced society.

The Wagner Act did not undertake the impossible task of specifying in precise and unmistakable language each incident which would constitute an unfair labor practice. On the contrary, that Act left to the Board the work of applying the Act's general prohibitory language in the light of the infinite combinations of events which might be charged as violative of its terms. Thus a "rigid scheme of remedies" is avoided and administrative flexibility within appropriate statutory limitations obtained to accomplish the dominant purpose of the legislation.[] So far as we are here concerned, that purpose is the right of employees to organize for mutual aid without employer interference. This is the principle of labor relations which the Board is to foster.

The gravamen of the objection of both *Republic* and *Le Tourneau* to the Board's orders is that they rest on a policy formulated without due administrative procedure. To be more specific it is that the Board cannot substitute its knowledge of industrial relations for substantive evidence. The contention is that there must be evidence before the Board to show that the rules and orders of the employers interfered with and discouraged union organization in the circumstances and situation of each company. Neither in the *Republic* nor the *Le Tourneau* cases can it properly be said that there was evidence or a finding that the plant's physical location made solicitation away from company property ineffective to reach prospective union members. Neither of these is like a mining or lumber camp where the employees pass their rest as well as their work time on the employer's premises, so that union organization must proceed upon the employer's premises or be seriously handicapped.

The National Labor Relations Act creates a system for the organization of labor with emphasis on collective bargaining by employees with employers in regard to labor relations which affect commerce. An essential part of that system is the provision for the prevention of unfair labor practices by the employer which might interfere with the guaranteed rights. . . .

An administrative agency with power after hearings to determine on the evidence in adversary proceedings whether violations of statutory commands have occurred may infer within the limits of the inquiry from the proven facts such conclusions as reasonably may be based upon the facts proven. One of the purposes which lead to the creation of such boards is to have decisions based upon evidential facts under the particular statute made by experienced officials with an adequate appreciation of the complexities of the subject which is entrusted to their administration.

In the *Republic Aviation Corporation* case the evidence showed that the petitioner was in early 1943 a non-urban manufacturing establishment for military production which employed thousands. It was growing rapidly. Trains and automobiles gathered daily many employees for the plant from an area on Long Island, certainly larger than walking distance. The rule against solicitation was introduced in evidence and the circumstances of its violation by the dismissed employee after warning was detailed.

As to the employees who were discharged for wearing the buttons of a union steward, the evidence showed in addition the discussion in regard to their right to wear the insignia when the union had not been recognized by the petitioner as the representative of the employees. Petitioner looked upon a steward as a union representative for the adjustment of grievances with the management after employer recognition of the stewards' union. Until such recognition petitioner felt that it would violate its neutrality in labor organization if it permitted the display of a steward button by an employee. From its point of view, such display represented to other employees that the union already was recognized.

No evidence was offered that any unusual conditions existed in labor relations, the plant location or otherwise to support any contention that conditions at this plant differed from those occurring normally at any other large establishment.

The *Le Tourneau Company of Georgia* case also is barren of special circumstances. The evidence which was introduced tends to prove the simple facts heretofore set out as to the circumstances surrounding the discharge of the two employees for distributing union circulars.

These were the facts upon which the Board reached its conclusions as to unfair labor practices. The Intermediate Report in the *Republic Aviation* case set out the reason why the rule against solicitation was considered inimical to the right of organization.[2]

This was approved by the Board. The Board's reasons for concluding that the petitioner's insistence that its employees refrain from wearing steward buttons appear at page 1187 of the report.[3] In the *Le Tourneau Company* case the discussion of the reasons underlying the findings was much more extended. We insert in the note below a quotation which shows the character of the Board's opinion.[4] Furthermore, in both opinions of the Board full citation of authorities was

---

[2] [n.6] 51 N.L.R.B. 1195: "Thus, under the conditions obtaining in January 1943, the respondent's employees, working long hours in a plant engaged entirely in war production and expanding with extreme rapidity, were entirely deprived of their normal right to 'full freedom of association' in the plant on their own time, the very time and place uniquely appropriate and almost solely available to them therefor. The respondent's rule is therefore in clear derogation of the rights of its employees guaranteed by the Act."

[3] [n.7] We quote an illustrative portion. 51 N.L.R.B. 1187–88: "We do not believe that the wearing of a steward button is a representation that the employer either approves or recognizes the union in question as the representative of the employees, especially when, as here, there is no competing labor organization in the plant. Furthermore, there is no evidence in the record herein that the respondent's employees so understood the steward buttons or that the appearance of union stewards in the plant affected the normal operation of the respondent's grievance procedure. On the other hand, the right of employees to wear union insignia at work has long been recognized as a reasonable and legitimate form of union activity, and the respondent's curtailment of that right is clearly violative of the Act."

[4] [n.8] 54 N.L.R.B. at 1259–60: "As the Circuit Court of Appeals for the Second Circuit has held, 'It is not every interference with property rights that is within the Fifth Amendment . . . . Inconvenience, or even some dislocation of property rights, may be necessary in order to safeguard the right to collective bargaining' The Board has frequently applied this principle in decisions involving varying sets of circumstances, where it has held that the employer's right to control his property does not permit him to deny access to his property to persons whose presence is necessary there to enable the employees effectively to exercise their right to self-organization and collective bargaining, and in those decisions which have reached the courts, the Board's position has been sustained. Similarly, the Board has held that, while it was 'within the province of an employer to promulgate and enforce a rule prohibiting union solicitation during working hours,' it was 'not within the province of an employer to promulgate and enforce a rule prohibiting union solicitation by an employee outside of working hours, although on

given, including *Matter of Peyton Packing Co.*, 49 N.L.R.B. 828, 50 N.L.R.B. 355, hereinafter referred to.

The Board has fairly, we think, explicated in these cases the theory which moved it to its conclusions in these cases. The excerpts from its opinions just quoted show this. The reasons why it has decided as it has are sufficiently set forth. We cannot agree, as Republic urges, that in these present cases reviewing courts are left to "sheer acceptance" of the Board's conclusions or that its formulation of policy is "cryptic."

Not only has the Board in these cases sufficiently expressed the theory upon which it concludes that rules against solicitation or prohibitions against the wearing of insignia must fall as interferences with union organization, but, in so far as rules against solicitation are concerned, it had theretofore succinctly expressed the requirements of proof which it considered appropriate to outweigh or overcome the presumption as to rules against solicitation. In the *Peyton Packing Company* case, 49 N.L.R.B. 828, at 843, hereinbefore referred to, the presumption adopted by the Board is set forth.[5]

Although this definite ruling appeared in the Board's decisions, no motion was made in the court by Republic or Le Tourneau after the Board's decisions for leave to introduce additional evidence to show unusual circumstances involving their plants or for other purposes. . . . We perceive no error in the Board's adoption of this presumption. The Board had previously considered similar rules in industrial establishments and the definitive form which the *Peyton Packing Company* decision gave to the presumption was the product of the Board's appraisal of normal conditions about industrial establishments. . . .

In the *Republic Aviation* case, petitioner urges that irrespective of the validity of the rule against solicitation, its application in this instance did not violate § 8(3) because the rule was not discriminatorily applied against union solicitation but was impartially enforced against all solicitors. It seems clear, however, that if a rule against solicitation is invalid as to union solicitation on the employer's premises during the employee's own time, a discharge because of violation of that rule discriminates within the meaning of § 8(3) in that it discourages membership in a labor organization.

Republic Aviation Corporation v. National Labor Relations Board is affirmed.

---

company property,' the latter restriction being deemed an unreasonable impediment to the exercise of the right to self-organization."

[5] [n.10] 49 N.L.R.B. at 843–44: "The Act, of course, does not prevent an employer from making and enforcing reasonable rules covering the conduct of employees on company time. Working time is for work. It is therefore within the province of an employer to promulgate and enforce a rule prohibiting union solicitation during working hours. Such a rule must be presumed to be valid in the absence of evidence that it was adopted for a discriminatory purpose. It is no less true that time outside working hours, whether before or after work, or during luncheon or rest periods, is an employee's time to use as he wishes without unreasonable restraint, although the employee is on company property. It is therefore not within the province of an employer to promulgate and enforce a rule prohibiting union solicitation by an employee outside of working hours, although on company property. Such a rule must be presumed to be an unreasonable impediment to self-organization and therefore discriminatory in the absence of evidence that special circumstances make the rule necessary in order to maintain production or discipline."

National Labor Relations Board v. Le Tourneau Company of Georgia is reversed.

JUSTICE ROBERTS dissents in each case.

POST PROBLEM DISCUSSION

1.   Following *Republic Aviation*, the NLRB has developed a presumption test to determine when employers can restrict employees' protected solicitations in the workplace. Where the *Republic Aviation* analysis applies, there is a presumption that an employer's attempt to ban solicitations that are outside of work areas and not during work time improperly restricts employees' Section 7 rights and, therefore, violates Section 8(a)(1). "Work time" are periods when employees are actually working, as opposed to breaks and other "down time." The other side of this presumption is that attempts to restrict solicitations in work areas or during work time is presumptively valid. Parties may rebut these presumptions with evidence of special circumstances. For instance, an employer may be able to implement broader restrictions on employee solicitations if there are security concerns or there is a significant impact on customers or clients. *See, e.g., NLRB v. Baptist Hospital, Inc.*, 442 U.S. 773, 786 (1979) (holding that employer could ban solicitation in "immediate patient care" areas, sitting rooms, and corridors of hospitals). Another key exception is that an employer cannot ban employee solicitations in a discriminatory manner. The meaning of "discrimination" in this context will be explored in more detail with the *Lechmere* and *Register-Guard* cases excerpted below.

This basic *Republic Aviation* presumption only applies to oral solicitations. Subsequent NLRB interpretations of *Republic Aviation* have concluded that written distributions, such as pamphlets, should be analyzed differently. *See Stoddard-Quirk Manufacturing Co.*, 138 N.L.R.B. 615 (1962). Under *Stoddard-Quirk*, an employer is presumptively allowed to restrict written distributions, even during non-work time, from virtually the entire workplace. The Board's theory is two-fold. First, the Board distinguished the purpose of oral solicitations, which require a back-and-forth discussion, from the purpose of written distributions, which is met as long as the employee can read it at some point. Second, the Board concluded that written distributions "carr[y] the potential of littering the employer's premises, [and] raise[] a hazard to production," which warranted giving employers more power to prevent such problems. *Id.* at 619. Thus, as long as employees have some opportunity to distribute written materials, the employer is largely allowed to prohibit them throughout the workplace. *See id.* at 620 (stating that an employer may have to allow distributions in parking lots and plant entrances or exits).

2.   Given what you now know, did Sarah violate the NLRA when she told the off-duty janitors and SEIU organizer to leave the mall? What about her order that the on-duty janitors leave the meeting and stop talking about the union while in the mall? Does your answer change if the janitors were on-duty, and not on break? If you found a problem with any of her actions, what could have Sarah lawfully have done differently to limit this type of communication?

3. What about the union buttons and hats in the problem? Would you characterize those as "solicitations," "distributions," or something else? *See Serv-Air, Inc. v. NLRB*, 395 F.2d 557 (10th Cir. 1968) ("The courts have generally held that the wearing of union insignia is a form of expression protected by § 7 rather than a form of solicitation.") (citing *Republic Aviation*, 324 U.S. at 802 n.7). Typically, the default rule is that employers cannot bar employees from wearing union buttons or other types of insignia absent special circumstances that make such restrictions necessary for production, discipline, or to protect customers. *See Meijer, Inc. v. NLRB*, 130 F.3d 1209, 1217 (6th Cir. 1997) (stressing "employee's near-absolute right to wear union insignia"); *Davison-Paxon Co. v. NLRB*, 462 F.2d 364 (5th Cir. 1972) (holding that employer could restrict the wearing of bright yellow campaign buttons in customer area of department store); *The Broadway*, 267 N.L.R.B. 385, 404 (1983).

4. Does the presence of customers in the mall's food court help the employer in the problem? What if the meeting was in an area where customers were buying goods? Or, what if the meeting took place in a hospital waiting room? The NLRB has given employers more leeway to restrict solicitations, even when employees are not working and not in their work area, when the solicitations might cause extra impact on the employers' operations. *See, e.g., Baptist Hospital*, 442 U.S. at 786.

5. What if, instead of telling the employees to stop a meeting, an employer merely implemented a new rule banning such meetings? Or the employer had an overly broad non-solicitation rule that it had yet to enforce? Usually, the NLRB concludes that a facially invalid anti-solicitation policy chills employee solicitations in violation of Section 8(a)(1). *See Palms Hotel & Casino*, 344 NLRB 1363 (2005) (concluding that anti-loitering rule was overly vague and could lead employees to believe that they could not engage in protected solicitations) (citing *Tri-County Medical Center*, 222 NLRB 1089, 1089 (1976)).

B. Non-Employee Access to the Workplace

LECHMERE, INC. v. NLRB
502 U.S. 527 (1992)

JUSTICE THOMAS delivered the opinion of the Court.

. . . This case stems from the efforts of Local 919 of the United Food and Commercial Workers Union, AFL-CIO, to organize employees at a retail store in Newington, Connecticut, owned and operated by petitioner Lechmere, Inc. The store is located in the Lechmere Shopping Plaza, which occupies a roughly rectangular tract measuring approximately 880 feet from north to south and 740 feet from east to west. Lechmere's store is situated at the Plaza's south end, with the main parking lot to its north. A strip of 13 smaller "satellite stores" not owned by Lechmere runs along the west side of the Plaza, facing the parking lot. To the Plaza's east (where the main entrance is located) runs the Berlin Turnpike, a four-lane divided highway. The parking lot, however, does not abut the Turnpike; they are separated by a 46-foot-wide grassy strip, broken only by the Plaza's entrance. The parking lot is owned jointly by Lechmere and the developer of the satellite stores. The grassy strip is public property (except for a four-foot-wide band adjoining the parking lot, which belongs to Lechmere).

The union began its campaign to organize the store's 200 employees, none of whom was represented by a union, in June, 1987. After a full-page advertisement in a local newspaper drew little response, nonemployee union organizers entered Lechmere's parking lot and began placing handbills on the windshields of cars parked in a corner of the lot used mostly by employees. Lechmere's manager immediately confronted the organizers, informed them that Lechmere prohibited solicitation or handbill distribution of any kind on its property,[6] and asked them to leave. They did so, and Lechmere personnel removed the handbills. The union organizers renewed this handbilling effort in the parking lot on several subsequent occasions; each time they were asked to leave, and the handbills were removed. The organizers then relocated to the public grassy strip, from where they attempted to pass out handbills to cars entering the lot during hours (before opening and after closing) when the drivers were assumed to be primarily store employees. For one month, the union organizers returned daily to the grassy strip to picket Lechmere; after that, they picketed intermittently for another six months. They also recorded the license plate numbers of cars parked in the employee parking area; with the cooperation of the Connecticut Department of Motor Vehicles, they thus secured the names and addresses of some 41 nonsupervisory employees (roughly 20 of the store's total). The union sent four mailings to these employees; it also made some attempts to contact them by phone or home visits. These mailings and visits resulted in one signed union authorization card.

Alleging that Lechmere had violated the National Labor Relations Act by barring the nonemployee organizers from its property, the union filed an unfair labor practice charge with respondent National Labor Relations Board (Board). Applying the criteria set forth by the Board in *Fairmont Hotel Co.*, 282 N.L.R.B. 139 (1986), an administrative law judge (ALJ) ruled in the union's favor. He recommended that Lechmere be ordered, among other things, to cease and desist from barring the union organizers from the parking lot . . . . The Board affirmed the ALJ's judgment and adopted the recommended order, applying the analysis set forth in its opinion in *Jean Country*, 291 N.L.R.B. 11 (1988), which had by then replaced the short-lived *Fairmont Hotel* approach. A divided panel of the United States Court of Appeals for the First Circuit denied Lechmere's petition for review and enforced the Board's order.

Section 7 of the NLRA provides in relevant part that "[e]mployees shall have the right to self-organization, to form, join, or assist labor organizations." Section 8(a)(1)

---

[6] [n.1] Lechmere had established this policy several years prior to the union's organizing efforts. The store's official policy statement provided, in relevant part:

> Non-associates [i.e., nonemployees] are prohibited from soliciting and distributing literature at all times anywhere on Company property, including parking lots. Non-associates have no right of access to the non-working areas and only to the public and selling areas of the store in connection with its public use.

On each door to the store Lechmere had posted a 6 in. by 8 in. sign reading: "TO THE PUBLIC. No Soliciting, Canvassing, Distribution of Literature or Trespassing by Non-Employees in or on Premises." Lechmere consistently enforced this policy inside the store, as well as on the parking lot (against, among others, the Salvation Army and the Girl Scouts).

of the Act, in turn, makes it an unfair labor practice for an employer "to interfere with, restrain, or coerce employees in the exercise of rights guaranteed in [Section 7]." By its plain terms, thus, the NLRA confers rights only on employees, not on unions or their nonemployee organizers. In *NLRB v. Babcock & Wilcox Co.*, 109 N.L.R.B. 485, 493–494 (1954), however, we recognized that insofar as the employees' "right of self-organization depends in some measure on [their] ability . . . to learn the advantages of self-organization from others," § 7 of the NLRA may, in certain limited circumstances, restrict an employer's right to exclude nonemployee union organizers from his property. It is the nature of those circumstances that we explore today.

Babcock arose out of union attempts to organize employees at a factory located on an isolated 100-acre tract. The company had a policy against solicitation and distribution of literature on its property, which it enforced against all groups. About 40% of the company's employees lived in a town of some 21,000 persons near the factory; the remainder were scattered over a 30-mile radius. Almost all employees drove to work in private cars and parked in a company lot that adjoined the fenced-in plant area. The parking lot could be reached only by a 100-yard-long driveway connecting it to a public highway. This driveway was mostly on company-owned land, except where it crossed a 31-foot-wide public right-of-way adjoining the highway. Union organizers attempted to distribute literature from this right-of-way. The union also secured the names and addresses of some 100 employees (20% of the total), and sent them three mailings. Still other employees were contacted by telephone or home visit.

The union successfully challenged the company's refusal to allow nonemployee organizers onto its property before the Board. While acknowledging that there were alternative, nontrespassory means whereby the union could communicate with employees, the Board held that contact at the workplace was preferable[:] "[T]he right to distribute is not absolute, but must be accommodated to the circumstances. Where it is impossible or unreasonably difficult for a union to distribute organizational literature to employees entirely off of the employer's premises, distribution on a nonworking area, such as the parking lot and the walkways between the parking lot and the gate, may be warranted." Concluding that traffic on the highway made it unsafe for the union organizers to distribute leaflets from the right-of-way, and that contacts through the mails, on the streets, at employees' homes, and over the telephone would be ineffective, the Board ordered the company to allow the organizers to distribute literature on its parking lot and exterior walkways.

The Court of Appeals for the Fifth Circuit refused to enforce the Board's order, and this Court affirmed. While recognizing that "the Board has a responsibility of 'applying the Act's general prohibitory language in the light of the infinite combinations of events which might be charged as violative of the terms,' " we explained that the Board had erred by failing to make the critical distinction between the organizing activities of employees (to whom 7 applies only derivatively). Thus, while "[n]o restriction may be placed on the employees' right to discuss self-organization *among themselves*, unless the employer can demonstrate that a restriction is necessary to maintain production or discipline," 351 U.S., at 113 (emphasis added) (citing *Republic Aviation Corp. v. NLRB*, "no such obligation is owed nonemployee organizers." As a rule, then, an employer cannot be compelled to allow distribution of union literature by nonemployee organizers on his property. As with many other rules, however, we recognized an exception. Where "the location of a plant and the living quarters of the employees place the employees beyond the reach of reasonable union efforts to communicate with them," employers' property rights may be "required to yield to the extent needed to permit communication of information on the right to organize." . . .

Jean Country . . . represents the Board's latest attempt to implement the rights guaranteed by § 7. It sets forth a three-factor balancing test:

> [I]n all access cases, our essential concern will be 1. the degree of impairment of the Section 7 right if access should be denied, as it balances against 2. the degree of impairment of the private property right if access should be granted. We view the consideration of 3. the availability of reasonably effective alternative means as especially significant in this balancing process.

The Board conceded that this analysis was unlikely to foster certainty and predictability in this corner of the law, but declared that, "as with other legal questions involving multiple factors, the 'nature of the problem, as revealed by unfolding variant situations, inevitably involves an evolutionary process for its rational response, not a quick, definitive formula as a comprehensive answer.' "

Citing its role "as the agency with responsibility for implementing national labor policy," the Board maintains in this case that is a reasonable interpretation of the NLRA entitled to judicial deference. It is certainly true, and we have long recognized, that the Board has the "special function of applying the general provisions of the Act to the complexities of industrial life." *NLRB v. Erie Resistor Corp.*, 373 U.S. 221, 236 (1963); see also *Phelps Dodge Corp. v. NLRB*, 313 U.S. 177, 196-197 (1941). . . . Before we reach any issue of deference to the Board, however, we must first determine whether *Jean Country* — at least as applied to nonemployee organizational trespassing — is consistent with our past interpretation of § 7.

In *Babcock*, as explained above, we held that the Act drew a distinction "of substance," between the union activities of employees and nonemployees. In cases involving *employee* activities, we noted with approval, the Board "balanced the conflicting interests of employees to receive information on self-organization on the company's property from fellow employees during nonworking time, with the employer's right to control the use of his property." In cases involving *nonemployee* activities (like those at issue in *Babcock* itself), however, the Board was not permitted to engage in that same balancing (and we reversed the Board for having done so). . . . *Babcock's* teaching is straightforward: § 7 simply does not protect nonemployee union organizers except in the rare case where "the inaccessibility of employees makes ineffective the reasonable attempts by nonemployees to communicate with them through the usual channels." Our reference to "reasonable" attempts was nothing more than a common sense recognition that unions need not engage in extraordinary feats to communicate with inaccessible employees - not an endorsement of the view (which we expressly rejected) that the Act protects "reasonable" trespasses. Where reasonable alternative means of access exist, § 7's guarantees do not authorize trespasses by nonemployee organizers, even (as we noted in *Babcock*) "under . . . reasonable regulations" established by the Board.

Jean Country, which applies broadly to "all access cases," misapprehends this critical point. . . . To say that our cases require accommodation between employees' and employers' rights is a true but incomplete statement, for the cases also go far in establishing the locus of that accommodation where nonemployee organizing is at issue. So long as nonemployee union organizers have reasonable access to employees outside an employer's property, the requisite accommodation has taken place. It is only where such access is infeasible that it becomes necessary and proper to take the accommodation inquiry to a second level, balancing the employees' and employers' rights . . . . At least as applied to nonemployees, *Jean Country* impermissibly conflates these two stages of the inquiry — thereby significantly eroding *Babcock's* general rule that "an employer may validly post his property against nonemployee distribution of union literature." We reaffirm that general rule today, and reject the Board's attempt to recast it as a multifactor balancing test.

The threshold inquiry in this case, then, is whether the facts here justify application of *Babcock's* inaccessibility exception. . . . As we have explained, the exception to Babcock's rule is a narrow one. It does not apply wherever nontrespassory access to employees may be cumbersome or less-than-ideally effective, but only where "the *location of a plant and the living quarters of the employees* place the employees *beyond the reach* of reasonable union efforts to communicate with them," 351 U.S., at 113 (emphasis added). Classic examples include logging camps; mining camps; and mountain resort hotels. [Citations omitted.] *Babcock's* exception was crafted precisely to protect the § 7 rights of those employees who, by virtue of their employment, are isolated from the ordinary flow of information that characterizes our society. The union's burden of establishing such isolation is, as we have explained, "a heavy one," and one not satisfied by mere conjecture or the expression of doubts concerning the effectiveness of nontrespassory means of communication.

The Board's conclusion in this case that the union had no reasonable means short of trespass to make Lechmere's employees aware of its organizational efforts is based on a misunderstanding of the limited scope of this exception. Because the employees do not reside on Lechmere's property, they are presumptively not "beyond the reach" of the union's message. Although the employees live in a large metropolitan area . . . , that fact does not in itself render them "inaccessible" in the sense contemplated by Babcock. Their accessibility is suggested by the union's success in contacting a substantial percentage of them directly, via mailings, phone calls, and home visits. Such direct contact, of course, is not a necessary element of "reasonably effective" communication; signs or advertising also may suffice. In this case, the union tried advertising in local newspapers; the Board said that this was not reasonably effective, because it was expensive and might not reach the employees. Whatever the merits of that conclusion, other alternative means of communication were readily available. Thus, signs (displayed, for example, from the public grassy strip adjoining Lechmere's parking lot) would have informed the employees about the union's organizational efforts. (Indeed, union organizers picketed the shopping center's main entrance for months as employees came and went every day.) *Access* to employees, not *success* in winning them over, is the critical issue — although success, or lack thereof, may be relevant in determining whether reasonable access exists. Because the union in this case failed to establish the existence of any "unique obstacles" that frustrated access to Lechmere's employees, the Board erred in concluding that Lechmere committed an unfair labor practice by barring the nonemployee organizers from its property.

The judgment of the First Circuit is therefore reversed, and enforcement of the Board's order denied.

JUSTICE WHITE, with whom JUSTICE BLACKMUN joins, dissenting.

. . . For several reasons, the Court errs in this case. First, that *Babcock* stated that inaccessibility would be a reason to grant access does not indicate that there would be no other circumstance that would warrant entry to the employer's parking lot and would satisfy the Court's admonition that accommodation must be made with as little destruction of property rights as is consistent with the right of employees to learn the advantages of self-organization from others. Of course, the union must show that its "reasonable efforts," without access, will not permit proper communication with employees. But I cannot believe that the Court in *Babcock* intended to confine the reach of such general considerations to the single circumstance that the Court now seizes upon. If the Court in *Babcock* indicated that nonemployee access to a logging camp would be required, it did not say that only in such situations could nonemployee access be permitted. Nor did *Babcock* require the Board to ignore the substantial difference between the entirely private parking lot of a secluded manufacturing plant and a shopping center lot which is open to the public without substantial limitation. Nor indeed did *Babcock* indicate that the Board could not consider the fact that employees' residences are scattered throughout a major metropolitan area; *Babcock* itself relied on the fact that the employees in that case lived in a compact area which made them easily accessible.

Moreover, the Court in Babcock recognized that actual communication with nonemployee organizers, not mere notice that an organizing campaign exists, is necessary to vindicate § 7 rights. If employees are entitled to learn from others the advantages of self-organization, it is singularly unpersuasive to suggest that the union has sufficient access for this purpose by being able to hold up signs from a public grassy strip adjacent to the highway leading to the parking lot.

Second, the Court's reading of *Babcock* is not the reading of that case reflected in later opinions of the Court. We have consistently declined to define the principle of *Babcock* as a general rule subject to narrow exceptions, and have instead repeatedly reaffirmed that the standard is a neutral and flexible rule of accommodation. [Citing *Hudgens v. NLRB*, 424 U.S. 507 (1976), and *Central Hardware Co. v. NLRB*, 407 U.S. 539, 544 (1972).] Our cases . . . are more consistent with the Jean Country view that reasonable alternatives are an important factor in finding the least destructive accommodation between 7 and property rights. . . .

Third, and more fundamentally, Babcock is at odds with modern concepts of deference to an administrative agency charged with administering a statute. See *Chevron U.S.A. Inc. v. Natural Resources Defense Council, Inc.*, 467 U.S. 837 (1984). When reviewing an agency's construction of a statute, we ask first whether Congress has spoken to the precise question at issue. If it has not, we do not simply impose our own construction on the statute; rather, we determine if the agency's view is based on a permissible construction of the statute. *Babcock* did not ask if Congress had specifically spoken to the issue of access by third parties, and did not purport to explain how the NLRA specifically dealt with what the access rule should be where third parties are concerned. If it had made such an inquiry, the only basis for finding statutory language that settled the issue would have been the language of § 7, which speaks only of the rights of employees; i.e., the Court might have found that § 7 extends no access rights at all to union representatives. But *Babcock* itself recognized that employees have a right to learn from others about self-organization, and itself recognized that, in some circumstances, § 7 and § 8 required the employer to grant the union access to parking lots. So have later Courts, and so does the Court today.

That being the case, the *Babcock* Court should have recognized that the Board's construction of the statute was a permissible one, and deferred to its judgment. Instead, the Court simply announced that, as far as access is concerned, third parties must be treated less favorably than employees. Furthermore, after issuing a construction of the statute different from that of the Board, rather than remanding to the Board to determine how third parties should be dealt with, the *Babcock* Court essentially took over the agency's job, not only by detailing how union organizer access should be determined, but also by announcing that the records before it did not contain facts that would satisfy the newly coined access rule.

Had a case like *Babcock* been first presented for decision under the law governing in 1991, I am quite sure that we would have deferred to the Board, or at least attempted to find sounder ground for not doing so. Furthermore, had the Board ruled that third parties must be treated differently than employees and held them to the standard that the Court now says *Babcock* mandated, it is clear enough that we also would have accepted that construction of the statute. But it is also clear, at least to me, that, if the Board later reworked that rule in the manner of *Jean Country*, we would also accept the Board's change of mind. . . .

Finally, the majority commits a concluding error in its application of the outdated standard of *Babcock* to review the Board's conclusion that there were no reasonable alternative means available to the union. . . . "The judicial role is narrow: . . . the Board's application of the rule, if supported by substantial evidence on the record as a whole, must be enforced." [Citation omitted.] The Board's conclusion as to reasonable alternatives in this case was supported by evidence in the record. Even if the majority cannot defer to that application, because of the depth of its objections to the rule applied by the NLRB, it should remand to the Board for a decision under the rule it arrives at today, rather than sitting in the place Congress has assigned to the Board. . . .

Under the law that governs today, it is *Babcock* that rests on questionable legal foundations. The Board's decision in *Jean Country*, by contrast, is both rational and consistent with the governing statute. The Court should therefore defer to the Board, rather than resurrecting and extending the reach of a decision which embodies principles which the law has long since passed by.

It is evident, therefore, that, in my view, the Court should defer to the Board's decision in Jean Country and its application of Jean Country in this case. With all due respect, I dissent.

Justice Stevens, dissenting [opinion omitted].

POST PROBLEM DISCUSSION

1. One issue that can arise from the Court's emphasis on the employee/nonemployee distinction is how to treat off-duty employees. For example, in our problem, imagine that some of the janitors promoting the union during the meeting were not scheduled to work that day. Is the employer's ability to stop the off-duty employees from soliciting any greater than its ability to stop on-duty employees? Generally, the answer is no. The NLRB typically extends the *Republic Aviation* analysis to off-duty employees because all employees have a direct Section 7 right to communicate with other employees about organizing and other protected subjects. *See Hillhaven Highland House*, 336 N.L.R.B. 646, 648 (2001), *enforced*, 344 F.3d 523 (6th Cir. 2003); *accord ITT Industries, Inc. v. NLRB*, 413 F.3d 64, 72–73 (D.C. Cir. 2005). The *Republic Aviation* presumption will apply even to employees who work at a different site for the same employer, although an employer's property interest will often be given more weight in that situation. *See Hillhaven*, 336 N.L.R.B. at 650. Finally, the NLRB will generally allow employers to restrict off-duty employees' access to working areas or the inside of a facility if that restriction is justified by valid business reasons, applies to all activities, and is disseminated to employees. *See Teletech Holdings, Inc.*, 333 N.L.R.B. No. 56, at 4 (2001); *Tri-County Medical Center*, 222 N.L.R.B. 1089, 1090 (1976).

2. Similar to the off-duty employee issue are situations in which employees solicit at their regular worksite, but the worksite is not owned by their employer. In one recent case, *New York New York Hotel & Casino*, 356 N.L.R.B. No. 119 (2011), *enforced*, 676 F.3d 193 (D.C. Cir. 2012), Ark was a food service provider that ran various restaurants at the New York New York Hotel and Casino in Las Vegas. During a campaign to unionize Ark, several Ark employees who regularly worked at New York New York distributed handbills outside of the hotel's main entrance and in front of two Ark restaurants inside the hotel. New York New York officials demanded that they leave and called the police — prompting a Section 8(a)(1) charge. After a back-and-forth with the D.C. Circuit, *see New York New York Hotel & Casino*, 334 N.L.R.B. 762 (2001), and *New York New York Hotel & Casino*, 334 N.L.R.B. 772 (2001), *enforcement denied by* 313 F.3d 585 (D.C. Cir. 2002), the NLRB — with one Member dissenting — issued a decision setting out a new test for the situation. Under that test:

> the property owner may lawfully exclude such employees [i.e., employees who are regularly employed on the property, doing work that is integral to the owner's business] only where the owner is able to demonstrate that their activity significantly interferes with his use of the property or where exclusion is justified by another legitimate business reason, including, but not limited to, the need to maintain production and discipline (as those terms have come to be defined in the Board's case law). Thus, any justification for exclusion that would be available to an employer of the

employees who sought to engage in Section 7 activity on the employer's property would also potentially be available to the nonemployer property owner, as would any justification derived from the property owner's interests in the efficient and productive use of the property.

356 NLRB No. 119, at ¶ 16. In effect, the NLRB will apply the *Republic Aviation* presumption to solicitations by employees that occur at those employees' regular place of work, even if the owner of the workplace is not their employer. In applying that test, the NLRB concluded that the hotel violated Section 8(a)(1). The D.C. Circuit was finally satisfied with this decision and enforced the NLRB's order. *See New York-New York, LLC v. NLRB*, 313 F.3d 585 (D.C. Cir. 2012).

3. What if New York New York had not asked the employees to leave directly, but only called the police to have them removed? Would the hotel have had a defense based on the First Amendment's guarantee of the right to petition the government? *See Venetian Casino Resort, LLC*, 357 N.L.R.B. No. 147 (2011) (concluding that the NLRB can find a Section 8(a)(1) violation for calling the police, despite the Supreme Court's *Noerr-Pennington* doctrine which protects some otherwise unlawful actions under the Petition Clause).

4. Does *Lechmere* require the NLRB to delve too much into state law? Under the NLRB's application of *Lechmere*, the first step in determining whether an employer lawfully excluded non-employee organizers is to examine whether the employer has a state property right to exclude people from the land in question. If not, the employer's attempt to remove non-employee solicitors — barring some special circumstance — is unlawful. *See Indio Grocery Outlet*, 323 N.L.R.B. 1138, 1141 (1997), *enforced sub nom. NLRB v. Calkins*, 187 F.3d 1080 (9th Cir. 1999). This can force the NLRB to engage in detailed analysis of state property law and result in divergent protection for solicitations depending on the jurisdiction. *See, e.g., Venetian Casino Resort, L.L.C. v. Local Joint Executive Bd.*, 257 F.3d 937, 942–43 (9th Cir. 2001) (holding that the employer lacked right to exclude organizers from a sidewalk that it built on its private property, because of an agreement it made with the city to get the road in front of its casino widened); *Food for Less*, 318 N.L.R.B. 646, 649–50 (1995) (concluding that the employer lacked the right to exclude organizers under state law, despite its ability to maintain the parking lot in question under its lease), *enforced in relevant part sub nom. O'Neil's Markets v. UFCW*, 95 F.3d 733, 739 (8th Cir. 1996). Indeed, in one case, the state law was so confusing that an appellate court asked the state supreme court to clarify the relevant law and, after the state court refused, the federal appellate court was forced to figure out the state property law for itself in order to resolve the NLRA issue before it. *See Waremart Foods*, 337 N.L.R.B. 289 (2001) (finding Section 8(a)(1) violation), *reviewed by* 333 F.3d 223 (D.C. Cir. 2003) (certifying question to California Supreme Court), and *enforcement denied*, 354 F.3d 870 (D.C. Cir. 2004). For a criticism of this reliance of state law, see Jeffrey M. Hirsch, *Taking State Property Rights Out of Federal Labor Law*, 47 B. C. L. REV. 891 (2006).

5. In part of *Lechmere* not excerpted above, the Court quoted with approval the following interpretation of its earlier *Babcock* decision: "To gain access, the union has the burden of showing that no other reasonable means of communicating its organizational message to the employees exists or that the employer's access rules

discriminate against union solicitation." 502 U.S. at 535 (emphasis omitted) (quoting *Sears, Roebuck & Co. v. Carpenters*, 436 U.S. 180, 205 (1978)); *see NLRB v. Babcock & Wilcox Co.*, 351 U.S. 105, 112 (1956). Thus, in cases where the employer might otherwise be allowed to exclude organizers, it will violate Section 8(a)(1) if one of two circumstances exist: 1) the organizers had no other reasonable means of communicating with employees and 2) the employer's exclusion was considered discriminatory. The first exception is relatively well, if narrowly, defined. In contrast, the second exception has resulted in a wide variety of interpretations. For an argument that *Lechmere* overly restricts employees' ability to communicate with one another, see Cynthia L. Estlund, *Labor, Property, and Sovereignty After Lechmere*, 46 STAN. L. REV. 305, 306 (1994); *see also* Jeffrey M. Hirsch, *Communication Breakdown: Reviving the Role of Discourse in the Regulation of Employee Collective Action*, 44 U.C. DAVIS L. REV. 1091 (2011) (discussing importance of communication to group action and criticizing *Lechmere* as ignoring that connection).

6.   What do you think "reasonable access" means? You might be forgiven if you take the view that that term implies some degree of access to employees that ensures that they are able to learn about unionization — the basis of the Section 7 rights at issue in these right-to-access cases. Indeed, *Lechmere* confirmed the idea put forth in *Babcock* that employees' interest in hearing initially about collective representation is such a vital part of their ability to freely decide whether to unionize that unions have a "derivative" Section 7 right to communicate with employees. However, *Lechmere* narrowed this right considerably. The Court stressed that "[a]ccess to employees, not *success* in winning them over, is the critical issue" and that as long as employees were not "beyond the reach" of unions solicitations through other means, there is no need for access to the worksite. 502 U.S. at 540 (citations omitted). The result has been that unions are virtually never able to use this exception save for extreme instances such as off-shore oil rigs or remote worksites where employees live on-site and are reachable only though direct access to the site. *See Nabors Alaska Drilling, Inc. v. NLRB*, 190 F.3d 1008 (9th Cir. 1999)

7.   Prior to *Lechmere*, the NLRB had concluded that employers could not, without special reasons, exclude non-employee organizers from certain property that is typically open to the public — much like a food court in our problem. *See Montgomery Ward & Co.*, 288 N.L.R.B. 126, 127 (1988). But the NLRB, feeling constrained by *Lechmere*, has overruled that approach. *See Farm Fresh*, 326 N.L.R.B. 997, 999 (1998), *petition for review granted on different grounds sub nom. UFCW v. NLRB*, 222 F.3d 1030, 1033–34 (D.C. Cir. 2000). That said, what if the employer allowed certain non-employees to solicit on its property, but not others, including unions? For instance, in our problem, imagine if the mall has previously permitted the Salvation Army and Girl Scouts to solicit in the food court. Given that it has already shown a willingness to allow certain non-employee solicitations, should the mall then be allowed to exclude union solicitors?

This question raises the discrimination exception to the *Lechmere* analysis (as discussed below in the material accompanying the *Register-Guard* decision, this discrimination exception arguably applies to *Republic Aviation* and *Lechmere* cases). Over the years, the NLRB and appellate courts have created numerous ways to interpret what "discrimination" means. The primary examples of these disparate interpretations of discrimination include employers who:

- provide access to all groups except for unions, *see Sandusky Mall Co.*, 329 N.L.R.B. 618, 620 (1999) ("[A]n employer that denies a union access while regularly allowing nonunion organizations to solicit and distribute on its property unlawfully discriminates against union solicitation."), *enforcement denied in relevant part*, 242 F.3d 682 (6th Cir. 2001); *Great American*, 322 N.L.R.B. 17, 24 (1996) (finding discrimination where employer excluded union organizers, but allowed gift-wrapping fundraisers, Salvation Army solicitations, auto sales, circus fliers, Chamber of Commerce information, and heart and cancer fund solicitations);

- allow only work-related or isolated charitable solicitations, but not unions, *see Lucille Salter Packard Children's Hospital*, 97 F.3d 583, 588–90 (D.C. Cir. 1996) (holding that excluding unions while allowing employee fringe-benefit program solicitations was not discriminatory, but excluding unions while permitting solicitations about home and automobile insurance, child and family services, and credit union membership was discriminatory);

- allow all charitable solicitations, but bar other non-work-related communications, including those related to unions, *see Lucille Salter*, 97 F.3d at 588 n.4 (noting that frequent charitable solicitations may provide basis for discrimination finding);

- favor one union over another or allow distributions by employers, but not unions, *see Cleveland Real Estate Partners v. NLRB*, 95 F.3d 457, 464–65 (6th Cir.1996); and

- bar union and other Section 7 communications, yet allow other communications of a similar character, *see Guardian Indus. Corp. v. NLRB*, 49 F.3d 317, 320 (7th Cir. 1995); *see also 6 West Ltd. Corp. v. NLRB*, 237 F.3d 767, 780 (7th Cir. 2001) (holding that employer did not discriminate by allowing "innocent" employee solicitations for Girl Scout cookies, Christmas ornaments, and other purposes that were beneficial to employees, but not allowing union solicitation by employees).

Recently, the NLRB shifted away from its previously broad view of what constitutes unlawful discrimination in its *Register-Guard* decision, which is excerpted below. As you read that decision, think about which interpretation the NLRB adopted. Also pay attention to the dissent's view. Because of the changed membership on the NLRB, by the time you read this, *Register-Guard* may be overruled and the dissent's view of discrimination, as well as the e-mail communications that are the focus of the case, may be controlling.

C. Electronic Communications

PROBLEM #2: UNION E-MAILS

After the meeting in the food court, the SEIU organizers wanted to maintain contacts with the janitors. Jane, a pro-union janitor, offered to e-mail some union materials to other janitors, using their mall e-mail addresses. The mall had provided all of its employees these e-mail addresses, which were associated with the mall's Internet account. The mall used the accounts to provide information to employees and had a computer at the mall that employees could use during their break times. Posted next to that computer was a "Computer Use Policy" that was also included in the employee handbook. That policy stated that "all mall computer systems and equipment are to be used for work-related reasons only. Any violation of this policy may result in disciplinary measures, including dismissal." In spite of this policy, employees regularly used the mall computer and their mall e-mail addresses to send messages on a variety of non-work-related subjects, including postings on items for sale, requests for donations to charitable organizations, and personal e-mails to other employees and to individuals not associated with the mall.

The day after Jane sent the union e-mail to other janitors, Sarah called the janitor into her office. Sarah asked Jane if she was aware of the Computer Use Policy; Jane said that she was, but that she was also aware of the many non-work-related e-mails that other employees frequently send. Sarah said that personal e-mails and occasional charitable and minor solicitations were one thing, but solicitations from outside organizations were something that the mall had never allowed. However, because of the confusion about what the policy actually covered, Sarah said that she would only give Jane a written warning for her personnel file.

Did Sarah have a right to restrict Jane's e-mails? As you read the following material consider the different challenges that Jane could make. Also consider how the NLRB's analysis of those challenges fit with the *Republic Aviation* and *Lechmere* cases, as well as the NLRA's policy goals.

PROBLEM MATERIALS

Jeffrey M. Hirsch, *Communication Breakdown: Reviving the Role of Discourse in the Regulation of Employee Collective Action*, 44 U.C. DAVIS L. REV. 1091 (2011)

Guard Publishing Co. (Register-Guard), 351 N.L.R.B. 1110 (2007)

Jeffrey M. Hirsch, *Communication Breakdown: Reviving the Role of Discourse in the Regulation of Employee Collective Action*
44 U.C. Davis L. Rev. 1091 (2011)[7]

The right to employee collective action is at the core of labor law. Before employees can exercise that right, however, they must overcome numerous problems that interfere with their ability to act together. Among the most serious of these collective-action problems are the restrictions on employee discourse, particularly the restrictions on employees' ability to access and discuss relevant information. Despite the significance of these problems, labor law has largely ignored the role of employee discourse in promoting collective action. If that core right is to have meaning, this failure must be rectified.

Many of the most pressing issues in labor law — such as unions' access to employer property, employees' right to use employer-provided e-mail, and employees' ability to choose a representative — center on attempts to restrict employee discourse. Although discourse has a major influence on employees' ability to act collectively in these instances, courts, agencies, and policymakers rarely mention it, and even when these decisionmakers acknowledge discourse, they badly undervalue its significance. . . .

Discourse — the act of people communicating with each other — is a central component of social interaction. Social interaction, in turn, is a necessary condition for groups to form and act collectively. Thus, without discourse there is no group action. All forms of discourse are not sufficient to prompt such action, however. It takes repeated interactions to establish the trust and feelings of shared interests that individuals require first to identify themselves as a group and, ultimately, act as one.

Despite the importance of discourse to collective action, labor law has continually dismissed the need for substantial employee communications. In case after case, the courts or federal labor agencies — particularly the [NLRB] — acknowledge that discourse has a role in collective action, but give protection for such a limited amount that they might as well not have bothered. Under this prevailing view, labor law need only prevent employers from barring all forms of communication to satisfy employees' right to collective action; courts have deemed even a mere theoretical opportunity to communicate sufficient. That view, however, is demonstrably untrue. As public choice theory, game theory, and psychological research show, collective action requires a significant level of discourse and information transference among individuals; mere sporadic or impersonal contacts are inadequate. Thus, to fulfill the rights embodied in the [NLRA] and other labor laws, there must be far more protection for employees' ability to communicate — protection for not only the frequency of communications but also the type. . . .

The importance of discourse has long been recognized in various aspects of work law. Whether as a condition for an economically efficient labor market, a prerequisite for the enforcement of employees' rights, or a means for opposing unlawful

---

[7] Copyright © 2011 by Jeffrey M. Hirsch. All rights reserved. Reprinted by permission.

employment practices, employees' ability to communicate and access information of various types has been a factor in many workplace policy debates. Yet in no area is the concern over discourse more prominent than labor law.

Labor law's relationship with discourse and information is unique among other work laws because those interests are integral to its fundamental concept: employees should be free to engage in collective action. As the text of the NLRA states, the right to collective action was the primary purpose of the statute:

It is hereby declared to be the policy of the United States to . . . encourag[e] the practice and procedure of collective bargaining and [to] protect[] the exercise by workers of full freedom of association, self-organization, and designation of representatives of their own choosing . . . . [Section 1 of the NLRA.]

From the early days of the statute, the NLRB and courts have noted the role of discourse and information in employees' exercise of their right to association, self-organization, representation, and other forms of collective action. These decisions implicitly recognized that labor law's guarantee of the right to engage in collective action necessarily depended on employees' ability to communicate among themselves and access enough information to decide whether and how to act together.

Although recognition of discourse's role in collective action has never fully vanished, over the last several decades, the NLRB and particularly the courts have increasingly dismissed the connection between the two. In case after case in which employer interests are weighed against employees' right to collective action, the need for discourse has frequently received little more than lip service. This disregard has substantially weakened employees' labor rights, for even where those rights are explicitly articulated in statutes or decisions, employees' inability to converse with each other often makes those rights useless. The cruel irony is that as the NLRB and courts have diminished the significance of discourse in overcoming collective-action problems, changes in the workplace have made those problems more acute.

Most modern employees face a very different environment than workers in the past. For instance, job security is much lower today, and employees spend less time with a given employer than before. This increase in job mobility makes collective action more difficult because it decreases both employees' long-term interest in improving work conditions at a given firm and their willingness to incur the costs of collective action for a job they may not have for long. The workplace has also become more diverse, which is largely beneficial, but makes it more difficult for employees to achieve consensus. Moreover, increased competition among firms, especially in the global economy, has fueled more employer resistance to demands for better work conditions. This resistance not only raises the risk of retaliation for employees who engage in collective action, but delays the possible benefits as well.

The enhanced complexity of the modern workplace also exacerbates a common problem for employees — a lack of relevant information. Information asymmetries affect many elements of employees' work life, including their ability to bargain with their employers and reach an economically efficient agreement. Similarly, information asymmetries can create significant barriers to employee collective action. If employees are unaware of the options or legal protections for acting collectively, they are unlikely even to consider such action, much less actually attempt it.

To be sure, employees who are unionized or have been part of a union organizing campaign will typically have some information about their legal protections, but these employees are a small portion of the overall workforce. The reality is that most employees are probably unaware of their right to engage in many types of collective action, such as sharing salary information with coworkers, much less the way in which they can exercise those rights. . . .

Among the more promising answers to the lack of protection for discourse in the workplace are the recent, extraordinary advances in communication technology. The increased availability and affordability of the Internet, e-mail, instant messaging, and other types of electronic communications have transformed employees' interactions with each other and their employers. This trend represents a substantial advance for workplace collective action, as the lower cost of communication and coordination can significantly enhance employees' ability to form and act as a group. Electronic communications may also be a means for employees to avoid some of the significant limits the NLRB and courts have imposed on workplace discourse.

According to the Department of Labor, approximately 40% of all workers used the Internet or e-mail at work in 2003. A private survey conducted a year later found that the use of e-mail at work was even higher, with over 80% of employees spending an hour or more e-mailing each day. Although the disparity in these numbers indicates the challenges in measuring e-mail use, the studies reveal a substantial reliance on workplace electronic communications, which has almost certainly increased in the intervening years. Although face-to-face discussions remain the ideal for organizing employees, electronic communications have increasingly become a second-best substitute — at least among employees who are frequent users of this technology. Because such workers are disproportionately young, the prevalence of workplace electronic communications will undoubtedly expand in the near future.

There are many reasons why e-mail and other electronic communications are becoming such an important part of employee collective-action efforts. Most obviously, general use of electronic communications has grown rapidly over the last couple of decades, and it is natural to see a parallel expansion in the workplace. Many employees may also believe that e-mail and other types of electronic communications can provide a veil of privacy — albeit one that is illusory. Further, for employees with access to their co-workers' e-mail addresses, electronic communications provide an easy and effective way to distribute information to a large number of people, many of whom may be difficult to reach by traditional means. Finally, electronic communications have been an increasingly important response to labor law restrictions on the use of more traditional discourse. . . .

One prominent illustration of electronic communications' value to collective action is reflected in union organizing strategies. Unions have the resources and experience necessary to take advantage of new technology, as well as a strong incentive to use these tools to avoid legal constraints on more direct communications. Thus, unions were quick to use the Internet to provide information to members and potential members. Building on those efforts, recent organizing campaigns have increasingly incorporated e-mail and other electronic communication strategies. Indeed, one union literally started in an Internet chat room and maintained all of its business meetings via electronic communications.

Technology's ability to enhance employee communication is significant but no panacea. Although helpful, electronic communications are not an equal substitute for face-to-face discussions. Personal interactions involve important social signals that give valuable information about the views of each participant. Those signals help the participants understand the beliefs of others and, in turn, help shape each participant's own views. This view-shaping function is a precursor to the development of a group or group action. Electronic communications, however, are often unable to replicate these effects.

Psychological research into the "saying-is-believing" phenomenon reveals why face-to-face communications are superior to electronic ones. In a typical saying-is-believing study, a speaker describes one person to an audience who is familiar with the described subject. The description starts with supplied passages that can be reasonably interpreted as either positive or negative, after which the speaker then provides her own descriptions of the subject. However, the speaker is told whether her audience likes or dislikes the subject. In repeated studies of this sort, speakers do two things. First, they adjust their descriptions to match what they were told about their audiences' like or dislike for the subject. Second, their own memory of the supplied description matches their audiences' views of the subject. The latter effect works as follows: after delays that range from as little as ten minutes to as long as several weeks, researchers asked speakers to repeat as accurately as they could the original, supplied descriptions. Speakers' memories of the ambiguous passages mirrored their audience-adjusted description, rather than the supplied description they read initially. This means that people not only adjust their message to fit an audience's view, but also alter their own interpretation of a subject to mesh with the views of their audience. For instance, one study showed that an eyewitness's memory of an event can change based on hearing another person's retelling of the witnessed event. This saying-is-believing effect can also manifest itself in different situations, including where the subject is an individual or a small group. The key is that a speaker and audience develop some form of interpersonal connection that results in a merging or sharing of beliefs.

The saying-is-believing effect illustrates why electronic communications cannot duplicate the interpersonal bonds that accompany face-to-face communications. The dynamic in face-to-face communications works in two directions; both the speaker and the audience influence each other. This influence is particularly strong where the speaker and audience are already part of a group, such as co-workers with a certain degree of familiarity and trust. Electronic communications can replicate some of this effect but not to the same extent. Additionally, face-to-face communications are better suited for applying social pressure or learning social norms. Groups, particularly smaller ones, may develop social norms, or impose social costs and rewards, that can often spur collective action where it might not otherwise occur. Again, electronic communications can convey some of these social considerations but to a lesser degree than personal contact.

This research's impact on labor law is two-fold. First, although electronic communications are an increasingly valuable category of employee discourse, they still have significant shortcomings compared to face-to-face communications. Second, this psychological research demonstrates the inaccuracy of the prevailing view that any single form of communication, no matter how impersonal, is sufficient to provide opportunities for employees to act together. Collective action often requires a substantial level of interaction among individuals, and while electronic communications can be an important part of that dynamic, they will rarely be sufficient.

In addition to the inherent shortcomings of electronic communications, their use, although ubiquitous in some workplaces, is rare or nonexistent in many others. The "digital divide" that has kept many low-income people from enjoying access to electronic communications is also seen in the workplace, particularly with blue-collar and service jobs. Moreover, even in workplaces dependent upon electronic communications, employees are often prohibited from using them to further their collective interests. In particular, the most common means for employees to communicate electronically involves the use of employer-owned computers or Internet service. As discussed in detail below, this has created a tension between employees' ability to communicate and employers' desire to limit use of their property. Indeed, as of 2005, at least 76% of employers currently had some type of policy restricting employees' use of e-mail at work.

Labor law is particularly well suited to govern the balance between these competing interests. Yet, for years the NLRB failed even to acknowledge that electronic communications might warrant a new approach to its regulation of workplace discourse. . . . Indeed, one of the more frustrating aspects of the NLRB's regulation of discourse in general is that it consistently has failed to account for changes in the workplace, whether they involve e-mail and other advances in communications, different physical workspaces, or employees' evolving job duties. These changes often create additional barriers to collective action, which makes the Board's restrictions on the rare innovations that actually enhance employee discourse all the more troubling. . . .

GUARD PUBLISHING CO. (REGISTER-GUARD)
351 N.L.R.B. 1110 (2007)

In this case, we consider several issues relating to employees' use of their employer's e-mail system for Section 7 purposes. First, we consider whether the Respondent violated Section 8(a)(1) by maintaining a policy prohibiting the use of e-mail for all "nonjob-related solicitations." Second, we consider whether the Respondent violated Section 8(a)(1) by discriminatorily enforcing that policy against union-related e-mails while allowing some personal e-mails, and Section 8(a)(3) and (1) by disciplining an employee for sending union-related e-mails. Finally, we consider whether the Respondent violated Section 8(a)(5) and (1) by insisting on an allegedly illegal bargaining proposal that would prohibit the use of e-mail for "union business."

After careful consideration, we hold that the Respondent's employees have no statutory right to use the Respondent's e-mail system for Section 7 purposes. We therefore find that the Respondent's policy prohibiting employee use of the system for "nonjob-related solicitations" did not violate Section 8(a)(1).

With respect to the Respondent's alleged discriminatory enforcement of the e-mail policy, we have carefully examined Board precedent on this issue. As fully set forth herein, we have decided to modify the Board's approach in discriminatory enforcement cases to clarify that discrimination under the Act means drawing a distinction along Section 7 lines. We then address the specific allegations in this case of discriminatory enforcement in accordance with this approach. . . .

II. Facts

The Respondent publishes a newspaper. The Union represents a unit of about 150 of the Respondent's employees. The parties' last collective-bargaining agreement was in effect from October 16, 1996, though April 30, 1999. When the record closed, the parties were negotiating, but had not yet reached a successor agreement.

In 1996, the Respondent began installing a new computer system, through which all newsroom employees and many (but not all) other unit employees had e-mail access. In October 1996, the Respondent implemented the "Communications Systems Policy" (CSP) at issue here. The policy governed employees' use of the Respondent's communications systems, including e-mail. The policy stated, in relevant part:

> Company communication systems and the equipment used to operate the communication system are owned and provided by the Company to assist in conducting the business of The Register-Guard. Communications systems are not to be used to solicit or proselytize for commercial ventures, religious or political causes, outside organizations, or other non-job-related solicitations.

The Respondent's employees use e-mail regularly for work-related matters. Throughout the relevant time period, the Respondent was aware that employees also used e-mail to send and receive personal messages. The record contains evidence of e-mails such as baby announcements, party invitations, and the occasional offer of sports tickets or request for services such as dog walking. However, there is no evidence that the employees used e-mail to solicit support for or participation in any outside cause or organization other than the United Way, for which the Respondent conducted a periodic charitable campaign.

Suzi Prozanski is a unit employee and the union president. In May and August 2000, Prozanski received two written warnings for sending three e-mails to unit employees at their Register-Guard e-mail addresses. The Respondent contends that the e-mails violated the CSP. . . .

[The first e-mail involved Prozanski's response to the employer's e-mail about a union rally. She wrote the e-mail on break, but sent it from her work station, and was given a written warning for violating the CSP for using e-mail to conduct union business. Prazanski sent the second and third e-mails, one of which asked employees to wear green to support the union and the other asked for participation in the union's entry in a parade, from a computer in the union's office in a different location. She again received written warnings for violating the CSP's ban against non-job-related solicitations.]

For the reasons set forth below, we agree with the judge that the Respondent did not violate Section 8(a)(1) by maintaining the CSP. We also agree with the judge that the Respondent's enforcement of the CSP with respect to Prozanski's May 4 e-mail was discriminatory and therefore violated Section 8(a)(1). Likewise, the written warning issued to Prozanski for the May 4 e-mail violated Section 8(a)(3) and (1). However, we reverse the judge and dismiss the allegations that the Respondent's application of the CSP to Prozanski's August 14 and 18 e-mails was discriminatory. We also find no 8(a)(3) violation as to Prozanski's discipline for those e-mails. . . .

A. Maintenance of the CSP

The CSP, in relevant part, prohibits employees from using the Respondent's e-mail system for any "nonjob-related solicitations." Consistent with a long line of cases governing employee use of employer-owned equipment, we find that the employees here had no statutory right to use the Respondent's e-mail system for Section 7 matters. Therefore, the Respondent did not violate Section 8(a)(1) by maintaining the CSP.

An employer has a "basic property right" to "regulate and restrict employee use of company property." *Union Carbide Corp. v. NLRB*, 714 F.2d 657, 663–664 (6th Cir. 1983). The Respondent's communications system, including its e-mail system, is the Respondent's property and was purchased by the Respondent for use in operating its business. The General Counsel concedes that the Respondent has a legitimate business interest in maintaining the efficient operation of its e-mail system, and that employers who have invested in an e-mail system have valid concerns about such issues as preserving server space, protecting against computer viruses and dissemination of confidential information, and avoiding company liability for employees' inappropriate e-mails.

Whether employees have a specific right under the Act to use an employer's e-mail system for Section 7 activity is an issue of first impression. In numerous cases, however, where the Board has addressed whether employees have the right to use other types of employer-owned property — such as bulletin boards, telephones, and televisions — for Section 7 communications, the Board has consistently held that there is "no statutory right . . . to use an employer's equipment or media," as long as the restrictions are nondiscriminatory. *Mid-Mountain Foods*, 332 NLRB 229, 230 (2000) (no statutory right to use the television in the respondent's breakroom to show a prounion campaign video), enfd. 269 F.3d 1075 (D.C. Cir. 2001). See also *Eaton Technologies*, 322 NLRB 848, 853 (1997) ("It is well established that there is no statutory right of employees or a union to use an employer's bulletin board."); *Champion International Corp.*, 303 NLRB 102, 109 (1991) (stating that an employer has "a basic right to regulate and restrict employee use of company property" such as a copy machine); *Churchill's Supermarkets*, 285 NLRB 138, 155 (1987) ("[A]n employer ha[s] every right to restrict the use of company telephones to business-related conversations . . . ."), enfd. 857 F.2d 1474 (6th Cir. 1988), cert. denied 490 U.S. 1046 (1989); *Union Carbide Corp.*, 259 NLRB 974, 980 (1981) (employer "could unquestionably bar its telephones to any personal use by employees"), enfd. in relevant part 714 F.2d 657 (6th Cir. 1983); *cf. Heath Co.*,

196 NLRB 134 (1972) (employer did not engage in objectionable conduct by refusing to allow prounion employees to use public address system to respond to antiunion broadcasts).

Our dissenting colleagues, however, contend that this well-settled principle — that employees have no statutory right to use an employer's equipment or media for Section 7 communications — should not apply to e-mail systems. They argue that the decisions cited above involving employer telephones — *Churchill's Supermarkets* and *Union Carbide* — were decided on discriminatory enforcement grounds, and therefore their language regarding an employer's right to ban nonbusiness use of its telephones was dicta. The Board, however, reaffirmed *Union Carbide* in *Mid-Mountain Foods*, supra, citing it for the specific principle that employees have no statutory right to use an employer's telephone for nonbusiness purposes.

Nevertheless, our dissenting colleagues assert that the issue of employees' use of their employer's e-mail system should be analyzed under *Republic Aviation Corp. v. NLRB*, 324 U.S. 793 (1945), by balancing employees' Section 7 rights and the employer's interest in maintaining discipline, and that a broad ban on employee nonwork-related e-mail communications should be presumptively unlawful absent a showing of special circumstances. We disagree and find the analytical framework *of Republic Aviation* inapplicable here. . . .

In contrast to the employer's policy at issue in *Republic Aviation*, the Respondent's CSP does not regulate traditional, face-to-face solicitation. Indeed, employees at the Respondent's workplace have the full panoply of rights to engage in oral solicitation on nonworking time and also to distribute literature on nonworking time in nonwork areas, pursuant to *Republic Aviation* and *Stoddard-Quirk*. What the employees seek here is use of the Respondent's communications equipment to engage in additional forms of communication beyond those that *Republic Aviation* found must be permitted. Yet, "Section 7 of the Act protects organizational rights . . . rather than particular means by which employees may seek to communicate." *Guardian Industries Corp. v. NLRB*, 49 F.3d 317, 318 (7th Cir. 1995); see also *NLRB v. Steelworkers (Nutone)*, 357 U.S. 357, 363–364 (1958) (The Act "does not command that labor organizations as a matter of law, under all circumstances, be protected in the use of every possible means of reaching the minds of individual workers, nor that they are entitled to use a medium of communications simply because the Employer is using it."). *Republic Aviation* requires the employer to yield its property interests to the extent necessary to ensure that employees will not be "entirely deprived," 324 U.S. at 801 fn. 6, of their ability to engage in Section 7 communications in the workplace on their own time. It does not require the most convenient or most effective means of conducting those communications, nor does it hold that employees have a statutory right to use an employer's equipment or devices for Section 7 communications. Indeed, the cases discussed above, in which the Board has found no Section 7 right to use an employer's equipment, were decided long after *Republic Aviation* and have been upheld by the courts.

The dissent contends that because the employees here are already rightfully on the Respondent's premises, only the Respondent's managerial interests — and not its property interests — are at stake. That would be true if the issue here concerned customary, face-to-face solicitation and distribution, activities that involve only the employees' own conduct during nonwork time and do not involve use of the employer's equipment. Being rightfully on the premises, however, confers no additional right on employees to use the employer's equipment for Section 7 purposes regardless of whether the employees are authorized to use that equipment for work purposes.

The dissent contends that e-mail has revolutionized business and personal communications and that, by failing to carve out an exception for it to settled principles regarding use of employer property, we are failing to adapt the Act to the changing patterns of industrial life. The dissent attempts to distinguish use of e-mail from other communication equipment based on e-mail's interactive nature and its ability to process thousands of communications simultaneously.

We recognize that e-mail has, of course, had a substantial impact on how people communicate, both at and away from the workplace. Moreover, e-mail has some differences from as well as some similarities to other communications methods, such as telephone systems. For example, as the dissent points out, transmission of an e-mail message, unlike a telephone conversation, does not normally "tie up" the line and prevent the simultaneous transmission of messages by others. On the other hand, e-mail messages are similar to telephone calls in many ways. Both enable virtually instant communication regardless of distance, both are transmitted electronically, usually through wires (sometimes the very same fiber-optic cables) over complex networks, and both require specialized electronic devices for their transmission. Although the widespread use of telephone systems has greatly impacted business communications, the Board has never found that employees have a general right to use their employer's telephone system for Section 7 communications.

In any event, regardless of the extent to which communication by e-mail systems is similar to or different from communication using other devices or systems, it is clear that use of the Respondent's e-mail system has not eliminated face-to-face communication among the Respondent's employees or reduced such communication to an insignificant level. Indeed, there is no contention in this case that the Respondent's employees rarely or never see each other in person or that they communicate with each other solely by electronic means. Thus, unlike our dissenting colleagues, we find that use of e-mail has not changed the pattern of industrial life at the Respondent's facility to the extent that the forms of workplace communication sanctioned in *Republic Aviation* have been rendered useless and that employee use of the Respondent's e-mail system for Section 7 purposes must therefore be mandated. Consequently, we find no basis in this case to refrain from applying the settled principle that, absent discrimination, employees have no statutory right to use an employer's equipment or media for Section 7 communications.[8]

---

[8] [n.12] Contrary to the dissent, in reaching this conclusion, we are not applying an "alternative means of communication" test appropriate only for questions of nonemployee access. *See Lechmere, Inc. v. NLRB*, 502 U.S. 527 (1992). Rather, we are merely examining whether, as asserted by the dissent, e-mail has so changed workplace communication that the Board should depart from settled precedent and order that the Respondent must permit employees to use its e-mail system to communicate regarding Sec. 7 matters. Such an analysis necessarily requires examination of whether the face-to-face solicitation and

Accordingly, we hold that the Respondent may lawfully bar employees' nonwork-related use of its e-mail system, unless the Respondent acts in a manner that discriminates against Section 7 activity.[9] As the CSP on its face does not discriminate against Section 7 activity, we find that the Respondent did not violate Section 8(a)(1) by maintaining the CSP.

B. Alleged Discriminatory Enforcement of the CSP

The judge found that the Respondent violated Section 8(a)(1) by discriminatorily enforcing the CSP to prohibit Prozanski's union-related e-mails while allowing other nonwork-related e-mails. We affirm the violation as to Prozanski's May 4 e-mail, but reverse and dismiss as to her August e-mails. In doing so, we modify Board law concerning discriminatory enforcement.

In finding that the Respondent discriminatorily enforced the CSP, the judge relied on evidence that the Respondent had permitted employees to use e-mail for various personal messages. Specifically, the record shows that the Respondent permitted e-mails such as jokes, baby announcements, party invitations, and the occasional offer of sports tickets or request for services such as dog walking. However, there is no evidence that the Respondent allowed employees (or anyone else) to use e-mail to solicit support for or participation in any outside cause or organization other than the United Way, for which the Respondent conducted a periodic charitable campaign.

Citing *Fleming Co.*, 336 NLRB 192 (2001), enf. denied 349 F.3d 968 (7th Cir. 2003), the judge found that "[i]f an employer allows employees to use its communications equipment for nonwork related purposes, it may not validly prohibit employee use of communications equipment for Section 7 purposes." We agree with the judge that the Board's decision in *Fleming* would support that proposition. However, having carefully examined current precedent, we find that the Board's approach in *Fleming* and other similar cases fails to adequately examine whether the employer's conduct discriminated against Section 7 activity.

In *Fleming*, the Board held that the employer violated Section 8(a)(1) by removing union literature from a bulletin board because the employer had allowed "a wide range of personal postings" including wedding announcements, birthday cards, and notices selling personal property such as cars and a television. There was no evidence that the employer had allowed postings for any outside clubs or organizations. Likewise, in *Guardian Industries*, 313 NLRB 1275 (1994), enf. denied 49 F.3d 317 (7th Cir. 1995), the Board found an 8(a)(1) violation where the employer allowed personal "swap and shop" postings but denied permission for union or other group postings, including those by the Red Cross and an employee credit union.

The Seventh Circuit denied enforcement in both cases. In *Guardian*, the court

---

distribution permitted under *Republic Aviation* no longer enable employees to communicate. As we find controlling here the principle that employees have no statutory right to use an employer's equipment or media for Sec. 7 communications, neither *Republic Aviation* nor *Lechmere* is applicable.

[9] [n.13] We do not pass on circumstances, not present here, in which there are no means of communication among employees at work other than e-mail.

started from the proposition that employers may control the activities of their employees in the workplace, "both as a matter of property rights (the employer owns the building) and of contract (employees agree to abide by the employer's rules as a condition of employment)." Although an employer, in enforcing its rules, may not discriminate against Section 7 activity, the court noted that the concept of discrimination involves the unequal treatment of equals. The court emphasized that the employer had never allowed employees to post notices of organizational meetings. Rather, the nonworkrelated postings permitted by the employer consisted almost entirely of "swap and shop" notices advertising personal items for sale. The court stated: "We must therefore ask in what sense it might be discriminatory to distinguish between for-sale notes and meeting announcements." The court ultimately concluded that "[a] rule banning all organizational notices (those of the Red Cross along with meetings pro and con unions) is impossible to understand as disparate treatment of unions."

In *Fleming*, the court reaffirmed its decision in *Guardian* and further stated:

> Just as we have recognized for-sale notices as a category of notices distinct from organizational notices (which would include union postings), we can now add the category of personal postings. The ALJ's factual finding that Fleming did not allow the posting of organizational material on its bulletin boards does not support the conclusion that Fleming violated Section 8(a)(1) by prohibiting the posting of union materials.

349 F.3d at 975.

We find that the Seventh Circuit's analysis, rather than existing Board precedent, better reflects the principle that discrimination means the unequal treatment of equals. Thus, in order to be unlawful, discrimination must be along Section 7 lines. In other words, unlawful discrimination consists of disparate treatment of activities or communications of a similar character because of their union or other Section 7-protected status. See, e.g., *Fleming*, supra, 349 F.3d at 975 ("[C]ourts should look for disparate treatment of union postings before finding that an employer violated Sec. 8(a)(1)."); *Lucile Salter Packard Children's Hospital at Stanford v. NLRB*, 97 F.3d 583, 587 (D.C. Cir. 1996) (charging party must demonstrate that "the employer treated nonunion solicitations differently than union solicitations").

For example, an employer clearly would violate the Act if it permitted employees to use e-mail to solicit for one union but not another, or if it permitted solicitation by antiunion employees but not by prounion employees.[10] In either case, the employer has drawn a line between permitted and prohibited activities on Section 7 grounds. However, nothing in the Act prohibits an employer from drawing lines on a non-Section 7 basis. That is, an employer may draw a line between charitable solicitations and noncharitable solicitations, between solicitations of a personal nature (e.g., a car for sale) and solicitations for the commercial sale of a product

---

[10] [n.17] On the other hand, an employer may use its own equipment to send antiunion messages, and still deny employees the opportunity to use that equipment for prounion messages. As noted above, employees are not entitled to use a certain method of communication just because the employer is using it. See *Nutone*, supra at 363–364.

(e.g., Avon products), between invitations for an organization and invitations of a personal nature, between solicitations and mere talk, and between business-related use and nonbusiness - related use. In each of these examples, the fact that union solicitation would fall on the prohibited side of the line does not establish that the rule discriminates along Section 7 lines.[11] For example, a rule that permitted charitable solicitations but not noncharitable solicitations would permit solicitations for the Red Cross and the Salvation Army, but it would prohibit solicitations for Avon and the union.

The dissent contends that our analysis is misplaced because, in 8(a)(1) cases, discrimination is not the essence of the violation. Rather, the dissent asserts that discrimination is relevant in 8(a)(1) cases merely because it weakens or exposes as pretextual the employer's business justification for its actions. In our view, the dissent overlooks the Supreme Court's inhospitable response to this theory and too readily writes off discrimination as the essential basis of many 8(a)(1) violations.

The dissent argues that denying employees access to the employer's e-mail system for union solicitations while permitting access for other types of messages undermines the employer's business justification and constitutes discrimination. This argument is at odds with Supreme Court precedent. In *NLRB v. Steelworkers*, 357 U.S. 357 (1958), the Court reviewed the Board's finding in *Avondale Mills*, 115 NLRB 840 (1956), that the employer violated Section 8(a)(1) when it denied employees worktime access to their coworkers for union solicitation while permitting supervisors to engage in antiunion solicitation on working time. Even though supervisors and employees were not similarly situated, the Board found the employer's rule discriminatory because it diminished the employees' ability to communicate their organizational message and the employer's exception for supervisors belied the working-time-is-for-work justification. The Supreme Court disagreed. Although the Court left the Board free in future cases to proceed on a theory of actual discrimination, it rejected the notion that a difference in treatment between any two groups not similarly situated that undermines the employer's asserted business justification violates Section 8(a)(1). According to the Court, there could be no unfair labor practice finding in such circumstances unless, in view of the available alternate channels of communication, the employer had truly diminished the ability of the labor organization involved to carry its message to the employees.

It is not surprising, therefore, that the dissent fails to acknowledge that many decisions require actual discrimination. For example, as the Board noted in *Salmon Run Shopping Center*, 348 NLRB 658 (2006), the Supreme Court has held that "an employer violates 8(a)(1) of the Act by prohibiting nonemployee distribution of union literature if its actions 'discriminate against the union by allowing other distribution.' " Id. at 658, quoting *NLRB v. Babcock & Wilcox Co.*, 351 U.S. 105, 112 (1956). After determining that the employer's decision to deny the union access was based "solely on the Union's status as a labor organization and its desire to engage in labor-related speech," the Board found in *Salmon Run* that "[s]uch discriminatory exclusion" violated Section 8(a)(1). *Salmon Run Shopping Center*, above at 659. . . .

---

[11] [n.18] Of course, if the evidence showed that the employer's motive for the line drawing was antiunion, then the action would be unlawful. There is no such evidence here. . . .

To be sure, the cases on which the dissent relies include language suggesting that the employers' unlawful, discriminatory conduct tended to undermine their asserted business justifications. However, the presence of such language in those cases does not negate the many cases that find discriminatory conduct violative of Section 8(a)(1) purely on the basis of the conduct's discriminatory nature.

We therefore adopt the position of the court in *Guardian* and *Fleming* that unlawful discrimination consists of disparate treatment of activities or communications of a similar character because of their union or other Section 7-protected status, and we shall apply this view in the present case and in future cases.[12] Accordingly, in determining whether the Respondent discriminatorily enforced the CSP, we must examine the types of e-mails allowed by the Respondent and ask whether they show discrimination along Section 7 lines.[13]

2. Application of the standard

Prozanski's August 14 e-mail urged all employees to wear green to support the Union. Her August 18 e-mail urged employees to participate in the Union's entry in a local parade. Both messages called for employees to take action in support of the Union. The evidence shows that the Respondent tolerated personal employee e-mail messages concerning social gatherings, jokes, baby announcements, and the occasional offer of sports tickets or other similar personal items. Notably, however, there is no evidence that the Respondent permitted employees to use e-mail to solicit other employees to support any group or organization. Thus, the Respondent's enforcement of the CSP with respect to the August 14 and 18 e-mails did not discriminate along Section 7 lines, and therefore did not violate Section 8(a)(1).[14]

---

[12] [n.21] Accordingly, we overrule the Board's decisions in *Fleming*, *Guardian*, and other similar cases to the extent they are inconsistent with our decision here. We note, however, that our view of "discrimination" is broader than that of some courts. See, e.g., *Cleveland Real Estate Partners v. NLRB*, 95 F.3d 457, 465 (6th Cir. 1996) (in case involving nonemployee access to an employer's premises, court defined "discrimination" as "favoring one union over another or allowing employer-related information while barring similar union-related information").

[13] [n.22] We also reject the dissent's assertion that our test, taken to its logical extreme, is a license for an employer to permit almost anything but union communication as long as the employer does not expressly say so. Indeed, the hypothetical postulated by the dissent shows the fallacy of this assertion. Thus, contrary to the dissent, a rule barring all nonwork-related solicitations by membership organizations certainly would not "permit employees to solicit on behalf of virtually anything except a union," given the vast number of membership organizations in which employees may participate.

[14] [n.24] The dissent asserts that there is no clear evidence that the Respondent ever enforced the CSP against anything other than union-related messages. However, there is no evidence that any employee had ever previously sent e-mails soliciting on behalf of *any* groups or organizations. Accordingly, given the absence of evidence that the Respondent permitted employees to use e-mail to solicit support for groups or organizations, we decline to find that the Respondent's barring of e-mail solicitation on behalf of the Union constituted disparate treatment of activities or communications of a similar character.

The dissent further argues that the Respondent's barring of e-mail solicitations on behalf of the Union was unlawful because the CSP barred all "nonjob-related" solicitations, but the Respondent — in practice — permitted personal e-mail messages, such as jokes, baby announcements, party invitations, and the occasional offer of sports tickets or request for services such as dog walking. We note, however, that the court of appeals in *Fleming Co.*, above, similarly found lawful the employer's removal of union literature from a bulletin board even though the employer's rule barring posting of all noncompany

Prozanski's May 4 e-mail, however, was not a solicitation. It did not call for action; it simply clarified the facts surrounding the Union's rally the day before. As noted above, the Respondent permitted a variety of nonwork-related e-mails other than solicitations. Indeed, the CSP itself prohibited only "nonjob-related solicitations," not all non-job-related communications. The only difference between Prozanski's May e-mail and the e-mails permitted by the Respondent is that Prozanski's e-mail was union-related. Accordingly, we find that the Respondent's enforcement of the CSP with respect to the May 4 e-mail discriminated along Section 7 lines and therefore violated Section 8(a)(1). . . .

[The NLRB also found that the employer violated Section 8(a)(3) when they gave Prozanski a warning because, as the employer official stated, an e-mail she sent was union-related. However, the NLRB found that the other two warnings were lawful because they were motivated by the fact that the e-mails were not job-related, rather than their relation to the union.]

MEMBERS LIEBMAN and WALSH, dissenting in part.

Today's decision confirms that the NLRB has become the "Rip Van Winkle of administrative agencies." *NLRB v. Thill, Inc.*, 980 F.2d 1137, 1142 (7th Cir. 1992). Only a Board that has been asleep for the past 20 years could fail to recognize that e-mail has revolutionized communication both within and outside the workplace. In 2007, one cannot reasonably contend, as the majority does, that an e-mail system is a piece of communications equipment to be treated just as the law treats bulletin boards, telephones, and pieces of scrap paper.

National labor policy must be responsive to the enormous technological changes that are taking place in our society. Where, as here, an employer has given employees access to e-mail for regular, routine use in their work, we would find that banning all nonwork-related "solicitations" is presumptively unlawful absent special circumstances. No special circumstances have been shown here. Accordingly, we dissent from the majority's holding that the Respondent's ban on using e-mail for "nonjob-related solicitations" was lawful.

We also dissent, in the strongest possible terms, from the majority's overruling of bedrock Board precedent about the meaning of discrimination as applied to Section 8(a)(1). Under the majority's new test, an employer does not violate Section 8(a)(1) by allowing employees to use an employer's equipment or media for a broad range of nonwork-related communications but not for Section 7 communications. We disagree, and therefore would also affirm the judge's finding that the Respondent violated Section 8(a)(3) and (1) by issuing written warnings to employee Suzy Prozanski for sending union-related e-mails. . . .

---

material was not enforced and posting of personal notices was routinely allowed.

A. Maintenance of the CSP

1. Legal framework governing Section 7 communications by employees in the workplace

The General Counsel contends that the CSP's prohibition on "nonjob-related solicitations" is unlawfully overbroad and violates Section 8(a)(1). The judge dismissed that allegation, and the majority affirms the dismissal. We dissent.

The issue in an 8(a)(1) case is whether the employer's conduct interferes with Section 7 rights. If so, the employer must demonstrate a legitimate business reason that outweighs the interference. . . .

Republic Aviation Corp. v. NLRB, 324 U.S. 793 (1945), is the seminal case balancing those interests with respect to oral solicitation in the workplace. The employer in *Republic Aviation* maintained a rule prohibiting solicitation anywhere on company property and discharged an employee for soliciting for the union during nonworking time. The Board adopted a presumption that restricting oral solicitation on nonworking time was unlawful, absent special circumstances. The Supreme Court affirmed the Board's finding that the employer's rule and its enforcement violated Section 8(a)(1). Although the solicitation occurred on the employer's property, the Court found that an insufficient justification to allow the employer to prohibit it. Rather, the Court endorsed the Board's reasoning that "[i]t is not every interference with property rights that is within the Fifth Amendment . . . . Inconvenience or even some dislocation of property rights, may be necessary in order to safeguard the right to collective bargaining." 324 U.S. at 802 fn. 8. Although an employer may make and enforce "reasonable rules" covering the conduct of employees on working time, "time outside working hours . . . is an employee's time to use as he wishes without unreasonable restraint, *although the employee is on company property.*" Id. at 803 fn. 10 (emphasis added). The Court upheld the Board's presumption that a rule banning solicitation during nonworking time is "an unreasonable impediment to self-organization . . . in the absence of evidence that special circumstances make the rule necessary in order to maintain production or discipline." Id. at 803 fn. 10.

Thus, the presumption adopted in *Republic Aviation* vindicates the right of employees to communicate in the workplace regarding Section 7 matters, subject to the employer's right to maintain production and discipline. Although the majority correctly notes that the rule in *Republic Aviation* itself involved a complete ban on solicitation on the employer's premises, the Board and courts have long since applied *Republic Aviation*'s principles to lesser restrictions on employee speech. See, e.g., *Beth Israel*, 437 U.S. at 492 (rule prohibiting solicitation and distribution in the hospital's patient-care and public areas; employer permitted those activities in employee locker rooms and restrooms); Times Publishing Co., 240 NLRB 1158 (1979) (rule prohibiting solicitation in "public areas" of the building), affd. 605 F.2d 847 (5th Cir. 1979); *Bankers Club, Inc.*, 218 NLRB 22, 27 (1975) (rule banning solicitation in "customer areas" of the respondent's restaurant).

The Supreme Court struck quite a different balance in cases involving nonemployees seeking to communicate with employees on the employer's premises. In a case involving distribution of union literature on an employer's property by nonemployee union organizers, the Court emphasized that "[a]ccommodation" between Section 7 rights and employer property rights "must be obtained with as little destruction of one as is consistent with the maintenance of the other." *NLRB v. Babcock & Wilcox*, 351 U.S. 105, 112 (1956). The Court held that an employer "may validly post his property against *nonemployee* distribution of union literature if reasonable efforts by the union through other available channels of communication will enable it to reach the employees with its message and if the employer's notice or order does not discriminate against the union by allowing other distribution." Id. (emphasis added). Distinguishing *Republic Aviation* on the basis that it involved communications by employees, the Court emphasized that "[t]he distinction [between employees and nonemployees] is one of substance. No restriction may be placed on the employees' right to discuss self-organization among themselves, unless the employer can demonstrate that a restriction is necessary to maintain production or discipline. But no such obligation is owed nonemployee organizers." Id. at 113. . . .

In short, the Board and courts have long protected employees' rights to engage in Section 7 communications at the workplace, even though the employees are on the employer's "property."

2. The Respondent's prohibition on all "nonjob-related solicitations" violated Section 8(a)(1)

Applying the foregoing principles, the General Counsel contends that employer rules restricting employee e-mail use must be evaluated under *Republic Aviation*, and that broad bans on employee e-mail use should be presumptively unlawful. The General Counsel emphasizes that e-mail has become the "natural gathering place" for employees to communicate in the workplace, and that e-mail sent and received on computers issued to employees for their use is not analogous to employer "equipment" such as bulletin boards, photocopiers, and public address systems.

The majority, however, finds the *Republic Aviation* framework inapplicable. Emphasizing the employer's "property" interest in its e-mail system, the majority reasons that, absent discriminatory treatment, employees have no Section 7 right to use employer personal property such as bulletin boards, television sets, and telephones. According to the majority, *Republic Aviation* ensures only that employees will not be "entirely deprived" of the ability to engage in any Section 7 communications in the workplace, but otherwise does not entitle employees to use their employer's equipment. Here, the majority asserts, the employees had other means of communication available.

We disagree. Indeed, we find that the General Counsel's approach is manifestly better suited to the role of e-mail in the modern workplace. "The responsibility to adapt the Act to changing patterns of industrial life is entrusted to the Board." *NLRB v. J. Weingarten*, 420 U.S. 251, 266 (1975). The majority's approach is flawed on several levels. First, it fails to recognize that e-mail has revolutionized business and personal communications, and that cases involving static pieces of "equipment" such as telephones and bulletin boards are easily distinguishable. Second, the majority's approach is based on an erroneous assumption that the Respondent's ownership of the computers gives it a "property" interest that is sufficient on its own to exclude Section 7 e-mails. Third, the majority's assertion that *Republic Aviation* created a "reasonable alternative means" test, even regarding employees who are already rightfully on the employer's property, is untenable.[15] . . .

Given the unique characteristics of e-mail and the way it has transformed modern communication, it is simply absurd to find an e-mail system analogous to a telephone, a television set, a bulletin board, or a slip of scrap paper. Nevertheless, that is what the majority does, relying on the Board's statements in prior cases that an employer may place nondiscriminatory restrictions on the nonwork-related use of such equipment and property. None of those "equipment" cases, however, involved sophisticated networks designed to accommodate thousands of multiple, simultaneous, interactive exchanges. Rather, they involved far more limited and finite resources. For example, if a union notice is posted on a bulletin board, the amount of space available for the employer to post its messages is reduced. If an employee is using a telephone for Section 7 or other nonworkrelated purposes, that telephone line is unavailable for others to use. Indeed, in *Churchill's Supermarkets*, 285 NLRB 138, 147 (1987), enfd. 857 F.2d 1471 (6th Cir. 1988), cert. denied 490 U.S. 1046 (1989), cited by the majority, the judge noted that the employer's "overriding consideration has always been that an employee should not tie up the phone lines" for personal use. Here, in contrast, the Respondent concedes that text e-mails impose no additional cost on the Respondent. At the time of the hearing in 2000, the Respondent's system was receiving as many as 4000 e-mail messages per day. One or more employees using the e-mail system would not preclude or interfere with simultaneous use by management or other employees. Furthermore, unlike a telephone, e-mail's versatility permits the sender of a message to reach a single recipient or multiple recipients simultaneously; allows the recipients to glimpse the subject matter of the message before deciding whether to read the message, delete it without reading it, or save it for later; and, once opened, allows the recipient to reply to the sender and/or other recipients, to engage in a realtime "conversation" with them, to forward the message to others, or to do nothing. Neither the telephone nor any other form of "equipment" addressed in the Board's prior cases shares these multidimensional characteristics.

The majority relies on the employer's ownership of the computer system as furnishing a "basic property right" to regulate e-mail use. But ownership, simpliciter, does not supply the Respondent with an absolute right to exclude Section 7 e-mails. The Respondent has already provided the computers and the e-mail capability to employees for regular and routine use to communicate at work. Thus, the employees are not only "rightfully" on the Respondent's real property, the building itself; they are rightfully on (using) the computer system. Moreover, an e-mail system and the messages traveling through it are not simply "equipment"; the Respondent does not own cyberspace.

---

[15] [n.6] We also disagree with the majority's characterization of our approach as "carv[ing] out an exception" to precedent. Our analysis is hardly novel. Rather, as explained below, we apply the decades-old principles that employees have a right to communicate in the workplace, that the Board must balance that right with the employer's right to protect its business interests, and that interference with employees' Section 7 rights is unlawful unless outweighed by a legitimate business interest. [Citations omitted.]

As the discussion above demonstrates, the existence of a "property right" does not end the inquiry — rather, it only begins it. The Respondent has not demonstrated how allowing employee e-mails on Section 7 matters interferes with its alleged property interest. To repeat, the Respondent already allows the employees to use the computers and e-mail system for work — and, for that matter, for personal messages. Additional text e-mails do not impose any additional costs on the Respondent. And e-mail systems, unlike older communications media, accommodate multiple, simultaneous users.

Common law involving computer "trespass," on which the Respondent relies, harms its case rather than helping it. Trespass cases illustrate that the mere use of a computer system to send e-mails does not interfere with the owner's property interest, absent some showing of harm to the system. The Restatement (Second) of Torts states in part: "The interest of a possessor of a chattel in its inviolability, unlike the similar interest of a possessor of land, is not given legal protection by an action for nominal damages for harmless intermeddlings with the chattel. In order that an actor who interferes with another's chattel may be liable, his conduct must affect some other and more important interest of the possessor." See Section 218, cmt. e. Where courts have allowed tort actions to go forward based on trespass to a computer system, they have relied on specific allegations of harm. Courts have dismissed claims where there was no such evidence.

As stated, the majority also reasons, based on the particular facts of *Republic Aviation*, that the Respondent need not yield its "property interests" here, because employees have alternative means to communicate in the workplace, such as oral in-person communication. In 2007, however, that train has already left the station: that is not how the courts and the Board have applied *Republic Aviation*, and the availability of alternative means is not relevant when dealing with employee-to-employee communications. The alternative-means test applies only to activity by *nonemployees* on the employer's property. See *Babcock & Wilcox*, supra at 112; *Lechmere, Inc. v. NLRB*, 502 U.S. 527 (1992). The distinction between employee and nonemployee activity is "one of substance." *Babcock & Wilcox*, supra at 113. If the absence of alternative means to communicate in the workplace were a prerequisite to employees' right to engage in Section 7 activity on employer property, presumably an employer could ban oral solicitation by employees in "work areas," or even everywhere except an employee breakroom, without any showing of special circumstances, because the employer would not have "entirely deprived" employees of the right to communicate on the premises. Of course, neither the Board nor the Supreme Court has ever placed such limits on Section 7 communication.

For all of the foregoing reasons, we reject the majority's conclusion that e-mail is just another piece of employer "equipment." Where, as here, the employer has given employees access to e-mail in the workplace for their regular use, we would find that banning all nonwork-related "solicitations" is presumptively unlawful absent special circumstances. This presumption recognizes employees' rights to discuss Section 7 matters using a resource that has been made available to them for routine workplace communication. Because the presumption is rebuttable, it also recognizes that an employer may have interests that justify a ban. For example, an employer might show that its server capacity is so limited that even text e-mails would interfere with its operation. An employer might also justify more limited restrictions on nonwork-related e-mails — such as prohibiting large attachments or audio/video segments — by demonstrating that such messages would interfere with the efficient functioning of the system. In addition, rules limiting nonwork-related e-mails to nonworking time would be presumptively lawful, just as with oral solicitations.

Here, the Respondent has shown no special circumstances for its ban on "nonjob-related solicitations," which on its face would prohibit even solicitations on nonworking time, without regard to the size of the message or its attachments, or whether the message would actually interfere with production or discipline. Accordingly, we would reverse the judge and find that the Respondent violated Section 8(a)(1) by maintaining the portion of the CSP that prohibits employees from using e-mail for "nonjob-related solicitations."

B. The Respondent's Enforcement of the CSP

Even assuming the maintenance of the CSP were lawful, the judge correctly found that the Respondent violated Section 8(a)(1) by discriminatorily enforcing it. The majority does not dispute that this result was correct under Board precedent. Instead, the majority overrules that precedent and announces a new, more limited conception of "discrimination," based on two decisions from the Seventh Circuit.

As explained below, we respectfully but emphatically disagree with the Seventh Circuit's analysis.[16] But even assuming we did not, the majority's application of its new test is flawed. Accordingly, we would affirm the judge's conclusion that the Respondent violated Section 8(a)(1) by discriminatorily enforcing the CSP to all three of Prozanski's union-related e-mails.

Section 7 grants employees the right "to engage in . . . concerted activities for the purpose of collective bargaining or other mutual aid or protection . . . ." An employer violates Section 8(a)(1) by "interfer[ing] with, restrain[ing], or coerc[ing] employees" in the exercise of that right. In particular, and in accord with the decadesold understanding of discrimination within the meaning of the National Labor Relations Act, the Board has long held that an employer violates that section by allowing employees to use an employer's equipment or other resources for nonwork-related purposes while prohibiting Section 7-related uses. . . .

Here, the record makes plain that the Respondent allowed employees to use e-mail for a broad range of nonwork-related messages, including e-mails requesting employees to participate in nonwork-related events. For example, employees and supervisors used e-mail to circulate jokes, baby announcements, and party invitations; to offer sports tickets; to seek a dog walker; to organize a poker group; and

---

[16] [n.19] As the Seventh Circuit itself has observed, it is not the obligation of the Board to "knuckle under to the first court of appeals (or the second, or even the twelfth) to rule adversely to the Board. The Supreme Court, not this circuit . . . is the supreme arbiter of the meaning of the laws enforced by the Board . . . ." *Nielsen Lithographing Co. v. NLRB*, 854 F.2d 1063, 1066 (1988). Rather, the court continued, the duty of the Board when faced with adverse circuit precedent is "to take a stance, to explain which decisions it agree[s] with and why, and to explore the possibility of intermediate solutions . . . . We do not follow stare decisis inflexibly; if the Board gives us a good reason to do so, we shall be happy to reexamine [our decisions]."

to make lunch plans. Yet, the Respondent enforced the CSP against Prozanski for sending three union-related messages. This is a clear 8(a)(1) violation under longstanding precedent.

The majority defines "unlawful discrimination" as "disparate treatment of activities or communications of a similar character because of their union or other Section 7-protected status." According to the majority, the employer "may draw a line between charitable solicitations and non-charitable solicitations, between solicitations of a personal nature . . . and solicitations for the commercial sale of a product . . . , between invitations for an organization and invitations of a personal nature, between solicitations and mere talk, and between business-related use and non-business-related use." Applying that standard to the record here, the majority finds that the Respondent permitted nonwork-related e-mails other than solicitations, but had never permitted solicitations to support any group or organization. Therefore, the majority concludes, the Respondent discriminated along Section 7 lines in applying the CSP to Prozanski's May 4 e-mail about the union rally (which was not a solicitation), but did not discriminate in applying the CSP to Prozanski's August 14 and 18 e-mails (which the majority finds were solicitations).

The majority decision is based on two Seventh Circuit cases: *Fleming Co. v. NLRB*, 349 F.3d 968 (7th Cir. 2003), denying enf. to 336 NLRB 192 (2001), and *Guardian Industries Corp. v. NLRB*, 49 F.3d 317 (7th Cir. 1995), denying enf. to 313 NLRB 1275 (1994). . . . In analyzing whether union postings were "equal to" "swap and shop" notices, the *Guardian* court relied on case law and hypotheticals involving the First and Fourteenth Amendments and ADEA. Thus, the court implicitly assumed that the "discriminatory" enforcement of a rule in violation of Section 8(a)(1) is analogous to "discrimination" in other contexts.

[However, u]nlike antidiscrimination statutes, the Act does not merely give employees the right to be free from discrimination based on union activity. It gives them the *affirmative* right to engage in concerted *group* action for mutual benefit and protection. Nor are employees' Section 7 rights dependent on a "public forum" analysis, as in *Perry*. Rather, in evaluating whether an employer's conduct violates Section 8(a)(1), the Board examines whether the conduct reasonably tended to interfere with those affirmative Section 7 rights. If so, the burden is on the employer to demonstrate a legitimate and substantial business justification for its conduct. Motive is not part of the analysis. Section 8(a)(3) separately prohibits discrimination with the motive to encourage or discourage union support.[17]

Therefore, by focusing on what types of activities are "equal" to Section 7 activities, the majority misses the point. In 8(a)(1) cases, the essence of the violation is not "discrimination." Rather, it is interference with employees' Section 7 rights. The Board's existing precedent on discriminatory enforcement — that an employer violates Section 8(a)(1) by allowing nonwork-related uses of its equipment while prohibiting Section 7 uses — is merely one application of Section 8(a)(1)'s core principles: that employees have a right to engage in Section 7 activity, and that

---

[17] [n.21] On that basis alone, we would have to reject the majority's definition of 8(a)(1) discriminatory enforcement as "disparate treatment of activities or communications of a similar character *because of their* union or other Section 7-protected status" (emphasis added). This improperly suggests that discriminatory motive is required — something even the Seventh Circuit does not propose.

interference with that right is unlawful unless the employer shows a business justification that outweighs the infringement. Discrimination, when it is present, is relevant simply because it weakens or exposes as pretextual the employer's business justification. . . .

[U]nder the basic Section 8(a)(1) principles discussed above, if an employer wants to "draw a line" between permitted and prohibited e-mails — or, for that matter, between permitted and prohibited bulletin board postings, telephone calls, or other uses of employer equipment or media — based on whether the employees are urging support for "groups" or "organizations," the employer must show some legitimate business reason for drawing that particular line, and that business justification must outweigh the interference with Section 7 rights. Otherwise, the employer's rule is completely antithetical to Section 7's protection of concerted activity. The Seventh Circuit and majority fail to engage in this analysis. In any event, the Respondent has not offered any such justification here.

Taken to its logical extreme, the majority's holding that an employer need only avoid "drawing a line on a Section 7 basis" is a license to permit almost anything but union communications, so long as the employer does not expressly say so.[18] It is no answer to say that a rule prohibiting all noncharitable solicitations or all solicitations for a group or organizations is not discriminatory because it would also prohibit selling Avon or Amway products. The Act does not protect against interference with those activities; it does protect against interference with Section 7 activity. Accordingly, we would adhere to precedent, which properly reflects that principle.

[The dissent then argued that, even under the majority's discrimination standard, the employer's enforcement of the CSP policy was unlawful. Subsequently, the D.C. Circuit agreed with the dissent's conclusion and held that all three of the warnings were unlawful; however, the court did not address the substance of the majority's new standards on e-mail communications and discrimination. *See* Guard Publishing Co. v. NLRB, 571 F.3d 53 (D.C. Cir. 2008).]

POST PROBLEM DISCUSSION

1. What do you think about the majority's refusal in *Register Guard* to extend the *Republic Aviation* framework to e-mails? The dissent stresses the employee/non-employee distinction that *Lechmere* used to differentiate employee communications from non-employee communications; under that distinction, the e-mails in *Register Guard* should have fallen under *Republic Aviation*. How does the majority avoid that result? Do you find that reasoning persuasive?

---

[18] [n.26] For example, an employer might prohibit all nonwork-related solicitations by membership organizations. Such a rule would extend privileges to employee solicitations on behalf of any commercial enterprise and many charities and other activities, but not to employee solicitations on behalf of the union representing the employees — the entity through which the employees have chosen to vindicate their Sec. 7 right to engage in concerted activity. In other words, the rule would permit employees to solicit on behalf of virtually anything *except* a union. Yet, on its face, this policy would not "draw the line" on Sec. 7 grounds, and would therefore be lawful. Such a result stands labor law on its head.

The majority notes that a line drawn out of antiunion motive will still be unlawful. As noted above, however, motive is not an element of this type of 8(a)(1) violation.

2. Professor Hirsch stresses the importance of giving employees ample opportunity to learn about and discuss unionization among themselves. Do you think that allowing employers to restrict electronic communications on their computer systems poses a significant threat to employees' ability to choose whether to unionize? What about our more traditional communication cases, such as *Republic Aviation* and *Lechmere* — does the current law adequately provide employees the chance to make a free and informed decision? *Cf.* Matthew Bodie, *Information and the Market for Union Representation*, 94 VA. L. REV. 1 (2008) (describing the information problems inherent in union campaigns, such as incentives for both unions and employers to overstate negative aspects of other, information asymmetries resulting from the difficulty in observing and predicting quality of union services, lack of competition among unions, absence of third-party sources of information, difficulty in ending union representation, lack of rules against misrepresentations, and lack of public confidence in NLRB's election procedure).

3. If the NLRB ends up reversing *Register Guard* and, as the dissent suggests, applies *Republic Aviation* to e-mails, are there are problems with using such an old test with new technology? For instance, remember the important distinction between oral solicitations and written distributions — how should e-mails be characterized? *See* General Counsel Advice Memorandum, Bureau of National Affairs, Case No. 5-CA-28860 (2000), http://www.nlrb.gov/research/memos/advice_ memos (recommending subject-matter based analysis for characterizing e-mails as either solicitations or distributions); *see also* Jeffrey M. Hirsch, *The Silicon Bullet: Will the Internet Kill the NLRA?*, 76 GEO. WASH. L. REV. 262 (2008) (criticizing Advice Memorandum's approach and arguing for modified *Republic Aviation*-like analysis for e-mails); Martin H. Malin & Henry H. Perritt, Jr., *The National Labor Relations Act in Cyberspace: Union Organizing in Electronic Workplaces*, 49 U. KAN. L. REV. 1, 3–4 (2000) (providing pre-*Register-Guard* view of e-mail regulation under the NLRA).

4. One of the bases for the majority's decision was that personal property is substantively different than real property. Are the differences between the two enough to warrant the stronger *Republic Aviation* protection for real property, but weaker protection for personal property? *See Register Guard*, 351 N.L.R.B. at 1126 (Members Liebman & Walsh, dissenting) (noting that real property warrants more protection under trespass law than personal property); Jeffrey M. Hirsch, *E-Mail and the Rip Van Winkle of Agencies: The NLRB's* Register-Guard *Decision, in* WORKPLACE PRIVACY: HERE AND ABROAD — PROCEEDINGS OF THE NEW YORK UNIVERSITY 61ST ANNUAL CONFERENCE ON LABOR (Jonathan Nash ed., 2010) (same).

5. In footnote 12, the majority states that its new test for e-mail communications is not the same as the *Lechmere* analysis; the dissent is less convinced. Do you think the majority's test is substantively different from *Lechmere*? Are there instances where restrictions on e-mail communications under this test will be treated differently from restrictions on non-employees' access to a worksite under *Lechmere*?

6. Consider the various interpretations of "discrimination" that you have read thus far. Which one seems the most appropriate to you and why? Note that although *Register Guard* involves a type of communication with an ostensibly unique

analysis, the decision's interpretation of discrimination could easily apply to *Republic Aviation* and *Lechmere* cases as well. In late 2010, the NLRB indicated its intent to address this issue in at least the *Lechmere* context by inviting amicus briefs in a related case, but the NLRB has not issued a decision in the case at the time of publication. *See Notice and Invitation to File Briefs in* Roundy's Inc., Case 30-CA-17185 (Nov. 12, 2010), https://www.nlrb.gov/sites/default/files/documents/236/roundys_notice_and_invitation.pdf.

SECTION 2   EMPLOYER SPEECH

PROBLEM #3: THE ELECTION CAMPAIGN: THE MALL'S CAPTIVE AUDIENCE MEETINGS

Concerned about what appeared to be increasing interest in the union, which had recently filed with the NLRB a successful petition for an election, Sarah began a series of weekly meetings for all janitors. Attendance at these meetings were mandatory for all janitors, whether or not they were scheduled to work that day, and they were paid for their time at the meetings. As became quickly apparent, the purpose of these meetings was to allow Sarah and other managers who participated to denigrate the union and push employees to vote against it. Among the arguments made by the managers were statements that the mall was already running on a very thin profit margin and that wage increases that the union said it could get the janitors would "threaten to bring down the mall." Sarah noted that another mall operated only ten miles away and that no employees there were unionized. She stated further that a lot of malls around the country contract out their janitorial work and that if a union came in making demands, "Northside might have to do the same and we couldn't guarantee that the contractor would still let the current janitors work here." Sarah and the other managers did not allow for any questions by the janitors.

Read the following material to determine whether Sarah ran afoul of the NLRA in her attempt to convince employees not to support the union. A broader consideration is the balance at issue in these cases. We spent the last section addressing the tension between employees' labor rights and employers' property rights. In this section, the employers' side of the balance involves an arguably weightier interest — their right to speak about union matters.

PROBLEM MATERIALS

Livingston Shirt Co., 107 N.L.R.B. 400 (1953)

NLRB v. United Steelworkers of America (Nutone Inc. & Avondale Mills), 357 U.S. 357 (1958)

NLRB v. Gissel Packing Co., 395 U.S. 575 (1969)

A.　Captive Audience Meetings

LIVINGSTON SHIRT CO.
107 N.L.R.B. 400 (1953)

. . . The Amalgamated [Clothing Workers of America] began an organizing drive among Respondent Livingston's employees sometime in March 1952. . . . Some success having been achieved by the Amalgamated, it filed a representation petition with the Board on April 15, 1952, seeking certification as the bargaining representative of Respondent Livingston's production and maintenance employees. . . .

Pursuant to a consent-election agreement, the first election was scheduled to be held on May 22, 1952, between 12 and 4 p. m. On May 21, at 11 a. m., during working hours, Migliore [then president of Respondent Livingston] made an antiunion, noncoercive speech to the assembled employees. One hour later, an employees' committee visited Migliore and requested that the Amalgamated be granted a similar opportunity to address an employee assembly. Migliore refused. Subsequently, on the morning of May 22, an Amalgamated representative requested an opportunity to reply to Migliore's speech. Migliore again refused. This election resulted in a defeat for the Amalgamated. The Regional Director, however, relying upon the Board's *Bonwit Teller* doctrine [*Bonwit Teller, Inc.*, 96 NLRB 608 (1951)], set the election aside.

A second election was scheduled for July 24, 1952, from 7 to 11 a. m. On July 21, at 11 a. m., during working hours, Migliore again spoke to the assembled employees. This speech, like the first, was antiunion but noncoercive. One hour after this speech, some employees requested that Respondent Livingston grant to the Amalgamated the opportunity to reply to Migliore's speech under similar circumstances. Migliore's answer to this request does not appear in the record. It can be assumed, however, that he denied this request; for, on two further occasions before the second election, Migliore did in fact deny the Amalgamated's reply requests, once in writing and once orally. This election resulted in another defeat for the Amalgamated. Once again, however, the Regional Director set aside the election in reliance upon the *Bonwit Teller* doctrine. . . .

It is true, as the General Counsel points out, that in the past the Board has held [under *Bonwit Teller* that] an employer's refusal to give the union equal opportunity to address its employees in the plant to be unlawful. In substance, that view rested on the belief that the employer exerted undue and unlawful influence upon the employees by monopolizing their workplace as a speechmaking platform. Board appraisal of the basic elements underlying this type of situation persuades us that the Act does not require the employer, absent unusual circumstances, to accede to such a union request.

A basic principle directly affecting any consideration of this question is that Section 8(c) of the Act specifically prohibits us from finding that an uncoercive speech, whenever delivered by the employer, constitutes an unfair labor practice. Therefore, any attempt to rationalize a proscription against an employer who makes a privileged speech must necessarily be rested on the theory that the employer's vice is not in making the speech but in denying the union an opportunity to reply on company premises. But to say that conduct which is privileged gives rise to an obligation on the part of the employer to accord an equal opportunity for the union to reply under like circumstances, on pain of being found guilty of unlawful conduct, seems to us an untenable basis for a finding of unfair labor practices. If the privilege of free speech is to be given real meaning, it cannot be qualified by grafting upon it conditions which are tantamount to negation.

It is conceded by everyone that Congress intended that both employers and unions should be free to attempt by speech or otherwise to influence and persuade employees in their ultimate choice, so long as the persuasion is not violative of the express provisions of the Act; and we find nothing in the statute which even hints at any congressional intent to restrict an employer in the use of his own premises for the purpose of airing his views. On the contrary, an employer's premises are the natural forum for him just as the union hall is the inviolable forum for the union to assemble and address employees. We do not believe that unions will be unduly hindered in their right to carry on organizational activities by our refusal to open up to them the employer's premises for group meetings, particularly since this is an area from which they have traditionally been excluded, and there remains open to them all the customary means for communicating with employees. These include individual contact with employees on the employer's premises outside working hours (absent, of course, a privileged broad no-solicitation rule), solicitation while entering and leaving the premises, at their homes, and at union meetings. These are time-honored and traditional means by which unions have conducted their organizational campaigns, and experience shows that they are fully adequate to accomplish unionization and accord employees their rights under the Act to freely choose a bargaining agent.

In the original *Bonwit Teller* case, the Board, as then constituted, found that a "fundamental consideration" in support of its decision was the right of employees under Section 7 to "hear both sides under circumstances which approximate equality." We have no quarrel with this principle, but we think that it is to be achieved not by administratively grafting new limbs on the statute, but by a strict enforcement of those provisions of the statute which afford employers the right of free and uncoercive speech and grants employees the protected right to join labor unions free from coercion or discrimination. The majority in *Bonwit Teller* did not cite, nor have we been able to find, any support in the statutory language or legislative history for holding that the employer who exercises his own admitted rights under the statute thereby incurs an affirmative obligation to donate his premises and working time to the union for the purpose of propagandizing the employees.

We agree that both parties to a labor dispute have the equal right to disseminate their point of view, but our disagreement with the old majority and our dissenting colleague stems from the fact that we do not think one party must be so strangely openhearted as to underwrite the campaign of the other. We reject the idea that the union has a statutory right to assemble and make campaign speeches to employees on the employer's premises and at the employer's expense. We see no real distinction in principle between this and admitting an employer to the union hall for the purpose of making an antiunion speech, a suggestion which our dissenting colleague would doubtless view with abhorrence. We believe that the equality of opportunity which the parties have a right to enjoy is that which comes from the lawful use of both the union and the employer of the customary fora and media available to each of them. It is not to be realistically achieved by attempting, as was done in *Bonwit Teller*, to make the facilities of the one available to the other. . . .

Our dissenting colleague, as his opinion shows, directs his main attack, not at our conclusion herein, but at our holding in *Peerless Plywood* [, 107 N.L.R.B. 427 (1953)], a representation case in which we prescribe, as an election rule, a prohibition against employer speeches to employees on his premises during working hours within 24 hours prior to a scheduled Board election. The dissenting member attacks this rule on the ground that it "extinguishes" the employer's right of free speech. Aside from the foreignness of such an argument coming from one who espouses *Bonwit Teller*, we do not believe that this criticism, which is relevant only to *Peerless Plywood*, and not to this decision, has real validity. The rule laid down in *Peerless Plywood* is a rule of conduct governing Board elections and, in our opinion, constitutes a narrow and reasonable limitation designed to facilitate the holding of free elections in the atmosphere of relative tranquility conducive to a sober choice of representative. It is beyond question a much more limited and, in our view, a more reasonable and practicable qualification on absolute freedom of speech than *Bonwit Teller*. It should, perhaps, be pointed out that, even during the 24-hour period, the employer and the union still have the right to use all lawful means of persuasion, including speech, subject only to the one qualification that they cannot assemble employees on company premises during working hours for the purpose of addressing them en masse. They may issue statements, talk to individual employees, write letters to them, or even invite them to listen to a speech on or off the employer's premises, so long as the occasion is on the employees' own time and their attendance is voluntary.

We would be less than candid if we did not concede that the imposition of the 24-hour rule in election cases gives rise to the argument that we are deviating from the strict logic of our decision in this case. But we consider this "departure" as both a minor and a necessary one. As Justice Holmes so aptly said, "The life of the law has not been logic; it has been experience." And, for reasons more fully set forth in *Peerless Plywood*, we believe that experience in holding elections has shown that elections are likely to more truly reflect employee desires if the employees are afforded a brief breathing spell from employer or, indeed, union speeches at their place of work during working hours immediately before the election. This will not in our opinion unduly restrict employers and unions in their right to publicize their point of view, but will at the same time provide a measure of protection for the employee, whose rights are after all paramount, from last-minute blandishments which he may feel compelled to hear and which may becloud his judgment and interfere with his thoughtful weighing of the issues involved. With this rule in election cases, we see no reason in law or equity for seeking to impose further restraints. This is a rule of practical labor relations governing the conduct of elections. We do not think that it seriously impinges on the principle laid down in this unfair labor practice case.

Accordingly, we are convinced that, absent special circumstances as hereinafter indicated, there is nothing improper in an employer refusing to grant to the union a right equal to his own in his plant. We rule therefore that, in the absence of either an unlawful broad no-solicitation rule (prohibiting union access to company premises on other than working time) or a privileged no-solicitation rule (broad, but not unlawful because of the character of the business), an employer does not commit an unfair labor practice if he makes a preelection speech on company time and premises to his employees and denies the union's request for an opportunity to reply. . . .

[The opinions of MEMBER PETERSON, concurring, and MEMBER MURDOCK, dissenting in part, are omitted.]

NLRB v. UNITED STEELWORKERS OF AMERICA
(Nutone Inc. & Avondale Mills)
357 U.S. 357 (1958)

MR. JUSTICE FRANKFURTER delivered the opinion of the Court.

These two cases, argued in succession, are controlled by the same considerations and will be disposed of in a single opinion. In one case the National Labor Relations Board ruled that it was not an unfair labor practice for an employer to enforce against his employees a no-solicitation rule, in itself concededly valid, while the employer was himself engaged in anti-union solicitation in a context of separate unfair labor practices. This ruling was reversed by a Court of Appeals. In the second case the Board on the basis of similar facts, except that the employer's anti-union solicitation by itself constituted a separate unfair labor practice, found the enforcement of the rule to have been an unfair labor practice, but another Court of Appeals denied enforcement of the Board's order. . . .

No. 81. - In April of 1953 the respondent Steelworkers instituted a campaign to organize the employees of respondent NuTone, Inc., a manufacturer of electrical devices. In the early stages of the campaign, supervisory personnel of the company interrogated employees and solicited reports concerning the organizational activities of other employees. Several employees were discharged; the Board later found that the discharges had been the result of their organizational activities. In June the company began to distribute, through its supervisory personnel, literature that, although not coercive, was clearly anti-union in tenor. In August, while continuing to distribute such material, the company announced its intention of enforcing its rule against employees' posting signs or distributing literature on company property or soliciting or campaigning on company time. The rule, according to these posted announcements, applied to 'all employees-whether they are for or against the union.' Later the same month a representation election was held, which the Steelworkers lost. . . .

No. 289. — In the fall of 1954 the Textile Workers conducted an organizational campaign at several of the plants of respondent Avondale Mills. A number of individual employees were called before supervisory personnel of the company, on the ground that they had been soliciting union membership, and informed that such solicitation was in violation of plant rules and would not be tolerated in the future. The rule had not been promulgated in written form, but there was evidence that it had been previously invoked in a non-organizational context. During this same period, both in these interviews concerning the rule and at the employees' places of work, supervisory personnel interrogated employees concerning their organizational views and activities and solicited employees to withdraw their membership cards from the union. This conduct was in many cases accompanied by threats that the mill would close down or that various employee benefits would be lost if the mill should become organized. Subsequently three employees, each of whom had been informed of the no-solicitation rule, were laid off and eventually discharged for violating the rule. . . .

Employer rules prohibiting organizational solicitation are not in and of themselves violative of the Act, for they may duly serve production, order and discipline. *See Republic Aviation Corp. v. National Labor Relations Board*, 324 U.S. 793; *National Labor Relations Board v. Babcock & Wilcox Co.*, 351 U.S. 105. In neither of the cases before us did the party attacking the enforcement of the no-solicitation rule contest its validity. Nor is the claim made that an employer may not, under proper circumstances, engage in non-coercive anti-union solicitation; indeed, his right to do so is protected by the so-called 'employer free speech' provision of s 8(c) of the Act. Contrariwise, as both cases before us show, coercive anti-union solicitation and other similar conduct run afoul of the Act and constitute unfair labor practices irrespective of the bearing of such practices on enforcement of a no-solicitation rule. The very narrow and almost abstract question here derives from the claim that, when the employer himself engages in anti-union solicitation that if engaged in by employees would constitute a violation of the rule — particularly when his solicitation is coercive or accompanied by other unfair labor practices — his enforcement of an otherwise valid no-solicitation rule against the employees is itself an unfair labor practice. . . .

There is no indication in the record in either of these cases that the employees, or the union on their behalf, requested the employer, himself engaging in anti-union solicitation, to make an exception to the rule for pro-union solicitation. There is evidence in both cases that the employers had in the past made exceptions to their rules for charitable solicitation. Notwithstanding the clear anti-union bias of both employers, it is not for us to conclude as a matter of law — although it might well have been open to the Board to conclude as a matter of industrial experience — that a request for a similar qualification upon the rule for organizational solicitation would have been rejected. Certainly the employer is not obliged voluntarily and without any request to offer the use of his facilities and the time of his employees for pro-union solicitation. He may very well be wary of a charge that he is interfering with, or contributing support to, a labor organization in violation of s 8(a)(2) of the Act.

No attempt was made in either of these cases to make a showing that the no-solicitation rules truly diminished the ability of the labor organizations involved to carry their message to the employees. Just as that is a vital consideration in determining the validity of a no-solicitation rule, *see Republic Aviation Corp. v. National Labor Relations Board, supra*, 324 U.S. at pages 797–798; *National Labor Relations Board v. Babcock & Wilcox Co., supra*, 351 U.S. at page 112, it is highly relevant in determining whether a valid rule has been fairly applied. Of course the rules had the effect of closing off one channel of communication; but the

Taft-Hartley Act does not command that labor organizations as a matter of abstract law, under all circumstances, be protected in the use of every possible means of reaching the minds of individual workers, nor that they are entitled to use a medium of communication simply because the employer is using it. No such mechanical answers will avail for the solution of this non-mechanical, complex problem in labor-management relations. If, by virtue of the location of the plant and of the facilities and resources available to the union, the opportunities for effectively reaching the employees with a pro-union message, in spite of a no-solicitation rule, are at least as great as the employer's ability to promote the legally authorized expression of his anti-union views, there is no basis for invalidating these 'otherwise valid' rules. The Board, in determining whether or not the enforcement of such a rule in the circumstances of an individual case is an unfair labor practice, may find relevant alternative channels, available for communications on the right to organize. When this important issue is not even raised before the Board and no evidence bearing on it adduced, the concrete basis for appraising the significance of the employer's conduct is wanting.

We do not at all imply that the enforcement of a valid no-solicitation rule by an employer who is at the same time engaging in anti-union solicitation may not constitute an unfair labor practice. All we hold is that there must be some basis, in the actualities of industrial relations, for such a finding. The records in both cases — the issues raised in the proceedings — are barren of the ingredients for such a finding.

Judgment in No. 81 reversed in part and affirmed in part and cause remanded with directions; judgment in No. 289 affirmed.

MR. CHIEF JUSTICE WARREN (joined by JUSTICES BLACK and DOUGLAS) dissenting in part and concurring in part.

These two cases concern the issue of whether the enforcement of company rules preventing union solicitation or distribution is an unfair labor practice when concurrent with this enforcement the employer embarks on a program of advocacy against the union. Contrary to what is stated in the opinion of the Court, I do not believe that both these cases are controlled by the same considerations. The pivotal distinction is that in National Labor Relations Board v. Avondale Mills the employer's antiunion activities were coercive in nature, while in National Labor Relations Board v. United Steelworkers they were not. . . .

In Avondale Mills this Court affirms the judgment of the Court of Appeals, which refused to enforce that portion of an order of the National Labor Relations Board which held that enforcement of the company's rule against solicitation on the premises during working hours was an unfair labor practice contrary to Section 8(a)(1) of the National Labor Relations Act. I cannot agree with the conclusion of the majority that the record is insufficient to sustain the action of the Board. Their conclusion depends on two circumstances. The first is the failure of the union or the employees to request the employer not to enforce his antisolicitation rule during the union organizing campaign. This is a slender reed. . . . [T]here was in fact no rule against solicitation on the premises during working hours and that the rule was invoked solely as an antiunion measure. None of these conclusions was disturbed by the court below, which merely held that the invocation of the rule under these facts was part of the employer's right to oppose the union. The majority thus attaches significance, where the Board did not, to the fact that the union failed to request the company to grant for the union's benefit an exception to a rule that was promulgated to keep the union out.

The second circumstance on which the majority relies is the failure of the Board to make findings that reasonable alternatives were not open to the union in the face of the no-solicitation rule. Admittedly, evidence and findings of this nature were elements in cases where the validity of employer no-solicitation and no-distribution rules was in issue. *See National Labor Relations Board v. Babcock & Wilcox Co.*, 351 U.S. 105; *Republic Aviation Corp. v. National Labor Relations Board*, 324 U.S. 793. However, there has heretofore been no indication that such evidence and findings were indispensable elements to every case in which these employer rules were being examined. In contrast to Babcock and Republic Aviation we are not concerned here with the validity of these rules per se. The no-solicitation rule under examination here may well be valid if fairly applied. But the Board held that it was not fairly applied on account of its link to the company's campaign of coercion, and the evidence and findings on that issue are far more relevant to this case than a discussion of the site of the plant, the nature of the surrounding area, and the places of residence of the workers.

While praising 'the Board's special understanding of these industrial situations,' the majority opinion reverses the Board on the very sort of issues that are within its special competence. An examination of the record shows that the Board has already carefully apprized itself of the interests of both sides in this controversy. An employer has forbidden his employees to engage in union solicitation within the plant during working hours. He contemporaneously engages in a campaign of coercive antiunion solicitation during those same working hours. The validity of both practices — the enforcement of the no-solicitation rule and the coercive antiunion solicitation — comes into question, for they are not separable. Under one set of circumstances the no-solicitation rule may be valid. However, the determination as to whether an employer's antiunion activities are an unfair labor practice depends on the context in which those activities occur, and no-solicitation rules are to be subjected to the same kind of scrutiny. Employees during working hours are the classic captive audience. At the very moment the employees in this case were under the greatest degree of control by their employer, they were forced to listen to denunciations of the union coupled with clear references to the personal disasters that would ensue if the union succeeded or if the particular employee continued to solicit for the union. These threats were themselves held to be unfair labor practices by the Board, and that holding was enforced by the Court of Appeals and is not in issue here. During this same working time the unionized employees, who under Section 7 of the National Labor Relations Act have a right to engage in concerted activity, were unable, due to their employer's own rule, to try to overcome the effect of his activities even though those activities were in violation of Section 8(a)(1) of the Act. It is not necessary to suggest that in all circumstances a union must have the same facilities and opportunity to solicit employees as the employer has in opposing the union. However, the plant premises and working time are such decisive factors during a labor dispute that when an employer denies them to the union and at the same time pursues his own program of coercion on the premises and during working hours, this denial is by itself an interference with the rights guaranteed in Section 7 of the Act and hence contrary to Section 8(a)(1). . . .

POST PROBLEM DISCUSSION

1.   Which rule — *Bonwit Teller* or *Livingston Shirt* — do you think best balances employees' right to freely choose whether to unionize and employers' right to express an opinion about that choice? Does the *Peerless Plywood* 24-hour limitation alleviate any of the concerns that you might have? How effective is the 24-hour limitation given that it only applies to mandatory group meetings — not voluntary groups meetings or mandatory individual discussions? For criticisms of the *Livingston Shirt* approach and suggestions for overcoming it, *see* Paul M. Secunda, *The Contemporary "Fist Inside the Velvet Glove": Employer Captive Audience Meetings Under the NLRA*, 5 FIU L. Rev. 385 (2010); David J. Doorey, *The Medium and the "Anti-Union" Message: "Forced Listening" and Captive Audience Meetings*, 29 Comp. Lab. L. & Pol'y J. 79 (2008) (discussing Canadian experience); and Paul M. Secunda, *Toward the Viability of State-Based Legislation To Address Workplace Captive Audience Meetings in the United States*, 29 Comp. Lab. L. & Pol'y J. 209 (2008).

2.   Since *Livingston Shirt*, captive audience meetings have become a common and prevalent technique in employer attempts to resist unionization. A recent study found that employers use captive audience meetings in 89% of all elections — on average 10.4 meetings in each election. *See* Kate Bronfenbrenner, *No Holds Barred: The Intensification of Employer Opposition to Organizing* 10 (Econ. Policy Inst. Briefing Paper No. 235, 2009) (survey of 1999–2003 campaigns), http://epi.3cdn.net/edc3b3dc172dd1094f_0ym6ii96d.pdf. There is a reason for this high number: these meetings are extremely effective, with recent estimates finding that unions win 73% of elections that lacked captive audience meetings, but only 47% of elections in which such meetings occurred. *Id.*

3.   In our problem, is there an issue with the mandatory nature of the meetings? In other words, should a pro-union employee who has already made up her mind be required to sit through such a meeting? The answer, according to the NLRB, is yes. *See Litton Systems, Inc.*, 173 N.L.R.B. 1024, 1030–1031 (1968) (interpreting *Livingston Shirt*); *see also 2 Sisters Food Group, Inc.*, 357 N.L.R.B. No. 168, at *20 (2011) (Member Becker, dissenting) (arguing for new rule what would prohibit "[a]n express or implied threat of discipline for not listening to the employer's speech" because such conduct "indisputably adds to the speech the element of coercion that takes it outside the protection of both the First Amendment and Section 8(c) and permits it to serve as grounds for overturning the results of an election"). Do you agree with this precedent or with Member Becker's argument to the contrary? *See also* Paul M. Secunda, *The Future of Board Doctrine on Captive Audience Speeches*, 87 Ind. L.J. 123 (2012) (providing analysis supporting Becker's approach in *2 Sisters*).

4.   What about Sarah's refusal to take questions during the meeting? If the legality of captive audience meetings is, in part, to provide employees with needed information about unionization, isn't it important to allow employees to seek

clarification or make comments? *See Roadway Package System, Inc.*, 302 N.L.R.B. 961, 977–78 (1991); Woolworth F.W., 251 N.L.R.B. 1111, 1113 (1980) (concluding that employers cannot forbid all questions — which are usually protected activity — during a captive audience meeting, but can bar questions that are intended to disrupt the meeting, are made in bad faith, or are part of violent actions), enforced, 655 F.2d 151 (8th Cir. 1981).

5. The Court states in *Nutone & Avondale Mills* that unions have equal opportunity to communicate with employees. Does this strike you as valid? Does the subsequent *Lechmere* doctrine affect that analysis?

B. Threats or Predictions?

NLRB v. GISSEL PACKING CO.
395 U.S. 575 (1969)

Mr. Chief Justice Warren delivered the opinion of the Court.

These [three consolidated] cases involve the extent of an employer's duty under the National Labor Relations Act to recognize a union that bases its claim to representative status solely on the possession of union authorization cards, and the steps an employer may take, particularly with regard to the scope and content of statements he may make, in legitimately resisting such card-based recognition. . . .[19]

In [the case from the First Circuit], the factual pattern was quite similar. The petitioner, a producer of mill rolls, wire, and related products at two plants in Holyoke, Massachusetts, was shut down for some three months in 1952 as the result of a strike over contract negotiations with the American Wire Weavers Protective Association, the representative of petitioner's journeymen and apprentice wire weavers from 1933 to 1952. The Company subsequently reopened without a union contract, and its employees remained unrepresented through 1964, when the Company was acquired by an Ohio corporation, with the Company's former president continuing as head of the Holyoke, Massachusetts, division. In July 1965, the International Brotherhood of Teamsters, Local Union No. 404, began an organizing campaign among petitioner's Holyoke employees . . . .

When petitioner's president first learned of the Union's drive in July, he talked with all of his employees in an effort to dissuade them from joining a union. He particularly emphasized the results of the long 1952 strike, which he claimed 'almost put our company out of business,' and expressed worry that the employees were forgetting the 'lessons of the past.' He emphasized, secondly, that the Company was still on 'thin ice' financially, that the Union's 'only weapon is to strike,' and that a strike 'could lead to the closing of the plant,' since the parent company had ample manufacturing facilities elsewhere. He noted, thirdly, that because of their age and the limited usefulness of their skills outside their craft, the employees might not be able to find re-employment if they lost their jobs as a result of a strike. Finally, he

---

[19] [Eds.: This excerpt addresses only the latter issue; the former will be discussed in Chapter 6.]

warned those who did not believe that the plant could go out of business to 'look around Holyoke and see a lot of them out of business.' The president sent letters to the same effect to the employees in early November, emphasizing that the parent company had no reason to stay in Massachusetts if profits went down.

During the two or three weeks immediately prior to the election on December 9, the president sent the employees a pamphlet captioned: 'Do you want another 13-week strike?' stating, inter alia, that: 'We have no doubt that the Teamsters Union can again close the Wire Weaving Department and the entire plant by a strike. We have no hopes that the Teamsters Union Bosses will not call a strike. . . . The Teamsters Union is a strike happy outfit.' Similar communications followed in late November, including one stressing the Teamsters' 'hoodlum control.' Two days before the election, the Company sent out another pamphlet that was entitled: 'Let's Look at the Record,' and that purported to be an obituary of companies in the Holyoke-Springfield, Massachusetts, area that had allegedly gone out of business because of union demands, eliminating some 3,500 jobs; the first page carried a large cartoon showing the preparation of a grave for the Sinclair Company and other headstones containing the names of other plants allegedly victimized by the unions. Finally, on the day before the election, the president made another personal appeal to his employees to reject the Union. He repeated that the Company's financial condition was precarious; that a possible strike would jeopardize the continued operation of the plant; and that age and lack of education would make re-employment difficult. The Union lost the election 7-6, and then filed both objections to the election and unfair labor practice charges which were consolidated for hearing before the trial examiner.

The Board agreed with the trial examiner that the president's communications with his employees, when considered as a whole, 'reasonably tended to convey to the employees the belief or impression that selection of the Union in the forthcoming election could lead (the Company) to close its plant, or to the transfer of the weaving production, with the resultant loss of jobs to the wire weavers.' Thus, the Board found that under the 'totality of the circumstances' petitioner's activities constituted a violation of [Section] 8(a)(1) of the Act. The Board further agreed with the trial examiner that petitioner's activities, because they 'also interfered with the exercise of a free and untrammeled choice in the election,' and 'tended to foreclose the possibility' of holding a fair election, required that the election be set aside. . . . On appeal, the Court of Appeals for the First Circuit sustained the Board's findings and conclusions and enforced its order in full. . . .

We consider [] petitioner Sinclair's First Amendment challenge to the holding of the Board and the Court of Appeals for the First Circuit. At the outset we note that the question raised here most often arises in the context of a nascent union organizational drive, where employers must be careful in waging their antiunion campaign. As to conduct generally, the above-noted gradations of unfair labor practices, with their varying consequences, create certain hazards for employers when they seek to estimate or resist unionization efforts. But so long as the differences involve conduct easily avoided, such as discharge, surveillance, and coercive interrogation, we do not think that employers can complain that the distinctions are unreasonably difficult to follow. Where an employer's antiunion efforts consist of speech alone, however, the difficulties raised are not so easily resolved. The Board has eliminated some of the problem areas by no longer requiring an employer to show affirmative reasons for insisting on an election and by permitting him to make reasonable inquiries. We do not decide, of course, whether these allowances are mandatory. But we do note that an employer's free speech right to communicate his views to his employees is firmly established and cannot be infringed by a union or the Board. Thus, [Section 8(c)] merely implements the First Amendment by requiring that the expression of 'any views, argument, or opinion' shall not be 'evidence of an unfair labor practice,' so long as such expression contains 'no threat of reprisal or force or promise of benefit' in violation of s 8(a)(1). Section 8(a)(1), in turn, prohibits interference, restraint or coercion of employees in the exercise of their right to self-organization.

Any assessment of the precise scope of employer expression, of course, must be made in the context of its labor relations setting. Thus, an employer's rights cannot outweigh the equal rights of the employees to associate freely, as those rights are embodied in [Section] 7 and protected by [Section] 8(a)(1) and the proviso to [Section] 8(c). And any balancing of those rights must take into account the economic dependence of the employees on their employers, and the necessary tendency of the former, because of that relationship, to pick up intended implications of the latter that might be more readily dismissed by a more disinterested ear. Stating these obvious principles is but another way of recognizing that what is basically at stake is the establishment of a nonpermanent, limited relationship between the employer, his economically dependent employee and his union agent, not the election of legislators or the enactment of legislation whereby that relationship is ultimately defined and where the independent voter may be freer to listen more objectively and employers as a class freer to talk.

Within this framework, we must reject the Company's challenge to the decision below and the findings of the Board on which is was based. The standards used below for evaluating the impact of an employer's statements are not seriously questioned by petitioner and we see no need to tamper with them here. Thus, an employer is free to communicate to his employees any of his general views about unionism or any of his specific views about a particular union, so long as the communications do not contain a 'threat of reprisal or force or promise of benefit.' He may even make a prediction as to the precise effects he believes unionization will have on his company. In such a case, however, the prediction must be carefully phrased on the basis of objective fact to convey an employer's belief as to demonstrably probable consequences beyond his control or to convey a management decision already arrived at to close the plant in case of unionization. *See Textile Workers v. Darlington Mfg. Co.*, 380 U.S. 263, 274, n. 20 (1965). If there is any implication that an employer may or may not take action solely on his own initiative for reasons unrelated to economic necessities and known only to him, the statement is no longer a reasonable prediction based on available facts but a threat of retaliation based on misrepresentation and coercion, and as such without the protection of the First Amendment. We therefore agree with the court below that '(c)onveyance of the employer's belief, even though sincere, that unionization will or may result in the closing of the plant is not a statement of fact unless, which is most improbable, the eventuality of closing is capable of proof.' As stated elsewhere, an employer is free only to tell 'what he reasonably believes will be the likely economic consequences of unionization that are outside his control,' and not 'threats of economic reprisal to be taken solely on his own volition.' *NLRB v. River Togs, Inc.*, 382 F.2d 198, 202 (2d Cir. 1967).

Equally valid was the finding by the court and the Board that petitioner's statements and communications were not cast as a prediction of 'demonstrable 'economic consequences,'" but rather as a threat of retaliatory action. The Board found that petitioner's speeches, pamphlets, leaflets, and letters conveyed the following message: that the company was in a precarious financial condition; that the 'strike-happy' union would in all likelihood have to obtain its potentially unreasonable demands by striking, the probable result of which would be a plant shutdown, as the past history of labor relations in the area indicated; and that the employees in such a case would have great difficulty finding employment elsewhere. In carrying out its duty to focus on the question: '(W)hat did the speaker intend and the listener understand?' (A. Cox, Law and the National Labor Policy 44 (1960)), the Board could reasonably conclude that the intended and understood import of that message was not to predict that unionization would inevitably cause the plant to close but to threaten to throw employees out of work regardless of the economic realities. In this connection, we need go no further than to point out (1) that petitioner had no support for its basic assumption that the union, which had not yet even presented any demands, would have to strike to be heard, and that it admitted at the hearing that it had no basis for attributing other plant closings in the area to unionism; and (2) that the Board has often found that employees, who are particularly sensitive to rumors of plant closings, take such hints as coercive threats rather than honest forecasts.

Petitioner argues that the line between so-called permitted predictions and proscribed threats is too vague to stand up under traditional First Amendment analysis and that the Board's discretion to curtail free speech rights is correspondingly too uncontrolled. It is true that a reviewing court must recognize the Board's competence in the first instance to judge the impact of utterances made in the context of the employer-employee relationship, *see NLRB v. Virginia Electric & Power Co.*, 314 U.S. 469, 479 (1941). But an employer, who has control over that relationship and therefore knows it best, cannot be heard to complain that he is without an adequate guide for his behavior. He can easily make his views known without engaging in "brinkmanship" when it becomes all too easy to 'overstep and tumble (over) the brink,' *Wausau Steel Corp. v. NLRB*, 377 F.2d 369, 372 (C.A.7th Cir. 1967). At the least he can avoid coercive speech simply by avoiding conscious overstatements he has reason to believe will mislead his employees.

For the foregoing reasons, we affirm the judgment of the Court of Appeals for the First Circuit in No. 585 . . . .

It is so ordered.

POST PROBLEM DISCUSSION

1.   We learned in *Darlington* that, under most conditions, an employer does not violate the NLRA by closing down when faced with a union victory. Given that holding, how does the Court hold that a mere *threat* of closure is unlawful? In other words, why isn't an actual closure, with an actual loss of jobs, treated as more

serious than a threat of closure and job loss? *See Crown Cork & Seal Co. v. NLRB*, 36 F.3d 1130, (D.C. Cir. 1994) (finding no violation); *TRW-United Greenfield Division v. NLRB*, 637 F.2d 410, 415 (5th Cir. 1981) (finding violation); *Savers*, 337 N.L.R.B. 1039 (2002) (finding no violation).

2. In our problem, how relevant is it that Sarah said only that the mall "might" have to contract out work? Is the use of a less certain word than "will" enough to avoid classification as an unlawful threat? *Compare Tellepsen Pipelines Services Co.*, 335 N.L.R.B. 1232, 1233 (2001) (finding violation because of surrounding circumstances, with dissent on this question), *enforced in part on relevant grounds*, 320 F.3d 554, 564 (6th Cir. 2003), *with CPP Pinkerton*, 309 N.L.R.B. 723, 724 (1992) (refusing to order new election).

3. What if Sarah was the company CEO or other high-ranking official? *See Impact Industries*, 285 N.L.R.B. 5, 6 (1987) (An "employer's unlawful conduct is heightened when it is committed by the highest-level management official."), *remanded on other grounds*, 847 F.2d 379 (7th Cir. 1988). What if she made the statements to a friend — would that relationship make the statements more or less threatening? *See Tellepsen Pipelines*, 320 F.3d at 564 (holding that close personal relationship not determinative; must still look at totality of circumstances); *NLRB v. Big Three Industries Gas & Equipment*, 579 F.2d 304, 311 (5th Cir. 1978) (holding that warnings "cast as friendly advice from a familiar associate might be more credible, hence more offensive to [Section] 8(a)(1) than generalized utterances by distant Company officials").

4. What if Sarah had told the janitors that if the union wins, the mall would have to "bargain from scratch"? Is this simply a factual statement reflecting the possibility that all issues are possible subjects of bargaining or a threat to take away benefits that the janitors currently enjoy if they vote for a union? *See Shaw's Supermarkets, Inc. v. NLRB*, 884 F.2d 34, 37–41 (1st Cir. 1989) (describing numerous "bargaining from scratch" cases, either as possible threats under Section 8(a)(1) or as evidence of a failure to bargain in good faith).

5. For the background on the *Gissel* cases, see Laura J. Cooper & Dennis R. Nolan, *The Story of* NLRB v. Gissel Packing: *The Practical Limits of Paternalism*, *in* LABOR LAW STORIES 191 (Laura J. Cooper & Catherine L. Fisk, eds. 2005).

SECTION 3   FACTUAL MISREPRESENTATION

PROBLEM #4: THE ELECTION CAMPAIGN: ALTERED SAMPLE BALLOTS

As is the typical practice before an election, the NLRB required the mall to post official election notices from the agency in various places, such as the employee lounge. In addition to notifying employees of some of their NLRA rights, the notices contain a sample of the ballot that will be used in the upcoming election, including "yes" and "no" boxes next to the union's name. During the union's meeting with the janitors, it printed fliers that contained the same sample ballot except that there was a computer-generated "x" in the yes box. Later, an unidentified individual used a pencil to mark the yes box on all of the posted election notices in the mall.

Should the defaced ballot be grounds to overturn the election if the union wins? As you read the NLRB's approach to cases like this, ask yourself whether you share its view about the effect that campaign misrepresentations have on employees.

PROBLEM MATERIALS

Midland National Life Insurance Co., 263 N.L.R.B. 127 (1982)

MIDLAND NATIONAL LIFE INSURANCE CO.
263 N.L.R.B. 127 (1982)

. . . [A] complaint was issued against the Employer alleging that since on or about March 27, 1978, the Employer had violated Section 8(a)(1) of the Act by engaging in various specified acts which restrained, coerced, and interfered with its employees in the exercise of their rights under the Act. . . . A hearing was held before an administrative law judge who issued a Decision finding that the Employer had committed unfair labor practices as alleged, that the Employer had engaged in objectionable conduct affecting the results of the election [in which the union lost by a vote of 75 to 127], and that accordingly a second election should be held. . . . Pursuant to the Board's Order of August 9, 1979, the Regional Director held a second election on October 16, 1980. . . . The tally of ballots shows that of approximately 239 eligible voters, 107 cast ballots for the Petitioner, 107 cast ballots against the Petitioner [union]. . . .

The facts are not complex. On the afternoon of October 15, 1980, the day before the election, the Employer distributed campaign literature to its employees with their paychecks. One of the distributions was a six-page document which included photographs and text depicting three local employers and their involvements with the Petitioner. The document also contained a reproduction of a portion of the Petitioner's 1979 financial report (hereinafter LMRDA report) submitted to the Department of Labor pursuant to the provisions of the Labor Management Reporting and Disclosure Act of 1959. The Petitioner learned of the document the next morning, 3-1/2 hours before the polls were to open.

The first subject of the document, Meilman Food, Inc., was portrayed in "recent" pictures as a deserted facility, and was described in accompanying text as follows: "They too employed between 200 and 300 employees. This Local 304A struck this plant — violence ensued. *Now all of the workers are gone!* What did the Local 304A do for them? Where is the 304A union job security?" Jack Smith, the Petitioner's business representative, testified that Local 304A, the Petitioner, had been the representative of Meilman's employees, but that neither the Petitioner nor Meilman's employees had been on strike when the plant closed. He added that the employees had been working for at least 1 1/2 years following the strike and prior to the closure of the facility.

The second and third employers pictured and discussed in the document were Luther Manor Nursing Home and Blue Cross/Blue Shield. The text accompanying the pictures of Luther Manor explained that:

> [a]lmost a year ago this same union that tells you they will "make job
> security" (we believe you are the only ones who can do that) and will get you
> more pay, told the employees of LUTHER MANOR (again, here in Sioux
> Falls) . . . the union would get them a contract with job security and more
> money. Unfortunately Local 304A did not tell the Luther Manor employees
> what year or century they were talking about. Today the employees have no
> contract. Most of the union leaders left to work elsewhere. Their job
> security is the same (depends upon the individual as it always has). There
> has been no change or increase in wages or hours. The union has sent in
> three different sets of negotiators. Again, promises and performance are
> two different things. All wages, fringes, working conditions are remaining
> the same while negotiations continue.

The text accompanying the pictures of Blue Cross stated that "this same Local
union won an election at Blue Cross/Blue Shield after promising less restrictive
policies, better pay and more job security. Since the election a good percentage of
its former employees are no longer working there. Ask them! The employees have
been offered a wage increase — *next year* of 5% . . . ."

Smith testified that the Petitioner took over negotiations at Luther Manor and at
Blue Cross on or about July 1, 1980, after the Petitioner had merged with Retail
Clerks, Local 1665, and that Retail Clerks, Local 1665, not the Petitioner, had
conducted the prior negotiations and won the election at Blue Cross.

Assessing the statements concerning these local employers, the Hearing Officer
concluded that, in its description of Meilman Food, the Employer intended to instill
in the minds of its employees the false impression that the Petitioner had conducted
a strike at Meilman, that violence had ensued, and that, as a direct result of the
strike, all of the employees at Meilman were terminated. Evaluating the statements
about Luther Manor and Blue Cross, the Hearing Officer found that the Employer
had misrepresented the labor organization involved, and had implied that the
Petitioner was an ineffectual and inefficient bargaining representative who would
cause employees to suffer.

The Employer's distribution also included a portion of the Petitioner's 1979
LMRDA report which listed information concerning the Petitioner's assets, liabilities, and cash receipts and disbursements for the reporting period. Three entries on
the reproduced page were underlined: total receipts, reported at $508,946; dis-
bursements "On Behalf of Individual Members," reported at zero; and total
disbursements, reported at $492,701. Other entries on the reproduced page showed
disbursements of $93,185 to officers, and $22,662 to employees. The accompanying
text stated that $141,000 of the Petitioner's funds went to "union officers and
officials and those who worked for them," and that "NOTHING — according to the
report they filed with the U.S. Government was spent 'on behalf of the individual
members.' "

The Hearing Officer found that the report actually showed that the Petitioner
disbursed only $115,847 to its officers and employees, a difference of $25,000, and
that the Employer's statement attributed 19 percent more in income to the officials

and employees than was actually received. He further found that, while the report showed that no sums had been spent "on behalf of the individual members," the instructions for the LMRDA report require that entry to reflect disbursements for "other than normal operating purposes," and that the Employer failed to include this fact in its distribution.

In accordance with his findings outlined above, the Hearing Officer concluded that the document distributed by the Employer contained numerous misrepresentations of fact of a substantial nature designed to portray the Petitioner as an organization staffed by highly paid officials and employees who were ineffectual as bargaining representatives, and that as a consequence employees would suffer with respect to job security and compensation. The Hearing Officer also determined that the document was distributed on the afternoon before the election, that the Petitioner did not become aware of it until approximately 10 a.m. election day, 2-1/2 hours before the preelection conference and 3-1/2 hours before the polls were to open, and that, owing to the nature of the misrepresentations, the Petitioner did not have sufficient time to respond effectively. Applying the standard found in *General Knit of California, Inc.*, [239 NLRB 619 (1978),] and *Hollywood Ceramics Company, Inc.*, [140 NLRB 221 (1962),] the Hearing Officer accordingly recommended that the objection be sustained and that a third election be directed.

We have decided to reject the Hearing Officer's recommendations and to certify the results of the election. We do so because, after painstaking evaluation and careful consideration, we have resolved to return to the sound rule announced in *Shopping Kart Food Market, Inc.*, [228 NLRB 1311 (1977),] and to overrule *General Knit* and *Hollywood Ceramics*. . . .

Overruling prior cases which indicated that intent to mislead was an element of the standard, [in *Hollywood Ceramics Company, Inc.*, 140 NLRB 221 (1962),] the Board stated that "an election should be set aside only where there has been a misrepresentation or other similar campaign trickery, which involves a substantial departure from the truth, at a time which prevents the other party or parties from making an effective reply, so that the misrepresentation, whether deliberate or not, may reasonably be expected to have a significant impact on the election." *Id.* at 224.

In 1977, after 15 years of experience under this rule, a majority of the Board decided in *Shopping Kart Food Market, Inc.*, 228 NLRB 1311 (1977), to overrule *Hollywood Ceramics* . . . . Thus, the Board stated that it would "no longer probe into the truth or falsity of the parties' campaign statements," but would instead recognize and rely on employees "as mature individuals who are capable of recognizing campaign propaganda for what it is and discounting it." *Id.* at 1311, 1313. Consistent with this view, the majority also held that the Board would intervene "in instances where a party has engaged in such deceptive campaign practices as improperly involving the Board and its processes, or the use of forged documents which render the voters unable to recognize the propaganda for what it is." *Id.* at 1313.

A scant 20 months later, the Board reversed itself, overruled *Shopping Kart*, and reinstated the *Hollywood Ceramics* standard. *General Knit of California, Inc.*, 239 NLRB 619 (1978). Finding that the rule propounded in *Shopping Kart* was "inconsistent with [the Board's] responsibility to insure fair elections," the Board stated that "there are certain circumstances where a particular misrepresentation . . . may materially affect an election," and that such an election should be set aside "in order to maintain the integrity of Board elections and there by protect employee free choice." *Id.* at 620. . . .

By returning to the sound principles espoused in *Shopping Kart*, not only do we alleviate the many difficulties attending the *Hollywood Ceramics* rule, but we also insure the certainty and finality of election results, and minimize unwarranted and dilatory claims attacking those results. . . . As was found in *Shopping Kart*, although the adoption of the *Hollywood Ceramics* rule "was premised on assuring employee free choice its administration has in fact tended to impede the attainment of that goal. The ill effects of the rule include extensive analysis of campaign propaganda, restriction of free speech, variance in application as between the Board and the courts, increasing litigation, and a resulting decrease in the finality of election results." [228 N.L.R.B. at 1312.]

In sharp contrast to the *Hollywood Ceramics* standard, *Shopping Kart* "draws a clear line between what is and what is not objectionable." [*General Knit of California, Inc.*, 239 NLRB 619, 629 (1978) (Member Penello, dissenting).] Thus, "elections will be set aside 'not on the basis of the *substance* of the representation, but the deceptive *manner* in which it was made.' . . . As long as the campaign material is what it purports to be, i.e., mere propaganda of a particular party, the Board would leave the task of evaluating its contents solely to the employees." *Id.* Where, due to forgery, no voter could recognize the propaganda "for what it is," Board intervention is warranted. Further, unlike *Hollywood Ceramics*, the rule in *Shopping Kart* lends itself to definite results which are both predictable and speedy. The incentive for protracted litigation is greatly reduced, as is the possibility of disagreement between the Board and the courts. Because objections alleging false or inaccurate statements can be summarily rejected at the first stage of Board proceedings, the opportunity for delay is almost nonexistent. Finally, the rule in *Shopping Kart* "furthers the goal of consistent and equitable adjudications" by applying uniformly to the objections of both unions and employers.

In addition to finding the *Hollywood Ceramics* rule to be unwieldy and counterproductive, we also consider it to have an unrealistic view of the ability of voters to assess misleading campaign propaganda. As is clear from an examination of our treatment of misrepresentations under the Wagner Act, the Board had long viewed employees as aware that parties to a campaign are seeking to achieve certain results and to promote their own goals. Employees, knowing these interests, could not help but greet the various claims made during a campaign with natural skepticism. The "protectionism" propounded by the *Hollywood Ceramics* rule is simply not warranted. On the contrary, as we found in *Shopping Kart*, "we believe that Board rules in this area must be based on a view of employees as mature individuals who are capable of recognizing campaign propaganda for what it is and discounting it." . . .

In sum, we rule today that we will no longer probe into the truth or falsity of the parties' campaign statements, and that we will not set elections aside on the basis of misleading campaign statements. We will, however, intervene in cases where a party has used forged documents which render the voters unable to recognize propaganda for what it is. Thus, we will set an election aside not because of the substance of the representation, but because of the deceptive manner in which it was made, a manner which renders employees unable to evaluate the forgery for what it is. As was the case in *Shopping Kart*, we will continue to protect against other campaign conduct, such as threats, promises, or the like, which interferes with employee free choice.

Accordingly, inasmuch as the Petitioner's objection alleges nothing more than misrepresentations, it is hereby overruled. Because the tally of ballots shows that the Petitioner failed to receive a majority of the valid ballots cast, we shall certify the results.

MEMBERS FANNING and JENKINS, dissenting:

. . . In return for the illusory benefits of speed and a speculative lightening of its workload, the majority today errs in relinquishing the Board's obligation to put some limits on fraud and deceit as campaign tools. It is apparent that the system contemplated by Section 9 of the Act for representation elections has survived reasonably well during the decades in which the Board has taken a role in insuring the integrity of its elections. Indeed, the majority does not suggest deregulating the election process other than with respect to misrepresentations. In this connection, we are especially puzzled by the distinction the majority draws between forgery, which it will regulate, and other kinds of fraud, which it will not. The majority states that forgeries "render the voters unable to recognize the propaganda for what it is." Yet it is precisely the Board's traditional perception that there are some misrepresentations which employees can recognize "for what they are" and others which, in the Board's considered judgment, they cannot, that has made the *Hollywood Ceramics* doctrine so effective. In place of this approach, under which judgments take into account the facts of each case, the majority creates an irrebuttable presumption that employees can recognize all misrepresentations, however opaque and deceptive, except forgeries. Employees' free choice in elections, the only reason we run elections, must necessarily be inhibited, distorted, and frustrated by this new rule. To the majority, this is less important than the freedom to engage in lies, trickery, and fraud. Under the new rule, important election issues will be ignored in favor of irresponsible charges and deceit. Under *Hollywood Ceramics*, the Board did not attempt to sanitize elections completely but only to keep the campaign propaganda within reasonable bounds. Those bounds have now disappeared. Why?

Albeit today's American employees may be better educated, in the formal sense, than those of previous generations, and may be in certain respects more sophisti-cated, we do not honor them by abandoning them utterly to the mercies of unscrupulous campaigners, including the expert cadre of professional opinion molders who devise campaigns for many of our representation elections. In political campaigns, which are conducted over a much longer period of time and are subject to extensive media scrutiny, the voters have ready access to independent sources of information concerning the issues. In representation campaigns, they do not. Thus, it has been observed that: "Promises are often written on the wind, but statements of fact are the stuff upon which men and women make serious value judgments . . . , and rank and file employees must largely depend on the company and the union to provide the data . . . ." [*J. I. Case* v. *N.L.R.B.*, 555 F.2d 202, 205 (8th Cir. 1977).] As we said in our dissent in *Shopping Kart*, the very high level of participation in Board elections as compared with political elections speaks well for the Board's role in insuring a measure of responsibility in campaigning. On the other hand, absent some external restraint, the campaigners will have little incentive to refrain from any last-minute deceptions that might work to their short-term advantage.

In sum, we are able to agree with the majority on very little. But one point of agreement is the majority's statement that, "The sole question facing us here is how [the fair and free choice of a bargaining representative] is best assured." For the reasons set forth above, and also for the reasons set forth in *General Knit* and our dissent in *Shopping Kart*, we find it impossible to answer that question by abandoning one of the most effective means the Board has yet devised for assuring that desired result. . . .

POST PROBLEM DISCUSSION

1.   How does *Midland*, as well as its predecessors, fit with the "laboratory conditions" of *General Shoe*? Do you think that union elections are similar to political elections and therefore warrant a more hands-off approach, or are the differences between the two substantial enough to justify the need for increased regulation. *See Midland*, 263 N.L.R.B. at 134–35 (Members Fanning & Jenkins, dissenting). Why or why not?

In a similar vein, how much effect do you think misrepresentations have on the outcome of elections? Are employees likely, as the NLRB states in *Midland*, to simply view most misrepresentations as typical campaign tactics or is there a real risk of swaying opinion based on factors that are not true?

2.   Consider the altered ballots in our problem. Should they warrant a new election? Are the ballots permissible campaign propaganda? Or do the ballots rise to the level of a forgery or other similarly hidden alteration? If it's the latter, "the Board will examine 'the nature and contents of the document,' as well as 'the circumstances of [its] distribution' to determine 'whether it was likely to give employees the misleading impression that the Board favored [one side] in the election.'" *Kwik Care Ltd. v. NLRB*, 82 F.3d 1122, 1128 (D.C. Cir. 1996) (quoting *3-Day Blinds*, 299 N.L.R.B. 110, 111 n.7 (1990)).

3.   The NLRB is especially sensitive about the alteration of its official documents, as this risks the appearance that the agency has a stake in the union winning or losing. *See Riveredge Hospital*, 264 N.L.R.B. 1094, 1095 (1982) (noting that the *Midland* test will still apply to misrepresentations of NLRB actions), *enforced as modified sub nom. NLRB v. Affiliated Midwest Hospital, Inc.*, 789 F.2d 524 (7th Cir. 1986). After many years of making case-by-case determinations regarding alterations of its notices, the NLRB now explicitly states in its notice of election that it does not endorse parties; if an altered document — including sample ballots distributed to employees — still contains that notice, the NLRB will generally find the alteration to be obvious propaganda. *See Ryder Memorial Hospital*, 351 N.L.R.B. 214, 216 (2007). If the notice is removed, the NLRB will use its normal analysis, as described in Note #2.

SECTION 4   PROVIDING OR PROMISING BENEFITS

PROBLEM #5: THE ELECTION CAMPAIGN: A VISIT FROM THE CORPORATE PRESIDENT AND A UNION RAFFLE

Northside Mall is owned by a large multinational company, Malls of the World, which is headquartered in London, England. The CEO of Malls of the World, Sir Rowland Warren, tries to visit each of his company's numerous malls every year or two. During these brief visits, Sir Rowland would usually walk through the mall and meet with its managers. Ten months after his last visit to the Northside Mall, Sir Rowland made another visit. During his tour of the mall, he stopped to talk with a few of the janitors and asked them if there were any problems that they wanted to talk about. Some of the janitors talked about the upcoming election and the complaints that had prompted interest in the union. Sir Rowland asked the employees if they would give him time to deal with these problems and told them that he would do a better job communicating with them about any issues they had with management at the mall. A week later, Sir Rowland sent an e-mail to all of the janitors that acknowledged their complaints, promised to look into them, and asked whether they thought that the mall should have new management.

Around the same time, the union had been holding periodic meetings at its office for the employees to learn more about the union, express their complaints about the mall management, and socialize. During these meetings, the union provided free pizza and soft drinks to the janitors. In addition, the union started a raffle that would provide the winner with an iPod Shuffle (which cost $49 at the time). Every time a janitor attended a union meeting, he or she would get an additional entry in the raffle. The union promised that on the day after the election — no matter whether it won or lost — it would draw one name from all the entries to determine the winner of the iPod.

Read the following material to determine whether Sir Roland or the union did anything inappropriate given the upcoming election. As you formulate your answer, think about how that answer would play out under different election outcomes — for instance, the union winning by a small margin or losing by a large margin. One way to judge the legal analysis in this area is to ask yourself whether the behavior in our problem should warrant vacating these hypothetical election outcomes.

PROBLEM MATERIALS

NLRB v. Exchange Parts Co., 375 U.S. 405 (1964)

NLRB v. Savair Manufacturing Co., 414 U.S. 270 (1973)

NLRB v. EXCHANGE PARTS CO.
375 U.S. 405 (1964)

Mr. Justice Harlan delivered the opinion of the Court.

This case presents a question concerning the limitations which [Section] 8(a)(1) of the National Labor Relations Act . . . places on the right of an employer to confer economic benefits on his employees shortly before a representation election. The precise issue is whether that section prohibits the conferral of such benefits, without more, where the employer's purpose is to affect the outcome of the election. . . .

The respondent, Exchange Parts Company, is engaged in the business of rebuilding automobile parts in Fort Worth, Texas. Prior to November 1959 its employees were not represented by a union. On November 9, 1959, the International Brotherhood of Boilermakers, Iron Shipbuilders, Blacksmiths, Forgers and Helpers, AFL-CIO, advised Exchange Parts that the union was conducting an organizational campaign at the plant and that a majority of the employees had designated the union as their bargaining representative. On November 16 the union petitioned the Labor Board for a representation election. The Board conducted a hearing on December 29, and on February 19, 1960, issued an order directing that an election be held. The election was held on March 18, 1960.

At two meetings on November 4 and 5, 1959, C. V. McDonald, the Vice-President and General Manager of Exchange Parts, announced to the employees that their "floating holiday" in 1959 would fall on December 26 and that there would be an additional "floating holiday" in 1960. On February 25, six days after the Board issued its election order, Exchange Parts held a dinner for employees at which Vice-President McDonald told the employees that they could decide whether the extra day of vacation in 1960 would be a "floating holiday" or would be taken on their birthdays. The employees voted for the latter. McDonald also referred to the forthcoming representation election as one in which, in the words of the trial examiner, the employees would "determine whether . . . (they) wished to hand over their right to speak and act for themselves." He stated that the union had distorted some of the facts and pointed out the benefits obtained by the employees without a union. He urged all the employees to vote in the election.

On March 4 Exchange Parts sent its employees a letter which spoke of "the Empty Promises of the Union" and "the *fact* that *it is the Company that puts things in your envelope* . . . ." After mentioning a number of benefits, the letter said: "The Union can't put any of those things in your envelope-*only the Company can do that.*" Further on, the letter stated: ". . . (I)t didn't take a Union to get any of those things and . . . it won't take a Union to get additional improvements in the future." Accompanying the letter was a detailed statement of the benefits granted by the company since 1949 and an estimate of the monetary value of such benefits to the employees. Included in the statement of benefits for 1960 were the birthday holiday, a new system for computing overtime during holiday weeks which had the effect of increasing wages for those weeks, and a new vacation schedule which enabled employees to extend their vacations by sandwiching them between two weekends. Although Exchange Parts asserts that the policy behind the latter two benefits was established earlier, it is clear that the letter of March 4 was the first general announcement of the changes to the employees. In the ensuing election the union lost.

The Board, affirming the findings of the trial examiner, found that the announcement of the birthday holiday and the grant and announcement of overtime and vacation benefits were arranged by Exchange Parts with the intention of inducing the employees to vote against the union. It found that this conduct violated [Section] 8(a)(1) of the National Labor Relations Act and issued an appropriate order. On the Board's petition for enforcement of the order, the Court of Appeals rejected the finding that the announcement of the birthday holiday was timed to influence the outcome of the election. It accepted the Board's findings with respect to the overtime and vacation benefits, and the propriety of those findings is not in controversy here. However, noting that 'the benefits were put into effect unconditionally on a permanent basis, and no one has suggested that there was any implication the benefits would be withdrawn if the workers voted for the union,' the court denied enforcement of the Board's order. It believed that it was not an unfair labor practice under [Section] 8(a)(1) for an employer to grant benefits to its employees in these circumstances. . . .

We think the Court of Appeals was mistaken in concluding that the conferral of employee benefits while a representation election is pending, for the purpose of inducing employees to vote against the union, does not "interfere with" the protected right to organize.

The broad purpose of [Section] 8(a)(1) is to establish "the right of employees to organize for mutual aid without employer interference." *Republic Aviation Corp. v. N.L.R.B.*, 324 U.S. 793, 798. We have no doubt that it prohibits not only intrusive threats and promises but also conduct immediately favorable to employees which is undertaken with the express purpose of impinging upon their freedom of choice for or against unionization and is reasonably calculated to have that effect. In *Medo Photo Supply Corp. v. N.L.R.B.*, 321 U.S. 678, this Court said: "The action of employees with respect to the choice of their bargaining agents may be induced by favors bestowed by the employer as well as by his threats or domination." Although in that case there was already a designated bargaining agent and the offer of "favors" was in response to a suggestion of the employees that they would leave the union if favors were bestowed, the principles which dictated the result there are fully applicable here. The danger inherent in well-timed increases in benefits is the suggestion of a fist inside the velvet glove. Employees are not likely to miss the inference that the source of benefits now conferred is also the source from which future benefits must flow and which may dry up if it is not obliged. The danger may be diminished if, as in this case, the benefits are conferred permanently and unconditionally. But the absence of conditions or threats pertaining to the particular benefits conferred would be of controlling significance only if it could be presumed that no question of additional benefits or renegotiation of existing benefits would arise in the future; and, of course, no such presumption is tenable. . . .

It is true, as the court below pointed out, that in most cases of this kind the increase in benefits could be regarded as "one part of an overall program of interference and restraint by the employer," and that in this case the questioned conduct stood in isolation. Other unlawful conduct may often be an indication of the motive behind a grant of benefits while an election is pending, and to that extent it is relevant to the legality of the grant; but when as here the motive is otherwise established, an employer is not free to violate [Section] 8(a)(1) by conferring benefits simply because it refrains from other, more obvious violations. We cannot agree with the Court of Appeals that enforcement of the Board's order will have the "ironic" result of "discouraging benefits for labor." The beneficence of an employer is likely to be ephemeral if prompted by a threat of unionization which is subsequently removed. Insulating the right of collective organization from calculated good will of this sort deprives employees of little that has lasting value.

Reversed.

NLRB v. SAVAIR MANUFACTURING CO.
414 U.S. 270 (1973)

Mr. Justice Douglas delivered the opinion of the Court.

The National Labor Relations Board . . . conducted an election by secret ballot among the production and maintenance employees of respondent at the request of the Mechanics Educational Society of America (hereafter Union). . . . The Union won the election by a vote of 22-20.

Respondent filed objections to the election, but after an evidentiary hearing a hearing officer found against respondent and the Board certified the Union as the representative of the employees in that unit. Respondent, however, refused to bargain. . . . The Board sustained the [refusal to bargain] allegations and ordered respondent to bargain with the Union. The Court of Appeals denied enforcement of the order. We granted the petition for certiorari [and w]e affirm.

It appeared that prior to the election, "recognition slips" were circulated among employees. An employee who signed the slip before the election[20] became a member of the Union and would not have to pay what at times was called an 'initiation fee' and at times a "fine." If the Union was voted in, those who had not signed a recognition slip would have to pay.

The actual solicitation of signatures on the "recognition slips" was not done by Union officials. Union officials, however, explained to employees at meetings that those who signed the slips would not be required to pay an initiation fee, while those who did not would have to pay. Those officials also picked out some five employees to do the soliciting and authorized them to explain the Union's initiation-fee policy. Those solicited were told that there would be no initiation fee charged those who signed the slip before the election. Under the bylaws of the Union, an initiation fee apparently was not to be higher than $10; but the employees who testified at the hearing (1) did not know how large the fee would be and (2) said that their understanding was that the fee was a "fine" or an "assessment."

---

[20] [n.4] . . . The Court of Appeals read the Hearing Officer's Report to state that the waiver was limited to those signing up before the election, as do we. . . . The Board argues that unions have a valid interest in waiving the initiation fee when the union has not yet been chosen as a bargaining representative, because "(e)mployees otherwise sympathetic to the union might well have been reluctant to pay out money before the union had done anything for them. Waiver of the (initiation fees) would remove this artificial obstacle to their endorsement of the union.' See Amalgamated endorsement of the union." *See Amalgamated Clothing Workers v. NLRB*, 345 F.2d 264, 268 (CA2 1969). While this union interest is legitimate, the Board's argument ignores the fact that this interest can be preserved as well by waiver of initiation fees available not only to those who have signed up with the union before an election but also to those who join after the election. The limitation imposed by the union in this case — to those joining before the election — is necessary only because it serves the additional purpose of affecting the Union organizational campaign and the election.

One employee, Donald Bridgeman, testified that he signed the slip to avoid paying the "fine" if the Union won. He got the message directly from an employee picked by the Union to solicit signatures on the "slips." So did Thomas Rice, another employee.

The Board originally took the position that pre-election solicitation of memberships by a union with a promise to waive the initiation fee of the union was not consistent with a fair and free choice of bargaining representatives. *Lobue Bros.*, 109 N.L.R.B. 1182. Later in *DIT-MCO, Inc.*, 163 N.L.R.B. 1019, the Board explained its changed position as follows:

> We shall assume, arguendo, that employees who sign cards when offered a waiver of initiation fees do so solely because no cost is thus involved; that they in fact do not at that point really want the union to be their bargaining representative. The error of the Lobue premise can be readily seen upon a review of the consequences of such employees casting votes for or against union representation. Initially, it is obvious that employees who have received or been promised free memberships will not be required to pay an initiation fee, whatever the outcome of the vote. If the union wins the election, there is by postulate no obligation; and if the union loses, there is still no obligation, because compulsion to pay an initiation fee arises under the Act only when a union becomes the employees' representative and negotiates a valid union-security agreement. Thus, whatever kindly feeling toward the union may be generated by the cost-reduction offer, when consideration is given only to the question of initiation fees, it is completely illogical to characterize as improper inducement or coercion to vote "Yes" a waiver of something that can be avoided simply by voting "No."

> The illogic of *Lobue* does not become any more logical when other consequences of a vote for representation are considered. Thus, employees know that if a majority vote for the union, it will be their exclusive representative, and, provided a valid union-security provision is negotiated, they will be obliged to pay dues as a condition of employment. Thus, viewed solely as a financial matter, a "no" vote will help to avoid any subsequent obligations, a "yes" may well help to incur such obligations. In these circumstances, an employee who did not want the union to represent him would hardly be likely to vote for the union just because there would be no initial cost involved in obtaining membership. Since an election resulting in the union's defeat would entail not only no initial cost, but also insure that no dues would have to be paid as a condition of employment, the financial inducement, if a factor at all, would be in the direction of a vote against the union, rather than for it.

Id., at 1021–1022.

We are asked to respect the expertise of the Board on this issue, giving it leeway to alter or modify its policy in light of its ongoing experience with the problem. . . . But in this case two opposed groups are in contention: one composed of those who want a union and the other, of those who prefer not to have one. The Board in its *DIT-MCO* opinion says "it is completely illogical to characterize as improper inducement or coercion" a waiver of initiation fees for those who vote "yes" when the whole problem can be avoided by voting "no." 163 N.L.R.B., at 1021–1022. But the Board's analysis ignores the realities of the situation.

Whatever his true intentions, an employee who signs a recognition slip prior to an election is indicating to other workers that he supports the union. His outward manifestation of support must often serve as a useful campaign tool in the union's hands to convince other employees to vote for the union, if only because many employees respect their coworkers' views on the unionization issue. By permitting the union to offer to waive an initiation fee for those employees signing a recognition slip prior to the election, the Board allows the union to buy endorsements and paint a false portrait of employee support during its election campaign.

That influence may well have been felt here for, as noted, there were 28 who signed up with the Union before the election petition was filed with the Board and either seven or eight more who signed up before the election. We do not believe that the statutory policy of fair elections prescribed in the *Tower* case permits endorsements, whether for or against the union, to be bought and sold in this fashion.

In addition, while it is correct that the employee who signs a recognition slip is not legally bound to vote for the union and has not promised to do so in any formal sense, certainly there may be some employees who would feel obliged to carry through on their stated intention to support the union. And on the facts of this case, the change of just one vote would have resulted in a 21-21 election rather than a 22-20 election.

Any procedure requiring a "fair" election must honor the right of those who oppose a union as well as those who favor it. The Act is wholly neutral when it comes to that basic choice. . . . An employer who promises to increase the fringe benefits by $10 for each employee who votes against the union, if the union loses the election, would cross the forbidden line under our decisions. *See NLRB v. Exchange Parts Co.*, 375 U.S. 405 . . . .

Whether it would be an "unfair" labor practice for a union to promise a special benefit to those who sign up for a union seems not to have been squarely resolved. The right of a free choice is, however, inherent in the principles reflected in [Section] 9(c)(1)(A).

When the dissent says that "(t)he special inducement is to sign the card, not to vote for the union" and that treating the two choices as one is untenable, it overlooks cases like *NLRB v. Gissel Packing Co.*, 395 U.S. 575. There we held that the gathering of authorization cards from a majority of the employees in the bargaining unit may entitle the union to represent the employees for collective-bargaining purposes, even though there has been and will be no election, and that rejection of that authorization by the employer is an unfair labor practice. Where the solicitation of cards is represented as being solely for the purpose of obtaining an election, a contrary result is indicated. Thus the solicitation of authorization cards may serve one of two ends. Of course, when an election is contemplated, an employee does not become a member of the union merely by signing a card. But prior to the election if the union receives overwhelming support, the pro-union group may decide to treat the union authorization cards as authorizing it to conduct collective bargaining without an election. The latent potential of that alternative use of authorization cards cautions us to treat the solicitation of authorization cards in exchange for consideration of fringe benefits granted by the union as a separate step protected by the same kind of moral standard that governs elections themselves.

The Board in its supervision of union elections may not sanction procedures that cast their weight for the choice of a union and against a nonunion shop or for a nonunion shop and against a union.

In the *Exchange Parts* case we said that, although the benefits granted by the employer were permanent and unconditional, employees were "not likely to miss the inference that the source of benefits now conferred is also the source from which future benefits must flow and which may dry up if it is not obliged." 375 U.S., at 409. If we respect, as we must, the statutory right of employees to resist efforts to unionize a plant, we cannot assume that unions exercising powers are wholly benign towards their antagonists whether they be nonunion protagonists or the employer. The failure to sign a recognition slip may well seem ominous to nonunionists who fear that if they do not sign they will face a wrathful union regime, should the union win. That influence may well have had a decisive impact in this case where a change of one vote would have changed the result.

Affirmed.

MR. JUSTICE WHITE, with whom MR. JUSTICE BRENNAN and MR. JUSTICE BLACKMUN join, dissenting.

It is well established that an "unconditional" offer to waive initiation fees, where the waiver offer is left open for some period of time after the election, is not coercive and does not constitute an unfair labor practice. . . . The existence of the initiation fee is created by the union and represents a self-imposed barrier to entry.[21] There is no evidence that the fee is normally imposed for the sole purpose of removing it during a labor campaign. A different case might be put if the union purported to remove a nonexistent fee or artificially inflated the fee so as to misrepresent the benefit tendered by its removal. Similarly, it is established that the union can promise employees to obtain wage increases or other benefits if it is elected as a bargaining representative.

In the instant case, an offer which by its terms expires with the conclusion of the election is a form of economic inducement. But insofar as the offer might affect the calculation of costs and benefits of joining the union, its effect is the same as an offer which does not expire until sometime after the election. The inability to distinguish between these two situations, at least where small fees are involved and where the sole source of concern is pure financial inducement, led the Board to conclude in *DIT-MCO* that "an employee who did not want the union to represent him would

---

[21] [n.3] The role of the initiation fee has been described by one writer as follows: "Initiation fees serve several sorts of union purposes. First, of course they are a source of revenue, which is occasionally expendable however during an organization drive when the union is anxious to induce workers to join the union. Second, the initiation fee represents for the older member a kind of equity payment by the new member to compensate, at least partially, for the efforts that others have put into building the union . . . ." J. Barbash, The Practice of Unionism 79 (1956).

hardly he likely to vote for the union just because there would be no initial cost involved in obtaining membership." 163 N.L.R.B., at 1022.

The majority places heavy reliance on the supposed analogy between the waiver of fees in this case and an actual increase in benefits made by an employer during the course of an election campaign. *NLRB v. Exchange Parts Co.*, 375 U.S. 405 (1964). . . . A number of important differences exist between that case and the instant one. First, the employer actually gave his employees substantial increased benefits, whereas here the benefit is only contingent and small; the union glove is not very velvet. Secondly, in the union context, the fist is missing. When the employer increased benefits, the threat was made "that the source of benefits now conferred is also the source from which future benefits must flow and which may dry up if it is not obliged." *Ibid.* The Union, on the other hand, since it was not the representative of the employees, and would not be if it were unsuccessful in the election, could not make the same threat by offering a benefit which it would take away if it lost the election. A union can only make its own victory more desirable in the minds of the employees. . . .

The special inducement is to sign the card, not to vote for the union. The majority decision collapses these two choices into one, and is thus untenable. The majority assumes, contrary to fact, that the employee has joined the Union by signing the authorization card. This is only true, however, if the Union wins the election and signs a collective contract, and the employee can still seek to prevent that outcome by casting his vote against the Union in a secret ballot. The testimony was clear that if the Union loses the election, the employee who signs the card incurs no obligation to the Union. . . .

Since the case for coercion arising out of the conditional offer is speculative, and since the alteration of the calculus of costs and benefits is marginal where a small fee is involved, the issue here resolves into the proper allocation of institutional responsibility between an administrative agency and a reviewing court. . . . There is certainly a conflicting interest between the union's right to make itself attractive to employees without misrepresentation and the employee's unfettered choice to vote for or against the union. I think it is rational for the Board to conclude on the basis of the facts presented that the decision of the Union to waive small fees was not coercive within the meaning of [Section] 7. I, therefore, respectfully dissent.

POST PROBLEM DISCUSSION

1. Why is an employer penalized for improving work conditions? Isn't that exactly what the employees want? Or put another way, are you as convinced as the NLRB and Supreme Court that employees would almost always view such improvements as threatening?

2. Although changes in the terms and conditions of work that occur during a union campaign are presumptively unlawful under the *Exchange Parts* line of cases, there are exceptions. In particular, if an employer is able to provide a valid business reason for the change, it may be able to avoid an unfair labor practice finding. *See The Register Guard*, 344 N.L.R.B. 1142, 1142 (2005) (stating that employer can rebut presumption with a "persuasive business reason demonstrating that the timing of the grant of benefits was governed by factors other than the union

campaign"). *See also* Note #8, below. A common example is when an employer planned to implement a change before the union came on the scene. *See Grouse Mountain Associates II*, 333 N.L.R.B. 1322, 1324 (2001) (noting general rule that employer must implement expected benefit as if the union wasn't on the scene, although the employer can postpone implementation if it makes clear to employees that the benefit will occur no matter the outcome of the vote and that the sole reason for postponement is to avoid the appearance of influencing the election), *enforced*, 56 Fed. Appx. 811 (9th Cir. 2003); *KMST-TV, Channel 46*, 302 N.L.R.B. 381, 382 (1991).

What if the employer has typically implemented raises every year? Must the employer hold off from implementing raises while there is a union campaign? Or, must the employer implement raises during the campaign? The best way to approach issues like these is to identify the status quo. The safest course for an employer is to maintain its previous practices during a union campaign, although that task may be easier said than done. *See NLRB v. Curwood Inc.*, 397 F.3d 548, 556 (7th Cir. 2005); *Atlantic Forest Products*, 282 N.L.R.B. 855, 858 (1987). For instance, what if the annual raises are based on the employer's discretion rather than a predictable set of factors? *Eastern Maine Medical Center*, 253 N.L.R.B. 224, 242 (1980) (noting that employer doesn't have to implement raise if it regularly had discretion over whether a raise would occur every year, but does have to implement a raise if raises were expected and amount was discretionary), *enforced*, 658 F.2d 1 (1st Cir. 1981). Given the difficulty in predicting whether implementing a raise — or not implementing a raise — might be considered unlawful, what if anything could the employer do to protect itself from an unfair labor practice complaint?

3. In *Exchange Parts*, the Court held that the NLRA prohibits "conduct immediately favorable to employees which is undertaken with the express purpose of impinging upon their freedom of choice for or against unionization and is reasonably calculated to have that effect." 375 U.S. at 490; *see also The Register Guard*, 344 N.L.R.B. at 1142. Is this stress on motive consistent with what you've learned about Section 8(a)(1)?

4. Think about Sir Rowland's conduct in the problem — are there any potential grants of benefits? A good way to approach a question like this is to consider what, if anything, has changed from the period before the union campaign to the critical period after the union has filed a valid election petition. For instance, Sir Rowland appears to be paying more attention to employee concerns, even to the extent of promises to investigate and respond to complaints. Such a change is usually referred to as a "solicitation of grievances." Given that Sir Rowland has not actually made any changes in the employees' terms and conditions or employment, nor promised any changes other than to look into the issues, should his solicitation of grievances be considered an unlawful benefit? *See NLRB v. V & S Schuler Engineering, Inc.*, 309 F.3d 362, 372 (6th Cir. 2002) (enforcing NLRB finding of a Section 8(a)(1) violation for unprecedented solicitation of grievances); *The Register Guard*, 344 N.L.R.B. at 1143 ("[A]bsent a prior practice of doing so, an employer's solicitation of grievances during a union campaign, accompanied by a promise, express or implied, to remedy such grievances, creates an inference that the employer is promising to redress the problems.").

5. In *Savair*, the Court compares the union's waiver of initiation fees to the benefits the employer provided in *Exchange Parts*. Do you find that comparison convincing or is there a substantial difference between union and employer conduct? For instance, is the dissent in *Savair* correct when it states that the "union glove is not very velvet" and "in the union context, the fist is missing"?

6. What if the union in *Savair* had waived initiation fees both before and after the election? The NLRB typically finds such waivers to be lawful, *see U-Haul Co. of Nevada, Inc. v. NLRB*, 490 F.3d 957, 962 (D.C. Cir. 2007), but are they really that different?

7. What about the union raffle in our problem? Should the possibility of receiving a $49 iPod constitute an unlawful benefit? The NLRB will consider a raffle to be unlawful and warranting a new election if participation in the raffle is tied to voting or being on site for a union election, or if the raffle occurs within 24 hours of an election. *See Atlantic Limousine, Inc.*, 331 N.L.R.B. 1025, 1029 (2000) (stressing also that the NLRB will continue to allow the distribution of parties "T-shirts, hats, buttons, stickers, or other items bearing a message or insignia, that have no significant intrinsic value"). But what about raffles, like the one in our problem, that do not occur so close to an election? *See id.* at 1029 n.13 (refusing to apply per se rule against such raffles, which are analyzed based on whether they "improperly affect employee free choice" or merely allow a party "to identify employees who might or might not be sympathetic, and thus to learn where to direct additional pressure or campaign efforts").

8. What about the free food provided by the union in our problem? In *Atlantic Limousine, Inc.*, 331 N.L.R.B. at 1030–31, the NLRB reiterated its reliance on its normal set of factors for determining whether a benefit warrants a new election: "1) the size of the benefit conferred in relation to the stated purpose for granting it; (2) the number of employees receiving it; (3) how employees reasonably would view the purpose of the benefit; and (4) the timing of the benefit." *B&D Plastics*, 302 N.L.R.B. 245, 245 (1991). Examples cited by the NLRB in *Atlantic Limousine* include a half-day party held by the employer the day before an election, *Chicagoland Television News*, 328 N.L.R.B. 367 (1999) (not objectionable because the cost was not excessive and there was a history of such events); distribution of Thanksgiving turkeys and a Christmas party during the critical period, *Jacqueline Cochran, Inc.*, 177 N.L.R.B. 837 (1969) (not objectionable);, and a $8,000 brunch held by an employer for employees and guests, with gifts, entertainment, Santa Claus visits for children, and other perks, *Chicago Tribune*, 326 N.L.R.B. 1057 (1998) (objectionable).

9. Should a union be permitted to file a lawsuit on behalf of employees during the critical period? Previously, the NLRB had determined that a union can investigate, prepare, and file lawsuits for employees, without charge, during the critical period. *See Novotel New York*, 321 N.L.R.B. 624 (1996). The NLRB found that these lawsuits were fundamentally different from other union-provided benefits, but the D.C. Circuit refused to enforce that rule. *See Freund Baking Co. v. NLRB*, 165 F.3d 928 (D.C. Cir. 1999). In light of the court's objections, the NLRB reconsidered its *Novotel* rule in *Stericycle, Inc.*, 357 N.L.R.B. No. 61 (2011), concluding that "a union ordinarily engages in objectionable conduct warranting a

second election by financing a lawsuit filed during the critical period, which states claims under Federal or State wage and hours laws or other similar employment law claims on behalf of employees in the unit." Chairman Liebman dissented on this issue because, among other things, the rule would require employees to choose between a union election and a suit to enforce their employment law rights. The NLRB also further defined the boundaries of permissible and impermissible assistance and stated that it was lawful for a union to "inform employees about their rights [under labor and employment laws], assist them in identifying violations, urge them to seek relief, and even refer them to competent counsel [which may file suit during the critical period as long as there is no union funding] without casting into question subsequent election results." Member Hayes dissented on this point because of a concern that it will be reversed by appellate courts and because it provides unions with a "manual on how they can provide gratuitous benefits to voters before and during the critical period without engaging in objectionable conduct." Which side of these issues do you think has the better argument?

SECTION 5   SURVEILLANCE

PROBLEM #6: I ALWAYS FEEL LIKE SOMEBODY'S WATCHING ME

As the union campaign continued, Sarah began to hear more rumors about union meetings with an increasing number of janitors in attendance. In an attempt to test the veracity of the rumors, she told Jane, an openly pro-union janitor, that she knew all about the union meeting on the previous evening and that the turnout sounded good. Jane just laughed and responded, "It depends on whose version of good you mean."

Unlawful impression of surveillance →

Soon thereafter, Sarah began to collect information that the mall regularly gathers from its array of video cameras. Although Sarah normally doesn't involve herself with these security cameras unless there is a specific problem, she started to review video footage during the periods surrounding the janitors' break time, when Sarah believed much of the on-site union discussions occurred. She also asked the mall's IT department to forward to her any e-mails that contained the word "union." The IT department regularly scanned employees' e-mails for a list of "red flag" words that might indicate possibly workplace harassment or violence, but they had never looked for union-related messages before.

As you read the following material, think about the various ways that Sarah might have gotten into trouble and what she could have done differently. Note that surveillance issues are generally more straightforward than the other types of misconduct that we've studied in this chapter. Consider why that's the case and whether you think it makes sense.

PROBLEM MATERIALS

F.W. Woolworth Co., 310 N.L.R.B. 1197 (1993)

F.W. WOOLWORTH CO.
310 N.L.R.B. 1197 (1993)

By Chairman Stephens and Members Devaney and Oviatt

. . . Contrary to our dissenting colleague, we agree with the judge that the Respondent violated Section 8(a)(1) of the Act by photographing and videotaping employees. The judge found that the Respondent's off-duty employees were engaged in protected union activities when they stationed themselves in the general area of the Respondent's store entrances in order to distribute handbills to potential customers and appeal to them to shop elsewhere during the labor dispute with the Respondent. The judge specifically found that handbillers did not block store entrances. The judge further found that at most some handbillers stood in front of store entrances, but that customers were able to walk around the handbillers. The judge additionally found unsupported the Respondent's assertion that large contingents of handbillers gathered in front of the entrances. Indeed, the Respondent's district manager Kovar testified that the handbillers moved to the side when he requested they do so. No misconduct by the handbillers is asserted by the Respondent other than their location.

As the judge recognized, the Board has long held that absent proper justification, the photographing of employees engaged in protected concerted activities violates the Act because it has a tendency to intimidate. *Waco, Inc.*, 273 N.L.R.B. 746, 747 (1984), and cases cited therein. Here, the record provides no basis for the Respondent reasonably to have anticipated misconduct by those handbilling, and there is no evidence that misconduct did, in fact, occur. Unlike our dissenting colleague, we adhere to the principle that photographing in the mere belief that "something 'might' happen does not justify Respondent's conduct when balanced against the tendency of that conduct to interfere with employees' right to engage in concerted activity." *Flambeau Plastics Corp.*, 167 N.L.R.B. 735, 743 (1967), enfd. 401 F.2d 128, 136 (7th Cir. 1968). Accord: *NLRB v. Colonial Haven Nursing Home*, 542 F.2d 691, 701 (7th Cir. 1976) ("the Board may properly require a company to provide solid justification for its resort to anticipatory photographing").

. . . Finally, [some of] the cases our dissenting colleague cites . . . are not "analogous" because they are based on the principle that an employer's "mere observation" of open, public union activity on or near its property does not constitute unlawful surveillance. When an employer's surveillance activity constitutes more than "mere observation," the Board has found a violation of the Act. E.g., *Gupta Permold Corp.*, 289 N.L.R.B. 1234 fn. 2 (1988); *Baddour*, 281 N.L.R.B. 546, 548 (1986), enfd. 848 F.2d 193 (6th Cir. 1988). Photographing and videotaping clearly constitute more than "mere observation" because such pictorial recordkeeping tends to create fear among employees of future reprisals. *Waco*, supra.

Accordingly, for all these reasons, we adopt the judge's finding that the Respondent violated Section 8(a)(1) of the Act by photographing and videotaping employees engaged in union activities without proper justification.

MEMBER OVIATT, dissenting in part [opinion omitted].

POST PROBLEM DISCUSSION

1.   Consider our problem and Sarah's review of the videos. Is that an activity that would tend to chill employees' Section 7 rights or interfere with an election? The presumption noted in *F.W. Woolworth* for photography applies generally to other types of surveillance. Thus, there is a presumption that surveillance of protected activity is unlawful unless the employer can show that it had a legitimate reason for doing so. *See Ingram Book Co.*, 315 N.L.R.B. 515, 518 (1994) (driving by employees waiting to meet with union representatives).

Suspected theft?
Employee review?
⌐→

2.   What types of situations do you think would provide the employer with a rebuttal to this presumption? Do you think any of these situations would be of use to Sarah? *See, e.g., National Steel & Shipbuilding Co. v. NLRB*, 156 F.3d 1268, 1271 (D.C. Cir. 1998) (citing examples of conduct that will mitigate surveillance's tendency to coerce: legitimate security interests, gathering evidence for legal proceedings, and reasonable anticipation of misconduct). Can you think of other examples?

3.   What if an employer is observing protected activity, but the employees are unaware of the surveillance — for instance, a supervisor driving through the parking lot of a restaurant where employees are meeting to see whose cars are there. Can employees be coerced or threatened by activity that they don't know about? The NLRB has said yes; do you agree? *See Easter Seals Connecticut, Inc.*, 345 N.L.R.B. 836, 849 (2005).

4.   Consider Sarah's comment that she had heard about the union meeting the night before, even though she was nowhere near the meeting and hadn't talked to anyone about it. She obviously hasn't engaged in actual surveillance, but should her comment alone be prohibited? If so, why?

This question gets at the concept of the "impression of surveillance." The NLRB has concluded that giving employees the impression that they are being watched while engaged in protected activity, even if they are not, may be unlawfully coercive. The test for when unlawful impression of surveillance exists is based on whether, "under all the relevant circumstances, reasonable employees would assume from [the employer's action or statement] that their union or other protected activities had been placed under surveillance." *Frontier Telephone of Rochester, Inc.*, 344 N.L.R.B. 1270, 1276 (2006), *enforced*, 181 Fed. Appx. 85 (2d Cir. 2006); *Grouse Mountain Associates II*, 333 N.L.R.B. 1322, 1322–23 (2001), *enforced*, 56 Fed. Appx. 811 (9th Cir. 2003).

Probably if
filtering exclusively
for the word "union."
If investigating
sexual harassment
then probably not.

5.   Does monitoring of e-mail or Internet usage count as unlawful surveillance? Remember that the NLRB, in *Register-Guard*, concluded that employers have substantial control over their electronic communications property. Does this extend to employers' monitoring of employees' e-mail and Internet usage on the employer's equipment or servers? What if the employer's monitoring was intended to discover behavior that might constitute unlawful sexual harassment, but also allowed supervisors to see messages about union-related activity? *See* Jeffrey M. Hirsch, *The Silicon Bullet: Will the Internet Kill the NLRA?*, 76 GEO. WASH. L. REV. 262

(2008) (discussing issue and suggesting that filtering programs could provide solution in many cases); *cf.* Trustees of Columbia University in the City of New York, 350 N.L.R.B. 574, 576 (2007) (noting that requiring employers to provide e-mail address as part of their *Excelsior* duty to provide election eligibility list raises the question whether employers could "continue existing e-mail monitoring programs without engaging in unlawful surveillance").

6. What if the union is the party videotaping the employees, rather than the employer? We've seen already that both employer and union benefits are analyzed similarly — should the same be true for surveillance? The NLRB used to take a more lenient view of union photography and videotaping under the theory that such conduct is less likely to be coercive if done by a union; however, in its 3-2 decision in *Randell Warehouse of Arizona, Inc.*, 347 N.L.R.B. 591 (2006), the NLRB changed course and extended the employer photography and videotaping analysis to union surveillance. Thus, union videotaping creates a presumption of unlawfulness that can be rebutted if the union gave a timely and valid explanation of the surveillance to the employees. *Id.* at 591, 596 (noting that photography and videotaping are less justified than unions' normal solicitation of support because they make a permanent record of the employees' views and the purpose of the photography or videotaping is rarely obvious).

[handwritten margin note: Potential for blackmail by the unions.]

SECTION 6 INTERROGATION AND POLLING

PROBLEM #7: THE ELECTION CAMPAIGN: QUESTIONS FROM A SUPERVISOR

One day, several janitors called in sick, leaving the mall far short of the coverage that it needed. Sarah began calling off-duty janitors to find someone to fill in, but without much luck. One janitor that Sarah contacted was James, a high-school student working at the mall during the summer. James said that he would be willing to come in, but his car had broken down and he had no way to get to the mall. Sarah was so desperate for help that she offered to pick him up and bring him home after his shift. During the ride home, Sarah and James talked about random non-job-related matters, until Sarah asked if James "knew anything about the union." James, who had not publically expressed any views about the campaign, responded that he didn't know anything and Sarah didn't ask anything more about the union.

[handwritten margin note: Possibly ULP but probably not. ① Background ② Nature of info ③ Identity of questioner ④ Place/method of interrogation]

Sarah had another conversation with a janitor that referenced the union. This time it was with a janitor named Bill, a union supporter with whom Sarah was friendly because their children were in the same class together. One day, while chatting at a playground during a playdate with their children, Sarah asked Bill, "Are you all really serious about this union thing? Do you really think that it can get you what you want in this economy?" Bill answered that the janitors were "serious as a heart attack" and that based on all the trash they had to clean up every day, the mall was doing well enough to pay them more. Sarah simply said "we'll see," and they didn't talk about the campaign any more.

[handwritten margin note: Doesn't seem to be a threat. Also a friendly conversation.]

This is not okay

① To determine truth of claimed majority.

② Was communicated

③ Assurance against reprisal.

④ NOT SECRET

⑤ Maybe engaged in ULP with comment to Bill.

But apply totality of circumstances test.

Finally, concerned about her impressions regarding the strength of the union campaign, Sarah sought to determine once and for all how much support the union had among the janitors. For several days, Sarah greeted janitors as they stamped their time-cards at the start of each shift. With a clipboard in hand, she asked each janitor whether they believed that the union had support from a majority of employees and whether each janitor individually thought the union could get them something that they didn't have already. Sarah told each janitor that she didn't care what their answer was and no janitor would be punished for their answer or refusal to answer; she stressed that the only reason she was asking was that the union had been bragging that it was going to win and she wanted to know how seriously to take that claim.

Was Sarah allowed to engage in these various interactions with employees? As you read the following cases, think about both the employer's and the employees' interests — and which of those interests predominates in the NLRB's analyses.

PROBLEM MATERIALS

Struknes Construction Co., 165 N.L.R.B. 1062 (1967)

Sunnyvale Medical Clinic, 277 N.L.R.B. 1217 (1985)

STRUKNES CONSTRUCTION CO.
165 N.L.R.B. 1062 (1967)

So many Section 7 cases begin w/ a supervisor asking about union sympathies.

. . . In our view any attempt by an employer to ascertain employee views and sympathies regarding unionism generally tends to cause fear of reprisal in the mind of the employee if he replies in favor of unionism and, therefore, tends to impinge on his Section 7 rights. As we have pointed out, "An employer cannot discriminate against union adherents without first determining who they are." [*Cannon Electric*, 151 NLRB 1465, 1468.] That such employee fear is not without foundation is demonstrated by the innumerable cases in which the prelude to discrimination was the employer's inquiries as to the union sympathies of his employees.

It was the Board's original view that an employer's poll of his employees was in and of itself coercive and therefore a *per se* violation of Section 8(a)(1). [*Blue Flash Express, Inc.*, 109 NLRB 591 (1954).] . . . [O]ur experience since *Blue Flash* indicates that that rule has not operated to discourage intimidation of employees by employer polls.

Ways for an employer to verify a unions majority status.

As recent Board decisions have emphasized, there are clearly uncoercive methods for an employer to verify a union's majority status. An employer faced with a union demand for recognition may normally refrain from according recognition; he may also request proof of majority status; or he may file a petition, or suggest that the union do so, and await the outcome of a Board election.

We have therefore determined, in the light of all the foregoing considerations, and in accord with the court's remand, to adopt the following revision of the *Blue Flash* criteria:

> Absent unusual circumstances, the polling of employees by an employer will be violative of Section 8(a)(1) of the Act unless the following safeguards

are observed: (1) the purpose of the poll is to determine the truth of a union's claim of majority, (2) this purpose is communicated to the employees, (3) assurances against reprisal are given, (4) the employees are polled by secret ballot, and (5) the employer has not engaged in unfair labor practices or otherwise created a coercive atmosphere.

The purpose of the polling in these circumstances is clearly relevant to an issue raised by a union's claim for recognition and is therefore lawful. The requirement that the lawful purpose be communicated to the employees, along with assurances against reprisal, is designed to allay any fear of discrimination which might otherwise arise from the polling, and any tendency to interfere with employees' Section 7 rights. Secrecy of the ballot will give further assurance that reprisals cannot be taken against employees because the views of each individual will not be known. And the absence of employer unfair labor practices or other conduct creating a coercive atmosphere will serve as a further warranty to the employees that the poll does not have some unlawful object, contrary to the lawful purpose stated by the employer. In accord with presumptive rules applied by the Board with court approval in other situations, this rule is designed to effectuate the purposes of the Act by maintaining a reasonable balance between the protection of employee rights and legitimate interests of employers.

On the other hand, a poll taken while a petition for a Board election is pending does not, in our view, serve any legitimate interest of the employer that would not be better served by the forthcoming Board election. In accord with long-established Board policy, therefore, such polls will continue to be found violative of Section 8(a)(1) of the Act.

Cant poll while petition for Board election pending.

B. *The Polling Issue in the Instant Case*

The record establishes that the Union organized the employees at the Respondent's construction jobsite in July and August 1963. The Respondent, although aware of the Union's organizing, did not interfere and, in fact, hired men it knew to be members of the Union. By August 7, 1963, a majority of the 26 employees had become members of the Union, but some had joined while employed at other projects years before, and some were delinquent in their dues payments. The Union's first demand for recognition and a contract was made on August 7, upon the Respondent's attorney, as Struksnes himself was out of town. The attorney informed Struksnes of this demand upon his return. Two days later, the Respondent by letter asked the Union, "in preparation to discuss your labor agreement," about the number of employees who were members "as of a specific date." The Union replied that it represented 20 employees.

On August 13, Struksnes and two supervisors polled the employees, asking them to sign a paper indicating whether they wanted the Respondent "to bargain with and sign a contract with" the Union, and assuring them that it made no difference to the Respondent how they voted. The results of this poll were that 15 signed in the "No" column, 9 in the "Yes" column, and 1 refused to sign. The Respondent then informed the Union that a majority of the employees did not want it to negotiate with the Union. . . .

In view of the failure of the Respondent to inform its employees of the purpose of the poll and the nonsecret manner in which the employees were polled, the Respondent's conduct would probably be found unlawful if this case were now before us for an initial determination under the new rule. We are satisfied, however, that in the special circumstances of this case no remedial order is warranted. Thus the poll previously was found lawful by the Board under the *Blue Flash* rule, which was in effect at the time the events herein occurred. Moreover, as the court noted in its opinion, the work at the jobsite where the poll was taken apparently was scheduled to be concluded within 3 months after these events took place, which was more than 3 years ago. All things considered, we find in these circumstances that effectuation of the purposes of the Act does not require a remedial order. Accordingly, we shall reaffirm the Board's original Decision and Order dismissing the complaint in its entirety.

SUNNYVALE MEDICAL CLINIC
277 N.L.R.B. 1217 (1985)

. . . The judge found, inter alia, that Respondent's personnel director Sandra Easterly did not unlawfully interrogate employee Tracie Rothweiler. For the reasons set forth below, we affirm the judge's finding.

Rothweiler and fellow employee Pam Gardner went on their own initiative to Easterly's office to take care of unrelated individual personnel matters. When Gardner finished the discussion of her matter with Easterly, Rothweiler gave Easterly a completed union dues-deduction authorization card. As Gardner and Rothweiler were leaving Easterly's office, Easterly asked Rothweiler to remain. Gardner left, and Easterly closed the office door.

Easterly asked Rothweiler why she had joined the Union. Rothweiler replied that she felt that the employees needed help. Easterly asked Rothweiler if it was anything personal against Easterly. Rothweiler replied that it was not. Easterly explained to Rothweiler that the Employer wanted the Union out of the clinic. Easterly told Rothweiler that just because she had joined the Union did not mean that the employees would necessarily get what they wanted. Easterly asked Rothweiler why the employees had not gone to her (Easterly). Rothweiler replied that they had, and that nothing was being done. The conversation then ended.

Rothweiler characterized her conversation with Easterly as "friendly" and "casual" and her relationship with Easterly as "friendly."

In dismissing the allegation in this regard, the judge applied the longstanding test, recently reiterated in *Rossmore House*, [269 NLRB 1176 (1984), affd. 760 F.2d 1006 (9th Cir. 1985),] for evaluating whether interrogations violate the Act: whether under all the circumstances the interrogation reasonably tends to restrain, coerce, or interfere with rights guaranteed by the Act. We agree with the judge's analysis, even though Rothweiler, unlike the questioned employee in *Rossmore House*, is not an open and active union supporter.

The specific purpose of the Board's decision in *Rossmore House* was to reject the per se approach to the interrogation of open and active union supporters about their union sympathies. Thus, the Board expressly overruled a particular line of cases "to the extent they [found] that an employer's questioning open and active union supporters about their union sentiments, in the absence of threats or promises, necessarily [violates the Act]." [269 NLRB at 1177–1178.].

However, an important additional purpose of the Board's decision in *Rossmore House* was to signal disapproval of a per se approach to allegedly unlawful interrogations in general, and to return to a case-by-case analysis which takes into account the circumstances surrounding an alleged interrogation and does not ignore the reality of the workplace. In this regard, *Blue Flash* [*Express, Inc.*, 109 NLRB 591 (1954),] the Board case relied on in *Rossmore House* in rejecting a per se approach to interrogation in general, did not involve the interrogation of open and active union supporters. Instead, unit members, whose sympathies were unknown to the employer, were individually questioned by the employer in an attempt to evaluate the union's claim of majority status. In setting forth the totality of circumstances test, the Board stated:

> The rule which we adopt will require the Trial Examiners and the Board to carefully weigh and evaluate the evidence in such case [sic], but that is what we believe the statute requires us to do. The only alternatives, both of which we reject, are either to find all interrogation per se unlawful, or to find that interrogation under all circumstances is permissible under the statute.

[109 NLRB at 594.]

The rule of *Blue Flash*, with its rejection of per se alternatives, is the central underlying rationale of the *Rossmore House* decision. For this reason, we find the judge properly applied the totality of circumstances test to the alleged unlawful interrogation of employee Rothweiler, even though she was not an open and active union adherent. We further find that he correctly concluded that no violation of the Act occurred.

The Board in *Rossmore House* outlined some areas of inquiry that may be considered in applying the *Blue Flash* test, stressing that these and other relevant factors were not to be mechanically applied in each case. Thus, the Board mentioned the background, the nature of information sought, the identity of the questioner, and the place and method of interrogation. Applying the *Blue Flash* test here, we find, as did the judge, that the circumstances surrounding Easterly's questioning of Rothweiler are devoid of the elements of coercion necessary for finding a violation.

First, although Rothweiler was not an open and active union supporter, she also was not an employee especially intent on keeping her support for the Union hidden from the Respondent. In this regard, Rothweiler's decision to authorize the deduction of union dues and her presentation of her authorization card directly to Easterly (when according to Easterly such cards were normally presented through the Union) imply Rothweiler's willingness to make the Respondent aware of her support for the Union. While we do not place undue weight on this factor, we nevertheless find it is relevant in evaluating the full context of the questioning at issue here. Second, there is no history of employer hostility towards or discrimination against union supporters. While Easterly told Rothweiler that Respondent wanted the Union "out of the clinic," there is no showing that the Respondent took or threatened any adverse action against employees in futherance of its desire to operate without the Union. Third, the nature of the questions was general and nonthreatening: why Rothweiler joined the Union, whether she did so because of anything personal against Easterly, and why the employees had not come directly to Easterly. As the judge points out, it did not reasonably appear from the nature of these questions that Easterly was seeking to obtain information from Rothweiler on which she might in turn take adverse action against employees. Fourth, Easterly and Rothweiler had a friendly relationship, and their conversation in question was casual and amicable. Taking all these factors into consideration, we find that the conversation between Rothweiler and Easterly is one instance of lawful, casual questioning which, under the circumstances, might be expected to occur between supervisors and employees who work closely together. Accordingly, we affirm the judge's dismissal of this allegation. . . .

MEMBER DENNIS, dissenting in part.

Contrary to my colleagues and the judge, I find that the Respondent violated Section 8(a)(1) of the Act by interrogating employee Tracie Rothweiler. . . .

In finding that Easterly's interrogation of Rothweiler did not violate Section 8(a)(1), my colleagues stray from the principles established in *Rossmore House*, 269 NLRB 1176 (1984), affd. 760 F.2d 1006 (9th Cir. 1985). My colleagues purport to apply the longstanding test, reconfirmed in *Rossmore House*, of "whether under all of the circumstances the interrogation reasonably tends to restrain, coerce, or interfere with rights guaranteed by the Act." In professing to apply the test, however, they de-emphasize the principal "circumstance" addressed in *Rossmore House* — whether the employee questioned is a self-proclaimed union adherent — and rely instead on lesser, or secondary, criteria. . . .

Ordinarily, an employer's questioning an employee who is not a self-proclaimed union adherent *does* "tend to restrain, coerce, or interfere" with statutory rights. Because the employee has not chosen voluntarily to disclose his union activities or beliefs, the employer's prying into this sensitive subject necessarily chills the employee's freedom of action. It should be the exceptional case, not the routine one, in which, based on secondary criteria alone, an employee who has not volunteered his views may be questioned about his union activities or beliefs.

In the instant case the judge found — and my colleagues do not dispute — that Rothweiler was not a self-proclaimed union adherent. Because Rothweiler was not a self-proclaimed union adherent, the employer's questioning her was inherently coercive absent some unusual additional circumstances.

Turning to the circumstances my colleagues address, they misapply the secondary criteria as well. My colleagues find no history of employer hostility against union supporters, despite Easterly's announcement to Rothweiler in the very conversation in question that the Respondent wanted the Union "out." The judge and my colleagues dismiss as "general and nonthreatening" Easterly's bluntly questioning Rothweiler about why she wanted the Union. I am not persuaded by my colleagues' reliance on the judge's finding that Easterly and Rothweiler were on a friendly basis and the discussion was quite informal. Whatever friendliness and informality attended the incident only added subtle pressure to Easterly's coercive questioning, because Easterly suggested that Rothweiler's activities might be a personal affront and queried why the employees had not come to her before turning to the Union. Nor can my colleagues and the judge effectively minimize the facts that Easterly was the Respondent's personnel director, a significant position within management vis-a-vis employees, and that the questioning occurred in Easterly's office. Although Rothweiler entered Easterly's office with another employee, Easterly waited until that employee left, closed the door, and then asked Rothweiler why she wanted the Union. Easterly then told her that the Respondent wanted the Union "out."

Under the instant circumstances, I find Easterly's questioning Rothweiler coercive and in violation of Section 8(a)(1) of the Act.

POST PROBLEM DISCUSSION

1. As discussed in Chapter 6, there are special considerations when polling is used to gauge whether an incumbent union still retains support from a majority of employees. Traditionally, an employer needs evidence showing that it had "good faith reasonable doubt" regarding the union's majority support. *See Allentown Mack Sales & Service, Inc. v. NLRB*, 522 U.S. 359 (1998). More recently, the NLRB in *Levitz Furniture Co. of the Pacific, Inc.*, 333 N.L.R.B. 717 (2001), altered its policy on when employers can take certain actions that question unions' support, such as petitioning for an election or unilaterally withdrawing recognition. In *Levitz*, the NLRB said, "we shall leave to a later case whether the current good-faith doubt (uncertainty) standard for polling should be changed." *Id.* at 723. It appears that the NLRB is still using the previous good faith reasonable doubt standard, but it is unclear whether that practice will continue. *See Wisconsin Porcelain, Inc.*, 349 N.L.R.B. 151, 151 & n.4 (2007). Keep this polling question in mind when you read *Allentown Mack* and *Levitz* later.

[handwritten margin note: Good Faith/ Reasonable Doubt standard could change with a new Board.]

2. Consider our problem — which scenario looks like it might be considered interrogation under the NLRB's factor test? Are there any circumstances that might suggest that the questions are *not* coercive? For instance, does it matter that Sarah and Bill were friends? If so, which way does that fact cut? *See* Note 3 in Section 2, above. What if either James or Bill testified that they did not feel threatened or coerced by Sarah's questions? Is that testimony relevant in interrogation cases; if so, how relevant is it and, if not, should it be? What about the conversation between Sarah and Jane in Problem #6?

3. What about questions that don't directly address an employees' union sympathies? For instance, employers sometimes want employees to appear in anti-union campaign videos. Does the attempt to seek volunteers for an anti-union video equate to polling under *Struknes*? *See Allegheny Ludlum Corp. v. NLRB*, 301 F.3d 167, 176 (3d Cir. 2002) (agreeing with NLRB that request was equivalent to polling and thereby requiring *Struknes*-like steps before asking).

4. Does Sarah's questions to all of the janitors qualify as a "poll"? If so, should it be considered lawful under the *Struknes/Blue Flash* analysis?

5. What if, instead of an employer polling the employees, the union does so? In *Randell Warehouse*, the NLRB concluded that employer and union surveillance

should be analyzed equally — is polling different? Should it be? *See Enterprise Leasing Company-Southeast, LLC*, 357 N.L.R.B. No. 159, at *3 (2011) (noting that "[e]mployers and unions . . . are held to different standards in evaluating the coerciveness of polling; although employer polling is generally assumed to be coercive and therefore unlawful, union polling is generally recognized as lawful activity . . . [because, among other things,] unions are required to poll in order to obtain the showing of interest that is a prerequisite to a Board-supervised election").

Chapter 6

SELECTING AND DESELECTING THE BARGAINING REPRESENTATIVE

There are three ways a union can be selected as the bargaining representative for a group of employees. First, the union or the employer can petition the Board to start the election process under Section 9(c) of the Act. On the other hand, a group of employees can ask their employer to voluntarily recognize their union. Finally, as discussed in Section 4 below, the Board can order bargaining between the parties in cases where there are pervasive and severe unfair labor practices by the employer. Prior to 1947, employers were not permitted to file an election petition; however, the Taft-Hartley Amendments added 9(c)(1)(B) to afford employers that right.

This Chapter is divided into five sections. Section 1 spells out the reasons why the Board will not hold a representation election. Assuming that no such grounds exist, Section 2 considers what groups of employees make up an "appropriate bargaining unit" for purposes of Section 9 of the NLRA. After an election is held, sometimes one of the parties disagrees with the results. Section 3 discusses the ways in which parties can challenge the outcome of an election and seek a new one, and Section 4 discusses the limited circumstances under which the NLRB can order the parties to bargain even if the union has not won an election. Finally, Section 5 explores ways in which employees or an employer can remove a union from its role as bargaining representative.

SECTION 1   GROUNDS FOR NOT HOLDING AN ELECTION

As a general matter, there is a three-step procedure for certifying a union as the bargaining representative for a unit of employees. First, a representation petition may be filed by either interested employees or by an employer (a sample form is available at this web link: https://www.nlrb.gov/sites/default/files/documents/48/nlrbform502.pdf). Second, the appropriate regional office investigates to determine if "a question of representation" exists. In this context, a "question of representation" means that a substantial number of employees wish to be represented by the union for purposes of collective bargaining. This means that at least 30% of the proposed bargaining unit have requested that the union act as their bargaining representative — the requests typically occur through signed authorization cards. A regional office usually handles this process with the aid of a hearing. If the Board finds a "question concerning representation" exists, it directs that an election take place. Parties can also avoid the hearing process by agreeing in advance to a consent election if there are no controversies concerning, for example, who should be in the appropriate bargaining unit. See Chapter 2 for more details of this process.

On the other hand, there are at least three grounds for not proceeding with an election.

1.   Lack of support from employees for union

Substantial Interest

To reiterate, to file an election petition, the union needs authorization cards or other similar showings of support from at least 30% of the employees in the proposed bargaining union. This is often referred to as a showing of "substantial interest."

Historically, unions will not file an election petition until they receive authorization cards from at least 60% of the employees in the unit. This is because, as we saw in Chapter 5, employer campaigns tend to cause unions to lose support during the average eight weeks between the filing of the petition and holding of the election. The NLRB recently proposed and instituted some election reform rules to shorten the time of the representation campaigns. Unions see quicker elections as a key to winning more representation elections.

The employer has no right to challenge the regional office's substantial interest determination. If there is another union (a so-called intervening union) that seeks to represent the same unit of employees, that intervening union must show at least 10% support to block a consent election agreement or only needs one authorization card to get on the ballot. However, suffice to say, if an intervening union only has one or a few authorization cards, they are not likely to prevail during the election.

2.   The commission of an unremedied ULP: the blocking charge policy

Sometimes, a union will file blocking charges to stop an election from taking place until pending unfair labor practice charges (ULPs) are remedied. The general rule is that the Board will not hold an election until those pending ULPs are decided one way or another. However, the Board has discretion whether to apply the policy and may decide not to if the pending ULPs are minor.

3.   The election bars: certification bar, voluntary recognition bar, and contract bar

The Supreme Court and the NLRA establish an irrebuttable presumption of majority status in the first year following a Board certified election. Once the bar to election expires, the union retains a rebuttable presumption of majority status which the employer or employees can seek to rebut through various types of evidence (see Section 5 below).

a. Certification Bar

To impart stability, Board rules bar another investigation by the regional office for a "reasonable time" after a union has been certified the representative of a group of employees. This is referred to as the certification bar rule and usually last for one year. The certification bar may be tolled while an employer fails to recognize or bargain with a union.

[handwritten margin note: only applies if union wins election]

b. Election Bar

On the other hand, the Taft-Hartley Amendments added a similar bar under Section 9(c)(3) of the Act to prohibits an election within one year of another election. This is called the election bar rule. The difference between the election bar and the certification bar is that the certification bar only applies if the union wins the election and is certified, whereas the election bar prevents another election from taking place within a year regardless of whether the union wins or loses an election.

c. Contract Bar and Its Exceptions

In addition to the certification bar and the election bar, the existence of a valid collective-bargaining agreement prevents an election from taking place for up to three years under the contract bar rule. The rule is meant to stabilize existing bargaining relationships. The contract bar only applies if the contract is in writing and lawfully executed by all parties. It applies only as long as a valid contract is in force, for a maximum of three years. Thus, for example, even if the collective bargaining agreement is for four or five years, the maximum length of the contract bar is three years.

Additionally, for a decertification petition (see Section 5 below) to be filed by an employer, a group of employees, or a rival union, the petition must be filed in a narrow "window" or "open" period. That window is open no more than 90 days, but no less than 60 days, prior to the expiration of the collective-bargaining agreement (in the health care context, the time period is modified to no more than 120 days, but no less than 90 days). The 60 days period following the closing of this window to the expiration of the CBA is referred to as the "insulated period," when stable bargaining is promoted and no further petitions may be filed. Once the contract expires, however, decertification petitions are then again permitted until a new contract is executed by the parties. Moreover, if the parties agree to a new collective-bargaining agreement before the open period occurs, the NLRB will allow petitions during the open period that would have existed under the previous agreement.

There are three general exceptions to the application of the contract bar. One exception occurs when a union is unable or unwilling to represent employees. Under this defunctness exception, the existence of a contract between the parties would not prevent an election. Similarly, under the schism exception, if a local union votes in open meeting to disaffiliate from its parent union due to intra-union conflict, the contract bar may no longer apply. Finally, under the changed operations exception, the contract bar does not apply when the operations of the company have substantially changed due to expansion or other changes in the company's operations. Additionally, the contract bar ceases to apply where, after an indefinite period of closing, an employer resumes operations with new employees. *See El Torito-La Fiesta Restaurants, Inc. v. NLRB*, 929 F.2d 490 (9th Cir. 1991). On the other hand, this exception to the contract bar rule does not apply when the shutdown is temporary and the character of the bargaining unit work remains the same.

d. Voluntary Recognition Bar

For forty years, the voluntary recognition bar stated that there could be no election for a reasonable time, but for at least six months, after an employer voluntarily recognized a union. As the Board has observed, "[v]oluntary recognition must be based on evidence of majority support for representation. Absent majority support, voluntary recognition is unlawful." *See Lamon's Gasket Co.*, 357 NLRB No. 72 (2011). As far as what constitutes "evidence of majority support":

> The evidence of majority support that must underlie voluntary recognition may take many forms. The *Dana* [*Corp.*, 351 N.L.R.B. No. 28 (2007),] majority referred to voluntary recognition as "card-based recognition," but that is an inaccurate or, at least, a drastically underinclusive characterization. Voluntary recognition may be, and has been, based on evidence of majority support as informal as employees walking into the owner's office and stating they wish to be represented by a union, and as formal as a secret-ballot election conducted by a third party such as the American Arbitration Association.

In 2007, the Bush II Board in *Dana Corp.*, 351 N.L.R.B. No. 28 (2007), held that employees may file a decertification petition up to 45 days after an employer voluntarily recognizes a union. Only after employees have 45-days notice of their right to file a decertification petition may a recognition bar of at least six months then prevent an election from taking place. However, in *Lamon's Gasket Co.*, 357 N.L.R.B. No. 72 (2011), the Obama Board went back to the original rule that a decertification petition will be barred "for a reasonable period of time (of at least six months) after voluntary recognition." In changing back to the traditional rule, the *Lamon's Gasket* majority observed:

> [T]he extraordinary process established in *Dana* was, fundamentally, grounded on a suspicion that the employee choice which must precede any voluntary recognition is often not free and uncoerced, despite the law's requirement that it be so. The evidence now before us as a result of administering the *Dana* decision during the past 4 years demonstrates that the suspicion underlying the decision was unfounded. Without an adequate foundation, *Dana* thus imposed an extraordinary notice requirement, informing employees only of their right to reconsider their choice to be represented, under a statute commanding that the Board remain strictly neutral in relation to that choice.

So, under current law, once the employer voluntary recognizes a union, a subsequent election is barred for at least six months.

PROBLEM #1: THE NEW NLRB ELECTIONS RULES[1]

One of the NLRB's primary responsibilities is to hold secret ballot elections so that employees can decide whether they wish to be represented by a labor union or, if already represented, to remove the union or replace it with another. The Board recently voted to change some pre- and post-election procedures to reduce unnecessary litigation, adopting parts of a broader proposal to modernize and streamline the election process.

When an election petition is filed, the NLRB typically works with the parties to quickly secure an agreement to schedule an election, setting the date, time, and location, and describing the appropriate voting group. In the few cases in which the parties can't reach an agreement, the NLRB's regional office conducts a pre-election hearing. The new rule primarily addresses that pre-election hearing process, as well as some post-election appeal procedures. It contains six procedural amendments.

1. Defining the Scope of the Pre-Election Hearing. Under the National Labor Relations Act, pre-election hearings are intended to determine if there is a "question concerning representation," that is, a question as to whether the employees covered by the petition form an appropriate bargaining unit or whether the petition cannot be processed based on an exception spelled out in the NLRA. Currently, parties raise issues at pre-election hearings not related to this question, such as whether individual employees, who do not form a significant percentage of the bargaining unit, should be allowed to vote in an election. These issues are litigated at great length and expense, despite usually having no effect on the final result because the disputed individuals' eligibility only becomes an issue if their votes would have made a difference in the final outcome of the election. The first amendment alters 29 C.F.R. § 102.64 of the Board's current Rules to state that the statutory purpose of the hearing is to determine a question concerning represen-tation and amends Section 102.66(a) to give the hearing officer the discretion to limit the hearing to matters that support a party's contentions and that are relevant to the existence of a question concerning representation.

2. Limiting Post-Hearing Briefs. The second amendment alters Section 102.66(d) of the Rules to give hearing officers the discretion to control the filing, subject matter, and timing of any post-hearing briefs. This amendment was adopted because most cases involve only routine issues based on well-known principles of NLRA law. In these cases, Regional Directors are fully capable of reaching fair and sound decisions based on the hearing record and the parties' closing arguments. Briefing adds little to the decision-making process, but adds significantly to the parties' litigation expenses. Allowing hearing officers to limit post-hearing briefs to difficult or novel issues, the new rules minimize delay and impose less of a financial burden on the parties.

3. Consolidating Pre- and Post-Election Appeals. The third amendment alters

---

[1] Taken directly from the NLRB website, at https://www.nlrb.gov/node/3608 (last visited Mar. 7, 2012).

Sections 102.67 and 102.69 to eliminate the need for parties to file multiple appeals which often prove to be a waste of time and money. Under the current rules, parties must file one appeal to seek Board review of pre-election issues, e.g. whether there is a question of representation, and another, separate appeal to seek Board review of post-election issues. Another example involves challenges to voter eligibility and objections to a party's conduct during the course of the election. Appeals concerning pre-election issues must be filed before the election. Often though, the Board defers a decision concerning these issues until after the election. If the party filing the pre-election appeal wins the election, the appeal becomes moot. The third amendment consolidates the two appeals into a single post-election procedure, which saves the parties from having to file and brief appeals that may be useless based on the outcome of the election. This change also conforms NLRB procedures with the ordinary rules found in both state and federal courts, which limit interlocutory appeals.

4.   Eliminating the 25-Day Waiting Period. The fourth amendment follows directly from the third by removing the 25-day waiting period after a regional director's pre-election decision issues. Under the current rules, Section 101.21(d) recommends that the regional director refrain from setting an election date sooner than 25 days after issuing the decision based on the pre-election hearing. The purpose of this 25-day waiting period was to allow the Board sufficient time to consider any requests for review of the regional director's decision, which the Board almost never granted. Also, because the new rules consolidate pre- and post-election appeals, this 25-day waiting period no longer serves any purpose.

5.   Establishing a Standard for Interlocutory Appeals. The fifth amendment also takes aim at the problem of multiple appeals to the Board in a single case by altering Section 102.65(c) of the Rules. The current rules fail to establish any standard for the filing of interlocutory appeals concerning individual rulings by hearing officers or regional directors during the course of a pre-election hearing. As a result, parties may, and have, filed numerous appeals in a single case regarding discrete rulings as to what evidence may, or may not, be permitted. The new rules make clear that the Board will grant such interlocutory appeals only under "extraordinary circumstances where it appears that the issue will otherwise evade review." A party is no longer required to seek an interlocutory appeal to preserve an issue for review after an election. Again, the new rules conform NLRB procedures with the rules found in both state and federal courts.

6.   Establishing Standards for Post-Election Procedures. The sixth amendment deals with post-election procedures. In particular, the amendment to Sections 102.62(b) and 102.69 codifies the long-established practice in which regional directors decide challenges and objections to elections through an investigation without a hearing when there are no substantial or material factual issues in dispute. The amendment also makes Board review of the regional directors' decisions discretionary. This change will require parties to identify significant prejudicial error by the regional director or some other compelling reason for Board review allowing the Board to devote its limited time to cases where its review is warranted.

In its original notice of proposed rulemaking, the NLRB proposed many other amendments as part of a broader modernization of the election process. These amendments, among other things, would have standardized deadlines across the country and allowed for the electronic filing of petitions. The Board set those portions of the proposal aside for possible future consideration.

*   *   *

What are the advantages of these new rules? Do you see why union groups have generally supported these rules, while management groups have opposed them? What do you think the management group objections are? How should these differences be addressed by the NLRB, if not through the current election rules?

POST PROBLEM DISCUSSION

1.   In *Chamber of Commerce v. NLRB*, Case No. 11-02262 (D.D.C.) (filed Dec. 20, 2011), the Chamber of Commerce sued the NLRB over what it called the Board's "ambush election rules." They go on to argue:

> [The new election rules] will make it significantly more difficult for employers, especially small employers, to respond to union campaigns . . . . The rule drastically speeds up the election process, depriving employers of a fair opportunity to explain to employees the costs of unionizing and curbing employers' opportunities to bring legal challenges to proposed representation elections.

Case details can be found here: http://www.chamberlitigation.com/chamber-commerce-et-al-v-national-labor-relations-board. On May 14, 2012, the district court invalidated the new election rules, finding no Board quorum ever existed for the vote that adopted the rules. *See* www.nlrb.gov/sites/default/files/documents/494/ddc_decision.pdf. In response to the court's decision, the NLRB has temporarily suspended implementation of these election rule changes. Does the Chamber of Commerce make a policy argument or a legal argument? How might the manner in which the argument is characterized make a difference? If a legal argument, on what parts of the NLRA do their arguments rest? Does Section 9 require the old election procedure? Or is it that employers believe their free speech rights under Section 8(c) are being undermined by these new rules? *See* https://www.federalregister.gov/articles/2012/04/30/201210263/representation-case-procedures (concurrence by Chairman Pearce and dissent by Member Hayes to new election rules).

2.   Prior to the current version of the election rules, the Obama Board had advanced even more sweeping election rules. Professor Hirsch wrote on the Workplace Prof Blog on June 21, 2011 that:

> The NLRB just announced today that it [has] published several proposed election rules. They're potentially a big deal . . . . The proposals would, according to the Board:
>
> (1)   Allow for electronic filing of election petitions and other documents.
>
> (2)   Ensure that employees, employers and unions receive and ex-

change timely information they need to understand and participate in the representation case process.

(3) Standardize timeframes for parties to resolve or litigate issues before and after elections.

(4) Require parties to identify issues and describe evidence soon after an election petition is filed to facilitate resolution and eliminate unnecessary litigation.

(5) Defer litigation of most voter eligibility issues until after the election.

(6) Require employers to provide a final voter list in electronic form soon after the scheduling of an election, including voters' telephone numbers and email addresses when available.

(7) Consolidate all election-related appeals to the Board into a single post-election appeals process and thereby eliminate delay in holding elections currently attributable to the possibility of pre-election appeals.

(8) Make Board review of post-election decisions discretionary rather than mandatory.

. . . The attempt to streamline the election process — pushing challenges to the post-election period is particularly significant — could significantly reduce the critical period after an election petition is filed and the election is held. This, of course, is the time where employers can aggressively fight the union campaign, often with success. What's interesting is that the rules could move the Board closer to the "quick election" proposals that came out of the EFCA debate and are used in some provinces in Canada.

Jeffrey M. Hirsch, *NLRB Proposed Election Rules* (June 21, 2011), at http://lawprofessors.typepad.com/laborprof_blog/2011/06/nlrb-proposed-election-rules.html (last visited Mar. 7, 2012).

* * *

Now consider the NLRB's initial list of proposals and the ones that are part of the election rule. Why do you think the NLRB decided not to go forward with some of these rules? What were the arguments? Some of the ones not pushed seem to include pretty straightforward reforms like, "[a]llowing for electronic filing of election petitions and other documents." Why do you think this reform was temporarily withdrawn?

SECTION 2 THE MEANING OF "APPROPRIATE BARGAINING UNIT"

Section 9(a) states that, "[r]epresentatives designated . . . by the majority of *employees in a unit appropriate for such purposes* . . . shall be the exclusive representatives of all the employees." (Emphasis added). It is for the Board to determine what group of jobs should make up the bargaining unit for purposes of the election. In making this determination, there are four basic ground rules:

1. The unit is comprised of jobs or job classifications, not particular persons working at those jobs at any particular time.

2. An "appropriate bargaining unit" is really an "appropriate election unit" since employees represented in different election units may choose to negotiate as a larger unit.

3. A determination of the appropriate bargaining unit by the Board is not a prerequisite to bargaining, as the union and company may voluntarily agree on the bargaining unit and begin negotiations.

4. The Board must only delineate an *appropriate* bargaining unit, not the best or most optimal.

Sub-sections 9(b) & (c) offer little guidance as to how the Board should make unit determinations. They prescribe only four limitations:

1. 9(b)(1) provides that both professional and non-professional employees may joined into one unit. However, professionals must vote by majority to be included in a unit with non-professionals.

2. 9(b)(2) gives "craft" employees the right to be represented in a unit separate from non-craft employees.

3. 9(b)(3) separates security guards into different units and unions than non-guard employees.

4. 9(c)(5) states that the extent to which employees have organized together in the past is not controlling to the unit determination.

There is always a tension between the type of bargaining units employers prefer and those that unions prefer. In general, unions tend to favor smaller units, while employers prefer larger ones. Unions favor smaller units because the individual employees are more effectively represented, and they are easier to organize because the larger, more diversified unit increases conflicts of interest.

In a large percentage of cases, the appropriate unit is determined voluntarily by the parties through a consent election agreement. In the cases where the parties cannot come to an agreement, the Regional Director (through a designated hearing officer) will conduct a formal hearing and make the ultimate decision, which can only be challenged on narrow grounds. The terminology used in these situations is that the Regional Director "directs an election."

The Board, in making its unit determinations, seeks an employee group that is united by a community of interest, which is neither too large and embraces too many different economic interests, nor too small and hinders the bargaining power of the union. Generally, the community of interest standard is quite vague, although eleven factors have been identified:

(handwritten note: Community of Interest Standard)

1. Similarity in the scale and manner of determining earnings

2. Conditions of employment

3. Similarity in the kind of work performed

4. Similarity in the qualifications, skills, and training of the employees

5. Frequency of contact or interchange among the employees

6. Geographic proximity

7. Continuity or integration of production processes

8. Common supervision and determination of labor-relations policy

9. History of collective bargaining

10. Desires of the affected employees

11. Extent of union organization

See NLRB v. Purnell's Pride, Inc., 609 F.2d 1153 (5th Cir. 1980).

The community of interest standard has been most divisive in the health care industry. The Board resolved this issue in 1989 through the formal rulemaking process. The Court examined the Board's power to adopt such a rule under Section 6 of the Act in *American Hospital Association v. NLRB*, 499 U.S. 606 (1991). The Court upheld the Board rule that, absent extraordinary circumstances, there are presumptively eight recognized bargaining units in acute health care cases. The extraordinary circumstance exception applies automatically to acute care hospitals where the eight-unit rule would produce a unit of five or fewer employees. Non-acute care health facilities are not covered by this rule; however, the NLRB used to apply a special analysis to those facilities. *See Park Manor Care Center*, 305 N.L.R.B. 872 (1991). Recently, the NLRB eliminated that special analysis and concluded that non-acute care facilities should fall under the general bargaining unit analysis. *See Specialty Healthcare & Rehabilitation Center of Mobile*, 357 N.L.R.B. No. 83 (2011).

Another frequently litigated issue is how to treat employees who work for companies with multiple locations. Generally, the NLRB may find that an appropriate unit includes: (1) all employees in a company; (2) only employees within a geographic location; or (3) employees within a single plant, store, or office. Although the Board takes into consideration a host of factors, the key factor is the interests of the parties concerned. Often, although not always, that analysis leads to a conclusion that a single-facility unit is appropriate. So, for instance, in *Sav-On Drugs*, 138 N.L.R.B. 1032 (1962), the Board found that a single retail store owned by a company with several stores constituted an appropriate bargaining unit. A couple of years later, the Board held in *Frisch's Big Boy Ill-Mar, Inc.*, 147 N.L.R.B. 551 (1964), that a single retail store in a chain-store operation is "presumptively appropriate." Finally, as far as multi-plant operations, the Board in *Dixie Belle Mills*, 139 N.L.R.B. 629 (1962), established a similar one-plant presumption for a company operating multiple plants, some within twenty miles of each other, which is still widely followed by the Board today. In 1995, the NLRB proposed a rule that would have codified the single-plant presumption, but withdrew the proposal in 1998 after Congress repeatedly attached budgetary riders prohibiting the rule's promulgation.

PROBLEM #2: HOLY APPROPRIATE BARGAINING UNIT, BATMAN!

Stevens Soccer supply has fifteen stores within a thirty mile radius in Metro Gotham. The stores are not highly centralized, and individual store managers have plenty of discretion, especially with regard to employment matters. Unless some larger issue of corporate policy is at issue, the individual stores run without interference from corporate headquarters. That being said, before a union filed a recent representation petition, there had been no history of collective bargaining, either on a single-store or multi-store basis. The Regional Director approved a unit of employees from only one store in East Gotham, and a majority of those employees voted for the union in an NLRB-run election.

A.   May the Board certify this unit of employees, even though all the chain stores are collectively owned?

B.   Change the facts of the problem slightly — now there are twenty-one Stevens Soccer stores, not only in Metro Gotham, but also in seven neighboring states. However, what if the store managers have little discretion, particularly with employment matters, in running stores? Also, what if there was a high degree of centralized administration, the stores were all quite similar, and there was a history of multi-store bargaining units?

PROBLEM MATERIALS

NLRB v. Chicago Health & Tennis Clubs, Inc., 567 F.2d 331 (7th Cir. 1977)

NLRB v. CHICAGO HEALTH & TENNIS CLUBS, INC.
567 F.2d 331 (7th Cir. 1977)

SWYGERT, CIRCUIT JUDGE.

In the two cases before us, the National Labor Relations Board ("the Board") petitions for enforcement of its orders directing each of the respondents to cease and desist from refusing to bargain collectively with the union which had been certified as the exclusive bargaining representative. These two cases have been consolidated for this opinion because they present the identical legal issue: whether the Board abused its discretion in certifying a single retail store as an appropriate unit for collective bargaining where such store constitutes only one of a chain of stores owned and operated by the company in the Chicago metropolitan area. For the reasons set forth, we grant the petition in Chicago Health Clubs and deny enforcement in Saxon Paint.

I

(A) Parties

No. 77-1227. Chicago Health & Tennis Clubs is an Illinois corporation engaged in the sale of club memberships and providing services of exercise training and weight loss counseling for its members. It operates sixteen clubs in the Chicago metropolitan area (Chicago and suburbs). Its central office is located in Chicago's central business district and all clubs are within a 28-mile radius of this office.

No. 77-1504. Saxon Paint & Home Care Centers is an Illinois corporation engaged in the retail sale of paint, wallpaper, and home decorating supplies. It owns and operates twenty-one stores in the Chicago metropolitan area (Cook County). In addition, Saxon has seven other stores in Illinois, Indiana, and Wisconsin. Although these seven stores are operated by separate corporate entities, they are owned in part by the same stockholders and are operated through a single managerial hierarchy. All of the Chicago metropolitan area stores are within a 30-mile radius of each other.

(B) Procedural History

The procedural history of the two cases is similar and therefore a single description suffices. The proceeding began when the Retail Clerks Union, Retail Clerks International Association, AFL-CIO-CLC filed a petition for representation seeking a unit limited to the employees of a single store in the company's chain. The company opposed the petition, contending that the only appropriate unit could consist of all its employees working in all its chain stores in the Chicago metropolitan area. Following a hearing, the Regional Director found that a single store constituted an appropriate bargaining unit. The Board denied the company's request for a review of the Director's decision.

An election was held in which a majority of the employees designated the Retail Clerks Union as their collective bargaining agent. The Director certified the union as the exclusive bargaining representative and shortly thereafter the union requested the company to bargain. The company refused on the ground that the unit found by the Board was inappropriate. The union then filed an unfair labor practice charge, alleging an unlawful refusal to bargain. Complaints issued and in its answer the company admitted its refusal to bargain, reasserting the inappropriateness of the designated unit.

The Board granted the General Counsel's motion for summary judgment, finding that each company violated section 8(a)(1) and (a)(5) of the Act by refusing to recognize and bargain with the union. On these two petitions for enforcement, each company reasserts its challenge to the unit determination. Since the companies defend solely on the grounds that the unit determinations were inappropriate, and since they concede that they refused to bargain, it is undisputed that the companies violated section 8(a)(1) and (a) (5) of the Act if the Board's unit determinations were correct.

II

The primary responsibility for determining the appropriateness of a unit for collective bargaining rests with the Board. It is given broad discretion in determining bargaining units "to assure to employees the fullest freedom in exercising the rights guaranteed by ([the Act])." The Board is not required to select the most appropriate bargaining unit in a given factual situation; it need choose only an appropriate unit within the range of appropriate units. It follows that Board unit determinations are rarely to be disturbed.

Board determines appropriateness of a unit. Given broad discretion.

↓

Assure rights.

Although Board determinations are subject to limited review, they are not immune from judicial scrutiny. We must bear in mind that section 10(e) of the Act clothes the courts of appeals with authority to enter decrees "enforcing, modifying, and enforcing as so modified, or setting aside in whole or in part the order of the Board." Indeed, the Supreme Court has held that we are not " 'to stand aside and rubber-stamp' Board determinations that run contrary to the language or tenor of the Act." Accordingly, we have the responsibility of determining whether the Board's unit determinations were unreasonable, arbitrarily or capriciously made, or unsupported by substantial evidence.

In making unit determinations, the Board must effect the policy of the Act to assure employees the fullest freedom in exercising their rights, yet at the same time "respect the interest of an integrated multi-unit employer in maintaining enterprise-wide labor relations." In reaching its decision, the Board considers several criteria, no single factor alone being determinative. These factors include:

(a) geographic proximity of the stores in relation to each other; *(Almost identical)*

(b) history of collective bargaining or unionization;

(c) extent of employee interchange between various stores;

(d) functional integration of operations; and

(e) centralization of management, particularly in regard to central control of personnel and labor relations.

As the geographic proximity of the stores in the two cases before us is almost identical, our decision whether to grant the petitions for enforcement must rest on an analysis of the other factors.

One further item deserves note before proceeding to a discussion of the individual cases. Although the Board has vacillated in deciding the proper scope of a bargaining unit in the retail chain industry, it has apparently now adopted the administrative policy that a single store is "presumptively an appropriate unit for bargaining." That presumption, however, is not conclusive and "may be overcome where factors are present in a particular case which would counter the appropriateness of a single store unit. . . ."

single store policy

↓

Not conclusive

We turn now to the two cases before us.

(A) Saxon Paint, No. 77-1504

Although the Board recognized that the Chicago area Saxon stores exhibited "a high degree of centralized administration," it nevertheless found a single store unit appropriate. In large part, the Board based its unit determination on the role of the local store manager, adopting the Regional Director's finding that "substantial responsibility is invested in the Employer's store managers." We believe that the Board exaggerated the control exercised by the store manager over labor and administrative matters and hold that the Board's finding that the store manager possesses autonomy and authority is not supported by substantial evidence.

'The evidence in the record clearly establishes that Saxon is a highly integrated operation. Each Saxon store is similar in all respects to each of the other Saxon stores in Cook County. All of the stores are open on the same days and at the same times. They sell the same merchandise at the same price and the physical layout of each store is similar. Special sales and promotions are held at the same time in each store with the same sale prices being charged. Advertising covers the entire metropolitan area and is prepared by headquarters as are store signs and window displays. The stores are "as much alike in this respect as peas in a pod."

Personnel and labor relations policies for the Saxon stores are also centrally administered, being formulated by the personnel director who maintains his office at corporate headquarters. Payrolls, accounts, personnel files, and other records are maintained at the general office. Employee job classifications are the same at each store, and employees within a particular classification perform the same duties and are required to have the same skills and experience. Employees within the same classification, experience, and seniority receive the same wages. A uniform fringe benefit program is maintained at each store, and store employees enjoy company-wide seniority.

The actual operations of the Cook County stores are also highly centralized. Under the vice president of operations are three district managers who are responsible for assuring that all stores within their respective districts are being operated in full compliance with the policies and procedures formulated at headquarters, including personnel and labor relations policies. These district managers visit the stores within their district on the average of every two days and maintain further contact with the individual stores through frequent telephone calls and written memoranda. In addition, the company maintains a messenger service which visits each metropolitan area store daily.

At the store level and below the district managers, the company employs fourteen store managers in all three districts. Seven of these managers are assigned to single stores, the remaining seven managers are each assigned to two stores. The evidence establishes that, contrary to the Board's conclusion, these store managers have limited involvement in the store's non-labor business activities. The individual store managers have no authority to commit the employer's credit, purchase or order merchandise and supplies, arrange for repair or maintenance work, change prices, or resolve customer complaints. At best it can be said that it is the responsibility of the store managers to implement the company's policies and procedures within the individual stores.

The store managers' involvement in labor relations and personnel matters is also severely limited. They have no authority to do any of the following: (a) hire new employees; (b) grant promotions, wage increases or changes in job classifications; (c) discharge or suspend employees for disciplinary reasons; (d) lay-off employees; (e) handle employee grievances; (f) grant requests for vacations or leaves of absence; (g) permanently or temporarily transfer employees between any of the stores; and (h) post the weekly work schedule without prior approval by the district manager. While the store manager may offer recommendations in certain of these areas, the record shows that these recommendations, even in such key areas as employee discharge, may not be followed. Furthermore, in certain areas such as promotion and wage increases, the store manager may not even be consulted before a decision is made. As the Second Circuit noted in NLRB v. Solis Theatre Corp., 403 F.2d 381, 383 (2d Cir. 1968):

> It appears, therefore, that instead of being in a decision making position, the "manager" has little or no authority on labor policy but is subject to detailed instructions from the central office.

That Saxon is completely integrated functionally is best illustrated by its hiring and training practices. Hiring is done almost exclusively through the corporate offices. Job applications are taken and interviews are held at the personnel office. The store manager may interview an applicant only after the applicant has first interviewed with the personnel director and then the district manager. Applicants may be rejected and new employees hired, however, without prior consultation with or participation by the store manager.

Similarly, the training of new employees comes under the primary jurisdiction of the central personnel department. The company issues manuals to all new employees and provides them with formal training, lasting from one to two weeks, at its corporate headquarters. In sum, it is apparent that there is no local autonomy among the individual stores and that the store managers lack the authority to resolve issues which would be subject to collective bargaining.

That Saxon's business is both centralized and integrated and that the individual stores lack meaningful identity as a self-contained unit is further supported by the numbers of employee transfers, both temporary and permanent, among the metropolitan area stores. During a thirteen month period and discounting employees not covered in the unit, eighteen percent of all employees were transferred permanently among the Chicago stores. Additional testimony showed that temporary transfers frequently occur, almost on a daily basis. While this alone may be insufficient to negate a single store unit, we cannot agree with the Board's finding that "the degree of employee interchange [was] too inconsequential and insubstantial to rebut the appropriateness of a single store unit," particularly when this factor is considered in light of all of the other factors.

That a single store is inappropriate here is further shown by the history of collective bargaining. The pattern of unionization both at stores in other regions and at stores within the Chicago metropolitan area has always been district wide. Since 1966, the employees at the company's two Hammond, Indiana stores have been represented by another local of the Retail Clerks Union. These employees are covered by one collective bargaining agreement between the union and the company. Both present and past agreements have stated that the unit it covers is "all present and future retail establishments of the Company situated within the Gary, Indiana metropolitan area, including the County of Lake." A similar clause was contained in the agreement with the employees from the company's store in Rockford, Illinois.

The record also reveals that the Retail Clerks Union once petitioned the Board for a representation election among all of the company's Chicago metropolitan area stores. An election was conducted in 1965 among the then existing five Saxon stores. A second election, held in 1967, also included a sixth Saxon store which was opened during the intervening period of time. We agree that this bargaining history is not controlling because the elections were conducted pursuant to an agreement between the union and the company. But we cannot agree that this history is entitled to little or no weight for, at a minimum, it shows that the union previously considered and treated all of the company's stores in the Chicago metropolitan area as a single unit . . . .

For the reasons herein stated, we conclude that the Board's determination that a single Saxon store was an appropriate bargaining unit is not supported by substantial evidence and therefore is arbitrary and unreasonable. Accordingly, the Board's order is set aside and enforcement is denied

(B) Chicago Health Clubs, No. 77-1227

Chicago Health Clubs is, at first sight, quite similar factually to Saxon Paint. The company's sixteen stores (clubs) are in a similar geographic proximity to each other. Many of its operations and procedures are centralized.

Other similarities are readily apparent. Chicago Health Clubs has two area supervisors (similar to Saxon's district managers) who oversee its sixteen clubs. These supervisors visit their respective clubs two or three times a week and maintain frequent telephone contact. Despite these similarities, we conclude that substantial evidence supports the Board's finding that a single club is an appropriate bargaining unit.

Notably absent in this case is any prior history of collective bargaining. In addition, the extent of employee interchange among the various clubs is minimal. Furthermore, there are significant differences in the functional integration of the clubs, the extent to which the company is centralized, and the degree of autonomy of the local club managers.

Unlike the Saxon stores which are virtually identical with each other, Chicago Health Clubs operates at least three types of clubs. Some clubs exclusively serve women, others serve men on one day and women on another. Still others serve men and women on the same day. The clubs also differ in the type of facilities available. Some have handball courts, others have swimming pools. One has a tennis court.

Although many aspects of the company's operations and procedures are centralized, they are not as highly centralized as in Saxon Paint. For example, even though official personnel and payroll records are maintained at the central office, each club manager also maintains records detailing needed information about the club employees. Similarly, the central office controls the advertising for all sixteen clubs, but the advertising may be directed at only one geographical area or may be on behalf of only one of the clubs.

Also unlike the store managers in Saxon Paint, the club managers exercise a marked degree of control over personnel and labor relations matters. Applicants apply at the individual clubs and are interviewed by the club manager without further interview by the area supervisor. Part-time employees, a large number if not a majority of all employees, are hired and fired by the club manager without consultation with the area supervisor. Although full-time employees are hired with the approval of the area supervisor, the decision is based on the applicant's interview with the club manager. In hiring, the club manager sets the wage rate for new employees within the perimeters determined by the area supervisor.

Autonomy for managers.

Additionally, unlike the store managers in Saxon Paint, the club managers here exercise considerable disciplinary authority over rank-and-file employees. A club manager may reprimand employees without prior approval. Moreover, in extreme cases, the club manager has the authority to discharge or suspend employees without prior consultation with the area supervisor.

The club manager exercises control over the working conditions of employees in many other respects. For example, the club manager handles employee complaints and grievances about wages and hours, schedules vacations, grants or denies overtime, decides whether employees may take their lunch break on or off the premises, administers the local payroll system, and trains employees in exercise instruction and sales. Thus, unlike Saxon Paint . . . , much of the day-to-day employment activities are supervised directly by the local club manager "without significant interference" by the central corporate organization.

Based on the autonomy of the club manager, the insubstantial amount of employee interchange among the metropolitan clubs, and the absence of any collective bargaining history, we conclude that the Board's determination that a single store was an appropriate bargaining unit is reasonable in light of all the facts presented in this case. Since Chicago Health Clubs has admitted its refusal to bargain with the union representing this single club, we accordingly enforce the Board's order.

In summary, the Board's order in No. 77-1227 shall be enforced. Enforcement of the Board's order in No. 77-1504 is denied.

POST PROBLEM DISCUSSION

1. Does *Chicago Health* suggest that the level of discretion afforded to individual store managers, particularly on issues involving the employees, is the most important factor in your answer in Problem 2? Perhaps, but it also seems that the centralization of payroll records and personnel files would work against the single-store unit.

2. Leased (or contingent employees) have become a fixture in modern labor and employment law. These employees include persons who are under contract to one employer, which in turn "leases" or "supplies" them to a second employer. A good example involves temporary employment agencies.

This relationship creates a unique situation where both employers have control over various work conditions that unions typically bargain over. The Board in *Greenhoot, Inc.*, 205 N.L.R.B. 250 (1973), held that employees "supplied" to various construction companies by a building management company would not constitute a multiemployer unit even if they formed a single bargaining unit, unless each construction company consented to such an arrangement. On the other hand, in *Lee Hospital*, 300 N.L.R.B. 947 (1990), the Board held that where various employers' employees were organizing and leased employees sought to join their bargaining unit, the leased employees would not be included in the bargaining unit without the consent of the contractor because a multiemployer unit would be created.

3. In *General Electric Co. v. NLRB*, 412 F.2d 512 (2d Cir. 1969), the court considered whether the union could form a mixed-union negotiating committee with representatives from seven other unions that represented other employees of the employer. At the time, General Electric's (GE) employees were represented by over 80 unions comprised of roughly 150 bargaining units. Eight of the international unions, led by the International Union of Electricians (IUE), formed a bargaining committee because each felt GE was playing one against the other in the individual negotiations. Although a representative of each union was present at the negotiating table, only IUE had voting privileges to consent to an agreement.

The court found that such coordinated bargaining was permissible, so long as such bargaining was not done in bad faith. Sanctioning coordinated bargaining does not mean that unions may negotiate on behalf of one another's employees; it only holds that the representatives of other unions may be present at such negotiations.

4. Forty percent of American workers are covered by collective bargaining agreements negotiated on a multiemployer basis. This practice is common in the clothing and service industries, where the union principally wants to gain more leverage in negotiations, and in the construction, longshore and maritime industries, where work for one employer is often short-lived and it makes sense for employers to band together. Further, in these situations, the international union often negotiates a master CBA, and subsidiary agreements may be negotiated at individual companies with local unions. In general, the Board has signed off on multiemployer agreements. If these agreements are consensually agreed upon, individual companies may withdraw up until the time bargaining begins. *See Charles D. Bonanno Linen Service, Inc. v. NLRB*, 454 U.S. 404 (1982) (holding that a bargaining impasse generally does not justify an employer's withdrawal from a multiemployer bargaining agreement).

SECTION 3 REPRESENTATION PROCEEDING REVIEW

On its face, the NLRA has no provision allowing for direct judicial review of Board decisions made in connection with representation election proceedings. For instance, there is no direct review of an appropriate bargaining unit decision.

This is because courts have jurisdiction over "final orders" under Section 10(f), and representation proceedings are not considered final orders. Therefore, since final orders are only issued as part of an unfair labor practice proceeding (ULP) proceeding, a party wanting review of a representational matter must commit an

ULP in order to get judicial review of the representation matter.

In practice, this process usually involves an employer's refusal to bargain with the union, once the union has been certified as the bargaining representative. This forces the union to file an ULP alleging a violation of Section 8(a)(5). This procedure is referred to as a "technical 8(a)(5)" unfair labor practice. On the other hand, a union can seek review of a some representational issues by committing unlawful recognitional picketing under Section 8(b)(7)(C).

If the employer's or union's claim is valid, and the election was improper or the bargaining unit was inappropriate, then the Board will not find an 8(a)(5) or 8(b)(7)(C) violation. Instead, it will set aside the election and order a rerun election. On review, Board decisions on representational issues are afforded great deference.

Leedom v. Kyne, 358 U.S. 184 (1958), makes clear that Congress generally did not permit direct judicial review of representation decisions. It was thought that such proceedings would delay the commencement of collective bargaining between the parties, which would unnecessarily lead to additional industrial strife. Although the *Leedom* Court first stated that Section 9(d) of the NLRA only permits limited judicial review of representation decisions that are connected to ULPs committed by the parties, it nevertheless went on to create an exception.

Under this exception, district courts may directly review Board decisions where the Board is accused of misinterpreting the statute. The majority in *Leedom* reasoned that the absence of federal jurisdiction in these types of cases would result in the obliteration of rights given to employees by Congress, which employees could not otherwise vindicate.

In a later case, *Boire v. Greyhound Corp.*, 376 U.S. 473 (1964), the Supreme Court illustrated exactly how narrow the *Leedom* exception is by limiting its terms to situations which turn solely on the construction of the statute, and not encompassing situations concerning Board assessment of particular facts under the law.

SECTION 4   GISSEL BARGAINING ORDERS

A union may secure collective bargaining status through three methods. Two of these methods have already been discussed: voluntary employer recognition and Board elections.

In *Gissel Packing Co.*, the Court upheld a third way for unions to secure bargaining status — through a Gissel Bargaining Order (GBO). You should be already familiar with the facts of *Gissel Packing* case as it was discussed earlier in the book in Chapter 5.

PROBLEM #3: NON-MAJORITY BARGAINING ORDERS

During an organizational campaign, the employer, Books Inc., committed numerous and egregious unfair labor practices against the union, the United Paper Workers (UPW). These ULPs took the form of interrogating employees who supported the union, firing those who refused to stop supporting the union, and making explicit threats against the rest of the bargaining unit if they insisted on voting for the union. After hearing testimony, an ALJ found that Books, Inc. violated Section 8(a)(1) and Section 8(a)(3).

As part of the testimony in the case, one union official had stated that he and others had formally requested that Books, Inc. voluntary recognize the union. The union presented authorization cards from 45% of the employees in the unit, saying that they wanted the union to represent them for purposes of collective bargaining. The company not only refused the request for voluntary recognition, but also took no further action.

The union then filed a petition for a representation election. It was during the organizational campaign that many of the above-mentioned ULPs were committed by the employer against the union and its supporters. Even though Books, Inc. has been found in violation of the Act, the UPW despaired that a rerun election could no longer be fair or measure whether the employees truly wished to be represented by the UPW. Consequently, the UPW asked the ALJ for a Gissel Bargaining Order, requiring Books Inc. to initiate collective bargaining with it. The ALJ refused and ordered that the election to be rerun. The union lost the election 60-40.

A. You work on the staff of one of the Members of the NLRB who has been assigned to look over the ALJ's decision. Can the Board order a Gissel Bargaining Order under current law?

B. Can the employer refuse to voluntary recognize the union and also refuse to file an election petition itself?

C. When you tell your Board member how this case comes out under current law, your Board Member is none too pleased. Make the best argument for changing the law in this context under Subpart (A) and (B), above.

PROBLEM MATERIALS

NLRB v. Gissel Packing Co., 395 U.S. 575 (1969)

Linden Lumber Division, Summer & Co. v. NLRB, 419 U.S. 301 (1974)

Gourmet Foods, Inc. v. Warehouse Employees of St. Paul, 270 N.L.R.B. 578 (1984)

NLRB v. GISSEL PACKING CO.
395 U.S. 575 (1969)

CHIEF JUSTICE WARREN delivered the opinion of the Court.

These cases involve the extent of an employer's duty under the National Labor Relations Act to recognize a union that bases its claim to representative status solely on the possession of union authorization cards, and the steps an employer may take, particularly with regard to the scope and content of statements he may make, in legitimately resisting such card-based recognition. The specific questions facing us here are whether the duty to bargain can arise without a Board election under the Act; whether union authorization cards, if obtained from a majority of employees without misrepresentation or coercion, are reliable enough generally to provide a valid, alternate route to majority status; whether a bargaining order is an appropriate and authorized remedy where an employer rejects a card majority while at the same time committing unfair practices that tend to undermine the union's majority and make a fair election an unlikely possibility; and whether certain specific statements made by an employer to his employees constituted such an election-voiding unfair labor practice and thus fell outside the protection of the First Amendment and s 8(c) of the Act. For reasons given below, we answer each of these questions in the affirmative.

. . . II

. . . [T]he Board asks us to approve its current practice, which is briefly as follows. When confronted by a recognition demand based on possession of cards allegedly signed by a majority of his employees, an employer need not grant recognition immediately, but may, unless he has knowledge independently of the cards that the union has a majority, decline the union's request and insist on an election, either by requesting the union to file an election petition or by filing such a petition himself under s 9(c)(1)(B). If, however, the employer commits independent and substantial unfair labor practices disruptive of election conditions, the Board may withhold the election or set it aside, and issue instead a bargaining order as a remedy for the various violations. A bargaining order will not issue of course, if the union obtained the cards through misrepresentation or coercion or if the employer's unfair labor practices are unrelated generally to the representation campaign . . . .

III

A.

The first issue facing us is whether a union can establish a bargaining obligation by means other than a Board election and whether the validity of alternate routes to majority status, such as cards, was affected by the 1947 Taft-Hartley amendments. The most commonly traveled route for a union to obtain recognition as the exclusive bargaining representative of an unorganized group of employees is through the Board's election and certification procedures under s 9(c) of the Act; it is also, from the Board's point of view, the preferred route. A union is not limited to a Board election, however, for, in addition to s 9, the present Act provides in s 8(a)(5), as did the Wagner Act in s 8(5), that '(i)t shall be an unfair labor practice for an employer . . . to refuse to bargain collectively with the representatives of his employees, subject to the provisions of section 9(a).' Since s 9(a), in both the Wagner Act and the present Act, refers to the representative as the one 'designated or selected' by a majority of the employees without specifying precisely how that representative is to be chosen, it was early recognized that an employer had a duty to bargain whenever the union representative presented 'convincing evidence of majority support.' Almost from the inception of the Act, then, it was recognized that a union did not have to be certified as the winner of a Board election to invoke a bargaining obligation; it could establish majority status by other means under the unfair labor practice provision of s 8(a)(5) — by showing convincing support, for instance, by a union-called strike or strike vote, or, as here, by possession of cards signed by a majority of the employees authorizing the union to represent them for collective bargaining purposes . . . .

B.

. . . The Board itself has recognized, and continues to do so here, that secret elections are generally the most satisfactory-indeed the preferred-method of ascertaining whether a union has majority support. The acknowledged superiority of the election process, however, does not mean that cards are thereby rendered totally invalid, for where an employer engages in conduct disruptive of the election process, cards may be the most effective-perhaps the only-way of assuring employee choice. As for misrepresentation, in any specific case of alleged irregularity in the solicitation of the cards, the proper course is to apply the Board's customary standards . . . and rule that there was no majority if the standards were not satisfied. It does not follow that because there are some instances of irregularity, the cards can never be used; otherwise, an employer could put off his bargaining obligation indefinitely through continuing interference with elections . . . .

[W]e think it sufficient to point out that employees should be bound by the clear language of what they sign unless that language is deliberately and clearly canceled by a union adherent with words calculated to direct the signer to disregard and forget the language above his signature. There is nothing inconsistent in handing an employee a card that says the signer authorizes the union to represent him and then telling him that the card will probably be used first to get an election. Elections have been, after all, and will continue to be, held in the vast majority of cases; the union will still have to have the signatures of 30% of the employees when an employer rejects a bargaining demand and insists that the union seek an election. We cannot agree with the employers here that employees as a rule are too unsophisticated to be bound by what they sign unless expressly told that their act of signing represents something else . . . .

C.

Remaining before us is the propriety of a bargaining order as a remedy for a s 8(a)(5) refusal to bargain where an employer has committed independent unfair labor practices which have made the holding of a fair election unlikely or which have in fact undermined a union's majority and caused an election to be set aside. We have long held that the Board is not limited to a cease-and-desist order in such cases, but has the authority to issue a bargaining order without first requiring the union to show that it has been able to maintain its majority status. And we have held the Board has the same authority even where it is clear that the union, which once had possession of cards from a majority of the employees, represents only a minority when the bargaining order is entered. We see no reason now to withdraw this authority from the Board. If the Board could enter only a cease-and-desist order and direct an election or a rerun, it would in effect be rewarding the employer and allowing him 'to profit from (his) own wrongful refusal to bargain,' while at the same time severely curtailing the employees' right freely to determine whether they desire a representative. The employer could continue to delay or disrupt the election processes and put off indefinitely his obligation to bargain; and any election held under these circumstances would not be likely to demonstrate the employees' true, undistorted desires . . . .

Before considering whether the bargaining orders were appropriately entered in these cases, we should summarize the factors that go into such a determination. Despite our reversal of the Fourth Circuit below . . . on all major issues, the actual area of disagreement between our position here and that of the Fourth Circuit is not large as a practical matter. While refusing to validate the general use of a bargaining order in reliance on cards, the Fourth Circuit nevertheless left open the possibility of imposing a bargaining order, without need of inquiry into majority status on the basis of cards or otherwise, in 'exceptional' cases marked by 'outrageous' and 'pervasive' unfair labor practices. Such an order would be an appropriate remedy for those practices, the court noted, if they are of 'such a nature that their coercive effects cannot be eliminated by the application of traditional remedies, with the result that a fair and reliable election cannot be had.' The Board itself, we should add, has long had a similar policy of issuing a bargaining order, in the absence of a s 8(a)(5) violation or even a bargaining demand, when that was the only available, effective remedy for substantial unfair labor practices.

The only effect of our holding here is to approve the Board's use of the bargaining order in less extraordinary cases marked by less pervasive practices which nonetheless still have the tendency to undermine majority strength and impede the election processes. The Board's authority to issue such an order on a lesser showing of employer misconduct is appropriate, we should reemphasize, where there is also a showing that at one point the union had a majority; in such a case, of course, effectuating ascertainable employee free choice becomes as important a goal as deterring employer misbehavior. In fashioning a remedy in the exercise of its discretion, then, the Board can properly take into consideration the extensiveness of an employer's unfair practices in terms of their past effect on election conditions and the likelihood of their recurrence in the future. If the Board finds that the possibility of erasing the effects of past practices and of ensuring a fair election (or a fair rerun) by the use of traditional remedies, though present, is slight and that employee sentiment once expressed through cards would, on balance, be better protected by a bargaining order, then such an order should issue.

We emphasize that under the Board's remedial power there is still a third category of minor or less extensive unfair labor practices, which, because of their minimal impact on the election machinery, will not sustain a bargaining order. There is, the Board says, no per se rule that the commission of any unfair practice will automatically result in a s 8(a)(5) violation and the issuance of an order to bargain.

LINDEN LUMBER DIVISION, SUMMER & CO. v. NLRB
419 U.S. 301 (1974)

JUSTICE DOUGLAS delivered the opinion of the Court.

These cases present a question expressly reserved in NLRB v. Gissel Packing Co., 395 U.S. 575, 595, 601 n. 18 (1969).

In Linden respondent union obtained authorization cards from a majority of petitioner's employees and demanded that it be recognized as the collective-bargaining representative of those employees. Linden said it doubted the union's claimed majority status and suggested the union petition the Board for an election. The union filed such a petition with the Board but later withdrew it when Linden declined to enter a consent election agreement or abide by an election, on the ground that respondent union's organizational campaign had been improperly assisted by company supervisors. Respondent union thereupon renewed its demand for collective bargaining; and again Linden declined, saying that the union's claimed membership had been improperly influenced by supervisors. Thereupon respondent union struck for recognition as the bargaining representative and shortly filed a charge of unfair labor practice against Linden based on its refusal to bargain.

There is no charge that Linden engaged in an unfair labor practice apart from its refusal to bargain. The Board held that Linden should not be guilty of an unfair labor practice solely on the basis 'of its refusal to accept evidence of majority status other than the results of a Board election.' . . .

The Board has at least some expertise in these matters and its judgment is that an employer's petition for an election, though permissible, is not the required course. It points out in its brief here that an employer wanting to gain delay can draw a petition to elicit protests by the union, and the thought that an employer petition would obviate litigation over the sufficiency of the union's showing of interest is in its purview apparently not well taken. A union petition to be sure must be backed by a 30% showing of employee interest. But the sufficiency of such a showing is not litigable by the parties.

In light of the statutory scheme and the practical administrative procedural questions involved, we cannot say that the Board's decision that the union should go forward and ask for an election on the employer's refusal to recognize the authorization cards was arbitrary and capricious or an abuse of discretion.

In sum, we sustain the Board in holding that, unless an employer has engaged in an unfair labor practice that impairs the electoral process, a union with authorization cards purporting to represent a majority of the employees, which is refused recognition, has the burden of taking the next step in invoking the Board's election procedure.

GOURMET FOODS, INC. v. WAREHOUSE EMPLOYEES OF ST. PAUL

270 N.L.R.B. 578 (1984)

By Chairman Dotson and Members Zimmerman, Hunter, and Dennis

As fully set forth in the attached decision, the judge found that the Respondent committed numerous 8(a)(3) and (1) violations. We agree with his findings.

We also agree with the judge that the General Counsel failed to demonstrate the Union's majority status and hence failed to support its argument for a remedial bargaining order predicated on majority status . . . .

Having determined that the Union was not at any relevant time the majority representative of the Respondent's employees in an appropriate unit, the judge apparently considered the matter of a bargaining order remedy foreclosed. He found it unnecessary to determine whether the Respondent's misconduct would have warranted a bargaining order remedy had majority status been demonstrated. Further, while referring to the Supreme Court's dictum in *NLRB v. Gissel Packing Co.*, about "imposing a bargaining order, without need of inquiry into majority status . . . in 'exceptional' cases marked by 'outrageous' and 'pervasive' unfair labor practices," the judge refrained from examining the appropriateness of granting a nonmajority bargaining order, apparently because the General Counsel did not specifically raise the issue.

The Charging Party contends that a bargaining order remedy is warranted here, even absent a showing of the Union's majority status, because of what it characterizes as the Respondent's "outrageous" and "pervasive" unfair labor practices. Had majority status been demonstrated we would have agreed with both the General Counsel and the Charging Party that a remedial bargaining order was warranted. The Respondent embarked on an approximately 5-month campaign of unfair labor practices almost immediately after it learned of the likelihood its employees would seek union representation. The campaign intensified following the Union's withdrawal of an election petition and continued throughout an unfair labor practice strike and the period of reinstatement. The violations here include discriminatory discharge; discriminatory discipline; threats of discharge and plant closure; and the retaliatory imposition of harsher working conditions. All these violations directly affected a number of employees. The impact of the violations was likely heightened by the relatively small size of the unit and by their orchestration and commission by high-level management officials and supervisory personnel. The Respondent's president's statement early in the campaign that he "would do anything to keep a union out" coupled with the continuation and intensification of unfair labor practices indicates the Respondent's predisposition to engage in unlawful misconduct in response to union activities. Given the circumstances of this case, we would in all likelihood have found that the possibility of erasing its effects and ensuring a fair election by the use of traditional remedies was slight and that the sentiment of a majority of the employees, reflected by valid authorization cards, would probably have been better protected by a bargaining order than by an election. We do not, however, now determine whether we would have viewed the

Respondent's misconduct as an "exceptional" case, within the description of the *Gissel* category one, that is, "marked by 'outrageous' and 'pervasive' unfair labor practices" and "so coercive that, even in the absence of an 8(a)(5) violation, a bargaining order would have been necessary to repair the unlawful effects" of the misconduct. The Board's post-*Gissel* cases show an array of factual circumstances that have been determined to fall within the *Gissel* category one, including some which appear of equivalent or less severity than the circumstances involved here and some which are of clearly greater severity. Under these circumstances, we are not disposed to decide this case on the narrower issue of a *Gissel* category determination since we have come to the conclusion that we would, under no circumstances, issue a nonmajority bargaining order . . . .

II.

Although we have stated our conclusions and general endorsement of certain positions, we consider it incumbent to further explicate the course of our analysis. We start with the authority Congress granted the Board to remedy unfair labor practices under Section 10(c) "to take such affirmative action . . . as will effectuate the policies of this Act." That authority though undeniably "broad" and "subject to limited judicial review" has been recognized as limited when its exercise would "violate a fundamental premise on which the Act is based."

In *H. K. Porter*, the fundamental premise violated was freedom of contract. There a Board order affirmed by the Court of Appeals for the D.C. Circuit required an employer to grant a union a contractual dues-checkoff provision in response to the employer's refusal to bargain in good faith about the provision. As described by Member Penello in *United Dairy I*, the Supreme Court "rejected the court of appeals' approach of balancing conflicting policy considerations and declined to examine the merits of the remedy" and found that the Board lacked the power to impose the remedy in dispute as that authority resided solely with Congress. He drew what we consider to be several convincing analogies between *H. K. Porter* and the issue involved here. Thus, in both cases (1) "it is claimed that the Board can issue a remedial order that conflicts with a fundamental principle of the Act," (2) "it is argued that violation of the basic precept must be tolerated in order to further the policy of the Act of securing employees' rights to bargain collectively," and (3) "support for the extraordinary remedy is allegedly found in the inadequacy of less dramatic measures and Respondent's prior violations of the Act." We agree with Member Penello that "the policy of majority rule . . . cannot be seriously contended to be . . . any less fundamental than freedom of contract," and that the rationale of *H. K. Porter* must be applied here.

The principle of majority rule is written into Section 9(a) of the National Labor Relations Act: "Representatives designated or selected . . . *by the majority of the employees* in a unit . . . shall be the exclusive representatives of all the employees in such unit for the purposes of collective bargaining . . . ." (Emphasis added.) It is this standard of majority rule that enables the Act's policies of "protecting the exercise by workers of . . . designation of representatives of their own choosing" and "encouraging the practice and procedures of collective bargaining" to be realized. For it is the culmination of choice by *a majority of employees* that leads to the process of collective bargaining; the choice by a majority gives legitimacy and effectiveness to a union's role as exclusive bargaining representative and correlatively gives rise to an employer's obligation to deal exclusively with that representative. As Senator Wagner stated in support of the bill which became the foundation for our current Act: "[C]ollective bargaining can be really effective only when workers are sufficiently solidified in their interests to make one agreement covering all. This is possible only by means of majority rule." In Senate debate on the bill, Senator Wagner further stated:

> Collective bargaining is not an artificial procedure devoted to an unknown end. Its object is the making of agreements which will stabilize employment conditions and promote fair working standards. It is well-nigh universally recognized that it is practically impossible to apply two or more sets of agreements to one unit of workers at the same time or to apply the terms of one agreement to only a portion of the workers in a single unit. For this reason *collective bargaining means majority rule*. This rule is conducive not only to agreements, but also to friendly relations. Workers find it easier to approach their employers in a spirit of good will if they are not torn by internal dissent. And employers, wherever majority rule has been given a fair chance, have discovered it more profitable to deal with a single group than to be harassed by a constant series of negotiations with rival factions. Majority rule makes it clear that the guaranty of the right of employees to bargain collectively through representatives of their own choosing must not be misapplied so as to permit employers to interfere with the practical effectuation of that right by bargaining with individuals or minority groups in their own behalf *after representatives have been picked by the majority to represent all*. [Emphasis added.] . . .

We reiterate simply that the undesirable and unacceptable results of forsaking the majority rule principle and granting a nonmajority bargaining order remedy are governmental imposition of a choice of representative in lieu of governmental protection of the right to choose that representative and the negative impact of such imposition on the public's perception of the Board as an impartial agency. We have considered the essential policy argument of Board proponents of nonmajority bargaining orders, i.e., that "where the employer's misconduct has prevented the ascertainment of the wishes of the majority . . . the only effective remedy to offset this unlawful action is a bargaining order." We seriously question however whether a nonmajority bargaining order, in practice, is an effective remedy. The bargaining environment established at the Board's instigation alone does not replicate that which arises from employees' impetus. What is lacking is the leverage normally possessed by exclusive bargaining representatives that derives from unions' and employers' knowledge that a majority of employees at one time, in some form, united in their support for a union and may do so again in support of bargaining demands. To gain that leverage, employees may be called on to demonstrate active support for a representative in a far more open way than a secret-ballot election. Accordingly, in imposing a representative on employees, the Board may be changing only the sphere of employees' choice. And yet the Board can be no more certain that, in this new sphere of employee choice, employees can more freely exercise their choice without regard to any lingering effects of massive unfair labor practices than it can be if a new election is directed after the Board has applied traditional as well as appropriate extraordinary remedies. The Board can be certain, however, of the possibility that it is forcing a majority of employees who do not have an interest in participating in the collective-bargaining process into that process and, potentially and consequently, into undesired terms and conditions of employment negotiated by an unchosen representative. Given these policy considerations we do not believe we would ever be justified in granting a nonmajority bargaining order remedy.

While we have determined that nonmajority bargaining orders cannot be considered a remedial option, we emphasize that in response to flagrant and repeated violations of the statute we will continue to impose all appropriate traditional and extraordinary remedies at our disposal. In this case, for example, in addition to adopting those remedies recommended by the judge, we shall also require the Respondent to mail copies of the notice to employees to all those employees who have been on the payroll since 10 October 1980. That is the date when the Respondent began its campaign of unfair labor practices. Because this case involves extensive violations which, as the judge found, exhibit "a general disregard for the employees' fundamental rights," we thereby seek to ensure that all of the Respondent's employees who may have been directly affected by the violations or by knowledge of the violations throughout the long period this case has been pending are assured that such unlawful acts are being remedied and will not be repeated.

MEMBER DENNIS, concurring [opinion omitted].

MEMBER ZIMMERMAN, dissenting [opinion omitted].

POST PROBLEM DISCUSSION

1. The Board in *Gourmet Foods* found that a "non-majority bargaining order" is beyond the Board's power. Further, even if the Board had the power to issue such orders, it should refrain from doing so as it violates the Section 7 right of employee free choice and may also cause an employer to engage in a Section 8(a)(2) violation of domination and assistance. Member Zimmerman, in dissent, stated that the "non-majority bargaining order" may be the only protection employees have against employers that commit egregious ULPs to ensure that the organizing union never gets majority support. Who has the better argument? Should the Board reverse course in this area of labor law?

2. Note the defining characteristic of a *Gissel* case: the union cannot show that it has majority support. In *Gissel*, the Supreme Court breaks down potential bargaining order cases into three categories of cases:

I. Exceptional Cases (rare) — The Court affirmed earlier precedent, which held the Board may issue a bargaining order where the employer committed independent and egregious ULPs that made holding a fair election unlikely or that undermined the union's majority causing an election to be set aside.

II.   Less Extraordinary Cases — The Court held that the Board may issue a bargaining order where the employer commits ULPs sufficient "to undermine majority strength and impede the election processes."

III.   Minor or Less Extensive Cases — The Court notes here that the Board has stated there is no *per se* rule that a bargaining order will result if the employer commits an 8(a)(5) violation. Therefore, if an employer commits a ULP, but it does not preclude a fair election, then a bargaining order is not a permissible remedy. Instead, the election will be ordered rerun.

In *Gissel*, the Court suggested that a *Gissel I* bargaining order could issue even though the union, in contrast to *Gissel II* orders, could not show that it had majority support prior to the commission of the ULPs. After *Gourmet Foods*, is there any real difference between *Gissel I* and *Gissel II* cases?

Does it make sense for the Court to differentiate egregious ULPs and technical ULPs? Empirical studies are mixed on whether the commission of ULPs during election campaigns has any effect on election outcomes. *Compare* Julies G. Getman, Stephen B. Goldberg & Jeanne B. Herman, Union Representation Elections: Law and Reality (1976) (finding that unlawful campaigning has no greater effect on employer voting behavior in a union representation election than does lawful campaigning), *with* John-Paul Ferguson *The Eyes of the Needles: A Sequential Model of Union Organizing Drives, 1999–2004*, 62 Indus. & Lab. Rel. Rev. 3 (2008) (contending that commission of ULP has more of an impact on whether an election is held than on how votes were cast).

3.   One could argue that waiting for a Gissel Bargaining Order (GBO) might not be the most expeditious way to secure bargaining rights for a union. Consider how long the litigation may take before a GBO issues. Indeed, if the Court were seeking to cure the employer's refusal to bargain, why not just give more credence to authorization cards?*Linden Lumber*, in making the union file an election petition in response to an employer refusal to recognize the union, seems to also push unions away from the GBO route and towards the "preferred" election process.

4.   While the Court in *Gissel* upheld the Board's use of bargaining orders in certain circumstances, it left the establishment of criteria up to the Board. After *Gissel*, however, the Board chose to determine if GBOs were needed on a case-by-case basis without establishing any guidelines. The Second Circuit, in *NLRB v. General Stencils, Inc.*, 438 F.2d 894 (2d Cir. 1971), took exception to this loose standard of evaluation, and requested that the Board establish firm guidelines to add consistency to their decisions. Although the majority of the Board failed to address the Second Circuit's concern, Chairman Miller dissented to point out two violations that necessitate a GBO: (1) an employer's grant of significant benefits during the organizational campaign; and (2) repeated 8(a)(3) violations by the employer. These have become known as "hallmark" violations that often warrant a GBO.

5.   In discussing employee "free choice," compare the *Gissel* Court's statements: (1) "Where an employer engages in conduct disruptive of the election process, cards may be the most effective — perhaps the only — way of assuring free choice," suggesting non-majority bargaining orders do not effectuate "free choice"; and (2)

the Board majority's statement in *Gourmet Foods*, "the majority rule principle is such an integral part of the Act's current substance and procedure that it must be adhered to." Which is correct?

6.   In dissent in *Linden Lumber*, Justice Stewart emphasized that Section 9(a) of the Act states that a union shall be the exclusive bargaining representative of the employees if "designated or selected" by a majority, but the Act never specifies how the employees must go about selecting their representative. Therefore, the employees should be able to designate their representative by a majority, regardless of the method used to show support. The burden then would fall on the employer, who may disagree with the showing, to petition for an election under Section 9(c)(1)(B). Agree?

7.   There is an on-going debate about whether *Linden Lumber* should be legislatively overruled, because representation elections typically take around five weeks between the filing of the petition and the holding of the election. The Commission on the Future of Worker-Management Relations (Dunlop Commission) suggested that this time delay increases industrial strikes by promoting an adversarial workplace environment. The Commission proposed that representation elections "should be conducted as promptly as administratively feasible, typically within two weeks." Interestingly, most provinces in Canada provide for such quick or snap elections — usually five to seven days, although in practice the time period is usually longer. Should the United States adopt such a rule? Do the Board's new election rules, discussed in Section 1, qualify as a snap election?

SECTION 5   WITHDRAWAL OF UNION RECOGNITION

Employers and disaffected employees can achieve decertification of the incumbent union through a number of methods. On the one hand, employers and employees can both file a decertification petition with the Board upon a showing of substantial interest. On the other hand, an employer can seek to unilaterally withdrawal recognition.

Unilateral withdrawal of recognition simply means the employer on its own ceases to recognize the union, leaving the union to restore recognition by filing a ULP under Section 8(a)(5) for failure to bargain in good faith. Unilateral withdrawal, at least historically, could be done through: (1) the employer having objective evidence in fact that the union no longer enjoyed majority status, or (2) by the employee having good faith doubt of the union's majority support based on objective considerations. Not surprisingly, employers have preferred to unilaterally withdraw recognition because of the lengthy delay between the filing of the decertification petition and the actual decertification election. This dynamic forces the employer to recognize the union much longer than it would like. Additionally, the union can delay the election further by filing blocking ULP charges (discussed in Section 1 above).

PROBLEM #4: BOXING OUT THE UNION

Baran Box Supplies has had enough with its union, Local 23. Baran Box is sick of negotiating ridiculously lucrative contracts and having to go through never-ending grievance arbitrations with whiny workers. Bevin Rynders, a life-long anti-union worker and member of Local 23, tells the president of Baran Box, Cob Hurley, that he believes that a majority of the 50 workers in the bargaining unit no longer support Local 23.

A.   As counsel for Baran Box, what would you advise the company to do if they want to legally withdraw recognition from the union?

B.   How would your answer change if this situation happened before the Board's decision in *Levitz Furniture* and the U.S. Supreme Court's decision in *Allentown Mack*, discussed below?

PROBLEM MATERIALS

Douglas E. Ray, *Withdrawal of Recognition After Curtin-Matheson: A House Built On Sand*, 25 U.S.F. L. Rev. 265 (1991)

Allentown Mack Sales and Services, Inc. v. NLRB, 522 U.S. 359 (1998)

Levitz Furniture Co., 333 N.L.R.B. 717 (2001)

Douglas E. Ray, *Withdrawal of Recognition After Curtin-Matheson: A House Built On Sand*
25 U.S.F. L. Rev. 265 (1991)[2]

. . . Under a test little altered over the past forty years, the NLRB allows an employer to withdraw recognition from a union and refuse to bargain further with that union if it can establish either that the union did not in fact enjoy majority support of the workers at the time of the refusal to bargain, or that it had a good faith doubt as to the union's continued majority status. Under this doctrine, the issue of whether the union retains its representative status is tested in lengthy and often unpredictable unfair labor practice proceedings which measure both the employer's good faith and the sufficiency of its evidence. The continued viability of the withdrawal of recognition doctrine is the subject of this article.

. . . I. Legislative and Decisional History

Although the NLRB has applied its withdrawal of recognition doctrine for over forty years, there is nothing in the legislative history of the NLRA, as amended, nor in past decisions of the United States Supreme Court, that would preclude the NLRB from reconsidering or revoking the good faith doubt test. The concept of withdrawing recognition based on an employer's good faith doubt as to the union's continued majority status has not yet been specifically addressed by Congress. The issue was first raised in 1947, however, when Congress considered providing

---

employees with the right to petition the NLRB for an election to decertify their union as part of the Taft-Hartley Amendments. The context in which the issue was raised suggests that the NLRB could have eliminated the withdrawal of recognition doctrine after these amendments were enacted . . . .

In 1947, Congress passed the Labor Management Relations (Taft-Hartley) Act, which amended the NLRA to specifically provide employees the right to petition for an election to determine whether their current collective bargaining representative continued to represent a majority . . . .

[T]he NLRB, [however,] reverted to a posture that seemed to indicate that the amendments to the NLRA did not preclude resort to the withdrawal of recognition doctrine. In its 1951 Celanese Corp. of America decision, the NLRB applied a good faith doubt test to justify the employer's refusal to bargain with the union after a strike which resulted in a workforce consisting primarily of strike replacements and former strikers who had crossed the picket line. As NLRB members Houston and Murdock pointed out in dissent, the majority's focus was more on the alleged good faith of the employer than on the weight of the objective evidence. It appears that the NLRB, having opposed decertification as the means to test continued majority status, ultimately chose to ignore the possibility that Congress had attempted to replace withdrawal of recognition with decertification. Instead, it merely continued on the course its chairman had told Congress he preferred.

It is apparent that Congress did not specifically approve or codify the NLRB's practice of allowing an employer to withdraw recognition from the representative of its employees. Indeed, it enacted an alternative. Nor has the United States Supreme Court limited the NLRB's discretion to reconsider the doctrine. In [NLRB v. Curtin Matheson Scientific, Inc., 494 U.S. 775 (1990)], for example, the Court notes its longstanding position that it is the NLRB which has primary responsibility for developing and applying national labor policy and that, on these grounds, it accords Board rules "considerable deference." The Court noted further that "a Board rule is entitled to deference even if it represents a departure from the Board's prior policy."

In footnote eight of the Curtin Matheson opinion, the Court acknowledges that the AFL-CIO, as amicus curiae, was urging the Court to reject the good faith doubt standard. Noting that it had "never expressly considered the validity of the good-faith doubt standard," the Court declined to address the issue, as its resolution was not necessary to decide the case and because both parties to the case had assumed the validity of the standard. Justice Blackmun, in his dissenting opinion, was even clearer, stating that "this Court has never held that the Board is required by statute to recognize the good-faith doubt defense, and the Board's power to eliminate that defense remains an open question."

Earlier decisions of the Court, too, have recognized that the NLRB applies the good faith doubt test through exercise of its broad discretionary authority, but these decisions have not expressly ruled on its validity or the NLRB's power to amend or eliminate it.

II. *Curtin Matheson*

NLRB v. Curtin Matheson Scientific, Inc. was decided by the United States Supreme Court on April 17, 1990 on writ of certiorari to the United States Court of Appeals for the Fifth Circuit. The Supreme Court reversed the judgment of the court of appeals, holding that the NLRB has discretion to refuse to adopt a presumption that striker replacements oppose the union when evaluating whether an employer has a good faith and objectively based doubt of a union's continued majority support.

The *Curtin Matheson* action arose when the collective bargaining agreement between a Teamsters Union local ("Union") and the employer expired on May 21, 1979. A strike began on June 12. The Union ended its strike on July 16, offering to accept the employer's May 25 final contract offer. Four days later, the employer informed the Union that its May 25 offer was no longer available, withdrew recognition, and refused to bargain further. On July 20, 1979, when the employer withdrew recognition and refused to bargain further, the bargaining unit consisted of nineteen strikers, twenty-five permanent replacements and five employees who had been crossing the picket line from the beginning of the strike. The NLRB ultimately concluded that the employer's evidence was "insufficient to rebut the presumption of the Union's continuing majority status." Crucial to this determination was the NLRB's adherence to the rationale of its 1987 decision in *Station KKHI* that no presumptions ought be made as to whether or not strike replacements support the Union. The NLRB ordered the employer to bargain with the Union on demand, provide information requested by the Union, to execute an agreement on the terms accepted by the union which had been improperly withdrawn by the employer, and to make employees whole for any losses suffered as a result of the employer's failure to execute a contract . . . .

In an opinion by Justice Marshall, the United States Supreme Court held that the NLRB's refusal to presume that strike replacements opposed the union was rational and consistent with the NLRA and, therefore, reversed the judgment of the Fifth Circuit, remanding for further proceedings . . . .

Justice Marshall's opinion for the Court notes the NLRB has long held that after expiration of a union's one year irrebuttable presumption of majority support, the presumption of majority support may be rebutted by an employer which shows that, at the time it refuses to bargain, "either (1) the union did not in fact enjoy majority support, or (2) the employer had a 'good faith' doubt founded on a sufficient objective basis, of the union's majority support." Justice Marshall then traced the NLRB's checkered history when assessing the union sentiments of employees hired to replace strikers, citing cases arising between 1959 and 1968 that appeared to adopt a presumption that replacements did not support the union, cases arising between 1974 and 1980 that established a presumption that replacements did support the union and, finally, the 1987 *Station KKHI* case in which the NLRB held that it would not apply any presumption regarding the union sentiments of replacements but, rather, would determine their views on a case-by-case basis.

After reviewing the facts and history of the *Curtin Matheson* case, Justice Marshall first discussed the Court's traditional deference to NLRB rules, stating that the Court "will uphold a Board rule as long as it is rational and consistent with the Act . . . even if [the Court] would have formulated a different rule had [the Court] sat on the Board." He noted, too, that even rules that constitute a departure from prior NLRB policy are entitled to deference. Justice Marshall rejected the employer's assertion that the NLRB's approach constituted an "unexplained abandonment of the good faith doubt test," describing the no presumption approach as one that considers the particular circumstances of each strike.

The Court then found the NLRB's no presumption approach to be "rational as an empirical matter." Justice Marshall stated the NLRB could conclude reasonably that in some circumstances replacements may desire union representation, analogizing replacement workers to strikers forced to abandon a strike and cross the picket line due to financial pressures.

In response to arguments that strikers and replacements have diametrically opposed interests because unions will attempt to return strikers to their jobs, thus displacing replacements, Justice Marshall noted that unions do not inevitably demand displacement of all strike replacements, and that much will depend on the extent of union bargaining power. Justice Marshall stated: "Because the circumstances of each strike and the leverage of each union will vary greatly, it was not irrational for the Board to reject the antiunion presumption and adopt a case-by-case approach in determining replacements' union sentiments." The Court approvingly noted the NLRB's willingness to consider as relevant indicia of union support evidence of picket line violence during a strike and attempts by the union to oust replacements. Justice Marshall also stated that even if replacements often may oppose the union, it was not irrational for the NLRB to determine that the probability was not sufficient to justify an antiunion presumption. Further, Justice Marshall noted that the NLRB's approach is supported by the NLRA's policy of achieving industrial peace, because it limits the employer's ability to oust the union and promotes negotiated settlement. In contrast, an antiunion presumption may encourage an employer to avoid bargaining in order to use the strike as a means of removing the union. He also found it "rational for the Board to conclude, then, that adoption of the antiunion presumption could chill employees' exercise of their right to strike." . . . .

IV. The Problem of Inconsistent Adjudication

. . . C. Employer's Petition for Election

Employer-filed petitions for election present another area that has led to inconsistent and illogical results. The NLRB has held that, after expiration of the certification year, an employer may file a petition for election under section 9(c)(1)(B) of the NLRA to test the continued majority status of the incumbent union. Although it would have been possible for the NLRB to limit section 9(c)(1)(B) to initial representation situations rather than expanding it to attack the status of incumbent unions, the Board rejected this approach in its 1949 *In re Whitney's* decision.

In *In re Whitney's*, the employer filed an election petition under section 9(c)(1)(B) and refused to bargain further with the incumbent union upon the expiration of the collective bargaining agreement. The union argued that the employer should not be allowed to file a petition "except 'where one or more hitherto unrecognized labor organizations have presented to him a claim to be recognized.' " The NLRB rejected this contention, treating the union's request for renewal of the contract as "a claim to be recognized" and ordered an election.

Despite the seemingly obvious advantages of the election process, current NLRB policy does not encourage an employer to file an election petition rather than withdrawing recognition unilaterally. Instead, filing an election petition is made to seem equally, if not more, difficult.

Since its 1966 decision in *United States Gypsum Co.*, the NLRB has held that an employer petitioning for election where there is an incumbent union must (1) establish the union's claim for continued recognition; and (2) "demonstrate by objective considerations that it has some reasonable grounds for believing that the union has lost its majority status since its certification."

After analyzing the legislative history of the 1947 amendment to the NLRA, the NLRB's opinion was that Congress, in enacting section 9(c)(1)(B), did not intend to allow an employer, acting without good faith doubt of a union's majority status, to repeatedly obtain elections. In the NLRB's view, to do so would disrupt collective bargaining and frustrate industrial stability.

Several commentators have attacked this situation and argued that the test for obtaining an election should be relaxed to more readily enable an employer that doubts a union's status to file its own petition for election. This proposal has a certain surface appeal. An election would surely be more reliable, and the costs to all that accompany the delay of unfair labor practice proceedings could be minimized. When the test for obtaining an election is the same as the test for withdrawing recognition, however, the employer has little incentive for an election.

Despite the obvious logic of this approach, it attacks the wrong side of the equation. The problem is not with *United States Gypsum Co.*, which protects industrial stability and employees' rights to continued representation from frivolous and unfounded attack. It should not be easy for an employer to obtain an election based on its alleged doubts when Congress has clearly given the employees themselves the right to file a decertification petition and protect their rights without any interference from the employer.

Thus, the blame for the inconsistency and the irrationality of having the same test for obtaining elections and for withdrawing recognition does not lie with the sensible restrictions the NLRB has placed on the election petition but, rather, with those rules which allow an employer to withdraw recognition on the basis of good faith doubt. If the NLRB chooses to interpret section 9(c)(1)(B) to allow an employer to file an election petition to test an incumbent union's majority status, there is no reason to allow the employer the alternative of testing the union's status through lengthy and unpredictable unfair labor practice proceedings . . . .

ALLENTOWN MACK SALES AND SERVICES, INC. v. NLRB
522 U.S. 359 (1998)

Justice Scalia delivered the opinion of the Court.

Under longstanding precedent of the National Labor Relations Board, an employer who believes that an incumbent union no longer enjoys the support of a majority of its employees has three options: to request a formal, Board-supervised election, to withdraw recognition from the union and refuse to bargain, or to conduct an internal poll of employee support for the union. The Board has held that the latter two are unfair labor practices unless the employer can show that it had a "good-faith reasonable doubt" about the union's majority support . . . .

I

Mack Trucks, Inc., had a factory branch in Allentown, Pennsylvania, whose service and parts employees were represented by Local Lodge 724 of the International Association of Machinists and Aerospace Workers, AFL-CIO (Local 724). Mack notified its Allentown managers in May 1990 that it intended to sell the branch, and several of those managers formed Allentown Mack Sales & Service, Inc., the petitioner here, which purchased the assets of the business on December 20, 1990, and began to operate it as an independent dealership. From December 21, 1990, to January 1, 1991, Allentown hired 32 of the original 45 Mack employees.

During the period before and immediately after the sale, a number of Mack employees made statements to the prospective owners of Allentown Mack Sales suggesting that the incumbent union had lost support among employees in the bargaining unit. In job interviews, eight employees made statements indicating, or at least arguably indicating, that they personally no longer supported the union. In addition, Ron Mohr, a member of the union's bargaining committee and shop steward for the Mack Trucks service department, told an Allentown manager that it was his feeling that the employees did not want a union, and that "with a new company, if a vote was taken, the Union would lose." And Kermit Bloch, who worked for Mack Trucks as a mechanic on the night shift, told a manager that the entire night shift (then five or six employees) did not want the union.

On January 2, 1991, Local 724 asked Allentown Mack Sales to recognize it as the employees' collective-bargaining representative, and to begin negotiations for a contract. The new employer rejected that request by letter dated January 25, claiming a "good faith doubt as to support of the Union among the employees." . . .

II

Allentown challenges the Board's decision in this case on several grounds . . . . Second, Allentown argues that the record evidence clearly demonstrates that it had a good-faith reasonable doubt about the union's claim to majority support. Finally, it asserts that the Board has, *sub silentio* (and presumably in violation of law), abandoned the "reasonable doubt" prong of its polling standard, and recognizes an employer's "reasonable doubt" only if a majority of the unit employees renounce the union . . . .

III

. . . [W]e must clear up some semantic confusion. The Board asserted at argument that the word "doubt" may mean either "uncertainty" or "disbelief," and that its polling standard uses the word only in the latter sense. We cannot accept that linguistic revisionism. "Doubt" is precisely that sort of "disbelief" (failure to believe) which consists of an uncertainty rather than a belief in the opposite. If the subject at issue were the existence of God, for example, "doubt" would be the disbelief of the agnostic, not of the atheist. A doubt is an uncertain, tentative, or provisional disbelief. See, *e.g.*, Webster's New International Dictionary 776 (2d ed.1949) (def. 1: "A fluctuation of mind arising from defect of knowledge or evidence; uncertainty of judgment or mind; unsettled state of opinion concerning the reality of an event, or the truth of an assertion, etc."); 1 The New Shorter Oxford English Dictionary 734 (1993) (def. 1: "Uncertainty as to the truth or reality of something or as to the wisdom of a course of action; occasion or room for uncertainty"); American Heritage Dictionary 555 (3d ed.1992) (def. 1: "A lack of certainty that often leads to irresolution").

The question presented for review, therefore, is whether, on the evidence presented to the Board, a reasonable jury could have found that Allentown lacked a genuine, reasonable uncertainty about whether Local 724 enjoyed the continuing support of a majority of unit employees. In our view, the answer is no. The Board's finding to the contrary rests on a refusal to credit probative circumstantial evidence, and on evidentiary demands that go beyond the substantive standard the Board purports to apply.

The Board adopted the ALJ's finding that 6 of Allentown's 32 employees had made "statements which could be used as objective considerations supporting a good-faith reasonable doubt as to continued majority status by the Union." (These included, for example, the statement of Rusty Hoffman that "he did not want to work in a union shop," and "would try to find another job if he had to work with the Union.") The Board seemingly also accepted (though this is not essential to our analysis) the ALJ's willingness to assume that the statement of a seventh employee (to the effect that he "did not feel comfortable with the Union and thought it was a waste of $35 a month,") supported good-faith reasonable doubt of his support for the union-as in our view it unquestionably does. And it presumably accepted the ALJ's assessment that "7 of 32, or roughly 20 percent of the involved employees" was not alone sufficient to create "an objective reasonable doubt of union majority support." The Board did not specify how many express disavowals would have been enough to establish reasonable doubt, but the number must presumably be less than 16 (half of the bargaining unit), since that would establish reasonable *certainty*. Still, we would not say that 20% first-hand-confirmed opposition (even with no countering evidence of union support) is alone enough to *require* a conclusion of reasonable doubt. But there was much more.

For one thing, the ALJ and the Board totally disregarded the effect upon Allentown of the statement of an eighth employee, Dennis Marsh, who said that "he was not being represented for the $35 he was paying." The ALJ, whose findings were adopted by the Board, said that this statement "seems more an expression of a desire for better representation than one for no representation at all." It seems to us that it is, more accurately, simply an expression of dissatisfaction with the union's performance-which *could* reflect the speaker's desire that the union represent him more effectively, but *could also* reflect the speaker's desire to save his $35 and get rid of the union. The statement would assuredly engender an *uncertainty* whether the speaker supported the union, and so could not be entirely ignored.

But the most significant evidence excluded from consideration by the Board consisted of statements of two employees regarding not merely their own support of the union, but support among the work force in general. Kermit Bloch, who worked on the night shift, told an Allentown manager "the entire night shift did not want the Union." The ALJ refused to credit this, because "Bloch did not testify and thus could not explain how he formed his opinion about the views of his fellow employees." Unsubstantiated assertions that other employees do not support the union certainly do not establish *the fact of that disfavor* with the degree of reliability ordinarily demanded in legal proceedings . . . .

Another employee who gave information concerning overall support for the union was Ron Mohr, who told Allentown managers that "if a vote was taken, the Union would lose" and that "it was his feeling that the employees did not want a union." The ALJ again objected irrelevantly that "there is no evidence with respect to how he gained this knowledge." In addition, the Board held that Allentown "could not legitimately rely on [the statement] as a basis for doubting the Union's majority status," because Mohr was "referring to Mack's existing employee complement, not to the individuals who were later hired by [Allentown]." This basis for disregarding Mohr's statements is wholly irrational . . . .

It must be borne in mind that the issue here is not whether Mohr's statement clearly establishes a majority in opposition to the union, but whether it contributes to a reasonable uncertainty whether a majority in favor of the union existed. We think it surely does . . . .

Accepting the Board's apparent (and in our view inescapable) concession that Allentown received reliable information that 7 of the bargaining-unit employees did not support the union, the remaining 25 would have had to support the union by a margin of 17 to 8-a ratio of more than 2 to 1-if the union commanded majority support. The statements of Bloch and Mohr would cause anyone to doubt that degree of support, and neither the Board nor the ALJ discussed any evidence that Allentown should have weighed on the other side . . . . Giving fair weight to Allentown's circumstantial evidence, we think it quite impossible for a rational factfinder to avoid the conclusion that Allentown had reasonable, good-faith grounds to doubt-to be *uncertain about*-the union's retention of majority support.

IV

That conclusion would make this a fairly straightforward administrative-law case, except for the contention that the Board's factfinding here was not an aberration. Allentown asserts that, although "the Board continues to cite the words of the good faith doubt branch of its withdrawal of recognition standard," a systematic review of the Board's decisions will reveal that "it has in practice eliminated the good faith doubt branch in favor of a strict head count." The Board denies (not too persuasively) that it has insisted upon a strict head count, but does defend its factfinding in this case by saying that it has regularly rejected similarly persuasive demonstrations of reasonable good-faith doubt in prior decisions . . . .

It is certainly conceivable that an adjudicating agency might consistently require a particular substantive standard to be established by a quantity or character of evidence so far beyond what reason and logic would require as to make it apparent that the *announced* standard is not *really* the effective one. And it is conceivable that in certain categories of cases an adjudicating agency which purports to be applying a preponderance standard of proof might so consistently demand in fact more than a preponderance, that all should be on notice from its case law that the genuine burden of proof is more than a preponderance. The question arises, then, whether, if that should be the situation that obtains here, we ought to measure the evidentiary support for the Board's decision against the standards consistently applied rather than the standards recited. As a theoretical matter (and leaving aside the question of legal authority), the Board could certainly have raised the bar for . . . withdrawal of recognition by imposing a more stringent requirement than the reasonable-doubt test, or by adopting a formal requirement that employers establish their reasonable doubt by more than a preponderance of the evidence. Would it make any difference if the Board achieved precisely the same result by formally leaving in place the reasonable-doubt and preponderance standards, but consistently applying them as though they meant something other than what they say? We think it would . . . .

Reasoned decisionmaking, in which the rule announced is the rule applied, promotes sound results, and unreasoned decisionmaking the opposite. The evil of a decision that applies a standard other than the one it enunciates spreads in both directions, preventing both consistent application of the law by subordinate agency personnel (notably ALJ's), and effective review of the law by the courts . . . .

Because reasoned decisionmaking demands it, and because the systemic consequences of any other approach are unacceptable, the Board must be required to apply in fact the clearly understood legal standards that it enunciates in principle, such as good-faith reasonable doubt and preponderance of the evidence. Reviewing courts are entitled to take those standards to mean what they say, and to conduct substantial-evidence review on that basis. Even the most consistent and hence predictable Board departure from proper application of those standards will not alter the legal rule by which the agency's factfinding is to be judged.

The Board can, of course, forthrightly and explicitly adopt counterfactual evidentiary presumptions (which are in effect substantive rules of law) as a way of furthering particular legal or policy goals-for example, the Board's irrebuttable presumption of majority support for the union during the year following certification. The Board might also be justified in forthrightly and explicitly adopting a rule of evidence that categorically excludes certain testimony on policy grounds, without reference to its inherent probative value. (Such clearly announced rules of law or of evidentiary exclusion would of course be subject to judicial review for their reasonableness and their compatibility with the Act.) That is not the sort of Board action at issue here, however, but rather the Board's allegedly systematic undervaluation of certain evidence, or allegedly systematic exaggeration of what the evidence must prove . . . . When the Board purports to be engaged in simple factfinding, unconstrained by substantive presumptions or evidentiary rules of exclusion, it is not free to prescribe what inferences from the evidence it will accept and reject, but must draw all those inferences that the evidence fairly demands. "Substantial evidence" review exists precisely to ensure that the Board achieves minimal compliance with this obligation, which is the foundation of all honest and legitimate adjudication.

For the foregoing reasons, we need not determine whether the Board has consistently rejected or discounted probative evidence so as to cause "good-faith reasonable doubt" or "preponderance of the evidence" to mean something more than what the terms connote. The line of precedents relied on by the ALJ and the Court of Appeals could not render irrelevant to the Board's decision, and hence to our review, any evidence that tends to establish the existence of a good-faith reasonable doubt . . . .

We conclude that the Board's "reasonable doubt" test for employer polls is facially rational and consistent with the Act. But the Board's factual finding that Allentown Mack Sales lacked such a doubt is not supported by substantial evidence on the record as a whole. The judgment of the Court of Appeals for the District of Columbia Circuit is therefore reversed, and the case is remanded with instructions to deny enforcement.

LEVITZ FURNITURE CO.
333 N.L.R.B. 717 (2001)

By CHAIRMAN TRUESDALE and MEMBERS LIEBMAN, HURTGEN, and WALSH

In this case we reconsider whether, and under what circumstances, an employer may lawfully withdraw recognition unilaterally from an incumbent union. The Board has long held that an employer may withdraw recognition by showing either that the union has actually lost the support of a majority of the bargaining unit employees or that it has a good-faith doubt, based on objective considerations, of the union's continued majority status. On the same showing of good-faith doubt, an employer may test an incumbent union's majority status by petitioning for a Board-conducted (RM) election, or by polling its employees to ascertain their union sentiments.

The General Counsel, the Charging Party Union, and the AFL-CIO as amicus curiae urge the Board to abandon the *Celanese* rule and prohibit employers from withdrawing recognition except pursuant to the results of a Board-conducted election. They also oppose lowering the standard that employers must meet to obtain RM elections. Employers urge the Board to retain the *Celanese* rule but to lower the standard for processing RM petitions.

While this case was pending, the Supreme Court issued *Allentown Mack Sales & Service v. NLRB*, 522 U.S. 359 (1998), which addressed the Board's good-faith doubt standard. The Court held that maintaining a unitary standard for an employer's withdrawal of recognition, filing an RM petition, and polling its employees was rational, but indicated that the Board also could rationally adopt a nonunitary standard, including, in theory, imposing more stringent requirements for withdrawal of recognition. The Court also held that the Board's "good-faith doubt" standard must be interpreted to permit the employer to act where it has a "reasonable uncertainty" of the union's majority status, rejecting the Board's argument that the standard required a good-faith disbelief of the union's majority support.

In addressing the arguments concerning the *Celanese* rule and the standards for holding RM elections, then, we must take into account the Court's teachings in *Allentown Mack.* In particular, we must avoid the confusion over terminology which the Court identified in our application of the good-faith doubt standard.

After careful consideration, we have concluded that there are compelling legal and policy reasons why employers should not be allowed to withdraw recognition merely because they harbor uncertainty or even disbelief concerning unions' majority status. We therefore hold that an employer may unilaterally withdraw recognition from an incumbent union only where the union has actually lost the support of the majority of the bargaining unit employees, and we overrule *Celanese* and its progeny insofar as they permit withdrawal on the basis of good-faith doubt. Under our new standard, an employer can defeat a postwithdrawal refusal to bargain allegation if it shows, as a defense, the union's actual loss of majority status.

We have also decided to allow employers to obtain RM elections by demonstrating good-faith reasonable *uncertainty* (rather than *disbelief*) as to unions' continuing majority status. We adopt this standard to enable employers who seek to test a union's majority status to use the Board's election procedures — in our view the most reliable measure of union support — rather than the more disruptive process of unilateral withdrawal of recognition . . . .

MEMBER HURTGEN, concurring [opinion omitted].

POST PROBLEM DISCUSSION

1. In one of the earlier employer withdrawal of recognition cases, *Brooks v. NLRB*, 348 U.S. 96 (1954), the union won the election (8 to 5) and was certified by the Board. A week later, a majority of employees (9 of 13) submitted a handwritten letter renouncing their support of the union. Relying on this letter, the employer refused to bargain, and the union brought a Section 8(a)(5) ULP.

The Board found the employer violated Section 8(a)(5) and ordered the employer to bargain with the union. The Ninth Circuit enforced the Board's order. The Supreme Court affirmed the Ninth Circuit. In so holding, the Court reviewed several new rules following the Taft-Hartley Amendments of 1947. First, under Section 9(c)(1)(A) of the Act, employees can petition the Board for a decertification election. Second, under Section 9(c)(1)(B), an employer may petition the Board for an election if it has a good faith doubt as to the continuing majority status of the union or in the face of conflicting claims of majority status by rival unions. Finally,

Section 9(c)(3) makes clear that after a valid certification or decertification election, the Board cannot order a second election within one year (discussed in Section 1 above as the "election bar").

Based on these amendments, the Court found that an employer is precluded from refusing to bargain with a union certified as the employee's representative after a valid election, even if the employer has doubt as to the union's majority status. In other words, the Court established an irrebuttable presumption of majority status in the first year following a Board-certified election. This is known as the "certification bar" and unlike the "election bar," is recognized as a matter of case law.

After the certification year is over, the employer may request an election or refuse to bargain under the new *Levitz* standards. In other words, after the certification year, there is only a rebuttable presumption of continuing majority status. The contract bar also sets up an irrebuttable presumption, and that presumption only becomes rebuttable after the first three years of the collective-bargaining agreement.

Historically, an employer could overcome the presumption of continuing majority status by affirmatively proving that the union has lost majority support *or* by showing that their refusal to bargain was based on "good-faith and reasonably grounded doubt of the union's continued majority status." Further, the employer's doubt had to be based on "objective considerations," and the employer's refusal must not have been intended "to undermine the union." Essentially, this standard means that the employer's refusal to continue to recognize the union must be advanced free of employer ULPs.

2. In *NLRB v. Curtin Matheson Scientific, Inc.*, 494 U.S. 775 (1990), discussed in Dean Ray's excerpt above, the Supreme Court addressed whether the Board should presume that striker replacements would not support the union, in determining whether an employer had reasonable doubt as to the union's continuing majority status. As will be discussed in Chapter 9, a striker replacement is a person who is hired to replace union workers who are on strike.

The Court upheld the Board's determination that, as a matter of policy, an antiunion presumption would impair the union's right to strike and no universal generalizations can be made about replacement workers' sentiments that would justify a presumption for or against the union. Why does the Court say no generalizations can be made in this situation? What is the threat to union representation if the antiunion presumption for striker replacements were adopted? One objection is that if the presumption were adopted, the employer could hire more replacements than strikers, which would destroy majority support of the union. If this happened, a strike would essentially be an illusory economic weapon.

3. In *Allentown Mack*, the Supreme Court determined that a reasonable jury could not have found that Allentown Mack lacked a "genuine, reasonable uncertainty" about the union's continuing majority support. Therefore, the Court overturned the Board finding to the contrary because, according to the Court, the Board failed to properly weigh the relevant evidence. Prior to *Allentown Mack*, an employer's "good faith doubt" had to be "based on objective considerations." Under

this new standard, all the employer needs is a "genuine reasonable uncertainty" to withdraw recognition. Is there a meaningful difference between the two standards?

Justice Breyer dissented on this point, because he disagreed with the Court's upheaval of the good faith doubt with objective consideration standard, which he argued has been uniformly applied for a number of decades. Instead, he maintained that the new standard makes it easier for an employer to withdraw recognition. He also argued the majority is substituting its judgment for that of the Board's, instead of affording the Board proper deference under administrative law deference standards.

4. Not happy with the *Allentown Mack* decision, the Board revisited the good faith doubt standard in *Levitz Furniture*. There, the Board adopted a different and more demanding standard for unilateral withdrawal of recognition of an incumbent union than for the filing of an employer petition. This move again corresponds with the Board's preference for elections.

More specifically, the Board overruled the "good faith doubt" standard for unilaterally withdrawals, and held "an employer may unilateral withdraw recognition from an incumbent union only where the union has actually lost the support of the majority of the bargaining unit employees," (or in other words, the employer must have objective evidence in fact). The burden rests on the employer to overcome the presumption of continuing majority support. How can the Board disagree with the Supreme Court? Is this permissible? Does it matter that this was a Board-created standard in the first place?

Following the Supreme Court's lead in *Allentown Mack*, the Board in *Levitz Furniture* lowered the standard needed for filing an employer decertification petition to "reasonable uncertainty" as to majority support. "Reasonable uncertainty" can be established by anti-union petitions and firsthand statements. Employee statements about other employee's views are also accepted. Do you think this type of evidence is reliable enough to throw a stable industrial relationship into turmoil?

5. Although excerpted out of the *Allentown Mack* case, there is also an issue when an employer wishes to take a poll of its employees to determine whether the union still maintains majority support (polling was discussed previously in Chapter 5). Under *Allentown Mack*, good faith doubt is sufficient to justify an employer's polling of employees. Although *Levitz Furniture*, as discussed above, abandoned the "good faith doubt" standard and created a higher standard (objective evidence in fact) for unilateral withdrawal of recognition, the Board expressly left open whether the *Allentown Mack* uncertainty standard would continue to control whether an employer might poll their employees on union beliefs. As discussed in Chapter 5, it appears that the NLRB is still using the good faith doubt standard, but it is unclear whether that practice will continue. *See Wisconsin Porcelain, Inc.*, 349 N.L.R.B. 151, 151 & n.4 (2007).

6. Although it appeared at one point that the Bush Board was ready to reconsider its *Levitz Furniture* decision, *see* Paul M. Secunda, *Withdrawal of Union Recognition Standard About to Change?* Workplace Prof Blog (Aug. 24, 2007), http://lawprofessors.typepad.com/laborprof_blog/2007/08/withdrawal-of-u.

html, the standard has not yet been overturned. This might have been because the D.C. Circuit soon thereafter upheld the *Levitz Furniture* withdrawal of recognition standard in *Highlands Hospital Corp. v. NLRB*, 508 F.3d 28 (D.C. Cir. 2007).

7. The remedy for an improper withdrawal of recognition was discussed by the D.C. Circuit in *Caterair International v. NLRB*, 22 F.3d 1114 (D.C. Cir. 1994). In that case, evidence existed that management had exercised pervasive influence in procuring employee signatures for a union decertification petition. Although the court found the employer conduct to be unlawful, it found that a Board order affirmatively requiring the employer to bargain with the union and barring union decertification was inappropriate. In coming to this conclusion, the court distinguished between a cease and desist order and an affirmative bargaining order:

> Although it might to the layman seem like lawyerly overkill to require Caterair simultaneously to cease refusing to bargain *and* to bargain upon request, the cease and desist and affirmative bargaining orders have very different legal and practical consequences. We have previously recognized that an affirmative bargaining order is an "extreme remedy," because according to time-honored Board practice it comes accompanied by a decertification bar that prevents employees from challenging the Union's majority status for at least "a reasonable period." The statute does not mandate that a decertification bar accompany a bargaining order, and the Supreme Court has neither required nor disclaimed its use. Nor do we. However, the Board has long followed the practice of distinguishing between affirmative bargaining orders on the one hand and remedial cease and desist orders that have the effect of compelling bargaining on the other, requiring a decertification bar for a reasonable period of time in the former, but not the latter, context.

> Despite its employee-protective effects in certain circumstances, for example in safeguarding a fragile union against the lingering effects of massive employer coercion, a decertification bar, whatever its duration, also prevents employees from exercising their right to dislodge the union however their sentiments about it may change. Decertification bars thus touch at the very heart of employees' rights under the National Labor Relations Act, and may have the effect of squelching, albeit temporarily, the right of employees "to form, join, or assist labor organizations [and] to bargain collectively through representatives of their own choosing." Because "effectuating ascertainable employee free choice [is] as important a goal as deterring employer misbehavior," we have consistently required some indication from the Board that it has engaged in that "balancing which is an essential component of any valid exercise of discretion" of employee rights against union protection before imposing an affirmative bargaining order.

Id. at 1121–22. Because the Board in *Caterair* did not undertake the requisite balancing, the court remanded back to the Board the issue of whether the affirmative bargaining order was appropriate. On remand, the Board concluded:

> [W]e reaffirm our longstanding policy that an affirmative bargaining order is the standard appropriate remedy for the restoration of the status

quo after an employer's unlawful withdrawal of recognition from an incumbent union and subsequent refusal to bargain. Furthermore, having once considered and balanced the critical statutory policies and rights relevant to this remedy, we find no need to engage in a case-by-case factual analysis to justify its imposition. Finally, we shall adhere to our traditional multifactor test for determining the "reasonable period of time" for protected bargaining in each case.

See Caterair International, 322 N.L.R.B. 64 (1996).

Chapter 7

EXCLUSIVITY AND THE DUTY TO BARGAIN IN GOOD FAITH

Synopsis

Although all unfair labor practices are integral to the NLRA's policies, if you were forced to choose the one that best epitomized the purposes underlying the statute, it would be the duty to bargain. That duty embodies the NLRA's goal of "encouraging practices fundamental to the friendly adjustment of industrial disputes arising out of differences as to wages, hours, or other working conditions, and by restoring equality of bargaining power between employers and employees." Section 1 of the NLRA.

The provisions enforcing the duty to bargain are Section 8(a)(5), which makes it an unfair labor practice for an employer "to refuse to bargain collectively with the representatives of his employees," and Section 8(b)(3), which imposes the same duty on unions "to bargain collectively with an employer." Duty to bargain cases will always cite Sections 8(a)(5) or (b)(3), but the real analysis come from Section 8(d), which defines the duty "to bargain collectively." We'll take a more thorough look at that definition later in this chapter, but the basic duty to bargain is defined by Section 8(d) as "the mutual obligation of the employer and the representative to meet at reasonable times and confer in good faith with respect to wages, hours, and other terms and conditions of employment."

This duty to bargain in good faith is deceptively straightforward. For instance, what does "wages, hours, and other terms and conditions of employment" cover? In Chapter 8, we'll explore that issue, which goes to the *topics* that parties must bargain over. But first, we'll address the *process* of bargaining. In other words, assuming that a covered (or "mandatory") topic is on the table, did the parties bargain over it in good faith? Don't let the "process" description fool you — these questions go to the heart of the NLRA's vision of labor relations.

SECTION 1   DIRECT DEALING

Look again at Section 8(a)(5). Notice that it describes an employer's duty to bargain "with the representatives of his employees." Section 8(d) says something similar by framing the duty to bargain as an obligation "of the employer and the representative." But did you notice that someone is missing? The employees. Because employees' interests are paramount in bargaining, their substitution with a union may strike you as odd, but it shouldn't. The NLRA intended for employees' duly selected representative to be just that, their representative. For a union to beveffective, it must be able to deal with the employer on its own, without being undermined by other parties purporting to represent the interests of employees.

This type of representation is referred to as "exclusive representation," which is guaranteed by Section 9(a), excerpted below. This exclusivity can seem unfamiliar to many law students — and lawyers — who are often more accustomed to discussing individual rights. But exclusive, collective representation is a defining characteristic of labor law. To see why, read on.

PROBLEM #1: ARE YOU READY FOR SOME KICKBALL?

The National Kickball League ("NKL") is an entity that oversees a national league of separately owned professional kickball teams. For the first few years of the league's existence, each player had a separate one-year employment agreement with each team. These agreements shared much in common, although in some instances there were significant variations regarding pay and other work conditions, such as guarantees for playing time. As the league became more successful, the players felt that they were not enjoying as much of the revenue as they deserved. Ultimately, several players helped form an independent union, the National Kickball League Players Association (NKLPA). A contentious campaign followed, but eventually the NLRB held an election in which a bare majority of players from every team chose the NKLPA to represent them.

Soon after the election, the NKLPA asked the league, which was representing the teams in their dealings with the union, to begin negotiations for a collective-bargaining agreement. The league stated that the teams would be happy to bargain, but would not discuss any subjects that were covered by the players' individual agreements until they expired, which would occur in nine months. The union responded by filing a charge alleging that the refusal to bargain over those subjects violated Section 8(a)(5).

The individual agreements finally expired while the charge was pending at the NLRB and the league, true to its word, began bargaining with the union. However, a group of star players who had strongly opposed the union in the election were dissatisfied with the union's bargaining strategy. In particular, they believed that the union showed too much willingness to allow a salary cap that would reduce the highest-paid players' salaries. Ultimately, these players disclaimed any interest in union representation and asked to bargain their own agreements with their teams.

As you read the following material, consider how the league should respond to the star players and the union's unfair labor practice charge. Pay special attention to *why* the NLRA provides the answer that is does and what that answer says about American labor law generally.

PROBLEM MATERIALS

Section 9(a) of the NLRA, 29 U.S.C. § 259(a)

James J. Brudney, *A Famous Victory: Collective Bargaining Protections and the Statutory Aging Process*, 74 N.C. L. REV. 939 (1996)

Emporium Capwell Co. v. Western Addition Community Organization, 420 U.S. 50 (1975)

SECTION 9(A) OF THE NLRA
29 U.S.C. § 259(a)

[Exclusive representatives; employees' adjustment of grievances directly with employer] Representatives designated or selected for the purposes of collective bargaining by the majority of the employees in a unit appropriate for such purposes, shall be the exclusive representatives of all the employees in such unit for the purposes of collective bargaining in respect to rates of pay, wages, hours of employment, or other conditions of employment: *Provided*, That any individual employee or a group of employees shall have the right at any time to present grievances to their employer and to have such grievances adjusted, without the intervention of the bargaining representative, as long as the adjustment is not inconsistent with the terms of a collective-bargaining contract or agreement then in effect: *Provided further*, That the bargaining representative has been given opportunity to be present at such adjustment.

James J. Brudney, *A Famous Victory: Collective Bargaining Protections and the Statutory Aging Process*
74 N.C. L. REV. 939 (1996)[1]

. . . 1. A Novel Emphasis on Collective Bargaining

When Congress passed the Wagner Act in 1935, it set forth a national labor policy shaped heavily by the economic exigencies of the times. In the midst of a major depression, the Act announced a policy of "encouraging the practice and procedure of collective bargaining" in order to achieve certain overriding legislative goals. [Section 1 of the NLRA.] Statutory recognition for collective bargaining was meant to address the twin objectives of promoting industrial peace and restoring mass purchasing power, objectives that were linked closely to prevailing ideas about how to achieve national economic recovery.

Faced with industrial unrest on a large if not unprecedented scale, the Wagner Act's chief proponents contended that federal protection for collective bargaining would reduce the costly effects of conflict between management and workers. While labor-management disputes were regarded as inevitable, proponents viewed government facilitation of the collective bargaining process as creating a more nearly equal balance of power that would channel many of these disputes into negotiated solutions.

Collective bargaining also was central to the Act's declared effort to address the underconsumption that was exacerbating the business depression. Leading supporters in Congress maintained that increases in mass purchasing power were essential to the short-term revival and long-term health of the economy. The growth of collective bargaining would produce substantial economic improvement for workers, which in turn would help the nation to spend its way out of the depression.

In addition to improving the country's economic future, the enforceable recognition of collective bargaining was justified as promoting basic fairness and as democratizing the workplace. Supporters insisted that protecting employees' freedom to organize and bargain collectively was "a matter of simple justice" needed to offset employers' concentration of economic power.[2] Senator Wagner, pointing to recent government-sanctioned increases in industrial combinations, urged that "[i]n order that the strong may not take advantage of the weak, every group must be equally strong."[3] Proponents also extolled the virtues of industrial democracy, drawing support from the analogous political right to representation. By providing for workers' voices to be part of industrial decisionmaking, the bill furthered the "inherent" American right of democratic self-government in the workplace, and thereby effectively discouraged more extreme challenges to the social order.

These four major legislative goals — reducing industrial strife, restoring mass purchasing power, promoting a fairer distribution of economic resources, and furthering self-government by employees — did not receive equal billing in the congressional debates leading up to enactment of the NLRA. While disputes persist as to the priority and weight that should be given to each goal in understanding the Act's meaning, what is important for present purposes is that all four goals were predicated on the virtues of collective action in the workplace. To be sure, achieving the status of a collectively bargained agreement redounds to the benefit of individual workers, insofar as it offers them greater economic rewards and participatory opportunities. But the Act's emphasis on the collective nature of this negotiated status entailed a subordination of traditional individualistic perspectives.

Statutory recognition of collectively bargained terms and conditions of employment meant that individuals gave up their contractual freedom to negotiate their own job conditions. The enforceable nature of this recognition meant — again departing from traditional contract law — that employers were compelled to bargain in good faith with this collectively constituted entity. The recognized primacy of collective bargaining also supplanted historical notions that individuals should take moral and legal responsibility for decisionmaking in the economic arena.

---

[2] [n.26] Hearings Before the Committee on Education and Labor on S. 1958, 74th Cong., 1st Sess. 126 [hereinafter Hearings] (statement of Lloyd K. Garrison, Dean of The University of Wisconsin Law School and former chair of pre-NLRA National Labor Relations Board), reprinted in 1 Legis. Hist., supra note 22, at 1505–06 . . . .

[3] [n.27] Hearings, supra note 26, at 34–35, reprinted in 1 Legis. Hist., supra note 22, at 1410–11 . . . .

The creation of collectively defined rights and responsibilities for the nation's private workplaces was a novel development in federal labor law, only dimly foreshadowed by earlier federal interventions. At the same time, the shift in emphasis toward collective decisionmaking and collective responsibility was part of a broader change in federal policy that extended to other aspects of the economy as part of the New Deal. The National Industrial Recovery Act (NIRA) inaugurated a system of "fair competition" codes, formulated by trade associations and other industry groups to regulate trade practices and certain minimum working standards. By suspending the enforcement of antitrust laws, Congress in the NIRA eschewed traditional notions of competition among individual firms, and instead embraced collective action by businesses to set prices and control production.

Similarly, the Agricultural Adjustment Acts of 1933 and 1938 (AAA) authorized the Secretary of Agriculture to sanction collective action by farmers and agricultural processors in lieu of free market competition among individual producers. . . . The federal government's active promotion of co-determination by various economic subgroups marked a major policy change from the pre-New Deal orientation toward individual self-determination in the economic arena. . . .

The bill that became the Wagner Act originally identified four employer unfair labor practices but did not prohibit employer refusals to bargain collectively with the employees' designated representative. Senator Wagner explained the omission by stating that the employees' explicit right to organize and bargain collectively imposed an implicit duty on the employer to bargain with the employees' chosen representative, and that the absence of an explicit unfair labor practice was due simply to "the difficulty of setting forth this matter precisely in statutory language."[4] Undaunted by the problems associated with drafting an enforceable duty to bargain, supporters of the bill pushed for such language to be added. During the hearings, Francis Biddle, chair of the current nonstatutory labor board, proposed to add a fifth employer unfair labor practice . . . . Testimony from Biddle and others who had served on the labor board emphasized the practical necessity of an explicit employer obligation if the new law was to foster genuine efforts by employers to reach an agreement through collective bargaining. The Biddle amendment was adopted by both Senate and House committees and incorporated into the Act; its language, now in section 8(a)(5), remains unchanged to this day. . . .

[Professor Brudney next describes his empirical study, which found that appellate courts were much less likely to uphold NLRB orders in cases involving an employer's argument that it had good faith doubt as to the union's majority status (see Chapter 6) and an affirmative bargaining order to remedy an employer's unlawful refusal to bargain with a union. Professor Brudney explains this divergence as "a persistent conflict in values. The Board gives primary weight to preserving the stability of bargaining relationships, or establishing those relationships, based on earlier evidence of majority employee support. By contrast, the courts tend to worry more about the risk of retaining, or imposing, a representative that current employees may not want."]

---

[4] [n.48] Hearings, supra note 26, at 43 (statement of Sen. Wagner), reprinted in 1 Legis. Hist., supra note 22, at 1419 . . . .

EMPORIUM CAPWELL CO. v. WESTERN ADDITION COMMUNITY ORGANIZATION
420 U.S. 50 (1975)

Opinion of the Court by MR. JUSTICE MARSHALL.

. . . This litigation presents the question whether, in light of the national policy against racial discrimination in employment, the National Labor Relations Act protects concerted activity by a group of minority employees to bargain with their employer over issues of employment discrimination. The National Labor Relations Board held that the employees could not circumvent their elected representative to engage in such bargaining. The Court of Appeals for the District of Columbia Circuit reversed and remanded, holding that in certain circumstances the activity would be protected . . . . We now reverse.

The Emporium Capwell Co. (Company) operates a department store in San Francisco. At all times relevant to this litigation it was a party to the collective-bargaining agreement negotiated by the San Francisco Retailer's Council, of which it was a member, and the Department Store Employees Union (Union) which represented all stock and marking area employees of the Company. The agreement, in which the Union was recognized as the sole collective-bargaining agency for all covered employees, prohibited employment discrimination by reason of race, color, creed, national origin, age, or sex, as well as union activity. It had a no-strike or lockout clause, and it established grievance and arbitration machinery for processing any claimed violation of the contract, including a violation of the antidiscrimination clause.

On April 3, 1968, a group of Company employees covered by the agreement met with the secretary-treasurer of the Union, Walter Johnson, to present a list of grievances including a claim that the Company was discriminating on the basis of race in making assignments and promotions. The Union official agreed to take certain of the grievances and to investigate the charge of racial discrimination. He appointed an investigating committee and prepared a report on the employees' grievances, which he submitted to the Retailer's Council and which the Council in turn referred to the Company. The report described "the possibility of racial discrimination" as perhaps the most important issue raised by the employees and termed the situation at the Company as potentially explosive if corrective action were not taken. . . .

Shortly after receiving the report, the Company's labor relations director met with Union representatives and agreed to "look into the matter" of discrimination and see what needed to be done. Apparently unsatisfied with these representations, the Union held a meeting in September attended by Union officials, Company employees, and representatives of the California Fair Employment Practices Committee (FEPC) and the local anti-poverty agency. The secretary-treasurer of the Union announced that the Union had concluded that the Company was discriminating, and that it would process every such grievance through to arbitration if necessary. Testimony about the Company's practices was taken and transcribed by a court reporter, and the next day the Union notified the Company of its formal charge and demanded that the joint union-management Adjustment Board be convened "to hear the entire case."

At the September meeting some of the Company's employees had expressed their view that the contract procedures were inadequate to handle a systemic grievance of this sort; they suggested that the Union instead begin picketing the store in protest. Johnson explained that the collective agreement bound the Union to its processes and expressed his view that successful grievants would be helping not only themselves but all others who might be the victims of invidious discrimination as well. The FEPC and antipoverty agency representatives offered the same advice. Nonetheless, when the Adjustment Board meeting convened on October 16, James Joseph Hollins, Tom Hawkins, and two other employees whose testimony the Union had intended to elicit refused to participate in the grievance procedure. Instead, Hollins read a statement objecting to reliance on correction of individual inequities as an approach to the problem of discrimination at the store and demanding that the president of the Company meet with the four protestants to work out a broader agreement for dealing with the issue as they saw it. The four employees then walked out of the hearing.

Hollins attempted to discuss the question of racial discrimination with the Company president shortly after the incidents of October 16. The president refused to be drawn into such a discussion but suggested to Hollins that he see the personnel director about the matter. Hollins, who had spoken to the personnel director before, made no effort to do so again. Rather, he and Hawkins and several other dissident employees held a press conference on October 22 at which they denounced the store's employment policy as racist, reiterated their desire to deal directly with "the top management" of the Company over minority employment conditions, and announced their intention to picket and institute a boycott of the store. On Saturday, November 2, Hollins, Hawkins, and at least two other employees picketed the store throughout the day and distributed at the entrance handbills urging consumers not to patronize the store.[5] Johnson encountered the picketing employees, again urged them to rely on the grievance process, and warned that they might be fired for their activities. The pickets, however, were not dissuaded, and they continued to press their demand to deal directly with the Company president.

On November 7, Hollins and Hawkins were given written warnings that a repetition of the picketing or public statements about the Company could lead to

---

[5] [n.2] The full text of the handbill read:

"* * * BEWARE * * * BEWARE * * * BEWARE * * *'EMPORIUM SHOPPERS 'Boycott Is On' 'Boycott Is On' 'Boycott Is On' For years at The Emporium black, brown, yellow and red people have worked at the lowest jobs, at the lowest levels. Time and time again we have seen intelligent, hard working brothers and sisters denied promotions and respect. 'The Emporium is a 20th Century colonial plantation. The brothers and sisters are being treated the same way as our brothers are being treated in the slave mines of Africa. 'Whenever the racist pig at The Emporium injures or harms a black sister or brother, they injure and insult all black people. THE EMPORIUM MUST PAY FOR THESE INSULTS. Therefore, we encourage all of our people to take their money out of this racist store, until black people have full employment and are promoted justly through out The Emporium. 'We welcome the support of our brothers and sisters from the churches, unions, sororities, fraternities, social clubs, Afro-American Institute, Black Panther Party, W.A.C.O. and the Poor Peoples Institute.'

their discharge. When the conduct was repeated the following Saturday, the two employees were fired.

Western Addition Community Organization (hereinafter respondent), a local civil rights association of which Hollins and Hawkins were members, filed a charge against the Company with the National Labor Relations Board. . . . After a hearing, the NLRB Trial Examiner found that the discharged employees had believed in good faith that the Company was discriminating against minority employees, and that they had resorted to concerted activity on the basis of that belief. He concluded, however, that their activity was not protected by [Section] 7 of the Act and that their discharges did not, therefore, violate [Section] 8(a)(1).

The Board, after oral argument, adopted the findings and conclusions of its Trial Examiner and dismissed the complaint. Among the findings adopted by the Board was that the discharged employees' course of conduct "was no mere presentation of a grievance but nothing short of a demand that the (Company) bargain with the picketing employees for the entire group of minority employees."

The Board concluded that protection of such an attempt to bargain would undermine the statutory system of bargaining through an exclusive, elected representative, impede elected unions' efforts at bettering the working conditions of minority employees, "and place on the Employer an unreasonable burden of attempting to placate self-designated representatives of minority groups while abiding by the terms of a valid bargaining agreement and attempting in good faith to meet whatever demands the bargaining representative put forth under that agreement."[6] . . .

[The Court of Appeals] was of the view that concerted activity directed against racial discrimination enjoys a "unique status by virtue of the national labor policy against discrimination, as expressed in both the NLRA, and in Title VII of the Civil Rights Act of 1964, and that the Board had not adequately taken account of the necessity to accommodate the exclusive bargaining principle of the NLRA to the national policy of protecting action taken in opposition to discrimination from employer retaliation." The court recognized that protection of the minority-group concerted activity involved in this case would interfere to some extent with the orderly collective-bargaining process, but it considered the disruptive effect on that process to be outweighed where protection of minority activity is necessary to full and immediate realization of the policy against discrimination. In formulating a standard for distinguishing between protected and unprotected activity, the majority held that the "Board should inquire, in cases such as this, whether the union was actually remedying the discrimination to the fullest extent possible, by the most expedient and efficacious means. Where the union's efforts fall short of this high standard, the minority group's concerted activities cannot lose (their) section 7 protection." . . .

---

[6] [n.6] The Board considered but stopped short of resolving the question of whether the employees' invective and call for a boycott of the Company bespoke so malicious an attempt to harm their employer as to deprive them of the protection of the Act. The Board decision is therefore grounded squarely on the view that a minority group member may not bypass the Union and bargain directly over matters affecting minority employees, and not at all on the tactics used in this particular attempt to obtain such bargaining. . . .

Section 7 affirmatively guarantees employees the most basic rights of industrial self-determination . . . . These are, for the most part, collective rights, rights to act in concert with one's fellow employees; they are protected not for their own sake but as an instrument of the national labor policy of minimizing industrial strife "by encouraging the practice and procedure of collective bargaining." [Section 1.]

Central to the policy of fostering collective bargaining, where the employees elect that course, is the principle of majority rule. If the majority of a unit chooses union representation, the NLRA permits it to bargain with its employer to make union membership a condition of employment, thereby imposing its choice upon the minority. In establishing a regime of majority rule, Congress sought to secure to all members of the unit the benefits of their collective strength and bargaining power, in full awareness that the superior strength of some individuals or groups might be subordinated to the interest of the majority. As a result, "(t)he complete satisfaction of all who are represented is hardly to be expected." Ford Motor Co. v. Huffman, 345 U.S. 330, 338 (1953).

The Court most recently had occasion to re-examine the underpinnings of the majoritarian principle in NLRB v. Allis-Chalmers Mfg. Co., 388 U.S. 175[, 180] (1967) . . . :

> National labor policy has been built on the premise that by pooling their economic strength and acting through a labor organization freely chosen by the majority, the employees of an appropriate unit have the most effective means of bargaining for improvements in wages, hours, and working conditions. The policy therefore extinguishes the individual employee's power to order his own relations with his employer and creates a power vested in the chosen representative to act in the interests of all employees. "Congress has seen fit to clothe the bargaining representative with powers comparable to those possessed by a legislative body both to create and restrict the rights of those whom it represents . . . ." *Steele v. Louisville & N.R. Co.*, 323 U.S. 192, 202. Thus only the union may contract the employee's terms and conditions of employment, and provisions for processing his grievances; the union may even bargain away his right to strike during the contract term . . . .

In vesting the representatives of the majority with this broad power Congress did not, of course, authorize a tyranny of the majority over minority interests. First, it confined the exercise of these powers to the context of a "unit appropriate for the purposes of collective bargaining," i.e., a group of employees with a sufficient commonality of circumstances to ensure against the submergence of a minority with distinctively different interests in the terms and conditions of their employment. Second, it undertook in the 1959 Landrum-Griffin amendments to assure that minority voices are heard as they are in the functioning of a democratic institution. Third, we have held, by the very nature of the exclusive bargaining representative's status as representative of all unit employees, Congress implicitly imposed upon it a duty fairly and in good faith to represent the interests of minorities within the unit. And the Board has taken the position that a union's refusal to process grievances against racial discrimination, in violation of that duty, is an unfair labor practice. Indeed, the Board has ordered a union implicated by a collective-bargaining agreement in discrimination with an employer to propose specific contractual provisions to prohibit racial discrimination.

Against this background of long and consistent adherence to the principle of exclusive representation tempered by safeguards for the protection of minority interests, respondent urges this Court to fashion a limited exception to that principle: employees who seek to bargain separately with their employer as to the elimination of racially discriminatory employment practices peculiarly affecting them, should be free from the constraints of the exclusivity principle of s 9(a). Essentially because established procedures under Title VII or, as in this case, a grievance machinery, are too time consuming, the national labor policy against discrimination requires this exception, respondent argues, and its adoption would not unduly compromise the legitimate interests of either unions or employers.

Plainly, national labor policy embodies the principles of nondiscrimination as a matter of highest priority, and it is a commonplace that we must construe the NLRA in light of the broad national labor policy of which it is a part. These general principles do not aid respondent, however, as it is far from clear that separate bargaining is necessary to help eliminate discrimination. Indeed, as the facts of this litigation demonstrate, the proposed remedy might have just the opposite effect. The collective-bargaining agreement involved here prohibited without qualification all manner of invidious discrimination and made any claimed violation a grievable issue. The grievance procedure is directed precisely at determining whether discrimination has occurred. . . .

The decision by a handful of employees to bypass the grievance procedure in favor of attempting to bargain with their employer, by contrast, may or may not be predicated upon the actual existence of discrimination. An employer confronted with bargaining demands from each of several minority groups would not necessarily, or even probably, be able to agree to remedial steps satisfactory to all at once. Competing claims on the employer's ability to accommodate each group's demands, e.g., for reassignments and promotions to a limited number of positions, could only set one group against the other even if it is not the employer's intention to divide and overcome them. Having divided themselves, the minority employees will not be in position to advance their cause unless it be by recourse seriatim to economic coercion, which can only have the effect of further dividing them along racial or other lines. Nor is the situation materially different where, as apparently happened here, self-designated representatives purport to speak for all groups that might consider themselves to be victims of discrimination. Even if in actual bargaining the various groups did not perceive their interests as divergent and further subdivide themselves, the employer would be bound to bargain with them in a field largely pre-empted by the current collective-bargaining agreement with the elected bargaining representative. . . . The potential for conflict between the minority and other employees in this situation is manifest. With each group able to enforce its conflicting demands — the incumbent employees by resort to contractual processes and the minority employees by economic coercion — the probability of strife and deadlock, is high; the likelihood of making headway against discriminatory practices would be minimal. . . .

[The Court then rejected the argument that Title VII's anti-retaliation provision required an unfair labor practice based on the terminations; according to the Court, a violation of Title VII is to be remedied by that statute and does not mean that the NLRA is necessarily implicated.]

Mr. Justice Douglas, dissenting.

The Court's opinion makes these Union members-and others similarly situated-prisoners of the Union. The law, I think, was designed to prevent that tragic consequence. Hence, I dissent. . . .

The Board has held that the employees were unprotected because they sought to confront the employer outside the grievance process, which was under Union control. The Court upholds the Board, on the view that this result is commanded by the principle of 'exclusive representation' embodied in [Section] 9 of the NLRA. But in the area of racial discrimination the Union is hardly in a position to demand exclusive control, for the employee's right to nondiscriminatory treatment does not depend upon Union demand but is based on the law. . . .

The law should facilitate the involvement of unions in the quest for racial equality in employment, but it should not make the individual a prisoner of the union. While employees may reasonably be required to approach the union first, as a kind of "exhaustion" requirement before resorting to economic protest, they should not be under continued inhibition when it becomes apparent that the union response is inadequate. The Court of Appeals held that the employees should be protected from discharge unless the Board found on remand that the Union had been prosecuting their complaints "to the fullest extent possible, by the most expedient and efficacious means." I would not disturb this standard. Union conduct can be oppressive even if not made in bad faith. The inertia of weak-kneed, docile union leadership can be as devastating to the cause of racial equality as aggressive subversion. Continued submission by employees to such a regime should not be demanded. . . .

POST PROBLEM DISCUSSION

1.   Consider our problem. Given the holding in *Emporium Capwell*, are teams permitted to bargain with the star players? What about the union's initial unfair labor practice charge — was the league on solid ground in refusing to bargain over terms covered by individual agreements? The problem is based on the facts of *J.I. Case Co. v. NLRB*, 321 U.S. 332 (1944). In its decision, the Supreme Court rejected the employer's attempt to avoid bargaining based on its individual agreements with employees. According to the Court:

> Individual contracts no matter what the circumstances that justify their execution or what their terms, may not be availed of to defeat or delay the procedures prescribed by the National Labor Relations Act looking to collective bargaining, nor to exclude the contracting employee from a duly ascertained bargaining unit; nor may they be used to forestall bargaining or to limit or condition the terms of the collective agreement. . . .
>
> It is equally clear since the collective trade agreement is to serve the purpose contemplated by the Act, the individual contract cannot be

effective as a waiver of any benefit to which the employee otherwise would be entitled under the trade agreement. The very purpose of providing by statute for the collective agreement is to supersede the terms of separate agreements of employees with terms which reflect the strength and bargaining power and serve the welfare of the group. Its benefits and advantages are open to every employee of the represented unit, whatever the type or terms of his pre-existing contract of employment.

But it is urged that some employees may lose by the collective agreement, that an individual workman may sometimes have, or be capable of getting, better terms than those obtainable by the group and that his freedom of contract must be respected on that account. We are not called upon to say that under no circumstances can an individual enforce an agreement more advantageous than a collective agreement, but we find the mere possibility that such agreements might be made no ground for holding generally that individual contracts may survive or surmount collective ones. The practice and philosophy of collective bargaining looks with suspicion on such individual advantages.

Id. at 337–38. *J.I. Case*, as well as *Emporium Capwell*, illustrate the prohibition against "direct dealing." By bargaining directly with employees, rather than with the union, the employer violates its duty to bargain in good faith with employees' duly selected representative.

Given the prohibition against direct dealing, how do you account for contract negotiations in sports? All of the major professional sports leagues are unionized, yet all have individual player contracts negotiated by the players' own agents. Is this legal?

2. What exactly did the employees in *Emporium Capwell* do that left them unprotected by the NLRA? Put another way, if you were counseling the employees from the beginning, what would you have suggested they do differently? *See, e.g., East Chicago Rehabilitation Center v. NLRB*, 710 F.2d 397 (7th Cir. 1983) (holding that Section 7 protected a "wildcat strike" — a strike that lacks union approval — where employees did not seek negotiations with their employer).

3. What about Section 9(a)'s proviso? Could the employees in *Emporium Capwell* merely be exercising their "right at any time to present grievances to their employer and to have such grievances adjusted, without the intervention of the bargaining representative, as long as the adjustment is not inconsistent with the terms of a collective-bargaining contract or agreement then in effect"? The Court rejected that argument, holding that:

Respondent [Union] clearly misapprehends the nature of the "right" conferred by this section. The intendment of the proviso is to permit employees to present grievances and to authorize the employer to entertain them without opening itself to liability for dealing directly with employees in derogation of the duty to bargain only with the exclusive bargaining representative, a violation of [Section] 8(a)(5). The Act nowhere protects this "right" by making it an unfair labor practice for an employer to refuse to entertain such a presentation, nor can it be read to authorize resort to economic coercion. . . . If the employees' activity in the present litigation is to be deemed protected, therefore, it must be so by reason of the reading given to the main part of [Section] 9(a), in light of Title VII and the national policy against employment discrimination, and not by burdening the proviso to that section with a load it was not meant to carry.

420 U.S. at 61 n.12

4. "Members-only" bargaining refers to an employer bargaining with a union that represents a minority of workers. Members-only agreements existed in the years soon after the Wagner's Act enactment and are generally thought to be legal, as long as the employer consents. But recently, several unions filed petitions with the NLRB that argued that the NLRA *required* members-only bargaining and asked the Board to promulgate a rule to that effect. *See generally* National Labor Relations Board, Office of the General Counsel, Advice Memorandum, Dick's Sporting Goods, Case No. 6-CA-24821 (Jun. 22, 2006), http://mynlrb.nlrb.gov/link/document.aspx/09031d45800da97d; CHARLES J. MORRIS, THE BLUE EAGLE AT WORK: RECLAIMING DEMOCRATIC RIGHTS IN THE AMERICAN WORKPLACE (2005). The NLRB denied the petitions because of more pressing demands on agency resources, but did not pass judgment on their merits.

5. As a review, what do you think of the issue noted in footnote 6 of *Emporium Capwell*? In other words, do you think the handbill quoted in footnote 2 would create a loyalty problem under *Jefferson Standard*, discussed in Chapter 4?

6. For more on the background of the *Emporium Capwell* case, see Calvin Sharpe, Marion Crane & Reuel Schiller, *The Story of* Emporium Capwell: *Civil Rights, Collective Action, and the Constraints of Union Power, in* LABOR LAW STORIES (Laura J. Cooper & Catherine L. Fisk, eds., 2005).

SECTION 2   BARGAINING TACTICS

It's not always the case that a party openly refuses to bargain with the other. At times, a party may actually engage in discussions. The question is then whether those discussions constitute good faith bargaining. As you might expect, the line between bad faith and good faith bargaining is quite blurry. This is especially true given that neither party has to agree to anything and that labor bargaining can be extremely antagonistic. How much antagonism is allowed will be the focus of our next section.

Two major tactics that often lead to claims of bad faith bargaining are the use of economic pressure and merely going through the motions (or "surface bargaining"). We will first tackle economic pressure.

A.   Economic Pressure

One thing that the NLRA did not do is outlaw economic pressure. Indeed, Section 13 of the NLRA expressly protects employees' right to strike. This reflects the view that economic pressure is often part and parcel of labor relations. That said, there are exceptions. Whether the use of economic pressure during bargaining should be one of those exceptions is our current question.

PROBLEM #2: BY-THE-BOOK

Central Atlanta Power ("CAT Power") is a private company that provides green power, primarily hydroelectric, to residential homes in downtown Atlanta. Among CAT Power's units was a group of employees who provided regular maintenance of power lines and emergency services when trees interfered with a power line. The employees were represented by a union, which was negotiating a new collective-bargaining agreement with the employer.

Although the parties had agreed to numerous terms, they were far apart with regard to several significant issues such as CAT Power's demand for more employee contributions to the company health insurance plan and the union's demand for higher pay. In an attempt to pressure CAT Power, the union implemented a campaign that it called "By-the-Book." The campaign generally encouraged the employees to follow the employer's policies to their letter, even when informal practices were different. Examples from the campaign included: doing exactly, but no more than what they were told; reporting to work at the exact minute they were scheduled; parking work trucks at company facilities at day's end, rather than at home, which slowed their ability to respond to after-hours emergencies; and informing customers of their right to get their meters checked for accuracy. The employees also refused to accept voluntary overtime requests.

CAT Power is alleging that the By-the-Book campaign is an unlawful "slowdown" and is threatening to fire any employee who follows it. Read the following to see whether the employer is justified in its position. One larger issue to contemplate is your view of collective bargaining. Should the NLRB use a strong hand to reign in harsh bargaining tactics or is a more hands-off approach better?

PROBLEM MATERIALS

NLRB v. Insurance Agents' Union, 361 U.S. 477 (1960)

NLRB v. INSURANCE AGENTS' UNION
361 U.S. 477 (1960)

MR. JUSTICE BRENNAN delivered the opinion of the Court.

This case presents an important issue of the scope of the National Labor Relations Board's authority under [Section] 8(b)(3) of the National Labor Relations Act, which provides that "It shall be an unfair labor practice for a labor organization or its agents . . . to refuse to bargain collectively with an employer, provided it is the representative of his employees . . . ." The precise question is whether the Board may find that a union, which confers with an employer with the desire of reaching agreement on contract terms, has nevertheless refused to bargain collectively, thus violating that provision, solely and simply because during the negotiations it seeks to put economic pressure on the employer to yield to its bargaining demands by sponsoring on-the-job conduct designed to interfere with the carrying on of the employer's business

Since 1949 the respondent Insurance Agents' International Union and the

Prudential Insurance Company of America have negotiated collective bargaining agreements covering district agents employed by Prudential in 35 States and the District of Columbia. . . . In January 1956 Prudential and the union began the negotiation of a new contract to replace an agreement expiring in the following March. Bargaining was carried on continuously for six months before the terms of the new contract were agreed upon on July 17, 1956. It is not questioned that, if it stood alone, the record of negotiations would establish that the union conferred in good faith for the purpose and with the desire of reaching agreement with Prudential on a contract.

However, in April 1956, Prudential filed a [Section] 8(b)(3) charge of refusal to bargain collectively against the union. The charge was based upon actions of the union and its members outside the conference room, occurring after the old contract expired in March. The union had announced in February that if agreement on the terms of the new contract was not reached when the old contract expired, the union members would then participate in a "Work Without a Contract" program — which meant that they would engage in certain planned, concerted on-the-job activities designed to harass the company.

A complaint of violation of [Section] 8(b)(3) issued on the charge and hearings began before the bargaining was concluded. It was developed in the evidence that the union's harassing tactics involved activities by the member agents such as these: refusal for a time to solicit new business, and refusal (after the writing of new business was resumed) to comply with the company's reporting procedures; refusal to participate in the company's "May Policyholders' Month Campaign"; reporting late at district offices the days the agents were scheduled to attend them, and refusing to perform customary duties at the offices, instead engaging there in "sit-in-mornings," "doing what comes naturally" and leaving at noon as a group; absenting themselves from special business conferences arranged by the company; picketing and distributing leaflets outside the various offices of the company on specified days and hours as directed by the union; distributing leaflets each day to policyholders and others and soliciting policyholders' signatures on petitions directed to the company; and presenting the signed policyholders' petitions to the company at its home office while simultaneously engaging in mass demonstrations there. . . .

[T]he Board's view is that irrespective of the union's good faith in conferring with the employer at the bargaining table for the purpose and with the desire of reaching agreement on contract terms, its tactics during the course of the negotiations constituted per se a violation of [Section] 8(b)(3). Accordingly, as is said in the Board's brief, "The issue here . . . comes down to whether the Board is authorized under the Act to hold that such tactics, which the Act does not specifically forbid but Section 7 does not protect, support a finding of a failure to bargain in good faith as required by Section 8(b)(3)."

First. The bill which became the Wagner Act included no provision specifically imposing a duty on either party to bargain collectively. Senator Wagner thought that the bill required bargaining in good faith without such a provision. However, the Senate Committee in charge of the bill concluded that it was desirable to include a provision making it an unfair labor practice for an employer to refuse to bargain collectively in order to assure that the Act would achieve its primary objective of requiring an employer to recognize a union selected by his employees as their representative. It was believed that other rights guaranteed by the Act would not be meaningful if the employer was not under obligation to confer with the union in an effort to arrive at the terms of an agreement. . . .

However, the nature of the duty to bargain in good faith thus imposed upon employers by [Section] 8(5) of the original Act [now Section 8(a)(5)] was not sweepingly conceived. The Chairman of the Senate Committee declared: "When the employees have chosen their organization, when they have selected their representatives, all the bill proposes to do is to escort them to the door of their employer and say, 'Here they are, the legal representatives of your employees.' What happens behind those doors is not inquired into, and the bill does not seek to inquire into it." [Senator Walsh, at 79 Cong. Rec. 7660.]

The limitation implied by the last sentence has not been in practice maintained — practically, it could hardly have been — but the underlying purpose of the remark has remained the most basic purpose of the statutory provision. That purpose is the making effective of the duty of management to extend recognition to the union; the duty of management to bargain in good faith is essentially a corollary of its duty to recognize the union. Decisions under this provision reflect this. . . . And as suggested, the requirement of collective bargaining, although so premised, necessarily led beyond the door of, and into, the conference room. The first annual report of the Board declared: "Collective bargaining is something more the mere meeting of an employer with the representatives of his employees; the essential thing is rather the serious intent to adjust differences and to reach an acceptable common ground. . . . The Board has repeatedly asserted that good faith on the part of the employer is an essential ingredient of collective bargaining." [1 N.L.R.B. Ann. Rep., pp. 85–86.] . . . Collective bargaining, then, is not simply an occasion for purely formal meetings between management and labor, while each maintains an attitude of "take it or leave it"; it presupposes a desire to reach ultimate agreement, to enter into a collective bargaining contract. . . .

But at the same time, Congress was generally not concerned with the substantive terms on which the parties contracted. Obviously there is tension between the principle that the parties need not contract on any specific terms and a practical enforcement of the principle that they are bound to deal with each other in a serious attempt to resolve differences and reach a common ground. And in fact criticism of the Board's application of the 'good-faith' test arose from the belief that it was forcing employers to yield to union demands if they were to avoid a successful charge of unfair labor practice. Thus, in 1947 in Congress the fear was expressed that the Board had "gone very far, in the guise of determining whether or not employers had bargained in good faith, in setting itself up as the judge of what concessions an employer must make and of the proposals and counterproposals that he may or may not make." H.R. Rep. No. 245, 80th Cong., 1st Sess., p. 19. Since the Board was not viewed by Congress as an agency which should exercise its powers to arbitrate the parties' substantive solutions of the issues in their bargaining, a check on this apprehended trend was provided by writing the good-faith test of bargaining into [Section] 8(d) of the Act. That section defines collective bargaining as follows:

For the purposes of this section, to bargain collectively is the performance of the mutual obligation of the employer and the representative of the employees to meet at reasonable times and confer in good faith with respect to wages, hours, and other terms and conditions of employment, or the negotiation of an agreement, or any question arising thereunder, and the execution of a written contract incorporating any agreement reached if requested by either party, but such obligation does not compel either party to agree to a proposal or require the making of a concession . . . .

The same problems as to whether positions taken at the bargaining table violate the good-faith test continue to arise under the Act as amended. But it remains clear that [Section] 8(d) was an attempt by Congress to prevent the Board from controlling the settling of the terms of collective bargaining agreements.

Second. At the same time as it was statutorily defining the duty to bargain collectively, Congress, by adding [Section] 8(b)(3) of the Act through the Taft-Hartley amendments, imposed that duty on labor organizations. Unions obviously are formed for the very purpose of bargaining collectively; but the legislative history makes it plain that Congress was wary of the position of some unions, and wanted to ensure that they would approach the bargaining table with the same attitude of willingness to reach an agreement as had been enjoined on management earlier. It intended to prevent employee representatives from putting forth the same "take it or leave it" attitude that had been condemned in management.

Third. It is apparent from the legislative history of the whole Act that the policy of Congress is to impose a mutual duty upon the parties to confer in good faith with a desire to reach agreement, in the belief that such an approach from both sides of the table promotes the over-all design of achieving industrial peace. Discussion conducted under that standard of good faith may narrow the issues, making the real demands of the parties clearer to each other, and perhaps to themselves, and may encourage an attitude of settlement through give and take. The mainstream of cases before the Board and in the courts reviewing its orders, under the provisions fixing the duty to bargain collectively, is concerned with insuring that the parties approach the bargaining table with this attitude. But apart from this essential standard of conduct, Congress intended that the parties should have wide latitude in their negotiations, unrestricted by any governmental power to regulate the substantive solution of their differences.

We believe that the Board's approach in this case-unless it can be defended, in terms of [Section] 8(b)(3), as resting on some unique character of the union tactics involved here-must be taken as proceeding from an erroneous view of collective bargaining. It must be realized that collective bargaining, under a system where the Government does not attempt to control the results of negotiations, cannot be equated with an academic collective search for truth — or even with what might be thought to be the ideal of one. The parties — even granting the modification of views that may come from a realization of economic interdependence — still proceed from contrary and to an extent antagonistic viewpoints and concepts of self-interest. The system has not reached the ideal of the philosophic notion that perfect understanding among people would lead to perfect agreement among them on values. The presence of economic weapons in reserve, and their actual exercise on occasion by the parties, is part and parcel of the system that the Wagner and Taft-Hartley Acts have recognized. Abstract logical analysis might find inconsistency between the command of the statute to negotiate toward an agreement in good faith and the legitimacy of the use of economic weapons, frequently having the most serious effect upon individual workers and productive enterprises, to induce one party to come to the terms desired by the other. But the truth of the matter is that at the present statutory stage of our national labor relations policy, the two factors — necessity for good-faith bargaining between parties, and the availability of economic pressure devices to each to make the other party incline to agree on one's terms — exist side by side. . . .

For similar reasons, we think the Board's approach involves an intrusion into the substantive aspects of the bargaining process-again, unless there is some specific warrant for its condemnation of the precise tactics involved here. The scope of [Section] 8(b)(3) and the limitations on Board power which were the design of [Section] 8(d) are exceeded, we hold, by inferring a lack of good faith not from any deficiencies of the union's performance at the bargaining table by reason of its attempted use of economic pressure, but solely and simply because tactics designed to exert economic pressure were employed during the course of the good-faith negotiations. Thus the Board in the guise of determining good or bad faith in negotiations could regulate what economic weapons a party might summon to its aid. And if the Board could regulate the choice of economic weapons that may be used as part of collective bargaining, it would be in a position to exercise considerable influence upon the substantive terms on which the parties contract. As the parties' own devices became more limited, the Government might have to enter even more directly into the negotiation of collective agreements. Our labor policy is not presently erected on a foundation of government control of the results of negotiations. Nor does it contain a charter for the National Labor Relations Board to act at large in equalizing disparities of bargaining power between employer and union.

Fourth. The use of economic pressure, as we have indicated, is of itself not at all inconsistent with the duty of bargaining in good faith. But in three cases in recent years, the Board has assumed the power to label particular union economic weapons inconsistent with that duty. . . . The Board freely (and we think correctly) conceded here that a "total" strike called by the union would not have subjected it to sanctions under [Section] 8(b)(3), at least if it were called after the old contract, with its no-strike clause, had expired. The Board's opinion in the instant case is not so unequivocal as this concession (and therefore perhaps more logical). But in the light of it and the principles we have enunciated, we must evaluate the claim of the Board to power, under [Section] 8(b)(3), to distinguish among various economic pressure tactics and brand the ones at bar inconsistent with good-faith collective bargaining. We conclude its claim is without foundation.

(a) The Board contends that the distinction between a total strike and the conduct at bar is that a total strike is a concerted activity protected against employer interference by [Sections] 7 and 8(a)(1) of the Act, while the activity at bar is not a protected concerted activity. We may agree arguendo with the Board that this Court's decision in the Briggs-Stratton case, *International Union, U.A.W., A.F. of L., Local 232 v. Wisconsin Employers Relations Board*, 336 U.S. 245, establishes that the employee conduct here was not a protected concerted activity. On this assumption the employer could have discharged or taken other appropriate disciplinary action against the employees participating in these "slow-down," "sit-in," and arguably unprotected disloyal tactics. But surely that a union activity is not protected against disciplinary action does not mean that it constitutes a refusal to bargain in good faith. The reason why the ordinary economic strike is not evidence of a failure to bargain in good faith is not that it constitutes a protected activity but that, as we have developed, there is simply no inconsistency between the application of economic pressure and good-faith collective bargaining. . . . There is little logic in assuming that because Congress was willing to allow employers to use self-help against union tactics, if they were willing to face the economic consequences of its use, it also impliedly declared these tactics unlawful as a matter of federal law. Our problem remains that of construing [Section] 8(b)(3)'s terms, and we do not see how the availability of self-help to the employer has anything to do with the matter.

(b) The Board contends that because an orthodox "total" strike is "traditional" its use must be taken as being consistent with [Section] 8(b)(3); but since the tactics here are not "traditional" or "normal," they need not be so viewed. . . . It may be that the tactics used here deserve condemnation, but this would not justify attempting to pour that condemnation into a vessel not designed to hold it. The same may be said for the Board's contention that these activities, as opposed to a "normal" strike, are inconsistent with [Section] 8(b)(3) because they offer maximum pressure on the employer at minimum economic cost to the union. One may doubt whether this was so here, but the matter does not turn on that. Surely it cannot be said that the only economic weapons consistent with good-faith bargaining are those which minimize the pressure on the other party or maximize the disadvantage to the party using them. The catalog of union and employer weapons that might thus fall under ban would be most extensive.

Fifth. These distinctions essayed by the Board here, and the lack of relationship to the statutory standard inherent in them, confirm us in our conclusion that the judgment of the Court of Appeals, setting aside the order of the Board, must be affirmed. For they make clear to us that when the Board moves in this area, with only [Section] 8(b)(3) for support, it is functioning as an arbiter of the sort of economic weapons the parties can use in seeking to gain acceptance of their bargaining demands. It has sought to introduce some standard of properly "balanced" bargaining power, or some new distinction of justifiable and unjustifiable, proper and "abusive" economic weapons into the collective bargaining duty imposed by the Act. The Board's assertion of power under [Section] 8(b)(3) allows it to sit in judgment upon every economic weapon the parties to a labor contract negotiation employ, judging it on the very general standard of that section, not drafted with reference to specific forms of economic pressure. We have expressed our belief that this amounts to the Board's entrance into the substantive aspects of the bargaining process to an extent Congress has not countenanced.

It is one thing to say that the Board has been afforded flexibility to determine, for example, whether an employer's disciplinary action taken against specific workers is permissible or not, or whether a party's conduct at the bargaining table evidences a real desire to come into agreement. . . . It is quite another matter, however, to say that the Board has been afforded flexibility in picking and choosing which economic devices of labor and management shall be branded as unlawful. . . .

MR. JUSTICE FRANKFURTER, concurring, which MR. JUSTICE HARLAN and MR. JUSTICE WHITTAKER join [opinion omitted].

POST PROBLEM DISCUSSION

1.   Do you think *Insurance Agents* helps the By-the-Book campaign in our problem? In other words, are the employees' actions, often referred to as "work-to-rule" tactics, the same as the slowdown in *Insurance Agents*? When considering that question, remember that there are two sub-issues to address: whether the campaign is protected and whether the campaign is unlawful. What aspects of the campaign are most helpful to the employer's argument that it is both unlawful and unprotected? Are there additional facts that you would like to know? *Cf. Central Illinois Public Service Co.*, 326 N.L.R.B. 928 (1998) (assuming but not deciding, in case upon which the problem was based, that the conduct was protected), *request for review denied sub nom. Electrical Workers Local 702 v. NLRB*, 215 F.3d 11 (D.C. Cir. 2000).

2.   How is it possible that the Court held the slowdown in *Insurance Agents* to be unprotected, but the union managed to avoid an unfair labor practice finding?

3.   Does it make sense that full strikes are protected, but partial strikes are not? Given that partial strikes are often less disruptive and allow the employer to maintain operations, how does the Court defend its position in *Insurance Agents*?

4.   For more background on *Insurance Agents* (and the *Truitt* case in Section 3 of this chapter), see Kenneth G. Dau-Schmidt, *The Story of* Truitt Manufacturing Co. *and* NLRB v. Insurance Agents' International Union: *The Duty To Bargain in Good Faith, in* LABOR LAW STORIES (Laura J. Cooper & Catherine L. Fisk, eds., 2005). Also see Chapters 4 and 9 for more discussion of slowdowns.

B.   Surface Bargaining

Our next bargaining tactic centers on situations in which a party, on the surface, appears to be bargaining. But, upon closer inspection, the party is merely going through the motions and has no real interest in reaching an agreement. These "surface bargaining" cases are among the most difficult to decide because the relevant factors rarely point clearly in one direction or the other. Parties are allowed to bargain hard, and they often do. So trying to separate lawful hard bargaining from unlawful surface bargaining is not easy and often leads reasonable minds to disagree.

PROBLEM #3: DO YOU WANT KETCHUP WITH THAT?

Kondiment King is a company that makes individual packets of ketchup and mustard that are used in fast food restaurants. Recently, Kondiment King's employees voted for union representation in an NLRB-run election and the parties began bargaining for an initial collective-bargaining agreement. The initial meetings did not go well, as Kondiment King's owner repeatedly expressed displeasure with the union, including the statement that "the union's only objective was to collect dues, and I wish there could be another vote because I don't think the employees really want the union." However, after a meeting with his attorney, the owner stopped making similar comments. Yet, the parties could come to little agreement; the union in particular objected to several proposals and positions made by Kondiment King:

- a recognition clause that would state that the employer "recognizes the right of the union to walk away from their obligation to represent the employees after one year from the election and that the employer for one year following the election;"

- a termination date for the agreement that would occur one year after it became effective;

- a management rights clause that would give Kondiment King "sole and exclusive rights" over: hiring, promotions, demotions, layoffs; establishing or adjusting work shifts; transferring or relocating operations; establishing or abolishing job positions; and determining and promulgating workplace policies;

- a clause that would give supervisors final authority to grant raises;

- a proposal that would eliminate sick leave and half of the current paid holidays;

- a refusal to agree to an arbitration system; and

- a refusal to allow dues checkoff.

After reading the following material, ask yourself whether the union had reason to be upset and, if so, which aspects of the bargaining troubled you the most.

PROBLEM MATERIALS

Movie, *Live Nude Girls Unite!* (2000) (documentary that shows difficulties in forming union and negotiating a first contract at San Francisco's Lusty Lady)[7]

NLRB v. American National Insurance Co., 343 U.S. 395 (1952)

Garden Ridge Management, Inc., 347 N.L.R.B. 131 (2006)

NLRB v. AMERICAN NATIONAL INSURANCE CO.
343 U.S. 395 (1952)

Mr. Chief Justice Vinson delivered the opinion of the Court.

This case arises out of a complaint that respondent refused to bargain collectively with the representatives of its employees as required under the National Labor

---

[7] As the name implies, this is not a family-friendly film; however, it is not gratuitously sexual.

Relations Act, as amended.

The Office Employees International Union A.F. of L., Local No. 27, certified by the National Labor Relations Board as the exclusive bargaining representative of respondent's office employees, requested a meeting with respondent for the purpose of negotiating an agreement governing employment relations. At the first meetings, beginning on November 30, 1948, the Union submitted a proposed contract covering wages, hours, promotions, vacations and other provisions commonly found in collective bargaining agreements, including a clause establishing a procedure for settling grievances arising under the contract by successive appeals to management with ultimate resort to an arbitrator.

On January 10, 1949, following a recess for study of the Union's contract proposals, respondent objected to the provisions calling for unlimited arbitration. To meet this objection, respondent proposed a so-called management functions clause listing matters such as promotions, discipline and work scheduling as the responsibility of management and excluding such matters from arbitration. The Union's representative took the position "as soon as (he) heard (the proposed clause)" that the Union would not agree to such a clause so long as it covered matters subject to the duty to bargain collectively under the Labor Act.

Several further bargaining sessions were held without reaching agreement on the Union's proposal or respondent's counterproposal to unlimited arbitration. As a result, the management functions clause was "by-passed" for bargaining on other terms of the Union's contract proposal. On January 17, 1949, respondent stated in writing its agreement with some of the terms proposed by the Union and, where there was disagreement, respondent offered counter-proposals, including a clause entitled "Functions and Prerogatives of Management" along the lines suggested at the meeting of January 10th. The Union objected to the portion of the clause providing:

> The right to select and hire, to promote to a better position, to discharge, demote or discipline for cause, and to maintain discipline and efficiency of employees and to determine the schedules of work is recognized by both union and company as the proper responsibility and prerogative of management to be held and exercised by the company, and while it is agreed that an employee feeling himself to have been aggrieved by any decision of the company in respect to such matters, or the union in his behalf, shall have the right to have such decision reviewed by top management officials of the company under the grievance machinery hereinafter set forth, it is further agreed that the final decision of the company made by such top management officials shall not be further reviewable by arbitration.

At this stage of the negotiations, the National Labor Relations Board filed a complaint against respondent based on the Union's charge that respondent had refused to bargain as required by the Labor Act and was thereby guilty of interfering with the rights of its employees guaranteed by Section 7 of the Act and of unfair labor practices under Sections 8(a)(1) and 8(a)(5) of the Act. While the proceeding was pending, negotiations between the Union and respondent continued with the management functions clause remaining an obstacle to agreement. During the negotiations, respondent established new night shifts and introduced a new system of lunch hours without consulting the Union.

On May 19, 1949, a Union representative offered a second contract proposal which included a management functions clause containing much of the language found in respondent's second counterproposal, quoted above, with the vital difference that questions arising under the Union's proposed clause would be subject to arbitration as in the case of other grievances. Finally, on January 13, 1950, after the Trial Examiner had issued his report but before decision by the Board, an agreement between the Union and respondent was signed. The agreement contained a management functions clause that rendered nonarbitrable matters of discipline, work schedules and other matters covered by the clause. The subject of promotions and demotions was deleted from the clause and made the subject of a special clause establishing a union-management committee to pass upon promotion matters.

While these negotiations were in progress, the Board's Trial Examiner conducted hearings on the Union's complaint. The Examiner held that respondent had a right to bargain for inclusion of a management functions clause in a contract. However, upon review of the entire negotiations, including respondent's unilateral action in changing working conditions during the bargaining, the Examiner found that from and after November 30, 1948, respondent had refused to bargain in a good faith effort to reach agreement. The Examiner recommended that respondent be ordered in general terms to bargain collectively with the Union.

The Board agreed with the Trial Examiner that respondent had not bargained in a good faith effort to reach an agreement with the Union. But the Board rejected the Examiner's views on an employer's right to bargain for a management functions clause and held that respondent's action in bargaining for inclusion of any such clause "constituted, quite (apart from) Respondent's demonstrated bad faith, per se violations of Section 8(a)(5) and (1)." Accordingly, the Board not only ordered respondent in general terms to bargain collectively with the Union, but also included in its order a paragraph designed to prohibit bargaining for any management functions clause covering a condition of employment. . . .

First. The National Labor Relations Act is designed to promote industrial peace by encouraging the making of voluntary agreements governing relations between unions and employers. The Act does not compel any agreement whatsoever between employees and employers. Nor does the Act regulate the substantive terms governing wages, hours and working conditions which are incorporated in an agreement. The theory of the Act is that the making of voluntary labor agreements is encouraged by protecting employees' rights to organize for collective bargaining and by imposing on labor and management the mutual obligation to bargain collectively.

Enforcement of the obligation to bargain collectively is crucial to the statutory scheme. And, as has long been recognized, performance of the duty to bargain requires more than a willingness to enter upon a sterile discussion of union-management differences. . . . The duty to bargain collectively, implicit in the Wagner Act as introduced in Congress, was made express by the insertion of the fifth employer unfair labor practice accompanied by an explanation of the purpose and meaning of the phrase "bargain collectively in a good faith effort to reach an agreement."[8] This understanding of the duty to bargain collectively has been accepted and applied throughout the administration of the Wagner Act by the National Labor Relations Board and the Courts of Appeal.

In 1947, the fear was expressed in Congress that the Board "has gone very far, in the guise of determining whether or not employers had bargained in good faith, in setting itself up as the judge of what concessions an employer must make and of the proposals and counter-proposals that he may or may not make." Accordingly, the Hartley Bill, passed by the House, eliminated the good faith test and expressly provided that the duty to bargain collectively did not require submission of counter-proposals. As amended in the Senate and passed as the Taft-Hartley Act, the good faith test of bargaining was retained and written into Section 8(d) of the National Labor Relations Act. That Section contains the express provision that the obligation to bargain collectively does not compel either party to agree to a proposal or require the making of a concession. . . .

Second. The Board offers in support of the portion of its order before this Court a theory quite apart from the test of good faith bargaining prescribed in Section 8(d) of the Act, a theory that respondent's bargaining for a management functions clause as a counterproposal to the Union's demand for unlimited arbitration was, "per se," a violation of the Act.

Counsel for the Board do not contend that a management functions clause covering some conditions of employment is an illegal contract term. . . . Without intimating any opinion as to the form of management functions clause proposed by respondent in this case or the desirability of including any such clause in a labor agreement, it is manifest that bargaining for management functions clauses is common collective bargaining practice.

If the Board is correct, an employer violates the Act by bargaining for a management functions clause touching any condition of employment without regard to the traditions of bargaining in the particular industry or such other evidence of good faith as the fact in this case that respondent's clause was offered as a counterproposal to the Union's demand for unlimited arbitration. The Board's argument is a technical one for it is conceded that respondent would not be guilty of an unfair labor practice if, instead of proposing a clause that removed some matters from arbitration, it simply refused in good faith to agree to the Union

---

[8] [n. 10] . . . The insertion of Section 8(5) [8(a)(5)] was described by the Senate Committee as follows:

> The committee wishes to dispel any possible false impression that this bill is designed to compel the making of agreements or to permit governmental supervision of their terms. It must be stressed that the duty to bargain collectively does not carry with it the duty to reach an agreement, because the essence of collective bargaining is that either party shall be free to decide whether proposals made to it are satisfactory. But, after deliberation, the committee has concluded that this fifth unfair labor practice should be inserted in the bill. It seems clear that a guarantee of the right of employees to bargain collectively through representatives of their own choosing is a mere delusion if it is not accompanied by the correlative duty on the part of the other party to recognize such representatives as they have been designated (whether as individuals or labor organizations) and to negotiate with them in a bona fide effort to arrive at a collective bargaining agreement. . . .

S. Rep. No.573, 74th Cong., 1st Sess. 12 (1935).

proposal for unlimited arbitration. The argument starts with a finding, not challenged by the court below or by respondent, that at least some of the matters covered by the management functions clause proposed by respondent are "conditions of employment" which are appropriate subjects of collective bargaining under [Section] 8(a)(5), 8(d) and 9(a) of the Act. The Board considers that employer bargaining for a clause under which management retains initial responsibility for work scheduling, a "condition of employment," for the duration of the contract is an unfair labor practice because it is "in derogation of" employees' statutory rights to bargain collectively as to conditions of employment.[9]

Conceding that there is nothing unlawful in including a management functions clause in a labor agreement, the Board would permit an employer to "propose" such a clause. But the Board would forbid bargaining for any such clause when the Union declines to accept the proposal, even where the clause is offered as a counterproposal to a Union demand for unlimited arbitration. Ignoring the nature of the Union's demand in this case, the Board takes the position that employers subject to the Act must agree to include in any labor agreement provisions establishing fixed standards for work schedules or any other condition of employment. An employer would be permitted to bargain as to the content of the standard so long as he agrees to freeze a standard into a contract. Bargaining for more flexible treatment of such matters would be denied employers even though the result may be contrary to common collective bargaining practice in the industry. . . .

Congress provided expressly that the Board should not pass upon the desirability of the substantive terms of labor agreements. Whether a contract should contain a clause fixing standards for such matters as work scheduling or should provide for more flexible treatment of such matters is an issue for determination across the bargaining table, not by the Board. If the latter approach is agreed upon, the extent of union and management participation in the administration of such matters is itself a condition of employment to be settled by bargaining.

Accordingly, we reject the Board's holding that bargaining for the management functions clause proposed by respondent was, per se, an unfair labor practice. Any fears the Board may entertain that use of management functions clauses will lead to evasion of an employer's duty to bargain collectively as to "rates of pay, wages, hours and conditions of employment" do not justify condemning all bargaining for management functions clauses covering any "condition of employment" as per se violations of the Act. The duty to bargain collectively is to be enforced by application of the good faith bargaining standards of Section 8(d) to the facts of each case rather than by prohibiting all employers in every industry from bargaining for management functions clauses altogether.

Third. The court below correctly applied the statutory standard of good faith bargaining to the facts of this case. It held that the evidence, viewed as a whole does not show that respondent refused to bargain in good faith by reason of its bargaining for a management functions clause as a counterproposal to the Union's

---

[9] [n.22] The Board's argument would seem to prevent an employer from bargaining for a "no-strike" clause, commonly found in labor agreements, requiring a union to [forgo] for the duration of the contract the right to strike expressly granted by Section 7 of the Act. . . .

demand for unlimited arbitration. . . . *Affirmed.*

MR. JUSTICE MINTON, with whom MR. JUSTICE BLACK and MR. JUSTICE DOUGLAS join, dissenting:

I do not see how this case is solved by telling the National Labor Relations Board that since some "management functions" clauses are valid (which the Board freely admits), respondent was not guilty of an unfair labor practice in this case. The record is replete with evidence that respondent insisted on a clause which would classify the control over certain conditions of employment as a management prerogative, and that the insistence took the form of a refusal to reach a settlement unless the Union accepted the clause. The Court of Appeals agreed that respondent was "steadfast" in this demand. Therefore, this case is one where the employer came into the bargaining room with a demand that certain topics upon which it had a duty to bargain were to be removed from the agenda-that was the price the Union had to pay to gain a contract. There is all the difference between the hypothetical "management functions" clauses envisioned by the majority and this "management functions" clause as there is between waiver and coercion. No one suggests that an employer is guilty of an unfair labor practice when it proposes that it be given unilateral control over certain working conditions and the union accepts the proposal in return for various other benefits. But where, as here, the employer tells the union that the only way to obtain a contract as to wages is to agree not to bargain about certain other working conditions, the employer has refused to bargain about those other working conditions. There is more than a semantic difference between a proposal that the union waive certain rights and a demand that the union give up those rights as a condition precedent to enjoying other rights. . . .

GARDEN RIDGE MANAGEMENT, INC.
347 N.L.R.B. 131 (2006)

By CHAIRMAN BATTISTA and MEMBERS LIEBMAN and SCHAUMBER

. . . The facts . . . are as follows. The Union was certified as the bargaining representative of the Respondent's employees on April 22, 2002. The parties began negotiations for a collective-bargaining agreement on May 15.[10] They negotiated on 20 occasions over 11 months, reaching tentative agreement on 28 articles. During these negotiations, the Union asked on approximately eight occasions that the Respondent meet with it more frequently. The Respondent refused each of these requests without explaining to the Union why it did not wish to meet more often. The final negotiation session occurred on April 7, 2003. In late April 2003, the Respondent received a petition from its employees indicating that a majority of unit

---

[10] [n.5] The parties reached tentative agreement on articles addressing military leave, contract duration, visitation rights, articles of agreement, recognition, new employees, bulletin boards, funeral/bereavement leave, arbitration, management rights, bonds, jury duty, legality/stability of agreement, grievance procedure, seniority, extra contract agreement, no oral or implied agreement, uniforms, examinations, wage classifications (but no wage rate), wash rooms and lunch rooms, attendance, automatic payroll deposit, election day leave, employee discount, intent and purpose, sick personnel, and substance abuse control.

employees no longer wanted the Union to represent them. Based on the employees' petition, the Respondent withdrew its recognition of the Union on April 25, 2003.

The judge found that the Respondent violated Section 8(a)(5) and (1) by refusing to meet with the Union at reasonable times, by engaging in surface bargaining, and by withdrawing recognition from the Union. . . . As discussed below, we affirm only the judge's finding that the Respondent did not meet at reasonable times as required by Section 8(d), and we shall dismiss the remaining allegations of 8(a)(5) and (1) misconduct.

We agree with the judge . . . that the Respondent violated Section 8(a)(5) by refusing to meet with the Union at reasonable times. The parties met approximately every 3 weeks from the time negotiations began until the last bargaining session in April 2003, for a total of about 20 bargaining sessions. The Union repeatedly requested additional bargaining sessions based on its dissatisfaction with the pace of negotiations, but the Respondent failed to accommodate any of those requests. The Union first requested that the parties meet on a more frequent basis at the fourth bargaining session, held on June 27, when union negotiators stated their concern that the parties were "not getting anywhere" and asked if the Respondent would be willing to meet several days in a row. The Respondent's Chief Negotiator Christopher Antone told the Union that additional meetings would probably not be possible, but that he would check on it.

At the next bargaining session on July 18, union negotiators again asserted that things were moving along too slowly and suggested that the Respondent was stalling the negotiations. The Respondent denied the accusation. During the rest of 2002, the Union continued to press for more frequent bargaining sessions and to express its concern that the parties were not meeting frequently enough to make any progress toward an agreement. For example, in discussing future meeting dates during a meeting on August 15, union negotiator Douglas Ellison told the Respondent that the parties were not meeting enough. On October 29, union negotiator Robert Bridges asked the Respondent if they could "string meeting dates together" because they "were not getting anywhere in negotiations." In all, the Union made such statements to the Respondent during 8 of the 12 bargaining sessions conducted between July and December. The Respondent consistently refused the Union's requests without offering any explanation as to why it could not meet on a more frequent basis. The only comment made to the Union relative to this refusal came from Chief Negotiator Antone at the October 29 bargaining session, where he stated that he enjoyed taking time off between sessions to contemplate what had happened during negotiations. At the hearing, the Respondent proffered no reason for its refusal to meet more often with the Union.

Section 8(d) of the Act requires that an "employer and the representative of the employees . . . meet at reasonable times and confer in good faith with respect to wages, hours, and other terms and conditions of employment . . . ." The Board considers the totality of the circumstances when determining whether a party has satisfied its duty to meet at reasonable times. Our inquiry is not limited to an examination of the number of bargaining sessions held. Here, on balance, we find that the Respondent violated its duty to meet at reasonable times.

We first acknowledge that the Respondent met with the Union on 20 occasions over 11 months and reached agreement on a host of issues. We also acknowledge that, as discussed below, the General Counsel failed to satisfy his burden of proving that the Respondent bargained in bad faith. However, despite the parties' progress in negotiations, significant issues remained outstanding, and the Union made repeated requests in 2002 for more frequent bargaining sessions. The Respondent summarily refused each of these requests without explaining its unwillingness to the Union or the Board. . . . [W]e rely heavily on the Respondent's repeated, unexplained refusals in finding that the Respondent violated its duty under Section 8(d) to meet at reasonable times.[11]

Contrary to the judge and our dissenting colleague, we do not find that the Respondent violated Section 8(a)(5) and (1) by engaging in surface bargaining. Recognizing that this is a close case, we nonetheless find that the General Counsel failed to prove by a preponderance of the evidence that the Respondent did not intend to reach agreement with the Union, an essential aspect of a surface-bargaining allegation. . . .

Good-faith bargaining "presupposes a desire to reach ultimate agreement, to enter into a collective bargaining contract." *NLRB v. Insurance Agents' Union*, 361 U.S. 477, 485 (1960). "The Board's task in cases alleging bad-faith bargaining is the often difficult one of determining a party's intent from the aggregate of its conduct." *Reichhold Chemicals*, 288 N.L.R.B. 69, 69 (1988), *enforcement denied in part on other grounds*, 906 F.2d 719 (D.C. Cir. 1990). "From the context of an employer's total conduct, it must be decided whether the employer is engaging in hard but lawful bargaining to achieve a contract that it considers desirable or is unlawfully endeavoring to frustrate the possibility of reaching agreement." *Public Service Co. of Oklahoma (PSO)*, 334 N.L.R.B. 487 (2001), *enforced*, 318 F.3d 1373 (10th Cir. 2003).

The General Counsel argues that he proved that the Respondent harbored an intent to avoid reaching agreement by introducing evidence of: (1) the content and timing of the Respondent's bargaining proposals; (2) the frequency of the bargaining sessions; and (3) certain precertification statements made by two of the Respondent's officials. We find that the General Counsel failed to satisfy his burden.

The sole proposal relied on by the judge to show unlawful intent was a proposal seeking the Union's agreement to refrain from organizing certain non-bargaining-unit employees. But, as acknowledged by the dissent, the Board has found such

---

[11] [n.7] Under different circumstances, such a frequency of negotiations might satisfy a party's duty to meet at reasonable times. Cf. *Honaker*, 147 N.L.R.B. 1184 (1964) (finding that employer acted lawfully in meeting on 11 occasions over 5 months); *Boaz Carpet*, 280 N.L.R.B. 40 (1986) (finding that employer satisfied its duties under Sec. 8(d) where it met on 13 occasions over 12 months). *Honaker* and *Boaz Carpet* are distinguishable from this case, however. Neither case presented a situation where, as here, the employer refused the union's repeated requests for additional meetings with no apparent basis for the refusal. *Radiator Specialty Co. v. NLRB*, 336 F.2d 495 (4th Cir. 1964), also relied on by the Respondent, is likewise distinguishable. In that case the court overruled the Board's finding of a violation due to the *union's* conduct during negotiations. *Id.* at 500. Noting that the union had engaged in personal attacks on the employer's negotiator, and also had attempted to hinder production and break up meetings, the court found that the employer's continuance of bargaining in spite of the union's conduct demonstrated the employer's good faith. In contrast, there is no evidence or claim that the Union here has engaged in misconduct.

agreements are permissible. Thus, there is nothing unlawful about the Respondent's proposal on this issue and hence nothing which evidences an intent not to reach an agreement.

The General Counsel also argues that the Respondent's management-rights proposals demonstrate an intent to avoid reaching agreement. We disagree. The Respondent proposed a broad management-rights clause. The Union voiced its opposition to several features of the Respondent's proposal. In response, the Respondent modified its proposal to eliminate the objectionable features, while simultaneously informing the Union that it might propose the substance of those features in separate articles. The parties agreed on the language of the management-rights clause that day. Consistent with its notice, the Respondent did propose the separate articles at the next bargaining session. The language that had been objected to was changed. The Respondent's effort to secure agreement, where possible, while voicing its intent not to retreat from the substance of its bargaining position, is not inconsistent with an intent to reach agreement.

There is no basis in the record for our colleague's assertion that the withdrawal of the broader proposal and resubmission of more specific ones was a tactic calculated to stretch out bargaining by revisiting matters that had been resolved. To the contrary, the Union rejected the broad management-rights proposal when it was introduced. In response, the Respondent isolated provisions that the Union found objectionable and removed them, reserving the right to make additional proposals to the clause as negotiations progressed. The judge found that no inference of bad faith could be derived from the substance of the more specific proposals that the Respondent submitted at the next bargaining session. These new proposals cannot fairly be compared, as our colleague suggests, to the tactics of "pretending to concede on some matter particularly objectionable to the Union, while retaining essentially the same provision in another clause in the Respondent's overall contract proposal (or transferring the provision to another clause)." *Prentice Hall, Inc.*, 290 N.L.R.B. 646, 646 (1988). With fair notice before its prompt submission of the more narrowly tailored proposals, no inference of slight-of-hand gamesmanship is warranted. Nor has it been shown that the change to the more narrowly tailored proposals created "additional challenges to reaching agreement." Our colleague can only assert that they "may well have" done so.

We decline to infer an intent to avoid reaching agreement from the Respondent's failure to meet more frequently. As stated above, the Respondent negotiated with the Union on 20 occasions over 11 months and reached agreement on significant issues. Though we found, above, that the Respondent's refusals to meet more frequently violated its duty to meet at reasonable times, we did so in large part because they were unexplained. We do not think that the frequency of bargaining sessions warrants an inference of unlawful motive in this case.

Section 8(d) requires a party to "meet at reasonable times" and to "confer in good faith." The former obligation refers to the frequency of meetings under the circumstances; the latter refers to the willingness to reach an accord on bargainable matters that are in dispute. Thus, the fact that a party does not meet with sufficient frequency does not necessarily mean that it does not wish to agree to a contract. In the instant case, the failure to meet is unexplained by the Respondent. Indeed, that is the principal basis on which the violation is premised. But, that is quite different from a finding that the failure to meet more frequently was for the unlawful purpose of avoiding an agreement.

The judge also relied on statements made by two of the Respondent's managers prior to the representation election, as evidence of bad-faith bargaining. Before the Union was certified, a manager asked Human Resources Vice President Kevin Rutherford what the environment would look like if the Union won the election. Rutherford replied that "we would basically tie the union up at the bargaining table and we would not come to an agreement." On a separate occasion before the election, Senior Vice President Dan Ferguson told a manager that, if the Union was voted in, "there's all kinds of things that we could do, and . . . the bargaining would go on and the union is not going to get anything that we don't want to give them." We interpret Ferguson's statement, made to a manager, as indicating nothing more than the fact that the law does not require a party to make concessions or to agree to particular proposals. Rutherford's statement is more troublesome. Ultimately, however, we conclude that Rutherford's statement does not demonstrate that the Respondent simply went through the motions of bargaining, rather than seeking, through bargaining, to reach an agreement. We emphasize that these statements were made during an election campaign, *before* the Union was certified. We also note that the judge found that Ferguson, not Rutherford, "called the shots" during negotiations. Further, agreement was reached during negotiations on many substantive contract provisions. In these circumstances, while we do not condone Rutherford's isolated comment, it is insufficient to satisfy the General Counsel's burden of proof when considered in light of all of the evidence regarding the parties' negotiations. . . .

MEMBER LIEBMAN, dissenting in part.

Because this case involves a new bargaining relationship and negotiations for a first contract, the Board should "exercise special care in monitoring the . . . bargaining process and closely scrutinize behavior which 'reflects a cast of mind against reaching agreement.'" Good-faith bargaining, of course, "presupposes a desire . . . to enter into a collective bargaining contract." *NLRB v. Insurance Agents' Union*, 361 U.S. 477, 485 (1960). Even before the union election had occurred, the Respondent had expressed its intent to engage in surface bargaining. The Respondent followed through on this intent by deliberately frustrating the bargaining process: introducing proposals that were likely to prolong negotiations, while at the same time failing to devote sufficient time to bargaining. Predictably, the Union, which had failed to produce a contract, lost majority support — and by then the Union's certification year, which insulated it from challenges to its representative status, had run out. Failing to grasp the significance of the Respondent's conduct as a whole, the majority finds only that the Respondent unlawfully refused to meet with the Union at reasonable times. While this violation of Section 8(a)(5) was enough, by itself, to taint the Respondent's withdrawal of recognition from the Union (contrary to the majority), the record also demonstrates that the Respondent engaged in surface bargaining.

The Board has recently summarized the test to be applied in surface-bargaining cases like this one:

> In determining whether a party has violated its statutory obligation to bargain in good faith, the Board examines the totality of the party's conduct, both at and away from the bargaining table . . . .

> The Board considers several factors when evaluating a party's conduct for evidence of surface bargaining. These include *delaying tactics*, the nature of the bargaining demands, unilateral changes in mandatory subjects of bargaining, efforts to bypass the union, failure to designate an agent with sufficient bargaining authority, *withdrawal of already-agreed-upon provisions*, and arbitrary scheduling of meetings. It has never been required that a respondent must have engaged in each of those enumerated activities before it can be concluded that bargaining has not been conducted in good faith. . . . [R]ather, a respondent will be found to have violated the Act when its conduct in its entirety reflects an intention on its part to avoid reaching an agreement.

Regency Service Carts, 345 N.L.R.B. No. 44, at ¶ 1-2 (2005) (citations and footnote omitted; emphasis added). The record here, considered in its entirety, establishes that the Respondent never intended to reach an overall agreement with the Union. . . .

Acknowledging that this is a "close case," the majority nevertheless concludes that there is no connection between the Respondent's failure to meet more frequently and the surface-bargaining allegation. But surely the only reasonable inference to draw from the Respondent's failure to meet at reasonable times — a failure that is otherwise entirely unexplained — is that the Respondent did not wish to reach an agreement. The two alleged violations are not separate, but inextricably linked.[12]

Further, as the judge correctly found, the Respondent's continued advancement of proposals that would require protracted negotiations, while at the same time inexplicably and invariably refusing the Union's requests for additional bargaining sessions, demonstrated that the Respondent was not serious about reaching an agreement. . . .

In finding that the Respondent bargained in good faith, the majority cites the number of times the Respondent met with the Union and the number of items tentatively agreed upon, without properly considering the Respondent's overall conduct.

The majority's reliance on the number of times the parties met is hard to understand, given the unanimous finding that the Respondent violated the Act by refusing to meet with the Union at reasonable times. Even more perplexing is the majority's reliance on the claim that the Respondent's refusals to meet more

---

[12] [n.5] The majority is incorrect in suggesting that Sec. 8(d) of the Act itself supports viewing the requirement to "meet at reasonable times" and the requirement to "confer in good faith" as somehow distinct. . . . The "meet" and "confer" requirements must be seen as interrelated components of the statutory duty to bargain collectively. As the facts of this case confirm, the two requirements cannot be separated without undercutting the duty to bargain.

frequently with the Union did not occur during the last several months of negotiations and the period closer to the withdrawal of recognition. The Union's ongoing requests for additional bargaining during the latter half of 2002 were steadfastly disregarded by the Respondent. Surely the Union simply gave up asking, rather than continue to make futile requests. If anything, as noted by the judge, the time periods between negotiation sessions actually *increased* during the final months of negotiations.

Further, although the Respondent and Union tentatively agreed on a number of issues, no agreement was reached on such significant issues as wages and health care. Indeed, the record shows that the parties engaged in few, if any, substantive discussions with regard to these issues. Ultimately, the parties never came close to reaching a collective-bargaining agreement. . . .

In this case, it is the employees who are the true losers. They selected a collective-bargaining representative, but faced a hostile Employer who was determined from the outset never to reach an agreement with the Union. As a result, they understandably lost faith in the collective-bargaining process. But for the Respondent's actions, this would not have happened. Such conduct should not go unremedied. Accordingly, I dissent.

POST PROBLEM DISCUSSION

1.   Do you think that the employer's tactics in our problem crossed the line into surface bargaining? Imagine that you represent the employer, which told you that it wanted to take the hardest stance against the union that it legally could. What, if any, of its tactics would you change? *See Burrows Paper Corp.*, 332 N.L.R.B. 82 (2000) (finding, in case similar to problem, that the employer engaged in surface bargaining). As you are considering this question, remember that although parties must bargain in good faith, Section 8(d) expressly states that "such obligation does not compel either party to agree to a proposal or require the making of a concession."

2.   Broad management rights clauses can signal a surface bargaining problem, especially when combined with a zipper clause (see Chapter 13 for more discussion of zipper clauses). *See Eastern Maine Medical Center v. NLRB*, 658 F.2d 1, 11–12 (1st Cir. 1981). However, as you can see from the *American National Insurance* and *Garden Ridge* cases, the surrounding facts will play a large role in determining whether a management rights proposal will lead to a surface bargaining finding. *See Chevron Oil Co.*, 261 N.L.R.B. 44 (1982) (finding that broad management rights clause was lawful hard bargaining), *enforced sub nom. Oil, Chemical & Atomic Workers v. NLRB*, 701 F.2d 172 (5th Cir. 1983) (Table). Do you agree with the outcome of both of the excerpted cases? If you had to pick one to reverse, which one would it be, and why? How does the management rights clause in our problem compare?

3.   One aspect of the *Burrows* case involved the employer's early proposal to eliminate virtually all current benefits and to bargain from that point. This is similar to comments that employers sometimes make to "bargain from scratch." Should this position be evidence of surface bargaining or merely hard, but lawful, bargaining? *See Shaw's Supermarkets, Inc. v. NLRB*, 884 F.2d 34, 37–41 (1st Cir. 1989)

(providing detailed examination of NLRB precedent in "bargaining from scratch" cases); *cf. TRW-United Greenfield Division v. NLRB*, 637 F.2d 410, 420 (5th Cir. 1981) (holding, in case involving pre-election threats, that " '[b]argaining from scratch' statements are objectionable when, in context, they effectively threaten employees with a loss of existing benefits and leave them with the impression that what they may ultimately receive depends in large measure on what the union can induce the [e]mployer to restore").

4. Consider some other bargaining tactics that, while not being per se violations, should serve as a "red flag" for possible surface bargaining. One that was mentioned in *Garden Ridge* is "regressive bargaining," in which a party backs away from a position that it had proposed or already agreed to. Regressive bargaining can be indicative of bad faith when there is not a good explanation for the reversal. *See San Antonio Machine & Supply Corp. v. NLRB*, 363 F.2d 633, 641 (5th Cir. 1966). Another is an employer's insistence on not having a dues checkoff system, which imposes no significant costs on employers. *See Sweeney & Co. v. NLRB*, 437 F.2d 1127, 1135–35 (5th Cir. 1971). Anti-union comments and contemporaneous unfair labor practices are also a potential problem. *See Bryant & Stratton Business Institute, Inc. v. NLRB*, 140 F.3d 169, 184 (2d Cir. 1998). A case that provides a good analysis of several typical red flags is *NLRB v. A-1 King Size Sandwiches, Inc.*, 732 F.2d 872 (11th Cir. 1984).

What about the one-year term proposed in our problem? One year is shorter than most collective-bargaining agreements, but should it be evidence of bad faith bargaining and why? *See Huck Manufacturing Co.*, 693 F.2d at 1188 (5th Cir. 1982) (holding that "insistence on a contract drafted to expire on the certification anniversary tends to evidence bad faith").

5. Imagine an employer that has a long bargaining history with a union. The employer, tired of initial bargaining sessions that produced more drama than actual negotiation, decided to embark on a new approach. Under this approach, the employer sought to come up with an initial, fair proposal to the union; the employer considered this a firm offer that it would not alter absent new information. Also assume that the vast majority of employees would consider the proposal fair. Did the employer satisfy its duty to bargain in good faith? In *NLRB v. General Electric Co.*, 418 F.2d 736 (2d Cir. 1969), the Second Circuit held that GE's similar "Boulwarism" strategy was unlawful. How do you think the court justified this holding, and do you agree?

6. Does the surface bargaining doctrine unfairly hurt parties that are in a strong bargaining position? If, for instance, an employer bargained with a union in an industry and area with high unemployment, should it be careful not to use all of its power? Or, are there ways for a party bargaining from a position of strength to ensure that it won't face a surface bargaining finding?

7. Of particular concern is a new union's ability to negotiate a so-called "first contract" with an employer. New unions are frequently under severe pressure from employees to provide quick results, but often face significant resistance from employers who just failed in their recent attempt to resist unionization. Add to this the lack of an pre-existing bargaining relationship and it should come as no surprise that most new unions fail to negotiate a first contract within the first couple of years.

See Susan J. T. Johnson, *First Contract Arbitration: Effects on Bargaining and Work Stoppages*, 63 INDUS. & LAB. REL. 585, 585 Table 1 (2010) (finding that between 2000–2004, the percentage of new unions that obtained first contracts within two fiscal years of certification varied from 42% to 45%); JOHN-PAUL FERGUSON & THOMAS A. KOCHAN, SEQUENTIAL FAILURES IN WORKERS' RIGHT TO ORGANIZE 1 (2008) (finding that between 2000–2004, the percentage of new unions that obtained first contracts within one year of certification was 38%, and that only 56% of unions ever negotiate a first contract), *available at* http://www.americanrightsatwork.org/dmdocuments/sequential_failures_in_workers_right_to_organize_3_25_2008.pdf.

The Employee Free Choice Act ("EFCA") tried to address this first contract problem. EFCA would have required negotiations, at a union's request, within ten days of certification. If ninety days of negotiations pass without an agreement, either party would be able to request mediation before the Federal Mediation and Conciliation Service ("FMCS"). Most significantly, if mediation failed after thirty days, then the dispute would go to mandatory arbitration, which would lead to a two-year binding agreement. Mandatory arbitration would have been a major change in NLRA law, as the Supreme Court has long held that the NLRB lacks power to force parties to agree to anything, even as a remedy for a failure to bargain in good faith. *See H.K. Porter Co. v. NLRB*, 397 U.S. 99 (1970) (holding that the NLRB could not order an employer to agree to a dues checkoff provision that it had resisted in bad faith because "allowing the Board to compel agreement when the parties themselves are unable to agree would violate the fundamental premise on which the Act is based — private bargaining under governmental supervision of the procedure alone, without any official compulsion over the actual terms of the contract"). For discussions of EFCA's potential effect on first contract negotiations, see William B. Gould IV, *New Labor Law Reform Variations on an Old Theme: Is the Employee Free Choice Act the Answer?*, 70 LA. L. REV. 1, 17–27 (2009); Catherine L. Fisk & Adam R. Pulver, *First Contract Arbitration and the Employee Free Choice Act*, 70 LA. L. REV. 47 (2009).

EFCA would have also allowed for fines of up to $20,000 for serious unfair labor practices during a union campaign or push for a first contract. Among other things, this new ability to fine would have helped address the NLRB's current refusal to issue "make whole" relief during contract negotiations. *See Ex-Cell-O Corp.*, 185 N.L.R.B. 107 (1970) (refusing to compensate employees based on hypothetical agreement because it would violate *H.K. Porter*). *But see International Union of Electrical, Radio & Machine Workers (Tiidee Products, Inc.) v. NLRB*, 426 F.2d 1243, 1249 (D.C. Cir. 1970) (holding that solely prospective orders may be inadequate in egregious cases and that make-whole relief may be appropriate).

Given the problems inherent in reaching a first contract, do you think a cease and desist order is a sufficient remedy?

SECTION 3   DUTY TO PROVIDE INFORMATION

Our next topic involves a less direct failure to bargain in good faith. Think about if you were a union negotiator bargaining over a new collective-bargaining agreement. Consider what type of information you would need or want to satisfy your duty to bargain on behalf of employees, including perhaps employee records and the company's finances. Often, that information is in the hands of the employer, which may not be keen on giving it to you. This section addresses whether the refusal to provide information to the other side constitutes a failure to bargain in good faith.

PROBLEM #4: A NOTE FROM YOUR DOCTOR

Kondiment King, from Problem #3, eventually settled its differences with the union and signed a collective-bargaining agreement. As part of the agreement's "Excessive Absentee and Tardiness" provision, an employee must provide a doctor's slip for any absence or late arrival that is due to a medical condition. Failure to provide a valid slip will result in a point being awarded; the accumulation of points can lead to various types of disciplinary action.

Zach Lenin was an employee and union steward. He had heard complaints from several employees that Kondiment King was enforcing the doctor slip policy unfairly. For example, one complaint was that some supervisors did not require their friends to provide doctor slips, while other employees were required to do so. In order to determine whether those claims were valid, Lenin asked Kondiment King to provide all of the doctor slips from the previous six months, as well as records of all the sick leave taken over the same time period. The employer's HR Director declined, saying that the doctor slips included confidential medical information and that she would not release them unless the union got signed medical-release forms from each employee with a slip.

Lenin responded by filing a grievance on behalf of the complaining employees; the grievance alleged that the employer violated the collective-bargaining agreement through its uneven enforcement of the doctor slip policy. While the grievance was pending, Lenin e-mailed the HR Director:

> In order to prepare for the grievance, I am requesting a list of the names of all employees who have had doctor slips over the past six months, and copies of each doctor slip for those employees. Doctor slips that have any medical information directly stating diagnosis, treatment, or medication given should have said information blocked out. All other information should be kept intact.

The HR Director responded:

> Your request is denied. If you want slips, you must get a signed authorization from each employee permitting the company to release medical information. Also, providing the doctor slips is a laborious and expensive process. We will undertake that only if the union is willing to pay for it.

Read the following material and determine how the union should respond. As you formulate your answer, ask yourself which party is most looking out for the employees' interests and whether that should matter.

PROBLEM MATERIALS

NLRB v. Truitt Manufacturing Co., 351 U.S. 149 (1956)

Detroit Edison Co. v. NLRB, 440 U.S. 301 (1979)

NLRB v. TRUITT MANUFACTURING CO.
351 U.S. 149 (1956)

MR. JUSTICE BLACK delivered the opinion of the Court.

. . . The question presented by this case is whether the National Labor Relations Board may find that an employer has not bargained in good faith where the employer claims it cannot afford to pay higher wages but refuses requests to produce information substantiating its claim.

The dispute here arose when a union representing certain of respondent's employees asked for a wage increase of 10 cents per hour. The company answered that it could not afford to pay such an increase, it was undercapitalized, had never paid dividends, and that an increase of more than 2 1/2 cents per hour would put it out of business. The union asked the company to produce some evidence substantiating these statements, requesting permission to have a certified public accountant examine the company's books, financial data, etc. This request being denied, the union asked that the company submit "full and complete information with respect to its financial standing and profits," insisting that such information was pertinent and essential for the employees to determine whether or not they should continue to press their demand for a wage increase. A union official testified before the trial examiner that "(W)e were wanting anything relating to the Company's position, any records or what have you, books, accounting sheets, cost expenditures, what not, anything to back the Company's position that they were unable to give any more money." The company refused all the requests, relying solely on the statement that "the information . . . is not pertinent to this discussion and the company declines to give you such information; You have no legal right to such."

On the basis of these facts the National Labor Relations Board found that the company had "failed to bargain in good faith with respect to wages in violation of Section 8(a)(5) of the Act." 110 N.L.R.B. 856. The Board ordered the company to supply the union with such information as would "substantiate the Respondent's position of its economic inability to pay the requested wage increase." The Court of Appeals refused to enforce the Board's order . . . .

The company raised no objection to the Board's order on the ground that the scope of information required was too broad or that disclosure would put an undue burden on the company. Its major argument throughout has been that the information requested was irrelevant to the bargaining process and related to matters exclusively within the province of management. Thus we lay to one side the suggestion by the company here that the Board's order might be unduly burdensome or injurious to its business. In any event, the Board has heretofore taken the position in cases such as this that "It is sufficient if the information is made available in a manner not so burdensome or time consuming as to impede the process of bargaining." [*Old Line Life Ins. Co.*, 96 N.L.R.B. 499, 503; *Cincinnati Steel Castings Co.*, 86 N.L.R.B. 592, 593.] And in this case the Board has held substantiation of the company's position requires no more than "reasonable proof."

We think that in determining whether the obligation of good-faith bargaining has been met the Board has a right to consider an employer's refusal to give information about its financial status. While Congress did not compel agreement between employers and bargaining representatives, it did require collective bargaining in the hope that agreements would result. Section 204(a)(1) of the [LMRA] admonishes both employers and employees to "exert every reasonable effort to make and maintain agreements concerning rates of pay, hours, and working conditions . . . ." In their effort to reach an agreement here both the union and the company treated the company's ability to pay increased wages as highly relevant. The ability of an employer to increase wages without injury to his business is a commonly considered factor in wage negotiations. Claims for increased wages have sometimes been abandoned because of an employer's unsatisfactory business condition; employees have even voted to accept wage decreases because of such conditions.

Good-faith bargaining necessarily requires that claims made by either bargainer should be honest claims. This is true about an asserted inability to pay an increase in wages. If such an argument is important enough to present in the give and take of bargaining, it is important enough to require some sort of proof of its accuracy. And it would certainly not be farfetched for a trier of fact to reach the conclusion that bargaining lacks good faith when an employer mechanically repeats a claim of inability to pay without making the slightest effort to substantiate the claim. . . . This was the position of the Board when the Taft-Hartley Act was passed in 1947 and has been its position ever since. We agree with the Board that a refusal to attempt to substantiate a claim of inability to pay increased wages may support a finding of a failure to bargain in good faith.

The Board concluded that under the facts and circumstances of this case the respondent was guilty of an unfair labor practice in failing to bargain in good faith. We see no reason to disturb the findings of the Board. We do not hold, however, that in every case in which economic inability is raised as an argument against increased wages it automatically follows that the employees are entitled to substantiating evidence. Each case must turn upon its particular facts. The inquiry must always be whether or not under the circumstances of the particular case the statutory obligation to bargain in good faith has been met. Since we conclude that there is support in the record for the conclusion of the Board here that respondent did not bargain in good faith, it was error for the Court of Appeals to set aside the Board's order and deny enforcement.

Reversed.

Mr. Justice Frankfurter, whom Mr. Justice Clark and Mr. Justice Harlan join, concurring in part and dissenting in part.

[Section 8(a)(5) and 8(d)] obligate the parties to make an honest effort to come to terms; they are required to try to reach an agreement in good faith. 'Good faith' means more than merely going through the motions of negotiating; it is inconsistent with a predetermined resolve not to budge from an initial position. But it is not necessarily incompatible with stubbornness or even with what to an outsider may seem unreasonableness. A determination of good faith or of want of good faith normally can rest only on an inference based upon more or less persuasive manifestations of another's state of mind. The previous relations of the parties, antecedent events explaining behavior at the bargaining table, and the course of negotiations constitute the raw facts for reaching such a determination. The appropriate inferences to be drawn from what is often confused and tangled testimony about all this makes a finding of absence of good faith one for the judgment of the Labor Board, unless the record as a whole leaves such judgment without reasonable foundation.

An examination of the Board's opinion and the position taken by its counsel here disclose that the Board did not so conceive the issue of good-faith bargaining in this case. The totality of the conduct of the negotiation was apparently deemed irrelevant to the question; one fact alone disposed of the case. "(I)t is settled law (the Board concluded), that when an employer seeks to justify the refusal of a wage increase upon an economic basis, as did the Respondent herein, good-faith bargaining under the Act requires that upon request the employer attempt to substantiate its economic position by reasonable proof." 110 N.L.R.B. 856.

This is to make a rule of law out of one item — even if a weighty item — of the evidence. There is no warrant for this. . . .

The Labor Board itself has not always approached "good faith" and the disclosure question in such a mechanical fashion. In *Southern Saddlery Co.*, 90 N.L.R.B. 1205, the Board also found that [Section] 8(a)(5) had been violated. But how differently the Board there considered its function.

". . . In applying [the] definition of good faith bargaining to any situation, the Board examines the Respondent's conduct as a whole for a clear indication as to whether the latter has refused to bargain in good faith, and the Board usually does not rely upon any one factor as conclusive evidence that the Respondent did not genuinely try to reach an agreement." 90 N.L.R.B. 1205, 1206.

The Board found other factors in the *Southern Saddlery* case. The employer had made no counter-proposals or efforts to compromise the controversy." Such specific evidence is not indispensable, for a study of all the evidence in a record may disclose a mood indicative of a determination not to bargain. That is for the Board to decide. It is a process of inference-drawing, however, very different from the ultra vires law-making of the Board in this case.

Since the Board applied the wrong standard here, by ruling that Truitt's failure to supply financial information to the union constituted per se a refusal to bargain in good faith, the case should be returned to the Board. There is substantial evidence in the record which indicates that Truitt tried to reach an agreement. It offered a 2 1/2-cent wage increase, it expressed willingness to discuss with the union "at any time the problem of how our wages compare with those of our competition," and it continued throughout to meet and discuss the controversy with the union . . .

To reverse the Court of Appeals without remanding the case to the Board for further proceedings, implies that the Board would have reached the same conclusion in applying the right rule of law that it did in applying a wrong one. I cannot make such a forecast. I would return the case to the Board so that it may apply the relevant standard for determining "good faith."

DETROIT EDISON CO. v. NLRB
440 U.S. 301 (1979)

Mr. Justice Stewart delivered the opinion of the Court.

. . . In this case an employer was brought before the National Labor Relations Board to answer a complaint that it had violated this statutory duty when it refused to disclose certain information about employee aptitude tests requested by a union in order to prepare for arbitration of a grievance. The employer supplied the union with much of the information requested, but refused to disclose three items: the actual test questions, the actual employee answer sheets, and the scores linked with the names of the employees who received them. The Board, concluding that all the items requested were relevant to the grievance and would be useful to the union in processing it, ordered the employer to turn over all of the materials directly to the union, subject to certain restrictions on the union's use of the information. A divided Court of Appeals for the Sixth Circuit ordered enforcement of the Board's order without modification. . . .

This is apparently the first case in which the Board has held that an employer's duty to provide relevant information to the employees' bargaining representative includes the duty to disclose tests and test scores achieved by named employees in a statistically validated psychological aptitude testing program administered by the employer. Psychological aptitude testing is a widely used employee selection and promotion device in both private industry and government. Test secrecy is concededly critical to the validity of any such program, and confidentiality of scores is undeniably important to the examinees. The underlying question is whether the Board's order, enforced without modification by the Court of Appeals, adequately accommodated these concerns.

The petitioner, Detroit Edison Co. (hereinafter Company), is a public utility engaged in the generation and distribution of electric power in Michigan. Since about 1943, the Utility Workers Union of America, Local 223, AFL-CIO (Union) has represented certain of the Company's employees. At the time of the hearing in this case, one of the units represented by the Union was a unit of operating and maintenance employees at the Company's plant in Monroe, Mich. The Union was certified as the exclusive bargaining agent for employees in that unit in 1971, and it was agreed that these employees would be covered by a pre-existing collective-bargaining agreement, one of the provisions of which specified that promotions within a given unit were to be based on seniority "whenever reasonable qualifications and abilities of the employees being considered are not significantly different." Management decisions to bypass employees with greater seniority were subject to the collective agreement's grievance machinery, including ultimate arbitration, whenever a claim was made that the bypass had been arbitrary or discriminatory.

The aptitude tests at issue were used by the Company to screen applicants for the job classification of "Instrument Man B." An Instrument Man is responsible for installing, maintaining, repairing, calibrating, testing, and adjusting the powerplant instrumentation. The position of Instrument Man B, although at the lowest starting grade under the contract and usually requiring on-the-job training, was regarded by the Company as a critical job because it involved activities vital to the operation of the plant. . . .

The Company administered the tests to applicants with the express commitment that each applicant's test score would remain confidential. Tests and test scores were kept in the offices of the Company's industrial psychologists who, as members of the American Psychological Association, deemed themselves ethically bound not to disclose test information to unauthorized persons. Under this policy, the Company's psychologists did not reveal the tests or report actual test numerical scores to management or to employee representatives. The psychologists would, however, if an individual examinee so requested, review the test questions and answers with that individual.

The present dispute had its beginnings in 1971 when the Company invited bids from employees to fill six Instrument Man B openings at the Monroe plant. Ten Monroe unit employees applied. None received a score designated as "acceptable," and all were on that basis rejected. The jobs were eventually filled by applicants from outside the Monroe plant bargaining unit.

The Union filed a grievance on behalf of the Monroe applicants, claiming that the new testing procedure was unfair and that the Company had bypassed senior employees in violation of the collective-bargaining agreement. The grievance was rejected by the Company at all levels, and the Union took it to arbitration. In preparation for the arbitration, the Union requested the Company to turn over various materials related to the Instrument Man B testing program. The Company furnished the Union with copies of test-validation studies performed by its industrial psychologists and with a report by an outside consultant on the Company's entire testing program. It refused, however, to release the actual test battery, the applicants' test papers, and their scores, maintaining that complete confidentiality of these materials was necessary in order to insure the future integrity of the tests and to protect the privacy interests of the examinees.

The Union then filed with the Board the unfair labor practice charge involved in this case. The charge alleged that the information withheld by the Company was relevant and necessary to the arbitration of the grievance, "including the ascertainment of promotion criteria, the veracity of the scoring and grading of the examination and the testing procedures, and the job relatedness of the test(s) to the Instrument Man B classification." . . .

During the course of the arbitration . . . the Company did disclose the raw scores of those who had taken the test, with the names of the examinees deleted. In addition, it provided the Union with sample questions indicative of the types of questions appearing on the test battery and with detailed information about its scoring procedures. It also offered to turn over the scores of any employee who would sign a waiver releasing the Company psychologist from his pledge of confidentiality. The Union declined to seek such releases. . . .

Several months later the Board issued a complaint based on the Union's unfair labor practice charge. At the outset of the hearing before the Administrative Law Judge, the Company offered to turn over the test battery and answer sheets to an industrial psychologist selected by the Union for an independent evaluation, stating that disclosure to an intermediary obligated to preserve test secrecy would satisfy its concern that direct disclosure to the Union would inevitably result in dissemination of the questions. The Union rejected this compromise. . . .

The Board, and the Court of Appeals for the Sixth Circuit in its decision enforcing the Board's order, ordered the Company to turn over all the material directly to the Union. They concluded that the Union should be able to determine for itself whether it needed a psychologist to interpret the test battery and answer sheets. Both recognized the Company's interest in maintaining the security of the tests, but both reasoned that appropriate restrictions on the Union's use of the materials would protect this interest.[13] Neither was receptive to the Company's claim that employee privacy and the professional obligations of the Company's industrial psychologists should outweigh the Union request for the employee-linked scores. . . .

Two issues . . . are presented on this record. The first concerns the Board's choice of a remedy for the Company's failure to disclose copies of the test battery and answer sheets. The second, and related, question concerns the propriety of the Board's conclusion that the Company committed an unfair labor practice when it refused to disclose, without a written consent from the individual employees, the test scores linked with the employee names.

We turn first to the question whether the Board abused its remedial discretion when it ordered the Company to deliver directly to the Union the copies of the test battery and answer sheets. The Company's position, stripped of the argument that it had no duty at all to disclose these materials, is as follows: It urges that disclosure directly to the Union would carry with it a substantial risk that the test questions would be disseminated. Since it spent considerable time and money validating the Instrument Man B tests and since its tests depend for reliability upon the Examinee's lack of advance preparation, it contends that the harm of dissemination would not be trivial. The future validity of the tests is tied to secrecy, and disclosure to employees would not only threaten the Company's investment but would also leave the Company with no valid means of measuring employee aptitude. . . .

In his brief on behalf of the Board, the Solicitor General has acknowledged the existence of a strong public policy against disclosure of employment aptitude tests

---

[13] [n.9] The Board, although it ordered the Company to supply the tests and answer sheets directly to the Union, incorporated by reference the Administrative Law Judge's restrictions on the Union's use of the materials. Under those restrictions, the Union was given the right "to use the tests and the information contained therein to the extent necessary to process and arbitrate the grievances, but not to copy the tests, or otherwise use them for the purpose of disclosing the tests or the questions to employees who have in the past, or who may in the future take these tests, or to anyone (other than the arbitrator) who may advise the employees of the contents of the tests." After the conclusion of the arbitration, the Union was required to return "all copies of the battery of tests" to the Company. The Court of Appeals, in enforcing the Board's order, stated that the "restrictions on use of the materials and obligation to return them to Detroit Edison are part of the decision and order which we enforce." 560 F.2d 722, 726.

. . . . He urges, however, that the Board's order can be justified on the grounds that the Union's institutional interests militate against improper disclosure, and that the specific protective provisions in the Board's order will safeguard the integrity of the tests. . . . We do not find these justifications persuasive.

A union's bare assertion that it needs information to process a grievance does not automatically oblige the employer to supply all the information in the manner requested. The duty to supply information under § 8(a)(5) turns upon "the circumstances of the particular case," *NLRB v. Truitt Mfg. Co.*, 351 U.S., at 153, and much the same may be said for the type of disclosure that will satisfy that duty. Throughout this proceeding, the reasonableness of the Company's concern for test secrecy has been essentially conceded. The finding by the Board that this concern did not outweigh the Union's interest in exploring the fairness of the Company's criteria for promotion did not carry with it any suggestion that the concern itself was not legitimate and substantial. Indeed, on this record-which has established the Company's freedom under the collective contract to use aptitude tests as a criterion for promotion, the empirical validity of the tests, and the relationship between secrecy and test validity-the strength of the Company's concern has been abundantly demonstrated. The Board has cited no principle of national labor policy to warrant a remedy that would unnecessarily disserve this interest, and we are unable to identify one.

It is obvious that the remedy selected by the Board does not adequately protect the security of the tests. The restrictions barring the Union from taking any action that might cause the tests to fall into the hands of employees who have taken or are likely to take them are only as effective as the sanctions available to enforce them. In this instance, there is substantial doubt whether the Union would be subject to a contempt citation were it to ignore the restrictions [because it was not a party to the enforcement proceeding in the Court of Appeals.] . . . Effective sanctions at the Board level are similarly problematic. To be sure, the Board's General Counsel could theoretically bring a separate unfair labor practice charge against the Union, but he could also in his unreviewable discretion refuse to issue such a complaint. Moreover, the Union clearly would not be accountable in either contempt or unfair labor practice proceedings for the most realistic vice inherent in the Board's remedy — the danger of inadvertent leaks. . . . The Board in this case having identified no justification for a remedy granting such scant protection to the Company's undisputed and important interests in test secrecy, we hold that the Board abused its discretion in ordering the Company to turn over the test battery and answer sheets directly to the Union.

The dispute over Union access to the actual scores received by named employees is in a somewhat different procedural posture, since the Company did on this issue preserve its objections to the basic finding that it had violated its duty under § 8(a)(5) when it refused disclosure. The Company argues that even if the scores were relevant to the Union's grievance (which it vigorously disputes), the Union's need for the information was not sufficiently weighty to require breach of the promise of confidentiality to the examinees, breach of its industrial psychologists' code of professional ethics, and potential embarrassment and harassment of at least some of the examinees. The Board responds that this information does satisfy the appropriate standard of "relevance," and that the Company having "unilaterally" chosen to make a promise of confidentiality to the examinees, cannot rely on that promise to defend against a request for relevant information. The professional obligations of the Company's psychologists, it argues, must give way to paramount federal law. Finally, it dismisses as speculative the contention that employees with low scores might be embarrassed or harassed.

We may accept for the sake of this discussion the finding that the employee scores were of potential relevance to the Union's grievance, as well as the position of the Board that the federal statutory duty to disclose relevant information cannot be defeated by the ethical standards of a private group. Nevertheless we agree with the Company that its willingness to disclose these scores only upon receipt of consents from the examinees satisfied its statutory obligations under § 8(a)(5).

The Board's position appears to rest on the proposition that union interests in arguably relevant information must always predominate over all other interests, however, legitimate. But such an absolute rule has never been established,[14] and we decline to adopt such a rule here. There are situations in which an employer's conditional offer to disclose may be warranted. This we believe is one.

The sensitivity of any human being to disclosure of information that may be taken to bear on his or her basic competence is sufficiently well known to be an appropriate subject of judicial notice. There is nothing in this record to suggest that the Company promised the examinees that their scores would remain confidential in order to further parochial concerns or to frustrate subsequent Union attempts to process employee grievances. And it has not been suggested at any point in this proceeding that the Company's unilateral promise of confidentiality was in itself violative of the terms of the collective-bargaining agreement. Indeed, the Company presented evidence that disclosure of individual scores had in the past resulted in the harassment of some lower scoring examinees who had, as a result, left the Company.

Under these circumstances, any possible impairment of the function of the Union in processing the grievances of employees is more than justified by the interests served in conditioning the disclosure of the test scores upon the consent of the very employees whose grievance is being processed. The burden on the Union in this instance is minimal. The Company's interest in preserving employee confidence in the testing program is well founded.

In light of the sensitive nature of testing information, the minimal burden that compliance with the Company's offer would have placed on the Union, and the total absence of evidence that the Company had fabricated concern for employee confidentiality only to frustrate the Union in the discharge of its responsibilities, we

---

[14] [n.14] See *Emeryville Research Center, Shell Development Co. v. NLRB*, 441 F.2d 880 (CA9 1971) (refusal to supply relevant salary information in precise form demanded did not constitute violation of § 8(a)(5) when company's proposed alternatives were responsive to union's need); *Shell Oil Co. v. NLRB*, 457 F.2d 615 (CA9 1975) (refusal to supply employee names without employee consent not unlawful when company had well-founded fear that nonstriking employees would be harassed); cf. *Kroger Co. v. NLRB*, 399 F.2d 455 (CA6 1968) (no disclosure of operating ratio data when, under circumstances, interests of employer predominated); *United Aircraft Corp.*, 192 N.L.R.B. 382, 390 (1971) (employer acted reasonably in refusing to honor generalized request for employee medical records without employee's permission), modified on other grounds, *Machinists v. United Aircraft Corp.*, 534 F.2d 422 (CA2 1975).

are unable to sustain the Board in its conclusion that the Company, in resisting an unconsented-to disclosure of individual test results, violated the statutory obligation to bargain in good faith. Accordingly, we hold that the order requiring the Company unconditionally to disclose the employee scores to the Union was erroneous. . . .

[Opinion of JUSTICE STEVENS, concurring in part and dissenting in part, and the opinion of JUSTICE WHITE, with whom JUSTICE BRENNAN and JUSTICE MARSHALL join, and with whom JUSTICE STEVENS joins as to Part I, dissenting, is omitted.]

POST PROBLEM DISCUSSION

1. Generally, the duty to provide information centers first on an inquiry into whether the information is relevant to the union's duties as the employees' representative. *See Detroit Edison Co. v. NLRB*, 440 U.S. 301, 303 (1979). This has been described as a discovery-type standard in which the union need only show that the "desired information was relevant, and that it would be of use to the union in carrying out its statutory duties and responsibilities." *NLRB v. Acme Industrial Co.*, 385 U.S. 432, 437 (1977) (holding that employer had duty to provide information needed to pursue grievance). If the information is relevant, then the employer has a presumptive duty to provide the information. As seen in *Detroit Edison*, the employer can rebut that presumption by showing that the information is confidential or otherwise involves special circumstances that weighs against disclosure.

A similar standard exists for unions under Section 8(b)(3). An employer can establish relevance by showing that the requested information is needed to fulfill its duties under a collective-bargaining agreement or to monitor the union's compliance with the agreement. *See SEIU, Local 715*, 355 N.L.R.B. No. 65, at 12 (2010); *Local One-L, Amalgamated Lithographers of America*, 352 N.L.R.B. No. 114, at 15–16 (2008) (stating that "[i]nformation pertaining to the terms and conditions of employment of the bargaining unit is presumptively relevant").

2. What about the situation in our problem? Are the employer's refusals to provide the doctor slips lawful? *See Norris, a Dover Resources Co. v. NLRB*, 417 F.3d 1161 (10th Cir. 2005) (holding that the employer unlawfully refused to provide slips with medical information redacted). Assuming that the union was entitled to the slips, can the employer demand payment for gathering the information? *See Tower Books*, 273 N.L.R.B. 671, 671 (1984) (concluding that "the cost and burden of compliance ordinarily will not justify an initial, categorical refusal to supply relevant data, but that '[i]f there are substantial costs involved in compiling the information in the precise form at the intervals requested by the Union, the parties must bargain in good faith as to who shall bear such costs' ") (quoting *Food Employer Council*, 197 N.L.R.B. 651, 651 (1972)), *enforced sub nom. Queen Anne Record Sales, Inc. v. NLRB*, 772 F.2d 913 (9th Cir. 1985) (Table).

3. Looking at another aspect of our problem, assume that the union's first request for the doctor slips was too broad and the employer was justified in its refusal. If the union still wants the information, who has the obligation to suggest an alternative? *See United States Testing Co. v. NLRB*, 160 F.3d 14, 21 (D.C. Cir. 1998) (holding that the employer has the obligation to propose an alternative that would accommodate both confidentiality concerns and the union's need for the information because the employer is "in the better position to propose how best it

can respond to a union request for information"); *Keauhou Beach Hotel*, 298 N.L.R.B. 702, 702 (1990). Do you agree with this obligation?

4. It can be difficult to determine when an employer has made an "inability to pay" claim. After appellate courts resisted the NLRB's initial attempt to apply *Truitt* to situations where the employer argued that lower labor costs were needed to maintain competitiveness, the NLRB moved closer to a "magic words" formulation that requires an employer to provide financial information only when it states that it would be unable to pay for the union's demands during the term of the agreement. *See Nielsen Lithographing Co.*, 305 N.L.R.B. 697 (1991) (Nielsen II), *petition for review denied sub nom. Graphic Communications International Union, Local 508 O-K-I, AFL-CIO v. NLRB*, 977 F.2d 1168 (7th Cir. 1991). In *Nielsen II*, the NLRB explained:

> that an employer's expressed view that its current economic position vis-à-vis competitors would lead to an eventual inability to pay beyond the intended contract term is quite different from an employer's insistence that a union's current bargaining demands are precluded by its condition at the present time or within the intended contract term. . . . The difference between the two types of claims is critical. The employer who claims a present inability to pay, or a prospective inability to pay during the life of the contract being negotiated, is claiming essentially that it cannot pay. By contrast, the employer who claims only economic difficulties or business losses or the prospect of layoffs is simply saying that it does not want to pay.

For a general discussion of the NLRB's approach in this area, see *ConAgra, Inc. v. NLRB*, 117 F.3d 1435, 1436 (D.C. Cir. 1997); *see also* William B. Gould IV, *New Labor Law Reform Variations on an Old Theme: Is the Employee Free Choice Act the Answer?*, 70 LA. L. REV. 1, 21–22 (2009) (criticizing "magic words" analysis); Keith N. Hylton, *An Economic Theory of the Duty To Bargain*, 83 GEO. L.J. 19, 45–49 (1994); Clifford R. Oviatt, Jr., *The Bush NLRB in Perspective: Does the Playing Field Need Leveling?*, 11 HOFSTRA LAB. L.J. 47, 51–56 (1993).

5. Do the NLRB and Court really expect both sides in labor negotiations to make "honest claims"? Do the parties expect the other to do so? Given that much of the NLRA recognizes that bargaining can be an antagonistic process, why not allow for some level of dishonesty? Take an employer's exaggerated claim of financial distress, such as the statement that "if employees aren't willing to contribute $5 more a month for health benefits, I'm not sure we can stay open." Should that be a violation of Section 8(a)(5) or merely be viewed as part of the normal bargaining process?

SECTION 4 IMPASSE

Our final procedural issue delves into situations where the parties appear to be deadlocked, which is referred to as an "impasse." As you will soon see, determining whether negotiations are truly at an impasse substantially affects what the parties can do next.

In a system that requires only a good faith attempt to reach an agreement, rather than an agreement itself, impasse is not an unusual occurrence. Parties can reach a point where, despite their honest efforts, they simply can't come to an agreement; this is the time when we often see strikes and other types of high-profile pressure. But what about the employer's business operations? Can it start implementing decisions that alter work conditions without the union's consent, or does it need to wait until tempers cool and then head back to the bargaining table? The answer can have a profound effect on parties' negotiating strength and strategy.

PROBLEM #5: I'M GOING TO TAKE MY BALL AND GO HOME!

Return to the National Kickball League ("NKL") and National Kickball League Players Association ("NKLPA") from Problem #1. Many years have past and the league is now extremely popular and profitable. The relationship between the NKL and NKLPA has improved as well, and the owners and players have been parties to multiple, successive collective-bargaining agreements. However, the most recent agreement is due to expire soon, and negotiations over a new agreements have become acrimonious.

A central issue in the bargaining was the owners' insistence on a salary cap, which would limit the total amount each team could spend on salaries. This was an attempt by owners to lower costs and make player spending more equitable, but the players strongly opposed the proposal because it would decrease their compensation. Unable to reach a compromise, the players went on strike in August, the middle of the season. The owners responded by cancelling the remainder of the season and negotiations continued through the Fall and Winter.

The players proposed a tax system as an alternative to the salary cap; under the system, the highest-spending teams would pay a "tax" that would be paid to the lowest-spending teams. The owners responded with their own tax plan and many counterproposals were made by both sides. Ultimately, in December, the owners announced that they were making their last, final offer. The union made another counterproposal, which the owners rejected. Despite the union's request, the owners did not make another counteroffer and instead implemented their last offer.

Should the owners have been allowed to stop bargaining and unilaterally implement their proposal? Read on to find out. As you contemplate your answer, ask how the rules in this area affect parties' bargaining strategy.

PROBLEM MATERIALS

NLRB v. Katz, 369 U.S. 736 (1962)

NLRB v. KATZ
369 U.S. 736 (1962)

MR. JUSTICE BRENNAN delivered the opinion of the Court.

Is it a violation of the duty "to bargain collectively" imposed by [Section] 8(a)(5) of the National Labor Relations Act for an employer, without first consulting a union with which it is carrying on bona fide contract negotiations, to institute changes regarding matters which are subjects of mandatory bargaining under [Section] 8(d) and which are in fact under discussion? The National Labor Relations Board answered the question affirmatively in this case, in a decision which expressly disclaimed any finding that the totality of the respondents' conduct manifested bad faith in the pending negotiations. A divided panel of the Court of Appeals for the Second Circuit denied enforcement of the Board's cease-and-desist order, finding in our decision in *National Labor Relations Board v. Insurance Agents' Union*, 361 U.S. 477 [(1960)], a broad rule that the statutory duty to bargain cannot be held to be violated, when bargaining is in fact being carried on, without a finding of the respondent's subjective bad faith in negotiating. . . .

We find nothing in the Board's decision inconsistent with *Insurance Agents* and hold that the Court of Appeals erred in refusing to enforce the Board's order.

The respondents are partners engaged in steel fabricating under the firm name of Williamsburg Steel Products Company. Following a consent election in a unit consisting of all technical employees at the company's plant, the Board, on July 5, 1956, certified as their collective bargaining representative Local 66 of the Architectural and Engineering Guild, American Federation of Technical Engineers, AFL-CIO. The Board simultaneously certified the union as representative of similar units at five other companies which, with the respondent company, were members of the Hollow Metal Door & Buck Association. The certifications related to separate units at the several plants and did not purport to establish a multi-employer bargaining unit. . . . [The parties negotiated on at least eleven different occasions from August 30, 1956 to May 13, 1957. On April 16, 1957, the union filed an unfair labor practice charge, upon which the General Counsel's complaint later issued.]

As amended and amplified at the hearing and construed by the Board, the complaint's charge of unfair labor practices particularly referred to three acts by the company: unilaterally granting numerous merit increases in October 1956 and January 1957; unilaterally announcing a change in sick-leave policy in March 1957; and unilaterally instituting a new system of automatic wage increases during April 1957. As the ensuing litigation has developed, the company has defended against the charges along two fronts: First, it asserts that the unilateral changes occurred after a bargaining impasse had developed through the union's fault in adopting obstructive tactics.[15] According to the Board, however, "the evidence is clear that the Respondent undertook its unilateral actions before negotiations were discontinued in May 1957, or before, as we find on the record, the existence of any possible impasse." 126 N.L.R.B., at 289–290. There is ample support in the record considered as a whole for this finding of fact . . . .

The second line of defense was that the Board could not hinge a conclusion that [Section] 8(a)(5) had been violated on unilateral actions alone, without making a finding of the employer's subjective bad faith at the bargaining table; and that the unilateral actions were merely evidence relevant to the issue of subjective good faith. . . .

The duty "to bargain collectively" enjoined by [Section] 8(a)(5) is defined by [Section] 8(d) as the duty to "meet . . . and confer in good faith with respect to wages, hours, and other terms and conditions of employment." Clearly, the duty thus defined may be violated without a general failure of subjective good faith; for there is no occasion to consider the issue of good faith if a party has refused even to negotiate *in fact* — "to meet . . . and confer" — about any of the mandatory subjects. A refusal to negotiate *in fact* as to any subject which is within [Section] 8(d), and about which the union seeks to negotiate, violates [Section] 8(a)(5) though the employer has every desire to reach agreement with the union upon an over-all collective agreement and earnestly and in all good faith bargains to that end. We hold that an employer's unilateral change in conditions of employment under negotiation is similarly a violation of [Section] 8(a) (5), for it is a circumvention of the duty to negotiate which frustrates the objectives of [Section] 8(a)(5) much as does a flat refusal.

The unilateral actions of the respondent illustrate the policy and practical considerations which support our conclusion.

We consider first the matter of sick leave. A sick-leave plan had been in effect since May 1956, under which employees were allowed ten paid sick-leave days annually and could accumulate half the unused days, or up to five days each year. Changes in the plan were sought and proposals and counterproposals had come up at three bargaining conferences. In March 1957, the company, without first notifying or consulting the union, announced changes in the plan, which reduced from ten to five the number of paid sick-leave days per year, but allowed accumulation of twice the unused days, thus increasing to ten the number of days which might be carried over. This action plainly frustrated the statutory objective

---

[15] [n.7] Particularizations of this charge [include] . . . that the conduct of negotiations by the union created unrest impairing the efficiency of the company's operations and causing valued employees to quit. . . . The unrest seems to have been a concomitant of the assertion by the employees of their rights to organize and negotiate a collective agreement, and could not justify a refusal of the company to bargain, at least in the absence of conduct of the union which amounted to an unfair labor practice. The Examiner rejected the company's offer to prove union-instigated slowdowns. But such proof would not have justified the company's refusal to bargain. Since, as we held in *National Labor Relations Board v. Insurance Agents' Union*, the Board may not brand partial strike activity as illegitimate and forbid its use in support of bargaining, an employer cannot be free to refuse to negotiate when the union resorts to such tactics. Engaging in partial strikes is not inherently inconsistent with a continued willingness to negotiate; and as long as there is such willingness and no impasse has developed, the employer's obligation continues.

of establishing working conditions through bargaining. Some employees might view the change to be a diminution of benefits. Others, more interested in accumulating sick-leave days, might regard the change as an improvement. If one view or the other clearly prevailed among the employees, the unilateral action might well mean that the employer had either uselessly dissipated trading material or aggravated the sick-leave issue. On the other hand, if the employees were more evenly divided on the merits of the company's changes, the union negotiators, beset by conflicting factions, might be led to adopt a protective vagueness on the issue of sick leave, which also would inhibit the useful discussion contemplated by Congress in imposing the specific obligation to bargain collectively.

Other considerations appear from consideration of the respondents' unilateral action in increasing wages. At the April 4, 1957, meeting the employers offered, and the union rejected, a three-year contract with an immediate across-the-board increase of $7.50 per week, to be followed at the end of the first year and again at the end of the second by further increases of $5 for employees earning less than $90 at those times. Shortly thereafter, without having advised or consulted with the union, the company announced a new system of automatic wage increases whereby there would be an increase of $5 every three months up to $74.99 per week; an increase of $5 every six months between $75 and $90 per week; and a merit review every six months for employees earning over $90 per week. It is clear at a glance that the automatic wage increase system which was instituted unilaterally was considerably more generous than that which had shortly theretofore been offered to and rejected by the union. Such action conclusively manifested bad faith in the negotiations, and so would have violated [Section] 8(a)(5) even on the Court of Appeals' interpretation, though no additional evidence of bad faith appeared. An employer is not required to lead with his best offer; he is free to bargain. But even after an impasse is reached he has no license to grant wage increases greater than any he has ever offered the union at the bargaining table, for such action is necessarily inconsistent with a sincere desire to conclude an agreement with the union.[16]

The respondents' third unilateral action related to merit increases, which are also a subject of mandatory bargaining. The matter of merit increases had been raised at three of the conferences during 1956 but no final understanding had been reached. In January 1957, the company, without notice to the union, granted merit increases to 20 employees out of the approximately 50 in the unit, the increases ranging between $2 and $10. This action too must be viewed as tantamount to an outright refusal to negotiate on that subject, and therefore as a violation of [Section] 8(a)(5), unless the fact that the January raises were in line with the company's long-standing practice of granting quarterly or semiannual merit reviews-in effect, were a mere continuation of the status quo-differentiates them from the wage increases and the changes in the sick-leave plan. We do not think it does. Whatever might be the case as to so-called "merit raises" which are in fact simply automatic increases to which the employer has already committed himself, the raises here in

---

[16] [n.12] Of course, there is no resemblance between this situation and one wherein an employer, after notice and consultation, "unilaterally" institutes a wage increase identical with one which the union has rejected as too low. See *National Labor Relations Board v. Bradley Washfountain Co.*, 7 Cir., 192 F.2d 144, 150–152; *National Labor Relations Board v. Landis Tool Co.*, 3 Cir., 193 F.2d 279.

question were in no sense automatic, but were informed by a large measure of discretion. There simply is no way in such case for a union to know whether or not there has been a substantial departure from past practice, and therefore the union may properly insist that the company negotiate as to the procedures and criteria for determining such increases.

It is apparent from what we have said why we see nothing in *Insurance Agents* contrary to the Board's decision. The union in that case had not in any way whatever foreclosed discussion of any issue, by unilateral actions or otherwise. The conduct complained of consisted of partial-strike tactics designed to put pressure on the employer to come to terms with the union negotiators. We held that Congress had not, in [Section] 8(b)(3), the counterpart of [Section] 8(a)(5), empowered the Board to pass judgment on the legitimacy of any particular economic weapon used in support of genuine negotiations. But the Board is authorized to order the cessation of behavior which is in effect a refusal to negotiate, or which directly obstructs or inhibits the actual process of discussion, or which reflects a cast of mind against reaching agreement. Unilateral action by an employer without prior discussion with the union does amount to a refusal to negotiate about the affected conditions of employment under negotiation, and must of necessity obstruct bargaining, contrary to the congressional policy. It will often disclose an unwillingness to agree with the union. It will rarely be justified by any reason of substance. It follows that the Board may hold such unilateral action to be an unfair labor practice in violation of [Section] 8(a)(5), without also finding the employer guilty of over-all subjective bad faith. While we do not foreclose the possibility that there might be circumstances which the Board could or should accept as excusing or justifying unilateral action, no such case is presented here. . . .

POST PROBLEM DISCUSSION

1.   The first step in a case like *Katz* is to determine whether an impasse exists (or second step after determining that the subject of a unilateral change was a mandatory subject of bargaining, as discussed later in Chapter 8). This is a highly fact-specific question that reasonable minds often differ over. In *Taft Broadcasting Co.*, 163 N.L.R.B. 475 (1967), the NLRB listed several factors that would help determine whether there was an impasse or, to put another way, "good-faith negotiations have exhausted the prospects of concluding an agreement":

> Whether a bargaining impasse exists is a matter of judgment. The bargaining history, the good faith of the parties in negotiations, the length of the negotiations, the importance of the issue or issues as to which there is disagreement, the contemporaneous understanding of the parties as to the state of negotiations are all relevant factors to be considered in deciding whether an impasse in bargaining existed.

Id. at 478; *see also Arrow Automotive Industries, Inc.*, 284 N.L.R.B. 487, 490 (1987) (considering whether the parties have treated their proposals as being final), *enforcement denied on other grounds*, 853 F.2d 223 (4th Cir. 1988).

Be aware that it is the position of the NLRB and virtually every appellate court that impasse involves a deadlock over an entire agreement, rather than a single issue. The Fifth Circuit is the lone hold-out on this issue, as it will find an impasse if the employer notifies the union of even a single intended change and gives the union an opportunity to respond. NLRB v. Pinkston-Hollar Construction Services, Inc., 954 F.2d 306, 311–312 (5th Cir. 1992). In *Duffy Tool & Stamping, L.L.C. v. NLRB*, 233 F.3d 995, 998 (7th Cir. 2000) (citing cases), Judge Posner described the split and, in a strong criticism of the Fifth Circuit's "partial impasse" rule, helped explain why the NLRB stands by its view that a total impasse is required:

> The [Fifth Circuit's] position would empty the duty to bargain of meaning, and this in two respects: (1) by removing issues from the bargaining agenda early in the bargaining process, it would make it less likely for the parties to find common ground; (2) by enabling the employer to paint the union as impotent, it would embolden him to hold out for a deal so unfavorable to the union as to preclude agreement.

The full *Duffy Tool* decision is worth reading, as it fleshes out these two points in a way that underscores why the *Katz* rule is an important facet of the duty to bargain.

2. Given the *Taft Broadcasting* test, do you think that the NKL in our problem violated its duty to bargain when it implemented the salary cap? What factors do you find most relevant to your conclusion? Which factors are most problematic?

Baseball fans will recognize that our problem is based on the 1994–1995 Major League Baseball strike. In that case, the NLRB decided by a 3-2 vote to seek a Section 10(j) injunction stopping the league from unilaterally implementing its salary cap proposal, as well as a salary arbitration and other proposals, because it found that those were mandatory subjects and no impasse had occurred. The judge in that case was now-U.S. Supreme Court Justice Sonia Sotomayor, who issued the injunction. *See Silverman v. Major League Baseball Player Relations Commission, Inc.*, 880 F. Supp. 246 (S.D.N.Y. 1995), affirmed 67 F.3d 1054 (2d Cir. 1995). The parties soon thereafter agreed not to engage in work stoppages and eventually reached a new agreement. For a description of the NLRB's involvement with the strike from the chairman at the time, see William B. Gould IV, *The 1994-'95 Baseball Strike and the National Labor Relations Board, in* REVERSING FIELD: EXAMINING COMMERCIALIZATION, LABOR, GENDER, AND RACE IN THE 21ST CENTURY SPORTS LAW (andré douglas pond cummings & Anne Marie Lofaso eds., 2010).

3. Preventing an employer from unilaterally implementing changes in mandatory subjects of bargaining while the parties are still negotiating is one thing. But it doesn't necessarily follow that once an impasse has occurred, the employer should be able to make changes. One explanation by the Board for allowing unilateral implementation in this situation is that it may help break the impasse. *See McClatchy Newspapers, Inc. v. NLRB*, 131 F.3d 1026, 1032 & n.4 (D.C. Cir. 1997). Do you agree? Are there alternatives that you think would better promote collective bargaining?

4. Once there is an impasse, can an employer implement *any* proposal? For example, in our problem, could the NKL implement a salary cap that was significantly more restrictive than anything it proposed? What about a change that was significantly *better* than its proposals? The general answer to both scenarios is no. Why do you think that is? *See NLRB v. Katz*, 369 U.S. 736, 745 (1962) ("But even

after an impasse is reached he has no license to grant wage increases greater than any he has ever offered the union at the bargaining table, for such action is necessarily inconsistent with a sincere desire to conclude an agreement with the union."); *McClatchy Newspapers*, 131 F.3d at 1031–34 (approving NLRB exception to general rule where employer implemented new merit-pay system that gave it sole discretion and removed the union from future merit-pay determinations; also concluding that employer cannot unilaterally implement no-strike requirement because it undermined fundamental right without valid union waiver).

Chapter 8

SUBJECTS OF COLLECTIVE BARGAINING

Synopsis

Having discussed the qualitative aspects of the duty to bargain in good faith in the previous chapter, i.e., "in what manner," this chapter considers the quantitative side of the duty to bargain in good faith, i.e., "what topics."

In Section 1, this Chapter discusses the general test for differentiating between mandatory subjects of bargaining under Section 8(d), over which the parties must bargain to impasse, and permissive subjects of bargaining, over which the party never need to bargain. From there, Section 2 explores whether employers have the duty to bargain in good faith over managerial decisions, like subcontracting and partial closings, that also have a significant impact on the terms and conditions of employment. Finally, Section 3 considers the ongoing debate concerning whether employers must bargain with the union over the decision to relocate a facility.

SECTION 1 MANDATORY v. PERMISSIVE SUBJECTS OF BARGAINING

In addition to deciding whether the parties' bargaining have been conducted in good faith, there is also the question of which subjects the parties must bargain over.

In this regard, there are two settled rules in deciding which subjects must be bargained over:

1. The duty to bargain under Section 8(d) extends to each and every subject relating to the "rates of pay, wages, hour of employment, or other conditions or employment." An unfair labor practice (ULP) is committed by the employer under Section 8(a)(5), or by the union under Section 8(b)(3), if the employer or union to refuses to bargain about such "mandatory" subjects.

2. As to the other subjects that fall outside this statutory language, there is no corresponding duty to bargain. Indeed, insisting on bargaining about these "non-mandatory" or "permissive subjects" is a per se violation of Section 8(a)(5) or 8(b)(3).

Further elaboration of what subjects must be bargained over was provided in *NLRB v. American National Insurance Co.*, 343 U.S. 395 (1952), discussed in more detail in Chapter 7. In that case, the U.S. Supreme Court appeared to draw the line in a way that permitted employers to expand their control by drafting expansive management rights provisions in collective-bargaining agreements (CBAs). By permitting these provisions, the Court narrowed the set of topics that fall into the category of joint management-union responsibility.

In *American National Insurance*, the parties attempted to negotiate an employment relations clause. Under this clause, the union proposed an unlimited arbitration provision, which provided that all grievances would be settled by arbitration. The employer's counter-proposal contained a management functions clause, which excluded from the arbitration process matters such as promotions, discipline and work scheduling as the responsibility of management and excluding such matters from arbitration. The NLRB found that the employer had not bargained in good faith and that the employer's insistence on the management functions clause was a per se violation of 8(a)(5), because it manifested bad faith.

The Supreme Court, however, refused to enforce the Board's order. In so doing, the Court observed that Congress added Section 8(d) through the Taft-Hartley amendments in an effort to promote industrial peace through voluntary agreements. At the same time, the Board is not permitted to compel agreements under the language of Section 8(d), which expressly states that the obligation to bargain in good faith "does not compel either party to agree to a proposal or require the making of a concession."

Because the Court in *American National Insurance Co.* found that bargaining for management function clauses is empirically a common collective-bargaining practice, whether such a clause should be included should be left for negotiations at the bargaining table and not decided by the Board. In short, the employer had not bargained in bad faith by insisting on a provision that would give it exclusive authority to determine a number of workplace issues.

In dissent, Justice Minton argued that the employer's demand acted to remove certain topics from the bargaining agenda that the parties had a statutory duty to bargain over. Justice Minton maintained that the employer's demand for a broad management functions clause effectually forced the union to agree to give up the right to bargain over subjects included in the clause to persuade the employer to bargain over other subjects related to working conditions. Of course, the rejoinder would be that if the union feels strongly enough about not agreeing to the management clause, they could always go on strike and force the issue.

In all, *American National Insurance Co.* appears to stand for the proposition that as long as the employer engages in good faith bargaining, it is permitted to engage in hard bargaining and stand firm on its proposals. The difference between refusing to engage in the process at all, which is clearly a violation of the bargain in good faith, and coming to the bargaining table but firmly insisting on a proposal, is that in the latter instance there is at least the possibility for some negotiated settlement to emerge. Furthermore, even if there is hard bargaining that does not lead to a compromise, economic weapons can be deployed once impasse has occurred.

PROBLEM #1: TESTING THE MANDATORY-PERMISSIVE DISTINCTION

An impasse exits between the parties to a collective-bargaining negotiation. On the one side, the Union insists that the Employer should agree to terminate any employee who does not join the Union within 30 days of employment, to consult the Union before it makes any major capital investments to improve its facilities, and to pay a higher percentage of health care benefits for current retired employees. The Employer refuses to accede to any of these demands.

On the other side, the Employer wants the Union to agree to a standard wage rate for all employees it represents to help the Employer more effectively compete with its competitors, and to give the Employer unilateral authority to set hours and work policies under a broad management rights clause. The Union refuses to accede to these demands. On July 1, believing that further negotiations with the Union are futile, the Employer unilaterally implements its proposals.

Has the Employer violated Section 8(a)(5) of the Act? Has the Union violated Section 8(b)(3)?

PROBLEM MATERIALS

NLRB v. Wooster Division of Borg-Warner Corp., 356 U.S. 342 (1958)

Johnson-Bateman Co. v. International Association of Machinists, 295 N.L.R.B. 180 (1989)

NLRB v. WOOSTER DIVISION OF BORG-WARNER CORP.
356 U.S. 342 (1958)

Mr. Justice Burton delivered the opinion of the Court.

In these cases an employer insisted that its collective-bargaining contract with certain of its employees include: (1) a "ballot" clause calling for a prestrike secret vote of those employees (union and nonunion) as to the employer's last offer, and (2) a "recognition" clause which excluded, as a party to the contract, the International Union which had been certified by the National Labor Relations Board as the employees' exclusive bargaining agent, and substituted for it the agent's uncertified local affiliate. The Board held that the employer's insistence upon either of such clauses amounted to a refusal to bargain, in violation of s 8(a)(5) of the National Labor Relations Act, as amended. The issue turns on whether either of these clauses comes within the scope of mandatory collective bargaining as defined in s 8(d) of the Act. For the reasons hereafter stated, we agree with the Board that neither clause comes within that definition. Therefore, we sustain the Board's order directing the employer to cease insisting upon either clause as a condition precedent to accepting any collective-bargaining contract.

Late in 1952, the International Union, United Automobile, Aircraft and Agricultural Implement Workers of America, CIO (here called International) was certified by the Board to the Wooster (Ohio) Division of the Borg-Warner Corporation (here called the company) as the elected representative of an appropriate unit of the company's employees. Shortly thereafter, International chartered Local No. 1239, UAW-CIO (here called the Local). Together the unions presented the company with a comprehensive collective-bargaining agreement. In the "recognition" clause, the unions described themselves as both the "International Union, United Automobile, Aircraft and Agricultural Implement Workers of America and its Local Union No. 1239, U.A.W.-C.I.O. . . ."

The company submitted a counterproposal which recognized as the sole repre- sentative of the employees "Local Union 1239, affiliated with the International Union, United Automobile, Aircraft and Agricultural Implement Workers of America (UAW-CIO)." The unions' negotiators objected because such a clause disregarded the Board's certification of International as the employees' represen- tative. The negotiators declared that the employees would accept no agreement which excluded International as a party.

The company's counterproposal also contained the "ballot" clause, quoted in full in the margin. In summary, this clause provided that, as to all nonarbitrable issues (which eventually included modification, amendment or termination of the contract), there would be a 30-day negotiation period after which, before the union could strike, there would have to be a secret ballot taken among all employees in the unit (union and nonunion) on the company's last offer. In the event a majority of the employees rejected the company's last offer, the company would have an opportu- nity, within 72 hours, of making a new proposal and having a vote on it prior to any strike. The unions' negotiators announced they would not accept this clause "under any conditions."

From the time that the company first proposed these clauses, the employees' representatives thus made it clear that each was wholly unacceptable. The company's representatives made it equally clear that no agreement would be entered into by it unless the agreement contained both clauses. In view of this impasse, there was little further discussion of the clauses, although the parties continued to bargain as to other matters. The company submitted a "package" proposal covering economic issues but made the offer contingent upon the satisfactory settlement of "all other issues . . . ." The "package" included both of the controversial clauses. On March 15, 1953, the unions rejected that proposal and the membership voted to strike on March 20 unless a settlement were reached by then. None was reached and the unions struck. Negotiations, nevertheless, contin- ued. On April 21, the unions asked the company whether the latter would withdraw its demand for the "ballot" and "recognition" clauses if the unions accepted all other pending requirements of the company. The company declined and again insisted upon acceptance of its "package," including both clauses. Finally, on May 5, the Local, upon the recommendation of International, gave in and entered into an agreement containing both controversial clauses.

In the meantime, International had filed charges with the Board claiming that the company, by the above conduct, was guilty of an unfair labor practice within the meaning of s 8(a)(5) of the Act. The trial examiner found no bad faith on either side. However, he found that the company had made it a condition precedent to its acceptance of any agreement that the agreement include both the "ballot" and the "recognition" clauses. For that reason, he recommended that the company be found guilty of a per se unfair labor practice in violation of s 8(a)(5). He reasoned that, because each of the controversial clauses was outside of the scope of mandatory bargaining as defined in s 8(d) of the Act, the company's insistence upon them, against the permissible opposition of the unions, amounted to a refusal to bargain as to the mandatory subjects of collective bargaining. The Board, with two members dissenting, adopted the recommendations of the examiner. In response to the Board's petition to enforce its order, the Court of Appeals set aside that portion of the order relating to the "ballot" clause, but upheld the Board's order as to the "recognition" clause.

. . . We turn first to the relevant provisions of the statute. Section 8(a)(5) makes it an unfair labor practice for an employer "to refuse to bargain collectively with the representatives of his employees . . . ." Section 8(d) defines collective bargaining as follows:

"(d) For the purposes of this section, to bargain collectively is the performance of the mutual obligation of the employer and the representative of the employees to meet at reasonable times and confer in good faith with respect to wages, hours, and other terms and conditions of employment, or the negotiation of an agreement, or any question arising thereunder, and the execution of a written contract incorporating any agreement reached if requested by either party, but such obligation does not compel either party to agree to a proposal or require the making of a concession . . . ."

Read together, these provisions establish the obligation of the employer and the representative of its employees to bargain with each other in good faith with respect to "wages, hours, and other terms and conditions of employment . . . ." The duty is limited to those subjects, and within that area neither party is legally obligated to yield. As to other matters, however, each party is free to bargain or not to bargain, and to agree or not to agree.

The company's good faith has met the requirements of the statute as to the subjects of mandatory bargaining. But that good faith does not license the employer to refuse to enter into agreements on the ground that they do not include some proposal which is not a mandatory subject of bargaining. We agree with the Board that such conduct is, in substance, a refusal to bargain about the subjects that are within the scope of mandatory bargaining. This does not mean that bargaining is to be confined to the statutory subjects. Each of the two controversial clauses is lawful in itself. Each would be enforceable if agreed to by the unions. But it does not follow that, because the company may propose these clauses, it can lawfully insist upon them as a condition to any agreement.

Since it is lawful it insist upon matters within the scope of mandatory bargaining and unlawful to insist upon matters without, the issue here is whether either the "valid" or the "recognition" clause is a subject within the phrase "wages, hours, and other terms and conditions of employment" which defines mandatory bargaining. The "ballot" clause is not within that definition. It relates only to the procedure to be followed by the employees among themselves before their representative may call a strike or refuse a final offer. It settles no term or condition of employment-it merely calls for an advisory vote of the employees. It is not a partial "no-strike" clause. A "no-strike" clause prohibits the employees from striking during the life of the contract. It regulates the relations between the employer and the employees. The "ballot" clause, on the other hand, deals only with relations between the employees and their unions. It substantially modifies the collective-bargaining system provided for in the statute by weakening the independence of the "representative" chosen by the employees. It enables the employer, in effect, to deal with its employees rather than with their statutory representative.

The "recognition" clause likewise does not come within the definition of mandatory bargaining. The statute requires the company to bargain with the certified representative of its employees. It is an evasion of that duty to insist that the certified agent not be a party to the collective-bargaining contract. The Act does not prohibit the voluntary addition of a party, but that does not authorize the employer to exclude the certified representative from the contract . . . .

Mr. Justice Frankfurter joins this opinion insofar as it holds that insistence by the company on the "recognition" clause, in conflict with the provisions of the Act requiring an employer to bargain with the representative of his employees, constituted an unfair labor practice. He agrees with the views of Mr. Justice Harlan regarding the "ballot" clause. The subject matter of that clause is not so clearly outside the reasonable range of industrial bargaining as to establish a refusal to bargain in good faith, and is not prohibited simply because not deemed to be within the rather vague scope of the obligatory provisions of s 8(d).

Mr. Justice Harlan, whom Mr. Justice Clark and Mr. Justice Whittaker join, concurring in part and dissenting in part.

I agree that the company's insistence on the "recognition" clause constituted an unfair labor practice, but reach that conclusion by a different route from that taken by the Court. However, in light of the finding below that the company bargained in "good faith," I dissent from the view that its insistence on the "ballot" clause can support the charge of an unfair labor practice.

Over twenty years ago this Court said in its first decision under the Wagner Act: "The theory of the act is that free opportunity for negotiation with accredited representatives of employees is likely to promote industrial peace and may bring about the adjustments and agreements which the act in itself does not attempt to compel." Today's decision proceeds on assumptions which I deem incompatible with this basic philosophy of the original labor Act, which has retained its vitality under the amendments effected by the Taft-Hartley Act. I fear that the decision may open the door to an intrusion by the Board into the substantive aspects of the bargaining process which goes beyond anything contemplated by the National Labor Relations Act or suggested in this Court's prior decisions under it.

The Court considers both the "ballot" and "recognition" clauses to be outside the scope of the mandatory bargaining provisions of s 8(d) of the Act, which in connection with ss 8(a)(5) and 8(b)(3) imposes an obligation on an employer and a union to ". . . confer in good faith with respect to wages, hours, and other terms and conditions of employment . . . ." From this conclusion it is said to follow that although the company was free to "propose" these clauses and "bargain" over them, it could not "insist" on their inclusion in the collective bargaining contract as the price of agreement, and that such insistence was a per se unfair labor practice because it was tantamount to a refusal to bargain on "mandatory" subjects. At the same time the Court accepts the Trial Examiner's unchallenged finding that the company had bargained in "good faith," both with reference to these clauses and all other subjects, and holds that the clauses are lawful in themselves and ". . . would be enforceable if agreed to by the unions."

Preliminarily, I must state that I am unable to grasp a concept of "bargaining" which enables one to "propose" a particular point, but not to "insist" on it as a condition to agreement. The right to bargain becomes illusory if one is not free to press a proposal in good faith to the point of insistence. Surely adoption of so inherently vague and fluid a standard is apt to inhibit the entire bargaining process because of a party's fear that strenuous argument might shade into forbidden insistence and thereby produce a charge of an unfair labor practice. This watered-down notion of "bargaining" which the Court imports into the Act with reference to matters not within the scope of s 8(d) appears as foreign to the labor field as it would be to the commercial world. To me all of this adds up to saying that the Act limits effective "bargaining" to subjects within the three fields referred to in s 8(d), that is "wages, hours, and other terms and conditions of employment," even though the Court expressly disclaims so holding . . . .

I

. . . I therefore cannot escape the view that today's decision is deeply inconsistent with legislative intention and this Court's precedents. The Act sought to compel management and labor to meet and bargain in good faith as to certain topics. This is the affirmative requirement of s 8(d) which the Board is specifically empowered to enforce, but I see no warrant for inferring from it any power in the Board to prohibit bargaining in good faith as to lawful matters not included in s 8(d). The Court reasons that such conduct on the part of the employer, when carried to the point of insistence, is in substance equivalent to a refusal to bargain as to the statutory subjects, but I cannot understand how this can be said over the Trial Examiner's unequivocal finding that the employer did in fact bargain in "good faith," not only over the disputed clauses but also over the statutory subjects.

It must not be forgotten that the Act requires bargaining, not agreement, for the obligation to bargain ". . . does not compel either party to agree to a proposal or require the making of a concession." s 8(d). Here the employer concededly bargained but simply refused to agree until the union would accept what the Court holds would have been a lawful contract provision. It may be that an employer or union, by adamant insistence in good faith upon a provision which is not a statutory subject under s 8(d), does in fact require the other party to bargain over it. But this effect is traceable to the economic power of the employer or union in the circumstances of a given situation and should not affect our construction of the Act. If one thing is clear, it is that the Board was not viewed by Congress as an agency which should exercise its powers to aid a party to collective bargaining which was in an economically disadvantageous position . . . .

Of course an employer or union cannot insist upon a clause which would be illegal under the Act's provisions, or conduct itself so as to contravene specific requirements of the Act. But here the Court recognizes, as it must, that the [ballot] clause is lawful under the Act, and I think it clear that the company's insistence upon it violated no statutory duty to which it was subject.

II.

The company's insistence on the "recognition" clause, which had the effect of excluding the International Union as a party signatory to agreement and making Local 1239 the sole contracting party on the union side, presents a different problem. In my opinion the company's action in this regard did constitute an unfair labor practice since it contravened specific requirements of the Act.

Section 8(a)(5) makes it an unfair labor practice for an employer not to bargain collectively "with the representatives of his employees." Such representatives are those who have been chosen by a majority of the employees of the appropriate unit, and they constitute ". . . the exclusive representatives of all the employees in such unit for the purposes of collective bargaining . . . ." s 9(a). The Board under s 9(c) is authorized to direct a representation election and certify its results. The employer's duty to bargain with the representatives includes not merely the obligation to confer in good faith, but also ". . . the execution of a written contract incorporating any agreement reached if requested . . ." by the employees' repre-sentatives. s 8(d). I think it hardly debatable that this language must be read to require the company, if so requested, to sign any agreement reached with the same representative with which it is required to bargain. By conditioning agreement upon a change in signatory from the certified exclusive bargaining representative, the company here in effect violated this duty.

I would affirm the judgment of the Court of Appeals in both cases and require the Board to modify its cease and desist order so as to allow the company to bargain over the "ballot" clause.

JOHNSON-BATEMAN CO. v. INTERNATIONAL ASSOCIATION OF MACHINISTS
295 N.L.R.B. 180 (1989)

By Chairman Stephens and Members Johansen, Cracraft, Higgins, and Devaney.

. . . I. Facts

. . . On December 1, 1986, the Respondent, without notifying or bargaining with the Union, posted the following notice:

ATTENTION ALL EMPLOYEES:

AS OF DECEMBER 1, 1986, ANY INJURIES REQUIRING TREAT-MENT WILL NOW BE ACCOMPANIED BY A DRUG/ALCOHOL TEST.

THANK YOU, MANAGEMENT

On December 4, the Union notified the Respondent in writing that: "The Union is not in agreement with [the above] policy; neither have we been contacted to negotiate such a policy." The Union requested the Respondent not to implement this policy and to remove the above-posted notice. The Respondent did not reply to the Union's December 4 letter, and it did not grant either of the Union's requests. Rather, the Respondent implemented the policy as announced. . . .

III. Analysis and Conclusions

A. *Drug/Alcohol Testing*

1. Mandatory subject of bargaining

A threshold issue, not directly addressed by the judge, and one of first impression for the Board, is whether drug/alcohol testing of current employees is a mandatory subject of bargaining.

Sections 8(a)(5) and 8(b)(3) of the Act, in conjunction with Section 8(d), essentially mandate employers and designated collective-bargaining representatives to bargain in good faith with each other about wages, hours, and other terms and conditions of employment. Generally, it is an unfair labor practice for an employer whose employees are represented for collective-bargaining purposes to make changes in mandatory subjects of bargaining without first providing the collective-bargaining representative with an opportunity to bargain with the employer about such proposed changes.

We find that the Respondent's newly imposed requirement of drug/alcohol testing for employees who require medical treatment for work injuries is a mandatory subject of bargaining. In *Ford Motor Co. v. NLRB*,[441 U.S. 488 (1979,] the Supreme Court described mandatory subjects of bargaining as such matters that are "plainly germane to the 'working environment' " and "not among those 'managerial decisions, which lie at the core of entrepreneurial control.' " Applying these standards to the issue before us, we find the drug/alcohol testing requirement to be both germane to the working environment, and outside the scope of managerial decisions lying at the core of entrepreneurial control.

As to the first factor — germane to the working environment — the drug/alcohol testing requirement is most closely analogous to physical examinations and polygraph testing, both of which the Board has found to be mandatory subjects of bargaining.

In *Medicenter*, [*Mid-South Hospital*, 221 N.L.R.B. 670 (1975),] the employer was alleged to have violated Section 8(a)(5) of the Act when it unilaterally instituted polygraph testing of all employees in an attempt to find which, if any of them were responsible for certain acts of vandalism that had been occurring at the employer's facility. The Board majority found that "a change of this nature in the method by which Respondent investigated suspected employee misconduct is a change in the 'terms and conditions' of employment." More specifically, the Board majority . . . emphasized that the introduction of polygraph testing in the employer's investigatory methodology substantially varied both the mode of investigation and the character of proof on which an employee's job security might depend. Thus, "the test itself substantially altered the existing terms and conditions of employment and constituted a subject of mandatory bargaining."

The analysis as to why the polygraph testing in *Medicenter* was a mandatory subject of bargaining is applicable to the drug/alcohol testing requirement at issue in the instant case. The record establishes that the Respondent implemented the drug/alcohol testing requirement because of an increasingly high number of workplace accidents, resulting in sharply increasing insurance rates. According to the Respondent's vice president, Larry Johnson, "we felt that there was a good probability that there was drugs involved with the significant amount of the accidents that we were experiencing, and that we were wanting some way to enforce our . . . drug policies that we have in our Company rules" (i.e., according to Johnson, the written rules against use or possession of alcohol on company premises or company time or reporting for work while under the influence of alcohol or drugs). Violation of these rules, as set forth above, is punishable by discipline, including discharge. Thus, in accordance with the Respondent's written policies: (1) employees who require medical treatment for work injuries must undergo drug/ alcohol testing; (2) the results of such testing might establish that the injured employee has violated the Respondent's drug/alcohol policies; (3) violation of those policies could result in the discharge or other discipline of the injured employee. Accordingly, the record firmly establishes that the drug/alcohol testing requirement is a condition of employment because it has the potential to affect the continued employment of employees who become subject to it.

In this regard, the drug/alcohol testing requirement is materially similar to the polygraph testing requirement found to be a mandatory subject of bargaining in *Medicenter*. Here, as with the investigation of vandalism in *Medicenter*, there has been a change in the method by which the Respondent investigates possible employee responsibility for a sharp increase in workplace accidents, and, like the employer in *Medicenter*, the Respondent has introduced relatively sophisticated technology, substantially varying both the mode of the investigation and the character of proof on which an employee's job security might depend.

In light of the above considerations, therefore, we conclude that the drug/alcohol testing requirement is entirely "germane to the working environment," as that term was applied by the Court in *Ford Motor Co.*, and thus, to that extent, it is a mandatory subject of bargaining.

The second criterion considered by the Supreme Court in *Ford Motor Co.* is that the subject in question not be among those managerial decisions that lie at the core of entrepreneurial control. In its discussion of this subject, the Court relied on the concurring opinion of Justice Stewart in *Fibreboard Corp.* [*v. NLRB*, 379 U.S. 203, 222–223 (1964)]:

> Nothing the Court holds today should be understood as imposing a duty to bargain collectively regarding such managerial decisions, which lie at the core of entrepreneurial control. Decisions concerning the commitment of investment capital and the basic scope of the enterprise are not in themselves primarily about conditions of employment, though the effect of

the decision may be necessarily to terminate employment. If, as I think clear, the purpose of § 8(d) is to describe a limited area subject to the duty of collective bargaining, those management decisions which are fundamental to the basic direction of a corporate enterprise or which impinge only indirectly upon employment security should be excluded from that area.

We find that the Respondent's drug/alcohol testing requirement is not among that class of managerial decisions that lie at the core of entrepreneurial control. Here again, the Board majority's treatment of this question in *Medicenter* is applicable to the instant case. There, the Board majority affirmed the judge's application of the standards set forth in Justice Stewart's concurring opinion in *Fibreboard*, and found, in agreement with the judge, that:

> The institution of a polygraph test is not entrepreneurial in character, is not fundamental to the basic direction of the enterprise, and does not impinge only indirectly upon employment security. It is, rather, a change in an important facet of the workaday life of employees, a change in personnel policy freighted with potentially serious implications for the employees which in no way touches the discretionary "core of entrepreneurial control."

The same can be said of the institution of drug/alcohol testing. It does not involve the commitment of investment capital and cannot otherwise be characterized as a decision taken with a view toward changing the scope or nature of the Respondent's enterprise. It is rather a more limited decision directed toward reducing workplace accidents and attendant insurance rates. Accordingly, we conclude that the instant drug/alcohol testing requirement is a mandatory subject of bargaining . . . .

POST PROBLEM DISCUSSION

1.   Under *Borg-Warner*, a party may insist to impasse on the inclusion or exclusion of any clause that is a mandatory subject of bargaining under Section 8(d). However, if a party insists to impasse on a clause that is not a mandatory subject of bargaining, then the party violates either Section 8(a)(5) or Section 8(b)(3). Justice Harlan, for his part, could not articulate the difference between insisting on a subject of bargaining and merely bargaining over it. Can you?

While the Court suggests that insistence on non-mandatory topics is dilatory and detracts from bargaining over substantive issues, does this approach ignore the importance of the typical "give and take" involved in negotiations that helps the parties to agree on a variety of topics? By unilaterally allowing one party to remove subjects from bargaining, through a refusal to bargain over non-mandatory subjects, has the Court frustrated the overall purpose of getting the parties to negotiate through their disagreements?

2.   The Court in *Borg-Warner* stated that the "ballot" clause is a non-mandatory subject of bargaining because it relates only to procedures by the employees among themselves before they can strike, as opposed to procedures that involve the employer-employee relationship, like "no-strike" clauses. In other words, the "ballot" clause settles no "terms or conditions of employment," it merely provides for an advisory vote. The Court also found the "recognition" clause was not a mandatory subject of bargaining because the NLRA requires the employer to

bargain with a certified representative, which was the international union in this case, not the local affiliate.

3. How does *Borg-Warner* and *Johnson-Bateman* assist you in deciding whether the union or company in the Problem have violated their duties to bargain in good faith?

4. What advice should an attorney give to a client who desires a non-mandatory concession? One possibility: the client should not insist on any specific term or condition at the bargaining table if it could be argued that the term or condition involves a non-mandatory subject of bargaining. Instead, the client should attempt to achieve the desired outcome by insisting on very favorable terms for mandatory subjects, while signaling that he or she may be willing to reduce these demands if the other party agrees to discuss and consent to the desired non-mandatory term or condition.

5. In *Borg-Warner*, is Justice Burton or Justice Harlan more accurate in their interpretation of the Act as it relates to collective bargaining? It appears that the principal difference between their views centers on the breadth each affords Section 8(d)'s phrase "other terms and conditions of employment." Justice Burton interprets the phrase narrowly to exclude topics that are not mandatory subjects of bargaining. Justice Harlan, on the other hand, interprets the phrase broadly, because he puts a heavy emphasis on the parties coming to an agreement without outside interference.

6. In all, *Borg-Warner* and the cases that follow establish three bargaining subject categories: (1) mandatory; (2) permissive; and (3) illegal. The distinction is made to determine several bargaining tactics:

(a) Whether a party must bargain in good faith if requested. If the subject is mandatory, a party must bargain in good faith.

(b) Whether pertinent information must be disclosed. If the subject is mandatory, a party must disclose related pertinent information.

(c) Whether unilateral action may be taken without bargaining to impasse. If the subject is mandatory, a party cannot take unilateral action until it bargains to impasse (see Chapter 7).

(d) Whether insistence backed by economic force is lawful. If the subject is mandatory, a party may use economic weapons to insist.

Under which category do you think the recognition clause in *Borg-Warner* falls?

7. In *Johnson-Bateman*, the employer insisted on a provision that required drug and alcohol tests anytime an employee was injured and required treatment. The Board held that such a provision was a mandatory subject of bargaining because it was "germane to the working environment" and a "condition of employment." The Board reasoned that the provision satisfied the mandatory criteria because it had the potential to affect the continued employment of employees who become subject to it.

The Board in *Colgate-Palmolive Co.*, 323 N.L.R.B. 515 (1997), found that video surveillance equipment in the workplace is analogous to drug tests or polygraphs;

therefore, under *Johnson-Bateman*, the use of such equipment was a mandatory subject of bargaining because it was "germane to the workplace." The D.C. Circuit took this a step further in *Brewers & Maltsters, Local 6 v. NLRB*, 414 F.3d 36 (D.C. Cir. 2005), where it held that cameras in an elevator motor room violated Section 8(a)(5) because the employer did not bargain with the union over the installation of the cameras, and because there were no applicable exceptions to the general rule that internal security is a mandatory subject of bargaining.

8.   Can an employer insist on provisions creating a health care committee of bargaining unit members and keeping contract terms in place in the event the contract expires without a replacement? The Board in *ServiceNet, Inc.*, 340 N.L.R.B. 1245 (2003), held that an employer may not insist on the two clauses because they are non-mandatory subjects of bargaining. The Eleventh Circuit in *Georgia Power Co. v. NLRB*, 427 F.3d 1354 (11th Cir. 2005), held that an employer's unilateral creation of an employee-management Workplace Ethics Program, which created a parallel system to the grievance procedure for dealing with employee complaints, was a term and condition of employment. Therefore, the employer violated Section 8(a)(5) by refusing to bargain over the program with the union.

9.   In *Allied Chemical& Alkali Workers v. Pittsburgh Plate Glass Co.*, 404 U.S. 157 (1971), the issue was whether a mid-term unilateral modification that concerned the benefits of already retired employees constituted a ULP. The Board found that retirement benefits were part of the mandatory bargaining obligation and that the employer committed a ULP by not bargaining. The Sixth Circuit refused to enforce the Board's order, and the Supreme Court affirmed. The Supreme Court reasoned that retirees are not statutory employees under Section 2(3) of the NLRA and, as a result, retirees cannot be part of the certified bargaining unit.

Further, the Court reasoned, even if retirees were bargaining unit employees, their retiree benefits were not mandatory subjects of bargaining because such subjects are limited to negotiating the relationship between the employer and the employees. Because retiree benefits do not concern this relationship, they are not mandatory.

SECTION 2   DUTY TO BARGAIN OVER SUBCONTRACTING AND PARTIAL CLOSINGS

Particularly challenging duty to bargain issues arise when the employer engages in management decisions that can be seen as lying at the entrepreneurial core of the business. Take, for instance, the issue of whether an employer can subcontract out bargaining unit work or shut down a part of its business without discussing the topic with the union. As will be seen, in these cases, the Board makes a distinction between "decision bargaining" and "effects bargaining." Moreover, the Supreme Court has developed a test that focuses on the amenability of the subject to the bargaining process.

PROBLEM #2: WHEN THE LIGHTS GO OUT IN MILWAUKEE

Lenz Lights Inc. (LLI), a unionized firm, has decided to close one of its distribution centers in Milwaukee because of the impact of the global economic recession. LLI believes Milwaukee is a small enough city that it can be serviced by its two remaining distribution centers. LLI declined to bargain with the Union over the closure, but did meet with the Union negotiator to verify that workers could bump less senior truck workers at the other distribution centers in order of seniority, in accordance with the applicable collective-bargaining agreement. Does the Union have any ULP claims against LLI for the closing of one its Milwaukee distribution facilities?

PROBLEM MATERIALS

Fibreboard Paper Products Co. v. NLRB, 379 U.S. 203 (1964)

First National Maintenance Corp. v. NLRB, 452 U.S. 666 (1981)

Theodore J. St. Antoine, *Legal Barriers to Worker Participation In Management Decision Making*, 58 Tul. L. Rev. 1301 (1984)

FIBREBOARD PAPER PRODUCTS CO. v. NLRB
379 U.S. 203 (1964)

Mr. Chief Justice Warren delivered the opinion of the Court.

This case involves the obligation of an employer and the representative of his employees under ss 8(a)(5), 8(d) and 9(a) of the National Labor Relations Act to "confer in good faith with respect to wages, hours, and other terms and conditions of employment." The primary issue is whether the "contracting out" of work being performed by employees in the bargaining unit is a statutory subject of collective bargaining under those sections.

Petitioner, Fibreboard Paper Products Corporation (the Company), has a manufacturing plant in Emeryville, California. Since 1937 the East Bay Union Machinists, Local 1304, United Steelworkers of America, AFL-CIO (the Union) has been the exclusive bargaining representative for a unit of the Company's maintenance employees . . . .

The Company, concerned with the high cost of its maintenance operation, had undertaken a study of the possibility of effecting cost savings by engaging an independent contractor to do the maintenance work. At the July 27, meeting, the Company informed the Union that it had determined that substantial savings could be effected by contracting out the work upon expiration of its collective bargaining agreements with the various labor organizations representing its maintenance employees. The Company delivered to the Union representatives a letter which stated in pertinent part:

> For some time we have been seriously considering the question of letting out our Emeryville maintenance work to an independent contractor, and have now reached a definite decision to do so effective August 1, 1959.

In these circumstances, we are sure you will realize that negotiation of a new contract would be pointless. However, if you have any questions, we will be glad to discuss them with you. . . .

We agree with the Court of Appeals that, on the facts of this case, the "contracting out" of the work previously performed by members of an existing bargaining unit is a subject about which the National Labor Relations Act requires employers and the representatives of their employees to bargain collectively. We also agree with the Court of Appeals that the Board did not exceed its remedial powers in directing the Company to resume its maintenance operations, reinstate the employees with back pay, and bargain with the Union.

I.

. . . Because of the limited grant of certiorari, we are concerned here only with whether the subject upon which the employer allegedly refused to bargain-contracting out of plant maintenance work previously performed by employees in the bargaining unit, which the employees were capable of continuing to perform-is covered by the phrase "terms and conditions of employment" within the meaning of s 8(d).

The subject matter of the present dispute is well within the literal meaning of the phrase "terms and conditions of employment." A stipulation with respect to the contracting out of work performed by members of the bargaining unit might appropriately be called a "condition of employment." The words even more plainly cover termination of employment which, as the facts of this case indicate, necessarily results from the contracting out of work performed by members of the established bargaining unit.

The inclusion of "contracting out" within the statutory scope of collective bargaining also seems well designed to effectuate the purposes of the National Labor Relations Act. One of the primary purposes of the Act is to promote the peaceful settlement of industrial disputes by subjecting labor-management controversies to the mediatory influence of negotiation. The Act was framed with an awareness that refusals to confer and negotiate had been one of the most prolific causes of industrial strife. To hold, as the Board has done, that contracting out is a mandatory subject of collective bargaining would promote the fundamental purpose of the Act by bringing a problem of vital concern to labor and management within the framework established by Congress as most conducive to industrial peace.

The conclusion that "contracting out" is a statutory subject of collective bargaining is further reinforced by industrial practices in this country. While not determinative, it is appropriate to look to industrial bargaining practices in appraising the propriety of including a particular subject within the scope of mandatory bargaining. Industrial experience is not only reflective of the interests of labor and management in the subject matter but is also indicative of the amenability of such subjects to the collective bargaining process. Experience illustrates that contracting out in one form or another has been brought, widely and successfully, within the collective bargaining framework. Provisions relating to contracting out exist in numerous collective bargaining agreements, and "(c)ontracting out work is the basis of many grievances; and that type of claim is grist in the mills of the arbitrators." . . .

The facts of the present case illustrate the propriety of submitting the dispute to collective negotiation. The Company's decision to contract out the maintenance work did not alter the Company's basic operation. The maintenance work still had to be performed in the plant. No capital investment was contemplated; the Company merely replaced existing employees with those of an independent contractor to do the same work under similar conditions of employment. Therefore, to require the employer to bargain about the matter would not significantly abridge his freedom to manage the business.

The Company was concerned with the high cost of its maintenance operation. It was induced to contract out the work by assurances from independent contractors that economies could be derived by reducing the work force, decreasing fringe benefits, and eliminating overtime payments. These have long been regarded as matters peculiarly suitable for resolution within the collective bargaining frame-work, and industrial experience demonstrates that collective negotiation has been highly successful in achieving peaceful accommodation of the conflicting interests. Yet, it is contended that when an employer can effect cost savings in these respects by contracting the work out, there is no need to attempt to achieve similar economies through negotiation with existing employees or to provide them with an opportunity to negotiate a mutually acceptable alternative. The short answer is that, although it is not possible to say whether a satisfactory solution could be reached, national labor policy is founded upon the congressional determination that the chances are good enough to warrant subjecting such issues to the process of collective negotiation.

The appropriateness of the collective bargaining process for resolving such issues was apparently recognized by the Company. In explaining its decision to contract out the maintenance work, the Company pointed out that in the same plant other unions "had joined hands with management in an effort to bring about an economical and efficient operation," but "we had not been able to attain that in our discussions with this particular Local." Accordingly, based on past bargaining experience with this union, the Company unilaterally contracted out the work. While "the Act does not encourage a party to engage in fruitless marathon discussions at the expense of frank statement and support of his position, it at least demands that the issue be submitted to the mediatory influence of collective negotiations. As the Court of Appeals pointed out, "(i)t is not necessary that it be likely or probable that the union will yield or supply a feasible solution but rather that the union be afforded an opportunity to meet management's legitimate complaints that its maintenance was unduly costly."

We are thus not expanding the scope of mandatory bargaining to hold, as we do now, that the type of "contracting out" involved in this case-the replacement of employees in the existing bargaining unit with those of an independent contractor to do the same work under similar conditions of employment-is a statutory subject of collective bargaining under s 8(d). Our decision need not and does not encompass other forms of "contracting out" or "subcontracting" which arise daily in our complex economy . . . .

Mr. Justice Goldberg took no part in the consideration or decision of this case.

Mr. Justice Stewart, with whom Mr. Justice Douglas and Mr. Justice Harlan join, concurring.

Viewed broadly, the question before us stirs large issues. The Court purports to limit its decision to "the facts of this case." But the Court's opinion radiates implications of such disturbing breadth that I am persuaded to file this separate statement of my own views.

Section 8(a)(5) of the National Labor Relations Act, as amended, makes it an unfair labor practice for an employer to "refuse to bargain collectively with the representatives of his employees." Collective bargaining is defined in s 8(d) as:

> the performance of the mutual obligation of the employer and the representative of the employees to meet at reasonable times and confer in good faith with respect to wages, hours, and other terms and conditions of employment.

The question posed is whether the particular decision sought to be made unilaterally by the employer in this case is a subject of mandatory collective bargaining within the statutory phrase "terms and conditions of employment." That is all the Court decides. The Court most assuredly does not decide that every managerial decision which necessarily terminates an individual's employment is subject to the duty to bargain. Nor does the Court decide that subcontracting decisions are as a general matter subject to that duty. The Court holds no more than that this employer's decision to subcontract this work, involving "the replacement of employees in the existing bargaining unit with those of an independent contractor to do the same work under similar conditions of employment," is subject to the duty to bargain collectively. Within the narrow limitations implicit in the specific facts of this case, I agree with the Court's decision . . . .

The basic question is whether the employer failed to "confer in good faith with respect to . . . terms and conditions of employment" in unilaterally deciding to subcontract this work. This question goes to the scope of the employer's duty in the absence of a collective bargaining agreement. It is true, as the Court's opinion points out, that industrial experience may be useful in determining the proper scope of the duty to bargain. But data showing that many labor contracts refer to subcontracting or that subcontracting grievances are frequently referred to arbitrators under collective bargaining agreements, while not wholly irrelevant, do not have much real bearing, for such data may indicate no more than that the parties have often considered it mutually advantageous to bargain over these issues on a permissive basis. In any event, the ultimate question is the scope of the duty to bargain defined by the statutory language.

It is important to note that the words of the statute are words of limitation. The National Labor Relations Act does not say that the employer and employees are bound to confer upon any subject which interests either of them; the specification of wages, hours, and other terms and conditions of employment defines a limited category of issues subject to compulsory bargaining. The limiting purpose of the statute's language is made clear by the legislative history of the present Act. As originally passed, the Wagner Act contained no definition of the duty to bargain collectively. In the 1947 revision of the Act, the House bill contained a detailed but limited list of subjects of the duty to bargain, excluding all others. In conference the present language was substituted for the House's detailed specification. While the language thus incorporated in the 1947 legislation as enacted is not so stringent as that contained in the House bill, it nonetheless adopts the same basic approach in seeking to define a limited class of bargainable issues.

The phrase "conditions of employment" is no doubt susceptible of diverse interpretations. At the extreme, the phrase could be construed to apply to any subject which is insisted upon as a prerequisite for continued employment. Such an interpretation, which would in effect place the compulsion of the Board behind any and all bargaining demands, would be contrary to the intent of Congress, as reflected in this legislative history. Yet there are passages in the Court's opinion today which suggest just such an expansive interpretation, for the Court's opinion seems to imply that any issue which may reasonably divide an employer and his employees must be the subject of compulsory collective bargaining. Only a narrower concept of "conditions of employment" will serve the statutory purpose of delineating a limited category of issues which are subject to the duty to bargain collectively. Seeking to effect this purpose, at least seven circuits have interpreted the statutory language to exclude various kinds of management decisions from the scope of the duty to bargain. In common parlance, the conditions of a person's employment are most obviously the various physical dimensions of his working environment. What one's hours are to be, what amount of work is expected during those hours, what periods of relief are available, what safety practices are observed, would all seem conditions of one's employment. There are other less tangible but no less important characteristics of a person's employment which might also be deemed "conditions'- most prominently the characteristic involved in this case, the security of one's employment. On one view of the matter, it can be argued that the question whether there is to be a job is not a condition of employment; the question is not one of imposing conditions on employment, but the more fundamental question whether there is to be employment at all. However, it is clear that the Board and the courts have on numerous occasions recognized that union demands for provisions limiting an employer's power to discharge employees are mandatorily bargainable. Thus, freedom from discriminatory discharge, seniority rights, the imposition of a compulsory retirement age, have been recognized as subjects upon which an employer must bargain, although all of these concern the very existence of the employment itself.

While employment security has thus properly been recognized in various circumstances as a condition of employment, it surely does not follow that every decision which may affect job security is a subject of compulsory collective bargaining. Many decisions made by management affect the job security of employees. Decisions concerning the volume and kind of advertising expenditures, product design, the manner of financing, and sales, all may bear upon the security of the workers" jobs. Yet it is hardly conceivable that such decisions so involve "conditions of employment" that they must be negotiated with the employees' bargaining representative.

In many of these areas the impact of a particular management decision upon job security may be extremely indirect and uncertain, and this alone may be sufficient reason to conclude that such decisions are not "with respect to . . . conditions of employment." Yet there are other areas where decisions by management may quite clearly imperil job security, or indeed terminate employment entirely. An enterprise may decide to invest in labor-saving machinery. Another may resolve to liquidate its assets and go out of business. Nothing the Court holds today should be understood as imposing a duty to bargain collectively regarding such managerial decisions, which lie at the core of entrepreneurial control. Decisions concerning the commitment of investment capital and the basic scope of the enterprise are not in themselves primarily about conditions of employment, though the effect of the decision may be necessarily to terminate employment. If, as I think clear, the purpose of s 8(d) is to describe a limited area subject to the duty of collective bargaining, those management decisions which are fundamental to the basic direction of a corporate enterprise or which impinge only indirectly upon employment security should be excluded from that area.

Applying these concepts to the case at hand, I do not believe that an employer's subcontracting practices are, as a general matter, in themselves conditions of employment. Upon any definition of the statutory terms short of the most expansive, such practices are not conditions-tangible or intangible-of any person's employment. The question remains whether this particular kind of subcontracting decision comes within the employer's duty to bargain. On the facts of this case, I join the Court's judgment, because all that is involved is the substitution of one group of workers for another to perform the same task in the same plant under the ultimate control of the same employer. The question whether the employer may discharge one group of workers and substitute another for them is closely analogous to many other situations within the traditional framework of collective bargaining. Compulsory retirement, layoffs according to seniority, assignment of work among potentially eligible groups within the plant-all involve similar questions of discharge and work assignment, and all have been recognized as subjects of compulsory collective bargaining.

Analytically, this case is not far from that which would be presented if the employer had merely discharged all its employees and replaced them with other workers willing to work on the same job in the same plant without the various fringe benefits so costly to the company. While such a situation might well be considered a s 8(a)(3) violation upon a finding that the employer discriminated against the discharged employees because of their union affiliation, it would be equally possible to regard the employer's action as a unilateral act frustrating negotiation on the underlying questions of work scheduling and remuneration, and so an evasion of its duty to bargain on these questions, which are concededly subject to compulsory collective bargaining. Similarly, had the employer in this case chosen to bargain with the union about the proposed subcontract, negotiations would have inevitably turned to the underlying questions of cost, which prompted the subcontracting. Insofar as the employer frustrated collective bargaining with respect to these concededly bargaining issues by its unilateral act of subcontracting this work, it can properly be found to have violated its statutory duty under s 8(a)(5).

This kind of subcontracting falls short or such larger entrepreneurial questions as what shall be produced, how capital shall be invested in fixed assets, or what the basic scope of the enterprise shall be. In my view, the Court's decision in this case has nothing to do with whether any aspects of those larger issues could under any circumstances be considered subjects of compulsory collective bargaining under the present law.

I am fully aware that in this era of automation and onrushing technological change, no problems in the domestic economy are of greater concern than those involving job security and employment stability. Because of the potentially cruel impact upon the lives and fortunes of the working men and women of the Nation, these problems have understandably engaged the solicitous attention of government, of responsible private business, and particularly of organized labor. It is possible that in meeting these problems Congress may eventually decide to give organized labor or government a far heavier hand in controlling what until now have been considered the prerogatives of private business management. That path would mark a sharp departure from the traditional principles of a free enterprise economy. Whether we should follow it is, within constitutional limitations, for Congress to choose. But it is a path which Congress certainly did not choose when it enacted the Taft-Hartley Act.

FIRST NATIONAL MAINTENANCE CORP. v. NLRB
452 U.S. 666 (1981)

JUSTICE BLACKMUN delivered the opinion of the Court.

Must an employer, under its duty to bargain in good faith "with respect to wages, hours, and other terms and conditions of employment," §§ 8(d) and 8(a)(5) of the National Labor Relations Act (Act) negotiate with the certified representative of its employees over its decision to close a part of its business? In this case, the National Labor Relations Board (Board) imposed such a duty on petitioner with respect to its decision to terminate a contract with a customer, and the United States Court of Appeals, although differing over the appropriate rationale, enforced its order.

I

Petitioner, First National Maintenance Corporation (FNM), is a New York corporation engaged in the business of providing housekeeping, cleaning, maintenance, and related services for commercial customers in the New York City area. It supplies each of its customers, at the customer's premises, contracted-for labor force and supervision in return for reimbursement of its labor costs (gross salaries, FICA and FUTA taxes, and insurance) and payment of a set fee. It contracts for and hires personnel separately for each customer, and it does not transfer employees between locations.

During the spring of 1977, petitioner was performing maintenance work for the Greenpark Care Center, a nursing home in Brooklyn. Its written agreement dated April 28, 1976, with Greenpark specified that Greenpark "shall furnish all tools, equipment [sic], materials, and supplies," and would pay petitioner weekly "the sum of five hundred dollars plus the gross weekly payroll and fringe benefits." App. in No. 79-4167 (CA2), pp. 43, 44. Its weekly fee, however, had been reduced to $250 effective November 1, 1976. *Id.*, at 46. The contract prohibited Greenpark from hiring any of petitioner's employees during the term of the contract and for 90 days thereafter. *Id.*, at 44. Petitioner employed approximately 35 workers in its Greenpark operation.

Petitioner's business relationship with Greenpark, seemingly, was not very remunerative or smooth. In March 1977, Greenpark gave petitioner the 30 days' written notice of cancellation specified by the contract, because of "lack of efficiency." This cancellation did not become effective, for FNM's work continued after the expiration of that 30-day period. Petitioner, however, became aware that it was losing money at Greenpark. On June 30, by telephone, it asked that its weekly fee be restored at the $500 figure and, on July 6, it informed Greenpark in writing that it would discontinue its operations there on August 1 unless the increase were granted. By telegram on July 25, petitioner gave final notice of termination.

While FNM was experiencing these difficulties, District 1199, National Union of Hospital and Health Care Employees, Retail, Wholesale and Department Store Union, AFL-CIO (union), was conducting an organization campaign among petitioner's Greenpark employees. On March 31, 1977, at a Board-conducted election, a majority of the employees selected the union as their bargaining agent. On July 12, the union's vice president, Edward Wecker, wrote petitioner, notifying it of the certification and of the union's right to bargain, and stating: "We look forward to meeting with you or your representative for that purpose. Please advise when it will be convenient." Petitioner neither responded nor sought to consult with the union.

On July 28, petitioner notified its Greenpark employees that they would be discharged three days later. Wecker immediately telephoned petitioner's secretary-treasurer, Leonard Marsh, to request a delay for the purpose of bargaining. Marsh refused the offer to bargain and told Wecker that the termination of the Greenpark operation was purely a matter of money, and final, and that the 30 days' notice provision of the Greenpark contract made staying on beyond August 1 prohibitively expensive. Wecker discussed the matter with Greenpark's management that same day, but was unable to obtain a waiver of the notice provision. Greenpark also was unwilling itself to hire the FNM employees because of the contract's 90-day limitation on hiring. With nothing but perfunctory further discussion, petitioner on July 31 discontinued its Greenpark operation and discharged the employees . . . .

II

A fundamental aim of the National Labor Relations Act is the establishment and maintenance of industrial peace to preserve the flow of interstate commerce. Central to achievement of this purpose is the promotion of collective bargaining as a method of defusing and channeling conflict between labor and management. Congress ensured that collective bargaining would go forward by creating the Board and giving it the power to condemn as unfair labor practices certain conduct by unions and employers that it deemed deleterious to the process, including the refusal "to bargain collectively."

Although parties are free to bargain about any legal subject, Congress has limited the mandate or duty to bargain to matters of "wages, hours, and other terms and conditions of employment." A unilateral change as to a subject within this category violates the statutory duty to bargain and is subject to the Board's remedial order. Conversely, both employer and union may bargain to impasse over these matters and use the economic weapons at their disposal to attempt to secure their respective aims. Congress deliberately left the words "wages, hours, and other terms and conditions of employment" without further definition, for it did not intend to deprive the Board of the power further to define those terms in light of specific industrial practices.

Nonetheless, in establishing what issues must be submitted to the process of bargaining, Congress had no expectation that the elected union representative would become an equal partner in the running of the business enterprise in which the union's members are employed. Despite the deliberate open-endedness of the statutory language, there is an undeniable limit to the subjects about which bargaining must take place:

> "Section 8(a) of the Act, of course, does not immutably fix a list of subjects for mandatory bargaining. . . . But it does establish a limitation against which proposed topics must be measured. In general terms, the limitation includes only issues that settle an aspect of the relationship between the employer and the employees."

Some management decisions, such as choice of advertising and promotion, product type and design, and financing arrangements, have only an indirect and attenuated impact on the employment relationship. Other management decisions, such as the order of succession of layoffs and recalls, production quotas, and work rules, are almost exclusively "an aspect of the relationship" between employer and employee. The present case concerns a third type of management decision, one that had a direct impact on employment, since jobs were inexorably eliminated by the termination, but had as its focus only the economic profitability of the contract with Greenpark, a concern under these facts wholly apart from the employment relationship. This decision, involving a change in the scope and direction of the enterprise, is akin to the decision whether to be in business at all, "not in [itself] primarily about conditions of employment, though the effect of the decision may be necessarily to terminate employment." At the same time, this decision touches on a matter of central and pressing concern to the union and its member employees: the possibility of continued employment and the retention of the employees' very jobs.

Petitioner contends it had no duty to bargain about its decision to terminate its operations at Greenpark. This contention requires that we determine whether the decision itself should be considered part of petitioner's retained freedom to manage its affairs unrelated to employment. The aim of labeling a matter a mandatory subject of bargaining, rather than simply permitting, but not requiring, bargaining, is to "promote the fundamental purpose of the Act by bringing a problem of vital concern to labor and management within the framework established by Congress as most conducive to industrial peace." The concept of mandatory bargaining is premised on the belief that collective discussions backed by the parties' economic weapons will result in decisions that are better for both management and labor and for society as a whole. This will be true, however, only if the subject proposed for discussion is amenable to resolution through the bargaining process. Management must be free from the constraints of the bargaining process to the extent essential for the running of a profitable business. It also must have some degree of certainty beforehand as to when it may proceed to reach decisions without fear of later evaluations labeling its conduct an unfair labor practice. Congress did not explicitly state what issues of mutual concern to union and management it intended to exclude from mandatory bargaining. Nonetheless, in view of an employer's need for unencumbered decisionmaking, bargaining over management decisions that have a substantial impact on the continued availability of employment should be required only if the benefit, for labor-management relations and the collective-bargaining process, outweighs the burden placed on the conduct of the business.

The Court in *Fibreboard* implicitly engaged in this analysis with regard to a decision to subcontract for maintenance work previously done by unit employees. Holding the employer's decision a subject of mandatory bargaining, the Court relied not only on the "literal meaning" of the statutory words, but also reasoned:

> The Company's decision to contract out the maintenance work did not alter the Company's basic operation. The maintenance work still had to be performed in the plant. No capital investment was contemplated; the Company merely replaced existing employees with those of an independent contractor to do the same work under similar conditions of employment. Therefore, to require the employer to bargain about the matter would not significantly abridge his freedom to manage the business.

The Court also emphasized that a desire to reduce labor costs, which it considered a matter "peculiarly suitable for resolution within the collective bargaining framework," was at the base of the employer's decision to subcontract:

> It was induced to contract out the work by assurances from independent contractors that economies could be derived by reducing the work force, decreasing fringe benefits, and eliminating overtime payments. These have long been regarded as matters peculiarly suitable for resolution within the collective bargaining framework, and industrial experience demonstrates that collective negotiation has been highly successful in achieving peaceful accommodation of the conflicting interests.

The prevalence of bargaining over "contracting out" as a matter of industrial practice generally was taken as further proof of the "amenability of such subjects to the collective bargaining process."

With this approach in mind, we turn to the specific issue at hand: an economically motivated decision to shut down part of a business.

III

A

Both union and management regard control of the decision to shut down an operation with the utmost seriousness. As has been noted, however, the Act is not intended to serve either party's individual interest, but to foster in a neutral manner a system in which the conflict between these interests may be resolved. It seems particularly important, therefore, to consider whether requiring bargaining over this sort of decision will advance the neutral purposes of the Act.

A union's interest in participating in the decision to close a particular facility or part of an employer's operations springs from its legitimate concern over job security. The Court has observed: "The words of [§ 8(d)] . . . plainly cover termination of employment which . . . necessarily results" from closing an operation. The union's practical purpose in participating, however, will be largely uniform: it will seek to delay or halt the closing. No doubt it will be impelled, in seeking these ends, to offer concessions, information, and alternatives that might be helpful to management or forestall or prevent the termination of jobs. It is unlikely, however, that requiring bargaining over the decision itself, as well as its effects, will augment this flow of information and suggestions. There is no dispute that the union must be given a significant opportunity to bargain about these matters of job security as part of the "effects" bargaining mandated by § 8(a)(5). And, under § 8(a)(5), bargaining over the effects of a decision must be conducted in a meaningful manner and at a meaningful time, and the Board may impose sanctions to insure its adequacy. A union, by pursuing such bargaining rights, may achieve valuable concessions from an employer engaged in a partial closing. It also may secure in contract negotiations provisions implementing rights to notice, information, and fair bargaining.

Moreover, the union's legitimate interest in fair dealing is protected by § 8(a)(3), which prohibits partial closings motivated by antiunion animus, when done to gain an unfair advantage. Under § 8(a)(3) the Board may inquire into the motivations behind a partial closing. An employer may not simply shut down part of its business and mask its desire to weaken and circumvent the union by labeling its decision "purely economic."

Thus, although the union has a natural concern that a partial closing decision not be hastily or unnecessarily entered into, it has some control over the effects of the decision and indirectly may ensure that the decision itself is deliberately considered. It also has direct protection against a partial closing decision that is motivated by an intent to harm a union.

Management's interest in whether it should discuss a decision of this kind is much more complex and varies with the particular circumstances. If labor costs are an important factor in a failing operation and the decision to close, management will have an incentive to confer voluntarily with the union to seek concessions that may make continuing the business profitable. At other times, management may have great need for speed, flexibility, and secrecy in meeting business opportunities and exigencies. It may face significant tax or securities consequences that hinge on confidentiality, the timing of a plant closing, or a reorganization of the corporate structure. The publicity incident to the normal process of bargaining may injure the possibility of a successful transition or increase the economic damage to the business. The employer also may have no feasible alternative to the closing, and even good-faith bargaining over it may both be futile and cause the employer additional loss.

There is an important difference, also, between permitted bargaining and mandated bargaining. Labeling this type of decision mandatory could afford a union a powerful tool for achieving delay, a power that might be used to thwart management's intentions in a manner unrelated to any feasible solution the union might propose. In addition, many of the cases before the Board have involved, as this one did, not simply a refusal to bargain over the decision, but a refusal to bargain at all, often coupled with other unfair labor practices. In these cases, the employer's action gave the Board reason to order remedial relief apart from access to the decisionmaking process. It is not clear that a union would be equally dissatisfied if an employer performed all its bargaining obligations apart from the additional remedy sought here.

While evidence of current labor practice is only an indication of what is feasible through collective bargaining, and not a binding guide, that evidence supports the apparent imbalance weighing against mandatory bargaining. We note that provisions giving unions a right to participate in the decisionmaking process concerning alteration of the scope of an enterprise appear to be relatively rare. Provisions concerning notice and "effects" bargaining are more prevalent . . . .

We conclude that the harm likely to be done to an employer's need to operate freely in deciding whether to shut down part of its business purely for economic reasons outweighs the incremental benefit that might be gained through the union's participation in making the decision, and we hold that the decision itself is *not* part of § (d)'s "terms and conditions," over which Congress has mandated bargaining.

B

In order to illustrate the limits of our holding, we turn again to the specific facts of this case. First, we note that when petitioner decided to terminate its Greenpark contract, it had no intention to replace the discharged employees or to move that operation elsewhere. Petitioner's sole purpose was to reduce its economic loss, and the union made no claim of antiunion animus. In addition, petitioner's dispute with Greenpark was solely over the size of the management fee Greenpark was willing to pay. The union had no control or authority over that fee. The most that the union could have offered would have been advice and concessions that Greenpark, the third party upon whom rested the success or failure of the contract, had no duty even to consider. These facts in particular distinguish this case from the subcontracting issue presented in *Fibreboard*. Further, the union was not selected as the bargaining representative or certified until well after petitioner's economic difficulties at Greenpark had begun. We thus are not faced with an employer's abrogation of ongoing negotiations or an existing bargaining agreement. Finally, while petitioner's business enterprise did not involve the investment of large amounts of capital in single locations, we do not believe that the absence of "significant investment or withdrawal of capital," is crucial. The decision to halt work at this specific location represented a significant change in petitioner's operations, a change not unlike opening a new line of business or going out of business entirely
. . . .

JUSTICE BRENNAN, with whom JUSTICE MARSHALL joins, dissenting [opinion omitted].

Theodore J. St. Antoine, *Legal Barriers to Worker Participation in Management Decision Making*
58 TUL. L. REV. 1301 (1984)[1]

I. Introduction: The Statutory Duty to Bargain

Collective bargaining lies at the heart of the union-management relationship. It is the end and purpose of the whole effort to protect employees against reprisals when they form an organization to represent them in dealing with their employers. Collective bargaining is grounded in the belief that industrial strife will be checked, and the workers' lot bettered, if workers are given an effective voice in determining the conditions of their employment My thesis is that federal law, even while placing the force of government behind collective bargaining, has so artificially confined its scope that the process has been seriously impeded from achieving its full potential.

One of the most disarmingly simple provisions of the National Labor Relations Act (NLRA) is section 8(a)(5), which makes it an unfair labor practice for an employer "to refuse to bargain collectively" with a union representing its employees. Strangely, Senator Wagner's original "labor disputes" bill, as reported from committee in 1934, contained no explicit requirement of collective bargaining, although the Senator believed it was implicit in the employees' right to organize. Some felt that imposing a statutory duty to bargain would amount to no more than a pious exhortation. Sumner Slichter, for example, caustically likened it to legislating "that the lions and lambs shall not fail to exert every reasonable effort to lie down together." Other labor experts took a different tack, opposing "legislation by implication" and insisting that failure to mandate collective bargaining "omits the very guts" of the organizational process. The views of the latter prevailed and their recommended language was accepted.

Yet what exactly had been done was left uncertain. The NLRA's two leading proponents diverged sharply over the meaning of the duty to bargain. Senator Wagner, the Act's sponsor, thought it would obligate an employer to "negotiate in good faith" and "make every reasonable effort to reach an agreement." Senator Walsh, the chairman of the Senate Labor Committee, felt instead that the parties would merely be required to get together, to meet and confer. "The bill," said he, "does not go beyond the office door." These contrasting positions presaged a long and continuing debate. An influential pair of articles in 1950 by Archibald Cox and John Dunlop insisted that the Wagner Act was concerned with *organization for bargaining* — not with the scope of the ensuing negotiations." They lamented that the NLRB, with judicial endorsement, had embarked on the mission of "defining the scope of collective bargaining." Eventually, nevertheless, Senator Wagner's concept of a duty to bargain in good faith prevailed. Even so, as late as 1961 a distinguished labor study group branded the bargaining requirement "unrealistic," adding that "the provision designed to bring 'good faith' have become a tactical

---

weapon used in many situations as a means of harassment."

Over the years, however, there has been increasing evidence that the statute has had a positive practical effect, including voluntary compliance by management. One survey revealed that successful bargaining relationships were eventually established in seventy-five percent of the cases sampled that were pursued to a final Board order as well as in ninety percent of the cases that were voluntarily adjusted after the issuance of a complaint. Although a recalcitrant offender can drag his heels with impunity, because a Board order to bargain operates only prospectively and ordinarily does not furnish any monetary relief, the majority of American employers and unions are law-abiding. However hard it may be to identify "good faith" and to classify legally such particular tactics as "take-it-or-leave-it" bargaining, it would seem almost perverse at this late date to deny that, overall, the statutory duty to negotiate has had a salutary impact.

Nonetheless, important problems remain. This paper will focus on one of the most crucial: the subject matter about which the NLRA mandates bargaining.

II. Mandatory Subjects of Bargaining

The pro-union Congress that passed the Wagner Act in 1935 and imposed thereby the duty to bargain did not see fit to define that duty. This lack was remedied, in a manner of speaking, by the pro-management Congress that enacted the Taft-Hartley amendments in 1947. A code of union unfair labor practices was adopted, and unions, like employers, were made subject to a duty to bargain. A new section, section 8(d), was added to the NLRA, declaring that to "bargain collectively" meant the "mutual obligation" of employer and union to confer "in good faith" with respect to "wages, hours, and other terms and conditions of employment." Section 8(d) also took pains to state that no party would be under a compulsion to "agree to a proposal" or make any concessions. If the House of Representatives had its way, the statute would have been much more specific, even definitive, in enumerating the subjects of bargaining. In so doing, the Act would have made clear, as the House Labor Committee put it, that a union had "no right to bargain with the employer about . . . how he shall manage his business . . . ."

The more general language that was finally adopted was seen as a confirmation of the course that the Labor Board had been following. That course was for the Board itself to define for employers and unions the "mandatory" subjects of bargaining about which either party could be required to negotiate at the behest of the other. Moreover, if a topic was mandatory, a party could require an agreement on it as the price of any contract. Stated differently, negotiations could be carried to the point of impasse or stalemate on such an issue. Matters outside this charmed circle of mandatory subjects were merely "permissive." The parties could negotiate concerning such topics if both sides were willing, but neither party could insist on bargaining over them if the other party objected. These permissive topics could not be the basis for an impasse or deadlock in negotiations.

The Supreme Court was eventually called upon to appraise this scheme in *NLRB v. Wooster Div. of Borg-Warner Corp.* The facts of *Borg-Warner* were curiously atypical. An employer demanded that its collective bargaining agreement contain, *inter alia,* a clause requiring a vote of the employees by secret ballot before the union could go on strike. A majority of the Supreme Court held first that the "ballot" clause related to a matter of purely internal union concern, and was thus not a mandatory subject of bargaining. Then, in a step not logically necessitated by section 8(d) and highly dubious as a matter of healthy industrial relations, the Court agreed with the NLRB that the employer's insistence on a "permissive" clause as a condition of agreement amounted in effect to an unlawful refusal to bargain on mandatory subjects.

At least two other approaches might have made more sense. I am told the lead attorney for the company in *Borg-Warner* seriously considered arguing for the most straight-forward solution, which would have been the obliteration of the whole mandatory-permissive distinction. Under this approach, any topic put on the table by either party would have triggered the duty of good faith negotiating. The other party, it should be emphasized, would never be obligated to agree, only to bargain. Why, after all, should a federal agency, rather than the parties themselves, determine whether a particular item is so important that it is worth a strike or a lockout? The subject matter of collective bargaining ought to be flexible rather than frozen into rigid molds by governmental fiat. Furthermore, the Board's doctrine encourages hypocrisy in negotiations. If a party deeply desires a concession on a permissive subject that may not legally be carried to impasse, it will be tempted to hang the bargaining up on a false issue that happens to enjoy official approbation as a mandatory topic. Candor would have been enhanced by a different rule, and unresolved disputes would have been recognized for what they ordinarily become in any case — matters to be decided by economic muscle.

Making all topics subject to the duty (and therefore the right) of good faith bargaining would of course have won the case for the employer in *Borg-Warner.* But it is readily understandable why the employer there shrank from such strong medicine. Ordinarily it would be the union, not the employer, that would profit most from an expanded range of negotiations. The right to force good faith bargaining on any topic would enable the union to demand bargaining over those most sensitive of issues, basic business decisions now classified as managerial prerogatives. On the other hand, even the prospect of bargaining to an impasse over a business decision would not be the worst thing that could happen to an employer from the viewpoint of the sophisticated management attorney.

Much worse is to be told, after the fact, that a business decision unilaterally implemented without prior negotiation with the union involved a mandatory subject of bargaining, and that the unilateral change therefore constituted an unfair labor practice that must now be undone at some substantial expense to the company. Such indeed was the ill fortune of numerous employers during the 1960's, when the NLRB significantly enlarged the scope of required bargaining. The wiser course might well have been to end the confusion and uncertainty by treating all lawful subjects as mandatory. But that was the road not taken.

A second, more modest approach would also have allowed the employer in *Borg-Warner* to prevail. That was the position adopted by Justice Harlan and three other Justices, who would have retained the mandatory-permissive distinction, but with a difference. Either party would still be required to bargain to an impasse about mandatory subjects but not about permissive subjects, as is the case under the existing law. At the same time, however, either party under the Harlan formulation could persist in pursuing any lawful demand, regardless of how the Board might categorize it, and could refuse to contract absent agreement on that item. In short, Justice Harlan read section 8(d) of the NLRA to mean what it says, and only that: A party is obligated to bargain about wages, hours, and working conditions, but an insistence on bargaining about more is not the equivalent of a refusal to bargain about a mandatory subject. A union, for example, could dismiss out of hand an employer's demand for a secret-ballot strike vote procedure, but the employer would not commit an unfair labor practice if it remained adamant.

Either of these two approaches would probably have comported better with the realities of collective bargaining than does the law as now propounded. If it is too late in the day to press for fundamental revisions, at least a recognition of past missteps may help guide our future course aright.

III. Managerial Decisions and Employee Job Security

The mandatory subjects of bargaining are wages, hours, and working conditions. It is now well established that wages include compensation in almost every conceivable form, from straight hourly wages through the most complex pension plan, not to mention the traditional Christmas turkey. Hours cover not only the total number of hours in a day or a week, but also the times of particular shifts, the scheduling of overtime, and the like. Working conditions plainly encompass such physical aspects of the job as heat and cold, dirt and noise, lighting, safety hazard, and other assorted stresses and strains. But over the last two decades, the most controversial issue concerning the duty to bargain has been the extent to which employers must negotiate about managerial decisions that result in a shrinkage of job opportunities for employees. Under the *Borg-Warner* rubric, the crucial question is whether a subject is classified as a condition of employment or as a management right.

For a long time the NLRB held that in the absence of anti-union animus, employers were not required to bargain over decisions to subcontract, relocate operations, or introduce technological improvements. Their only requirement was to negotiate regarding the *effects* of such decisions on the employees displaced. Layoff schedules, severance pay, and transfer rights were thus bargainable, but the basic decision to discontinue or change an operation was not. Under the so-called Kennedy-Johnson Board, however, a whole range of managerial decisions were reclassified as mandatory subjects of bargaining. These included decisions to terminate a department and subcontract its work, decisions to consolidate operations through automation, and decisions to close one plant of a multiplant enterprise. The key seems to have been whether the employer's action would result in a "significant impairment of job tenure, employment security, or reasonably anticipated work opportunities for those in the bargaining unit."

In *Fibreboard Paper Products Corp. v. NLRB*, the Supreme Court gave limited approval to this shift of direction. The Court sustained a bargaining order issued when a manufacturer wished to subcontract out its maintenance work within a plant. The Court emphasized that the subcontracting did not alter the company's "basic operation" or require any "capital investment." It simply involved a replacement of one group of employees with another group to do the same work in the same place under the same general supervision. Bargaining would not "significantly abridge" the employer's "freedom to manage the business."

One court of appeals, elaborating on this rationale, held that there was no duty to bargain about subcontracting involving a "change in the capital structure." Other courts of appeals, in cases of partial shutdowns and relocations, attempted to balance such factors as the severity of any adverse impact on unit jobs, the extent and urgency of the employer's economic need, and the likelihood that bargaining would be productive. This approach had the attraction of maximizing fairness in individual situations, but it could often lead to uncertainty and unpredictability.

In 1981 the Supreme Court reconsidered the problem, with puzzling results. In *First National Maintenance Corp. v. NLRB*, the Court held that a maintenance firm did not have to bargain when it decided to terminate an unprofitable contract to provide janitorial services to a nursing home. The Court first stated broadly that an employer has no duty to bargain about a decision "to shut down part of its business purely for economic reasons." It then pointed out that in this particular case the operation was not being moved elsewhere and the laid-off employees were not going to be replaced, the employer's dispute with the nursing home concerned the size of a management fee over which the union had no control, and because the union had only recently been certified there was no disruption of an ongoing relationship. The decision thus leaves unanswered many questions regarding the more typical instance of a partial closing or the removal of a plant to a new location.

The problem in such instances is how to reconcile management's interest in running its own business as it sees fit with the workers' claim to a voice in shaping their industrial lives. Before I set forth my own views on how such a reconciliation may be effectuated, one further important technical distinction must be understood. Whether a particular item is a mandatory subject of bargaining may arise in two quite different contexts. First, the union may be seeking a certain provision, either as part of a new labor contract that is open for negotiation or as an addition to an existing agreement in mid-term. Second, an employer may wish to make a unilateral change in its operations, either in the absence of or in the face of a current collective agreement, without first having to bargain with the union about the matter. In both of these contexts the Supreme Court has apparently assumed, with little or no analysis, that the scope or ambit of mandatory subjects is the same. That is to say, if the item in question is one about which the union could demand bargaining, then generically it is the sort of matter that an employer may not unilaterally change at any time without prior notice to the union and good faith efforts to negotiate an agreement concerning it. This doctrine is susceptible of several refinements depending on the terms of the existing agreement, the extent of pre-contract discussion, and the scope of any union waivers or management rights clauses. For our purposes, however, the important point is that in determining the range of mandatory subjects of bargaining, we are not merely deciding what the parties are obligated to deal with at the time a contract is initially negotiated. To a significant degree we are also deciding what limits shall be imposed on the employer's freedom and business flexibility during the two or three years of the contract's life. Let us now turn to the principles and practicalities that should be considered in making that determination.

IV. Actual and Potential Impact of Collective Bargaining

Imposing a duty to bargain about managerial decisions such as plant removals, technological innovation, and subcontracting (or "outsourcing," to use the current jargon) would obviously delay transactions, reduce business adaptability, and perhaps interfere with the confidentiality of negotiations with third parties. In some instances bargaining would be doomed in advance as a futile exercise. Nonetheless, the closer we move toward recognizing that employees may have something akin to a property interest in their jobs, the more apparent it may become that not even the employer's legitimate regard for profit-making or the public's justified concern for a productive economy should totally override the workers' claim to a voice in the decisions of ongoing enterprises that will vitally affect their future employment opportunities. A moral value is arguably at stake in determining whether employees may be treated as pawns in management decisions. On a crasser, tactical level, a leading management attorney of my acquaintance once said that long before the Supreme Court's decision on in-plant subcontracting, he *"Fibreboarded"* the unions he dealt with simply as a matter of sound personnel relations.

From the workers' perspective, the opportunity to bargain before a decision is made could be crucial. Unions will lose considerable leverage in bargaining about even the effects of a business change if the employer can present them with a *fait accompli* in the change itself. Oftentimes negotiations may benefit both parties by producing a less drastic solution than a shutdown or a relocation. For example, one of the most dramatic moments during the 1982 Ford-UAW negotiations occurred when a union representative from the plant level and his opposite number from the management side agreed that not once had the two of them failed to find a way to adjust operations so as to keep work within the shop and not have it contracted out. At the very least, bargaining may serve a therapeutic purpose. As the Supreme Court stated in *Fibreboard*, in words that might sound platitudinous but for the grim historical reality behind them, the NLRA "was framed with an awareness that refusals to confer and negotiate had been one of the most prolific causes of industrial strife."

Despite these advantages of collective bargaining, neither organized labor nor collective bargaining has ever enjoyed full acceptance in this country. Unions are feared by many employers and distrusted by much of the public. Their support today even among workers is lower than at any time during the past half century. For several years they have lost over fifty percent of all the representation elections conducted by the NLRB, and their membership has shrunk to only one-fifth of the total labor force [eds. now 7% in 2012], not even half the proportionate strength of unions in most of Western Europe.

There is keen irony here. Ours is the most conservative, least ideological of all labor movements, traditionally committed to the capitalistic system and to the principle that management should have the primary responsibility for managing. Yet employers will pay millions of dollars to experts in "union avoidance" in order to maintain their nonunion status. In part this resistance is attributable to the highly decentralized character of American industrial relations. Because of this decentralization, an employer typically must confront a union on a one-to-one basis, without the protective shield of an association to negotiate on behalf of all or substantially all the firms in a particular industry, as is true in Western Europe. In part the resistance to union organization here may result, among both employers and workers, from ingrained American attitudes of rugged individualism and the ideal of the classless society.

In any event, it seems plain that aversion to unionism can hardly be supported by a dispassionate analysis of the actual impact of collective bargaining in this country. Indeed, for many years labor economists wrangled over whether *any* significant economic effect could be demonstrated. Today, however, there is an emerging consensus, which was reflected in a volume produced in 1981 by the Industrial Relations Research Association. This volume assessed U.S. industrial relations over the last three decades, during which time collective bargaining could be said to have come of age. To no one's surprise, unionism was not found to have brought about any substantial redistribution of wealth as between labor and capital. It has achieved a wage level that is roughly ten to twenty percent higher for union workers, but that differential is largely offset by increased efficiency and greater productivity in unionized firms. Furthermore, unions have not been an initiating cause of inflation in the post-World War II period, although they may have hampered efforts to combat it. Last, to mention a point that I must concede is at least superficially damaging to my thesis, union workers generally find less satisfaction in their jobs than do similarly situated nonunion workers. On the other hand, union members are more likely to say they would never consider changing jobs. Perhaps the solution to this paradox, as suggested by Richard Freeman and James Medoff, is that "the collective voice of unionism provides workers with a channel for expressing their preferences to management and that this increases their willingness to complain about undesirable conditions."

For many observers of the labor scene, the major achievement of collective bargaining has not been economic at all. It has been the creation of the grievance and arbitration system, a formalized procedure whereby labor and management may resolve disputes arising during the term of a collective agreement, either by voluntary settlements between the parties themselves or by reference to an impartial outsider, without resort to economic force or court litigation. The mere existence of a grievance and arbitration system helps to eradicate such former abuses as favoritism, arbitrary or ill-informed decisionmaking, and outright discrimination in the workplace.

My conclusion from these facts is that collective bargaining has promoted both industrial peace and broader worker participation in the governance of the shop, while simultaneously stimulating higher productivity and causing only modest dislocations in the economy generally. At the same time I believe that the true potential of collective bargaining has not been tapped. Because law serves such an important legitimating function in our society, collective bargaining may have been seriously undermined when the courts began to cut back the scope of mandatory bargaining to exclude managerial decisions even though they might have a substantial effect on employees' job security.

Peter Pestillo, Ford Motor Company's able, dynamic vice-president for labor relations, has mused: "U.S. labor relations are too little people-driven and too much law-driven." That may be regrettable, but it seems the reality. Ironically, the legal duty to bargain is now more hindrance than help to a well-entrenched union. Without it, the union could demand bargaining on anything it wished; with it, bargaining is by leave of the employer on everything outside the prescribed list of "wages, hours, and other terms and conditions of employment." Far better, it seems to me, would have been an open-ended mandate that lets the parties themselves decide what their vital interests are. The only exclusions from compulsory bargaining that I would readily admit are matters going to the very existence or identity of the negotiating parties, such as the membership of a corporation's board of directors, and perhaps the integrity of their internal structure and procedure. Those limitations would preserve the holding in *Borg-Warner*, which adopted the mandatory-permissive dichotomy in the first place . . . .

POST PROBLEM DISCUSSION

1.   Going back to Problem #2, did LLI commit a Section 8(a)(5) violation when it closed one of its distribution facilities without first bargaining with the union?

2.   The *Fibreboard* Court reasoned that the contracting of work was of immediate concern to both parties, and it was amenable to being resolved successfully through collective bargaining without intruding on the employer's freedom to manage the business. The Court limited its holding to the facts of this case by stating that "the type of 'contracting out' involved in this case — the replacement of employees in the existing bargaining unit with those of an independent contractor to do the same work under similar conditions of employment — is a statutory subject of collective bargaining."

3.   Justice Stewart's concurrence in *Fibreboard*, which narrowed the scope of Section 8(d), was adopted by later courts, including *First National Maintenance*. Justice Stewart sought to make clear that the Court's holding was narrow, as he wanted to ensure that it did not encroach into areas that are exclusively within management's purview. Based on the notion that Section 8(d) was added by Taft-Hartley to limit the areas subject to the duty to collective bargaining, Justice Stewart developed three categories of managerial decisions:

A.   Decisions that have a direct impact on employment, such as hours of work, layoffs, discharges, retirement and seniority, have no entrepreneurial implications, and are therefore mandatory subjects of bargaining.

B.   Decisions that indirectly and in an uncertain way affect job security, such as advertising expenditures, product design, manner of financing, and sales programs, are non-mandatory or permissive subjects of bargaining due to their indirection and uncertainty.

C.   Decisions that directly imperil job security of the employees, but because they "lie at the core of entrepreneurial control" are non-mandatory subjects of bargaining. Examples include investing in labor saving machinery or liquidating business assets or going out of business. The *First*

National Maintenance case provides a working example of this third category of cases.

4. Under *Fibreboard*, must an employer bargain over subcontracting when no members of the unit are laid off or replaced? The First Circuit in *Sociedad Española v. NLRB*, 414 F.3d 158 (1st Cir. 2005), found that that there is no requirement that workers be laid off or replaced for subcontracting to be a mandatory subject of bargaining.

5. Although subcontracting is a mandatory subject of bargaining, the union may waive its statutory right to bargain over the issue by contracting it away in the CBA, usually through a management rights clause. Another form of waiver involves the employer's past practice, sometimes called the safe-harbor exception. The Board in *Westinghouse Electric Corp.*, 150 N.L.R.B. 1574 (1965) looked at several factors, including whether the employer followed the *status quo* in subcontracting work and whether the union had an opportunity to bargain over the practice.

6. Is an employer obligated to bargain with the union over temporary workers, a class of workers not included in the bargaining unit, who are hired to replace outgoing members of the bargaining unit? In *St. George Warehouse, Inc. v. NLRB*, 420 F.3d 294 (3d Cir. 2005), the court held that the employer was required to bargain with the union over the policy of replacing bargaining unit employees with temporary workers. The court relied on the ALJ's findings that the employer instituted the policy of hiring temporary workers to replace direct hires after the election of the union, but before the Board certified the election.

7. Do you agree with Professor St. Antoine that collective bargaining under the NLRA would be better without the mandatory/permissive distinction? Would such a bargaining regime more likely favor unions or employers?

8. Clearly, Professor St. Antoine believes that *First National Maintenance* did more harm than good as far as bringing clarity to the bargaining obligation under Section 8(a)(5). The Court held that the employer did not need to bargain over its decision to partially close its business at the Greenpark location. The decision seemed to turn on the reason that the employer terminated its contract with a nursing home and then had to terminate the workers: because the fee paid to the employer was too low. The union had no ability to make the nursing home pay a higher fee, so the Court concluded the decision to close this unit was not amenable to bargaining. Is this right? Is the Court's conclusion that the union would have nothing to offer the employer in negotiations convincing? For instance, because the contract between the employer and the nursing home was terminated due to "unprofitability," isn't possible that the employer and the union could have come to an agreement that lowered wages and costs enough to make another contract between the employer and the nursing home desirable to all parties involved?

9. After *First National Maintenance*, the Board and many courts focus on whether the issue is amenable to bargaining. In other words, could the union make concessions or otherwise negotiate with the employer in order to make the employer change its mind?

10. The Court in *First National Maintenance* reversed the Board on the question of decision-making, but affirmed the Board on bargaining over the effects

of the partial closing on the employees. Effects bargaining, as Professor St. Antoine points out, includes bargaining over matters such as layoff schedules, severance pay, and reassignment to other jobs within the same company. In fact, the employer in this case did bargain with the union over the effect of the closing and the parties reached an agreement on severance pay.

11. The Court in *First National Maintenance* adopted Justice Stewart's analytical approach in his *Fibreboard* concurrence, with slight modifications. The Court found that *First National Maintenance* fell within the third category of management decisions — decisions that directly imperil job security of the employees, but because they "lie at the core of entrepreneurial control," are non-mandatory subjects of bargaining. Additionally, the Court established a balancing test to discern when entrepreneurial decisions are mandatory subjects of bargaining and when they are permissive. In this regard, the Court stated that, "bargaining over management decisions that have a substantial impact on the continued availability of employment should be required only if the benefit, for labor-management relations and the collective bargaining process, outweighs the burden placed on the conduct of the business." Do you agree that this test appears to favor management sovereignty because a tie goes to management?

SECTION 3   RUNAWAY SHOPS

PROBLEM #3: SWEET HOME MISSALABAMA, WHERE THE SKIES ARE SO BLUE[2]

Davis Trucks manufactured flatbed and dump trailers at its Easthumberland, Wisota plant until late 2005. The plant had been unionized since 1967. The previous contract between the union and the company ran from March 4, 2002 until March 1, 2005. In that contract, the union made concessions because the plant had not been profitable, but by early 2005, the plant had regained profitability. Indeed, the operating profit for the first six months of 2005 was $1,500,000.

All was not well at the Easthumberland plant, however. In February of 2005, the union and the company started to negotiate a new collective bargaining agreement. The company wanted the ability to subcontract work and to mandate overtime. The company asserted that these provisions would allow Davis to meet the increasing demand for its trailers. The union wanted to regain some of the benefits it had conceded in the last contract. Consequently, it asked for wage increases while opposing the subcontracting and mandatory overtime provisions. Tensions rose when the company instituted a new attendance policy, which permitted the company to fire workers for fewer unexcused absences. The company refused the union's demand to bargain about the new policy.

The company president, Mark Marilyn, said that he would shut down the plant if the parties could not reach an agreement on subcontracting and mandatory overtime. The company's lead negotiator told the union that the company had to decide whether to keep the plant in Easthumberland or move it to another state. If

---

[2] This fact pattern is based on *Dorsey Trailers, Inc. v. NLRB*, 233 F.3d 831 (4th Cir. 2000).

subcontracting and mandatory overtime were not allowed, he said, the company would probably shut down the plant and move its operations to another facility. The plant manager told supervisors to tell employees that if employees went on strike, the plant would close. He later emphasized to a group of workers that closing the plant was "not a threat, it's a promise, but you didn't hear it from me."

On June 26, 2005, the employees went on strike. In response, the company began to look at other options to fill the work orders that were back-logged due to the strike. On September 25, the company investigated purchasing a new facility in Reagansville, Missalabama. The company found that the economics of the Reagansville plant surpassed the Northumberland plant in nearly all respects. By October 5, the company agreed to buy the Reagansville plant.

On October 9, the company informed the union of the impending purchase of the Reagansville plant, and of the possibility of closing the Easthumberland facility and relocating the work to Reagansville. The company made clear that the continued operation of the Easthumberland facility was open to bargaining, but that the union had to agree to some thirty-one concessions to keep the plant in Easthumberland. These included a five-year contract with an immediate twenty percent wage cut followed by a wage freeze for the duration of the contract. On November 9, the company notified the union that it was closing the plant. By the end of the year, the company shut down the Easthumberland facility. All employees were terminated. The Reagansville plant had a total net loss of $1,500,000 in 2006.

(1) Did the relocation of plant without bargaining to impasse violate Section 8(a)(5)?

(2) If the employer engaged in an unfair labor practice in relocating the plant without bargaining, did that violation warrant an order requiring the employer to reopen the closed plant?

PROBLEM MATERIALS

United Food & Commercial Workers, Local 150-A v. NLRB (Dubuque Packing Co.), 1 F.3d 24 (D.C. Cir. 1993)

Dorsey Trailers, Inc. v. NLRB, 233 F.3d 831 (4th Cir. 2000)

UNITED FOOD & COMMERCIAL WORKERS, LOCAL 150-A v. NLRB (Dubuque Packing Co.)
1 F.3d 24 (D.C. Cir. 1993)

BUCKLEY, CIRCUIT JUDGE:

Dubuque Packing Company petitions for review of a National Labor Relations Board order holding that it committed unfair labor practices by breaching its duty to bargain with its union regarding the relocation of its "hog kill and cut" operations. We hold that the new standard adopted by the Board for evaluating such claims is an acceptable reading of the National Labor Relations Act and Supreme Court precedents; that the Board's finding that Dubuque owed a duty to bargain was supported by substantial evidence; and that the Board properly applied its new test retroactively to the facts of this case. Hence, we deny Dubuque's petition and enforce the Board's remedial order . . . .

I. Background

A. Facts and Procedural History

. . . Beginning about 1977, the Dubuque Packing Company, a processor and packager of beef and pork, began losing money at its Dubuque, Iowa, home plant. In 1978, Dubuque won an agreement from the plant's workers, who were represented by the United Food and Commercial Workers International Union ("UFCW"), requiring the workers to produce at higher rates in return for a one-time cash payment. In August 1980, Dubuque extracted concessions worth approximately $5 million per annum in return for a pledge that it would not ask for further concessions before the September 1, 1982, expiration of the union contract then in effect. In March 1981, however, it again requested concessions, this time in the form of additional productivity increases in its hog kill department.

On March 30, 1981, the events at issue here began to unfold. On that date, Dubuque gave six-months' notice, as required by its labor contract, of its intention to close its hog kill and cut operations at Dubuque. Various maneuvers between the company and the UFCW ensued, culminating in the union's rejection of a wage freeze aimed at keeping the Dubuque hog kill and cut operation open. The following day, June 10, 1981, the company announced that it was considering relocating-rather than closing-its hog kill and cut department, and that it was also considering relocating up to 900 Dubuque plant pork processing jobs. The UFCW responded by requesting detailed financial information from Dubuque, which the company refused to provide. Dubuque then advised its employees in writing that they could save their jobs by approving its wage freeze proposal. On June 28, 1981, the wage freeze was resubmitted to the workers for a vote, accompanied by the union leadership's recommendation that it be rejected until Dubuque opened its books. The workers voted overwhelmingly with their union and against the company. Three days later, Dubuque informed the union that its decision to close the hog kill and cut department was "irrevocable."

Over the next few months, Dubuque and the UFCW continued to negotiate over Dubuque's proposed relocation of its pork processing operations. On October 1, 1981, Dubuque opened a hog kill and cut operation at its newly acquired Rochelle, Illinois, plant and, two days later, eliminated approximately 530 hog kill and cut jobs at the Dubuque plant . . . .

B. Legal Framework

The critical question in this litigation is whether Dubuque's relocation of its hog kill and cut operation constitutes a mandatory subject of bargaining under the National Labor Relations Act. Although parties to collective bargaining agreements are free to bargain about any legal subject, Congress has imposed on employers and unions "a mandate or duty" to bargain about certain issues. Any "unilateral change as to a subject within this category violates the statutory duty to bargain and is

[handwritten marginalia: Does relocation constitute mandatory subject of bargaining?]

① Whether relocation constitutes a "term or condition" of employment

② If so is it ULP under 8(a)(5).

subject to the Board's remedial order." . . .

The narrow issue in this case is whether a plant relocation such as the one executed by Dubuque constitutes a "term[ ] [or] condition[ ] of employment" under section 8(d) of Act; if it does, then Dubuque's failure to bargain in good faith over the relocation constitutes an unfair labor practice under section 8(a)(5). The two critical Supreme Court decisions interpreting "terms and conditions of employment" for these purposes are *First National Maintenance Corp. v. NLRB*, 452 U.S. 666 (1981), which held that an employer's decision to close a part of its business is not a mandatory subject of bargaining, and *Fibreboard Paper Products Corp. v. NLRB*, 379 U.S. 203 (1964), which held that the replacement of union labor with subcontracted workers is.

II. Discussion

A. Dubuque's Petition . . .

Dubuque argues that the Board's new test improperly interprets Supreme Court precedent, that it was improperly applied to these facts, and that the Board erred by retroactively applying its new test to this case. We disagree on all counts.

1. The Legality of the Board's New Test

. . . In determining whether a particular decision is sufficiently related to employment that it must be bargained over, *First National Maintenance* announced and applied a three-part taxonomy:

> Some management decisions, such as choice of advertising and promotion, product type and design, and financing arrangements, have only an indirect and attenuated impact on the employment relationship. Other management decisions, such as the order of succession of layoffs and recalls, production quotas, and work rules, are almost exclusively "an aspect of the relationship" between employer and employee. The present case concerns a third type of management decision, one that had a direct impact on employment, since jobs were inexorably eliminated by the termination, but had as its focus only the economic profitability of the [employer's] contract with [its customer], a concern under these facts wholly apart from the employment relationship. This decision, involving a change in the scope and direction of the enterprise, is akin to the decision whether to be in business at all, "not in [itself] primarily about conditions of employment, though the effect of the decision may be necessarily to terminate employment." At the same time, this decision touches on a matter of central and pressing concern to the union and its member employees: the possibility of continued employment and the retention of the employees' very jobs . . . .

In these proceedings, the Board set out to enunciate a new legal test "guided by the principles set forth in *First National Maintenance*." It adopted the following standard for determining whether "a decision to relocate [bargaining] unit work," is a mandatory subject of bargaining:

Initially, the burden is on the [NLRB] General Counsel to establish that the employer's decision involved a relocation of unit work unaccompanied by a basic change in the nature of the employer's operation. If the General Counsel successfully carries his burden in this regard, he will have established prima facie that the employer's relocation decision is a mandatory subject of bargaining. At this juncture, the employer may produce evidence rebutting the prima facie case by establishing that the work performed at the new location varies significantly from the work performed at the former plant, establishing that the work performed at the former plant is to be discontinued entirely and not moved to the new location, or establishing that the employer's decision involves a change in the scope and direction of the enterprise. Alternatively, the employer may proffer a defense to show by a preponderance of the evidence: (1) that labor costs (direct and/or indirect) were not a factor in the decision, or (2) that even if labor costs were a factor in the decision, the union could not have offered labor cost concessions that could have changed the employer's decision to relocate . . . .

The Board's test involves three distinct layers of analysis. First, the test recognizes a category of decisions lying "at the core of entrepreneurial control," in which employers may unilaterally take action. Specifically, the test exempts from the duty to bargain relocations involving (1) "a basic change in the nature of the employer's operation," (2) "a change in the scope and direction of the enterprise," (3) situations in which "the work performed at the new location varies significantly from the work performed at the former plant," or (4) situations in which "the work performed at the former plant is to be discontinued entirely and not moved to the new location."

This language would appear broad enough to cover key entrepreneurial decisions such as setting the scale (e.g., the quantity of product produced) and scope (e.g., the type of product produced) of the employer's operations, and determining the basic method of production. Moreover, as to these issues, the Board's test requires an analysis based on the objective differences between the employer's old and new operations. It asks whether various types of "basic change," "change," "vari[ance]," or "discontinu[ance]" were involved in the relocation. Where such objective differences appear, an entrepreneurial decision is deemed to have been taken, and the employer is permitted to relocate without negotiating.

The second layer of the Board's analysis is a subjective one. Under this heading, the relevant question is whether "labor costs (direct and/or indirect) were . . . a factor" in the employer's relocation decision. As illustrated by the Board, this analysis will distinguish relocations motivated by labor costs from those motivated by other perceived advantages of the new location.

The third layer includes a futility provision. As we shall see below, the Board permits an employer to relocate without negotiating where its union either would not or could not offer sufficient concessions to change its decision. Also, the Board has pledged to consider circumstances such as the need to implement a relocation "expeditiously" in determining whether bargaining over a relocation has reached "a bona fide impasse," that is, the point at which a party may act unilaterally.

Dubuque objects that the Board's test is inconsistent with *First National Maintenance*. Its argument tends toward the proposition that a *per se* rule exempting relocation decisions from the duty to bargain is implicit in *First National Maintenance* 's reasoning, if not its holding. Dubuque's general objection is that the Board's test is insufficiently protective of management prerogatives, both on its face and because it is not capable of certainty in application. Dubuque pointedly reminds us that *First National Maintenance* held that employers "must have some degree of certainty beforehand" as to which decisions are and are not subject to a bargaining duty. More specifically, Dubuque argues that relocation decisions must be exempt from the duty to bargain because they involve the reallocation of capital, observing that allocations of capital are "core managerial decisions."

We pause to emphasize that our analysis of the Board's test is premised on our resolution of an important ambiguity in the Board's statement of its second affirmative defense. As stated by the Board, that defense requires an employer to establish that "the union *could not* have offered labor cost concessions that *could* have changed the employer's decision to relocate." On its face, this language might be read as an impossibility exception-a provision allowing an employer to eschew negotiations only if its union could not possibly have changed the relocation decision no matter how accommodating the union might have been at the bargaining table. This reading is strengthened by the Board's illustration of the defense, which involves a case in which an employer "would not remain at the present plant because . . . the costs for modernization of equipment or environmental controls were greater than [the value of] any labor cost concessions the union *could* offer."

Despite this evidence, we think this defense was intended to cover situations in which bargaining would be futile, as well as ones in which it would be impossible for the union to persuade the employer to rescind its relocation decision. Immediately after setting forth its test and the above illustration, the Board stated that under the second affirmative defense, "an employer would have a bargaining obligation *if the union could and would* offer concessions that approximate, meet, or exceed the anticipated costs or benefits that prompted the relocation decision." Furthermore, in the next succeeding sentence and a footnote appended to it, the Board stated:

> *As an evidentiary matter*, an employer might establish that it has no decision bargaining obligation, *even without discussing the union's position* on concessions, if the wage and benefit costs of the unit employees were already so low that it was clear on the basis of those figures alone that the employees could not make up the difference. For example, if a relocation of unit work would save an employer a projected $10.5 million in costs for equipment modernization and environmental controls (quite apart from any labor costs), and if the employer's present labor costs totaled $10 million, then even if the employees were willing to work for free, the union could not offer sufficient labor cost concessions to offset the equipment and environmental savings.

We gather from this that showing the impossibility of obtaining sufficient concessions is simply one means of demonstrating the futility of bargaining *as an evidentiary matter*. And we note that the Board's aside to the effect that an employer might establish that it has no bargaining obligation, "even without discussing the union's position on concessions," implies that an employer might also establish the same proposition through a discussion of "the union's position on concessions." As we read it, the Board's test holds that no duty to bargain exists where bargaining would be futile-either because the union was unable to offer sufficient concessions, or because it was unwilling to do so.

Viewing the Board's test through the lens of this interpretation, we find it sufficiently protective of an employer's prerogative to manage its business. Under *First National Maintenance*, employers may be required to negotiate management decisions where "the benefit, for labor-management relations and the collective-bargaining process, outweighs the burden placed on the conduct of the business. The Board's test exempts from the duty to negotiate relocations that, viewed objectively, are entrepreneurial in nature. It exempts decisions that, viewed subjectively, were motivated by something other than labor costs. And it explicitly excuses employers from attempting to negotiate when doing so would be futile or impossible. What is left are relocations that leave the firm occupying much the same entrepreneurial position as previously, that were taken because of the cost of labor, and that offer a realistic hope for a negotiated settlement. The Board's determination that bargaining over such decisions promises benefits outweighing the "burden[s] placed on the conduct of [an employer's] business" was in no way unreasonable.

Similarly, the Board was also justified in finding that its test accords with Supreme Court precedent. A relocation satisfying the three layers of the Board's test will resemble the subcontracting decision held subject to a mandatory bargaining duty in *Fibreboard* in three distinct ways: Because of the new test's objective component, such a relocation will not "alter the Company's basic operation," because of the new test's subjective component, "a desire to reduce labor costs" will lie "at the base of the employer's decision," (discussing *Fibreboard*); and because of the new test's exclusion of situations in which bargaining would be futile, there will be some prospect of resolving the relocation dispute "within the collective bargaining framework." Like its balancing of burdens and benefits, the Board's finding that its test accords with precedent is fully defensible . . . .

2. The Application of the Board's Test to Dubuque

Dubuque next contends that the Board improperly applied its test to the facts of this case and that under the new standard, properly applied, its actions did not give rise to a bargaining duty. In addressing this contention, we are required by statute to uphold "the findings of the Board with respect to questions of fact if supported by substantial evidence on the record considered as a whole."

Dubuque objects, first, to the Board's finding that its relocation did not constitute a change in the scope and direction of its business. It relies for support on the ALJ's finding that the Rochelle plant was a "smaller, newer, more modern . . . , better laid out" facility and his conclusion "that [Dubuque's] relocation of the hog kill and cut to Rochelle clearly turned on a fundamental change in the scope, nature, and direction of [its] business of which labor costs were but a single important factor." The Board rejected this conclusion, stating that "[t]here is no evidence that the relocation decision was accompanied by a basic change in the nature of the employer's operation."

The Board's position enjoys ample support in the record. In fact, its rejection of the ALJ's conclusion is specifically supported by the ALJ's findings. The ALJ stated that Dubuque used the Rochelle facility to substantially replace the Dubuque facility. As production in Rochelle increased, there was a corresponding reduction at Dubuque until the hog kill and cut processing departments and related operations there were completely phased out. Larry J. Tangeman, general plant superintendent at Dubuque, became superintendent of the Rochelle facility and about 13 members of Dubuque management also were transferred to Rochelle, as was certain production equipment. The purposes of the Rochelle plant, to slaughter hogs, dress carcasses, and to process pork into hams, bacon, and sausage, were the same as at the Dubuque plant . . . .

Dubuque's second contention is that because "the record . . . is very clear that the union 'would not' offer labor concessions," bargaining would have been futile; hence it was not required . . . .

While we agree that our precedent, like the Board's test, relieves employers from any duty to bargain in the face of a union's adamantine intransigence, that principle has no bearing here. As counsel for the UFCW pointed out at oral argument, the UFCW "could, would, and did" accept concessions-in 1978, in August 1980, and again in October 1981-all in a vain attempt to keep the Dubuque facility open. Indeed, the vote that led to Dubuque's "irrevocable" decision to relocate was not a vote to categorically refuse Dubuque's overtures, but a vote to insist on financial disclosure as a prelude to bargaining. The Board's finding that good-faith bargaining between Dubuque and the UFCW might not have been futile was substantially supported by the record . . . .

DORSEY TRAILERS, INC. v. NLRB
233 F.3d 831 (4th Cir. 2000)

WILKINSON, CHIEF JUDGE:

Dorsey Trailers, Inc. appeals a National Labor Relations Board decision finding that the company committed various labor violations at its plant in Northumberland, Pennsylvania. The Board ordered the company to, among other things, cease and desist from the ongoing labor violations and reopen its Northumberland plant. We find that substantial evidence supports the NLRB's conclusions regarding some of the company's violations of Sections 8(a)(1), 8(a)(3), and 8(a)(5) of the National Labor Relations Act. We hold, however, that Dorsey Trailers did not violate Section 8(a)(3) by closing the plant, and it did not violate Section 8(a)(5) by failing to bargain to impasse with the union on the plant's relocation. Furthermore, we find the NLRB's restoration order beyond the Board's remedial power given the remaining violations. Because the decision of where to locate a business lies at the core of entrepreneurial discretion, enforcement of the NLRB's order shall be granted in part and denied in part. On remand, the order shall be modified in conformity with this decision.

. . . II.

The National Labor Relations Act is designed to encourage individual employees to join labor unions and bargain collectively, while at the same time ensuring that a company can control the functioning of its business. One of the fundamental purposes of the Act is to promote the peaceful settlement of industrial disputes by prohibiting employers from engaging in unfair labor practices and by promoting the collective bargaining process . . .

Section 8(a)(5) makes it an unfair labor practice for an employer "to refuse to bargain collectively with the representatives of his employees . . . ." The obligation to bargain collectively is further defined in Section 8(d) of the Act, which directs the union and the employer to "confer in good faith with respect to wages, hours, and other terms and conditions of employment. . . ." Matters falling within the category of wages, hours, and other terms or conditions of employment are mandatory subjects of bargaining. An employer commits an unfair labor practice under Section 8(a)(5) when it makes a unilateral change or otherwise fails to bargain in good faith on any mandatory subject.

III.

A.

. . . Under Section 8(a)(1), the NLRB General Counsel presented a strong case that the company: 1) threatened the workers with plant closure and job loss if the union went on strike; 2) told workers that it would close the facility because it had no time to waste on negotiations; 3) directed employees to bring grievances to supervisors before going to the union; and 4) told workers not to talk to the union during working hours without a supervisor's approval. Accordingly, substantial evidence exists that the company violated Section 8(a)(1) in these four respects. The record also indicates that the company unilaterally changed its attendance policy and refused to furnish the union with information relating to employee attendance. Substantial evidence thus supports the Board's finding that the company violated Sections 8(a)(5) and (1) in these two respects . . . .

C.

The company argues that it did not violate Section 8(a)(5) when it failed to bargain to impasse with the union on the plant relocation. Dorsey Trailers now concedes that it did not bargain to impasse on this point. The question, therefore, turns on whether the plant relocation was a "term or condition of employment," and thus a mandatory subject of bargaining. For the reasons that follow, we hold that it was not.

The Supreme Court's decision in *First National Maintenance v. NLRB* provides our starting point. *First National Maintenance* concerned a company that closed one of its facilities and terminated all of its workers there three weeks after the union attempted to bargain with the company. In *First National Maintenance*, the Supreme Court held that a company's decision to eliminate part of its business is not a term or condition of employment, and therefore not a mandatory subject of bargaining. Because "Congress had no expectation that the elected union representative would become an equal partner in the running of the business enterprise in which the union's members are employed," partial closings are not mandatory subjects of bargaining. Indeed, the Court stated that a business needs "some degree of certainty beforehand as to when it may proceed to reach decisions without fear of later evaluations labeling its conduct an unfair labor practice."

Although the Court in *First National Maintenance* did not have to reach the question of whether a plant relocation is a term or condition of employment, this court made clear in *Arrow Automotive Indus. v. NLRB* that the reasoning of *First National Maintenance* encompassed plant relocations. *Arrow* involved a company that remanufactured automobile and truck parts. It operated four plants: one each in Massachusetts, South Carolina, Arkansas, and California. Each plant made identical products. After the Massachusetts plant went on strike, the company relocated the Massachusetts operations to the pre-existing facility in South Carolina. The company found that the South Carolina plant could "more efficiently" perform the work previously done at the Massachusetts facility.

This circuit held that the move to South Carolina was not a term or condition of employment, and therefore not a mandatory subject of bargaining. *Arrow* noted that *First National Maintenance* "established a per se rule that an employer has no duty to bargain over a decision to close part of its business." *Arrow* emphasized, however, that the reasoning of *First National Maintenance* was not limited to partial closings. Rather, the *Arrow* court's "conclusion that [the company's] closing decision was not a mandatory subject of bargaining is not dependent on the 'partial closing' label." In *Arrow*, the company's actions, "however they might be labeled, were not a subject of mandatory bargaining when examined in light of the analysis set forth by the Supreme Court." We emphasized, in fact, that cases were not "to be resolved by placing decisions within rigid categories such as 'partial closing,' 'relocation,' or 'consolidation.' "

The reasoning behind such conclusions is straightforward. The ability to decide where to commit "investment capital" is so "fundamental to the basic direction of a corporate enterprise" that a plant relocation is not a term or condition of employment, and thus not a Section 8(a)(5) obligation. If the decision of where to locate a plant is, as the Supreme Court says, a core entrepreneurial decision, then the "benefit for labor-management relations and the collective bargaining process" cannot be deemed to outweigh "the burden placed on the conduct of the business." The benefit to the collective bargaining process is limited because just like partial closings, the plant relocation decision is not "amenable to resolution through the bargaining process." On the other side of the ledger, the burden to the company remains high. A company would lose the freedom to decide where to locate its business and where to invest finite capital resources. In this case, Dorsey Trailers had to spend a significant amount of capital to buy its new Cartersville plant and to move its equipment there.

The Act itself provides support for the conclusion that a plant relocation is not a mandatory subject of bargaining. Certainly, there is no support in the statute for fitting plant relocations within the terms of Section 8(d). A plant relocation that results in termination may affect the "tenure" of employment, but tenure is not the same thing as a "term or condition of employment." In the Act, the word "tenure" includes length of employment. Tenure, or length, of employment is pointedly not one of the elements included in the mandatory bargaining obligation, which is triggered by Section 8(d) of the Act.

This distinction between the concept of "tenure" and that of "terms and conditions of employment" is borne out by other sections of the statute. Section 8(a)(3), for instance, makes it an unfair labor practice to discriminate "in regard to hire or tenure of employment *or* any term or condition of employment . . . ." Section 8(a)(3) thus distinguishes "tenure" from a "term or condition of employ-ment." Indeed, the Supreme Court itself has recognized this distinction. This statutory separation of "tenure" from "term or condition of employment" suggests tenure is not synonymous with terms and conditions of employment under Section 8(a)(3).

To hold, therefore, that a plant closure or relocation or like decision that affects the tenure of employees is a term or condition of employment under Section 8(d) would do violence both to the Supreme Court's decision in *First National Maintenance* and to the language of the Act. Bargaining over the effects of a decision to close or relocate the plant, by contrast, is a mandatory subject of bargaining precisely because the effects of the decision concern matters such as severance pay and retirement benefits. Section 8(d) specifically includes these matters and others like them because they are "wages, hours, and other terms and conditions of employment." On the other hand, the language of the statute suggests that "terms and conditions of employment" need not include entrepreneurial decisions that have the effect of necessarily terminating employment.

Of course, to recognize the statutory distinction is not to ride it for all it is worth. If, however, Congress meant to include such traditional management decisions as plant closures and relocations within the set of bargainable obligations, it stopped far short of saying so in Section 8(d). To rest such a far-reaching bargaining obligation on such a thin statutory reed would have judges expand the contours of the NLRA beyond all proper bounds. "Terms and conditions of employment" is simply not an all-inclusive phrase. Indeed, another circuit has already held that Dorsey Trailers' decision to subcontract part of its work to the company that previously operated the Cartersville facility was not a mandatory subject of bargaining.

The NLRB General Counsel argues, however, that *Dubuque Packing Co.*, 303 NLRB 386 (1991), compels the result that the plant relocation is a mandatory subject of bargaining. We disagree. *Dubuque Packing* is simply incompatible with our decision in *Arrow.* Indeed, in *Arrow* we specifically disapproved of *Otis Elevator Company*, 269 NLRB 891 (1984) (*Otis II*), which was the predecessor of *Dubuque Packing. Dubuque Packing*, just like *Otis II*, is "flatly inconsistent with *First National Maintenance.* Where an employer closes down part of its operation . . . the Court has made clear that bargaining over the decision is not required." Moreover, *Dubuque Packing* posits a false dichotomy between economic and labor costs. Under *Arrow*, however, economic reasons for moving "are not reasons distinct and apart from a desire to decrease labor costs." Indeed, labor costs are "inescapably" a part of the economic calculus that a company must consider in deciding whether to relocate.

The union contends that *Arrow* is distinguishable because *Arrow* did not involve a claim of anti-union animus. This distinction is unavailing. The phrase "terms and conditions of employment" does not magically change meaning with the infusion of anti-union animus. Section 8(a)(5) simply does not cover plant relocations or partial closings. This does not mean, of course, that the union and the General Counsel are without a remedy for anti-union animus. The relevant section to redress this animus is the broader language of Section 8(a)(3), not the more circumscribed text of Section 8(d) and 8(a)(5). Furthermore, the union can certainly protect its interest through bargaining over the effects of the decision to relocate, which is a mandatory subject of bargaining under Section 8(a)(5). And, of course, nothing in the Act prevents permissive bargaining over a closure or relocation decision. What we decline to do, however, is to expand the scope of mandatory or impasse bargaining to matters which the relevant statutory sections do not include. Because a plant relocation is not a term or condition of employment, the company did not violate Section 8(a)(5) by failing to bargain to impasse on the work transfer.

D.

The Board used its remedial powers under § 10(c) to order the restoration of operations at the Northumberland plant. *See* 29 U.S.C. § 160(c) (giving Board the power to issue an order requiring company "to cease and desist from such unfair labor practice, and to take such affirmative action including reinstatement of employees . . . as will effectuate the policies of" the NLRA). The company alleges that requiring it to reopen the plant will cause an undue economic burden. We have found that the company did not commit an unfair labor practice by moving the plant from Northumberland to Cartersville or by failing to bargain to impasse about the move. Consequently, the Board's order is not supportable given the remaining violations of the Act.

Indeed, the Supreme Court warned that restoration orders "trench [ ] . . . closely upon otherwise legitimate employer prerogatives." When a company must expend significant funds or make new capital investments to restore operations, the order will be unduly burdensome given its economic cost. Restoration orders to reopen a facility are presumptively suspect given the substantial cost in both human and monetary terms. In this case, the unfair labor practices that have been upheld come nowhere close to allowing the Board to order such a draconian remedy.

IV.

The decision of where to locate a business is fundamentally a managerial decision. Companies must account for the costs of operating a facility as well as the benefits of working in a particular place. Thus a company is under no statutory obligation to bargain about judgments that lie at the entrepreneurial heart of an enterprise. In this case, the company made its decision to relocate its plant for a variety of economic reasons. Although Dorsey Trailers violated the Act in the ways we have recounted, it did not do so by relocating its plant to a more favorable business environment or by failing to bargain to impasse about the move. Accordingly, enforcement of the Board's order is granted in part and denied in part. On remand, the order shall be modified to conform with this decision.

POST PROBLEM DISCUSSION

1. The issue in *Dubuque Packing, Dorsey Trailers*, and Problem #3 is whether the relocation of a plant constitutes a mandatory subject of bargaining. In answering this question, courts seem to suggest that relocation is either more like subcontracting in *Fibreboard*, and thus bargaining is required, or more like the partial closing in *First National Maintenance*, and bargaining is not required. Which court's reasoning is more persuasive? Does the *Dubuque Packing* test do a good job of accommodating the employer's entrepreneurial control concerns with preserving a place for the collective bargaining process to work?

2. In *Regal Cinemas, Inc. v. NLRB*, 317 F.3d 300 (D.C. Cir. 2003), the court applied the *Dubuque Packing* test to a case where the employer terminated union jobs and gave the union members' work to managers. The Board and the D.C. Circuit found that the work was the same, the work was being performed under similar conditions, and the change was made not because of technology but due to labor costs. Therefore, the court concluded that the decision was a mandatory bargaining subject.

3. Does the *Dubuque Packing* burden shifting test adequately achieve the NLRB's stated goals? Although the Board arguably achieved its objective in promulgating this test, its inherent complexity and subjectivity suggest there will remain a lack of clarity for labor market participants.

4. Should the NLRB extend the *Dubuque Packing* test to all major corporate decisions? For instance, the Board in *Mid-State Ready Mix*, 307 N.L.R.B. 809 (1992), found that an employer who terminated unionized employees and transferred their work to subcontractors engaged in *Fibreboard* subcontracting and committed an unfair labor practice by failing to negotiate with the union before restructuring the work.

5. Of course, as seen above, the Fourth Circuit (covering Virginia, North Carolina, and South Carolina) in *Dorsey Trailers* disagreed with the *Dubuque Packing* standards. The court found that an employer that closed one of its facilities and moved the work to another, non-union, facility was not required to bargain with the union, because the relocation involved a decision about the withdrawal and location of capital resources. The court went even further, stating that it did not believe that plant relocations could be based on factors that had nothing to do with labor costs. Agree? Does the geographical location of the courts or the cultural background of the judges help to explain the diametrically-opposed outcomes in these cases?

6. The Worker Adjustment and Retraining Notification Act, 29 U.S.C. §§ 2101-2108 (WARN Act), applies to employers with 100 or more employees and provides notice and other protections for covered employees in certain mass layoff and plant closing scenarios. Basically, an employer must give employees six-month's notice or its equivalent whenever a statutory "plant closing" or "mass layoff" occurs.

7. As far as bargaining remedies, the Supreme Court held in *H.K. Porter Co. v. NLRB*, 397 U.S. 99 (1970), that the Board could not order a company to grant the union a contract clause providing for the checkoff of union dues. The Board has power to make parties negotiate, but it does not have power to compel a company to agree to any substantive provisions, no matter how egregious the employer's conduct. Although Section 8(d) does not expressly address remedies, the Court held that the same considerations that led to Section 8(d) compelled the conclusion that the Board does not have remedial power to force contract provisions between the parties. Given *H.K. Porter*, what is to prevent a company from negotiating in bad faith if they only face a cease and desist order from the Board? Indeed, because the remedies available after *H.K. Porter* are so minimal, why should employers even bother challenging a Section 8(a)(5) finding against them?

8. On the other hand, if a company withdraws in bad faith proposals it once agreed to, *TNT USA, Inc. v. NLRB*, 208 F.3d 362 (2d Cir. 2000), stands for the proposition that the NLRB may order an employer to reinstate the proposals. The court reasoned that the "order [to accept terms] did not compel agreement but merely required employer to reinstate proposal it previously voluntarily presented." Is this decision consistent with *H.K. Porter*?

9. In another bargaining remedies case, *Ex-Cell-O Corporation*, 185 N.L.R.B. 107 (1970), the United Auto Workers (UAW) demanded recognition, the company refused, the union petitioned for an election and won, and the company still refused to bargain. It was not disputed that the company violated Section 8(a)(5), but the issue of an appropriate remedy remained. The Trial Examiner (now called the ALJ) recommended that the Board issue a compensatory order, awarding back pay for the unlawful refusal to bargain. The Board "reluctantly conclude[d]" that the Trial Examiner overstepped his authority in issuing the remedial order, even though the Board agreed that the remedies available for Section 8(a)(5) violations were inadequate.

The Board reasoned that compensatory orders were not permitted because they constituted an impermissible penalty, and punitive damages were not provided for under the NLRA. The Board found this to be a punitive damage award, because the order imposed a large financial obligation on a company that had a debatable issue as to whether it should be required to bargain. The order would have punished the company for pursuing the representation question beyond the Board and to the courts.

As far requiring contractual terms, the Board found the compensatory order would have operated retroactively to impose financial liability on an employer flowing from a presumed contractual agreement. According to the Board, it is for Congress to provide such additional remedies, not the agency.

10. In a very fractured opinion, the Fourth Circuit Court of Appeals in *Fieldcrest Cannon, Inc. v. NLRB*, 97 F. 3d 65 (4th Cir. 1996), enforced a Board order for a slew of remedies, but not the order for a 1% wage increase. One of the judges would have allowed such an increase, even after taking *H.K. Porter* into account, because the company did more than just refuse to bargain. Indeed, "[t]he Board *additionally* found that Fieldcrest's creation of an unprecedented wage disparity amounted to a completely separate kind of unfair labor practice: discrimi-

natory withholding of a 'wage increase from its represented employees in order to discourage support for the Union.' " Should such egregious employer conduct permit more significant remedies under Section 10(c)?

Chapter 9

STRIKES, LOCKOUTS, AND EMPLOYER RESPONSES TO UNION CONCERTED ACTIVITY

Our previous discussions of protected union activity leads to an important question: what actions may employers take in response to these union tactics?

In Section 1, this Chapter discusses the right to strike under Section 13 of the Act and the employer's ability to permanently replace workers who decide to strike. From there, Section 2 explores other types of actions that employers have taken in response to union picketing, boycotting, and striking, including the use of super-seniority systems and offensive bargaining lockouts. Finally, Section 3 considers the modern *Great Dane* framework under Section 8(a)(3) and inherently destructive conduct.

SECTION 1   STRIKES AND PERMANENT REPLACEMENTS

Wages and terms of employment are determined by the parties, not by the government. Collective bargaining works because negotiations narrow the issues between the parties, and the threat of a work stoppage looms over the parties. At the last minute, the union has to decide whether to compromise or go on strike, and the employer has to decide whether to compromise or lock out its employees. If a strike or lockout occurs, there will only be a settlement if the costs of not settling become greater than the costs of accepting the terms of the proposal.

Particularly challenging strike issues arise when dealing with industries where strikes become intolerable to the public long before they become intolerable to the parties. For instance, with national emergencies, Sections 206 through 210 of Labor Management Relations Act (Taft-Hartley Act) sets forth detailed procedures to govern strikes that are deemed to constitute a national emergency. The President can impanel a Board of Inquiry if the strike will imperil the national health or safety. After investigation, the President can ask the Attorney General to petition the federal court for a 60-day injunction. The injunction must be dissolved after 80 days. These procedures have been held constitutional by the Supreme Court. The most recent use of these procedures occurred in 2002, when the Bush II administration sought an injunction stopping a lockout of longshoreman. A court granted the injunction based on its finding that the lockout caused a national emergency by delaying shipments of goods through the 29 affected West Coast ports.

Even when a work stoppage doesn't constitute a national emergency, the NLRA attempts to avoid the economic disruption caused by strikes and lockouts. This policy fosters voluntary settlements of disputes through, among other things, Section 8(d)'s elaborate notification and cooling off procedures in Section 8(d).

Section 8(d)(1) requires written notice sixty days prior to expiration of a collective-bargaining agreement if a party wants to terminate or modify the CBA. Section 8(d)(2) requires the party to meet and confer with the other party for the purpose of negotiating a new CBA or modifying the current CBA. Section 8(d)(3) next requires that thirty days after the initial notice, the parties must notify the Federal Mediation and Conciliation Service (FMCS) of the pending dispute. The parties, however, are not currently required to mediate with the FMCS. Finally, Section 8(d)(4) states that parties must not strike for sixty days after notification under Section 8(d)(1), and failure to comply with this rule violates the duty to bargain in good faith under Section 8(a)(5).

There are additional special rules for health care institutions as result of the 1974 amendments to the NLRA. These institutions, because of patient health concerns, must mediate with FMCS under Sections 8(d) and 8(g) of the Act, and in this context, there is also the ability to appoint an impartial Board of Inquiry to investigate.

PROBLEM 1: IS THE RIGHT TO STRIKE IN THE U.S. ILLUSORY?

Local 13 of the Amalgamated Widget Makers is involved in a difficult negotiation with their employer, Widget Busters. The negotiations have broken down over employee pension contributions and the employer's refusal to agree to a dues-checkoff provision to withhold union membership fees from workers' paychecks.

After an impasse has been declared over these issues, the company lawfully and unilaterally implements its last best offer on these issues. In response, all Local 13 workers walk off the job and begin an economic strike against Widget Busters. The next day, Widget Busters places an ad in the newspaper, offering to hire new workers on a permanent basis to replace the striking workers. A week later, the company has permanently replaced all striking workers.

A group of Local 13 workers, still out on strike, think that the company's actions are tantamount to firing them in violation of Sections 8(a)(1) and 8(a)(3) of the Act. Are they correct? What is the difference between being permanently replaced and being terminated?

PROBLEM MATERIALS

NLRB v. Mackay Radio & Telegraph Co., 304 U.S. 333 (U.S. 1938)

Laidlaw Corp., 171 N.L.R.B. 1366 (1968)

Paul M. Secunda, *Politics Not As Usual: Inherently Destructive Conduct, Institutional Collegiality, and the National Labor Relations Board*, 32 FLA. ST. U. L. REV. 51 (2004)

NLRB v. MACKAY RADIO & TELEGRAPH CO.
304 U.S. 333 (1938)

JUSTICE ROBERTS delivered the opinion of the Court.

The Circuit Court of Appeals refused to decree enforcement of an order of the National Labor Relations Board . . . .

The respondent, a California corporation, is engaged in the transmission and receipt of telegraph, radio, cable, and other messages between points in California and points in other states and foreign countries. It maintains an office in San Francisco for the transaction of its business wherein it employs upwards of sixty supervisors, operators and clerks, many of whom are members of Local No. 3 of the American Radio Telegraphists Association, a national labor organization; the membership of the local comprising 'point-to-point' or land operators employed by respondent at San Francisco. Affiliated with the national organization also were locals whose members are exclusively marine operators who work upon ocean-going vessels. The respondent, at its San Francisco office, dealt with committees of Local No. 3; and its parent company, whose headquarters were in New York, dealt with representatives of the national organization. Demand was made by the latter for the execution of agreements respecting terms and conditions of employment of marine and point-to-point operators. On several occasions when representatives of the union conferred with officers of the respondent and its parent company the latter requested postponement of discussion of the proposed agreements and the union acceded to the requests. In September, 1935, the union pressed for immediate execution of agreements and took the position that no contract would be concluded by the one class of operators unless an agreement were simultaneously made with the other.

Local No. 3 sent a representative to New York to be in touch with the negotiations and he kept its officers advised as to what there occurred. The local adopted a resolution to the effect that if satisfactory terms were not obtained by September 23 a strike of the San Francisco point-to-point operators should be called. The national officers determined on a general strike in view of the unsatisfactory state of the negotiations. This fact was communicated to Local No. 3 by its representative in New York and the local officers called out the employees of the San Francisco office. At midnight Friday, October 4, 1935, all the men there employed went on strike. The respondent, in order to maintain service, brought employees from its Los Angeles office and others from the New York and Chicago offices of the parent company to fill the strikers' places.

Although none of the San Francisco strikers returned to work Saturday, Sunday, or Monday, the strike proved unsuccessful in other parts of the country and, by Monday evening, October 7th, a number of the men became convinced that it would fail and that they had better return to work before their places were filled with new employees. One of them telephoned the respondent's traffic supervisor Monday evening to inquire whether the men might return. He was told that the respondent would take them back and it was arranged that the official should meet the employees at a downtown hotel and make a statement to them. Before leaving the company's office for this purpose the supervisor consulted with his superior, who told him that the men might return to work in their former positions but that, as the company had promised eleven men brought to San Francisco they might remain if they so desired, the supervisor would have to handle the return of the striking employees in such fashion as not to displace any of the new men who desired to continue in San Francisco. A little later the supervisor met two of the striking employees and gave them a list of all the strikers together with their addresses, and the telephone numbers of those who had telephones, and it was arranged that these two employees should telephone the strikers to come to a meeting at the Hotel Bellevue in the early hours of Tuesday, October 8th. In furnishing this list the supervisor stated that the men could return to work in a body but he checked off the names of eleven strikers who he said would have to file applications for reinstatement which applications would be subject to the approval of an executive of the company in New York.

Because of this statement the two employees, in notifying the strikers of the proposed meeting, with the knowledge of the supervisor, omitted to communicate with the eleven men whose names had been checked off. Thirty-six men attended the meeting. Some of the eleven in question heard of it and attended. The supervisor appeared at the meeting and reiterated his statement that the men could go back to work at once but read from a list the names of the eleven who would be required to file applications for reinstatement to be passed upon in New York. Those present at the meeting voted on the question of immediately returning to work and the proposition was carried. Most of the men left the meeting and went to the respondent's office Tuesday morning, October 8th, where on that day they resumed their usual duties. Then or shortly thereafter six of the eleven in question took their places and resumed their work without challenge. It turned out that only five of the new men brought to San Francisco desired to stay.

Five strikers who were prominent in the activities of the union and in connection with the strike, whose names appeared upon the list of eleven, reported at the office at various times between Tuesday and Thursday. Each of them was told that he would have to fill out an application for employment; that the roll of employees was complete, and that his application would be considered in connection with any vacancy that might thereafter occur. These men not having been reinstated in the course of three weeks, the secretary of Local No. 3 presented a charge to the National Labor Relations Board that the respondent had violated section 8(1) and (3) [now 8(a)(1) and (a)(3)] of the National Labor Relations Act. Thereupon the Board filed a complaint charging that the respondent had discharged and was refusing to employ the five men who had not been reinstated to their positions for the reason that they had joined and assisted the labor organization known as Local No. 3 and had engaged in concerted activities with other employees of the respondent for the purpose of collective bargaining and other mutual aid and protection; that by such discharge respondent had interfered with, restrained, and coerced the employees in the exercise of their rights guaranteed by section 7 of the

National Labor Relations Act and so had been guilty of an unfair labor practice within the meaning of section 8(1) of the act. The complaint further alleged that the discharge of these men was a discrimination in respect of their hire and tenure of employment and a discouragement of membership in Local No. 3, and thus an unfair labor practice within the meaning of section 8(3) of the act . . . .

We hold that we have jurisdiction; that the Board's order is within its competence and does not contravene any provision of the Constitution . . . .

The strikers remained employees under section 2(3) of the act, which provides: 'The term 'employee' shall include . . . any individual whose work has ceased as a consequence of, or in connection with, any current labor dispute or because of any unfair labor practice, and who has not obtained any other regular and substantially equivalent employment . . . .' Within this definition the strikers remained employees for the purpose of the act and were protected against the unfair labor practices denounced by it.

. . . It is contended that the Board lacked jurisdiction because respondent was at no time guilty of any unfair labor practice. Section 8 of the act denominates as such practice action by an employer to interfere with, restrain, or coerce employees in the exercise of their rights to organize, to form, join, or assist labor organizations, and to engage in concerted activities for the purpose of collective bargaining or other mutual aid or protection, or 'by discrimination in regard to . . . tenure of employment or any term or condition of employment to encourage or discourage membership in any labor organization . . . .' There is no evidence and no finding that the respondent was guilty of any unfair labor practice in connection with the negotiations in New York. On the contrary, it affirmatively appears that the respondent was negotiating with the authorized representatives of the union. Nor was it an unfair labor practice to replace the striking employees with others in an effort to carry on the business. Although section 13 of the act, provides, 'Nothing in this Act (chapter) shall be construed so as to interfere with or impede or diminish in any way the right to strike,' it does not follow that an employer, guilty of no act denounced by the statute, has lost the right to protect and continue his business by supplying places left vacant by strikers. And he is not bound to discharge those hired to fill the places of strikers, upon the election of the latter to resume their employment, in order to create places for them. The assurance by respondent to those who accepted employment during the strike that if they so desired their places might be permanent was not an unfair labor practice, nor was it such to reinstate only so many of the strikers as there were vacant places to be filled. But the claim put forward is that the unfair labor practice indulged by the respondent was discrimination in reinstating striking employees by keeping out certain of them for the sole reason that they had been active in the union. As we have said, the strikers retained, under the act, the status of employees. Any such discrimination in putting them back to work is, therefore, prohibiting by section 8.

. . . The Board's findings as to discrimination are supported by evidence. We shall not attempt a discussion of the conflicting claims as to the proper conclusions to be drawn from the testimony. There was evidence, which the Board credited, that several of the five men in question were told that their union activities made them undesirable to their employer; and that some of them did not return to work with the great body of the men at 6 o'clock on Tuesday morning because they understood they would not be allowed to go to work until the superior officials had passed upon their applications. When they did apply at times between Tuesday morning and Thursday they were each told that the quota was full and that their applications could not be granted in any event until a vacancy occurred. This was on the ground that five of the eleven new men remained at work in San Francisco. On the other hand, six of the eleven strikers listed for separate treatment who reported for work early Tuesday morning, or within the next day or so, were permitted to go back to work and were not compelled to await the approval of their applications. It appears that all of the men who had been on strike signed applications for re-employment shortly after their resumption of work. The Board found, and we cannot say that its finding is unsupported, that, in taking back six of the eleven men and excluding five who were active union men, the respondent's officials discriminated against the latter on account of their union activities and that the excuse given that they did not apply until after the quota was full was an afterthought and not the true reason for the discrimination against them.

As we have said, the respondent was not bound to displace men hired to take the strikers' places in order to provide positions for them. It might have refused reinstatement on the grounds of skill or ability, but the Board found that it did not do so. It might have resorted to any one of a number of methods of determining which of its striking employees would have to wait because five men had taken permanent positions during the strike, but it is found that the preparation and use of the list, and the action taken by respondent, was with the purpose to discriminate against those most active in the union. There is evidence to support these findings . . . .

The judgment of the Circuit Court of Appeals is reversed, and the cause is remanded to that court for further proceedings in conformity with this opinion. So ordered.

Reversed and remanded.

JUSTICE CARDOZO and JUSTICE REED took no part in the consideration or decision of this case.

LAIDLAW CORP.
171 N.L.R.B. 1366 (1968)

. . . The Board has reviewed the rulings of the Trial Examiner made at the hearing and finds that no prejudicial error was committed. The rulings are hereby affirmed. The Board has considered the Trial Examiner's Decision, the exceptions and briefs, and the entire record in the case, and hereby adopts the findings, conclusions, and recommendations of the Trial Examiner as modified herein.

In affirming the Trial Examiner we take particular note of that part of his Decision which in effect holds that replaced economic strikers who have made an unconditional application for reinstatement, and who have continued to make known their availability for employment, are entitled to full reinstatement to fill positions left by the departure of permanent replacements. In arriving at this conclusion, we specifically find that Respondent has not shown any legitimate and substantial business justification for not offering full reinstatement to these strikers and, that, accordingly, the failure to make such an offer constitutes an unfair labor practice even without regard to Respondent's intent or union animus.

The facts surrounding the issues of reinstatement rights are relatively free from dispute. On January 10, 1966, the Union voted to reject the Company's wage offer and notified the Company of an intent to strike on January 12. As noted by the Trial Examiner, on the day before the strike Plant Manager Johnston read a speech to employees emphasizing that if they went out on a strike and were replaced, "you LOSE FOREVER your right to employment by this company." On January 12 approximately 70 employees began the strike with the pickets bearing signs indicating that the strike was for "fair wages."

One of the strikers was William Massey, an employee since 1961. On January 14 Massey made an unconditional request for reinstatement but was told his job had been filled and that if he were reemployed it would be as a new employee at the rate of $1.895 per hour as opposed to the $1.995 Massey made before the strike. On January 18 Massey was called by the Company and asked to return, as a vacancy had occurred in his classification. Massey was offered his old rate of pay, but was informed he would otherwise be treated as a new employee, without his seniority and vacation rights. When he expressed concern about these terms, Plant Manager Johnston promised to see that the rights were restored in 60 days, but reiterated that Massey would have to come back as a new employee. Under these circumstances Massey refused to return and continued on strike.

At a union meeting on February 10, attended by about 50 of the employees, the strikers voted to return to work. On Friday, February 11, Union Representative Rains and some 40 strikers appeared at the plant and made an unconditional request to return to work. The unconditional offer to return was made on behalf of all the strikers, not just those who accompanied Rains. In addition, each of the workers who accompanied Rains presented a signed statement offering to return immediately and unconditionally. After consulting his attorney, Plant Manager Johnston read a prepared statement to the effect that many of the strikers had been "permanently replaced and are not entitled to reinstatement," and that those for whom there was a job would be notified on or before Monday. The Trial Examiner found, and we agree, that as of February 11 the strike was an economic one, and that as of that date all but five of the economic strikers' jobs were filled by replacements who were assured of permanent status if their work proved satisfactory. As the five strikers who were not replaced were thereafter offered jobs, Respondent's actions were proper and not in violation of the Act.

In addition to the written applications for reinstatement which were submitted on February 11, other written applications were made, between February 11 and 21, by about 16 employees who had not been present at the February 11 meeting. On the dates these later applications were received Respondent checked to see if vacancies existed at that time, and, if they did, some of the applicants were hired. However, new applicants were hired if the vacancies exceeded the number of striker applicants. By February 22 a total of 10 strikers had been reinstated and 8 others had been offered reinstatement, but had declined and remained on strike. The

Respondent did not check over the earlier reinstatement applications of February 11 before making new hires, and reinstatement applications were considered only on the date of application. Plant Manager Johnston's testimony established that this hiring policy was newly inaugurated after the strike and apparently conformed with and implemented Respondent's previously voiced threat that once replaced, strikers "lose forever" their right to employment by the Company. Beginning on February 16 Respondent sent strikers, except those who had been reinstated or had declined reinstatement, termination notices that they had been replaced as of the date of their written reinstatement applications and that no jobs were available. However, Respondent continued to advertise for permanent help and a number of new employees were hired due to turnover, which included the departure of some permanent replacements.

At a union meeting on February 20 a group of strikers who had been reinstated, or offered reinstatement, protested the employment termination notices to the strikers and the failure to reinstate the bulk of the strikers. The employees decided to renew their strike over this alleged unfair labor practice and on February 21, 16 of them continued or rejoined the strike. Thereafter, no other strikers were offered reinstatement . . . .

We concur in the conclusions of the Trial Examiner and in the relief granted Respondent's employees. In so doing we rely particularly on the principles set forth in *N.L.R.B.* v. *Fleetwood Trailer Co.*, in which the Supreme Court discussed the rights of economic strikers to reinstatement and the responsibility of employers to fully reinstate economic strikers, absent "legitimate and substantial business justifications," in a situation where production increased and more jobs were reestablished.

In *Fleetwood*, the employer was held to have violated the Act by failing to reinstate strikers and by hiring new employees for jobs which were reestablished when the employer resumed full production some 2 months after the strikers applied for reinstatement. In so finding, the Court pointed out that by virtue of Section 2(3) of the Act, an individual whose work ceases due to a labor dispute remains an employee if he has not obtained other regular or substantially equivalent employment, and that an employer refusing to reinstate strikers must show that the action was due to legitimate and substantial business justification. The Court further held that the burden of proving such justification was on the employer and also pointed out that the primary responsibility for striking a proper balance between the asserted business justifications and the invasion of employee rights rests with the Board rather than the courts. The Court also noted that an act so destructive of employee rights, without legitimate business justification, is an unfair labor practice without reference to intent or improper motivation. Furthermore, the Court explicitly rejected the argument, asserted by the employer in *Fleetwood* and relied upon by the Respondent in the instant case, that reinstatement rights are determined at the time of initial application.

It was clearly error to hold that the right of the strikers to reinstatement expired on August 20, when they first applied. *This basic right to jobs cannot depend on job availability as of the moment when applications are filed.* The right to reinstatement does not depend upon technicalities relating to application. On the contrary, *the status of the striker as an employee continues until he has obtained "other regular and substantially equivalent employment."* [Emphasis supplied.]

Application of these principles to the case before us makes it evident that the results reached by the Trial Examiner were correct, even though he did not have the benefit of the Supreme Court's *Fleetwood* decision, which issued subsequently.

Thus, in the case of Massey, he remained an employee when he rejoined the strike after his first effort to be reinstated was rejected even though at that particular moment he had been replaced. The right to reinstatement did not expire when the original application was made. When the position again became vacant, Massey, an economic striker who was still an employee, was available and entitled to full reinstatement unless there were legitimate and substantial business justifications for the failure to offer complete reinstatement. However, it is evident that no such justifications existed, for in fact Respondent needed and desired Massey's services, and it was Respondent who sought out Massey when the vacancy occurred. But its offer of employment as a new employee or as an employee with less than rights accorded by full reinstatement (such as denial of seniority) was wholly unrelated to any of its economic needs, could only penalize Massey for engaging in concerted activity, was inherently destructive of employee interests, and thus was unresponsive to the requirements of the statute. In these circumstances there was no valid reason why Massey should not have been offered complete reinstatement, and Respondent's failure to do so was in violation of Section 8(a)(3) and (1) of the Act.

Similarly, we are guided by *Fleetwood* and *Great Dane* in our consideration of the strikers whom Respondent terminated and did not recall after their application for reinstatement on February 11 and thereafter. As in the case of Massey, they remained employees, and their right to reinstatement did not expire on the date they first applied, even though replacements filled most of the positions at the precise time they sought reinstatement. As employees with outstanding unconditional applications for reinstatement at the time the strike changed into an unfair labor practice strike, on and after February 11, these strikers were entitled to full reinstatement as vacancies arose in their old positions. This conclusion was foreshadowed long ago by, and is consistent with, the Supreme Court's decision in *N.L.R.B.* v. *Mackay Radio & Telegraph Co.*

Furthermore, we would so hold even if we did not concur in the Trial Examiner's finding that the strike was converted from an economic to an unfair labor practice strike on February 11. As economic strikers their situation would have been essentially the same as Massey's; i.e., they remained employees who had offered to abandon the strike and who were available to fill openings as such arose. As Respondent brought forward no evidence of business justification for refusing to reinstate these experienced employees while continuing to advertise for and hire new unskilled employees, we find such conduct was inherently destructive of employee rights. This right of reinstatement continued to exist so long as the strikers had not abandoned the employ of Respondent for other substantial and equivalent employment. Moreover, having signified their intent to return by their unconditional application for reinstatement and by their continuing presence, it was incumbent on Respondent to seek them out as positions were vacated. Having failed to fulfill its obligation to reinstate the employees to their jobs as vacancies arose, the Respondent thereby violated Section 8(a)(3) and (1) of the Act . . . .

We hold, therefore, that economic strikers who unconditionally apply for reinstatement at a time when their positions are filled by permanent replacements: (1) remain employees; and (2) are entitled to full reinstatement upon the departure of replacements unless they have in the meantime acquired regular and substantially equivalent employment, or the employer can sustain his burden of proof that the failure to offer full reinstatement was for legitimate and substantial business reasons.

Paul M. Secunda, *Politics Not As Usual: Inherently Destructive Conduct, Institutional Collegiality, and the National Labor Relations Board*
32 FLA. ST. U. L. REV. 51 (2004)[1]

. . . B. Section 8(a)(3) Cases Under the Wagner Act

. . . 2. NLRB v. Mackay Radio & Telegraph Co.

[T]he Supreme Court again considered section 8(a)(3) in the well-known case of *NLRB v. Mackay Radio & Telegraph Co.* In *Mackay Radio*, the company responded to strike activity on the part of its employees by replacing them during the strike with new employees and then by refusing to displace these replacements once the strike had ended. The employer maintained that it had permanently replaced the strikers not for any anti-union reasons, but for the legitimate reason of continuing its business operations during the strike.

Mackay Radio, therefore, represented a classic case of union discouragement without specific evidence of discrimination. At this point in the doctrinal development of section 8(a)(3), however, the Court was unable, or perhaps unwilling, to infer the necessary unlawful intent from the sheer colossal effect such action had on the strikers and their union. The problem for the Court was that in the absence of specific evidence of anti-union intent, it was extremely difficult to determine which motivation played the dominant role in determining the employer's conduct vis-à-vis its striking workers.

Apparently reluctant to engage in this intricate analytical exercise, the Supreme Court avoided the issue lurking in *Mackay Radio* and instead was contented to assume there was no unlawful discrimination under section 8(a)(3) based on the employer's mere protestations of innocence. Inferring anti-union intent from the injurious consequences of employer conduct on employee rights under the Act would have to wait another day.

---

3. Republic Aviation Corp. v. NLRB

Indeed, it was not until seven years later, in *Republic Aviation Corp. v. NLRB*, that the Court appeared tentatively to take this next step and find a section 8(a)(3) violation in a case where specific evidence of unlawful employer intent was lacking. In *Republic Aviation*, there were two instances of employees being terminated for engaging in union solicitation activities in violation of two different companies' strictly enforced no-solicitation policies. Having found that the companies' no-solicitation policies violated section 8(a)(1) by impermissibly interfering with employees' section 7 rights to organize, the Court then found "that if a rule against solicitation is invalid as to union solicitation on the employer's premises during the employee's own time, a discharge because of violation of that rule discriminates within the meaning of Section 8[(a)](3) in that it discourages membership in a labor organization."

Republic Aviation's innovation was that there could be an unfair labor practice under section 8(a)(3) in the absence of specific evidence of employer anti-union intent. As a Supreme Court Justice explained in a subsequent section 8(a)(3) case: "A finding of [employer] motivation [in *Republic Aviation*] . . . [was] unnecessary because there was no employer showing of a nondiscriminatory purpose for applying the rule to union solicitation during the employees' free time." [Local 357, Int'l Bhd. of Teamsters v. NLRB, 365 U.S. 667, 680 (1961) (Harlan, J., concurring)]. The seeds of the inherently destructive standard had thus been sown.

POST PROBLEM DISCUSSION

1. Here, it is important to distinguish between the uncontroversial holding of *Mackay Radio* and what the case has come to stand for, which is controversial. As an initial matter, not bringing back active union members after a strike because of their activity is clear discrimination in violation of Section 8(a)(3). However, *Mackay Radio* has come to stand for the proposition that an employer may permanently replace striking workers and does not have to remove them once the economic strike is over. How does permanent replacement differ from termination?

Laidlaw Corp. continues to stand for the proposition that employers may hire permanent replacements under *Mackay Radio* and replacements are permitted to keep their jobs even after the economic strike is over. However, an employee's status as a statutory employee under Section 2(3) of the Act means that they retain their seniority, and upon an unconditional offer to return to work and an appropriate vacancy, they go to the front of the queue. On the other hand, if the striking employee finds substantially equivalent work elsewhere, they no longer have these *Laidlaw* rights. Practically speaking, then, how useful are *Laidlaw* rights? How long can an average employee wait after being replaced before having to look for substantially equivalent employment?

2. In Ontario, permanent replacement is generally not permitted, but temporarily replacing workers during a strike is. If you were an employer trying to survive a strike by your employees, why might you argue that temporary replacements will not permit you to carry on your business during the strike? Do you think many experienced workers would apply for a job they knew was only temporary?

3. As noted before, the NLRA seeks to find a balance between employer and employee interests. Does *Mackay Radio*'s sanctioning of permanent replacement workers go too far in chilling employees' willingness to exercise their rights to strike? Or are management attorneys correct that the threat of permanent replacements limits unreasonable union demands and that employers should have the right to run their work places as they see fit, which includes being able to hire other employees (if they can find the appropriate skilled labor) needed to keep their business running?

4. In Problem #1, would your legal advice change if there was either inferential or direct evidence that the strikers were not being brought back to punish them for engaging in protected concerted activity under Sections 7 and 13?

5. There are two categories of strikes: economic strikes, which was the subject of *Mackay Radio*, and unfair labor practice strikes. The distinction between the two has significant consequences. ULP strikers, those who go out on strike at least in part to protest alleged unfair labor practices by the employer, can be temporarily, but not permanently, replaced. The argument is that ULP strikers should be able to get their jobs back immediately after the strike is over so that the employer does not gain anything from engaging in unlawful activity. With regard to voting in certification or decertification elections, the Board also treats ULP strikers more favorably than economic strikers. Although both ULP strikers and economic strikers can vote, economic strikers' right to vote expires if the election is held more than twelve months after the strike begins. Also, replacement workers hired during an economic strike may vote, while those hired during an unfair labor practice strike may not.

To complicate matters, an economic strike may be converted to a ULP strike (e.g., in *Laidlaw*, an economic strike over bargaining demands was converted into an ULP strike when the union voted to renew its original strike to protest the employer's firing of employees seeking reinstatement). Finally, in the event that strikers have engaged in unprotected activity, courts have historically been more favorable to the ULP striker's rights to reinstatement. The Board has reasoned that a ULP striker who engages in unprotected activity should not be automatically denied reinstatement because the employer's ULP might have been so bad as to provoke the employee to commit the illegality. Reinstatement may be the only way to prevent the employer from benefitting from the ULP.

6. A number of bills have been introduced to legislatively overrule *Mackay Radio*, the most recent of which was defeated by congressional Republicans in 1994. President Clinton sought to use his executive order authority to prohibit permanent replacements from being used where federal contracts were involved, but this executive order was later ruled invalid by the D.C. Circuit Court. *See Chamber of Commerce of the United States v. Reich*, 74 F.3d 1322 (D.C. Cir. 1996).

7. In *Belknap v. Hale*, 463 U.S. 491 (1983), the Supreme Court held that permanent replacements who lost their jobs as a result of a strike settlement agreement between the company and union could bring state tort and contract claims against the company. The company argued that the NLRA preempted any such state common law claims, but the Court disagreed. (We will learn more about preemption in Chapter 11.) On one hand, *Belknap* might make employers less likely

to promise permanent positions to replacements unless they are absolutely sure that a subsequent strike settlement agreement will not require strikers to get their jobs back. On the other hand, strikes might be harder to settle if employers have already made these promises and the union will not end the strike until it can ensure that strikers will get their jobs back.

8.   Although the use of permanent replacements by employers has been lawful since the late 1930s, the Supreme Court did not reaffirm its *Mackay Radio* holding until *Erie Resistor* (discussed below) in 1963. Even then, permanent replacements did not become a normal part of industrial life in the United States until the 1980s. A number of commentators believe that it was the firing of some 11,000 air traffic controllers by President Reagan in 1981 that led to frequent use of this tactic in the private sector and the subsequent precipitous decline in the number of strikes in the United States. *See* Michael H. LeRoy, *Lockouts Involving Replacement Workers: An Empirical Public Policy Analysis and Proposal to Balance Economic Weapons Under the NLRA*, 74 WASH. U. L.Q. 981, 985 (1996); Joseph P. Norelli, *Permanent Replacements: Time For A New Look?*, 24 LAB. LAW. 97, 99 (2008-09).

SECTION 2   SUPER-SENIORITY AND LOCKOUTS

In addition to using permanent replacements, employers have sought to employ other responses to protected union activity. Some have been found lawful, while others have been found unlawful. As you read the problem materials, ask yourself: what are the important differences between legitimate and illegitimate employer responses to union concerted activity?

PROBLEM 2: KEEP ON KNOCKIN', BUT YOU CAN'T COME IN

Ball Bearings, Inc. (BBI) is in the midst of a nasty worker stoppage with the union that represents its engineering employees. BBI locked out its engineers when they refused to agree to a substantial benefit and pay cut.

In order to convince replacement workers to come work in this volatile environment, the company offered replacement employees both a permanent job and three years of additional seniority to protect them from future layoffs.

You are counsel to BBI. Advise BBI whether the lockout was lawful and whether this super-seniority arrangement violates the NLRA.

PROBLEM MATERIAL

NLRB v. Erie Resistor Corp., 373 U.S. 221 (1963)

American Ship Building Co. v. NLRB, 380 U.S. 300 (1965)

Paul M. Secunda, *Politics Not As Usual: Inherently Destructive Conduct, Institutional Collegiality, and the National Labor Relations Board*, 32 FLA. ST. U. L. REV. 51 (2004)

NLRB v. ERIE RESISTOR CORP.
373 U.S. 221 (1963)

JUSTICE WHITE delivered the opinion of the Court.

The question before us is whether an employer commits an unfair labor practice under s 8(a) of the National Labor Relations Act, when he extends a 20-year seniority credit to strike replacements and strikers who leave the strike and return to work . . . .

Erie Resistor Corporation and Local 613 of the International Union of Electrical Radio and Machine Workers were bound by a collective bargaining agreement which was due to expire on March 31, 1959. In January 1959, both parties met to negotiate new terms but, after extensive bargaining, they were unable to reach agreement. Upon expiration of the contract, the union, in support of its contract demands, called a strike which was joined by all of the 478 employees in the unit.

The company, under intense competition and subject to insistent demands from its customers to maintain deliveries, decided to continue production operations. Transferring clerks, engineers and other nonunit employees to production jobs, the company managed to keep production at about 15% to 30% of normal during the month of April. On May 3, however, the company notified the union members that it intended to begin hiring replacements and that strikers would retain their jobs until replaced. The plant was located in an area classified by the United States Department of Labor as one of severe unemployment and the company had in fact received applications for employment as early as a week or two after the strike began.

Replacements were told that they would not be laid off or discharged at the end of the strike. To implement that assurance, particularly in view of the 450 employees already laid off on March 31, the company notified the union that it intended to accord the replacements some form of super-seniority. At regular bargaining sessions between the company and union, the union made it clear that, in its view, no matter what form the super-seniority plan might take, it would necessarily work an illegal discrimination against the strikers. As negotiations advanced on other issues, it became evident that super-seniority was fast becoming the focal point of disagreement. On May 28, the company informed the union that it had decided to award 20 years' additional seniority both to replacements and to strikers who returned to work, which would be available only for credit against future layoffs and which could not be used for other employee benefits based on years of service. The strikers, at a union meeting the next day, unanimously resolved to continue striking now in protest against the proposed plan as well.

The company made its first official announcement of the super-seniority plan on June 10, and by June 14, 34 new employees, 47 employees recalled from layoff status and 23 returning strikers had accepted production jobs. The union, now under great pressure, offered to give up some of its contract demands if the company would abandon super-seniority or go to arbitration on the question, but the company refused. In the following week, 64 strikers returned to work and 21 replacements took jobs, bringing the total to 102 replacements and recalled workers and 87 returned strikers. When the number of returning strikers went up to 125 during the following week, the union capitulated. A new labor agreement on the remaining economic issues was executed on July 17, and an accompanying settlement agreement was signed providing that the company's replacement and job assurance policy should be resolved by the National Labor Relations Board and the federal courts but was to remain in effect pending final disposition.

Following the strike's termination, the company reinstated those strikers whose jobs had not been filled (all but 129 were returned to their jobs). At about the same time, the union received some 173 resignations from membership. By September of 1959, the production unit work force had reached a high of 442 employees, but by May of 1960, the work force had gradually slipped back to 240. Many employees laid off during this cut back period were reinstated strikers whose seniority was insufficient to retain their jobs as a consequence of the company's super-seniority policy.

The union filed a charge with the National Labor Relations Board alleging that awarding super-seniority during the course of the strike constituted an unfair labor practice and that the subsequent layoff of the recalled strikers pursuant to such a plan was unlawful . . . . The Board rejected the argument that super-seniority granted during a strike is a legitimate corollary of the employer's right of replacement under National Labor Relations Board v. Mackay Radio & Tel. Co., and detailed at some length the factors which to it indicated that "super-seniority is a form of discrimination extending far beyond the employer's right of replacement sanctioned by Mackay, and is, moreover, in direct conflict with the express provisions of the Act prohibiting discrimination." Having put aside Mackay, the Board went on to deny "that specific evidence of Respondent's discriminatory motivation is required to establish the alleged violations of the Act . . . .

The Court of Appeals rejected as unsupportable the rationale of the Board that a preferential seniority policy is illegal however motivated . . . .

We think the Court of Appeals erred in hold that, in the absence of a finding of specific illegal intent, a legitimate business purpose is always a defense to an unfair labor practice charge. Cases in this Court dealing with unfair labor practices have recognized the relevance and importance of showing the employer's intent or motive to discriminate or to interfere with union rights. But specific evidence of such subjective intent is "not an indispensable element of proof of violation." "Some conduct may by its very nature contain the implications of the required intent; the natural foreseeable consequences of certain action may warrant the inference. . . . The existence of discrimination may at times be inferred by the Board, for "it is permissible to draw on experience in factual inquiries." Local 357, International Brotherhood of Teamsters, Chauffeurs, Warehousemen and Helpers of America v. National Labor Relations Board.

Though the intent necessary for an unfair labor practice may be shown in different ways, proving it in one manner may have far different weight and far different consequences than proving it in another. When specific evidence of a subjective intent to discriminate or to encourage or discourage union membership is shown, and found, many otherwise innocent or ambiguous actions which are normally incident to the conduct of a business may, without more, be converted into unfair labor practices. Such proof itself is normally sufficient to destroy the employer's claim of a legitimate business purpose, if one is made, and provides strong support to a finding that there is interference with union rights or that union membership will be discouraged. Conduct which on its face appears to serve legitimate business ends in these cases is wholly impeached by the showing of an intent to encroach upon protected rights. The employer's claim of legitimacy is totally dispelled.

The outcome may well be the same when intent is founded upon the inherently discriminatory or destructive nature of the conduct itself. The employer in such cases must be held to intend the very consequences which foreseeably and inescapably flow from his actions and if he fails to explain away, to justify or to characterize his actions as something different than they appear on their face, an unfair labor practice charge is made out. Radio Officers Union of Commercial Telegraphers Union, A.F.L. v. National Labor Relations Board. But, as often happens, the employer may counter by claiming that his actions were taken in the pursuit of legitimate business ends and that his dominant purpose was not to discriminate or to invade union rights but to accomplish business objectives acceptable under the Act. Nevertheless, his conduct does speak for itself-it is discriminatory and it does discourage union membership and whatever the claimed overriding justification may be, it carries with it unavoidable consequences which the employer not only foresaw but which he must have intended. As is not uncommon in human experience, such situations present a complex of motives and preferring one motive to another is in reality the far more delicate task, reflected in part in decisions of this Court, of weighing the interests of employees in concerted activity against the interest of the employer in operating his business in a particular manner and of balancing in the light of the Act and its policy the intended consequences upon employee rights against the business ends to be served by the employer's conduct. This essentially is the teaching of the Court's prior cases dealing with this problem and, in our view, the Board did not depart from it.

The Board made a detailed assessment of super-seniority and, it its experienced eye, such a plan had the following characteristics:

(1)   Super-seniority affects the tenure of all strikers whereas permanent replacement, proper under Mackay, affects only those who are, in actuality, replaced. It is one thing to say that a striker is subject to loss of his job at the strike's end but quite another to hold that in addition to the threat of replacement, all strikers will at best return to their jobs with seniority inferior to that of the replacements and of those who left the strike.

(2)   A super-seniority award necessarily operates to the detriment of those who participated in the strike as compared to nonstrikers.

(3)   Super-seniority made available to striking bargaining unit employees as well as to new employees is in effect offering individual benefits to the strikers to induce them to abandon the strike.

(4)   Extending the benefits of super-seniority to striking bargaining unit employees as well as to new replacements deals a crippling blow to the strike effort. At one stroke, those with low seniority have the opportunity

to obtain the job security which ordinarily only long years of service can bring, while conversely, the accumulated seniority of older employees is seriously diluted. This combination of threat and promise could be expected to undermine the strikers' mutual interest and place the entire strike effort in jeopardy. The history of this strike and its virtual collapse following the announcement of the plan emphasize the grave repercussions of super-seniority.

(5) Super-seniority renders future bargaining difficult, if not impossible, for the collective bargaining representative. Unlike the replacement granted in Mackay which ceases to be an issue once the strike is over, the plan here creates a cleavage in the plant continuing long after the strike is ended. Employees are henceforth divided into two camps: those who stayed with the union and those who returned before the end of the strike and thereby gained extra seniority. This breach is reemphasized with each subsequent layoff and stands as an ever-present reminder of the dangers connected with striking and with union activities in general.

In the light of this analysis, super-seniority by its very terms operates to discriminate between strikers and non-strikers, both during and after a strike, and its destructive impact upon the strike and union activity cannot be doubted. The origin of the plan, as respondent insists, may have been to keep production going and it may have been necessary to offer super-seniority to attract replacements and induce union members to leave the strike. But if this is true, accomplishment of respondent's business purpose inexorably was contingent upon attracting sufficient replacements and strikers by offering preferential inducements to those who worked as opposed to those who struck. We think the Board was entitled to treat this case as involving conduct which carried its own indicia of intent and which is barred by the Act unless saved from illegality by an overriding business purpose justifying the invasion of union rights. The Board concluded that the business purpose asserted was insufficient to insulate the super-seniority plan from the reach of s 8(a)(1) and s 8(a)(3), and we turn now to a review of that conclusion.

The Court of Appeals and respondent rely upon *Mackay* as precluding the result reached by the Board but we are not persuaded. Under the decision in that case an employer may operate his plant during a strike and at its conclusion need not discharge those who worked during the strike in order to make way for returning strikers. It may be, as the Court of Appeals said, that "such a replacement policy is obviously discriminatory and may tend to discourage union membership." But Mackay did not deal with super-seniority, with its effects upon all strikers, whether replaced or not, or with its powerful impact upon a strike itself. Because the employer's interest must be deemed to outweigh the damage to concerted activities caused by permanently replacing strikers does not mean it also outweighs the far greater encroachment resulting from super-seniority in addition to permanent replacement.

We have no intention of questioning the continuing vitality of the Mackay rule, but we are not prepared to extend it to the situation we have here. To do so would require us to set aside the Board's considered judgment that the Act and its underlying policy require, in the present context, giving more weight to the harm wrought by super-seniority than to the interest of the employer in operating its plant during the strike by utilizing this particular means of attracting replacements. We find nothing in the Act or its legislative history to indicate that super-seniority is necessarily an acceptable method of resisting the economic impact of a strike, nor do we find anything inconsistent with the result which the Board reached. On the contrary, these sources are wholly consistent with, and lend full support to, the conclusion of the Board.

Section 7 guarantees, and s 8(a)(1) protects from employer interference the rights of employees to engage in concerted activities, which, as Congress as indicated include the right to strike. Under s 8(a)(3), it is unlawful for an employer by discrimination in terms of employment to discourage "membership in any labor organization," which includes discouraging participation in concerted activities. Section 13 makes clear that although the strike weapon is not an unqualified right, nothing in the Act except as specifically provided is to be construed to interfere with this means of redress, and s 2(3) preserves to strikers their unfilled positions and status as employees during the pendency of a strike. This repeated solicitude for the right to strike is predicated upon the conclusion that a strike when legitimately employed is an economic weapon which in great measure implements and supports the principles of the collective bargaining system.

While Congress has from time to time revamped and redirected national labor policy, its concern for the integrity of the strike weapon has remained constant. Thus when Congress chose to qualify the use of the strike, it did so by prescribing the limits and conditions of the abridgment in exacting detail, . . . and by preserving the positive command of s 13 that the right to strike is to be given a generous interpretation within the scope of the labor Act. The courts have likewise repeatedly recognized and effectuated the strong interest of federal labor policy in the legitimate use of the strike.

Accordingly, in view of the deference paid the strike weapon by the federal labor laws and the devastating consequences upon it which the Board found was and would be precipitated by respondent's inherently discriminatory super-seniority plan, we cannot say the Board erred in the balance which it struck here . . . . Here, as in other cases, we must recognize the Board's special function of applying the general provisions of the Act to the complexities of industrial life, and of "(appraising) carefully the interests of both sides of any labor management controversy in the diverse circumstances of particular cases" from its special understanding of "the actualities of industrial relations." "The ultimate problem is the balancing of the conflicting legitimate interests. The function of striking that balance to effectuate national labor policy is often a difficult and delicate responsibility, which the Congress committed primarily to the National Labor Relations Board, subject to limited judicial review."

Consequently, because the Board's judgment was that the claimed business purpose would not outweigh the necessary harm to employee rights-a judgment which we sustain-it could properly put aside evidence of respondent's motive and decline to find whether the conduct was or was not prompted by the claimed business purpose . . . .

JUSTICE HARLAN, concurring.

I agree with the Court that the Board's conclusions respecting this 20-year "super-seniority" plan were justified without inquiry into the respondents' motives. However, I do not think that the same thing would necessarily be true in all circumstances, as for example with a plan providing for a much shorter period of extra seniority. Being unsure whether the Court intends to hold that the Board has power to outlaw all such plans, irrespective of the employer's motives and other circumstances, or only to sustain its action in the particular circumstances of this case, I concur in the judgment.

AMERICAN SHIP BUILDING CO. v. NLRB
380 U.S. 300 (1965)

JUSTICE STEWART delivered the opinion of the Court.

The American Ship Building Company seeks review of a decision of the United States Court of Appeals for the District of Columbia enforcing an order of the National Labor Relations Board which found that the company had committed an unfair labor practice under ss 8(a)(1) and 8(a)(3) of the National Labor Relations Act. The question presented is that expressly reserved in National Labor Relations Board v. Truck Drivers Local Union; namely, whether an employer commits an unfair labor practice under these sections of the Act when he temporarily lays off or "locks out" his employees during a labor dispute to bring economic pressure in support of his bargaining position . . . .

The American Ship Building Company operates four shipyards on the Great Lakes-at Chicago, at Buffalo, and at Toledo and Lorain, Ohio. The company is primarily engaged in the repairing of ships, a highly seasonal business concentrated in the winter months when the freezing of the Great Lakes renders shipping impossible. What limited business is obtained during the shipping season is frequently such that speed of execution is of the utmost importance to minimize immobilization of the ships.

Since 1952 the employer has engaged in collective bargaining with a group of eight unions. Prior to the negotiations here in question, the employer had contracted with the unions on five occasions, each agreement having been preceded by a strike. The particular chapter of the collective bargaining history with which we are concerned opened shortly before May 1, 1961, when the unions notified the company of their intention to seek modification of the current contract, due to expire on August 1.

At the initial bargaining meeting on June 6, 1961, the company took the position that its competitive situation would not allow increased compensation. The unions countered with demands for increased fringe benefits and some unspecified wage increase. Several meetings were held in June and early July during which negotiations focused upon the fringe benefit questions without any substantial progress. At the last meeting, the parties resolved to call in the Federal Mediation and Conciliation Service, which set the next meeting for July 19. At this meeting, the unions first unveiled their demand for a 20-cent-an-hour wage increase and proposed a six-month extension of the contract pending continued negotiations. The employer rejected the proposed extension because it would have led to expiration during the peak season . . . .

Thus on August 9, after extended negotiations, the parties separated without having resolved substantial differences on the central issues dividing them and without having specific plans for further attempts to resolve them-a situation which the trial examiner found was an impasse. Throughout the negotiations, the employer displayed anxiety as to the unions' strike plans, fearing that the unions would call a strike as soon as a ship entered the Chicago yard or delay negotiations into the winter to increase strike leverage. The union negotiator consistently insisted that it was his intention to reach an agreement without calling a strike; however, he did concede incomplete control over the workers-a fact borne out by the occurrence of a wildcat strike in February 1961. Because of the danger of an unauthorized strike and the consistent and deliberate use of strikes in prior negotiations, the employer remained apprehensive of the possibility of a work stoppage.

In light of the failure to reach an agreement and the lack of available work, the employer decided to lay off certain of his workers. On August 11 the employees received a notice which read: "Because of the labor dispute which has been unresolved since August 1, 1961, you are laid off until further notice." The Chicago yard was completely shut down and all but two employees laid off at the Toledo yard. A large force was retained at Lorain to complete a major piece of work there and the employees in the Buffalo yard were gradually laid off as miscellaneous tasks were completed. Negotiations were resumed shortly after these layoffs and continued for the following two months until a two-year contract was agreed upon on October 27. The employees were recalled the following day.

Upon claims filed by the unions, the General Counsel of the Board issued a complaint charging the employer with violations of ss 8(a)(1), (a)(3), and (a) (5). . . .

A three-to-two majority of the Board rejected the trial examiner's conclusion that the employer could reasonably anticipate a strike. Finding the unions' assurances sufficient to dispel any such apprehension, the Board was able to find only one purpose underlying the layoff: a desire to bring economic pressure to secure prompt settlement of the dispute on favorable terms. The Board did not question the examiner's finding that the layoffs had not occurred until after a bargaining impasse had been reached. Nor did the Board remotely suggest that the company's decision to lay off its employees was based either on union hostility or on a desire to avoid its bargaining obligations under the Act. The Board concluded that the employer "by curtailing its operations at the South Chicago yard with the consequent layoff of the employees, coerced employees in the exercise of their bargaining rights in violation of Section 8(a)(1) of the Act, and discriminated against its employees within the meaning of Section 8(a)(3) of the Act." . . .

The Board has, however, exempted certain classes of lockouts from proscription. "Accordingly, it has held that lockouts are permissible to safeguard against . . . loss where there is reasonable ground for believing that a strike was threatened or imminent." Developing this distinction in its rulings, the Board has approved lockouts designed to prevent seizure of a plant by a sitdown strike, Link-Belt Co.;

to forestall repetitive disruptions of an integrated operation by "quickie" strikes, International Shoe Co.; to avoid spoilage of materials which would result from a sudden work stoppage, Duluth Bottling Assn.; and to avert the immobilization of automobiles brought in for repair. In another distinct class of cases the Board has sanctioned the use of the lockout by a multiemployer bargaining unit as a response to a whipsaw strike against one of its members. Buffalo Linen Supply Co., 109 N.L.R.B. 447, rev'd, sub. nom. Truck Drivers Local Union, etc. v. National Labor Relations Board.

In analyzing the status of the bargaining lockout under ss 8(a)(1) and (3) of the National Labor Relations Act, it is important that the practice with which we are here concerned be distinguished from other forms of temporary separation from employment. No one would deny that an employer is free to shut down his enterprise temporarily for reasons of renovation or lack of profitable work unrelated to his collective bargaining situation. Similarly, we put to one side cases where the Board has concluded on the basis of substantial evidence that the employer has used a lockout as a means to injure a labor organization or to evade his duty to bargain collectively. What we are here concerned with is the use of a temporary layoff of employees solely as a means to bring economic pressure to bear in support of the employer's bargaining position, after an impasse has been reached. This is the only issue before us, and all that we decide.

To establish that this practice is a violation of s 8(a)(1), it must be shown that the employer has interfered with, restrained, or coerced employees in the exercise of some right protected by s 7 of the Act. The Board's position is premised on the view that the lockout interferes with two of the rights guaranteed by s 7: the right to bargain collectively and the right to strike. In the Board's view, the use of the lockout "punishes" employees for the presentation of and adherence to demands made by their bargaining representatives and so coerces them in the exercise of their right to bargain collectively. It is important to note that there is here no allegation that the employer used the lockout in the service of designs inimical to the process of collective bargaining. There was no evidence and no finding that the employer was hostile to its employees' banding together for collective bargaining or that the lockout was designed to discipline them for doing so. It is therefore inaccurate to say that the employer's intention was to destroy of frustrate the process of collective bargaining. What can be said is that it intended to resist the demands made of it in the negotiations and to secure modification of these demands. We cannot see that this intention is in any way inconsistent with the employees' rights to bargain collectively.

Moreover, there is no indication, either as a general matter or in this specific case, that the lockout will necessarily destroy the unions' capacity for effective and responsible representation. The unions here involved have vigorously represented the employees since 1952, and there is nothing to show that their ability to do so has been impaired by the lockout. Nor is the lockout one of those acts which are demonstrably so destructive of collective bargaining that the Board need not inquire into employer motivation, as might be the case, for example, if an employer permanently discharged his unionized staff and replaced them with employees known to be possessed of a violent antiunion animus. Cf. National Labor Relations Board v. Erie Resistor Corp. The lockout may well dissuade employees from adhering to the position which they initially adopted in the bargaining, but he right to bargain collectively does not entail any "right" to insist on one's position free from economic disadvantage. Proper analysis of the problem demands that the simple intention to support the employer's bargaining position as to compensation and the like be distinguished from a hostility to the process of collective bargaining which could suffice to render a lockout unlawful. See National Labor Relations Board v. Brown.

The Board has taken the complementary view that the lockout interferes with the right to strike protected under ss 7 and 13 of the Act in that it allows the employer to pre-empt the possibility of a strike and thus leave the union with "nothing to strike against." Insofar as this means that once employees are locked out, they are deprived of their right to call a strike against the employer because he is already shut down, the argument is wholly specious, for the work stoppage which would have been the object of the strike has in fact occurred. It is true that recognition of the lockout deprives the union of exclusive control of the timing and duration of work stoppages calculated to influence the result of collective bargaining negotiations, but there is nothing in the statute which would imply that the right to strike "carries with it" the right exclusively to determine the timing and duration of all work stoppages. The right to strike as commonly understood is the right to cease work-nothing more. No doubt a union's bargaining power would be enhanced if it possessed not only the simple right to strike but also the power exclusively to determine when work stoppages should occur, but the Act's provisions are not indefinitely elastic, content-free forms to be shaped in whatever manner the Board might think best conforms to the proper balance of bargaining power.

Thus, we cannot see that the employer's use of a lockout solely in support of a legitimate bargaining position is in any way inconsistent with the right to bargain collectively or with the right to strike. Accordingly, we conclude that on the basis of the findings made by the Board in this case, there has been no violation of s 8(a)(1).

Section 8(a)(3) prohibits discrimination in regard to tenure or other conditions of employment to discourage union membership. Under the words of the statute there must be both discrimination and a resulting discouragement of union membership. It has long been established that a finding of violation under this section will normally turn on the employer's motivation. Thus when the employer discharges a union leader who has broken shop rules, the problem posed is to determine whether the employer has acted purely in disinterested defense of shop discipline or has sought to damage employee organization. It is likely that the discharge will naturally tend to discourage union membership in both cases, because of the loss of union leadership and the employees' suspicion of the employer's true intention. But we have consistently construed the section to leave unscathed a wide range of employer actions taken to serve legitimate business interests in some significant fashion, even though the act committed may tend to discourage union membership. See, e.g., National Labor Relations Board v. Mackay Radio & Telegraph Co. Such a construction of s 8(a)(3) is essential if due protection is to be accorded the employer's right to manage his enterprise.

This is not to deny that there are some practices which are inherently so prejudicial to union interests and so devoid of significant economic justification that no specific evidence of intent to discourage union membership or other antiunion animus is required. In some cases, it may be that the employer's conduct carries with it an inference of unlawful intention so compelling that it is justifiable to disbelieve the employer's protestations of innocent purpose. Thus where many have broken a shop rule, but only union leaders have been discharged, the Board need not listen too long to the plea that shop discipline was simply being enforced. In other situations, we have described the process as the "far more delicate task . . . of weighing the interests of employees in concerted activity against the interest of the employer in operating his business in a particular manner . . . ."

But this lockout does not fall into that category of cases arising under s 8(a)(3) in which the Board may truncate its inquiry into employer motivation. As this case well shows, use of the lockout does not carry with it any necessary implication that the employer acted to discourage union membership or otherwise discriminate against union members as such. The purpose and effect of the lockout were only to bring pressure upon the union to modify its demands. Similarly, it does not appear that the natural tendency of the lockout is severely to discourage union membership while serving no significant employer interest. In fact, it is difficult to understand what tendency to discourage union membership or otherwise discriminate against union members was perceived by the Board. There is no claim that the employer locked out only union members, or locked out any employee simply because he was a union member; nor is it alleged that the employer conditioned rehiring upon resignation from the union. It is true that the employees suffered economic disadvantage because of their union's insistence on demands unacceptable to the employer, but this is also true of many steps which an employer may take during a bargaining conflict, and the existence of an arguable possibility that someone may feel himself discouraged in his union membership or discriminated against by reason of that membership cannot suffice to label them violations of s 8(a)(3) absent some unlawful intention. The employer's permanent replacement of strikers (National Labor Relations Board v. Mackay Radio & Telegraph Co.), his unilateral imposition of terms, or his simple refusal to make a concession which would terminate a strike-all impose economic disadvantage during a bargaining conflict, but none is necessarily a violation of s 8(a)(3).

To find a violation of s 8(a)(3), then, the Board must find that the employer acted for a proscribed purpose. Indeed, the Board itself has always recognized that certain "operative" or "economic" purposes would justify a lockout. But the Board has erred in ruling that only these purposes will remove a lockout from the ambit of s 8(a)(3), for that section requires an intention to discourage union membership or otherwise discriminate against the union. There was not the slightest evidence and there was no finding that the employer was actuated by a desire to discourage membership in the union as distinguished from a desire to affect the outcome of the particular negotiations in which it was involved. We recognize that the "union membership" which is not to be discouraged refers to more than the payment of dues and that measures taken to discourage participation in protected union activities may be found to come within the proscription. However, there is nothing in the Act which gives employees the right to insist on their contract demands, free from the sort of economic disadvantage which frequently attends bargaining disputes. Therefore, we conclude that where the intention proven is merely to bring about a settlement of a labor dispute on favorable terms, no violation of s 8(a)(3) is shown . . . .

There is of course no question that the Board is entitled to the greatest deference in recognition of its special competence in dealing with labor problems. In many areas its evaluation of the competing interests of employer and employee should unquestionably be given conclusive effect in determining the application of ss 8(a)(1), (3), and (5). However, we think that the Board construes its functions too expansively when it claims general authority to define national labor policy by balancing the competing interests of labor and management.

While a primary purpose of the National Labor Relations Act was to redress the perceived imbalance of economic power between labor and management, it sought to accomplish that result by conferring certain affirmative rights on employees and by placing certain enumerated restrictions on the activities of employers. The Act prohibited acts which interfered with, restrained, or coerced employees in the exercise of their rights to organize a union, to bargain collectively, and to strike; it proscribed discrimination in regard to tenure and other conditions of employment to discourage membership in any labor organization. The central purpose of these provisions was to protect employee self-organization and the process of collective bargaining from disruptive interferences by employers. Having protected employee organization in countervailance to the employers' bargaining power, and having established a system of collective bargaining whereby the newly coequal adversaries might resolve their disputes, the Act also contemplated resort to economic weapons should more peaceful measures not avail. Sections 8(a)(1) and (3) do not give the Board a general authority to assess the relative economic power of the adversaries in the bargaining process and to deny weapons to one party or the other because of its assessment of that party's bargaining power. In this case the Board has, in essence, denied the use of the bargaining lockout to the employer because of its conviction that use of this device would give the employer "too much power." In so doing, the Board has stretched ss 8(a)(1) and (3) far beyond their functions of protecting the rights of employee organization and collective bargaining . . . .

Reversed.

Justice White, concurring in the result [opinion omitted].

Justice Goldberg, with whom The Chief Justice joins, concurring in the result [opinion omitted].

Paul M. Secunda, *Politics Not As Usual: Inherently Destructive Conduct, Institutional Collegiality, and the National Labor Relations Board*
32 FLA. ST. U. L. REV. 51 (2004)[2]

. . . D. Inferential Section 8(a)(3) Cases Since Taft-Hartley

1. Radio Officers' Union v. NLRB

After enactment of the Taft-Hartley Amendments, the Supreme Court turned its attention to reexamine a question left open by the *Republic Aviation* decision: Under what other circumstances may a violation of section 8(a)(3) be found in the absence of specific evidence of employer anti-union intent? In 1954, the Supreme Court sought to clarify this issue in *Radio Officers' Union v. NLRB*, a case in which, pursuant to a collective bargaining agreement, a company had agreed to grant retroactive wage increases and vacation payments to union members, but not to nonunion members . . . . [T]he Court, relying in part on *Republic Aviation*, . . . commented that "specific evidence of intent to encourage or discourage is not an indispensable element of proof of violation of § 8(a)(3)," and that the mere proof of certain types of discriminatory conduct satisfies the intent requirement. In other words, some employer conduct so inherently encourages or discourages union membership that specific proof of intent is unnecessary and intent is presumed.

According to the Court, this was not a novel concept, but "an application of the common-law rule that a man is held to intend the foreseeable consequences of his conduct." When the "natural" consequence of an employer's conduct is to discourage or encourage union activity, an employer's response that it was not its "true purpose" to interfere with its employees' section 7 rights will be unavailing. In *Radio Officers' Union (Gaynor News)*, the employer was found to have committed an unfair labor practice under section 8(a)(3) because in the Court's judgment the employer's discriminatory action of granting better benefits to union members inevitably caused the encouragement of union membership; that is, unlawful intent could be inferred based on the foreseeable consequences of such conduct on employees' rights under the Act.

Although the *Radio Officers' Union* Court reaffirmed the general rule that anti-union motivation must be proven in a section 8(a)(3) case, it recognized an exception to this general rule on the basis of the foreseeable consequences that employer conduct could have on employee rights under the Act. In cases involving the exception, illicit motivation could be inferred from the destructive impact of such conduct on employee rights under the Act. As made apparent by subsequent inferential section 8(a)(3) cases, the problem introduced by this conduct-speaks-for-itself formulation is that it is not always clear what the foreseeable consequences of employer conduct are. Nailing down the "natural" or "foreseeable" consequences of an employer's action is far from a straightforward exercise; it is fraught with all kinds of subjective decisions about cause and effect. In any event, *Radio Officers'*

Union explicitly recognized the validity of inferential section 8(a)(3) cases for the first time and unmistakably laid the analytical foundation for the inherently-destructive-conduct standard . . . .

4. NLRB v. Brown

To make matters even more confusing, another inferential section 8(a)(3) case concerning an employer lockout scenario was decided by the Supreme Court on the very same day as *American Ship Building.* Yet this case, *NLRB v. Brown*, set forth a standard for the inherently-destructive-conduct determination with some important differences.

In *Brown*, the Court considered whether an employer member of a multiemployer bargaining unit faced with a whipsaw strike could lock out its employees and temporarily hire replacement workers until the strike ended. As in *American Ship Building*, there was no specific evidence of unlawful intent, so the Court had to consider whether unlawful intent could be inferred from the impact of the employer's conduct on employee rights under the Act.

The *Brown* Court set forth the applicable inherently-destructive-conduct standard in the following manner: "[W]hen an employer practice is inherently destructive of employee rights and is not justified by the service of important business ends, no specific evidence of intent to discourage union membership is necessary to establish a violation of § 8(a)(3)." In such instances, the Court found that inherently destructive conduct "could not be saved from illegality by an asserted overriding business purpose pursued in good faith." However, where "the tendency to discourage union membership is comparatively slight, and the employers' conduct is reasonably adapted to achieve legitimate business ends," the Court required improper motivation on the part of the employer to be established by independent evidence. Applying these standards, the Court found the use of a lockout with temporary replacements in the context of a whipsaw strike to have only a comparatively slight tendency to discourage union membership. In other words, the preservation of the multiemployer bargaining unit was a "legitimate business end" which was not unlawful under the Act because the action only had a comparatively slight impact on employee rights under the Act. Under these circumstances, the Court required specific evidence of antiunion intent before it would characterize employer action as an unfair labor practice. Finding no such intent, the Court held that the employer had not committed an unfair labor practice.

The *Brown* decision for the first time expressly divided employer conduct having a discriminatory effect on employee rights under the Act into two groups: conduct which had an inherently destructive impact on employee rights and conduct which had a comparatively slight impact on employee rights. Although the Court explained its comparatively-slight-impact conclusion in *Brown*, there was no attempt by the Court to establish prospective rules for making this distinction in the future. The decision in *Brown* also seemed to solidify the importance of an employer's business reasons for its action as part of the inherently-destructive-conduct test, although it was still unclear which party had the burden of showing that such legitimate business ends existed or how substantial the showing had to be for the employer's reasons to be immune from attack.

POST PROBLEM DISCUSSION

1. In *Erie Resistor*, the Supreme Court explored the relationship between an employer's business justifications and "conduct which spoke for itself" in the context of an employer's plan to extend a 20-year super-seniority credit to strike replacement workers and strike breakers (or "cross-overs"). Does the Court's holding mean that all super-seniority plans, even shorter ones, are per se unlawful? How are employers supposed to lure replacement workers and encourage union employees to cross the picket line, if not through such enticements?

2. All of the cases discussed above seem to recognize that there are two interests at stake — the right of the employer to run its business during the strike or lockout and employees' right to strike under Section 13 and to engage in concerted protected activity for mutual aid and protection under Section 7. In *Erie Resistor*, the Court commented that the NLRB should undertake the delicate task:

> of weighing the interests of employees in concerted activity against the interest of the employer in operating his business in a particular manner and of balancing in the light of the Act and its policy the intended consequences upon employee rights against the business ends to be served by the employer's conduct.

What does that mean, and how does this test get applied practically?

3. Can it be argued that super-seniority is worse than hiring permanent replacements because it affects the tenure of all strikers, operates to the detriment of all strikers, induces abandonment of the strike, deals a blow to the strike effort, and creates a division in the workforce that continues after the strike has ended? Can't lockouts do the same thing if some employees are brought back to work early because they agree with the employer? In other words, is such a partial lockout strategy any less destructive of the collective-bargaining process than using permanent replacements?

4. Does *American Ship Building* represent a much more employer-friendly approach to the enterprise of inferring unlawful intent on the part of employers? It seems that as long as the employer has some economic justification for its actions, the Board will be precluded from inferring unlawful intent based on the impact that the employer's actions have on employee rights. Does this holding severely limit the manner in which the Board is able to balance employer and employee competing interests in Section 8(a)(3) cases?

5. A whipsaw strike occurs in a multi-employer bargaining unit where a union strikes a single employer within that unit. Meanwhile, the unstruck competitors are able to go about business as usual, which puts further pressure on the struck employer. When the struck employer meets the strikers' demands, the strike will move to another employer within the unit. As a defense to the whipsaw strike tactic, the multi-employer unit may choose to temporarily lock out employees of the unstruck facilities as a legitimate employer response. See *NLRB v. Truck Drivers Local No. 449 (Buffalo Linen Supply Co.)*, 353 U.S. 87 (1957).

6. An employer does not violate the Act when it institutes a lockout in response to a union's "inside game" tactics, such as "working-to-rule" (e.g., not accepting

overtime opportunities, not performing duties outside of their job classification, and presenting all grievances as a group). *See Local 702, IBEW v. NLRB*, 215 F.3d 11 (D.C. Cir. 2000) (holding lockout permissible in such circumstances). See Chapter 7 for more discussion of work-to-rule tactics.

7.   Should employers be able to initiate a lockout and then use temporary replacements? The D.C. Circuit held in *International Brotherhood of Boilermakers, Local 88 v. NLRB*, 858 F.2d 756 (D.C. Cir. 1988), that the hiring of temporary workers during a lockout was not an unfair labor practice. In coming to this conclusion, the court observed that the Act does not guarantee employees a bargain, only the right to bargain. Thus, it was not unlawful for an employer to strengthen its own bargaining position by hiring temporary workers during a lockout. Do you agree? Can an employer hire permanent replacements during a lockout? Why or why not?

SECTION 3   THE *GREAT DANE* FRAMEWORK AND INHERENTLY DESTRUCTIVE CONDUCT UNDER SECTION 8(a)(3)

PROBLEM 3: THE 30% RULE[3]

An employer had a policy under which it refused to hire new employees whose previous wages were 30% higher or lower than the employer's starting wage. Although this policy had its greatest effect on former union employees who had made greater wages in the past, the employer maintained that it had a legitimate and substantial business reason for the rule: evidence showed that employees who satisfied this rule were less likely to quit. The employer also maintained that the impact of the 30% rule on union members' Section 7 rights was "comparatively slight."

Does the 30% rule violate Section 8(a)(3) by discriminating against those employees who are, or have been, affiliated with a union? Does the NLRA incorporate a "disparate impact model" of discrimination as in Title VII of the Civil Rights Act of 1964?

PROBLEM MATERIALS

Paul M. Secunda, *Politics Not As Usual: Inherently Destructive Conduct, Institutional Collegiality, and the National Labor Relations Board*, 32 Fla. St. U. L. Rev. 51 (2004)

Local 15 IBEW v. NLRB, 429 F.3d 651 (7th Cir. 2005)

---

[3]   This problem is based on *Contractor's Labor Pool, Inc. v. NLRB*, 323 F.3d 1051 (D.C. Cir. 2003).

Paul M. Secunda, *Politics Not As Usual: Inherently Destructive Conduct, Institutional Collegiality, and the National Labor Relations Board*
32 Fla. St. U. L. Rev. 51 (2004)[4]

. . . E. *Great Dane* and the Inherently-Destructive-Conduct Standard

On June 12, 1967, the Supreme Court decided *NLRB v. Great Dane Trailers, Inc.*, once and for all hoping to close the book on the proper test to apply in inferential section 8(a)(3) cases. Rejecting outright the business-friendly inherently-destructive-conduct standard enunciated in *American Ship Building*, the Court in *Great Dane* embraced the "inherently destructive"/"comparatively slight" dichotomy set forth in *Brown*, but with an important twist.

Great Dane involved a case in which an employer refused to pay striking employees vacation benefits which had accrued under the terms of the expired collective bargaining agreement, while simultaneously announcing its intention to pay these same vacation "benefits to striker replacements, returning strikers, and nonstrikers who had been at work on a certain date during the strike." Because there was no specific evidence that the employer's actions against the strikers were motivated by anti-union intent, the Court again considered whether such intent could be inferred based on the impact the conduct had on employee rights under the Act. Synthesizing the holdings of previous inferential section 8(a)(3) cases, the Court divided all inferential cases into two categories:

> First, if it can reasonably be concluded that the employer's discriminatory conduct was "inherently destructive" of important employee rights, no proof of an antiunion motivation is needed and the Board can find an unfair labor practice even if the employer introduces evidence that the conduct was motivated by business considerations.

> Second, if the adverse effect of the discriminatory conduct on employee rights is "comparatively slight," an antiunion motivation must be proved to sustain the charge *if* the employer has come forward with evidence of legitimate and substantial business justifications for the conduct.

The important twist came in the seemingly innocuous concluding sentence of the same paragraph of the Court's decision:

> Thus, *in either situation*, once it has been proved that the employer engaged in discriminatory conduct which could have adversely affected employee rights to *some* extent, the burden is upon the employer to establish that he was motivated by legitimate objectives since proof of motivation is most accessible to him.

Because the Court concluded in *Great Dane* that the employer had not met its initial burden of proving that it had legitimate and substantial reasons for treating strikers differently than other workers in their eligibility for vacation benefits, "it

---

[was] not necessary for [the Court] to decide the degree to which the challenged conduct might have affected employee rights." Instead, the Court found a violation of section 8(a)(3) based on the fact that the necessary antiunion intent could be inferred from employer conduct which "carr[ied] a potential for adverse effect upon employee rights" and which was not supported by any "evidence of a proper motivation . . . in the record."

Thus, on one hand, the Supreme Court in *Great Dane* appeared to divide the universe of employer discriminatory conduct in inferential section 8(a)(3) cases into either inherently destructive or comparatively slight conduct; there was no undistributed middle. On the other hand, placing the initial burden on the employer to prove that it had legitimate and substantial justifications for its conduct clearly made the "inherently destructive"/ "comparatively slight" characterization unnecessary in some inferential cases. *Great Dane* was one such case, and its precedent, as will be demonstrated below, certainly offered a clear guidepost for the Board and other courts to follow in future inherently-destructive-conduct decisions.

F. The Aftermath of Great Dane

1. Subsequent Supreme Court and Appellate Cases Applying the Inherently-Destructive-Conduct Standard

To this day, the Supreme Court has still not supplied clear prospective rules for deciding when employer conduct has an inherently destructive impact versus a comparatively slight impact. In *NLRB v. Fleetwood Trailer Co.*, the Court's first inferential section 8(a)(3) case after *Great Dane*, the Court avoided the inherently-destructive-conduct determination in much the same manner as the *Great Dane* Court. Having found that refusing to reinstate replaced strikers had "some" discriminatory effect on employee rights, the *Fleetwood Trailer* Court searched the record in vain for legitimate and substantial reasons for the employer not to reinstate the former strikers. Finding none, the Court was able under the *Great Dane* framework to infer anti-union intent in violation of section 8(a)(3) without needing to categorize the conduct as inherently destructive or comparatively slight. Therefore, *Fleetwood Trailer* shed no further light on the logic behind the "inherently destructive"/"comparatively slight" dichotomy.

In the only other Supreme Court case to discuss an inferential section 8(a)(3) scenario since *Fleetwood Trailer, Metropolitan Edison Co. v. NLRB*, the Court found an employer's selective discipline of union officers to be inherently destructive of employee rights under the Act and, therefore, violative of section 8(a)(3) of the Act. In doing so, however, the Court merely affirmed the Board's conclusions and failed to shed any more light on how the inherently-destructive-conduct determination should be made.

Because the Supreme Court has not established clear-cut standards for determining when employer conduct reaches the inherently-destructive-conduct threshold, appellate courts reviewing Board decisions have been left to fend for themselves in these types of cases. In the resulting analytical vacuum, reviewing courts have had to analogize to the relatively few cases where the Supreme Court has found conduct to be inherently destructive and have employed different standards for making the inherently-destructive-conduct determination. Under this ad hoc approach, it is hardly surprising that different appellate courts have come to inconsistent conclusions when reviewing a Board's determination that certain employer conduct is inherently destructive.

2. The Board's Application of the Inherently-Destructive-Conduct Standard

Since *Great Dane*, the Board has also struggled in determining the contours of inherently destructive employer conduct. Nevertheless, the Board appears to have most frequently (though far from always) found conduct to be inherently destructive in cases in which the employer's actions distinguish among workers based on participation in protected activities, and where employer actions discourage the process of collective bargaining by making it appear to be a futile exercise in the eyes of employees. On the other hand, the Board has generally found employer conduct to have a comparatively slight impact on employee rights in cases in which employers have locked out their employees and used temporary replacement workers. Additionally, many Board decisions, mimicking the *Great Dane* decision itself, do not even reach the inherently-destructive-conduct determination. Such cases involve fact patterns where there have been changes in the work force during a strike and striker reinstatement rights are at issue and where there has been a withholding of accrued benefits from employees during a labor dispute.

Recently, the Board has attempted to formulate standards for the inherently-destructive-conduct determination by distilling several fundamental guiding principles based on past Supreme Court inferential section 8(a)(3) cases. In *International Paper Co.*, the Board considered whether permanently subcontracting out bargaining unit work during a lockout constituted inherently destructive conduct. The Board applied four "guiding principles" to make this determination:

1. The severity of the harm suffered by employees as well as the severity of the impact on the statutory right being exercised;

2. The temporal nature of the conduct in question;

3. Whether the employer's conduct demonstrated hostility to the process of collective bargaining as opposed to a simple intention to support its bargaining position as to compensation and other matters; and

4. Whether employer conduct "discourage[d] collective bargaining in the sense of making it seem a futile exercise in the eyes of employees."

Applying these four guiding principles to the permanent subcontracting scenario under review, the Board concluded that the conduct in question had an inherently destructive impact on employee rights because all four of these guiding principles were violated by the employer's conduct.

Nevertheless, *International Paper* fails to clarify what conduct has an inherently destructive impact and what conduct has a comparatively slight impact. The guiding principles set forth in *International Paper* appear redundant to a large extent and do little more than put in one place Supreme Court reasoning that had existed prior to the Board's decision. Just as there was little guidance as to what conduct constituted inherently destructive conduct prior to *International* Paper, those questions appear no more resolved merely because the Board combined all the various Supreme Court rationales.

Moreover, the Board's *International Paper* decision appears to make the all-too-common mistake of characterizing employer conduct as inherently destructive, even though there was no finding that the employer had a legitimate and substantial justification for its conduct. *Great Dane*, however, makes abundantly clear that once some discriminatory effect on employee rights has been found and no legitimate and substantial justification for the employer's conduct can be located in the record, unlawful intent can be inferred to support a section 8(a)(3) violation without the conduct having to be further labeled inherently destructive or comparatively slight.

3. Remaining Issues Surrounding the Inherently-Destructive-Conduct Standard

Having examined in extensive detail the doctrinal framework surrounding the inherently-destructive-conduct standard in inferential section 8(a)(3) cases, the primary problem with its current iteration under *Great Dane* seems clear. The inherently-destructive-conduct standard would appear, even under *International Paper*'s guiding principles, to give unguided discretion to Board Members to determine whether discriminatory intent should be inferred from employer conduct. It is anyone's guess what conduct is, and what conduct is not, "inherently destructive"; you might as well ask a Great Dane.

One commentator has even suggested that Board Members in these cases are often left to defend their decisions with no more than an unpersuasive "I know it when I see it" rejoinder. Indeed, without knowing anything more about these cases, there is every reason to assume that Republican Board Members will be less likely to infer unlawful intent on the part of employers, while Democratic Board Members may be more likely to do so — the end consequence being "[j]udgment which bends with the political winds." In short, these inherently-destructive-conduct cases appear to present ample opportunity for Board Members to base the "inherently destructive"/"comparatively slight" distinction on their personal political preferences, rather than on the merits of the case.

Whether the Board is really applying the inherently-destructive-conduct standard in a blatantly political manner can only be discerned through empirical study of the Board's inherently-destructive-conduct cases. Such a study will help clarify exactly how this highly indeterminate standard has been applied in practice by the Board. Empirical findings that indicate the Board is implementing this standard in a consistent, nonpartisan basis will no doubt bolster the Board's credibility by reassuring both management and labor that industrial justice may still be obtained at the NLRB.

[The article then conducts an empirical study of all Board inherently destructive cases between 1968 and 2003, and concludes, counter-intuitively, that there is a surprising amount of decisional consistency in these cases. The decisional consistency appears to be based on notions of institutional collegiality among Board members and short-hand presumptions that Board members employ in frequently recurring fact situations.]

LOCAL 15 IBEW v. NLRB
429 F. 3d 651 (7th Cir. 2005)

FLAUM, CHIEF JUDGE.

Petitioner Local 15, International Brotherhood of Electrical Workers, AFL-CIO ("Union") petitions this Court for review of an order of the National Labor Relations Board ("NLRB" or "Board") finding that the Intervenor, Midwest Generation, EME, LLC ("Midwest"), did not violate sections 8(a)(1) and (3) of the National Labor Relations Act ("NLRA"). Because substantial evidence did not support the Board's decision, we reverse the holding and remand to the Board to determine whether Midwest's unfair labor practices render the current collective bargaining agreement void.

I. Background

The Union began an economic strike against Midwest on June 28, 2001, over stalled negotiations for a new collective bargaining agreement. Approximately 1150 workers went on strike. Eight employees refused to strike ("non-participants"). During the course of the strike, 47 employees who were part of the Union made individual offers to return to work ("crossovers"). Midwest accepted each of these offers and reinstated the individual employees. Sixteen employees crossed the picket line in July, and thirty-one crossed between August 1 and August 30. Six additional employees made offers to return to work shortly before the strike ended on August 31. Midwest returned these last six crossovers to the workforce between September 1 and September 6. In all, a combination of sixty-one crossovers and non-participants offered to return to the workforce before the end of the strike.

Midwest continued to operate during the course of the strike, relying upon supervisors, contractors, and some temporary replacement employees. Midwest hired no permanent replacements. No evidence that the sixty-one non-participants and crossovers were necessary to maintain operations during the strike was submitted. Employees who returned to work were not questioned concerning their status in the Union and Midwest did not encourage or assist any employee in resigning from the Union.

On Friday, August 31, 2001, after failing to reach a collective bargaining agreement, the Union members voted to end their strike and offered to return to work unconditionally. Midwest initially gave no response to this offer, but on September 6, 2001, Midwest informed the Union that it was instituting a lockout. The Union alleges that the purpose of the six-day delay in announcing the lockout was to process the last six crossovers.

The lockout did not include those sixty-one workers who offered to return to work before the Union made its unconditional offer on August 31. Midwest locked out any employee who sought to return to work after the Union had voted to end the strike; and the lockout continued until the parties reached a collective bargaining agreement. The announced purpose of the lockout was to exert pressure upon the Union to meet Midwest's contract demands.

On October 3, 2001, the Union voted on Midwest's "final offer." The Union informed Midwest that it believed if the NLRB later found Midwest had committed an unfair labor practice during the lockout, the contract would be "void because the Company's unfair labor practice[s] . . . coerced the employees into accepting it. Nothing the Union or its representatives say or do should be interpreted as a waiver of this position." On October 3, 2001, the Union rejected the offer. The Union sent a similar notification letter before a second vote on the same contract. On the second vote, the contract passed easily. The lockout officially ended on Monday, October 22, 2001 . . . .

Although at times all but eight of the approximately 1,150 workers were on strike, Midwest maintained normal operations throughout the strike and lockout. Midwest contends that the non-strikers and crossovers "helped the company weather the work stoppage's effects." Midwest also contends that the sixty-one employees had "abandoned an economic strike undertaken for the express purpose of supporting the Union's bargaining demands." . . .

II. Discussion

A. Standard of Review/Method of Analysis

Board Rulings are "entitled to considerable deference so long as [they are] rational and consistent with the [National Labor Relations] Act." This Court, however, is not "obliged to stand aside and rubberstamp [its] affirmance of administrative decisions that [it] deem[s] inconsistent with a statutory mandate or that frustrate the congressional policy underlying a statute."

. . . The basic procedure to evaluate whether a company has engaged in an unfair labor practice was first outlined by the Supreme Court in NLRB v. Great Dane Trailers, Inc.

The first question in the Great Dane framework is whether the employer's conduct is "inherently destructive of important employee rights." Actions that harm the collective bargaining process, interfere with employees' right to strike, or are taken against employees based upon union status are "inherently destructive." To be "inherently destructive," the effect on the collective bargaining process must be more than temporary; it must instead establish a barrier to future collective bargaining. If an action by an employer is inherently destructive of important rights, no proof of an anti-union motivation is needed.

A harmful action by an employer that is not inherently destructive is classified as "comparatively slight." These two categories, "inherently destructive" harm and "comparatively slight" harm, make up the two prongs of the Great Dane framework. Under the first prong of the Great Dane test ("inherently destructive"), an employer's actions are submitted to a stringent test. Such actions are permissible only if after balancing business justifications against employee rights, the business justification is found to be superior. Under the second prong of the *Great Dane* test, ("comparatively slight"), an employer's actions are more likely to be justified. "[A] finding of comparatively slight harm calls for a threshold test of business justification, rather than a balancing of interests." If an individual employer's actions cannot be justified under the comparatively slight harm standard, which requires a legitimate and substantial business justification, they clearly cannot be justified under the "inherently destructive" standard. Under either prong, once it has been established that the employer's conduct negatively affects protected section 7 rights, the key question for the Board, informed by *Great Dane*, is whether the employer can state a business justification for its actions. If an employer can show no legitimate and substantial business justification, the lockout is presumptively an unfair labor practice under either prong of the *Great Dane* analysis.

Thus, the question of whether a "legitimate and substantial" business justification exists is a threshold question, properly asked prior to any decision as to whether an action is "comparatively slight" or "inherently destructive" under *Great Dane*. If a legitimate and substantial business justification is found for an employer's action, the question of whether the harm caused was "inherently destructive" or "comparatively slight" is then examined and the *Great Dane* analysis proceeds.

B. Failure to Prove a Business Justification

. . . A "legitimate and substantial" business justification must have a non-frivolous purpose. The issue then is whether Midwest has shown that its lockout had any business justification that was neither frivolous nor based upon an impermissible violation of section 7 rights.

The Board's majority opinion advanced two arguments in support of its finding that Midwest instituted the partial lockout for the valid purpose of "bringing economic pressure to bear in support of its legitimate bargaining position." First, the Board stated that partial lockouts are legal "when justified by operational needs and without regard to union membership status." Second, the Board concluded that locking out only those participating in the strike on August 31 was a lawful means of pressuring holdouts to abandon their bargaining position . . . .

1. Operational needs did not justify the partial lockout.

Prior to the Board's decision, Midwest offered no proof that its operational needs justified the partial lockout. Indeed, the record indicates that Midwest's operational needs were being "successfully maintained . . . through the efforts of supervisory personnel, contractors, and some temporary replacement employees . . . .

Every indication in the stipulated facts is that the crossovers and non-strikers were unnecessary to the continuation of business operations. Midwest and the majority opinion of the Board charge the dissent with advocating for a standard of "indispensab[ility] to continued operations in order to be retained" during a partial lockout . . . .

In any event, a standard less demanding than "indispensable" cannot provide employers with carte blanche to lock out employees of their choosing without regard to seniority or any other criteria. Such an approach would allow employers acting under the guise of maintaining business operations to engage in exactly the type of action Midwest undertook: punishing those who stood with the Union and rewarding those who crossed picket lines.

Demanding more than Midwest's labeling of its conduct as "necessary for business operations" does not establish strike-hiring practices that are difficult for employers to comply with. Instead, it merely avoids creating a "business operations" exception with no limiting principle, which would sanction discriminatory conduct by an employer where the employer chooses to announce its position as "necessary for business operations" without evidence supporting such a need. Simply put, to justify a partial lockout on the basis of operational need, an employer must provide a reasonable basis for finding some employees necessary to continue operations and others unnecessary.

2. The partial lockout was not justified as a lawful means of economically pressuring holdouts.

Throughout the course of this litigation, Midwest contended that it allowed the non-strikers and crossovers to return to work because they "had removed themselves from the Union's economic action," making it unnecessary to pressure them into abandoning the Union's bargaining position. This allegation rests on the proposition that "working for a struck employer may, without more, be equated with abandonment of the Union's bargaining demands." This assumption is fatally flawed. There can be several reasons why an employee might choose to cross a picket line. Abandonment of the Union's bargaining demands is merely one possible explanation, standing alongside individual financial motivations, personal relationships with employers, indifference, an attempt to impress management, etc. Midwest has failed to offer any direct correlation between employees' non-participation in a strike and lack of support for the Union's demands.

Midwest claims that it was unnecessary to lock out the crossovers and non-strikers because they had taken "affirmative action in derogation of the Union's bargaining position." Any business justification that relies upon workers having "removed themselves from the Union's economic action," or argues that by returning to their jobs, workers had abandoned their demands cannot carry the day in this case. When Midwest announced the selective lockout, all of the employees in the bargaining unit had removed themselves from the economic strike by offering to return to work. The only distinction between employees was whether an individual worker had made his or her offer to return as part of the Union's action or individually.

Midwest argues that an employee who has returned to work no longer demonstrates a commitment to the Union's position. Therefore, no economic pressure against such an employee is required. What Midwest fails to note is that at the time of the lockout, all employees had offered to return to work . . . .

The Board also justified the use of a partial lockout on the basis that "there is nothing in the law that requires an employer to use maximum economic pressure."

While this statement is a truism, it does not address the relevant question before the Board. The burden remains upon the employer to prove that it had a legitimate and substantial basis for its actions. In this case, the Board appears to find sufficient any reason presented by Midwest without evidence of a "legitimate and substantial" basis for distinguishing between those employees it locked out and those it did not.

Both the NLRB and the Fifth Circuit have found that an employer "may not discriminate against certain employees merely because it anticipates that they will honor a picket line or otherwise engage in protected activity." An employer's discriminatory lockout on the basis of a protected activity is unlawful even when it is supportive of an employer's bargaining position.

Lockouts are not all protected. . . . The Seventh Circuit in *Inland Trucking Co. v. N.L.R.B.*, held that an employer violated Section 8(a)(1) and (3) by locking out its employees and continuing operation with the use of new hires. The *American Ship Building* rule does not give the employer license to pick and choose among its employees and suspend those whose protected picket line activities are most damaging to it. The mere selection of such an employee from among all those in the unit for suspension is per se discriminatory . . . .

In the context of collective bargaining negotiations, nearly all employer actions are attempts to win an economic battle. Merely because retribution against strikers may be effective does not make such actions legitimate and substantial. The fact that employers have acted with the "best judgment as to the interests of their business . . . has not been deemed an absolute defense to an unfair labor practice charge."

Based on the record presented in this appeal, there is no line that can be drawn between those employees that agreed to return to work before August 31 and those employees who agreed to return to their positions after August 31. As of the time of the lockout, every employee had made an unconditional offer to return to work. Without a valid basis for distinction between those locked out and those allowed to work, Midwest's claim of a legitimate and substantial business justification fails
. . . .

A partial lockout is a significant measure that requires a justification beyond economic effectiveness. The fact that employees could avoid partial lockouts by agreeing to employer demands would in effect validate all partial lockouts. Undoubtedly, this would render ineffective the requirement of a legitimate and substantial business justification for discriminatory employer action and would be in derogation of nearly four decades of employee protection.

III. Conclusion

For the reasons set forth above, we Reverse the findings of the Board and Remand to the Board with instructions to find that the partial lockout was an unfair labor practice . . . .

POST PROBLEM DISCUSSION

1.   More important than *Great Dane's* holding is the standard that it provides. In particular, the Court put forth the "inherently destructive"/"comparatively slight" framework for systemic, inferential Section 8(a)(3) discrimination cases. This is the framework to apply whenever there is an employer response to union protected concerted activity, unless there is evidence of bad intent. In this latter case, the *Wright Line* test, discussed in Chapter 3, is applied.

It is important to point out here that by placing the initial burden on the employer to prove that it had a legitimate and substantial justification for its conduct towards the union, sometimes the Board will not have to engage in an analysis of whether that conduct had an inherently destructive or comparatively slight impact on employees' Section 7 rights. This is because if the Board concludes there is not a legitimate and substantial justification for the employer action, the Board can find a Section 8(a)(3) violation without going any further. Indeed, this was the mode of analysis in both *Great Dane* itself and the *Laidlaw* case.

2.   In *Local 15*, when the employer locked out employees who did not cross the picket line, but allowed those who crossed to return to work (a partial lockout), the court held that: 1) the partial lockout was not justified by operational needs, 2) the partial lockout was not justified as a lawful means of applying economic pressure, and 3) the employer, in the alternative, exhibited anti-union animus. Interestingly, and significantly, the court ruled against the employer, not based on an inherently destructive/comparatively slight characterization, but because the employer failed to meet its initial burden of showing that it had substantial and legitimate justifications for its partial lockout. Does this case come out the same way under the old *American Ship Building* standard?

3.   *Bunting Bearings Corp.*, 343 N.L.R.B. 479 (2004), involved an employer that tried to strengthen its bargaining position and put pressure on non-probationary employees, who were union members, by not locking out probationary employees, who were not union members. The Board concluded that this pressure was lawful so long as the decision whether to lock out was based on the employees' probationary status and not their union status. Does this make sense?

4.   In *Church Homes, Inc.*, 350 N.L.R.B. 214 (2007), enforced, 303 Fed. Appx. 998 (2d Cir. 2008), the employer replaced the entire striking workforce with permanent replacements. The rub was that they kept the existence of the permanent replacements secret until all the replacements had been successfully hired. Does keeping the union in the dark about its intentions to replace the entire workforce violate the Act? Recall the importance of *Laidlaw* rights and the *Fleetwood Trailer* case mentioned in the Secunda excerpt.

Even though the Board found the conduct unlawful, the Second Circuit opinion points out that secrecy may not amount to an independent unlawful purpose based on factors such as the employer: (1) demonstrating an ongoing willingness to negotiate a contract with the union; (2) agreeing to a request by the Mayor of Hartford that it stop hiring additional permanent replacements while his strike mediation efforts were ongoing; and (3) soliciting the union's input on how best to recall strikers who had not been permanently replaced, and then following the union's suggestions.

5.   Focusing on the impact of the 30% rule in Problem #3, Dean Rebecca White has compared the "conduct speaks for itself" doctrine to an immature type of disparate impact analysis, a type of employment discrimination theory recognized under Title VII. *See* Rebecca Hanner White, *Modern Discrimination Theory and the National Labor Relations Act*, 39 Wm. & Mary L. Rev. 99, 101 (1997). The disparate impact theory allows an employer to be held liable in some instances for the discriminatory effect of its facially nondiscriminatory policies. Nevertheless, the court in *Contractors Labor Pool*, the case upon which the problem is based, found that a disparate impact model of discrimination based on notions of employee equality is incongruent with the animus model of discrimination established under the NLRA.

6.   In *Trans World Airlines v. Independent Federation of Flight Attendants*, 489 U.S. 426 (1989), a case decided under the Railway Labor Act (RLA), the Supreme Court applied the same *Great Dane* framework. Striking flight attendants had asked the airline to oust junior cross-over employees to prevent those strikebreakers from having greater seniority. Not only did seniority impact future layoff decisions, but also determined who was able to bid for more attractive flight routes. The Court ruled that TWA was not required to lay off cross-over flight attendants to reinstate striking flight attendants with greater seniority.

The Court reasoned that the airline's policy of retaining junior employees who chose not to honor the strike was comparable to hiring permanent replacements, because the tactic put pressure on the strikers to abandon the strike. In their dissent, Justices Brennan and Marshall argued that *Erie Resistor* should be read to prevent employers from placing junior cross-over employees in positions that, if not for the strike, they would not be eligible for given their lack of seniority. Who do you think has the better argument?

7.   Coming full circle, does *Mackay Radio* come out differently under *Great Dane*? You should first ask whether the employer has a legitimate and substantial reason for hiring permanent replacements. If the answer is yes, then the next issue is whether the use of permanent replacement has an inherently destructive impact or comparatively slight impact on workers' Section 7 rights. This is also disputable, but a comparison to the factors considered in the super-seniority context in *Erie Resistor* may be helpful.

Chapter 10

PICKETING, BOYCOTTS, AND UNION SECONDARY ACTIVITY

Synopsis

When a dispute exists between employees who are in a union, or in the process of forming a union, and their employer, we refer to that as a primary labor dispute. There are primary pickets, primary boycotts, and primary strikes. On the other hand, when a group of employees, in a union or not, bring economic pressure to bear on an employer that is not their own, we refer to this as a secondary dispute. Probably most well known of these types of actions is the secondary boycott.

Before considering the treatment of these types of activities under the NLRA, Section 1 of this Chapter first explores whether unions have any constitutional protections when they engage in picketing or strike activities. Section 2 next discusses the primary activity of recognition picketing, where a group of employees picket their employer in order to pressure it to recognize their union. Since 1959, recognitional picketing has been regulated by Section 8(b)(7) of the NLRA. Section 3 then explores secondary boycott issues under Section 8(b)(4). This Chapter concludes with a consideration of consumer appeals and corporate campaigns, where employees place pressure on the consuming public to cease doing business with the employer with whom they have a dispute. This area of labor law is also regulated by Section 8(b)(4).

SECTION 1   CONSTITUTIONAL LIMITATIONS ON THE RIGHT TO STRIKE AND PICKET

Before considering statutory picketing issues under Sections 8(b)(4) and 8(b)(7), a little doctrinal ground-clearing is necessary. The U.S. constitutional due process protections of the Fifth and Fourteenth Amendments and the free speech protections of the First and Fourteenth Amendments potentially affect state and federal governments' power to limit the union's use of concerted activity, such as pickets and strikes.

That being said, there has been little litigation concerning how the Fifth and Fourteenth due process protections apply to strike actions as distinguished from picketing. The leading case on the constitutional right to strike under the substantive due process provisions of the Fourteenth Amendment is *Dorchy v. Kansas*, 272 U.S. 306 (1926). The case concerned a Kansas statute that made it a crime for mining employees to induce other employees to quit their jobs in order to slow down or stop the mining operations. Because he organized an unfair labor practice strike against the employer, the vice president of the union was sentenced to imprisonment and fined under the statute. The Supreme Court upheld the statute in *Dorchy*, finding that employees do not have an absolute right to strike under the Constitution. Since then, no case has directly examined whether an employee's interest in striking is entitled to some degree of constitutional protection.

[handwritten note: EEs do not have absolute right to strike under Constitution]

While employees' constitutional right to strike remains unclear, the Court has spoken much more clearly as to whether employee picketing is protected speech under the First and Fourteenth Amendments. In *Thornhill v. Alabama*, 310 U.S. 88 (1940), a picketer was prosecuted under a state law forbidding any picketing that had the purpose of influencing or inducing others not do business with a company. In reversing the picketer's convictions, the Court equated picketing with pure political speech, indicating that laws limiting the right to picket infringe on the employees' right to inform the public about the facts of a labor dispute. The Court also rejected the idea that picketing is inherently intimidating and violent or that the state's interest in curbing merely economic injury to the picketed employer is sufficiently important.

However, in *International Brotherhood of Teamsters, Local 695 v. Vogt, Inc.*, 354 U.S. 284 (1957), the Court shifted its approach. The Court acknowledged that picketing has coercive elements to it, is not pure political speech as it was characterized in *Thornhill*, and, therefore, cannot be completely free from state regulation. Factually, Vogt concerned a scenario where a union was picketing the entrance of a non-unionized plant to drum up employee support for the union. The picketing caused union truck drivers employed by other companies not to deliver goods to the company. As a result of the economic injury, the employer sought to enjoin the picketing under a Wisconsin law that prohibited this type of coercive picketing.

The *Vogt* Court found that picketing always consists of more than just conveying a message through speech because every picket has coercive elements. Picketing involves the patrolling of a particular area and the mere presence of a picket line may induce some sort of action irrespective of the ideas being disseminated (e.g., the union truck drivers refusing to enter Vogt's gates). Because states can regulate the conduct associated with picketing, the Court held that even a peaceful picket can be enjoined when it is counter to valid state policy.

Although it is true that labor picketers also may make their views known by less intrusive means, those means may not be as effective. These alternate means, like handbilling or leafleting, are generally considered pure speech and not subject to the same types of regulation as picketing. For instance, in *Edward J. DeBartolo Corp. v. Florida Gulf Coast Building & Construction Trades Council*, 485 U.S. 568 (1988), the Court considered whether leafleting should be protected by the First Amendment. In that case, a union passed out handbills encouraging shoppers not to do business with a mall's stores because the owner of the mall had hired a building contractor that allegedly did not pay its employees fair wages and fringe benefits. The Court concluded that because there was no indication that handbilling, in the absence of picketing, coerces secondary employers, the conduct could not be regulated. The Court reasoned that if a mall store was to lose business because a potential customer read the handbill, the loss of business would be the result of "mere persuasion" and not because the customer was intimidated from entering the store by a picket line. Ultimately, the Court held that unlike picketing, which has coercive elements to it, handbilling is more akin to pure communication and is entitled to more First Amendment protection.

In seeking to dissuade customers to do business with a picketed employer, unions have become quite creative in their methods. In *Tucker v. City of Fairfield*, 398 F.3d 457 (6th Cir. 2005), the union employed an inflatable rat during a labor protest. The use of the rat was held to be protected First Amendment expression. However, a labor dispute-oriented mock funeral procession was held not to be protected First Amendment expression because it contained elements of picketing, including patrolling with a coffin and a union representative dressed as the grim reaper. *See Kentov v. Sheet Metal Workers*, 418 F.3d 1259 (11th Cir. 2005). *But see Sheet Metal Workers v. NLRB*, 491 F.3d 429 (D.C. Cir. 2007) (concluding that mock funerals were not overly coercive or intimidating and thus was constitutionally protected). Yet another case, *Overstreet v. United Brotherhood of Carpenters*, 409 F.3d 1199 (9th Cir. 2005), found protected First Amendment expression for a large, stationary banner that was employed by the union to shame an employer for failing to follow union guidelines on wage rates.

Finally, a last category of First Amendment cases involves union picketing in areas open to the public, such as common areas at shopping malls. In *Hudgens v. NLRB*, 424 U.S. 507 (1976), the question posed to the Court was whether the owner of a shopping mall violated the free speech provisions of the First Amendment when it threatened to call the police if leafleters did not leave the premises. The union members were peacefully distributing handbills encouraging shoppers not to do business with mall stores because the mall owner did business with a contractor that did not hire union employees. In considering the First Amendment issue, the Court held that free speech can be abridged because the shopping mall does not take the place of a town center and is thus not a public forum, but a privately owned space. However, in a later California case, *Fashion Valley Mall, LLC v. NLRB*, 42 Cal.4th 850 (Cal. 2007), the California Supreme Court held that the state constitution provided great protection than the First Amendment and considered shopping malls to be public forums. Consequently, the mall prohibition against union leafleting in that case was found to be an impermissible content-based restriction on speech.

SECTION 2   RECOGNITIONAL PICKETING UNDER SECTION 8(b)(7)

Having considered constitutional protections for picketing, what type of statutory protection for picketing exists under the NLRA? As we shall see, just because an activity is not protected by the Constitution does not mean that statutory protections are unavailable.

The amount of protection that is afforded picketing under the NLRA depends on the purpose for which picketing is being employed. The enactment of Section 8(b)(7) in the Landrum Griffin Act of 1959 placed restrictions on organizational and recognitional picketing, but also provided an exception for informational picketing and a procedure for expedited elections.

PROBLEM #1: CAN I GET SOME RECOGNITION HERE?[1]

The NLRB General Counsel alleges that the Retail Clerks Union picketed a retail market owned by CityMart for the unlawful object of obtaining recognition as the employees' collective-bargaining representative in violation of Section 8(b)(7)(C) of the NLRA.

The Union acknowledges engaging in picketing, and that such picketing continued for more than 30 days without a representation petition being filed. The Union, however, insists that it never sought recognition, nor engaged in conduct tantamount to seeking recognition from CityMart, and insists that at all times the picketing was conducted to persuade CityMart to meet area standards regarding wages and working conditions. The union, however, never directly sought information from CityMart as to the wage rate being paid.

The picket signs that appeared at CityMart stated: "This market is unfair because they do not pay the prevailing wage rates or benefits paid by other markets in this area." As a result of this picketing, deliveries by CityMart suppliers ceased at this store.

1.   Have the Retail Clerks committed a Section 8(b)(7)(C) unfair labor practice?

2.   Can the union claim that the publicity picketing proviso to Section 8(b)(7)(C) protects them from ULP charges?

PROBLEM MATERIALS

Lee Modjeska, *Recognition Picketing Under the NLRA*, 35 U. FLA. L. REV. 633 (1983)

Hod Carriers Local 840 (Blinne Construction Co.), 135 N.L.R.B. 1153 (1962)

Lee Modjeska, *Recognition Picketing Under the NLRA*
35 U. FLA. L. REV. 633 (1983)[2]

INTRODUCTION

Long ago, Justice Holmes articulated the broad socioeconomic considerations underlying national labor policy:

---

[1] This Problem is based on Retail Clerks International Association, Local Union No. 899 (State-Mart Inc.), 166 N.L.R.B. 818 (1967).

[2] Copyright © 1983 by University of Florida Law Review. All rights reserved. Reprinted with permission.

[O]ne of the eternal conflicts out of which life is made up is that between the effort of every man to get the most he can for his services, and that of society, disguised under the name of capital, to get his services for the least possible return. Combination on the one side is patent and powerful. Combination on the other is the necessary and desirable counterpart, if the battle is to be carried on in a fair and equal way.

Peaceful picketing is a potent union weapon in this battle. To protect labor's right to use this weapon for organization or recognition while checking potential abuses inherent in its unrestrained exercise, Congress amended the National Labor Relations Act in 1959. The amendment, section 8(b)(7), provides 'a comprehensive code governing organizational strikes and picketing . . . .' Congress enacted this section to ensure employees freedom of choice in selecting a bargaining representative.

From its inception, section 8(b)(7) has raised difficult problems of interpretation and harmonization. It continues to be one of the most intricate and opaque strands in the web of national labor policy. To unravel some of these intricacies, this article will trace the section's evolution, reviewing its construction and application by the courts and the National Labor Relations Board (the Board). Board procedures for resolving alleged violations of the section will also be examined. The current state of the law pertaining to organizational picketing will be analyzed, and problem areas in application of the section identified.

EXPLICATION OF THE STATUTE

Section 8(b)(7) bars a union from picketing for recognition or organization in certain circumstances. Subsection (A) bans organizational or recognitional picketing when the employer has lawfully recognized another union and questions concerning representation cannot appropriately be raised. Subsection (B) bars such picketing when a valid Board election has been held within the preceding twelve months. Subsection (C) provides that when picketing for recognition or organization is not barred by subsections (A) or (B), such picketing may not exceed thirty days unless a representation petition is filed within that period.

If no such petition is filed, picketing beyond thirty days is an unfair labor practice. Filing a timely petition stays the limitation and the picketing may continue pending the outcome of the petition. The first proviso to subsection (C) expedites the procedure. It requires a Board directed and certified election once a timely petition has been filed. The second proviso to subsection (C) affords an immunity to certain kinds of informational picketing when subsections (A) and (B) do not apply. This immunity is withheld when the object of the informational picketing is to interfere with deliveries to the picketed employer.

The 'comprehensive code' contained in section 8(b)(7) is designed to further the orderly resolution of disputes over representation of employees by requiring settlement through Board procedures rather than coercive picketing. The Board's Rules and Regulations and Statements of Procedure implement the section. A case is given priority status and promptly investigated upon the filing of a charge that a union has violated section 8(b)(7). If after investigation the charge appears to have merit, the Regional Director issues a complaint and simultaneously applies to the federal district court for an injunction against the picketing. However, when a union that has filed a 'timely' election petition is charged with violating subsection (C), the Regional Director suspends proceedings on the unfair labor practice charge and investigates the petition. If the Regional Director decides an election is warranted and no issues require a prior hearing, he will direct an election to be held in an appropriate unit of employees. Any party aggrieved by the Regional Director's direction of the election may seek review by filing with the Board a request for special permission to appeal the Regional Director's action. The Board may order a stay of the election if appropriate. After the election, and after disposition of any challenges to election procedures, the Regional Director issues a certification of the election results.

If the picketing union loses the election but nevertheless continues picketing for recognition or organization, it is subject to restraint under section 8(b)(7)(B) because an election was held within the past twelve months. Accordingly, the employer may file a new unfair labor practice charge alleging violation of section 8(b)(7)(B). Upon investigating the charge and finding it meritorious, the Regional Director may issue a complaint and concurrently seek to enjoin the picketing. In the subsequent section 8(b)(7)(B) proceeding, the initial question is whether the post-election picketing has the proscribed object of recognition or organization. With an affirmative finding the inquiry becomes whether there was a 'valid election.' In the new proceeding, all questions relating to the validity of the election, including the Regional Director's propriety of directing it, are open to Board and judicial review . . . .

Proscribed Objects: Organization and Recognition

Section 8(b)(7) proscribes picketing when 'an object' of the picketing is to force an employer 'to recognize or bargain with a labor organization,' or to force employees to select the union as their bargaining representative. The section prohibits picketing only when one of the objects is organization or recognition. Because section 8(b)(7) uses the phrase 'an object,' so long as *one* of the union's objectives is illegal the existence of other legitimate objectives is immaterial. Conversely, picketing conducted solely to protest an employee's discharge and secure his reinstatement is not illegal. When an employer alleges an 8(b)(7) violation, the Board must first ascertain whether the union's conduct constitutes picketing. If so, the Board must then determine the object of the picketing.

Picketing solely for the purpose of protesting substandard wages and achieving area wage standards does not violate section 8(b)(7) because the picketing's object is not for recognition or organization. Determining whether picketing is directed only to area standards is often problematic. The Board considers various factors to determine whether a union is engaged in permissible area standards picketing or is using area standards as a pretext for recognition. For example, the Board examines whether the union actually investigated the employer's wages and benefits, or whether there were 'adequate, reasonably reliable, external sources to substantiate the union's conclusion' that the employer's economic package was substandard. The Board also considers whether the union requested the employer to furnish information irrelevant to area standards. Another factor in the Board's determination is whether the union's demands of the employer were broader than necessary for compliance with area standards.

The Board has recognized that a union may alter its picketing objectives. Thus, a union's original recognitional object does not preclude a finding that later picketing was for the permissible purpose of maintaining area standards. ' When a union follows a disclaimer with the cessation of picketing for a significant period of time and engages in no other conduct inconsistent with its disavowal of representative interest, the Board has been more inclined to conclude that the union has abandoned its present recognitional objective.' . . .

Unreasonable Duration and Expedited Election

Section 8(b)(7)(C) provides that when subsections (A) and (B) do not bar picketing for recognition or organization, such picketing is limited to a reasonable period. This reasonable period may not exceed thirty days unless a representation petition is filed within that period. If no petition is filed, picketing beyond the reasonable period is an unfair labor practice. To avoid prolonged picketing, the first proviso to subsection (C) expedites the election procedure specifying that when a timely petition has been filed, 'the Board shall forthwith, without regard to the provisions of section 9(c)(1) or the absence of a showing of a substantial interest on the part of the labor organization, direct an election in such unit as the Board finds to be appropriate and shall certify the results thereof.'

The purpose of section 8(b)(7)(C) is to afford a union a reasonable opportunity to use picketing as an organizational device. Thereafter, the Board may hold an election to determine whether a majority of the employees want the union as its representative. Although the section sets thirty days as the maximum picketing period without filing a representation petition the Board may fix shorter periods as 'reasonable.' In assessing whether a shorter period is reasonable, the Board may consider the particular circumstances, such as pre-Act picketing, violence or perishable goods. In some instances, the Board has found picketing to be unreasonable *ab initio*: when the picketing union is statutorily disabled from representing the unit . . . .

Employer unfair labor practices are not an automatic defense to a charge of a section 8(b)(7) violation. Nonetheless, employer unfair labor practices which prompt a union's picketing for recognition or organizational purposes are not completely irrelevant under section 8(b)(7). Section 8(b)(7)(A) bans picketing where the employer 'has lawfully recognized in accordance with this Act any other labor organization.' Under section 8(b)(7)(A), the picketing union can defeat an unfair labor practice charge by proving that the incumbent union had been supported by the employer in violation of section 8(a)(2).

Furthermore, section 8(b)(7)(C) makes the right to continue picketing beyond a reasonable period of time contingent upon a prompt determination of the representation question in a Board election. The election must be valid under Board standards for the election results to have meaning. A valid election cannot be conducted when current, unremedied employer unfair labor practices might affect employee free choice. Curtailing the union's right to continue picketing based on the results of such an election could encourage the employer to commit unfair labor practices to assure the union's defeat.

In *International Hod Carriers, Local 840 (C. A. Blinne Construction Co.)*, the Board analyzed the effect of employer unfair labor practices on a union's section 8(b)(7)(C) obligation to file a representation petition as a prelude to an expedited election when picketing for longer than thirty days. The union argued that when an employer commits unfair labor practices the Board should waive the filing requirement because the resulting expedited election would be tainted by unfair labor practices. Holding that unfair labor practice charges did not relieve the union of its obligation to file a representation petition, the Board found the union's fears groundless. If the unfair practice charges were meritorious, the expedited election would be delayed until an uncoerced election could be held. On the other hand, if the charge of employer unfair labor practices were found baseless, an expedited election would quickly follow in accordance with Congress' direction.

The Board concluded that unless a representation petition is filed within a reasonable period of time, the picketing will violate subsection (C) notwithstanding the employer's unfair labor practices. Even if a timely petition is filed, it nonetheless may be 'blocked' by the employer's unfair labor practices. If the union files charges concerning the employer's conduct and the Board determines the charges have merit, no election would be held on the petition until the unfair labor practices were remedied. The union could continue picketing in the interim, but steps to check the picketing could not be taken under 8(b)(7)(B) until the union lost in a valid election.

Informational Picketing Exception

Subsection 8(b)(7)(C) proscribes picketing for recognition or organization when a petition for an election has not been filed within a reasonable time from the commencement of picketing. The second proviso to section 8(b)(7)(C) carves out a significant exception to this general ban on recognition and organizational picketing. The proviso allows picketing for recognition or organization under two specified conditions. First, the picketing must be for the purpose of truthfully advising the public that the picketed employer 'does not employ members of, or have a contract with a labor organization.' Under the second condition, the picketing cannot interfere with deliveries to or the performance of other services at the picketed premises by employees of other employers.

The Board's focus in determining whether the picketing causes delivery inter-ruptions or work stoppages at the picketed premises is on the actual impact upon the employer's business. The question, in the Board's view is 'whether the picketing has disrupted, interfered with, or curtailed the employer's business.' The proviso's protection is lost only if the picketing results in numerous delivery stoppages or compels the employer to modify his normal dealings with suppliers. Picketing for other purposes is not within the ambit of section 8(b)(7) and thus is not proscribed by the second proviso even when it causes delivery stoppage. Furthermore, the proviso does not exempt picketing that is otherwise banned by subsections (A) and (B).

The second proviso essentially reflects a congressional compromise sanctioning 'publicity picketing' and prohibiting 'signal picketing.' Publicity picketing seeks to enlist the consuming public's support for the picket's cause. Signal picketing, on the other hand, is primarily intended to inform union members that their unions are invoking organized economic action against the picketed employer. As noted by the Second Circuit, 'this proviso gives the union freedom to appeal to the unorganized public for spontaneous popular pressure upon an employer; it is intended, however, to exclude the invocation of pressure by organized labor groups or members of unions, as such.'

APPRAISAL OF THE STATUTE: CONSTITUTIONAL CONSIDERATIONS

Recognitional or organizational picketing has been virtually prohibited by section 8(b)(7) as the preceding discussion indicates. Picketing which is not subject to prohibition is severely limited in duration. Only an innocuous form of informational picketing is seemingly preserved, and even that protection is forfeited where adverse effects occur. Section 8(b)(7) thus goes 'beyond the Taft-Hartley Act to legislate a comprehensive code governing' recognitional and organizational picketing.

Such a sweeping governmental prohibition of peaceful picketing raises questions of unconstitutional abridgement of first amendment rights of freedom of speech and assembly. It may be too late in the decisional day, however, for such questions to be considered seriously. At one time the Supreme Court broadly assimilated peaceful picketing into the freedom of speech and assembly protected under the fourteenth amendment.

In later years the Court retreated from this broad equation with the development of the unlawful purpose doctrine. The Court found that picketing encompassed more than the communication of ideas. While picketing had publicity aspects, it was also a signal to organized labor for economic action. The act of picketing was more likely to induce action than the message conveyed. The signal aspects therefore justified curtailment of picketing which contravened legitimate governmental purposes.

The Court thus upheld state injunctions against picketing when the manner or object of the picketing was contrary to a valid state policy. Moreover, the Court held that Congress similarly had the power to regulate and curtail peaceful picketing. Given this federal and state power to curtail picketing that contravenes legitimate governmental purposes, first amendment challenges to section 8(b)(7) have been uniformly unsuccessful. In upholding the constitutionality of the section, courts have relied upon the unlawful purpose doctrine, the Act's safeguards protecting 'pure' free speech, and the section's lack of oppression in its practical impact.

One legitimate governmental purpose which, if contravened, justifies curtailing picketing is ensuring employee freedom of choice in selecting a bargaining representative. Section 8(b)(7) implements this policy by channeling representation questions into the NLRB election processes and away from the recognitional and organizational pressures of the picket line. While the representational question is pending, the right to continue recognition or organization picketing may be preserved despite any signal effects of the picketing. The right to engage in publicity (informational) non-effects picketing is also clearly preserved in this period, as well as in other non-(A) or (B) situations. In this regard, then, a balance between a legitimate governmental purpose and free speech is made.

Section 8(b)(7) further implements the governmental policy of securing employee free choice by insulating that choice from picketing pressures once the selection is made. Thus, sections 8(b)(7)(A) and (B) provide for periods of absolute repose following election or contract execution. During these periods both signal recognition or organization picketing and publicity recognition or organization picketing is banned. In these situations the constitutional balance is less even.

Even during the (A) and (B) periods of repose, however, the union remains free to engage in nonrecognition or organization publicity picketing. For example, the union may engage in area standards picketing. Free speech rights are somewhat preserved when the union's interest is in publicizing an employer's noncompliance with union economic *standards*. Free speech rights are limited, however, when the union's interest is in publicizing the employer's non-union or other union *status*.

Because the union may disseminate information in (A) and (B) periods through means other than picketing suggests that its first amendment rights are preserved to some extent. The right to engage in publicity other than picketing, however, may be so meaningless a form of communication as to be no right at all. This is especially so where such conduct as handbilling and stationary signs is deemed picketing under 8(b)(7).

Arguably, the constitutional balance in (A) and (B) situations is restored when the employer's interests are added to the governmental side of the scale. The dispositive question is whether Congress has a legitimate governmental purpose in insulating employers not only from all signal and effects-publicity (informational) recognition in (A) and (B) situations, but also from all such non-effects publicity picketing.

From the standpoint of both private and public interests, Congress clearly has a legitimate purpose in protecting the employer against certain coercive picketing. Property and industrial peace considerations are particularly significant. Such purpose certainly justifies the employer protections accorded in (C) situations when signal picketing is limited to a reasonable period not to exceed thirty days, or to a confined, expedited election period. Beyond that, effects-recognition or organization publicity picketing is proscribed. Non-effects publicity picketing may continue indefinitely, however, until it is subsumed in (A) or (B) situations. The governmental purpose of protecting employers against certain picketing also justifies a ban on signal or effects-publicity picketing in (A) and (B) situations.

Absent coercive pressures there is no legitimately vindicatable employer interest that justifies the ban on non-effects publicity picketing. Employer reassertion of the employee free choice rights previously discussed does not magnify the weight already accorded those separate rights. Consideration of employer interests on the government's side thus fails to repair the constitutional imbalance suggested in (A) and (B) situations.

In short, it is doubtful that legitimate governmental purposes warrant the prohibitions of (A) and (B) against non-effects publicity picketing. Absent signal harm, the mere existence of a recognitional or organizational object would not seem to predominate over the speech elements. A distinction should be made between information, non-effects recognition or organization picketing, and signal or informational effects recognition or organization picketing. Implicit in this distinction is the proposition that informational, non-effects picketing is not intended to force immediate recognition during a period when such object cannot lawfully be granted . . . .

HOD CARRIERS LOCAL 840 (BLINNE CONSTRUCTION CO.)
135 N.L.R.B. 1153 (1962)

. . . II.

Before proceeding to determine the application of Section 8(b)(7) (C) to the facts of the instant case, it is essential to note the interplay of the several subsections of Section 8(b)(7), of which subparagraph (C) is only a constituent part.

The section as a whole, as is apparent from its opening phrases, prescribes limitations only on picketing for an object of "recognition" or "bargaining" (both of which terms will hereinafter be subsumed under the single term "recognition") or for an object of organization. Picketing for other objects is not proscribed by this section. Moreover, not all picketing for recognition or organization is proscribed. A "currently certified" union may picket for recognition or organization of employees for whom it is certified. And even a union which is not certified is barred from recognition or organization picketing only in three general areas. The first area, defined in subparagraph (A) of Section 8(b)(7), relates to situations where another union has been lawfully recognized and a question concerning representation cannot appropriately be raised. The second area, defined in subparagraph (B), relates to situations where, within the preceding 12 months, a "valid election" has been held.

The intent of subparagraphs (A) and (B) is fairly clear. Congress concluded that where a union has been lawfully recognized and a question concerning representation cannot appropriately be raised, or where the employees within the preceding 12 months have made known their views concerning representation, both the employer and employees are entitled to immunity from recognition or organization picketing for prescribed periods.

Congress did not stop there, however. Deeply concerned with other abuses, most particularly "blackmail" picketing, Congress concluded that it would be salutary to impose even further limitations on picketing for recognition or organization. Accordingly, subparagraph (C) provides that even where such picketing is not barred by the provisions of (A) or (B) so that picketing for recognition or organization would otherwise be permissible, such picketing is limited to a reasonable period not to exceed 30 days unless a representation petition is filed prior to the expiration of that period. Absent the filing of such a timely petition, continuation of the picketing beyond the reasonable period becomes an unfair labor practice. On the other hand, the filing of a timely petition stays the limitation and

[handwritten margin notes:]
Currently certified union may picket for recognition or org. of EEs for whom its certified.

Union not cert barred:
① Where another union lawfully recognized & a question on rep cant be raised.
② sits where w/n 12 months an election held.

Even when picketing not barred by (A) or (B)
↓
cant exceed 30 days w/o rep petition. w/o pet then ULP.

picketing may continue pending the processing of the petition. Even here, however, Congress by the addition of the first proviso to subparagraph (C) made it possible to foreshorten the period of permissible picketing by directing the holding of an expedited election pursuant to the representation petition.

The expedited election procedure is applicable, of course, only in a Section 8(b)(7)(C) proceeding, i.e., where an 8(b)(7)(C) unfair labor practice charge has been filed. Congress rejected efforts to amend the provisions of Section 9(c) of the Act so as to dispense generally with preelection hearings. Thus, in the absence of an 8(b)(7)(C) unfair labor practice charge, a union will not be enabled to obtain an expedited election by the mere device of engaging in recognition or organization picketing and filing a representation petition. And on the other hand, a picketing union which files a representation petition pursuant to the mandate of Section 8(b)(7)(C) and to avoid its sanctions will not be propelled into an expedited election, which it may not desire, merely because it has filed such a petition. In both the above situations, the normal representation procedures are applicable; the showing of a substantial interest will be required, and the preelection hearing directed in Section 9(c)(1) will be held.

This, in our considered judgment, puts the expedited election procedure prescribed in the first proviso to subparagraph C in its proper and intended focus. That procedure was devised to shield aggrieved employers and employees from the adverse effects of prolonged recognition or organization picketing. Absent such a grievance, it was not designed either to benefit or to handicap picketing activity. . . . "If [the first proviso] were intended to confer a primary or independent right to an expedited election entirely separated from the statutory scheme, it would seem that such intention would have manifested itself in a more forthright manner, rather than in the shy seclusion of Section 8(b)(7)(C)."

Subparagraphs (B) and (C) serve different purposes. But it is especially significant to note their interrelationship. Congress was particularly concerned, even where picketing for recognition or organization was otherwise permissible, that the question concerning representation which gave rise to the picketing be resolved as quickly as possible. It was for this reason that it provided for the filing of a petition pursuant to which the Board could direct an expedited election in which the employees could freely indicate their desires as to representation. If, in the free exercise of their choice, they designate the picketing union as their bargaining representative, that union will be certified and it will by the express terms of Section 8(b)(7) be exonerated from the strictures of that section. If, conversely, the employees reject the picketing union, that union will be barred from picketing for 12 months thereafter under the provisions of subparagraph (B).

The scheme which Congress thus devised represents what that legislative body deemed a practical accommodation between the right of a union to engage in legitimate picketing for recognition or organization and abuse of that right. One caveat must be noted in that regard. The congressional scheme is, perforce, based on the premise that the election to be conducted under the first proviso to subparagraph (C) represents the free and uncoerced choice of the employee electorate. Absent such a free and uncoerced choice, the underlying question concerning representation is not resolved and, more particularly, subparagraph (B) which turns on the holding of a "valid election" does not become operative.

There remains to be considered only the second proviso to subparagraph (C). In sum, that proviso removes the time limitation imposed upon, and preserves the legality of, recognition or organization picketing falling within the ambit of subparagraph (C), where that picketing merely advises the public that an employer does not employ members of, or have a contract with, a union unless an effect of such picketing is to halt pickups or deliveries, or the performance of services. Needless to add, picketing which meets the requirements of the proviso also renders the expedited election procedure inapplicable.

Except for the final clause in Section 8(b)(7) which provides that nothing in that section shall be construed to permit any act otherwise proscribed under Section 8(b) of the Act, the foregoing sums up the limitations imposed upon recognition or organization picketing by the Landrum-Griffin amendments. However, at the risk of laboring the obvious, it is important to note that structurally, as well as grammatically, subparagraphs (A), (B), and (C) are subordinate to and controlled by the opening phrases of Section 8(b)(7). In other words, the thrust of all the Section 8(b)(7) provisions is only upon picketing for an object of recognition or organization, and not upon picketing for other objects. Similarly, both structurally and grammatically, the two provisos in subparagraph (C) appertain only to the situation defined in the principal clause of that subparagraph.

III.

Having outlined, in concededly broad strokes, the statutory framework of Section 8(b)(7) and particularly subparagraph (C) thereof, we may appropriately turn to a consideration of the instant case which presents issues going to the heart of that legislation.

The relevant facts may be briefly stated. On February 2, 1960, all three common laborers employed by Blinne at the Fort Leonard Wood jobsite signed cards designating the Union to represent them for purposes of collective bargaining. The next day the Union demanded that Blinne recognize the Union as the bargaining agent for the three laborers. Blinne not only refused recognition but told the Union it would transfer one of the laborers, Wann, in order to destroy the Union's majority. Blinne carried out this threat and transferred Wann 5 days later, on February 8. Following this refusal to recognize the Union and the transfer of Wann the Union started picketing at Fort Wood. The picketing, which began on February 8, immediately following the transfer of Wann, had three announced objectives: (1) recognition of the Union; (2) payment of the Davis-Bacon scale of wages; and (3) protest against Blinne's unfair labor practices in refusing to recognize the Union and in threatening to transfer and transferring Wann.

The picketing continued, with interruptions due to bad weather, until at least March 11, 1960, a period of more than 30 days from the date the picketing commenced. The picketing was peaceful, only one picket was on duty, and the picket sign he carried read "C. A. Blinne Construction Company, unfair." The three laborers on the job (one was the replacement for Wann) struck when the picketing started.

The Union, of course, was not the certified bargaining representative of the employees. Moreover, no representation petition was filed during the more than 30 days in which picketing was taking place. On March 1, however, about 3 weeks after the picketing commenced and well within the statutory 30-day period, the Union filed unfair labor practice charges against Blinne, alleging violations of Section 8(a)(1), (2), (3), and (5). On March 22, the Regional Director dismissed the 8(a)(2) and (5) charges, whereupon the Union forthwith filed a representation petition under Section 9(c) of the Act.

Subsequently, on April 20, the Regional Director approved a unilateral settlement agreement with Blinne with respect to the Section 8(a)(1) and (3) charges which had not been dismissed. In the settlement agreement, Blinne neither admitted nor denied that it had committed unfair labor practices.

General Counsel argues that a violation of Section 8(b)(7)(C) has occurred within the literal terms of that provision because (1) the Union's picketing was concededly for an object of obtaining recognition; (2) the Union was not currently certified as the representative of the employees involved; and (3) no petition for representation was filed within 30 days of the commencement of the picketing. Inasmuch as the Union made no contention that its recognition picketing was "informational" within the meaning of the second proviso to subparagraph (C) or that it otherwise comported with the strictures of that proviso, General Counsel contends that a finding of unfair labor practice is required.

Respondent Union, for its part, points to the manifest inequity of such a finding and argues that Congress could not have intended so incongruous a result. In essence, its position is that it was entitled to recognition because it represented all the employees in the appropriate unit, that Blinne by a series of unfair labor practices deprived the Union and the employees it sought to represent of fundamental rights guaranteed by the Act, and that the impact of a finding adverse to the Union would be to punish the innocent and reward the wrongdoer. More specifically, Respondent argues that Section 8(b)(7)(C) was not intended to apply to picketing by a majority union and that, in any event, Blinne's unfair labor practices exonerated it from the statutory requirement of filing a timely representation petition . . . .

IV.

As already noted, Respondent advances two major contentions. The first is that Section 8(b)(7)(C) does not apple to picketing by a majority union in an appropriate unit; the second is that employer unfair labor practices are a defense to a charge of an 8(b)(7) violation. We deal with the contentions in that order.

A. *The contention that Section 8(b)(7)(C) does not proscribe picketing for recognition or organization by a majority union*

Respondent, urging the self-evident proposition that a statute should be read as a whole, argues that Section 8(b)(7)(C) was not designed to prohibit picketing for recognition by a union enjoying majority status in an appropriate unit. Such picketing is for a lawful purpose inasmuch as Sections 8(a)(5) and 9(a) of the Act specifically impose upon an employer the duty to recognize and bargain with a union which enjoys that status. Accordingly, Respondent contends, absent express language requiring such a result, Section 8(b)(7)(C) should not be read in derogation of the duty so imposed.

There is grave doubt that the argument here made is apposite in this case. But, assuming its relevance, we find it to be without merit. To be sure, the legislative history is replete with references that Congress in framing the 1959 amendments was primarily concerned with "blackmail" picketing where the picketing union represented none or few of the employees whose allegiance it sought. Legislative references susceptible to an interpretation that Congress was concerned with the evils of majority picketing are sparse. Yet it cannot be gainsaid that Section 8(b)(7) by its explicit language exempts only "currently certified" unions from its proscriptions. Cautious as we should be to avoid a mechanical reading of statutory terms in involved legislative enactments, it is difficult to avoid giving the quoted words, essentially words of art, their natural construction. Moreover, such a construction is consonant with the underlying statutory scheme which is to resolve disputed issues of majority status, whenever possible, by the machinery of a Board election. Absent unfair labor practices or preelection misconduct warranting the setting aside of the election, majority unions will presumably not be prejudiced by such resolution. On the other hand, the admitted difficulties of determining majority status without such an election are obviated by this construction.

Congress was presumably aware of these considerations. In any event, there would seem to be here no valid considerations requiring that Congress be assumed to have intended a broader exemption than the one it actually afforded.

B. *The contention that employer unfair labor practices are a defense to a charge of a Section 8(b)(7)(C) violation*

We turn now to the second issue, namely, whether employer unfair labor practices are a defense to an 8(b)(7)(C) violation. As set forth in the original Decision and Order, the Union argues that Blinne was engaged in unfair labor practices within the meaning of Section 8(a)(1) and (3) of the Act; that it filed appropriate unfair labor practice charges against Blinne within a reasonable period of time after the commencement of the picketing; that it filed a representation petition as soon as the 8(a)(2) and (5) allegations of the charges were dismissed; that the 8(a)(1) and (3) allegations were in effect sustained and a settlement agreement was subsequently entered into with the approval of the Board; and that, therefore, this sequence of events should satisfy the requirements of Section 8(b)(7)(C).

The majority of the Board in the original Decision and Order rejected this argument. Pointing out that the representation petition was concededly filed more than 30 days after the commencement of the picketing, the majority concluded that the clear terms of Section 8(b)(4)(C) had been violated.

The majority also addressed itself specifically to the Union's contention that Section 8(b)(7)(C) could not have been intended by Congress to apply where an employer unfair labor practice had occurred. Its opinion alludes to the fact that the then Senator, now President, Kennedy had proposed statutory language to the effect that any employer unfair labor practice would be a defense to a charge of an 8(b)(7) violation both with respect to an application to the courts for a temporary restraining order and with respect to the unfair labor practice proceeding itself. The majority noted that the Congress did not adopt this proposal but instead limited itself merely to the insertion of a proviso in Section 10(l) prohibiting the application for a restraining order under Section 8(b)(7)(C) if there was reason to believe that a Section 8(a)(2) violation existed. Accordingly, the majority concluded that Congress had specifically rejected the very contention which Respondent urged.

The dissenting member in the original Decision and Order took sharp issue with the majority. In his view, the majority failed to "look to the provisions of the whole law and its object and policy." Conceding that Section 8(b)(7)(C) in terms outlawed recognition picketing for more than 30 days unless a representation petition was filed, he emphasized that the cited section also provided for an expedited election if such a petition was filed. The purpose of the election is to obtain a free and uncoerced expression of the employees' desires as to their representation. Where unfair labor practices have taken place, however, such a free and uncoerced expression is precluded and the filing of a representation petition would be a futility. Indeed, consistent Board practice, presumably known to Congress, is to stay representation proceedings and elections thereunder until the effect of existing unremedied unfair labor practices is dissipated. Accordingly, the dissenting member concluded that the failure of a picketing union to file a timely petition in the face of employer unfair labor practices should not be made the basis for a finding of a violation under Section 8(b)(7)(C) of the Act.

The dissenting opinion likewise did not find the majority's reliance upon the proviso to Section 10(l) persuasive. On the basis of the relevant legislative history, the dissent concluded that this proviso was intended merely to implement Section 8(b)(7)(A) of the Act, that is, to insure that a union which was the beneficiary of a "sweetheart agreement" with an employer could not derive the benefit of injunctive relief that would otherwise be accorded by virtue of the provisions of subparagraph (A).

In retrospect, both the majority and dissenting opinions are not without logic or respectable foundation. Certainly, the narrow proviso embodied in Section 10(l), and the failure to embrace a proposal that would exempt recognition and organization picketing from the Section 8(b)(7)(C) bar where employer unfair labor practices had been committed, suggest that Congress was reluctant to grant such an exemption. Conversely, as the dissenting opinion argues, to hold that employer unfair labor practices sufficient to affect the results of an election are irrelevant in an 8(b)(7)(C) context seems incongruous and inconsistent with the overall scheme of the Act.

Fortified by the advantages of hindsight and added deliberation as to the ramifications of the majority and minority opinions, we are now of the view that neither opinion affords a complete answer to the question here presented. It seems fair to say that Congress was unwilling to write an exemption into Section 8(b)(7)(C) dispensing with the necessity for filing a representation petition wherever employer unfair labor practices were alleged. The fact that the bill as ultimately enacted by the Congress did not contain the amendment to Section 10(l) which the Senate had adopted in S. 1555 cogently establishes that this reluctance was not due to oversight. On the other hand, it strains credulity to believe that Congress proposed to make the rights of union and employees turn upon the results of an election which, because of the existence of unremedied unfair labor practices, is unlikely to reflect the true wishes of the employees.

We do not find ourselves impaled on the horns of this dilemma. Upon careful reappraisal of the statutory scheme we are satisfied that Congress meant to require, and did require, in an 8(b)(7)(C) situation, that a representation petition be filed within a reasonable period, not to exceed 30 days. By this device machinery can quickly be set in motion to resolve by a free and fair election the underlying question concerning representation out of which the picketing arises. This is the normal situation, and the situation which the statute is basically designed to serve.

There is legitimate concern, however, with the abnormal situation, that is, the situation where because of unremedied unfair labor practices a free and fair election cannot be held. We believe Congress anticipated this contingency also. Thus, we find no mandate in the legislative scheme to compel the holding of an election pursuant to a representation petition where, because of unremedied unfair labor practices or for other valid reason, a free and uncoerced election cannot be held. On the contrary, the interrelated provisions of subparagraphs (B) and (C), by their respective references to a "valid election" and to a "certif[ication of] results" presuppose that Congress contemplated only a fair and free election. Only after such an election could the Board certify the results and only after such an election could the salutary provisions of subparagraph (B) become operative.

In our view, therefore, Congress intended that, except to the limited extent set forth in the first proviso, the Board in 8(b)(7)(C) cases follow the tried and familiar procedures it typically follows in representation cases where unfair labor practice charges are filed. That procedure, as already set forth, is to hold the representation case in abeyance and refrain from holding an election pending the resolution of the unfair labor practice charges. Thus, the fears that the statutory requirement for filing a timely petition will compel a union which has been the victim of unfair labor practices to undergo a coerced election are groundless. No action will be taken on that petition while unfair labor practice charges are pending, and until a valid election is held pursuant to that petition, the union's right to picket under the statutory scheme is unimpaired.

On the other side of the coin, it may safely be assumed that groundless unfair labor practice charges in this area, because of the statutory priority accorded Section 8(b)(7) violations, will be quickly dismissed. Following such dismissal an election can be directed forthwith upon the subsisting petition, thereby effectuating the congressional purpose. Moreover, the fact that a timely petition is on file will protect the innocent union, which through a mistake of fact or law has filed a groundless unfair labor practice charge, from a finding of an 8(b)(7)(C) violation. Thus, the policy of the entire Act is effectuated and all rights guaranteed by its several provisions are appropriately safeguarded.

The facts of the instant case may be utilized to demonstrate the practical operation of the legislative scheme. Here the union had filed unfair labor practice charges alleging violations by the employer of Section 8(a)(1), (2), (3), and (5) of the

Act. General Counsel found the allegations of 8(a)(2) and (5) violations groundless. Hence had these allegations stood alone and had a timely petition been on file, an election could have been directed forthwith and the underlying question concerning representation out of which the picketing arose could have been resolved pursuant to the statutory scheme. The failure to file a timely petition frustrated that scheme.

On the other hand, the Section 8(a)(1) and (3) charges were found meritorious. Under these circumstances, and again consistent with uniform practice, no election would have been directed notwithstanding the currency of a timely petition; the petition would be held in abeyance pending a satisfactory resolution of the unfair labor practice charges. The aggrieved union's right to picket would not be abated in the interim and the sole prejudice to the employer would be the delay engendered by its own unfair labor practices. The absence of a timely petition, however, precludes disposition of the underlying question concerning representation which thus remains unresolved even after the Section 8(a)(1) and (3) charges are satisfactorily disposed of. Accordingly, to condone the refusal to file a timely petition in such situations would be to condone the flouting of a legislative judgment. Moreover, and most important, to impose a lesser requirement would fly in the face of the public interest which prompted that judgment.

Conclusion

Because we read Section 8(b)(7)(C) as requiring in the instant case the filing of a timely petition and because such a petition was admittedly not filed until more than 30 days after the commencement of the picketing, we find that Respondent violated Section 8(b)(7)(C) of the Act. As previously noted, it is undisputed that "an object" of the picketing was for recognition. It affords Respondent no comfort that its picketing was also in protest against the discriminatory transfer of an employee and against payment of wages at a rate lower than that prescribed by law. Had Respondent confined its picketing to these objectives rather than, as it did, include a demand for recognition, we believe none of the provisions of Section 8(b)(7) would be applicable. Under the circumstances here, however, Section 8(b)(7)(C) is applicable.

Accordingly, having concluded as in the original decision herein that a violation of Section 8(b)(7)(C) has occurred, albeit for differing reasons, we reaffirm the Order entered therein.

POST PROBLEM DISCUSSION

1.   The Modjeska article excerpt and *Blinne Construction Co.* both nicely set out the interrelation and structure of subparagraphs A, B, and C of Section 8(b)(7). As the Board indicates, there is little controversy concerning subparagraphs A and B, which cover various bars to election and certification. Subparagraph C was enacted to prevent blackmail picketing by a non-majority union — a picket for recognition that disrupts the employer's business for an extended period until the employer gives in to the union's demands. Of course, an employer gives in cannot voluntarily recognize a non-majority union. To do so would violate Section 8(a)(2).

2. *Blinne* addresses two questions. Where an election petition is not filed within thirty days after recognitional picketing commences, as is required by Section 8(b)(7), can the union still avoid an unfair labor practice charge if 1) the union engaging in such conduct is a majority union in an appropriate unit; or 2) the employer has engaged in unfair labor practices during the course of the recognitional picketing? The Board held that Section 8(b)(7)(C) applies equally to a majority union picketing for recognition even though the purpose of the Subsection was to eliminate blackmail picketing by minority unions. This outcome is consistent with encouraging the parties to utilize the election procedures contained within the Act.

Also, the fact that an unfair labor practice is committed during the thirty-day recognitional picketing period does not excuse the requirement for the timely filing of an election petition by the expiration of that period. For example, the union in *Blinne* should have filed both the unfair labor practice charge and the petition for recognition at the same time. The election likely would not have been held before the resolution of the unfair labor practice charges, under the NLRB's "blocking charge" policy (see Chapter 6), so there was no need to fear that the union would have been subject to a premature election. Moreover, had the strike's aim been just to protest the unlawful transfer of the employee, and not also for recognition, Section 8(b)(7) would not have been an issue.

3. Why, in Problem #1, is it so important to determine whether the employee conduct is for the purpose of informing the public that CityMart does not pay area standard wages? Would such picketing be subject to the restrictions under Section 8(b)(7)? If not, how does the Modjeska excerpt explain why the Act treats different types of picketing differently?

It is well established that picketing for area standards, as distinguished from picketing for recognition or for a collective-bargaining agreement, is lawful and not regulated by Section 8(b)(7). When a union states that it is picketing for area standards, the Board will inquire whether the stated purpose is merely pretextual and the union is really unlawfully picketing for recognition. *See Retail Clerks Local 899 (State-Mart, Inc.)*, 166 N.L.R.B. 818 (1967) (noting that "a union might picket for equal wages or for equivalent costs, but when it undertakes to go beyond this and to dictate what benefits are to be granted, it is attempting to engage in *pro tanto* bargaining to gain benefits for employees which it does not claim to represent."). In *State-Mart Inc.*, because the picketers expressly demanded equivalent benefits, the Board concluded that the union was actually attempting to bargain for the employees.

4. Unions can seek neutrality agreements or card-check agreements as a way to gain recognition. What if a union pickets an employer to sign a neutrality or card-check agreement? Would such picketing be characterized as recognitional and thus, subject to Section 8(b)(7)(C)? If so, and the employer refuses to sign these agreements after thirty days, the union would have to file an election petition and forgo the neutrality or card-check route.

5. A related issue to those addressed in *Blinne* is whether informational (also called publicity) picketing under the second proviso of Subparagraph C must be purely informational or may be recognitional and informational at the same time.

Under *Smitley v. NLRB*, 327 F.2d 351 (9th Cir. 1964), a picket may be recognitional and informational and still receive the protections offered by Subparagraph C as long as the picket does not have the effect of causing work stoppages or causing others to stop doing business with the struck employer.

6. In *NLRB v. Local 3, International Brotherhood of Electrical Workers*, 317 F.2d 193 (2d Cir. 1963), after a contractor who dealt with a different union was awarded a contract to renovate a post office, Local 3 began picketing the side and rear delivery areas of the post office — areas not accessible to the general public. At least twice, the picketers blocked the contractor from receiving deliveries from other companies. The picketing union stated that the purpose of the picketing was to make the General Services Administration (GSA) give the federal contract to a contractor that recognized the union or, in the alternative, to simply oust the picketed contractor. At issue was whether a union may engage in recognitional picketing against an employer that has chosen to perform a contract with a different union.

The *Local 3* Court responded that lawful publicity picketing covers the dissemination of certain allowed messages designed to influence members of the unorganized public, as individuals. This type of picketing is permitted because the impact on the employer through such individuals is weak, indirect, and not that coercive. On the other hand, if the union engaged in "signal picketing" to other labor groups to obtain their support for their action against the employer, such picketing is not permitted under the second proviso of Section 8(b)(7)(C), because of its much greater impact on the business of the employer.

In short, informational picketing to members of the public is normally allowed unless it causes significant disruptions to the employer's business. At that point, the picketing becomes "signal picketing" — signaling to others workers not to work for the struck company, which is not permitted by the Act.

SECTION 3   SECONDARY BOYCOTTS UNDER SECTION 8(b)(4)

In the Section, we discuss secondary boycotts under Section 8(b)(4) of the NLRA. An initial secondary boycott provision was added by the Taft-Hartley Amendments in 1947, Section 8(b)(4)(A) (a provision dealing with consumer boycotts, added by the Landrum-Griffin Act in 1959, will be discussed in Section 4 of this Chapter). A secondary boycott is the application of economic pressure upon a person with whom the union has no dispute regarding its terms of employment in order to induce that "secondary employer" to cease doing business with another employer ("the primary employer") with whom the union does have such a dispute. Under Section 8(b)(4)(A), secondary boycotts are generally considered to be a union unfair labor practice.

Thus, an important characterization under Section 8(b)(4)(A) is whether the employer is a primary or secondary employer. This is usually easy to figure out, but there are some more challenging issues on the periphery as will be seen in the Problem Materials below. But as a general rule, a primary strike, boycott, or picketing is lawful if they are otherwise protected activity under Section 7. On the other hand, secondary strikes, boycotts, and picketing are generally unlawful regardless of whether they would otherwise be protected activity under Section 7.

In addition to creating this new unfair labor practice, Congress provided employers different remedial and injunctive relief against unions that violated the new provision. Section 303 of the Labor Management Relations Act (LMRA) provides a federal tort action that allows compensatory damages as a remedy for unlawful secondary boycotts. Additionally, under Section 10(l) of the NLRA (added by the Taft-Hartley Amendments), the NLRB's General Counsel is required to give priority to these types of violations and must seek a federal preliminary injunction, even before a hearing on the merits. Unlike injunctive relief under Section 10(j), which applies to most other unfair labor practices under the Act, and for which Board approval is necessary, the 10(l) injunction does not require the Board's blessing.

PROBLEM #2: SECONDARY BOYCOTTING BRADGELINA

Brad Jolie Safari Supplies (BJSS) is in the business of outfitting adventurers around the world with clothes and other necessary provisions. When its production workers go out on strike, BJSS contracts with Angelina Pitt Safari Goods (APSG) to make the goods that BJSS can no longer make itself. The striking workers picket at both BJSS and APSG, where the BJSS goods are now being manufactured. APSG files unfair labor practice charges against the union.

1.   What result?

2.   Does your answer change if APSG independently ends up obtaining most of BJSS' business as a result of the strike?

3.   Can BJSS keep the union from picketing at all of its facilities' gates by setting up a separate gate just for independent contractors who do work on the BJSS premises?

PROBLEM MATERIALS

NLRB v. Denver Building & Construction Trades Council, 341 U.S. 675 (1951)

Sailors Union of the Pacific (Moore Dry Dock Co.), 92 N.L.R.B. 547 (1950)

Douds v. Metropolitan Federation of Architects, 75 F. Supp. 672 (S.D.N.Y. 1948)

Local 761, International Union of Electrical, Radio, and Machine Workers v. NLRB, 366 U.S. 667 (1961)

NLRB v. DENVER BUILDING & CONSTRUCTION TRADES COUNCIL
341 U.S. 675 (1951)

Mr. Justice Burton delivered the opinion of the Court.

Strike
↓
Object to force
gen con to terminate
contract w/ certain sub

The principal question here is whether a labor organization committed an unfair labor practice, within the meaning of § 8(b)(4)(A) of the National Labor Relations Act by engaging in a strike, an object of which was to force the general contractor on a construction project to terminate its contract with a certain subcontractor on that project. For the reasons hereafter stated, we hold that such an unfair labor practice was committed.

In September, 1947, Doose & Lintner was the general contractor for the construction of a commercial building in Denver, Colorado. It awarded a subcontract for electrical work on the building, in an estimated amount of $2,300, to Gould & Preisner, a firm which for 20 years had employed nonunion workmen on construction work in that city. The latter's employees proved to be the only nonunion workmen on the project. Those of the general contractor and of the other subcontractors were members of unions affiliated with the respondent Denver Building and Construction Trades Council (here called the Council).

In November a representative of one of those unions told Gould that he did not see how the job could progress with Gould's nonunion men on it. Gould insisted that they would complete the electrical work unless bodily put off. The representative replied that the situation would be difficult for both Gould & Preisner and Doose & Lintner.

January 8, 1948, the Council's Board of Business Agents instructed the Council's representative "to place a picket on the job stating that the job was unfair" to it. In keeping with the Council's practice, each affiliate was notified of that decision. That notice was a signal in the nature of an order to the members of the affiliated unions to leave the job and remain away until otherwise ordered. Representatives of the Council and each of the respondent unions visited the project and reminded the contractor that Gould & Preisner employed nonunion workmen and said that union men could not work on the job with nonunion men. They further advised that if Gould & Preisner's men did work on the job, the Council and its affiliates would put a picket on it to notify their members that nonunion men were working on it and that the job was unfair. All parties stood their ground.

January 9, the Council posted a picket at the project carrying a placard stating "This Job Unfair to Denver Building and Construction Trades Council." He was paid by the Council and his picketing continued from January 9 through January 22. During that time the only persons who reported for work were the nonunion electricians of Gould & Preisner. January 22, before Gould & Preisner had completed its subcontract, the general contractor notified it to get off the job so that Doose & Lintner could continue with the project. January 23, the Council removed its picket and shortly thereafter the union employees resumed work on the project. Gould & Preisner protested this treatment but its workmen were denied entrance to the job . . . .

III. The Secondary Boycott.-We now reach the merits. They require a study of the objectives of the strike and a determination whether the strike came within the definition of an unfair labor practice stated in § 8(b)(4)(A) . . . .

While § 8(b)(4) does not expressly mention "primary" or "secondary" disputes, strikes or boycotts, that section often is referred to in the Act's legislative history as one of the Act's "secondary boycott sections." . . .

A. We must first determine whether the strike in this case had a proscribed object . . . . In the background of the instant case there was a longstanding labor dispute between the Council and Gould & Preisner due to the latter's practice of employing nonunion workmen on construction jobs in Denver. The respondent labor organizations contend that they engaged in a primary dispute with Doose & Lintner alone, and that they sought simply to force Doose & Lintner to make the project an all-union job. If there had been no contract between Doose & Lintner and Gould & Preisner there might be substance in their contention that the dispute involved no boycott. If, for example, Doose & Lintner had been doing all the electrical work on this project through its own nonunion employees, it could have replaced them with union men and thus disposed of the dispute.

However, the existence of the Gould & Preisner subcontract presented a materially different situation. The nonunion employees were employees of Gould & Preisner. The only way that respondents could attain their purpose was to force Gould & Preisner itself off the job. This, in turn, could be done only through Doose & Lintner's termination of Gould & Preisner's subcontract. The result is that the Council's strike, in order to attain its ultimate purpose, must have included among its objects that of forcing Doose & Lintner to terminate that subcontract. On that point, the Board adopted the following finding: "That an object, if not the only object, of what transpired with respect to . . . Doose & Lintner was to force or require them to cease doing business with Gould & Preisner seems scarcely open to question, in view of all of the facts. And it is clear at least as to Doose & Lintner, that that purpose was achieved."

We accept this crucial finding. It was an object of the strike to force the contractor to terminate Gould & Preisner's subcontract.

B. We hold also that a strike with such an object was an unfair labor practice within the meaning of § 8(b)(4)(A) . . . .

We agree with the Board also in its conclusion that the fact that the contractor and subcontractor were engaged on the some construction project, and that the contractor had some supervision over the subcontractor's work, did not eliminate the status of each as an independent contractor or make the employees of one the employees of the other. The business relationship between independent contractors is too well established in the law to be overridden without clear language doing so. The Board found that the relationship between Doose & Lintner and Gould & ← DoBIS* Preisner was one of "doing business" and we find no adequate reason for upsetting that conclusion.

Finally, § 8(c) safeguarding freedom of speech has no significant application to the picket's placard in this case. Section 8(c) does not apply to a mere signal by a labor organization to its members, or to the members of its affiliates, to engage in an unfair labor practice such as a strike proscribed by § 8(b)(4)(A). That the placard was merely such a signal, tantamount to a direction to strike, was found by the Board. ". . . the issues in this case turn upon acts by labor organizations which are tantamount to directions and instructions to their members to engage in strike action. The protection afforded by Section 8(c) of the Act to the expression of "any views, argument or opinion" does not pertain where, as here, the issues raised under Section 8(b)(4)(A) turn on official directions or instructions to a union's own members.'

The further conclusion that § 8(c) does not immunize action against the specific provisions of § 8(b)(4)(A) has been announced in other cases.

Not only are the findings of the Board conclusive with respect to questions of fact in this field when supported by substantial evidence on the record as a whole, but the Board's interpretation of the Act and the Board's application of it in doubtful situations are entitled to weight. In the views of the Board as applied to this case we find conformity with the dual congressional objectives of preserving the right of labor organizations to bring pressure to bear on offending employers in primary labor disputes and of shielding unoffending employers and others from pressures in controversies not their own.

For these reasons we conclude that the conduct of respondents constituted an unfair labor practice within the meaning of § 8(b)(4)(A). The judgment of the Court of Appeals accordingly is reversed and the case is remanded to it for procedure not inconsistent with this opinion.

MR. JUSTICE JACKSON would affirm the judgment of the Court of Appeals.

MR. JUSTICE DOUGLAS, with whom MR. JUSTICE REED joins, dissenting.

The employment of union and nonunion men on the same job is a basic protest in trade union history. That was the protest here. The union was not out to destroy the contractor because of his antiunion attitude. The union was not pursuing the contractor to other jobs. All the union asked was that union men not be compelled to work alongside nonunion men on the same job. As Judge Rifkind stated in an analogous case, "the union was not extending its activity to a front remote from the immediate dispute but to one intimately and indeed inextricably united to it."

The picketing would undoubtedly have been legal if there had been no subcontractor involved-if the general contractor had put nonunion men on the job. The presence of a subcontractor does not alter one whit the realities of the situation; the protest of the union is precisely the same. In each the union was trying to protect the job on which union men were employed. If that is forbidden, the Taft-Hartley Act makes the right to strike, guaranteed by § 13, dependent on fortuitous business arrangements that have no significance so far as the evils of the secondary boycott are concerned. I would give scope to both § 8(b)(4) and § 13 by reading the restrictions of § 8(b)(4) to reach the case where an industrial dispute spreads from the job to another front.

SAILORS UNION OF THE PACIFIC
(MOORE DRY DOCK CO.)
92 N.L.R.B. 547 (1950)

. . . Section 8 (b)(4)(A) is aimed at secondary boycotts and secondary strike activities. It was not intended to proscribe primary action by a union having a legitimate labor dispute with an employer. Picketing at the premises of a primary employer is traditionally recognized as primary action even though it is "necessarily designed to induce and encourage third persons to cease doing business with the picketed employer." . . .

[I]f Samsoc, the owner of the S. S. *Phopho*, had had a dock of its own in California to which the *Phopho* had been tied up while undergoing conversion by Moore Dry Dock employees, picketing by the [Union] at the dock site would unquestionably have constituted *primary* action, even though the Respondent might have expected that the picketing would be more effective in persuading Moore employees not to work on the ship than to persuade the seamen aboard the *Phopho* to quit that vessel. The difficulty in the present case arises therefore, not because of any difference in picketing objectives, but from the fact that the *Phopho* was not tied up at its own dock, but at that of Moore, while the picketing was going on in front of the Moore premises.

In the usual case, the *situs* of a labor dispute is the premises of the primary employer. Picketing of the premises is also picketing of the *situs* . . . . But in some cases the *situs* of the dispute may not be limited to a fixed location; it may be ambulatory . . . . [W]e hold in the present case that, as the *Phopho* was the place of employment of the seamen, it was the *situs* of the dispute between Samsoc and the [Union] over working conditions aboard that vessel.

When the *situs* is ambulatory, it may come to rest temporarily at the premises of another employer. The perplexing question is: Does the right to picket follow the *situs* while it is stationed at the premises of a secondary employer, when the only way to picket that *situs* is in front of the secondary employer's premises? Admittedly, no easy answer is possible. Essentially the problem is one of balancing the right of a union to picket at the site of its dispute as against the right of a secondary employer to be free from picketing in a controversy in which it is not directly involved.

When a secondary employer is harboring the *situs* of a dispute between a union and a primary employer, the right of neither the union to picket nor of the secondary employer to be free from picketing can be absolute. The enmeshing of premises and *situs* qualifies both rights. In the kind of situation that exists in this case, we believe that picketing of the premises of a secondary employer is primary if it meets the following conditions: (a) The picketing is strictly limited to times when the *situs* of dispute is located on the secondary employer's premises; (b) at the time of the picketing the primary employer is engaged in its normal business at the *situs;* (c) the picketting is limited to places reasonably close to the location of the *situs;* and (d) the picketing discloses clearly that the dispute is with the primary employer. All these conditions were met in the present case.

(a) During the entire period of the picketing the *Phopho* was tied up at a dock in the Moore shipyard.

(b) Under its contract with Samsoc, Moore agreed to permit the former to put a crew on board the *Phopho* for training purposes during the last 2 weeks before the vessel's delivery to Samsoc. At the time the picketing started on February 17, 1950, 90 percent of the conversion job had been completed, practically the entire crew had been hired, the ship's oil bunkers had been filled, and other stores were shortly to be put aboard. The various members of the crew commenced work as soon as they reported aboard the *Phopho*. Those in the deck department did painting and cleaning up; those in the steward's department, cooking and cleaning up; and those in the engine department, oiling and cleaning up. The crew were thus getting the ship ready for sea. They were on board to serve the purposes of Samsoc, the *Phopho's* owners, and not Moore. The normal business of a ship does not only begin with its departure on a scheduled voyage. The multitudinous steps of preparation, including hiring and training a crew and putting stores aboard, are as much a part of the normal business of a ship as the voyage itself. We find, therefore, that during the entire period of the picketing, the *Phopho* was engaged in its normal business.

(c) Before placing its pickets outside the entrance to the Moore shipyard, the Union asked, but was refused, permission to place its pickets at the dock where the *Phopho* was tied up. The [Union] therefore posted its pickets at the yard entrance which, as the parties stipulated, was as close to the *Phopho* as they could get under the circumstances.

(d) Finally, by its picketing and other conduct the Respondent was scrupulously careful to indicate that its dispute was solely with the primary employer, the owners of the *Phopho*. Thus the signs carried by the pickets said only that the *Phopho* was unfair to the [Union]. The *Phopho* and not Moore was declared "hot." Similarly, in asking cooperation of other unions, the [Union] clearly revealed that its dispute was with the *Phopho*. Finally, Moore's own witnesses admitted that no attempt was made to interfere with other work in progress in the Moore yard.

We believe that our dissenting colleagues' expressions of alarm are based on a misunderstanding of our decision. We are not holding, as the dissenters seem to think, that a union which has a dispute with a shipowner over working conditions of seamen aboard a ship may lawfully picket the premises of an independent shipyard to which the shipowner has delivered his vessel for overhaul and repair. We are only holding that, if a shipyard permits the owner of a vessel to use its dock for the purpose of readying the ship for its regular voyage by hiring and training a crew and putting stores aboard ship, a union representing seamen may then, within the careful limitations laid down in this decision, lawfully picket in front of the shipyard premises to advertise its dispute with the shipowner.

It is true, of course, that the *Phopho* was delivered to the Moore yard for conversion into a bulk gypsum carrier. But Moore in its contract agreed that "During the last two weeks, . . . [the *Phopho's*] Owner shall have the right to put a crew on board the vessel for training purposes, provided, however, that such crew shall not interfere in any way with the work of conversion." Samsoc (the *Phopho's* owner) availed itself of this contract privilege. When it did, Moore and Samsoc were simultaneously engaged in their separate businesses in the Moore yard.

The dissent finds it "logically" difficult to believe in this duality. We find no such difficulty. Nor did Moore, apparently, when it included the above clause in its contract. Indeed, from a practical standpoint, there was a strong reason why Samsoc should ready the ship for sea while the conversion work was still going on. A laid-up ship does not earn money. By completing training and preparation for sea while the ship was still undergoing conversion, the lay-up time was reduced, with a consequent money saving to owner Samsoc.

Under the circumstances of this case, we therefore find that the picketing practice followed by the Respondent was primary and not secondary and therefore did not violate Section 8(b)(4)(A) of the Act . . . .

DOUDS v. METROPOLITAN FEDERATION OF ARCHITECTS
75 F. Supp. 672 (S.D.N.Y. 1948)

RIFKIND, DISTRICT JUDGE.

This is a petition brought by Charles T. Douds, Regional Director of the Second Region of the National Labor Relations Board to enjoin the respondent, Metropolitan Federation of Architects, Engineers, Chemists and Technicians, Local 231, United Office & Professional Workers of America, C.I.O., from engaging in certain activities alleged to be in violation of Section 8(b)(4)(A) of the National Labor Relations Act. Project Engineering Company, a partnership, is the "charging party," and has asked for, and received permission to intervene . . . .

Ebasco Services, Inc. is a corporation engaged, since 1905, in the business of supplying engineering services, such as planning and designing and drafting plans, for industrial and public utility installations. During the year ending September 1, 1947, the respondent union was the bargaining agent for Ebasco's employees. On that day the agreement between Ebasco and the union expired. A new agreement was not reached and a strike against Ebasco was commenced on September 5, 1947.

James P. O'Donnell and Guy M. Barbolini in 1946 organized a partnership, styled Project Engineering Company, herein called "Project". Its business is identical with Ebasco's — planning and designing and drafting plans for industrial installations although they seem to have specialized in chemical and petroleum plants. The partnership had an inception completely independent of Ebasco or its influence. There is no common ownership of any kind. It was through Project's solicitations that Ebasco first employed the partnership. An open contract dated December 19, 1946 marked the beginning of their business relations.

Prior to August, 1946, Ebasco never subcontracted any of its work. Subsequent to that date it subcontracted some of its work. At the time the strike was called, part of Ebasco's work had been let out to Project. An appreciable percentage of Project's business for some months antedating the strike consisted of work secured from Ebasco. After the strike had begun, an even greater percentage — about 75% — of its work was Ebasco's. Some work, which had been begun by Ebasco's workers, was transferred, after the commencement of the strike, in an unfinished condition to Project for completion.

In a brochure printed and distributed by Ebasco before the strike to its prospective customers, Ebasco represented itself as having available the services of a number of draftsmen and designers, which included the personnel of Project and of other subcontractors. The contract price of all the work done by Project for Ebasco was computed by adding to the compensation of the men engaged on Ebasco work a factor for overhead and profits. In their business relationship it was the practice of Project to furnish Ebasco with time sheets, showing the number of hours each of the former's employees spent on Ebasco work. Ebasco's statements to its customers contained the time spent by technicians, with no distinction made between the work done by Ebasco employees and subcontractors' employees.

Ebasco supervisory personnel made regular visits to Project to oversee the work on the subcontracts. After the strike was called and the work subcontracted increased, these visits increased in frequency and numbers of personnel involved. Ebasco supervisory personnel, whose subordinates were on strike, continued to supervise their "jobs", at Project's plant, where such work had been transferred. The working hours of Project employees were increased after the commencement of the Ebasco strike.

Delegations representing the respondent union approached the charging party on more than one occasion and asked, among other things, that it refuse to accept work which had come "off the boards" of Ebasco.

On October 28, 1947, respondent union ordered Project picketed and such picketing has continued since that day. The pickets carry signs which denominate Project a scab shop for Ebasco. A number of resignations at Project are attributable to the picketing.

The number of pickets has usually been reasonable and the picketing was ordinarily unaccompanied by violence. However, on a number of occasions, to wit, October 28, November 6 and November 25, there was picketing by 35 men or more. Such occasions were marked by pushing, kicking and blocking the entrance way to the building. Epithets such as "scab," "louse", "rat" and others were hurled at Project employees by the pickets. On those occasions the assistance of the police was requested by Project employees and order was promptly restored. Project continues to do engineering work for Ebasco — the kind of work which Ebasco employees themselves would be doing if they were not striking . . . .

One of the prohibitions of Section 8(b)(4)(A) of the Act is: "It shall be an unfair labor practice for a labor organization . . . to . . . encourage the employees of any employer to engage in, a strike . . . where an object thereof is . . . requiring . . . any . . . person . . . to cease doing business with any other person."

Is Project "doing business" with Ebasco within the meaning of the Act? The term is not defined in the Act itself. Section 2 contains thirteen definitions, but none of doing business. The term itself has, of course, received a vast amount of judicial construction but always in context so different that it is pointless to explore that field for help in construing the term in the present context. Nor is it possible to attach legal consequences to all the relationships which the dictionary meaning of the term embraces. So to do would destroy the Act by driving it to absurdity. To give such broad scope to the term would, for instance, reach out to and include the business relation between an employee of the primary employer (Ebasco, in this case) and the primary employer, or the business relationship between a primary employer and a professional supplier of strike-breakers. Certainly it is an object of very many strikes and picket lines to induce a reduction in the struck employer's business by an appeal to customers — "any person" — to cease dealing with the employer. This is one of the most conspicuous weapons employed in many labor disputes. The effect of a strike would be vastly attenuated if its appeals were limited to the employer's conscience. I shall proceed on the assumption, warranted by the history of the Act, that it was not the intent of Congress to ban such activity, although the words of the statute, given their broadest meaning, may seem to reach it. Moreover, such broad construction would probably run afoul of Section 13 of the Act, which reads: "Sec. 13. Nothing in this Act, except as specifically provided for herein, shall be construed so as either to interfere with or impede or diminish in any way the right to strike, or to affect the limitations or qualifications on that right."

. . .

Examination of these expositions of Congressional purpose indicates that the provision was understood to outlaw what was theretofore known as a secondary boycott. It is to the history of the secondary boycott, therefore, that attention should be directed and it is in the light of that history that the term "doing business" should be evaluated.

When the term is read with the aid of the glossary provided by the law of secondary boycott it becomes quite clear that Project cannot claim to be a victim of that weapon in labor's arsenal. To suggest that Project had no interest in the dispute between Ebasco and its employees is to look at the form and remain blind to substance. In every meaningful sense it had made itself party to the contest. Manifestly it was not an innocent bystander, nor a neutral. It was firmly allied to Ebasco and it was its conduct as ally of Ebasco which directly provoked the union's action.

Significant is the unique character of the contract between Ebasco and Project. Ebasco did not retain the professional services of Project. Ebasco "bought" from Project, in the words of the basic contract, "services of your designers and draftsmen . . . to work under the direction and supervision of the Purchaser." The purchase price consisted of the actual wages paid by Project plus a factor for overhead and profit. In practice the terms and implications of the agreement were fully spelled out. Ebasco supplied both direction and supervision of a detailed and pervasive character. It established the maximum wage rates for which it would be charged. Invoices were in terms of man-hours, employee by employee. Daily tally was taken of the number of men at work on Ebasco assignments and communicated to Ebasco. The final product, the plans and drawings, were placed upon forms supplied by Ebasco, bearing its name, and were thus delivered to Ebasco's clients as Ebasco's work. In advertising its services to the industries which it served Ebasco held itself out as "having available" a number of designers and draftsmen which included those employed by Project.

True enough, the contract prescribes that "all employees furnished by the seller shall at all times be and remain employees of the seller". I do not, however, draw therefrom the inference advocated by the petitioner and the charging party. The very need for such a provision emphasizes the realization of the parties that they were doing business on terms which cast a shadow of doubt upon the identity of the employer. Without question, Ebasco and Project were free to contract who, as between themselves, should be subject to the burden and possessed of the privileges that attach to the employer of those on Project's payroll. But the law is not foreclosed by such agreements to examine the reality relevant to the purposes of a particular statute.

I am unable to hold that corporate ownership or insulation of legal interests between two business can be conclusive as to neutrality or disinterestedness in a labor dispute.

The evidence is abundant that Project's employees did work, which, but for the strike of Ebasco's employees, would have been done by Ebasco. The economic effect upon Ebasco's employees was precisely that which would flow from Ebasco's hiring strikebreakers to work on its own premises. The conduct of the union in inducing Project's employees to strike is not different in kind from its conduct in inducing Ebasco's employees to strike. If the latter is not amenable to judicial restraint, neither is the former. In encouraging a strike at Project the union was not extending its activity to a front remote from the immediate dispute but to one intimately and indeed inextricably united to it . . . .

The case at bar is not an instance of a secondary boycott . . . .

LOCAL 761, INTERNATIONAL UNION OF ELECTRICAL, RADIO AND MACHINE WORKERS v. NLRB
366 U.S. 667 (1961)

MR. JUSTICE FRANKFURTER delivered the opinion of the Court.

Local 761 of the International Union of Electrical, Radio and Machine Workers, AFL-CIO, was charged with a violation of § 8(b)(4)(A) of the National Labor Relations Act, upon the following facts.

General Electric Corporation operates a plant outside of Louisville, Kentucky, where it manufactures washers, dryers, and other electrical household appliances. The square-shaped, thousand-acre, unfenced plant is known as Appliance Park. A large drainage ditch makes ingress and egress impossible except over five roadways across culverts, designated as gates.

Since 1954, General Electric sought to confine the employees of independent contractors, described hereafter, who work on the premises of the Park, to the use of Gate 3-A and confine its use to them. The undisputed reason for doing so was to insulate General Electric employees from the frequent labor disputes in which the contractors were involved. Gate 3-A is 550 feet away from the nearest entrance available for General Electric employees, suppliers, and deliverymen. Although anyone can pass the gate without challenge, the roadway leads to a guardhouse where identification must be presented. Vehicle stickers of various shapes and colors enable a guard to check on sight whether a vehicle is authorized to use Gate 3-A. Since January 1958, a prominent sign has been posted at the gate which states:

"Gate 3-A For Employees Of Contractors Only-G.E. Employees Use Other Gates." On rare occasions, it appears, a General Electric employee was allowed to pass the guardhouse, but such occurrence was in violation of company instructions. There was no proof of any unauthorized attempts to pass the gate during the strike in question.

The independent contractors are utilized for a great variety of tasks on the Appliance Park premises. Some do construction work on new buildings; some install and repair ventilating and heating equipment; some engage in retooling and rearranging operations necessary to the manufacture of new models; others do "general maintenance work." These services are contracted to outside employers either because the company's employees lack the necessary skill or manpower, or because the work can be done more economically by independent contractors. The latter reason determined the contracting of maintenance work for which the Central Maintenance department of the company bid competitively with the contractors. While some of the work done by these contractors had on occasion been previously performed by Central Maintenance, the findings do not disclose the number of employees of independent contractors who were performing these routine maintenance services, as compared with those who were doing specialized work of a capital-improvement nature.

The Union, petitioner here, is the certified bargaining representative for the production and maintenance workers who constitute approximately 7,600 of the 10, 500 employees of General Electric at Appliance Park. On July 27, 1958, the Union called a strike because of 24 unsettled grievances with the company. Picketing occurred at all the gates, including Gate 3-A, and continued until August 9 when an injunction was issued by a Federal District Court. The signs carried by the pickets at all gates read: "Local 761 On Strike G.E. Unfair." Because of the picketing, almost all of the employees of independent contractors refused to enter the company premises.

Neither the legality of the strike or of the picketing at any of the gates except 3-A nor the peaceful nature of the picketing is in dispute. The sole claim is that the picketing before the gate exclusively used by employees of independent contractors was conduct proscribed by § 8(b)(4)(A) . . . .

I.

Section 8(b)(4)(A) of the National Labor Relations Act provides that it shall be an unfair labor practice for a labor organization

'. . . to engage in, or to induce or encourage the employees of any employer to engage in, a strike or a concerted refusal in the course of their employment to use, manufacture, process, transport, or otherwise handle or work on any goods, articles, materials, or commodities or to perform any services, where an object thereof is: (A) forcing or requiring . . . any employer or other person . . . to cease doing business with any other person . . . .'

This provision could not be literally construed; otherwise it would ban most strikes historically considered to be lawful, so-called primary activity. "While

§ 8(b)(4) does not expressly mention "primary" or "secondary" disputes, strikes or boycotts, that section often is referred to in the Act's legislative history as one of the Act's "secondary boycott sections. " 'Congress did not seek by § 8(b)(4), to interfere with the ordinary strike . . . ." The impact of the section was directed toward what is known as the secondary boycott whose "sanctions bear, not upon the employer who alone is a party to the dispute, but upon some third party who has no concern in it. Thus the section "left a striking labor organization free to use persuasion, including picketing, not only on the primary employer and his employees but on numerous others. Among these were secondary employers who were customers or suppliers of the primary employer and persons dealing with them . . . and even employees of secondary employers so long as the labor organization did not . . . "induce or encourage the employees of any employer to engage, in a strike or a concerted refusal in the course of their employment" . . . .'

But not all so-called secondary boycotts were outlawed in § 8(b)(4)(A). "The section does not speak generally of secondary boycotts. It describes and condemns specific union conduct directed to specific objectives. Employees must be induced; they must be induced to engage in a strike or concerted refusal; an object must be to force or require their employer or another person to cease doing business with a third person. Thus, much that might argumentatively be found to fall within the broad and somewhat vague concept of secondary boycott is not in terms prohibited."

Important as is the distinction between legitimate "primary activity" and banned "secondary activity," it does not present a glaringly bright line. The objectives of any picketing include a desire to influence others from withholding from the employer their services or trade. "(I)ntended or not, sought for or not, aimed for or not, employees of neutral employers do take action sympathetic with strikers and do put pressure on their own employers." "It is clear that, when a union pickets an employer with whom it has a dispute, it hopes, even if it does not intend, that all persons will honor the picket line, and that hope encompasses the employees of neutral employers who may in the course of their employment (deliverymen and the like) have to enter the premises." "Almost all picketing, even at the situs of the primary employer and surely at that of the secondary, hopes to achieve the forbidden objective, whatever other motives there may be and however small the chances of success." But picketing which induces secondary employees to respect a picket line is not the equivalent of picketing which has an object of inducing those employees to engage in concerted conduct against their employer in order to force him to refuse to deal with the struck employer.

However difficult the drawing of lines more nice than obvious, the statute compels the task. Accordingly, the Board and the courts have attempted to devise reasonable criteria drawing heavily upon the means to which a union resorts in promoting its cause. Although "(n)o rigid rule which would make . . . (a) few factors conclusive is contained in or deducible from the statute," "(I)n the absence of admissions by the union of an illegal intent, the nature of acts performed shows the intent." . . .

III.

. . . With due regard to the relation between the Board's function and the scope of judicial review of its rulings, the question is whether the Board may apply the Dry Dock criteria so as to make unlawful picketing at a gate utilized exclusively by employees of independent contractors who work on the struck employer's premises. The effect of such a holding would not bar the union from picketing at all gates used by the employees, suppliers, and customers of the struck employer. Of course an employer may not, by removing all his employees from the situs of the strike, bar the union from publicizing its cause. The basis of the Board's decision in this case would not remotely have that effect, nor any such tendency for the future.

The Union claims that, if the Board's ruling is upheld, employers will be free to erect separate gates for deliveries, customers, and replacement workers which will be immunized from picketing. This fear is baseless. The key to the problem is found in the type of work that is being performed by those who use the separate gate. It is significant that the Board has since applied its rationale, first stated in the present case, only to situations where the independent workers were performing tasks unconnected to the normal operations of the struck employer-usually construction work on his buildings. In such situations, the indicated limitations on picketing activity respect the balance of competing interests that Congress has required the Board to enforce. On the other hand, if a separate gate were devised for regular plant deliveries, the barring of picketing at that location would make a clear invasion on traditional primary activity of appealing to neutral employees whose tasks aid the employer's everyday operations. The 1959 Amendments to the National Labor Relations Act, which removed the word "concerted" from the boycott provisions, included a proviso that "nothing contained in this clause (B) shall be construed to make unlawful, where not otherwise unlawful, any primary strike or primary picketing." The proviso was directed against the fear that the removal of "concerted" from the statute might be interpreted so that "the picketing at the factory violates section 8(b)(4)(A) because the pickets induce the truck drivers employed by the trucker not to perform their usual services where an object is to compel the trucking firm not to do business with the . . . manufacturer during the strike."

In a case similar to the one now before us, the Court of Appeals for the Second Circuit sustained the Board in its application of § 8(b)(4)(A) to a separate gate situation. "There must be a separate gate marked and set apart from other gates; the work done by the men who use the gate must be unrelated to the normal operations of the employer and the work must be of a kind that would not, if done when the plant were engaged in its regular operations, necessitate curtailing those operations." These seem to us controlling considerations.

IV.

The foregoing course of reasoning would require that the judgment below sustaining the Board's order be affirmed but for one consideration, even though this consideration may turn out not to affect the result. The legal path by which the Board and the Court of Appeals reached their decisions did not take into account that if Gate 3-A was in fact used by employees of independent contractors who performed conventional maintenance work necessary to the normal operations of General Electric, the use of the gate would have been a mingled one outside the bar of § 8(b)(4)(A). In short, such mixed use of this portion of the struck employer's premises would not bar picketing rights of the striking employees. While the record shows some such mingled use, it sheds no light on its extent. It may well turn out to be that the instances of these maintenance tasks were so insubstantial as to be treated by the Board as de minimis. We cannot here guess at the quantitative aspect of this problem. It calls for Board determination. For determination of the questions thus raised, the case must be remanded by the Court of Appeals to the Board.

Reversed.

[THE CHIEF JUSTICE and MR. JUSTICE BLACK concurred in the result, and MR. JUSTICE DOUGLAS dissented.]

POST PROBLEM DISCUSSION

1.   As can be seen from the four cases above, the answer to the Problem questions depend on which case applies. Does the Problem present a common situs, ambulatory situs, or neither type of boycotting scenario? Does the ally doctrine of *Douds* apply? How about the reserved gate rationale of *Local 761*?

2.   In *Denver Building*, the Supreme Court agreed with the subcontractor that forcing the general contractor to cease doing business with it because of its non-union status was an illegal secondary boycott. This is because the Court found that economic pressure was being applied to a neutral (the general contractor) who had no working dispute with the union. Is the general contractor a true neutral in this labor dispute? Does the treatment of the general contractor as a neutral employer make sense giving the economic realities of the situation (see Justice Douglas' dissent in this regard). Isn't it more accurate to say that the general contractor and subcontractors are allies under the *Douds* analysis? Interestingly, a legislative override of the *Denver Building* case was vetoed in 1975 by President Ford.

3.   Does Section 8(b)(4)(B) prohibit a union from engaging in picketing of one employer in order to pressure another employer to recognize and bargain with the union as the certified representative of that employer's employees? In *Visiting Nurse Health System, Inc.*, 336 N.L.R.B. 421 (2001), a union threatened to picket and leaflet the United Way of Metropolitan Atlanta, a neutral employer, to pressure another employer (VNHS) to recognize and bargain with the union. The Board concluded that such a situation did not amount to a secondary boycott because VNHS had a duty to bargain with the union, which the Board had certified as the collective-bargaining representative of a unit of VNHS's employees.

4.   Ambulatory situs cases under *Moore Dry Dock* ask which standards should apply when the labor dispute moves from one location or situs to another. In *Moore Dry Dock*, the Board found that a number of factors must be met in order to make picketing the premises of a secondary employer primary in nature. These *Moore Dry Dock* standards have also been applied to common-situs situations where the

primary and secondary employers are working at the same site, such as a large construction project. There is a right to picket the primary employer in these common-situs situations as long as the action does not violate the *Moore Dry Dock* standards. Consider how the *Moore Dry Dock* standards would have applied in the *Denver Building* case if the union had picketed the primary employer (the subcontractor), rather than the secondary employer (the general contractor).

5.   The ally doctrine discussed in *Douds* is also related to the alter ego doctrine. The alter ego doctrine determines whether a secondary employer that shares common ownership, common management, interrelation of operations and common or central control of labor relations with the primary employer should be treated as the primary employer. Common situations that arise under this doctrine include picketing the office of a parent company while engaging in a secondary strike of the subsidiary, and picketing different branches or divisions of a larger company. The answer in both of these situations usually is based on how interrelated the various companies are.

6.   One principle that emerges from the *Douds* case is that a third-party employer that does work which, but for the strike, would have been done by employees of the struck employer may be lawfully picketed without running afoul of the secondary boycott provisions. Picketing at the premises of secondary employer in this case is permitted because the secondary employer performing the struck work has become, in effect, an ally of the struck, primary employer. However, an important distinction must be made here: an employer does not make itself a party to the dispute with the primary employer by taking over the business that the strike has prevented the primary employer from doing. The ally doctrine is triggered only when the primary employer hires a secondary employer to do work that would otherwise have been done by strikers. Competition is fine, collusion is not.

7.   A hot cargo agreement is a secondary boycott provision in a collective-bargaining agreement that requires employers to disaffiliate with certain non-union companies or that permits employees not to handle products from a struck or non-union company. Hot cargo agreements constitute an unlawful secondary boycott under Section 8(e) of the NLRA. In essence, Section 8(e) prevents unions from accomplishing through contract that which Section 8(b)(4) prohibits them from accomplishing through other secondary means (e.g., boycotts, picketing, or strikes).

8.   The last case in this series, *Local 761*, concerns the use of reserved gates. When a neutral employer is on the property of a primary employer, the primary employer sometime sets up a reserved gate where only the employees and suppliers of the primary employer can enter. The union must picket at this gate as long as the reserved nature of the gate is maintained or else face charges of secondary boycott. Once the reserved gate is established, it must be monitored to make sure there are no violations of the rule.

If the primary employer uses gates reserved for neutrals, depending on the extent of that use, the reserve gate system may be disregarded. If a reserve gate is tainted in this matter, the employer may rehabilitate it by expanding its efforts to enforce limitation on the use of the gates and notifying the union that the gates have been reestablished and will be enforced in the future.

Also, if a contractor doing work for a primary employer helps the struck primary continue operations (like an ally), the union may still picket a gate reserved for that contractor. Alternatively, if a contractor's work is not equivalent to performing struck work, such as constructing a new building on the premises of the primary employer, the union may not picket a gate for the contractor, as it is truly a secondary employer.

9.   Overall, there are three situs situations in secondary boycott cases:

a.   Primary Employees on Ambulatory Secondary Property — analyzed under *Moore Dry Dock*

b.   Secondary Employees on Primary Property — analyzed under *Local 761*

c.   Primary and Secondary Share Same Property (Common Situs) — analyzed under *Moore Dry Dock*

SECTION 4   CONSUMER APPEALS AND CORPORATE CAMPAIGNS

The 1959 Landrum-Griffin Amendments added new secondary boycott provisions that concern so-called consumer appeals or corporate campaigns. The relevant statutory language is found at Section 8(b)(4)(B). The provision is concerned with preventing unions from using a consumer boycott to threaten a secondary employer to cease doing business with a primary employer. See *NLRB v. Servette*, 377 U.S. 46 (1964). If this is not the objective of a consumer boycott, then Section 8(b)(4) does not apply.

These consumer appeals generally occur in two different circumstances: (1) picketing or handbilling (i.e., leafleting) at a secondary employer's site in order to persuade members of the public not to buy struck goods; or (2) picketing or handbilling at a secondary site in order to persuade members of the public not to do business with secondary employers that are somehow connected to a primary employer. In both of these types of cases, First Amendment free speech concerns are front and center. The question is what limits the NLRA can put on this union pressure without running afoul of First Amendment free speech principles.

As with recognition picketing under Section 8(b)(7), Section 8(b)(4)(B) also has an exception for non-picketing activities that merely publicize "that a product or products are produced by an employer with whom the labor organization has a primary dispute and are distributed by another employer." There has been some controversy about what it means to "produce goods" in order to fall within this statutory language. The Supreme Court, in *NLRB v. Servette*, 377 U.S. 46 (1964), made clear that for purpose of this provision an employer can be a producer without actually producing the goods as long as the employer perform services which are essential to the production and distribution of consumer goods.

The meaning of "distributed" under the publicity proviso has also been in contention. In *Edward J. De Bartolo Corp. v. NLRB*, 463 U.S. 147 (1983) (*DeBartolo I*) (note that this is a different *DeBartolo* decision than the one from 1988 discussed below, although both cases arose from the same set of facts), a mall owner hired a general contractor, H.J. High Construction, to construct a department store in the mall. The union handbilled the mall's entrances, asking customers not to shop at any stores in the mall until the mall owner agreed to use a contractor that paid union wages. The Court concluded that the publicity provision of 8(b)(4) did not apply because the mall and its stores (except for the department store) were one step removed from the primary employer, H.J. High. According to the Court, "[t]o treat DeBartolo and the shopping center cotenants as vulnerable to handbilling because they all 'symbiotically' derived benefit from High's construction work 'would have almost stripped the distribution requirement of its limiting effect.'" In other words, the mall stores in no way "distributed" H.J. High's "products," and so the handbilling calling for a boycott of the stores did not fall within the protection of Section 8(b)(4)'s publicity proviso.

PROBLEM #3: "OCEAN GASOLINE MADE BY SCABS"[3]

The Union, while on strike against the Ocean Refining Division of the Wod Chemical Company in Ocean City, Michigan, picketed six gas stations in the surrounding area. The stations, as the Board stated, derived "their revenues largely from the sale of this gasoline, marketed under the trade name of 'Ocean.' The picket signs asked consumers to Boycott Ocean gasoline."

The percentage of Ocean gas revenues to the stations' total revenues was approximately as follows: Of the $280,000 gross annual revenue of one station, 81% to 86% came from the sale of Ocean gas; about 85% of the gross sales of $140,000 at a second; at a third station, in operation only about six months, 97.5% of its $40,000 gross revenues was due to Ocean gas. A fourth station had gross revenues of $68,000, of which 91% came from "Ocean gas and oil and other Wod products such as radiator sealer, brake fluid, and windshield solvent." At a fifth station, 98% of its gross revenues of $45,000 was attributable to Ocean gas. At the sixth station, a tire dealership, 60% to 65% of its $1,200,000 in gross revenues came from fuel sales.

The picketing of the six retail gas stations was peaceful and did not cause any employee to stop working, did not interfere with deliveries or pickups, and did not obstruct customer from coming and going. The pickets stationed themselves on sidewalk locations away from entrances or exit driveways and they did not appear until the station opened and departed before it closed. Pickets limited their appeal to the struck product "Ocean gasoline." The legends on the picket signs generally stated: "Don't Buy Ocean Gas," "Boycott Ocean Gas," and "Ocean Gasoline Made by Scabs."

Has the union violated the consumer appeal provisions of Section 8(b)(4) of the Act?

[3] Based on *Local 14055, United Steelworkers v. NLRB (Dow Chemical Co.)*, 524 F.2d 853 (D.C. Cir. 1975), vacated and remanded, 429 U.S. 807 (1976).

PROBLEM MATERIALS

NLRB v. Fruit & Vegetable Packers & Warehouseman, Local 760 (Tree Fruits), 377 U.S. 58 (1964)

NLRB v. Retail Store Employees Union Local No. 1001 (Safeco Title Insurance Co.), 447 U.S. 607 (1980)

Edward J. DeBartolo Corp. v. Florida Gulf Coast Building & Construction Trades Council, 485 U.S. 568 (1988)

NLRB v. FRUIT & VEGETABLE PACKERS & WAREHOUSEMAN, LOCAL 760 (TREE FRUITS)
377 U.S. 58 (1964)

MR. JUSTICE BRENNAN delivered the opinion of the Court.

Under § 8(b)(4)(ii)(B) of the National Labor Relations Act, it is an unfair labor practice for a union "to threaten, coerce, or restrain any person," with the object of "forcing or requiring any person to cease using, selling, handling, transporting, or otherwise dealing in the products of any other producer . . . or to cease doing business with any other person . . . ." A proviso excepts, however, "publicity, other than picketing, for the purpose of truthfully advising the public . . . that a product or products are produced by an employer with whom the labor organization has a primary dispute and are distributed by another employer, as long as such publicity does not have an effect of inducing any individual employed by any person other than the primary employer in the course of his employment to refuse to pick up, deliver, or transport any goods, or not to perform any services, at the establishment of the employer engaged in such distribution." The question in this case is whether the respondent unions violated this section when they limited their secondary picketing of retail stores to an appeal to the customers of the stores not to buy the products of certain firms against which one of the respondents was on strike.

Respondent Local 760 called a strike against fruit packers and warehousemen doing business in Yakima, Washington. The struck firms sold Washington State apples to the Safeway chain of retail stores in and about Seattle, Washington. Local 760, aided by respondent Joint Council, instituted a consumer boycott against the apples in support of the strike. They placed pickets who walked back and forth before the customers' entrances of 46 Safeway stores in Seattle. The pickets-two at each of 45 stores and three at the 46th store-wore placards and distributed handbills which appealed to Safeway customers, and to the public generally, to refrain from buying Washington State apples, which were only one of numerous food products sold in the stores . . . .

The Board's reading of the statute-that the legislative history and the phrase "other than picketing" in the proviso reveal a congressional purpose to outlaw all picketing directed at customers at a secondary site-necessarily rested on the finding that Congress determined that such picketing always threatens, coerces or restrains the secondary employer. We therefore have a special responsibility to examine the legislative history for confirmation that Congress made that determination. Throughout the history of federal regulation of labor relations, Congress has consistently refused to prohibit peaceful picketing except where it is used as a means to achieve specific ends which experience has shown are undesirable. "In the sensitive area of peaceful picketing Congress has dealt explicitly with isolated evils which experience has established flow from such picketing." We have recognized this congressional practice and have not ascribed to Congress a purpose to outlaw peaceful picketing unless "there is the clearest indication in the legislative history," ibid., that Congress intended to do so as regards the particular ends of the picketing under review. Both the congressional policy and our adherence to this principle of interpretation reflect concern that a broad ban against peaceful picketing might collide with the guarantees of the First Amendment.

We have examined the legislative history of the amendments to § 8(b)(4), and conclude that it does not reflect with the requisite clarity a congressional plan to proscribe all peaceful consumer picketing at secondary sites, and, particularly, any concern with peaceful picketing when it is limited, as here, to persuading Safeway customers not to buy Washington State apples when they traded in the Safeway stores. All that the legislative history shows in the way of an "isolated evil" believed to require proscription of peaceful consumer picketing at secondary sites was its use to persuade the customers of the secondary employer to cease trading with him in order to force him to cease dealing with, or to put pressure upon, the primary employer. This narrow focus reflects the difference between such conduct and peaceful picketing at the secondary site directed only at the struck product. In the latter case, the union's appeal to the public is confined to its dispute with the primary employer, since the public is not asked to withhold its patronage from the secondary employer, but only to boycott the primary employer's goods. On the other hand, a union appeal to the public at the secondary site not to trade at all with the secondary employer goes beyond the goods of the primary employer, and seeks the public's assistance in forcing the secondary employer to cooperate with the union in its primary dispute. This is not to say that this distinction was expressly alluded to in the debates. It is to say, however, that the consumer picketing carried on in this case is not attended by the abuses at which the statute was directed.

The story of the 1959 amendments . . . begins with the original § 8(b)(4) of the National Labor Relations Act. Its prohibition, in pertinent part, was confined to the inducing or encouraging of "the employees of any employer to engage in, a strike or a concerted refusal . . . to . . . handle . . . any goods . . ." of a primary employer. This proved to be inept language. Three major loopholes were revealed. Since only inducement of "employees" was proscribed, direct inducement of a supervisor or the secondary employer by threats of labor trouble was not prohibited. Since only a "strike or a concerted refusal" was prohibited, pressure upon a single employee was not forbidden. Finally, railroads, airlines and municipalities were not "employers" under the Act and therefore inducement or encouragement of their employees was not unlawful . . . .

· Peaceful consumer picketing to shut off all trade with the secondary employer unless he aids the union in its dispute with the primary employer, is poles apart from such picketing which only persuades his customers not to buy the struck product. The proviso indicates no more than that the Senate conferees' constitutional doubts led Congress to authorize publicity other than picketing which persuades the customers of a secondary employer to stop all trading with him, but not such publicity which has the effect of cutting off his deliveries or inducing his employees to cease work. On the other hand, picketing which persuades the customers of a secondary employer to stop all trading with him was also to be barred.

In sum, the legislative history does not support the Board's finding that Congress meant to prohibit all consumer picketing at a secondary site, having determined that such picketing necessarily threatened, coerced or restrained the secondary employer. Rather, the history shows that Congress was following its usual practice of legislating against peaceful picketing only to curb "isolated evils."

This distinction is opposed as "unrealistic" because, it is urged, all picketing automatically provokes the public to stay away from the picketed establishment. The public will, it is said, neither read the signs and handbills, nor note the explicit injunction that "This is not a strike against any store or market." Be that as it may, our holding today simply takes note of the fact that Congress has never adopted a broad condemnation of peaceful picketing, such as that urged upon us by petitioners, and an intention to do so is not revealed with that "clearest indication in the legislative history," which we require.

We come then to the question whether the picketing in this case, confined as it was to persuading customers to cease buying the product of the primary employer, falls within the area of secondary consumer picketing which Congress did clearly indicate its intention to prohibit under § 8(b)(4)(ii). We hold that it did not fall within that area, and therefore did not "threaten, coerce, or restrain" Safeway. While any diminution in Safeway's purchases of apples due to a drop in consumer demand might be said to be a result which causes respondents' picketing to fall literally within the statutory prohibition, "it is a familiar rule that a thing may be within the letter of the statute and yet not within the statute, because not within its spirit nor within the intention of its makers." When consumer picketing is employed only to persuade customers not to buy the struck product, the union's appeal is closely confined to the primary dispute. The site of the appeal is expanded to include the premises of the secondary employer, but if the appeal succeeds, the secondary employer's purchases from the struck firms are decreased only because the public has diminished its purchases of the struck product. On the other hand, when consumer picketing is employed to persuade customers not to trade at all with the secondary employer, the latter stops buying the struck product, not because of a falling demand, but in response to pressure designed to inflict injury on his business generally. In such case, the union does more than merely follow the struck product; it creates a separate dispute with the secondary employer.

We disagree therefore with the Court of Appeals that the test of "to threaten, coerce, or restrain" for the purposes of this case is whether Safeway suffered or was likely to suffer economic loss. A violation of § 8(b)(4)(ii)(B) would not be established, merely because respondents' picketing was effective to reduce Safeway's sales of Washington State apples, even if this led or might lead Safeway to drop the item as a poor seller.

NLRB v. RETAIL STORE EMPLOYEES UNION LOCAL NO. 1001 (SAFECO TITLE INSURANCE CO.)
447 U.S. 607 (1980)

MR. JUSTICE POWELL delivered the opinion of the Court.

The question is whether § 8(b)(4)(ii)(B) of the National Labor Relations Act forbids secondary picketing against a struck product when such picketing predictably encourages consumers to boycott a neutral party's business.

I

Safeco Title Insurance Co. underwrites real estate title insurance in the State of Washington. It maintains close business relationships with five local title companies. The companies search land titles, perform escrow services, and sell title insurance. Over 90% of their gross incomes derives from the sale of Safeco insurance. Safeco has substantial stockholdings in each title company, and at least one Safeco officer serves on each company's board of directors. Safeco, however, has no control over the companies' daily operations. It does not direct their personnel policies, and it never exchanges employees with them.

Local 1001 of the Retail Store Employees Union became the certified bargaining representative for certain Safeco employees in 1974. When contract negotiations between Safeco and the Union reached an impasse, the employees went on strike. The Union did not confine picketing to Safeco's office in Seattle. The Union also picketed each of the five local title companies. The pickets carried signs declaring that Safeco had no contract with the Union, and they distributed handbills asking consumers to support the strike by canceling their Safeco policies.

Safeco and one of the title companies filed complaints with the National Labor Relations Board. They charged that the Union had engaged in an unfair labor practice by picketing in order to promote a secondary boycott against the title companies. The Board agreed. It found the title companies to be neutral in the dispute between Safeco and the Union. The Board then concluded that the Union's picketing violated § 8(b)(4)(ii)(B) of the National Labor Relations Act. The Union had directed its appeal against Safeco insurance policies. But since the sale of those policies accounted for substantially all of the title companies' business, the Board found that the Union's action was "reasonably calculated to induce customers not to patronize the neutral parties at all." The Board therefore rejected the Union's reliance upon *NLRB v. Fruit Packers*, 377 U.S. 58 (1964) (*Tree Fruits*), which held that § 8(b)(4)(ii)(B) allows secondary picketing against a struck product. It ordered the Union to cease picketing and to take limited corrective action . . . .

II

Section 8(b)(4)(ii)(B) of the National Labor Relations Act makes it "an unfair labor practice for a labor organization . . . to threaten, coerce, or restrain" a person not party to a labor dispute "where . . . an object thereof is . . . forcing or requiring [him] to cease using, selling, handling, transporting, or otherwise dealing in the products of any other producer . . . or to cease doing business with any other person . . . ."

In *Tree Fruits*, the Court held that § 8(b)(4)(ii)(B) does not prohibit all peaceful picketing at secondary sites. There, a union striking certain Washington fruit packers picketed large supermarkets in order to persuade consumers not to buy Washington apples. Concerned that a broad ban against such picketing might run afoul of the First Amendment, the Court found the statute directed to an " 'isolated evil.' " The evil was use of secondary picketing "to persuade the customers of the secondary employer to cease trading with him in order to force him to cease dealing with, or to put pressure upon, the primary employer." Congress intended to protect secondary parties from pressures that might embroil them in the labor disputes of others, but not to shield them from business losses caused by a campaign that successfully persuades consumers "to boycott the primary employer's goods." Thus, the Court drew a distinction between picketing "to shut off all trade with the secondary employer unless he aids the union in its dispute with the primary employer" and picketing that "only persuades his customers not to buy the struck product." The picketing in that case, which "merely follow[ed] the struck product," did not " 'threaten, coerce, or restrain' " the secondary party within the meaning of § 8(b)(4)(ii)(B).

Although *Tree Fruits* suggested that secondary picketing against a struck product and secondary picketing against a neutral party were "poles apart," the courts soon discovered that product picketing could have the same effect as an illegal secondary boycott . . . .

. . . The product picketed in *Tree Fruits* was but one item among the many that made up the retailer's trade. If the appeal against such a product succeeds, the Court observed, it simply induces the neutral retailer to reduce his orders for the product or "to drop the item as a poor seller." The decline in sales attributable to consumer rejection of the struck product puts pressure upon the primary employer, and the marginal injury to the neutral retailer is purely incidental to the product boycott. The neutral therefore has little reason to become involved in the labor dispute. In this case, on the other hand, the title companies sell only the primary employer's product and perform the services associated with it. Secondary picketing against consumption of the primary product leaves responsive consumers no realistic option other than to boycott the title companies altogether. If the appeal succeeds, each company "stops buying the struck product, not because of a falling demand, but in response to pressure designed to inflict injury on [its] business generally." Thus, "the union does more than merely follow the struck product; it creates a separate dispute with the secondary employer." Such an expansion of labor discord was one of the evils that Congress intended § 8(b)(4)(ii)(B) to prevent.

As long as secondary picketing only discourages consumption of a struck product, incidental injury to the neutral is a natural consequence of an effective primary boycott. But the Union's secondary appeal against the central product sold by the title companies in this case is "reasonably calculated to induce customers not to patronize the neutral parties at all." The resulting injury to their businesses is distinctly different from the injury that the Court considered in *Tree Fruits*. Product picketing that reasonably can be expected to threaten neutral parties with ruin or substantial loss simply does not square with the language or the purpose of § 8(b)(4)(ii)(B). Since successful secondary picketing would put the title companies to a choice between their survival and the severance of their ties with Safeco, the picketing plainly violates the statutory ban on the coercion of neutrals with the object of "forcing or requiring [them] to cease . . . dealing in the [primary] produc[t] . . . or to cease doing business with" the primary employer.

III

The Court of Appeals suggested that application of § 8(b)(4)(ii)(B) to the picketing in this case might violate the First Amendment. We think not. Although the Court recognized in *Tree Fruits* that the Constitution might not permit "a broad ban against peaceful picketing," the Court left no doubt that Congress may prohibit secondary picketing calculated "to persuade the customers of the secondary employer to cease trading with him in order to force him to cease dealing with, or to put pressure upon, the primary employer." Such picketing spreads labor discord by coercing a neutral party to join the fray . . . . As applied to picketing that predictably encourages consumers to boycott a secondary business, § 8(b)(4)(ii)(B) imposes no impermissible restrictions upon constitutionally protected speech . . . .

[MR. JUSTICE BLACKMUN, concurring in part and concurring in the result, omitted].

[MR. JUSTICE STEVENS, concurring in part and concurring in the result, omitted].

MR. JUSTICE BRENNAN, with whom MR. JUSTICE WHITE and MR. JUSTICE MARSHALL join, dissenting.

Tree Fruits held that it was permissible under § 8(b)(4)(ii)(B) of the National Labor Relations Act (NLRA) for a union involved in a labor dispute with a primary employer to conduct peaceful picketing at a secondary site with the object of persuading consumers to boycott the primary employer's product. Today's decision stunts *Tree Fruits* by declaring that secondary site picketing is illegal when the primary employer's product at which it is aimed happens to be the only product which the secondary retailer distributes. I dissent.

The NLRA does not place the secondary site off limits to all consumer picketing over the dispute with the primary employer. The Act only prohibits a labor union from picketing to "coerce" a secondary firm into joining the union's struggle against the primary employer. But inasmuch as the secondary retailer is, by definition, at least partially dependent upon the sale of the primary employer's goods, the secondary firm will necessarily feel the pressure of labor activity pointed at the primary enterprise. Thus, the pivotal problem in secondary site picketing cases is determining when the pressure imposed by consumer picketing is illegitimate, and therefore deemed to "coerce" the secondary retailer.

Tree Fruits addressed this problem by focusing upon whether picketing at the secondary site is directed at the primary employer's product, or whether it more broadly exhorts customers to withhold patronage from the full range of goods carried by the secondary retailer, *including those goods originating from nonprimary sources.* The *Tree Fruits* test reflects the distinction between economic damage sustained by the secondary firm solely by virtue of its dependence upon the primary employer's goods, and injuries inflicted upon interests of the secondary firm that are unrelated to the primary dispute-injuries that are calculated to influence the secondary retailer's conduct with respect to the primary dispute.

The former sort of harm is simply the result of union success in its conflict with the primary employer. The secondary firm is hurt only insofar as it entwines its economic fate with that of the primary employer by carrying the latter's goods. To be sure, the secondary site may be a battleground; but the secondary retailer, in its own right, is not enlisted as a combatant.

The latter kind of economic harm to the secondary firm, however, does not involve merely the necessary commercial fallout from the primary dispute. Appeals to boycott nonprimary goods sold by a secondary retailer place more at stake for the retailer than the risk it has assumed by handling the primary employer's product. Four considerations indicate that this broader pressure is highly undesirable from the standpoint of labor policy. First, nonprimary product boycotts distort the strength of consumer response to the primary dispute; the secondary retailer's decision to continue purchasing the primary employer's line becomes a function of consumer reaction to the primary conflict *amplified* by the impact of the boycott upon nonprimary goods. Second, although it seems proper to compel the producer or retailer of an individual primary product to internalize the costs of labor conflict engendered in the course of the item's production, a nonprimary product boycott may unfairly impose multiple costs upon the secondary retailer who does not wish to terminate his relationship with the primary employer. Third, nonprimary product boycotts attack interests of the secondary firm that are not derivative of the interests of the primary enterprise; because the retailer thereby becomes an independent disputant, the primary labor controversy may be aggravated and complicated. Finally, by affecting the sales of nonprimary goods handled by the secondary firm, the disruptive effect of the primary dispute is felt even by those businesses that manufacture and sell nonprimary products to the secondary retailer.

These sound reasons support *Tree Fruits'* conclusion that the legality of secondary site picketing should turn upon whether the union pickets urge only a boycott of the primary employer's product. Concomitantly, *Tree Fruits* expressly rejected the notion that the coerciveness of picketing should depend upon the extent of loss suffered by the secondary firm through diminished purchases of the primary product. Nevertheless, the Court has now apparently abandoned the *Tree Fruits* approach, choosing instead to identify coerciveness with the percentage of the secondary firm's business made up by the primary product.

The conceptual underpinnings of this new standard are seriously flawed. The type of economic pressure exerted upon the secondary retailer by a primary product boycott is the same whatever the percentage of its business the primary product composes-in each case, a decline in sales at the secondary outlet may well lead either to a decrease in purchases from the primary employer or to product substitution. To be sure, the damaging effect of this pressure upon individual secondary firms will vary, but it is far from clear that the harmfulness of a primary product boycott is necessarily correlated with the percentage of the secondary firm's business the product constitutes. For example, a marginally profitable large retailer may handle a multiplicity of products, yet find the decrease in sales of a single, very profitable, primary product ruinous. A small healthy single product secondary retailer, on the other hand, might be able to sustain losses during a boycott, or substitute a comparable product.

Moreover, it is odd to treat the NLRA's prohibition against coercion of neutral secondary parties as a means of protecting single product secondary firms from the effects of a successful primary product boycott. A single product retailer will always suffer a degree of harm incident to a successful primary product boycott, whether or not the retailer becomes the focus of union activity. Thus, a ban on coercion of neutral businesses is mismatched to the goal of averting that harm. Far more sensible would be to read the statutory ban on coercion of neutral parties as shielding secondary firms from the injuries that ensue precisely because of union conduct aimed at them. Nonprimary product boycotts fall within this category because they are specifically targeted at the secondary retailer.

Unlike the *Tree Fruits* rule, the test formulated by the Court in this case is not rooted in the policy of maintaining secondary firm neutrality with respect to the primary dispute. There is no ground to believe that a single product secondary retailer is more prone than a multiproduct retailer to react to a primary product boycott by joining the union in its struggle against the primary employer. On the contrary, the single product secondary firm is likely to be the primary employer's strongest ally because of the alignment of their respective economic interests. Nor is it especially unfair to subject the single product retailer to a primary product boycott. Whatever the percentage of a retailer's business that is constituted by a given item, the retailer necessarily assumes the risks of interrupted supply or declining sales that follow when labor conflict embroils the manufacturer of the item.

By shifting its focus from the nature of the product boycotted to the composition of the secondary firm's business, today's decision substitutes a confusing and unsteady standard for *Tree Fruits'* clear approach to secondary site picketing. Labor unions will no longer be able to assure that their secondary site picketing is lawful by restricting advocacy of a boycott to the primary product, as ordained by *Tree Fruits*. Instead, picketers will be compelled to guess whether the primary product makes up a sufficient proportion of the retailer's business to trigger the displeasure of the courts or the Labor Relations Board. Indeed, the Court's general disapproval of "[p]roduct picketing that reasonably can be expected to threaten neutral parties with ruin or substantial loss . . . ," leaves one wondering whether unions will also have to inspect balance sheets to determine whether the primary product they wish to picket is too profitable for the secondary firm.

I continue to "disagree . . . that the test of 'to threaten, coerce, or restrain' . . . is whether [the secondary retailer] suffered or was likely to suffer economic loss." I would adhere to the primary product test. Accordingly, I dissent.

EDWARD J. DEBARTOLO CORP. v. FLORIDA GULF COAST BUILDING & CONSTRUCTION TRADES COUNCIL
485 U.S. 568 (1988)

JUSTICE WHITE delivered the opinion of the Court.

This case centers around the respondent union's peaceful handbilling of the businesses operating in a shopping mall in Tampa, Florida, owned by petitioner, the Edward J. DeBartolo Corporation (DeBartolo). The union's primary labor dispute was with H.J. High Construction Company (High) over alleged substandard wages and fringe benefits. High was retained by the H.J. Wilson Company (Wilson) to construct a department store in the mall, and neither DeBartolo nor any of the other 85 or so mall tenants had any contractual right to influence the selection of contractors.

The union, however, sought to obtain their influence upon Wilson and High by distributing handbills asking mall customers not to shop at any of the stores in the mall "until the Mall's owner publicly promises that all construction at the Mall will be done using contractors who pay their employees fair wages and fringe benefits." The handbills' message was that "[t]he payment of substandard wages not only diminishes the working person's ability to purchase with earned, rather than borrowed, dollars, but it also undercuts the wage standard of the entire community." The handbills made clear that the union was seeking only a consumer boycott against the other mall tenants, not a secondary strike by their employees. At all four entrances to the mall for about three weeks in December 1979, the union peacefully distributed the handbills without any accompanying picketing or patrolling.

After DeBartolo failed to convince the union to alter the language of the handbills to state that its dispute did not involve DeBartolo or the mall lessees other than Wilson and to limit its distribution to the immediate vicinity of Wilson's construction site, it filed a complaint with the National Labor Relations Board (Board), charging the union with engaging in unfair labor practices under § 8(b)(4) of the National Labor Relations Act (NLRA). The Board's General Counsel issued a complaint, but the Board eventually dismissed it, concluding that the handbilling was protected by the publicity proviso of § 8(b)(4). The Court of Appeals for the Fourth Circuit affirmed the Board, but this Court reversed in *Edward J. DeBartolo Corp. v. NLRB*, 463 U.S. 147 (1983). There, we concluded that the handbilling did not fall within the proviso's limited scope of exempting "publicity intended to inform the public that the primary employer's product is 'distributed by' the secondary employer" because DeBartolo and the other tenants, as opposed to Wilson, did not distribute products of High. Since there had not been a determination below whether the union's handbilling fell within the prohibition of § 8(b)(4), and, if so, whether it was protected by the First Amendment, we remanded the case . . . .

The Board, the agency entrusted by Congress with the authority to administer the NLRA, has the "special function of applying the general provisions of the Act to the complexities of industrial life." Here, the Board has construed § 8(b)(4) of the Act to cover handbilling at a mall entrance urging potential customers not to trade with any retailers in the mall, in order to exert pressure on the proprietor of the mall to influence a particular mall tenant not to do business with a nonunion construction contractor. That statutory interpretation by the Board would normally be entitled to deference unless that construction were clearly contrary to the intent of Congress.

Another rule of statutory construction, however, is pertinent here: where an otherwise acceptable construction of a statute would raise serious constitutional problems, the Court will construe the statute to avoid such problems unless such construction is plainly contrary to the intent of Congress . . . .

We agree with the Court of Appeals and respondents that this case calls for the invocation of the *Catholic Bishop* rule, for the Board's construction of the statute, as applied in this case, poses serious questions of the validity of § 8(b)(4) under the First Amendment. The handbills involved here truthfully revealed the existence of a labor dispute and urged potential customers of the mall to follow a wholly legal course of action, namely, not to patronize the retailers doing business in the mall. The handbilling was peaceful. No picketing or patrolling was involved. On its face, this was expressive activity arguing that substandard wages should be opposed by abstaining from shopping in a mall where such wages were paid. Had the union simply been leafleting the public generally, including those entering every shopping mall in town, pursuant to an annual educational effort against substandard pay, there is little doubt that legislative proscription of such leaflets would pose a substantial issue of validity under the First Amendment. The same may well be true in this case, although here the handbills called attention to a specific situation in the mall allegedly involving the payment of unacceptably low wages by a construction contractor.

That a labor union is the leafletter and that a labor dispute was involved does not foreclose this analysis. We do not suggest that communications by labor unions are never of the commercial speech variety and thereby entitled to a lesser degree of constitutional protection. The handbills involved here, however, do not appear to be typical commercial speech such as advertising the price of a product or arguing its merits, for they pressed the benefits of unionism to the community and the dangers of inadequate wages to the economy and the standard of living of the populace. Of course, commercial speech itself is protected by the First Amendment, and however these handbills are to be classified, the Court of Appeals was plainly correct in holding that the Board's construction would require deciding serious constitutional issues.

The Board was urged to construe the statute in light of the asserted constitutional considerations, but thought that it was constrained by its own prior authority and cases in the Courts of Appeals, as well as by the express language of the Act, to hold that § 8(b)(4) must be construed to forbid the handbilling involved here. Even if this construction of the Act were thought to be a permissible one, we are quite sure that in light of the traditional rule followed in *Catholic Bishop*, we must independently inquire whether there is another interpretation, not raising these serious constitutional concerns, that may fairly be ascribed to § 8(b)(4)(ii)(B) . . . .

We follow this course here and conclude, as did the Court of Appeals, that the section is open to a construction that obviates deciding whether a congressional prohibition of handbilling on the facts of this case would violate the First Amendment.

The case turns on whether handbilling such as involved here must be held to "threaten, coerce, or restrain any person" to cease doing business with another, within the meaning of § 8(b)(4)(ii)(B). We note first that "induc[ing] or encourag-[ing]" employees of the secondary employer to strike is proscribed by § 8(b)(4)(i). But more than mere persuasion is necessary to prove a violation of § 8(b)(4)(ii)(B): that section requires a showing of threats, coercion, or restraints. Those words, we have said, are "nonspecific, indeed vague," and should be interpreted with "caution" and not given a "broad sweep," and in applying § 8(b)(1)(A) they were not to be construed to reach peaceful recognitional picketing. Neither is there any necessity to construe such language to reach the handbills involved in this case. There is no suggestion that the leaflets had any coercive effect on customers of the mall. There was no violence, picketing, or patrolling and only an attempt to persuade customers not to shop in the mall . . . .

"[P]icketing is qualitatively 'different from other modes of communication,'" and *Safeco* noted that the picketing there actually threatened the neutral with ruin or substantial loss. As Justice Stevens pointed out in his concurrence in *Safeco*, picketing is "a mixture of conduct and communication" and the conduct element "often provides the most persuasive deterrent to third persons about to enter a business establishment." Handbills containing the same message, he observed, are "much less effective than labor picketing" because they "depend entirely on the persuasive force of the idea." . . .

In *Tree Fruits*, we could not discern with the "requisite clarity" that Congress intended to proscribe all peaceful consumer picketing at secondary sites. There is even less reason to find in the language of § 8(b)(4)(ii)(B), standing alone, any clear indication that handbilling, without picketing, "coerces" secondary employers. The loss of customers because they read a handbill urging them not to patronize a business, and not because they are intimidated by a line of picketers, is the result of mere persuasion, and the neutral who reacts is doing no more than what its customers honestly want it to do . . . .

It is nevertheless argued that the second proviso to § 8(b)(4) makes clear that that section, as amended in 1959, was intended to proscribe nonpicketing appeals such as handbilling urging a consumer boycott of a neutral employer. That proviso reads as follows:

> "*Provided further*, That for the purposes of this paragraph (4) only, nothing contained in such paragraph shall be construed to prohibit publicity, other than picketing, for the purpose of truthfully advising the public, including consumers and members of a labor organization, that a product or products are produced by an employer with whom the labor organization has a primary dispute and are distributed by another employer, as long as such publicity does not have an effect of inducing any individual employed by any person other than the primary employer in the course of his employment to refuse to pick up, deliver, or transport any goods, or not to perform any services, at the establishment of the employer engaged in such distribution."

By its terms, the proviso protects nonpicketing communications directed at customers of a distributor of goods produced by an employer with whom the union has a labor dispute. Because handbilling and other consumer appeals not involving such a distributor are not within the proviso, the argument goes, those appeals must be considered coercive within the meaning of § 8(b)(4)(ii)(B). Otherwise, it is said, the proviso is meaningless, for if handbilling and like communications are never coercive and within the reach of the section, there would have been no need whatsoever for the proviso.

This approach treats the proviso as establishing an exception to a prohibition that would otherwise reach the conduct excepted. But this proviso has a different ring to it. It states that § 8(b)(4) "shall not be construed" to forbid certain described nonpicketing publicity. That language need not be read as an exception. It may indicate only that without the proviso, the particular nonpicketing communication the proviso protects might have been considered to be coercive, even if other forms of publicity would not be. Section 8(b)(4), with its proviso, may thus be read as not covering nonpicketing publicity, including appeals to customers of a retailer as they approach the store, urging a complete boycott of the retailer because he handles products produced by nonunion shops.

The Board's reading of § 8(b)(4) would make an unfair labor practice out of any kind of publicity or communication to the public urging a consumer boycott of employers other than those the proviso specifically deals with. On the facts of this case, newspaper, radio, and television appeals not to patronize the mall would be prohibited; and it would be an unfair labor practice for unions in their own meetings to urge their members not to shop in the mall. Nor could a union's handbills simply urge not shopping at a department store because it is using a nonunion contractor, although the union could safely ask the store's customers not to buy there because it is selling mattresses not carrying the union label. It is difficult, to say the least, to fathom why Congress would consider appeals urging a boycott of a distributor of a nonunion product to be more deserving of protection than nonpicketing persuasion of customers of other neutral employers such as that involved in this case . . . .

In our view, interpreting § 8(b)(4) as not reaching the handbilling involved in this case is not foreclosed either by the language of the section or its legislative history. That construction makes unnecessary passing on the serious constitutional questions that would be raised by the Board's understanding of the statute. Accordingly, the judgment of the Court of Appeals is

Affirmed.

POST PROBLEM DISCUSSION

1.   *Tree Fruits* makes a distinction between pressure on the secondary employer to stop doing business with the primary employer, which is clearly an impermissible secondary boycott, and picketing concerning specific struck products which is closer to a primary dispute. That is, even though the clear language of the statute and legislative history seems to prohibit all secondary picketing of this type, and makes no distinction between picketing one item versus the whole store, the Court maintains that if the Court interpreted this section of the NLRA in any other way, these secondary boycott provisions would be violative of the Free Speech clause of

the First Amendment. Thus, under the principle that the Court should interpret a statutory clause so as not to be constitutionally unsound, *Tree Fruits* interprets 8(b)(4)(ii)(B) to allow consumer picketing where the union is only picketing one product and not the entire business of the secondary employer.

2. In the second case in this Section, *Safeco Title Insurance Co.*, the Supreme Court appears to be backing away from its reasoning in *Tree Fruits*, at least in situations where the secondary employer only has essentially one product and a boycott of that product would economically ruin the employer. The distinction between *Safeco* and *Tree Fruits* is apparently based on whether just one product in a store with thousands of product is being boycotted or whether the employer has essentially one product and the boycott could put the employer out of business. Does this distinction make sense? Is the situation in *Tree Fruits* any less coercive than that in the *Safeco* case? And if so, does the statute speak in degrees of coercion or just the mere fact that the behavior is coercive? In short, where does one draw the line between picketing one item out of many (likely permissible) and picketing one of only a few items (may not be permissible)? Also, isn't there an argument that the local title companies in *Safeco* are allies of Safeco and thus, primary employers for all intents and purposes?

3. Problem #3 points to the difficult question of how to distinguish cases that fall in the middle of the extreme circumstances in *Tree Fruits* and *Safeco*. In *Dow Chemical Co.*, 524 F.2d 853 (D.C. Cir. 1975), on which this Problem is based, the court held that the union's peaceful picketing of the gas stations asking consumers to boycott only named gasoline refined by the struck, primary employer was not unlawful, even though most of each station's gross revenue came from selling that gas. The case was later overturned and clearly *Safeco*, which hadn't yet been decided at the time of the D.C. Circuit's decision, does not permit ruin or substantial loss to the neutral retailer. But where does one draw the line? Is 98% of revenue enough to cause ruin or substantial loss? What about 85% or 42%?

4. In "merged product" cases, the product being struck loses its separate identity from the secondary employer's product. For instance, in *Local 142, Plumbers Union*, 133 N.L.R.B. 307 (1961), the Board found that the picketing of a refrigeration repair company, the primary employer, at a market had devolved into urging others not to do business with the market and therefore, was an unlawful secondary boycott. Similarly, in *Kroger Co. v. NLRB*, 647 F.2d 634 (6th Cir. 1980), the court held that boycotting paper bags made from the primary employer at the site of a neutral grocery store was an unlawful secondary boycott. According to the court, the grocery store's need to use paper bags meant that the store and the paper bag supplier lost their separate identity; thus, a successful boycott of the bags would require a boycott of the store as well. Given this reasoning, a union would have a hard time wording picket signs to avoid this result.

5. The *DeBartolo* case appears to make an important distinction between secondary consumer boycotts carried out through picketing and those carried out through leafleting. In construing 8(b)(4)(ii)(B), the Supreme Court found that unlike picketing, handbilling is typically not prohibited by the NLRA. This is because, unlike the coercion normally associated with picketing, handbilling is much more pure communication that is unlikely to threaten or coerce. Moreover, to construe

Section 8(b)(4)(ii)(B) as outlawing this type of peaceful handbilling would probably run afoul of the First Amendment.

6.   More recently, the full five-member Board, in *Carpenters Local 1506 (Eliason & Knuth of Arizona, Inc.)*, 355 N.L.R.B. No. 159 (2010), considered an issue of first impression: "does a union violate Section 8(b)(4)(ii)(B) . . . when, at a secondary employer's business, its agents display a large stationary banner announcing a 'labor dispute' and seeking to elicit 'shame on' the employer or persuade customers not to patronize the employer." In a 3-2 decision, the Board majority concluded that the union had not violated the Act because it peaceably displayed a message directed toward the public, the banner was stationary, no one patrolled or carried picket signs, and no one sought to keep persons out of the employer's business. Moreover, the Board contended that any other interpretation would create serious constitutional questions because such peaceful bannering implicates the core protections of the First Amendment. The dissenting Board Members maintained that the bannering by the union was equivalent to coercive picketing and should be enjoined as a secondary boycott.

7.   To sum up consumer appeals: (1) picketing is typically allowed where the union is just picketing one of many items distributed by the secondary employer, but not one of a few items; and (2) handbilling and stationary banners are allowed as long as they do not coerce secondary employers not to do business with the primary employer. Handbilling and bannering must be directed to the consuming public.

8.   Work assignment disputes, also called jurisdictional disputes, between competing unions are handled under Section 8(b)(4)(D). Such disputes arise when two unions are certified for different groups of employees that work for the same employer and the collective-bargaining agreements do not make clear which employees should undertake certain work. Section 8(b)(4)(D) "makes it an unfair labor practice for a labor union to induce a strike or a concerted refusal to work in order to compel an employer to assign particular work to employees represented by it rather than to employees represented by another union." *See NLRB v. Radio & Television Broadcast Engineers Union, Local 1212 (CBS)*, 364 U.S. 573, 574 (1961). However, Section 10(k) of the Act "emphasizes the belief of Congress that it is more important to industrial peace that jurisdictional disputes be settled permanently than it is that unfair labor practice sanctions for jurisdictional strikes be imposed upon unions." *Id.* Section 10(k) thus gives the Board power to hold hearings to determine how best to settle these jurisdictional disputes. More specifically, the Supreme Court held in the *CBS* case that the Board must decide these disputes on their merits and decide which union employees are entitled to the disputed work. However, Section 10(k) only permits government resolution of work assignment disputes in the event that private resolution of the dispute between the parties is unsuccessful.

Chapter 11

LABOR LAW PREEMPTION DOCTRINES

Synopsis

Section 1   Mandatory Preemption: *Garmon* Preemption

Section 2   Permissive Preemption: *Machinists* Preemption

Section 3   Section 301 Preemption

Labor law preemption has recently become a hot topic of debate with the recent decision of the United States Supreme Court in *Chamber of Commerce of United States of America v. Brown*, 554 U.S. 60 (2008) (holding that California statutes that prohibit grant recipients receiving more than $10,000 in state program funds from using such funds "to assist, promote, or deter union organizing" preempted by NLRA). This is because more states are increasingly passing their own labor relation laws due to unhappiness with current NLRA doctrines and congressional inability to change the Act.

These state laws cut both ways, with some state seeking to provide additional labor rights to workers, and some states seeking to take such rights away. *See, e.g., Attorney Generals of Four States Defy NLRB Threat to File Lawsuits over Amendments that would Prohibit Voluntary Recognition of Unions*, Wolters Kluwer Labor Relations and Wages Hours Update (Jan. 2011), http://business.cch.com/updates/laborWages/january2011.htm (discussing four states' (South Carolina, Utah, Arizona, and South Dakota) attempts to outlaw voluntary recognition as a valid route for union recognition). Recently, a district court in Arizona upheld a state secret ballot law against preemption attack. *See* Jeffrey M. Hirsch, *Judge Defers Suit on State Secret Ballot Laws*, WORKPLACE PROF. BLOG (Sept. 7, 2012), at http://lawprofessors.typepad.com/laborprof_blog/2012/09/judge-defers-suit-on-state-secret-ballot-laws.html

As Professor Secunda has written:

> When discussing current labor preemption doctrine in the United States, and the move to state-based legislative responses for what ills American labor relations law, one cannot avoid a sense of irony. When Congress initially enacted the NLRA in 1935, state courts and legislatures were very pro-employer, and the labor movement sought broad protections from the new federal labor laws. At the time, federal labor law sought to proactively encourage unionization and collective bargaining between employers and their employees.

> Starting with the enactment of the Taft-Hartley Amendments of 1947, however, the federal government's orientations toward unionization became

decidedly neutral, with the emphasis of the new amendment being on the employees' ability to exercise free choice "in laboratory conditions" to decide whether they wished to be represented by a union. Even more recently, with the increased politicization of the National Labor Relations Board, especially by the second Bush administration, federal labor law has been interpreted to favor employers of many issues considered essential to organized labor. The surprising upshot of all this labor history is that there has been an increasing push by the labor movement to decrease the scope of labor preemption to permit state legislation to provide union protections that federal labor law no longer does.

Paul M. Secunda, *Toward the Viability of State-Based Legislation to Address Workplace Captive Audience Meetings in the United States*, 29 Comp. Lab. L. & Pol'y J. 209, 229–30 (2008).

At its simplest level, labor preemption doctrine deals with the conflicts that arise between federal labor law and state labor laws and regulations. Where federal labor law is said to preempt state law, the state law in question, and the state court which seeks to enforce it, must give way in favor of the federal scheme. This preemption scheme is based on both Article VI of the federal constitution's Supremacy Clause, which states that federal law is the supreme law of the land, and on the Commerce Clause, which has been interpreted to give Congress an exclusive right to legislate in the labor relations area.

Consequently, Congress could, if it chose to do so, be the exclusive source of all labor relations law. Clearly, however, Congress has never chosen to exercise its power to the fullest extent. We know this because there are many state and local laws that explicitly apply to the workplace and others that have an impact on labor relations that would have no force if Congress chose to occupy the labor relations field exclusively. Indeed, even the NLRA contains one explicit exception to its normally robust preemption by allowing state right-to-work laws (see Chapter 12).

The problem in preemption law is that Congress has not been very helpful in delineating the exact extent to which federal labor law preempts state labor law:

> To clarify where the preemption line may lie, it is helpful to understand that the Supreme Court has set forth two guiding principles or themes in its labor preemption decisions: (1) the need to avoid conflicts in substantive rights; and (2) the need to protect the primary jurisdiction of the NLRB. With regard to guarding against conflict between state and federal labor law, state laws have been found preempted under at least four basic circumstances: (1) where state laws restrict or potentially restricts the exercise of rights under Section 7 of the NLRA, (2) where state laws permit or potentially permit conduct that is restricted by the unfair labor practice provisions of Section 8, (3) where state laws provide a different remedial scheme than federal labor law, and (4) where state laws seek to regulate activity that Congress purposefully chose to leave unregulated.

> On the other hand, the complementary doctrine of primary jurisdiction brings to bear familiar administrative law concepts. Most importantly, that Congress has created the NLRB to administer and implement the NLRB

and has granted primary jurisdiction to the NLRB, as the court of first resort, to adjudicate disputes that arise under the statute. This means that labor and management must first use the NLRB to resolve their labor relations disputes. This primary reliance on the NLRB is, in turn, premised on the NLRB's expertise and experience in resolving labor relations matters and on the importance of fashioning a coherent and uniform body of labor law by which parties can predicate their future conduct.

Secunda, *supra*, at 231–232.

This Chapter is divided into the three major labor preemption doctrines: (1) *Garmon* preemption; (2) *Machinists* preemption, and (3) Section 301 preemption.

SECTION 1   MANDATORY PREEMPTION: *GARMON* PREEMPTION

PROBLEM #1: WORKER FREEDOM LAWS AND CAPTIVE AUDIENCE MEETINGS, TAKE 1

Private-sector employers in the United States routinely hold mandatory workplace meetings during union organization campaigns to express anti-union views to their employees (see Chapter 5). Employees must attend these meetings at pain of discharge and may not be able to leave these meetings, ask questions, or espouse pro-union views. Indeed, these captive audience meetings are so effective that American employers are increasingly using this technique to also inform their employees about their political and religious views.

Because unions are generally not guaranteed access to employer property to share their pro-union message with employees, organized labor believes such meetings give employers the ability to effectively intimidate and harass employees during union organizational campaigns. It is therefore not surprising that unions would very much like to see such captive audience meetings prohibited.

As discussed in Chapter 5, the U.S. Supreme Court has long interpreted the NLRA as permitting employers to hold these captive audience meetings with their employees on labor-oriented issues. Although this has been the state of affairs for some time, there has been a recent push by organized labor to enact state laws that would prohibit employers from holding captive audience meetings concerning labor-related, political, or religious messages. Under the Worker Freedom Act (WFA), employers would not only be prohibited from holding mandatory sessions during work to express opinions on labor-related, political, and religious issues, but would be liable for retaliating against workers who reported the holding of such sessions or who were terminated for not attending such sessions.

Should Worker Freedom Act legislation be held preempted by federal labor law? The State of Oregon recently passed WFA legislation, and the Chamber of Commerce immediately challenged the law as preempted by the NLRA. You are a law clerk to a judge in the District Court for the District of Oregon. How would you write your bench memo to the judge in this case? For this Section, limit your analysis to the *Garmon* preemption issue.

PROBLEM MATERIALS

San Diego Building Trades Council v. Garmon, 359 U.S. 236 (1959)

Paul M. Secunda, *Toward the Viability of State-Based Legislation to Address Workplace Captive Audience Meetings in the United States*, 29 Comp. Lab. L. & Pol'y J. 209 (2008).

SAN DIEGO BUILDING TRADES COUNCIL v. GARMON
359 U.S. 236 (1959)

Mr. Justice Frankfurter delivered the opinion of the Court.

This case is before us for the second time. The present litigation began with a dispute between the petitioning unions and respondents, co-partners in the business of selling lumber and other materials in California. Respondents began an action in the Superior Court for the County of San Diego, asking for an injunction and damages. Upon hearing, the trial court found the following facts. In March of 1953 the unions sought from respondents an agreement to retain in their employ only those workers who were already members of the unions, or who applied for membership within thirty days. Respondents refused, claiming that none of their employees had shown a desire to join a union, and that, in any event, they could not accept such an arrangement until one of the unions had been designated by the employees as a collective bargaining agent. The unions began at once peacefully to picket the respondents' place of business, and to exert pressure on customers and suppliers in order to persuade them to stop dealing with respondents. The sole purpose of these pressures was to compel execution of the proposed contract. The unions contested this finding, claiming that the only purpose of their activities was to educate the workers and persuade them to become members. On the basis of its findings, the court enjoined the unions from picketing and from the use of other pressures to force an agreement, until one of them had been properly designated as a collective bargaining agent. The court also awarded $1,000 damages for losses found to have been sustained.

At the time the suit in the state court was started, respondents had begun a representation proceeding before the National Labor Relations Board. The Regional Director declined jurisdiction, presumably because the amount of interstate commerce involved did not meet the Board's monetary standards in taking jurisdiction.

On appeal, the California Supreme Court sustained the judgment of the Superior Court, holding that, since the National Labor Relations Board had declined to exercise its jurisdiction, the California courts had power over the dispute. They further decided that the conduct of the union constituted an unfair labor practice under s 8(b)(2) of the National Labor Relations Act, and hence was not privileged under California law. As the California court itself later pointed out this decision did not specify what law, state or federal, was the basis of the relief granted. Both state and federal law played a part but, "(a)ny distinction as between those laws was not thoroughly explored."

We granted certiorari . . . . [W]e held that the refusal of the National Labor Relations Board to assert jurisdiction did not leave with the States power over activities they otherwise would be pre-empted from regulating . . . .

On remand, the California court . . . set aside the injunction, but sustained the award of damages. After deciding that California had jurisdiction to award damages for injuries caused by the union's activities, the California court held that those activities constituted a tort based on an unfair labor practice under state law. In so holding the court relied on general tort provisions, . . . as well as state enactments dealing specifically with labor relations.

We again granted certiorari [a second time] to determine whether the California court had jurisdiction to award damages arising out of peaceful union activity which it could not enjoin.

The issue is a variant of a familiar theme . . . . The comprehensive regulation of industrial relations by Congress, novel federal legislation twenty-five years ago but now an integral part of our economic life, inevitably gave rise to difficult problems of federal-state relations. To be sure, in the abstract these problems came to us as ordinary questions of statutory construction. But they involved a more complicated and perceptive process than is conveyed by the delusive phrase, "ascertaining the intent of the legislature." Many of these problems probably could not have been, at all events were not, foreseen by the Congress. Others were only dimly perceived and their precise scope only vaguely defined. This Court was called upon to apply a new and complicated legislative scheme, the aims and social policy of which were drawn with broad strokes while the details had to be filled in, to no small extent, by the judicial process. Recently we indicated the task that was thus cast upon this Court in carrying out with fidelity the purposes of Congress, but doing so by giving application to congressional incompletion . . . .

The case before us concerns one of the most teasing and frequently litigated areas of industrial relations, the multitude of activities regulated by ss 7 and 8 of the National Labor Relations Act. These broad provisions govern both protected "concerted activities" and unfair labor practices. They regulate the vital, economic instruments of the strike and the picket line, and impinge on the clash of the still unsettled claims between employers and labor unions. The extent to which the variegated laws of the several States are displaced by a single, uniform, national rule has been a matter of frequent and recurring concern . . . .

In the area of regulation with which we are here concerned, the process thus described has contracted initial ambiguity and doubt and established guides for judgment by interested parties and certainly guides for decision. We state these principles in full realization that, in the course of a process of tentative, fragmentary illumination carried on over more than a decade during which the writers of opinions almost inevitably, because unconsciously, focus their primary attention on the facts of particular situations, language may have been used or views implied which do not completely harmonize with the clear pattern which the decisions have evolved. But it may safely be claimed that the basis and purport of a long series of adjudications have "translated into concreteness" the consistently applied principles which decide this case.

In determining the extent to which state regulation must yield to subordinating federal authority, we have been concerned with delimiting areas of potential conflict; potential conflict of rules of law, of remedy, and of administration. The nature of the judicial process precludes an ad hoc inquiry into the special problems of labor-management relations involved in a particular set of occurrences in order to ascertain the precise nature and degree of federal-state conflict there involved, and more particularly what exact mischief such a conflict would cause. Nor is it our business to attempt this. Such determinations inevitably depend upon judgments on the impact of these particular conflicts on the entire scheme of federal labor policy and administration. Our task is confined to dealing with classes of situations. To the National Labor Relations Board and to Congress must be left those precise and closely limited demarcations that can be adequately fashioned only by legislation and administration. We have necessarily been concerned with the potential conflict of two law-enforcing authorities, with the disharmonies inherent in two systems, one federal the other state, of inconsistent standards of substantive law and differing remedial schemes. But the unifying consideration of our decisions has been regard to the fact that Congress has entrusted administration of the labor policy for the Nation to a centralized administrative agency, armed with its own procedures, and equipped with its specialized knowledge and cumulative experience . . . .

Administration is more than a means of regulation; administration is regulation. We have been concerned with conflict in its broadest sense; conflict with a complex and interrelated federal scheme of law, remedy, and administration. Thus, judicial concern has necessarily focused on the nature of the activities which the States have sought to regulate, rather than on the method of regulation adopted. When the exercise of state power over a particular area of activity threatened interference with the clearly indicated policy of industrial relations, it has been judicially necessary to preclude the States from acting. However, due regard for the presuppositions of our embracing federal system, including the principle of diffusion of power not as a matter of doctrinaire localism but as a promoter of democracy, has required us not to find withdrawal from the States of power to regulate where the activity regulated was a merely peripheral concern of the Labor Management Relations Act. Or where the regulated conduct touched interests so deeply rooted in local feeling and responsibility that, in the absence of compelling congressional direction, we could not infer that Congress had deprived the States of the power to act.

When it is clear or may fairly be assumed that the activities which a State purports to regulate are protected by s 7 of the National Labor Relations Act, or constitute an unfair labor practice under s 8, due regard for the federal enactment requires that state jurisdiction must yield. To leave the States free to regulate conduct so plainly within the central aim of federal regulation involves too great a danger of conflict between power asserted by Congress and requirements imposed by state law. Nor has it mattered whether the States have acted through laws of broad general application rather than laws specifically directed towards the governance of industrial relations. Regardless of the mode adopted, to allow the States to control conduct which is the subject of national regulation would create potential frustration of national purposes.

At times it has not been clear whether the particular activity regulated by the States was governed by s 7 or s 8 or was, perhaps, outside both these sections. But courts are not primary tribunals to adjudicate such issues. It is essential to the administration of the Act that these determinations be left in the first instance to the National Labor Relations Board. What is outside the scope of this Court's authority cannot remain within a State's power and state jurisdiction too must yield to the exclusive primary competence of the Board.

The case before us is such a case. The adjudication in California has throughout been based on the assumption that the behavior of the petitioning unions constituted an unfair labor practice. This conclusion was derived by the California courts from the facts as well as from their view of the Act. It is not for us to decide whether the National Labor Relations Board would have, or should have, decided these questions in the same manner. When an activity is arguably subject to s 7 or s 8 of the Act, the States as well as the federal courts must defer to the exclusive competence of the National Labor Relations Board if the danger of state interference with national policy is to be averted.

To require the States to yield to the primary jurisdiction of the National Board does not ensure Board adjudication of the status of a disputed activity. If the Board decides, subject to appropriate federal judicial review, that conduct is protected by s 7, or prohibited by s 8, then the matter is at an end, and the States are ousted of all jurisdiction. Or, the Board may decide that an activity is neither protected nor prohibited, and thereby raise the question whether such activity may be regulated by the States. However, the Board may also fail to determine the status of the disputed conduct by declining to assert jurisdiction, or by refusal of the General Counsel to file a charge, or by adopting some other disposition which does not define the nature of the activity with unclouded legal significance . . . . It follows that the failure of the Board to define the legal significance under the Act of a particular activity does not give the States the power to act. In the absence of the Board's clear determination that an activity is neither protected nor prohibited or of compelling precedent applied to essentially undisputed facts, it is not for this Court to decide whether such activities are subject to state jurisdiction . . . . The governing consideration is that to allow the States to control activities that are potentially subject to federal regulation involves too great a danger of conflict with national labor policy.

In the light of these principles the case before us is clear. Since the National Labor Relations Board has not adjudicated the status of the conduct for which the State of California seeks to give a remedy in damages, and since such activity is arguably within the compass of s 7 or s 8 of the Act, the State's jurisdiction is displaced . . . .

Reversed.

MR. JUSTICE HARLAN, whom MR. JUSTICE CLARK, MR. JUSTICE WHITTAKER and MR. JUSTICE STEWART join, concurring [opinion omitted].

Paul M. Secunda, *Toward the Viability of State-Based Legislation to Address Workplace Captive Audience Meetings in the United States*
29 COMP. LAB. L. & POL'Y J. 209, 233–34 (2008)[1]

. . . III. The Current State of Federal Labor Preemption Doctrine

. . . A. A Brief Primer on American Labor Preemption Law

. . . 1. Garmon Preemption Analysis

The Supreme Court held in San Diego Trades Council v. Garmon that the NLRA preempts state laws that Section 7 protects or arguably protects or that Section 8 prohibits or arguably prohibits. The use of the word "arguably" underscores the breadth of Garmon preemption. Nevertheless, Workplace Freedom Act legislation would not appear to be subject to Garmon preemption. This is because the state law neither regulates employee activities that are actually or potentially protected under Section 7, nor does it permit employer activity that is actually or potentially prohibited under Section 8. More specifically, Section 7 only provides rights to employees and says nothing about employer's rights in the workplace. Section 7 is thus not even arguably implicated.

Similarly, there is nothing in Section 8 that arguably prohibits the states from outlawing captive audience speech on labor organizing. The unfair labor practices discussed therein only apply to employer or union interference, restraint of or coercion of employee's Section 7 rights. Even if one were to accept the view of some courts that Section 8(c) protects "employer rights" under the First Amendment to express views on unionization in a non-coercive manner to its employees, it does not speak to whether employers may mandatorily require employees to attend meetings to hear those views. Section 8(c) is just not applicable to the captive audience situation, since employers can still freely express their views to employees who chose to listen during workplace meetings without having to force their employees to be there. In short, workplace captive audience legislation is one of those "activities in labor relations [that] are neither protected nor prohibited by the NLRA and are therefore not preempted under Garmon."

POST PROBLEM DISCUSSION

1. Under *Garmon*, the NLRA preempts state regulation of conduct that is protected or prohibited by the Act, or that is arguably protected or prohibited by the Act. The Court in *Garmon* showed an unwillingness to resolve these disputes on an ad hoc basis. The preference is for a broad, prospective, categorical treatment of the preemption problem. Remember that preemption can apply where there is a conflict in substantive law or remedial schemes ("conflict preemption"), and where primary jurisdiction issues are involved (i.e., primary power to interpret labor

---

issues is set aside for the Board, often called "field preemption," because the NLRA "occupies the field" of labor law). It does not matter whether one is considering a specific law that deals with labor relations or just a rule of general application that only incidentally touches on labor relations. The focus of the *Garmon* preemption analysis is properly "on the nature of the activities which the States have sought to regulate, rather than the method of regulation adopted."

2.   Although *Garmon* preemption was supposed to provide a bright-line categorical rule for which state laws and regulations are preempted, the Court has recognized at least one significant exception: state regulation of mass picketing and threats of violence is permitted, although the conduct at issue is likely prohibited by Section 8 of the NLRA. This is because the conduct involves "interests so deeply rooted in local feeling and responsibility" that state regulation will not be preempted absent direct congressional direction (notice that the NLRA lacks any express preemption clause). *See UAW v. Russell*, 356 U.S. 634 (1958); *United Construction Workers v. Laburnum*, 347 U.S. 656 (1954). These types of cases typically involve conduct that amounts to a crime, an intentional tort, or both — where the state interest in regulation is strong and obvious.

3.   Over the years, the United States Supreme Court has addressed a number of cases under *Garmon* preemption principles, with some state actions being preempted and some not (under similar reasoning used in *Russell* and *Laburnum*). For instance, in *Amalgamated Association of Street, Electric Railway & Motor Coach Employees v. Lockridge*, 403 U.S. 274 (1971), the Court applied *Garmon* rather inflexibly. It held that a state court order reinstating a worker to union membership after he had been terminated for failing to pay union dues was preempted by the NLRA. The Court came to this conclusion because the state court's decision had to deal with contractual issues normally presented to the NLRB. In short, *Garmon* preemption applied because the union's conduct in the case was arguably prohibited by Section 8(b)(2), which applies when a union causes an employer to discriminate against an employee.

Conversely, in *Farmer v. United Brotherhood of Carpenters & Joiners, Local 25*, 430 U.S. 290 (1977), the Court concluded that the NLRA did not preempt a tort action brought in state court by a union member against the union to recover damages for intentional infliction of emotional distress. Because the state had a substantial interest in regulation of that conduct, the Court concluded that the state's interest did not threaten the federal regulatory scheme for labor law. *See also Linn v. Plant Guard Workers*, 383 U.S. 53 (1966) (holding that a Pinkerton manager's defamation claim against a union was not preempted because it did not involve protected activity under Section 7 and there was an overriding state interest in protecting residents from defamation).

4.   In yet another *Garmon* preemption case, *Sears, Roebuck & Co. v. San Diego District Council of Carpenters*, 436 U.S. 180 (1978), the union had picketed Sears' use of a non-union subcontractor to perform carpentry work in the store. A state court enjoined the picketing under state trespass law. Although the conduct could be seen as arguably prohibited recognitional picketing under Section 8(b)(7)(C), a prohibited jurisdictional dispute strike under Section 8(b)(4)(D), or arguably protected area standards picketing under Section 7, the Court held that the state

court action was not preempted under *Garmon.* Preemption did not exist because: (1) the issues before the state court would not be the same issues before the NLRB, and thus, the Board's primary jurisdiction was not implicated; and (2) the union could have had filed an unfair labor practice charge when Sears demanded the removal of the picket, but the union never filed a charge. Because the union had a fair opportunity to present the picketing issue to the Board, it had sufficient protection against the risk of error by the state court in coming to its trespass decision.

5.   *Garmon* conflict preemption principles have been found to apply in cases concerning the selection of bargaining representatives. In *Brown v. Hotel & Restaurant Employees, International Union Local 54,* 468 U.S. 491 (1984), the New Jersey Casino Control Commission ordered that the president and other officers of a union be removed from their offices because of their criminal convictions and association with members of organized crime. If the union refused, the Commission would bar the union from collecting dues from any of its members. On the issue of whether these state Casino Control Act provisions were preempted by the NLRA because they conflicted with Section 7 rights, the *Brown* Court found the law was not preempted because Congress has "indicated both that employees do not have an unqualified right to choose their union officials and that certain state disqualification requirements are compatible with Section 7." So the regulation of the qualifications of casino industry union officials was found not to conflict with Section 7, and the law was not preempted.

6.   In a case concerning collective bargaining rights, *Local 24, International Teamsters v. Oliver,* 358 U.S. 283 (1959), an owner-operator of a truck sought to have a minimum rental provision in the Teamsters collective-bargaining agreement voided under state antitrust law, because it limited his ability to lease his truck to various interstate trucking companies. The state court entered a permanent injunction against the minimum rental provision and the union responded by saying that the state court injunction was preempted by the NLRA. The court agreed with the Teamsters and found the state antitrust action preempted because the contract provision was a mandatory subject of bargaining under Section 8(d) and bargaining on this subject was a right of the employees protected by Section 7.

SECTION 2   PERMISSIVE PREEMPTION: *MACHINISTS* PREEMPTION

PROBLEM #2: WORKER FREEDOM LAWS AND CAPTIVE AUDIENCE MEETINGS, TAKE 2

Same facts as Problem #1. For this problem, your judge wants you to focus on whether the Oregon Worker Freedom Act is preempted under the *Machinists* preemption doctrine.

PROBLEM MATERIALS

Lodge 76, International Association of Machinists v. Wisconsin Employment Relations Commission, 427 U.S. 132 (1976)

Chamber of Commerce of the United States v. Brown, 554 U.S. 60 (2008)

Brief of Law Professors as Amicus Curiae in Support of Defendants' Opposition to Motion For Summary Judgment, Associated Oregon Industries v. Avakian, No. 3:09-CV-1494-MO (March 22, 2010)

LODGE 76, INTERNATIONAL ASSOCIATION OF MACHINISTS v. WISCONSIN EMPLOYMENT RELATIONS COMMISSION
427 U.S. 132 (1976)

MR. JUSTICE BRENNAN delivered the opinion of the Court.

The question to be decided in this case is whether federal labor policy pre-empts the authority of a state labor relations board to grant an employer covered by the National Labor Relations Act an order enjoining a union and its members from continuing to refuse to work overtime pursuant to a union policy to put economic pressure on the employer in negotiations for renewal of an expired collective-bargaining agreement.

A collective-bargaining agreement between petitioner Lodge 76 (Union) and respondent Kearney & Trecker Corp. (employer) was terminated by the employer pursuant to the terms of the agreement on June 19, 1971. Good-faith bargaining over the terms of a renewal agreement continued for over a year thereafter, finally resulting in the signing of a new agreement effective July 23, 1972. A particularly controverted issue during negotiations was the employer's demand that the provision of the expired agreement under which, as for the prior 17 years, the basic workday was seven and one-half hours, Monday through Friday, and the basic workweek was 37½ hours, be replaced with a new provision providing a basic workday of eight hours and a basic workweek of 40 hours, and that the terms on which overtime rates of pay were payable be changed accordingly.

A few days after the old agreement was terminated the employer unilaterally began to make changes in some conditions of employment provided in the expired contract, E. g., eliminating the checkoff of Union dues, eliminating the Union's office in the plant, and eliminating Union lost time. No immediate change was made in the basic workweek or workday, but in March 1972, the employer announced that it would unilaterally implement, as of March 13, 1972, its proposal for a 40-hour week and eight-hour day. The Union response was a membership meeting on March 7 at which strike action was authorized and a resolution was adopted binding Union members to refuse to work any overtime, defined as work in excess of seven and one-half hours in any day or 37½ hours in any week. Following the strike vote, the employer offered to "defer the implementation" of its workweek proposal if the Union would agree to call off the concerted refusal to work overtime. The Union, however, refused the offer and indicated its intent to continue the concerted ban on overtime. Thereafter, the employer did not make effective the proposed changes in the workday and workweek before the new agreement became effective on July 23, 1972. Although all but a very few employees complied with the Union's resolution against acceptance of overtime work during the negotiations, the employer did not discipline, or attempt to discipline, any employee for refusing to work overtime.

Instead, while negotiations continued, the employer filed a charge with the National Labor Relations Board that the Union's resolution violated s 8(b)(3) of the National Labor Relations Act. The Regional Director dismissed the charge . . . . However, the employer also filed a complaint before the Wisconsin Employment Relations Commission charging that the refusal to work overtime constituted an unfair labor practice under state law . . . The Commission thereupon entered an order that the Union, Inter alia, "[i]mmediately cease and desist from authorizing, encouraging or condoning any concerted refusal to accept overtime assignments . . . ." We reverse.

I

"The national . . . Act . . . leaves much to the states, though Congress has refrained from telling us how much. We must spell out from conflicting indications of congressional will the area in which state action is still permissible." Federal labor policy as reflected in the National Labor Relations Act has been construed not to preclude the States from regulating aspects of labor relations that involve "conduct touch[ing] interests so deeply rooted in local feeling and responsibility that . . . we could not infer that Congress had deprived the States of the power to act." Policing of actual or threatened violence to persons or destruction of property has been held most clearly a matter for the States. Similarly, the federal law governing labor relations does not withdraw "from the States . . . power to regulate where the activity regulated [is] a merely peripheral concern of the Labor Management Relations Act."

Cases that have held state authority to be pre-empted by federal law tend to fall into one of two categories: (1) those that reflect the concern that "one forum would enjoin, as illegal, conduct which the other forum would find legal" and (2) those that reflect the concern "that the [application of state law by] state courts would restrict the exercise of rights guaranteed by the Federal Acts." "[I]n referring to decisions holding state laws pre-empted by the NLRA, care must be taken to distinguish pre-emption based on federal protection of the conduct in question . . . from that based predominantly on the primary jurisdiction of the National Labor Relations Board . . . , although the two are often not easily separable." Each of these distinct aspects of labor law pre-emption has had its own history in our decisions, to which we now turn.

We consider first pre-emption based predominantly on the primary jurisdiction of the Board. This line of pre-emption analysis was developed in San Diego Unions v. Garmon . . . .

However, a second line of pre-emption analysis has been developed in cases focusing upon the crucial inquiry whether Congress intended that the conduct involved be unregulated because left "to be controlled by the free play of economic forces." . . .

For the Court soon recognized that a particular activity might be "protected" by federal law not only when it fell within s 7, but also when it was an activity that Congress intended to be "unrestricted by any governmental power to regulate" because it was among the permissible "economic weapons in reserve, . . . actual exercise [of which] on occasion by the parties, is part and parcel of the system that the Wagner and Taft-Hartley Acts have recognized." "[T]he legislative purpose may . . . dictate that certain activity 'neither protected nor prohibited' be deemed privileged against state regulation."

II

. . . The Court had earlier recognized in pre-emption cases that Congress meant to leave some activities unregulated and to be controlled by the free play of economic forces . . . .

> 'For a state to impinge on the area of labor combat designed to be free is quite as much an obstruction of federal policy as if the state were to declare picketing free for purposes or by methods which the federal Act prohibits.'

Although many of our past decisions concerning conduct left by Congress to the free play of economic forces address the question in the context of union and employee activities, self-help is of course also the prerogative of the employer because he, too, may properly employ economic weapons Congress meant to be unregulable . . . .

Whether self-help economic activities are employed by employer or union, the crucial inquiry regarding pre-emption is the same: whether "the exercise of plenary state authority to curtail or entirely prohibit self-help would frustrate effective implementation of the Act's processes."

III

There is simply no question that the Act's processes would be frustrated in the instant case were the State's ruling permitted to stand. The employer in this case invoked the Wisconsin law because it was unable to overcome the Union tactic with its own economic self-help means. Although it did employ economic weapons putting pressure on the Union when it terminated the previous agreement, it apparently lacked sufficient economic strength to secure its bargaining demands under "the balance of power between labor and management expressed in our national labor policy." But the economic weakness of the affected party cannot justify state aid contrary to federal law for, as we have developed, "the use of economic pressure by the parties to a labor dispute is not a grudging exception [under] . . . the [federal] Act; it is part and parcel of the process of collective bargaining." The state action in this case is not filling "a regulatory void which Congress plainly assumed would not exist," Rather, it is clear beyond question that Wisconsin "[entered] into the substantive aspects of the bargaining process to an extent Congress has not countenanced."

Our decisions hold that Congress meant that these activities, whether of employer or employees, were not to be regulable by States any more than by the NLRB, for neither States nor the Board is "afforded flexibility in picking and choosing which economic devices of labor and management shall be branded as unlawful." Rather, both are without authority to attempt to "introduce some standard of properly 'balanced' bargaining power' or to define "what economic sanctions might be permitted negotiating parties in an 'ideal' or 'balanced' state of collective bargaining." To sanction state regulation of such economic pressure deemed by the federal Act "desirabl[y] . . . left for the free play of contending economic forces, . . . is not merely [to fill] a gap [by] outlaw[ing] what federal law fails to outlaw; it is denying one party to an economic contest a weapon that Congress meant him to have available." Accordingly, such regulation by the State is impermissible because it " 'stands as an obstacle to the accomplishment and execution of the full purposes and objectives of Congress.' "

IV

. . . Our decisions . . . have made it abundantly clear that state attempts to influence the substantive terms of collective-bargaining agreements are as inconsistent with the federal regulatory scheme as are such attempts by the NLRB: "Since the federal law operates here, in an area where its authority is paramount, to leave the parties free, the inconsistent application of state law is necessarily outside the power of the State." And indubitably regulation, whether federal or State, of "the choice of economic weapons that may be used as part of collective bargaining [exerts] considerable influence upon the substantive terms on which the parties contract." The availability or not of economic weapons that federal law leaves the parties free to use cannot "depend upon the forum in which the [opponent] presses its claims." . . .

V

This survey of the extent to which federal labor policy and the federal Act have pre-empted state regulatory authority to police the use by employees and employers of peaceful methods of putting economic pressure upon one another compels the conclusion that the judgment of the Wisconsin Supreme Court must be reversed. It is not contended, and on the record could not be contended, that the Union policy against overtime work was enforced by violence or threats of intimidation or injury to property. Workers simply left the plant at the end of their workshift and refused to volunteer for or accept overtime or Saturday work . . . .

[W]e hold . . . that the Union's refusal to work overtime is peaceful conduct constituting activity which must be free of regulation by the States if the congressional intent in enacting the comprehensive federal law of labor relations is not to be frustrated, the judgment of the Wisconsin Supreme Court is

Reversed.

Mr. Justice Powell, with whom The Chief Justice joins, concurring [opinion omitted].

Mr. Justice Stevens, with whom Mr. Justice Stewart and Mr. Justice Rehnquist join, dissenting [opinion omitted].

CHAMBER OF COMMERCE OF THE UNITED STATES v. BROWN
554 U.S. 60 (2008)

Justice Stevens delivered the opinion of the Court.

A California statute known as "Assembly Bill 1889" (AB 1889) prohibits several classes of employers that receive state funds from using the funds "to assist, promote, or deter union organizing." The question presented to us is whether two of its provisions — § 16645.2, applicable to grant recipients, and § 16645.7, applicable to private employers receiving more than $10,000 in program funds in any year — are pre-empted by federal law mandating that certain zones of labor activity be unregulated.

I

As set forth in the preamble, the State of California enacted AB 1889 for the following purpose:

"It is the policy of the state not to interfere with an employee's choice about whether to join or to be represented by a labor union. For this reason, the state should not subsidize efforts by an employer to assist, promote, or deter union organizing. It is the intent of the Legislature in enacting this act to prohibit an employer from using state funds and facilities for the purpose of influencing employees to support or oppose unionization and to prohibit an employer from seeking to influence employees to support or oppose unionization while those employees are performing work on a state contract."

AB 1889 prohibits certain employers that receive state funds — whether by reimbursement, grant, contract, use of state property, or pursuant to a state program — from using such funds to "assist, promote, or deter union organizing." This prohibition encompasses "any attempt by an employer to influence the decision of its employees" regarding "[w]hether to support or oppose a labor organization" and "[w]hether to become a member of any labor organization." The statute specifies that the spending restriction applies to "any expense, including legal and consulting fees and salaries of supervisors and employees, incurred for . . . an activity to assist, promote, or deter union organizing."

Despite the neutral statement of policy quoted above, AB 1889 expressly exempts "activit[ies] performed" or "expense[s] incurred" in connection with certain undertakings that promote unionization, including "[a]llowing a labor organization or its representatives access to the employer's facilities or property," and "[n]egotiating, entering into, or carrying out a voluntary recognition agreement with a labor organization."

To ensure compliance with the grant and program restrictions at issue in this case, AB 1889 establishes a formidable enforcement scheme. Covered employers must certify that no state funds will be used for prohibited expenditures; the employer must also maintain and provide upon request "records sufficient to show that no state funds were used for those expenditures. If an employer commingles state and other funds, the statute presumes that any expenditures to assist, promote, or deter union organizing derive in part from state funds on a pro rata basis. Violators are liable to the State for the amount of funds used for prohibited purposes plus a civil penalty equal to twice the amount of those funds. Suspected violators may be sued by the state attorney general or any private taxpayer, and prevailing plaintiffs are "entitled to recover reasonable attorney's fees and costs."

II

In April 2002, several organizations whose members do business with the State of California (collectively, Chamber of Commerce), brought this action against the California Department of Health Services and appropriate state officials (collectively, the State) to enjoin enforcement of AB 1889. Two labor unions (collectively, AFL-CIO) intervened to defend the statute's validity . . . .

Although the NLRA itself contains no express pre-emption provision, we have held that Congress implicitly mandated two types of pre-emption as necessary to implement federal labor policy. The first, known as *Garmon* pre-emption, "is intended to preclude state interference with the National Labor Relations Board's interpretation and active enforcement of the 'integrated scheme of regulation' established by the NLRA." To this end, *Garmon* pre-emption forbids States to "regulate activity that the NLRA protects, prohibits, or arguably protects or prohibits." The second, known as *Machinists* pre-emption, forbids both the National Labor Relations Board (NLRB) and States to regulate conduct that Congress intended "be unregulated because left 'to be controlled by the free play of economic forces.'" *Machinists* pre-emption is based on the premise that "'Congress struck a balance of protection, prohibition, and laissez-faire in respect to union organization, collective bargaining, and labor disputes.'"

Today we hold that §§ 16645.2 and 16645.7 are pre-empted under *Machinists* because they regulate within "a zone protected and reserved for market freedom." We do not reach the question whether the provisions would also be pre-empted under *Garmon*.

III

As enacted in 1935, the NLRA, which was commonly known as the Wagner Act, did not include any provision that specifically addressed the intersection between employee organizational rights and employer speech rights. Rather, it was left to the NLRB, subject to review in federal court, to reconcile these interests in its construction of §§ 7 and 8. Section 7 provided that workers have the right to organize, to bargain collectively, and to engage in concerted activity for their mutual aid and protection. Section 8(1) made it an "unfair labor practice" for employers to "interfere with, restrain, or coerce employees in the exercise of the rights guaranteed in section 7."

Among the frequently litigated issues under the Wagner Act were charges that an employer's attempts to persuade employees not to join a union — or to join one favored by the employer rather than a rival — amounted to a form of coercion prohibited by § 8. The NLRB took the position that § 8 demanded complete employer neutrality during organizing campaigns, reasoning that any partisan employer speech about unions would interfere with the § 7 rights of employees. In 1941, this Court curtailed the NLRB's aggressive interpretation, clarifying that nothing in the NLRA prohibits an employer "from expressing its view on labor policies or problems" unless the employer's speech "in connection with other circumstances [amounts] to coercion within the meaning of the Act." We subsequently . . . recognize[ed] the First Amendment right of employers to engage in noncoercive speech about unionization. Notwithstanding these decisions, the NLRB continued to regulate employer speech too restrictively in the eyes of Congress.

Concerned that the Wagner Act had pushed the labor relations balance too far in favor of unions, Congress passed the Labor Management Relations Act, 1947 (Taft-Hartley Act). The Taft-Hartley Act amended §§ 7 and 8 in several key respects. First, it emphasized that employees "have the right to refrain from any or all" § 7 activities. Second, it added § 8(b), which prohibits unfair labor practices by unions. Third, it added § 8(c), which protects speech by both unions and employers from regulation by the NLRB. Specifically, § 8(c) provides:

> "The expressing of any views, argument, or opinion, or the dissemination thereof, whether in written, printed, graphic, or visual form, shall not constitute or be evidence of an unfair labor practice under any of the provisions of this subchapter, if such expression contains no threat of reprisal or force or promise of benefit."

From one vantage, § 8(c) "merely implements the First Amendment," in that it responded to particular constitutional rulings of the NLRB. But its enactment also manifested a "congressional intent to encourage free debate on issues dividing labor and management." It is indicative of how important Congress deemed such "free debate" that Congress amended the NLRA rather than leaving to the courts the task of correcting the NLRB's decisions on a case-by-case basis. We have characterized this policy judgment, which suffuses the NLRA as a whole, as "favoring uninhibited, robust, and wide-open debate in labor disputes," stressing that "freewheeling use of the written and spoken word . . . has been expressly fostered by Congress and approved by the NLRB."

Congress' express protection of free debate forcefully buttresses the preemption analysis in this case. Under *Machinists*, congressional intent to shield a zone of activity from regulation is usually found only "implicit[ly] in the structure of the Act," drawing on the notion that " '[w]hat Congress left unregulated is as important as the regulations that it imposed.' " In the case of noncoercive speech, however, the protection is both implicit and explicit. Sections 8(a) and 8(b) demonstrate that when Congress has sought to put limits on advocacy for or against union organization, it has expressly set forth the mechanisms for doing so.

Moreover, the amendment to § 7 calls attention to the right of employees to refuse to join unions, which implies an underlying right to receive information opposing unionization. Finally, the addition of § 8(c) expressly precludes regulation of speech about unionization "so long as the communications do not contain a 'threat of reprisal or force or promise of benefit.'"

The explicit direction from Congress to leave noncoercive speech unregulated makes this case easier, in at least one respect, than previous NLRA cases because it does not require us "to decipher the presumed intent of Congress in the face of that body's steadfast silence." California's policy judgment that partisan employer speech necessarily "interfere[s] with an employee's choice about whether to join or to be represented by a labor union," is the same policy judgment that the NLRB advanced under the Wagner Act, and that Congress renounced in the Taft-Hartley Act. To the extent §§ 16645.2 and 16645.7 actually further the express goal of AB 1889, the provisions are unequivocally pre-empted.

IV

The Court of Appeals concluded that *Machinists* did not pre-empt §§ 16645.2 and 16645.7 for three reasons: (1) The spending restrictions apply only to the *use* of state funds, (2) Congress did not leave the zone of activity free from *all* regulation, and (3) California modeled AB 1889 on federal statutes. We find none of these arguments persuasive.

Use of State Funds

In NLRA pre-emption cases, "'judicial concern has necessarily focused on the nature of the activities which the States have sought to regulate, rather than on the method of regulation adopted.'" California plainly could not directly regulate noncoercive speech about unionization by means of an express prohibition. It is equally clear that California may not indirectly regulate such conduct by imposing spending restrictions on the use of state funds . . . .

[I]n [*Building and Const. Trades Council of Metropolitan Dist. v. Associated Builders and Contractors of Massachusetts/Rhode Island, Inc. (Boston Harbor)*, 507 U.S. 218 (1993)], [we held] that the NLRA did not preclude a state agency supervising a construction project from requiring that contractors abide by a labor agreement. We explained that when a State acts as a "market participant with no interest in setting policy," as opposed to a "regulator," it does not offend the pre-emption principles of the NLRA. In finding that the state agency had acted as a market participant, we stressed that the challenged action "was specifically tailored to one particular job," and aimed "to ensure an efficient project that would be completed as quickly and effectively as possible at the lowest cost."

It is beyond dispute that California enacted AB 1889 in its capacity as a regulator rather than a market participant. AB 1889 is neither "specifically tailored to one particular job" nor a "legitimate response to state procurement constraints or to local economic needs." As the statute's preamble candidly acknowledges, the legislative purpose is not the efficient procurement of goods and services, but the furtherance of a labor policy. Although a State has a legitimate proprietary interest in ensuring that state funds are spent in accordance with the purposes for which they are appropriated, this is not the objective of AB 1889. In contrast to a neutral affirmative requirement that funds be spent solely for the purposes of the relevant grant or program, AB 1889 imposes a targeted negative restriction on employer speech about unionization. Furthermore, the statute does not even apply this constraint uniformly. Instead of forbidding the use of state funds for *all* employer advocacy regarding unionization, AB 1889 permits use of state funds for *select* employer advocacy activities that promote unions. Specifically, the statute exempts expenses incurred in connection with giving unions access to the workplace, and voluntarily recognizing unions without a secret ballot election . . . .

California's reliance on a "use" restriction rather than a "receipt" restriction "does not significantly lessen the inherent potential for conflict" between AB 1889 and the NLRA. AB 1889's enforcement mechanisms put considerable pressure on an employer either to forgo his "free speech right to communicate his views to his employees," or else to refuse the receipt of any state funds. In so doing, the statute impermissibly "predicat[es] benefits on refraining from conduct protected by federal labor law," and chills one side of "the robust debate which has been protected under the NLRA." . . .

NLRB Regulation

We have characterized *Machinists* pre-emption as "creat[ing] a zone free from all regulations, whether state or federal." Stressing that the NLRB has regulated employer speech that takes place on the eve of union elections, the Court of Appeals deemed *Machinists* inapplicable because "employer speech in the context of organizing" is not a zone of activity that Congress left free from "*all* regulation." See *Peerless Plywood Co.*, 107 N.L.R.B. 427, 429 (1953) (barring employers and unions alike from making election speeches on company time to massed assemblies of employees within the 24-hour period before an election)).

The NLRB has policed a narrow zone of speech to ensure free and fair elections under the aegis of § 9 of the NLRA. Whatever the NLRB's regulatory authority within special settings such as imminent elections, however, Congress has clearly denied it the authority to regulate the broader category of noncoercive speech encompassed by AB 1889. It is equally obvious that the NLRA deprives California of this authority, since " '[t]he States have no more authority than the Board to upset the balance that Congress has struck between labor and management.' "

Federal Statutes

Finally, the Court of Appeals reasoned that Congress could not have intended to pre-empt AB 1889 because Congress itself has imposed similar restrictions. Specifically, three federal statutes include provisions that forbid the use of particular grant and program funds "to assist, promote, or deter union organizing." We are not persuaded that these few isolated restrictions, plucked from the multitude of federal spending programs, were either intended to alter or did in fact alter the " 'wider contours of federal labor policy.' "

A federal statute will contract the pre-emptive scope of the NLRA if it demonstrates that "Congress has decided to tolerate a substantial measure of diversity" in the particular regulatory sphere. In *New York Telephone*, an employer challenged a state unemployment system that provided benefits to employees absent from work during lengthy strikes. The employer argued that the state system conflicted with the federal labor policy "of allowing the free play of economic forces to operate during the bargaining process." We upheld the statute on the basis that the legislative histories of the NLRA and the Social Security Act, which were enacted within six weeks of each other, confirmed that "Congress intended that the States be free to authorize, or to prohibit, such payments." Indeed, the tension between the Social Security Act and the NLRA suggested that the case could "be viewed as presenting a potential conflict between two federal statutes . . . rather than between federal and state regulatory statutes."

The three federal statutes relied on by the Court of Appeals neither conflict with the NLRA nor otherwise establish that Congress "decided to tolerate a substantial measure of diversity" in the regulation of employer speech. Unlike the States, Congress has the authority to create tailored exceptions to otherwise applicable federal policies, and (also unlike the States) it can do so in a manner that preserves national uniformity without opening the door to a 50 — state patchwork of inconsistent labor policies. Consequently, the mere fact that Congress has imposed targeted federal restrictions on union-related advocacy in certain limited contexts does not invite the States to override federal labor policy in other settings.

Had Congress enacted a federal version of AB 1889 that applied analogous spending restrictions to *all* federal grants or expenditures, the pre-emption question would be closer. But none of the cited statutes is government-wide in scope, none contains comparable remedial provisions, and none contains express pro-union exemptions . . . .

JUSTICE BREYER, with whom JUSTICE GINSBURG joins, dissenting [opinion omitted].

Brief of Law Professors as Amicus Curiae in Support of Defendants' Opposition to Motion For Summary Judgment, Associated Oregon Industries v. Avakian
No. 3:09-CV-1494-MO, March 22, 2010[2]

. . . II. *SUMMARY OF ARGUMENT*

A finding of NLRA preemption in this case would be both inconsistent with Congress' purposes in enacting the NLRA and with principles of federalism which give the states and federal government shared authority over the employment relationship.

---

[2] This amicus brief was written by Professor Secunda and joined by William B. Gould IV, the Charles A. Beardsley Professor of Law, Emeritus, at the Stanford Law School and former Chairman of the National Labor Relations Board; Michael H. Gottesman, a Professor of Law at the Georgetown University Law Center; Henry H. Drummonds, a Professor of Law at the Lewis & Clark Law School; and Joseph Slater, the Eugene N. Balk Professor of Law and Values at the University of Toledo College of Law.

Indeed, a number of well-known exceptions exist to the *Machinists* labor preemption doctrine, *Machinists v. Wisconsin Employment Relations Commission*, 427 U.S. 132 (1976), in the area of state police powers and the regulation of property rights. Under this line of cases, traditional areas of state concern are within the states' power to regulate and, therefore, not within the scope of NLRA preemption. There are two sources of applicable authority here: (1) the state can place property restrictions on the bundle of property rights that the state grants to its property owners and (2) the state can provide for minimum conditions in the workplace under its police powers. Consistent with Section 8(c) of the NLRA, employers can still inform employees of their views of unionization, but may not force employees into mandatory meetings to hear those views under [Oregon Senate Bill] SB 519. In short, this Court should find that Oregon has the inherent power to enact SB 519 and such promulgation is consistent with both the reach and purposes of the NLRA and the principles of federalism.

First, under United States Supreme Court precedent interpreting rights of states to continue to regulate property rights in the labor relations context, SB 519 is not preempted by the NLRA. The state can place property restrictions on the bundle of property rights that the state grants to its property owners — that is, the bundle of property rights that private property owners possess would not include the use of their property to compel attention to labor, political, or religious speech. In this manner, Oregon's legislation should be exempt from *Machinists* preemption based on the powers of the state to regulate property interests. This exception to preemption law derives directly from the U.S. Supreme Court's holding in *Lechmere Inc. v. NLRB*, 502 U.S. 527 (1992).

Second, a state can provide for minimum conditions in the workplace under its police powers. Congress could have chosen to occupy the field of labor relations law exclusively, but it has never exercised its full powers in this regard, leaving state and local government free to pass many state and local laws and regulations that apply to the workplace. In this regard, the Supreme Court has recognized an exception to *Machinists* preemption where the states "traditionally have had great latitude under their police powers to legislate as 'to the protection of the lives, limbs, health, comfort, and quiet of all persons.' " This power includes the "broad authority . . . to regulate the employment relationship to protect workers within the State." In such circumstances, minimum employment standards that are not in conflict with the Act survive preemption. Thus, mandated benefit laws, child labor laws, occupational safety and health laws, minimum wage laws, and state severance statutes have all survived NLRA preemption. Similarly, Oregon exercised appropriate power to enact SB 519 to prohibit employers from firing workers who refuse to attend captive audience meetings about their employer's political, religious, or union views.

Third, and finally, in this byzantine area of the law, a need exists to step back and provide a review of the shaky origins of the current preemption doctrine and its development into an incoherent, exception-riddled body of law which fails to point in any single direction. In fact, although *amici* agree with defendants that SB 519 is not preempted under current NLRA doctrine, the Court should also consider taking a rigorous analytical approach to labor preemption doctrine. In this regard, *amici* law professors assert that it is possible to understand labor preemption doctrine in a more coherent manner and come to the same conclusion with regard to the validity of SB 519. Under this sounder approach, once federal labor law is satisfied by permitting the free exchange of ideas on unionization between employers and their employees under Section 8(c), Oregon is then able to go beyond that federal floor and provide additional protections to employees to be free from these employer mandatory indoctrination sessions.

III. *ARGUMENT* . . . .

A. PRECEDENT INTERPRETING THE RIGHTS OF STATES TO CONTINUE TO REGULATE PROPERTY RIGHTS IN THE LABOR RELATIONS CONTEXT SUPPORTS THE CONCLUSION THAT SB 519 IS NOT PREEMPTED BY THE NLRA

The Supreme Court explained its holding in *Lechmere Inc. v. NLRB*, 502 U.S. 527 (1992), involving the relationship between federal labor law and state property regulation, in this manner:

> Without addressing the merits of petitioner's underlying claim, we note that petitioner appears to misconstrue *Lechmere Inc. v. N.L.R.B.* . . . . The right of employers to exclude union organizers from their private property emanates from state common law, and *while this right is not superseded by the NLRA*, nothing in the NLRA expressly protects it. To the contrary, this Court consistently has maintained that the NLRA may entitle union employees to obtain access to an employer's property under limited circumstances.

Thunder Basin Coal Co. v. Reich, 510 U.S. 200, 217 n.21 (1994) (emphasis added). Two critical points can be derived from this passage: (1) The NLRA left most state property rights intact even if they influence the balance of power in a labor dispute or the ability of the two sides to campaign; and (2) these same private property rights are also not protected by the NLRA. The latter point makes clear that *Garmon* preemption, is not implicated in these property rights situations or, put differently, situations where employers seek to use their property as they wish.

The first point above makes clear that *no* form of labor preemption, *Garmon* or *Machinists*, comes into play when states decide to modify the state law rights that were not displaced by the NLRA.

Indeed, the Supreme Court applied this very same principle to the advantage of employers in *Lechmere* where it found that non-employee union organizers generally had no right to access employer property to solicit for union membership. The right to exclude these organizers did not derive from federal labor law, but rather from the state-based property rights of the employers.

Thus, an employer can, consistent with federal labor law, use its state law property rights to its advantage in an organizing campaign, but a state is not barred from altering such rights. It is simply a matter of states, by statute, modifying the bundle of property rights that employers enjoy under state law. While there is a zone of federal prohibition, there is no zone of federal protection of an employer's right to exclude. If states wish to go further in restricting the employer's property rights, no federal interest is implicated. All of this is consistent with the understanding of the NLRB and federal courts that federal labor law operates against the background of state regulation of property rights.

The Oregon legislation in dispute only does precisely what the courts and Board have recognized is within the traditional prerogatives of the states to do in *Lechmere*. State law previously permitted employers to condition employment on their employees being compelled to attend meetings at work unrelated to job performance. SB 519 changes that by not permitting the employer to use its property to coerce employees to attend non-work related meetings. *Lechmere* permits this change in state property law because it stands for the proposition that the NLRA does not supersede the ability of states to regulate common law rights of property. As such, SB 519 was well within Oregon's power to enact.

B. CONSISTENT WITH NOTIONS OF FEDERALISM, OREGON MAY LEGISLATE MINIMUM CONDITIONS IN THE WORKPLACE UNDER ITS POLICE POWERS WHICH ARE NOT PREEMPTED BY THE NLRA

A state can provide for minimum conditions in the workplace under its police powers. Congress could have chosen to completely occupy the field of labor relations law, but it has never exercised its full powers in this regard, leaving the states free to pass many state and local laws and regulations that apply to the workplace. In this regard, the Supreme Court has recognized an exception to *Machinists* preemption where the states "traditionally have had great latitude under their police powers to legislate as 'to the protection of the lives, limbs, health, comfort, and quiet of all persons.' "

This power established in *Metropolitan Life* includes the "broad authority . . . to regulate the employment relationship to protect workers within the State." In such circumstances minimum employment standards that are not in conflict with the Act survive preemption. The Court has used similar language in cases under the Railway Labor Act: "We hold that the enactment by Congress of the Railway Labor Act was not a preemption of the field of regulating working conditions themselves and did not preclude the State . . . from making the order in question."

Thus, mandated benefit laws, child labor laws, occupational safety and health laws, minimum wage laws, and state severance laws have all survived NLRA preemption challenges. Similarly, states should be able to enact laws that prohibit employers from firing workers who refuse to attend captive audience meetings about the employer's political, religious, or union views. In doing so, the Oregon statute would be merely modifying the employment at will rule. It does not muzzle an employer during union election campaigns (as the California statute arguably did in *Chamber of Commerce v. Brown*, 128 S. Ct. 2408 (2008)); the employer can campaign generally against the union, and can continue to hold meetings with employees to discuss the employers views on religion, politics, or unions. The employer just cannot fire or otherwise discipline an employee who declines to attend or leaves such a meeting. In all, this is just another limited erosion of employment at will, similar to the common law's recognition of the tort of wrongful discharge in violation of public policy, or the many statutes which make discrimination against whistleblowers or retaliation unlawful.

Finally, the Oregon captive audience law does not single out meetings concerning unionization. It covers matters of personal conscience and belief: religion, political campaigns, and unionization. All of these concerns can involve highly charged and complex issues of personal preference and trust. Oregon's legislature and Governor have chosen to carve out a narrow exception to employment at will to address the perception that it is unfair to require employees to listen to their employers' views about subjects laden with ideological content. Whether this is a wise law or not is not the question. The question is whether this statute falls within the labor standards exception to *Machinists* preemption. Clearly it does.

Additionally, SB 519 is an example of permissible minimum conditions legislation because it applies to *all workers* in Oregon, union or non-union, and bars employers from disciplining or discharging them for refusing to listen to speech unrelated to their job performance. And like the other minimum conditions laws, this state law does not interfere with existing federal labor law because the NLRA does not protect employer coercive *conduct*. Most importantly, employers in Oregon are still able to communicate their views about unionization with their employees as Section 8(c) contemplates, but just are forbidden from forcing these same employees to listen on pain of losing their jobs or other benefits of employment. The right to speech *does not* include the right to compel someone to listen. Not under the First Amendment and certainly not under statutory law.

C. SB 519 DOES NOT REGULATE CONDUCT ON THE PROTECTED-PROHIBITED CONTINUUM AND THEREFORE, OREGON IS FREE TO PROVIDE ADDITIONAL PROTECTIONS FOR EMPLOYEES AGAINST CO-ERCIVE EMPLOYEE CONDUCT

Although this brief argues that SB 519 clearly survives labor law preemption under current labor preemption doctrine, this section seeks to provide an alternative and sounder doctrinal basis for finding SB 519 not preempted by federal labor law. As discussed above, a pro-preemption preference by the federal courts would be inconsistent with constitutional federalism.

Moreover, and quite simply, the current approach to labor law preemption under *Garmon* and *Machinist* preemption is overbroad. In this regard, a significant and overlooked distinction exists between different types of labor-oriented conduct which states seek to regulate. Specifically, some conduct, like picketing, lies on a "protected-prohibited continuum" which Congress has chosen to regulate in its entirety. Conduct on such a continuum is conduct that the NLRA protects up to a point and prohibits beyond that point. With regard to picketing, either it is protected as concerted activity for mutual aid and protection under Section 7 (because it enhances bargaining power) or it is prohibited conduct under Section 8 (as in the case of secondary picketing, because of its impact on the business of neutral employers). But all in all, Congress has chosen to completely occupy the field of employee picketing under federal labor law and it is for the National Labor Relations Board (NLRB or Board), not the states, to decide where the line exists on this picketing continuum between protected and prohibited conduct. Indeed, it is important that the NLRB make this determination between protected and prohibited picketing in a consistent, uniform matter so future exercise of these rights will not be chilled.

On the other hand, much other union conduct exists that does not lie completely on this protected-prohibited continuum. Conduct outside of this continuum is prohibited in some of its manifestations, but federal law does not protect it otherwise. In these situations, *amici* maintain that states should be free to regulate beyond the point which the federal labor law, and corresponding federal interest, no longer come into play. For instance, Congress and the courts have interpreted the NLRA to permit union access to employer property to address employees during organizational campaigns only when the union is completely unable to communicate with employees through other alternative means or where the employer discriminatorily restricts access to property. Beyond this extremely limited right to access employer property, federal labor law is silent on the ability of the employer to exclude union organizers from their property. *Lechmere* stands for the proposition that an employer's property interest almost always outweighs the competing derivative rights of non-employee, union organizers under Section 7 of the NLRA. But it does not stand to reason that the NLRA thereby confers upon employers a right they had not previously possessed: to be free of state laws concerning private property or minimum employment conditions wherever federal law did not create a right of union access.

Similarly, employer captive audience meetings also constitute conduct not on the "protected-prohibited continuum" and therefore, states are free to regulate it as a property interest or minimum employment condition beyond a certain point. So although federal labor law prohibits captive audience speech twenty-four hours before a representation election, it is silent on the ability of employers to hold such meetings before that time. Seen in this light, SB 519's flat prohibition on employer captive audience meeting on non-work topics is just a means by which Oregon has chosen to modify existing property interests and the doctrine of employment at will. So although Section 8(c) requires the minimum condition of allowing employers to share their views on unionization with their employees, once that point is reached, federal labor law is silent and federal interests are no longer implicated. It is at that point, consistent with notions of federalism, that states should be given the power to ensure that employers can no longer require employees to attend captive audience meetings on non-work issues.

Amici maintain that the federal courts are best able to undertake this needed clarification of labor preemption law because, in the absence of an express preemption provision in the NLRA, the Supreme Court has been the driving force in promulgating current labor preemption doctrine. By recognizing that employer captive audience meeting conduct is not completely on the prohibition-protection continuum, the end result would be a labor preemption doctrine that is more consistent with the purposes of NLRA in ensuring employee free choice and with the principles of federalism.

IV. *CONCLUSION*

For the reasons set forth above, the plaintiffs' motion for summary judgment should be denied.

POST PROBLEM DISCUSSION

1. *Machinist*, or permissive, preemption refers to permissible conduct that is neither prohibited nor protected by the NLRA. In *Machinists*, the union was engaging in partial strike activity by refusing to work overtime, and the state labor board enjoined this activity. The policy of federal labor law was to leave self-help activities available to the parties, subject only to the free play of economic forces. Therefore, the NLRA not only protects some conduct and prohibits other conduct, but it also leaves open a field of economic conflict that Congress intended to keep unregulated. Consequently, state interference with this scheme impermissibly alters the balance of power that occurs under this free play of economic forces and is preempted.

2. Does the opinion in *Chamber of Commerce v. Brown* mean that Worker Freedom Act laws, like the one Oregon passed, are preempted under *Machinists*? Or does the Law Professors' Amicus Brief persuasively argue that the expenditure of state money in *Brown* is sufficiently distinct from laws that prohibit the firing of employees for failing to attend labor-oriented captive audience meetings?

3. In *Golden State Transit Corp. v. City of Los Angeles*, 475 U.S. 608 (1986), the union argued that the city should not grant a franchise to a cab company until a labor dispute between the union and the cab company had been settled. The city subsequently conditioned renewal of franchise on the cab company's settlement of the labor dispute by a certain date. The Court held that city's action in conditioning the cab company's franchise renewal on settlement of the labor dispute was preempted by the NLRA under *Machinists*. More specifically, *Machinists* preemption precluded the city regulation because Congress intended the labor dispute between the parties to be unregulated, and consequently, the city was prohibited from imposing restrictions on either parties' use of economic weapons.

4. In a case concerning whether a Massachusetts mandated health insurance benefit law was preempted by the NLRA, the Court concluded unanimously that it was not. *See Metropolitan Life Insurance Co. v. Massachusetts*, 471 U.S. 724 (1985). The Court reasoned that, although state law required benefits plans to purchase benefits the parties to a collective-bargaining agreement did not wish to purchase, *Machinists* preemption was inapplicable. In this regard, the Court found that the Massachusetts mandated benefit law did not alter the balance of power between parties to a labor contract: "The evil Congress was addressing [in the NLRA] . . . was entirely unrelated to local or federal regulation establishing minimum terms of employment." Can the Worker Freedom Act legislation discussed in Problem #2 be similarly characterized as "minimum employment standards" legislation that is not subject to *Machinists* preemption?

5. Another interesting issue mentioned in *Chamber of Commerce v. Brown* was the question decided in *New York Telephone Co. v. New York State Department of Labor*, 440 U.S. 519 (1979): whether the NLRA prohibits states from paying unemployment compensation to strikers? New York law permits striking employees to collect unemployment benefits. In a highly fractured set of opinions, the Court ultimately concluded that the New York unemployment compensation scheme was not preempted by the NLRA. Although the provision of unemployment compensation to strikers altered the economic balance between labor and management, the

plurality opinion written by Justice Stevens found that Congress had the ability to prevent states from making this choice of providing unemployment compensation to strikers, but chose not to do so in enacting both the Wagner Act and the Social Security Act in 1935.

6. *Machinists* preemption has also been invoked where permanent replacements lose their jobs after companies reach a strike settlement agreement with the union that returns all striking employees to their previous jobs. In such circumstances, permanent replacements have brought state misrepresentation and breach of contract claims against the companies. In *Belknap, Inc. v. Hale*, 463 U.S. 491 (1983), the Supreme Court held that the permanent replacement's state law claims were not preempted under *Machinists*. More specifically, the Court concluded that allowing the contract claims would not impermissibly burden the employer's economic weapon of hiring permanent replacement workers during an economic strike. The Court observed in this regard: "It is one thing to hold that the federal law intended to leave the employer and the union free to use their economic weapons against one another, but it is quite another to hold that either the employer or union is also free to injure innocent third parties without regard to the normal rules of law governing those relationships."

SECTION 3   SECTION 301 PREEMPTION

The third, and final, preemption doctrine is Section 301 preemption. Section 301 of the Labor Management Relations Act (Taft-Hartley Act), provides a federal right of action for enforcement of collective-bargaining agreements. More specifically, Section 301 allows either an employer or union to sue or be sued in federal court based on an alleged breach of a provision in a collective-bargaining agreement. To promote uniformity in the interpretation of collective-bargaining agreements, federal common law governs in Section 301 cases. *See Textile Workers Union v. Lincoln Mills of Alabama*, 353 U.S. 448 (1957) (finding that Section 301 not only confers subject matter jurisdiction on the federal courts, but also directs the district courts to develop a federal common law of labor agreements).

Consequently, where a claim brought under state law requires an interpretation of a collective-bargaining agreement, Section 301 preemption requires that the state claim be preempted by federal common law. *See Allis-Chalmers Corp. v. Lueck*, 471 U.S. 202 (1985) (finding that Section 301 preempts a state-law tort action for bad-faith delay in making disability-benefit payments due under a collective-bargaining agreement because the state law claim is "inextricably intertwined" with consideration of the terms of the labor contract). Section 301 preemption is a type of complete preemption and operates even if there is not a federal question on the face of the complaint. *See Avco Corp. v. Machinists*, 390 U.S. 557 (1968). This area of labor law is so completely occupied by federal labor law that state-law contract claims will be read as if the plaintiff meant to file a Section 301 claim. *See Metropolitan Life Insurance Co. v. Taylor*, 481 U.S. 58, 63–64 (1987) ("One corollary of the well-pleaded complaint rule developed in the case law . . . is that Congress may so completely pre-empt a particular area that any civil complaint raising this select group of claims is necessarily federal in character. For 20 years, this Court has singled out claims pre-empted by § 301 of the LMRA for such special treatment.").

A more recent example of the Section 301 preemption analysis can be found in the Supreme Court case of *Lingle v. Norge Division of Magic Chef, Inc.*, 486 U.S. 399 (1988). There, the Court considered whether an employee covered by a collective-bargaining agreement that provided her with a contractual remedy for discharge may instead enforce her state law remedy for retaliatory discharge under the Illinois worker's compensation law. The Court concluded that such a state tort remedy was not preempted by Section 301. Although the state law analysis of the employee's retaliatory discharge claim might lead to examination of some of the same issues that come up when interpreting collective-bargaining agreements, "Section 301 pre-emption merely ensures that federal law will be the basis for interpreting collective-bargaining agreements, and says nothing about the substantive rights a State may provide to workers when adjudication of those rights does not depend upon the interpretation of such agreements." Because the state law claim in *Lingle* could be resolved without interpreting the agreement itself, and particularly without interpreting the "just cause" provision of the contract, the state claim was considered independent of the collective-bargaining agreement, and Section 301 preemption was found not to apply.

Chapter 12

WORKER RIGHTS IN A UNION

Synopsis

Section 1   The Duty of Fair Representation

Section 2   Union Security Clauses and State Right-To-Work Laws

Section 3   The Union's Right to Discipline its Members

Although the "practice and philosophy of collective bargaining looks with suspicion on . . . individual advantages," there are still protections for individual union members. As will be discussed in Section 1, the duty of fair representation (DFR), a judge-made doctrine not found specifically in the NLRA, provides some protection for employees against the power of their unions.

On the other side of the ledger, unions have the ability to collect union dues from their members and to discipline them when they engage in certain prohibited conduct. That being said, the NLRA permits states, as a result of the Taft-Hartley Amendments, to pass right-to-work (RTW) legislation which forbids unions from collecting any dues from objecting workers. These right-to-work laws are an express exception to the labor preemption doctrines that normally would prohibit such a law. As will be discussed below, some 23 states are RTW states, with Indiana becoming the most recent addition in 2012. RTW states tend to have low union density rates for at least two probable reasons: 1) RTW laws are more likely to pass in states that have a weak labor movement that is unable to muster the necessary political opposition, and 2) it is difficult for unions to organize and collectively bargaining where dissenting employees are permitted to receive union benefits without paying for them (i.e., "free ride").

Union dues and right-to-work provisions are the subject of Section 2. Section 3 concludes this chapter by considering the circumstances under which a union may permissibly discipline its members within the parameters of the NLRA.

SECTION 1   THE DUTY OF FAIR REPRESENTATION

It is inevitable that the interests of individual employees and small groups of employees must be subordinated to the whole under the exclusive representation principle in Section 9(a) of the NLRA (see Chapter 7). The question is: do these employees have any recourse when their interests conflict with the interests of the union majority? There are a number of ways by which an individual employee or minority group of employees could show displeasure with a union.

First, employees can always vote against a union during a representation campaign, but as we saw in Chapters 6 and 7, once the union is elected it becomes the exclusive representative of all employees, whether or not they voted for the union. After the various election, certification, and contract bars expire, dissatisfied employees could lead a campaign to decertify the union by filing a petition for a decertification election under Section 9(c) of the Act.

Second, even when the union becomes the certified representative of the bargaining unit, there are still Section 8(b) unfair labor practices that an individual employee may bring. For instance, if a union induced an employer to discipline or discharge an employee because he or she was not a member of the union, such union conduct would violate Section 8(b)(2). Indeed, if an individual suffers union-induced discipline separate and apart from membership issues, a Section 8(b)(1)(A) and a Section 8(b)(2) ULP still may be brought against the union. *See NLRB v. Miranda Fuel Co.*, 140 N.L.R.B. 181 (1962). However, history has shown that these types of ULPs have only been marginally effective in vindicating dissenting employees' rights under the NLRA.

Third, the Labor Management Disclosure and Reporting Act (the LMRDA or Landrum-Griffin Act of 1959), 29 U.S.C. §§ 401 et seq., provides some additional protections to individual employees through the development of a code for internal union affairs. The LMRDA focused on ensuring democratic processes within the union structure so that union members can, among other things, nominate their preferred candidates, run for office, and vote freely in union elections.

Yet, among all of individual employees' potential rights against their union, perhaps the most effective one is the duty of fair representation (DFR). If the union acts in an unfair, arbitrary, or discriminatory manner against an individual union employee in either the bargaining or grievance processing context, that employee may be able to bring a breach of the duty of fair representation claim against their union. This duty of fair representation was initially inferred in the RLA case of *Steele v. Louisville & N.R. Co.*, 323 U.S. 192 (1944) (discussed in Chapter 6).

In *Steele*, the Brotherhood of Locomotive Firemen and Engineers Union did not permit black employees to be members of the Union even though the Union exclusively represented all firemen and engineers working for the railroad. Indeed, the Union and 21 railroads entered into a collective-bargaining agreement whose purpose was to systematically eliminate all black employees in favor of white employees in the relevant railroad positions. Black employees had no notice of these provisions and did not participate in contract negotiations between the Union and the railroads.

Initially, the Supreme Court of Alabama found that the Union had no duty to protect the rights of minorities from discrimination or unfair treatment. The United States Supreme Court reversed, finding that the RLA imposes a duty on unions to fairly exercise their power to exclusive representation. In other words, the union cannot treat a certain group arbitrarily, in bad faith, or with hostile discrimination.

If there is a breach of the duty of fair representation, a court may award injunctions and monetary remedies where appropriate. Although *Steele* is an RLA case, this same duty of fair representation now also applies in the NLRA context. In *Ford Motor Co. v. Huffman*, 345 U.S. 330 (1953), the company provided additional seniority credits to members of the military. The Court held that the company's actions were lawful and did not breach any duty of fair representation because the seniority credits were allocated in good faith and served the legitimate purpose of giving employees seniority credit for military service.

DFR actions may be brought as unfair labor practices to the Board under Sections 8(b)(1)(A) or 8(b)(2). Additionally, such claims may be brought in federal court under a Section 301 action when grievants either lose their arbitration cases or the union refuses to bring the employee's grievance in the first place. Section 301, added by the Taft-Hartley Amendments in 1947, allows both employers and unions to sue or be sued for breaches of the collective bargaining contract. In a so-called "hybrid Section 301" action, the individual sues the union and the employer simultaneously: the union for breach of the duty of fair representation and the employer for breach of the collective-bargaining agreement. These types of claims are exceedingly difficult for individuals to win because they must prove and win both parts of the case. Moreover, it is often hard for individual employees to find attorneys willing to bring these types of claims because most labor attorneys have their allegiances either to management or to the unions. However, if an individual is successful in one of these federal court Section 301 claims, both compensatory and injunctive relief may be had, although not punitive damages.

DFR claims can be viewed as a necessity to protect dissenting individuals in a labor relations system that is based on principles of majoritarianism and exclusive representation. Indeed, DFR claims are one of the ways to mitigate individuals' loss of bargaining power under this scheme. As the following materials establish, the scope of the duty of fair representation changes depending upon in which role the union acts. Unions tend to have more latitude when bargaining a contract than when they are processing grievances under a contract.

PROBLEM #1: THE TALE OF THE DECEITFUL MOTEL CLERK[1]

A group of truck drivers were discharged for just cause by Sailor Motor Freight, Inc. (Sailor). Sailor claimed that the truck drivers falsified their expense reports after staying at a motel. The truck driver's union claimed the drivers were innocent and opposed the discharges, but the union did not present any evidence contradicting the company's documents that showed that the employees had submitted inflated expense reimbursement requests. The employees lost the arbitration.

Subsequently, the truck drivers retained their own attorney and sought rehearing based on information suggesting that the motel clerk recorded less than what was actually paid and kept the difference for himself. The arbitrator denied rehearing.

It later came to light that the motel clerk had lied and in fact pocketed the money as alleged by the truck drivers. The trucker drivers then filed a section 301 hybrid DFR claim against Sailor and the union. The truck drivers contended that the false charges brought against them could have been discovered with a minimum of investigation and argued that, because the union had not made that

---

[1] The facts of Problem #1 are taken directly from *Hines v. Anchor Motor Freight*, 424 U.S. 554 (1976).

minimal effort, it had violated its duty of fair representation.

1. Should the decision of the arbitrator against the employees still be found final and binding in light of these new facts?

2. Does it matter whether the union met professional standards of competency in not more fully investigating the charges against the truck drivers? Don't the facts just demonstrate at most bad judgment on the part of the union? If the union breached its duty, does that mean that the employer also breached the collective-bargaining agreement?

3. How would your answer change if these events had occurred while the employees were seeking to get the union to push for a more employee-protective expense reimbursement standard in the collective-bargaining agreement?

4. If the union breached the duty of fair representation and the employer breached the collective-bargaining agreement, how should damages between the union and the employer be apportioned?

PROBLEM MATERIALS

Vaca v. Sipes, 386 U.S. 171 (1967)

Air Line Pilots Association International v. O'Neill, 499 U.S. 65 (1991)

VACA v. SIPES
386 U.S. 171 (1967)

MR. JUSTICE WHITE delivered the opinion of the Court.

On February 13, 1962, Benjamin Owens filed this class action against petitioners, as officers and representatives of the National Brotherhood of Packinghouse Workers and of its Kansas City Local No. 12 (the Union), in the Circuit Court of Jackson County, Missouri. Owens, a Union member, alleged that he had been discharged from his employment at Swift & Company's (Swift) Kansas City Meat Packing Plant in violation of the collective bargaining agreement then in force between Swift and the Union, and that the Union had "arbitrarily, capriciously and without just or reasonable reason or cause" refused to take his grievance with Swift to arbitration under the fifth step of the bargaining agreement's grievance procedures . . . .

Although we conclude that state courts have jurisdiction in this type of case, we hold that federal law governs, that the governing federal standards were not applied here, and that the judgment of the Supreme Court of Missouri must accordingly be reversed.

I.

In mid-1959, Owens, a long-time high blood pressure patient, became sick and entered a hospital on sick leave from his employment with Swift. After a long rest during which his weight and blood pressure were reduced, Owens was certified by his family physician as fit to resume his heavy work in the packing plant. However, Swift's company doctor examined Owens upon his return and concluded that his blood pressure was too high to permit reinstatement. After securing a second authorization from another outside doctor, Owens returned to the plant, and a nurses permitted him to resume work on January 6, 1960. However, on January 8, when the doctor discovered Owens' return, he was permanently discharged on the ground of poor health.

Armed with his medical evidence of fitness, Owens then sought the Union's help in securing reinstatement, and a grievance was filed with Swift on his behalf. By mid-November 1960, the grievance had been processed through the third and into the fourth step of the grievance procedure established by the collective bargaining agreement. Swift adhered to its position that Owens' poor health justified his discharge, rejecting numerous medical reports of reduced blood pressure proffered by Owens and by the Union. Swift claimed that these reports were not based upon sufficiently thorough medical tests.

On February 6, 1961, the Union sent Owens to a new doctor at Union expense "to see if we could get some better medical evidence so that we could go to arbitration with his case." This examination did not support Owens' position. When the Union received the report, its executive board voted not to take the Owens grievance to arbitration because of insufficient medical evidence. Union officers suggested to Owens that he accept Swift's offer of referral to a rehabilitation center, and the grievance was suspended for that purpose. Owens rejected this alternative and demanded that the Union take his grievance to arbitration, but the Union refused. With his contractual remedies thus stalled at the fourth step, Owens brought this suit . . . .

II.

Petitioners challenge the jurisdiction of the Missouri courts on the ground that the alleged conduct of the Union was arguably an unfair labor practice and within the exclusive jurisdiction of the NLRB . . . . [W]e reject this argument.

It is now well established that, as the exclusive bargaining representative of the employees in Owens' bargaining unit, the Union had a statutory duty fairly to represent all of those employees, both in its collective bargaining with Swift, and in its enforcement of the resulting collective bargaining agreement. The statutory duty of fair representation was developed over 20 years ago in a series of cases involving alleged racial discrimination by unions certified as exclusive bargaining representatives under the Railway Labor Act, and was soon extended to unions certified under the N.L.R.A. Under this doctrine, the exclusive agent's statutory authority to represent all members of a designated unit includes a statutory obligation to serve the interests of all members without hostility or discrimination toward any, to exercise its discretion with complete good faith and honesty, and to avoid arbitrary conduct. It is obvious that Owens' complaint alleged a breach by the Union of a duty grounded in federal statutes, and that federal law therefore governs his cause of action . . . .

[W]e think the wrongfully discharged employee may bring an action against his employer in the face of a defense based upon the failure to exhaust contractual remedies, provided the employee can prove that the union as bargaining agent breached its duty of fair representation in its handling of the employee's grievance. We may assume for present purposes that such a breach of duty by the union is an unfair labor practice, as the NLRB and the Fifth Circuit have held. The employee's suit against the employer, however, remains a [section] 301 suit, and the jurisdiction of the courts is no more destroyed by the fact that the employee, as part and parcel of his [section] 301 action, finds it necessary to prove an unfair labor practice by the union, than it is by the fact that the suit may involve an unfair labor practice by the employer himself. The court is free to determine whether the employee is barred by the actions of his union representative, and, if not, to proceed with the case. And if, to facilitate his case, the employee joins the union as a defendant, the situation is not substantially changed . . . .

[I]t is obvious that the courts will be compelled to pass upon whether there has been a breach of the duty of fair representation in the context of many [section] 301 breach-of-contract actions. If a breach of duty by the union and a breach of contract by the employer are proven, the court must fashion an appropriate remedy. Presumably, in at least some cases, the union's breach of duty will have enhanced or contributed to the employee's injury. What possible sense could there be in a rule which would permit a court that has litigated the fault of employer and union to fashion a remedy only with respect to the employer? Under such a rule, either the employer would be compelled by the court to pay for the union's wrong-slight deterrence, indeed, to future union misconduct-or the injured employee would be forced to go to two tribunals to repair a single injury. Moreover, the Board would be compelled in many cases either to remedy injuries arising out of a breach of contract, a task which Congress has not assigned to it, or to leave the individual employee without remedy for the union's wrong . . . . [W]e [therefore] conclude that the courts may also fashion remedies for such a breach of duty . . . .

III.

Petitioners contend . . . that Owens failed to prove that the Union breached its duty of fair representation in its handling of Owens' grievance. Petitioners also argue that the Supreme Court of Missouri, in rejecting this contention, applied a standard that is inconsistent with governing principles of federal law with respect to the Union's duty to an individual employee in its processing of grievances under the collective bargaining agreement with Swift. We agree with both contentions.

A.

. . . A breach of the statutory duty of fair representation occurs only when a union's conduct toward a member of the collective bargaining unit is arbitrary, discriminatory, or in bad faith. There has been considerable debate over the extent of this duty in the context of a union's enforcement of the grievance and arbitration procedures in a collective bargaining agreement. Some have suggested that every individual employee should have the right to have his grievance taken to arbitration. Others have urged that the union be given substantial discretion (if the collective bargaining agreement so provides) to decide whether a grievance should be taken to arbitration, subject only to the duty to refrain from patently wrongful conduct such as racial discrimination or personal hostility.

Though we accept the proposition that a union may not arbitrarily ignore a meritorious grievance or process it in perfunctory fashion, we do not agree that the individual employee has an absolute right to have his grievance taken to arbitration regardless of the provisions of the applicable collective bargaining agreement. In L.M.R.A. § 203(d), Congress declared that "Final adjustment by a method agreed upon by the parties is . . . the desirable method for settlement of grievance disputes arising over the application or interpretation of an existing collective-bargaining agreement." In providing for a grievance and arbitration procedure which gives the union discretion to supervise the grievance machinery and to invoke arbitration, the employer and the union contemplate that each will endeavor in good faith to settle grievances short of arbitration. Through this settlement process, frivolous grievances are ended prior to the most costly and time-consuming step in the grievance procedures. Moreover, both sides are assured that similar complaints will be treated consistently, and major problem areas in the interpretation of the collective bargaining contract can be isolated and perhaps resolved. And finally, the settlement process furthers the interest of the union as statutory agent and as coauthor of the bargaining agreement in representing the employees in the enforcement of that agreement.

If the individual employee could compel arbitration of his grievance regardless of its merit, the settlement machinery provided by the contract would be substantially undermined, thus destroying the employer's confidence in the union's authority and returning the individual grievant to the vagaries of independent and unsystematic negotiation. Moreover, under such a rule, a significantly greater number of grievances would proceed to arbitration. This would greatly increase the cost of the grievance machinery and could so overburden the arbitration process as to prevent it from functioning successfully. It can well be doubted whether the parties to collective bargaining agreements would long continue to provide for detailed grievance and arbitration procedures of the kind encouraged by L.M.R.A. § 203(d), if their power to settle the majority of grievances short of the costlier and more time-consuming steps was limited by a rule permitting the grievant unilaterally to invoke arbitration. Nor do we see substantial danger to the interests of the individual employee if his statutory agent is given the contractual power honestly and in good faith to settle grievances short of arbitration. For these reasons, we conclude that a union does not breach its duty of fair representation, and thereby open up a suit by the employee for breach of contract, merely because it settled the grievance short of arbitration . . . .

B.

Applying the proper standard of union liability to the facts of this case, we cannot uphold the jury's award, for we conclude that as a matter of federal law the evidence does not support a verdict that the Union breached its duty of fair representation. As we have stated, Owens could not have established a breach of that duty merely by convincing the jury that he was in fact fit for work in 1960; he must also have proved arbitrary or bad-faith conduct on the part of the Union in processing his grievance. The evidence revealed that the Union diligently supervised the grievance into the fourth step of the bargaining agreement's procedure, with the Union's business representative serving as Owens' advocate throughout these steps. When Swift refused to reinstate Owens on the basis of his medical reports indicating reduced blood pressure, the Union sent him to another doctor of his own choice, at Union expense, in an attempt to amass persuasive medical evidence of Owens' fitness for work. When this examination proved unfavorable, the Union concluded that it could not establish a wrongful discharge. It then encouraged Swift to find light work for Owens at the plant. When this effort failed, the Union determined that arbitration would be fruitless and suggested to Owens that he accept Swift's offer to send him to a heart association for rehabilitation. At this point, Owens' grievance was suspended in the fourth step in the hope that he might be rehabilitated.

In administering the grievance and arbitration machinery as statutory agent of the employees, a union must, in good faith and in a nonarbitrary manner, make decisions as to the merits of particular grievances. In a case such as this, when Owens supplied the Union with medical evidence supporting his position, the Union might well have breached its duty had it ignored Owens' complaint or had it processed the grievance in a perfunctory manner. But here the Union processed the grievance into the fourth step, attempted to gather sufficient evidence to prove Owens' case, attempted to secure for Owens less vigorous work at the plant, and joined in the employer's efforts to have Owens rehabilitated. Only when these efforts all proved unsuccessful did the Union conclude both that arbitration would be fruitless and that the grievance should be dismissed. There was no evidence that any Union officer was personally hostile to Owens or that the Union acted at any time other than in good faith. Having concluded that the individual employee has no absolute right to have his grievance arbitrated under the collective bargaining agreement at issue, and that a breach of the duty of fair representation is not established merely by proof that the underlying grievance was meritorious, we must conclude that that duty was not breached here.

IV.

. . . The appropriate remedy for a breach of a union's duty of fair representation must vary with the circumstances of the particular breach. In this case, the employee's complaint was that the Union wrongfully failed to afford him the arbitration remedy against his employer established by the collective bargaining agreement. But the damages sought by Owens were primarily those suffered because of the employer's alleged breach of contract. Assuming for the moment that Owens had been wrongfully discharged, Swift's only defense to a direct action for breach of contract would have been the Union's failure to resort to arbitration, and if that failure was itself a violation of the Union's statutory duty to the employee, there is no reason to exempt the employer from contractual damages which he would otherwise have had to pay. The difficulty lies in fashioning an appropriate scheme of remedies.

Petitioners urge that an employee be restricted in such circumstances to a decree compelling the employer and the union to arbitrate the underlying grievance. It is true that the employee's action is based on the employer's alleged breach of contract plus the union's alleged wrongful failure to afford him his contractual remedy of arbitration. For this reason, an order compelling arbitration should be viewed as one of the available remedies when a breach of the union's duty is proved. But we see no reason inflexibly to require arbitration in all cases. In some cases, for example, at least part of the employee's damages may be attributable to the union's breach of duty, and an arbitrator may have no power under the bargaining agreement to award such damages against the union. In other cases, the arbitrable issues may be substantially resolved in the course of trying the fair representation controversy. In such situations, the court should be free to decide the contractual claim and to award the employee appropriate damages or equitable relief.

A more difficult question is, what portion of the employee's damages may be charged to the union: in particular, may an award against a union include, as it did here, damages attributable solely to the employer's breach of contract? We think not. Though the union has violated a statutory duty in failing to press the grievance, it is the employer's unrelated breach of contract which triggered the controversy and which caused this portion of the employee's damages. The employee should have no difficulty recovering these damages from the employer, who cannot, as we have explained, hide behind the union's wrongful failure to act; in fact, the employer may be (and probably should be) joined as a defendant in the fair representation suit. It could be a real hardship on the union to pay these damages, even if the union were given a right of indemnification against the employer. With the employee assured of direct recovery from the employer, we see no merit in requiring the union to pay the employer's share of the damages.

The governing principle, then, is to apportion liability between the employer and the union according to the damage caused by the fault of each. Thus, damages attributable solely to the employer's breach of contract should not be charged to the union, but increases if any in those damages caused by the union's refusal to process the grievance should not be charged to the employer. In this case, even if the Union had breached its duty, all or almost all of Owens' damages would still be attributable to his allegedly wrongful discharge by Swift. For these reasons, even if the Union here had properly been found liable for a breach of duty, it is clear that the damage award was improper.

Reversed.

Mr. Justice Fortas, with whom The Chief Justice and Mr. Justice Harlan join, concurring in the result [opinion omitted].

AIR LINE PILOTS ASSOCIATION INTERNATIONAL v. O'NEILL
499 U.S. 65 (1991)

Justice Stevens delivered the opinion of the Court.

We granted certiorari to clarify the standard that governs a claim that a union has breached its duty of fair representation in its negotiation of a back-to-work agreement terminating a strike. We hold that the rule announced in *Vaca v. Sipes*, 386 U.S. 171 (1967) — that a union breaches its duty of fair representation if its actions are either "arbitrary, discriminatory, or in bad faith" — applies to all union activity, including contract negotiation. We further hold that a union's actions are arbitrary only if, in light of the factual and legal landscape at the time of the union's actions, the union's behavior is so far outside a "wide range of reasonableness," as to be irrational.

I

This case arose out of a bitter confrontation between Continental Airlines, Inc. (Continental), and the union representing its pilots, the Air Line Pilots Association, International (ALPA). On September 24, 1983, Continental filed a petition for reorganization under Chapter 11 of the Bankruptcy Code. Immediately thereafter, with the approval of the Bankruptcy Court, Continental repudiated its collective-bargaining agreement with ALPA and unilaterally reduced its pilots' salaries and benefits by more than half. ALPA responded by calling a strike that lasted for over two years.

Of the approximately 2,000 pilots employed by Continental, all but about 200 supported the strike. By the time the strike ended, about 400 strikers had "crossed over" and been accepted for reemployment in order of reapplication. By trimming its operations and hiring about 1,000 replacements, Continental was able to continue in business. By August 1985, there were 1,600 working pilots and only 1,000 strikers.

The strike was acrimonious, punctuated by incidents of violence and the filing of a variety of lawsuits, charges, and countercharges. In August 1985, Continental notified ALPA that it was withdrawing recognition of ALPA as the collective-bargaining agent for its pilots. ALPA responded with a federal lawsuit alleging that Continental was unlawfully refusing to continue negotiations for a new collective-bargaining agreement. In this adversary context, on September 9, 1985, Continental posted its "Supplementary Base Vacancy Bid 1985–5" (85–5 bid) — an act that precipitated not only an end to the strike, but also the litigation that is now before us.

For many years Continental had used a "system bid" procedure for assigning pilots to new positions. Bids were typically posted well in advance in order to allow time for necessary training without interfering with current service. When a group of vacancies was posted, any pilot could submit a bid specifying his or her preferred position (captain, first officer, or second officer), base of operations, and aircraft type. In the past, vacant positions had been awarded on the basis of seniority, determined by the date the pilot first flew for Continental. The 85–5 bid covered an unusually large number of anticipated vacancies — 441 future captain and first officer positions and an undetermined number of second officer vacancies. Pilots were given nine days — until September 18, 1985 — to submit their bids.

Fearing that this bid might effectively lock the striking pilots out of jobs for the indefinite future, ALPA authorized the strikers to submit bids. Several hundred did so, as did several hundred working pilots. Although Continental initially accepted bids from both groups, it soon became concerned about the bona fides of the striking pilots' offers to return to work at a future date. It therefore challenged the strikers' bids in court and announced that all of the 85–5 bid positions had been awarded to working pilots.

At this juncture, ALPA intensified its negotiations for a complete settlement. ALPA's negotiating committee and Continental reached an agreement, which was entered as an order by the Bankruptcy Court on October 31, 1985. The agreement provided for an end to the strike, the disposition of all pending litigation, and reallocation of the positions covered by the 85–5 bid.

The agreement offered the striking pilots three options. Under the first, pilots who settled all outstanding claims with Continental were eligible to participate in the allocation of the 85–5 bid positions. Under the second option, pilots who elected not to return to work received severance pay of $4,000 per year of service (or $2,000 if they had been furloughed before the strike began). Under the third option, striking pilots retained their individual claims against Continental and were eligible to return to work only after all the first option pilots had been reinstated.

Pilots who chose the first option were thus entitled to some of the 85–5 bid positions that, according to Continental, had previously been awarded to working pilots. The first 100 captain positions were allocated to working pilots and the next 70 captain positions were awarded, in order of seniority, to returning strikers who chose option one. Thereafter, striking and nonstriking pilots were eligible for captain positions on a 1-to-1 ratio. The initial base and aircraft type for a returning striker was assigned by Continental, but the assignments for working pilots were determined by their bids. After the initial assignment, future changes in bases and equipment were determined by seniority, and striking pilots who were in active service when the strike began received seniority credit for the period of the strike.

II

Several months after the settlement, respondents, as representatives of a class of former striking pilots, brought this action against ALPA. In addition to raising other charges not before us, respondents alleged that the union had breached its duty of fair representation in negotiating and accepting the settlement. After extensive discovery, ALPA filed a motion for summary judgment. Opposing that motion, respondents identified four alleged breaches of duty, including the claim that "ALPA negotiated an agreement that arbitrarily discriminated against striking pilots." . . .

III

ALPA's central argument is that the duty of fair representation requires only that a union act in good faith and treat its members equally and in a nondiscriminatory fashion. The duty, the union argues, does not impose any obligation to provide *adequate* representation. The District Court found that there was no evidence that ALPA acted other than in good faith and without discrimination. Because of its view of the limited scope of the duty, ALPA contends that the District

Court's finding, which the Court of Appeals did not question, is sufficient to support summary judgment.

The union maintains, not without some merit, that its view that courts are not authorized to review the rationality of good-faith, nondiscriminatory union decisions is consonant with federal labor policy. The Government has generally regulated only "the *process* of collective bargaining," but relied on private negotiation between the parties to establish "their own charter for the ordering of industrial relations." As we stated in *NLRB v. Insurance Agents*, 361 U.S. 477 (1960), Congress "intended that the parties should have wide latitude in their negotiations, unrestricted by any governmental power to regulate the substantive solution of their differences."

There is, however, a critical difference between governmental modification of the terms of a private agreement and an examination of those terms in search for evidence that a union did not fairly and adequately represent its constituency. Our decisions have long recognized that the need for such an examination proceeds directly from the union's statutory role as exclusive bargaining agent. "[T]he exercise of a granted power to act in behalf of others involves the assumption toward them of a duty to exercise the power in their interest and behalf."

The duty of fair representation is thus akin to the duty owed by other fiduciaries to their beneficiaries. For example, some Members of the Court have analogized the duty a union owes to the employees it represents to the duty a trustee owes to trust beneficiaries. Others have likened the relationship between union and employee to that between attorney and client. The fair representation duty also parallels the responsibilities of corporate officers and directors toward shareholders. Just as these fiduciaries owe their beneficiaries a duty of care as well as a duty of loyalty, a union owes employees a duty to represent them adequately as well as honestly and in good faith.

ALPA suggests that a union need owe no enforceable duty of adequate representation because employees are protected from inadequate representation by the union political process. ALPA argues . . . that employees "do not need . . . protection against representation that is inept but not invidious" because if a "union does an incompetent job . . . its members can vote in new officers who will do a better job or they can vote in another union." In *Steele*, the case in which we first recognized the duty of fair representation, we also analogized a union's role to that of a legislature. Even legislatures, however, are subject to *some* judicial review of the rationality of their actions.

ALPA relies heavily on language in *Ford Motor Co. v. Huffman*, 345 U.S. 330 (1953), which, according to the union, suggests that no review of the substantive terms of a settlement between labor and management is permissible. In particular, ALPA stresses our comment in the case that "[a] wide range of reasonableness must be allowed a statutory bargaining representative in serving the unit it represents, subject always to complete good faith and honesty of purpose in the exercise of its discretion." Unlike ALPA, we do not read this passage to limit review of a union's actions to "good faith and honesty of purpose," but rather to recognize that a union's conduct must also be within "[a] wide range of reasonableness."

Although there is admittedly some variation in the way in which our opinions have described the unions' duty of fair representation, we have repeatedly identified three components of the duty, including a prohibition against "arbitrary" conduct. Writing for the Court in the leading case in this area of the law, Justice WHITE explained:

> "The statutory duty of fair representation was developed over 20 years ago in a series of cases involving alleged racial discrimination by unions certified as exclusive bargaining representatives under the Railway Labor Act, and was soon extended to unions certified under the N.L.R.A. Under this doctrine, the exclusive agent's statutory authority to represent all members of a designated unit includes a statutory obligation to serve the interests of all members without hostility or discrimination toward any, to exercise its discretion with complete good faith and honesty, and to avoid arbitrary conduct. It is obvious that Owens' complaint alleged a breach by the Union of a duty grounded in federal statutes, and that federal law therefore governs his cause of action." *Vaca v. Sipes*, 386 U.S. at 177.

This description of the "duty grounded in federal statutes" has been accepted without question by Congress and in a line of our decisions spanning almost a quarter of a century.

The union correctly points out, however, that virtually all of those cases can be distinguished because they involved contract administration or enforcement rather than contract negotiation. ALPA argues that the policy against substantive review of contract terms applies directly only in the negotiation area. Although this is a possible basis for distinction, none of our opinions has suggested that the duty is governed by a double standard. Indeed, we have repeatedly noted that the *Vaca v. Sipes* standard applies to "challenges leveled not only at a union's contract administration and enforcement efforts but at its negotiation activities as well." We have also held that the duty applies in other instances in which a union is acting in its representative role, such as when the union operates a hiring hall.

We doubt, moreover, that a bright line could be drawn between contract administration and contract negotiation. Industrial grievances may precipitate settlement negotiations leading to contract amendments, and some strikes and strike settlement agreements may focus entirely on questions of contract interpretation. Finally, some union activities subject to the duty of fair representation fall into neither category.

We are, therefore, satisfied that the Court of Appeals correctly concluded that the tripartite standard announced in *Vaca v. Sipes* applies to a union in its negotiating capacity . . . .

As we acknowledged above, Congress did not intend judicial review of a union's performance to permit the court to substitute its own view of the proper bargain for that reached by the union. Rather, Congress envisioned the relationship between the courts and labor unions as similar to that between the courts and the legislature. Any substantive examination of a union's performance, therefore, must be highly deferential, recognizing the wide latitude that negotiators need for the effective performance of their bargaining responsibilities. For that reason, the final product of the bargaining process may constitute evidence of a breach of duty only if it can be fairly characterized as so far outside a "wide range of reasonableness," that it is wholly "irrational" or "arbitrary." . . .

IV

The Court of Appeals placed great stress on the fact that the deal struck by ALPA was worse than the result the union would have obtained by unilateral termination of the strike. Indeed, the court held that a jury finding that the settlement was worse than surrender could alone support a judgment that the union had acted arbitrarily and irrationally. This holding unduly constrains the "wide range of reasonableness," within which unions may act without breaching their fair representation duty.

For purposes of decision, we may assume that the Court of Appeals was correct in its conclusion that, if ALPA had simply surrendered and voluntarily terminated the strike, the striking pilots would have been entitled to reemployment in the order of seniority. Moreover, we may assume that Continental would have responded to such action by rescinding its assignment of all of the 85–5 bid positions to working pilots. After all, it did rescind about half of those assignments pursuant to the terms of the settlement. Thus, we assume that the union made a bad settlement — one that was even worse than a unilateral termination of the strike.

Nevertheless, the settlement was by no means irrational. A settlement is not irrational simply because it turns out *in retrospect* to have been a bad settlement. Viewed in light of the legal landscape at the time of the settlement, ALPA's decision to settle rather than give up was certainly not illogical. At the time of the settlement, Continental had notified the union that all of the 85–5 bid positions had been awarded to working pilots and was maintaining that none of the strikers had any claim on any of those jobs . . . .

Given the background of determined resistance by Continental at all stages of this strike, it would certainly have been rational for ALPA to recognize the possibility that an attempted voluntary return to work would merely precipitate litigation over the right to the 85–5 bid positions. Because such a return would not have disposed of any of the individual claims of the pilots who ultimately elected option one or option two of the settlement, there was certainly a realistic possibility that Continental would not abandon its bargaining position without a complete settlement.

At the very least, the settlement produced certain and prompt access to a share of the new jobs and avoided the costs and risks associated with major litigation. Moreover, since almost a third of the striking pilots chose the lump-sum severance payment rather than reinstatement, the settlement was presumably more advantageous than a surrender to a significant number of striking pilots. In labor disputes, as in other kinds of litigation, even a bad settlement may be more advantageous in the long run than a good lawsuit. In all events, the resolution of the dispute over the 85–5 bid vacancies was well within the "wide range of reasonableness," that a union is allowed in its bargaining.

The suggestion that the "discrimination" between striking and working pilots represented a breach of the duty of fair representation also fails. If we are correct in our conclusion that it was rational for ALPA to accept a compromise between the claims of the two groups of pilots to the 85–5 bid positions, some form of allocation was inevitable. A rational compromise on the initial allocation of the positions was not invidious "discrimination" of the kind prohibited by the duty of fair representation . . . . The agreement here only provided the order and mechanism for the reintegration of the returning strikers but did not permanently alter the seniority system . . . .

The judgment of the Court of Appeals is reversed, and the case is remanded for further proceedings consistent with this opinion.

It is so ordered.

POST PROBLEM DISCUSSION

1.   In *Hines v. Anchor Motor Freight*, 424 U.S. 554 (1976), the case upon which Problem #1 is based, the Supreme Court reversed the lower court judgment for the employer on a 6-2 vote, and held that the collective-bargaining agreement's finality provisions were no defense. More specifically, the Court found that the union's subversion of the arbitration process, by failing to appropriately investigate the truck drivers' claims about the motel clerk, removed the bar that would normally apply when the arbitrator has already decided the case. Therefore, as far as the first question from Problem #1, although individual employees are not permitted to relitigate their discharge simply because new evidence is discovered after the arbitration decision, if the arbitration process itself is suffused with bad faith, arbitrary, or discriminatory conduct by the union, then the arbitration decision can be attacked in a DFR action. The Court concluded: "[The truck drivers,] if they prove an erroneous discharge, and the Union's breach of duty tainting the decision of the [arbitrator,] are entitled to an appropriate remedy against the employer as well as the Union . . . ."

2.   The *O'Neill* Court stated that the same DFR rules apply both to cases involving contract-making and grievance processing. From a practical standpoint, is that an accurate statement or does the union have more latitude in the collective-bargaining context? Consider this question in answering question #3 in Problem #1. The difference is thought to stem from the fact that in contract-making situations, the union acts like a legislature and needs a wide range of flexibility in negotiating a contract. On the other hand, grievance processing involves rights already vested in the employees through the collective-bargaining agreement, and unions are therefore thought to have less leeway in declining to process grievances. The *O'Neill* Court, although it suggested that the *Vaca* standard applies in the contract-making context, reinforced this difference by holding that agreements should only be reviewed for rationality, as is the case for legislative action. Under this standard, the *O'Neill* Court found the union's conduct was within the "wide range of reasonableness" even though it accepted a settlement that turned out to provide less for some employees than they would have received if the strike had simply been abandoned.

When a union administers a collective-bargaining agreement through grievance processing, it is thought to be acting more like an enforcement agency. Because such agencies are largely applying established rules, unions have less need for discretion when they are administering an agreement. Under *Vaca*, "[b]efore an employee can sue his employer under sec. 301 of the Act for a simple breach of his employment contract, the employee must prove not only that he attempted to exhaust his contractual remedies, but that his attempt to exhaust was frustrated by 'arbitrary, discriminatory, or bad faith' conduct on the part of the union." This DFR standard recognizes unions' gatekeeping function. Allowing unions discretion to decide whether to take a grievance to arbitration enhances the entire grievance-arbitration system by managing costs and ensuring that employees cannot make an end-run around the negotiated system.

3.   Overall, one can derive five grievance-related DFR standards under *Vaca*:

a.   a union's conduct cannot be arbitrary, discriminatory, or in bad faith;

b.   a union cannot arbitrarily ignore a grievance with merit or process that grievance carelessly;

c.   a union must work in good faith to resolve grievances with the employer;

d   a union must treat similar grievances consistently; and

e.   a union cannot base its grievance decisions on "patently wrongful conduct such as racial discrimination or personal hostility."

4.   As far as question #4 in Problem #1, the *Vaca* Court also established the union's and employer's liability for damages resulting from a successful hybrid Section 301 DFR action. Basically, each party is liable for the share of damages caused by their breaches: "damages attributable solely to the employer's breach of contract should not be charged to the union, but increases . . . in those damages caused by the union's refusal to process the grievance should not be charged to the employer." For instance, in *Bowen v. United States Postal Service*, 459 U.S. 212 (1983), the Court limited the damages apportioned to the employer to the date when the arbitration should have taken place if the union had appropriately brought the grievance. On the other hand, the union was fully responsible for the damages after the hypothetical arbitration date.

The *Bowen* dissent, written by Justice White, commented that, "[t]he union should well consider itself fortunate that this dispute proceeded to trial less than three years after the cessation of Bowen's employment. Most of the cases of this nature that have been reviewed by this Court have taken the better part of a decade to run their course . . . . Nor will the union have any readily apparent way to limit its constantly increasing liability." Is the dissent in *Bowen* right that because the employer could have reinstated Bowen at any time that, "it is bizarre to hold . . . that the relatively impotent union is *exclusively* liable for the bulk of the backpay[?]"

5.   On a procedural note, the Court has used the NLRA's six-month statute of limitations in these hybrid Section 301 suits against unions and employers. *See DelCostello v. International Brotherhood of Teamsters*, 462 U.S. 151 (1983) (citing Section 10(b)).

SECTION 2   UNION SECURITY CLAUSES AND STATE RIGHT-TO-WORK LAWS

Union security clauses are written provisions in a collective bargaining agreement which seek to obligate individual employees to support the union. This area of labor law involves the weighing of collective rights (including the importance of group strength and cohesion) against individual rights (including the rights of individuals under Section 7 to refrain from supporting any union).

The following materials show a growing trend, particularly from courts, of emphasizing individual rights over collective rights. Many see this trend as consistent with the Taft-Hartley Amendments' philosophy of bolstering employees' freedom to choose whether to join, form, or assist a labor organization.

Union security agreements come in a variety of forms — some legal and some illegal. The following five are the most common:

1. <u>Closed Shop Provisions</u>: Under these provisions, an employer agrees in the collective-bargaining agreement to only hire and retain union members as employees. These types of arrangements were made illegal in 1947 by the Taft-Hartley Amendments.

2. <u>Union Shop Provisions</u>: These provisions remove union membership as a precondition of employment. Instead, a union shop provision allows a period of time (e.g., 30 days) before a new employee must become a union member to keep his or her job.

3. <u>Agency Shop Provisions</u>: These types of provisions do not require "card-carrying" membership in the union as a precondition of employment or to keep a job. An agency shop provision only requires employees to pay initiation fees and union dues. This is union membership "whittled down to its financial core." As will be seen in the materials below, agency shop provisions only permit unions to collect dues germane to collective bargaining and the processing of grievances. This means that dissenting employees do not have to pay unions dues for political expenditures or other excludable expenses.

4. <u>Maintenance of Membership Provisions</u>: These provisions do not affect employees that do not join the union. However, a maintenance of membership provision requires union members to maintain their membership in good standing for the life of the collective-bargaining agreement.

5. <u>Dues Checkoff Provisions</u>: These provisions provide for payroll deduction of union dues (like withholding of taxes), which makes dues collection much easier for the union. As unions have seen when they lose dues checkoff through legislative enactment or through judicial sanctions, it is exceedingly difficult to track down and locate members to pay dues.

The legality of these union security provisions come under two provisos to Section 8(a)(3), which read in pertinent part:

> Provided, That nothing in this Act . . . shall preclude an employer from making an agreement with a labor organization . . . to require as a

condition of employment membership therein on or after the 30th day following the beginning of such employment or the effective date of such agreement whichever is later . . . .

Provided further, that no employer shall justify any discrimination against an employee for nonmembership in a labor organization (A) if he has reasonable grounds for believing that such membership was not available to the employee on the same terms and conditions generally applicable to other members, or (B) if he had reasonable grounds for believing that membership was denied or terminated for reasons other than the failure of the employee to tender the periodic dues and the initiation fees uniformly required as a condition of acquiring or retaining membership.

The upshot of these provisos is that closed shops are now illegal and other union security clauses must give 30 days for an employee to become a member of the union and such membership may be limited to nothing more than paying initiation fees and union dues. So union shop clauses requiring more formal types of membership obligations (e.g., attending meetings and observing strikes) are not permitted, whereas agency shop clauses requiring only financial support for the union's collective bargaining and contract administration responsibilities are allowed.

PROBLEM #2: SAFEGUARDING THE RIGHTS OF A DISSENTING ACTRESS[2]

The Screen Actors Guild (SAG or union) represents performers in the entertainment industry. In 2004, Riverside Productions (Riverside) signed a collective-bargaining agreement with SAG that made the union the exclusive representative of all of Riverside's performers. This agreement contained a union security clause that required the performers to be "a member of the Union in good standing." Tracking the language of Section 8(a)(3), the clause also provided:

The foregoing [section], requiring as a condition of employment membership in the Union, shall not apply until on or after the thirtieth day following the beginning of such employment or the effective date of this Agreement, whichever is the later; the Union and the Producers interpret this sentence to mean that membership in the Union cannot be required of any performer by a Producer as a condition of employment until thirty (30) days after his first employment as a performer in the motion picture industry . . . . The Producer shall not be held to have violated this paragraph if it employs a performer who is not a member of the Union in good standing . . . if the Producer has reasonable grounds for believing that membership in the Union was denied to such performer or such performer's membership in the Union was terminated for reasons other than the failure of the performer to tender the periodic dues and the initiation fee uniformly required as a condition of acquiring or retaining membership in the Union . . . .

---

[2] Problem #2's fact pattern is based on *Marquez v. Screen Actors Guild, Inc.*, 525 U.S. 33 (1998).

Veruca Salt, a part-time actress who had worked in the motion picture industry for more than 30 days, obtained a one-line role in an episode of Riverside's television series, Balled Medicine. Pursuant to the collective-bargaining agreement, Riverside called SAG to verify that Salt had complied with the union security clause. Based on the union's information, Riverside told Salt that she had to pay around $500 in SAG dues before she could work on the episode.

Salt was unable to get SAG to allow her to pay the union fees after she was paid by Riverside, and she lost the job.

(1) Does Salt have a duty of fair representation claim against SAG and Riverside for negotiating and enforcing a union security clause with two alleged basic flaws? First, Salt alleges the union security clause requires union "membership" and the payment of full fees and dues when those terms could not be legally enforced. Second, she alleges that the union security clause required the 30-day grace period provision to begin with any employment in the industry, which contravenes Section 8(a)(3)'s express language that requires employees to be given a 30-day grace period from the beginning of "such employment."

(2) Should the SAG collective-bargaining agreement have contained language that informed Salt of her right not to join the union and of her right to pay only dues that were tied to the union's representational activities?

(3) How would your answer change if this fact pattern occurred in a right-to-work state?

PROBLEM MATERIALS

NLRB v. General Motors Corp., 373 U.S. 734 (1963)

Communication Workers v. Beck, 487 U.S. 735 (1988)

Harry G. Hutchison, *Compulsory Unionism as a Fraternal Conceit? Free Choice for Workers: A History of the Right to Work Movement*, 7 U.C. Davis Bus. L.J. 3 (2006)

NLRB v. GENERAL MOTORS CORP.
373 U.S. 734 (1963)

Mr. Justice White delivered the opinion of the Court.

The issue here is whether an employer commits an unfair labor practice . . . when it refuses to bargain with a certified union over the union's proposal for the adoption of the "agency shop." More narrowly, since the employer is not obliged to bargain over a proposal that he commit an unfair labor practice, the question is whether the agency shop is an unfair labor practice under § 8(a)(3) of the Act or else is exempted from the prohibitions of that section by the proviso thereto. We have concluded that this type of arrangement does not constitute an unfair labor practice and that it is not prohibited by § 8.

Respondent's employees are represented by the United Automobile, Aerospace and Agricultural Implement Workers of America, UAW, in a single, multiplant company-wide unit. The 1958 agreement between union and company provides for maintenance of membership and the union shop. These provisions were not operative, however, in such States as Indiana where state law prohibited making union membership a condition of employment.

In June 1959, the Indiana intermediate appellate court held that an agency shop arrangement would not violate the state right-to-work law. As defined in that opinion, the term "agency shop" applies to an arrangement under which all employees are required as a condition of employment to pay dues to the union and pay the union's initiation fee, but they need not actually become union members. The union thereafter sent respondent a letter proposing the negotiation of a contractual provision covering Indiana plants "generally similar to that set forth" in the Meade case. Continued employment in the Indiana plants would be conditioned upon the payment of sums equal to the initiation fee and regular monthly dues paid by the union members. The intent of the proposal, the National Labor Relations Board concluded, was not to require membership but to make membership available at the employees' option and on nondiscriminatory terms. Employees choosing not to join would make the required payments and, in accordance with union custom, would share in union expenditures for strike benefits, educational and retired member benefits, and union publications and promotional activities, but they would not be entitled to attend union meetings, vote upon ratification of agreements negotiated by the union, or have a voice in the internal affairs of the union. The respondent made no counterproposal, but replied to the union's letter that the proposed agreement would violate the National Labor Relations Act and that respondent must therefore "respectfully decline to comply with your request for a meeting" to bargain over the proposal.

The union thereupon filed a complaint with the National Labor Relations Board against respondent for its alleged refusal to bargain in good faith. In the Board's view of the record, "the Union was not seeking to bargain over a clause requiring nonmember employees to pay sums equal to dues and fees as a condition of employment while at the same time maintaining a closed-union policy with respect to applicants for membership," since the proposal contemplated an arrangement in which "all employees are given the option of becoming, or refraining from becoming, members of the Union." Proceeding on this basis and putting aside the consequences of a closed-union policy upon the legality of the agency shop, the Board assessed the union's proposal as comporting fully with the congressional declaration of policy in favor of union-security contracts and therefore a mandatory subject as to which the Act obliged respondent to bargain in good faith. At the same time, it stated that it had "no doubt that an agency-shop agreement is a permissible form of union-security within the meaning of Sections 7 and 8(a)(3) of the Act." Accordingly, the Board ruled that respondent had committed an unfair labor practice by refusing to bargain in good faith with the certified bargaining representative of its employees, and it ordered respondent to bargain with the union over the proposed arrangement; no back-pay award is involved in this case . . . .

Section 8(3) under the Wagner Act was the predecessor to § 8(a)(3) of the present law. Like § 8(a)(3), § 8(3) forbade employers to discriminate against employees to compel them to join a union. Because it was feared that § 8(3) and § 7, if nothing were added to qualify them, might be held to outlaw union-security arrangements such as the closed shop, the proviso to § 8(3) was added expressly declaring:

'Provided, That nothing in this Act . . . or in any other statute of the United States, shall preclude an employer from making an agreement with a labor organization . . . to require as a condition of employment membership therein, if such labor organization is the representative of the employees as provided in section 9(a) . . . .'

The prevailing administrative and judicial view under the Wagner Act was or came to be that the proviso to § 8(3) covered both the closed and union shop, as well as less onerous union-security arrangements, if they were otherwise legal. The National Labor Relations Board construed the proviso as shielding from an unfair labor practice charge less severe forms of union-security arrangements than the closed or the union shop, including an arrangement in Public Service Co. of Colorado, 89 N.L.R.B. 418, requiring nonunion members to pay to the union $2 a month "for the support of the bargaining unit." And in Algona Plywood Co. v. Wisconsin Board, 336 U.S. 301, 307, which involved a maintenance of membership agreement, the Court, in commenting on petitioner's contention that the proviso of § 8(3) affirmatively protected arrangements within its scope, said of its purpose: "The short answer is that § 8(3) merely disclaims a national policy hostile to the closed shop or other forms of union-security agreement."

When Congress enacted the Taft-Hartley Act, it added the following to the language of the original proviso to § 8(3):

on or after the thirtieth day following the beginning of such employment or the effective date of such agreement, whichever is the later . . . . Provided further, That no employer shall justify any discrimination against an employee for non-membership in a labor organization (A) if he has reasonable grounds for believing that such membership was not available to the employee on the same terms and conditions generally applicable to other members, or (B) if he has reasonable grounds for believing that membership was denied or terminated for reasons other than the failure of the employee to tender the periodic dues and the initiation fees uniformly required as a condition of acquiring or retaining membership.

These additions were intended to accomplish twin purposes. On the one hand, the most serious abuses of compulsory unionism were eliminated by abolishing the closed shop. On the other hand, Congress recognized that in the absence of a union-security provision "many employees sharing the benefits of what unions are able to accomplish by collective bargaining will refuse to pay their share of the cost." Consequently, under the new law "employers would still be permitted to enter into agreements requiring all the employees in a given bargaining unit to become members 30 days after being hired," but "expulsion from a union cannot be a ground of compulsory discharge if the worker is not delinquent in paying his initiation fee or dues." The amendments were intended only to "remedy the most serious abuses of compulsory union membership and yet give employers and unions who feel that such agreements promoted stability by eliminating "free riders' the right to continue such arrangements." As far as the federal law was concerned, all employees could be required to pay their way. The bill "abolishes the closed shop but permits voluntary agreements for requiring such forms of compulsory membership as the union shop or maintenance of membership . . . ."

We find nothing in the legislative history of the Act indicating that Congress intended the amended proviso to § 8(a)(3) to validate only the union shop and simultaneously to abolish, in addition to the closed shop, all other union-security arrangements permissible under state law. There is much to be said for the Board's view that, if Congress desired in the Wagner Act to permit a closed or union shop and in the Taft-Hartley Act the union shop, then it also intended to preserve the status of less vigorous, less compulsory contracts which demanded less adherence to the union.

Respondent, however, relies upon the express words of the proviso which allow employment to be conditioned upon "membership": since the union's proposal here does not require actual membership but demands only initiation fees and monthly dues, it is not saved by the proviso. This position, of course, would reject administrative decisions concerning the scope of § 8(3) of the Wagner Act. More-over, the 1947 amendments not only abolished the closed shop but also made significant alterations in the meaning of "membership" for the purposes of union-security contracts. Under the second proviso to § 8(a)(3), the burdens of membership upon which employment may be conditioned are expressly limited to the payment of initiation fees and monthly dues. It is permissible to condition employment upon membership, but membership, insofar as it has significance to employment rights, may in turn be conditioned only upon payment of fees and dues. "Membership" as a condition of employment is whittled down to its financial core. This Court has said as much before in Radio Officers' Union v. Labor Board, 347 U.S. 17, 41:

> "This legislative history clearly indicates that Congress intended to prevent utilization of union security agreements for any purpose other than to compel payment of union dues and fees. Thus Congress recognized the validity of unions" concern about "free riders," i.e., employees who receive the benefits of union representation but are unwilling to contribute their fair share of financial support to such union, and gave unions the power to contract to meet that problem while withholding from unions the power to cause the discharge of employees for any other reason . . . .

We are therefore confident that the proposal made by the union here conditioned employment upon the practical equivalent of union "membership," as Congress used that term in the proviso to § 8(a)(3). The proposal for requiring the payment of dues and fees imposes no burdens not imposed by a permissible union shop contract and compels the performance of only those duties of membership which are enforceable by discharge under a union shop arrangement. If an employee in a union shop unit refuses to respect any union-imposed obligations other than the duty to pay dues and fees, and membership in the union is therefore denied or terminated, the condition of "membership" for § 8(a)(3) purposes is nevertheless satisfied and the employee may not be discharged for nonmembership even though he is not a formal member. Of course, if the union chooses to extend membership even though the employee will meet only the minimum financial burden, and refuses to support or "join" the union in any other affirmative way, the employee may have to become a "member" under a union shop contract, in the sense that the union may be able to place him on its rolls. The agency shop arrangement proposed here removes that choice from the union and places the option of membership in the employee while still requiring the same monetary support as does the union shop. Such a difference between the union and agency shop may be of great importance in some contexts, but for present purposes it is more formal than real. To the extent that it has any significance at all it serves, rather than violates, the desire of Congress to reduce the evils of compulsory unionism while allowing financial support for the bargaining agent.

In short, the employer categorically refused to bargain with the union over a proposal for an agreement within the proviso to § 8(a)(3) and as such lawful for the purposes of this case. By the same token, § 7, and derivatively § 8(a)(1), cannot be deemed to forbid the employer to enter such agreements, since it too is expressly limited by the § 8(a)(3) proviso. We hold that the employer was not excused from his duty to bargain over the proposal on the theory that his acceding to it would necessarily involve him in an unfair labor practice. Whether a different result obtains in States which have declared such arrangements unlawful is an issue still to be resolved in Retail Clerks Ass'n v. Schermerhorn, 373 U.S. 746, and one which is of no relevance here because Indiana law does not forbid the present contract proposal. In the context of this case, then, the employer cannot justify his refusal to bargain. He violated § 8(a)(5), and the Board properly ordered him to return to the bargaining table.

Reversed and remanded.

MR. JUSTICE GOLDBERG took no part in the consideration or decision of this case.

COMMUNICATION WORKERS v. BECK
487 U.S. 735 (1988)

BRENNAN, J., delivered the opinion of the Court, in which REHNQUIST, C.J., and WHITE, MARSHALL, and STEVENS, JJ., joined. BLACKMUN, J., filed an opinion, concurring in part and dissenting in part, in which O'CONNOR and SCALIA, JJ., joined. KENNEDY, J., took no part in the consideration or decision of the case.

Section 8(a)(3) of the National Labor Relations Act of 1935 (NLRA), permits an employer and an exclusive bargaining representative to enter into an agreement requiring all employees in the bargaining unit to pay periodic union dues and initiation fees as a condition of continued employment, whether or not the employees otherwise wish to become union members. Today we must decide whether this provision also permits a union, over the objections of dues-paying nonmember employees, to expend funds so collected on activities unrelated to collective bargaining, contract administration, or grievance adjustment, and, if so, whether such expenditures violate the union's duty of fair representation or the objecting employees' First Amendment rights.

I

In accordance with § 9 of the NLRA, a majority of the employees of American Telephone and Telegraph Company and several of its subsidiaries selected petitioner Communications Workers of America (CWA) as their exclusive bargaining representative. As such, the union is empowered to bargain collectively with the employer on behalf of all employees in the bargaining unit over wages, hours, and other terms and conditions of employment, § 9(a), and it accordingly enjoys "broad authority . . . in the negotiation and administration of [the] collective bargaining contract." This broad authority, however, is tempered by the union's "statutory obligation to serve the interests of all members without hostility or discrimination toward any," a duty that extends not only to the negotiation of the collective-bargaining agreement itself but also to the subsequent enforcement of that agreement, including the administration of any grievance procedure the agreement may establish. CWA chartered several local unions, copetitioners in this case, to assist it in discharging these statutory duties. In addition, at least in part to help defray the considerable costs it incurs in performing these tasks, CWA negotiated a union-security clause in the collective-bargaining agreement under which all represented employees, including those who do not wish to become union members, must pay the union "agency fees" in "amounts equal to the periodic dues" paid by union members. Under the clause, failure to tender the required fee may be grounds for discharge.

In June 1976, respondents, 20 employees who chose not to become union members, initiated this suit challenging CWA's use of their agency fees for purposes other than collective bargaining, contract administration, or grievance adjustment (hereinafter "collective-bargaining" or "representational" activities). Specifically, respondents alleged that the union's expenditure of their fees on activities such as organizing the employees of other employers, lobbying for labor legislation, and participating in social, charitable, and political events violated petitioners' duty of fair representation, § 8(a)(3) of the NLRA, the First Amendment, and various common-law fiduciary duties. In addition to declaratory relief, respondents sought an injunction barring petitioners from exacting fees above those necessary to finance collective-bargaining activities, as well as damages for the past collection of such excess fees . . . .

II

At the outset, we address briefly the jurisdictional question that divided the Court of Appeals. Respondents sought relief on three separate federal claims: that the exaction of fees beyond those necessary to finance collective-bargaining activities violates § 8(a)(3); that such exactions violate the judicially created duty of fair representation; and that such exactions violate respondents' First Amendment rights. We think it clear that the courts below properly exercised jurisdiction over the latter two claims, but that the National Labor Relations Board (NLRB or Board) had primary jurisdiction over respondents' § 8(a)(3) claim.

In *San Diego Building Trades Council v. Garmon*, 359 U.S. 236 (1959), we held that "[w]hen an activity is arguably subject to § 7 or § 8 of the [NLRA], the States *as well as the federal courts* must defer to the exclusive competence of the [Board] if the danger of state interference with national policy is to be averted." A simple recitation of respondents' § 8(a)(3) claim reveals that it falls squarely within the primary jurisdiction of the Board: respondents contend that, by collecting and using agency fees for nonrepresentational purposes, the union has contravened the express terms of § 8(a)(3), which, respondents argue, provides a limited authorization for the collection of only those fees necessary to finance collective-bargaining activities. There can be no doubt, therefore, that the challenged fee-collecting activity is "subject to" § 8.

While the five-judge plurality of the en banc court did not explain the basis of its jurisdictional holding, the panel majority concluded that because courts have jurisdiction over challenges to union-security clauses negotiated under § 2, Eleventh of the Railway Labor Act (RLA), Eleventh, which is in all material respects identical to § 8(a)(3), there must be a parity of federal jurisdiction over § 8(a)(3) claims. Unlike the NLRA, however, the RLA establishes no agency charged with administering its provisions, and instead leaves it to the courts to determine the validity of activities challenged under the Act. The primary jurisdiction of the NLRB, therefore, cannot be diminished by analogies to the RLA, for in this regard the two labor statutes do not parallel one another. The Court of Appeals erred, then, to the extent that it concluded it possessed jurisdiction to pass directly on respondents' § 8(a)(3) claim.

The court was not precluded, however, from deciding the merits of this claim insofar as such a decision was necessary to the disposition of respondents' duty-of-fair-representation challenge. Federal courts may resolve unfair labor practice questions that "emerge as collateral issues in suits brought under independent federal remedies," and one such remedy over which federal jurisdiction is well settled is the judicially implied duty of fair representation. This jurisdiction to adjudicate fair-representation claims encompasses challenges leveled not only at a union's contract administration and enforcement efforts, but at its negotiation activities as well. Employees, of course, may not circumvent the primary jurisdiction of the NLRB simply by casting statutory claims as violations of the union's duty of fair representation. Respondents, however, have done no such thing here; rather, they claim that the union failed to represent their interests fairly and without hostility by negotiating and enforcing an agreement that allows the exaction of funds for purposes that do not serve their interests and in some cases are contrary to their personal beliefs. The necessity of deciding the scope of § 8(a)(3) arises because *petitioners* seek to defend themselves on the ground that the statute authorizes precisely this type of agreement. Under these circumstances, the Court of Appeals had jurisdiction to decide the § 8(a)(3) question raised by respondents' duty-of-fair-representation claim.

III

Added as part of the Labor Management Relations Act, 1947, or Taft-Hartley Act, § 8(a)(3) makes it an unfair labor practice for an employer "by discrimination in regard to hire or tenure of employment . . . to encourage or discourage membership in any labor organization." The section contains two provisos without which all union-security clauses would fall within this otherwise broad condemnation: the first states that nothing in the Act "preclude[s] an employer from making an agreement with a labor organization . . . to require as a condition of employment membership therein" 30 days after the employee attains employment; the second, limiting the first, provides:

> "[N]o employer shall justify any discrimination against an employee for nonmembership in a labor organization (A) if he has reasonable grounds for believing that such membership was not available to the employee on the same terms and conditions generally applicable to other members, or (B) if he has reasonable grounds for believing that membership was denied or terminated for reasons other than the failure . . . to tender the periodic dues and the initiation fees uniformly required as a condition of acquiring or retaining membership."

Taken as a whole, § 8(a)(3) permits an employer and a union to enter into an agreement requiring all employees to become union members as a condition of continued employment, but the "membership" that may be so required has been "whittled down to its financial core." The statutory question presented in this case, then, is whether this "financial core" includes the obligation to support union activities beyond those germane to collective bargaining, contract administration, and grievance adjustment. We think it does not.

Although we have never before delineated the precise limits § 8(a)(3) places on the negotiation and enforcement of union-security agreements, the question the parties proffer is not an entirely new one. Over a quarter century ago we held that § 2, Eleventh of the RLA does not permit a union, over the objections of nonmembers, to expend compelled agency fees on political causes. *Machinists v. Street*, 367 U.S. 740 (1961). Because the NLRA and RLA differ in certain crucial respects, we have frequently warned that decisions construing the latter often provide only the roughest of guidance when interpreting the former. Our decision in *Street*, however, is far more than merely instructive here: we believe it is controlling, for § 8(a)(3) and § 2, Eleventh are in all material respects identical. Indeed, we have previously described the two provisions as "statutory equivalent[s]," *Ellis v. Railway Clerks*, 466 U.S. 435, 452, n. 13 (1984), and with good reason, because their nearly identical language reflects the fact that in both Congress authorized compulsory unionism only to the extent necessary to ensure that those who enjoy union-negotiated benefits contribute to their cost. Thus, in amending the RLA in 1951, Congress expressly modeled § 2, Eleventh on § 8(a)(3), which it had added to the NLRA only four years earlier, and repeatedly emphasized that it was extending "to railroad labor the same rights and privileges of the union shop that are contained in the Taft-Hartley Act." In these circumstances, we think it clear that Congress intended the same language to have the same meaning in both statutes.

A

Both the structure and purpose of § 8(a)(3) are best understood in light of the statute's historical origins. Prior to the enactment of the Taft-Hartley Act of 1947, § 8(a)(3) of the Wagner Act of 1935 (NLRA) permitted majority unions to negotiate "closed shop" agreements requiring employers to hire only persons who were already union members. By 1947, such agreements had come under increasing attack, and after extensive hearings Congress determined that the closed shop and the abuses associated with it "create[d] too great a barrier to free employment to be longer tolerated." The 1947 Congress was equally concerned, however, that without such agreements, many employees would reap the benefits that unions negotiated on their behalf without in any way contributing financial support to those efforts. As Senator Taft, one of the authors of the 1947 legislation, explained, "the argument . . . against abolishing the closed shop . . . is that if there is not a closed shop those not in the union will get a free ride, that the union does the work, gets the wages raised, then the man who does not pay dues rides along freely without any expense to himself." Thus, the Taft-Hartley Act was

> "intended to accomplish twin purposes. On the one hand, the most serious abuses of compulsory unionism were eliminated by abolishing the closed shop. On the other hand, Congress recognized that in the absence of a union-security provision 'many employees sharing the benefits of what unions are able to accomplish by collective bargaining will refuse to pay their share of the cost.' "

The legislative solution embodied in § 8(a)(3) allows employers to enter into agreements requiring all the employees in a given bargaining unit to become members 30 days after being hired as long as such membership is available to all workers on a nondiscriminatory basis, but it prohibits the mandatory discharge of an employee who is expelled from the union for any reason other than his or her failure to pay initiation fees or dues. As we have previously observed, Congress carefully tailored this solution to the evils at which it was aimed:

"Th[e] legislative history clearly indicates that Congress intended to prevent utilization of union security agreements for any purpose other than to compel payment of union dues and fees. Thus Congress recognized the validity of unions' concerns about 'free riders,' *i.e.*, employees who receive the benefits of union representation but are unwilling to contribute their *fair share* of financial support to such union, and gave unions the power to contract to meet *that problem* while withholding from unions the power to cause the discharge of employees for any other reason."

Indeed, "Congress' decision to allow union-security agreements *at all* reflects its concern that . . . the parties to a collective bargaining agreement be allowed to provide that there be no employees who are getting the benefits of union representation without paying for them."

This same concern over the resentment spawned by "free riders" in the railroad industry prompted Congress, four years after the passage of the Taft-Hartley Act, to amend the RLA. As the House Report explained, 75 to 80% of the 1.2 million railroad industry workers belonged to one or another of the railway unions. These unions, of course, were legally obligated to represent the interests of all workers, including those who did not become members thus nonunion workers were able, at no expense to themselves, to share in all the benefits the unions obtained through collective bargaining. Noting that the "principle of authorizing agreements for the union shop and the deduction of union dues has now become firmly established as a national policy for all industry subject to the Labor Management Relations Act of 1947," the House Report concluded that "[n]o sound reason exists for continuing to deny to labor organizations subject to the Railway Labor Act the right to negotiate agreements with railroads and airlines of a character permitted in the case of labor organizations in the other large industries of the country."

In drafting what was to become § 2, Eleventh, Congress did not look to § 8(a)(3) merely for guidance. Rather, as Senator Taft argued in support of the legislation, the amendment "inserts in the railway mediation law almost the exact provisions, so far as they fit, of the Taft-Hartley law, so that the conditions regarding the union shop and the check-off are carried into the relations between railroad unions and the railroads." This was the universal understanding, among both supporters and opponents, of the purpose and effect of the amendment. Indeed, railroad union representatives themselves proposed the amendment that incorporated in § 2, Eleventh, § 8(a)(3)'s prohibition against the discharge of employees who fail to obtain or maintain union membership for any reason other than nonpayment of periodic dues; in offering this proposal the unions argued, in terms echoing the language of the Senate Report accompanying the Taft-Hartley Act, that such a prohibition "remedies the alleged abuses of compulsory union membership . . . , yet makes possible the elimination of the 'free rider' and the sharing of the burden of maintenance by all of the beneficiaries of union activity."

In *Street* we concluded "that § 2, Eleventh contemplated compulsory unionism to force employees to share the costs of negotiating and administering collective agreements, and the costs of the adjustment and settlement of disputes," but that Congress did not intend "to provide the unions with a means for forcing employees, over their objection, to support political causes which they oppose." Construing the statute in light of this legislative history and purpose, we held that although § 2, Eleventh on its face authorizes the collection from nonmembers of "periodic dues, initiation fees, and assessments . . . *uniformly required* as a condition of acquiring or retaining membership" in a union, Eleventh (b), this authorization did not "ves[t] the unions with unlimited power to spend exacted money." We have since reaffirmed that "Congress' essential justification for authorizing the union shop" limits the expenditures that may properly be charged to nonmembers under § 2, Eleventh to those "necessarily or reasonably incurred for the purpose of performing the duties of an exclusive [bargaining] representative." Given the parallel purpose, structure, and language of § 8(a)(3), we must interpret that provision in the same manner. Like § 2, Eleventh, § 8(a)(3) permits the collection of "periodic dues and initiation fees uniformly required as a condition of acquiring or retaining membership" in the union, and like its counterpart in the RLA, § 8(a)(3) was designed to remedy the inequities posed by "free riders" who would otherwise unfairly profit from the Taft-Hartley Act's abolition of the closed shop. In the face of such statutory congruity, only the most compelling evidence could persuade us that Congress intended the nearly identical language of these two provisions to have different meanings. Petitioners have not proffered such evidence here.

B

(1)

Petitioners claim that the union-security provisions of the RLA and NLRA can and should be read differently in light of the vastly different history of unionism in the industries the two statutes regulate. Thus they note that in *Street* we emphasized the "long-standing tradition of voluntary unionism" in the railway industry prior to the 1951 amendment, and the fact that in 1934 Congress had expressly endorsed an "open shop" policy in the RLA. It was this historical background, petitioners contend, that led us to conclude that in amending the RLA in 1951, Congress "did not completely abandon the policy of full freedom of choice embodied in the 1934 Act, but rather made inroads on it for the limited purpose of eliminating the problems created by the 'free rider.' " The history of union security in industries governed by the NLRA was precisely the opposite: under the Wagner Act of 1935, all forms of compulsory unionism, including the closed shop, were permitted. Petitioners accordingly argue that the inroads Congress made in 1947 on the policy of compulsory unionism were likewise limited, and were designed to remedy only those "carefully-defined" abuses of the union shop system that Congress had expressly identified. Because agreements requiring the payment of uniform dues were not among these specified abuses, petitioners contend that § 8(a)(3) cannot plausibly be read to prohibit the collection of fees in excess of those necessary to cover the costs of collective bargaining.

We find this argument unpersuasive for several reasons. To begin with, the fact that Congress sought to remedy "the most serious abuses of compulsory union membership," hardly suggests that the Taft-Hartley Act effected only limited changes in union-security practices. Quite to the contrary, in *Street* we concluded that Congress' purpose in amending the RLA was "limited" precisely because Congress did not perceive voluntary unionism as the source of widespread and flagrant abuses, and thus modified the railroad industry's open shop system only to the extent necessary to eliminate the problems associated with "free riders." That Congress viewed the Wagner Act's regime of compulsory unionism as seriously flawed, on the other hand, indicates that its purposes in overhauling that system were, if anything, far less limited and not, as petitioners and the dissent contend, equally circumspect. Not surprisingly, therefore-and in stark contrast to petitioners' "limited inroads" theory-congressional opponents of the Taft-Hartley Act's union-security provisions understood the Act to provide only the most grudging authorization of such agreements, permitting "union-shop agreement[s] only under limited and administratively burdensome conditions." That understanding comports with our own recognition that "Congress' decision to allow union-security agreements *at all* reflects its concern that . . . the parties to a collective bargaining agreement be allowed to provide that there be no employees who are getting the benefits of union representation without paying for them." Congress thus did not set out in 1947 simply to tinker in some limited fashion with the NLRA's authorization of union-security agreements. Rather, to the extent Congress preserved the status quo, it did so because of the considerable evidence adduced at congressional hearings indicating that "such agreements promoted stability by eliminating 'free riders,' " and Congress accordingly "gave unions the power to contract to meet *that problem* while withholding from unions the power to cause the discharge of employees for any other reason." We therefore think it not only permissible but altogether proper to read § 8(a)(3), as we read § 2, Eleventh, in light of this animating principle.

Finally, however much union-security practices may have differed between the railway and NLRA-governed industries prior to 1951, it is abundantly clear that Congress itself understood its actions in 1947 and 1951 to have placed these respective industries on an equal footing insofar as compulsory unionism was concerned. Not only did the 1951 proponents of the union shop propose adding to the RLA language nearly identical to that of § 8(a)(3), they repeatedly insisted that the purpose of the amendment was to confer on railway unions precisely the same right to negotiate and enter into union-security agreements that all unions subject to the NLRA enjoyed. Indeed, a subtheme running throughout the comments of these supporters was that the inequity of permitting "free riders" in the railroad industry was especially egregious in view of the fact that the Taft-Hartley Act gave exclusive bargaining representatives in all other industries adequate means to redress such problems. It would surely come as a surprise to these legislators to learn that their efforts to provide these same means of redress to railway unions were frustrated by the very historical disparity they sought to eliminate.

(2)

Petitioners also rely on certain aspects of the Taft-Hartley Act's legislative history as evidence that Congress intended to permit the collection and use of full union dues, including those allocable to activities other than collective bargaining. Again, however, we find this history insufficient to compel a broader construction of § 8(a)(3) than that accorded § 2, Eleventh in *Street.*

First and foremost, petitioners point to the fact that Congress expressly considered proposals regulating union finances but ultimately placed only a few limitations on the collection and use of dues and fees, and otherwise left unions free to arrange their financial affairs as they saw fit. In light of this history and the specific prohibitions Congress did enact, petitioners argue that there is no warrant for implying any further limitations on the amount of dues equivalents that unions may collect or the manner in which they may use them. As originally passed, § 7(b) of the House bill guaranteed union members the "right to be free from unreasonable or discriminatory financial demands of" unions. Similarly, § 8(c) of the bill, the so-called "bill of rights for union members," set out 10 protections against arbitrary action by union officers, one of which made it an unfair labor practice for a union to impose initiation fees in excess of $25 without NLRB approval, or to fix dues in amounts that were unreasonable, nonuniform, or not approved by majority vote of the members. In addition, § 304 of the bill prohibited unions from making contributions to or expenditures on behalf of candidates for federal office. The conferees adopted the latter provision, and agreed to a prohibition on "excessive" initiation fees, but the Senate steadfastly resisted any further attempts to regulate internal union affairs . . . .

It simply does not follow from this that Congress left unions free to exact dues equivalents from nonmembers in any amount they please, no matter how unrelated those fees may be to collective-bargaining activities. On the contrary, the complete lack of congressional concern for the rights of nonmembers in the debate surrounding the House "bill of rights" is perfectly consistent with the view that Congress understood § 8(a)(3) to afford nonmembers adequate protection by authorizing the collection of only those fees necessary to finance collective-bargaining activities: because the amount of such fees would be fixed by their underlying purpose-defraying the costs of collective bargaining-Congress would have every reason to believe that the lack of any limitations on union dues was entirely irrelevant so far as the rights of nonmembers were concerned. In short, we think it far safer and far more appropriate to construe § 8(a)(3) in light of its legislative justification, *i.e.*, ensuring that nonmembers who obtain the benefits of union representation can be made to pay for them, than by drawing inferences from Congress' rejection of a proposal that did not address the rights of nonmembers at all.

Petitioners also deem it highly significant that prior to 1947 unions "rather typically" used their members' dues for a "variety of purposes . . . in addition to meeting the . . . costs of collective bargaining," and yet Congress, which was presumably well aware of the practice, in no way limited the uses to which unions could put fees collected from nonmembers. This silence, petitioners suggest, should be understood as congressional acquiescence in these practices. The short answer to this argument is that Congress was equally well aware of the same practices by railway unions, yet neither in *Street* nor in any of the cases that followed it have we deemed Congress' failure in § 2, Eleventh to prohibit or otherwise regulate such expenditures as an endorsement of fee collections unrelated to collective-bargaining expenses. We see no reason to give greater weight to Congress' silence in the NLRA than we did in the RLA, particularly where such silence is again perfectly consistent with the rationale underlying § 8(a)(3): prohibiting the collection of fees that are not germane to representational activities would have been redundant if Congress understood § 8(a)(3) simply to enable unions to charge nonmembers only for those activities that actually benefit them . . . .

(3)

We come then to petitioners' final reason for distinguishing *Street.* Five years prior to our decision in that case, we ruled in *Railway Employees v. Hanson*, 351 U.S. 225 (1956), that because the RLA pre-empts all state laws banning union-security agreements, the negotiation and enforcement of such provisions in railroad industry contracts involves "governmental action" and is therefore subject to constitutional limitations. Accordingly, in *Street* we interpreted § 2, Eleventh to avoid the serious constitutional question that would otherwise be raised by a construction permitting unions to expend governmentally compelled fees on political causes that nonmembers find objectionable. No such constitutional questions lurk here, petitioners contend, for § 14(b) of the NLRA expressly preserves the authority of States to outlaw union-security agreements. Thus, petitioners' argument runs, the federal pre-emption essential to *Hanson* 's finding of governmental action is missing in the NLRA context, and we therefore need not strain to avoid the plain meaning of § 8(a)(3) as we did with § 2, Eleventh.

We need not decide whether the exercise of rights permitted, though not compelled, by § 8(a)(3) involves state action. Even assuming that it does not, and that the NLRA and RLA therefore differ in this respect, we do not believe that the absence of any constitutional concerns in this case would warrant reading the nearly identical language of § 8(a)(3) and § 2, Eleventh differently. It is, of course, true that federal statutes are to be construed so as to avoid serious doubts as to their constitutionality, and that when faced with such doubts the Court will first determine whether it is fairly possible to interpret the statute in a manner that renders it constitutionally valid. But statutory construction may not be pressed " 'to the point of disingenuous evasion,' " and in avoiding constitutional questions the Court may not embrace a construction that "is plainly contrary to the intent of Congress." In *Street*, we concluded that our interpretation of § 2, Eleventh was "not only 'fairly possible' but entirely reasonable," and we have adhered to that interpretation since. We therefore decline to construe the language of § 8(a)(3) differently from that of § 2, Eleventh on the theory that our construction of the latter provision was merely constitutionally expedient. Congress enacted the two provisions for the same purpose, eliminating "free riders," and that purpose dictates our construction of § 8(a)(3) no less than it did that of § 2, Eleventh, regardless of whether the negotiation of union-security agreements under the NLRA partakes of governmental action.

IV

We conclude that § 8(a)(3), like its statutory equivalent, § 2, Eleventh of the RLA, authorizes the exaction of only those fees and dues necessary to "performing the duties of an exclusive representative of the employees in dealing with the employer on labor-management issues." . . .

JUSTICE BLACKMUN, with whom JUSTICE O'CONNOR and JUSTICE SCALIA join, concurring in part and dissenting in part.

. . . I cannot agree with [the majority's] resolution of the § 8(a)(3) issue. Without the decision in *Machinists v. Street*, 367 U.S. 740 (1961), involving the Railway Labor Act (RLA), the Court could not reach the result it does today. Our accepted mode of resolving statutory questions would not lead to a construction of § 8(a)(3) so foreign to that section's express language and legislative history, which show that Congress did not intend to limit either the amount of "agency fees" (or what the majority labels "dues-equivalents") a union may collect under a union-security agreement, or the union's expenditure of such funds. The Court's excessive reliance on *Street* to reach a contrary conclusion is manifested by its unique line of reasoning. No sooner is the language of § 8(a)(3) intoned, than the Court abandons all attempt at construction of *this* statute and leaps to its interpretation over a quarter century ago of another statute enacted by a different Congress, a statute with a distinct history and purpose. I am unwilling to offend our established doctrines of statutory construction and strain the meaning of the language used by Congress in § 8(a)(3), simply to conform § 8(a)(3)'s construction to the Court's interpretation of similar language in a different later-enacted statute, an interpretation which is itself "not without its difficulties." *Abood v. Detroit Board of Education*, 431 U.S. 209, 232 (1977) (characterizing the Court's decision in *Street*). I therefore dissent from Parts III and IV of the Court's opinion . . . .

Harry G. Hutchison, *Compulsory Unionism as a Fraternal Conceit? Free Choice for Workers: A History of the Right to Work Movement*
7 U.C. Davis Bus. L.J. 3 (2006)[3]

Introduction

One candid reporter offers this assessment, "I honestly believe it, and I'm ashamed to say it: the Labor movement is on life support." He later notes, "Where the hell is Moses when you need him? I mean parting the Red Sea is nothing compared to the challenges we face as a [labor] movement." This bracing appraisal corroborates evidence pointing to a steady decline in the unionized share of the U.S. work force, which comprised 7.9% of the private sector in 2004. After experiencing a steady increase in both wages and productivity over several decades, it appears that only thirty-five percent of non-unionized workers are interested in unionizing their workplace and only sixteen percent would definitely vote to unionize.

Membership woes generate growing fears of looming union irrelevance despite extensive counterfactual evidence substantiating persistent growth in union political influence and economic wealth. Notwithstanding the counterfactuals, academic observers offer similar pessimism, implying that many of the hopeful proposals for labor "reform" are nothing more than attempts to reshuffle the deck chairs on the Titanic. Such despondency has led some labor union proponents to contemplate the abolition of the National Labor Relations Act (NLRA). There appears to be gloom regarding labor's future, and this gloominess is attached to the expectant belief that unions exemplify and secure communal progress. Labor's current difficulties correspond with despair over the failure of the progressive agenda and signify that it is time to start over, as the economic and political conditions which have enabled the NLRA to succeed in the past have come to an end.

From a global perspective, these dire developments were foreseeable. More than 50 years ago, Jacques Ellul saw unions as largely technical entities which predictably trapped workers in compulsory organizations that diminished both their personalities and independence, despite the earlier hope by some that unions would act as a revolutionary force that would free workers from the bureaucratic power wielded by large organizations. Ellul insists that labor unions are best understood as institutions led by hierarchs who have an inadequate understanding of the unorganized workforce and the necessity of human liberty. Ellul's verdict, coupled with data on union density rates and other evidence justifying the labor movement's melancholy, substantiates Epstein's forecast that private sector unions will continue to lose ground because they no longer provide their membership with benefits that outweigh their costs.

With the publication of *Free Choice for Workers: a History of the Right to Work Movement*, George Leef reexamines labor unions and contests the justification offered in support of America's labor laws. Leef's perspective delegitimizes compulsory unionism on ethical and empirical grounds. "One dominant feature of this

---

system is the necessary abrogation of the contract at will," notes Richard Epstein, "for an employer is not allowed to dismiss any worker for engaging in union activities or expressing union sympathies." Such arrangements are customarily attached to progressive principles and ideals, and are "typically justified by an appeal to ideas of economic duress, employer exploitation, and inequality of bargaining power." Demonstrating that statutory compulsion fails to lead society on a pathway to progress, the book reveals that the road to serfdom can often be paved by bureaucratic regulation. Carefully examining history and contemporary events, Leef contributes to the richly textured debate about the normative role of unions in a putatively free society. Although F.A. Hayek accurately notes that "[c]ontemporary events differ from history in that we do not know the results they will produce," he also observes that we can discern tendencies. Leef's book provides a historical appraisal that helps society learn from the past, and explicates the capacity of principled ideals, embedded in fearless individuals, to trump historical tendencies favoring privileged and entrenched autocracies. George Leef's reassessment offers an essentially contractarian and liberal model of labor relations that focuses on a vision of individual rights which have a clearly defined, independent existence predating society. From this perspective, Leef specifies liberty as a desirable good in and of itself, which is then placed in harm's way by progressive ideals and constructs. In the essay that follows, I offer neither a meta-narrative on contractarianism nor a comprehensive refutation of the criticism of the contractarian model. Nevertheless, I contend that Leef supplies a highly pragmatic and strongly theoretical (if incomplete) argument against the tendency to see government as the solution to the "labor problem." . . .

I. The Origin of the Right to Work Movement and Right to Work Laws

Free Choice for Workers vindicates the commitment of courageous Americans to certain freedoms, such as freedom of conscience, freedom of association and freedom to say no to groups, values and actions that individuals find incompatible with their own beliefs. Implicit in this understanding of liberty is the notion of freedom from coercion, authoritarianism, violence and intimidation from those who hold contrary views. This understanding can be seen as controversial when the source of coercion is the government itself. Leef further incites controversy when he shows that the source of coercion is not direct government power, but private, putatively voluntary associations of workers that have attained legal rights and privileges. Under federal and various state laws, labor organizations can condition employment on the payment of union dues. Alternatively agency fees and workers are given the stark choice of paying up or losing their job. Since 1955, however, "there has been one organization dedicated to the principle that Americans should not be compelled to support unions and accept their supposed services against their wills," that organization being the National Right to Work Law Committee (NRWLC) and its progeny.

Free Choice for Workers breathes life into the contention that autocratic labor unions require a dedicated opponent. For example, while working for UPS, Rod Carter declined to participate in a 1997 strike that Teamsters Local 769 and the national Teamsters union called against his employer. "Top union officers ordered all drivers to cease working and support the strike, no matter their personal circumstances." Ignoring threats, he continued to work in order to support his family, which ultimately led to an attack by union militants. Severely punching and beating Carter, union militants stabbed him in the chest with an ice pick several times. How did the United States become a country in which citizens can be beaten as a result of working for a living? George Leef responds to this question by describing the evolution of America's labor cartel. This evolution includes the rejection of the common law and the extension of various privileges and immunities to labor organizations as part of a movement aimed at allowing unions "to be freer of the constraints that bind businessmen and everyone else, thereby allowing unions more latitude to use their aggressive tactics." Essential vehicles for the formation and preservation of labor cartels are statutory rules that: (1) grant unions the right of exclusive representation, (2) allow unions to deploy a selective incentive such as compulsory dues payments in the form of an agency, union or a closed shop and (3) subordinate individual workers' interest to the tyranny of the majority.

Once a union has been certified as the bargaining agent for a group of workers it typically has the power to bind all workers to a contract. Leef argues that this authority grants monopoly status to unions and eliminates the freedom of workers to make their own contracts. This practice operates contrary to the prudential judgment of Justice Brandeis, a long-time supporter of organized labor, supported restrictions on union power. Justice Brandeis stated that, "[t]he union attains success when it reaches the ideal condition and the ideal condition for a union is to be strong and stable, and yet to have in the trade outside of its ranks an appreciable number of men who are non-unionists . . . . Such a nucleus of unorganized labor will check oppression by the union as the union checks oppression by the employer." The notion of competition within the labor market sector is consistent with a principled conception of liberty, but is incompatible with America's labor history and labor laws.

A. Transforming the Common Law: American Labor History

Free Choice for Workers examines the creation and implementation of an interventionist and prescriptively collectivist model in American labor relations. Leef argues that "under the common law, there was no need for a special set of rules for labor relations because the law of contract and property rights was sufficient to handle any dispute that arose." Individual workers were "free to join labor organizations and seek to bargain as a group if they wanted to do so," and employers were permitted to "choose whether or not they would bargain with the representatives of a labor organization." While "union officials had sought preferential laws even before the era of the Great Depression," the depression triggered numerous proposals aimed at delimiting the common law both inside and outside the labor law arena. Herbert Hoover is frequently referred to as a clumsy *laissez-faire* proponent who refused to initiate government action needed to revitalize the crumbling economy from 1929 to 1932. In reality, President Hoover was an interventionist who set the stage for even greater government involvement during the Roosevelt administration. He approved the Norris-LaGuardia Act that gave union officials a good deal of what they wanted. The centerpiece of the legislation was its anti-injunction provision. Although some academic observers assert that "injunctions were unfairly suppressing workers in their attempt to improve their conditions . . . the empirical evidence . . . [shows] that injunctions were seldom issued except where there had been violence associated with a strike." Consistent with that observation, after the passage of the act, "the number of strikes, repeatedly accompanied by violence, *doubled* from 1932 to 1933 and continued to rise in following years."

Free Choice for Workers provides further evidence that government intervention can backfire. First Franklin Roosevelt was elected with energetic backing from union leaders. Second, Roosevelt's "Brain Trust" consisted of men who were admirers of European collectivism, in which strong unions were regarded as socially beneficial. Members of the "Brain Trust" were captivated by the paradoxical idea that high prices brought about prosperity, and hence believed that high wages would help the economy by giving workers more purchasing power. While Richard Vedder and Lowell Gallaway demonstrate the absurdity of this view, it is unmistakably clear that cartelization of both of business and labor became an accepted article of faith during the Roosevelt period. As Leef puts it, "The year 1934 was marked by numerous violent strikes in which the heads of unions sought to compel management to recognize and deal with them." This effort solidified and accelerated measures aimed at bringing cartelization to the labor market. Disruption in an already weak economy provided an attractive "industrial peace" rationale for the passage of new labor laws that culminated in the enactment of the Wagner Act of 1935. Explicitly attached to these laws were the contestable claims that the "inequality of bargaining power between employees who do not possess full freedom of association or actual liberty of contract, and employers who are organized in the corporate or other forms of ownership association substantially burdens and affects the flow of commerce, and tends to aggravate recurrent business depressions." Proponents of the NLRA also claimed that industrial peace would be advanced through compulsory union activity. Leef exposes the transformation of "industrial peace" reasoning into constitutional cover in the form of congressional power to regulate interstate commerce within the meaning of Article I, Section 8 of the United States Constitution.

The NLRA subordinated workers' freedom to choose their own employment arrangements to the insistent demand of union hierarchs for "union security." The Wagner Act, while proclaiming the employees right to self-organization, illogically "gave absolutely no legal protection to workers to *refrain* from participating in labor unions or collective bargaining." The Wagner Act also granted unions exclusive representation, because it provided them with a monopoly status and shredded "another basic American liberty - the freedom to make your own contracts." Although "[m]onopolies rarely last very long unless government intervenes to prevent competition with them," the Wagner Act authorized labor organizations to treat workers as a captive market to be exploited to benefit the preferences and self-interest of union hierarchs and outsiders with whom the union leadership has fashioned an ideological bond. In sum, the NLRA contained a number of provisions such as union security provisions, the right to exclusive representation, the absence of effective union democracy as well as the vindication of majoritarianism, that vitiated workers' freedom of association and free speech rights. Furthermore, the United States Supreme Court, far from acting as a guardian of freedom of speech, instead permitted the National Labor Relations Board (NLRB) to enact rules that "stifle [d] real speech by employers." Additionally, the NLRB restricted the property rights of employers through questionable statutory interpretations. Leef adverts to a number of Wagner Act deficiencies that endangered workers' freedom to choose, including the notion that once a union has been certified as the workers' bargaining agent, and it tends to act as such indefinitely, without having to face periodic reelection campaigns. Although decertification is possible, "[m]ost American workers who have union representation have never had the opportunity to vote on it themselves, since the union was certified before they were hired." Viewed collectively, these debatable rules expurgate common law principles and simultaneously prove that workers' autonomy and liberty interests were not the central concern for either those who drafted the legislation, or the National Labor Relations Board (NLRB).

B. Right to Work Laws and the Origins of the Right to Work Movement

In light of the benefits they received through the passage of the Norris-LaGuardia Act and the Wagner Act, unions flourished in the period between 1935 and 1947, and membership soared from three to fifteen million. In some heavily industrialized sectors, union membership comprised eighty percent of the workforce. This vision of expansive labor union power reached its pinnacle when John L. Lewis led coal miners in two prolonged and devastating strikes during World War II. In "response to the postwar deregulation of wages and prices in August 1945, 'major unions immediately demanded huge raises, thirty percent and more . . . [and] union leaders . . . threatened to shut the country down." "During and after World War II, the labor movement thus acted consistently with the objective of augmenting its power and expanding "its forced-dues empire." Illustrating the incoherence of the industrial peace justification for the NLRA, "[d]uring the war, union [leaders] ordered more than 13,000 strikes — many of them having nothing to do with wages and working conditions, but simply to expand their control over the labor market."

On the other hand, an embryonic movement led by opponents of "compulsory unionism succeeded in getting referenda placed on the 1944 general election ballots in Florida and Arkansas, asking voters to approve laws that would make contracts, which forced workers to choose between paying union dues and losing their jobs, illegal." Both measures were approved. A few years later, three more states added Right to Work protection for workers, and six additional states followed suit in 1947. Horrified, the labor movement filed suit culminating in two decisions by the United States Supreme Court to uphold state Right to Work law protection. Justice Hugo Black in a concurring opinion in one case stated,

> There cannot be wrung from a constitutional right of workers to assemble to discuss improvement of their own working standards, a further constitutional right to drive from remunerative employment all persons who will not or cannot participate in union assemblies.

With successful state referenda ratified by the United States Supreme Court, a vibrant grassroots movement aimed at blocking compulsory unionism in America began. The passage of the Taft-Hartley Act in 1947 via a Congressional override of President Truman's veto reinforced this grassroots movement. George Leef observes that the passage Taft-Hartley Amendments had little immediate effect on the growth of unionization. Instead, by 1953 unions grew to comprise thirty-six percent of private sector workers. Therefore, claims that the Taft-Hartley Act withdrew nearly all union advantages and reduced union density rates are not sustained by the empirical record. While the Taft-Hartley Act attempted a more balanced approach to labor relations than the Wagner Act by adding a list of union unfair labor practices such as coercion, discrimination and the use of secondary boycotts, the statute did not withdraw federal support for *most* of the characteristics of compulsory unionism.

Nonetheless, crucial for the right to work law movement was the addition of the following language:

> Nothing contained in the amendment made by subsection (a) shall be construed to authorize the execution or application of agreements requiring membership in a labor organization as a condition of employment in any State or Territory in which such execution or application is prohibited by State or Territorial law.

Leef argues, however, that the rights of workers to refrain from unionism could have been effectuated more effectively by simply abolishing the original (Wagner Act) statute. Although free rider claim have been used to maintain union coercion, Leef eviscerates such arguments by demonstrating that worker interests are not uniform. Without consent or interest uniformity among workers, the free rider pretext collapses. Because only the individual can assess the subjective benefits of union membership, represented workers who prefer to remain independent of a union are likely to become *forced* riders via union security agreements. Further, contrary to contentions by labor union advocates, Leef shows that unions have continued to exist in Right to Work law states despite the fact that workers can legally withdraw their support. Additionally, Leef convincingly argues that unions might act more responsibly if they had to compete for resources provided by working people.

Persistent union autocracy and violence continued to fuel the Right to Work movement. In 1953, the Teamsters Union organized taxicab companies across the nation and called a strike in Wichita, Kansas. The companies resisted and workers continued to go to work. The Teamsters responded by targeting such workers with stink bombs, bottles, paint, and gasoline bombs. The union continued to issue threats and the dispatch office of one company was dynamited. Violence continued to escalate. On the night of December 12, 1953, cab driver Deering Crowe was beaten with repeated blows to the face. This assault burst a malignant tumor. The operation required to repair Crowe's tumor was delayed, and he died leaving a widow and two children. This act of violence coincided with an ongoing debate in Kansas over a Right to Work bill that had been introduced in the legislature. Before his death, Crowe had become a compelling spokesperson for the law, and his story provoked Reed Larson to serve as the driving force in the American Right to Work Law movement.

In 1955 the National Right to Work Committee proclaimed that both its existence and its sole objective was the elimination of compulsory unionism. The committee announced the following goals: educate the public about the threats posed by compulsory unionism; encourage and support both employers and employees who resisted the adoption of union shops; assist workers who fought in the courts to protect their jobs from union initiated discharges; and provide information and material to the various state groups that were engaged in the fight against compulsory unionism. The Right to Work movement had to overcome the failure of politicians and large corporations to take a principled stand in favor of the liberty of workers. This failure contributed to funding problems, which were solved through direct mail efforts. Direct mail efforts produced hundreds of small individual contributions from workers and small businesses. The Right to Work Movement, however, lost five of six referenda campaigns during 1958. Because of these difficulties some considered the Right to Work effort dead, yet both the movement and its organization experienced a revival during the 1960s.

C. Defending Government Employees From Forced Unionism

Because it seemed impossible to bargain collectively with government in the 1950s, the labor movement focused much of its energy on unionizing the private sector workplace. This attitude changed in the 1960s and labor hierarchs realized that they had overlooked "a gold mine of workers who might become union dues payers." Union leaders decided not "to rely on persuasion to get more workers to join voluntarily." Leef illustrates the NRWLC's struggle to counter these efforts. The reluctance of politicians to place the liberty of interests of individual workers ahead of short-term political expediency contributed to the thorniness of this conflict. For example, in an effort to improve efficiency and take small steps toward privatizing the U.S. Postal service during the Nixon administration, Postmaster General Winton Blount agreed to compulsory unionism for postal workers. This agreement, if ratified, would have provided a foothold for unions to "install compulsory unionism throughout the federal government."

With 750,000 workers, the Post office "was the largest civilian employer in the United States." Approximately "twenty percent [of the workforce] had chosen not to join a union, a right that was protected under Executive Order 10988 issued by President Kennedy in 1962." This order "had been reiterated by President Nixon's Executive Order 11491 . . . in 1969." Nonetheless, Blount concealed his capitulation to AFL-CIO demands.

After discovering this surrender, the NRWLC launched an effective counterattack within the United States Chamber of Commerce, in similar business groups, and among significant contributors to Republican candidates. While the "postal service remains inefficient and mailing costs escalate faster than the rate of inflation, Congress with the assistance of the NRWLC, has continued to ban compulsory unionism within the Postal Service, and to advance the principle of individual liberty." Although the NRWLC has not always triumphed, its vigilant efforts against attempts to expand compulsory unionism within the federal government sector have been largely successful.

D. Rent Seeking in the Construction Industry and the Battle for "Reform"

Union activities in the construction industry included efforts to maximize both the number of job classifications and the number of jobs. Taken together, these efforts sought to maximize profits for union treasuries while providing economic rent for the labor movement. In cooperation with these objectives, unions turned their attention to common situs picketing, and other efforts aimed at stifling competition from nonunion shop operators. Most of these efforts, as John Gray might describe, involved politics in pursuit of special interests. In the past, labor officials used common situs picketing until "it was declared to be an unfair labor practice by the Supreme Court's ruling in *NLRB v. Denver Building & Construction Trades Council* in 1951." Craving the capacity to inflict economic damage on parties with whom the union did not have a dispute, unions sought a legislative solution. However, the National Right to Work Law Committee's fierce opposition led to the defeat of common situs picketing bills in 1975 and 1977.

Among other "reform" efforts, labor unions supported campaign finance initiatives. Clearly, "government financing of elections might tilt the playing field" because "union officials would still be free to support their favored candidates with hundreds of millions of dollars worth of 'in kind' services such as phone banks and get-out-the-vote drives." The NRWLC took action to prevent this initiative by working to intercept this legislation. Additional "reform" efforts included the enactment of laws, making it easier for unions to prevail in certification efforts before the National Labor Relations Board. Skillfully supporting legislative filibusters, the NRWLC facilitated the defeat of these "reforms."

E. Legal Defense Efforts

While the accomplishments of the NRWLC in the legislative arena have been noteworthy, its work in the litigation arena has been equally impressive. The latter arena remains crucial because autocratic union officials, often snub the law. "Over the years, thousands of workers have suffered violations of their rights, including physical violence and even death, because they . . . put their own desires and welfare above the demands of union autocrats." While union hierarchs discovered the irresistible temptation to engage in subordination, workers fell victim to intimidation. Archibald Cox describes this quandary clearly:

> Most men are reluctant to incur the financial cost in order to vindicate intangible rights. Individual workers who sue union officers run enormous risks, for there are many ways, legal as well as illegal, by which entrenched officials can 'take care of' recalcitrant members.

Union bullying requires an opponent with ample resources and sufficient motivation to lessen the odds. The National Right to Work Law Committee catalyzed the formation of a new entity — the National Right To Work Legal Defense Foundation (LDF). They are separate organizations, each with its own staff and sources of funding, but neither organization takes a partisan political position. The LDF takes cases involving misuse of compulsory union dues for political and ideological purposes as well as cases involving violations of workers' constitutional rights of free speech, assembly and other civil rights; violations of the merit principle in public employment and academic freedom in public education; injustices in the compulsory union hiring hall referral system; violations of existing protections against compulsory unionism, and cases involving union violence. Among the LDF''s most famous Supreme Court cases are *Abood v. Detroit Board of Education* and *Beck v. Communication Workers of America*. In *Beck*, the District Court ultimately found that "the collection and disbursement of agency fees for purposes other than collective bargaining violated the First Amendment rights of workers." Moreover, a special master appointed by the court found that the union spent nearly eighty percent of its income on political activities and other matters having nothing to do with collective bargaining. This finding is vital because such evidence, along with similar proof, extirpates persistent union free rider arguments in favor of compulsory unionism and mandatory dues payments.

The Supreme Court decision in *Beck*, upheld the district court's decision, but rested largely on the narrower claim that the union breached its duty of fair representation. The *Beck* decision provides a starting point for dissenting workers to take such claims either to court or to the NLRB. In light of the imbalance in economic resources favoring unions, the vindication of employee rights is rare. This is particularly true at the administrative agency level, since the NLRB appears driven by a political calculus that favors compulsory unionism. Accordingly, the Board has been reluctant to support workers' duty of fair representation rights, even when the United States Supreme Court has previously vindicated them. Indeed, the NLRB delayed for eight years before issuing it first post-*Beck* decision, *California Saw*.

Despite the challenges it faces, the Right to Work movement has been very effective. Verification comes in the form of counterattacks by America's labor hierarchy, with similar efforts by the American government's bureaucracy. The counterattack has taken the following forms: (A) a lawsuit filed by thirteen unions and the AFL-CIO asserting "Right to Work organizations were financing workers' lawsuits against unions with funds provided by 'interested employer,' conduct allegedly . . . prohibited by the Landrum-Griffin Act," (B) a labor union suit that sought to compel the disclosure of Right To Work contributors despite a Supreme Court decision preventing such disclosures in NAACP v. Alabama, (C) an Internal Revenue Service that challenged the LDF's charitable status which threatened the tax deductibility of contributions, (D) an aggressive effort led by the Chairman of the Federal Election Commission (FEC) who formerly served as the AFL-CIO's associate general counsel, who, "used the powers of office" to impede the Right to Work movement.

Among the NRWLC's cherished objectives is to pass statutes that extend the Right to Work principle to more states while concurrently defending statutes that are already in place. The AFL-CIO recognizes the benefits of combat through exhaustion, and its allies have introduced bills to repeal Right to Work laws in eight to ten states per year. On the litigation side, the LDF is embroiled in important efforts to prevent "top-down organizing." Since union leaders recognize that they are likely to lose fifty-percent of union certification votes and even if they prevail they may fail to successfully negotiate a collective bargaining agreement, labor leaders "have taken to pressuring management into forcing unionism on their employees whether they want it or not." In essence, labor and management join

together and agree they will support unionization. LDF lawsuits attack the legality of this trend in union organizing. On the legislative front the Right to Work Committee has remained vigilant against recent proposals to approve "unionization without a secret ballot vote of the workers," while continuing to support efforts aimed at protecting "workers against union coercion and abuse." Such efforts vindicate the observation that compulsory unionism is "antithetical to the American tradition of liberty and individual choice." Eighty percent "of the public believes that workers should not be compelled to belong to a union in order to hold a job." Nevertheless, the Right to Work movement will face persistent difficulty in translating the preferences of most Americans into a reality enjoyed by all workers
. . . .

POST PROBLEM DISCUSSION

1. *General Motors* makes clear that Section 8(a)(3) only protects agency fee agreements, under which unit employees need not become full members, but must tender periodic dues and initiation fees. Indeed, *General Motors* stands for the proposition that the only type of membership that may be enforced under the Act is the agency type situation ("membership whittled down to its financial core"), not the traditional union shop one.

2. Having decided that the NLRA allowed only agency shop provisions, the next question for the Court was whether individual dissenters could object to having their union dues used for political purposes with which they did not agree. The Court initially examined this question under the Railway Labor Act (RLA) in *International Association of Machinists v. Street*, 367 U.S. 740 (1961). Before 1951, no security agreements were allowed under the RLA. After that, the RLA was amended to provide in Section 2 Eleventh the same provisions found under the Taft-Hartley-modified version of Section 8(a)(3).

In *Street*, union dissenters challenged these RLA provisions on First Amendment grounds because they were being compelled to pay fees and dues, a substantial portion of which funded political campaigns for candidates whom they did not support and propagation of political ideas that they did not hold. Justice Brennan, writing for the majority, avoided the constitutional issue by construing the RLA to allow the dissenters not to have to pay union fees or dues used for political purposes they found objectionable.

On the other hand, union dues payments could be compelled to support collective bargaining, contract administration, and grievance processing. Justice Brennan maintained in *Street* that the primary purpose behind Section 2 Eleventh was to prevent nonmembers from free riding by receiving the benefits of union representation without paying. This problem was absent in the political context, and so compelled support there did not make sense.

3. Two years later, in *Railway Clerks v. Allen*, 373 U.S. 113 (1963), the Court held that only expenses germane to collective bargaining could be charged to nonmembers of the union. Even more recently, in *Ellis v. Brotherhood of Railway, Airline & Steamship Clerks*, 466 U.S. 435 (1984), the Court specified what kind of expenditures could be charged to nonmembers: "[T]est must be whether the challenged expenditures are necessarily or reasonably incurred for the purpose of

performing the duties of an exclusive representative of the employees in dealing with the employer on labor management issues . . . . Under this standard . . . . objecting employees may be compelled to pay their fair share of expenses of activities or undertakings normally or reasonably employed to implement or effectuate the duties of the union."

4.   It was not until 1988 that the *Street* decision and its progeny were extended formally by the Supreme Court to the NLRA. These dissenter rights are now referred to as *Beck* rights after *Communication Workers v. Beck*, 487 U.S. 735 (1988). As in *Street*, the Court avoided the constitutional issue by interpreting the NLRA to permit agency fees from dissidents only for purposes germane to collective bargaining. The *Beck* dissenters, led by Justice Blackmun, believed that the statutory history of the NLRA and RLA were different enough that agency fees under the NLRA should not be limited to purposes germane to collective bargaining.

5.   More recent Supreme Court cases have placed added glosses on union security clauses and dissenter rights under *Beck*. In *Locke v. Karass*, 555 U.S. 207 (2009), the Court held that a local union representing state employees in Maine could charge nonmembers a portion of an affiliation fee that the local union paid to its national union organization for litigation expenses incurred by other local units, as long as two conditions were met. First, the subject matter of the litigation had to be of the kind that would be chargeable if the litigation were local. Second, the litigation expenses had to be available to the local union at issue if it faced similar litigation in the future.

6.   *California Saw & Knife Works*, 320 N.L.R.B. 224 (1995), is the product of twelve consolidated cases that dealt with the obligation of the union to notify, and to provide opt-out procedures for, *Beck* dissenters. In *California Saw*, the Board established the following *Beck* procedures, which state that: (1) the union give a "*Beck* rights notice" to all newly hired nonmember employees at the time these employees are first obligated to pay union dues; (2) the union provide current employees a notice of their *Beck* rights; (3) the right to file a *Beck* objection could not be limited to a single month in the year; (4) dissenting employees may be properly charged for non-political dues for expenses incurred at the national level of the union; and (5) the union need not provide a unit-by-unit accounting for litigation outside the objector's unit. In the case itself, the NLRB found the form of notice given by the International Association of Machinists (IAM) in its monthly magazine to be legally adequate. However, in the future, the IAM would be required to use an independent, certified accountant to conduct an audit to verify the various expenses of the national and local unions.

7.   Problem #2 is based on *Marquez v. Screen Actor Guilds, Inc.*, 525 U.S. 33 (1998). The employee claimed that the union breached its duty of fair representation when it negotiated a union security clause that tracked the language of Section 8(a)(3) but did not explain the Supreme Court's interpretation of that language in cases like *General Motor* and *Beck*. In finding that the union had not violated its duty of fair representation, the Court concluded that negotiating a union security clause based on the express language of Section 8(a)(3) was far from arbitrary (the DFR standard under *O'Neill*). More specifically, the Court held that the union

security clause incorporated all the refinements that have become associated with the statutory language.

In other words, "[w]hen [the Court] interpreted § 8(a)(3) in *General Motors* and *Beck*, we held the section, fairly read, included the rights that we found. To the extent that these interpretations are not obvious, the relevant provisions of § 8(a)(3) have become terms of art; the words and phrasing of the section now encompass the rights that [the Court] announced in *General Motors* and *Beck*." In concurring, Justice Kennedy thought that certain union security clause language could facilitate deception of dissenting members' rights. Is this a valid concern? Could a collective-bargaining agreement that speaks in terms of "membership" or "member in good standing" without further definition mislead employees into believing that they could be terminated if they do not become full-fledged members of the union? *See Monson Trucking, Inc.*, 324 N.L.R.B. 933 (1997).

Should the NLRB or Department of Labor (which oversees unions' LMRDA reporting requirements) be more forceful in informing employees of their rights? Certain presidential administrations have sought greater dissemination of employees' *Beck* rights. Relatedly, the NLRB has recently promulgated a rule that would require employers to post a notice in their workplaces, such as those that exist for the Fair Labor Standards Act (minimum wage and overtime) and other employment laws. However, the notice did not mention employees' *Beck* rights and the NLRB's authority to require the notice is currently under challenge in court. For more information on the NLRB notice rule, see http://www.nlrb.gov/faq/poster.

8.   The excerpt from Professor Hutchinson provides a robust defense for the need for right-to-work state legislation and for related activities by the National Right to Work Committee and its Legal Defense Foundation. Right-to-work laws are state laws which generally provide that employees are not required to join a union as a condition of receiving or retaining a job. Section 14(b) of the NLRA specifically allows states to pass these laws without them being preempted by Section 8(a)(3) (as described in Chapter 11, without Section 14(b), there would be *Garmon* preemption). Twenty-three states, most recently Indiana in 2012, have enacted right-to-work laws.

Although right-to-work laws were initially thought to apply only to union shop agreements, in *Retail Clerks International Association, Local 1625 v. Schermerhorn*, 373 U.S. 746 (1963), the Supreme Court made clear that states can also prohibit agency shop agreements like the one in *General Motors*. The Court found that agency shop provisions were the practical equivalent of union shop provisions, requiring union membership within 30 days of becoming employed by an employer. As recent legislative battles illustrate, there continues to be a campaign to increase the number of right-to-work states. What are the arguments for and against right-to-work legislation? Professor Hutchinson focuses on individual choice and the ability of individual employees not to have any affiliation with a union. How does that notion coexist with the principle of exclusive representation enshrined in the Wagner Model of labor relations? Are right-to-work laws really just right-to-free-ride laws because unions must provide representation in right-to-work states to bargaining unit members who do not pay union dues? Is the solution to this quandary to permit unions not to provide representational services to these free-riding employees?

SECTION 3   THE UNION'S RIGHT TO DISCIPLINE ITS MEMBERS

The discipline of union members by their own union has become a complex, much-litigated area. It is clear that Section 7 of the NLRA protects individuals in their right to organize, collectively bargain and to engage in concerted activities. It is also true that because of the enactment of the Taft-Hartley Act in 1947, individuals also have the right to refrain from engaging in those activities. Additionally, the Labor Management Reporting and Disclosure Act of 1959 (LMDRA or Landrum-Griffin Act), 29 U.S.C. §§ 401 et seq., also has some provisions concerning union discipline of its members.

That right to refrain from joining a union found in Section 7 after Taft-Hartley is enforced by the unfair labor practice provision found in Section 8(b)(1)(A). There is a proviso to this section, however, that appears to give a union free reign in deciding who to admit to membership and who to exclude. The intersection between these rights to refrain from joining a union and the ability of a union to "coerce and threaten" their members through internal union rules is the subject of this Section.

PROBLEM #3: I DON'T WALK THE LINE[4]

The Union and a large airplane manufacturer, Heedlock Corp. (the Company), were parties to a two-year collective-bargaining agreement. When the agreement expired, the Union called an economic strike at the Company's Mardi Gras plant in New Orleans. Eighteen days later, the parties signed a new collective-bargaining agreement and the strikers returned to work. Both of the agreements contained maintenance-of-membership clauses that required Union members to retain their membership during the contract term. New employees were required to notify the Union and the Company within 40 days of accepting employment if they elected not to join the Union.

During the 18-day strike, 143 out of 1,900 bargaining unit employees crossed the picket lines and returned to work. All of these employees were Union members at the time the strike began, although some of them resigned either before or after crossing the picket lines. Soon thereafter, the Union brought charges against the cross-over employees for violating the International Union's constitution, which provided penalties for the "improper conduct of a member," which includes "(a)ccepting employment . . . in an establishment where a strike . . . exists." After the required union procedures, including notice and opportunity for a hearing, were followed all of the cross-overs were found guilty, fined $450, and barred from holding Union office for a period of five years. Although some of the fines were reduced and some cross-overs partially paid the Union, no union member paid the full $450. After warning the members to pay their fines or face the consequences,

---

[4] This Problem is derived from the fact pattern in *NLRB v. Boeing Co.*, 412 U.S. 67 (1973).

the Union filed suits in state court against nine individual cross-overs to collect the fines. These suits are still pending.

Later, the Company filed an unfair labor practice charge with the NLRB alleging that the attempted court enforcement of the fines violated Section 8(b)(1)(A) for two reasons. First, the Union committed an unfair labor practice by fining employees who had resigned from the Union. Second, with regard to the members who were validly fined, the amount of the fines was unreasonable.

Did the Union commit ULPs as alleged by the Company? Did Congress intend to give the Board authority to regulate the size of union fines and to establish standards with respect to a fine's reasonableness?

PROBLEM MATERIALS

Movie, *On the Waterfront* (1954)

NLRB v. Allis-Chalmers Manufacturing Co., 388 U.S. 175 (1967)

Scofield v. NLRB, 394 U.S. 423 (1969)

Roger Hartley, *National Labor Relations Board Control of Union Discipline and the Myth of Nonintervention*, 16 VT. L. REV. 11 (1991)

NLRB v. ALLIS-CHALMERS MANUFACTURING CO.
388 U.S. 175 (1967)

MR. JUSTICE BRENNAN delivered the opinion of the Court.

The question here is whether a union which threatened and imposed fines, and brought suit for their collection, against members who crossed the union's picket line and went to work during an authorized strike against their employer, committed the unfair labor practice under § 8(b)(1)(A) of the National Labor Relations Act of engaging in conduct "to restrain or coerce" employees in the exercise of their right guaranteed by § 7 to "refrain from" concerted activities.

Employees at the West Allis, and La Crosse, Wisconsin, plants of respondent Allis-Chalmers Manufacturing Company were represented by locals of the United Automobile Workers. Lawful economic strikes were conducted at both plants in support of new contract demands. In compliance with the UAW constitution, the strikes were called with the approval of the International Union after at least two-thirds of the members of each local voted by secret ballot to strike. Some members of each local crossed the picket lines and worked during the strikes. After the strikes were over, the locals brought proceedings against these members charging them with violation of the International constitution and bylaws. The charges were heard by local trial committees in proceedings at which the charged members were represented by counsel. No claim of unfairness in the proceedings is made. The trials resulted in each charged member being found guilty of "conduct unbecoming a Union member" and being fined in a sum from $20 to $100 . . . .

Allis-Chalmers filed unfair labor practice violation of § 8(b)(1)(A) . . . .

I.

The panel and the majority en banc of the Court of Appeals thought that reversal of the NLRB order would be required under a literal reading of §§ 7 and 8(b)(1)(A); under that reading union members who cross their own picket lines would be regarded as exercising their rights under § 7 to refrain from engaging in a particular concerted activity, and union discipline in the form of fines for such activity would therefore "restrain or coerce" in violation of § 8(b)(1)(A) if the section's proviso is read to sanction no form of discipline other than expulsion from the union. The panel rejected that literal reading. The majority en banc adopted it, stating that the panel "mistakenly took the position that such a literal reading was unwarranted in the light of the history and purposes" of the sections, and holding that "[T]he statutes in question present no ambiguities whatsoever, and therefore do not require recourse to legislative history for clarification."

It is highly unrealistic to regard § 8(b)(1), and particularly its words "restrain or coerce," as precisely and unambiguously covering the union conduct involved in this case. On its face court enforcement of fines imposed on members for violation of membership obligations is no more conduct to "restrain or coerce" satisfaction of such obligations than court enforcement of penalties imposed on citizens for violation of their obligations as citizens to pay income taxes, or court awards of damages against a contracting party for nonperformance of a contractual obligation voluntarily undertaken. But even if the inherent imprecision of the words "restrain or coerce" may be overlooked, recourse to legislative history to determine the sense in which Congress used the words is not foreclosed. We have only this Term again admonished that labor legislation is peculiarly the product of legislative compromise of strongly held views, and that legislative history may not be disregarded merely because it is arguable that a provision may unambiguously embrace conduct called in question. Indeed, we have applied that principle to the construction of § 8(b)(1)(A) itself in holding that the section must be construed in light of the fact that it "is only one of many interwoven sections in a complex Act, mindful of the manifest purpose of the Congress to fashion a coherent national labor policy."

National labor policy has been built on the premise that by pooling their economic strength and acting through a labor organization freely chosen by the majority, the employees of an appropriate unit have the most effective means of bargaining for improvements in wages, hours, and working conditions. The policy therefore extinguishes the individual employee's power to order his own relations with his employer and creates a power vested in the chosen representative to act in the interests of all employees. "Congress has seen fit to clothe the bargaining representative with powers comparable to those possessed by a legislative body both to create and restrict the rights of those whom it represents . . . ." Thus only the union may contract the employee's terms and conditions of employment, and provisions for processing his grievances; the union may even bargain away his right to strike during the contract term, and his right to refuse to cross a lawful picket line. The employee may disagree with many of the union decisions but is bound by them. "The majority-rule concept is today unquestionably at the center of our federal labor policy." "The complete satisfaction of all who are represented is hardly to be expected. A wide range of reasonableness must be allowed a statutory bargaining representative in serving the unit it represents, subject always to complete good faith and honesty of purpose in the exercise of its discretion."

It was because the national labor policy vested unions with power to order the relations of employees with their employer that this Court found it necessary to fashion the duty of fair representation. That duty "has stood as a bulwark to prevent arbitrary union conduct against individuals stripped of traditional forms of redress by the provisions of federal labor law." For the same reason Congress in the 1959 Landrum-Griffin amendments, enacted a code of fairness to assure democratic conduct of union affairs by provisions guaranteeing free speech and assembly, equal rights to vote in elections, to attend meetings, and to participate in the deliberations and voting upon the business conducted at the meetings.

Integral to this federal labor policy has been the power in the chosen union to protect against erosion its status under that policy through reasonable discipline of members who violate rules and regulations governing membership. That power is particularly vital when the members engage in strikes. The economic strike against the employer is the ultimate weapon in labor's arsenal for achieving agreement upon its terms, and "[t]he power to fine or expel strikebreakers is essential if the union is to be an effective bargaining agent . . . ." Provisions in union constitutions and bylaws for fines and expulsion of recalcitrants, including strikebreakers, are therefore common-place and were commonplace at the time of the Taft-Hartley amendments.

In addition, the judicial view current at the time § 8(b)(1)(A) was passed was that provisions defining punishable conduct and the procedures for trial and appeal constituted part of the contract between member and union and that "The courts' role is but to enforce the contract.' In International Association of Machinists v. Gonzales, 356 U.S. 617, 618, we recognized that "(t)his contractual conception of the relation between a member and his union widely prevails in this country . . . ." Although state courts were reluctant to intervene in internal union affairs, a body of law establishing standards of fairness in the enforcement of union discipline grew up around this contract doctrine.

To say that Congress meant in 1947 by the § 7 amendments and § 8(b)(1)(A) to strip unions of the power to fine members for strikebreaking, however lawful the strike vote, and however fair the disciplinary procedures and penalty, is to say that Congress preceded the Landrum-Griffin amendments with an even more pervasive regulation of the internal affairs of unions. It is also to attribute to Congress an intent at war with the understanding of the union-membership relation which has been at the heart of its effort "to fashion a coherent labor policy" and which has been a predicate underlying action by this Court and the state courts. More importantly, it is to say that Congress limited unions in the powers necessary to the discharge of their role as exclusive statutory bargaining agents by impairing the usefulness of labor's cherished strike weapon. It is no answer that the proviso to § 8(b)(1)(A) preserves to the union the power to expel the offending member. Where the union is strong and membership therefore valuable, to require expulsion of the member visits a far more severe penalty upon the member than a reasonable fine. Where the union is weak, and membership therefore of little value, the union faced with further depletion of its ranks may have no real choice except to condone the member's disobedience. Yet it is just such weak unions for which the power to execute union decisions taken for the benefit of all employees is most critical to effective discharge of its statutory function.

Congressional meaning is of course ordinarily to be discerned in the words Congress uses. But when the literal application of the imprecise words "restrain or coerce" Congress employed in § 8(b)(1)(A) produces the extraordinary results we have mentioned we should determine whether this meaning is confirmed in the legislative history of the section.

II.

The explicit wording of § 8(b)(2), which is concerned with union powers to affect a member's employment, is in sharp contrast with the imprecise words of § 8(b)(1)(A). Section 8(b)(2) limits union power to compel an employer to discharge a terminated member other than for "failure [of the employee] to tender the periodic dues and the initiation fees uniformly required as a condition of acquiring or retaining membership." It is significant that Congress expressly disclaimed in this connection any intention to interfere with union self-government or to regulate a union's internal affairs . . . .

What legislative materials there are dealing with § 8(b)(1)(A) contain not a single word referring to the application of its prohibitions to traditional internal union discipline in general, or disciplinary fines in particular. On the contrary there are a number of assurances by its sponsors that the section was not meant to regulate in internal affairs of unions . . . .

Cogent support for an interpretation of the body of § 8(b)(1) as not reaching the imposition of fines and attempts at court enforcement is the proviso to § 8(b)(1). It states that nothing in the section shall "impair the right of a labor organization to prescribe its own rules with respect to the acquisition or retention of membership therein . . . ." Senator Holland offered the proviso during debate and Senator Ball immediately accepted it, stating that it was not the intent of the sponsors in any way to regulate the internal affairs of unions. At the very least it can be said that the proviso preserves the rights of unions to impose fines, as a lesser penalty than expulsion, and to impose fines which carry the explicit or implicit threat of expulsion for nonpayment. Therefore, under the proviso the rule in the UAW constitution governing fines is valid and the fines themselves and expulsion for nonpayment would not be an unfair labor practice. Assuming that the proviso cannot also be read to authorize court enforcement of fines, a question we need not reach, the fact remains that to interpret the body of § 8(b)(1) to apply to the imposition and collection of fines would be to impute to Congress a concern with the permissible means of enforcement of union fines and to attribute to Congress a narrow and discreet interest in banning court enforcement of such fines. Yet there is not one word in the legislative history evidencing any such congressional concern. And, as we have pointed out, a distinction between court enforcement and expulsion would have been anomalous for several reasons. First, Congress was operating within the context of the "contract theory" of the union-member relationship which widely prevailed at that time. The efficacy of a contract is precisely its legal enforceability. A lawsuit is and has been the ordinary way by which performance of private money obligations is compelled. Second, as we have noted, such a distinction would visit upon the member of a strong union a potentially more severe punishment than court enforcement of fines, while impairing the bargaining facility of the weak union by requiring it either to condone misconduct or deplete its ranks.

There may be concern that court enforcement may permit the collection of unreasonably large fines. However, even were there evidence that Congress shared this concern, this would not justify reading the Act also to bar court enforcement of reasonable fines.

The 1959 Landrum-Griffin amendments, thought to be the first comprehensive regulation by Congress of the conduct of internal union affairs, also negate the reach given § 8(b)(1)(A) by the majority en banc below . . . . However, as another major step in an evolving pattern of regulation of union conduct, the 1959 Act is a relevant consideration. Courts may properly take into account the later Act when asked to extend the reach of the earlier Act's vague language to the limits which, read literally, the words might permit." In 1959, Congress did seek to protect union members in their relationship to the union by adopting measures to insure the provision of democratic processes in the conduct of union affairs and procedural due process to members subjected to discipline. Even then, some Senators emphasized that "in establishing and enforcing statutory standards great care should be taken not to undermine union self-government or weaken unions in their role as collective-bargaining agents." The Eighty-sixth Congress was thus plainly of the view that self-government was not regulated in 1947. Indeed, that Congress expressly recognized that a union member may be "fined, suspended, expelled, or otherwise disciplined," and enacted only procedural requirements to be observed. Moreover, Congress added a proviso to the guarantee of freedom of speech and assembly disclaiming any intent "to impair the right of a labor organization to adopt and enforce reasonable rules as to the responsibility of every member toward the organization as an institution . . . ."

The 1959 provisions are significant for still another reason. We have seen that the only indication in the debates over § 8(b)(1)(A) of a reach beyond organizational tactics which restrain or coerce nonmembers was Senator Taft's concern with arbitrary and undemocratic union leadership. The 1959 amendments are addressed to that concern. The kind of regulation of internal union affairs which Senator Taft said protected stockholders of a corporation, and made necessary a "right of protest against arbitrary powers which have been exercised by some of the labor union leaders." is embodied in the 1959 Act. The requirements of adherence to democratic principles, fair procedures and freedom of speech apply to the election of union officials and extend into all aspects of union affairs. In the present case the procedures followed for calling the strikes and disciplining the recalcitrant members fully comported with these requirements, and were in every way fair and democratic. Whether § 8(b)(1)(A) proscribes arbitrary imposition of fines, or punishment for disobedience of a fiat of a union leader, are matters not presented by this case, and upon which we express no view.

Thus this history of congressional action does not support a conclusion that the Taft-Hartley prohibitions against restraint or coercion of an employee to refrain from concerted activities included a prohibition against the imposition of fines on members who decline to honor an authorized strike and attempts to collect such fines. Rather, the contrary inference is more justified in light of the repeated refrain throughout the debates on § 8(b)(1)(A) and other sections that Congress did not propose any limitations with respect to the internal affairs of unions, aside from barring enforcement of a union's internal regulations to affect a member's employment status . . . .

Reversed.

MR. JUSTICE WHITE, concurring [opinion omitted].

MR. JUSTICE BLACK, whom MR. JUSTICE DOUGLAS, MR. JUSTICE HARLAN, and MR. JUSTICE STEWART join, dissenting.

The United Automobile Workers went on a lawful economic strike against the Allis-Chalmers Manufacturing Co. Some union members, refusing to engage in the concerted strike activities, crossed the picket lines and continued to work for Allis-Chalmers. The right to refrain from engaging in such "concerted activities" is guaranteed all employees by the language of § 7 of the National Labor Relations Act, and § 8(b)(1)(A) of the Act, makes it an unfair labor practice for a union to "restrain or coerce" employees in their exercise of their § 7 rights. Despite these emphatic guarantees of the Act, the union filed charges against the employees and imposed fines against those who had crossed its picket lines to go back to work. Though the proviso to § 8(b)(1)(A) preserves the union's "right . . . to prescribe its own rules with respect to the . . . retention of membership therein," the union did not attempt to exercise its right under the proviso to expel the disciplined members when they refused to pay the fines. Instead, it brought legal proceedings in state courts to compel the payment of the fines. The Court now affirms the Labor Board's action in refusing to find the union guilty of an unfair labor practice under § 8(b)(1)(A) for fining its members because they crossed its picket lines. I cannot agree and, therefore, would affirm the judgment of the Court of Appeals which set aside the Labor Board's order.

I.

. . . With no reliance on the proviso to § 8(b)(1)(A) or on the meaning of § 7, the Court's holding boils down to this: a court-enforced reasonable fine for nonparticipation in a strike does not "restrain or coerce" an employee in the exercise of his right not to participate in the strike. In holding as it does, the Court interprets the words "restrain or coerce" in a way directly opposed to their literal meaning, for the Court admits that fines are as coercive as penalties imposed on citizens for the nonpayment of taxes. Though Senator Taft, in answer to charges that these words were ambiguous, said their meaning "is perfectly clear," and though any union official with sufficient intelligence and learning to be chosen as such could hardly fail to comprehend the meaning of these plain, simple English words, the Court insists on finding an "inherent imprecision" in these words. And that characterization then allows the Court to resort to "[w]hat legislative materials there are." In doing so, the Court finds three significant things: (1) there is "not a single word" to indicate that § 8(b)(1)(A) was intended to apply to "traditional internal union discipline in general, or disciplinary fines in particular"; (2) the "repeated refrain" running through the debates on the section was that Congress did not intend to impose any limitations on the "internal affairs of unions"; (3) the Senators who supported the section were primarily concerned with union coercion during organizational drives and with union violence in general.

Even were I to agree with the Court's three observations about the legislative history of § 8(b)(1)(A), I do not think they alone justify disregarding the plain meaning of the section, and it seems perfectly clear to me that the Court does not think so either. The real reason for the Court's decision is its policy judgment that unions, especially weak ones, need the power to impose fines on strikebreakers and to enforce those fines in court. It is not enough, says the Court, that the unions have the power to expel those members who refuse to participate in a strike or who fail to pay fines imposed on them for such failure to participate; it is essential that weak unions have the choice between expulsion and court-enforced fines, simply because the latter are more effective in the sense of being more punitive. Though the entire mood of Congress in 1947 was to curtail the power of unions, as it had previously curtailed the power of employers, in order to equalize the power of the two, the Court is unwilling to believe that Congress intended to impair "the usefulness of labor's cherished strike weapon." I cannot agree with this conclusion or subscribe to the Court's unarticulated premise that the Court has power to add a new weapon to the union's economic arsenal whenever the Court believes that the union needs that weapon. That is a job for Congress, not this Court . . . .

VI.

The National Labor Relations Act, as originally passed and amended from time to time, is the work product of draftsmen skilled by long experience in labor affairs. These draftsmen thoroughly understood labor legislation terminology, especially the oft-used words "restrain or coerce." Sections 7 and 8 together bespeak a strong purpose of Congress to leave workers wholly free to determine in what concerted labor activities they will engage or decline to engage. This freedom of workers to go their own way in this field, completely unhampered by pressures of employers or unions, is and always has been a basic purpose of the labor legislation now under consideration. In my judgment it ill behooves this Court to strike so diligently to defeat this unequivocally declared purpose of Congress, merely because the Court believes that too much freedom of choice for workers will impair the effective power of unions. A court-enforced fine is certainly coercive, certainly affects the employee's job, and certainly is not a traditional method of internal union discipline. When applied by a union to an employee who has joined it as a condition of obtaining employment in a union shop, it defeats the provisions of the Act designed to prevent union security clauses from being used for purposes other than to compel payment of dues. In such a situation it cannot be justified on any theory that the employee has contracted away or waived his § 7 rights.

Where there is clear legislative history to justify it, courts often decline to follow the literal meaning of a statute. But this practice is fraught with dangers when the legislative history is at best brief, inconclusive, and ambiguous. This is precisely such a case, and I dissent because I am convinced that the Court has ignored the literal language of § 8(b)(1)(A) in order to give unions a power which the Court, but not Congress, thinks they need.

SCOFIELD v. NLRB
394 U.S. 423 (1969)

Mr. Justice White delivered the opinion of the Court.

Half the production employees of the Wisconsin Motor Corporation are paid on a piecework or incentive basis. They and the other employees are represented by respondent union, which has had contractual relations with the company since 1937. In 1938 the union initiated a ceiling on the production for which its members would accept immediate piecework pay. This was done at first by gentlemen's agreement among the members, but since 1944 by union rule enforceable by fines and expulsion. As the rule functions now, members may produce as much as they like each day, but may only draw pay up to the ceiling rate. The additional production is "banked" by the company; that is, wages due for it are retained by the company and paid out to the employee for days on which the production ceiling has not been reached because of machine breakdown or for some other reason. If the member demands to be paid in full each pay period over the ceiling rate the company will comply, but the union assesses a fine of $1 for each violation, and in cases of repeated violation may fine the member up to $100 for "conduct unbecoming a union member." Failure to pay the fine may lead to expulsion. As the trial examiner found, the company's complaint is not and cannot be that "the employee, for the pay he receives, has not given the requisite quid pro quo in production." Rather, the question is the extent to which the group will forgo for pay the rest periods it has bargained for, and the discipline which the union may invoke to achieve unity toward this end which, the trial examiner found, was "manifestly a matter affecting the interest of the group and in which its collective bargaining strength hinges upon the cooperation of its individual components."

The collective bargaining contract between employer and union defines a "machine rate" of hourly pay guaranteed to the employees. The piecework rate, as defined by the contract, is set at such a level that "the average competent operator working at a reasonable pace (as determined by a time study) shall earn not less than the machine rate of his assigned task." Allowances are made in the time study for setting up machinery, cleaning tools, fatigue, and personal needs. By ignoring these allowances or by speed and efficiency it is possible for an industrious employee to produce faster than the machine rate. If he does so, he is entitled to additional pay. Union members, however, are subject to the banking procedures imposed by the union rule.

The margin between the "machine" rate set by the contract and the ceiling rate set by the union was 10¢ per hour in 1944. As a result of collective bargaining between company and union over both the machine and ceiling rates, the margin has been increased to between 45¢ and 50¢, depending on the skill level of the job. The company has regularly urged the union to abandon the ceiling and has never agreed to refuse employees immediate pay for work done over the ceiling. However, the parties have bargained over the ceiling rate and the company has extracted from the union promises to increase the ceiling rate. The company opens its work records to the union to permit it to check compliance with the ceiling; pays union stewards for time spent in this checking activity as legitimate union business; and banks money for union members complying with the rule. The ceiling rate is also used in computing piece rate increases and in settling grievances.

This case arose in 1961 when a random card check by the union showed that petitioners, among other union members, had exceeded the ceiling. The union membership imposed fines of $50 to $100, and a year's suspension from the union. Petitioners refused to pay the fines, and the union brought suit in state court to collect the fines as a matter of local contract law. Petitioners then initiated charges before the National Labor Relations Board, arguing that union enforcement of its rule through the collection of fines was an unfair labor practice. Petitioners asserted that their right to refrain from "concerted activities," . . . was impaired by the union's effort to "restrain or coerce" them, in violation of NLRA, § 8(b)(1)(A). The trial examiner, after extensive findings, concluded that there was no violation of the Act, and his findings and recommendations were adopted by the Board, whose order was enforced by the Court of Appeals for the Seventh Circuit. We affirm . . . .

II.

Section 8(b)(1) makes it an unfair labor practice to "restrain or coerce (A) employees in the exercise of the rights guaranteed in (§ 7): Provided, That this paragraph shall not impair the right of a labor organization to prescribe its own rules with respect to the acquisition or retention of membership therein . . . ."

Based on the legislative history of the section, including its proviso, the Court in NLRB v. Allis-Chalmers Mfg. Co., 388 U.S. 175, 195 (1967), distinguished between internal and external enforcement of union rules and held that "Congress did not propose any limitations with respect to the internal affairs of unions, aside from barring enforcement of a union's internal regulations to affect a member's employment status." A union rule, duly adopted and not the arbitrary fiat of a union officer, forbidding the crossing of a picket line during a strike was therefore enforceable against voluntary union members by expulsion or a reasonable fine . . . .

This interpretation of § 8(b)(1) . . . was reinforced by the Landrum-Griffin Act of 1959 which, although it dealt with the internal affairs of unions, including the procedures for imposing fines or expulsion, did not purport to overturn or modify the Board's interpretation of § 8(b)(1). And it was this interpretation which the Board followed in Allis-Chalmers and in the case now before us.

Although the Board's construction of the section emphasizes the sanction imposed, rather than the rule itself, and does not involve the Board in judging the fairness or wisdom of particular union rules, it has become clear that if the rule invades or frustrates an overriding policy of the labor laws the rule may not be enforced, even by fine or expulsion, without violating § 8(b)(1). In both *Skura* and *Marine Workers*, the Board was concerned with union rules requiring a member to exhaust union remedies before filing an unfair labor practice charge with the Board. That rule, in the Board's view, frustrated the enforcement scheme established by the statute and the union would commit an unfair labor practice by fining or expelling members who violated the rule.

The *Marine Workers* case came here and the result reached by the Board was sustained, the Court agreeing that the rule in question was contrary to the plain policy of the Act to keep employees completely free from coercion against making complaints to the Board. Frustrating this policy was beyond the legitimate interest of the labor organization, at least where the member's complaint concerned conduct of the employer as well as the union.

Under this dual approach, § 8(b)(1) leaves a union free to enforce a properly adopted rule which reflects a legitimate union interest, impairs no policy Congress has imbedded in the labor laws, and is reasonably enforced against union members who are free to leave the union and escape the rule. This view of the statute must be applied here.

III.

In the case at hand, there is no showing in the record that the fines were unreasonable or the mere fiat of a union leader, or that the membership of petitioners in the union was involuntary. Moreover, the enforcement of the rule was not carried out through means unacceptable in themselves, such as violence or employer discrimination. It was enforced solely through the internal technique of union fines, collected by threat of expulsion or judicial action. The inquiry must therefore focus on the legitimacy of the union interest vindicated by the rule and the extent to which any policy of the Act may be violated by the union-imposed production ceiling.

As both the trial examiner and the Court of Appeals noted, union opposition to unlimited piecework pay systems is historic. Union apprehension, not without foundation, is that such systems will drive up employee productivity and in turn create pressures to lower the piecework rate so that at the new, higher level of output employees are earning little more than they did before. The fear is that the competitive pressure generated will endanger workers' health, foment jealousies, and reduce the work force. In addition, the findings of the trial examiner were that the ceiling served as a yardstick for the settlement of job allowance grievances, that it has played an important role in negotiating the minimum hourly rate and that it is the standard for "factoring" the hourly rate raises into the piecework rate. The view of the trial examiner was that "in terms of a union's traditional function of trying to serve the economic interests of the group as a whole, the Union has a very real, immediate, and direct interest in it."

It is doubtless true that the union rule in question here affects the interests of all three participants in the labor-management relation: employer, employee, and union. Although the enforcement of the rule is handled as an internal union matter, the rule has and was intended to have an impact beyond the confines of the union organization. But as *Allis-Chalmers* and *Marine Workers* made clear, it does not follow from this that the enforcement of the rule violates § 8(b)(1)(A), unless some impairment of a statutory labor policy can be shown.

The principal contention of the petitioners is that the rule impedes collective bargaining, a process nurtured in many ways by the Act. But surely this is not the case here. The union has never denied that the ceiling is a bargainable issue. It has never refused to bargain about it as far as this record shows. Indeed, the union has at various times agreed to raise its ceiling in return for an increase in the piece rate, and the ceiling has been regularly used to compute the new piece rate. In light of this bargaining history it can hardly be said that the union rule has removed this issue from the bargaining table. The company has repeatedly sought an agreement eliminating the piecework ceiling, an agreement which, had it been obtained, unquestionably would have been violated by the union rule. But the company could not attain this. Although, like the union, it could have pressed the point to impasse, followed by strike or lockout, it has never done so. Instead, it has signed contracts recognizing the ceiling, has tolerated it, and has cooperated in its administration by honoring requests by employees to bank their pay for over-ceiling work. We discern no basis in the statutory policy encouraging collective bargaining for giving the employer a better bargain than he has been able to strike at the bargaining table.

Nor does the union ceiling itself or compliance with it by union members violate the collective contract. The company and the union had agreed to an incentive pay scale, but they have also established a guaranteed minimum or machine rate considerably below the union ceiling and defined in the contract as the rate of production of an average, efficient worker. The contract therefore leaves in the hands of the employee the option of taking full advantage of his allowances, performing only as an average employee and not reaching even the ceiling rate. At least there is nothing before us to indicate that the company disciplines individuals who work at only the machine rate or individuals who produce more but who choose not to exceed the union ceiling. The same decision can be made collectively by the union. Although it has agreed in the contract to a pay scale for production in excess of ceiling, that fact in the context of this case does not support an inference that the union has agreed not to impose the ceiling or that its action in announcing one is somehow contrary to the contract. And if neither union nor member is in breach of contract for establishing and adhering to the ceiling, it is equally clear that the rule neither causes nor invites a contract violation by the employer who stands ready to pay an employee for his over-ceiling production or to bank it at his request . . . .

That the choice to remain a member results in differences between union members and other employees raises no serious issue under § 8(b)(2) and § 8(a) (3) of the Act, because the union has not induced the employer to discriminate against the member but has merely forbidden the member to take advantage of benefits which the employer stands willing to confer. Those sections are not aimed at completely internal union discipline of union members, even though the discipline may result in the member's refusal to accept work offered by the employer. Allis-Chalmers makes this quite clear.

The union rule here left the collective bargaining process unimpaired, breached no collective contract, required no pay for unperformed services, induced no discrimination by the employer against any class of employees, and represents no dereliction by the union of its duty of fair representation. In light of this, and the acceptable manner in which the rule was enforced, vindicating a legitimate union interest, it is impossible to say that it contravened any policy of the Act.

We affirm, holding that the union rule is valid and that its enforcement by reasonable fines does not constitute the restraint or coercion proscribed by § 8(b)(1)(A).

Affirmed.

MR. JUSTICE MARSHALL took no part in the consideration or decision of this case.

MR. JUSTICE BLACK, dissenting [opinion omitted].

Roger Hartley, *National Labor Relations Board Control of Union Discipline and the Myth of Nonintervention*
16 VT. L. REV. 11 (1991)[5]

INTRODUCTION

No brighter star shines in the firmament of national labor policy rhetoric than the promise to American workers of their right to designate union "representatives of their own choosing." The National Labor Relations Board (NLRB), recognizing this much heralded autonomy, professes a fierce commitment not to obstruct union members' right to choose their own leaders and otherwise oversee internal governance. Although the NLRB has publicly embraced a policy of nonintervention, an examination of its activities demonstrates that it has become a major regulator of internal union government. For example, the NLRB limits the membership majority's autonomy to determine eligibility to vote in internal union elections and hold union office, it monitors the union officer election campaign, and it constricts members' ability to compel union leaders to conform to the will of their constituencies.

This article explains how the NLRB, contrary to its protestations of noninterference with internal union affairs, has perfected its grip on union self-governance through control of the union disciplinary processes. The disparity between the Board's policies and its actions discredits the Board's proclaimed abstention.

Second, this article examines whether the NLRB overreaches its regulatory authority through its intervention in the officer selection and discipline processes. NLRB regulation of union discipline rests primarily on section 8(b)(1)(A) of the Labor Management Relations (Taft-Hartley) Act. The Board's early decisions under this section, as well as judicial precedent, defined a narrower role for NLRB intervention than the role presently claimed by the Board. Courts increasingly are rejecting the NLRB's assertion of broad regulatory authority. The Supreme Court's union discipline cases, decided over a decade ago, initiated these judicial misgivings. Moreover, the Supreme Court's more recent decisions in *Pattern Makers' League v. NLRB* and *Communication Workers v. Beck* require a reappraisal of expansive NLRB monitoring of internal union life. *Pattern Makers'* and *Beck* ring in a new era of voluntary unionism that demands acknowledgement.

Finally, this article addresses the various conflicting interests that underlie and oppose NLRB intervention in internal union affairs. The Board's decisions rarely discuss their practical impact on unions or their contribution to the national policy aspirations that unions be governed democratically and independently. The desirability of Board intervention, however, should be assessed by considering all of the legitimate conflicting interests raised: the individual rights at risk, the union majority's collective associational interests, and the wider public interest in union democratic self-government with minimal governmental interference.

As recently as 1973, the Chief Justice of the United States Supreme Court stated, "It is odd, to say the least, to find a union urging on us severe limitations on NLRB authority [because the NLRB lacks the requisite expertise]." However, in light of increasing NLRB control over the union disciplinary process, requests to limit NLRB authority seem less odd today. The NLRB has exceeded its authority by intervening in internal union affairs and it is time to reevaluate the appropriate limits on NLRB authority.

I. The Transformation of Section 8(b)(1)(A)

The United States has many laws regulating the selection of union officers. Title IV of the Labor Management Reporting and Disclosure Act of 1959 (LMRDA) explicitly regulates union officer elections. In addition, union members may initiate litigation directly under Title I of the LMRDA to challenge abuses of the officer selection process. Title I also regulates the discipline of union members, including union officers, with regard to their intra-union political activities. The NLRB has become an additional regulator of the internal union political process through its supervision of union discipline.

A union employs discipline to achieve various objectives. A monetary fine may be intended to punish or deter future breaches of obligations of union membership. A fine, however, carries no statement from the group that the individual recipient lacks continued worthiness to participate in union governance. When, however, a member is expelled or suspended from membership, barred from eligibility to be a candidate for union office, or precluded from attending union meetings for a set period, the union collective sends a different message. The union may deter and punish, but it also excludes the disciplined member from participation in the internal union political process.

Appreciation of the NLRB's role as intervenor in internal union political processes begins with an understanding that the Board's control over union member expulsion shifts the locus of authority outside the union because the NLRB determines leadership eligibility within the union. NLRB authority to regulate union discipline derives from section 8(b)(1)(A) of the Taft-Hartley Act. Section 8(b)(1)(A) prohibits union restraint or coercion of an employee's right to engage in or refrain from concerted activity for the purpose of collective bargaining or other mutual aid or protection. Section 8(b)(1)(A) provides, however, that the section shall not be interpreted to "impair the right of a labor organization to prescribe its own rules with respect to the acquisition or retention of membership in the union."

Section 8(b)(1)(A) seems to state unequivocally that the Board may not proscribe union member expulsion. Moreover, the Board may not bar the imposition of lesser forms of discipline that only affect one's "retention of membership," such as temporary suspension or ineligibility to be a candidate for office or to attend union meetings. Nevertheless, the NLRB now routinely bans union discipline that affects only membership rights.

A. The Original Interpretation

. . . The present interpretation of section 8(b)(1)(A) began to evolve in 1948 when the NLRB decided *National Maritime Union.* The issue raised was whether a union's attempt, through collective bargaining, to obtain an unlawful closed shop agreement violated section 8(b)(1)(A). In another case discussing *National Maritime,* the Board examined the section's legislative history and decided that, although Congress used the term "restraint and coercion" in section 8(b)(1)(A), the legislative scheme envisaged a narrow construction "limited to situations involving actual or threatened economic reprisals and physical violence by unions . . . to compel individuals to join a union or cooperate in a union's strike activities." The NLRB applied this vision of limited section 8(b)(1)(A) regulatory authority in *International Typographical Union (American Newspaper Publishers).* In that case, an international union allegedly threatened local unions and members with summary expulsion if they failed to engage in conduct inconsistent with their duty to bargain in good faith. Citing its decision in *National Maritime,* the Board dismissed all section 8(b)(1)(A) allegations. The Board held that "Congress unmistakenly intended to, and did, remove the application of a union's membership rules to its members from the proscriptions of Section 8(b)(1)(A), irrespective of any ulterior reasons motivating the union's application of such rules or the direct effect thereof on particular employees." . . .

B. The Board's 1964 Internal Union Affairs Trilogy

In 1964, the Board decided three pivotal cases. Two of these cases reached the Supreme Court. The third, while not reaching the Supreme Court, considered an issue that the Court resolved soon thereafter. These three cases highlight the Board's expansionist tendencies. Although the Board originally was committed to noninterference with internal union affairs, it reversed itself in the span of less than one year by accepting various limitations and exceptions that eventually blossomed into a rich source of authority to regulate internal union government.

The Board's landmark decision, *Local 283, UAW (Scofield),* held that, pursuant to section 8(b)(1)(A), it was lawful for a union to fine members for violating the union's production ceilings. The majority reasoned that section 8(b)(1)(A) prohibits only "unlawful . . . use of force, violence, physical obstruction or threats thereof to accomplish certain purposes associated with organizational activity and strikes." Even if section 8(b)(1)(A) has a broader reach, as the Supreme Court's decision in *ILGWU v. NLRB (Bernhard-Altmann Texas Corp.)* suggests, "internal union disciplines were not among the restraints intended to be encompassed by the section." The majority explained that even before the proviso was added to section 8(b)(1)(A), Senator Taft assured his colleagues that "the sponsors had no intention to interfere with a union's internal affairs." As the Board majority concluded,

[T]he Board has not been empowered by Congress to police a union decision that a member is or is not in good standing or to pass judgment on the penalties a union may impose on a member so long as the penalty does not impair the member's status as an employee. . . . [Otherwise] the Board . . . [must] sit in judgment on union standards of conduct for its members even though such standards are not enforced by threats affecting the member's job tenure or job opportunities.

Dissenting, Member Leedom sounded an alarm that has dominated the section 8(b)(1)(A) debate ever since. "Under my colleagues' reading of the proviso, it would appear that the Union can turn any employment matter or Section 7 right into an internal union affair simply by adopting a union rule or bylaw dealing with the subject and disciplining employees thereunder." Member Leedom cited a parade of horribles that he posited would be beyond the reach of section 8(b)(1)(A) under the majority's reasoning.

Concurring, Member Jenkins considered it appropriate for the NLRB to monitor the type of discipline imposed as well as the reason for its imposition. He concurred with the majority's conclusion, however, finding nothing in the Act regulating a union's authority to impose production ceilings. Hence, the union rule "cannot be said . . . to offend the Act even if it were . . . unreasonable . . . ."

Seven months later, in *Operating Engineers Local 138 (Charles S. Skura)*, the NLRB considered union discipline imposed for reasons offensive to the Act - filing unfair labor practice charges with the NLRB without first exhausting internal union remedies. Abandoning the view that section 8(b)(1)(A) is limited to violence or physical obstruction, or threats thereof, used to accomplish ends involving organizational activity and strikes, the Board unanimously held that union discipline may not "run counter to other recognized public policies . . . ." The Board then reasoned that there exists an "overriding public interest" that no private organization should be permitted to prevent or regulate access to the Board.

The Board's reasoning in *Skura*, that no private organization may impede Board processes, seems to encompass union attempts to regulate access to the Board through purely internal means, such as expulsion. This is so notwithstanding the Board's previous assurances that unions may expel members for any reason without violating section 8(b)(1)(A). Indeed, within a week of its *Skura* decision, the Board applied this reasoning to cases involving only expulsion from union membership.

Skura arguably is the most significant of all NLRB union discipline cases because it positions the Board as the dominant union discipline regulator. By claiming the power to invalidate any union discipline that contravenes "other recognized public policies," the Board controls the union disciplinary process because of its authority to define "public policies" and to adjudicate the issue of contravention. No union discipline can escape this net.

Two months after its decision in *Skura*, the Board decided the third of its 1964 trilogy: *Local 248, UAW (Allis-Chalmers)*. *Allis-Chalmers* raised the issue of whether section 8(b)(1)(A) proscribes the imposition of union fines on members for crossing lawful picket lines. Three members of the Board held that fining members who cross a lawful picket line "is a far cry from . . . *Skura*." The fine was within the "competence of the union to enforce" because it sought to promote a legitimate union interest - the preservation of the union's integrity during a strike, a "time of crisis for the union." Moreover, the fine did not interfere with the enforcement of the Act, as was the case in *Skura*, and the strike and picket lines were lawful.

The *Allis-Chalmers* majority should have stated that its reasoning was a "far cry" from *Scofield*, not from *Skura*. In *Scofield*, this same majority recognized a congressional intent mandating NLRB abstention from the regulation of internal union discipline when a member's employment status is not affected. *Skura* modified that approach in an exceptional context, when a union fined a member to deter access to the Board's unfair labor practice processes. Although the majority in *Allis-Chalmers* did not measure the union's actions by whether they override public policies, it, nevertheless, did note the legitimacy of the union's interest, the effect on the Act's administration, and the lawfulness of the strike and picketing. In addition, Member Jenkins, concurring, urged that the Board inquire into the procedural regularity of the discipline. Armed with the power to act as arbiter of legitimate motivations and procedures and to determine their effect on other public policies, the NLRB became the internal union discipline regulatory czar. Ultimately, the Supreme Court considered whether Congress intended to vest such power in the NLRB.

C. The Supreme Court's Union Discipline Cases

The first case to reach the Supreme Court was *NLRB v. Allis-Chalmers Manufacturing Co.* Four members of the Court agreed with the majority of the Board in *Local 283, UAW (Scofield)* that section 8(b)(1)(A) was not intended to regulate internal union affairs. By enacting section 8(b)(1)(A), "Congress did not propose any limitations with respect to the internal affairs of unions, aside from barring enforcement of a union's internal regulations to affect a member's employment status." . . .

. . . In *Scofield v. NLRB*, Court dicta transformed the simple logic of the Board's opinion into a formidable six part test. Justice White, writing for a seven member majority, acknowledged the holding of *Allis-Chalmers*, which was that Congress did not propose any limitations with respect to union enforcement of internal affairs aside from " 'barring enforcement of a union's internal regulations to affect a member's employment status.' " Yet, the Court added that "if the rule invades or frustrates an overriding policy of the labor laws, the rule may not be enforced, *even by fine or expulsion*, without violating section 8(b)(1) (A)." To these two limitations, the *Scofield* majority added four more: 1) the rule must be a "properly adopted rule," 2) it must "reflect a legitimate union interest," 3) it must be "reasonably enforced against union members who are free to leave the union and escape the rule," and 4) the amount of the union fine must not be "unreasonable."

It has been argued that *Scofield* turned *Allis-Chalmers* on its head and invited conflict: social conflict as to the bounds of legitimate union interests, judicial and political-administrative conflict (in and over the Board) as to what Congress had or had not imbedded in the law, and internecine conflicts among workers, some of them tempted to leave the unions and escape the rules at opportune times. After *Scofield*, much of the litigation revolved around the determination of which of the several limitations *Scofield* expressed would find a permanent home in section 8(b)(1)(A) . . . .

Pattern Makers' League v. NLRB signals a . . . retreat from *Scofield.* By holding that it was unlawful for a union to restrict members who wanted to resign from the union, the Court defined the sweep of the section 8(b)(1)(A) proviso. The Court reasoned that Congress intended that "a union should be free to 'refuse a man admission to the union, or *expel him from the union.*' " The Court did not suggest that the autonomy to expel members was dependent on whether the reason for the expulsion frustrated any policy in the Taft-Hartley Act or any other labor law.

The Supreme Court's retreat from *Scofield* is significant but, as yet, uncertain. The legitimacy of the Board's role as a dominant internal union affairs regulator depends on the *Scofield* dicta stating that the union majority may not enforce an obligation of union membership, by either fine or expulsion, if the union either has no legitimate interest for invoking the discipline, or the discipline frustrates overriding labor law policies . . . .

II. NLRB Intervention When Union Discipline Is Seen to Frustrate Labor Policies in the Taft-Hartley Act

A. The NLRB's Frustration of Congressional Intent

Since the Supreme Court's decision in *Scofield v. NLRB*, the NLRB has invalidated additional categories of union discipline because they frustrate overriding labor policies. Although the Board is tolerant of certain union disciplinary action, it prohibits other such action. For example, while the NLRB has held that a union does not violate the Act by expelling or suspending a member for filing a decertification petition with the Board, it also has held that a union may not impose a court enforceable fine for filing such a petition. Discipline for filing union security deauthorization petitions is similarly evaluated. The Board also bars a union from fining a member for supporting a rival union in order to oust the incumbent union; but the Board permits the union to expel such a member or bar the member from holding office. Still, the Board does not permit any discipline of members who file unit clarification petitions, reasoning that these are more akin to unfair labor practice charges than decertification petitions.

Permitting a union to expel for defensive purposes protects the union's interest in excluding disloyal members from its political community, and deprives dissident members access to the strategy and tactics of the union. Yet, by prohibiting fines, the Board becomes ensnared in the complex process of determining the motivation underlying the fine . . . .

Beyond the Board access cases, the NLRB controls union discipline to preserve the integrity of the Taft-Hartley Act labor policies in many additional ways. By failing to distinguish between fines and expulsion, the Board positions itself to influence eligibility to participate in the selection of union leaders. Moreover, by reserving to itself the decision of whether union discipline frustrates labor policy, the NLRB adds a new layer of restriction on a union's choice of economic weapons.

For example, nothing in the Act explicitly prohibits a union from inducing employees to strike in breach of a no-strike clause. Such inducement may subject the union to damages or to an injunction, but Congress has specifically chosen not to make a breach of a no-strike clause an unfair labor practice. Nevertheless, the Board views union inducement to breach a no-strike clause as an unfair labor practice when the inducement is effected through union discipline. The Board reasons that it is seeking to protect the sanctity of the collective bargaining agreement by disallowing such union discipline.

Most union discipline cases involving the breach of a no-strike clause arise in sympathy strike contexts. Whether the strike breaches the contract is usually a close question. Sometimes the Board cannot agree with its administrative law judge or even agree with its own prior ruling on the question in a given case. Yet the Board, superimposing its understanding of the contract, prohibits a union's expulsion in these circumstances. Consequently, the NLRB, and not the union members, determines who shall be eligible to nominate union officers, vote for such officers, and run for elective office. The NLRB thereby removes an economic weapon from the union's arsenal . . . .

The Board's use of section 8(b)(1)(A) to convert union economic weapons that Congress chose not to prohibit into conduct violative of section 8(b)(1)(A) is not what the Supreme Court intended in *Scofield*. In *NLRB v. Insurance Agents' Union*, decided prior to *Scofield*, the Court chastised the Board for attempting to use section 8(b)(3) of the Act to enlarge its regulatory power to restrict the parties' choice of economic weapons beyond those powers expressly provided by Congress. In *Insurance Agents'*, the Board attempted to prohibit a partial strike, used as leverage against the employer during bargaining, by making the union's inducement of the partial strike a violation of the duty to bargain in good faith. The Court condemned the NLRB's attempt to add to its arsenal of regulatory authority by using section 8(b)(3) of the Act to outlaw a union's inducement of partial strikes. Noting that "Congress has been rather specific when it has come to outlaw particular economic weapons on the part of unions and that . . . the activities here involved have never been specifically outlawed by Congress," the Court found that the NLRB has no license to determine the permissibility of partial strikes as economic weapons. The NLRB's attempt to amend the statute administratively frustrates a policy of the Act that some activities, left unregulated by Congress, are to be controlled by the parties themselves.

The principles spelled out in *Insurance Agents'* are violated by the Board's cases making it unlawful for a union to discipline a member for refusing to engage in a partial strike (i.e., for performing overtime). The Board created unfair labor practices from the same union economic weapons that the Court concluded Congress chose to leave unregulated by any governmental authority. The Court could not have intended in *Scofield* to permit the Board to accomplish through section 8(b)(1)(A) what it had denied the Board power to accomplish through section 8(b)(3) in *Insurance Agents'* . . . .

B. The NLRB's Failure to Consider Union Interests Adequately When Balancing Union Interests Against Overriding Labor Policies

. . . The new voluntary unionism guaranteed by *Pattern Makers' League v. NLRB* must now be factored into that balance. More than any other recent development in the field of union discipline, *Pattern Makers' League v. NLRB* protects the individual from the effects of majoritarian rule. The Supreme Court has required a reevaluation of union discipline cases which involve a member being able to escape the consequences of having joined the union. Resignation from the union permits the former member to choose not to engage in unprotected concerted activities and thereby avoid all risk of discipline. Certainly, the member who resigns forfeits the right to participate in the future governance of the union, but that is the exact choice *NLRB v. Allis-Chalmers Manufacturing Co.* and *Pattern Makers'* anticipate.

When balancing the interests of the individual, the membership majority, and the public, the fact that the membership majority chose to expel, rather than to fine, a member charged with violating a membership obligation is significant. This is required by the explicit guarantee of section 8(b)(1)(A), granting the majority the autonomy to expel. The Supreme Court endorsed this principle in *Allis-Chalmers*. In *Pattern Makers'*, the Court restated the principle that a union's choice of expulsion as a remedy for violating an obligation of membership should have a significant impact on the Board's decision. . . .

In short, *Scofield*, at a minimum, requires the Board to find that union discipline contravenes an "overriding" policy in our labor laws. Such a determination requires a balancing that must weigh the right to resign guaranteed by *Pattern Makers'*. However, the right to resign has its concomitant: the union's right to expel. Hence, in most cases, the union's choice of expulsion to enforce membership obligations should not be viewed as contrary to any overriding policy.

C. The Societal Need for Union Self-Governance

The NLRB's control of the unions' right to expel undermines an important national labor policy favoring democratically governed independent unions. Only the most substantial countervailing public interests may outweigh the membership majority's right to an independent democratic union, and the inherent power to decide who shall govern the union. This national commitment to democratic unions governed independently from the state is well established. Union democracy is necessary if unions are to perform their assigned societal functions. National labor policy is rooted in the conviction that workers have a right to a voice at the work place. The best way to secure that voice and give it effect is through a union that is responsive to membership's concerns.

Unions have at least two democratic functions. The first is to provide employees with the dignity gained from participating in industrial government. The second is to provide employees with an effective voice in the workplace by replacing the employer's arbitrary power with clearly established union rules and procedures contained in a collective agreement. To perform these functions effectively, unions must operate as democratic organizations. Outside the work place, unions stabilize workers' political power by representing them in the political arena. In order for this political voice to be truly representative, workers must control the direction and operation of their unions. "An effective internal political process provides such control and checks the misrepresentation of members' views. In this sense societal democracy depends on union democracy."

Unions also perform economic functions. They influence the amount of compensation a worker receives and its form. They provide job security and protect against capriciousness and error in personnel decisions. They also make the work environment healthier, both physically and psychologically. Moreover, unions' collective bargaining power decentralizes economic decisions . . . .

Unlike businesses, unions lack the "universal quantifier" of profit margin to gauge the efficiency of the leadership's bargaining goals. A union's internal political process replaces the market's influence by ensuring that union leadership is responsive to membership's needs. It also assures that a labor contract's benefits and burdens are distributed fairly.

The importance of union democratic governance should limit governmental intervention in internal union affairs. Unions cannot serve as "centres of power and instruments of control apart from the State," and collective bargaining cannot "shorten[] the reach of central legal control by establishing a separate structure of industrial government as an alternative to suffocating statism," unless unions remain independent, self-governing institutions. It is "because unions are among the important 'competing units of social and economic aggregation' that their independence from state control is so vital." The Senate Committee on Labor and Public Welfare summarized the underlying labor policy by stating that governmental interference should be avoided if it would "undermine union self-government . . . weaken unions in their role as collective bargaining agents, or cross over into the area of trade union licensing and destroy union independence."

When the NLRB prohibits expulsion in circumstances other than where necessary to protect an overriding public interest, it undermines union self-governance, reduces their effectiveness as collective bargaining agents, and destroys union independence. Self-governance is undermined because NLRB intervention encourages dissident members to look to the Board, rather than to the internal union political process, as the final arbiter of appropriate union policy. For example, if the NLRB permitted the union to discipline those who perform overtime work against the will of the membership majority, the dissident wishing to remain a union member would be forced to participate in the internal union political process and persuade the majority to amend the rules and allow overtime. When, however, the NLRB superimposes its will over that of the union majority, the dissident procures a political victory without expending any political effort. The interests of those members who worked diligently to persuade the majority to approve a no-overtime rule are overlooked. In short, when the NLRB substitutes its own processes for a union's internal political process, it enhances the importance of the former and undermines the latter.

The NLRB's union discipline cases have also weakened unions' collective bargaining ability. The NLRB has repeatedly prohibited the use of expulsion to discipline a member who refuses to participate in a concerted effort to counter employer power during a labor dispute. By limiting the unions' ability to discipline their members, these prohibitions weaken the unions' effectiveness as collective bargaining agents.

The NLRB's regulatory authority, which enables it to discipline unions when they act "irresponsibly," compromises the unions' independence. This is especially true because the NLRB's definition of "responsible" union behavior is primarily premised upon the Board's determination of whether the union conduct in question undermines national labor policy. As a result of this power, the NLRB has the ability to control, to a certain degree, who within the union is permitted to nominate officers, vote for such officers, and run for union office. This control puts the Board in a position to influence the outcome of union elections. The state's commitment to union independence is inconsistent with the Board possessing unbridled discretion to determine permissible and impermissible economic weapons, or to determine eligibility to participate in the selection of union leaders. Union independence is imperiled when an executive agency of government, and not Congress, is given the authority to define the scope of responsible union conduct . . . .

CONCLUSION

The NLRB continually claims noninterference in internal union affairs and this claim has become too soothing a shibboleth to be excised from its discourse. Nevertheless, it is important that the NLRB and the public understand the myth of nonintervention. Through control of union disciplinary processes, the Board regulates important aspects of internal union governance-such as member selection and direction of both appointed and elected union representatives. The NLRB has a direct impact upon internal union affairs in many other ways as well.

Some may be neither surprised nor alarmed to discover a government agency hiding behind rhetorical cover. If the Board's protestations of nonintervention shield or deflect its actions from scrutiny, an important check on the Board's authority is lost. Much of the Board's rhetoric of nonintervention in internal union affairs cannot survive scrutiny. The Board prohibits unions from disciplining members for filing unfair labor practices without first exhausting internal union remedies . . . . The implications of the post-*Scofield* cases need to be acknowledged and integrated within the Board's approach to union discipline cases.

The Board, in most opinions, draws no distinction between expulsion and other forms of union discipline. This violates the plain language of the proviso to section 8(b)(1)(A), and ignores both the legislative history of the section and Supreme Court precedent. By regulating expulsion, the Board becomes the final arbiter of whom the majority may exclude from governance. In the Board's cases, the possible impact of this regulatory authority is neither discussed nor even acknowledged . . . .

In short, many NLRB union discipline cases frustrate a basic tenet of national labor policy. Governmental regulation should not impinge upon the ability of unions to govern themselves, reduce their effectiveness as collective bargaining agents, or by licensing unions, destroy union independence. Over fifty years have passed since the Supreme Court chided the Board for attempting to expand its authority by regulating internal union affairs through administrative amendment of the Act. Nonetheless, the Board continues to go its own way, its actions often escaping scrutiny because of excessive judicial deference . . . .

The concept of voluntary unionism was firmly established by the decisions in *Pattern Makers' League v. NLRB* and *Communication Workers v. Beck.* Following that achievement, the next step is a recommitment to the right of union members, who have voluntarily accepted the obligations of membership, to govern their own institutions. Such an action would reconfirm this country's dedication to two of its basic national labor policies: respect for individual rights, and the collective right of the membership majority to participate in self-governing unions free from government regulation.

POST PROBLEM DISCUSSION

1. *Allis-Chalmers* poses the question whether a union rule that places a court-imposed fine on cross-overs is inconsistent with the employees' Section 7 rights and the prohibition found in Section 8(b)(1)(A). After a strike was over, the union fined members and sought to enforce these fines in state court when the members did not pay. Disagreeing with the Seventh Circuit, the Supreme Court found that neither the Board nor the courts have the right to interfere with internal union affairs. Only where the union seeks to interfere with the employee's employment may the court intervene under Section 8(b)(2) of the Act. Justice Brennan, writing for a 5-4 majority, looked beyond the literal statutory language and considered the legislative history behind these provisions in the Act. He maintained that the policy of labor law is to protect the union's representational status from being weakened by the defection of individual members. This policy is particularly vital when the membership engages in a strike and the union needs absolute adherence to its views in order to outlast the employer. Weak unions, in particular, need to be able to fine their members in order to be an effective collective-bargaining representative. In all, the Court found no ULP in *Allis-Chalmers* when the union fine cross-over members and then sought to enforce those fines in state court.

2. Justice Black penned a strong dissent in *Allis-Chalmers*. He argued that the court was engaging in judicial lawmaking to protect weak unions who need the ability to fine employees in order to keep the union together and keep the strike as a legitimate weapon. Justice Black stated that this concern was a question for the legislature and was not provided for in the language of the NLRA. He also criticized the majority for failing to recognize the practical and theoretical difference between a court-enforced fine and a fine enforced by expulsion or less drastic intra-union means. Finally, Justice Black maintained that individual members are unable to discern when they are just paying agency fee dues versus when they become full-fledged members of the union, subject to the union's rules. Does Justice Black have the better argument?

3. After deciding that the union can fine members who cross a picket line during a strike, the Supreme Court considered in the *Scofield* case whether the union can enforce an internal rule that penalizes a member who was covered by an incentive plan for working too hard and thereby undermining the rest of the union.

The Court found no Section 8(b)(1)(A) ULP because it concluded that this was just another internal union rule that helped the union ensure that work was available for the majority of members, that members were not overworked, and that jealousies were kept to a minimum. The rule from *Scofield* is that Board and courts will allow an internal union rule if it is: (1) "properly adopted through procedures;" (2) "reflects a legitimate union interest;" (3) "impairs no policy Congress has imbedded in the labor laws;" and (4) "is reasonably enforced against union members who are free to leave the union and escape the rule."

4. *Allis-Chalmers* and *Scofield* still left open at least three questions in the internal union discipline context: (1) how big can a union fine be and does it have to be reasonable (see *Boeing* case below); (2) can a union apply fines to non-members (no, it may not, *see Booster Lodge No. 405 v. NLRB*, 412 U.S. 84 (1973) (holding that when union members neither knew of nor had consented to any limitation on their right to resign from union, they were not properly subject to imposition of fines by union)); and (3) can a union keep a member from resigning from membership during a specific time period (i.e., like during a strike) (see discussion in Note 6 on *Pattern Makers*)?

The first question — the subject of Problem #3 — was answered in *NLRB v. Boeing Co.*, 412 U.S. 67 (1973). In *Boeing*, members who crossed the picket line were fined $450 dollars (they made $95-$145 a week) and could not hold union office for five years. The Court concluded that Congress did not give the Board authority to regulate the size of union fines or establish standards for their reasonableness. As long as the fines did not impact the employer-employee relationship, the Board could not delve into the union's motives in assessing the fines as part of its statutory duty. In any event, courts which are asked to enforce such fines will pass judgment on their reasonableness.

5. Does it make sense to balance union rights to discipline and employees' Section 7 rights to refrain from union involvement? Is the union discipline situation different from Section 8(a)(1) cases involving a similar balance between the property interests of employers and the statutory rights of union members to organize (e.g., *Republic Aviation* and *Lechmere*, discussed in Chapter 5)? For instance, is the employers' property right in these Section 8(a)(1) cases as substantial as the union's right to demand conformity from its members? *See NLRB v. Marine & Shipbuilding Workers*, 391 U.S. 418 (1968) (holding that a union unlawfully fired a member who failed to exhaust internal union remedies before filing a ULP because the punishment did not advance strong union interests and was inconsistent with labor policy providing access to the NLRB).

6. The final question that remained after *Allis-Chalmers* and *Scofield* was whether a union could prevent current members from resigning during a strike, which would prevent members from crossing over without violating the union's rule against members crossing picket lines. In *Pattern Makers' League of North America v. NLRB*, 473 U.S. 95 (1985), a union constitution provided that member-ship resignations were not permitted during a strike or when a strike was imminent. The union fined ten members who resigned during a strike before crossing the picket line. The Court agreed with the Board that the no-resignation clause violated Section 7 rights guaranteed under 8(b)(1)(A) because members should be free to

resign from a union when they want to, without penalty. Is this conclusion consistent with *Allis-Chalmers, Scofield,* and *Boeing?*

The Supreme Court's *Chevron, USA, Inc. v. Natural Resources Defense Council, Inc.*, 467 U.S. 837 (1984), principles also played a major role in the *Pattern Makers'* Court's deference to the Board's expert analysis. Under *Chevron*, a court must defer to the Board's interpretation of an ambiguous provision in the NLRA as long as it is reasonable. In *Pattern Makers'*, the Court held that the Board's finding of a ULP was reasonable because: (1) based on legislative history, the congressional purpose to preserve unions' control over their own internal affairs does not suggest an intent to authorize restrictions on the right to resign; (2) workers are traditionally allowed to resign; (3) *Scofield* was based on the fact that workers were free to resign if they did not like the incentive rate restriction in that case; and (4) although *Scofield* allowed unions to enforce rules that are not inconsistent with labor law policies, the union anti-resignation policy at issue was inconsistent with the NLRA's policy of voluntary unionism.

Justice Blackmun dissented in *Pattern Makers'* and utilized a contract theory to suggest that when union members signed up for membership, they agreed to the provision limiting their ability to resign during a strike. According to Justice Blackmun, these workers broke this promise at the expense of the union, and the union should be able to enforce the promise through use of a fine. Justice Blackmun also contended that the rule was an internal union rule not subject to interference by the Board. Of course, it is on this point that Professor Hartley in his article takes the Board and Court to task. Do you agree that decisions like *Pattern Makers'* represent an inappropriate intrusion of the Board and courts into internal union governance or are such decisions merely a vindication of dissenting union members' rights under Section 7? Do *Pattern Makers'* and *Beck* represent a completely new approach to internal union governance, as Professor Hartley suggests?

Chapter 13

ADVANCED ISSUES IN LABOR LAW

Synopsis

Up to this point, this book has covered most of the basic issues in private-sector labor law. This chapter examines issues that are typically more complex and are often intertwined with other areas of the law. However, this does not mean that these issues are merely peripheral to labor law. For instance, labor law practitioners frequently arbitrate disputes, but legal principles governing how to arbitrate cases, how the NLRB should treat arbitrations, and the role of courts in reviewing arbitrations can be quite complicated.

In addition to Section 1's discussion of the grievance and arbitration process, Section 2 will address the successorship doctrine — what happens when one employer buys or adopts parts of another, unionized, company. Next, Section 3 deals with advanced doctrines in collective bargaining, such as parties' ability to bargain while a collective-bargaining agreement is still in effect and parties' options once an agreement has expired. Finally, Section 4 will explore the intersection of labor law and antitrust law. This topic was an important feature in the most recent National Basketball Association and National Football League work stoppages, but it can arise in any industry.

SECTION 1   THE GRIEVANCE AND ARBITRATION PROCESS

In the vast majority of collective-bargaining agreements, employers and unions negotiate some type of grievance and arbitration process. This process is intended to provide a means to enforce the agreement simply, cheaply, and quickly. In particular, the parties can avoid the expense and disruption of court litigation and economic pressure, such as a strike or lockout.

Although the exact parameters of grievance and arbitration processes can differ, they generally follow a basic form. Take for example, a termination. Either on its own, or prompted by the terminated employee, the union will try to determine whether the termination violated some aspect of the collective-bargaining agreement, such as a seniority rule or anti-discrimination clause. If the union thinks a violation might have happened, it must then decide whether to file a grievance with the employer. The grievance procedure will usually have several steps up the chain of command, but it essentially involves the union asking the employer to reconsider its decision because of an alleged violation of the agreement.

Note that generally it is the union, not the employee, that has the power to pursue a grievance. (See also the discussion of a union's duty of fair representation in Chapter 12.) This reflects the collective nature of the grievance and arbitration process; although grievances frequently involve individuals, it is the entire unit's rights under the collective-bargaining agreement that is being protected. This system also allows the union to take a gatekeeping role by filtering out claims that are not valid or that are too weak to pursue. This gatekeeping function becomes particularly relevant in the next major phase that occurs once all of the grievance steps are completed and the parties are still not satisfied: arbitration.

Arbitration involves an informal trial-like hearing in front of a neutral arbitrator or set of arbitrators. These hearings are almost always, to varying degrees, cheaper, quicker, and less formal than judicial trials. There are many differences in arbitration procedures, which are beyond the scope of this book, but they all result in a decision that is binding on the parties. As we will see below, although there is very limited judicial review, an arbitration decision is almost always the last word. Moreover, arbitration is less formal than a judicial proceeding, but it still usually requires legal representation and therefore imposes additional costs on a union. That cost will often be part of a union's decision whether to file for arbitration, with the result being that some, typically weaker, claims are dropped. As long as the union makes that decision in a non-arbitrary, non-discriminatory manner, it will not violate its duty of fair representation (see Chapter 12).

An arbitrator's primary job is to determine whether a challenged action violates the collective-bargaining agreement. This typically involves interpreting contractual language, the parties' past practice, industry custom, and other factors to determine what the agreement requires and then applying that interpretation to the facts at issue — much like a judge who interprets a legal rule and then applies it to a given situation. Below, you will see some discussion of what arbitrators do, but be aware that a full discussion of how exactly an arbitrator goes about these functions is too complicated to delve into here.

PROBLEM #1: LAYOFFS, UP ON THE ROOF

TuffCoat is a company that manufactures roofing shingles at a single plant. Its manufacturing employees are represented by a union, which has signed a collective-bargaining agreement with TuffCoat. Among other things, the agreement includes a mandatory grievance and arbitration system, a no-strike/no-lockout clause, an anti-discrimination clause, and a seniority layoff provision. The layoff provision applies to any termination of more than five employees within a one-month period and requires that all layoffs shall be made in reverse seniority, unless TuffCoat can establish a valid business reason for making an exception. In other words, the company must lay off less senior employees first, unless special circumstances exist, such as a less senior employee having a particular set of needed skills.

Recently, TuffCoat has been facing serious economic pressure. The housing construction market has been declining, which has reduced demand for its products. At the same time, oil prices have been going up, which has increased the cost of making shingles because petroleum is a key ingredient. In the face of this economic pressure, TuffCoat informed the union that it needed to lay off 10% of its workforce (20 employees). As the collective-agreement allowed, TuffCoat selected which employees would be laid off. These selections tracked employees' seniority in all but one instance — Lynn, an employee with six months seniority, was selected even though another employee, Mark, with only three months seniority, kept his job. TuffCoat claimed that Mark had a higher education level than most employees and that he was hired in the hopes that he would work his way up to a managerial position. Lynn believed that this fact did not constitute a special circumstance under the agreement and that TuffCoat chose Mark over her because she was a woman and an active union supporter. She has complained to her union steward and wants the union to file a grievance on her behalf. As you read the following material, think about what the union and Lynn need to do to get her job back.

PROBLEM MATERIALS

Martin H. Malin, *The Evolving Schizophrenic Nature of Labor Arbitration*, 2010 J. Disp. Resol. 57

Section 301, Labor Management Relations Act, 29 U.S.C. § 301

United Steelworkers of America v. Warrior & Gulf Navigation Co., 363 U.S. 574 (1960)

Harry T. Edwards, *Deferral to Arbitration and Waiver of the Duty to Bargain: A Possible Way Out of Everlasting Confusion at the NLRB*, 46 Ohio St. L.J. 23 (1985)

NLRB, Office of the General Counsel, Division of Operations-Management, *Casehandling Regarding Application of* Spielberg/Olin *Standards*, Memorandum OM 10-13(CH), November 3, 2009

A. Why Have a Grievance and Arbitration Process?

Martin H. Malin, *The Evolving Schizophrenic Nature of Labor Arbitration*
2010 J. Disp. Resol. 57[1]

Collective bargaining agreements (CBAs) between unions and employers commonly provide for paid time off on specified holidays. Such agreements also commonly require that, to be eligible for holiday pay, employees must work their last regularly scheduled shift prior to and first regularly scheduled shift after the holiday. Assume that a holiday falls on a Friday. An employee is injured on the job through no fault of the employee on the Tuesday of the week containing the holiday.

---

[1] Copyright © 2010 by the Journal of Dispute Resolution. All rights reserved. Reprinted with permission.

The employee is taken to an employer-selected doctor for treatment. The doctor restricts the employee from working for the remainder of the week. The employee follows the doctor's orders and returns to work the following Monday. The employer denies the employee holiday pay for failing to work on Thursday, the employee's last regularly scheduled shift prior to the holiday. The employee feels that he or she has been treated unjustly and complains to the union. Such holiday pay disputes are common.

Under the typical CBA, the union will file a grievance on behalf of the employee protesting the denial of holiday pay. If the parties are unable to resolve the grievance through bilateral negotiations established in the CBA's grievance procedure, the union will demand that the dispute be submitted to a mutually selected neutral arbitrator whose decision will be final and binding on the parties.

Why is grievance arbitration the almost universal method contained in CBAs for resolving such claims? Section 301 of the Labor Management Relations Act confers jurisdiction on federal district courts to hear claims of breaches of contracts between employers and labor organizations. A union or an employee may bring a breach of contract claim under section 301. The amount of damages in the holiday pay dispute, however — one day's pay — would not justify the time or expense of a federal lawsuit. One might surmise that because many claims for breach of a CBA will be similarly of low value, the parties would rationally agree to devise a forum for adjudicating those claims that would be faster and less expensive than federal court litigation.

The speed and cost efficiency of grievance arbitration might explain why a union would want to provide for it, but an employer may rationally conclude that the high cost of litigation will deter the bringing of low-value claims. Why, then, do employers so readily agree to grievance and arbitration procedures in CBAs? The traditional answer has been that employers do not fear litigation in the absence of a grievance and arbitration procedure. They recognize that unions are not likely to sue; rather, unions are likely to resort to strikes or other job actions to enforce their contracts. Thus, grievance arbitration is unlike most other forms of arbitration that provide substitutes for litigation. As recognized by the Supreme Court in *United Steelworkers of America v. Warrior & Gulf Navigation Co.*, [363 U.S. 574 (1960)], one of three cases comprising the seminal *Steelworkers Trilogy*:[2]

> [A]rbitration is the substitute for industrial strife. Since arbitration of labor disputes has quite different functions from arbitration under an ordinary commercial agreement, the hostility evinced by courts towards arbitration of commercial agreements has no place here. For arbitration of labor disputes under collective bargaining agreements is part and parcel of the collective bargaining process itself. [*Warrior & Gulf*, 363 U.S. at 578.]

For a half century, the traditional view of labor arbitration has been that it is part of a private process of union-employer workplace self-governance and a substitute for workplace strife rather than a substitute for litigation. This view of labor arbitration reached its zenith in 1974 when the Supreme Court in *Alexander v.*

---

[2] [n.8] The other two cases are *United Steelworkers of Am. v. Am. Mfg. Co.*, 363 U.S. 564 (1960) and *United Steelworkers of Am. v. Enter. Wheel & Car Corp.*, 363 U.S. 593 (1960).

Gardner-Denver Co.[, 415 U.S. 36, 53 (1974)]. declared labor arbitration to be separate from and to operate independently of the public legal system. In *Gardner-Denver*, the Court held that employees need not resort to the CBA's grievance and arbitration procedure before bringing a lawsuit under Title VII of the Civil Rights Act of 1964 and may proceed with their lawsuits even though they have grieved and arbitrated under the CBA and lost. To the Court, the labor arbitration process was completely different from the public adjudication process. The Court observed:

> As the proctor of the bargain, the arbitrator's task is to effectuate the intent of the parties. His source of authority is the collective-bargaining agreement, and he must interpret and apply that agreement in accordance with the "industrial common law of the shop" and the various needs and desires of the parties. The arbitrator, however, has no general authority to invoke public laws that conflict with the bargain between the parties . . . . [415 U.S. at 53.][3] . . .

Congress enacted the National Labor Relations Act (NLRA) in 1935, as part of the New Deal reaction to the Great Depression. Part of the New Deal strategy was to more equitably distribute wealth and income, thereby spurring demand for goods and services and inoculating the economy against another depression. . . .

Congress could have pursued its goal of more equitable distribution of income by directly setting wages and terms and conditions of employment for workers. It chose not to do so. Instead, it opted for a much more conservative, laissez-faire approach. It empowered workers to pool their bargaining power through self-organization and to use that collective bargaining power to negotiate their own terms, which it presumed would be more equitable for workers than the terms the workers could secure individually. . . .

The system of collective bargaining produces a private agreement. Government may supervise the process, but it may not intervene in the substance of the negotiations. Grievance arbitration plays a critical role in this essentially private process. Arbitrators derive their authority from the parties, and arbitrators are responsible to the parties. As Harry Shulman, the first umpire for the Ford-UAW labor agreement and Dean of Yale Law School, observed, the underlying premise of American collective bargaining is "that wages and other conditions of employment be left to autonomous determination by employers and labor." [Harry Shulman,

---

[3] Elsewhere in this article, Professor Malin notes that:

On April 1, 2009, in *14 Penn Plaza, L.L.C. v. Pyett*, [556 U.S. 227 (2009),] the Court, in apparent disregard of a half century of precedent, held that a "collective-bargaining agreement that clearly and unmistakably requires union members to arbitrate Age Discrimination in Employment Act (ADEA) claims is enforceable as a matter of federal law." . . . The Court continued, "Parties generally favor arbitration precisely because of the economics of dispute resolution . . . . As in any contractual negotiation, a union may agree to the inclusion of an arbitration provision in a collective-bargaining agreement in return for other concessions from the employer." Completely absent from the Court's opinion in *Pyett* is any discussion of labor arbitration's role in a private system of workplace self-governance. Also absent is a half century of recognition that labor arbitration is a substitute for strikes and other workplace strife.

Id. at 58–59.

Reason, Contract, and Law in Labor Relations, 68 Harv. L. Rev. 999, 1000 (1955).]
Dean Schulman described and helped define the role of the arbitrator within this
autonomous system created by the parties:

> A proper conception of the arbitrator's function is basic. He is not a
> public tribunal imposed upon the parties by superior authority which the
> parties are obliged to accept. He has no general charter to administer
> justice for a community which transcends the parties. He is rather part of
> a system of self-government created by and confined to the parties. He
> serves their pleasure only, to administer the rule of law established by their
> collective bargaining agreement. They are entitled to demand that, at least
> on balance, his performance be satisfactory to them, and they can readily
> dispense with him if it is not. [*Id.* at 1016.]

In the *Steelworkers Trilogy*, the Supreme Court quoted Shulman's article and
relied upon his idea of arbitration as part of the parties' system of self-governance.
In these landmark decisions, in which the Court established the legal framework of
labor arbitration, the Court described the collective bargaining agreement as "an
effort to erect a system of industrial self-government." . . .

The collective bargaining process, which continues during the life of the CBA
through the grievance and arbitration procedure, enables the parties' relationship
"to be governed by an agreed-upon rule of law [rather than] leaving each and every
matter subject to a temporary resolution dependent solely upon the relative
strength, at any given moment, of the contending forces." [*Warrior & Gulf*, 363 U.S.
at 580.] The Court has characterized the grievance and arbitration procedure as the
quid pro quo for the union's agreement not to strike during the term of the CBA.
David Feller, whose briefs as a lawyer successfully arguing the *Trilogy* cases were
relied upon by the Court and who later became a renowned arbitrator and labor law
professor, has theorized that the true essence of a CBA consists of the grievance-
arbitration procedure and the no-strike clause. In other words, the union's
concession that it will not strike is the basis for the employer's concession that it will
be bound by the grievance and arbitration procedure.

The grievance and arbitration procedure prevents strikes and other job actions
in several ways. First, as illustrated by the hypothetical dispute over whether the
injured employee was entitled to holiday pay, unions would be more likely to resort
to job actions rather than litigation to resolve disputes that arise midcontract if
there were no provision for binding arbitration. Second, the availability of grievance
arbitration during the term of the CBA facilitates the parties' ability to reach
agreement on the CBA in the first instance by deferring potential disputes to
case-by-case negotiation through the grievance procedure with the understanding
that if the parties are unable to reach agreement in any particular case, they will be
bound by the decision of their mutually selected arbitrator.

Some matters cannot readily be reduced to specific, detailed contract provisions.
For example, parties likely would find it difficult to reach agreement on the specifics
of a detailed disciplinary code. Even if they could reach agreement, they would find
it highly impracticable to devise a code that would cover every circumstance of
employee misfeasance or malfeasance. To resolve such matters, parties routinely
agree that discipline and discharge will only be imposed for just cause. By so doing,

they leave refinement of this necessarily indefinite term to case-by-case negotiation through the grievance procedure, with ultimate resolution, in the absence of agreement in any particular case, by the arbitrator.

In other circumstances, parties find that they disagree in principle over how a particular term of employment should be governed but realize that their abstract disagreement may not result in disagreements in practice and is not worth a strike or otherwise impeding agreement on the terms of the CBA. For example, parties commonly provide that, in filling vacancies in a bargaining unit, qualifications will govern, but where candidates' qualifications are relatively equal, the senior candidate will prevail. This very common CBA provision often results from union and employer disagreement over the appropriate relative mix of qualifications and seniority in filling vacancies and recognition that the disagreement may never arise in practice, as the employer may end up deciding that the senior candidate is also the most qualified, or a rejected senior candidate may not want to pursue the matter. It makes no sense to preclude agreement on a CBA over an abstract dispute that may never develop into a real issue. The grievance and arbitration procedure enables the parties to defer their abstract disagreement to case-by-case negotiation with ultimate resolution by the arbitrator if it ever becomes a real issue, even though the parties recognize that they attach different meanings to the term "relatively equal." . . .

POST PROBLEM DISCUSSION

1.   Consider Lynn's complaint in our problem. What types of arguments do you think that she and the union can make in arguing that Mark should have been chosen for layoff instead of her? What other facts or information would you want to know in order to determine whether those arguments are likely to be successful?

2.   If Lynn is correct that she was chosen for layoff instead of Mark because she is a woman, she would have a valid claim under Title VII of the Civil Rights Act. However, as noted in the excerpt from Professor Malin, the Supreme Court has recently held that a collective-bargaining agreement can waive employees' right to sue under civil rights statutes. *See 14 Penn Plaza, L.L.C. v. Pyett*, 556 U.S. 227 (2009) (holding that courts should enforce a "collective-bargaining agreement that clearly and unmistakably requires union members to arbitrate Age Discrimination in Employment Act (ADEA) claims"). *Pyett* was a departure from a long-standing approach that did not allow collective-bargaining agreements to waive employees' non-NLRA statutory rights. Do you think that the advantages of a mandatory grievance and arbitration system, as well as collective representation generally, should outweigh employees' statutory right of action — or should the non-NLRA right of action prevail?

3.   Even if a union has the power to waive certain employee rights, how should the NLRB determine whether such a waiver occurred? The Supreme Court addressed this question in *Metropolitan Edison Co. v. NLRB*, 460 U.S. 693 (1983), where an employer gave union officials extra discipline for not actively opposing a wildcat strike that violated the parties' no-strike agreement. The employer argued that the no-strike agreement implicitly required the officials to affirmatively oppose a strike and waived their right not to face more severe discipline for a failure to take

such action. The Court rejected that argument, holding that "we will not infer from a general contractual provision that the parties intended to waive a statutorily protected right unless the undertaking is 'explicitly stated.' More succinctly, the waiver must be *clear and unmistakable*." *Id.* at 780 (emphasis added). However, there are limits to the "clear and unmistakable" standard, as a union is unable to waive certain employee rights, no matter how clear the waiver appears to be. *See, e.g.*, *NLRB v. Magnavox Co. of Tennessee*, 415 U.S. 322 (1974) (holding that the union cannot waive employees' workplace solicitation rights because it affects employees' freedom to choose their bargaining representative).

B.   The Arbitration-Court Relationship

Section 301, Labor Management Relations Act, *Suits By and Against Labor Organizations*
29 U.S.C. § 301

Sec. 301(a). Suits for violation of contracts between an employer and a labor organization representing employees in an industry affecting commerce as defined in this Act, or between any such labor organization, may be brought in any district court of the United States having jurisdiction of the parties, without respect to the amount in controversy or without regard to the citizenship of the parties. . . .

UNITED STEELWORKERS OF AMERICA v. WARRIOR & GULF NAVIGATION CO.
363 U.S. 574 (1960)

Opinion of the Court by MR. JUSTICE DOUGLAS, announced by MR. JUSTICE BRENNAN.

Respondent transports steel and steel products by barge and maintains a terminal at Chickasaw, Alabama, where it performs maintenance and repair work on its barges. The employees at that terminal constitute a bargaining unit covered by a collective bargaining agreement negotiated by petitioner union. Respondent between 1956 and 1958 laid off some employees, reducing the bargaining unit from 42 to 23 men. This reduction was due in part to respondent contracting maintenance work, previously done by its employees, to other companies. The latter used respondent's supervisors to lay out the work and hired some of the laid-off employees of respondent (at reduced wages). Some were in fact assigned to work on respondent's barges. A number of employees signed a grievance which petitioner presented to respondent . . . .

The collective agreement had both a "no strike" and a "no lockout" provision. It also had a grievance procedure which provided in relevant part as follows:

> Issues which conflict with any Federal statute in its application as established by Court procedure or matters which are strictly a function of management shall not be subject to arbitration under this section.

Should differences arise between the Company and the Union or its members employed by the Company as to the meaning and application of the provisions of this Agreement, or should any local trouble of any kind arise, there shall be no suspension of work on account of such differences but an earnest effort shall be made to settle such differences immediately in the following manner: [The agreement then set forth the details of its grievance and arbitration procedures.]

Settlement of this grievance was not had and respondent refused arbitration. This suit was then commenced by the union to compel it. . . .

The collective bargaining agreement states the rights and duties of the parties. It is more than a contract; it is a generalized code to govern a myriad of cases which the draftsmen cannot wholly anticipate. See Shulman, *Reason, Contract, and Law in Labor Relations*, 68 HARV. L. REV. 999, 1004–1005. The collective agreement covers the whole employment relationship. It calls into being a new common law-the common law of a particular industry or of a particular plant. As one observer has put it:[4]

(I)t is not unqualifiedly true that a collective-bargaining agreement is simply a document by which the union and employees have imposed upon management limited, express restrictions of its otherwise absolute right to manage the enterprise, so that an employee's claim must fail unless he can point to a specific contract provision upon which the claim is founded,. There are too many people, too many problems, too many unforeseeable contingencies to make the words of the contract the exclusive source of rights and duties. One cannot reduce all the rules governing a community like an industrial plant to fifteen or even fifty pages. Within the sphere of collective bargaining, the institutional characteristics and the governmental nature of the collective-bargaining process demand a common law of the shop which implements and furnishes the context of the agreement. We must assume that intelligent negotiators acknowledged so plain a need unless they stated a contrary rule in plain words.

A collective bargaining agreement is an effort to erect a system of industrial self-government. When most parties enter into contractual relationship they do so voluntarily, in the sense that there is no real compulsion to deal with one another, as opposed to dealing with other parties. This is not true of the labor agreement. The choice is generally not between entering or refusing to enter into a relationship, for that in all probability pre-exists the negotiations. Rather it is between having that relationship governed by an agreed-upon rule of law or leaving each and every matter subject to a temporary resolution dependent solely upon the relative strength, at any given moment, of the contending forces. The mature labor agreement may attempt to regulate all aspects of the complicated relationship, from the most crucial to the most minute over an extended period of time. Because of the compulsion to reach agreement and the breadth of the matters covered, as well as the need for a fairly concise and readable instrument, the product of negotiations (the written document) is, in the words of the late Dean Shulman, 'a compilation of

---

[4] [n.6] Cox, *Reflections Upon Labor Arbitration*, 72 Harv. L. Rev. 1482, 1498–1499 (1959).

diverse provisions: some provide objective criteria almost automatically applicable; some provide more or less specific standards which require reason and judgment in their application; and some do little more than leave problems to future consideration with an expression of hope and good faith.' Shulman, supra, at 1005. Gaps may be left to be filled in by reference to the practices of the particular industry and of the various shops covered by the agreement. Many of the specific practices which underlie the agreement may be unknown, except in hazy form, even to the negotiators. Courts and arbitration in the context of most commercial contracts are resorted to because there has been a breakdown in the working relationship of the parties; such resort is the unwanted exception. But the grievance machinery under a collective bargaining agreement is at the very heart of the system of industrial self-government. Arbitration is the means of solving the unforeseeable by molding a system of private law for all the problems which may arise and to provide for their solution in a way which will generally accord with the variant needs and desires of the parties. The processing of disputes through the grievance machinery is actually a vehicle by which meaning and content are given to the collective bargaining agreement.

Apart from matters that the parties specifically exclude, all of the questions on which the parties disagree must therefore come within the scope of the grievance and arbitration provisions of the collective agreement. The grievance procedure is, in other words, a part of the continuous collective bargaining process. It, rather than a strike, is the terminal point of a disagreement.

The labor arbitrator performs functions which are not normal to the courts; the considerations which help him fashion judgments may indeed by foreign to the competence of courts.

> "A proper conception of the arbitrator's function is basic. He is not a public tribunal imposed upon the parties by superior authority which the parties are obliged to accept. He has no general charter to administer justice for a community which transcends the parties. He is rather part of a system of self-government created by and confined to the parties. . . ." Shulman, supra, at 1016.

The labor arbitrator's source of law is not confined to the express provisions of the contract, as the industrial common law-the practices of the industry and the shop-is equally a part of the collective bargaining agreement although not expressed in it. The labor arbitrator is usually chosen because of the parties' confidence in his knowledge of the common law of the shop and their trust in his personal judgment to bring to bear considerations which are not expressed in the contract as criteria for judgment. The parties expect that his judgment of a particular grievance will reflect not only what the contract says but, insofar as the collective bargaining agreement permits, such factors as the effect upon productivity of a particular result, its consequence to the morale of the shop, his judgment whether tensions will be heightened or diminished. For the parties' objective in using the arbitration process is primarily to further their common goal of uninterrupted production under the agreement, to make the agreement serve their specialized needs. The ablest judge cannot be expected to bring the same experience and competence to bear upon the determination of a grievance, because he cannot be similarly informed.

The Congress, however, has by [Section] 301 of the Labor Management Relations Act, assigned the courts the duty of determining whether the reluctant party has breached his promise to arbitrate. For arbitration is a matter of contract and a party cannot be required to submit to arbitration any dispute which he has not agreed so to submit. Yet, to be consistent with congressional policy in favor of settlement of disputes by the parties through the machinery of arbitration, the judicial inquiry under [Section] 301 must be strictly confined to the question whether the reluctant party did agree to arbitrate the grievance or did agree to give the arbitrator power to make the award he made. An order to arbitrate the particular grievance should not be denied unless it may be said with positive assurance that the arbitration clause is not susceptible of an interpretation that covers the asserted dispute. Doubts should be resolved in favor of coverage . . . .

The grievance alleged that the contracting out was a violation of the collective bargaining agreement. There was, therefore, a dispute 'as to the meaning and application of the provisions of this Agreement' which the parties had agreed would be determined by arbitration.

The judiciary sits in these cases to bring into operation an arbitral process which substitutes a regime of peaceful settlement for the older regime of industrial conflict. Whether contracting out in the present case violated the agreement is the question. It is a question for the arbiter, not for the courts.

Reversed.

[Concurring opinion of Mr. Justice Brennan, joined by Mr. Justice Frankfurter and Mr. Justice Harlan, and dissenting opinion of Mr. Justice Whittaker, are omitted.]

POST PROBLEM DISCUSSION

1. *Warrior & Gulf* is part of the *"Steelworkers Trilogy."* This trilogy consists of three cases decided by the Supreme Court, all on the same day, that involved the Steelworkers union and its collectively bargained arbitration agreements. Before discussing the *Steelworkers Trilogy*, it is important to note its predecessor, *Textile Workers Union v. Lincoln Mills of Alabama*, 353 U.S. 448 (1957). In *Lincoln Mills*, the Supreme Court held that Section 301 not only gave federal courts jurisdiction over claims alleging breach of a collective-bargaining agreement, but also intended for federal common law to cover such claims. *Id.* at 457 (noting that state and federal courts had concurrent jurisdiction over Section 301 claims); *see also Local 174, Teamsters v. Lucas Flour Co.*, 369 U.S. 95, 101–02 (1962). The Court also rejected the argument that the Norris-LaGuardia Act prevented a federal court from compelling arbitration or enforcing an arbitration order with injunctive relief, such as enjoining a strike that violated a no-strike clause. *Lincoln Mills*, 353 U.S. at 458 (noting that the Norris-LaGuardia Act "denies injunctive relief to any person who has failed to make 'every reasonable effort' to settle the dispute by negotiation, mediation, or 'voluntary arbitration.' ") (quoting 29 U.S.C. § 108). See Chapter 1 for

a description of the Norris-LaGuardia Act.

Following *Lincoln Mills*, the NLRB and courts had to determine how they should analyze agreements to grieve and arbitrate disputes. Enter the *Steelworkers Trilogy.* In *United Steelworkers of America v. American Manufacturing Co.*, 363 U.S. 564, 567–68 (1960), the Court held that if the parties have agreed to arbitrate, the courts' role is generally limited to determining whether a claim, on its face, is governed by that agreement. The arbitrator is the entity to decide whether the claim has merit. *Id; see also Granite Rock Co. v. International Brotherhood of Teamsters*, 130 S. Ct. 2847 (2010) (holding that it is the court's role to determine when a collective-bargaining agreement was ratified and, therefore, when a no-strike clause contained in that agreement would require arbitration). As you just read, when a court is determining whether a dispute should go to arbitration, the *Warrior & Gulf* decision established a presumption of arbitrability.

Finally, in *United Steelworkers of America v. Enterprise Wheel & Car Corp.*, 363 U.S. 593 (1960), the Court addressed the standard of review when an arbitrator's award is challenged. Turning again to the policy favoring the arbitration of labor disputes, the Court held that judicial review of arbitration awards is quite limited, and that a court should affirm an arbitrator's decision as long as it "draws its essence from the CBA." *Id.* at 597; *see also Warrior & Gulf*, 363 U.S. at 581–82 (noting that arbitrator's source of law extends to "industrial common law," which includes the past practices of a given plant or industry).

2.   Imagine, in our problem, that the union struck in response to TuffCoat's termination of Lynn. TuffCoat then filed a Section 301 claim and sought damages from the union for a breach of the no-strike clause, as well as an injunction to stop the strike. As referenced in Note 1, the Court in *Lincoln Mills* held that courts have the power to enjoin a strike that violates a no-strike clause if the subject of the strike is covered by an arbitration agreement. *See also Buffalo Forge Co. v. United Steelworkers of America*, 428 U.S. 397, 407–08 (1976). A similar answer exists for the damages question; as long as the parties intended the object of the strike to be arbitrated, a court can order damages for breach of a no-strike clause. *See Lucas Flour*, 369 U.S. at 106.

3.   What if the union refused to pursue a grievance or arbitration on Lynn's behalf? Could she sue TuffCoat for violating her rights under the collective-bargaining agreement? *See Republic Steel Corp. v. Maddox*, 379 U.S. 650, 653 (1965) (permitting individual suits as long as the employee exhausted the grievance and arbitration process).

4.   For further recommendations on various aspects of the arbitration-court relationship, see Richard A. Bales, *The Arbitrability of Side and Settlement Agreements in the Collective Bargaining Context*, 105 W. VA. L. REV. 575 (2003), and Charles B. Craver, *Labor Arbitration as a Continuation of the Collective Bargaining Process*, 66 CHI.-KENT L. REV. 571 (1991).

C. The Arbitration-NLRB Relationship

The Supreme Court made clear in the *Steelworkers Trilogy* that federal labor policy favored the arbitration of disputes. However, that policy can bump up against the NLRB's exclusive authority to enforce the NLRA. When the subject of an alleged violation of a collective-bargaining agreement might also constitute an unfair labor practice under the NLRA, a question arises about whether and to what extent the NLRB should allow an arbitrator to decide the matter. This question arises in two situations: (1) before arbitration has concluded, which requires the NLRB to consider whether to back off the complaint and allow the arbitrator to handle the matter ("pre-arbitral" or "*Collyer*" deferral); and (2) after arbitration has concluded, which requires the NLRB to decide whether to examine the issue on its own or defer to the arbitrator's decision ("post-arbitral" or "*Spielberg/Olin*" deferral). In our problem, this deferral issue arises because of Lynn's claim that she was terminated in part because of her union activity — a possible Section 8(a)(3) unfair labor practice. If she filed an unfair labor practice charge, the NLRB would have to decide whether to allow an arbitrator to decide the case or, if there was already an arbitration decision on the issue, whether to follow it.

Harry T. Edwards, *Deferral to Arbitration and Waiver of the Duty to Bargain: A Possible Way Out of Everlasting Confusion at the NLRB*
46 Ohio St. L.J. 23 (1985)[5]

Although the NLRB has no authority to *enforce* private contracts, there is no doubt that the Board may construe the terms of an agreement either to determine their legality or to determine whether a party has violated its statutory duty to bargain. Thus, even though breach of contract is not an unfair labor practice under the NLRA, the Board does not exceed its jurisdiction when it construes a labor agreement in order to decide an unfair labor practice charge. Nonetheless, it was long ago recognized by the Board that it was contrary to the purposes of the NLRA "for the Board to assume the role of policing collective contracts between employers and labor organizations by attempting to decide whether disputes as to the meaning and administration of such contracts constitute unfair labor practices under the Act."[6] While the Board never has been consistent in its approach to deferral, there has been a historical acceptance of arbitration as a legitimate means of resolving labor disputes. Simply stated, the Board's willingness to defer to arbitration reflects "the underlying conviction that the parties to a collective-bargaining agreement are in the best position to resolve, with the help of a neutral third party if necessary, disputes concerning the correct interpretation of their contract."[7]

In 1955, in a seminal decision in *Spielberg Mfg. Co.*, [112 N.L.R.B. 1080 (1955)] the Board announced that it would defer to an arbitration award already rendered

[6] [n.12] *Consolidated Aircraft Corp.*, 47 N.L.R.B. 694, 706 (1943), *enforced in part*, 141 F.2d 785 (9th Cir. 1944).

[7] [n.13] *United Technologies Corp.*, 268 N.L.R.B. [557, 558 (1984).]

where (1) the arbitration proceedings appeared to be fair and regular, (2) all parties to the arbitration had agreed to be bound and (3) the decision of the arbitrator was not clearly repugnant to the purposes and policies of the NLRA. The deferral doctrine reached a critical highpoint with the Board's 1971 decision in *Collyer Insulated Wire*, [192 N.L.R.B. 837 (1971)], a case involving prospective deferral. In *Collyer*, the Board was faced with a complaint alleging that an employer had breached its duty to bargain under section 8(a)(5) by unilaterally changing certain wages and working conditions among unionized employees. Rather than decide the merits of the unfair labor practice charge, the Board dismissed the case in deference to the parties' contractual grievance-arbitration machinery.[8]

After *Collyer*, the deferral doctrine followed a rocky course. Initially, in *National Radio Co.*, [205 N.L.R.B. 1179 (1973),] the Board extended the doctrine to include cases charging unlawful interference, coercion, restraint or discrimination under sections 8(a)(1) and 8(a)(3). Subsequently, however, in *General American Transportation Corp.*, [228 N.L.R.B. 808 (1977),] the Board reversed *National Radio* and thereafter ceased deferring to arbitration in cases arising under sections 8(a)(1) and 8(a)(3). And, in the 1980 case of *Suburban Motor Freight, Inc.*, [247 N.L.R.B. 146 (1980),] the Board modified the *Spielberg* doctrine by declining to defer to an arbitration award unless the arbitrator had fully considered the unfair labor practice charge.

In light of these and other changes in the case law, the Board's policy on deferral often has appeared in disarray. Recent Board decisions, however, have sought to reimpose broad policies in favor of deferral and to give renewed life to *Spielberg*, *Collyer*, and *National Radio*.

Any discussion of the Board's current policy on deferral to arbitration must begin with *United Technologies Corp.*, a case decided early in 1984. In *United Technologies*, a worker filed an 8(a)(1) charge with the NLRB, claiming that her supervisor had unlawfully threatened her with disciplinary action if she persisted in processing a grievance. The employer sought deferral to arbitration on the grounds that the employee's charge was covered by a grievance-arbitration clause in a collective bargaining agreement. Following issuance of a complaint, an Administrative Law Judge (ALJ) declined to defer to arbitration because, under the then-existing rule of *General American Transportation*, deferral was restricted to cases involving claims of a breach of the duty to bargain under sections 8(a)(5) and 8(b)(3). In its review, however, the Board used *United Technologies* to overrule *General American Transportation*. Reasoning that its resources were limited and that the parties

---

[8] [n.17] In *United Technologies Corp.*, 268 N.L.R.B. [at 558], the Board described the *Collyer* doctrine as follows:

> The *Collyer* majority articulated several factors favoring deferral: The dispute arose within the confines of a long and productive collective-bargaining relationship; there was no claim of employer animosity to the employees' exercise of protected rights; the parties' contract provided for arbitration in a very broad range of disputes; the arbitration clause clearly encompassed the dispute at issue; the employer had asserted its willingness to utilize arbitration to resolve the dispute; and the dispute was eminently well suited to resolution by arbitration. In these circumstances, deferral to the arbitral process merely gave full effect to the parties' agreement to submit disputes to arbitration. In essence, the *Collyer* majority was holding the parties to their bargain by directing them to avoid substituting the Board's processes for their own mutually agreed-upon method for dispute resolution.

were in a better position to resolve contract disputes, the Board held that where a company and union provide for resolution of unfair labor practices through arbitration, they should be required to use these contractual mechanisms before resorting to the Board's processes. In essence, the Board returned to the principles announced in *National Radio*, requiring deferral to arbitration in 8(a)(1) and 8(a)(3) cases unless the union's interests are adverse to those of the complaining employee, or the employer's conduct demonstrates a rejection of the principles of collective bargaining, or the employer refuses to arbitrate, or it appears that arbitration would be futile.

On the same day that *United Technologies* was decided, the Board issued its decision in *Olin Corp.*, [268 N.L.R.B. 573 (1984),] announcing new standards for post-arbitral deferral. In *Olin*, a union official was implicated in a 'sick out' that followed a work assignment dispute. Relying on the collective bargaining agreement, the employer fired the union official and an arbitrator upheld the discharge. The union then filed an unfair labor practice charge under sections 8(a)(1) and (3), and an ALJ refused to defer to the arbitrator's decision. The ALJ noted that, although the issue had been raised during the arbitration proceeding, the arbitrator had made no serious effort to resolve the statutory questions posed by the grievance. The ALJ thus concluded that, under the precedent established by *Suburban Motor Freight*, he had no authority to defer to the arbitrator's judgment. The ALJ then went on to consider the merits of the unfair labor practice charge and found that no violation had occurred.

In affirming the ALJ's decision in *Olin*, the Board declined to reach the merits of the unfair labor practice charge and, instead, deferred to the arbitrator's judgment in the case. The Board expressly overruled *Suburban Motor Freight*, and held that in the future it would defer to arbitration decisions as long as (1) the contractual issue is *factually parallel* to the unfair labor practice issue; (2) the arbitrator was presented generally with the facts relevant to resolving the unfair labor practice; and (3) the award is not 'palpably wrong,' that is, the decision is 'susceptible to an interpretation consistent with the Act.' Under *Olin*, there is a strong presumption in favor of deference; the burden of overcoming this presumption clearly rests on the party seeking to avoid an arbitrator's decision. The decision in *Olin* also recognizes that under *Suburban Motor Freight* the Board had fallen prey to the temptation of reviewing the merits of unfair labor practice charges *before* deciding whether or not to defer. This approach completely frustrated the *Spielberg* policy of deference, leading to "overzealous dissection" of arbitration decisions and wasteful duplication of efforts in the adjudication of contract grievance disputes.

Under *United Technologies* and *Olin*, arbitration again will be the preferred forum for the resolution of contractual disputes between labor and management. This policy judgment by the Board appears both to be legally sound and to make eminently good practical sense. Congress and the courts have long recognized arbitration as one of the cornerstones of industrial peace. Indeed, in *United Technologies*, the Board relied on the Supreme Court's landmark decisions in *Textile Workers v. Lincoln Mills* and the *Steelworkers Trilogy*, to the effect that arbitration is an essential element of collective bargaining:

Where an employer and a union have voluntarily elected to create dispute resolution machinery culminating in final and binding arbitration, it is contrary to the basic principles of the Act for the Board to jump into the fray prior to an honest attempt by the parties to resolve their disputes through that machinery. For dispute resolution under the grievance-arbitration process is as much a part of collective bargaining as the act of negotiating the contract.

[*United Technologies Corp.*, 268 N.L.R.B. at 559.]

To the extent that recent Board decisions underscore and foster long-established principles emanating from *Lincoln Mills* and the *Steelworkers Trilogy*, it is difficult to find fault with these judgments in favor of deference or deferral to arbitration.

Clearly, then, there are a number of good reasons to support decisions favoring arbitration over the Board's own processes for the resolution of collective bargaining disputes. Nonetheless, I would argue that, even with respect to current NLRB case law, most Board decisions deferring to arbitration have been grounded on a faulty rationale. I would suggest that, because the parties to a bargaining relationship have provided for arbitration of their contract disputes, the Board has no role to play in most so-called "deferral" cases.

"Deferral" is simply an unfortunate misnomer that has contributed to the perpetual mischaracterization of contract grievance disputes. In the traditional *Collyer*-type case, the proper analysis is not one of deferral at all, but rather of waiver. Putting aside for the moment cases involving overriding public law questions (as under Title VII), individual rights and the duty of fair representation, I believe that when the parties negotiate a collective bargaining agreement and stipulate that they will arbitrate disputes arising under it, they have waived many of their statutory rights under the NLRA. The parties' agreement, in essence, supplants the statute as the source of many employee rights in the context of collective bargaining. . . .

This system comports fully with the strong national labor policy of promoting industrial peace through arbitration, and is grounded on the equally strong policy of freedom of contract. It has the additional advantages of eliminating uncertainty and wasteful duplication of adjudication efforts. Moreover, arbitration resolves disputes much more quickly than does litigation before the Board, and arbitrators are far more familiar with contract interpretation and the 'common law of the shop' than are members of the Board. Indeed, given the Board's historic tendency to follow the prevailing political winds, the contractual waiver doctrine insulates the collective bargaining parties' private ordering of their rights and responsibilities from meddle-some interference by this sometimes highly politicized body.

In advancing these views, I should emphasize that I am not addressing here those cases in which the union and employee interests are potentially adverse. The entire premise underlying the waiver theory is that of fair representation. As the Supreme Court made clear in *NLRB v. Magnavox*, [415 U.S. 322 (1974),] a union's waiver of employees' statutory rights in the economic sphere presupposes that the union fairly represents the interests of the workers. Thus, as the Court held in *Magnavox*, a union may not waive the employees' rights to choose a new bargaining representative, because on that particular issue the interests of the union and the workers diverge. It is therefore clear that when such situations arise, waiver is inappropriate. But these cases are rare, and can be handled by the Board when they do come up. . . .

Putting aside the cases of individual rights and the union's duty of fair representation, I believe that the collective bargaining agreement and arbitration clause supplant many statutory rights under the NLRA, and the Board therefore simply has no business intruding into what are essentially contractual disputes. In other words, in the context of bargaining disputes arising under a collective agreement, the Board's function is quite simple and extremely narrow: its sole task is to determine whether, with respect to *nonwaivable* issues, the parties' labor contract is illegal. For example, does the contract authorize hot cargo shipments in contravention of section 8(e)? Does it mandate a "closed shop" in violation of section 8(a)(3)? If so, then obviously the Board cannot defer to arbitration, since no public policy is served by allowing arbitrators to enforce illegal contracts. The parties have no authority to vitiate nonwaivable statutory rights or prohibitions by agreement or by resort to arbitration. However, with respect to the classical "economic" issues of collective bargaining, the Board should leave the parties to their own contractual dispute resolution machinery.

This same standard should be applied to post-arbitral decisions as well. The arbitrator's interpretation of the contract is, in essence, *part* of the contract. If the agreement, as the parties read it, is illegal — for example, if it is interpreted to require a 'closed shop' — then the arbitrator's award cannot be given effect. If the contract, as interpreted, is not illegal, the Board's inquiry should be at an end, and the award should stand. This suggested standard of post-arbitral review is far narrower than the 'repugnance' test currently employed by the Board. It results in true deference, in the sense that the Board in no way second-guesses the arbitrator's decision. The parties have bargained for the arbitrator's interpretation, and that interpretation is fully accepted. The Board conducts no independent review of the parties' bargaining history, nor does it engage in any contract interpretation of its own. It simply takes the contract as construed and determines whether it violates the NLRA in any way. . . .

NLRB, Office of the General Counsel Division of Operations-Management Casehandling Regarding Application of *Spielberg/Olin* Standards Memorandum OM 10-13(CH)
November 3, 2009
http://mynlrb.nlrb.gov/link/document.aspx/09031d458080ca54

As you are aware, under the *Spielberg/Olin* standards, the Board examines four factors in deciding whether to defer to an arbitration award.[9] In recent years, however, the Court of Appeals for the D.C. Circuit has questioned the Board's

---

[9] [n.1] Specifically, the Board considers whether (1) the arbitration proceedings were fair and regular; (2) all parties agreed to be bound; (3) the Arbitrator "considered" the unfair labor practice issue in that the contractual issue is "factually parallel" to the unfair labor practice issue and the arbitrator was presented generally with the facts relevant to resolving the unfair labor practice charge and (4) the resulting decision is not "clearly repugnant" to the Act. *Olin Corp.*, 268 N.L.R.B. 573, 573–574 [(1984)],

standards. Rather, the court has proposed that, with limited exceptions, a collective-bargaining agreement provision dealing with conduct protected by the Act, together with a grievance-arbitration clause covering disputes about such a provision constitutes an implied waiver of the statutory right in favor of the contractual provision. Consequently, no separate unfair labor practice issue remains for Board review. See *Plumbers & Pipefitters Local Union No. 520 v. NLRB*, 955 F.2d 744, 756 (D.C. Cir. 1992) (adopting waiver analysis as basis for review); *Titanium Metals Corp. v. NLRB*, 392 F.3d 439, 447 (D.C. Cir. 2004). Accordingly, the D.C. Circuit would limit administrative review to whether arbitral procedures were fair and regular and whether the Union violated its duty of fair representation in processing the grievance. *Plumbers & Pipefitters Local Union No. 520 v. NLRB*, 955 F.2d at 756.

The Supreme Court's recent decision in *14 Penn Plaza, LLC v. Steven Pyett*, 129 S. Ct. 1456 (2009), also has potential implications for the Board's deferral policy. There, the Court held that a union-negotiated agreement to arbitrate statutory employment discrimination claims is enforceable as long as any such union waiver of a judicial forum is expressed in clear and unmistakable terms. *Id.* at 1465, citing *Wright v. Universal Maritime Service Corp.*, 525 U.S. 70, 80 (1998). This conclusion may call into question the D.C. Circuit's theory that statutory rights may be impliedly waived. In addition, the *Pyett* Court's decision is premised on the arbitrator's authority and obligation to apply statutory, and not merely contractual, norms. *Id.* at 1471. This approach contrasts with the Board's more limited review of whether the arbitrator "considered" the unfair labor practice issue, that is, whether the arbitral question was factually parallel to the statutory issue and whether the arbitrator was presented generally with the facts relevant to resolving the unfair labor practice. *Olin Corp.*, 268 N.L.R.B. 573, 574 (1984).

The Supreme Court's and D.C Circuit's approaches do not compel a change to the traditional *Spielberg/Olin* standards of review. Nevertheless, they raise questions that the Board must answer as it decides whether to defer to an arbitral award. The need for refinement is also prominent because parties can always choose to seek review of a Board decision before the D.C. Circuit.

Accordingly, a new approach to cases involving arbitral deference may be warranted. That approach will be developed based upon a case-by-case review of submissions to the Division of Advice. In light of the importance of these issues, please submit to Advice all cases in which a Region recommends that the General Counsel reject deference to an arbitral award under the *Spielberg/Olin* framework.

POST PROBLEM DISCUSSION

1. Note that Harry Edwards, who authored the first piece and argued for a "waiver theory" of deferral, is currently "Judge Edwards" and the author of the D.C. Circuit decisions cited in the General Counsel's memorandum. Judge Edwards used to be a professor, and one of his specialties was labor law. If you practice labor law, you will quickly notice that NLRB opinions by Judge Edwards often garner

---

citing and clarifying *Spielberg Mfg. Co.*, 112 N.L.R.B. 1080.

significant respect from his colleagues on the D.C. Circuit, the NLRB, and labor law practitioners.

2.　　Thus far, the NLRB has not altered its traditional *Spielberg/Olin* analysis, as acknowledged in footnote 1 of the General Counsel's memorandum. *See Roadway Express, Inc.*, 335 N.L.R.B. No. 23 (2010). Professor Michael Harper agrees with much of Judge Edward's approach, but cautions that if the NLRB reconsiders its deferral analysis, it among other things:

> should not fully embrace the waiver theory for Board deferral as developed in Judge Edwards's opinions for panels of the District of Columbia Circuit Court of Appeals. These decisions reveal several flaws in the theory as articulated by Judge Edwards. First, Judge Edwards at least implicitly compromises the important requirement, confirmed by the Court in *Metropolitan Edison*, that a union waiver of a statutory right must be "clear and unmistakable." He does so by articulating a standard for Board deference requiring consideration only of whether the statutory right on which a claim was based was waivable and whether the grievance arbitration process was fair, but not whether the arbitration decision or settlement agreement actually found union authorization of a waiver or qualification of the right. . . .

Michael C. Harper, *A New Board Policy on Deferral to Arbitration: Acknowledging and Delimiting Union Waiver of Employee Statutory Rights*, 5 F.I.U. L. Rev. 685 (2010). Do you think the NLRB's current analysis or Judge Edward's waiver theory is the better approach?

SECTION 2　SUCCESSORSHIP

It is not unusual for a business to undergo a transformation. This transformation can take many forms, including closing the business or merely changing ownership. When the original business is unionized, the nature of the transformation becomes important. Take, for example, a mere change in ownership. If the same employees work in the same place and perform the same jobs, should the change in ownership also change the union's status as the employees' collective-bargaining representative? What about unresolved unfair labor practices with the "predecessor" employer — should the "successor" employer be liable? These questions, and more, fall under the NLRB's "successorship doctrine."

PROBLEM #2: APPLES AND ORANGES

Orchard Farms is a company with 1,000 employees that processes apples and oranges to make apple juice, applesauce, apple butter, and orange juice. The company has entered into a series of collective-bargaining agreements with the local cannery union. Recently, the owner and president of Orchard Farms made plans to retire within a year and decided to sell the company. She entered into an agreement with the Appleseed Corporation, which purchased Orchard Farms' processing plant, warehouse, and equipment. Appleseed continued to make apple juice and used the same equipment and production methods as Orchard Farms.

However, Appleseed decided not to produce applesauce, apple butter, or orange juice.

Appleseed began production three months after Orchard Farms shut down. Within the first year of its purchase of the Orchard Farms plant and equipment, Appleseed employed 70 people at the plant. Forty-five of those employees (approximately two-thirds of Appleseed's employees at the plant) were formerly employees of Orchard Farms. Appleseed paid those employees 20% less than Orchard Farms had and, unlike Orchard Farms, did not provide health insurance. The training also differed, as Orchard Farm employees learned how to make all of the company's products, while the Appleseed employees focused solely on apple juice production. Appleseed also employed seven former Orchard Farms managers, including the plant manager. Almost half of Appleseed's customers were also customers of Orchard Farms, and Appleseed's apple juice production and revenue were very similar to Orchard Farms'.

Two weeks after Appleseed began production, the union asked the company to extend the most recent Orchard Farms collective-bargaining agreement to all employees. After Appleseed refused, the union demanded that the company recognize the union and begin bargaining. Appleseed again refused. As you read the article excerpt below, ask yourself whether Appleseed's refusals were lawful.

PROBLEM MATERIALS

Keith N. Hylton & Maria O'Brien Hylton, *Rent Appropriation and the Labor Law Doctrine of Successorship*, 70 B.U. L. REV. 821 (1990)

Keith N. Hylton & Maria O'Brien Hylton, *Rent Appropriation and the Labor Law Doctrine of Successorship*
70 B.U. L. REV. 821 (1990)[10]

The modern successorship era began with the Supreme Court's decision in *John Wiley & Sons, Inc. v. Livingston*, [376 U.S. 543 (1964),] which marked a dramatic departure from prior successorship cases. *Wiley* involved a small publishing company, Interscience Publishers, Inc. ("Interscience"), which merged with Wiley & Sons, Inc. ("Wiley"). As a result of the merger Interscience ceased to exist. Claiming that Wiley was obligated to recognize the rights of Interscience employees under the existing agreement, the Union brought suit under section 301 of the Labor Management Relations Act (the "LMRA") to compel arbitration. These rights, the Union argued, included such things as seniority, pension contributions and severance pay.

Agreeing with the Union that Wiley was obligated to arbitrate regarding the alleged rights, a unanimous Supreme Court held that the arbitration provisions of a collective bargaining agreement survive a merger because employees must be protected from sudden changes in the employment relationship resulting from a regime that allows employers the unfettered right to acquire and divest themselves

---

[10] Copyright © 1990 by Keith N. Hylton & Maria O'Brien Hylton. All rights reserved. Reprinted with permission.

of business enterprises. Additionally, the Court stated that where a "substantial continuity of identity in the business enterprise" exists, a successor employer will be obligated to arbitrate with the union according to the terms of the bargaining agreement.

In *NLRB v. Burns International Security Services, Inc.*, [406 U.S. 272 (1972),] the Supreme Court appeared to back away from *Wiley* and the strong presumption favoring arbitration. The dispute in Burns arose when a security contract between the Wackenhut Corporation ("Wackenhut") and Lockheed Aircraft Service Company ("Lockheed") expired. Under the arrangement with Lockheed, Wackenhut had provided security guards represented by the recently certified United Plant Guard Union (the "UPG"). Lockheed solicited bids for a new security contract and eventually awarded it to Burns International Security Services ("Burns"). Burns provided Lockheed with a unit of forty-two guards, twenty-seven of whom were former Wackenhut employees. Burns refused a request from the UPG for recognition, recognizing instead the American Federation of Guards which already represented other Burns employees.

The UPG alleged violations of sections 8(a)(2) and 8(a)(5) of the [NLRA], claiming that Burns' recognition of the American Federation of Guards was unlawful, and that its failure to honor the Wackenhut contract resulted in an unlawful, unilateral change in employment conditions. The National Labor Relations Board (the "NLRB") determined that Burns was a successor employer and, as such, was obligated to recognize and bargain with the former Wackenhut employees' union representative. Relying on the *Wiley* decision, the NLRB further required Burns to adopt the substantive terms of the UPG's agreement with Wackenhut. The Supreme Court agreed with the NLRB that "where the bargaining unit remains unchanged and a majority of the employees hired by the new employer are represented by a recently certified bargaining agent there is little basis for faulting the NLRB's implementation by ordering the employer to bargain with the incumbent union." [406 U.S. at 281.]

As far as Burns' duty to bargain with the Union, the Supreme Court held that the duty arose when Burns hired a majority of holdover Wackenhut employees. In other words, Burns was free to establish initial terms and conditions of hiring. But, when a majority of the new work force came to consist of "holdover" employees and there was "substantial continuity" in the business enterprise, Burns became a successor and had to bargain. Notwithstanding this general rule, the Court noted that there may be times when it is "perfectly clear" that the successor employer intends to retain all of the predecessor's employees, and "it will be appropriate to have him initially consult with the employees' bargaining representative before he fixes terms."

In an apparent departure from *Wiley*, the Court concluded that Burns was under no obligation to assume the substantive terms of the Wackenhut-UPG contract. Specifically, the Court interpreted section 8(d) as prohibiting the NLRB from imposing substantive terms on an employer who was not a party to the contract. The Court distinguished *Wiley*, noting that, unlike *Burns*, that case involved a suit to compel arbitration under section 301 and that the Court had been particularly concerned with encouraging arbitration.

In 1973, the Court once again examined the obligations of a successor employer, this time in the context of liability for the unfair labor practices of the predecessor. In *Golden State Bottling Co. v. NLRB*, [414 U.S. 168 (1973),] the successor employer had purchased a beverage bottling and distribution operation with the knowledge that the predecessor had been ordered by the NLRB to rehire and compensate a former employee. The NLRB determined that the successor employer was obligated to rehire the individual and was jointly liable for the back pay award. The Supreme Court agreed, noting that industrial peace and reasonable employee expectations require that a successor with knowledge of outstanding unfair labor practices be required to remedy them.

One year later, the Court effectively overruled *Wiley* in *Howard Johnson Co. v. Detroit Local Joint Executive Board, Hotel & Restaurant Employees* [, 417 U.S. 249 (1974)]. *Howard Johnson* concerned a section 301 action brought by the Hotel and Restaurant Employees Union to compel arbitration by the new owner, Howard Johnson Co., ("Howard Johnson") under the predecessor's contract. In reversing the Sixth Circuit's order to arbitrate, the Court determined that there was no substantial continuity of identity in the work force since the predecessor's employees did not constitute a majority of the new complement of employees, and therefore, Howard Johnson had no duty to arbitrate. Furthermore, the Court disavowed the distinction made in *Burns* between an unfair labor practice proceeding and a section 301 action. The Court did, however, suggest that the Union might have moved to enjoin the predecessor from selling its assets to Howard Johnson on the grounds that the sale constituted a breach of the successorship clause contained in the collective bargaining agreement.

Notably, the majority pointedly contrasted the merger in *Wiley* with the straightforward sale of assets in *Howard Johnson*. In prior successorship cases the Court had never treated the nature of the underlying corporate transaction as a relevant consideration. Indeed, in *Golden State*, the Court refused "to adopt a mode of analysis requiring the NLRB to distinguish among mergers, consolidations, and purchases of assets . . . so long as there is a continuity in the employing industry . . . ." [414 U.S. at 182–83 n.5]. The emphasis on the nature of the underlying transaction in *Howard Johnson*, however, was relatively minor and proved to be short-lived. Ultimately, instead of adopting transaction-specific guidelines for applying the successorship doctrine, the Court focused on whether the predecessor survived the change in control.

The Court's opinions in *Burns* and *Howard Johnson* teach that the NLRB and federal courts must apply the "substantial continuity of identity" test when determining a successor's obligation in change of ownership cases. This test, which examines whether there is substantial continuity between the two business enterprises, is based on the facts and circumstances of each situation. The NLRB considers several factors in its successorship analysis including:

> (1) whether there has been a substantial continuity of the same business operations; (2) whether the new employer uses the same plant; (3) whether he has the same or substantially the same work force; (4) whether the same jobs exist[] under the same working conditions; (5) whether he employs the

same supervisors; (6) whether he uses the same machinery, equipment, and methods of production; and (7) whether he manufactures the same produc[t] or offer[s] the same services.

[*Georgetown Stainless Mfg. Corp.*, 198 N.L.R.B. 234, 236 (1972).]

The substantial continuity of identity test incorporates the requirement that there be continuity of the workforce. Thus, to satisfy the test the successor employer must have hired a majority of the predecessor's employees. The NLRB has adopted the "substantial and representative complement rule for fixing the moment when the determination as to the composition of the successor's work force is to be made." [*Fall River Dyeing & Finishing Corp. v. NLRB*, 482 U.S. 27, 47 (1987).] If at the moment fixed by the substantial and representative complement rule a majority of the new employer's workers had been employed by the previous employer "then the successor has an obligation to bargain with the union that represented these employees." [*Id.* at 47.]

The Court applied these doctrines in *Fall River Dyeing & Finishing Corp. v. NLRB*. This case concerned the Sterlingwale Corporation ("Sterlingwale"), a textile dyeing and manufacturing plant in Fall River, Massachusetts. Sterlingwale laid off all of its production employees in February, 1982 after some thirty years in business. The company retained a skeleton crew in order to complete remaining orders and to maintain its buildings and machinery. For many years, Sterlingwale's employees had been represented by the United Textile Workers of America ("the UTW"). The most recent employment contract expired on April 1, 1982 and embodied several concessions made by the UTW in response to Sterlingwale's financial problems. In the summer of 1982, Sterlingwale went out of business, making an assignment for the benefit of its creditors and hiring a professional liquidator to dispose of its assets. A new company, Fall River Dyeing & Finishing Corporation ("Fall River"), was formed "with the intention of engaging strictly in the commission-dyeing business and of taking advantage of the availability of Sterlingwale's assets and workforce." [*Id.* at 32.]

In September 1982, Fall River began operating out of its predecessor's facilities and hiring employees. October 19, 1982, the UTW requested that Fall River recognize it and commence bargaining negotiations. Fall River refused — at this time eighteen of its twenty-one employees were former Sterlingwale employees. By January 1983, Fall River had hired fifty-five employees, a number sufficient to fill one shift. Of these, thirty-six had worked for Sterlingwale. By April 1983, Fall River was operating with two full shifts and, for the first time, former Sterlingwale employees were outnumbered fifty-four to fifty-three.

The UTW filed an unfair labor practice charge with the NLRB alleging that Fall River had violated sections 8(a)(1) and 8(a)(5) of the [NLRA] by refusing to bargain. The Administrative Law Judge (the "ALJ")[, with the NLRB's agreement,] determined that Fall River, as a successor employer, was obliged to bargain with the UTW if it had hired a majority of Sterlingwale employees. Accordingly, the ALJ found that the Union's demand, originally made in October, was "of a continuing nature" and was still effective in January when former Sterlingwale employees constituted a majority of the "representative complement." [*Fall River Dyeing & Finishing Corp.*, 272 N.L.R.B. 839, 840 (1984).]

The Court of Appeals for the First Circuit enforced the NLRB's order, noting that "viewed from the employees' standpoint" there was no significant change in business operations. [*NLRB v. Fall River Dyeing & Finishing Corp.*, 775 F.2d 425, 430 (1st Cir. 1985).] In addition, the court found that both the NLRB's "representative complement" rule and "continuing demand" rule were reasonable and entitled to deference. [*Id.*]

The Supreme Court agreed that Fall River was a successor employer and that the *Burns* holding was not limited to situations in which a union had been recently certified. Moreover, the Court stated, a successor "is under no obligation to hire the employees of its predecessor, subject, of course, to the restriction that it not discriminate against union employees in its hiring." [482 U.S. at 80.] This approach places the potential successor in control of his destiny. The Court next examined the three basic rules the NLRB applies in successorship cases: (1) the "substantial continuity" rule for determining successorship status; (2) the "representative complement" rule for determining when an analysis of the successor's workforce should take place; and (3) the "continuing demand" rule preserving a union's demand to bargain until the "representative complement" is achieved.

The "substantial continuity" test compares the nature of the predecessor's overall enterprise with that of the successor and evaluates each enterprise from the employees' point of view. "This emphasis on the employees' perspective furthers the Act's policy of industrial peace. If the employees find themselves in essentially the same jobs after the employer transition and if their legitimate expectations in continued representation by their union are thwarted, their dissatisfaction may lead to labor unrest." [*Id.* at 43–44.] Applying the substantial continuity test, the Court compared the nature of Sterlingwale's overall enterprise with that of Fall River. Noting that Fall River continued to manufacture the same product line and that the employees worked at the same jobs and used the same machinery, the Court agreed that there was "substantial continuity" between Sterlingwale and Fall River.

The Court next turned to the "substantial and representative complement" rule. In upholding the NLRB's application of this rule, the Court noted that the rule was designed to balance the competing interests of maximum employee participation in choosing a bargaining representative and speedy representation for desirous employees. Moreover, because the employer is best situated to determine when normal production has begun and most job classifications have been filled, the Court concluded that the "substantial and representative complement" rule is not overly burdensome to employers.

Last, the Court held that the "continuing demand" rule was reasonable and, given the Union's lack of relationship with the successor, was the only practical way for the Union to trigger a duty to bargain. Because unions frequently will not be aware of the status of the successor's operations, many demands may be premature. The Court noted, however, that even a premature demand places "a minimal burden" on a successor who knows that the demand is only effective when a "representative complement" of employees are hired and the predecessor's employees constitute a majority of the workforce. The possibility raised in *Howard Johnson*, of analyzing successorship cases based on the nature of the underlying corporate transaction, did not affect the analysis in *Fall River*.

Justice Powell, joined by Justices Rehnquist and O'Connor, dissented in *Fall River*. Justice Powell focused on the "overwhelming" evidence of discontinuity including the long hiatus in operations and Fall River's refusal to purchase Sterlingwale's tradename, goodwill, or customer lists. Thus, the dissent suggests that where there is a lengthy interruption in production or other indicia of discontinuity this evidence should bar assertion of successor obligations. Both the *Fall River* majority and dissent suggest that the application of the substantial continuity test is likely to be affected by competing functional considerations regarding the social desirability of allowing unfettered freedom to acquire and transfer businesses and the protection of employee expectations. . . .

POST PROBLEM DISCUSSION

1. Consider our problem: should Appleseed be considered a successor to Orchard Farms? *See Harter Tomato Products Co. v. NLRB*, 133 F.3d 934 (D.C. Cir. 1998) (holding, in case similar to problem, that new employer was a successor).

2. Assume in our problem that Appleseed is the successor to Orchard Farms. Can Appleseed hire new employees, including former Orchard Farm employees, with less-favorable terms and conditions? *See NLRB v. Burns International Security Services, Inc.*, 406 U.S. 272, 294 (1972) (holding that successor is generally free to hire employees, even from predecessor, on its own terms). Does Appleseed have to bargain with the union? *See Fall River Dyeing & Finishing Corp. v. NLRB*, 482 U.S. 27, 38–41 (1987) (holding that the successor has a duty to bargain with the union if there is substantial continuity and a majority of its employees came from the predecessor).

Does Appleseed have to extend all or part of the Orchard Farms collective-bargaining agreement to its workforce? The answer to this question is still up in the air. *Burns* suggests that a successor is not bound by the substantive terms of the predecessor's collective-bargaining agreement, unless the successor assumes the agreement or is an alter-ego of the predecessor. However, relying on *Wiley*, some courts have held that a successor may be bound by the substantive terms of a collective-bargaining agreement, or at least its arbitration clause, simply through the substantial continuity test. For a good discussion of this issue, see *Ameristeel Corp. v. International Brotherhood of Teamsters*, 267 F.3d 264 (3rd Cir. 2001).

3. Although under *Burns*, a successor can usually hire employees under new terms, there are exceptions. *Burns*, itself, suggests that when a successor has actually hired all of its employees from the predecessor or made it "perfectly clear" that it plans to hire all of its employees from the predecessor, then it must first consult with the union before establishing the terms and conditions of employment. 406 U.S. at 294–95. Moreover, a corollary to *Burns'* holding that a successor can hire employees under new terms is that the successor is also generally free to hire whomever it wants. *See Burns*, 406 U.S. at 280. However, there are exceptions to this rule as well, especially under the prohibition against discrimination in Section 8(a)(3). *See Fall River*, 482 U.S. at 80; *Daufuskie Island Club and Resort, Inc.*, 328 N.L.R.B. 415 (1999), *enforced sub nom. International Union of Operating Engineers v. NLRB*, 221 F.3d 196 (D.C. Cir. 2000).

4.   With regard to note 3, why do you think that *Burns* required bargaining once a successor hired enough of the predecessor's employees to make them a majority of the workforce? Hint: think about why the duty turns on whether a "majority" of the successor's employees came from the predecessor.

5.   Imagine that a successor hires a majority of its employees from its predecessor and recognizes the union that represented those employees. After a few months, the successor believes that the union no longer has support from a majority of employees and wants to file for a decertification election. Should the union in this instance enjoy protection under the voluntary recognition bar (see Chapter 6)? This question is one that has been subject to flip-flops at the NLRB. The Clinton Board concluded that the voluntary recognition bar does apply, but the Bush Board overruled it. Later, in 2011, the Obama Board reinstated the Clinton Board's rule. *Compare UGL-UNICCO Service Co.*, 357 N.L.R.B. No. 76 (2011), and *St. Elizabeth's Manor, Inc.*, 329 N.L.R.B. 341 (1999), *with MV Transportation*, 337 N.L.R.B. 770 (2002).

SECTION 3   MID-TERM BARGAINING AND CONTRACT EXPIRATION

Although parties to a collective-bargaining agreement usually try to address all of the issues that they think will come up during the life of an agreement, no one has a crystal ball. Moreover, at times, parties may be aware that an issue could arise later but are unable or unwilling to reach an agreement. As a result, during the life of a collective-bargaining agreement, a party may try to change a term in the agreement or introduce a new issue that is not addressed by the agreement. This section will discuss the limits and responsibilities of parties in this situation.

A related issue occurs immediately after a collective-bargaining agreement ends without a new agreement taking over. In this situation, competing policies are often in tension. On one side is the parties' freedom of contract, which might lead you to conclude that once the agreement ends, all obligations under the agreement end as well. As you shall see, that is not generally true. The reason is one of the fundamental policies of labor law: promoting fruitful collective-bargaining. If a party, usually the employer, is able to simply walk away from established terms and conditions as soon as an agreement ends, employees' ability to seek beneficial bargaining can be significantly hampered. As a result, the NLRB and courts have typically extended the *Katz* duty to maintain current terms and conditions until negotiations have reached an impasse. But, as you will see, there are exceptions to this rule.

PROBLEM #3: FIGHTING AGAINST EXTRA PAY

Nurses at St. Elsewhere Hospital are represented by a union that has an active collective-bargaining agreement with the hospital. One of the terms in the agreement was called "Hours of Work and Extraordinary Pay" and stated that the hospital retained the "right to assign nurses as it deems appropriate, including when the hospital determines that additional work hours or nurses are needed; if nurses work such additional hours, they will receive 'extraordinary pay' for those hours" as calculated by an accompanying formula.

Eventually, the hospital realized that it had consistent nurse staffing shortages during various times of the year. As a response, the hospital implemented a new "incentive policy" that gave up to an additional $500 for any nurse who worked extra shifts during specified times of year. The hospital did not consult with the union over this policy, either during negotiations for the current collective-bargaining agreement or before the policy was implemented. The union now complains that the failure to consult prior to the policy's implementation was illegal. Is the union right?

PROBLEM MATERIALS

Milwaukee Spring Division (Milwaukee Spring II), 268 N.L.R.B. 601 (1984)

MILWAUKEE SPRING DIVISION (MILWAUKEE SPRING II)
268 N.L.R.B. 601 (1984)

On 22 October 1982 the National Labor Relations Board issued its Decision and Order in Milwaukee Spring I, finding that Respondent had engaged in unfair labor practices in violation of Section 8(a)(1), (3), and (5) and Section 8(d) of the National Labor Relations Act, as amended. The Board held that Respondent violated the Act by deciding without the Union's consent to transfer its assembly operations from its unionized Milwaukee Spring facility to its unorganized McHenry Spring facility during the term of a collective-bargaining agreement because of the comparatively higher labor costs under the agreement, and to lay off unit employees as a consequence of that decision. Respondent filed a petition for review of the Board's Decision and Order with the United States Court of Appeals for the Seventh Circuit, and the Board filed a cross-application for enforcement of its Order. On 4 August 1983 the court granted the Board's motion to remand this case to the Board for additional consideration. . . .

The Board has reconsidered its Decision and Order in light of the entire record and the oral arguments and has decided to reverse that decision and dismiss the complaint. . . .

The Union has represented Respondent's bargaining unit employees for a number of years. The most recent contract became effective on 1 April 1980, and remained in effect until at least 31 March 1983. The contract contains specific wage and benefits provisions. The contract also provides that the Company "recognizes the Union as the sole and exclusive collective bargaining agent for all production and maintenance employees in the Company's plant at Milwaukee, Wisconsin."

On 26 January 1982 Respondent asked the Union to forgo a scheduled wage increase and to grant other contract concessions. In March, because Respondent lost a major customer, it proposed to the Union relocating its assembly operations to the nonunionized McHenry facility, located in McHenry, Illinois, to obtain relief from the comparatively higher assembly labor costs at Milwaukee Spring. Respondent also advised the Union that it needed wage and benefit concessions to keep its molding operations in Milwaukee viable. On 23 March the Union rejected the proposed reduction in wages and benefits. On 29 March Respondent submitted to the Union a document entitled "Terms Upon Which Milwaukee Assembly Operations Will Be Retained in Milwaukee." On 4 April the Union rejected the Company's proposal for alternatives to relocation and declined to bargain further over the Company's decision to transfer its assembly operations. The Company then announced its decision to relocate the Milwaukee assembly operations to the McHenry facility.

The parties stipulated that the relocation decision was economically motivated and was not the result of union animus. The parties also stipulated that Respondent has satisfied its obligation to bargain with the Union over the decision to relocate the assembly operations and has been willing to engage in effects bargaining with the Union.[11]

Sections 8(a)(5) and 8(d) establish an employer's obligation to bargain in good faith with respect to "wages, hours, and other terms and conditions of employment." Generally, an employer may not unilaterally institute changes regarding these mandatory subjects before reaching a good-faith impasse in bargaining.[12] Section 8(d) imposes an additional requirement when a collective-bargaining agreement is in effect and an employer seeks to "modif[y] . . . the terms and conditions contained in" the contract: the employer must obtain the union's consent before implementing the change. If the employment conditions the employer seeks to change are not "contained in" the contract, however, the employer's obligation remains the general one of bargaining in good faith to impasse over the subject before instituting the proposed change.

Applying these principles to the instant case, before the Board may hold that Respondent violated Section 8(d), the Board first must identify a specific term "contained in" the contract that the Company's decision to relocate modified. In *Milwaukee Spring I*, the Board never specified the contract term that was modified by Respondent's decision to relocate the assembly operations. The Board's failure to do so is not surprising, for we have searched the contract in vain for a provision requiring bargaining unit work to remain in Milwaukee.

Milwaukee Spring I suggests, however, that the Board may have concluded that Respondent's relocation decision, because it was motivated by a desire to obtain relief from the Milwaukee contract's labor costs, modified that contract's wage and benefits provisions. We believe this reasoning is flawed. While it is true that the Company proposed modifying the wage and benefits provisions of the contract, the Union rejected the proposals. Following its failure to obtain the Union's consent, Respondent, in accord with Section 8(d), abandoned the proposals to modify the contract's wage and benefits provisions. Instead, Respondent decided to transfer the assembly operations to a different plant where different workers (who were not subject to the contract) would perform the work. In short, Respondent did not disturb the wages and benefits at its Milwaukee facility, and consequently did not violate Section 8(d) by modifying, without the Union's consent, the wage and

---

[11] [n.5] The parties' stipulation and the manner in which they briefed this case treat Respondent's relocation decision as a mandatory subject of bargaining. . . .

[12] [n.6] See *NLRB v. Katz*, 369 U.S. 736 (1962).

benefits provisions contained in the contract.

Nor do we find that Respondent's relocation decision modified the contract's recognition clause. . . . Language recognizing the Union as the bargaining agent "for all production and maintenance employees in the Company's plant at Milwaukee, Wisconsin," does not state that the functions that the unit performs must remain in Milwaukee. No doubt parties could draft such a clause; indeed, work-preservation clauses are commonplace. It is not for the Board, however, to create an implied work-preservation clause in every American labor agreement based on wage and benefits or recognition provisions, and we expressly decline to do so.

In sum, we find in the instant case that neither wage and benefits provisions nor the recognition clause contained in the collective-bargaining agreement preserves bargaining unit work at the Milwaukee facility for the duration of the contract, and that Respondent did not modify these contract terms when it decided to relocate its assembly operations. Further, we find that no other term contained in the contract restricts Respondent's decision-making regarding relocation.

Our dissenting colleague and the decision in *Milwaukee Spring I* fail to recognize that decision's substantial departure from NLRB textbook law that an employer need not obtain a union's consent on a matter not contained in the body of a collective-bargaining agreement even though the subject is a mandatory subject of bargaining. See, e.g., *Ozark Trailers*, 161 N.L.R.B. 561 (1966). Although the Board found a violation in *Ozark*, it did so grounded on the employer's failure to bargain over its decision to close a part of its operation during the collective-bargaining agreement, transfer equipment to another of its plants, and subcontract out work which had been performed at the Ozark plant. Even though the Board's ultimate conclusion in that case may not here survive the Supreme Court's analysis in *First National Corp.*, it is instructive to note the Board's recognition that the employer's obligation, absent a specific provision in the contract restricting its rights, was to *bargain* with the union over its decision:

> In the first place, however, as we have pointed out time and time again, an employer's obligation to bargain does not include the obligation to agree, but solely to engage in a full and frank discussion with the collective-bargaining representative in which a bona fide effort will be made to explore possible alternatives, if any, that may achieve a mutually satisfactory accommodation of the interests of both the employer and the employees. If such efforts fail, the employer is wholly free to make and effectuate his decision.

[161 NLRB at 568. Footnote omitted.] . . .

Accordingly, we conclude that Respondent's decision to relocate did not modify the collective-bargaining agreement in violation of Section 8(d). In view of the parties' stipulation that Respondent satisfied its obligation to bargain over the decision, we also conclude that Respondent did not violate Section 8(a)(5) . . . .

. . . *Milwaukee Spring I* discourage[s] truthful midterm bargaining over decisions to transfer unit work. Under [*Milwaukee Spring I*], an employer contemplating a plant relocation for several reasons, one of which is labor costs, would be likely to admit only the reasons unrelated to labor costs in order to avoid granting the union veto power over the decision. The union, unaware that labor costs were a factor in the employer's decision, would be unlikely to volunteer wage or other appropriate concessions. Even if the union offered to consider wage concessions, the employer might hesitate to discuss such suggestions for fear that bargaining with the union over the union's proposals would be used as evidence that labor costs had motivated the relocation decision.

We believe our holding today avoids this dilemma and will encourage the realistic and meaningful collective bargaining that the Act contemplates. Under our decision, an employer does not risk giving a union veto power over its decision regarding relocation and should therefore be willing to disclose all factors affecting its decision. Consequently, the union will be in a better position to evaluate whether to make concessions. Because both parties will no longer have an incentive to refrain from frank bargaining, the likelihood that they will be able to resolve their differences is greatly enhanced.

MEMBER ZIMMERMAN, dissenting [opinion omitted].

POST PROBLEM DISCUSSION

1. Midterm modifications can be confusing, as there are several different scenarios that might occur. These scenarios include:

   a. An employer's unilateral modification of a term that was not contained in the collective-bargaining agreement and was never discussed during bargaining. If the term is a permissive subject of bargaining, the unilateral change is lawful. *See Allied Chemical & Alkali Workers v. Pittsburgh Plate Glass Co.*, 404 U.S. 157, 188 (1971). However, if the term is a mandatory subject, then the unilateral change violates Section 8(a)(5). *See Jacobs Manufacturing Co.*, 94 N.L.R.B. 1214, 1215 (1951), *enforced*, 196 F.2d 680 (2d Cir. 1952). In addition, the usual *Katz* rule will still apply; thus, an employer can implement unilateral changes of mandatory subjects after impasse. *Milwaukee Springs II*, 268 N.L.R.B. at 602.

   b. An employer's unilateral change of a term that was not contained in the collective-bargaining agreement, but was discussed during negotiations. If the term was "fully discussed and consciously explored and [ ] the union consciously yielded or clearly and unmistakably waived its interest in the matter," then the change will be lawful no matter whether the term was a mandatory or permissive subject. *See Georgia Power Co.*, 325 N.L.R.B. 420, 420–21 (1998), *enforced mem.* 176 F.3d 494 (11th Cir. 1999). If these conditions do not apply, then the union will not be deemed to have waived its right to bargain over any mandatory subject.

   c. An employer's unilateral change of a term that was never discussed during bargaining and was not contained in the collective-bargaining agreement, which contains a "zipper clause." A zipper clause is an agreement by the parties to waive their right to bargain over certain terms. These clauses can vary in coverage, but generally they prevent a party from insisting on bargaining over new terms that are not in the agreement — in other words, the agreement is "zipped" up. These zipped up terms are not in the agreement because the terms were either already discussed and not included on purpose, or because the terms were not discussed at all. Generally, an employer cannot unilaterally change any term during the life of the agreement if the term covered by the zipper clause, even after there is an impasse. *See CBS Corp.*, 326 N.L.R.B. 861, 861–62 (1998) (concluding that, where a zipper clause clearly covered the subject at issue, "the Union could use the clause as a shield to resist efforts by the [employer] to re-raise the matter . . . and the [employer] could not use the clauses as a sword to change the status-quo as to this subject"); *see also VMI Cabinets*, 340 N.L.R.B. 1196, 1200 (2003).

2.   What about our problem — is the union correct that the hospital's unilateral implementation of the incentive policy violated the NLRA? What do you think the hospital will argue in response? *See Provena St. Joseph Medical Center*, 350 N.L.R.B. 808 (2007) (concluding, under similar facts and over a dissent, that the authority to provide extraordinary pay in the agreement was not a clear and unmistakable waiver of the union's right to bargain over a regular incentive pay policy). Also, as a review of past material (see Chapter 3), why would the union object to the hospital providing extra pay to the nurses?

3.   As noted in Chapter 9, Section 8(d) of the NLRA provides certain rules that cover the expiration of a collective-bargaining agreement. One rule covers the procedures required when a party wants to modify or terminate an agreement. Section 8(d) mandates that the party must give the other party notice of the desire to change or terminate at least 60 days before the expiration of the agreement (90 days if the employer is a health care institution). The party seeking a change must also agree to negotiate with the other party and notify relevant federal and state agencies set up to mediate labor disputes.

Probably the most important Section 8(d) requirement is that a party seeking change "continues in full force and effect, without resorting to strike or lockout, all the terms and conditions of the existing contract for a period of sixty days after such notice is given or until the expiration date of such contract, whichever occurs later." Section 8(d)(4). What this, in combination with the *Katz* doctrine, means in practice is that most mandatory subjects in an expired collective-bargaining agreement must remain in force until the parties have reached an impasse. *Litton Financial Printing Division v. NLRB*, 501 U.S. 190, 198 (1991); *Laborers Health & Welfare Trust Fund v. Advanced Lightweight Concrete Co.*, 484 U.S. 539, 544, n. 6 (1988). One exception occurs when the parties clearly and unmistakably state in the agreement that its terms will end when the agreement expires. *See Local Joint Executive Board of Las Vegas v. NLRB*, 540 F.3d 1072, 1080–81 (9th Cir. 2008); *Cauthorne Trucking v. Drivers, Local Union 639*, 256 N.L.R.B. 721, 722 (1981).

The NLRB also excludes certain, specific mandatory subjects from this rule, meaning that they will usually expire along with the agreement. These subjects include union security agreements, dues check off provisions, arbitration clauses, and no-strike clauses. *See Litton*, 501 U.S. at 199 (noting that union security and dues check off clauses are permitted by statute only in a collective-bargaining agreement, and that the right to strike and the right to seek adjudication are statutory rights that require a valid wavier). *But see Local Joint Executive Board of Las Vegas v. NLRB*, 309 F.3d 578, 585–86 (9th Cir. 2002) (questioning dues check off exclusion where no union security clauses existed).

4.   Related to note 3 is a post-agreement issue that often has a large impact on both the employer and employees: benefits given to retirees. The major case in the area is *UAW v. Yard-Man, Inc.*, 716 F.2d 1476 (6th Cir. 1983), in which the employer told its retirees that the health and life insurance benefits it had been providing under the terms of the collective-bargaining agreement would end when that agreement expired. The Sixth Circuit held that the termination of benefits violated the agreement because those benefits vested once employees retired while the agreement was still in effect. This will not be true in every instance, as that holding was based on an interpretation of the parties' contractual intent. However, the holding also ushered in what is called the "*Yard-Man* inference." Under this inference, "when the parties contract for benefits which accrue upon achievement of retiree status, there is an inference that the parties likely intended those benefits to continue as long as the beneficiary remains a retiree." *Id.* at 1482 (noting that retiree benefits are like "status benefits" that deserve a presumption of continuing status). Courts have since split on how much influence an inference in favor of vesting should play when interpreting whether the parties "clearly and unmistakably" indicated that the benefits should end with the agreement. *See* Richard L. Kaplan et al., *Retirees at Risk: The Precarious Promise of Post-Employment Health Benefits*, 9 YALE J. HEALTH POL'Y, L. & ETHICS 287, 306–09 (2009); *see generally* Catherine L. Fisk, Lochner *Redux: The Renaissance of Laissez-Faire Contract in the Federal Common Law of Employee Benefits*, 56 OHIO ST. L.J. 153 (1995).

SECTION 4   ANTITRUST

There may be no two areas of law that are more in conflict than antitrust and labor law. The central aim of antitrust law is to limit the ability of actors to join together and use their market power to create an anticompetitive advantage. The central aim of unions is to join together and, hopefully, create market power to obtain more compensation for employees than they would receive under perfectly competitive conditions. Something had to give. Accordingly, Congress and the Supreme Court eventually developed a labor exemption to the antitrust laws. Yet, how and when this exemption works can be quite complicated, and the answers to those questions can have a significant impact on unions and employers alike.

PROBLEM #4: KICKBALL LOCKOUT

The National Kickball League ("NKL") is an entity that oversees a national league of separately owned professional kickball teams. The kickball players are represented by a union, the National Kickball League Players Association ("NKLPA"). The league and union have been parties to multiple, successive collective-bargaining agreements over the years (the NKL acts as the bargaining representative on behalf of all of the teams, which have all consented to the NKL's representation). However, negotiations over a new agreement have turned contentious. There were many issues that the parties had yet to resolve, but the biggest issue was how to share the popular league's expanding share of revenue.

The players were aware that the team owners were planning on declaring a lockout as soon as the previous agreement expired. Thus, before that happened, the players voted to renounce their desire to have the NKLPA represent them and the union announced that it was "voluntarily decertifying." The NKL instituted a lockout the next day. Later that day, several star kickball players, such as Brady Brees and Priest Manning, sued the NKL alleging that the lockout was an attempt to price fix in violation of antitrust laws and sought an injunction against the lockout. After reading the material below, do you think kickball can be saved this season?

PROBLEM MATERIALS

Brown v. Pro Football, Inc., 518 U.S. 231 (1996)

BROWN v. PRO FOOTBALL, INC.
518 U.S. 231 (1996)

JUSTICE BREYER delivered the opinion of the Court.

The question in this case arises at the intersection of the Nation's labor and antitrust laws. A group of professional football players brought this antitrust suit against football club owners. The club owners had bargained with the players' union over a wage issue until they reached impasse. The owners then had agreed among themselves (but not with the union) to implement the terms of their own last best bargaining offer. The question before us is whether federal labor laws shield such an agreement from antitrust attack. We believe that they do. This Court has previously found in the labor laws an implicit antitrust exemption that applies where needed to make the collective-bargaining process work. Like the Court of Appeals, we conclude that this need makes the exemption applicable in this case.

We can state the relevant facts briefly. In 1987, a collective-bargaining agreement between the National Football League (NFL or League), a group of football clubs, and the NFL Players Association, a labor union, expired. The NFL and the Players Association began to negotiate a new contract. In March 1989, during the negotiations, the NFL adopted Resolution G-2, a plan that would permit each club to establish a "developmental squad" of up to six rookie or "first-year" players who, as free agents, had failed to secure a position on a regular player roster. Squad members would play in practice games and sometimes in regular games as substitutes for injured players. Resolution G-2 provided that the club owners would pay all squad members the same weekly salary.

The next month, April, the NFL presented the developmental squad plan to the Players Association. The NFL proposed a squad player salary of $1,000 per week. The Players Association disagreed. It insisted that the club owners give developmental squad players benefits and protections similar to those provided regular players, and that they leave individual squad members free to negotiate their own salaries.

Two months later, in June, negotiations on the issue of developmental squad salaries reached an impasse. The NFL then unilaterally implemented the developmental squad program by distributing to the clubs a uniform contract that embodied the terms of Resolution G-2 and the $1,000 proposed weekly salary. The League advised club owners that paying developmental squad players more or less than $1,000 per week would result in disciplinary action, including the loss of draft choices.

In May 1990, 235 developmental squad players brought this antitrust suit against the League and its member clubs. The players claimed that their employers' agreement to pay them a $1,000 weekly salary violated the Sherman Act. See 15 U.S.C. § 1 (forbidding agreements in restraint of trade).[13] The Federal District Court denied the employers' claim of exemption from the antitrust laws; it permitted the case to reach the jury; and it subsequently entered judgment on a jury treble-damages award that exceeded $30 million. The NFL and its member clubs appealed.

The Court of Appeals (by a split 2-to-1 vote) reversed. The majority interpreted the labor laws as "waiv[ing] antitrust liability for restraints on competition imposed through the collective-bargaining process, so long as such restraints operate primarily in a labor market characterized by collective bargaining." 50 F.3d 1041, 1056 (C.A.D.C.1995). The court held, consequently, that the club owners were immune from antitrust liability. We granted certiorari to review that determination. Although we do not interpret the exemption as broadly as did the Appeals Court, we nonetheless find the exemption applicable, and we affirm that court's immunity conclusion.

The immunity before us rests upon what this Court has called the "nonstatutory" labor exemption from the antitrust laws. *Connell Constr. Co. v. Plumbers*, 421 U.S. 616, 622 (1975); see also *Meat Cutters v. Jewel Tea Co.*, 381 U.S. 676 (1965); *Mine Workers v. Pennington*, 381 U.S. 657 (1965). The Court has implied this exemption from federal labor statutes, which set forth a national labor policy favoring free and private collective bargaining, see 29 U.S.C. § 151; *Teamsters v. Oliver*, 358 U.S. 283, 295 (1959); which require good-faith bargaining over wages, hours, and working conditions, see 29 U.S.C. §§ 158(a)(5), 158(d); *NLRB v. Wooster Div. of Borg-Warner Corp.*, 356 U.S. 342, 348–349 (1958); and which delegate related rulemaking and interpretive authority to the National Labor Relations Board (Board), see 29 U.S.C. § 153; *San Diego Building Trades Council v. Garmon*, 359 U.S. 236, 242–245 (1959).

This implicit exemption reflects both history and logic. As a matter of history, Congress intended the labor statutes (from which the Court has implied the exemption) in part to adopt the views of dissenting Justices in *Duplex Printing Press Co. v. Deering*, 254 U.S. 443 (1921), which Justices had urged the Court to interpret broadly a different *explicit* "statutory" labor exemption that Congress earlier (in 1914) had written directly into the antitrust laws. *Id.*, at 483–488 (Brandeis, J., joined by Holmes and Clarke, JJ., dissenting) (interpreting § 20 of the

---

[13] [Section 1 of the Sherman Act states that "[e]very contract, combination in the form of trust or otherwise, or conspiracy, in restraint of trade or commerce among the several States, or with foreign nations, is declared to be illegal. . . . 15 U.S.C. § 1."]

Clayton Act, 38 Stat. 738, 29 U.S.C. § 52); see also *United States v. Hutcheson*, 312 U.S. 219, 230–236 (1941) (discussing congressional reaction to *Duplex*). In the 1930's, when it subsequently enacted the labor statutes, Congress, as in 1914, hoped to prevent judicial use of antitrust law to resolve labor disputes — a kind of dispute normally inappropriate for antitrust law resolution. See *Jewel Tea, supra,* at 700–709 (opinion of Goldberg, J.) . . . . The implicit ("nonstatutory") exemption interprets the labor statutes in accordance with this intent, namely, as limiting an antitrust court's authority to determine, in the area of industrial conflict, what is or is not a "reasonable" practice. It thereby substitutes legislative and administrative labor-related determinations for judicial antitrust-related determinations as to the appropriate legal limits of industrial conflict.

As a matter of logic, it would be difficult, if not impossible, to require groups of employers and employees to bargain together, but at the same time to forbid them to make among themselves or with each other *any* of the competition-restricting agreements potentially necessary to make the process work or its results mutually acceptable. Thus, the implicit exemption recognizes that, to give effect to federal labor laws and policies and to allow meaningful collective bargaining to take place, some restraints on competition imposed through the bargaining process must be shielded from antitrust sanctions. See *Connell, supra,* at 622 (federal labor law's "goals" could "never" be achieved if ordinary anticompetitive effects of collective bargaining were held to violate the antitrust laws); *Jewel Tea, supra,* at 711 (national labor law scheme would be "virtually destroyed" by the routine imposition of antitrust penalties upon parties engaged in collective bargaining); *Pennington, supra,* at 665 (implicit exemption necessary to harmonize Sherman Act with "national policy . . . of promoting 'the peaceful settlement of industrial disputes by subjecting labor-management controversies to the mediatory influence of negotiation' ") (quoting *Fibreboard Paper Products Corp. v. NLRB*, 379 U.S. 203, 211 (1964)).

The petitioners and their supporters concede, as they must, the legal existence of the exemption we have described. They also concede that, where its application is necessary to make the statutorily authorized collective-bargaining process work as Congress intended, the exemption must apply both to employers and to employees. Nor does the dissent take issue with these basic principles. Consequently, the question before us is one of determining the exemption's scope: Does it apply to an agreement among several employers bargaining together to implement after impasse the terms of their last best good-faith wage offer? We assume that such conduct, as practiced in this case, is unobjectionable as a matter of labor law and policy. On that assumption, we conclude that the exemption applies.

Labor law itself regulates directly, and considerably, the kind of behavior here at issue — the postimpasse imposition of a proposed employment term concerning a mandatory subject of bargaining. Both the Board and the courts have held that, after impasse, labor law permits employers unilaterally to implement changes in pre-existing conditions, but only insofar as the new terms meet carefully circumscribed conditions. For example, the new terms must be "reasonably comprehended" within the employer's preimpasse proposals (typically the last rejected proposals), lest by imposing more or less favorable terms, the employer unfairly undermined the union's status. The collective-bargaining proceeding itself must be free of any unfair labor practice, such as an employer's failure to have bargained in good faith. These regulations reflect the fact that impasse and an accompanying implementation of proposals constitute an integral part of the bargaining process.

Although the case law we have cited focuses upon bargaining by a single employer, no one here has argued that labor law does, or should, treat multiemployer bargaining differently in this respect. Indeed, Board and court decisions suggest that the joint implementation of proposed terms after impasse is a familiar practice in the context of multiemployer bargaining. We proceed on that assumption.

Multiemployer bargaining itself is a well-established, important, pervasive method of collective bargaining, offering advantages to both management and labor. See Appendix, *infra* (multiemployer bargaining accounts for more than 40% of major collective-bargaining agreements, and is used in such industries as construction, transportation, retail trade, clothing manufacture, and real estate, as well as professional sports); *NLRB v. Truck Drivers*, 353 U.S. 87, 95 (1957) *(Buffalo Linen)* (Congress saw multiemployer bargaining as "a vital factor in the effectuation of the national policy of promoting labor peace through strengthened collective bargaining"); *Charles D. Bonanno Linen Service, Inc. v. NLRB*, 454 U.S. 404, 409, n. 3 (1982) *(Bonanno Linen)* (multiemployer bargaining benefits both management and labor, by saving bargaining resources, by encouraging development of industry-wide worker benefits programs that smaller employers could not otherwise afford, and by inhibiting employer competition at the workers' expense) . . . . The upshot is that the practice at issue here plays a significant role in a collective-bargaining process that itself constitutes an important part of the Nation's industrial relations system.

In these circumstances, to subject the practice to antitrust law is to require antitrust courts to answer a host of important practical questions about how collective bargaining over wages, hours, and working conditions is to proceed — the very result that the implicit labor exemption seeks to avoid. And it is to place in jeopardy some of the potentially beneficial labor-related effects that multiemployer bargaining can achieve. That is because unlike labor law, which sometimes welcomes anticompetitive agreements conducive to industrial harmony, antitrust law forbids all agreements among competitors (such as competing employers) that unreasonably lessen competition among or between them in virtually any respect whatsoever. Antitrust law also sometimes permits judges or juries to premise antitrust liability upon little more than uniform behavior among competitors, preceded by conversations implying that later uniformity might prove desirable, or accompanied by other conduct that in context suggests that each competitor failed to make an independent decision . . . .

If the antitrust laws apply, what are employers to do once impasse is reached? If all impose terms similar to their last joint offer, they invite an antitrust action premised upon identical behavior (along with prior or accompanying conversations) as tending to show a common understanding or agreement. If any, or all, of them individually impose terms that differ significantly from that offer, they invite an unfair labor practice charge. Indeed, how can employers safely discuss their offers together even before a bargaining impasse occurs? A preimpasse discussion about, say, the practical advantages or disadvantages of a particular proposal invites a later antitrust claim that they agreed to limit the kinds of action each would later take should an impasse occur. The same is true of postimpasse discussions aimed at renewed negotiations with the union. Nor would adherence to the terms of an expired collective-bargaining agreement eliminate a potentially plausible antitrust claim charging that they had "conspired" or tacitly "agreed" to do so, particularly if maintaining the status quo were not in the immediate economic self-interest of some. All this is to say that to permit antitrust liability here threatens to introduce instability and uncertainty into the collective-bargaining process, for antitrust law often forbids or discourages the kinds of joint discussions and behavior that the collective-bargaining process invites or requires.

We do not see any obvious answer to this problem. We recognize, as the Government suggests, that, in principle, antitrust courts might themselves try to evaluate particular kinds of employer understandings, finding them "reasonable" (hence lawful) where justified by collective-bargaining necessity. But any such evaluation means a web of detailed rules spun by many different nonexpert antitrust judges and juries, not a set of labor rules enforced by a single expert administrative body, namely the Board. The labor laws give the Board, not antitrust courts, primary responsibility for policing the collective-bargaining process. And one of their objectives was to take from antitrust courts the authority to determine, through application of the antitrust laws, what is socially or economically desirable collective-bargaining policy.

Both petitioners and their supporters advance several suggestions for drawing the exemption boundary line short of this case. We shall explain why we find them unsatisfactory.

Petitioners claim that the implicit exemption applies only to labor-management *agreements* — a limitation that they deduce from case-law language, see, *e.g.*, *Connell*, 421 U.S., at 622 (exemption for "some union-employer *agreements*") (emphasis added), and from a proposed principle — that the exemption must rest upon labor-management consent. The language, however, reflects only the fact that the cases previously before the Court involved collective-bargaining agreements; the language does not reflect the exemption's rationale.

Nor do we see how an exemption limited by petitioners' principle of labor-management consent could work. One cannot mean the principle literally — that the exemption applies only to understandings embodied in a collective-bargaining agreement — for the collective-bargaining process may take place before the making of any agreement or after an agreement has expired. Yet a multiemployer bargaining process itself necessarily involves many procedural and substantive understandings among participating employers as well as with the union. Petitioners cannot rescue their principle by claiming that the exemption applies only insofar as *both* labor and management consent to those understandings. Often labor will not (and should not) consent to certain common bargaining positions that employers intend to maintain. Similarly, labor need not consent to certain tactics that this Court has approved as part of the multiemployer bargaining process, such as unit-wide lockouts and the use of temporary replacements. . . .

The Government argues that the exemption should terminate at the point of impasse. After impasse, it says, "employers no longer have a duty under the labor laws to maintain the status quo," and "are free as a matter of labor law to negotiate individual arrangements on an interim basis with the union."

Employers, however, are not completely free at impasse to act independently. The multiemployer bargaining unit ordinarily remains intact; individual employers cannot withdraw. The duty to bargain survives; employers must stand ready to resume collective bargaining. And individual employers can negotiate individual interim agreements with the union only insofar as those agreements are consistent with "the duty to abide by the results of group bargaining." *Bonanno Linen, supra,* at 416. . . .

More importantly, the simple "impasse" line would not solve the basic problem we have described above. Labor law permits employers, after impasse, to engage in considerable joint behavior, including joint lockouts and replacement hiring. Indeed, as a general matter, labor law often limits employers to four options at impasse: (1) maintain the status quo, (2) implement their last offer, (3) lock out their workers (and either shut down or hire temporary replacements), or (4) negotiate separate interim agreements with the union. What is to happen if the parties cannot reach an interim agreement? The other alternatives are limited. Uniform employer conduct is likely. Uniformity — at least when accompanied by discussion of the matter — invites antitrust attack. And such attack would ask antitrust courts to decide the lawfulness of activities intimately related to the bargaining process. . . .

Petitioners and their supporters argue in the alternative for a rule that would exempt postimpasse agreement about bargaining "tactics," but not postimpasse agreement about substantive "terms," from the reach of antitrust. They recognize, however, that both the Board and the courts have said that employers can, and often do, employ the imposition of "terms" as a bargaining "tactic." See, *e.g., American Ship Building Co. v. NLRB*, 380 U.S. 300, 316 (1965) . . . . This concession as to joint "tactical" implementation would turn the presence of an antitrust exemption upon a determination of the employers' primary purpose or motive. But to ask antitrust courts, insulated from the bargaining process, to investigate an employer group's subjective motive is to ask them to conduct an inquiry often more amorphous than those we have previously discussed. And, in our view, a labor/antitrust line drawn on such a basis would too often raise the same related (previously discussed) problems. See . . . *Jewel Tea*, 381 U.S., at 716 (opinion of Goldberg, J.) (expressing concern about antitrust judges "roaming at large" through the bargaining process). . . .

Petitioners also say that irrespective of how the labor exemption applies elsewhere to multiemployer collective bargaining, professional sports is "special." We can understand how professional sports may be special in terms of, say, interest, excitement, or concern. But we do not understand how they are special in respect to labor law's antitrust exemption. We concede that the clubs that make up a professional sports league are not completely independent economic competitors, as they depend upon a degree of cooperation for economic survival. In the present context, however, that circumstance makes the league more like a single bargaining employer, which analogy seems irrelevant to the legal issue before us.

We also concede that football players often have special individual talents, and, unlike many unionized workers, they often negotiate their pay individually with their employers. But this characteristic seems simply a feature, like so many others, that might give employees (or employers) more (or less) bargaining power, that might lead some (or all) of them to favor a particular kind of bargaining, or that might lead to certain demands at the bargaining table. We do not see how it could make a critical legal difference in determining the underlying framework in which bargaining is to take place. Indeed, it would be odd to fashion an antitrust exemption that gave additional advantages to professional football players (by virtue of their superior bargaining power) that transport workers, coal miners, or meat packers would not enjoy.

The dissent points to other "unique features" of the parties' collective-bargaining relationship, which, in the dissent's view, make the case "atypical." It says, for example, that the employers imposed the restraint simply to enforce compliance with league-wide rules, and that the bargaining consisted of nothing more than the sending of a "notice," and therefore amounted only to "so-called" bargaining. Insofar as these features underlie an argument for looking to the employers' true purpose, we have already discussed them. Insofar as they suggest that there was not a genuine impasse, they fight the basic assumption upon which the District Court, the Court of Appeals, petitioners, and this Court rest the case. Ultimately, we cannot find a satisfactory basis for distinguishing football players from other organized workers. We therefore conclude that all must abide by the same legal rules.

For these reasons, we hold that the implicit ("nonstatutory") antitrust exemption applies to the employer conduct at issue here. That conduct took place during and immediately after a collective-bargaining negotiation. It grew out of, and was directly related to, the lawful operation of the bargaining process. It involved a matter that the parties were required to negotiate collectively. And it concerned only the parties to the collective-bargaining relationship.

Our holding is not intended to insulate from antitrust review every joint imposition of terms by employers, for an agreement among employers could be sufficiently distant in time and in circumstances from the collective-bargaining process that a rule permitting antitrust intervention would not significantly interfere with that process. See, *e.g.*, [*Brown*,] 50 F.3d, at 1057 (suggesting that exemption lasts until collapse of the collective-bargaining relationship, as evidenced by decertification of the union); *El Cerrito Mill & Lumber Co.*, 316 N.L.R.B., at 1006–1007 (suggesting that "extremely long" impasse, accompanied by "instability" or "defunctness" of multiemployer unit, might justify union withdrawal from group bargaining). We need not decide in this case whether, or where, within these extreme outer boundaries to draw that line. . . .

The judgment of the Court of Appeals is *affirmed*.

JUSTICE STEVENS, dissenting [opinion omitted].

POST PROBLEM DISCUSSION

1. How do you think the kickball players will fare in their attempt to enjoin the lockout? Is the lockout, itself, an agreement among the owners to eliminate competition that violates the Sherman Act absent immunity? Now imagine that the lockout lasted for the entire season and that during the off-season the owners implemented their proposed revenue-sharing plan and a salary cap that the union had rejected during negotiations. Would these actions fall under the possible limitations to the labor antitrust exemption that the Supreme Court discussed at the end of *Brown*?

As you might recognize, this problem is based on the 2011 National Football League lockout. The district court issued a preliminary injunction against the lockout, holding that the players were likely to win their argument that the lockout violated Section 1 of the Sherman Act. *See Brady v. National Football League*, 779 F. Supp. 2d 992, 1040–42 (D. Minn. 2011). However, the Eighth Circuit reversed the district court, albeit not on antitrust grounds. *See Brady v. National Football League*, 644 F.3d 661 (8th Cir. 2011) (holding that Norris-LaGuardia Act prevents an injunction against an employer's work stoppage). Unfortunately for labor and antitrust law fans, but fortunately for football fans, the NFL and the National Football League Players Association settled their dispute before the issue was litigated further.

2. Labor laws and antitrust laws, by their very nature, have been in conflict from the very beginning. Whereas antitrust laws are intended to foster marketplace competition and to limit the aggregation of private economic power, labor law gives its blessings to at least one sort of anticompetitive behavior — attempts by unions to control the labor market through organization and collective bargaining with employers. After the Sherman Antitrust Act was enacted in 1890 to prohibit conspiracies in restraint of trade primarily among cartels and trusts and monopolies, as we saw in Chapter 1, it was more often applied to labor unions to prevent them from boycotting employers that did not use union employees.

It was not until the enactment of the Norris-LaGuardia Act, which outlawed most labor injunctions, and the enactment of the Wagner Act, which stressed the importance of collective bargaining to industrial stability, that the antitrust laws were applied differently in labor disputes. More specifically, in 1941, the Court held that most union conduct was shielded by antitrust liability. *United States v. Hutcheson*, 312 U.S. 219 (1941). The following condition was set out, however: "So long as the union acts in self-interest and does not combine with non-labor groups," peaceful conduct in the course of a labor dispute is not covered by the Sherman Act. The protection afforded by *Hutcheson* is known as the "statutory exemption" based upon its reliance on various labor and antitrust laws. The statutory exemption is of limited use because it does not apply where there is collaboration between unions and employers. *See Allen Bradley Co. v. Local Union No. 3, IBEW*, 325 U.S. 797 (1945) (finding no statutory exemption where union and employer worked together to control the market for electrical contractors and electrical equipment manufacturing in New York City).

3. In two 1965 cases, the Supreme Court described a new type of exemption: the nonstatutory labor exemption. In *United Mine Workers of America v. Penning-*

ton, 381 U.S. 657 (1965), large coal mine companies and the mineworkers union agreed to a higher standard wage rate to push smaller coal mine companies out of business, a response to an oversupply of coal. The Court found that union did not act alone and so did not qualify for statutory immunity. But the Court found that a second kind of exemption applied, a nonstatutory labor exemption that harmonized antitrust law and national labor policy under the NLRA.

In *Local Union No. 189, Amalgamated Meat Cutters v. Jewel Tea Co.*, 381 U.S. 676 (1965), a multi-employer group and a union agreed to specific butcher hours and also sought to impose these hours on other butchers. Applying the nonstatutory labor exemption, the Court held that the interests of national labor policy outweighed those of antitrust law because even though the agreement addressed the product market by addressing hours of service, the union and employers were negotiating over mandatory subjects of bargaining. In other words, their agreement was intimately involved with wages, hours, and working conditions that were obtained through successful arms-length bargaining. Note, however, that the nonstatutory labor exemption adds a balancing test that provides additional uncertainty in this area of labor law.

4. More recently, in *Connell Construction Co. v. Plumbers and Steamfitters Local Union* 100, 421 U.S 616 (1975), the Court considered a case where a general contractor in Dallas subcontracted all of its work to union and nonunion subcontractors. The union picketed the general contractor so that it would give the work only to union subcontractors. The general contractor agreed to this arrangement, thereby establishing a hot cargo agreement in violation of NLRA Section 8(e). Addressing a federal antitrust challenge, the Court held that the subcontracting agreement between the union and the general contractor was not exempt from antitrust law. The statutory exception did not apply because it was an agreement between a union and an employer. Moreover, the Court held that the nonstatutory labor exemption did not apply because the antitrust interests in eliminating the anticompetitive effects of the hot cargo agreement in the case outweighed the labor law interests. In particular, the "substantial anticompetitive effects" of the agreement "would not follow naturally from the elimination of competition over wages and working conditions. [Thus, the agreement] contravenes antitrust policies to a degree not justified by congressional labor policy . . . ."

5. A more thorough history of antitrust law's application to labor activity and bargaining is too long to provide in detail here. If you are more curious about this doctrine's development, which is a fascinating one, good articles to start with include: Douglas L. Leslie, *Principles of Labor Antitrust*, 66 VA. L. REV. 1183 (1980); Theodore J. St. Antoine, Connell: *Antitrust Law at the Expense of Labor Law*, 62 VA. L. REV. 603 (1976); and Bernard D. Meltzer, *Labor Unions, Collective Bargaining, and the Antitrust Laws*, 32 U. CHI. L. REV. 659 (1965). Moreover, if the intersection of sports, labor, and antitrust law is of particular interest, a few articles to check out: are William B. Gould IV, *Labor Issues in Professional Sports: Reflections on Baseball, Labor and Antitrust Law*, 15 STAN. L. & POL'Y REV. 61 (2004); Michael H. Gottesman, *Union Summer: A Reawakened Interest in the Law of Labor?*, 1996 SUP. CT. REV. 285 (1996); and Gary R. Roberts, *Reconciling Federal Labor and Antitrust Policy: The Special Case of Sports League Labor Market Constraints*, 75 GEO. L.J. 19 (1986).

Appendix

NORRIS-LA GUARDIA (ANTI-INJUNCTION) ACT

Act of March 23, 1932, 47 Stat. 70, 29 U.S.C. §§ 101-15; F.C.A. 29 §§ 101-15

Be it enacted by the Senate and House of Representatives of the United States of America in Congress assembled, That no court of the United States, as herein defined, shall have jurisdiction to issue any restraining order or temporary or permanent injunction in a case involving or growing out of a labor dispute, except in strict conformity with the provisions of this Act; nor shall any such restraining order or temporary or permanent injunction be issued contrary to the public policy declared in this Act.

SEC. 2. In the interpretation of this Act and in determining the jurisdiction and authority of the courts of the United States, as such jurisdiction and authority are herein defined and limited, the public policy of the United States is hereby declared as follows:

"Whereas under prevailing economic conditions, developed with the aid of governmental authority for owners of property to organize in the corporate and other forms of ownership association, the individual unorganized worker is commonly helpless to exercise actual liberty of contract and to protect his freedom of labor, and thereby to obtain acceptable terms and conditions of employment, wherefore though he should be free to decline to associate with his fellows, it is necessary that he have full freedom of association, selforganization, and designation of representatives of his own choosing, to negotiate the terms and conditions of his employment, and that he shall be free from the interference, restraint, or coercion of employees of labor, or their agents, in the designation of such representatives or in self-organization or in other concerted activities for the purpose of collective bargaining or other mutual aid or protection; therefore, the following definitions of, and limitations upon, the jurisdiction and authority of the courts of the United States are hereby enacted."

SEC. 3. Any undertaking or promise, such as is described in this section, or any other undertaking or promise in conflict with the public policy declared in section 2 of this Act, is hereby declared to be contrary to the public policy of the United States, shall not be enforceable in any court of the United States and shall not afford any basis for the granting of legal or equitable relief by any such court, including specifically the following:

Every undertaking or promise hereafter made, whether written or oral, express or implied, constituting or contained in any contract or agreement of hiring or employment between any individual, firm, company, association, or corporation, and any employee or prospective employee of the same, whereby

(a) Either party to such contract or agreement undertakes or promises not to join, become, or remain a member of any labor organization or of any employer organization; or

(b) Either party to such contract or agreement undertakes or promises that he will withdraw from an employment relation in the event that he joins, becomes, or remains a member of any labor organization or of any employer organization.

SEC. 4. No court of the United States shall have jurisdiction to issue any restraining order or temporary or permanent injunction in any case involving or growing out of any labor dispute to prohibit any person or persons participating or interested in such dispute (as these terms are herein defined), from doing, whether singly or in concert, any of the following acts:

(a) Ceasing or refusing to perform any work or to remain in any relation of employment;

(b) Becoming or remaining a member of any labor organization or of any employer organization, regardless of any such undertaking or promise as is described in section 3 of this Act;

(c) Paying or giving to, or withholding from, any person participating or interested in such labor dispute, any strike or unemployment benefits or insurance, or other moneys or things of value;

(d) By all lawful means aiding any person participating or interested in any labor dispute who is being proceeded against in, or is prosecuting, any action or suit in any court of the United States or of any state;

(e) Giving publicity to the existence of, or the facts involved in, any labor dispute, whether by advertising, speaking, patrolling, or by any other method not involving fraud or violence;

(f) Assembling peaceably to act or to organize to act in promotion of their interests in a labor dispute;

(g) Advising or notifying any person of an intention to do any of the acts heretofore specified;

(h) Agreeing with other persons to do or not to do any of the acts heretofore specified; and

(i) Advising, urging, or otherwise causing or inducing without fraud or violence the acts heretofore specified, regardless of any such undertaking or promise as is described in section 3 of this Act.

SEC. 5. No court of the United States shall have jurisdiction to issue a restraining order or temporary or permanent injunction upon the ground that any of the persons participating or interested in a labor dispute constitute or are engaged in an unlawful combination or conspiracy because of the doing in concert of the acts enumerated in section 4 of this Act.

SEC. 6. No officer or member of any association or organization, and no association or organization participating or interested in a labor dispute, shall be held responsible or liable in any court of the United States for the unlawful acts of individual officers, members, or agents, except upon clear proof of actual participation in, or actual authorization of, such acts, or of ratification of such acts after actual knowledge thereof.

SEC. 7. No court of the United States shall have jurisdiction to issue a temporary or permanent injunction in any case involving or growing out of a labor dispute, as herein defined, except after hearing the testimony of witnesses in open court (with opportunity for cross-examination), in support of the allegations of a complaint made under oath, and testimony in opposition thereto, if offered, and except after findings of fact by the court, to the effect-

(a) That unlawful acts have been threatened and will be committed unless restrained or have been committed and will be continued unless restrained, but no injunction or temporary restraining order shall be issued on account of any threat or unlawful act excepting against the person or persons, association, or organization making the threat or committing the unlawful act or actually authorizing or ratifying the same after actual knowledge thereof;

(b) That substantial and irreparable injury to complainant's property will follow;

(c) That as to each item of relief granted greater injury will be inflicted upon complainant by the denial of relief than will be inflicted upon defendants by the granting of relief;

(d) That complainant has no adequate remedy at law; and

(e) That the public officers charged with the duty to protect complainant's property are unable or unwilling to furnish adequate protection.

Such hearing shall be held after due and personal notice thereof has been given, in such manner as the court shall direct, to all known persons against whom relief is sought, and also to the chief of those public officials of the county and city within which the unlawful acts have been threatened or committed charged with the duty to protect complainant's property: *Provided, however,* That if a complainant shall also allege that, unless a temporary restraining order shall be issued without notice, a substantial and irreparable injury to complainant's property will be unavoidable, such a temporary restraining order may be issued upon testimony under oath, sufficient, if sustained, to justify the court in issuing a temporary injunction upon a hearing after notice. Such temporary restraining order shall be effective for no longer than five days and shall become void at the expiration of said five days. No temporary restraining order or temporary injunction shall be issued except on condition that complainant shall first file an undertaking with adequate security in an amount to be fixed by the court sufficient to recompense those enjoined for any loss, expense, or damage caused by the improvident or erroneous issuance of such order or injunction, including all reasonable costs (together with a reasonable attorney's fee), and expense of defense against the order or against the granting of any injunctive relief sought in the same proceeding and subsequently denied by the court.

The undertaking herein mentioned shall be understood to signify an agreement entered into by the complainant and the surety upon which a decree may be rendered in the same suit or proceeding against said complainant and surety, upon a hearing to assess damages of which hearing complainant and surety shall have reasonable notice, the said complainant and surety submitting themselves to the jurisdiction of the court for that purpose. But nothing herein contained shall deprive any party having a claim or cause of action under or upon such undertaking from electing to pursue his ordinary remedy by suit at law or in equity.

SEC. 8. No restraining order or injunctive relief shall be granted to any complainant who has failed to comply with any obligation imposed by law which is involved in the labor dispute in question, or who has failed to make every reasonable effort to settle such dispute either by negotiation or with the aid of any available governmental machinery of mediation or voluntary arbitration.

SEC. 9. No restraining order or temporary or permanent injunction shall be granted in a case involving or growing out of a labor dispute, except on the basis of findings of fact made and filed by the court in the record of the case prior to the issuance of such restraining order or injunction; and every restraining order or injunction granted in a case involving or growing out of a labor dispute shall include only a prohibition of such specific act or acts as may be expressly complained of in the bill of complaint or petition filed in such case and as shall be expressly included in said findings of fact made and filed by the court as provided herein.

SEC. 10. Whenever any court of the United States shall issue or deny any temporary injunction in a case involving or growing out of a labor dispute, the court shall, upon the request of any party to the proceedings and on his filing the usual bond for costs, forthwith certify as in ordinary cases the record of the case to the circuit court of appeals for its review. Upon the filing of such record in the circuit court of appeals, the appeal shall be heard and the temporary injunctive order affirmed, modified, or set aside with the greatest possible expedition, giving the proceedings precedence over all other matters except older matters of the same character.

SEC. 11. In all cases arising under this Act in which a person shall be charged with contempt in a court of the United States (as herein defined), the accused shall enjoy the right to a speedy and public trial by an impartial jury of the state and district wherein the contempt shall have been committed: *Provided*, That this right shall not apply to contempts committed in the presence of the court or so near thereto as to interfere directly with the administration of justice or to apply to the misbehavior, misconduct, or disobedience of any officer of the court in respect to the writs, orders, or process of the court.*

SEC. 12. The defendant in any proceeding for contempt of court may file with the court a demand for the retirement of the judge sitting in the proceeding, if the contempt arises from an attack upon the character or conduct of such judge and if the attack occurred elsewhere than in the presence of the court or so near thereto as to interfere directly with the administration of justice. Upon the filing of any such demand the judge shall thereupon proceed no further, but another judge shall be designated in the same manner as is provided by law. The demand shall be filed prior to the hearing in the contempt proceeding.

SEC. 13. When used in this Act, and for the purposes of this Act-

(a) A case shall be held to involve or to grow out of a labor dispute when the case involves persons who are engaged in the same industry, trade, craft, or occupation; or have direct or indirect interests therein; or who are employees of the same employer; or who are members of the same or an affiliated organization of employers or employees; whether such dispute is (1) between one or more employers or associations of employers and one or more employees or associations of employees; (2) between one or more employers or associations of employers and one or more employers or associations of employers; or (3) between one or more employees or associations of employees and one or more employees or associations of employees; or when the case involves any conflicting or competing interests in a "labor dispute" (as hereinafter defined), of "persons participating or interested" therein (as hereinafter defined).

(b) A person or association shall be held to be a person participating or interested in a labor dispute if relief is sought against him or it, and if he or it is engaged in the same industry, trade, craft, or occupation in which such dispute occurs, or has a direct or indirect interest therein, or is a member, officer, or agent of any association composed in a whole or in part of employers or employees engaged in such industry, trade, craft, or occupation.

(c) The term "labor dispute" includes any controversy concerning terms or conditions of employment, or concerning the association or representation of persons in negotiating, fixing, maintaining, changing, or seeking to arrange terms or conditions of employment, regardless of whether or not the disputants stand in the proximate relation of employer and employee.

(d) The term "court of the United States" means any court of the United States whose jurisdiction has been or may be conferred or defined or limited by Act of Congress, including the courts of the District of Columbia.

SEC. 14. If any provision of this Act or the application thereof to any person or circumstance is held unconstitutional or otherwise invalid, the remaining provisions

---

* Sections 11 and 12 were repealed by the Act of June 25, 1948, 62 Stat. 862, effective September 1, 1948.

Sections 11 and 12 were repealed by the Act of June 25, 1948, 62 Stat. 862, effective September 1, 1948.

of the Act and the application of such provisions to other persons or circumstances shall not be affected thereby.

SEC. 15. All Acts and parts of Acts in conflict with the provisions of this Act are hereby repealed.

NATIONAL LABOR RELATIONS ACT*

49 Stat. 449 (1935), as amended by Pub. L. No. 101, 80th Cong., 1st Sess.,
1947, and Pub. L. No. 257, 86th Cong., 1st Sess., 1959;
29 U.S.C. §§ 151-69, F.C.A. 29 §§ 151-69

FINDINGS AND POLICIES

SEC. 1. The denial by *some* employers of the right of employees to organize and
the refusal by *some* employers to accept the procedure of collective bargaining lead
to strikes and other forms of industrial strife or unrest, which have the intent or the
necessary effect of burdening or obstructing commerce by (a) impairing the
efficiency, safety, or operation of the instrumentalities of commerce; (b) occurring in
the current of commerce; (c) materially affecting, restraining, or controlling the flow
of raw materials or manufactured or processed goods from or into the channels of
commerce, or the prices of such materials or goods in commerce; or (d) causing
diminution of employment and wages in such volume as substantially to impair or
disrupt the market for goods flowing from or into the channels of commerce.

The inequality of bargaining power between employees who do not possess full
freedom of association or actual liberty of contract, and employers who are
organized in the corporate or other forms of ownership association substantially
burdens and affects the flow of commerce, and tends to aggravate recurrent
business depressions, by depressing wage rates and the purchasing power of wage
earners in industry and by preventing the stabilization of competitive wage rates
and working conditions within and between industries.

Experience has proven that protection by law of the right of employees to
organize and bargain collectively safeguards commerce from injury, impairment, or
interruption, and promotes the flow of commerce by removing certain recognized
sources of industrial strife and unrest, by encouraging practices fundamental to the
friendly adjustment of industrial disputes arising out of differences as to wages,
hours, or other working conditions, and by restoring equality of bargaining power
between employers and employees.

*Experience has further demonstrated that certain practices by some labor
organizations, their officers, and members have the intent or the necessary effect of
burdening or obstructing commerce by preventing the free flow of goods in such
commerce through strikes and other forms of industrial unrest or through
concerted activities which impair the interest of the public in the free flow of such
commerce. The elimination of such practices is a necessary condition to the
assurance of the rights herein guaranteed.*

It is hereby declared to be the policy of the United States to eliminate the causes
of certain substantial obstructions to the free flow of commerce and to mitigate and
eliminate these obstructions when they have occurred by encouraging the practice
and procedure of collective bargaining and by protecting the exercise by workers of

---

* Material from the original act is printed in roman type; matter added by the Labor Management
Relations Act, 1947, is in italics; and matter added by the Labor Management Reporting and Disclosure
Act, 1959, is in boldface. Matter omitted by the Labor Management Relations Act, 1947, is in brackets
and that omitted by the Labor Management Reporting and Disclosure Act, 1959, is in double brackets.

full freedom of association, self-organization, and designation of representatives of their own choosing, for the purpose of negotiating the terms and conditions of their employment or other mutual aid or protection.

DEFINITIONS

SEC. 2. When used in this Act—

(1) The term "person" includes one or more individuals, labor organizations, partnerships, associations, corporations, legal representatives, trustees, trustees in cases under Title 11 of the United States Code, or receivers.

(2) The term "employer" includes any person acting [in the interest] *as an agent* of an employer, directly or indirectly, but shall not include the United States *or any wholly owned Government corporation, or any Federal Reserve Bank*, or any State or political subdivision thereof, or any person subject to the Railway Labor Act, as amended from time to time, or any labor organization (other than when acting as an employer), or anyone acting in the capacity of officer or agent of such labor organization.*

(3) The term "employee" shall include any employee, and shall not be limited to the employees of a particular employer, unless the Act explicitly states otherwise, and shall include any individual whose work has ceased as a consequence of, or in connection with, any current labor dispute or because of any unfair labor practice, and who has not obtained any other regular and substantially equivalent employment, but shall not include any individual employed as an agricultural laborer, or in the domestic service of any family or person at his home, or any individual employed by his parent or spouse, *or any individual having the status of an independent contractor, or any individual employed as a supervisor, or any individual employed by an employer subject to the Railway Labor Act, as amended from time to time, or by any other person who is not an employer as herein defined.*

(4) The term "representatives" includes any individual or labor organization.

(5) The term "labor organization" means any organization of any

kind, or any agency or employee representation committee or plan, in which employees participate and which exists for the purpose, in whole or in part, of dealing with employers concerning grievances, labor disputes, wages, rates of pay, hours of employment, or conditions of work.

(6) The term "commerce" means trade, traffic, commerce, transportation, or communication among the several States, or between the District of Columbia or any Territory of the United States and any State or other Territory, or between any foreign country and any State, Territory, or the District of Columbia, or within the District of Columbia or any Territory, or between points in the same State but

---

* The phrase, "or any corporation or association operating a hospital, if no part of the net earnings inures to the benefit of any private shareholder or individual," was added as an exclusion in section 2(2) by the Labor Management Relations Act. 1947, and was deleted by Public Law 93-360, 93d Congress, 2d Session, approved July 26, 1974.

through any other State or any Territory or the District of Columbia or any foreign country.

(7) The term "affecting commerce" means in commerce, or burdening or obstructing commerce or the free flow of commerce, or having led or tending to lead to a labor dispute burdening or obstructing commerce or the free flow of commerce.

(8) The term "unfair labor practice" means any unfair labor practice listed in section 8.

(9) The term "labor dispute" includes any controversy concerning terms, tenure or conditions of employment, or concerning the association or representation of persons in negotiating, fixing, maintaining, changing, or seeking to arrange terms or conditions of employment, regardless of whether the disputants stand in the proximate relation of employer and employee.

(10) The term "National Labor Relations Board" means the National Labor Relations Board provided for in section 3 of this Act.

(11) The term "supervisor" means any individual having authority, in the interest of the employer, to hire, transfer, suspend, lay off, recall, promote, discharge, assign, reward, or discipline other employees, or responsibly to direct them, or to adjust their grievances, or effectively to recommend such action, if in connection with the foregoing the exercise of such authority is not of a merely routine or clerical nature, but requires the use of independent judgment.

(12) The term "professional employee" means

(a) Any employee engaged in work (i) predominantly intellectual and varied in character as opposed to routine mental, manual, mechanical, or physical work; (ii) involving the consistent exercise of discretion and judgment in its performance; (iii) of such a character that the output produced or the result accomplished cannot be standardized in relation to a given period of time; (iv) requiring knowledge of an advanced type in a field of science or learning customarily acquired by a prolonged course of specialized intellectual instruction and study in an institution of higher learning or a hospital, as distinguished from a general academic education or from an apprenticeship or from training in the performance of routine mental, manual, or physical processes; or

(b) any employee, who (i) has completed the courses of specialized intellectual instruction and study described in clause (iv) of paragraph (a), and (ii) is performing related work under the supervision of a professional person to qualify himself to become a professional employee as defined in paragraph (a).

(13) In determining whether any person is acting as an "agent" of another person so as to make such other person responsible for his acts, the question of whether the specific acts performed were actually authorized or subsequently ratified shall not be controlling.

(14) The term "health care institution" shall include any hospital, convalescent hospital, health maintenance organization, health clinic, nursing home, extended care facility, or other institution devoted to the care of sick, infirm,

or aged persons.*

NATIONAL LABOR RELATIONS BOARD

SEC. 3. (a) *The National Labor Relations Board (hereinafter called the "Board") created by this Act prior to its amendment by the Labor Management Relations Act, 1947, is hereby continued as an agency of the United States, except that the Board shall consist of five instead of three members, appointed by the President by and with the advice and consent of the Senate. Of the two additional members so provided for, one shall be appointed for a term of five years and the other for a term of two years. Their successors, and the successors of the other members, shall be appointed for terms of five years each, excepting that any individual chosen to fill a vacancy shall be appointed only for the unexpired term of the member whom he shall succeed. The President shall designate one member to serve as Chairman of the Board. Any member of the Board may be removed by the President, upon notice and hearing, for neglect of duty or malfeasance in office, but for no other cause.*

(b) The Board is authorized to delegate to any group of three or more members any or all of the powers which it may itself exercise. **The Board is also authorized to delegate to its regional directors its powers under section 9 to determine the unit appropriate for the purpose of collective bargaining, to investigate and provide for hearings, and determine whether a question of representation exists, and to direct an election or take a secret ballot under subsection (c) or (e) of section 9 and certify the results thereof, except that upon the filing of a request therefor with the Board by any interested person, the Board may review any action of a regional director delegated to him under this paragraph, but such a review shall not, unless specifically ordered by the Board, operate as a stay of any action taken by the regional director.** *A vacancy in the Board shall not impair the right of the remaining members to exercise all of the powers of the Board, and three members of the Board shall, at all times, constitute a quorum of the Board, except that two member shall constitute a quorum of any group designated pursuant to the first sentence hereof. The Board shall have an official seal which shall be judicially noticed.*

(c) The Board shall at the close of each fiscal year make a report in writing to Congress and to the President [[*stating in detail the cases it has heard, the decisions it has rendered,*]] [*the names, salaries, and duties of all employees and officers in the employ or under the supervision of the Board,*]* [[*and an account of all moneys it has disbursed.*]] **summarizing significant case activities and operations for that fiscal year.**†

(d) *There shall be a General Counsel of the Board who shall be appointed by the President, by and with the advice and consent of the Senate, for a term of four years. The General Counsel of the Board shall exercise general supervision over all*

---

* Section 2(14) was added by Public Law 93-360, 93d Congress, 2d Session, approved July 26, 1974.

* The bracketed material was deleted by Public Law 93-608, 93d Congress, 2d Session, approved January 2, 1975.

† The bold language was added and the double-bracketed material was deleted by Public Law 97-375, 97th Congress, 2d Session, approved December 21, 1982.

attorneys employed by the Board (other than administrative law judges and legal assistants to Board members) and over the officers and employees in the regional offices. He shall have final authority, on behalf of the Board, in respect of the investigation of charges and issuance of complaints under section 10, and in respect of the prosecution of such complaints before the Board, and shall have such other duties as the Board may prescribe or as may be provided by law. **In case of a vacancy in the office of the General Counsel the President is authorized to designate the officer or employee who shall act as General Counsel during such vacancy, but no person or persons so designated shall so act (1) for more than forty days when the Congress is in session unless a nomination to fill such vacancy shall have been submitted to the Senate, or (2) after the adjournment sine die of the session of the Senate in which such nomination was submitted.**

SEC. 4. *(a) Each member of the Board and the General Counsel of the Board shall receive a salary of $12,000** a year, shall be eligible for reappointment, and shall not engage in any other business, vocation, or employment. The Board shall appoint an executive secretary, and such attorneys, examiners, and regional directors, and such other employees as it may from time to time find necessary for the proper performance of it duties. The Board may not employ any attorneys for the purpose of reviewing transcripts of hearing or preparing drafts of opinions except that any attorney employed for assignment as a legal assistant to any Board member may for such Board member review such transcripts and prepare such drafts. No trial examiner's report shall be reviewed, either before or after its publication, by any person other than a member of the Board or his legal assistant, and no trial examiner shall advise or consult with the Board with respect to exceptions taken to his findings, rulings, or recommendations. The Board may establish or utilize such regional, local, or other agencies, and utilize such voluntary and uncompensated services, as may from time to time be needed. Attorneys appointed under this section may, at the direction of the Board, appear for the represent the Board in any case in court. Nothing in this Act shall be construed to authorize the Board to appoint individuals for the purpose of conciliation or mediation, or for economic analysis.*

*(b) All of the expenses of the Board, including all necessary traveling and subsistence expenses outside the District of Columbia incurred by the members or employees of the Board under its orders, shall be allowed and paid on the presentation of itemized vouchers therefor approved by the Board or by any individual it designates for that purpose.**

SEC. 5. The principal office of the Board shall be in the District of Columbia, but it may meet and exercise any or all of its powers at any other place. The Board may, by one or more of its members or by such agents or agencies as it may designate, prosecute any inquiry necessary to its functions in any part of the United States. A member who participates in such an inquiry shall not be disqualified from subsequently participating in a decision of the Board in the same case.

** The annual salaries of the Board members and the General Counsel are now prescribed in the Federal Executive Salary Schedule.

* The italicized portion of Sections 3 and 4 shows those sections as rewritten by the 1947 amendments.

SEC. 6. The Board shall have authority from time to time to make, amend, and rescind, *in the manner prescribed by the Administrative Procedure Act*, such rules and regulations as may be necessary to carry out the provisions of this Act.

RIGHTS OF EMPLOYEES

SEC. 7. Employees shall have the right to self-organization, to form, join, or assist labor organizations, to bargain collectively through representatives of their own choosing, and to engage in *other* concerted activities for the purpose of collective bargaining or other mutual aid or protection, *and shall also have the right to refrain from any or all of such activities except to the extent that such right may be affected by an agreement requiring membership in a labor organization as a condition of employment as authorized in section 8(a)(3).*

UNFAIR LABOR PRACTICES

SEC. 8. (a) It shall be an unfair labor practice for an employer-

(1) to interfere with, restrain, or coerce employees in the exercise of the rights guaranteed in section 7;

(2) to dominate or interfere with the formation or administration of any labor organization or contribute financial or other support to it: *Provided*, That subject to rules and regulations made and published by the Board pursuant to section 6, an employer shall not be prohibited from permitting employees to confer with him during working hours without loss of time or pay;

(3) by discrimination in regard to hire or tenure of employment or any term or condition of employment to encourage or discourage membership in any labor organization: *Provided*, That nothing in this Act, or in any other statute of the United States, shall preclude an employer from making an agreement with a labor organization (not established, maintained, or assisted by any action defined in section 8(a) of this Act as an unfair labor practice) to require as a condition of employment membership therein *on or after the t hirtieth day following the beginning of such employment or the effective date of such agreement, whichever is the later,* (i) if such labor organization is the representative of the employees as provided in section 9(a), in the appropriate collective-bargaining unit covered by such agreement when made [[*and has at the time the agreement was made or within the preceding twelve months received from the Board a notice of compliance with section 9(f), (g), (h)*]] *and (ii) unless following an election held as provided in section 9(e) within one year preceding the effective date of such agreement, the Board shall have certified that at least a majority of the employees eligible to vote in such election have voted to rescind the authority of such labor organization to make such an agreement: Provided further, That no employer shall justify any discrimination against an employee for non-membership in a labor organization (A) if he has reasonable grounds for believing that such membership was not available to the employee on the same terms and conditions generally applicable to other members, or (B) if he has reasonable grounds for believing that membership was denied or terminated for reasons other than the failure of the employee to tender the periodic dues and the*

initiation fees uniformly required as a condition of acquiring or retaining membership;

(4) to discharge or otherwise discriminate against an employee because he has filed charges or given testimony under this Act;

(5) to refuse to bargain collectively with the representatives of his employees, subject to the provisions of section 9(a).

(b) It shall be an unfair labor practice for a labor organization or its agents-

(1) *to restrain or coerce (A) employees in the exercise of the rights guaranteed in section 7: Provided, That this paragraph shall not impair the right of a labor organization to prescribe its own rules with respect to the acquisition or retention of membership therein; or (B) an employer in the selection of his representatives for the purposes of collective bargaining or the adjustment of grievances;*

(2) *to cause or attempt to cause an employer to discriminate against an employee in violation of subsection (a)(3) or to discriminate against an employee with respect to whom membership in such organization has been denied or terminated on some ground other than his failure to tender the periodic dues and the initiation fees uniformly required as a condition of acquiring or retaining membership;*

(3) *to refuse to bargain collectively with an employer, provided it is the representative of his employees subject to the provisions of section 9(a);*

(4) *(i) to engage in, or to induce or encourage* [[*the employees of any employer*]] **any individual employed by any person engaged in commerce or in an industry affecting commerce** *to engage in, a strike or a* [[*concerted*]] *refusal in the course of* [[*their*]] **his** *employment to use, manufacture, process, transport, or otherwise handle or work on any goods, articles, materials, or commodities or to perform any services*[[,]]; **or (ii) to threaten, coerce, or restrain any person engaged in commerce or in an industry affecting commerce,** *where* **in either case** *an object thereof is:*

(A) forcing or requiring any employer or self-employed person to join any labor or employer organization or [[*any employer or other person to cease using, selling, handling, transporting, or otherwise dealing in the products of any other producer, processor, or manufacturer, or to cease doing business with any other person*]] **to enter into any agreement which is prohibited by section 8(e);**

(B) forcing or requiring any person to cease using, selling, handling, transporting, or otherwise dealing in the products of any other producer, processor, or manufacturer, or to cease doing business with any other person, or *forcing or requiring any other employer to recognize or bargain with a labor organization as the representative of its employees unless such labor organization has been certified as the representative of such employees under the provisions of section 9* [[;]]: **Provided, That nothing contained in this clause (B) shall be construed to make unlawful, where not otherwise unlawful, any primary strike or primary picketing;**

(C) forcing or requiring any employer to recognize or bargain with a particular labor organization as the representative of his employees if another labor organization has been certified as the representative of such employees under the provisions of section 9;

(D) forcing or requiring any employer to assign particular work to employees in a particular labor organization or in a particular trade, craft, or class rather than to employees in another labor organization or in another trade, craft, or class, unless such employer is failing to conform to an order or certification of the Board determining the bargaining representative for employees performing such work: Provided, That nothing contained in this subsection (b) shall be construed to make unlawful a refusal by any person to enter upon the premises of any employer (other than his own employer), if the employees of such employer are engaged in a strike ratified or approved by a representative of such employees whom such employer is required to recognize under this Act [[;]]: **Provided further, That for the purposes of this paragraph (4) only, nothing contained in such paragraph shall be construed to prohibit publicity, other than picketing, for the purpose of truthfully advising the public, including consumers and members of a labor organization, that a product or products are produced by an employer with whom the labor organization has a primary dispute and are distributed by another employer, as long as such publicity does not have an effect of inducing any individual employed by any person other than the primary employer in the course of his employment to refuse to pick up, deliver, or transport any goods, or not to perform any services, at the establishment of the employer engaged in such distributions;**

(5) to require of employees covered by an agreement authorized under subsection (a)(3) the payment, as a condition precedent to becoming a member of such organization, of a fee in an amount which the Board finds excessive or discriminatory under all the circumstances. In making such a finding, the Board shall consider, among other relevant factors, the practices and customs of labor organizations in the particular industry, and the wages currently paid to the employees affected; [[and]]

(6) to cause or attempt to cause an employer to pay or deliver or agree to pay or deliver any money or other thing of value, in the nature of an exaction, for services which are not performed or not to be performed [[.]]; **and**

(7) to picket or cause to be picketed, or threaten to picket or cause to be picketed, any employer where an object thereof is forcing or requiring an employer to recognize or bargain with a labor organization as the representative of his employees, or forcing or requiring the employees of an employer to accept or select such labor organization as their collective-bargaining representative, unless such labor organization is currently certified as the representative of such employees:

(A) where the employer has lawfully recognized in accordance with this Act any other labor organization and a question concerning representation may not appropriately be raised under section 9(c) of this Act,

(B) **where within the preceding twelve months a valid election under section 9(c) of this Act has been conducted, or**

(C) **where such picketing has been conducted without a petition under section 9(c) being filed within a reasonable period of time not to exceed thirty days from the commencement of such picketing: Provided, That when such a petition has been filed the Board shall forthwith, without regard to the provisions of section 9 (c)(1) or the absence of a showing of a substantial interest on the part of the labor organization, direct an election in such unit as the Board finds to be appropriate and shall certify the results thereof: Provided further, That nothing in this subparagraph (C) shall be construed to prohibit any picketing or other publicity for the purpose of truthfully advising the public (including consumers) that an employer does not employ members of, or have a contract with, a labor organization, unless an effect of such picketing is to induce any individual employed by any other person in the course of his employment, not to pick up, deliver or transport any goods or not to perform any services.**

Nothing in this paragraph (7) shall be construed to permit any act which would otherwise be an unfair labor practice under this section 8(b).

(c) The expressing of any views, argument, or opinion, or the dissemination thereof, whether in written, printed, graphic, or visual form, shall not constitute or be evidence of an unfair labor practice under any of the provisions of this Act, if such expression contains no threat of reprisal or force or promise of benefit.

(d) For the purposes of this section, to bargain collectively is the performance of the mutual obligation of the employer and the representative of the employees to meet at reasonable times and confer in good faith with respect to wages, hours, and other terms and conditions of employment, or the negotiation of an agreement, or any question arising thereunder, and the execution of a written contract incorporating any agreement reached if requested by either party, but such obligation does not compel either party to agree to a proposal or require the making of a concession: Provided, That where there is in effect a collective-bargaining contract covering employees in an industry affecting commerce, the duty to bargain collectively shall also mean that no party to such contract shall terminate or modify such contract, unless the party desiring such termination or modification-

(1) serves a written notice upon the other party to the contract of the proposed termination or modification sixty days prior to the expiration date thereof, or in the event such contract contains no expiration date, sixty days prior to the time it is proposed to make such termination or modification;

(2) offers to meet and confer with the other party for the purpose of negotiating a new contract or a contract containing the proposed modifications;

(3) notifies the Federal Mediation and Conciliation Service within thirty days after such notice of the existence of a dispute, and simultaneously therewith notifies any State or Territorial agency established to mediate and conciliate disputes within the State or Territory where the dispute occurred, provided no agreement has been reached by that time; and

(4) continues in full force and effect, without resorting to strike or lockout, all the terms and conditions of the existing contract for a period of sixty days after such notice is given or until the expiration date of such contract, whichever occurs later:

The duties imposed upon employers, employees, and labor organizations by paragraphs (2), (3), and (4) shall become inapplicable upon an intervening certification of the Board, under which the labor organization or individual, which is a party to the contract, has been superseded as or ceased to be the representative of the employees subject to the provisions of section 9(a), and the duties so imposed shall not be construed as requiring either party to discuss or agree to any modification of the terms and conditions contained in a contract for a fixed period, if such modification is to become effective before such terms and conditions can be reopened under the provisions of the contract. Any employee who engages in a strike within any notice period specified in this subsection, or who engages in any strike within the appropriate period specified in subsection (g) of this section, *shall lose his status as an employee of the employer engaged in the particular labor dispute, for the purposes of sections 8, 9, and 10 of this Act, as amended, but such loss of status for such employee shall terminate if and when he is reemployed by such employer.* Whenever the collective bargaining involves employees of a health care institution, the provisions of this section 8(d) shall be modified as follows:

(A) The notice of section 8(d)(1) shall be ninety days; the notice of section 8(d)(3) shall be sixty days; and the contract period of section 8(d)(4) shall be ninety days.

(B) Where the bargaining is for an initial agreement

following certification or recognition, at least thirty days' notice of the existence of a dispute shall be given by the labor organization to the agencies as set forth in section 8(d)(3).

(C) After notice is given to the Federal Mediation and Conciliation Service under either clause (A) or (B) of this sentence, the Service shall promptly communicate with the parties and use its best efforts, by mediation and conciliation, to bring them to agreement. The parties shall participate fully and promptly in such meetings as may be undertaken by the Service for the purpose of aiding in a settlement of the dispute.*

(e) It shall be an unfair labor practice for any labor organization and any employer to enter into any contract or agreement, express or implied, whereby such employer ceases or refrains or agrees to cease or refrain from handling, using, selling, transporting or otherwise dealing in any of the products of any other employer, or to cease doing business with any other person, and any contract or agreement entered into heretofore or hereafter containing such an agreement shall be to such extent unenforcible and void: Provided, That nothing in this subsection (e) shall apply to an agreement between a labor organization and an employer in the construction industry relating to the

---

* Material in roman type was added by Public Law 93-360, 93d Congress, 2d Session, approved July 26, 1974.

contracting or subcontracting of work to be done at the site of the construction, alteration, painting, or repair of a building, structure, or other work: Provided further, That for the purposes of this subsection (e) and section 8(b)(4)(B) the terms "any employer", "any person engaged in commerce or an industry affecting commerce", and "any person" when used in relation to the terms "any other producer, processor, or manufacturer", "any other employer", or "any other person" shall not include persons in the relation of a jobber, manufacturer, contractor, or subcontractor working on the goods or premises of the jobber or manufacturer or performing parts of an integrated process of production in the apparel and clothing industry: Provided further, That nothing in this Act shall prohibit the enforcement of any agreement which is within the foregoing exception.

(f) It shall not be an unfair labor practice under subsections (a) and (b) of this section for an employer engaged primarily in the building and construction industry to make an agreement covering employees engaged (or who, upon their employment, will be engaged) in the building and construction industry with a labor organization of which building and construction employees are members (not established, maintained, or assisted by any action defined in section 8 (a) of this Act as an unfair labor practice) because (1) the majority status of such labor organization has not been established under the provisions of section 9 of this Act prior to the making of such agreement, or (2) such agreement requires as a condition of employment, membership in such labor organization after the seventh day following the beginning of such employment or the effective date of the agreement, whichever is later, or (3) such agreement requires the employer to notify such labor organization of opportunities for employment which such employer, or gives such labor organization an opportunity to refer qualified applicants for such employment, or (4) such agreement specifies minimum training or experience qualifications for employment or provides for priority in opportunities for employment based upon length of service with such employer, in the industry or in the particular geographical area: Provided, That nothing in this subsection shall set aside the final proviso to section 8(a)(3) of this Act: Provided further, That any agreement which would be invalid, but for clause (1) of this subsection, shall not be a bar to a petition filed pursuant to section 9(c) or 9(e).*

(g) A labor organization before engaging in any strike, picketing, or other concerted refusal to work at any health care institution shall, not less than ten days prior to such action, notify the institution in writing and the Federal Mediation and Conciliation Service of that intention, except that in the case of bargaining for an initial agreement following certification or recognition the notice required by this subsection shall not be given until the expiration of the period specified in clause (B) of the last sentence of section 8(d) of this Act. The notice shall state the date and

---

* Section 8(f) was inserted in the Act by subsection (a) of Section 705 of Public Law 86-257. Section 705(b) provides:

"Nothing contained in the amendment made by subsection (a) shall be construed as authorizing the execution or application of agreements requiring membership in a labor organization as a condition of employment in any State or Territory in which such execution or application is prohibited by State or Territorial law."

time that such action will commence. The notice, once given, may be extended by the written agreement of both parties.*

REPRESENTATIVES AND ELECTIONS

SEC. 9. (a) Representatives designated or selected for the purposes of collective bargaining by the majority of the employees in a unit appropriate for such purposes, shall be the exclusive representatives of all the employees in such unit for the purposes of collective bargaining in respect to rates of pay, wages, hours of employment, or other conditions of employment: *Provided,* That any individual employee or a group of employees shall have the right at any time to present grievances to their employer *and to have such grievances adjusted, without the intervention of the bargaining representative, as long as the adjustment is not inconsistent with the terms of a collective-bargaining contract or agreement then in effect: Provided further, That the bargaining representative has been given opportunity to be present at such adjustment.*

(b) The Board shall decide in each case whether, in order to assure to employees the fullest freedom in exercising the rights guaranteed by this Act, the unit appropriate for the purposes of collective bargaining shall be the employer unit, craft unit, plant unit, or subdivision thereof: *Provided, That the Board shall not (1) decide that any unit is appropriate for such purposes if such unit includes both professional employees and employees who are not professional employees unless a majority of such professional employees vote for inclusion in such unit; or (2) decide that any craft unit is inappropriate for such purposes on the ground that a different unit has been established by a prior Board determination, unless a majority of the employees in the proposed craft unit vote against separate representation or (3) decide that any unit is appropriate for such purposes if it includes, together with other employees, any individual employed as a guard to enforce against employees and other persons rules to protect property of the employer or to protect the safety of persons on the employer's premises; but no labor organization shall be certified as the representative of employees in a bargaining unit of guards if such organization admits to membership, or is affiliated directly or indirectly with an organization which admits to membership, employees other than guards.*

[(c) Whenever a question affecting commerce arises concerning the representation of employees, the Board may investigate such controversy and certify to the parties, in writing, the name or names of the representatives that have been designated or selected. In any such investigation, the Board shall provide for an appropriate hearing upon due notice, either in conjunction with a proceeding under section 10 or otherwise, and may take a secret ballot of employees, or utilize any other suitable method to ascertain such representatives.]

(c)

    (1) Whenever a petition shall have been filed, in accordance with such regulations as may be prescribed by the Board-

---

* Section 8(g) was added by Public Law 93-360, 93d Congress, 2d Session, approved July 26, 1974.

(A) by an employee or group of employees or any individual or labor organization acting in their behalf alleging that a substantial number of employees (i) wish to be represented for collective bargaining and that their employer declines to recognize their representative as the representative defined in section 9(a), or (ii) assert that the individual or labor organization, which has been certified or is being currently recognized by their employer as the bargaining representative, is no longer a representative as defined in section 9(a); or

(B) by an employer, alleging that one or more individuals or labor organizations have presented to him a claim to be recognized as the representative defined in section 9(a); the Board shall investigate such petition and if it has reasonable cause to believe that a question of representation affecting commerce exists shall provide for an appropriate hearing upon due notice. Such hearing may be conducted by an officer or employee of the regional office, who shall not make any recommendations with respect thereto. If the Board finds upon the record of such hearing that such a question of representation exists, it shall direct an election by secret ballot and shall certify the results thereof.

(2) In determining whether or not a question of representation affecting commerce exists, the same regulations and rules of decision shall apply irrespective of the identity of the persons filing the petition or the kind of relief sought and in no case shall the Board deny a labor organization a place on the ballot by reason of an order with respect to such labor organization or its predecessor not issued in conformity with section 10(c).

(3) No election shall be directed in any bargaining unit or any subdivision within which, in the preceding twelve-month period, a valid election shall have been held. Employees [[on]] **engaged in an economic** *strike who are not entitled to reinstatement shall [[not]] be eligible to vote [[.]]* **under such regulations as the Board shall find are consistent with the purposes and provisions of this Act in any election conducted within twelve months after the commencement of the strike.** *In any election where none of the choices on the ballot receives a majority, a run-off shall be conducted, the ballot providing for a selection between the two choices receiving the largest and second largest number of valid votes cast in the election.*

(4) Nothing in this section shall be construed to prohibit the waiving of hearings by stipulation for the purpose of a consent election in conformity with regulations and rules of decision of the Board.

(5) In determining whether a unit is appropriate for the purposes specified in subsection (b) the extent to which the employees have organized shall not be controlling.

(d) Whenever an order of the Board made pursuant to section 10(c) is based in whole or in part upon facts certified following an investigation pursuant to subsection (c) of this section and there is a petition for the enforcement or review of such order, such certification and the record of such investigation shall be included in the transcript of the entire record required to be filed under section

10(e) or 10(f), and thereupon the decree of the court enforcing, modifying, or setting aside in whole or in part the order of the Board shall be made and entered upon the pleadings, testimony, and proceedings set forth in such transcript.

[(e)(1) Upon the filing with the Board by a labor organization, which is the representative of employees as provided in section 9(a), of a petition alleging that 30 per centum or more of the employees within a unit claimed to be appropriate for such purposes desire to authorize such labor organization to make an agreement with the employer of such employees requiring membership in such labor organization as a condition of employment in such unit, upon an appropriate showing thereof the Board shall, if no question of representation exists, take a secret ballot of such employees, and shall certify the results thereof to such labor organization and to the employer.]*

(e)

(1) Upon the filing with the Board, by 30 per centum or more of the employees in a bargaining unit covered by an agreement between their employer and a labor organization made pursuant to section 8(a)(3), of a petition alleging they desire that such authority be rescinded, the Board shall take a secret ballot of the employees in such unit and certify the results thereof to such labor organization and to the employer.

(2) No election shall be conducted pursuant to this subsection in any bargaining unit or any subdivision within which, in the preceding twelve-month period, a valid election shall have been held.

[[(f) No investigation shall be made by the Board of any question affecting commerce concerning the representation of employees, raised by a labor organization under subsection (c) of this section, and no complaint shall be issued pursuant to a charge made by a labor organization under subsection (b) of section 10, unless such labor organization and any national or i nternational labor organization of which such labor organization is an affiliate or constituent unit (A) shall have prior thereto filed with the Secretary of Labor copies of its constitution and bylaws and a report, in such form as the Secretary may prescribe, showing-

(1) the name of such labor organization and the address of its principal place of business;

(2) the names, titles, and compensation and allowances of its three principal officers and of any of its other officers or agents whose aggregate compensation and allowances for the preceding year exceeded $5,000, and the amount of the compensation and allowances paid to each such officer or agent during such year;

(3) the manner in which the officers and agents referred to in clause (2) were elected, appointed, or otherwise selected;

(4) the initiation fee or fees which new members are required to pay on becoming members of such labor organization;

* Repealed by Public Law 189, 82d Congress, 1st Session, approved October 22, 1951, which also renumbered the two following subsections and made minor changes in present subsection (e)(1).

(5) the regular dues or fees which members are required to pay in order to remain members in good standing of such labor organization;

(6) a detailed statement of, or reference to provisions of its constitution and by-laws showing the procedure followed with respect to, (a) qualification for or restrictions on membership, (b) election of officers and stewards, (c) calling of regular and special meetings, (d) levying of assessments, (e) imposition of fines, (f) authorization for bargaining demands, (g) ratification of contract terms, (h) authorization for strikes, (i) authorization for disbursement of union funds, (j) audit of union financial transactions, (k) participation in insurance or other benefit plans, and (l) expulsion of members and the grounds therefor; and (B) can show that prior thereto it has-

(1) filed with the Secretary of Labor, in such form as the Secretary may prescribe, a report showing all of (a) its receipts of any kind and the sources of such receipts, (b) its total assets and liabilities as of the end of its last fiscal year, (c) the disbursements made by it during such fiscal year, including the purposes for which made; and

(2) furnished to all of the members of such labor organization copies of the financial report required by paragraph (1) hereof to be filed with the Secretary of Labor.]]

[[(g) It shall be the obligation of all labor organizations to file annually with the Secretary of Labor, in such form as the Secretary of Labor may prescribe, reports bringing up to date the information required to be supplied in the initial filing by subsection (f)(A) of this section, and to file with the Secretary of Labor and furnish to its members annually financial reports in the form and manner prescribed in subsection (f)(B). No labor organization shall be eligible for certification under this section as the representative of any employees, and no complaint shall issue under section 10 with respect to a charge filed by a labor organization unless it can show that it and any national or international labor organization of which it is an affiliate or constituent unit has complied with its obligations under this subsection.]]

[[(h) No investigation shall be made by the Board of any question affecting commerce concerning the representation of employees, raised by a labor organization under subsection (c) of this section, and no complaint shall be issued pursuant to a charge made by a labor organization under subsection (b) of section 10, unless there is on file with the Board an affidavit executed contemporaneously or within the preceding twelve-month period by each officer of such labor organization and the officers of any national or international labor organization of which it is an affiliate or constituent unit that he is not a member of the Communist Party or affiliated with such party, and that he does not believe in, and is not a member of or supports any organization that believes in or teaches, the overthrow of the United States Government by force or by any illegal or unconstitutional methods. The provisions of section 35 A of the Criminal Code shall be applicable in respect to such affidavits.]]

PREVENTION OF UNFAIR LABOR PRACTICES

SEC. 10. (a) The Board is empowered, as hereinafter provided, to prevent any person from engaging in any unfair labor practice (listed in section 8) affecting commerce. This power shall not be affected by any other means of adjustment or prevention that has been or may be established by agreement, law, or otherwise: *Provided, That the Board is empowered by agreement with any agency of any State or Territory to cede to such agency jurisdiction over any cases in any industry (other than mining, manufacturing, communications, and transportation except where predominantly local in character) even though such cases may involve labor disputes affecting commerce, unless the provision of the State or Territorial statute applicable to the determination of such cases by such agency is inconsistent with the corresponding provision of this Act or has received a construction inconsistent therewith.*

(b) Whenever it is charged that any person has engaged in or is engaging in any such unfair labor practice, the Board, or any agent or agency designated by the Board for such purposes, shall have power to issue and cause to be served upon such person a complaint stating the charges in that respect, and containing a notice of hearing before the Board or a member thereof, or before a designated agent or agency, at a place therein fixed, not less than five days after the serving of said complaint: *Provided, That no complaint shall issue based upon any unfair labor practice occurring more than six months prior to the filing of the charge with the Board and the service of a copy thereof upon the person against whom such charge is made, unless the person aggrieved thereby was prevented from filing such charge by reason of service in the armed forces in which event the six-month period shall be computed from the day of his discharge.* Any such complaint may be amended by the member, agent, or agency conducting the hearing or the Board in its discretion at any time prior to the issuance of an order based thereon. The person so complained of shall have the right to file an answer to the original or amended complaint and to appear in person or otherwise and give testimony at the place and time fixed in the complaint. In the discretion of the member, agent, or agency conducting the hearing or the Board, any other person may be allowed to intervene in the said proceeding and to present testimony. [In any such proceeding the rules of evidence prevailing in courts of law or equity shall not be controlling.] *Any such proceeding shall, so far as practicable, be conducted in accordance with the rules of evidence applicable in the district courts of the United States under the rules of civil procedure for the district courts of the United States, adopted by the Supreme Court of the United States pursuant to section 2072 of Title 28.*

(c) The testimony taken by such member, agent, or agency or the Board shall be reduced to writing and filed with the Board. Thereafter, in its discretion, the Board upon notice may take further testimony or hear argument. If upon [all] *the preponderance of* the testimony taken the Board shall be of the opinion that any person named in the complaint has engaged in or is engaging in any such unfair labor practice, then the Board shall state its findings of fact and shall issue and cause to be served on such person an order requiring such person to cease and desist from such unfair labor practice, and to take such affirmative action including reinstatement of employees with or without back pay, as will effectuate the policies of this Act: *Provided, That where an order directs reinstatement of an employee, back pay may be required of the employer or labor organization, as the case may be, responsible for the discrimination suffered by him: And provided further, That in determining whether a complaint shall issue alleging a violation of section 8(a)(1) or section 8(a)(2), and in deciding such cases, the same regulations and rules of decision shall apply irrespective of whether or not the labor organization affected is affiliated with a labor organization national or international in scope. Such order may further require such person to make reports from time to time showing the extent to which it has complied with the order.* If upon [all] *the preponderance of* the testimony taken the Board shall not be of the opinion that the person named in the complaint has engaged in or is engaging in any such unfair labor practice, then the Board shall state its findings of fact and shall issue an order dismissing the said complaint. *No order of the Board shall require the reinstatement of any individual as an employee who has been suspended or discharged, or the payment to him of any back pay, if such individual was suspended or discharged for cause. In case the evidence is presented before a member of the Board, or before an administrative law judge or judges thereof, such member, or such judge or judges, as the case may be, shall issue and cause to be served on the parties to the proceeding a proposed report, together with a recommended order, which shall be filed with the Board, and if no exceptions are filed within twenty days after service thereof upon such parties, or within such further period as the Board may authorize, such recommended order shall become the order of the Board and become effective as therein prescribed.*

(d) Until *a transcript of* the record in a case shall have been filed in a court, as hereinafter provided, the Board may at any time, upon reasonable notice and in such manner as it shall deem proper, modify or set aside, in whole or in part, any finding or other made or issued by it.

(e) The Board shall have power to petition any court of appeals of the United States, or if all the courts of appeals to which application may be made are in vacation, any district court of the United States, within any circuit or district, respectively, wherein the unfair labor practice in question occurred or wherein such person resides or transacts business, for the enforcement of such order and for appropriate temporary relief or restraining order, and shall file in the court the record in the proceedings, as provided in section 2112 of title 28, United States Code. Upon the filing of such petition, the court shall cause notice thereof to be served upon such person, and thereupon shall have jurisdiction of the proceeding and of the question determined therein, and shall have power to grant such temporary relief or restraining order as it deems just and proper, and to make and enter a decree enforcing, modifying, and enforcing as so modified, or setting aside in whole or in part the order of the Board. No objection that has not been urged before the Board, its member, agent, or agency, shall be considered by the court, unless the failure or neglect to urge such objection shall be excused because of extraordinary circumstances. The findings of the Board with respect to questions of fact if supported by *substantial* evidence *on the record considered as a whole* shall be conclusive. If either party shall apply to the court for leave to adduce additional evidence and shall show to the satisfaction of the court that such additional evidence is material and that there were reasonable grounds for the failure to adduce such evidence in the hearing before the Board, its member, agent, or agency, the court may order such additional evidence to be taken before the Board, its member, agent, or agency, and to be made a part of the record. The Board may modify its findings as to the facts, or make new findings, by reason of additional evidence so taken and filed, and it shall file such modified or new findings, which findings with respect to questions of fact if supported by substantial evidence on the record considered as a whole shall be conclusive, and shall file its recommendations, if any, for the modification or setting aside of its original order. Upon the filing of the record with it the jurisdiction of the court shall be exclusive and its judgment and decree shall be final, except that the same shall be subject to review by the appropriate United States court of appeals if application was made to the district court as hereinbefore provided, and by the Supreme Court of the United States upon writ of certiorari or certification as provided in section 1254 of title 28.

(f) Any person aggrieved by a final order of the Board granting or denying in whole or in part the relief sought may obtain a review of such order in any circuit court of appeals of the United States in the circuit wherein the unfair labor practice in question was alleged to have been engaged in or wherein such person resides or transacts business, or in the United States Court of Appeals for the District of Columbia, by filing in such court a written petition praying that the order of the Board be modified or set aside. A copy of such petition shall be forth with transmitted by the clerk of the court to the Board, and thereupon the aggrieved party shall file in the court the record in the proceeding, certified by the Board, as provided in section 2112 of title 28, United States Code. Upon the filing of such petition, the court shall proceed in the same manner as in the case of an application by the Board under subsection (e) of this section, and shall have the same jurisdiction to grant to the Board such temporary relief or restraining order as it deems just and proper, and in like manner to make and enter a decree enforcing, modifying, and enforcing as so modified, or setting aside in whole or in part the order of the Board; the findings of the Board with respect to questions of fact if supported by *substantial* evidence *on the record considered as a whole* shall in like manner be conclusive.

(g) The commencement of proceedings under subsection (e) or (f) of this section shall not, unless specifically ordered by the court, operate as a stay of the Board's order.

(h) When granting appropriate temporary relief or a restraining order, or making and entering a decree enforcing, modifying, and enforcing as so modified, or setting aside in whole or in part an order of the Board, as provided in this section, the jurisdiction of courts sitting in equity shall not be limited by the Act entitled "An Act to amend the Judicial Code and to define and limit the jurisdiction of courts sitting in equity, and for other purposes," approved March 23, 1932 (U.S.C., title 29, secs. 101-115).

(i) Petitions filed under this Act shall be heard expeditiously, and if possible within ten days after they have been docketed.*

---

*   Subsection 10(i) was repealed by Public Law 98-620, 98th Congress, 2d Session, approved November 8, 1984.

(j) The Board shall have power, upon issuance of a complaint as provided in subsection (b) charging that any person has engaged in or is engaging in an unfair labor practice, to petition any district court of the United States (including the District Court of the United States for the District of Columbia), within any district wherein the unfair labor practice in question is alleged to have occurred or wherein such person resides or transacts business, for appropriate temporary relief or restraining order. Upon the filing of any such petition the court shall cause notice thereof to be served upon such person, and thereupon shall have jurisdiction to grant to the Board such temporary relief or restraining order as it deems just and proper.

(k) Whenever it is charged that any person has engaged in an unfair labor practice within the meaning of paragraph (4)(D) of section 8(b), the Board

is empowered and directed to hear and determine the dispute out of which such unfair labor practice shall have arisen, unless, within ten days after notice that such charge has been filed, the parties to such dispute submit to the Board satisfactory evidence that they have adjusted, or agreed upon methods for the voluntary adjustment of, the dispute. Upon compliance by the parties to the dispute with the decision of the Board or upon such voluntary adjustment of the dispute, such charge shall be dismissed.

(l) Whenever it is charged that any person has engaged in an unfair labor practice within the meaning of paragraph (4)(A), (B), or (C) of section 8(b), **or section 8(e) or section 8(b)(7),** *the preliminary investigation of such charge shall be made forthwith and given priority over all other cases except cases of like character in the office where it is filed or to which it is referred. If, after such investigation, the officer or regional attorney to whom the matter may be referred has reasonable cause to believe such charge is true and that a complaint should issue, he shall, on behalf of the Board, petition any district court of the United States (including the District Court of the United States for the District of Columbia) within any district where the unfair labor practice in question has occurred, is alleged to have occurred, or wherein such person resides or transacts business, for appropriate injunctive relief pending the final adjudication of the Board with respect to such matter. Upon the filing of any such petition the district court shall have jurisdiction to grant such injunctive relief or temporary restraining order as it deems just and proper, notwithstanding any other provision of law: Provided further, That no temporary restraining order shall be issued without notice unless a petition alleges that substantial and irreparable injury to the charging party will be unavoidable and such temporary restraining order shall be effective for no longer than five days and will become void at the expiration of such period [[.]]:* **Provided further, That such officer or regional attorney shall not apply for any restraining order under section 8(b)(7) if a charge against the employer under section 8(a)(2) has been filed and after the preliminary investigation, he has reasonable cause to believe that such charge is true and that a complaint should issue.** *Upon filing of any such petition the courts shall cause notice thereof to be served upon any person involved in the charge and such person, including the charging party, shall be given an opportunity to appear by counsel and present any relevant testimony: Provided further, That for the purposes of this subsection district courts shall be*

deemed to have jurisdiction of a labor organization (1) in the district in which such organization maintains its principal office, or (2) in any district in which its duly authorized officers or agents are engaged in promoting or protecting the interests of employee members. The service of legal process upon such officer or agent shall constitute service upon the labor organization and make such organization a party to the suit. In situations where such relief is appropriate the procedure specified herein shall apply to charges with respect to section 8(b)(4)(D).

(m) Whenever it is charged that any person has engaged in an unfair labor practice within the meaning of subsection (a)(3) or (b)(2) of section 8, such charge shall be given priority over all other cases except cases of like character in the office where it is filed or to which it is referred and cases given priority under subsection (1).

INVESTIGATORY POWERS

SEC. 11. For the purpose of all hearings and investigations, which, in the opinion of the Board, are necessary and proper for the exercise of the powers vested in it by section 9 and section 10-

(1) The Board, or its duly authorized agents or agencies, shall at all reasonable times have access to, for the purpose of examination, and the right to copy any evidence of any person being investigated or proceeded against that relates to any matter under investigation or in question. The Board, or any member thereof, shall upon application of any party to such proceedings, forthwith issue to such party subpenas requiring the attendance and testimony of witnesses or the production of any evidence in such proceeding or investigation requested in such application. Within five days after the service of a subpena on any person requiring the production of any evidence in his possession or under his control, such person may petition the Board to revoke, and the Board shall revoke, such subpena if in its opinion the evidence whose production is required does not relate to any matter under investigation, or any matter in question in such proceedings, or if in its opinion such subpena does not describe with sufficient particularity the evidence whose production is required. Any member of the Board, or any agent or agency designated by the Board for such purposes, may administer oaths and affirmations, examine witnesses, and receive evidence. Such attendance of witnesses and the production of such evidence may be required from any place in the United States or any Territory or possession thereof, at any designated place of hearing.

(2) In case of contumacy or refusal to obey a subpena issued to any person, any district court of the United States or the United States courts of any Territory or possession, within the jurisdiction of which the inquiry is carried on or within the jurisdiction of which said person guilty of contumacy or refusal to obey is found or resides or transacts business, upon application by the Board shall have jurisdiction to issue to such person an order requiring such person to appear before the Board, its member, agent, or agency, there to produce evidence if so ordered, or there to give testimony touching the matter under investigation or in question; and any failure to obey such order of the court may be punished by said court as a contempt thereof.

(3) No person shall be excused from attending and testifying or from producing books, records, correspondence, documents, or other evidence in obedience to the subpena of the Board, on the ground that the testimony or evidence required of him may tend to incriminate him or subject him to a penalty or forfeiture; but no individual shall be prosecuted or subjected to any penalty or forfeiture for or on account of any transaction, matter, or thing concerning which he is compelled, after having claimed his privilege against self-incrimination, to testify or produce evidence, except that such individual so testifying shall not be exempt from prosecution and punishment for perjury committed in so testifying.*

(4) Complaints, orders, and other process and papers of the Board,

its member, agent, or agency, may be served either personally or by registered or certified mail or by telegraph or by leaving a copy thereof at the principal office or place of business of the person required to be served. The verified return by the individual so serving the same setting forth the manner of such service shall be proof of the same, and the return post office receipt or telegraph receipt therefor when registered or certified and mailed or telegraphed as aforesaid shall be proof of service of the same. Witnesses summoned before the Board, its member, agent, or agency, shall be paid the same fees and mileage that are paid witnesses in the courts of the United States, and witnesses whose depositions are taken and the persons taking the same shall severally be entitled to the same fees as are paid for like services in the courts of the United States.

(5) All process of any court to which application may be made

under this Act may be served in the judicial district wherein the defendant or other person required to be served resides or may be found.

(6) The several departments and agencies of the Government,

when directed by the President, shall furnish the Board, upon its request, all records, papers, and information in their possession relating to any matter before the Board.

SEC. 12. Any person who shall willfully resist, prevent, impede, or interfere with any member of the Board or any of its agents or agencies in the performance of duties pursuant to this Act shall be punished by a fine of not more than $5,000 or by imprisonment for not more than one year, or both.

LIMITATIONS

SEC. 13. Nothing in this Act, *except as specifically provided for herein*, shall be construed so as either to interfere with or impede or diminish in any way the right to strike, *or to affect the limitations or qualifications on that right*.

SEC. 14. (a) *Nothing herein shall prohibit any individual employed as a supervisor from becoming or remaining a member of a labor organization, but no employer subject to this Act shall be compelled to deem individuals defined herein*

---

* Section 11(3) was repealed by Public Law 91-452, 91st Congress, 2d Session, approved October 15, 1970, which added 18 U.S.C. §§ 6001, 6002, and 6004 to cover the immunity of witnesses in administrative proceedings.

as supervisors as employees for the purpose of any law, either national or local, relating to collective bargaining.

(b) Nothing in this Act shall be construed as authorizing the execution or application of agreements requiring membership in a labor organization as a condition of employment in any State or Territory in which such execution or application is prohibited by State or Territorial law.

(c)

(1) The Board, in its discretion, may, by rule of decision or by published rules adopted pursuant to the Administrative Procedure Act, decline to assert jurisdiction over any labor dispute involving any class or category of employers, where, in the opinion of the Board, the effect of such labor dispute on commerce is not sufficiently substantial to warrant the exercise of its jurisdiction: Provided, That the Board shall not decline to assert jurisdiction over any labor dispute over which it would assert jurisdiction under the standards prevailing upon August 1, 1959.

(2) Nothing in this Act shall be deemed to prevent or bar any agency or the courts of any State or Territory (including the Commonwealth of Puerto Rico, Guam, and the Virgin Islands), from assuming and asserting jurisdiction over labor disputes over which the Board declines, pursuant to paragraph (1) of this subsection, to assert jurisdiction.

SEC. 15. *Wherever the application of the provisions of section 272 of chapter 10 of the Act entitled "An Act to establish a uniform system of bankruptcy throughout the United States", approved July 1, 1898, and Acts amendatory thereof and supplementary thereto (U.S.C., title 11, sec. 672), conflicts with the application of the provisions of this Act, this Act shall prevail: Provided, That in any situation where the provisions of this Act cannot be validly enforced, the provisions of such other Acts shall remain in full force and effect.*

SEC. 16. If any provision of this Act, or the application of such provision to any person or circumstances, shall be held invalid, the remainder of this Act, or the application of such provision to persons or circumstances other than those as to which it is held invalid, shall not be affected thereby.

SEC. 17. This Act may be cited as the "National Labor Relations Act".

SEC. 18. No petition entertained, no investigation made, no election held, and no certification issued by the National Labor Relations Board, under any of the provisions of section 9 of the National Labor Relations Act, as amended, shall be invalid by reason of the failure of the Congress of Industrial Organizations to have complied with the requirements of section 9(f), (g), or (h) of the aforesaid Act prior to December 22, 1949, or by reason of the failure of the American Federation of Labor to have complied with the provisions of section 9 (f), (g), or (h) of the aforesaid Act prior to November 7, 1947: Provided, That no liability shall be imposed under any provision of this Act upon any person for failure to honor any election or certificate referred to above, prior to the effective date of this amendment: Provided, however, That this proviso shall not have the effect of setting aside or in any way affecting judgments or decrees heretofore entered under section 10(e) or (f) and which have become final.

INDIVIDUALS WITH RELIGIOUS CONVICTIONS

SEC. 19. Any employee who is a member of and adheres to established and traditional tenets or teachings of a bona fide religion, body, or sect which has historically held conscientious objections to joining or financially supporting labor organizations shall not be required to join or financially support any labor organization as a condition of employment; except that such employee may be required in a contract between such employees' employer and a labor organization in lieu of periodic dues and initiation fees, to pay sums equal to such dues and initiation fees to a nonreligious, nonlabor organization charitable fund exempt from taxation under section 501(c)(3) of title 26 of the Internal Revenue Code, chosen by such employee from a list of at least three such funds, designated in such contract or if the contract fails to designate such funds, then to any such fund chosen by the employee. If such employee who holds conscientious objections pursuant to this section requests the labor organization to pursue the grievance-arbitration procedure on the employee's behalf, the labor organization is authorized to charge the employee for the reasonable cost of using such procedure.[*]

EFFECTIVE DATE OF CERTAIN CHANGES[†]

SEC. 102. *No provision of this title shall be deemed to make an unfair labor practice any act which was performed prior to the date of the enactment of this Act which did not constitute an unfair labor practice prior thereto, and the provisions of section 8(a)(3) and section 8(b)(2) of the National Labor Relations Act as amended by this title shall not make an unfair labor practice the performance of any obligation under a collective-bargaining agreement entered into prior to the date of the enactment of this Act, or (in the case of an agreement for a period of not more than one year) entered into on or after such date of enactment, but prior to the effective date of this title, if the performance of such obligation would not have constituted an unfair labor practice under section 8 (3) of the National Labor Relations Act prior to the effective date of this title, unless such agreement was renewed or extended subsequent thereto.*

SEC. 103. *No provisions of this title shall affect any certification of representatives or any determination as to the appropriate collective-bargaining unit, which was made under section 9 of the National Labor Relations Act prior to the effective date of this title until one year after the date of such certification or if, in respect of any such certification, a collective-bargaining contract was entered into prior to*

---

[*] Sec. 19, added August 25, 1974, by P.L. 93-360, 93rd Congress, appears as amended December 24, 1980, by P.L. 96-593, 96th Congress.

[†] The effective date referred to in Sections 102, 103, and 104 is August 22, 1947. The effective date of most of the 1959 amendments was Nov. 13, 1959. Sections 201(d) and (e) of the Labor-Management Reporting and Disclosure Act of 1959 which repealed Sections 9(f), (g), and (h) of the NLRA, as amended, and Section 505 of the LMRDA which amended Section 302 of the LMRA, 1947, took effect September 14, 1959.

the effective date of this title, until the end of the contract period or until one year after such date, whichever first occurs.

SEC. 104. *The amendments made by this title shall take effect sixty days after the date of the enactment of this Act, except that the authority of the President to appoint certain officers conferred upon him by section 3 of the National Labor Relations Act as amended by this title may be exercised forthwith.*

LABOR MANAGEMENT RELATIONS ACT*
Pub. L. No. 101, 80th Cong., 1st Sess., 1947, 61 Stat. 136, as amended by
Pub. L. No. 257, 86th Cong., 1st Sess., 1959; 29 U.S.C. §§ 141-67, 171-97,
F.C.A. 29 §§ 141-67, 171-97

AN ACT

To amend the National Labor Relations Act, to provide additional facilities for the mediation of labor disputes affecting commerce, to equalize legal responsibilities of labor organizations and employers, and for other purposes.

Be it enacted by the Senate and House of Representatives of the United States of America in Congress assembled,

SHORT TITLE AND DECLARATION OF POLICY

SEC. 1. (a) This Act may be cited as the "Labor Management Relations Act, 1947."

(b) Industrial strife which interferes with the normal flow of commerce and with the full production of articles and commodities for commerce, can be avoided or substantially minimized if employers, employees, and labor organizations each recognize under law one another's legitimate rights in their relations with each other, and above all recognize under law that neither party has any right in its relations with any other to engage in acts or practices which jeopardize the public health, safety, or interest.

It is the purpose and policy of this Act, in order to promote the full flow of commerce, to prescribe the legitimate rights of both employees and employers in their relations affecting commerce, to provide orderly and peaceful procedures for preventing the interference by either with the legitimate rights of the other, to protect the rights of individual employees in their relations with labor organizations whose activities affect commerce, to define and proscribe practices on the part of labor and management which affect commerce and are inimical to the general welfare, and to protect the rights of the public in connection with labor disputes affecting commerce.

TITLE I

AMENDMENT OF NATIONAL LABOR RELATIONS ACT

SEC. 101. The National Labor Relations Act is hereby amended to read as follows:

. . . .

[The text of the National Labor Relations Act as amended appears at p. 1, *supra*.]

---

* Portions of the Act which have been eliminated by the Labor-Management Reporting and Disclosure Act of 1959, Public Law 86-257, are enclosed by brackets; provisions which have been added to the Act are in boldface; and unchanged portions are shown in roman type.

TITLE II
CONCICLIATION OF LABOR DISPUTES IN INDUSTRIES AFFECTING COMMERCE;

NATIONAL EMERGENCIES

SEC. 201. That it is the policy of the United States that-

(a) sound and stable industrial peace and the advancement of the

general welfare, health, and safety of the Nation and of the best interest of employers and employees can most satisfactorily be secured by the settlement of issues between employers and employees through the processes of conference and collective bargaining between employers and the representatives of their employees;

(b) the settlement of issues between employers and employees through collective bargaining may be advanced by making available full and adequate governmental facilities for conciliation, mediation, and voluntary arbitration to aid and encourage employers and the representatives of their employees to reach and maintain agreements concerning rates of pay, hours, and working conditions, and to make all reasonable efforts to settle their differences by mutual agreement reached through conferences and collective bargaining or by such methods as may be provided for in any applicable agreement for the settlement of disputes; and

(c) certain controversies which arise between parties to collective-bargaining agreements may be avoided or minimized by making available full and adequate governmental facilities for furnishing assistance to employers and the representatives of their employees in formulating for inclusion within such agreements provision for adequate notice of any proposed changes in the terms of such agreements, for the final adjustment of grievances or questions regarding the application or interpretation of such agreements, and other provisions designed to prevent the subsequent arising of such controversies.

SEC. 202. (a) There is hereby created an independent agency to be known as the Federal Mediation and Conciliation Service (herein referred to as the "Service," except that for sixty days after the date of the enactment of this Act such term shall refer to the Conciliation Service of the Department of Labor). The Service shall be under the direction of a Federal Mediation and Conciliation Director (hereinafter referred to as the "Director"), who shall be appointed by the President by and with the advice and consent of the Senate. The Director shall receive compensation at the rate of $12,000* per annum. The Director shall not engage in any other business, vocation, or employment.

(b) The Director is authorized, subject to the civil-service laws, to appoint such clerical and other personnel as may be necessary for the execution of the functions of the Service, and shall fix their compensation in accordance with the Classification Act of 1923, as amended, and may, without regard to the provisions of the

---

* The annual salary of the Director is now prescribed in the Federal Executive Salary Schedule.

civil-service laws and the Classification Act of 1923, as amended, appoint and fix the compensation of such conciliators and mediators as may be necessary to carry out the functions of the Service. The Director is authorized to make such expenditures for supplies, facilities, and services as he deems necessary. Such expenditures shall be allowed and paid upon presentation of itemized vouchers therefor approved by the Director or by any employee designated by him for that purpose.

(c) The principal office of the Service shall be in the District of Columbia, but the Director may establish regional offices convenient to localities in which labor controversies are likely to arise. The Director may by order, subject to revocation at any time, delegate any authority and discretion conferred upon him by this Act to any regional director, or other officer or employee of the Service. The Director may establish suitable procedures for cooperation with State and local mediation agencies. The Director shall make an annual report in writing to Congress at the end of the fiscal year.

(d) All mediation and conciliation functions of the Secretary of Labor or the United States Conciliation Service under section 8 of the Act entitled "An Act to create a Department of Labor," approved March 4, 1913 (U.S.C., title 29, sec. 51), and all functions of the United States Conciliation Service under any other law are hereby transferred to the Federal Mediation and Conciliation Service, together with the personnel and records of the United States Conciliation Service. Such transfer shall take effect upon the sixtieth day after the date of enactment of this Act. Such transfer shall not affect any proceedings pending before the United States Conciliation Service or any certification, order, rule, or regulation thereto-fore made by it or by the Secretary of Labor. The Director and the Service shall not be subject in any way to the jurisdiction or authority of the Secretary of Labor or any official or division of the Department of Labor.

FUNCTIONS OF THE SERVICE

SEC. 203. (a) It shall be the duty of the Service, in order to prevent or minimize interruptions of the free flow of commerce growing out of labor disputes, to assist parties to labor disputes in industries affecting commerce to settle such disputes through conciliation and mediation.

(b) The Service may proffer its services in any labor dispute in any industry affecting commerce, either upon its own motion or upon the request of one or more of the parties to the dispute, whenever in its judgment such dispute threatens to cause a substantial interruption of commerce. The Director and the Service are directed to avoid attempting to mediate disputes which would have only a minor effect on interstate commerce if State or other conciliation services are available to the parties. Whenever the Service does proffer its services in any dispute, it shall be the duty of the Service promptly to put itself in communication with the parties and to use its best efforts, by mediation and conciliation, to bring them to agreement.

(c) If the Director is not able to bring the parties to agreement by conciliation within a reasonable time, he shall seek to induce the parties voluntarily to seek other means of settling the dispute without resort to strike, lock-out, or other coercion, including submission to the employees in the bargaining unit of the employer's last offer of settlement for approval or rejection in a secret ballot. The failure or refusal of either party to agree to any procedure suggested by the Director shall not be deemed a violation of any duty or obligation imposed by this Act.

(d) Final adjustment by a method agreed upon by the parties is hereby declared to be the desirable method for settlement of grievance disputes arising over the application or interpretation of an existing collectivebargaining agreement. The Service is directed to make its conciliation and mediation services available in the settlement of such grievance disputes only as a last resort and in exceptional cases.

(e) The Service is authorized and directed to encourage and support the establishment and operation of joint labor management activities conducted by plant, area, and industrywide committees designed to improve labor management relationships, job security and organizational effectiveness, in accordance with the provisions of section 205A.*

SEC. 204. (a) In order to prevent or minimize interruptions of the free flow of commerce growing out of labor disputes, employers and employees and their representatives, in any industry affecting commerce, shall-

(1) exert every reasonable effort to make and maintain agreements concerning rates of pay, hours, and working conditions, including provision for adequate notice of any proposed change in the terms of such agreements;

(2) whenever a dispute arises over the terms or application of a collective-bargaining agreement and a conference is requested by a party or prospective party thereto, arrange promptly for such a conference to be held and endeavor in such conference to settle such dispute expeditiously; and

(3) in case such dispute is not settled by conference, participate fully and promptly in such meetings as may be undertaken by the Service under this Act for the purpose of aiding in a settlement of the dispute.

SEC. 205. (a) There is hereby created a National Labor-Management Panel which shall be composed of twelve members appointed by the President, six of whom shall be selected from among persons outstanding in the field of management and six of whom shall be selected from among persons outstanding in the field of labor. Each member shall hold office for a term of three years, except that any member appointed to fill a vacancy occurring prior to the expiration of the term for which his predecessor was appointed shall be appointed for the remainder of such term, and the terms of office of the members first taking office shall expire, as designated by the President at the time of appointment, four at the end of the first year, four at the end of the second year, and four at the end of the third year after the date of appointment. Members of the panel, when serving on business of the panel, shall be paid compensation at the rate of $25 per day, and shall also be entitled to receive an allowance for actual and necessary

---

* Subsection (e) was added by Public Law 95-524, 95th Congress, 2d Session, approved October 27, 1978.

travel and subsistence expenses while so serving away from their places of residence.

(b) It shall be the duty of the panel, at the request of the Director, to advise in the avoidance of industrial controversies and the manner in which mediation and voluntary adjustment shall be administered, particularly with reference to controversies affecting the general welfare of the country.

SEC. 205A. (a)(1) The Service is authorized and directed to provide assistance in the establishment and operation of plant, area and industrywide labor management committees which-

(A) have been organized jointly by employers and labor organizations representing employees in that plant, area, or industry; and

(B) are established for the purpose of improving labor management relationships, job security, organizational effectiveness, enhancing economic development or involving workers in decisions affecting their jobs including improving communication with respect to subjects of mutual interest and concern.

(2) The Service is authorized and directed to enter into contracts and to make grants, where necessary or appropriate, to fulfill its responsibilities under this section.

(b)

(1) No grant may be made, no contract may be entered into and no other assistance may be provided under the provisions of this section to a plant labor management committee unless the employees in that plant are represented by a labor organization and there is in effect at that plant a collective bargaining agreement.

(2) No grant may be made, no contract may be entered into and no other assistance may be provided under the provisions of this section to an area or industrywide labor management committee unless its participants include any labor organizations certified or recognized as the representative of the employees of an employer participating in such committee. Nothing in this clause shall prohibit participation in an area or industrywide committee by an employer whose employees are not represented by a labor organization.

(3) No grant may be made under the provisions of this section to any labor management committee which the Service finds to have as one of its purposes the discouragement of the exercise of rights contained in section 7 of the National Labor Relations Act (29 U.S.C. 157), or the interference with collective bargaining in any plant, or industry.

(c) The Service shall carry out the provisions of this section through an office established for that purpose.

(d) There are authorized to be appropriated to carry out the provisions of this section $10,000,000 for the fiscal year 1979, and such sums as may be necessary thereafter.*

NATIONAL EMERGENCIES

SEC. 206. Whenever in the opinion of the President of the United States, a threatened or actual strike or lock-out affecting an entire industry or a substantial part thereof engaged in trade, commerce, transportation, transmission, or communication among the several States or with foreign nations, or engaged in the production of goods for commerce, will, if permitted to occur or to continue, imperil the national health or safety, he may appoint a board of inquiry to inquire into the issues involved in the dispute and to make a written report to him within such time as he shall prescribe. Such report shall include a statement of the facts with respect to the dispute, including each party's statement of its position but shall not contain any recommendations. The President shall file a copy of such report with the Service and shall make its contents available to the public.

SEC. 207. (a) A board of inquiry shall be composed of a chairman and such other members as the President shall determine, and shall have power to sit and act in any place within the United States and to conduct such hearings either in public or in private, as it may deem necessary or proper, to ascertain the facts with respect to the causes and circumstances of the dispute.

(b) Members of a board of inquiry shall receive compensation at the rate of $50 for each day actually spent by them in the work of the board, together with necessary travel and subsistence expenses.

(c) For the purpose of any hearing or inquiry conducted by any board appointed under this title, the provisions of sections 9 and 10 (relating to the attendance of witnesses and the production of books, papers, and documents) of the Federal Trade Commission Act of September 16, 1914, as amended (U.S.C. 19, title 15, secs. 49 and 50, as amended), are hereby made applicable to the powers and duties of such board.

SEC. 208. (a) Upon receiving a report from a board of inquiry the President may direct the Attorney General to petition any district court of the United States having jurisdiction of the parties to enjoin such strike or lock-out or the continuing thereof, and if the court finds that such threatened or actual strike or lock-out-

(i) affects an entire industry or a substantial part thereof engaged in trade, commerce, transportation, transmission, or communication among the several States or with foreign nations, or engaged in the production of goods for commerce; and

(ii) if permitted to occur or to continue, will imperil the national health or safety, it shall have jurisdiction to enjoin any such strike or lock-out, or the continuing thereof, and to make such other orders as may be appropriate.

---

* Section 205A was added by Public Law 95-524, 95th Congress, 2d Session, approved October 27, 1978.

(b) In any case, the provisions of the Act of March 23, 1932, entitled "An Act to amend the Judicial Code and to define and limit the jurisdiction of courts sitting in equity, and for other purposes," shall not be applicable.

(c) The order or orders of the court shall be subject to review by the appropriate circuit court of appeals and by the Supreme Court upon writ of certiorari or certification as provided in sections 239 and 240 of the Judicial Code, as amended (U.S.C., title 29, secs. 346 and 347).

SEC. 209. (a) Whenever a district court has issued an order under section 208 enjoining acts or practices which imperil or threaten to imperil the national health or safety, it shall be the duty of the parties to the labor dispute giving rise to such order to make every effort to adjust and settle their differences, with the assistance of the Service created by this Act. Neither party shall be under any duty to accept, in whole or in part, any proposal of settlement made by the Service.

(b) Upon the issuance of such order, the President shall reconvene the board of inquiry which has previously reported with respect to the dispute. At the end of a sixty-day period (unless the dispute has been settled by that time), the board of inquiry shall report to the President the current position of the parties and the efforts which have been made for settlement, and shall include a statement by each party of its position and a statement of the employer's last offer of settlement. The President shall make such report available to the public. The National Labor Relations Board, within the succeeding fifteen days, shall take a secret ballot of the employees of each employer involved in the dispute on the question of whether they wish to accept the final offer of settlement made by their employer as stated by him and shall certify the results thereof to the Attorney General within five days thereafter.

SEC. 210. Upon the certification of the results of such ballot or upon a settlement being reached, whichever happen sooner, the Attorney General shall move the court to discharge the injunction, which motion shall then be granted and the injunction discharged. When such motion is granted, the President shall submit to the Congress a full and comprehensive report of the proceedings, including the findings of the board of inquiry and the ballot taken by the National Labor Relations Board, together with such recommendations as he may see fit to make for consideration and appropriate action.

COMPILATION OF COLLECTIVE-BARGAINING AGREEMENTS, ETC.

SEC. 211. (a) For the guidance and information of interested representatives of employers, employees, and the general public, the Bureau of Labor Statistics of the Department of Labor shall maintain a file of copies of all available collectivebargaining agreements and other available agreements and actions thereunder settling or adjusting labor disputes. Such file shall be open to inspection under appropriate conditions prescribed by the Secretary of Labor, except that no specific information submitted in confidence shall be disclosed.

(b) The Bureau of Labor Statistics in the Department of Labor is authorized to furnish upon request of the Service, or employers, employees, or their representatives, all available data and factual information which may aid in the settlement of any labor dispute, except that no specific information submitted in confidence shall be disclosed.

EXEMPTION OF RAILWAY LABOR ACT

SEC. 212. The provisions of this title shall not be applicable with respect to any matter which is subject to the provisions of the Railway Labor Act, as amended from time to time.

CONCILIATION OF LABOR DISPUTES IN THE HEALTH CARE INDUSTRY

SEC. 213. (a) If, in the opinion of the Director of the Federal Mediation and Conciliation Service a threatened or actual strike or lockout affecting a health care institution will, if permitted to occur or to continue, substantially interrupt the delivery of health care in the locality concerned, the Director may further assist in the resolution of the impasse by establishing within 30 days after the notice to the Federal Mediation and Conciliation Service under clause (A) of the last sentence of section 8(d) (which is required by clause (3) of such section 8(d)), or within 10 days after the notice under clause (B), an impartial Board of Inquiry to investigate the issues involved in the dispute and to make a written report thereon to the parties within fifteen (15) days after the establishment of such a Board. The written report shall contain the findings of fact together with the Board's recommendations for settling the dispute, with the objective of achieving a prompt, peaceful and just settlement of the dispute. Each such Board shall be composed of such number of individuals as the Director may deem desirable. No member appointed under this section shall have any interest or involvement in the health care institutions or the employee organizations involved in the dispute.

(b)

(1)

Members of any board established under this section who are otherwise employed by the Federal Government shall serve without compensation but shall be reimbursed for travel, subsistence, and other necessary expenses incurred by them in carrying out its duties under this section.

(2) Members of any board established under this section who are not subject to paragraph (1) shall receive compensation at a rate prescribed by the Director but not to exceed the daily rate prescribed for GS-18 of the General Schedule under section 5332 of title 5, United States Code, including travel for each day they are engaged in the performance of their duties under this section and shall be entitled to reimbursement for travel, subsistence, and other necessary expenses incurred by them in carrying out their duties under this section.

(c) After the establishment of a board under subsection (a) of this section and for 15 days after any such board has issued its report, no change in the status quo in effect prior to the expiration of the contract in the case of negotiations for a contract renewal, or in effect prior to the time of the impasse in the case of an initial bargaining negotiation, except by agreement, shall be made by the parties to the controversy.

(d) There are authorized to be appropriated such sums as may be necessary to carry out the provisions of this section.*

TITLE III

SUITS BY AND AGAINST LABOR ORGANIZATIONS

SEC. 301. (a) Suits for violation of contracts between an employer and a labor organization representing employees in an industry affecting commerce as defined in this Act, or between any such labor organizations, may be brought in any district court of the United States having jurisdiction of the parties, without respect to the amount in controversy or without regard to the citizenship of the parties.

(b) Any labor organization which represents employees in an industry affecting commerce as defined in this Act and any employer whose activities affect commerce as defined in this Act shall be bound by the acts of its agents. Any such labor organization may sue or be sued as an entity and in behalf of the employees whom it represents in the courts of the United States. Any money judgment against a labor organization in a district court of the United States shall be enforceable only against the organization as an entity and against its assets, and shall not be enforceable against any individual member or his assets.

(c) For the purposes of actions and proceedings by or against labor organizations in the district courts of the United States, district courts shall be deemed to have jurisdiction of a labor organization (1) in the district in which such organization maintains its principal office, or (2) in any district in which its duly authorized officers or agents are engaged in representing or acting for employee members.

(d) The service of summons, subpena, or other legal process of any court of the United States upon an officer or agent of a labor organization, in his capacity as such, shall constitute service upon the labor organization.

(e) For the purposes of this section, in determining whether any person is acting as an "agent" of another person so as to make such other person responsible for his acts, the question of whether the specific acts performed were actually authorized or subsequently ratified shall not be controlling.

RESTRICTIONS ON PAYMENTS TO EMPLOYEE REPRESENTATIVES

SEC. 302. (a) It shall be unlawful for any employer **or association of employers or any person who acts as a labor relations expert, adviser, or consultant to an employer or who acts in the interest of an employer** to pay, **lend**, or deliver, or [to] agree to pay, **lend**, or deliver, any money or other thing of value-

(1) to any representative of any of his employees who are employed in an industry affecting commerce[.]; **or**

---

* Section 213 was added by Public Law 93-360, 93d Congress, 2d Session, approved July 26, 1974.

(2) to any labor organization, or any officer or employee thereof, which represents, seeks to represent, or would admit to membership, any of the employees of such employer who are employed in an industry affecting commerce; or

(3) to any employee or group or committee of employees of such employer employed in an industry affecting commerce in excess of their normal compensation for the purpose of causing such employee or group or committee directly or indirectly to influence any other employees in the exercise of the right to organize and bargain collectively through representatives of their own choosing; or

(4) to any officer or employee of a labor organization engaged in an industry affecting commerce with intent to influence him in respect to any of his actions, decisions, or duties as a representative of employees or as such officer or employee of such labor organization.

(b)

(1) It shall be unlawful for any [representative of any employees who are employed in an industry affecting commerce] person to request, demand, receive, or accept, or [to] agree to receive or accept, [from the employer of such employees] any payment, loan, or delivery of any money or other thing of value[.] prohibited by subsection (a).

(2) It shall be unlawful for any labor organization, or for any person acting as an officer, agent, representative or employee of such labor organization, to demand or accept from the operator of any motor vehicle (as defined in part II of the Interstate Commerce Act) employed in the transportation of property in commerce, or the employer of any such operator, any money or other thing of value payable to such organization or to an officer, agent, representative or employee thereof as a fee or charge for the unloading, or in connection with the unloading, of the cargo of such vehicle: Provided, That nothing in this paragraph shall be construed to make unlawful any payment by an employer to any of his employees as compensation for their services as employees.

(c) The provisions of this section shall not be applicable (1) [with] in respect to any money or other thing of value payable by an employer to any of his employees whose established duties include acting openly for such employer in matters of labor relations or personnel administration or to any representative of his employees, or to any officer or employee of a labor organization, who is also an employee or former employee of such employer, as compensation for, or by reason of, his service[s] as an employee of such employer; (2) with respect to the payment or delivery of any money or other thing of value in satisfaction of a judgment of any court or a decision or award of an arbitrator or impartial chairman or in compromise, adjustment, settlement, or release of any claim, complaint, grievance, or dispute in the absence of fraud or duress; (3) with respect to the sale or purchase of an article or commodity at the prevailing market price in the regular course of business; (4) with respect to money deducted from the wages of employees in payment of membership dues in a labor organization: Provided, That the employer has received from each employee, on whose account such deductions are made, a written assignment which shall not be irrevocable for a period of more than one year, or beyond the termination date of the applicable collective agreement, whichever occurs sooner; [or] (5) with respect to money or other thing of value paid to a trust fund established by such representative, for the sole and exclusive benefit of the employees of such employer, and their families and dependents (or of such employees, families, and dependents jointly with the employees of other employers making similar payments, and their families and dependents): Provided, That (A) such payments are held in trust for the purpose of paying, either from principal or income or both, for the benefit of employees, their families and dependents, for medical or hospital care, pensions on retirement or death of employees, compensation for injuries or illness resulting from occupational activity or insurance to provide any of the foregoing, or unemployment benefits or life insurance, disability and sickness insurance, or accident insurance; (B) the detailed basis on which such payments are to be made is specified in a written agreement with the employer, and employees and employers are equally represented in the administration of such fund, together with such neutral persons as the representatives of the employers and the representatives of [the] employees may agree upon and in the event the employer and employee groups deadlock on the administration of such fund and there are no neutral persons empowered to break such deadlock, such agreement provides that the two groups shall agree on an impartial umpire to decide such dispute, or in event of their failure to agree within a reasonable length of time, an impartial umpire to decide such dispute shall, on petition of either group, be appointed by the district court of the United States for the district where the trust fund has its principal office, and shall also contain provisions for an annual audit of the trust fund, a statement of the results of which shall be available for inspection by interested persons at the principal office of the trust fund and at such other places as may be designated in such written agreement; and (C) such payments as are intended to be used for the purpose of providing pensions or annuities for employees are made to a separate trust which provides that the funds held therein cannot be used for any purpose other than paying such pensions or annuities [.]; **(6) with respect to money or other thing of value paid by any employer to a trust fund established by such representative for the purpose of pooled vacation, holiday, severance or similar benefits, or defraying costs of apprenticeship or other training programs: Provided, That the requirements of clause (B) of the proviso to clause (5) of this subsection, shall apply to such trust funds;** or (7) with respect to money or other thing of value paid by any employer to a pooled or individual trust fund established by such representative for the purpose of (A) scholarships for the benefit of employees, their families, and dependents for study at educational institutions, or (B) child care centers for pre-school and school age dependents of employees: *Provided,* That no labor organization or employer shall be required to bargain on the establishment of any such trust fund, and refusal to do so shall not constitute an unfair labor practice: *Provided further,* That the requirements of clause (B) of the proviso to clause (5) of this subsection shall apply to such trust funds; or (8) with respect to money or any other thing of value paid by any employer to a trust fund established by such representative for the purpose of defraying the costs of legal services for employees, their families, and dependents for counsel or plan of their choice: *Provided,* that the requirements of clause (B) of the proviso to clause (5) of this subsection shall apply to such trust funds: *Provided further*, that no such legal services shall be furnished: (A) to initiate any proceeding directed (i) against any such employer or its officers or agents except in workman's compensation cases, or (ii) against such labor organization, or its parent or subordinate bodies, or their officers or agents, or (iii) against any other employer or labor organization, or their officers or agents, in any matter arising under the National Labor Relations Act, as amended, or this Act; and (B) in any proceeding where a labor organization would be prohibited from defraying the costs of legal services by the provisions of the LaborManagement Reporting and Disclosure Act of 1959; or (9) with respect to money or other things of value paid by an employer to a plant, area or industrywide labor management committee established for one or more of the purposes set forth in section 5(b) [sic; 6(b)] of the Labor Management Cooperation Act of 1978.*

(d)

(1) Any person who participates in a transaction involving a payment, loan, or delivery of money or other thing of value to a labor organization in payment of membership dues or to a joint labor-management trust fund as defined by clause (B) of the proviso to clause (5) of subsection (c) of this section or to a plant, area, or industry-wide labor-management committee that is received and used by such labor organization, trust fund, or committee, which transaction does not satisfy all the applicable requirements of subsections (c)(4) through (c)(9) of this section, and willfully and with intent to benefit himself or to benefit other persons he knows are not permitted to receive a payment, loan, money, or other thing of value under subsections (c)(4) through (c)(9) violates this subsection, shall, upon conviction thereof, be guilty of a felony and be subject to a fine of not more than $15,000, or imprisoned for not more than five years, or both; but if the value of the amount of money or thing of value involved in any violation of the provisions of this section does not exceed $1,000, such person shall be guilty of a misdemeanor and be subject to a fine of not more than $10,000, or imprisoned for not more than one year, or both.

(2) Except for violations involving transactions covered by subsection (d)(1) of this section, any person who willfully violates this section shall, upon conviction thereof, be guilty of a felony and be subject to a fine of not more than $15,000, or imprisoned for not more than five years, or both; but if the value of the amount of money or thing of value involved in any violation of the provisions of this section does not exceed $1,000, such person shall be guilty of a misdemeanor and be subject to a fine of not more than $10,000, or imprisoned for not more than one year, or both.

(e) The district courts of the United States and the United States courts of the Territories and possessions shall have jurisdiction, for cause shown, and subject to

---

* Subsection (c)(7) was added by Public Law 91-86, 91st Congress, 1st Session, approved October 14, 1969. Subsection (c)(8) was added by Public Law 93-95, 91st Congress, 1st Session, approved August 15, 1973. Subsection (c)(9) was added by Public Law 95-524, 95th Congress, 2d Session, approved October 27, 1978.

Subsection (d) was substantially amended by Public Law 98-473, 98th Congress, 2d Session, approved October 12, 1984.

the provisions of section 17 (relating to notice to opposite party) of the Act entitled "An Act to supplement existing laws against unlawful restraints and monopolies, and for other purposes," approved October 15, 1914, as amended (U.S.C., title 28, section 381), to restrain violations of this section, without regard to the provisions of sections 6 and 20 of such Act of October 15, 1914, as amended (U.S.C., title 15, section 17, and title 29, section 52), and the provisions of the Act entitled "An Act to amend the Judicial Code and to define and limit the jurisdiction of courts sitting in equity, and for other purposes," approved March 23, 1932 (U.S.C., title 29, sections 101-115).

(f) This section shall not apply to any contract in force on the date of enactment of this Act, until the expiration of such contract, or until July 1, 1948, whichever first occurs.

(g) Compliance with the restrictions contained in subsection (c)(5) (B) upon contributions to trust funds, otherwise lawful, shall not be applicable to contributions to such trust funds established by collective agreement prior to January 1, 1946, nor shall subsection (c)(5)(A) be construed as prohibiting contributions to such trust funds if prior to January 1, 1947, such funds contained provisions for pooled vacation benefits.

BOYCOTTS AND OTHER UNLAWFUL COMBINATIONS

SEC. 303. (a) It shall be unlawful, for the purpose[s] of this section only, in an industry or activity affecting commerce, for any labor organization to engage in [, or to induce or encourage the employees of any employer to engage in, a strike or a concerted refusal in the course of their employment to use, manufacture, process, transport, or otherwise handle or work on any goods, articles, materials, or commodities or to perform any services, where an object thereof is-]

[(1) forcing or requiring any employer or self-employed person to join any labor or employer organization or any employer or other person to cease using, selling, handling, transporting, or otherwise dealing in the products of any other producer, processor, or manufacturer, or to cease doing business with any other person;]

[(2) forcing or requiring any other employer to recognize or bargain with a labor organization as the representative of his employees unless such labor organization has been certified as the representative of such employees under the provisions of section 9 of the National Labor Relations Act;]

[(3) forcing or requiring any employer to recognize or bargain with a particular labor organization as the representative of his employees if another labor organization has been certified as the representative of such employees under the provisions of section 9 of the National Labor Relations Act;]

[(4) forcing or requiring any employer to assign particular work to employees in a particular labor organization or in a particular trade, craft, or class rather than to employees in another labor organization or in another trade, craft, or class unless such employer is failing to conform to an order or certification of the National Labor Relations Board determining the bargaining representative for employees performing such work. Nothing contained in this subsection shall be construed to make unlawful a refusal by any person to enter upon the premises of any employer (other than his own employer), if the employees of such employer are engaged in a strike ratified or approved by a representative of such employees whom such employer is required to recognize under the National Labor Relations Act.]

any activity or conduct defined as an unfair labor practice in section 8(b)(4) of the National Labor Relations Act, as amended.

(b) Whoever shall be injured in his business or property by reason

of any violation of subsection (a) may sue therefor in any district court of the United States subject to the limitations and provisions of section 301 hereof without respect to the amount in controversy, or in any other court having jurisdiction of the parties, and shall recover the damages by him sustained and the cost of the suit.

TABLE OF CASES

[References are to pages]

[References are to pages]

[References are to pages]

[References are to pages]

[References are to pages]

INDEX

[References are to sections.]

A

[References are to sections.]

[References are to sections.]

[References are to sections.]